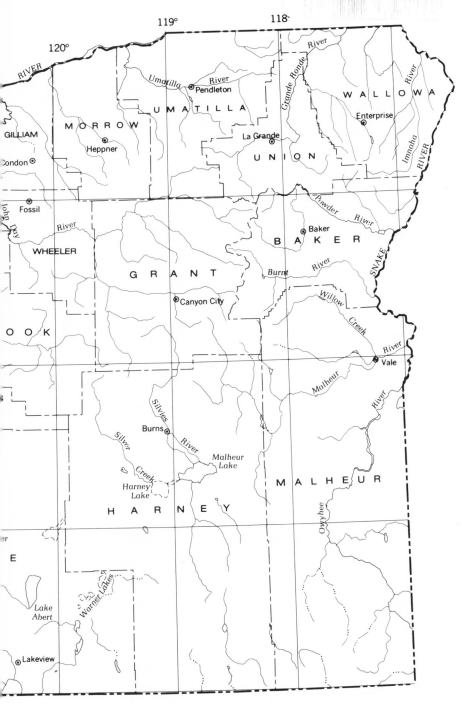

120°   119°   118°

RIVER

GILLIAM

Condon

Fossil

WHEELER

OOK

MORROW

Heppner

Umatilla   River
Pendleton

UMATILLA

La Grande

UNION

Grande Ronde   River

WALLOWA

Enterprise

Imnaha   RIVER

John Day   River

GRANT

Canyon City

BAKER

Baker

Powder   River

Burnt   River

SNAKE   RIVER

Willow   Creek

Vale   River

Malheur   River

River

Silvies   River

Burns

Silver   Creek

Malheur
Lake

Harney
Lake

HARNEY

MALHEUR

Owyhee

er

Lake
Abert

Warner Lakes

Lakeview

E

Oregon Geographic Names

Oregon Geographic Names

Lewis A. McArthur

FIFTH EDITION
Revised & Enlarged by
Lewis L. McArthur

Western Imprints
The Press of the Oregon Historical Society
1982

Library of Congress Cataloging in Publication Data

McArthur, Lewis A. (Lewis Ankeny), 1883 – 1951.
  Oregon geographic names.

  Includes index.
  1. Names, Geographical—Oregon. 2. Oregon—History,
Local. I. McArthur, Lewis L. II. Title.
F874.M16   1982   917.95'003'21   82-18808
ISBN 0-87595-113-9
ISBN 0-87595-114-7 (pbk.)

First Edition, 1928
Second Edition, Revised and Enlarged, 1944
Third Edition, Revised and Enlarged, 1952
Fourth Edition, Revised and Enlarged, 1974
Fifth Edition, Revised and Enlarged, 1982
Copyright, 1928 and 1944, by Lewis A. McArthur
Copyright, 1952, 1974 and 1982, by Lewis L. McArthur

Printed in the United States of America

Introduction

Lewis A. McArthur was born in The Dalles on April 27, 1883. The son of Lewis Linn and Harriet Nesmith McArthur, he had an early association with Oregon history through both grandfathers. William P. McArthur made the earliest government survey of the northern Pacific Coast including the mouth of the Columbia River. James W. Nesmith, father of Harriet Nesmith, came to Oregon in the emigration of 1843 and was long active on the political scene of territorial government and early statehood.

McArthur was educated at the Portland Academy and graduated from the University of California in 1908. During his college years he worked for the *Oregonian* when Harvey Scott was editor and after graduation he spent two years with the then young Oregon Electric Railway under Guy W. Talbot. In 1910 Talbot left to found the Pacific Power & Light Company and McArthur came as one of the first employees. He was appointed Vice-President and General Manager in 1923 and continued with the company until his retirement in 1946.

Governor Oswald West appointed him to the Oregon Geographic Board in 1914 and he became secretary in 1916, a position he occupied until illness forced him to resign in 1949. During the period between the first two world wars the thoughts of a volume on Oregon place names jelled and resulted in the first edition in 1928. The research for this work was a wonderful combination—reading the oldest journals of Northwest explorers, traders, trappers, naturalists and military men, and conversing with many pioneers who had been on the ground when some of Oregon's early history was made. Lewis A. McArthur never passed up an opportunity to question anyone who might add to his knowledge of local history.

McArthur was active in many fields besides the electric utility business. He was an advisor to government agencies engaged in topographic mapping and primary surveying. He was an avid stamp and book collector and served as president and for many years as director of the Oregon Historical Society. After he relinquished the position of General Manager of the Pacific Power & Light Company in 1936, he still traveled extensively throughout the state. In due course he brought out a second edition of *Oregon Geographic Names* in 1944 and finally a third in 1952. His first wife, Mary Lawrence Hewett, died in 1943 and in 1946 he married Nellie Pipes, the long-time librarian of the Oregon Historical Society. In 1950 McArthur's health began to fail rapidly and he died on November 8, 1951 in Portland. However, he had completed all the text for the third edition which was put in final form by Nellie P. McArthur.

The present compiler is his son, Lewis L. McArthur. The original text has been changed only as necessary corrections and revisions required. Every effort has been made to maintain the original style and there is intentionally no distinction between new and original material. The preface to the 1944 edition was reprinted for 1952 and then modified slightly for the 1974 edition. The major change in the present preface is the complete and accurate revision of the tables of language of origin and type of name.

This edition of *Oregon Geographic Names* is published by the Oregon Historical Society working through and in cooperation with Executive Director Thomas Vaughan and the society Publications Committee. A volume such as this is beyond the capabilities of one person. It is not possible to list all the individuals who have provided or checked information but credit in the text is given in many instances while the staff of the Oregon Historical Society has given generously of their time. The type composition was done by Nelson Composition Systems of San Bruno, California. In 1974 Mr. Gordon Nelson placed the text on magnetic tape including coding for biographical and geographical indexing. This has decimated the time spent on tedious proof-reading and largely eliminated new errors occurring in reset, unchanged text. It has also permitted search programs to standardize style and abreviations. Miss Priscilla Knuth, editor of the *Oregon Historical Quarterly,* has been a constant source of knowledge, especially on early military and Indian matters. Credit must also be given to Bruce Hamilton of the publications staff and the members of the Oregon Geographic Names Board for their continued support.

L. L. McA.

Preface to the Fifth Edition

The origins of geographic names in Oregon may be traced roughly to six periods in the history of the state, and in most instances the names themselves indicate approximately the epoch in which they were applied. The six periods may be described as follows:

First—The period of aboriginal Indian life which is reflected in Oregon by the existence of a considerable number of Indian place names, some of which were applied by the Indians themselves, and some later by the whites. These names are characterized by Willamette and Tualatin, approximations of the Indian name of the feature or the area including it.

Second—The period of exploration. Along the coast this resulted in names strongly Spanish with an English admixture such as Heceta Head, Cape Blanco, Cape Meares and Mt. Hood. Overland exploration, influenced by the fur trade, brought English and French names such as Astoria, John Day and The Dalles.

Third—The pioneer period resulting in the application of a large number of eastern place names to Oregon communities, generally for sentimental reasons, and also resulting in the use of many pioneer family names for Oregon features such as streams and mountains. During this period a number of political subdivisions were named for well-known national figures who may or may not have played a part in Oregon's development. Examples of this period include the eastern names Portland and Salem, Eugene and Roseburg for pioneer settlers and Linn and Washington counties for national figures. "Pioneer" settlements in many parts of eastern and central Oregon, of course, occurred in different decades than those in the western part of the state.

Fourth—The Indian wars and the mining periods caused the application of the names of soldiers and also the picturesque nomenclature that always follows the early pursuit of gold. Howluk Butte and Steens Mountain and Althouse Creek, Steamboat Creek and Luckyboy are typical.

Fifth—The Homestead era. During the fifty years between 1875 and 1925, nine million acres qualified for final entry and thousands of family names were applied to creeks and buttes. There was also a multiple application of names generic to the land laws and the farming and grazing occupations such as School Section Creek, Homestead, Freezeout Ridge and Dipping Vat Creek.

Sixth—The modern period of made-up names, real estate phraseology and the current efforts to apply a suitable historic or Indian name to something that bears an unsatisfactory title. Vanport, Wood Village and Lincoln City represent the first two groups while Kelley Point, Salishan and many other examples demonstrate a laudable trend on the part of most public and private bodies currently applying new names.

The U S Geological Survey has now completed the preliminary draft of the Geographic Names Information System, or GNIS, for Oregon. This lists slightly less than 32,000 names currently shown on their Oregon quadrangles. However, they have only studied the current maps published as of early 1981. The compiler has made lists for all quadrangles including those in the advance stages of pre-publication as of early 1982 and the name total approaches 35,000. This figure covers more than 90% of the state so it is reasonable to assume that it will not be far from the final total. After eliminating the innumerable Beaver, Bear, Sheep, Rock, Sand, Squaw (why is Brave so conspicuous by its absence), Fish, Huckleberry and the like, there are probably 15,000 features worthy of serious study. The writer has information under headings covering approximately 5000 total features or about a third of the more important ones in the state. From an historical point of view, it is apparent that practically all the best-known names of the state are mentioned.

Because the book is on magnetic tape, it has been simple to code each entry with language of origin and type of name. The language divisions, with three additions, are those used by the late Lewis A. McArthur for the second edition in 1944.

Language of Origin	Percent
English	81.0
Indian	8.3
German	2.1
French	1.4
Spanish	1.4
Greek	.5
Hawaiian	.—
Latin	.3
Portuguese	.1
Hebrew	.5
Norse	.6
Italian	.3
Oriental	.2
Made-up	2.7
Unknown	.5
Total	100.0

These language divisions are not adequate for a serious study and do not consider such knotty questions as when is *Johnson* English and when Nordic or is *Schultz* still German if the family had been in the United States for 200 years before coming to Oregon. The writer hopes to enlist the help of competent linguists so that this subject may be properly addressed in the next edition.

The majority of Oregon place names are descriptive in their application. The following table gives the percentage of names listed in this book:

	Percent
Descriptive	59.5
Honorary	26.2
Arbitrary	6.6
Complimentary	4.2
Unknown	3.5
Total	100.0

It may be said in explanation of this table that it has not always been easy to draw the line between the first two classes. It is the belief of the compiler that if a stream flows through the donation land claim of Balthasar Jones, a pioneer of 1850, and that the stream was named Jones Creek about the time Mr. Jones settled on the land, then the name is just as surely descriptive as though it was Gold Creek or Blue Creek. The matter of honoring Balthasar Jones was not considered when the stream began to be called Jones Creek. The whole business was a matter of descriptive convenience. On the other hand, the name Lake Abert is classified as being honorary, because Colonel Abert was a well-known army officer who did not live in the vicinity of the lake. Captain Fremont named the lake in honor of his superior. It seems to the compiler that there should be a clear distinction between these two classes of names, although there are some cases where the segregation has been difficult.

The compiler has listed as complimentary those names of places and features that were bestowed to keep in mind the name of places and features in another state or country, such as Portland, Oswego, Mount Horeb and many others.

It is apparent that as more names are studied, the percentage of descriptive applications will increase, as most of the unimportant names are purely descriptive.

Errors of fact have an irritating way of creeping into a work of this sort. Every effort has been made to check all the data published, but notwithstanding this, mistakes frequently occur, and there are probably not a few herein that have not been detected. Even government archives are not infallible. Donation land claim records in the branch land office show many inconsistencies, and affidavits of a claimant made but a few months apart bear gross disagreements in dates of birth and marriage and other data. The pioneers did not worry much about such matters and did not forsee the difficulties that would befall an investigator a century and a quarter later. Other fruitful sources of error are the printed reminiscences of popular "oldest living residents," who do not realize that they cannot remember so well as they did fifty years ago.

Records of the Oregon provisional and territorial governments are not always consistent in the spellings of geographic names. Sometimes the forms used in the manuscript bills as passed are not the same as the styles used in the printed session laws and journals. Official records give both Tuality and Twality as the name of one of Oregon's original four districts and when the name was changed to Washington County, the printed law used the spelling Tualitz, possibly a printer's error. The writer has not found it possible to reconcile all these discrepancies.

Similar difficulties are found in the records of Oregon post offices. Some of the records must be used with caution. *Caveat lector.* These records, kept at Washington, run back for over a century, and some of the entries are almost indecipherable. Then there are cases where post office records are continued from one book to another, and in the transfer minor changes have been made in the spellings of the names of the post offices and sometimes in the names of the postmasters. There are other places where it is almost impossible to follow the history of eastern Oregon post offices that have been in different counties at different times. Some post offices and postmasters jumped about like fleas.

Currently post offices are being continually discontinued and established. The writer has endeavored to show the post office information current as of January 1, 1982 but statements in the text to the effect that names are used by Oregon post offices must be accepted in a general sense and not as of any particular date unless specified.

A good deal of nonsense has been written about the meaning of Indian names. The compiler has known and respected many Indians and it has been his experience that they were principally concerned in getting a living amidst hard circumstances. It seems improbable that Oregon Indians ever made up geographic names because of "moonlight filtering through trees," "sunshine dancing on the water," "rose petals floating on water" and "water rippling over pebbles." Competent researchers have found that most Indian names were based on much more practical and everyday matters.

A few abbreviations have been used to save space. Some of these agencies have had name variations other than those shown but the current abbreviation is used regardless of the actual initials at the time referred to in the text. They are listed below along with pertinent comments. Other abbreviations are self-explanatory.

USBGN—The United States Board on Geographic Names, formerly the United States Geographic Board.

OGNB—Oregon Geographic Names Board, formerly the Oregon Geographic Board.

USGS—United States Geological Survey.

USFS—United States Forest Service.

USCE—United States Corps of Engineers.

USC&GS—United States Coast and Geodetic Survey, formerly the United States Coast Survey.

OHS—Oregon Historical Society.

OHQ—Oregon Historical Society Quarterly.

OGN—Oregon Geographic Names, 1928 edition.

OPA—Oregon Pioneer Association.

OSHD—Oregon State Highway Division, formerly Oregon State Highway Department.

BLM—Bureau of Land Management.

USBR—United States Bureau of Reclamation.

CPO—Community post office.

Where there is historical significance to a distinction, the present abbreviation has not been used and the name is presented in full such as the U. S. Topographical Engineers in connection with Fremont. There have also been many changes in the corporate organization and names of railroads. The most prominent example is the new Burlington Northern Inc., that includes the Great Northern Railway, Northern Pacific Railroad, Oregon Electric Railway and several others. An effort has been made to use the modern name for present stations and current text but in most historic references the original name is retained.

The compiler hopes that a sixth edition of this book may be forthcoming at some future date, and with that in mind corrections and suggestions are earnestly requested. Correspondence addressed to Lewis L. McArthur, Oregon Historical Society, 1230 SW Park Avenue, Portland, Oregon 97205, will be welcomed.

Portland, Oregon, 1982   Lewis L. McArthur

Oregon Geographic Names

Oregon Geographic Names

Abberdeen, Linn County. Efforts to learn the reason for this odd name for a Linn County post office have not been fruitful. No real Aberdonian would waste the extra letter in the spelling, and the style must have been selected by someone other than a Scot. Abberdeen post office was established June 13, 1892, with Mary Flauger postmaster. The office was closed April 24, 1894, and the business turned over to Lacomb post office. About 1890 one John Flaugher started a store at his home about eight miles east of Lebanon and applied for a post office which was supposed to have been named in compliment to a former home, Aberdeen, Michigan. The compiler has been unable to find a place called Aberdeen, Michigan, in available records, but there may have been one about 1890.

Abbot Creek, Jefferson County. Abbot Creek flows into Metolius River from the west about twelve miles southeast of Mount Jefferson. It was formerly called Eagle Creek, one of many of that name in Oregon. In 1930 Robert W. Sawyer of Bend recommended that the name of the stream be changed to Abbot Creek to commemorate Henry Larcom Abbot, who as a young lieutenant in the United States Army attached to the Pacific Railroad Surveys, passed along its banks on September 28, 1855. The change was made by decision of USBGN. Abbot had a long and distinguished career. He was born in Massachusetts in 1831 and was graduated from West Point in 1854. He served with distinction in the Civil War and reached the brevet rank of major-general of volunteers, awarded "for gallant and meritorious conduct during the Rebellion." After the war his activities covered a wide range of military engineering, and he retired in 1895 only to serve for another three decades as a consultant to the government and to private enterprises. He died in 1927. The USFS has applied the name Abbot Butte to a point, elevation 4318 feet, in the northwest corner of township 12 south, range 9 east. It is just west of Abbot Creek and was named on that account. See also Camp Abbot.

Abbot Pass, Clackamas and Wasco counties. In 1935 the USFS renamed the old High Rock road for Henry Larcom Abbot who crossed the Cascade Range westbound near Clear Lake on October 8, 1855. For further information regarding Abbot see under Abbot Creek. Abbot's route ran from Clear Lake to Dry Meadow to Fryingpan Lake while Abbot Road crosses at Abbot Pass some five miles to the south. Between Fryingpan Lake and High Rock both the road and Abbot's 1855 route pass through Abbott Burn which, as noted under that heading, was named during the 1890s for James Abbott. One faction claims that Abbot Pass takes its name from the road and is thus spelled correctly while another says it was really the sheep crossing and should be spelled Abbott for the Wapinitia sheep man. The mass confusion resulting from the proximity of Abbot and Abbott was further compounded by the frequent misspelling of both names so the

USBGN in *Decision List 7102* settled on the form Abbot. The road to Hell must be paved with the same good intentions had by people who bestow honorary names.

Abbott Burn, Clackamas County. Abbott Burn was named for James Abbott, a well-known stockman of Wapinitia. It is near the headwaters of Salmon River.

Abbott Butte, Douglas and Jackson counties. The following quotation from a letter by Captain O. C. Applegate, of Klamath Falls, indicates the origin of this name: "In very early times Hiram Abbott, usually known as Hi. Abbott, was, I believe, a resident of Big Butte Creek, or of that vicinity, and had some employment, as a sub-agent, perhaps, with the Rogue River Indians. He never was in any way connected with the Indian service on the Klamath reservation. I am of the impression that Abbott Butte on the Umpqua divide was named for him." The spelling Abbot is wrong.

Abernethy Creek, Clackamas County. This stream rises at an elevation of about 1100 feet ten miles southeast of Oregon City, and flows into the Willamette River at Oregon City. It was named for George Abernethy, first governor of Oregon under the provisional government. He was elected to this position on June 3, 1845. He died on May 2, 1877. He was long engaged in the mercantile business in Oregon City. His biography appears in OPA *Transactions* for 1886. See also Scott's *History of the Oregon Country*. George Abernethy once owned the island in the Willamette River at the edge of Willamette Falls at Oregon City. It was formerly known as Governors Island but is now known as Abernethy Island. In 1924 Professor Edwin T. Hodge of the University of Oregon applied the name Abernethy Island to a geographic feature in the lava fields near McKenzie Pass. This was also in commemoration of Governor Abernethy. The Southern Pacific Company has selected the name Abernethy for a station in Lane County on the Cascade line in honor of Governor George Abernethy.

Abert Rim, Lake County. Abert Rim is one of the impressive fault scarps of Oregon, and is said to have a height of 2000 feet above Lake Abert. The upper 600 feet is practically vertical cliff. This rim is named for Lake Abert, which lies at its western foot. For the origin of the name Lake Abert, see under that heading. Captain John C. Fremont visited the lake and rim on December 20, 1843, and wrote quite accurately of this rim, as well as of others in south central Oregon. Abert Rim and surrounding country are well described in USGS WSP 220. The highest part of the rim is just east of the south end of Lake Abert.

Abes Mountain, Douglas County. According to Fred Asam, this mountain five miles southeast of Red Butte was named for Abraham Wilson, an early resident of the area and a packer for the USFS during the 1920s.

Abiqua Creek, Marion County. Abiqua Creek rises in the west slope of the Cascade Range, and joins Pudding River about three miles northwest of Silverton. It was on the Abiqua Creek that a skirmish or battle was fought in March, 1848, and several Indians were killed. Thirty years later there was lively disagreement between various old timers who either minimized, maximized or equivocated the extent of the engagement and the casulties. For a discussion of this battle by John Minto, see the *Oregonian*, March 12, 1877;

by James W. Nesmith, *ibid*, March 15, 1877; by John Minto, March 20, 1877; by A. F. Johnson, March 22, 1877; by John Warnock, April 3, 1877. The most extensive research on the subject is contained in Down's *A History of the Silverton Country*, page 47. The compiler of these notes has been unable to learn the meaning of the Indian name Abiqua. It may have referred to a small tribe or to a camping place along the stream. The USBGN has decided on the spelling of Abiqua. The accent is on the first syllable.

Ace Williams Mountain, Douglas County. This prominent nose above the north bank of Little River three miles southeast of Glide was named for Asa Williams who took up a donation land claim at its base in 1854. The spelling of the first name has been corrupted for many years.

Acker Rock, Douglas County. This point south of South Umpqua River near the headwaters is the site of a USFS lookout and has an elevation of 4112 feet. It was named for Hiram L. Acker, originally from Texas, who settled at nearby Tallow Butte in 1913.

Acton, Morrow County. Acton was a post office on Butter Creek in the east part of the county and about 16 miles north-northeast of Heppner. This post office was established July 11, 1879, with John Barker first postmaster. With one exception it remained in service until June 19, 1888. It was not far from the place called Pine City and was probably in the east or northeast part of township 1 north, range 27 east. It may have been named for a family but the compiler has not been able to get further information about it. However, it should be noted that there are a good many places elsewhere named Acton and the locality in Morrow County may have received its name by transfer.

Acton Gulch, Malheur County. Acton Gulch empties into Lake Owyhee from the west. It was named for Roy and Orin Acton who built and operated a wild horse trap in this canyon.

Ada, Lane County. The post office of Ada was named for Miss Ada Wilkes, a daughter of an old-time resident. Ada Wilkes was subsequently Mrs. Ada Cleveland. Ada post office was established in 1892 on the Douglas County list.

Adair Village, Benton County. The post office at Adair Village owes its name to Camp Adair. At the conclusion of World War II the status of Camp Adair changed and the name was no longer suited for a post office. Adair Village post office was established September 1, 1947.

Adams, Umatilla County. This town is about 13 miles northeast of Pendleton on Wildhorse Creek. It was named for John F. Adams, part of whose homestead is now included in the town. The post office was established July 9, 1883, with Wm. H. McCoy postmaster.

Adams Creek, Wallowa County. This stream drains Ice Lake and flows into West Fork Wallowa River about four miles south of Wallowa Lake. It was formerly known as Fall Creek, but USFS officials changed the name to Adams Creek to avoid confusion with other Fall creeks. J. H. Horner of Enterprise informed the writer in 1931 that the present name commemorates one Tom Adams who had some mining claims on the stream.

Adams Mountain, Lane County. Adams Mountain, elevation 4955 feet, is in the southwest part of township 22 south, range 1 east. It was named for Oscar P. Adams, an early resident of Lane County. For short article about Adams by Jack Howard, see Cottage Grove *Sentinel*, March 28, 1929. For biography, see Hines' *Illustrated History of the State of Oregon*, page 485. Adams was born in Pennsylvania in 1828 and came to Oregon in 1854. After mining and other activities, he settled on a farm at what is now Cottage Grove in 1858. He spent much time prospecting and mining in the Calapooya Mountains and Adams Mountain was named on that account.

Adamsville, Morrow County. Adamsville post office was established April 15, 1884, with Silas W. Miles first postmaster. It was discontinued June 30, 1885. Old maps show the place in the vicinity of the present site of Hardman.

Adel, Lake County. Adel is a post office on Deep Creek where it debouches into Warner Valley. C. A. Moore, in a communication in the *Oregonian* on September 18, 1926, says the office was named by Bert Sessions, who owned the land where it was first established in 1896. He named it for a former sweetheart. A more intriguing source is suggested by Judge Virgil Langtry of Portland who states that Mrs. Jacob Messner, an early settler in the Warner Valley, had recalled to her grandchildren that the name was a compliment to Leda, a cow of many virtues belonging to a local resident. Since the spelling was reversed, one can only assume the compliment was back-handed.

Adkisson Creek, Wasco County. Joshua Adkisson came from Virginia and settled near Boyd in 1894. Adkisson Creek empties into Butler Canyon north of Tygh Valley.

Adobe Camp, Harney County. Adobe Camp was a very small military installation established on Silvies River in Harney Valley September 18, 1865, by Captain L. L. Williams of H Company, First Oregon Volunteer Infantry. See Oregon Adjutant General's *Report*, 1865-66, page 82. A plat of level ground was laid off about 25 yards square, protected with a sod wall 30 inches high, with an inside ditch 30 inches deep. The compiler does not know the exact location of the camp, but it seems to have been near what was later called Camp Wright. See under that heading. Camp Wright was established October 3, 1865, and it may be assumed that Captain Williams abandoned Adobe Camp at that time.

Adrian, Malheur County. When a branch of the Oregon Short Line Railroad was built into this part of the county, there was a post office called Riverview on the east side of Snake River, and railroad officials did not desire to have a station of the same name on the west side. Reuben McCreary, who platted the townsite of Riverview on the west side, suggested that if that name was unsatisfactory, the name Adrian be used, which was adopted by the railroad on February 13, 1913. This was to commemorate his birthplace, Adrian, Hancock County, Illinois. Riverview post office with its descriptive name was established on the east side of the river on August 22, 1911, with John E. Holley postmaster. About 1915 the office was moved west across the river to the vicinity of Adrian station, and the name of the office was changed to Adrian on November 10, 1919. Earlier editions of this book ascribe the name to James Adrian, a local sheepman, but Adrian did not arrive in the area until 1916.

Agate Beach, Lincoln County. This is a descriptive name. The sea beach between Newport and Yaquina Head has long been noted for the very fine agates found there. Dealers in Newport make a specialty of cutting and polishing these stones.

Agate Desert, Jackson County. Agate Desert is northeast of Central Point and just south of Rogue River. It was named for the minerals found there in some abundance. It is not a desert in the exact sense of the word. Some of Agate Desert was used for the development of Camp White in World War II. On February 13, 1901, a post office with the name Agate was established in the area, with Jefferson S. Grigsby first and only postmaster. The office was closed April 30, 1907, and the area was then served from Central Point.

Agency Creek, Polk and Yamhill counties. Agency Creek rises on the east slope of the Coast Range, and flows for the greater part of its length in Yamhill County, joining Yamhill River near Grand Ronde. It was named because of the United States Indian Agency at Grand Ronde, which was established in pioneer days.

Agency Hill, Klamath County. This is a prominent landmark just north of Klamath Indian Agency. The Klamath Indian name is *Yanaldi*, which describes the ridge extending from Klamath Agency to a point north of Fort Klamath.

Agency Lake, Klamath County. This name is generally used in referring to the north arm of Upper Klamath Lake, so called because of the Klamath Indian Agency nearby.

Agency Plains, Jefferson County. These plains lie at an elevation of from 2300 to 2400 feet, and are bordered on the west by the Deschutes River and on the east by Mud Springs Creek. They were so named because they were near the agency of the Warm Springs Indian Reservation.

Agness, Curry County. Agness post office was established October 16, 1897, and was named for the daughter of Amaziah Aubery, the first postmaster. Agness is situated on Rogue River. Amaziah Aubery was born in northern California December 24, 1865, and came to Curry County in 1883. He married Rachel Fry on February 22, 1887. It is said that the name was improperly reported to the postal authorities, hence the unusual spelling.

Ahalapam Cinder Field, Deschutes and Lane counties. This cinder field lies on the summit of the Cascade Range just north of the Three Sisters. It was named in 1924 by Professor Edwin T. Hodge of the University of Oregon. Ahalapam is one of the forms of the Indian name *Santiam*, and was used because the Santiam River possibly at one time headed in the region.

Aims, Clackamas County. Aims is the name of a locality about five miles airline northeast of Sandy, north of Bull Run River and just within Clackamas County. Aims post office was established January 11, 1886, with Eleazor S. Bramhall first postmaster. The office was closed August 31, 1907. In August, 1946, Harry E. Bramhall of Troutdale wrote the compiler that it was first planned to call this post office Bramhall, but it was concluded that the name was too long. Since it was the hope or aim of the local residents to develop a substantial community, it was concluded to adopt the name Aims, which was done. The spelling Aims is that used in postal records, and by USGS, but in recent years road signs have been installed with the spelling Ames. Mr. Bramhall, who does not approve the style Ames, says that the name Aims was proposed by Lloyd C. Lowe.

Ainsworth, Sherman County. Ainsworth is a locality just east of the mouth of Deschutes River. It has had several names. In 1909 the Harriman system began the construction of a railroad south from the Columbia River up the Deschutes Canyon into central Oregon, and the construction was carried on by the Des Chutes Railroad Company. The point of departure from the main line of the Oregon Railroad & Navigation Company was called Deschutes Junction. The junction was about a mile and a half east of the station called Deschutes, now Miller. When the railroads reached central Oregon, a station Deschutes was established a few miles north of Bend. This called for new names for the older stations, so Deschutes was changed to Miller and Deschutes Junction was changed to Sherman, because it was in Sherman County. The change to Sherman was made in 1912. This name later caused confusion with other stations named Sherman in Oregon and elsewhere, so in October, 1930, the station was renamed Ainsworth. This was in honor of Captain J. C. Ainsworth.

Captain Ainsworth was one of the most prominent of Oregon's pioneer citizens. He was born in Ohio on June 6, 1822, and came to Oregon in 1850. As a youth he became acquainted with steamboat activity on the Mississippi River. After reaching Oregon he became interested in transportation. He was the leading spirit in the founding of the Oregon Steam Navigation Company. He moved to Oakland, California, in 1880, and died near that city on December 30, 1893. His son, John C. Ainsworth, became a prominent Oregon business man and gave freely of his time to public affairs.

In 1936 much of the branch line up Deschutes River was scrapped, and the junction at Ainsworth was abandoned. However, the locality is still known as Ainsworth. For editorial comment about Captain Ainsworth, see the *Oregonian*, December 31, 1893.

Ainsworth State Park, Multnomah County. The original tract of this park was donated to the state by John C. and Alice H. Ainsworth. Ainsworth was the son of Captain J. C. Ainsworth mentioned above.

Airlie, Polk County. This was the southern terminus of the narrow gauge line of the Oregonian Railway Company, Limited. The tracks were subsequently widened to standard gauge, and the property acquired by the Southern Pacific Company. The station was named for the Earl of Airlie in Scotland. He was president of the Oregonian Railway Company, Limited, and visited Oregon during the course of construction. Most of the track on the Airlie branch was taken out in 1929.

Ajax, Gilliam County. Ajax is a locality about sixteen miles airline northwest of Condon, between Ferry and Devils canyons. It supported a post office at one time, but now there is not much in the place. The office operated intermittently from 1888 to 1921. There is a story to the effect that a cowboy named Gardner volunteered to carry the mail in the new office, without pay, and that he suggested the name for the steamer *Ajax*. Gardner had come to Oregon from California on that ship and had a sentimental interest in the name.

Alamo, Grant County. Alamo, a Spanish word meaning poplar or cottonwood tree, was made famous in American history in 1836 when a small band of Texans was annihilated by Mexican troops. The Texans were defending their positions in the Alamo Chapel in San Antonio. As a result of this encounter the name Alamo has been used in many places throughout the country. Alamo post office was about six or seven miles by road southwest of Granite and is said to have been named for the Alamo mine nearby. The compiler cannot determine if the mine was named for the local tree growth or by someone interested in Texas history. In any event the post office was established May 19, 1900, with Fred McCoy first postmaster. Available records are incomplete and the compiler cannot tell when the office was discontinued, though it did not have a long life, perhaps not much after 1905.

Albany, Linn County. "Albany was founded in 1848 by Walter and Thomas Monteith, named after Albany, New York" (Bancroft's *History of Oregon*, volume II, page 716). The first settler arrived in 1846, (*Oregonian*, November 18, 1888). The Monteiths bought the squatter's claim to the townsite in 1848 from Hiram Smeed for $400 and a horse. The first house in Albany, then the finest residence in Oregon, was built in 1849 by Monteith brothers, at Washington and Second streets. The first store was established in 1849. The town of Takenah was started in 1849, near Albany, and by act of January 12, 1854 (*Oregon Session Laws*, page 27), the legislature gave that name to both towns, but in 1855, the name Albany was restored by the legislature. The first school was operated in 1851, the first flour mill in 1852. The first steamboat arrived in 1852. For additional information about the Monteiths and early history of Albany, see *Oregon Journal*, December 5, 1925, editorial page. C. H. Stewart of Albany calls attention to the fact that Bancroft's statement that Albany was named at the request of James P. Millar cannot be true because Millar did not arrive in Albany until 1851. Postal records indicate that Albany post office was established on January 8, 1850, with John Burkhart first postmaster. The name of the office was changed to New Albany on November 4, 1850. At this point the record becomes confused. It shows that James P. Millar became postmaster on January 3, 1852, on which date the name was changed back to Albany. However another entry shows that Millar became postmaster on January 3, 1853, and the name was changed on that date. It is probable that the second entry is correct and that the clerk forgot about the new year when he wrote the entry dated January 3, 1852. James H. Foster became postmaster at Albany on July 16, 1853. In 1925 George H. Himes wrote that Takenah, the name applied in 1849 to the locality of Albany, was an Indian word which referred to a hole in the ground, apparently near the mouth of Calapooia River where the current had cut away the bank.

Albee, Umatilla County. A post office with the name Snipe was established in this locality on June 17, 1881, undoubtedly taking its name from nearby Snipe Creek. John H. Clifford was postmaster. On April 17, 1882, the name was changed to Alba and in 1887 a plat for the community was filed using the same form. *Alba* is the Latin word for white. Sometime near the turn of the century the place became known as Albee for the Albee brothers, well-known local stockmen, and on July 30, 1907 the name of the post office was changed to conform. The compiler does not know the reason for this discrepancy in names. Possibly the land was platted with an old family name, at a time when Albee was spelled Alba. Possibly the similarity of names is merely a coincidence. Albee, like many other small communities in eastern Oregon, has suffered the ravages of time beginning with the depression of the 1930s and accelerating during World War II. The post office was closed on October 31, 1943 and now all that remains are a few weatherbeaten buildings entirely on private property. Barbara Curtin gives the current situation in an article in the *Oregonian,* September 20, 1976, page B1.

Alberson, Harney County. For more than a score of years Alberson was a post office on the extreme east edge of Harney County, in the locality of township 30 south, range 36 east. As with similar offices, it was moved around a little. The office was established September 20, 1907 with William E. Alberson first of nine postmasters. The office was named in honor of the official, who was an early settler in the vicinity of Juniper Lake. The office was discontinued September 29, 1930.

Albert, Clatsop County. Albert was a small community and post office on the upper reaches of Blind Slough a little to the south of Aldrich Point. The office was established September 11, 1901, with Nels Haglund first postmaster. The place was named for Albert Berglund, who was the second postmaster. The office was closed out on September 15, 1913, with all papers to Blind Slough.

Albina, Multnomah County. Albina is now a part of Portland, but it was originally a separate municipality. It was laid out in 1872 and incorporated in 1887. Portland, East Portland and Albina were consolidated in 1891. It was named for Albina V. Page, the wife of William W. Page, by Edwin Russell, one-time manager of the Bank of British Columbia in Portland. Page, a native of Virginia, came to Oregon in 1857 and died in Portland in 1897. Albina was settled upon (donation land claim) by James L. Loring and Joseph Delay. Litigation between them was won by Delay, who sold to W. W. Page, Edwin Russell and George H. Williams, who laid out the town. It was later purchased by William Reid and J. B. Montgomery, and settlement began in 1874. Albina post office was in service from 1876 to 1892.

Alco Creek, Jackson County. Alco Creek flows into Elk Creek about eight miles airline northeast of Trail, and Alco Rock, elevation 4479 feet, is a little to the north of the headwaters of the stream. According to D. W. Pence of Eagle Point, these features were named for an early settler, about whom little seems to be known. He had a place near the mouth of Alco Creek. On May 1, 1896, a post office was established for the locality, with the name Alcoe and with Richard P. Winsly postmaster, but the office was never actually put in operation, and Winsly's appointment was rescinded June 24, 1896.

Alder Slope, Wallowa County. Alder Slope is a well known part of the Wallowa Valley, lying southwest of Enterprise and at the base of Wallowa Mountains. Alder was one of the first communities in the valley. It was named for the alder trees that grew around the Beecher cabin. The first church in Wallowa Valley, Quaker, was built at Alder about 1888. The townsite was platted in 1886, but the newer community of Enterprise drew the trade and now Alder is mostly a memory, with Alder Slope as its legacy. The name alder has been used in many places in Oregon, and in the western part of the state generally refers to the presence of the red alder, *Alnus rubra*. In the eastern part of the state the name alder is more likely to refer to mountain alder, *Alnus tenuifolia,* or white alder, *Alnus rhombifolia*. Alder post office, the third in what is now Wallowa County, was established April 5, 1878, with Henry Beecher first postmaster. The office was discontinued October 9, 1890.

Alder Springs. Lane County. Alder Springs is a place on McKenzie Highway about 15 miles east of McKenzie Bridge and for a very long time it has been a popular spot. In early days it was sometimes called Isom Corral. In the summer of 1898 Claude Branton and Courtland Green were helping a man named John Linn drive some stock from the Cobb place near Sisters, west over McKenzie Pass into the Willamette Valley. It turned out that the word "helping" was euphemistic, to say the least. On the evening of June 15, 1898, while the party was camped at Alder Springs, Branton shot and killed Linn with a revolver. Branton was later tried and convicted for his part in the affair. He was hanged at Eugene, May 12, 1899. Green turned state's evidence and pleaded guilty to a charge of murder in the second degree. He was sentenced to life imprisonment, but was pardoned after a time. A remarkable fact about the murder transpired at the trial. After Linn was killed, he was buried and a fire built over his grave. As they sat by the fire, one of the assassins performed on the Jew's harp while the other furnished vocal music. They did not have the aid of the radio in those days.

Aldrich Point, Clatsop County. This point was named for R. E. Aldrich who at one time lived there and had a small mercantile establishment. In pioneer days it was known as Cathlamet Point for the Cathlamet Indians. For information about that name see under Cathlamet Bay.

Alecs Butte, Yamhill County. Alexander Carson, generally known as Alec Carson and sometimes called Essen, was a well-known western hunter and trapper in very early days. Mrs. Alice B. Maloney has put together some bits of his biography which are printed in *OHQ*, volume XXXIX, page 16. Carson was on the upper Missouri River as early as 1807. He was for a time a member of Wilson Price Hunt's party traveling west in 1810. In 1814 he appears to have been trapping in the Willamette Valley and was classed as a "freeman" or free American trapper not connected with the British fur companies. He was in Peter Skene Ogden's brigade that trapped the Snake country in 1824-25. Indians killed him at the small hill now known as Alecs Butte in 1836. This butte is about a mile and a half south of Yamhill, west of the Tualatin Valley Highway and east of North Yamhill River. In 1944 it was part of the William Fryer farm. The compiler has an original letter from T. J. Hubbard of Fairfield to James W. Nesmith, dated September 24, 1858, telling about the murder of Carson. The substance of the letter is that in April or May, 1836, Carson, then sick, spent two or three weeks at Hubbard's home. He had with him his Nefalitin (Tualatin) Indian trapper Boney, Boney's wife and Boney's son, twelve or fourteen years old. Carson had confidence in the Indian. When he was well enough to travel, the party of four set out and camped the first night at Ellicks Butte (now Alecs Butte). In the night Boney compelled his son to murder the sleeping Carson with a shotgun. Other Indians were at the camp and they plundered Carson's property. Click-kowin, a part Tillamook Indian, had a hand in the murder and shared in the plunder. He was later shot by Waaninkapah, chief of the Nefalitins. Hubbard said he never knew why Boney committed the crime, which was the first to mar the friendly feeling between Indians and whites in the Willamette Valley.

Alexander Butte, Douglas County. Alexander Butte is northwest of Dillard, and has an elevation of about 1600 feet. It was named for David Alexander, an early settler, who lived near its foot.

Alfalfa, Deschutes County. Alfalfa is a well-known district in Deschutes County about fifteen miles east of Bend, named for the forage crop grown there under irrigation. Alfalfa post office was established January 29, 1912, with Sibyl C. Walker first of several postmasters. The office was closed December 26, 1922, and the business was turned over to Bend. The compiler does not know who named the place, but the name is appropriate.

Alford, Linn County. Alford is a station on the Southern Pacific line between Halsey and Harrisburg. It bears the name of Thomas Alford, a pioneer of 1850, upon whose donation land claim it is situated. The station was originally known as Muddy, on account of Muddy Creek, which flows nearby. The name of the creek appears in the *Oregonian* as early as November 7, 1857. A post office was established in this locality in February, 1874, with the name Muddy Station. It was in service about a year. Liverpool was the name of a post office that served the area in 1877-79. The name of the railroad station was changed from Muddy to Alford some time after 1900.

Algoma, Klamath County. This town was named for the Algoma Lumber Company. The name is said to be an Indian word formed from *Algonquin* and *goma*, meaning Algonquin waters. Various forms of the name have been used in several states.

Alicel, Union County. Alicel is a station on the Joseph branch of the Union Pacific Railroad. It is reported that when this branch line was built about 1890 Charles Ladd, a local resident, had the station named for his wife, Alice Ladd. After the death of Mr. Ladd his widow married a Mr. Tucker and subsequently lived in Seattle. Alicel is in the Grande Ronde Valley.

Alkali Lake, Lake County. This playa occupies the south part of a broad shallow basin northeast of Lake Abert. The water is highly concentrated, the dissolved salts averaging 10 per cent of the weight of the total brine. This lake, together with many other lakes, playas and streams, received its name on account of the alkaline salts dissolved in the water.

Allegany, Coos County. Allegheny is the modern spelling of a Delaware Indian word for the Allegheny and Ohio rivers. The word is used for many features in the United States, including the Allegheny Mountains in the eastern United States, and for a county, city and river in Pennsylvania. There are several variations of the spelling. This post office was established March 25, 1893, with Wm. Vincamp first postmaster. The compiler has been unable to learn why the spelling of the place in Oregon, Allegany, differs from the form generally used, Allegheny.

Allen Canyon, Wasco County. The old Free Bridge Road in eastern Wasco County descended the upper part of this canyon which was named for John W. Allen. Allen bought government land nearby in 1884.

Allen Creek, Josephine County. Allen Creek is southwest of Grants Pass. It was named for Lafayette Allen who took up a homestead land claim on its banks in 1867.

Allen Creek, Tillamook County. Allen Creek is the main watercourse through Camp Meriwether. It was named by the Boy Scouts to honor E. E. Allen Sr. Allen came to Sandlake in 1905 and for years the Boy Scouts maintained a supply point on his property at the end of the automobile road.

Allingham Guard Station, Jefferson County. This forest guard station and USFS forest camp of the same name are on the site of the oldest known homestead in the upper Metolius River area, filed by David W. Allingham prior to the establishment of Camp Sherman.

Alma, Lane County. Alma is in the southwest part of Lane County on the Siuslaw River. On March 13, 1919, Mrs. W. H. Weatherson of Portland wrote the editor of the Eugene *Register* that Alma was named for Alma Johnson, daughter of Arthur and Alice Johnson, early settlers in the community. Before 1928, A. H. Hinkson of Eugene, who was familiar with the history of the place, informed the compiler that the name was selected by A. P. Condray. Condray was the first postmaster and the post office was established in 1888. *Alma* is a Latin word meaning kind or bountiful.

Almeda, Josephine County. Almeda post office, serving a place on Rogue River about fifteen miles northwest of Merlin, was named for the Almeda mine nearby. On February 27, 1947, A. E. Voorhies, publisher of the Grants Pass *Courier*, wrote the compiler that the mine was named about 1904 or 1905 by J. F. Wickham, who promoted and owned the copper property. The name was given in compliment to Miss Almeda Hand, niece of Mr. Wickham. Almeda Hand was then a little girl living in Spokane. Almeda post office was established February 15, 1912, and was discontinued July 15, 1920. Josephine Donoghue was the first of three postmasters.

Aloha, Washington County. Aloha is a community just west of Beaverton. Robert Caples named the place in 1912. The meaning of the Hawaiian word *Aloha* is varied according to the relationship existing between the persons using the word and also depending upon the time of day it is used and whether it is at a meeting or a departure. It also depends to a certain extent upon what conversation took place just previous to its use and the gesture which ofttimes accompanies it. On meeting anyone in the morning the use of the word indicates "good morning" and in the evening "good evening," but on leaving at night it means "good night." If it is used at the time of departure on a journey it means "farewell," and it is also very generally used as an affectionate greeting even when addressed to strangers.

Aloysius, Josephine County. Aloysius post office apparently operated at the Leonard ranch in the Althouse district. Mary E. Leonard was the postmaster. Aloysius post office was established July 12, 1888, and was discontinued November 30, 1889. The available business was turned over to Althouse. James T. Chinnock, long a student of southern Oregon history, wrote from Grants Pass in April, 1948, substantially as follows: "Lawrence Leonard and Mary Ellen Leonard, his wife, were pioneer settlers in the Illinois Valley in Josephine County. Lawrence Leonard was a native of Ireland, his wife of Ohio. They owned several farms and also mining property. Among the children was William Aloysius Leonard, born in 1875, died in 1915. Aloysius post office was established in 1888 with Mrs. Leonard postmaster, and I am sure the establishment was given the middle name of this son." Aloysius is the patron saint of the young, and his name is frequently given to Catholic children.

Alpha, Lane County. The post office at Alpha was established in 1890, and was named for Alpha Lundy, the daughter of the first postmaster, Mrs. Flora B. Lundy. Alpha is the first letter of the Greek alphabet.

Alpine, Benton County. This little settlement was named because of its location near the top of one of the foothills of the Coast Range. The situation is not particularly alpine in character but is attractive nevertheless. The community took its name from the Alpine School. This school had been operated with the name for several years prior to the time the community was started. The post office was established in 1912, according to information furnished by the postmaster in 1926.

Alpine, Morrow County. Just what there was to suggest the name Alpine for a post office in eastern Morrow County about 20 miles north of Heppner the compiler cannot imagine, but that is the record. This office was established October 3, 1884, with G. H. Parsell first postmaster. It continued in service until July 27, 1894, when it was closed out to Galloway, a nearby office. A directory for 1886 says Alpine was a special supply post office, but there is no explanation of the term. The compiler's recollection of the locality is that it is not alpine in character, and the name may have been brought in from elsewhere. As of 1940 a diagram of Morrow County shows a precinct called Alpine in the northeast part of the county.

Alsea, Benton County. The name Alseya Settlement appears on the Surveyor General's map of 1855. The legend stretches along the river, and the center of the settlement is a little to the west of the present community Alsea. This is the earliest appearance of the name for the place that the compiler has been able to locate. It was not until July, 1871, that Alsea post office was established, with Thomas Russell postmaster. The early history of the locality is largely concerned with the difficulties of communication and transportation. Some of these problems are set out in an article in *OHQ*, volume XLIV, page 56, by J. F. Santee and F. B. Warfield, with the title "Account of Early Pioneering in the Alsea Valley." Paul V. Wustrow became postmaster on March 30, 1876, and held the position until May 28, 1898, nearly a quarter of a century. Colonel Wustrow was a well-known character in the Alsea Valley and was of European birth and up-bringing, but whether Russian or German, the compiler cannot learn. He is said to have coined the name Waldport at the request of David Ruble, who founded that community. For information about the origin of the name Alsea see under Alsea River.

Alsea River, Benton and Lincoln counties. *Alsea* is said to be a corruption of *Alsi*, the name of a Yakonan tribe that lived at the mouth of Alsea River. Lewis and Clark give *Ulseah*. Duflot de Mofras gives *Alsiias* in his *Exploration*, 1844, volume II, page 335. Wm. P. McArthur gives *Alseya* on his chart accompanying the report of the U.S. Coast Survey for 1851. The name has many variations, but there is no doubt that it was originally pronounced with three syllables, and not with two as at present. Alsea River rises in the Coast Range and flows into Alsea Bay at Waldport. The town of Alsea is in the southwest part of Benton County.

Altamont, Josephine County. Altamont is Spanish for high mountain. Altamont post office was established April 16, 1884, with Benjamin M. Parker first and only postmaster. The office was closed June 21, 1886. The available geographic information about this place is meagre, but perhaps sufficient for its importance. Early gazetteers show a place called Alta and also Altamont at a point on the railroad about twenty-one miles north of Grants Pass and that was doubtless the location of the post office mentioned above. There had been an earlier post office named Leland near the highway crossing on Grave Creek about four miles east of the railroad. After Altamont post office was closed in 1886, Leland office was moved west to the railroad, but the exact date of this move cannot be determined from the records. The compiler thinks it was in the early 1890s. It seems probable that the location of the old Altamont office and the present Leland railroad station were in approximately the same place.

Altamont, Klamath County. This community is just southeast of Klamath Falls, and is said to have been named for Altamont, the famous racehorse. It was applied to the locality by Jay Beach, a prominent horseman. Altamont post office was in service from January, 1895, to February, 1902, with George W. Smith postmaster.

Althouse Creek, Josephine County. Althouse Creek and Althouse Mountain near the Oregon-California line were named for the Althouse brothers of Albany. They were pioneer prospectors and miners in southern Oregon. Althouse post office was established near the lower reaches of Althouse Creek in October, 1877, with Charles H. Beach first postmaster. This office was in service for about thirty years.

Alvadore, Lane County. Alvadore is a town about 10 miles northwest of Eugene and about a mile northeast of Fern Ridge dam. It was formerly on a branch line of the Southern Pacific. It was named for Alvadore Welch of Portland, a public utility promoter and manager, who built the Portland, Eugene and Eastern Railway through the community. The railway was later acquired by the Southern Pacific Company, and in 1936 the track in this vicinity was torn up. Welch died in 1931.

Alville, Gilliam County. Alville is a place about eight miles airline northwest of Condon that has from time to time had a post office. An office called Igo was established early in 1891 with J. J. Fix postmaster. It was in operation either at or near the present site of Alville until the end of 1892.

Alville post office was opened early in 1901 and was named for the first postmaster Allen McConnell. Alville is near the head of Ferry Canyon.

Alvord Lake, Harney County. This is an alkali lake of varying size near the south end of Steens Mountain, from which it receives its main water supply through Wildhorse Creek. In wet weather the lake overflows Alvord Desert, a playa to the north which occupies a large part of Alvord Valley. These geographic features were named by then Captain George B. Currey of the First Oregon Cavalry, during the Snake War of 1864 for Brigadier-General Benjamin Alvord of the U.S. Army. He was paymaster of the Department of Oregon, 1854-62. In 1861-65 he was in command of the Department of Oregon. He was born at Rutland, Vermont, August 8, 1813; died October 16, 1884. He was held in high esteem in the Pacific Northwest, and Indian depredations in eastern Oregon, after his departure, made his absence all the more regrettable. For a biographical sketch, see the *Oregonian*, March 3, 1865. See also under Camp Alvord in this book. A post office with the name Alvord was in service in this area from August, 1874, to April, 1881. J. G. Abbott was the first postmaster.

Amazon Creek, Lane County. This is a small stream with a big name. Amazon Creek flows through the southwest part of Eugene and its waters eventually reach the Long Tom River. The compiler has been unable to get the facts about the original application of the name, but it was suggested by R. V. Mills of the University of Oregon that it was because the creek widened out over such a large area of flat lands during flood stages.

Amelia City, Malheur County. The U. S. Engineer map of the Department of the Columbia, 1885, shows Amelia City at the north end of Malheur County, a little east of the town of Malheur. It was a mushroom mining town in the locality of Mormon Basin. J. Tracy Barton, in *OHQ*, volume XLIII, page 228, gives a little of the history of Amelia City and says that the place was named for Amelia Koontz, a preacher's daughter, who eloped with a miner. The new diggings had not yet been named, and local enthusiasts could not resist the chance to honor the young bride. However, it must be recorded that another origin of the name has been suggested. Amelia Young is said to have been Brigham Young's favorite wife, and her name has been perpetuated in several places on that account. Many years ago the compiler was told that Amelia City was named for Mrs. Young because it was in the vicinity of Mormon Basin. The matter is of little consequence today as Amelia City is hardly a ghost town, less than that, if possible.

Ames Creek, Linn County. Ames Creek, near Sweet Home, is named for a family of early settlers. Lowell Ames, Sr., came to the Sweet Home area in 1852 and sired a family of six sons. According to *History of Linn County,* page 66, the family as a whole is entitled to credit for the name.

Amine Peak, Wheeler County. Amine Peak, elevation 3486 feet, is in the west part of the county, about 11 miles southeast of Clarno, airline. Amine Canyon drains northwest toward John Day River. These two features were named for Harriet Amine Saltzman, member of a well-known pioneer family at Burnt Ranch in early days. This information was furnished in 1931 by Jay Saltzman, a brother of Miss Saltzman. The spelling Aymine is wrong.

Amity, Yamhill County. This name was the result of an amicable settlement of a local school dispute. Amity was the name of a school, first applied in 1849 by Ahio S. Watt, pioneer of 1848. who was the first teacher in a log building that was built by two rival communities which were seeking school advantages. The post office was established July 6, 1852, with Jerome B. Walling postmaster.

Amity Hills, Yamhill County. Amity Hills are a northern spur or extension from the Eola Hills. They are separated from Eola Hills by a pass between Amity and Hopewell. This pass has an elevation of 451 feet. Amity Hills have an elevation of 880 feet in their northwestern part. They were named for the town of Amity, nearby. These hills are also known as Yamhill Mountains, but that name does not reflect the best use. See under Eola Hills.

Amos, Lane County. Amos is a locality on one of the tributaries of Coast Fork Willamette River at a point fourteen miles south of Cottage Grove. The post office was in service from April 23, 1898, to November 1, 1902, with John Sutherland postmaster. The end of the post office was brought about by moving it two miles and changing the name to London. Sutherland continued as postmaster at London. In February, 1947, Mrs. George A. Powell of Eugene, a daughter of John Sutherland, wrote the compiler that Amos post office was named for one of her brothers, John Amos Sutherland. In 1902 Sutherland moved north two miles to the place previously called London. Levi Geer had developed a mineral spring at London and apparently Geer selected the name London, though the compiler does not know why. When the Amos post office was moved to London, the name was changed to fit the new location. Sutherland and Geer operated a general store at London, and for a time at least the office was in one corner of the store with Emma Sutherland, now Mrs. Powell, assistant postmaster in charge. London post office continued in service until January 15, 1919, when it was closed out to Cottage Grove.

Amota Butte, Lake County. This butte is south of the Paulina Mountains, in the extreme northwest corner of the county, near Indian Butte. It is named with the Chinook jargon word for strawberry, presumably because the plant grows on the butte.

Ana River, Lake County. Ana River is a short, spring-fed stream that flows into the north end of Summer Lake. W. H. Byars, who surveyed the lands bordering on the lake named the river for his small daughter, later Mrs. S. W. Thompson of Salem. Byars was a well-known pioneer resident of Oregon, and was surveyor general from 1890 to 1894.

Anchor, Douglas County. The name Anchor was given to this post office by Miss Charity Thomas, and was suggested by the fact that the Thomas family used an anchor for its stock brand. Several names were sent to the postal authorities, who selected the word Anchor. Miss Thomas later married Paul Ludwig and was living in Yoncalla in 1926. The post office at Anchor was established February 3, 1906, with James W. Thomas postmaster. The Thomas ranch was known as Meadows Ranch. Many years ago there was a post office at this place called Binger but it was discontinued.

Anderson, Josephine County. Anderson or Anderson Station was one of the famous old stopping places on the stage road about two miles north of Selma. This was on the route of travel between Grants Pass and Crescent City and is now on the Redwood Highway. The Anderson family was well known. Anderson post office was established June 6, 1889, with Mary Anderson postmaster. The name of the office was changed to Selma on July 10, 1897. The office may have been moved to the new location at that time.

Anderson Creek, Lane County. Anderson Creek flows into the upper reaches of Dorena Reservoir. Alfred J. Anderson homesteaded near its mouth in 1889.

Anderson Creek, Lincoln County. In September, 1945, Andrew L. Porter of Newport told the compiler that Anderson Creek was named for Carl Anderson who had a homestead in the northwest quarter of section 4, township 11 south, range 11 west. Anderson lived near the stream for many years and was well known. Anderson Creek flows into Big Creek just northeast of Newport.

Anderson Lake, Lake County. This lake is one of the Warner Lakes. It is said to have been named for Thomas A. Anderson, a nearby resident.

Anderson Spring, Jefferson County. Anderson Spring southwest of Ashwood was named for Christian G. Anderson who settled there prior to World War I.

Anderson Spring, Crater Lake National Park, Klamath County. This spring is about a mile east of Kerr Notch in the southeast rim of Crater Lake and is one of the sources of Sand Creek. It has an elevation of approximately 6800 feet. It was named for Frank M. Anderson by Captain O. C. Applegate in 1888.

Anderson Valley, Harney County. Anderson Valley is so called because one G. W. "Doc" Anderson lived therein. It is about 25 miles southeast of Malheur Lake. Anderson post office was established in 1908.

Andrews, Harney County. This post office was named for Peter Andrews, who settled in the Wildhorse Valley about 1890. The post office was established in that year.

Andy Creek, Lane County. Andy Creek runs into Fall Creek from the south about ten miles east of Winberry. The creek and Chichester Falls near its mouth are both named for Andrew Chichester, a homesteader along Fall Creek in the 1890s.

Aneroid Lake, Wallowa County. Aneroid Lake and Aneroid Point, one of the high peaks of the Wallowa Mountains, are among the show places of northern Oregon. The lake was named in the fall of 1897 by Hoffman Philip, at that time a member of a party making an investigation for the United States Fish Commission. He made a barometric determination of the elevation of the lake, using an aneroid barometer, and applied the name on that account. These facts are related in a letter by Philip, printed in the Enterprise *Chieftain* for November 16, 1933. At that time Philip was American minister to Norway and the letter was written from the American legation at Oslo. It is an interesting coincidence that prior to 1897 the lake appears to have been called Anna Royal Lake, but the reasons given for the name Anna Royal are not as conclusive as they might be. J. H. Horner, long a student of Wallowa history, told the compiler that the name was applied

in 1893 in honor of Miss Anna Royal of Walla Walla, who was the first
white woman to climb up to the lake. The compiler has also been furnished
with the spelling Anna Royl. However, in the story printed in the *Chieftain*,
mentioned above, it is said that the name was applied by a Professor M. G.
Royal, who attended a teachers' institute at Joseph in 1893 and was the
guest of J. D. McCully. His mother's name was Mary Ann (Stanley) Royal,
and it is said he named the lake for her. The compiler has been unable to
reconcile all these discrepancies. The name Aneroid is now so well-estab-
lished that it seems improbable that it will be supplanted by the older style.

Angell Peak, Baker and Grant counties. Angell Peak, elevation approximately 8675 feet, is situated at the summit of the Blue Mountains, a little to
the south of the junction of Union, Grant and Baker counties. Angell Peak
was named by the USFS to honor Albert G. Angell, a member of the service
in Oregon for nearly thirty years. More than half of that time he spent on
the Whitman National Forest. He also served on the Deschutes National
Forest and at the regional office in Portland up to the time of his death in
1941.

Anglersvale, Tillamook County. The post office Anglersvale was first
called Firglen. It was established with that name on September 8, 1916,
with L. S. Miller postmaster. The name was changed to Anglersvale in
November, 1916, and the office was closed in February, 1919. According to
J. H. Scott of Nehalem, Miller was a civil engineer connected with the
Pacific Railway and Navigation Company. A fishing camp was established
on Nehalem River about opposite the mouth of Cook Creek. The place was
first called Firglen, though the records show that some tracts were platted
with the name Minnehaha. There were accommodations for fishermen
who traveled to the place by rail and thus furnished traffic for the railroad.
The change of name to Anglersvale was because it was thought to be a
name that would be better advertising. As the automobile came into greater
use, fishermen were diverted to other streams. Anglersvale was at or close
to the place now known as Batterson.

Angora, Lincoln County. Angora post office which was a few miles
west of Alsea was named for the goats raised in the vicinity. It was in the
southeast part of township 13 south, range 9 west, on or near Fall Creek at
a point not far above the mouth of that stream. The office was established
March 11, 1899, with Otto Dieckhoff first postmaster, and was discontinued June 29, 1907.

Anidem, Linn County. Anidem is one of those names which was
formed by spelling another word backward. Oregon has had a number of
post offices with this type of name. Most of them have faded from the
picture. Anidem was established January 10, 1896, with William B. Lawler
first postmaster at the old location of Quartzville when mining activity was
resumed nearby. Lawler was apparently the principal in Lawler's Gold
Mines, Ltd., the company which undertook the revival. Albert Burch was
the manager and he gives further details in *OHQ*, volume XLIII, page 108.
The post office was discontinued June 16, 1902. Lawler had previously
lived at a community or locality called Medina, possibly in Colorado. Why
he chose to burden his mining development with such an odd name as
Anidem is a mystery to the compiler. In 1906 there were approximately a

dozen post offices in the United States with the name Medina but none in
Colorado. However, there may have been a Medina mine in Colorado.
These post offices were probably all named for Medina in Arabia, although
it is of course possible that in some cases the name Medina was of Spanish
origin. The compiler does not know why the name Medina turned out to be
so popular in the United States.

Ankeny Bottom, Marion County. This bottom has a general elevation
of about 200 feet and is situated on the east bank of the Willamette River
just north of the mouth of the Santiam River. It was named for Henry E.
Ankeny, son of Captain A. P. Ankeny, who developed a farm there in the
1870s. Henry E. Ankeny was born in West Virginia in 1844, came to Oregon in 1850 with his father, and died December 21, 1906. See Carey's *History of Oregon*, volume II, page 538. Ankeny post office was at or near the
Ankeny home on the northeast edge of Ankeny Bottom. It was established
in February, 1889. The name of the office was changed to Sidney in May,
1894, and moved about a mile west to a new location.

Anlauf, Douglas County. This is a station north of Drain, on the Siskiyou line of the Southern Pacific Company. It was named for a pioneer
family of the vicinity. The post office was established May 1, 1901, with
James A. Sterling first postmaster.

Annie Creek, Crater Lake National Park, Klamath County. This
stream, together with Annie Spring, which is its principal source, was
named for Miss Annie Gaines in 1865. She and Mrs. O. T. Brown were the
first white women to descend to the waters of Crater Lake. She always
spelled her name Annie. Miss Gaines was later Mrs. Augustus C. Schwatka
of Salem, hence a sister-in-law of Frederick Schwatka, the arctic explorer.
Authorities at one time used the spelling Anna, but the USBGN has officially adopted the style Annie.

Annie Creek, Lane County. Annie Creek rises southeast of Fairview
Peak in the Bohemia district. It was named for Annie Oglesby, an early
resident. Loren Hunt told the writer in 1968 that the nearby Noonday
Mine was originally named Annie Mine but he was unable to explain the
change, which occurred many years ago.

Anns Butte, Deschutes County. This butte is just west of the confluence of Deschutes River and Little Deschutes River south of Bend. It was
named for Ann Markel who taught at Bend High School just after the turn
of the century. Miss Markel tried homesteading near the butte and later
married Vernon Forbes, one of the first legislators from Deschutes County.

Anoka, Columbia County. This post office was situated on the Ralph
Rogers homestead on Pebble Creek two or three miles above an earlier
office called Pebble. The only postmaster at Anoka was Mrs. Ralph Rogers,
the same person as Mrs. Lou A. Rogers, mother of Nelson Rogers, Oregon's late state forester. The office was in service from August 9, 1902,
until April 30, 1907. Omar C. Spencer reports that the office was named at
the request of one Randolph, who had had post office experience at
Anoka, the well-known place in Minnesota on the Mississippi River, a little
upstream from Minneapolis. There are several places of this name in the
United States. Anoka is obviously an Indian word and it is said to mean "on
both sides of."

Antelope, Wasco County. Antelope Valley was probably named in 1862 by members of the party of Joseph H. Sherar, while packing supplies in to the John Day mines. See Bancroft's *History of Oregon,* volume I, page 787. There were many antelope in central Oregon in pioneer days, hence the name. Antelope post office was established August 7, 1871, and Howard Maupin was first postmaster, the office taking its name from the valley. In 1862 the Sherar party also named Muddy Creek, Cherry Creek, Burnt Ranch and laid the foundation for Bakeoven.

Anthony Lakes, Baker and Union counties. These lakes form a source of Anthony Fork, a tributary of North Powder River. The lakes were at one time known as North Powder Lakes, but the USBGN has officially decided on Anthony Lakes. The compiler has been unable to get the origin of the name Anthony. A post office called Anthony was in service in Baker County from 1903 to 1907, but the compiler does not know its location.

Antler, Lake County. Antler was a pioneer post office in Lake County that went out of service many years ago. In October, 1945, J. O. Jewett of the *Lake County Examiner-Tribune* was kind enough to look into the history of this office and as a result, was able to report as follows: "The first Antler post office was established in December, 1875, with B. S. Chandler postmaster. Chandler was a native of Ohio and an early settler in Wisconsin and served in the Civil War. Chandler State Park bears his name. The post office was in the Crooked Creek district about a half mile north of the present ranchhouse of Dr. W. Hayden Fisk of Lakeview, and in 1945 the remains of the old log cabin still stand there, about fifteen miles north of Lakeview. This office was operated until April, 1879. Later, citizens living in that community wanted to reroute the stage line to include a stop there, so it was necessary to reestablish the office. This was done in November, 1891, with R. A. Paxton postmaster. This office was a few miles further north on Loveless Creek about the site of the present Fred Reynolds ranch. This office was closed in October, 1892." While there is no direct evidence as to the origin of the name, it is probable that Mr. Chandler had some deer horns on the premises, possibly nailed above the front door of the cabin.

Antoken Creek, Wasco County. This stream is on the Warm Springs Indian Reservation in the east part of the Mutton Mountains. It flows into Deschutes River. In May, 1943, the compiler was informed by J. E. Elliott of the Warm Springs Agency that the creek bears the name of an Indian who lived near its mouth many years ago and who died in 1905. Indians report that the word has no special meaning.

Antone, Wheeler County. This place was named in the early 1890s for Antone Francisco, a pioneer settler. He was of Portuguese descent. The post office was established in September, 1894.

Apiary, Columbia County. One of the most remarkable names in Oregon geographic history is Apiary, for a place about eight miles southwest of Rainier. Apiary post office was established August 28, 1889, with David M. Dorsey first postmaster. The office was closed on March 24, 1924. The office was so named because Dorsey had a bee ranch.

Apple Creek, Douglas County. Apple Creek flows into North Umpqua River four miles east of Steamboat and is the site of the USFS Forest Camp of the same name. Jessie Wright of Cap's Illahee stated in 1967 that many years ago a USFS construction crew was camped nearby and George Collins, the cook, began to prepare dried apples for supper. Collins' experience as a cook must have been largely theoretical as he made no provision for the increase in volume. The creek was named for the surfeit which it carried away.

Applegate Butte, Klamath County. Applegate Butte and Little Applegate Butte nearby are on the Klamath Indian Reservation, east of Fort Klamath. They bear the name of Philip Applegate, a grandson of General E. L. Applegate, a member of one of Oregon's prominent pioneer families. Philip Applegate was long a forester in the Klamath country.

Applegate Peak, Crater Lake National Park, Klamath County. This peak is on the south rim of Crater Lake and is just above Vidae Cliff. It has an elevation of 8135 feet and was named for Captain O. C. Applegate of Klamath Falls. Oliver Cromwell Applegate was born in what is now Polk County, June 11, 1845, son of Lindsay Applegate. He performed important service during the Modoc War and was Indian agent at Fort Klamath for a number of years. He had great influence over the Indians and did much to promote their welfare. He was a much respected citizen of Klamath Falls, where he lived for many years, and where he died October 11, 1938.

Applegate River, Jackson and Josephine counties. Applegate River and its tributaries rise in the Siskiyou Mountains. It flows into Rogue River west of Grants Pass. The valley through which it flows is known as the Applegate district, and there is a post office called Applegate in Jackson County. Applegate is an honored name in Oregon history. Jesse, Lindsay and Charles Applegate came to Oregon from Missouri in 1843, and for many years were prominent in pioneer affairs. Jesse and Lindsay Applegate went into southern Oregon on an exploring expedition in 1846, particulars of which may be found in Lindsay Applegate's account in *OHQ*, March, 1921 and also in Carey's *History of Oregon,* page 444. In 1848, Lindsay Applegate was a member of a party of Willamette Valley settlers who visited the Rogue River Valley in southern Oregon on the way to the mines in California. This party prospected on the stream now known as Applegate River, which was named in compliment to Lindsay Applegate. See *OHQ,* volume XXII, page 3.

Appleton, Wallowa County. This post office was established in September, 1902, and operated until July, 1913, with Miranda Rebecca Applegate postmaster. She homesteaded the land where the post office was situated about two miles east of Flora. It was planned to have the office named for Miranda Applegate but that was not possible because there was already an Applegate post office in Oregon. Accordingly a suitable name was coined by using part of the name Applegate.

Arago, Coos County. Arago post office is about six miles south of Coquille. In May, 1927, Mrs. T. P. Hanly of Bandon informed the compiler that Arago was named by her father, the late Henry Schroder, for Cape Arago. The office was not named for a racehorse, as is sometimes asserted. The community was formerly called Halls Prairie, but postal authorities were unwilling to accept a name of two words.

Arant Point, Crater Lake National Park, Klamath County. This point, with an elevation of 6815 feet, is about one mile south of Annie Spring. It was named for William F. Arant of Klamath Falls, formerly superintendent of the park. Arant died on November 23, 1927. For his obituary, see the *Oregonian,* December 4, 1927, section I, page 8.

Arata, Multnomah County. Arata was the name of a station about a mile east of Fairview on the electric interurban line. The station was named for a local resident, S. A. Arata, who operated a farm nearby. The railway was torn up some years ago and the station was abandoned. The location is shown on the USGS map of the Troutdale quadrangle, 1918 edition. S. A. Arata was born in Genoa in 1864 and came to the United States in 1871. He came to Oregon about 1883, and for many years was in the grocery business in Portland. He retired in 1910 and moved to his farm. He died May 3, 1948, in Portland.

Arcadia, Malheur County. Arcadia post office was established on the Malheur County list on November 11, 1896, with Theodore T. Danielson first of six postmasters. The office remained in service with short interruptions until May 26, 1908, when it was closed out to Nyssa. The office, which was named for the pastoral area of Greece, was a few miles north of Nyssa, and served the K. S. & D. orchard area. The K. S. & D. Fruit and Land Company was promoted by Messrs Keisel, Shilling and Danielson, who projected the development about 1890 and incorporated the company about 1897. There were some 1320 acres of land in the project, under the Owyhee ditch, and it was planned to develop an extensive fruit growing and processing community. The promoters selected the name Arcadia in the expectation that life on the project would be ideal. For more information, see *History of Baker, Malheur and Harney Counties,* page 553. The compiler has been informed that the plan for a fruit growing community was abandoned many years ago and the land was later devoted to the general crops grown in the area.

Arcadia, Wallowa County. Thomas Gwillim was an early settler in Wallowa County, and like several others, he was so impressed by the character of his surroundings that he tried to express his appreciation by applying a romantic name to a post office. Arcadia office was established January 8, 1887, with Gwillim postmaster. It operated until January, 1897, at a point a little to the northwest of the present site of Zumwalt. Arcadia, a region in Greece, was noted for its pastoral, peaceful simplicity.

Arch Cape, Clatstop County. This cape is in the extreme southwest part of the county, at the south end of Cannon Beach. It was named because of the natural arch in the rocks. Arch Cape post office was established June 27, 1912, with William C. Adams first postmaster. It was discontinued August 31, 1913, but has been reestablished.

Ardenwald, Clackamas County. Ardenwald was named about 1888 for Arden M. Rockwood, whose father owned the site of the community and platted it. *Wald* is German for a wood, and the combination name was used because of the woods in the neighborhood, and because of the name Rockwood. Arden was a family name.

Argenti, Marion County. Argenti townsite was near Silver Creek about a dozen miles southeast and upstream from Silverton, very close to Silver Creek Falls. Argenti post office was established in April, 1889, with George A. Lehman first of six postmasters. The office was closed in September, 1904, with all papers to Sublimity. There is a local story in Silverton and in Salem to the effect that Herbert Hoover, then a resident of Salem, worked as a chainman on the survey party that laid out the original townsite. See Dean Collins' story in the *Oregon Journal*, April 19, 1940. It is said that there was a post office, store, blacksmith shop, hotel and two sawmills in the place, but these establishments have completely disappeared. *Argenti* is a Latin word meaning "of silver," a name obviously suggested by Silver Creek nearby.

Arkansas Hollow, Wallowa County. This small valley empties into Swamp Creek about eight miles north of Enterprise. James T. Baker, formerly of Madison County, Arkansas, homesteaded there in the early 1890s and the place was named for his former home.

Arko, Wallowa County. Arko was at one time a post office, but was discontinued some years ago. The place was in the north end of the county, a few miles northwest of Troy. It was named by Mary C. Loy for Arkoe, Nodaway County, Missouri, but the spelling was somehow changed.

Arleta, Multnomah County. Arleta is part of Portland. It was named for Arleta Potter, daughter of T. B. Potter of the Potter-Chapin Realty Company, which put the addition on the market.

Arlington, Gilliam County. This town is on the south bank of the Columbia River at the mouth of Alkali Canyon. In pioneer days the place was known as Alkali. The post office at Alkali, which was then in Wasco County, was established on November 7, 1881. Local residents did not consider the name Alkali suitable for a growing community, and at a town meeting N. A. Cornish suggested that the town be named Arlington, supposedly because there were a number of southerners living in the community at the time and it was the home of General Robert E. Lee. However, an ulterior motive lay hidden, for many years later his daughter, Nellie C. Cornish, in *Miss Aunt Nellie*, page 28, says the name was selected to honor her father whose full name was Nathan Arlington Cornish. Cornish apparently neglected to mention this connection and the honor went unknown, at least during his lifetime. The name of the community Alkali was changed to Arlington by an act passed at a special session of the legislature and approved November 20, 1885 and the Post Office Department conformed on December 31, 1885.

Armet, Lane County. Armet was a station on the original Southern Pacific Cascade line between Lowell and Oakridge. The place was formerly called Blakelyville, which was the name of the post office, but the railroad adopted the name Eula for the station. See under Eula for the history of these names. The post office was later changed to Eula, but by that time the railroad found there was confusion between Eula and Eola, so about 1925 the station name was changed to Armet, the name of a head armor used in the middle ages. This name was selected arbitrarily by railroad officials. Properly the word is accented on the first syllable, but the name of the station is accented on the last syllable. Eula post office was taken out of service in the fall of 1943. The railroad was relocated when Lookout Point Dam was completed but the name survives on Armet Creek.

Armin, Wallowa County. Armin is said to have been named for one Armin Bodmer, of the Wallowa Valley, at a time when he was courting a young widow, Affie B. Hanna, who lived in the place.

Armitage, Lane County. Armitage was named for George H. Armitage, an early settler nearby. He was born in New York in 1824, and came to Oregon in 1848, by way of California. For his biography, see Walling's *History of Lane County*, page 490. He operated the first ferry across the McKenzie River. For editorial about his public services, see the *Oregonian*, August 4, 1928. McKenzie post office was established on January 21, 1854, with George H. Armitage postmaster. It was apparently near the present site of Armitage station. The office was discontinued in October, 1859.

Armstrong Creek, Grant County. This stream is near Galena. It was named for W. W. Armstrong, a pioneer resident of the neighborhood. He was a veteran of the Civil War, and came to Oregon with government troops in 1866, and was for a time stationed at Camp Logan, near what is now Strawberry Mountain. He was a resident of Grant County for many years.

Army Hill, Douglas County. Army Hill is an elevation of sand on the west bank of Umpqua River, two miles north of its mouth. It was named because of the soldiers at Fort Umpqua. Fort Umpqua was a post at Umpqua City from 1856 to 1862. Umpqua City was a pioneer trading post near the mouth of Umpqua River.

Arnold Ice Cave, Deschutes County. Arnold Ice Cave has been so known for a number of years, and the name is apparently established. However, the late Robert B. Gould of Bend told the writer that the name of Arnold came to be applied to this cave as a result of the misreading of a county road sign, which bore directions for Arnold (ranch) and the ice cave. Visitors combined the two names on the signboard, with the result that "Arnold Ice Cave" is now well known by that name. For additional information about the naming of this cave see editorial in Bend *Bulletin*, April 18, 1927.

Arock, Malheur County. This name was first applied in May, 1922, and the post office was established in 1926. The name was suggested by T. Townley Garlick, because of the proximity of a large rock bearing picture writing, supposedly of Indian origin.

Arrastra Creek, Jackson County. An arrastra is a crude mill for grinding ore. The operation generally consists of dragging heavy stones over the ore, which has been placed in the bottom of a pit. The grinding stones are moved around by beams operated by mules or horses. There were a good many arrastras in southern Oregon in the days of the quartz mining, and Arrastra Creek was named for such a mill. The stream is tributary to Wagner Creek south of Talent.

Arrow, Lake County. Arrow post office was another office that was in operation during the days of the homesteaders in northern Lake County. It was situated a few miles northeast of Silver Lake, and is said to have been named for the Indian arrowheads found in the vicinity. The office was established May 21, 1910, with Edith Reigel postmaster. It was discontinued February 28, 1918.

Arrowwood Point, Crook County. Arrowwood Point is the highest peak at the east end of the Maury Mountains southeast of Prineville. At one time this point was called Maury Mountain, which was confusing because the east-west range is called Maury Mountains. Accordingly about 1932, when it was planned to make a lookout development on the peak, the name was changed to Arrowwood Point, because of the presence of arrowwood shrubs on the summit. This shrub is the *Philadelphus lewisii* or syringa, also called Lewis mock orange.

Arthur, Baker County. Arthur was the name selected for a post office in the north part of the county to the northeast of Keating. The office was established as a result of mining activity in the Balm Creek area. It was in service from February 25, 1929, to June 30, 1930, when it was closed to Keating. The writer does not know the activities of the mining industry mentioned. The name Arthur was derived from W. J. Arthur, more generally known as Johnny Arthur.

Arthur, Multnomah County. In earlier days a well-known Multnomah County post office was Arthur on the west shore of Sauvie Island a little north of Holbrook. This office was established July 26, 1880, with Mary Taylor postmaster. The office was closed November 30, 1904, apparently as the result of the extension of rural free delivery. Mary Taylor was the only postmaster the place ever had. A good deal of effort has been made trying to learn the origin of this name, but with no result. The place was not named for President Chester A. Arthur because he was not president when the office was established, in fact he had not even been elected vice-president. The office was established about the time the Republicans nominated the Garfield-Arthur ticket in Chicago in the summer of 1880, and it may have been named because Arthur's name was in the news, but this is just a guess.

Asbestos, Jackson County. Asbestos locality and post office were named for the fireproofing material, deposits of which are to be found in the north part of Jackson County. The post office was established August 15, 1893, with May Sackett first postmaster. It was closed August 31, 1918, with papers to Beagle. It was situated in township 33 south, range 2 west, near Evans Creek. F. W. Libbey of the State Department of Geology and Mineral Industries calls the attention of the compiler to the fact that the word asbestos is a commercial term rather than a definite mineral name. There are a number of minerals which are called asbestos, the most important of which is chrysotile, a fibrous variety of serpentine. Fibrous tremolite, another type of asbestos, is known to occur in Jackson County.

Aschoff Buttes, Clackamas County. These buttes lie about five miles east of Marmot and are north of Little Sandy River. They were named for Adolf Aschoff, who was born in Germany May 21, 1849, emigrated to the United States in 1869 and came to Oregon in 1882. He settled at what is now Marmot on March 16, 1883 and was for many years a prominent guide and forester in that part of the state. He was an enthusiastic advocate of all things tending to preserve and popularize the scenic features of Oregon.

He died in Portland on May 16, 1930. For obituary, see *Oregon Journal*, May 17, 1930. See also under Marmot.

Ash, Douglas County. This post office was established July 24, 1894, and the first postmaster was Charles L. Parker. The postoffice department asked for a short name and he suggested Ash as there were many of those trees in the vicinity.

Ashland, Jackson County. Ashland was named by Abel D. Hellman, whose birthplace was Ashland County, Ohio. Matthew P. Deady is authority for the statement that the town was named in honor of Henry Clay's birthplace, which was near Ashland, Virginia (Deady letter in the *Oregonian*, May 13, 1884). Both explanations are possibly correct. Hellman was born in 1824. The town in Oregon was named in 1852 (Walling's *History of Southern Oregon*). The flour mill was built by Abel D. Hellman, John Hellman, Eber Emery, Jacob Emery and James Cardwell. Ashland Mills in 1855 is described by T. J. Dryer, *Oregonian*, June 23, 1855; see also April 4, 1903. For notes on Ashland in 1855, *ibid.*, February 2, 1855. Ashland Mills post office was established on May 17, 1855, with Abel D. Hellman first postmaster. Hellman and associates built a sawmill before they built the flour mill and supplied lumber to the Jacksonville mines. For further information, see article by Fred Lockley in the *Oregon Journal* for May 2, 1928, editorial page. The name of the post office was changed to Ashland June 14, 1871.

Ashwood, Jefferson County. Near Ashwood is a butte known as Ash Butte because of the volcanic ash deposits on its sides. When the post office was established about 1898, the word Ash was combined with Wood to form the name. This was done to honor Whitfield T. Wood, who settled in the vicinity in the 1870s. His son, James Wood, was the first postmaster.

Aspen Lake, Klamath County. Aspen Lake is west of Upper Klamath Lake, and is fed by streams from the east side of Aspen Butte. These features and others so named in the state are distinguished by the presence of that beautiful tree, the quaking aspen, or *Populus tremuloides*. In *The American Fur Trade of the Far West*, General H. M. Chittenden says: "Another species of the genus populus was the *Populus tremuloides*, the quaking asp, or the *tremble* of the French. The superstitious voyageurs thought this was the wood of which the Cross was made and that ever since the crucifixion its leaves have exhibited that constant tremulous appearance which has given rise to the name. The wood of the quaking asp was preferred by the trappers as a fuel for cooking, because it had little odor and did not taint the meat."

Astoria, Clatsop County. The name Astoria is full of historic significance, for about it is woven the story of the discovery, exploration and development of the great Oregon country. It was near here that Captain Robert Gray discovered the mouth of the Columbia River and gave to the United States its claim to the title of the territory. It was near here that Lewis and Clark passed the winter of 1805-6 and it was here that the first commercial settlement of Americans was made on the Pacific Coast in 1811. This settlement was the direct result of the organization of the Pacific Fur Company in 1810 by John Jacob Astor of New York, and it was fitting that his name should be given to the company's initial enterprise. John

Jacob Astor was born in Germany in 1763, and after four years in London,
came to New York when he was 20. By his energy and industry he grew to
be a leading figure in the commercial life of the city, where he died on
March 29, 1848, leaving a large fortune. The bibliography of John Jacob
Astor's relations with Oregon is unusually large. Washington Irving's *Astoria*,
published in 1836, is picturesque in style, but gives a good general
account of Astor's enterprise. The first chapters of Scott's *History of the Oregon
Country* treat of the founding of Astoria quite fully, and include many
references invaluable to those interested in the matter. The Astor party on
the ship *Tonquin* arrived off the mouth of the Columbia River on March 22,
1811, and after two disastrous days of strenuous effort, succeeded in landing in the estuary. Three weeks later, April 12, the party began to build a
post and bestowed upon it the name of the originator and chief owner of
the enterprise. The place was called Astoria until the fall of 1813, when it
was taken over by the British, and rechristened Fort George. See Carey's
History of Oregon, page 246. Fort George it remained until it was nominally
returned to the United States in 1818. The name Astoria was gradually
restored with pioneer settlement. Attention is called to the fact that the first
trading post at Astoria is sometimes called Fort Astor rather than Astoria.
The compiler has never found any authority for the name Fort Astor.
Lewis and Clark hibernated on what is now known as Lewis and Clark
River, a few miles southwest of the present city of Astoria. Their camp was
called Fort Clatsop. The city of Astoria is situated on a peninsula between
the Columbia River on the north and Youngs Bay on the south, and the
high ridge in between is known as Coxcomb Hill. It has an extreme eleva-
tion of 595 feet at the bench mark in the base of the Astoria Column.
Astoria post office was established on March 9, 1847, with John M. Shively
first postmaster. This was the first American post office on the Pacific
Coast. Statements to the effect that the first post office at Astoria was in the
John Adair house do not seem to be correct. General Adair got to Astoria
in April, 1849, more than two years after the post office was established.
On April 10, 1852, General Adair wrote to Joseph Lane as follows: "When
I came to the country, or shortly after, you know Shively, who was postmas-
ter and resided on the hill at Fort George, left for the mines, leaving no one
to take care of the office. . . . McClure, who was one of Shively's bonds-
men, would not allow a mail bag to go into his house and demanded of the
P.M. Genl an immediate release as surety. I consented to take the poor
bantling." John Adair became postmaster on November 8, 1849; Butler
Anderson on November 11, 1850, and Sam'l A. Seymore on May 27, 1852.
These data are from postal records at Washington, D. C.

Athena, Umatilla County. This town is about half way between Walla
Walla and Pendleton. For many years it was known as Centerville. The
name caused confusion with Centerville in Washington County, and also
with Centerville in Klickitat County, Washington. In 1889 the town authorities decided on a change and asked D. W. Jarvis, local school principal, to
suggest a new name. Jarvis, being of a romantic and classical turn of mind,
suggested Athena, which was adopted. Athena was one of the most important goddesses of Greek mythology, and with Zeus and Apollo represented

the embodiment of all divine power. She was the goddess of counsel, war, female arts and industries. In Italy she was known as Minerva. The post office of Centerville was established October 11, 1878, with Wm. T. Cook as first postmaster. The name was changed to Athena May 16, 1889.

Athey Canyon, Polk County. This canyon is on the west slope of Eola Hills about two miles northeast of McCoy. It was named for a pioneer family of the north Willamette Valley.

Attwell Creek, Hood River County. This stream near Cascade Locks was named for Roger G. Attwell and his wife Mary, pioneer settlers. Attwell was born in New York City and arrived in Oregon in August, 1852. He settled near the present site of Cascade Locks on April 12, 1853. See land office certificate 5041.

Atwood, Morrow County. When Atwood post office was established on October 22, 1883, it was on the Umatilla County list. Morrow County had not yet been organized. Henry C. Thompson was the first postmaster and with a short intermission this office ran along until November 20, 1888. Whether it was always in what is now Morrow County the compiler cannot tell. It was on Butter Creek which, in that locality, is very close to the Morrow-Umatilla county line. The office may have been in the two counties at different times but when it was discontinued it certainly was in Morrow County.

Auburn, Baker County. Gold was found on Griffin Creek in October, 1861, and within a few weeks the eastern Oregon gold rush was in full fever. Thousands of miners and prospectors poured into the Blue Mountains and also into parts of Idaho where there were similar discoveries. A camp sprang up in the Blue Canyon district a little south of Griffin Creek. This camp was about eight miles airline southwest of the present city of Baker, and it rapidly became one of the largest settlements in eastern Oregon. A paragraph from Isaac Hiatt's *Thirty-one Years in Baker County,* page 30, gives the following account of the founding of the place: "On the 13th of June, 1862, a meeting was called by Wm. H. Packwood, Ed Cranston, Geo. Hall and others at which time it was resolved to lay out a town to be called Auburn, and the next day a street was located from Freezeout gulch to Blue canon, and building lots taken on each side, and in a short time a number of buildings were put up and Auburn assumed the usual appearance of a new mining town. The diggings in that vicinity were thereafter called the Auburn mines." Many interesting stories have been written about the rise and fall of this camp, which is now not even a ghost town, but the compiler has never seen any information about the reason for the application of the name. Upward of twenty-five places in the United States have been named with the word made famous by Oliver Goldsmith in the first line of his *Deserted Village,* a name that turned out to be truly prophetic as far as the Oregon camp was concerned. According to Irving L. Rand of Portland there were no buildings left in Auburn, Oregon, in 1945. Many miners came to eastern Oregon from the Sierra Nevada region of California and the compiler is of the opinion that Auburn, Oregon, was named for the well-known California mining town, which was in turn named by miners who came from Auburn, New York. The compiler admits he has no evidence to support this theory but it is pleasing to contemplate. It is a matter of interest that there is a place called Blue Canyon in the Sierra Nevada not very many miles northeast of Auburn, California. There is nothing on modern maps to recall the mining camp of Auburn except the Auburn Ditch now used for irrigation. The post office at Auburn, Oregon, was established November 1, 1862, with William F. McCrary first postmaster. This was the first post office in northeastern Oregon. It was in operation continuously until October 31, 1903. See also under Baker.

Audison Creek, Wallowa County. This stream empties into Saddle Gulch in township 2 south, range 49 east. It bears the name of George Audison, hunter and trapper, who had a dugout there in the early 1880s.

Audrey, Baker County. Audrey post office was established in March, 1902, and was discontinued in April, 1918. The first postmaster was Lemuel D. King. The writer has been told that the office was named for Audrey King, daughter of the first postmaster. This office was in the extreme southwest corner of township 11 south, range 37 east, on North Fork Burnt River about nine miles southeast of Whitney, at the old King ranch and stage stop. Miss Audrey King married Charles Davidson. She was appointed postmaster at Audrey in August, 1912, after her marriage, and served until the office was discontinued as of April 15, 1918. In 1949 it was reported that the Davidsons were then living in Salem.

Augur Creek, Lake County. There are two streams of this name in Lake County. One is immediately northwest of Lakeview and flows into Thomas Creek. The other is twenty miles further northwest and empties into Chewaucan River via Dairy Creek. The compiler is certain both were named for Captain C. C. Augur, U.S. Army, who was a participant in early Indian wars in Oregon. The names were doubtless applied during the Snake War in 1864. C. C. Augur was born in 1821, and graduated from West Point. During the Civil War he became major-general of volunteers, and was a brigadier-general in the regular establishment. He died in 1898.

Augusta, Baker County. Augusta post office operated from August 10, 1871, to October 11, 1872, with William T. Atkeson postmaster. The office was on Eagle Creek not far from the place later called Sanger, and is said to have been named for a Miss Augusta Parkwood, the first unmarried woman resident. See under Sanger.

Augusta Creek, Lane County. Augusta Creek is an important tributary of South Fork McKenzie River, flowing in from the south. It was named for Miss Augusta Young, daughter of Carl Young, an early day forest ranger in the McKenzie River country. Augusta Young was later Mrs. Starr.

Aumsville, Marion County. This community is on the site of Henry L. Turner's pioneer farm, and Turner and his sons and son-in-law, Amos M. Davis, built a flour mill there, and for a time the place was called Hoggum, because there were so many pigs about. Before the mill was completed, Amos Davis died, on December 26, 1863. Turner was very fond of his son-in-law, who was generally called Aumus, and after Amos' death, he named the place Aumsville. Post Office authorities state that the first post office was called Condit, and was established July 10, 1862, with Cyrenius Condit postmaster. The name of the office was changed to Aumsville March 11,

1868, with John W. Cusick postmaster. The Condit post office was first on the Condit property about three miles southwest of the present site of Aumsville. About 1865 it was moved about a mile and a half west to the William Morris place. It was moved to Aumsville when the name was changed in 1868.

Aurora, Marion County. Aurora was the center of a German colony, and is now on the main line of the Southern Pacific Company and also on the Pacific Highway East about 28 miles from Portland. The town was founded by Dr. William Keil March 20, 1857, and was named for his daughter. Keil was born in Prussia in 1811 and died in 1877. The colony was founded in 1855, coming from Bethel, Missouri, where Dr. Keil founded a colony in 1845. After his death, private property succeeded his community system. See Scott's *History of the Oregon Country*, volume II, page 324, which refers to several articles on the subject. Aurora Mills post office was established December 30, 1857, with William Keil first postmaster. The name was changed to Aurora on December 10, 1894.

Austin, Grant County. This community was named for Mr. and Mrs. Minot Austin, early settlers, who operated a small store and hotel not far from the present site of the town. The post office was established in 1888.

Austin Creek, Tillamook County. Austin Creek flows into Little Nestucca River about three miles above Meda. It was named for Henry Austin who homesteaded nearby in 1903.

Austin Hot Springs, Clackamas County. In 1903 Seth Austen patented 151 acres on Clackamas River three miles above the mouth of Collawash River. The hot springs on this plot as well as the point and meadow to the west were all named for him, but the incorrect spelling Austin now prevails.

Avery, Benton County. This is a station on the Southern Pacific Company line about two miles south of Corvallis. It was named for Joseph C. Avery, a pioneer of 1845. He was the first owner of the site of Corvallis, which was then known as Marysville, and he sold the first town lots in 1849. Avery was a prominent and progressive citizen engaged in farming and mercantile business and was appointed postal agent for Oregon and Washington in 1853. He was several times a member of the Oregon legislature. He was born in Pennsylvania in 1817 and died at Corvallis June 16, 1876. See under Corvallis.

Awbrey Mountain, Jefferson County. This butte, at one time known as Sheep Rock, is in the extreme southeast part of the county, northeast of Grizzly. It bears the name of a pioneer stockman, Marshall Clay Awbrey, who was born at Camden, Ray County, Missouri, on January 16, 1829, and died at Soldiers' Home, Roseburg, on January 16, 1921. He served in the Mexican War, came to Oregon in 1850 and also served in the Rogue River Indian War. He began operations in central Oregon in the late 1860s. Awbrey Heights are just west of Bend and form a butte with an elevation of 4234 feet, covered with scattered timber. These heights together with Awbrey Falls on the Deschutes River several miles north of Tumalo were also named for Marshall C. Awbrey.

Axehandle Spring, Jefferson County. Axehandle Spring and Axehandle Ridge are eastward of Ashwood, and the general locality was once known as Axehandle. Later on the name Donnybrook was used as the result of a little social affair in Calf Gulch, but the post office is called Kilts. The reader will find entertaining information under those headings. The following quotation from an editorial by Phil Brogan in the Bend *Bulletin*, April 20, 1943, tells of the origin of the name Axehandle: "Shortly before the turn of the century, the community, then in Crook County, was known as Axehandle, named by wood haulers from Antelope community who secured fuel in the western spur of the Blue Mountains. One of their stopping places was a big spring. Old timers say some of the first wood haulers past the place found a broken axe handle and named the water hole Axehandle spring. The name gradually extended to the entire community, to take in the Bannon, Morgan, McLennan, Brogan, Eades, Crowley and Creegan ranches."

Axtell, Lincoln County. Axtell was the name of a post office on Yachats River in the extreme south part of the county, about six or seven miles east of Yachats, applied in compliment to a local family. The office was established in May, 1891, with John D. Axtell first postmaster. The office was closed in August, 1903, with papers to Waldport. The compiler visited the area in 1968 and noted that while nothing is left to mark the locality, the USFS has constructed a small fish ladder near the mouth of Axtell Creek. This, one of the marked exhibits on the Cape Perpetua Auto Tour, is a typical example of a minor stream improvement to better spawning access.

Ayers Canyon, Morrow County. Thomas W. Ayers settled where this canyon empties into Butter Creek south of Service Buttes. Ayers was born in Iowa in 1840 and came to Oregon in 1862. He moved to the Butter Creek area with several brothers and sisters in the 1860s.

Azalea, Douglas County. Douglas County is noted for its azaleas and this post office was named on account of their abundance in that locality. There are two well-known members of the *Ericaceae* of this type in Oregon, the *Azalea occidentalis* or western azalea, and *Azaleastrum albiflorum*, or small white. The name Azalea has been used for post offices in Douglas County at two separate times and places, and the post offices Starvout, Booth and Azalea have at different times all served more or less the same territory in upper Cow Creek Valley. Starvout post office was established February 18, 1888, with H. L. Miser postmaster. The name of the place was changed to Booth on August 24, 1907, probably because the name Starvout was suggestive of an unsatisfactory locality. The name of Booth post office was changed to Azalea on May 6, 1914. In the meantime there had been another Azalea post office which was established October 17, 1899, with Joseph A. Wharton first postmaster. This post office was discontinued September 30, 1909. The postmaster at Azalea in 1925 told the writer that Mrs. Maggie Picket suggested the present name of Azalea for the former Booth post office. The writer does not know who suggested the name of the original Azalea post office, which is shown on the 1900 postal map at a point on Cow Creek about ten miles southwest of Riddle.

Baby Rock, Lane County. This rock is on the southwest shoulder of Heckletooth Mountain, and above the track of the Southern Pacific Company just southeast of Oakridge. It was named by the Indians. Mrs. Lina A. Flock has given the compiler an unusual legend about the name. Indians who slept near the rock were believed to have been bitten by some animals that left the footprints of a baby. The wounds were fatal. Finally two Indians determined to exterminate these peculiar animals, and hiding in the rocks above, they surprised the visitors, jumping down on them and covering them with blankets in such a way that they could not escape. The animals were twisted in the blankets and burned up. Indian Charlie Tufti would never go near this rock. Mrs. Flock's grandfather, Fred Warner, was of the opinion that the peculiar animals were porcupines, which make tracks not unlike a small baby. Indians asserted that the baby tracks remained about the rock for many years, hence the name.

Baca Lake, Harney County. This is a small overflow lake near Donner und Blitzen River south of Malheur Lake. It has an elevation of about 4160 feet. *Baca,* or *vaca,* is the Spanish word for cow, and the lake was named by Mrs. Dolly Kiger because so many cattle watered there.

Bachelor Butte, Deschutes County. Bachelor Butte has an elevation of 9060 feet as determined by the USGS, and is one of the imposing isolated peaks of the middle Cascade Range of Oregon. It is just southeast of the Three Sisters and receives its name because it stands apart from them. John C. Todd of Bend told the compiler in 1928 that in early days Bachelor Butte was frequently called Brother Jonathan, in contradistinction to the Three Sisters.

Bachelor Flat, Columbia County. According to a news story in the St. Helens *Mist*, June 28, 1929, Bachelor Flat was named because of the presence of so many unmarried men in the locality, which is about three miles southwest of St. Helens. The news story contains an interview with Charles Gable, who in 1880, settled near the present Bachelor Flat School. Gable relates that there were five or six young bachelors in the neighborhood, who were cronies, and that at a gathering one night he suggested the name Bachelor Flat, which has prevailed through many years.

Bacona, Washington County. This community is in the extreme north part of the county. When the post office was established in May, 1897, it was named for a family of early residents by the name of Bacon.

Bade, Umatilla County. Bade is a station on the Union Pacific Railroad between Milton and Weston. It was named for William G. Bade, a nearby resident. For many years this station was called Bates, and it is said this was because a German section foreman misinterpreted Bade's name in transmitting it to the railroad company headquarters.

Badger, Sherman County. Badger, a post office in what is now Sherman County, was not named for the animal that burrows in the ground, but for Thomas R. Badger, the postmaster. Badger post office was established on the Wasco County list on December 19, 1882. The name of the office was changed to DeMoss Springs on August 5, 1887, with Thomas J. Cocking as the new postmaster. Early in December, 1945, Giles L. French of Moro undertook to get together some of the history of the Badger office. According to Mr. French, Thomas Badger and a brother Ephraim came to what is now Sherman County from Illinois. They left after a few years but their later history is not available to Mr. French. In any event, Thomas Badger had his post office down Barnum Canyon a few miles from Moro. This would make the Badger place about a half mile south and west of DeMoss Springs. Doubtless the office was moved at the time the name was changed.

Badger Creek, Hood River and Wasco counties. The badger, *Taxidea americana*, is so plentiful throughout Oregon, especially in that part east of the Cascade Range, that it is not surprising that many geographic features were named for it. Badger holes are in evidence in many localities, and Badger creeks are particularly plentiful. The creek mentioned at the head of this paragraph has its source in Badger Lake, in Hood River County, with an elevation of 4472 feet. A mile southeast is Badger Butte, with an elevation of 5981 feet, a well-known landmark.

Bagby Hot Springs, Clackamas County. These springs are in township 7 south, range 5 east. They were named for Robert W. Bagby, a prospector and miner who frequented this part of the state. He lived between Molalla and Wilhoit. He died on October 8, 1927. For his obituary, see the *Oregonian,* October 9, 1927, section I, page 17. The spelling Bagsby is wrong.

Bagnell, Curry County. In pioneer days a man named William Bagnell operated a ferry on Rogue River about five miles northeast of Gold Beach, then known as Ellensburg. The compiler has been unable to get much of Bagnell's history. On June 7, 1894, Bagnell post office was established at the ferry, with John R. Miller first and only postmaster. The office was closed to Gold Beach, April 4, 1895.

Bailey Butte, Wheeler County. This butte just west of Mitchell was named for Ezekiel Bailey who settled there in the 1880s.

Bailey Butte, Wheeler County. Bailey Butte in the West Branch country was named before the turn of the century for early settler Lee Bailey.

Bailey Hill, Lane County. This hill southwest of Eugene was named for John Bailey who settled there in 1857. The land was originally the donation land claim of Jackson Wright, Bailey's brother-in-law.

Bailey Mountain, Curry County. Bailey Mountain, elevation 3920 feet, is about 12 miles airline west of Kerby. The following quotation is from a statement made by the USFS to the USBGN, which adopted the name December 4, 1941: "The name suggested is in honor of one of the first miners to settle in this area. He had a claim and built a cabin nearby that is still known as Bailey Cabin. The date of his death is unknown."

Baird, Gilliam County. Baird post office was established December 8, 1884, and was named for J. C. Baird, the first and only postmaster. The office was discontinued February 8, 1886. In March, 1948, J. D. Weed of Condon wrote the compiler that he came to Gilliam County on January 17, 1899, and lived that winter at Shutler. Mr. Weed says that the Junction House was situated at Shutler Station and he was told in early days there was a post office there called Baird. The Junction House was the point where emigrants from the east traveling the Oregon Trail reached Alkali Canyon. From this point the Oregon Trail went westward up Alkali Canyon and along Rock Creek to John Day River.

Baiseley Creek, Baker County. Baiseley Creek near Pleasant Valley was named for James Baiseley who discovered gold in the area in 1893.

The Baiseley family were well-known Baker County prospectors in the early days.

Bakeoven, Wasco County. During pioneer gold excitement in Canyon City, an enterprising trader started from The Dalles with a pack train of flour. After crossing the Deschutes River Indians drove off his horses in the night and left him with his supplies. He constructed a rough clay and stone bakeoven and made bread which he sold to miners and prospectors going to the mines. The old oven was in existence for many years after the owner abandoned it. H. H. Bancroft, in his *History of Oregon*, volume I, page 787, says that the baker was a German and that the event occurred when Joseph H. Sherar took a party to the mines in 1862. The post office of Bakeoven was established December 1, 1875, with Mrs. Ellen Burgess first postmaster.

Baker, Baker County. Baker was originally known as Baker City and it was, of course, named for Baker County. The post office was first established on March 27, 1866, with William F. McCrary as postmaster. In 1911 the name of the post office was changed to Baker to conform to the new style adopted by the incorporated community. For additional information about the origin of the name see under Baker County and also editorial in the *Oregonian*, November 13, 1925, page 14. McCrary was the first postmaster at Auburn post office, which was established November 1, 1862. It is reported that McCrary moved the office to the present site of Baker in the fall of 1865 and opened a variety store. Whatever the facts are about this unauthorized move, the Baker City office was established March 27, 1866, with McCrary postmaster. Despite McCrary's move, Auburn continued to have a post office until October, 1903.

Baker Bridge, Clackamas County. This bridge was named for Horace Baker, who took up a donation land claim nearby in pioneer days. His land office certificate was number 4967. The bridge is near Carver.

Baker Canyon, Morrow County. Baker Canyon empties into Eightmile Canyon. It was named for Lorin D. Baker who settled there at the turn of the century.

Baker County. Baker County was created September 22, 1862, by the state legislature (*General Laws* of 1862, page 112). It was made from the eastern part of Wasco County. It was named for Edward Dickinson Baker (1808-61) who was elected United States senator from Oregon in 1860. He was killed at Balls Bluff just after he had been appointed a major-general. His biography appears in the *Oregonian* January 15, 1875, by Tom Merry; May 31, 1908, by Clark E. Carr; January 19, 1896. He first came to Oregon in December, 1859, and, in the following February, moved his family to Oregon. For the narrative of his death, *ibid.*, July 16, 1893, page 4; October 21, 1906, page 49; tribute to his strong oratorical power, *ibid.*, April 5, 1899, page 3, by P. B. Johnson; reminiscences of Baker, by George H. Williams, *ibid.*, July 29, 1906, page 41; Baker's speech in Union Square, New York, in April, 1861, *ibid.*, May 30, 1906, page 8; his oration over the body of Senator Broderick, *ibid.*, October 14, 1883; his reply to Breckenridge, *ibid.*, July 30, 1905, page 43; description of the grave of E. D. Baker at San Francisco, *ibid.*, March 13, 1892; June 4, 1872, page 3. For biographical narrative, by William D. Fenton, see *OHQ*, volume IX, pages 1-23. For a description of Baker County in 1880 see the *Oregonian* for December 28, 1880; in 1885, *ibid.*, October 19, 1885, by Alfred Holman; in 1881, *ibid.*, December 6, 1881, by George H. Atkinson. Details concerning the origin of Oregon counties may be obtained from *OHQ*, volume XI, No. 1, for March, 1910, which contains an address on the subject by Frederick V. Holman.

Baker Creek, Yamhill County. Baker Creek rises in the Coast Range and flows east to Panther Creek just west of North Yamhill River. It was named for John G. Baker who was born in Kentucky in 1818 and came to Oregon in 1843. He settled just north of the present site of McMinnville and for six years was sheriff of Yamhill County under the provisional and territorial governments.

Baker Gulch, Wallowa County. Baker Gulch drains into Joseph Creek in township 4 north, range 45 east. It was named for James, Sam and John Baker who had a hunting camp there in the 1890s. They were the sons of James T. Baker of Arkansas Hollow.

Bakersfield, Washington County. Bakersfield post office was about five miles northwest of Thatcher. It was named in compliment to the family of the only postmaster, Sylvia S. Baker. The office was established December 2, 1899, and was ordered closed to Thatcher, December 16, 1901.

Balch Creek, Multnomah County. Danford Balch settled near what is now Willamette Heights in Portland in 1850. Balch was hanged October 17, 1859, for killing his son-in-law, Mortimer Stump, on the Stark Street ferry. For history of the tragedy of the Balch family, see Scott's *History of the Oregon Country*, volume III, page 352, and also story in *Oregonian* August 14, 1938, magazine section. Balch creek was named for this family. At one time the creek furnished the city water supply.

Bald Mountain, Curry County. Bald Mountain, elevation 2967 feet, is a prominent point about ten miles airline southeast of Port Orford, and has been so called since the days of the mining excitement in the 1850s. Glisan in *Journal of Army Life* uses the name on March 15, 1856, and it is apparent that the name was in vogue before that date. On modern maps, Bald Mountain is the northwest end of a prominent ridge and Rocky Peak, elevation 3023 feet, is at the southeast end and about a mile away. It is possible that in early days the name Bald Mountain was applied to the ridge rather than to either of the two points. Davidson, in *Coast Pilot*, 1889, describes these features, though the wording is not entirely clear. He seems to call the northwest peak Pilot Knob and the southeast point Bald Peak, with an elevation of 3056 feet. He describes the ridge as a double peak above all the immediate mountains, and says the Indian name was *Chus-suggel*. In early days the expression Pilot Knob was used by mariners to describe all of the ridge referred to at the beginning of this paragraph. Preston's *Map of Oregon*, 1856, has the name Pilot Knob applied to the entire ridge, but that does not agree with Glisan.

Bald Peter, Jefferson County. Bald Peter, elevation 6540 feet, is a conspicuous landmark on the Warm Springs Indian Reservation about six miles east of Mount Jefferson. This mountain bears a descriptive name sometimes applied by surveyors to points, rocky at the top and bare of timber. While this name may be derived directly from the Latin word *petrus*, meaning rock, it is more probably an allusion to Saint Peter, the rock on which the church was founded. There is another point called Bald Peter Butte, elevation 3725 feet, on the north boundary of the reservation in Wasco County, doubtless named for the same reason.

Bald Peter, Linn County. J. L. Gilbert, an early postmaster at Berlin, stated that this Bald Peter with its barren top was not given the generic name described above, but rather was specifically for Peter Powell who took a donation land claim on McDowell Creek. The compiler has never seen a picture of Mr. Powell but assumes he suffered from a common affliction of the American male. Bald Peter Creek, a tributary of Crabtree Creek, rises on its north slopes.

Baldock Slough, Baker County. Baldock Slough is one of the channels of Powder River north of Baker. Hiatt, in *Thirty-one Years in Baker County*, page 36, has an account of William Baldock, who came into the Baker Valley from Colorado in the fall of 1862. He was attracted by the fine stand of wild hay growing in the valley, and worked up a market for it in Auburn. He got a scythe from some source and made pitchforks from forked willow sticks. He harvested the hay and found ready buyers in the mining camps. Baldock Slough was named for this man or some member of his family.

Baldwin Creek, Hood River County. Baldwin Creek drains the northeast part of upper Hood River Valley, and flows into East Fork Hood River. It was named for S. M. Baldwin, who, in 1878, homesteaded a tract through which the stream flows.

Baldwin Hills, Jefferson County. The hills west of Hay Creek were named for Dr. David Baldwin who established the Baldwin Sheep and Land Company in 1873. This was the beginning of the famous Hay Creek Ranch. For further information see *East of the Cascades* by Phil Brogan and *OHQ*, volume XXXIX, page 384.

Baldy Lake, Grant County. This is a small lake on the north slope of Ireland Mountain, so named because at one time Ireland Mountain was known as Bald Mountain.

Ballard Landing, Baker County. Ballard Landing is a place on Snake River in the extreme northeast corner of Baker County, named for a local resident. A post office with the name Landing was in operation in this locality from December 22, 1900, until May 10, 1904, with Eli F. Ballard postmaster.

Ballston, Polk County. Ballston was named for Isaac Ball who took up a donation land claim where the town now stands. The post office was originally established as Ballsville on September 19, 1878, with Andrew N. Martin postmaster. The name was changed to Ballston on July 19, 1880. Isaac Ball was one of the early champions of the west side narrow gauge railroad project. See *OHQ*, volume XX, page 144.

Balm, Tillamook County. Several varieties of cottonwood trees are called balm or balm-of-Gilead, and in consequence the name Balm has been applied geographically to places inhabited by these trees. A post office named Balm was in operation in Tillamook County from May, 1897, until December, 1911. Everett R. Bales was the first postmaster. The office was on Foley Creek, not far above the mouth and about two miles southeast of

Mohler. The office moved about, depending on the postmaster. The office is supposed to have been named for some balm trees, which are not common in that part of Oregon, but the compiler does not know which variety. Mohler post office was established the day the Balm office was closed and it may be assumed that the Balm office was moved to Mohler and the name changed.

Balm Mountain, Douglas County. Balm Mountain is in the northeastern part of the county in the Calapooya Mountains and has an elevation of 6088 feet. It was named for a brushy plant known as mountain balm, or mountain lilac, *Ceanothus velutinus*. This plant is also called snow bush and sticky laurel.

Baltimore Rock, Coos County. Baltimore Rock is south of the entrance to Coos Bay and north of Cape Arago, not far from the lighthouse. George Davidson, in *Coast Pilot*, 1889, says it was named because the schooner *Baltimore* struck on it and was wrecked.

Ban, Multnomah County. Ban was a station north of Linnton. It was named for Shinzaburo Ban, a prominent Japanese merchant of Portland who also operated a shingle mill near the station. Ban was born in Tokyo and came to the United States in 1891 when he was thirty-seven years old and had already had a successful career in Japan. For further information about early Japanese settlers in Oregon see Barbara Yasui's article, "The Nikkei in Oregon, 1834-1940", *OHQ*, volume LXXVI, page 229 *et seq.*

Bancroft, Coos County. It is reported that the Post Office Department named this office, but the reason is not known. The post office was established July 28, 1891, with Burrel R. Banning first postmaster.

Bandon, Coos County. Bandon is a community on the south side of the mouth of the Coquille River. It was named by George Bennett who settled not far from the present town in 1873. Bennett was a native of Ireland and named the new city for Bandon, on Bandon River, County Cork, Ireland. He married Katherine Ann Scott Harrison, and three children were born to them, two of whom have been prominent citizens of Coos County. Bandon was almost completely destroyed by fire on September 26, 1936, but has been rebuilt. For historical sketch of Bandon, see the *Oregonian*, September 28, 1936. For history of Bandon and Coquille River by George Bennett, see *OHQ*, volume XXVIII, page 311, and volume XXIX, page 20. An Englishman, William Davidson, known locally as Billy Buckhorn, is said to have been the first resident. Bandon post office was established September 12, 1877, with John Lewis first of a long line of postmasters.

Bangor, Coos County. Bangor was a townsite laid out on the west side of Pony Slough, now within the city of North Bend. "Major" L. D. Kinney, who came to Coos Bay about May, 1902, from Maine, promoted the townsite and also expected to build a belt line railroad at Coos Bay and a railroad from Coos Bay to the Willamette Valley. The promotions did not mature. Bangor was named for Kinney's former home in Maine. A post office with the name Bangor was established November 8, 1902, with Edwin H. Wall postmaster. The office was never in active operation and the order was rescinded March 10, 1903.

Banks, Washington County. Banks was named in compliment to Robert Banks, a pioneer resident, and his father, John Banks. The name is said to have been selected by Joe Schulmerich and Joed Hartley. Banks post office was established January 21, 1902, with Ewell S. Turner first postmaster. It was at first planned to name the office Turner, probably for the first postmaster, but this could not be done because of duplication with Turner in Marion County. Banks post office was discontinued in December, 1904, and the business was turned over to Greenville. Early in 1907 the Greenville office was moved north a few miles to the location of the old Banks office. Local residents petitioned to have the old name Banks restored, which was done in April, 1907.

Bannister Creek, Lane County. This creek flows into Lookout Point Lake. A. J. Briem, in his notes on file at the OHS, says that the stream was named because an iron bar was installed near its mouth as a bannister to help travellers across an awkward spot.

Bannock Ridge, Malheur County. Bannock Ridge is west of the site of Rockville. In 1978 Alfred McConnell of Ontario, who was raised in the area, provided the following information about the name. In the early days some Indians stole a particularly fine stallion from the Ruby Ranch. The ranch hands chased them north to Cow Lakes where the Indians, allegedly Bannocks, turned the horse loose. However, their pursuers followed them up onto what is now Bannock Ridge and killed them. The Bannocks or Bannacks were a subdivision of the Shoshone Nation centered in eastern Idaho. After an abortive uprising in the winter of 1862-63, they were placed on Fort Hall Reservation but numbers of them continued to summer on Camas Prairie in southwest Idaho. In 1878 there was a second uprising under Chief Buffalo Horn. During a protracted summer campaign troops under the command of Major-General O. O. Howard pursued them through southeast Oregon and north through Grant County into the Blue Mountains. Defeated in several battles, the Indians dispersed in the fall and eventually returned to Fort Hall. Mark V. Weatherford gives many details in *Bannack-Piute War, The Campaign and Battles.*

Bar Creek, Douglas County. William J. and Hugh A. Barr settled on this creek in Camas Valley shortly after the Civil War. The Barr brothers found the fertile, isolated valley a fine spot to make money—literally, but they made a hasty departure after they were discovered minting their own coins from lead.

Barber, Lincoln County. Barber post office was established March 30, 1911, and was discontinued January 31, 1912. Clarinda Barber was the only postmaster in the history of the establishment. The compiler is informed that the office was at or near the mouth of Wolf Creek, on Elk Creek about three miles downstream from Harlan. It was named in compliment to the family of the postmaster.

Barbra, Clatsop County. Barbra is an unusual name for a place but that is the way it is in postal records. Barbra was in the extreme south part of Clatsop County, on North Fork Nehalem River, near the middle of section 28, township 4 north, range 9 west. In recent years the Markham and Callow logging camp was in operation a little to the northeast on the Necanicum Highway. Barbra post office was established May 24, 1892, with

Thomas Mitchell the first and only postmaster. The office was closed May 26, 1900, with papers to Nehalem. Mrs. Rose West Johnson, RFD Warrenton, Oregon, wrote that Barbra post office was named for the wife of the postmaster, Thomas Mitchell. The Johnsons were old timers on Clatsop Plains and recalled the days when carriers took the mail through from Seaside to Nehalem.

Bare Creek, Wallowa County. This stream flows into Imnaha River from the west in township 2 north, range 48 east. It was named for Ike N. Bare who settled on its banks about 1887. He came into the Wallowa Valley in the late 1870s, according to J. H. Horner of Enterprise, and formerly lived in Iowa and Colorado. Bare was a typical frontiersman and also a rustic fiddler and minstrel. Bare Creek was once known as Fall Creek, but that name has sunk into disuse.

Bare Island, Klamath County. This island is in Upper Klamath Lake not far from Modoc Point. It was so named because it was bare of any considerable stand of timber. The Klamath Indian name of this island was *Aushme*. Those Indians had a legend that it was created by one of their deities who threw a game-stick into the lake.

Barite, Wheeler County. Barite was a name once used for a post office in the extreme southeast corner of the county, probably on or near Birch Creek southeast of Antone. Barite post office was established March 22, 1901, with Reuben Fields postmaster. The office was closed August 20, 1906. Barite, also called barytes and heavy spar, is sulphate of barium, frequently used in paint making. In December, 1945, F. W. Libbey, director of the State Department of Geology and Mineral Industries, wrote the compiler that he had no knowledge of barite in the locality mentioned, but as it is not an uncommon mineral, it is quite possible that it could have been found there.

Bark Cabin Creek, Grant County. Bark Cabin Creek is a tributary of South Fork Murderers Creek about twenty-five miles southwest of John Day. So called because an old trapper's cabin by the creek was covered with bark from nearby trees, the name Dark Cabin is incorrect.

Bark Creek, Benton County. Bark Creek flows northward from the foothills of Marys Peak. In 1937 Mark Phinney of Philomath interviewed Jerry E. Henkle, a well-known Benton County pioneer, who said the stream was named in the spring of 1856 by a party of neighbors looking for grazing land. They tried to cross this stream at a place so miry that they had to lay large pieces of fir bark to keep their horses from sinking. They called the stream Bark Creek.

Barkley Spring, Klamath County. Barkley Spring is on the east shore of Upper Klamath Lake between Algoma and Modoc Point. It is a well-known locality, and bears the name of James Barkley, native of Ireland, who served at Fort Klamath as sergeant in C Company, 1st Oregon Cavalry and was discharged there about 1866. He lived in a small cabin near the spring for some years, then moved to a home in Yonna Valley. Still later he was thrown from a cart near the spring and killed.

Barklow Mountain, Coos and Curry counties. This mountain with an elevation of 3559 feet was named for a well-known pioneer family of Coos County.

Barlow, Clackamas County. Barlow is on the main line of the Southern Pacific Company in Clackamas County, and also on the Pacific Highway East. It was named for William Barlow. He was a son of Samuel K. Barlow, who opened the Barlow Road. William Barlow's reminiscences are in *OHQ*, volume XIII, page 240, where it is stated that he was born October 26, 1822, in Marion County, Indiana, and it was in that state that his father had married Susannah Lee. The Barlows came to Oregon in 1845, traveling over the Cascade Range by what was later known as the Barlow Road, and arrived in Oregon City Christmas night. William Barlow engaged in various enterprises, and among other things, started the first black walnut trees grown in Oregon in 1859. Samuel K. Barlow bought the donation land claim of Thomas McKay on September 17, 1850, and afterwards sold this place to his son William. The railroad was built through the place in 1870, and the station was named for William Barlow. For additional information about the Barlow family, see article by Fred Lockley, editorial page of the *Oregon Journal*, December 24, 1937.

Barlow Creek, Hood River and Wasco counties. This stream bears the name of Samuel K. Barlow, the builder of Barlow Road. See under Barlow Road heading for additional information. The Barlow Road followed along Barlow Creek between White River and Barlow Pass. For discussion of the use of the name Zigzag, describing this creek, see *OHQ*, volume XIX, page 75. The early use of the name Zigzag instead of Barlow for this stream seems to the compiler improbable.

Barlow Road, Clackamas and Wasco counties. The Barlow Road was named for Samuel Kimbrough Barlow, a pioneer of 1845, who developed the first made road in the state of Oregon. For a description of the difficulties the Barlows had getting over the Cascade Range on what was later the Barlow Road, see *OHQ*, volume XIII, page 240. For a history of the road itself, see *ibid.*, page 287. For story about the road and a map, see *Sunday Oregonian*, magazine section, May 29, 1938. Barlow started the work when he came over with the emigration, and finished it the following year. From the summit of the Cascade Range westward to Sandy the Mount Hood Loop Highway is in substantially the same location as the Barlow Road, though modern engineering has solved some of Samuel K. Barlow's greatest difficulties. East of the summit the Barlow Road has been in disuse for many years for a considerable distance down the eastern slope, especially where it traversed the canyon of White River. The Oak Grove Road from Salmon River Meadows to Wapinitia was not a part of the original Barlow Road, though frequently spoken of as such. On July 27, 1925, a memorial tablet was dedicated to Samuel Kimbrough Barlow at a point on the Mount Hood Loop Highway just east of Government Camp. This tablet, which is on a large boulder, was unveiled in 1923 but could not be put in place then owing to difficulties over the title to the site. On the same boulder is another tablet dedicated to Susannah Lee Barlow, wife of S. K. Barlow. Samuel K. Barlow was born in Nicholas County, Kentucky, on January 24, 1792. He died at Canemah, Oregon, July 14, 1867, and is buried beside his wife at Barlow.

Barnegat, Tillamook County. Barnegat is one of Oregon's ghost post offices, although the name is still used occasionally to refer to a locality on the narrow neck of land south of Bayocean. In September, 1943, O. K. Tittle of Tillamook wrote the compiler that Barnegat post office was first situated about two miles south of the place where the Bayocean Hotel was built later. The office was established at the instigation of A. B. Hallock, who was the first postmaster. When Hallock died October 30, 1892, the office was moved a mile south to the Bert Biggs place and was operated by Mrs. Biggs, who was a daughter of Webley Hauxhurst. It is said that Hallock named Barnegat for his former home on the Atlantic Coast. The only Barnegat on the Atlantic Coast is of course Barnegat Bay, a well-known inlet on the shore of New Jersey north of Atlantic City. However, the biography of Hallock in the files of the Oregon Historical Society fails to show that he ever lived close to the Atlantic Ocean. In 1929 H. C. Sutherland of Portland told the compiler that his father, Thomas A. Sutherland, went shooting on Tillamook Bay in the 1870s and named Barnegat Bay, Tillamook County, because of similar activity on Barnegat Bay in New Jersey. It was the impression of the Sutherland family that Thomas A. Sutherland applied the name to the southwest part of Tillamook Bay and not to a place on land. Barnegat Bay in New Jersey is said to have been named by Henry Hudson with the Dutch word "breaker's inlet." Barnegat post office in Tillamook County was not established until 1891, and it is possible that the post office was named for the Barnegat Bay designated by Sutherland. The name of this office was changed from Barnegat to Bayocean in February, 1909.

Barnes, Crook County. For some years, Barnes was a post office in the south part of Crook County. The office was discontinued July 31, 1925, and mail was then handled through Roberts post office. Barnes office was named for Harry Barnes as it was established at his ranch in May, 1909, and he was the first postmaster.

Barnes Butte, Crook County. Barnes Butte is a spur or ridge extending from the foothills just northeast of Prineville. It was named for Elisha Barnes, a pioneer resident of Prineville.

Barnes Road, Multnomah County. This road leads westward from the head of West Burnside Street, in Portland. It was named for William Barnes, who came to Oregon in 1861, and took up land west of Portland in Washington County. He died April 4, 1909. An electric railway was opened up Barnes Road in 1893, but service was abandoned in the fall of that year. Traces of the old line are still visible. Barnes Heights in Portland got its name from the same source.

Barnes Valley, Klamath County. Barnes Valley is in the extreme southeast part of the county, very close to the Lake County line. In fact it is probable that part of the valley is in Lake County. Early in 1948 Miss Frances L. Barnes, of Portland, wrote that the valley was named for her uncle, Captain James Thornton Barnes, and that she lived thereabouts as a small child over sixty years ago. Captain James Thornton Barnes was born near Little Orleans, Indiana, in 1819, and later moved with his family to Missouri. He served in the Mexican War, went to California in 1850 and came to Oregon in 1851 to join his brother, Daniel P. Barnes, a pioneer of 1847. James T. Barnes served in the Rogue River War and reached the rank of captain. For many years he was actively engaged in stock business in the Goose Lake and the Sprague River valleys. He died May 18, 1889, at Jacksonville.

Barnesdale, Tillamook County. Miss Lucy E. Doughty, Bay City, told the compiler that this place, which does not now have a post office, was named for Frank Barnes, who settled in the valley of Foley Creek about 1910. Barnesdale post office was established April 18, 1912, with Frank Barnes first postmaster. The office was discontinued June 15, 1925.

Barnett, Gilliam County. This is a railroad station south of Arlington. The correct spelling is Barnett and not Burnett, as is shown on some maps.

Barney, Crook County. Barney post office was in operation from September 6, 1913, to January 15, 1918, with William A. Barney postmaster, and the office was named in his honor. The place was on the upper reaches of Mill Creek, about where the stream crosses the line between township 13 south, ranges 17 and 18 east. The Barney homestead was in section 25, township 13 south, range 17 east. The office served a small sawmill community about a mile north up Mill Creek. It is reported that most of the improvements were later destroyed by fire.

Barnhart, Umatilla County. The following information is paraphrased from a letter written the compiler by George A. Hartman of Pendleton, in 1947: Jeremiah Barnhart probably lived on the land ten miles west of Pendleton when the railroad established a siding, and his name was applied to the station. He did not homestead the place. He and Bob Thompson were partners in the sheep business for a number of years prior to the death of Thompson, who was killed by a sheepherder about 1894. The siding is on the Union Pacific Railroad and close to Umatilla River. A post office named Barnhart was established May 20, 1897, with Stella Jackson postmaster. This office was never in service and the order for its establishment was rescinded.

Barnhouse Spring, Wheeler County. This spring in section 2, township 13 south, range 23 east, bears the name of Jacob L. Barnhouse who homesteaded on the upper reaches of Mac Creek in 1905.

Barnum Canyon, Sherman County. Henry Barnum was one of the first settlers in the vicinity of Moro. He moved to this part of what then was Wasco County about 1867 and became a prominent early citizen.

Barr Creek, Jackson County. Mrs. Frances Aiken Pearson, who was born in Prospect in 1885, told the compiler that this creek was named because of a cattle bar to prevent livestock straying from the adjacent Red Blanket Ranch.

Barren Valley, Malheur County. Barren Valley lies between South Fork Malheur River and Owyhee River southwest of Crowley. Louis Scholl, a draftsman and cartographer, accompanied Wallen in 1859 and was with Steen's expedition in 1860 when it passed through this area. It is not named in any known account, but when Scholl returned to The Dalles in the fall of 1863, he prepared from memory for Brigadier-General Benjamin Alvord a "Map of Major Steen's Field Notes of 1860" to be used in the following spring's campaign. This shows Barren Valley north of Alvord Valley but there is nothing to indicate the name was used prior to 1863. Lieutenant

John Bowen accompanied Captains Currey and Drake during the 1864 expeditions and Barren Valley does appear on his map. This was enough to fix the name although Williamson's map of the late 1860s shows Banner Valley, probably a typographical error. The descriptive name will appear appropriate to anyone familiar with the local geography.

Barrett, Hood River County. Dr. P. G. Barrett settled in the Hood River Valley in 1871, and for many years was the only physician in the valley and popular throughout the entire territory. He lived about three-quarters of a mile south of the site of Barrett School, and at one time all the west side of the Hood River Valley was known as the Barrett District. He died in 1900. Barrett Spur on the north side of Mount Hood was also named for Dr. Barrett. Mrs Barrett was interested in botany. She died in New York in 1924, aged 92 years.

Barrett, Umatilla County. This is a station on the Union Pacific Railroad just west of Milton. C. A. Barrett, a pioneer stock raiser of the county, owned land at this point and the station was named for him. For Barrett's reminiscences of pioneer and farming conditions in this section of Oregon, see *OHQ*, volume XVI, page 343.

Barron, Jackson County. Barron was a post office about ten miles southeast of Ashland, near to, but possibly not actually on the Southern Pacific railroad. It was named for a local family. The office was established June 18, 1875, with James Tyler first postmaster. That was of course before the railroad was built. The office was closed October 15, 1910.

Barstow, Multnomah County. This station on the Oregon Electric Railway, just east of Garden Home, was named for W. S. Barstow, of New York City, a prominent engineer and public utility operator, who was interested in the construction of the railroad. He died on December 26, 1942, at Great Neck, Long Island.

Bartlett, Wallowa County. Bartlett was named for Theron A. Bartlett, who owned the land on which the post office was situated. The office was established on May 14, 1904, and Bartlett was the first postmaster.

Barton, Clackamas County. This place was named for Barton, Wisconsin, by an old resident, E. H. Burghardt, who had formerly lived there. He settled near the mouth of Deep Creek and started a small flour mill and store, and later had the post office established with the name of his old home in the East. His daughter, Mrs. Anna Burghardt Davis, was living at Tangent, Oregon, in 1925. Her father was born in 1851 and died in 1912. He came to Oregon about 1876. Barton post office was established May 16, 1896, with Burghardt first postmaster.

Barton Lake, Harney County. Barton Lake was named for an early settler, William Barton. It is about ten miles south of Malheur Lake.

Bartrum Rocks, Douglas County. These two prominent rocks form a double summit about eight miles east of Steamboat. They were named for Smith C. Bartrum an early USFS employee and first supervisor of the Umpqua National Forest when it was formed in 1905.

Barview, Tillamook County. This community was named in 1884 by L. C. Smith. It is just north of the bar at the entrance to Tillamook Bay and affords a fine view of the bay, bar and ocean. The style Barview has been adopted by the USBGN and not Bar View.

Basche Ditch, Baker County. Basche Ditch near Keating was named for the Peter Basche family. Basche was an early settler whose family is still well known in Baker County.

Basey Canyon, Morrow County. Basey Canyon south of Heppner was named for Isaac Basey who settled there in the 1880s.

Bashaw Creek, Marion County. Bashaw Creek drains Ankeny Bottom in the extreme southwest part of the county and flows into the Willamette River. It was named for Joseph Bashaw who was born in France in 1820 and settled on the land October 1, 1851. The Land Office plat of this township indicates the spelling Bashan, but this is an error as the original application for the donation land claim is made out Bashaw.

Basin, Grant County. Butler Basin is a prominent expansion of the John Day Canyon just north of Picture Gorge and is notable for being the site of some of the most remarkable of the John Day fossil beds. A post office with the name Basin was established in this area on July 10, 1907, with William B. Bales postmaster. The office was closed out to Dayville in April, 1916. It was about seven miles south of Kimberly.

Baskett Slough, Polk County. This slough originates in the intermittent Boyle Lakes about two miles northwest of Rickreall. It flows eastward several miles and joins Mud Slough. It was named for George J. Baskett who was born in Kentucky in 1817 and who settled on a donation land claim near this slough in October, 1850. Baskett spelled his name with two "t's" as indicated and this style of name for this geographic feature has been officially adopted by the USBGN.

Bastendorff Beach, Coos County. Bastendorff Beach is on the west part of Coos Head, south of the entrance to Coos Bay. It bears the name of a local family. The spelling Bastendorff appears in signatures to deeds in the files of the Oregon State Highway Commission.

Bates, Grant County. This post office is in the east part of the county near Austin. It was named for Paul C. Bates, an insurance man of Portland. Bates was instrumental in negotiating the purchase of timber lands by the Oregon Lumber Company, and when that company began operations, it suggested the name of Bates for the post office. Paul C. Bates was born in Massachusetts in 1874 and came to Portland in 1896. He died in Portland February 4, 1943. For obituary, see the *Oregonian,* February 6, 1943. For biography, see Carey's *History of Oregon,* volume III, page 20.

Bates Butte, Deschutes County. Bates Butte is west of Deschutes River and north of Fall River. It received its name from George Bates, a homesteader who settled nearby.

Batterson, Tillamook County. The railroad station Batterson on Nehalem River about six miles east of Mohler bears the name of S. M. Batterson, a local landowner. See under the heading Anglersvale.

Battle Ax, Marion County. This mountain is in the eastern end of the county on the western slopes of the Cascade Range, and has an elevation of 5547 feet. There are two stories as to how it received its name. One is to the effect that it is sharp and has the appearance of a battle ax, while the other is that it was named by an old woodsman of the North Santiam Valley for a brand of chewing tobacco which was popular in the 1890s, and which he used liberally while exploring in the neighborhood of the mountain.

Battle Bar, Curry County. On April 27, 1856, there took place one of those indecisive skirmishes that characterized the Rogue River Indian War of 1855-56. This fight lasted all day. The Oregon volunteers were on the north side of Rogue River about a mile west of what is now the east boundary of Curry County. The Indians, men, women and children were on a bar on the south bank of the river, now called Battle Bar, in section 17, township 33 south, range 9 west. Neither side was able to cross the river so the combatants spent the time taking pot shots. See Walling's *History of Southern Oregon,* pages 266-68.

Battle Creek, Clatsop County. This stream is situated about six miles southeast of Astoria on the Tucker Creek road. J. B. Kilmore of Astoria informed the compiler that it was named because of a boundary dispute between two farmers.

Battle Creek, Douglas County. This tributary of Twelvemile Creek south of Camas Valley was named for one of the many skirmishes between settlers and Indians in the early days. The trouble was precipitated when local braves stole a horse belonging to Nancy Martindale, the daughter of a Camas Valley founder. The renegades were overtaken at this creek as they fled south towards Rogue River.

Battle Creek, Grant County. This stream flows into John Day River west of Dayville. J. E. Snow told the compiler that about 1870 two bands of Indians had a fight about two miles up this creek, near the canyon, hence the name.

Battle Creek, Jackson County. Battle Creek and Battle Mountain are in the northwest part of the county near the headwaters of Evans Creek. These features are named for the battle of Evans Creek, fought against Rogue River Indians in this locality August 24, 1853.

Battle Creek, Marion County. This stream heads on the east slopes of Prospect Hill about eight miles south of Salem and flows eastward to Mill Creek near Turner. Its name commemorates one of the few conflicts between settlers and Indians in the Willamette Valley. It was at a point near this stream that a party of Oregon Rangers engaged in a minor encounter with a band of eastern Oregon Indians in June, 1846, as a result of cattle depredations. Only one Indian was killed in the excitement, and peace was finally restored by gifts.

Battle Creek, Wallowa County. This small stream flows into Snake River in township 3 south, range 49 east, east of Lookout Mountain. It was named because of a squabble and fight between two old prospectors who were living near its mouth in the early 1880s. Each went up and down the river to tell his version of the row, and other prospectors soon had a name for the creek.

Battle Mountain, Umatilla County. Battle Mountain, about 25 miles south of Pilot Rock on the Pendleton-John Day Highway, was named for a fight of whites against Indians in 1878, said to have been the last of such battles in Oregon.

Battle Ridge, Crook and Wheeler counties. Battle Ridge is at the county line between Crook and Wheeler counties and just southwest of the headwaters of Beaverdam Creek. It is mostly in township 15 south, range 25 east, in Crook County. The ridge is said to have received its name as a result of the shooting of a large number of W. R. Mascall's sheep by cattlemen in the range wars in the 1890s.

Battle Rock, Curry County. This historic landmark is at the shore line of Port Orford and is a massive block of rock standing well above the water. In June, 1851, Captain William Tichenor, who was at that time in command of the steamer *Sea Gull* operating between the Columbia River and San Francisco, endeavored to establish a commercial enterprise at Port Orford. He engaged J. M. Kirkpatrick and a number of others to go to Port Orford where the party was landed and provisioned on what is now known as Battle Rock. The party was besieged by Indians and an actual battle was fought on June 10, 1851, at which time seventeen Indians were killed, mostly by fire from a small cannon. Kirkpatrick and his party finally succeeded in stealing away from the rock after several days' siege and made their way north along the coast until they reached settlements of the whites. When Captain Tichenor's representative returned by sea he found the contingent gone and assumed it had been murdered by the Indians. For an account of this battle see *Pioneer History of Coos and Curry Counties,* Chapter III, which consists of a statement by Captain Kirkpatrick.

Batts Meadow, Hood River County. This meadow near Blue Ridge on West Fork Hood River was named for Batt Senecal, an old time USFS ranger at Dufur. Senecal ran horses in the area.

Baty Butte, Clackamas County. Baty Butte is near the headwaters of a branch of Molalla River. It was named for Andrew Jackson Baty. He was a farmer who lived on Dickey Prairie, about five miles southeast of Molalla. He was a pioneer settler in this locality, and spent much of his time hunting in the Cascade Range. This mountain was named for him, probably by the USGS party which prepared the maps accompanying Professional Paper Number 9, *Forest Conditions in the Cascade Range Forest Reserve,* Washington, 1903. The mountain was at one time known as Whitespot.

Baxter Creek, Tillamook County. This stream was named for William T. Baxter, a pioneer of Oregon, who settled in Tillamook County about 1871. The stream is a tributary to Kilchis River.

Bay City, Tillamook County. For many years that part of Tillamook County around Bay City has been known as "down the bay," and when the county was first organized, the voting precinct for that section was called Bay Precinct. The town was established in 1888 and named by Winfield S. Cone. It is said that Cone came from Bay City, Michigan, and that he thus had a double reason for naming Bay City, Oregon, as he did. The post office at Bay City was established June 17, 1889, with Onslow Young first postmaster.

Bayocean, Tillamook County. This place was on the long neck of land lying between Tillamook Bay and Pacific Ocean. It was named in 1907 by the Potter-Chapin Realty Company of Portland, which established it as a summer resort, and named it because of its proximity to the two features mentioned. Bayocean post office was established in February 1909, by change of name from Barnegat. See under that heading.

Bays. The important bays and harbors of the Pacific Ocean in Oregon from north to south, are: Columbia River, Nehalem River, Tillamook Bay, Netarts Bay, Nestucca Bay, Siletz Bay, Yaquina Bay, Alsea Bay, Siuslaw

River, Umpqua River, Coos Bay, Coquille River, Port Orford and Chetco Cove. It is an interesting fact that while most of the capes and headlands of Oregon were discovered and named before Lewis and Clark arrived, few of the harbors had been seen by white men up to that time. On August 17, 1775, Captain Bruno Heceta anchored off the mouth of the Columbia River, the entrance to which he gave the name of *La Asuncion*, apparently because of the celebration of the *Asuncion de Nuestra Senora*, or the Assumption, on August 15. Although the currents led him to believe he was near a river, he did not make the entrance, and thus lost the honor of discovering the Columbia. He named the north cape of the entrance *Cabo San Roque* and the south *Cabo Frondoso*, now Point Adams. John Meares was the next explorer to make any important mention of Oregon bays and harbors. For details of Meares' voyage off the Oregon coast see the information under Cape Meares. Meares passed the mouth of the Columbia on July 6, 1788, and while he recognized the fact that he was off a bay, he failed to identify the place as the mouth of a river. By nightfall of the same day he discovered and named Quicksand Bay, and while he says that the bay had a sand bar closing its mouth, yet his other observations indicate without much doubt that he had found Tillamook Bay. During the same year Captain John Kendrick and Captain Robert Gray brought the first American fur trading enterprise to the north Pacific Coast in the *Columbia Rediviva* and the *Lady Washington*. Robert Haswell, second mate of the *Lady Washington*, kept a diary, but notwithstanding the latitudes and landmarks mentioned along the Oregon coast, it is impossible to trace the course of the vessel with accuracy. Bancroft, in his *History of the Northwest Coast*, volume I, page 188, indicates some of the difficulties in interpreting the writing. It is possible that Alsea Bay or Yaquina Bay was seen by the ship. On August 12, 1788, the *Lady Washington* anchored off Tillamook Bay. On August 14 the ship crossed the bar, and at first the Americans had no trouble with the natives but on August 16, the Indians made a murderous assault and killed a member of the crew. Two days later the ship got away, and in his diary Haswell makes the following observation: "Murderers Harbour, for so it was named, is I suppose the entrance of the river of the West it is by no means a safe place for aney but a very small vessel to enter the shoal at its entrance being so aucwardly situated the passage so narrow and the tide so strong it is scarce possible to avoid the dangers." Data on other bays in Oregon will be found under their respective headings.

Bayview, Lincoln County. Bayview is on the northeast part of Alsea Bay. The post office was established about 1901, and the name was chosen by Daniel M. Oakland, the first postmaster, because of the view of Alsea Bay that could be had from where the office then stood.

B. C. Creek, Wallowa County. This stream is near the south end of Wallowa Lake and drains B. C. Basin. It bears the initials of Breedan and Camp, who located some silver claims in the basin about 1905.

Beagle, Jackson County. Beagle was named for William Beagle, an early settler and one-time postmaster. The community is a few miles north of Upper Table Rock and west of Rogue River.

Beagle Creek, Union County. Beagle Creek near Medical Springs, bears the name of one Beagle who kept a little inn on the stream in 1864, on the pack trail between Columbia River and the Boise mines. Oliver H. P. Beagle came to Oregon in 1843 when he was eleven years old and had many stirring adventures, some of which are described in an article by Fred Lockley in the *Oregon Journal* for July 13, 1927. He operated a pack train in northeast Oregon in the 1860s and he and his wife lived there for a time. Beagle Creek was probably named for him.

Beal, Klamath County. This station on the Burlington Northern Inc., seven miles south of La Pine was named for Pearley Beal whose homestead was next to the station.

Beale Canyon, Umatilla County. Beale Canyon is about eight miles southeast of Nye in West Birch Creek drainage. Charles W. Beale settled there in 1886.

Beals Creek, Douglas County. This creek rises north of Beals Mountain and flows into South Umpqua River. Both features were named for Oliver N. Beals who was born in Crawford County, Indiana in 1839 and took up a land claim along the creek in 1868. Numerous maps use Beal but the form Beals is correct. The USBGN affirms this in *Decision List 6801*.

Bear Creek, Jackson County. This is an important tributary of Rogue River, draining the valley in which Medford and Ashland are situated. It was for some years known as Stuart Creek, but is now called by a name of little significance. Stuart Creek, and Camp Stuart, a pioneer military establishment, were named by then Captain George B. McClellan, for his brother officer Captain James Stuart, who died June 18, 1851, not far from the stream. Stuart was wounded the day before near Rogue River while leading a charge against a band of hostile Indians. For additional data, see under Camp Stuart. For story about the origin of the name Bear for this creek, see the *Oregonian*, November 9, 1913. Bear Creek flows through Medford, and that city was named for the middle ford of the stream.

Bear Creek, Wallowa County. This important tributary of Wallowa River heads in the Wallowa Mountains in township 3 south, range 43 east, and flows into the Wallowa just west of the town of Wallowa. The name, Bear Creek, for this stream has been adopted by the USBGN. The principal tributary of Bear Creek is Little Bear Creek, flowing in from the east. Pioneer settlers in the Wallowa Valley found many bears along this stream. The wild animals were very destructive of cattle.

Bear Creek, Wallowa County. This stream heads near the Oregon-Washington state line and flows southeast into Grande Ronde River in township 6 north, range 43 east. In 1931 J. H. Horner told the compiler that the stream was named by a sheepherder employed by Judge Chester F. Miller of Dayton, Washington, who ran into nine bears all at one time frolicking on its banks. This sounds like a record.

Bear Flat, Wallowa County. Bear Flat is about on the line between township 1 north, ranges 48 and 49 east, on the ridge between Horse and Pumpkin creeks. It was named because Ben Johnson and Waldo Chase killed several bears there, among them two grizzlies. Charles and Guy Horner built the first cabin and corrals on this flat, according to information from J. H. Horner in 1931.

Bear Gulch, Wallowa County. Bear Gulch is an important canyon in the east part of township 1 south, range 47 east, and empties into Little

Sheep Creek. It was named by George A. Wilson who had a remarkable experience with a bear in this gulch. Wilson's dogs chased a bear, and the excited animal jumped on a pack horse. This was too much for the patient nag, who bucked the bear off and then scattered the pack down the canyon. Wilson was a stock man with a place at the mouth of the gulch.

Bear Island, Benton County. This island in Willamette River, and Bear Chute just to the east, were named for Owen Bear, a nearby pioneer settler. The record of his donation land claim is in land office certificate 327.

Bear Paw Forest Camp, Wasco County. Tom Carter of the USFS told the compiler in 1969 that this forest camp on US 26 is so named because a skinned out bear paw was found nearby when the site was selected in the 1920s.

Beardsley Bar, Marion County. Beardsley Bar is on the east bank of Willamette River, about three miles northwest of Salem. It was named for W. W. Beardsley, who owned a farm near the bar.

Bearway Meadow, Wheeler County. In 1969 George W. Nelson who was raised in Mitchell told the compiler the curious origin of this name west of Waterman. During the 1860s a man called Berry Way robbed and killed a packer named Gallagher. Way escaped with a large quantity of gold and while he was later caught and hanged, the loot was never recovered. He said before his execution that it was hidden in a meadow marked by blazed trees west of where Waterman now stands. Nelson said that he was well acquainted with this meadow and the two trees and when he was a boy, it was still called Berry Way Meadow. The treasure has proven as elusive as the gold at Neahkahnie or the Bluebucket Mine. For more information on outlaws see Judith K. Kenny's article in Pendleton *East Oregonian*, September 3, 1959.

Beatty, Klamath County. Annie E. Taylor, postmaster at Beatty, reported in 1925 that this place was named for the Rev. J. L. Beatty, a missionary who lived in that section of the Klamath Indian Reservation. Beatty is on Sprague River, on the highway between Klamath Falls and Lakeview.

Beatys Butte, Harney County. This prominent butte is in the southwest part of the county, and Beatys Springs are nearby. These features were named during Colonel C. S. Drew's Owyhee Reconnoissance with the 1st Oregon Cavalry in 1864, and serve to perpetuate the memory of Sergeant A. M. Beaty, who is especially mentioned in Drew's report for the zealous performance of his duties. The USC&GS gives the elevation of this butte as 7916 feet.

Beaver, Tillamook County. It is not surprising that the name of the animal that exercised such influence in the history of the West should be attached to so many geographic features. There are three post offices in Oregon with Beaver as the dominant part of the name, and a score of creeks, mountains and buttes. The American beaver (*Castor canadensis* and its sub-species) occupied a wide field on this continent and existed in great numbers. Beavers are heavily built, and are covered with long, coarse hairs overlying the short, dense and silky underfur to which beaver skins owe their value. The abundance and high value of this fur had a great influence in the early exploration and development of North America. Beaver skins were the one ready product of the western world which the merchants elsewhere were eager to purchase, and as a consequence the competition in trapping was keen to the point where it caused international complications. Beaver skins passed as a standard of barter. Beavers belong to the rodent family, a group notable for low mental powers. Beavers are an exception to this rule, however. They have extraordinary intelligence, though probably not as great as sometimes stated. They apparently understand something about hydraulic operations and save themselves much labor by digging canals for floating and transporting sticks and branches needed for food. They live entirely on twigs and bark, and have a gnawing capacity that is startling. There appears to be no truth in the reports that they use their flat tails as trowels, and they do not transport mud thereon. This is done by means of their front paws. The beaver is considered to be a symbol of industry, and pioneers of Oregon were quick to associate this idea with the new commonwealth. The first money was known as "Beaver Money."

Beaver Creek, Clackamas County. The name of Beaver Creek community was first used for a school district in the early 1850s, and came from the name of the stream that flows into the Willamette River near New Era. Beaver Creek community is south of Oregon City and is a rather loosely defined area or district adjacent to the stream. In 1945 its commercial activity was centered at the Beaver Creek crossroads, elevation 528 feet, where the Beavercreek post office was in operation. The postal history of this area is complex. A post office named Beaver was established in December, 1868, with James K. Graham postmaster. The office was closed in September, 1871. Beaver post office was reestablished in March, 1882, with C. F. Vonderahe first postmaster, and operated until February, 1883. In 1945 the writer was told that this office was near the present locality of the Carus School. A post office called Mink was in service from February, 1886, until May, 1894. This office was about three miles southeast of the present Beaver Creek store, possibly on the Highland road. It was named by using an adaptation of the name of a local family, Moehnke, for Charles Moehnke was at one time postmaster of the office. The locality around the Mink post office was later served by an office called Shubel, which was operated from December 1897, until September, 1904, with Gustav A. Shubel postmaster. In the early 1890s a post office named Beaver Creek was established, although the writer does not know its exact location. The name was changed to Beavercreek, probably in 1896. This office was in operation well after the turn of the century, and during its later life it may have been at the Beaver Creek store. Joseph R. Hoff took over this store and petitioned for a post office. An office with the name Hoff was established in April, 1916, with Hoff postmaster. Later Hoff disposed of the store and the name of the office was changed to Beavercreek December 15, 1922, and that was the style used in 1945. There are streams called Beaver Creek in almost every county in the state. The beaver were very numerous through early days in Oregon, a fact that is attested by examination of the journals of the various fur hunters. For instance, on Sunday, April 22, 1827, Peter

Skene Ogden mentioned in his diary that McKay had taken 735 beaver and otter skins on two small streams discharging into Clammitte (Klamath) River in about three weeks. No wonder we have so many Beaver creeks, and so few beaver.

Beaver Hill, Coos County. For well over half a century Beaver Hill has been a well-known name in western Oregon because of its application to the Beaver Hill coal mine about 12 miles airline south of the city of Coos Bay. The mining community Beaver Hill had a railroad, but never had a post office with its own name. The place is shown with fidelity on the USGS atlas sheet of the Coos Bay area mapped in 1895-96, but there is nothing on the map to indicate that the name was used for a hill or other topographic feature. The name was obviously applied because the mine is or was on one of the upper tributaries of Beaver Slough which drains south into Coquille River. There is a good deal of interesting information about the mine in the Nineteenth Annual Report of the USGS, from the pen of Dr. J. S. Diller. In 1942-43 the Coos Bay area was remapped by the USGS and the locality of Beaver Hill mine is shown on the northeast part of the Bandon atlas sheet, but the topographic engineers report that little is left of the place, and the only thing to identify it is a bench mark in the east part of section 17, township 27 south, range 13 west. It is about two miles airline west of Coaledo. If the mine is ever reopened doubtless it will be in the news. Mrs. Mary M. Randleman of Coquille, authority on the history of that part of Oregon, calls attention to the fact that Preuss post office was established at the mining community of Beaver Hill, April 17, 1917, with Cora E. Holmes first of two postmasters. The office was discontinued February 15, 1924. Preuss post office was named for Rosa Preuss, a school teacher of the neighborhood. It is probable that the post office department would not accept the name Beaver Hill because of possible confusion with other post offices such as Beaverton, Beavercreek, *et al.*

Beaver Landing, Columbia County. Beaver Landing was the name of a short-lived post office established March 21, 1879, and discontinued on May 1 of the same year. Jacob S. Rinearson was the only postmaster and it may be assumed that the post office was somewhere near the Rinearson place northwest of Rainier. There has been a railway station in this locality called Rinearson and of course Rinearson Slough is well known. Beaver Landing was doubtless named because it provided an easy way of getting from the Columbia River up to the headwaters of Beaver Creek in the hills above the river.

Beaver Marsh, Klamath County. Beaver Marsh is a place on The Dalles-California Highway about six miles south of Chemult, prominent since the days of stagecoaches and freight wagons in central Oregon. The topographic feature bears a descriptive name. The community has never had a robust growth, as may be seen from its postal history. Beaver Marsh post office was established June 30, 1927, and was discontinued August 22, 1928. William Zumbrunn was the only postmaster. Miller Creek flows through the place.

Beaverton, Washington County. Beaverton received its name because of the existence nearby of a large body of beaverdam land. Soil of this character was sought for by pioneer settlers because of its productivity. The town was laid out in 1869 by George Betts, Joshua Welch, Charles Angel, W. P. Watson and others. Beaverton post office was established in March, 1872, with George W. Betts, first postmaster.

Beckley, Harney County. Beckley is in Catlow Valley, and in 1911 Charles D. Beckley started a general store where the post office was established in April, 1912. The community was named for Beckley.

Bedfield, Klamath County. Bedfield, a locality in the Poe Valley a few miles southeast of Olene, was named for Bedfield, near Framlingham, Suffolk, England. Edward Freuer came to Klamath County from the Bedfield in Suffolk in 1882 and engaged in the stock business. He named his new home in compliment to his former English home, and when a post office was established in March, 1892, Freuer was the postmaster and named the office, which was in his house at first. The post office was in operation until August, 1909. The Freuer place was also called the Seven-springs Ranch.

Bedrock Creek, Clackamas County. Ralph Lewis told the writer that he named this creek west of Bull Run Lake about 1906 because of the smooth, exposed bedrock on its flat bottom. He added that the creek he named was nearer Thunder Rock but later mapmakers affixed the name permanently to the stream north of Blazed Alder Butte.

Beech Creek, Grant County. This post office is about ten miles north of Mount Vernon. B. C. Trobridge of John Day, who settled in the John Day Valley July 19, 1862, wrote the compiler that Beech Creek was named for a pioneer settler who lived near the mouth of the stream. The post office was established January 26, 1900, by James T. Berry, and it seemed appropriate to name it after Beech Creek because it was near the headwaters of that stream.

Beeler Ridge, Wallowa County. This ridge is just west of Imnaha River. It was named for Jake Beeler, of Joseph, a freighter.

Beerman Creek, Clatsop County. Beerman Creek flows into Necanicum River south of Seaside. It was named for Fred Beerman, who took up a donation land claim in the vicinity.

Beetle Spring, Crook County. A story in the Prineville *Central Oregonian,* September 11, 1969, attributed to Fred Houston, says that the USFS established a beetle control camp at this spring in the early 1930s.

Beetles Rest Spring, Klamath County. This is the well-known spring at Klamath Agency. The stream formed by this spring is quite short. The Klamath Indian name for the stream was *Tgulutcham Kshuteleh.* The first part of the name is descriptive of a small beetle with a green or purple shell. The second part of the name indicates to "live underneath or live below," indicating that the beetles lived in this particular locality. The stream flows into Crooked Creek.

Belknap Crater, Deschutes and Linn counties. This is one of the important features of the Cascade Range, and lies just north of McKenzie Pass. The crater and its enormous lava fields are easily seen from the McKenzie Highway and produce a spectacle that is awe inspiring to say the least. The crater has an elevation of 6877 feet. It was named for J. H. Belknap, an early resident along the McKenzie River, and a son of R. S. Belknap who developed Belknap Springs. J. H. Belknap was interested in the toll road that was built over McKenzie Pass in the early 1870s.

Belknap Springs, Lane County. R. S. Belknap located these springs in November, 1869, and conceived a plan for developing them. They now bear his name. Salt Springs post office was established October 26, 1874, with Belknap postmaster. The name of the office was changed to Belknaps Springs June 15, 1875. About 1891 the name was changed to Belknap Springs.

Bell Canyon, Morrow County. This canyon north of Willow Creek and east of Lexington was named for Frank E. Bell who took up land near its head in 1889.

Bellamy, Lincoln County. Information about Bellamy post office is unsatisfactory, but the following data are the best that the compiler can lay hands on. Bellamy office was established May 24, 1898, with Ola A. Tveitmoe first postmaster. The office was four or five miles north of Toledo on the road to Siletz and the postal facilities were intended for a small colony of Scandinavians living in the vicinity. It was closed to Toledo on June 15, 1899. The compiler has had no success in getting the reason for the selection of the name for this office. It may have been intended to compliment a local resident or even someone living at a distance.

Belle, Lane County. Belle post office was established at the main forks of Indian Creek in western Lane County on August 25, 1906, with Daisy Belle Wilkinson first and only postmaster. The office was closed August 31, 1908. Belle post office of 1906 was in the same locality as Hermann post office when that office was first established in 1889. In January 1947, Smith L. Taylor of McKenzie Bridge, formerly a resident of western Lane County, informed the compiler that Belle post office was named with the postmaster's middle name.

Belle Passi, Marion County. This is one of Oregon's ghost towns, situated about a mile south of Woodburn. The name came before the public in February, 1942, as the result of the erection of an historical marker by members of Belle Passi chapter of the Daughters of the American Revolution of Woodburn. The marker is on the Pacific Highway East, and commemorates the establishment of a pioneer community that eventually succumbed probably because of the development of Woodburn, which had the advantage of railroad service. The Rev. Neill Johnson located at the place about 1851. He was a member of the Cumberland Presbyterian denomination, and he soon built a church and later a school. In 1857 a contract was let to carry mail by stage from Portland to Sacramento, and this furnished an opportunity for a post office. Johnson suggested the name Groveland for a place in Illinois, but authorities objected because the name was too common. The Oregon Historical Society has a letter written by John L. Johnson, son of Neill Johnson, in which it is said that Johnson then recommended a name he had found, possibly in Humboldt's *Cosmos*, describing a place in Italy. J. L. Johnson gives this as Bell Passi, meaning good pass or beautiful place. Now the place in Italy, which is on the island of Sicily, is Belpasso. The post office in Marion County was officially Belpassi. The younger Johnson calls it Bell Passi and the marker uses the spelling Belle Passi. This selection of styles seems reasonably ample. Postal authorities inform the compiler that the post office at Belpassi was established on June 15, 1860. The name was changed to Gervais on November 6, 1871.

Belle Vue Point, Multnomah County. This point is on the east shore of Sauvie Island and the west bank of Columbia River, just north of the mouth of Willamette River. The name Belle Vue Point was adopted for this feature by USBGN on February 7, 1934. Belle Vue Point was named by Lt. W. R. Broughton, R. N., of the Vancouver expedition, on October 29, 1792. It seems certain that at that time the arrangement of islands and channels at the mouth of Willamette River differed from the condition that now exists. About 1930 Mr. J. Neilson Barry of Portland made an extensive study of the problem and it was his conclusion that the locality that now bears the name Belle Vue Point was the proper place. Federal agencies accepted his recommendations.

Bellevue, Yamhill County. This community is on the Salmon River Highway about nine miles southwest of McMinnville. The name is descriptive but the compiler does not know who applied it. The place is on the Hathaway Yocum donation land claim. Yocum came to Oregon in 1851 from Illinois. Records at the Oregon Historical Society indicate that Bellevue was settled about 1860. Muddy post office was established in this locality in May, 1855, with George Davis postmaster. It may have been on Muddy Creek a little northeast of Bellevue. The name was changed to Bellevue in April, 1869. The records do not indicate exactly where pioneer post offices were situated and frequently they were moved around to fit the convenience of the postmasters.

Bellfountain, Benton County. H. L. Mack, county clerk of Benton County, informed the compiler in December, 1926, that he lived in Bellfountain for thirteen years and there was no question in his mind but that it was named for a town of the same name in Ohio by local residents who had previously lived in the Ohio town. In Ohio the name is spelled Bellefontaine. A post office called Dusty was established in this locality December 6, 1895, with Helen Elgin first postmaster. The name of the office was not satisfactory, for obvious reasons. Postal records are not entirely clear, but it seems apparent that the name of the office was changed to Bellfountain July 31, 1902. The office was closed in January, 1905.

Belmont, Douglas County. Belmont post office was named with the middle name of Durward Belmont Hunt, the first and only postmaster. The office was established July 5, 1913, and was discontinued August 15, 1914. Durward B. Hunt, then living at Redmond, wrote on February 28, 1947, substantially as follows: "Belmont post office was situated in section 31, township 24 south, range 3 west, on the Nathaniel H. Rone homestead, thirteen miles east of Oakland. As far as I know the name Durward Belmont originated in the novel *Lena Rivers,* written by Mary J. Holmes."

Beltz Dike, Tillamook County. F. A. Beltz, a lumberman and former county judge, built this dike in the 1930s to drain his ranch bordering Sand Lake.

Ben Jones Bridge, Lincoln County. This concrete structure carries the Oregon Coast Highway over Rocky Creek north of Newport. It is named for the late Ben F. Jones, who is considered to be the father of the plan to build the coast highway. The span was dedicated to Jones' memory on September 17, 1927. For account of dedication and picture, see the *Oregonian,* September 18, 1927, section I, page 1.

Bend, Deschutes County. This city derived its name from Farewell Bend, a point on the Deschutes River, which received its descriptive name because it was at this place travelers over the pioneer roads had their last view of the river. For a considerable distance Deschutes River occupies a canyon in central Oregon, and there are comparatively few places where it would have been easy in pioneer days to get a wagon down to the water's edge and ford the stream. The most accessible of these places, and the point where a canyon was not in evidence was at a pronounced double bend in the river where the city of Bend is now situated. It afforded a good place to camp in pleasant surroundings. It is certain that it was thus used in the days of the emigrations, but just how early cannot now be determined. It was also used when the road was opened over McKenzie Pass. The place began to be known as Farewell Bend, and the name was appropriate irrespective of the destination of the traveler, north, south, east or west. This origin of the name has been objected to on the ground that emigrant travelers would not say farewell when they meant goodbye, for farewell meant a place where the fare was good. Nevertheless the compiler is of the opinion that farewell in the sense of goodbye was not an uncommon use of the word, and meant that the emigrants were sorry to leave the pleasant spot. Bend was platted by Pilot Butte Development Company, and the plat was filed for record on June 7, 1904. The history of Bend post office is a little complex, and is given under the heading Deschutes in this volume. See also under Pilot Butte. In November, 1927, Captain O. C. Applegate of Klamath Falls informed the compiler that the Warm Springs Indian name for the ford where the city of Bend is now situated was *Wychick.* Captain Applegate was unable to secure a translation of the word.

Bend Glacier, Deschutes County. This glacier lies on the north slope of Broken Top. It was named in 1924 by Professor Edwin T. Hodge of the University of Oregon in honor of the city of Bend.

Bendire Creek, Malheur County. Bendire Creek and Bendire Mountain are in the north end of the county and were named for Captain and Brevet Major Charles Bendire, U.S.A. Major Bendire was a noted ornithologist and pursued the study of bird life in many parts of the Pacific Northwest. After retirement from the army he was honorary curator of the department of Oology of the National Museum at Washington. He was the author of *Life Histories of North American Birds,* published in special bulletins of the Smithsonian Institution in 1892 and 1895.

Beneke Creek, Clatsop County. Beneke Creek flows into Fishhawk Creek from the north at Jewell. The name has been spelled in various styles, but recent government maps use the form Beneke. The name is that of a family of early settlers and the spelling Beneke is furnished by county authorities.

Benham Falls, Deschutes County. These falls were named for J. R. Benham, who filed on land nearby about 1885. The government rejected his filing. Benham was born in Oregon, and settled in Prineville in 1876.

He moved to what is now Deschutes County in 1879. The falls were named for Benham by a Mr. Hutchinson, who was at the time promoting central Oregon irrigation enterprises.

Benjamin Spring, Wallowa County. This is a spring on the Summit Trail about a half mile north of Lookout Mountain in township 3 south, range 49 east. The spring was named for Benjamin Marks, a pioneer settler, who died in 1913. The name has been approved by decision of the USBGN.

Bennett Butte, Coos County. This butte, elevation 2185 feet, is in Coos County near the northeast corner of Curry County. It is a well-known point about 10 miles east of the Pacific Ocean. In November, 1943, Mrs. Mary M. Randleman of Coquille wrote the compiler that the mountain was probably named during the Coos County gold rush. Two prospectors, Hudson and Bennett, operated in the locality and the butte was apparently named for Bennett. The butte was a meeting place for Indians, as it was on the dividing line between tribal hunting grounds. Mrs. Randleman was also authority for the statement that Bennett Prairie, near the mouth of Johnson Creek, was named for the same miner.

Bennett Creek, Lane County. This creek is tributary from the west to Coast Fork Willamette River. It originates in the hills north of Cottage Grove and flows into the Coast Fork just north of McFarland Butte. It was named for Scott Bennett, a landowner near its banks.

Bennett Pass, Hood River County. This pass is the highest point on the Mount Hood Loop Highway, and has an elevation of 4673 feet. It lies about six miles southeast of Mount Hood on the ridge dividing the drainage of Hood River from White River. It is not on the main summit of the Cascade Range. The pass was named for one Samuel Bennett, a Wasco County stockman.

Bennett Rock, Douglas County. Combs in *God Made A Valley,* page 59, says this peak north of Camas Valley was named for J. W. Bennett, a solitary resident with an unexplained and unending supply of gold dust.

Benson Glacier, Union and Wallowa counties. Benson Glacier is an ice field on the northeast and east sides of Eagle Cap in the Wallowa Mountains. It is impossible to determine from existing knowledge just what county it is in. It was named about 1914 by a party of climbers and the name was suggested by Clyde B. Aitchison in compliment to Governor Benson. Frank W. Benson was born at San Jose, California, March 20, 1858. He came to Oregon with his parents in 1864 and except for a short time lived most of his life in Douglas County. He taught school, and was county clerk from 1892 to 1896. He served as secretary of state for Oregon from January 15, 1907, until his death on April 14, 1911. During that time he was governor from March 2, 1909, to June 17, 1910. He was a citizen of high character, and was greatly esteemed.

Benson Plateau, Multnomah County. This high ground east of Eagle Creek and Benson State Park near Multnomah Falls both honor Simon Benson, pioneer lumberman and philanthropist. Benson was born in Norway October 8, 1852, and came to Oregon in 1878 after an interlude in Wisconsin. For the ensuing thirty years he pursued the lumber business with diligence and perseverance and amassed a considerable fortune. In 1910 he sold his timber interests and devoted his time to business and philanthropic affairs. He was an early member of the State Highway Commission and a strong advocate of good roads. He purchased the property that includes Benson State Park and donated it to the city of Portland who later conveyed it to the OSHD and the USFS. His other benefactions included the well-known bronze drinking fountains in Portland and $100,000 to School District #1 which was used to start Benson Polytechnic School. Benson died in Beverly Hills, California on August 5, 1942. For further information and comment see the *Oregon Journal* of the same date.

Benton County. Benton County, which is in the west part of the Willamette Valley, was created December 23, 1847, by the provisional legislature (*General and Special Laws of* 1843-9, page 50). It was named in honor of Thomas Hart Benton, who was born in North Carolina on March 14, 1782, and died in Washington, D.C., April 10, 1858. For 30 years he was a member of the United States Senate from Missouri, and one of the great events of his active life was his espousal, with his colleague, Senator Lewis F. Linn, of the extension of the control of the United States into the Oregon country. For an excellent short biography of Senator Benton, see the *Encyclopedia Britannica*. See also Scott's *History of the Oregon Country*. Benton County has an area according to the U. S. Bureau of the Census of 647 square miles, and an excellent map of the county is published in the Benton County Soil Survey by the U. S. Bureau of Soils of the Department of Agriculture.

Berdugo, Harney County. Berdugo post office was situated in the Catlow Valley near the Roaring Springs Ranch and was named for Joaquin "Chino" Berdugo, one of Peter French's early vaqueros. The post office was established August 17, 1915, with Rita M. Kiphart first and only postmaster. The office was closed September 29, 1927, with papers to Blitzen.

Berkley, Lane County. Berkley post office was established March 1, 1907, with David B. Allison first and only postmaster. The office was closed December 31, 1908, but the record fails to show what other office fell heir to the business. Berkley post office was situated a little northnortheast of the present location of Noti. The place was named with the second name of the postmaster, David Berkley Allison.

Berkley, Umatilla County. Berkley post office was named for a small community in Boone County, Iowa. The Umatilla County office was in the farm home of Thomas Coleman Gettings, who, with his family, came from Iowa to Umatilla County in 1902. Berkley post office was established July 1903, and operated until February 28, 1905. It was in section 20, of township 4 north, range 37 east, about ten miles east of Weston.

Berlin, Linn County. Berlin is a community near Hamilton Creek, about seven miles southeast of Lebanon. In the early days of the county the Bellingers, Burrells and other pioneer families living in the vicinity were admirers of fine racing stock. The annual fair at Albany did not seem to satisfy their sporting spirit, so they began to hold their own races near the residence of Mr. Burrell. Burrell entertained all comers with true western hospitality. Finally the attendance was so large that he was forced to make a charge for meals and his home was referred to as Burrell's Inn. When the post office was established it was decided to name the place Burl Inn. This was cumbersome and the consolidation, Berlin, was adopted. Early in October, 1944, residents of Berlin were astonished to learn that arrangements had been made to change the name of their community to Distomo for the place in Greece so horribly treated by the Germans. This change in name, to be accompanied by a blast of nation-wide radio and other publicity, was said to be in the interest of democracy, but the promoters of the plan were not sufficiently interested in practical democracy to ask the local residents for their views about the business. These local citizens promptly organized a democratic revolt and the scheme was abandoned. A project to change all the names in this country so as to eliminate those commemorating places and people of nations with which the United States had at one time or another been at war would have surprising results.

Berry, Marion County. Berry was a station on North Santiam River a few miles southwest of Detroit. It was named for a family of early settlers on the river. Berry post office was established June 8, 1893, with Ira S. Hatfield first of four postmasters. The office was closed January 13, 1906.

Berry Creek, Benton and Polk counties. This creek flows through the donation land claim of Thomas W. Berry, and it was named for him. The record of his claim is in land office certificate 2323. Berry Creek is southeast of Airlie.

Berry Creek, Marion County. This stream was named for Press Berry, an early resident in the North Santiam Valley. Berry Creek flows into North Santiam River southwest of Detroit.

Bertha, Multnomah County. This was the name of a railroad station on the Southern Pacific West Side branch southwest of Portland where the line entered the Tualatin Valley. It was named for Mrs. Bertha Koehler of Portland, wife of Richard Koehler, for many years manager of the Southern Pacific Lines in Oregon and their predecessors. The early name of the community and later the post office was Hillsdale, but the railroad was unwilling to adopt that name for the station on account of possible confusion with Hillsboro on the same line. See editorial page of Portland *Telegram,* January 18, 1926. This section of track has been abandoned and Bertha station is a thing of the past. Mrs. Koehler died in Portland November 20, 1943. For many years after the West Side railroad was built, the station on the watershed between the Willamette and Tualatin drainage was called Summit, but there were several other places in Oregon known as Summit, and this fact led railroad authorities to change the name. The change from Summit to Bertha took place about 1890.

Bessie Butte, Deschutes County. Bessie Butte, 4768 feet high, is ten miles south of Bend east of Lava Butte. It was named for Bessie Wilkinson, the second telephone operator in Bend, who in common with numerous other local residents applied for a homestead near the city.

Besters Ford, Tillamook County. About 1880 Stephen D. Bester took up land on Wilson River about five miles east of Tillamook and for many years the Bester family made the place its home. A ford was developed for the use of settlers further up the stream and later when a wagon road was

built the Besters kept the toll gate. An interesting account of these matters
is contained in a letter by Frank D. Bester printed on the editorial page of
the *Oregonian*, April 8, 1945. As a youth, Frank Bester, son of Stephen,
operated a boat at the ford and accommodated the travel. This ford was a
mile downstream from the new Wilson River Highway bridge over Wilson
River.

Bethany, Marion County. Bethany is a community about two miles
west of Silverton on the road west to Chemawa. The locality was named in
pioneer days, possibly as early as April, 1851, when Bethany Christian
Church was organized. However, Silverton outgrew Bethany. Bethany
School serves to keep the name alive. For a history of the locality and of a
proposed college, see Salem *Statesman*, October 30, 1931. See also Down's
History of the Silverton Country. Efforts made by members of the Christian
Church to establish a college or institution at Bethany failed for lack of
funds. The churches continued their interest in the project and it is possi-
ble that the development of Bethel Institute at Bethel in Polk County was a
result of the earlier effort. Bethany is a Hebrew word meaning "House of
Poverty" and the name was applied to a place in Palestine not far from
Jerusalem. The word has been used as a placename in many parts of the
United States, frequently as part of some church activity.

Bethany, Washington County. The name Bethany is applied to a crossroads trading center about four miles northwest of Cedar Mill, but in earlier days Bethany was at the crossroads about two miles northeast of the
present community of that name. Ulrich Gerber came to Oregon from
Switzerland in the middle 1870s and settled on North Plains in the south
part of section 17, township 1 north, range 1 west. He was instrumental in
getting Bethany post office established in July, 1878, at a point about a mile
east of the present Bethany School. He suggested the name and was the
first postmaster. The office was later moved to the crossroads on the west
line of section 19. Bethany post office was discontinued in 1904 but the
name for the community is still in use. A Presbyterian church stands at the
northwest corner of the original Bethany crossroads of Ulrich Gerber. The
Bethany Baptist Church is about a mile south of these crossroads.

Bethel, Polk County. All that remains of this community is a school,
situated at the base of the Eola Hills about a mile east of McCoy. Bethel is in
a little vale called Plum Valley, and the locality was named in 1846 by the
Rev. Glen O. Burnett for Bethel Church in Missouri where he had served
as pastor. John E. Smith's booklet *Bethel*, published by the author in 1941,
gives an account of this and subsequent events. Dr. Nathaniel Hudson
settled nearby in 1851 and in 1852 opened Bethel Academy, a private
undertaking. Bethel Academy was short lived. In 1854 Dr. Hudson moved
to a new claim west of Dallas. In 1855 G. O. Burnett and Amos Harvey
organized a new school called Bethel Institute. A building was erected and
the institute opened in October of that year. In January, 1856, the legislature officially chartered the school with the name Bethel Institute and it
operated with that name until October, 1860, when the legislature granted
a new charter with the name Bethel College. The college failed financially
in 1861, and efforts to turn it over to the Christian Church were unsuccessful. See under Monmouth. Bethel Institute and Bethel College seem to

have been community affairs and while the Christian Church gave moral
support, it does not appear that the church actually furnished funds.
Bethel is a Hebrew word meaning "House of God." The name was applied
to a holy city of Palestine originally known as Luz.

Bethel School, Marion County. Bethel School is on the south side of
the penitentiary road about six miles east of the business section of Salem.
In early days Dan Early operated a sawmill in this locality, cutting some of
the fine timber that grew there. Soon after the mill was torn down a group
of Dunkards settled in the place and built a church on the site of the mill.
This they called the Bethel Church. The Dunkards lived a quiet life there
for some years but the group gradually dwindled to the point where the
church could no longer be maintained. The building was sold to the newly
formed Bethel school district, made up from parts of other districts. The
old building was used until about 1925, when a new school was built. There
is more information about the name and place in a short neighborhood
story by Mrs. J. R. Carruthers in the Salem *Statesman,* October 1, 1931.

Betzen, Lane County. Betzen station on the Southern Pacific between
Mapleton and Cushman was named for Betty Zentner, daughter of one of
the engineers on the construction of the railroad.

Beulah, Malheur County. Beulah was named for Beulah Arnold,
daughter of the first postmaster. She was later Mrs. Roy S. Rutherford.
Beulah post office was established December 16, 1884, with Thomas L.
Arnold first postmaster. The use of Miss Arnold's name is said to have been
suggested by a family friend, J. C. Roberts, an early stockman of the Harney Valley.

Beverly Beach, Lincoln County. Beverly Beach is a small community
north of Yaquina Head and Beverly Beach State Park adjoins it on the
north. In 1981 Florence May Christy sent the compiler the following statement giving the origin of the name. "During the early nineteen thirties my
husband, Curtis F. Christy, and I owned the property which is now known
as Beverly Beach, Lincoln County, Oregon. Our goal was to establish a
small seaside community on this property. In choosing a name for this site
my daughter Florence Daneene Christy Pearson, who at that time was a
small child, was asked what she would like to call the community. Her favorite doll at that time was named Beverly, and her choice of that name established the location as Beverly Beach, which it has remained to this day."

Bewley Creek, Tillamook County. This branch of Tillamook River carries the name of J. C. Bewley, an early settler and one time deputy U. S.
Marshal.

Bible Creek, Tillamook and Yamhill counties. A. S. Bible was born in
Tennessee March 16, 1834. He established a store in Sheridan in 1879 and
was also a merchant in Willamina. He retired from these activities in 1898.
See *Portrait and Biographical Record of the Willamette Valley,* page 570. He
operated a ranch near the Tillamook-Yamhill line north of Willamina and
the names Bible Ranch and Bible Creek resulted from this activity. The
stream flows into Nestucca River.

Biddle Pass, Jefferson County. Biddle Pass, elevation about 5450 feet,
is due east of Mount Jefferson. East of the pass the ground rises sharply to
the southeast to form Bald Peter, a well-known landmark on the Warm

Springs Indian Reservation. In 1920, Henry J. Biddle of Portland and Vancouver, who was an enthusiastic sportsman and naturalist, decided to investigate the feasibility of building a trail around the east base of Mount Jefferson. He made up a small party, including himself, Charles C. Giebeler of Detroit, the compiler of these notes and three amiable packhorses. As the result of two weeks in the field, enlivened by minor misadventures, excessively rough lava fields, fallen timber, boulders and yellowjackets, Mr. Biddle concluded that the territory was not suitable for the type of construction he had in mind. The party camped at the south end of the pass on the night of August 14, 1920, and went through the pass next day. At that time there was no evidence that a white man had been there before. Mr. Biddle died September 27, 1928, and the compiler suggested to the USBGN that the pass should be named in his honor, which was done on March 6, 1929.

Big Butte, Jackson County. Big Butte post office took its name from Big Butte Creek. The post office was established May 9, 1878 with George W. King first postmaster. Henry H. Pope was appointed postmaster July 11, 1882, and John A. Obenchain on October 6, 1888. The office was closed to Brownsboro on March 31, 1908. It is reported to the compiler that Big Butte post office was moved several times, though it was generally in the neighborhood of township 35 south, range 2 east.

Big Butte Creek, Jackson County. Mount McLoughlin was known by the early settlers in the Rogue River Valley as Snowy Butte. Big Butte Creek had its rise near Snowy Butte and was so named on that account. It flows into Rogue River. A smaller stream rising in the same vicinity was christened Little Butte Creek. The name Butte Creek when applied to Big Butte Creek is incorrect.

Big Canyon, Wallowa County. This canyon carries Deer Creek which flows into Wallowa River just east of Minam. It has been shown with various names on older maps, including Bear Creek, Deep Canyon Creek, Little Minam Creek and Sheep Creek. The USBGN once named this Big Canyon Creek but changed to Big Canyon and Deer Creek in *Decision List 6601*.

Big Creek, Clatsop County. Big Creek has been known by that name for many years, and yet at one time it must have had another name. Old maps show it as Tillasana Creek, changed later to Tilly Ann Creek and even Tilly Jane Creek. The writer has been unable to determine where these older names originated. H. S. Lyman in *OHQ*, volume I, number 4, says that the Indian name for the locality near Knappa was *Tle-las-qua*, which may have been the same as *Tillasana*.

Big Eddy, Wasco County. Big Eddy was at the western end of the obstructions in the Columbia River at The Dalles. It was at this point that travelers and freight began the portage around these obstructions. As far as the writer can determine the name was not used in the days of exploration but probably came into use at the time of gold discoveries in eastern Oregon just after 1860.

Big Hole, Lake County. Big Hole is a sunken spot in the northwest part of the county, with an area of about a quarter of a square mile. It is roughly circular, and its bottom is about three hundred feet below the surrounding land level. The name well describes it. Big Hole Butte lies just to the northeast.

Big Meadows, Curry County. This descriptive name for an area in the northeast part of Curry County has been in use since the days of the Rogue River Indian War of 1855-56. Big Meadows are near the southeast corner of township 32 south, range 10 west, about two miles airline north of Rogue River. Fort Lamerick was established in this locality May 1, 1865. According to L. J. Cooper, USFS ranger at Galice, this stockade was near the quarter-corner between sections 1 and 2, township 33 south, range 10 west. The Big Meadows referred to above are not the same as Big Meadows at the Big Bend of Rogue River near Illahe, where there was a sharp engagement with the Indians at the end of May, 1856.

Big Noise Creek, Clatsop County. This stream is about 20 miles east of Astoria. It was named in early days because of the fact that there was a sluice gate near its mouth used to control the water for floating logs. This sluice gate made an excessive noise and the stream was named on that account.

Big Prairie, Lane County. Big Prairie post office was probably the first post office in the upper valley of Middle Fork Willamette River. This office was established July 14, 1873, with Addison Black first postmaster. The office operated until December 10, 1879, with one intermission. The name was descriptive of the locality. Old maps show Big Prairie at or near the present locality of Westfir. The modern name for the plateau northeast of Westfir is High Prairie, and that was probably the reason for the name of the post office. The compiler does not know if the post office Big Prairie was near the Middle Fork or up on the plateau.

Big Rayborn Canyon, Umatilla County. Big and Little Rayborn canyons were both named for William Rayborn who in 1903 bought land on the north slope of Weston Mountain.

Biggs, Sherman County. Biggs is a station on the Union Pacific Railroad main line at what was the junction with the now abandoned branch south into Sherman County. It was named for a nearby landowner, W. H. Biggs, who was born in Belmont County, Ohio, May 12, 1831 and who came to Sherman County in 1880. The small local community is known as Biggs Junction because this is where US 97, running north and south, makes an important intersection with I84.

Biggs Cove, Tillamook County. Biggs Cove is in Tillamook Bay just northeast of the town of Cape Meares. It was named for John A. Biggs who came from Kansas and settled in Tillamook County about 1885. Biggs was a son-in-law of Webley Hauxhurst who came to Oregon with Ewing Young in 1834.

Billy Meadows, Wallowa County. These meadows are about 25 miles northeast of Enterprise. They were named in the 1880s for William Smith, better known as Billy. He was a pioneer sheepherder employed by R. Frank Stubblefield and is said to have been a native of England.

Bilyeu Creek, Linn County. This stream rises on the northwest slope of Snow Peak and flows northwestward into Thomas Creek. It bears the name of the Bilyeu family, members of which have lived on its banks since 1852. The stream is sometimes called Neal Creek, but that is not the name originally applied.

Bingen Gap, Hood River County. This is the geologic name for the cut four miles long and 2000 feet deep that the Columbia River has made through the Bingen anticline. Both the gap and the anticline were named for Bingen, Washington, situated in the gap on the north bank. The town in turn was named for the famous German city Bingen on the Rhine.

Binger, Douglas County. The place once called Binger was in the upper Cow Creek Valley, near The Meadows and also near the place later called Anchor. Binger post office was established July 16, 1894, with Isaac N. French postmaster. The office was closed September 20, 1902, and mail was sent to Galesville. Binger Hermann was representative in Congress from the first Oregon district when the office was established and it may be assumed that it was named in compliment to him.

Bingham Creek, Douglas County. Bingham Creek is tributary to Middle Fork Coquille River south of Camas Valley. It was named for Samuel Bingham who homesteaded nearby in 1876.

Bingham Lake, Klamath County. Bingham Lake is south of Crescent Lake. It was named for Cy J. Bingham, for many years connected with the USFS and later sheriff of Grant County.

Bingham Mountain, Coos County. This mountain which has an elevation of 2287 feet, is in the valley of South Fork Coquille River. It was named for Isaac Bingham, a pioneer settler, and a conspicuous figure in the Indian fighting near Port Orford.

Bingham Springs, Umatilla County. Bingham Springs are in the east part of the county, on Umatilla River, eight miles east of Gibbon, and well up in the Blue Mountains. The springs have had a number of names. In earlier days the style Warm Springs was generally used for the place and a man named Tip Parrent is said to have owned or operated them. The 30 by 50 foot main building was built about 1864 of square hewn tamarack logs, but whether this work was done by Parrent or others is not known. Early in the 1880s Parrent sold the establishment to John B. Purdy who added the kitchen and dining wing, and secured a post office called Purdy on June 9, 1881, with William Parrent postmaster. This sounds as if Tip Parrent and William Parrent were the same man. Purdy became postmaster August 7, 1882, and ran the office until September 17, 1891, when it was closed. During Purdy's ownership, the place was known as Purdy Springs. The place was for a time a station on the Thomas and Ruckel stage line through the Blue Mountains, and there was a toll gate at the stage house. About 1892 Dr. John E. Bingham of Walla Walla bought the springs and changed the name to Bingham Springs. A number of improvements were made and the place served as a popular resort for Portland, Pendleton and Walla Walla people. The writer of these lines spent many happy days there swimming in the pool, fishing in the Umatilla River and setting up pins in the bowling alley for guests who were willing to spend small sums for the service. The Union Pacific Railroad changed the name of Gibbon station to Bingham Springs, but the post office at Gibbon, which served the springs, continued with the name Gibbon. After the turn of the century the springs were called Wenaha Springs, probably for the Wenaha River in the Blue Mountains, but the name Bingham Springs has been restored and is in use at this writing. Many years ago the railroad changed the name of its station from Bingham Springs back to Gibbon.

Birch Gulch, Wallowa County. Birch Gulch drains into Snake River in township 4 north, range 49 east. The place is named for the birch trees that grow there. These trees are probably the red birch, sometimes called the water birch, *Betula fontinalis.*

Bird Butte, Clackamas and Wasco counties. This butte is in the Cascade Range, north of Frog Lake. It was named for George Bird, a forest ranger, who bled to death nearby as the result of an accident.

Birdseye Creek, Jackson County. This stream flows into Rogue River two miles south of the town of Rogue River. It was named for David Birdseye, a pioneer settler near its mouth.

Birkenfeld, Columbia County. Anton Birkenfeld, a native of Germany, settled in the Nehalem Valley in 1886 and founded the community of Birkenfeld about 1910. The place was named for him.

Bishop Creek, Columbia County. This stream, tributary to Tide Creek from the southwest, is sometimes shown on maps as Bashop Creek. In 1943, Wales Wood of Saint Helens wrote that the correct spelling was Bishop. Wood got his information from James Anlicker of Goble, member of a pioneer family of Columbia County, who was conversant with the matter.

Bishop Meadows, Wallowa County. These meadows are in township 3 north, range 42 east, and were named for Oliver N. Bishop who settled in the middle Wallowa Valley in the 1880s. He wintered stock on the meadows, as there was a good crop of wild hay there.

Bissell, Clackamas County. In 1927 it was reported by old residents that this town was named for W. S. Bissell who was postmaster general of the United States from 1893 to 1895. Wilson Shannon Bissell was born in New London, New York, in 1847, and when appointed to the cabinet was a practicing lawyer at Buffalo where he was a partner of Grover Cleveland. During his incumbency as postmaster general a number of improvements were made in the postal service, including a cut in transcontinental mail time, and the turning over to the Bureau of Engraving and Printing the work of printing postage stamps, previously done by private agencies. In 1902 he was made chancellor of the University of Buffalo, and died in 1903.

Bitter Lick, Jackson County. Bitter Lick is in the north part of the county about four miles northwest of Persist. The name is descriptive, and was given because of the strong taste of a fairly large spring. Bitterlick Creek, which took its name from the lick, flows southward into Elk Creek at a point close to Bitter Lick.

Blachly, Lane County. Blachly is three miles from Triangle Lake, a well-known place in the Coast Range. Residents of the neighborhood formerly received their mail at Franklin post office, now discontinued. The office at Blachly was established June 27, 1892, and named for William Blachly, a local resident. William Blachly was born in Illinois in 1844 and came to Oregon in 1854. He died at Blachly on February 16, 1934. See the *Oregonian,* February 19, 1934, page 8.

Black Butte, Deschutes and Jefferson counties. This imposing butte is one of the most important landmarks in the Deschutes Valley, not only on account of its characteristic dark color, but also on account of its symmetry.

It stands well apart from the peaks of the Cascade Range, and has an elevation of 6415 feet, with a USFS lookout at the summit, which is in Jefferson County. From its north base flows the Metolius River, full bodied from a giant spring. It is not known who named Black Butte, but the title is fitting. It had this name as early as 1855, and an interesting picture of it is shown in Pacific Railroad Surveys *Reports*, volume VI, page 90. In the diary of Lt. Henry L. Abbot in *OHQ* volume XXXIII, page 19, Black Butte is called Pivot Mountain, also an appropriate name. Abbot was one of the engineers connected with the Pacific Railroad Surveys. He did not use the name Pivot Mountain in the printed report, but Black Butte.

Black Butte, Deschutes County. In 1970 a subsidiary of Brooks Scanlon Lumber Company began development of a resort community on the site of the old Black Butte Ranch directly south of Black Butte. The first inhabitants took up residence in 1971 and Black Butte post office was established September 16, 1971 with Wendell Clore first postmaster.

Black Butte, Lane County. The geographic feature Black Butte is at the headwaters of Coast Fork Willamette River, about 20 miles south of Cottage Grove. The mountain was named for its characteristic color. A post office named Harris was established near the butte on December 28, 1898, with William Harris postmaster, and it was named in compliment to the official. On August 10, 1901, the name of the office was changed to Blackbutte and it operated with that name until August 31, 1957.

Black Hills, Klamath County. These hills occupy a number of square miles in the southeastern part of Klamath Indian Reservation and were named on account of their characteristic color. They have a maximum elevation of about 6300 feet.

Black Place, Jefferson County. This ranch northeast of Sampson Mountain was the homestead of Addison Black about the turn of the century.

Black Rock, Polk County. Black Rock is on the western end of a branch line of the Southern Pacific Company extending southwest from Dallas. It is on the Little Luckiamute River. It is generally believed this town was named because of a ledge of black shale rock which is exposed nearby.

Blackhorse Canyon, Morrow County. Legend has it that in the early days this canyon east of Lexington was the range of a horse rancher named Wade. Wade had one trait in common with Henry Ford; he didn't care what color a horse was as long as it was black.

Blackhorse Creek, Wallowa County. Blackhorse Creek flows into Imnaha River in the extreme southwest corner of township 4 south, range 48 east. It was named in the late 1890s by Horace J. Butler for a horse that strayed into the canyon and wintered there.

Blacklock Point, Curry County. M. S. Brainard wrote the author in 1967 that this point north of Cape Blanco was named for John Blacklock who was born in Scotland and lived near the point for many years. He died in Bandon on June 8, 1905.

Blackmore Creek, Wallowa County. Blackmore Creek is a small stream flowing into Imnaha River in township 1 south, range 48 east. It was named for Fred Blackmore, a homesteader.

Blacks Island, Douglas County. Blacks Island is a small, marshy tract of land in the mouth of Smith River northeast of Reedsport. The Southern Pacific Company railroad trestle crosses the west end of the island. The name is said to be in commemoration of Arthur Black of the Jedediah S. Smith party which was massacred by the Indians in this vicinity on July 14, 1828. Black was one of the four who escaped. Fifteen members of the Smith party were killed. Black escaped alone and made his way to the Tillamook country, thence to Vancouver. For details of this outrage, see under Smith River. The compiler does not know who applied the name Blacks Island or when it was done, but it is in general use.

Blacksmith Shop Well, Morrow County. This well in Sand Hollow just east of Finley Buttes supplied water for the field blacksmith shop and corral maintained by John S. Kilkenny. Completed in 1904, it was the first drilled well in Morrow County and was 290 feet to water. For a full account of Kilkenny and his many Irish Morrow County contemporaries see *"Shamrocks and Shepherds"* by John F. Kilkenny, *OHQ,* June 1968.

Blaine, Curry County. Blaine post office is listed in Curry County for a few months in 1891. It was closed to Ophir. Eliza Woodruff was the only postmaster. The compiler has not been able to turn up much information about this office although it seems probable that it was named for James G. Blaine, candidate for the presidency of the United States in 1884. The Woodruff family lived not far from Ophir but early residents of the locality are of the opinion that Blaine post office was never in actual operation. That, of course, may be true.

Blaine, Tillamook County. Blaine is on the Nestucca River. It was named by the first postmaster, William Smith, for James G. Blaine (1830-1893), at one time republican candidate for the presidency of the United States. Smith was appointed postmaster of Blaine in 1892 by John Wanamaker.

Blair Lake, Lane County. Blair Lake northeast of Oakridge was named for Frank Blair of Lowell, who at one time ran some cattle near the lake. He is said to have discovered it.

Blake Flat, Wheeler County. Grover C. Blake was born in West Virginia in February 1884. He came west with his family via Kansas and Colorado and then emigrated to Oregon in 1904. He settled near West Branch and took up a homestead on the flat that bears his name. In May 1909, Blake went to work for the USFS and served in various locations until his retirement in 1944. His reminiscences, *Blazing Oregon Trails,* contain a wealth of information about early days in Wheeler County.

Blakeley, Umatilla County. This station was originally called Eastland for Robert E. Eastland, who received a patent to land nearby on March 30, 1880. The name was later changed to Blakeley for William M. Blakeley, a wheat grower in the vicinity.

Blakes, Baker County. This station east of Huntington was named for Thomas J. Blake of the Iron Dyke mine at Homestead, who was instrumental in securing the construction of the Homestead branch of the Union Pacific Railroad.

Blalock, Gilliam County. Blalock is a station on the Union Pacific Railroad west of Arlington. It was here that Dr. Nelson G. Blalock, a pioneer citizen of Walla Walla and a veteran of the Civil War, hoped to develop an extensive horticultural establishment along the south bank of the Columbia River. Blalock died in Walla Walla March 14, 1913, aged 77 years. The flat land along the river suitable for agriculture was inundated in 1968 by the pool behind John Day Dam and there is now little to recall Dr. Blalock's hopes.

Blalock Mountain, Umatilla County. Blalock Mountain lies in the northeast part of Umatilla County, between North and South forks of Walla Walla River. It has an elevation of over 4500 feet. It was named for Dr. Nelson G. Blalock whose name is attached to the community of Blalock, Gilliam County. For information about Dr. Blalock see under that heading. At one time Dr. Blalock cut timber and wood on top of Blalock Mountain and flumed it down into the two forks of the Walla Walla River. It is on that account that Blalock Mountain bears its name.

Bland Mountain, Douglas County. This peak is near the confluence of Days Creek and South Umpqua River and the creek of the same name rises on its south slopes. The 1860 census lists Henry and Mary Beckworth Bland and children including John, age 8 months. Records of the BLM also show that Henry M. Bland homesteaded along the creek in 1863. These items are mentioned in detail because Reinhart in *The Golden Frontier,* page 149, mentions staying near Days Creek with John Bland and his wife, the eldest Beckworth girl, in 1858. It seems probable that the father may have been called John by his wife or friends but that this ceased after the birth of their son.

Blann Meadow, Wheeler County. Blann Meadow southwest of Waterman was the location of the homestead taken by Isaac Blann in 1890.

Blanton, Grant County. Blanton was a post office in Bear Valley named for David Blanton, the first postmaster. The office was established June 9, 1888, and was closed September 14, 1891. It was reestablished March 15, 1892, with Madison Waddell postmaster and was closed again June 12, 1895. In September, 1946, Edward I. Southworth of Seneca wrote the compiler that the Blanton post office was on the old Burns-Canyon City stage road about four miles north of the present town of Seneca.

Blazed Alder Creek, Clackamas and Multnomah counties. This creek received its name from a 24 inch blazed alder tree near its confluence with Bull Run River. The tree was a bench mark established during the early City of Portland watershed surveys. Blazed Alder Creek rises on the slopes of Blazed Alder Butte but Ralph Lewis of Parkdale said that the butte took its name from the creek. He was in the area during the 1906 fire and stated that the butte was then already so named.

Blevins Spring, Wheeler County. This spring north of Derr Meadows was named for Jim Blevins, an early employee of the Fopiano Ranch.

Blind Slough, Clatsop County. Blind Slough opens off the Prairie Channel of the Columbia River about halfway between Knappa and Brownsmead. The slough wanders about a good deal and gets nowhere in particular. One fair sized branch pinches out suddenly and that was probably the reason for the name. Blind Slough post office was established near this water on May 2, 1910, with John W. Crow first of four postmasters. The office was closed out to Brownsmead December 15, 1924.

Blitzen, Harney County. This post office was named for the Donner und Blitzen River which flows nearby. The river was named during the Snake War of 1864, when troops under the command of Colonel George B. Currey crossed it during a thunder storm, and gave to it the German name for thunder and lightning.

Blitzen Butte, Douglas County. USFS ranger Fred Asam named this summit a mile east of Thunder Mountain. Asam was born in Austria and came to this country as a young man so he applied the German word for lightning to match the nearby Thunder.

Blizzard Ridge, Jefferson County. This ridge was named on a winter day about 1900 by John O'Kelly of the OK Ranch. O'Kelly was headed south towards home when he encountered such a severe snowstorm that he had to return to Ashwood.

Blodgett, Benton County. Blodgett is said to have been named for a pioneer settler, William Blodgett. The post office was established with the name of Emrick early in April, 1888, with James A. Wood first postmaster. The name was changed to Blodgett on May 8 of the same year. Emrick was the name of a local family.

Bloody Run, Josephine County. This stream is three miles east of Grants Pass. It was so called because of an incident in the Rogue River Indian War in the 1850s. In 1944 W. A. Moxley of Lebanon wrote that there was a sharp skirmish at this point and one of the white men, separated from his companions, was shot while he was stooping to get a drink from the stream. His blood ran into the water and this gave rise to the name of the run.

Blooming, Washington County. Blooming is a locality about two miles south of Cornelius but not a commercial community. Many years ago it was known as the German Settlement. In December, 1945, Ed Demmin of Hillsboro wrote the compiler that the Rev. Mr. Paul of the Lutheran Church wanted a better name for the community and selected the title Blooming, which he thought descriptive of the floral conditions and pleasant prospects generally. Blooming post office was established February 27, 1895, with Heinrich Paul first postmaster. The office was closed November 28, 1904, because of the extension of rural delivery. The writer has been told that it was a residence post office, not in a store. It seems probable that the man who named the place was the same person as the first postmaster, but the compiler has no proof of it.

Bloomington, Polk County. Postal authorities have informed the compiler that this post office was established May 25, 1852 with Eli W. Foster first postmaster. Preston's *Map of Oregon* of 1856 shows Bloomington in the site of the community now known as Parker. Bloomington post office was closed in June, 1863. The descriptive name seems to have been tinctured with too much optimism.

Bloucher, Hood River County. This is a station on the Mt. Hood Railroad west of Odell. It was named for H. E. Bloucher, a local resident.

Blowout Creek, Linn County. This creek flows into Detroit Reservoir.

It was named because of a great landslide nearby resembling a blowout of the mountainside.

Blowout Creek, Wallowa County. Blowout Creek empties into Bear Creek in the southeast part of township 2 south, range 42 east. It was named by Leander McCubbin and others who camped near the stream in pioneer days and had trouble getting a fire started because the wind blew so hard.

Blue Box Pass, Wasco County. This point is on US 26 about one mile south of Frog Lake and one and one half miles south of Wapinitia Pass through the Cascade Range. Blue Box Pass has an elevation 4024 feet and is some seventy feet higher than the main pass. The word pass is a misnomer since here the highway merely crosses the ridge separating Frog Lake and Clear Lake drainage as it follows this ridge to the south. Ivan M. Woolley in *"Mt Hood or Bust: The Old Road," OHQ,* volume LX, page 54, says that the Clackamas Lake road turned off at this point and the location was marked by and named for a blue box containing a USFS telephone.

Blue Lake, Multnomah County. This Blue Lake in the extreme southeast corner of the county was named by Pete and Jim Odell and Jake Lenz. They were on a hunting expedition when they looked down from above and said that the lake looked exactly like a blue huckleberry.

Blue Mountain, Umatilla County. This is a station on the Union Pacific Railroad southwest of Milton. It is on Dry Creek just north of the horseshoe curve made by the railroad in getting from Weston down into the Walla Walla Valley. When the railroad was being extended south from Walla Walla it was for some time dead-ended at Blue Mountain, and as the station was the last one on the way into the Blue Mountains, it was named for those features, although no one seems to know just why the singular form was used.

Blue Mountains. The Blue Mountains constitute one of the largest uplifts in the state and the main range together with its spurs and offshoots extends into several counties. The backbone of the Blue Mountains begins in Grant County and runs northward through Baker, Union, Umatilla and Wallowa counties in Oregon and into Walla Walla, Columbia, Garfield and Asotin counties in Washington. The Blue Mountains are separated from the Wallowa Mountains in northeastern Oregon by Powder River and Grande Ronde River. The highest point in the Blue Mountains is Rock Creek Butte, a peak on Elkhorn Ridge a few miles west of Baker. Rock Creek Butte has an elevation of 9097 feet. Strawberry Mountain near Prairie City is the highest peak in the southwest part of the Blue Mountains. It has an elevation of 9052 feet. One of the first references to these mountains is by Gabriel Franchere, one of the Astorians. On arriving at the Walla Walla River, he wrote: "A range of mountains was visible to the S. E., about fifty or sixty miles off." He does not give the mountains a name. On July 9, 1811, David Thompson of the North West Company of Montreal, refers to them as Shawpatin Mountains, but in his entry for August 8, 1811, he says: "Beginning of course to see the Blue Mountains between the Shawpatin and the Snake Indians." In a footnote, T. C. Elliott, editor of the Thompson Journal, says: "Apparently the first record of this name Blue as applied to these mountains." (*OHQ*, volume XV, pages 57 and 121.) Alexander Ross, J. K. Townsend, David Douglas, Peter Skene Ogden, John Work and other early travelers continued to use the name Blue Mountains. One of the early references is by the Rev. Gustavus Hines (*Oregon: Its History, Condition and Prospects*, 1851, page 323): "As you approach the Blue Mountains on the south, particularly on the Umatilla and Walla Walla rivers, the hills disappear, and you find yourself passing over a beautiful and level country, about twenty-five or thirty miles broad, on the farther borders of which rise with indescribable beauty and grandeur, that range which, from its azure-like appearance, has been called the 'Blue Mountains.' "

Blue River, Lane County. Blue River is remarkable in color, and is well named. The Blue River mines were discovered in 1863, and the stream was doubtless named about that time. Large stamp-mills were installed, but the ore was low grade, and the mills have not been operated for many years. See the *Oregonian*, December 8, 1863; November 2 and December 17, 1889 and July 3, 1897. Blue River post office is near the mouth of Blue River where that stream flows into the McKenzie. It was established January 18, 1886, with J. M. Davis first postmaster.

Bluebucket Creek, Grant and Harney counties. This stream rises just west of Antelope Mountain in the southeastern part of Grant County, and after flowing through Antelope Swale in Harney County, joins a tributary of Malheur River. The name has been applied in recent years to preserve an interesting Oregon romance. The mystery of the location of the real Bluebucket Creek will probably never be solved. Members of the Meek party of 1845 picked up yellow pebbles and hung them under a wagon in a blue wooden bucket. The bucket was either lost or abandoned later, and it was not until some time had elapsed that the emigrants realized that they had possibly found gold. An interesting discussion of the episode and possible locations of Bluebucket Creek may be found in Scott's *History of the Oregon Country*, volume III, page 336. It is generally thought that the discovery must have been on a tributary of either the John Day or Malheur River, though suggestions that the locality was near Steens Mountain and also Tygh Valley have also been advanced. Columns have been written on the subject. As far as the writer knows there is nothing to connect the name of the stream in Harney County with the gold discovery, but it is used to preserve the tradition, and may not be far from the true locality.

Bluejoint Lake, Lake County. This is one of the lakes of the Warner Valley. It was named for the bluejoint grass that grows nearby in great profusion.

Bly, Klamath County. *Bly* was a word of the Klamath Indians meaning up or high. According to Captain O. C. Applegate of Klamath Falls, it meant the old village *up* Sprague River from Yainax. White people appropriated the name and applied it to a town east of the Klamath Indian Reservation. A. S. Gatschet in his *Dictionary of the Klamath Language* (U. S. Geographical and Geological Survey, Washington, D. C., 1890) gives the word as *p'lai*, and says that it meant among other things the Sprague River Valley and sometimes simply the Sprague River as distinguished from the lower country along the Williamson River. *P'laikni* were people living high up, or along the upper reaches of Sprague River. *P'laikni* was also used to mean heavenly, or the Christian God. A post office called Sprague River was established in this vicinity on November 12, 1873, with John W. Gearhart first postmaster. The name of the office was changed to Bly January 31, 1883.

Blybach, Tillamook County. Blybach post office was on Nehalem River, about four or five miles east of what is now Mohler, about a half a mile east of the place later called Foss and just east of the E. H. Lindsey ranch. It was established September 5, 1892, and was named for the postmaster, Hattie Blybach. The office was closed March 5, 1896.

Boardman, Morrow County. Boardman is a station on the Union Pacific Railroad not far from the Columbia River. It was named for Sam Boardman, a well-known resident of Oregon. Boardman has an elevation of 281 feet. S. H. Boardman was born in Lowell, Massachusetts, and for some years followed the construction and engineering business. In 1903, while stationed at Leadville, Colorado, he became interested in the Pacific Northwest and came to Oregon. He got a job with A. M. Drake at Bend, but on the way to central Oregon, he ran into smallpox at Shaniko, and lost interest in the Deschutes country. He returned to Portland. In the same year he filed on a homestead where the town of Boardman is now situated. For thirteen years Sam and Mrs. Boardman snuffed sand and worked to develop irrigated land. At odd times he was engaged in railroad and highway construction and Mrs. Boardman taught school to help with the expenses. The town was platted in 1916. S. H. Boardman was continually interested in the phenomena of nature, and as a result of employment by the Oregon State Highway Department about 1916, he put his attention to roadside improvement and state park development. He was engaged in this activity for many years and the splendid results of his work are too well known to require comment. Boardman died on January 26, 1953. See *Oregon Journal*, January 27, 1953. In the 1960s the town of Boardman was relocated to the south during the construction of the John Day Dam and much of the original townsite is now covered by Lake Umatilla.

Boaz Mountain, Jackson County. Boaz Mountain, elevation about 3500 feet, is in the south part of township 39 south, range 3 west. It was named for Kinder Boaz who homesteaded nearby in 1876. The name is sometimes spelled Boaze in official records.

Bob Creek, Wallowa County. Bob Creek flows into Snake River in section 10, township 3 north, range 50 east. J. H. Horner of Enterprise told the compiler in 1928 that the stream was named because Lu Knapper and some companions had an experience with several wildcats in this canyon in the late 1880s.

Boeckman Creek, Clackamas and Washington counties. Boeckman Creek flows into Willamette River just east of Wilsonville. It was named for Ernest A. Boeckmann who settled there in 1875.

Bohemia, Lane County. Bohemia Mountain in the Bohemia mining district is a well-known geographic feature in eastern Lane County. It was named for a wandering prospector and miner called Bohemia Johnson. For nearly thirty years there was a Bohemia post office serving this neighborhood. The office was established on the Douglas County list on April 26, 1893, with John B. McGee first of seven postmasters. The office oscillated back and forth between Douglas County and Lane County and for the last fifteen years of its life it was in Lane County. It was discontinued December 7, 1922, with mail to Disston. It is possible that some of the change in county lists was due to the moving of the Douglas-Lane boundary in this area.

Bohemia Mountain, Lane County. This mountain is one of the summits of the Calapooya Mountains, a spur of the Cascade Range, and is in what is generally referred to as the Bohemia mining district. It was named for a wandering mountaineer and prospector, James Johnson, who was supposed to have been born in Bohemia. He was popularly known as "Bohemia" Johnson. He discovered the Bohemia mines in 1863. See the *Oregonian*, January 20, 1900, and Scott's *History of the Oregon Country*, volume I, page 343.

Bohna, Malheur County. Railroad company records indicate that this station near Malheur River was named for Ernest Bohna, who formerly owned land nearby. The siding is between Juntura and Harper.

Boiler Bay, Lincoln County. From time to time the *Oregonian* prints an editorial about an Oregon geographic name. These editorials, which are of nice reading length, are frequently erudite and accurate, but beyond all that, they are always sprightly. Such an editorial appeared on November 10, 1942, and the secondary subject was Boiler Bay, though the title was otherwise. Boiler Bay, as many people know, is a little more than a mile north of Depoe Bay and is bounded on the west by a long, low promontory known as Government Point. The bay takes its name from a marine boiler "fast on a rocky shoal that is prolific of butter clams at low tide." The boiler and a shaft are the remains of a small freighter, the *J. Marhoffer*, built at Aberdeen, Washington, in 1907, and engaged in the coastwise trade. She was lost on May 18, 1910, enroute from San Francisco to the Columbia River, as the result of the explosion of a gasoline torch. The skipper brought the flaming ship to shore, and the crew, with one exception, was saved. The cook died of exposure. The captain had his wife along, and there are stories to the effect that she greatly inspired the shipwrecked sailors by her courage. A letter in the *Oregonian* for January 10, 1943, says that the early name for Boiler Bay was Briggs Landing for a pioneer family. However, a bay and a landing are not exactly the same thing.

Boiling Point, Umatilla County. Boiling Point, elevation about 3250 feet, was a place on old US 30 on Emigrant Hill southeast of Pendleton. It got its name because it was the locality where the old teapot automobiles began to boil over on a hot day. Boiling Point post office was in service from November, 1932, to December, 1935. Arthur G. Greer was the only postmaster. The fire under this community was extinguished when it was bypassed by the new highway, I80N.

Bolan Creek, Josephine County. For many years this creek and other nearby features have been known variously as Bolan, Bollon or Bolland. After an early investigation of this supposed Indian name, the USBGN adopted the present spelling. However, the publication of the Reinhart recollections, *The Golden Frontier,* provides a different source. Reinhart describes how he and several others crossed the divide from Althouse Creek in 1853 and built a small community at the forks of Sucker Creek. Their buildings, including a bowling alley, were all burned in 1855 by the Indians. Reinhart returned in 1857 to what he says was then known as Bowling Creek where he staked a claim and constructed another alley. His description of how three men carried thirty balls and twenty pins over the divide from Althouse Creek convinces the compiler that in those days men were strong of purpose as well as back.

Bolon Island, Douglas County. Bolon Island is in the Umpqua River north of Reedsport. This island has apparently had several names including Bone, Bowline and Dewars, but Warren P. Reed of Reedsport says that there is no doubt but that it was originally called after a settler by the name of Bolon. The USBGN has adopted the form Bolon.

Bolt, Jackson County. Bolt is on the south side of Rogue River about six miles east of the west boundary of Jackson County, at the point where the Pacific Highway crosses Foots Creek. This place together with Bolt Mountain on the Applegate River about seven miles southwest of Grants Pass, was named for John Bolt, a member of the firm of Kubli and Bolt, pioneer packers and merchants of southern Oregon.

Bonanza, Klamath County. *Bonanza* is a Spanish word meaning prosperity. This place is said to have been named because of a number of fine springs in the vicinity. Good water is always a source of prosperity in a country that needs irrigation.

Boner Flat, Wallowa County. Boner Flat is in the Wallowa Mountains, in the east part of township 5 south, range 45 east. It bears the name of George W. Boner who ranged sheep in the vicinity about 1889. Boner Spring in township 3 north, range 45 east, is named for the same man. The spelling Bonner is wrong.

Boneyard Creek, Wallowa County. This stream flows into Sheep Creek in section 16, township 1 south, range 48 east. One Charles Holmes lost most of his cattle in the canyon during a hard winter in the 1890s and the bleached bones became a landmark.

Bonifer, Umatilla County. Bonifer is a railroad station about two and a half miles southeast of Gibbon. It bears the name of a well-known rancher of the vicinity. The station was named in 1928.

Bonita, Lane County. *Bonita* is a Spanish word meaning pretty. The compiler does not know why it was applied to a Lane County post office on Brice Creek. It may have been in compliment to a girl or possibly because of a pleasing outlook. Bonita post office was established March 2, 1904, and operated until February 20, 1908. Fred W. Lee was the first postmaster. Bonita was a little to the southeast of the center of township 22 south, range 1 east.

Bonita, Washington County. This was a station on the Oregon Electric Railway a short distance south of Tigard. It was named by a local resident, Geo. W. Cassaday, who was of a romantic turn of mind and selected the Spanish word for pretty or graceful.

Bonneville, Multnomah County. This is an historic spot in Oregon, and for many decades it was a popular picnic grounds for people living along the Columbia River between Portland and The Dalles. The railroad company maintained an "eating house" at Bonneville, where tired travelers paid a modest sum for all they could eat. The station was named for Captain (later Brigadier General) Benjamin L. E. Bonneville, the hero of Washington Irving's *The Adventures of Captain Bonneville*. He was born in France in 1795, graduated from West Point and fought with gallantry through the Mexican War. He explored the west from 1832-5, and visited many parts of Oregon and may have been the first white man to go into the Wallowa country. He died in 1878. For details of his life and travels see Scott's *History of the Oregon Country*, volume I, pages 170 and 297. The locality of Bonneville has become nationally known as the site of the Bonneville Dam, construction of which was started in September, 1933, by the USCE. The main features are a dam, a powerhouse, a ship lock and fishways. The dam is across the main or north channel of the Columbia River and is 1090 feet long. The powerhouse stands across the channel south of Bradford Island and contains generators with a total rated capacity of 518,400 kilowatts. The ship lock is south of the powerhouse and is 76 feet wide by 500 feet long. At normal river stage the lift is 59 feet. For details of construction and equipment of Bonneville Dam, see article by Col. C. R. Moore, *Oregon Blue Book, 1941-1942*, page 191. In 1925 the USBGN, at the suggestion of J. Neilson Barry of Portland, applied the name of Mount Bonneville to a conspicuous peak about three miles south of Wallowa Lake, previously known as Middle Mountain.

Bonney Butte, Hood River County. This butte is in the extreme southwest part of the county, and has an elevation of 5593 feet. Just east of it is Bonney Meadow. These two features were named for a Wasco County stockman, Augustus A. Bonney. He was born in Marion County, Oregon, April 14, 1849, graduated from Willamette University in 1871, and settled in Tygh Valley in 1875.

Boones Ferry, Clackamas County. Alphonso Boone brought his family to Oregon in 1846 by the Applegate route. He was a grandson of Daniel Boone. About 1847, his son Jesse V. Boone, began to operate a ferry across the Willamette River just east of the present site of the Oregon Electric Railway bridge at Wilsonville. A road leading south from Portland to this ferry was, and still is, known as Boones Ferry road. Another son, Alphonso D. Boone, became associated with his brother Jesse in the ferry. Jesse was killed in 1872. Chloe Donnelly Boone, daughter of Alphonso Boone, married George L. Curry, one time governor of Oregon, for whom Curry County was named. For post office history, see under Wilsonville.

Booneville Channel, Benton County. This is a branch of the Willamette River flowing on the west side of John Smith Island and Kiger Island, a few miles south of Corvallis. Early maps of the Willamette Valley show the community of Booneville near this point and it is presumed that the channel was named for this community. The name should not be spelled Boonesville.

Boot Creek, Wasco County. Boot Creek is tributary to Ward Creek west of Antelope. J. A. Rooper of Antelope told the author it was named for one Booten who ranched near its mouth in the early days. He was unable to explain the elision.

Booth, Douglas County. Booth is a station on the Southern Pacific Company line from Eugene to Coos Bay. It is near the extreme south end of Siltcoos Lake. In June, 1948, Mrs. F. K. Davis of Eugene, daughter of the late Robert A. Booth, wrote the compiler that this station was named for her father. He was one of the most prominent western Oregon lumber men and was a founder of the Booth-Kelly Lumber Company of Eugene and elsewhere. Mrs. Davis wrote that R. A. Booth and A. C. Dixon of Eugene bought an island in Siltcoos Lake and that was the reason the railroad station was named Booth. The railroad station was named prior to 1918 but the compiler does not know just when. Booth post office was established near the railroad station in September, 1934, with Mrs. Clara P. Law first postmaster. It is reported that there has been some lumbering activity at this place. The post office has been discontinued but the compiler does not know the date. The place called Booth in western Douglas County should not be confused with Booth post office in the upper Cow Creek valley, which was named for Winfield S. Booth. That post office was in service from 1907 to 1914. It had previously been called Starvout and in 1914 the name of the office was changed to Azalea.

Booth, Josephine County. Booth was named for its postmaster, Henry E. Booth. The office was established January 22, 1897, and was closed December 31, 1898. An old map shows the place on Rogue River a few miles northwest of Grants Pass and about the same distance southwest of Merlin. The writer does not know the reason for the establishment.

Booth Hill, Hood River County. Named for George Booth, an early settler in the Hood River Valley, who is said to have set out the first commercial orchard in the valley and who sent 20 boxes of Newtowns to the Buffalo fair in 1901 and received a gold medal and sold the apples for $7 a box. It is reported that Booth settled near the foot of the hill in 1885. For many years travelers hesitated to attempt the muddy road up Booth Hill in the winter, but the Mount Hood Loop Highway has solved the difficulty with some change in location from the old road.

Boren Creek, Lane County. Boren Creek flows into Martin Creek about a mile east of Divide. It was named for Charles Boren who took a donation land claim in the vicinity. Boren came to Oregon in 1853 from Illinois.

Boring, Clackamas County. The town of Boring was named for W. H. Boring, an old resident of the neighborhood. The district was known to old settlers as the Boring neighborhood, and in 1903 a townsite was platted and called Boring Junction. The Post Office Department and the builders of the interurban railway adopted Boring as the name of the community.

Bosley Butte, Curry County. Bosley Butte is in the southwest part of the county. F. S. Moore of Gold Beach informed the compiler that this peak was named for Julia Bosley, a young woman, who in early days was a member of a party that made a trip to the large prairies lying south of and extending across to the east side of the peak. Miss Bosley was one of the few of the party to ascend to the top of the mountain and it was named in her honor.

Boston Mills, Linn County. About 1858 R. C. Finley and associates established a community and grist mill on Calapooia River about a mile and a half east of the present town of Shedd. They called the place Boston Mills, presumably because one or more of the proprietors came from the Massachusetts city. A small butte nearby was named Bunker Hill. The community became a stage stop and made a little growth. Boston Mills post office was established on September 22, 1869, with William Simmons postmaster. Efforts to get the railroad through the place were unsuccessful and Boston Mills began to decline. The railroad was built through Shedd and the post office was moved to that place and the name changed to Shedds on August 28, 1871. Shedds post office was changed to Shedd in 1915.

Boswell Springs, Douglas County. Boswell Springs are situated just west of the Pacific Highway at a point about three miles south of Drain. They were named for the owner, Captain Benjamin D. Boswell. Boswell post office was established April 9, 1895, with B. F. Sanders postmaster. The office was closed sometime between 1906 and 1909, but the writer cannot tell the exact date.

Boulder Creek, Marion County. Boulder Creek flows into the North Santiam River east of Detroit. Boulder Creek was named in 1874 by T. W. Davenport of the Marion County road surveying party. See *OHQ,* volume IV, page 248.

Boundary Creek, Douglas County. This tributary of Little River was named by USFS ranger Fred Asam because of its location near the National Forest boundary. The boundary was subsequently moved east near Wolf Creek.

Boundary Creek, Lane County. Boundary Creek is so named because it flows into Fall Creek near the west boundary of the Willamette National Forest.

Bour, Josephine County. The mining locality called Bour was given the family name of David, John and George Bour who were engaged in placer operations shortly after the turn of the century. Bour post office was established in May, 1906, with Geneva M. Bour first postmaster. The office was discontinued in February, 1907. The Bour placer was situated on Illinois River about midway between the mouths of Deer Creek and Josephine Creek, a little downstream from Kerby. Nobody seems to know whether the post office was ever in actual operation or merely authorized. George Bour, living near Kerby in 1948, is of the opinion that the post office never was in service.

Bourbon, Sherman County. Bourbon was a station on the Union Pacific Railroad, originally the Columbia Southern, about seven or eight miles southeast of Grass Valley. The station was established for a wheat shipping point. Giles French of Moro wrote the compiler about this name on June 1, 1946, as follows: "The name originated directly from that of the famous early-day tipple, which has been preserved to this time and is, in normal times, in conflict with Scotch and Rye. Bourbon you will recognize as the drink of the frontier, the product of good American corn, the elixir of the common man. Some say that when the first construction crew went to Bourbon to stake out the site of the first warehouse they found a bottle that once contained Bourbon and named the place for that reason. Another story is that the crew built the warehouse a little askew of the railroad and the reason for such lack of constructive ability was laid to a superabundance of Bourbon. Bourbon attained some local fame during World War I because Charles (Puss) Schwartz, an elderly bachelor, retired from farming, always gave his occupation as an employee of the 'shipyards at Bourbon.' Even yet Grass Valley residents use it as an occasional excuse for their vagrancy." The compiler thinks that Mr. French is well acquainted with the subject and that this account should be given great weight. It is pleasing to know that these historic names are being preserved in Sherman County.

Bourne, Baker County. Bourne was named for Jonathan Bourne, Jr., of Portland, who was at one time interested in eastern Oregon mines. He was United States senator from Oregon from 1907 to 1913. He was born in New Bedford, Mass., February 23, 1855, and graduated from Harvard in 1877. He came to Portland in the following year and in 1880 was admitted to the Oregon bar. After his term in the Senate, he lived in Washington, D. C., and died there September 1, 1940. Bourne post office was established in March, 1895, and discontinued May 31, 1927.

Bowden Crater, Malheur County. Bowden Crater is a characteristic volcanic vent in the south-central part of the county about six miles northeast of the old Bowden ranch on Rattlesnake Creek. The crater got its name from the ranch, and the title was applied by Dr. Israel C. Russell of the USGS about 1902. See USGS Bulletin 217, *Geology of Southwestern Idaho and Southeastern Oregon,* page 57. Dr. Russell gives an interesting description of this crater, which is unusual in that there seems to be a complete absence of the products of explosive eruptions such as lapilli and volcanic bombs. Bowden Crater is an isolated example of volcanism and Dr. Russell says that the adjacent lava flow, covering about a hundred square miles, apparently all came from the single crater. In 1902 the remains of the raised rim of the central elevation of Bowden Crater was about 600 feet in diameter enclosing a basin about 40 feet deep. The Bowden ranch was on Rattlesnake Creek a little to the south of the center of township 34 south, range 41 east. A post office named Bowdens was in operation here from October, 1890, until April, 1898. John B. Bowden was the first postmaster.

Bowen Valley, Baker County. Powder River passes through Bowen Valley just south of Baker. The valley was named for Ira B. Bowen who had a ranch there and a sawmill near Auburn. Ira B. Bowen and his brother, John P., were among the earliest settlers in Baker County.

Bowers Slough, Benton County. This slough joins Willamette River from the north about four miles west of Albany. Two brothers of the name of Bowers lived in this vicinity in pioneer days and the slough was named for them.

Bowlus Hill, Umatilla County. This hill is just north of the forks of Walla Walla River. It was named for Lewis Bowlus, a nearby landowner.

Bowman Creek, Curry County. Bowman Creek flows into Pacific Ocean north of Cape Ferrelo. It was named for Jonas W. Bowman, an early day blacksmith in Langlois, who homesteaded on the creek in 1879.

Bowman Creek, Umatilla County. Bowman Creek flows into Camas Creek near the Union County line. Henry Bowman took up land near its mouth in 1883.

Bowman Creek, Wallowa County. Bowman Creek is in township 3 south, range 43 east, and flows into Lostine River. It was named for Robert B. Bowman, who traveled over the trail along the stream to get to his mining claim. This was an old elk trail, and in early days the stream was sometimes called Elk Trail Creek.

Bowman Dam, Crook County. In 1961 Crooked River was dammed southeast of Prineville creating Prineville Reservoir. In 1973 at the instigation of a number of Crook County residents, the dam was named to honor Arthur R. Bowman who was born in Kansas in 1882 and moved to Prineville before World War I. He was active in many local affairs including reclamation work and was a member of both the Oregon and National Reclamation Associations where he was a strong supporter of the Crooked River Project. He died in Bend in 1970.

Box, Benton and Lincoln counties. A post office with the terse name Box was established on the Lincoln County list January 28, 1897, with Mary J. Grier first postmaster. It was on or near Lobster Creek in the extreme southeast corner of the county. This office seems to have oscillated back and forth across the Benton-Lincoln county line, for it was first in one county, then the other. It was on the Benton County list as of July 21, 1906, but the writer cannot learn what happened to it after that except that it was not a post office in 1913. Polk's *Oregon and Washington Gazetteer* for 1907-08 says that the locality served by Box post office was frequently called Lobster Valley. John E. Davis of the Oregon Department of Agriculture at Salem has been kind enough to send in the following story: "Before the post office was established a big box was placed beside the road and when any of the neighbors went to or from Alsea, the nearest post office, they carried the mail for all in Lobster Valley. Mail for those in the valley was placed in this box, from which it found its way into the various homes. None of the names first submitted for the post office was acceptable to the department and it occurred to someone to call it Box. This information came from Thomas Taylor who was postmaster at two different times."

Boyd, Wasco County. This name is reported as being derived from T. P. Boyd who settled in the vicinity about 1883 and with his sons operated a flour mill. When the post office was established March 6, 1884, G. H. Barnett, a local merchant, suggested the name of Boyd as being both short and appropriate. John E. Barnett was the first postmaster.

Boyer, Lincoln and Tillamook counties. John and Julia Boyer were among the early settlers on Salmon River and they operated the Salmon River toll road 1908-1920. The predecessor of this toll road was called the Elk Trail and it was used at a much earlier date. A post office called Boyer was established August 18, 1910, with Mervin O. Boyer first of three postmasters. The compiler is informed that M. O. Boyer was a son of John Boyer and that the post office was in John Boyer's house. It was in the extreme north end of Lincoln County, probably not more than a mile from the county line. This office was discontinued March 31, 1915. At a much later date the name Boyer was applied to a community on the Salmon River Highway in the extreme southeast corner of Tillamook County and about four miles northeast of the former Boyer post office. This little community

now called Boyer is about a half mile northeast of the stone monument
erected on the highway in 1926 to John and Julia Boyer. It is where the
highway crosses Little Nestucca River. Boyer community does not have a
post office as this paragraph is written in May, 1948. For information about
Salmon River Highway and John Boyer, see Leslie M. Scott's article "Military Beginnings of the Salmon River Highway," *OHQ*, September, 1934.

Boyle Lakes, Polk County. These are intermittent ponds about two
miles northwest of Rickreall, and they are generally dry in summer. They
were named for Dr. James W. Boyle, a pioneer of Oregon, who was born in
Virginia in 1815, and came to this state in 1845. Dr. Boyle settled on the
land near these lakes in 1850. He married Josephine P. Ford. For additional information about Dr. Boyle, see article by Fred Lockley on editorial
page of *Oregon Journal*, July 27, 1927.

Bracket Mountain, Clackamas County. This mountain, elevation 5018
feet, is in township 6 south, range 5 east. It was named by W. B. Osborn,
Jr., of the USFS, because it resembled a printer's bracket, or brace, placed
horizontally with the point up, as follows:

Bradbury, Columbia County. This station and a slough in the Columbia River nearby were named for C. A. Bradbury, an early settler. Wilkes
shows this slough as Kinak Passage, in an atlas accompanying *U.S. Exploring
Expedition*, Volume XXIII, Hydrography, but does not explain the name.
The name of the railroad station was later changed to Locoda. For information about C. A. Bradbury, see Fred Lockley's story in the *Oregon Journal*,
April 15, 1945.

Braden, Umatilla County. Braden post office was in operation on the
extreme north border of the county from March, 1891, to September,
1891. Jennie Braden was the postmaster. The post office was a room in the
Braden home, which was on the lower Walla Walla road about four miles
north of Milton. The house disappeared some years ago. It was near what
was later called the Engel Chapel. It was in section 15, township 6 north,
range 45 east.

Bradetich Well, Deschutes County. Bradetich Well in Millican Valley
was named for George and John Bradetich who established the Pine Mountain spread of Black Angus cattle. The two brothers came from southern
Europe and started a small dairy farm in Bend. After this had grown to be
one of the best known in the state, the brothers began their beef cattle
operation. In 1969 George was still active and running the ranch with his
son Phil.

Bradford Island, Multnomah County. This island in the Columbia
River has become very well known as a result of the Bonneville Dam. The
south end of the dam itself is on the island, and much of the fish ladder
structure. The north end of the powerhouse is also on the island. The
island was named for Daniel F. and Putnam Bradford, brothers, who were
pioneer steamboat operators on the Columbia River. Among other things
they rebuilt the portage road at the Cascades in 1856. Later another por-

tage road was built on the south side of the river, and eventually both were absorbed by the Oregon Steam Navigation Company. For details of fight with Indians on this island see OPA *Transactions* for 1896. Assertions that Bradford Island is the Strawberry Island of Lewis and Clark are not substantiated by the maps of the explorers. It is apparent from both text and maps that Lewis and Clark used the name Brant Island for what is now known as Bradford Island. Their Strawberry Island is now Hamilton Island, close to the north bank. However, on the return journey, Patrick Gass used the name Strawberry Island in error for what was then Brant Island, now Bradford. This was on the evening of April 9, 1806. The Astorians had the Gass journals but not those of Lewis and Clark, and as a result applied the name Strawberry Island to the wrong landmark. This error has been perpetuated by several subsequent editors and writers.

Bradley Creek, Douglas County. John V. Bradley came to the Glide area in 1858 and took up a land claim near the mouth of this creek in 1864.

Bradley Trail, Douglas County. This trail is a well-known route of travel along the North Umpqua River in the eastern part of the county. It was named for William Bradley, a pioneer trapper and mountain stockman, who is said to have been born near Oakland, and to have worked his way into the headwaters of the North Umpqua River as early as 1875, when he was a young man. He traded deer meat and hides with the Indians, taking ponies in return, which he sold in Eugene and other points. This trade opened up a trail across the Cascade Range, which has ever since been known as the Bradley Trail, and much of it has been put on modern standards by the USFS. Bradley Creek, a tributary of the North Umpqua rising west of Windigo Butte, also bears the name of the same man. Bradley was killed by a horse in 1909, dying near his lonely cabin at Illahe.

Bradwood, Clatsop County. The Bradley-Woodard Lumber Co. was incorporated July 15, 1930, and one of its activities was the development of a mill and community on the south bank of the Columbia River about two miles upstream from Clifton. The name of the new town, Bradwood, was made synthetically from the name of the company.

Brandt, Douglas County. This station on the Southern Pacific Company line in Cow Creek canyon was probably named for one of the Brandt family whose three members working in various capacities for the early Oregon and California Railroad included Superintendent John Brandt, Jr.

Brandy Bar, Douglas County. Brandy Bar is in Umpqua River about fifteen miles east of Reedsport. On August 6, 1850, the schooner *Samuel Roberts* of the Klamath Exploring Expedition grounded on this bar and the party was forced to spend the night there. There was some brandy aboard the ship which was used too freely during the night to the exasperation of the owner. The place was called Brandy Bar because of this incident. See *OHQ*, volume XVII, page 355.

Braunsport, Columbia County. Braunsport post office was established in November, 1891, with Johann B. Braun postmaster. The office operated under Braun's guidance until November 9, 1901, when it was discontinued. In December, 1945, Omar C. Spencer of the Portland bar wrote the compiler that Braunsport was on Beaver Creek approximately five miles southwest of Vernonia, and that it was named for the first postmaster, who was a native of Germany. Mr. Spencer added the historical fact that there was a school at this place called Braunsport School, where he, Mr. Spencer, taught four months during the summer of 1897. An Army map of the Vernonia quadrangle shows Beaver Creek School in the approximate location of the old locality of Braunsport. The place on the map shown as Braun is a little to the northeast of Braunsport.

Bravo Creek, Curry County. This tributary of North Fork Chetco River was named for cattleman John C. Bravo who came to this area in 1892 from Switzerland.

Bray Mountain, Coos County. Bray Mountain is near the headwaters of Johnson Creek ten miles southwest of Powers. Dodge in *Pioneer History of Coos and Curry Counties* has several references to Iredel Bray. He says that Bray was a member of the "Coarse Gold" Johnson party that discovered gold on Johnson Creek in 1854 and that he subsequently had a cabin nearby during the Indian troubles of 1855. The diary of John Evans, the discoverer of the Port Orford meteorite, under date of Sunday, July 19, 1856, tells of meeting Bray near what is now the Powers Ranch and that Bray invited the party to partake of two freshly killed bear hanging in his cabin. Bray later patented a homestead near the present community of Powers.

Bray Point, Lane County. Bray Point was named for a local family. The promontory is about a third of a mile south of Bob Creek and just north of Agate Creek. While not large, Bray Point presents a bold front to the sea and affords a fine view to travelers on the Oregon Coast Highway.

Braymill, Klamath County. This post office had a comparatively short life. The name of the office was coined by taking the last name of W. M. Bray, principal owner of the Sprague River Company, which operated a sawmill at that point, and combining it with the word "mill". Surely ingenuity could go no further. Braymill station was formerly called Meva.

Breeds Flat, Wasco County. In 1902 Walter L. Breed filed for a homestead on this flat between the forks of Mill Creek.

Breitenbush, Marion County. Breitenbush post office and Breitenbush Hot Springs, on Breitenbush River about ten miles northeast and upstream from Detroit, got their names from the river. Breitenbush post office was established March 21, 1928 with Merle D. Bruckman postmaster.

Breitenbush River, Marion County. John Minto's account of the 1873 exploring party in *OHQ*, volume IV, page 248, says that this river was named for John Breitenbush, a pioneer hunter who preceded them in the North Santiam River region. He gives no other information about the man but *Reminiscences of Southern Oregon Pioneers* contains a 1938 interview with Frederick R. Breitenbusher who was born at Buena Vista in 1862. Breitenbusher says that the pioneer hunter was his father, Lewis Breitenbusher, who crossed the plains in 1849 and after living in Buena Vista, moved to Linn County where he stayed for twelve years. The form Breitenbush has been firmly established since Minto's time.

Brenner Canyon, Morrow County. This canyon which empties into Rhea Creek was probably named for John E. Brenner who filed for a homestead there about the time of World War I. Brenner was the son or grandson of Peter Brenner, an early Morrow County settler, who came to the Eightmile area in the 1880s.

Brewer Ranch, Lake County. Ellsbury Brewer took up the land where this ranch stands on Bridge Creek prior to World War I.

Brewer Reservoir, Jefferson County. In 1874 William Brewer took a homestead where Awbrey Creek joins Hay Creek. Hay Creek was later dammed and the reservoir is named for this early settler.

Brewster, Linn County. This station north of Lebanon was named for Alexander Brewster, on whose land it was situated.

Brice Creek, Lane County. This stream rises on the western slopes of the Cascade Range and flows into Row River. It was named for Frank Brass, a prospector of early days. Brass fell into the stream on a prospecting trip and a companion named the creek for him. Time has brought about the change in spelling. The stream was formerly called Frank Brice Creek, but in 1943, the USBGN, in the interest of simplicity adopted the style Brice Creek. Brice Creek seems to be the form used locally.

Bridal Veil Falls, Multnomah County. The romantically inclined never fail to name at least one important waterfall in a state Bridal Veil. The falls in Oregon bearing this name are quite attractive during the higher stages of water, even though they are to a certain extent obscured by the bridge of the Columbia River Highway. They have borne this name since pioneer days. There is a community nearby named Bridal Veil. The creek forming the falls is also known as Bridal Veil Creek. It heads on Larch Mountain.

Bridge, Coos County. Bridge is a post office and community on Middle Fork Coquille River about eleven miles east of Myrtle Point, named for a nearby bridge over the stream. A post office named Angora served this locality, in part, in earlier days. It was established in August, 1883, and was closed in May, 1894. Bridge post office was established July 6, 1894, with Thomas E. Manly postmaster. An effort was made to call the reestablished office Angora but for some reason the Post Office Department did not approve of the suggestion. It seems probable that the office at Bridge was not in the same place as the former office of Angora, but the records are not clear.

Bridge Creek, Grant County. Bridge Creek lay along the first route of travel from northeastern Oregon into the John Day mines. This route was at first nothing more than a trail. During the mining excitement of the early 1860s, the packers made some improvements so their work could be carried on more expeditiously, and among other things they built some pole bridges over what is now Bridge Creek. This fact gave rise to the name. The stream is southwest of Austin.

Bridge Creek, Marion County. Bridge Creek is a stream southwest of Silverton, the waters of which find their way into Abiqua Creek, but the compiler does not know just how. He has been told that the stream was named in pioneer days because of a convenient bridge, but he does not know its location. Bridge Creek post office was established near this stream in November, 1919, and operated until November, 1923, when it was closed to Hullt. Edward Trenter was the only postmaster. This office was a little to the east of Hullt, near the north quartercorner of section 9, township 8 south, range 2 east. It was very close to the old Bridge Creek school and the two establishments were both named for the stream. In 1932-33 a new post office called Cedar Camp was in service in the same location with Mrs. Edith M. Filer, postmaster. Cedar Camp was apparently named because of the cedar lumber and shingle making in the vicinity.

Bridge Creek, Wheeler County. This stream heads in the mountains in the south part of the county, and flows into John Day River. One branch flows through Mitchell. H. H. Bancroft in his *History of Oregon,* volume I, page 787, says that it was named because Shoeman and Wadley, California prospectors, built a small bridge over it of juniper logs, while enroute to the John Day mines. This was about 1862. On July 2, 1868, a post office named Bridge Creek was established in what is now Wheeler County with Alfred Sutton postmaster. Sutton was a prominent Wasco and Wheeler county pioneer. Sutton Mountain north of Mitchell bears his name. Bridge Creek post office, which was finally closed in 1882, was on the Sutton place, which was very close to the mouth of the stream, where it joined John Day River.

Bridgeport, Baker County. C. A. Moore, of Baker, in a letter in the *Oregonian,* August 7, 1926, page 8, gives the early history of this community. In 1861-63 considerable placer gold was discovered at Clark Creek, several miles southeast of Bridgeport. Supplies were packed from Baker over the old Creighton road, crossing Burnt River near where Hereford now is, and then down the river on the south side to these mines, where there were some stores and a post office. Bridgeport is on the south bank of the river, which could not then be forded. The need for a wagon road and a shorter route to Clark Creek led Dr. Jacob M. Boyd and James W. Virtue and associates, in 1868, to begin the construction of a toll road from Baker to what is now Bridgeport, and in 1869 this road was made passable for the entire distance. At the south end of the road, where it crossed the river, there was a bridge some 200 feet long, and since this was the terminus of the toll road, it was decided to call the place Bridgeport.

Bridgeport, Polk County. Bridgeport is an unorganized locality on Little Luckiamute River about three miles east or downstream from Falls City. It is said to have been named for a pioneer bridge over the stream, but the compiler does not know the exact location of the structure. Bridge Port post office was established June 1, 1854, with Samuel T. Scott first postmaster. The name of the office was very soon changed to Bridgeport. It continued in operation until January 13, 1874.

Briedwell, Yamhill County. Briedwell was a station on the Oregonian Railway narrow gauge line, later the Southern Pacific, at a point about two miles west of Amity, in the south part of the county. It was named for John W. Briedwell, a local resident, who was the first postmaster. Briedwell post office was established August 16, 1887, and discontinued October 31, 1888. Recent maps show a Briedwell School at this place, but the rest of the community is a thing of the past.

Briem Creek, Lane County. Briem Creek on the south slopes of Hehe Mountain about ten miles south of Blue River was named for Alfred J. Briem, USFS district ranger in the area for 17 years.

Briggs Landing, Lincoln County. Briggs Landing, in Boiler Bay, was named for Joe Briggs, who lived nearby.

Briggson, Umatilla County. Briggson post office served an area about eight miles east-southeast and up in the Blue Mountains from Weston in what is known as the Wildhorse Mountain district. One Dan Briggs fostered the idea of an office in this locality, but it was decided to put it at the McCorkell place rather than at the Briggs ranch, as Briggs lived too far back in the mountains. However, when the office was established, it was named in his honor. Briggson post office was established June 2, 1896, with William McCorkell first and only postmaster. The office was closed April 30, 1909, with papers to Weston.

Brigham Creek, Wallowa County. Brigham Creek flows into Bear Gulch from the west in section 26, township 1 south, range 47 east. It was named in pioneer days because of an event that suggested Mormonism, hence the use of Brigham Young's first name.

Brighton, Tillamook County. This post office and railroad station are near the mouth of Nehalem River, in the northwest part of the county. The town was platted about 1910 with the name of Brighton Beach although it is not directly on the ocean. This place, together with many others in the United States, was named for Brighton, the fashionable seashore resort on the south coast of England.

Brightwood, Clackamas County. Brightwood is said to have been named by a Mr. Alcorn, a property owner, because of the pleasing effect of the sun shining on the cottonwood trees in the spring. The first local post office was called Salmon, because it was very close to Salmon River, a stream named in pioneer days. Salmon post office was established in April, 1891, with Winnie McIntyre first postmaster. The name of this office was changed to Brightwood on May 6, 1910. Brightwood is about a quarter of a mile east of Salmon River on the old Mount Hood Loop Highway. The compiler does not know if the post office was moved this distance when the name was changed in 1910, or at some other time.

Bristow Prairie, Lane County. This prairie on the summit of the Calapooya Mountains was named for Elijah Bristow, the founder of Pleasant Hill, near Goshen. See under Pleasant Hill. Bristow used to go hunting on the prairie. He was born in Virginia in 1788, and came to Oregon in 1846. For his biography see Walling's *History of Lane County,* page 475.

Britt Creek, Douglas County. In 1887 William Britt homesteaded at the mouth of this creek a mile west of Idleyld Park on North Umpqua River.

Britten, Baker County. Britten was a post office in the mining district in the Blue Mountains between Baker and Sumpter, named for a local family. The office was established September 25, 1884, with Elizabeth E. Britten postmaster. Britten post office was discontinued May 9, 1893.

Broadacres, Marion County. About the time the Oregon Electric was opened for service between Portland and Salem in 1908, a station with the descriptive name Broadacres was established at a point about three miles west of Hubbard. There was not a great deal of business there at first, but in a few years it was necessary to have a post office. This office called Broadacres was opened in June, 1914, and was discontinued in December, 1928, with the business turned over to Hubbard. John R. Foulds was the first postmaster.

Broadbent, Coos County. Broadbent was named for C. E. Broadbent, who built a cheese factory in the community some time prior to the date the post office was established, which was in 1916.

Broadmead, Polk County. Mead is the Anglo-Saxon word for meadow, and Broadmead means Broadmeadow. The post office was established January 8, 1915, with Wm. H. Morris postmaster.

Broady Creek, Wallowa County. This stream is in the northeast part of the county. It was named for a broad-horned cow that belonged to Tom Green. She ranged along this stream.

Brock Creek, Lane County. This creek is fifteen miles northeast of Oakridge. It was named for Stewart Brock who ran cattle nearby before the turn of the century.

Brockway, Douglas County. Brockway, a little to the southwest of Roseburg, was once known as Civil Bend, a name said to refer to the boisterous activity of visitors to the horseraces. Civil Bend post office was in service from September, 1881, to October, 1888. When the office was reestablished in 1889, postal authorities objected to a name with two words, so a new name was selected in honor of B. B. Brockway, a pioneer resident. See under Civil Bend.

Brogan, Malheur County. This town was started by D. M. Brogan and was given his name in 1909. It is in the northern part of the country at the north end of the Union Pacific Railroad Company's branch from Vale.

Brogan Creek, Crook County. Phil Brogan of Bend informed the compiler in 1970 that this tributary of East Fork Mill Creek was named for his great uncle, Tom Brogan of Antelope, who used the area for summer graze. The tenor of those times is cogently described by Mr. Brogan's comment, "He was a stern old guy, and I certainly earned my $1 a day, plus board and bunk".

Broken Hand, Deschutes County. This prominent gendarme or rock outcrop is on the east ridge of Broken Top about one and one half miles east of the summit. It has an elevation of 8376 feet. In 1966 Judge John F. Kilkenny proposed the name to honor Thomas "Broken Hand" Fitzpatrick who passed through central Oregon as a scout with Fremont in the fall of 1843. Fitzpatrick, though a man of many accomplishments, is less remembered than his friends and contemporaries who included Smith, Meek, Carson and Bridger. He was with the party that discovered South Pass in 1824 and he served as scout and guide for Father DeSmet, Fremont, Kearney and numerous others. Later he was Indian Agent for the Upper Platte and arranged the council of 1851 at Fort Laramie. Fitzpatrick was born in Ireland in 1799 and died in Washington D.C., February 7, 1854. He acquired his nickname early in his career when a rifle exploded and crippled his left hand. Hafen and Ghent have an excellent biography in *Broken Hand, The Story of Thomas Fitzpatrick, Chief of the Mountain Men*.

Broken Top, Deschutes County. Although badly shattered, this mountain is one of the important peaks in the Cascade Range. It is southeast of South Sister and has an elevation of 9165 feet. From the aspect of its jagged summit it is not difficult to see why it was named. On its northern slope is Bend Glacier, on its south slope is Crook Glacier.

Brokencot Creek, Curry County. This stream is in the southeast part of the county in the Siskiyou Mountains. It rises east of Chetco Peak, and flows northward into Chetco River. It was named for Brokencot Camp, an old stopping place near its headwaters, distinguished by some worn out camp equipment.

Brookings, Curry County. Brookings was founded about 1908 as a company town for the Brookings Lumber & Box Company. John E. Brookings was president and as chief executive officer lived on the Pacific Coast, while his cousin, Robert S. Brookings, provided the major financial support. Robert Brookings lived in the east and devoted much of his time to semi-diplomatic missions and support of the arts. It was he who hired Bernard Maybeck, a San Francisco architect later involved in the Panama-Pacific Exposition, to lay out the townsite, certainly the only early plat in Oregon to receive the attention of such a qualified professional. Brookings post office was established January 4, 1913.

Brooks, Marion County. This is a station on the main line of the Southern Pacific Company nine miles north of Salem. It was named for Linus Brooks, who was born in Ohio in 1805, and came to Oregon from Illinois in 1850 and settled near the present site of the community. For additional information about the Brooks family see editorial page of the *Oregon Journal,* June 25, 1927.

Brooks Meadows, Hood River County. Brooks Meadows are drained by one of the branches of Dog River. These meadows were named for Caleb G. Brooks, who began to run cattle there about 1877. Brooks was a native of Iowa, and came to The Dalles with his family about 1870. He died in 1899, but his sons continued to use Brooks Meadows for cattle until about 1920.

Brooten Mountain, Tillamook County. Brooten Mountain has an elevation of 533 feet and forms the high ground east of Pacific City and south of Nestucca River. Shortly after World War I, H. H. Brooten uncovered a deposit of fossil kelp at the base of this mountain. He capitalized upon it through an advertising campaign worthy of the television claims of modern headache remedies and customers came from far and near to soak in the odoriferous baths. The name is all that remains to show for Mr. Brooten's enterprise.

Brothers, Deschutes County. Brothers is on the Central Oregon Highway between Bend and Burns, in the southeast part of the county. Brothers post office was established in September 1913, with Patrick H. Coffey first postmaster. There were several fraternal family groups that settled in the area of whom the various Stenkamp brothers comprised one of the more notable. Apparently the community was named for the many homesteading brothers and not in contradistinction to Sisters, the community northwest of Bend.

Broughton, Lane County. Broughton post office was named for the family of Thomas Broughton, the first and only postmaster. He was appointed May 8, 1891, and served until May 1, 1893. Despite diligent effort the compiler has been unable to get information about the location of this post office.

Broughton Bluff, Multnomah County. Lieutenant William Robert Broughton, commander of the armed tender *Chatham* of the Vancouver expedition, explored the Columbia River in the fall of 1792, and as far as known, was the first white man to visit the vicinity of the mouth of Willamette River. Broughton reached a point east of Troutdale on October 30, 1792. He wrote quite accurately of the geography of the mouth of Sandy River, and his maps, though on a small scale, were carefully made. The bluff east of Troutdale has always been a prominent landmark, but bore no name until 1926, when at the request of the Girl Scouts of Portland, the USBGN officially adopted for it the name of Broughton Bluff. William Robert Broughton was born in England in 1762. He entered the Royal Navy at an early age and in 1776 after the battle of Bunker Hill he and his commanding officer, while engaging in a salvage operation, were captured by American troops. After the war he served in various capacities and in 1791 in command of the *Chatham,* discovered and named the Chatham Islands off New Zealand. His subsequent activities with Vancouver are well known. In later years he continued exploration and in 1797 was wrecked off the coast of Formosa with his ship *Providence*. Broughton then served in the Java Sea, retired as captain and died in Italy in 1821. For further details of his life, see Meany's *Vancouver's Discovery of Puget Sound,* page 264.

In the summer of 1974, Sir Charles Madden visited Portland to open the Oregon Historical Society's memorable Cook Exhibition. To commemorate the exploration by the British Navy, he participated in naming Chatham Island and Broughton Reach in the Columbia River. Broughton Reach is the stretch of the river running east from Flag Island where Broughton looked upstream for fifteen miles and saw that the Columbia did not rise on Mount Hood but extended far inland.

Brower, Multnomah County. Brower was the name of a post office in the hills about two miles south-southeast of Bridal Veil and at the north base of Pepper Mountain. It was named for George W. Brower who had a logging and lumber business thereabouts in the 1890s. Brower post office was established December 20, 1889, with Robert C. Bell first postmaster. The compiler does not know the closing date, but it was probably about 1895.

Brown, Benton County. Brown post office was established July 5, 1902, with Clara Huggins first and only postmaster. The office was closed March 10, 1903. Robert Johnson informed the compiler that the office was situated at the home of William and Clara Huggins on the Brown place some eight or ten miles southwest of Corvallis.

Brown Meadows, Wallowa County. These meadows are in section 16, township 4 north, range 41 east. They bear the name of John Brown, a homesteader.

Brown Mountain, Wallowa County. This is a high peak in the Wallowa Mountains northwest of Eagle Cap. It was named because of its characteristic color near the top.

Brownlee, Baker County. Two men named Brown and Lee, uncle and nephew, settled on the Idaho side of Snake River in the 1860s. Later on, the men established a ferry across the river and when the railroad was built down the Oregon side, the company named the station Brownlee. Brownlee post office was established December 17, 1910, and operated intermittently until July 1943. In 1959 the Idaho Power Company completed Brownlee Dam. This 395 foot high dam forms a slackwater pool extending to within ten miles of Weiser and has a maximum generating capacity of 450,000 kilowatts.

Browns Mountain, Deschutes County. Browns Mountain, elevation 5330 feet, is south of Crane Prairie, and Browns Creek is nearby. These features were named for John A. Brown, a negro homesteader who settled in the neighborhood. Brown was a trapper and hunter and also ran some stock. C. J. Keefer is authority for the statement that he always paid his bills in gold which led to the notion that gold was buried near the homestead. Brown died in Prineville in 1903 but rumors of buried treasure near Crane Prairie have been more durable.

Brownsboro, Jackson County. This place was named in 1853 for Henry R. Brown, on whose land the community was established. Brownsboro is on Little Butte Creek. A post office was established in the locality in February, 1873, with the name Brownsborough and with John Bilger first of a long list of postmasters. The name of the office was changed to Brownsboro on June 25, 1892.

Brownsmead, Clatsop County. This community has developed on the bank of the Columbia River as the result of diking and reclamation, carried on by W. G. Brown, a well-known engineer of Portland. His name coupled with the Anglo-Saxon word for meadow formed the name of the community. It was formerly known as Brody.

Brownsville, Linn County. Brownsville is on the Calapooia River near the foothills of the Cascade Range, and has an elevation of 356 feet. It was laid out in 1853, and named by James Blakely in honor of Hugh L. Brown, who started the first store there. Both these men were pioneers of 1846. Blakely built the first house in the fall of 1846. For biography and portrait of Blakely, see the *Oregonian*, April 17, 1901, page 10. For description of Brownsville in 1889, *ibid.*, January 18, 1890. For description in 1894, *ibid.*, January 1, 1895, page 11. Postal records show that Brownsville post office was established on January 8, 1850, with the name Calapooya with H. H. Spalding first postmaster. This was changed to Brownsville on May 18, 1859.

Browntown, Josephine County. This place is a relic of the past. It was a mining town on Althouse Creek, about three miles south of Holland. Walling, in his *History of Southern Oregon,* page 455 says that it was named for one Webfoot Brown, the pioneer Brown of the vicinity, and that at one time the place had 500 inhabitants.

Bruce, Benton County. Bruce is the name of a small community on the Pacific Highway West about ten miles south of Corvallis. It is on the Major James Bruce land claim and was named on that account. A post office named Bruce was established in July, 1900, with Lucinda Norwood first postmaster. The office was closed in May, 1905.

Bruces Bones Creek, Curry County. John Quiner of the OSHD told of the naming of this creek north of Cape Ferrelo. In the 1950s Bruce Schilling was a chainman with the crew completing the survey for the new alignment of US 101. At the end of the day when the crew started to leave, Schilling headed in the wrong direction and because of the heavy brush had considerable difficulty finding his way out of the deep gully. The rest of the party saw him but could not make themselves heard over the sound of the surf. Ron Brazeau, the transitman, then commented that they would find Bruce's parched bones next spring when they returned. No doubt the story bore considerable repeating and the name was soon firmly fixed.

Brush Creek, Curry County. Brush Creek drains an area southeast of Port Orford and flows into Pacific Ocean just north of Humbug Mountain. It seems to be the consensus in Curry County that this stream was named for Gilbert Brush, a young Texan, who was a member of the T'Vault exploring party in those parts in 1851. To say that he had hairraising adventures is apposite, since Coquille Indians "lifted" part of his scalp. See Bancroft's *History of Oregon*, volume II, pages 196-200, and Dodge's *Pioneer History of Coos and Curry Counties*, page 26. Preston's *Map of Oregon*, 1856, shows this stream as Savage Creek, but Preston possibly confused it with Euchre Creek, a little further south, which George Davidson, in *Coast Pilot*, 1889 says was called Savage Creek. See under Euchre Creek. Preston's knowledge of Curry County geography was necessarily sketchy.

Brush College, Polk County. Brush College is situated in the southeast part of the Eola Hills. It was named because of the character of the nearby ground cover. For story about Brush College school and community by Mrs. W. N. Crawford see Salem *Statesman*, October 8, 1931.

Brushy Creek, Wallowa County. Brushy Creek flows into Little Sheep Creek about twelve miles east of Enterprise. It was named because of the unusually dense brush growing along its banks. The first homesteader on this stream was William Waln.

Bryan Creek, Yamhill County. Bryan Creek in the Chehalem Valley was probably named for Tom Bryan who farmed the lower reaches in the early days. Bryan was one of nine sons of Francis and Sarah Bryan who lived north of Newberg. All the sons as well as two daughters married into local pioneer families so the name was well known.

Bryant Lake, Linn County. This is a small slough lake about a mile west of Albany. It was named for Hub Bryant, a pioneer resident. Bryant Park, in Albany, was given to the city by the same man. He owned considerable land in the vicinity of the lake.

Buchanan, Harney County. Buchanan is a locality about twenty miles east of Burns on the Central Oregon Highway where the highway begins to climb up out of Harney Valley. The place bears the name of a local family. Buchanan post office was established on May 1, 1911, with Hattie E. Buchanan first postmaster. The office was closed June 30, 1919, but the place is still referred to as Buchanan. For biography of Joseph W. and Hattie E. Buchanan, see *History of Baker, Grant, Malheur and Harney Counties*, page 715.

Buck Creek, Multnomah County. This stream flows into Sandy River just north of Gordon Creek. It has also been known as Trapper Creek, but the USGS has adopted the name Buck Creek, which seems to represent the best local use.

Buck Fork, Douglas County. Buck Fork was the name of a post office on Buck Fork, a tributary of North Myrtle Creek. Fred Asam, an early USFS ranger, homesteaded nearby before the creek was named and was one of the settlers instrumental in establishing the office. During a discussion regarding a name, Asam remarked "I have just killed a forked horn buck. Why not call it Buck Fork?" The office was in operation from September, 1910, until August 1927. Nearby Buck Peak was apparently named for the stream.

Buck Island, Klamath County. Buck Island is near the lower end of Upper Klamath Lake. It is one of many features in Oregon named for some event connected with a deer. In pioneer days it was called Rattlesnake Island.

Buck Peak, Hood River and Multnomah counties. This peak west of Lost Lake was named in July, 1906 by R. S. Shelley of the USFS. Shelley and Ralph Lewis were locating trail and came across a large buck sunning himself near the summit.

Buck Rock, Jackson County. Buck Rock is a well-known landmark northeast of Trail. It was named in 1860 by Albert Winkel, a pioneer hunter and trapper. Its top was frequented by deer.

Bucket Lake, Baker County. Bucket Lake is west of Elkhorn Peak. Herbert Ensminger of Haines stated in 1968 that in 1920 he, Raymond Ward and Omar Maxwell stocked Bucket Lake and nearby Rock Creek Lake with trout. The fish were trucked to Eilertson Meadow and taken the rest of the way by pack train. Bucket Lake was already so called because of the bucket like basin it is in.

Buckhorn Springs, Wallowa County. Buckhorn Springs are well known. They are in township 3 north, range 48 east. The place was frequented by deer and many horns were shed there. Campers found the horns and made piles of them.

Buckneck Mountain, Douglas County. This mountain is on the divide between Rogue River and North Umpqua River, northwest of Crater Lake, and has an elevation of 6173 feet. The origin of the name is not known, but it was applied by a sheepherder some time prior to 1906.

Buckskin Peak, Curry and Josephine counties. This peak, elevation 3925 feet, is in the Siskiyou Mountains about 6 1/4 miles north of the Oregon-California state line. The summit of the peak is covered with the so-called "buckskin boulders." They are of many sizes but all of peculiar buckskin color.

Budd Creek, Coos County. Budd Creek bears the name of an early settler. It flows into Cunningham Creek northwest of Coquille.

Buell, Polk County. Buell is in the northern part of the county, and was named for Elias Buell, who started a mill there and a small store in pioneer days. Elias Buell's land office certificate was numbered 4165. Buell post office was established in March, 1900.

Buena Vista, Polk County. The compiler is informed by E. M. Croisan, of Salem, that Buena Vista was named by his grandfather, Reason B. Hall, whose donation land claim formed the site of the community. Hall was born in Georgia in 1791, and settled on his land claim in 1847. He named Buena Vista about 1850, because some of his relatives participated in the battle of Buena Vista in Mexico. About the time he named the community, he started Halls Ferry across Willamette River. James A. O'Neal built a warehouse in Buena Vista, the first mercantile establishment, about 1850. Later one of Reason Hall's sons started another Halls Ferry north of Independence. *Buena Vista* is Spanish for beautiful view or good view.

Buffalo, Lake County. Buffalo was a post office in the northeast part of the county, just northwest of the center of township 27 south, range 21 east, about a dozen miles east of Christmas Lake. It was established April 11, 1913, with Samuel W. Stanton first of four postmasters. The office was discontinued June 29, 1918. A news item in the *Lake County Examiner,* Lakeview, February 13, 1947, says that the office was named because a nearby juniper tree was so shaped that it looked like a buffalo. The story is credited to S. V. Carroll, well-known resident of the county.

Buford Creek, Wallowa County. This stream rises in Oregon a little north of Flora, and flows northward into Washington, where it drains into Grande Ronde River. It was named for Park Buford, a pioneer settler nearby. The locality became important because Buford Canyon was used for the highway from Enterprise to Lewiston. Park Buford is reported to have died as a result of rattlesnake bite, which he received while reaching under his cabin trying to find a pup.

Bug Butte, Klamath County. On March 1, 1926, L. D. Arnold of the Indian Field Service wrote the USBGN from Klamath Agency as follows: "Bug Butte, not Big Butte, is a newly coined name for the butte two miles southeast of Council Butte in sections 24 and 25. It has been so named because bark beetles have in the past five years killed nearly all the pine trees." This insect is the western pine beetle, *Dendroctonus brevicomis.* See Essig's *Insects of Western North America,* page 514, and news article in Bend *Bulletin,* July 14, 1927.

Bug Creek, Wheeler County. This small creek in the Ochoco National Forest just north of the Crook County line was named by USFS ranger Grover Blake before World War I. He had an insect control camp on the creek with about sixty men cutting and peeling lodge pole pines infected with the pine bark bug.

Bugby Hole, Clatsop County. Bugby Hole is the name of a very deep place in the Columbia River about midway between Wauna and Bradwood, close under the precipitous cliffs to the west of the stream. There is a railway flag stop nearby known as Bugby Hole. In September, 1943, Seth F. Michael of the USCE office in Portland wrote the compiler that Bugby Hole was named for an earlyday settler who carried on some logging operations in the vicinity. Bugby Hole has a depth of over 100 feet at low water and is remarkable on that account.

Bull Mountain, Washington County. This mountain is situated about three miles southwest of Tigard and has an elevation of 711 feet. G. W. Tefft of Beaverton told the writer in 1927 that it was named for a band of wild cattle that ranged on the hill in pioneer days. These cattle were gradually killed off with the exception of one bull and thus the descriptive name was attached to the hill in question.

Bull of the Woods, Marion County. This peak, elevation 5510 feet, is in the northeast part of the county but a short distance from the Clackamas

County line. One account asserts it was named for a nearby mining claim or prospect but Ron Burnett in an article in *Mazama,* April, 1979, page 3, relates that William R. Bagby of the hot springs family once shot a large bull elk and told his friends, "I got the Bull of the woods". Regardless of the application, "Bull of the woods" is an old logger's term. Walter F. McCulloch in *Woods Words,* page 21, gives three definitions all relating to big or important men in the logging industry.

Bull Run Lake, Clackamas and Multnomah counties. Will G. Steel is authority for the statement that the Klickitat Indian name for Bull Run Lake was *Gohabedikt,* meaning Loon Lake. It is not surprising that such a name was not used by white men. The lake undoubtedly received its present name from Bull Run River, not *vice versa.* The compiler has no evidence that the lake was called Chitwood for an old settler, as it seems improbable that anyone could have settled in such a locality. Bull Run Lake has an area of about .6 of a square mile, and an elevation of 3161 feet. The outlet is through underground springs forming Bull Run River, but a dam now regulates part of the leakage. Contrary to general belief, no drainage from melting snow or ice on Mount Hood enters Bull Run drainage basin. A chemical description of the water may be secured from USGS *WSP 363.* The intake of Portland water supply is about 20 miles down stream from the lake. Economically, Bull Run Lake is the most important lake in Oregon, for it is the source of water supply for about a third of the population of the state.

Bull Run River, Clackamas and Multnomah counties. George H. Himes, late curator of the Oregon Historical Society, said the name of Portland's water supply, Bull Run, may have started from the presence of wild cattle on that river in the pioneer period (1849-55). According to Charles B. Talbot, who arrived in Oregon in 1849, cattle escaped from immigrants in that vicinity and ran wild a number of years. The place was called by the settlers Bull Run. For further history of the name Bull Run, see the *Oregonian,* March 29, April 5, 1897, page 8; July 30, 1901, page 12. The locality called Bull Run is about three miles northeast of Sandy, in Clackamas County, and near Bull Run River. The first post office was Unavilla, established in May, 1893. The compiler does not know the reason for selecting this odd word. The name was changed to Bullrun in November, 1895, and to Camp Namanu in January, 1939. See under that heading.

Bullard Creek, Lake County. M. W. Bullard moved into the Goose Lake Valley in 1869 and settled at the present site of Lakeview. Bullard Creek and Bullard Canyon, just east of the town, bear his name. For a description of his activities, see *History of Central Oregon,* page 844. Bullard Creek and the Bullard ranch played a prominent part in the county seat squabble of 1876. The legislature created Lake County in October, 1874, and named Linkville, now Klamath Falls, temporary county seat until an election to be held June 5, 1876, at which time a permanent county seat was to be selected by majority vote. At the appointed election Bullard Creek rolled up a count of 120 against 88 for Linkville, but 120 was not a majority of the 384 votes cast. About 75 votes were cast for Goose Lake, Goose Lake Valley, Bullard's Ranch and Bullard's Creek in Goose Lake, which were not counted for Bullard Creek. On August 10, 1876, the county commissioners ordered the scattered votes to be included in the Bullard Creek total and directed that the county seat be set up at the Bullard house. However, the county clerk would not comply. In accordance with the legislative act, the election was held again on November 7, 1876. By that time the town of Lakeview had been organized, and it carried the election. Six years later the people of Linkville and the Klamath Valley succeeded in getting a county of their own cut off from Lake, and called it Klamath.

Bullards, Coos County. This town is near the mouth of Coquille River and was named for Robert W. Bullard, who was born in Iowa November 26, 1857, and died July 11, 1925. In 1882 he established a general merchandise store at what is now Bullards, and also a ferry across the river. The post office was named for him. He came to Coos County in 1877. He married Malinda A. Hamblock.

Bulldog Rock, Douglas County. This rock is near the summit of the Calapooya Mountains in the northeastern part of the county and has an elevation of 5801 feet. It was named by USFS Supervisor E. H. McDaniels on account of the prominence with which the bluff stood out from its immediate surroundings, in defiance of the elements.

Bullock Creek, Douglas County. This creek flows into Jackson Creek above South Umpqua River. It was named for William A. Bullock who homesteaded there in the 1890s.

Bully Creek, Malheur County. There are several stories concerning the origin of the name of this stream, all apparently revolving around the fact that when a man fell into its waters many years ago, his friends stood about and cried out "Bully! Bully!" T. T. Geer, in the *Oregonian,* February 9, 1921, says that during a debate on a bill to change the name of the stream in the legislature in 1889, David P. Thompson told the story and said that the incident happened while he, Thompson, was engaged in surveying townships for the government. In a letter in the *Oregonian,* April 21, 1927, Glen Livingston relates the story, saying that it came from D. P. Thompson and that it applied to Bull Run River. On April 27, 1927, Henry E. Reed, in the *Oregonian,* replied to Livingston, saying that the incident did not happen on Bull Run River. He says that Thompson told him it happened to some soldiers in the 1850s. The legislature of 1889 changed the name of this stream from Bully Creek to Alder Creek and Thompson was a member of the house of representatives at the time. It seems probable to the compiler that the story told by Governor Geer is the correct one, and that the incident happened while Thompson was surveying. It does not seem probable that there were soldiers on Bully Creek in the 1850s. Despite the act of the legislature, the name of the stream has remained Bully Creek, and it is universally so known. The act is printed on page 158 of the *Laws of Oregon,* fifteenth legislative assembly, 1889. A post office called Bully was established near this stream April 3, 1882, with Nancy Kime first postmaster. This office did not operate continuously. The name was changed to Westfall in February, 1889. The office was doubtless moved from time to time.

Bunchgrass Creek, Wasco County. This stream is in the extreme northwest part of the Warm Springs Indian Reservation, and flows into Warm Springs River. There are a number of geographic features in Oregon named for bunchgrass, a valuable natural forage of the eastern part of

Oregon. Charles V. Piper lists two varieties: *Festuca ovina ingrata,* the blue bunchgrass of the prairies, which is densely tufted, and *Agropyron spicatum,* the wheat bunchgrass which is taller and grows generally on dry hills.

Buncom, Jackson County. Buncom was a community at the confluence of Sterling Creek and Little Applegate River. The post office was established December 5, 1896 with J. Parks first postmaster, and closed December 15, 1917. There is little left of the town in 1980. Dean Saltmarsh of Jackson County, in an interview with Kay Atwood in 1975, said that the name was a mispronunciation of the name of a local settler by Chinese miners. The settler's actual name has long been forgotten.

Bunker Hill, Coos County. Bunker Hill is a neighborhood in the south part of the city of Coos Bay, and is remarkable for the fact that it was not named for the historic spot in Boston. Prior to 1900 it was just another timbered hill rising above tidewater near the mouth of Coalbank Slough. It was called Bunker Hill because of the coal bunkers nearby and the application of the name came without formality. About 1906 the area was platted for homes by the Flanagan estate and the title Bunker Hill seemed natural. The coal bunkers were principally on Isthmus Slough to the east of Bunker Hill, but there were also some on Coalbank Slough to the west. It was here that the ocean vessels took on their cargoes of coal from the Newport mines.

Bunker Hill, Linn County. About 1858 R. C. Finley and associates established a community and grist mill on Calapooia River about a mile and a half east of the present town of Shedd. The locality was called Boston Mills. Just southeast of the site of the Finley enterprises was a small butte, which took the name Bunker Hill because it was so close to the Boston Mills. This little butte is about a half mile west of Saddle Butte and south of the east-west road.

Bunker Hill, Marion County. Bunker Hill is one of the highest points in the group of hills south of Salem. It has an elevation of 956 feet, and lies about two miles west of the Pacific Highway East and a mile north of Ankeny Bottom. In a letter written to Ladd & Bush, Bankers, dated February 1, 1915, John W. Jory gives information about the origin of this name. The letter was published in the *Ladd & Bush Quarterly,* April, 1915. Jory wrote that in pioneer days Bunker Hill was known as Bald Hill to distinguish it from other hills in the vicinity. He was of the opinion that the name was changed to Bunker Hill either by Perry Watson or by Henry E. Ankeny. The name Bunker Hill has been in general use since about 1870. Stories to the effect that the hill may have been named for a local resident seem to be erroneous, and Bunker Hill near Boston, famous in the American Revolution, is no doubt the origin of the name.

Bunyard Creek, Lake County. Bunyard Creek flows into Silver Creek near the town of Silver Lake. It was named for Jesse Bunyard, one of the very early homesteaders in the area, who was born in Missouri October 2, 1843. He came west with his mother in 1854 and settled in Umatilla County in 1866. In 1876 he moved to Silver Lake where he took up his homestead along this creek. He is reported to have sowed the first crop of grain in the Silver Lake area.

Burghardts Mill, Clackamas County. This little settlement is about a mile west of Barton and is near Clackamas River. It was named for Ernest H. Burghardt, one of the early settlers in that community. It was he who secured the establishment of the Barton post office. The mill is occasionally referred to as Burkhards Mill but that form is incorrect. For additional information see under Barton.

Burkemont, Baker County. Burkemont is a locality in the extreme northern part of the county, about 20 miles northeast of Baker. It was named for Judge Thomas Carrick Burke, who was at one time interested in mining development at that place and was later a resident of Portland and collector of customs.

Burleson, Lake County. Burleson post office was established May 25, 1914, with Mima E. Petit postmaster and was in operation until January 31, 1915. It was named in compliment to Albert S. Burleson, postmaster general from 1913 until 1921. The office was about 16 miles east-northeast of the town of Silver Lake.

Burlington, Linn County. In March, 1947, Leslie L. Haskin of Newport, a student of Linn County history, wrote the compiler in substance as follows: "It is commonly said the town of Burlington was renamed and called Peoria. This is not correct. The town of Burlington was started in 1851 with a ferry run by John Smith and a store by John Donald. The townsite was mapped by James Freeman in 1853. The place had at that time two dwellings, two stores, one smithy and a ferry. However, the river silted up and spoiled the boat landings. Because boats found no suitable landing places, they passed the town and it died. The site of Burlington was the better part of a mile down the river from Peoria, and they were two different towns. Some buildings were moved from Burlington to Peoria." Burlington post office was established November 17, 1855, with William M. McCorkle postmaster. The name of the office was changed to Peoria November 7, 1857, and it was doubtless moved to the new location about that time. There had been some settlement at Peoria as early as 1851, but active growth did not follow until later. Mr. J. C. Irvine writes from Lebanon that Burlington, Oregon, was on the donation land claim of his grandfather, James Martin, who came to Oregon in 1852. It was in sections 5,6,7 and 8, township 13 south, range 4 west. Mr. Irvine says that before coming to Oregon his grandfather farmed for some twenty years near Little York, Illinois. The nearest market town was Burlington, Iowa. It is a matter of family tradition that Burlington, Oregon, was named for Burlington, Iowa.

Burlington, Multnomah County. Burlington is the name of a community north of Portland. The plat was filed for record March 24, 1909, by Ruth Trust Company. Herman Wittenberg was president of the company and named the place Burlington, but it is not known why he selected that name.

Burma, Lane County. Burma is an operating station on the Southern Pacific railroad north of Eugene, and was established to help clear trains at the north end of Eugene Yard. Traffic became congested at this point in 1941, and when the station was put in service, the name was selected because of the traffic bottleneck then existing on the great Burma Road between India and China. Burma station was officially established by the railroad on November 27, 1942, but it was actually put in service about the beginning of 1942.

Burns, Harney County. This community was named for Robert Burns by George McGowan, a pioneer resident who was a great admirer of the Scottish poet. Elevation 4148 feet. In February, 1943, Archie McGowan of Burns furnished the compiler with some data about his father, George McGowan, who moved into the Harney Valley from the Willamette Valley in May, 1882. George McGowan first stopped at the little settlement of Egan, about two and a half miles southwest of the present site of Burns, and engaged in the mercantile business. He soon decided to enlarge his business and move to a new location. He took Peter Stenger into partnership in the fall of 1883, and the two established themselves at the present locality of Burns, one reason being that it was nearer the Stenger ranch. Stenger wanted to name the new place Stenger, but McGowan thought otherwise, calling attention to the fact that Stenger was frequently pronounced Stinger, and the name Stingertown would be bad advertising. McGowan finally suggested Burns, and early in 1884 the community was established with the name. George McGowan died in Portland January 31, 1930, aged 85 years. For story of hanging of portrait of George McGowan in new Burns post office, see Burns *Times-Herald,* June 13, 1941. Egan post office was established July 31, 1882, with George McGowan postmaster. The name was changed to Burns January 22, 1884. The name Egan is said to have been that of a local Indian celebrity.

Burnside, Clatsop County. David Burnside, for whom this place was named, was a native of Ireland. He came to the United States about 1825, and was naturalized in April, 1832. He arrived in Oregon in 1847. He married Mary Ann, last name not given, in Philadelphia, in August, 1853. He settled on his donation land claim in 1855, and the nearby station was subsequently named on this account. His land office certificate was numbered 3606. Marys Creek in Clatsop County was named for his wife.

Burnt Bridge Creek, Lane County. Burnt Bridge Creek flows into Middle Fork Willamette River a few miles below Westfir. According to C. B. McFarland of Oakridge, the name came into use as a result of the Dead Mountain fire of 1910, which destroyed the wagon bridge over the stream. The name Burnt Ridge Creek is wrong.

Burnt Ranch, Wheeler County. Burnt Ranch is a place on the south bank of the John Day River at the extreme western edge of Wheeler County. The name was applied in 1866. The ranch was on the old military road from The Dalles to Canyon City. The buildings were burned during an Indian uprising and from that time the place was known by its present name. The original Burnt Ranch was near the mouth of Bridge Creek, but the post office moves about, depending upon the home of the postmaster. At one time the office was far enough west to be in Jefferson County. Burnt Ranch post office was established January 15, 1883, by change of name from Grade. Addie S. Masterson was the first postmaster.

Burnt River, Baker County. Burnt River is an important stream rising in the Blue Mountains and draining the south part of the county. It joins Snake River east of Huntington. Exact information about its name is not available, and there are two theories about the matter, one being that Burnt River was so called because of the burned timber along its banks and the other because of the burned looking rocks, especially along the lower reaches. As far as the writer knows, the first mention of Burnt River is in the Peter Skene Ogden journals for Friday, October 28, 1825. T. C. Elliott was of the opinion that the name came from the burned woods, because fur-traders reached the upper parts of the stream first where the burned looking rocks are not so much in evidence. During the times in question the stream was frequently mentioned as the *Riviere Brule*, by the French-Canadians. It is of course evident that the traders named the stream, and that pioneers proceeding along the lower part of the river 25 years later had nothing to do with it, though they doubtless thought the name was appropriate because of the dry character of the country they traversed. Mr. Elliott thought that the name was probably first applied to the river by Donald McKenzie possibly as early as 1818. See *OHQ*, volume XIII, page 71. For many references about the name Burnt River, see *Discovery of the Oregon Trail* (Stuart's Narrative edited by Rollins), pages 79 and 95. In the first edition of *Astoria*, volume II, page 122, Burnt River is appropriately called Woodpile Creek apparently on account of driftwood accumulations. The compiler has seen later editions of *Astoria* with this name spelled Woodvile, a meaningless error.

Burnt Woods, Lincoln County. This post office is in the eastern part of Lincoln County, near Tumtum River, where the remains of forest fires are still much in evidence. The office was established in 1919, and a list of suggested names was sent to the Post Office Department. On the list was Burnt Woods, proposed by H. G. Downing, and this was the name chosen by the authorities.

Burnt Woods, Washington County. Washington County has had more than its share of forest fires and it is not surprising that there was once a post office in the county called Burnt Woods. This office was a mile or so north of the place called Glenwood, as Glenwood was situated in 1945. Burnt Woods post office was established September 12, 1879, with Mrs. Mary J. Evans postmaster. The office was closed September 17, 1883. Later a post office named Glenwood was organized to serve the same general locality, but it may not have been in exactly the same place. Glenwood post office was subsequently moved a couple of miles south to a site on Gales Creek.

Burroughs, Umatilla County. The compiler has been unable to get much information about Burroughs post office, except that it was in service from May 10, 1893, to July 12, 1895, with Barney F. Hogue the only postmaster. Hogue is said to have lived in Coombs Canyon four miles west of Sparks Station, southwest of Pendleton, in a locality sometimes referred to as Burroughs. There was a smithy and some other buildings in the locality. Postal records show that a post office called Bissell was established with Benjamin L. Burroughs postmaster on April 27, 1893, but Bissell post office was never in operation. Judging from available information Burroughs post office was in the same neighborhood as the Bissell office and was named for the Bissell postmaster.

Bus Point, Wasco County. Eric Gordon of the USFS named this point in section 19, township 4 south, range 11 east, for Lewis D. "Bus" Reavis who worked for Gordon in the 1920s. Dr. Reavis told the writer in 1969 that he had just topped a 120 foot tree to prepare a fire lookout platform and his boss named the spot in his honor.

Bush, Marion County. Bush is the name of a station on the Burlington Northern in north Salem. It commemorates Asahel Bush, the prominent editor and publisher of the Salem *Statesman* during the second half of the nineteenth century. Bush was born in Massachusetts in 1824 and came to Oregon in 1850. He was associated with W. S. Ladd in the Salem Ladd & Bush Bank and was influential in the Democratic Party. He died in Salem on December 23, 1913. The Bush house in Salem is listed in the National Register of Historic Places and is the central feature of Bush Pasture Park.

Bushnell Creek, Douglas County. This creek above Tenmile was named for Linus Bushnell who took up a donation land claim there in 1854. Bushnell Rock, northwest of Tenmile, was apparently named for Archie L. Bushnell, a more recent member of the family.

Buster Butte, Lane County. This butte and other features of the same name are on Steamboat Creek near the summit of the Calapooya Mountains. They were named in 1921 by USFS ranger Fred Asam for his faithful old packhorse, Buster.

Butcher Knife Ridge, Hood River County. Ralph Lewis of Parkdale told the writer that this ridge east of Lost Lake was named about 1900 because Pete Lenz remarked to hunting companions that the brush on this ridge was so thick you couldn't stick a butcherknife into it.

Butcherknife Creek, Wallowa County. One day in the early 1890s Jack Shields and Dick and Alex Warnock found an old butcherknife on this stream, and named the creek on that account. Butcherknife Creek is a tributary of Lightning Creek.

Butler, Polk County. On February 16, 1861, a post office with the name Grand Ronde was established in the north part of Polk County, at the site of Fort Yamhill. Benjamin Simpson, an Indian agent, was the first postmaster, and the area served was about a half mile north of the present locality of Valley Junction. On October 3, 1894, this office was moved about three miles northwest to Grand Ronde Agency in Yamhill County, but without change of name. This move left the Fort Yamhill area without a post office. A new office was established in the locality, with the name Butler, on March 16, 1895, and with J. C. Ellis first of two postmasters. The office was named in compliment to Judge N. L. Butler of Dallas, who owned a large farm nearby. According to Mr. Ellis the farm was then being operated by James Shepherd, and Shepherd suggested the use of the name. Butler post office was discontinued June 30, 1911.

Butler Basin, Grant and Wheeler counties. This is a large basin in the John Day Valley north of Picture Gorge. It was named for an early settler, Frank Butler, a one-armed rancher who lived in a little cabin near the present site of Cants Ranch. Butler was the only resident of the basin in 1877. The name Upper Basin is occasionally used for this geographic feature, but Butler Basin seems to be the generally accepted form. There was once a post office in this locality called Basin.

Butler Canyon, Wasco County. US 197 follows Butler Canyon from

Tygh Valley north to Tygh Ridge summit. Jonathan Butler was born in Illinois in 1833 and came to Oregon and Wasco County with his family. Butler settled near Kingsley and helped develop the road in the canyon that bears his name.

Butler Mountain, Wheeler County. Butler Mountain lies just north of Richmond. It was named for two brothers, John D. and George O. Butler who raised stock in the Richmond area before the turn of the century. The two had adjoining homesteads on the north slopes of the mountain.

Butte, Lake County. Butte post office was on the east border of the county line a little south of Wagontire Mountain. The office was established December 21, 1911, with Josiah E. Pope first postmaster. This was at the time that many dry farmers and homesteaders were coming into central Oregon. The office was closed October 31, 1922, and the mail was then handled through Wagontire office. Butte post office was named for a well-known point, Elk Butte, near the east border of township 27 south, range 22 east.

Butte Creek, Clackamas and Marion counties. Down, in *A History of the Silverton Country,* says that Butte Creek was probably named for Graves Butte, or Lone Tree Butte, so called because at its summit was a gigantic fir. The butte is now known as Mount Angel. Butte Creek was so known in the days of pioneer settlement. A post office with the name Bute Creek was operated from January to November, 1851, with Jeremiah Jack postmaster. This office was reestablished with the name Butte Creek in 1867, and the name was changed to Marquam in November, 1889.

Butte Creek, Wallowa County. J. H. Horner of Enterprise told the compiler in 1931 that the Indians called the locality of this stream *Tuscowall-a me,* meaning a place where the owls lived. In early days the stream was called Owl Creek, but the name was gradually changed to Butte Creek because it rises near Oregon Butte in Columbia County, Washington. Butte Creek flows south into Oregon and drains into Wenaha River in township 6 north, range 41 east.

Butte Creek, Wheeler County. This stream rises near Fossil and flows into John Day River. It was so named because of Black Butte, a prominent point near its source, which serves as a landmark. Black Butte has an elevation of about 4000 feet and is about two miles northeast of Fossil.

Butte Disappointment, Lane County. Butte Disappointment is on the north side of Middle Fork Willamette River, east and northeast of Lowell. It has a maximum elevation of 2409 feet and is a very prominent landmark. Walling in his *Illustrated History of Lane County* gives an account of the naming of this feature. In 1848 a party of settlers led by Elijah Bristow of Pleasant Hill undertook a foray against marauding Indians. The posse tried to ascend the river on the northeast bank, but was blocked by Fall Creek, which was in flood. The settlers mistook Fall Creek for the main stream, and returned to the Hills place, crossed the river and followed up the southwest bank. When they reached a point about opposite the present site of Lowell, they found to their disappointment that they were on the wrong side of the Middle Fork. They could not proceed on that side and had to give up the expedition. Because of this episode the name Butte Disappointment was applied to the prominent hill on the north side. A post office named Butte Disappointment was established May 8, 1872, with Samuel Handsaker, postmaster. It was at or near the present site of Dexter and was named for the prominent point a few miles eastward. The name of the office was changed to Dexter on July 19, 1875.

Butte Falls, Jackson County. Settlers in the Rogue River Valley refered to Mount McLoughlin as Snowy Butte, and the two main streams draining to the northwest from that mountain were known as Big and Little Butte creeks. At the falls on Big Butte Creek a settlement sprang up that took its name from the natural feature.

Butter Creek, Umatilla County. Butter Creek is a tributary of Umatilla River, and the old pioneer road crossed it west of Echo. See Scott's *History of the Oregon Country,* volume III, page 316. The writer has heard of two theories about the origin of the name. The diary of John T. Kerns, published in OPA *Transactions* for 1914, says under date of September 9, 1852, that Butter Creek was named because some volunteers took butter from the stores during the Cayuse War. Miss L. C. McKay, for many years a resident of eastern Oregon, confirmed this statement, and informed the writer that the butter was taken from the officers' mess so the enlisted men could have hot cakes. The other story is to the effect that a party of pioneers found some stale butter on the banks of the stream. The writer has no confirmation of this story.

Butterfield, Clatsop County. Butterfield was a station just north of Gearhart. It was named for Charles Butterfield, who married Margaret Gearhart, daughter of a Clatsop Plains pioneer.

Buttermilk Creek, Benton County. This very small stream flows southward through Philomath into Marys River. A letter printed in the Philomath *Review* for January 15, 1942, signed by F. S. Minshall, gives the origin of the name. Many years ago a creamery did a thriving business on the banks of this brook, and ran its surplus buttermilk into the drain. This activity was of no great consequence in the cold months of the year, but in summer, the resulting stench aroused local residents to indignation. A septic tank was installed, but it overflowed. Farmers carried away the surplus milk for hog feed, but they could not carry away the odor. A "Smelling Committee" was appointed by the council, but as is frequently the case with committees, little was done. Finally the creamery got into financial trouble and closed, thus bringing an end to the business. The name Buttermilk Creek remains, however.

Butteville, Marion County. Butteville is on the east bank of the Willamette River in the extreme north part of the county and has an elevation of 103 feet. It was named for a well-known hill about a mile to the southwest, called by the early settlers on French Prairie *La Butte,* a form of name still used by the USGS on its map of the Sherwood quadrangle, which shows the geography of this region. *La Butte* has an elevation of 427 feet. Butteville was laid out prior to 1850 by Abernethy and Beers. The Oregon Electric Railway has a station called Butteville about two miles east of the town. This station was formerly called Chopunnish, a northwest Indian name, but was changed to Butteville to avoid confusion. Postal officials inform the compiler that Butteville post office was established with the name Champoeg on April 9, 1850, with F. X. Matthieu first postmaster. The name was changed to Buteville September 9, 1850, and to Butteville probably in the 1860s, although the date of this change is not clear in the records. The office was discontinued in the summer of 1905.

Button Springs, Lake County. Lee Button was a pioneer homesteader northeast of Fort Rock. He is mentioned in Charles H. Sternberg's *Life of a Fossil Hunter.* Sternberg was in the locality in 1877. Button Springs are in township 23 south, range 16 east, and they have given their name to the Button Springs Ranch, which is well known in Lake County. The springs were not named because of their size or shape.

Buxton, Washington County. Henry T. Buxton settled in this place in 1884, and was appointed its first postmaster in 1886. He was a son of Henry Buxton, a pioneer of 1841, and the town was named for his family.

Byars Creek, Marion County. This creek flows into Breitenbush River northeast of Detroit. Byars Creek and Byars Mountain nearby were named for W. H. Byars, surveyor general for Oregon from 1890 to 1894.

Bybee Bridge, Jackson County. This bridge crosses Rogue River not far from Upper Table Rock. It was named for William Bybee who operated a ferry at this point for many years in the early days. In addition, Bybee ran sheep in the upper Rogue River valley and Bybee Creek in the northeast corner of the county also bears his name.

Bybee Lake, Multnomah County. This is a small overflow lake on the south bank of Columbia River north of St. Johns. It was named for James Bybee. According to land office certificate 2234, Bybee was born in Kentucky on December 1, 1827, and arrived in Oregon in the fall of 1850. He settled on his claim near Columbia River in the fall of 1853, and made final proof in November, 1859, and was then unmarried. The lake was largely on his property, and not on that of James F. Bybee, a pioneer of 1845, who was a nearby settler.

Byrds Point, Wheeler County. This prominent bluff above Burnt Ranch was named for William Byrd who homesteaded nearby in 1882.

Byron Creek, Douglas County. In 1853 John Byron took up a donation land claim along this creek south of Olalla.

Cabbage Hill, Umatilla County. The notion that the Oregon Trail comes down Cabbage Hill into Umatilla Valley east of Pendleton does not seem to be borne out by facts. The highway traverses and descends Emigrant Hill and is not on Cabbage Hill at all. Cabbage Hill is a long spur extending southwest from Emigrant Hill, ending at Table Rock above McKay Creek. Cabbage Hill School is about a mile south of the Oregon Trail. The geography of this locality is shown on the USGS topographic map of the Cabbage Hill quadrangle. In March, 1946, the compiler received a letter from Mrs. J. E. Jones of Elgin containing a statement by her uncle, G. L. Dunn of Gibbon, about the naming of Cabbage Hill. Dunn says that in the fall of 1897 he was herding sheep on the hill above North Fork McKay Creek and he named the locality Cabbage Hill because of a prominent cabbage patch near the top of the slope. This name was soon adopted by the local residents and has been in use ever since. Dunn says the cabbages were on land farmed by one Huderman.

Cabin Creek, Douglas County. This stream flows into Calapooya Creek near Oakland. Both the Southern Pacific Company line and the

Pacific Highway follow Cabin Creek between Oakland and Rice Hill. It is said that the Rev. J. A. Cornwall built a cabin on this stream in the fall of 1846, in which he and his family spent the following winter. This is believed to have been the first cabin built in Douglas County by citizens of the United States, and the stream was named for it.

Cable Cove, Baker County. Cable Cove is well up in the Blue Mountains in the northwest part of the county. Cable Cove is drained by Silver Creek. These names were applied as a result of mining activities long ago. Cable Cove was named for a man who used that spelling. The compiler does not know his first name but he was prominent in mining development. It is said that other members of the family spelled the name Cabel. For a time there was a post office in the vicinity of Cable Cove which was operated with the name Cableville. Cableville post office was established October 24, 1901, with Thomas Costello the first of five postmasters. The office was discontinued in May, 1909.

Cache Creek, Wallowa County. This creek flows into Snake River in township 6 north, range 47 east, in the extreme northeast of Oregon. It was named by A. C. Smith, a pioneer of the Wallowa Valley. He and some companions were scouting in the neighborhood in the 1870s and found Indian caches on a bar at the mouth of the stream.

Cadle Butte, Crook County. Cadle Butte south of Veazie Creek has an elevation of 5106 feet. It was named for John F. Cadle who homesteaded on Ochoco Creek at the turn of the century.

Cahill Creek, Clackamas County. This is a short stream that flows northward into Beaver Creek about two miles east of New Era. It bears the name of Enos Cahill, who was born in Ohio in 1844, a Union soldier in the Civil War and later a homesteader on the banks of this stream. He held a number of public offices in Clackamas County and died in 1913. He was favorably remembered in the neighborhood, and in 1941 a group of former students of Leland School asked to have his name applied to this stream which has its source in a number of springs on the Cahill homestead. The name has been adopted by USBGN.

Cain Creek, Lane County. Cain Creek flows into Lookout Point Lake. John and Henry Cain both homesteaded along Middle Fork Willamette River in the 1890s but A. J. Briem, in his notes on file at the OHS, says the stream was probably named for John Cain.

Cairn Basin, Hood River County. Cairn Basin is a secluded alpine meadow just east of Cathedral Ridge on Mount Hood and the site of one of the stone shelters on the Timberline Trail. It takes its name from the large cairn constructed in 1922 by C. Edward Graves and the Hood River exploring party. At various times the cairn fell into disrepair but in the late sixties a group of Crag Rats undertook periodic maintenance.

Cake, Malheur County. Cake post office was in the extreme north part of the county, almost on the watershed between Burnt River and Malheur River, and at the head of Mormon Basin. The office was established to serve the headquarters of the Rainbow mine, and the mine itself was just over the line in Baker County. Cake was the name of a Portland business man who was interested in the development of the property. Cake post office was established February 3, 1917, with Isaac Blumauer first postmaster. Carl H. Connet was the second postmaster, and he wrote from Albany in August, 1946, giving some information about the place. The office was closed in March, 1920. It was reestablished June 21, 1922, with the name Rainbow Mine, but the compiler does not know the closing date of this office. The mine was named because of association with the place where the pot of gold was supposed to be. There has been a change of the county boundary in this locality, but it is not clear just how it affects the information recorded above.

Calamut Lake, Douglas County. Calamut Lake is in the extreme northeast part of the county. The writer has been unable to secure definite information as to how it got its name, but it seems probable that it may have been an early form of Klamath, and may have been so called by emigrants. The form of spelling here used is that adopted by the USBGN.

Calapooia River, Linn County. Calapooia River rises in the western slopes of the Cascade Range and joins the Willamette River at Albany. The name has the same origin as Calapooya in Douglas County. However, the territorial Linn County Court established the spelling Calapooia at its first session July 1, 1850, and this form has since been used locally. The OGNB confirmed this spelling on December 7, 1962 and the USBGN in *Decision List 6401.*

Calapooya Mountains, Douglas and Lane counties. These mountains are a westward spur of the Cascade Range and constitute the watershed between the Willamette and Umpqua rivers. Calapooya Mountains join the Cascade Range at Cowhorn Mountain with an elevation of 7666 feet in the northeast corner of Douglas County. The Indians of the Willamette Valley were of the *Kalapooian* family. Calapooya Mountains bear the name. See Lewis' *Tribes of the Columbia Valley,* page 178. The Calapooya Indians were indolent and peaceful, and not disposed to trade *(ibid.)* The name is given as *Calapoosie* by David Douglas in his journals, *OHQ,* volume VI, page 85; *Col-lap-poh-yea-ass,* by Alexander Ross, in *Adventures of the First Settlers on the Oregon,* pages 235, 236; *Call-law-poh-yea-as,* in his *Fur Hunters of the Far West,* volume I, page 108; *Kala-pooyhas,* in Townsend's *Narrative,* page 175; *Callapuya,* by Wilkes. Lewis and Clark give *Collapoewah;* Parker's journal gives *Calapooa;* Lee and Frost *Calapooyas. Calapooya* is properly the name of a division of the *Kalapooian* family formerly living between Willamette and Umpqua rivers. The USBGN has adopted the spelling Calapooya. Calapooya Creek rises on the south slopes of Calapooya Mountains in Douglas County and flows through Oakland and joins the Umpqua River at Umpqua. The origin of the name of the stream is the same as that of the Calapooya Mountains.

Caldwell Creek, Clackamas County. Caldwell Creek is a small tributary of Henry Creek from the north just east of Rhododendron. In January, 1980, John C. Caldwell of Oregon City wrote the compiler and told how this creek got its name. His father, J. B. "Boots" Caldwell, was an Oregon City business man who would often spend weekends at his father in law's cottage in Rhododendron. A regular diversion was to spend a few solitary hours fishing some small stream in the neighborhood and the one now called Caldwell Creek was a favorite. One day in the 1930s Caldwell was visiting a friend, Ralph S. Milln, deputy surveyor of Clackamas County.

Milln was busy putting the finishing touches on a new map and said "Boots, how would you like to have a creek named for you? I have a lot of them that need names." The fishing stream came at once to mind and the name was applied forthwith. Naming regulations were less involved in those days and the few federal rules were often bent.

Calf Gulch, Jefferson County. Calf Gulch is east of Ashwood, in the Donnybrook country, and is the veritable place where an event took place that gave Donnybrook its name. The general locality was once called Axe-handle, and additional information will be found under that heading. The Bend *Bulletin*, April 20, 1943, says editorially: "...one of the community's names, Donnybrook, was derived from a little social affair in Calf gulch, where guns, as well as axe handles, were used, and one man, Tom Kinney, received a bullet wound." See also under Donnybrook and Kilts. Calf Gulch was named during the days of pioneer stockmen, but the compiler does not know the exact reason.

California Gulch, Baker County. California Gulch, which is about ten miles airline southwest of Baker, drains south into Powder River. It is just a little west of the famous pioneer mining camp of Auburn. It was named in the eastern Oregon gold rush of the early 1860s because of the presence of many California miners in that part of the diggings. Hiatt in his *Thirty-one Years in Baker County* has a good deal to say about the rivalry between the visitors from California, called Tarheads, and the Oregonians, dubbed Webfeet.

Calimus, Klamath County. The Southern Pacific Company formerly had a station named Sprague in Klamath County, but in 1926 changed the name to Calimus to avoid duplication. The name Calimus was taken from Calimus Butte.

Calimus Butte, Klamath County. This is an important landmark near the center of the Klamath Indian Reservation and is used as a lookout station. Captain O. C. Applegate, authority on the Klamath country, said the origin of the name was obscure. One Klamath Indian told him it meant Flat Butte.

Calor, Klamath County. Calor is a station on the Southern Pacific Company Cascade Line just north of the Oregon-California state line. The name is synthetic and was made up from parts of the names of the two states. There are many of these combination names in the United States.

Calvert, Douglas County. Calvert post office was established May 3, 1892, with Mrs. John (Laura V.) Applegate first and only postmaster. The office was closed September 5, 1894, and the business turned over to Louis post office. Calvert was about four miles east of Yoncalla in Scott Valley on what had been the R. M. Kelly donation land claim. Mrs. Applegate planned to name the office Scott Valley, but postal authorities objected to a name with two words and also because it was so nearly the same as Scottsburg in the same county. It was then planned to name the office Kelly, but this was unacceptable to the authorities because of duplication. At length Calvert was selected. It is reported that Calvert was a family name in the Applegate clan.

Camas Valley, Douglas County. The word Camas is used to describe geographic features in many parts of Oregon, including Camas Valley in

Douglas County, Camas Swale in Lane County, Camas Swale in Douglas County, Camas Creek in Umatilla County, and others. The name is taken from that of a favorite food of the western Indians, the *Camassia* bulb, a plant related to the scilla. The word was derived from the Nootka Indian word *Chamass*, meaning "fruit" or "sweet." It was adopted into the Chinook jargon as camas, kamass, lacmass, and lakamass. The locality of Camas Valley was a place where the Indians gathered supplies of the sweetish bulbs of the blue-flowered "Lakamass."

Cambrai, Wasco County. Cambrai is a station on the Burlington Northern Inc. just south of Maupin. The 1961 Oregon Trunk Gold Spike issue of the Spokane Portland and Seattle Railway *Dope Bucket* states that Cambrai was a coined word with no local significance originated in 1917 when the station was named. The compiler does not know why the name came to be applied but it was much in the news in the late fall of 1917. The battle of Cambrai was a major engagement between the English and Germans during World War I. It commenced on November 20, 1917 and was centered about the French town of that name.

Camelot Lake, Deschutes County. Ray Engels, then USFS ranger at McKenzie Bridge, thought that the lake basin southwest of Wickiup Plain must resemble the jousting fields of King Arthur's time. He thus named two of the lakes Camelot and Lancelot.

Camp Abbot, Deschutes County. On December 4, 1942, the War Department announced that an army engineer replacement and training center would be named Camp Abbot, in honor of Brigadier-General Henry Larcom Abbot. Abbot's distinguished career is described in this volume under the heading Abbot Creek. On September 2, 1855, in command of a detached party engaged on one of the projects of the Pacific Railroad Surveys, he camped on the site of the engineer center. Camp Abbot was dedicated on September 2, 1943, and was in active service for about a year.

Camp Adair, Benton and Polk counties. Henry Rodney Adair was a scion of a prominent Oregon pioneer family and was a native of Astoria. He was graduated from West Point and became a lieutenant of cavalry in the regular army. He was killed at Carrizal, Mexico, about 90 miles south of El Paso, June 21, 1916, when Mexican soldiers made a surprise attack on a small detachment of American troops. Lieutenant Adair conducted a spirited defense but the few troopers in his immediate vicinity were greatly outnumbered and many were killed. Camp Adair, on the west side of the Willamette Valley north of Corvallis, contained about 50,000 acres and was built in 1942-43 as a training center for World War II. It was formally dedicated September 4, 1943, although occupied by troops for some time prior to that date. See news articles in the *Oregonian,* August 27, 1943, and the *Oregon Journal,* September 4, 1943. The camp was named in honor of Lieutenant Adair. Camp Adair post office was established June 1, 1942. It was discontinued May 23, 1946.

Camp Alden, Jackson County. After the battle of Evans Creek, August 24, 1853, which was an important event in the Rogue River Indian outbreak, General Lane put the white soldiers into a camp at Hailey Ferry near Upper Table Rock. This camp was called Camp Alden in compliment to Captain Bradford Ripley Alden of the Fourth U. S. Infantry, who had been severely wounded on Evans Creek. After a few weeks, Fort Lane supplanted Camp Alden. The exact location of Camp Alden is not known. Hailey Ferry later became Bybee Ferry. Walling's statement in *History of Southern Oregon*, page 220, to the effect that Alden died from the effect of his wound two years later is not borne out by Heitman's *Historical Register*, which gives the date as September 10, 1870.

Camp Alvord, Malheur County. Camp Alvord was established in June, 1864, in what is now known as Alvord Valley at the east base of Steens Mountain just south of Little Alvord Creek. Lieutenant J. A. Waymire and troops of the First Oregon Volunteer Cavalry had camped in the locality early in the year and had dug some rifle-pits during an engagement with the Indians. In June, Captain George B. Currey of the same regiment, in command of cavalry and infantry, found these pits and used the site until September for an establishment which he called Camp Alvord in compliment to Brigadier-General Benjamin Alvord. For a history of Alvord, see under Alvord Lake. Currey caused some additional earthworks to be thrown up in the form of a star, but the compiler has been unable to learn of any permanent structures. The Oregon Adjutant General's *Report,* 1865-66, says this camp was broken up late in September, 1864. On August 31, 1865, Major W. V. Rinehart, commanding the First Oregon Volunteer Infantry at Fort Klamath, issued a letter order to Captain F. B. Sprague directing him to take a detachment of the regiment to the Alvord Valley and establish Camp Alvord on Horse Creek in a position with "natural advantages, such as security against attack, and the severities of winter, its healthfulness, and convenience to wood, water, and grass." The Horse Creek mentioned is now called Wildhorse Creek. Sprague found Captain Borland of the same regiment already encamped on Horse Creek at a site probably near the northeast corner of section 26, township 35 south, range 33 east, by the mouth of the canyon about one and one half miles northeast of Andrews. Camp Alvord was used until June, 1866, when on the recommendation of Major-General F. Steele, commanding the Department of the Columbia, it was evacuated and the troops moved about twenty-five miles southeast to a spot on Whitehorse Creek along the Chico Road. The new post was called Camp C. F. Smith. See under that heading.

Camp Baker, Jackson County. Alice A. Sargent wrote a short account of Camp Baker in the Medford *Mail-Tribune* September 13, 1931. The camp was established in 1862 and was garrisoned by part of the First Oregon Volunteer Cavalry. It was named in honor of Major-General E. D. Baker who was killed at the battle of Balls Bluff in 1861. See under Baker County. The site of Camp Baker was about a half a mile west of Phoenix. The various buildings were built of hewn pine logs. Coleman Creek flowed between the mess hall and the stables. In 1931 there were a few mouldering logs to mark the spot. The compiler does not know when the camp was evacuated but it was used as late as 1865. In January, 1944, T. V. Williams of Medford wrote the compiler that the D.A.R. marker for Camp Baker stands about 75 feet west of Coleman Creek on the south side of the east-west road through the middle of section 16, township 38 south, range 1 west.

Camp Barlow, Clackamas County. Camp Barlow is mentioned in official military records, but it does not seem to have been a formal establishment and was perhaps not more than a campground. It was used in the 1860s as a place of enlistment or rendezvous for Oregon volunteers. Tradition at Oregon City says that the camp was on the property of William Barlow adjacent to Molalla River, or just northeast of the present community of Barlow. In March, 1944, William Tull of Canby reported that his grandfather, William S. Tull, was one of the first to enlist at Camp Barlow, and that Mrs. William Barlow served dinner to the recruiting staff the first day. The record shows that William Tull, aged 18, enlisted in E Company of the First Oregon Volunteer Cavalry on February 5, 1862. Camp Barlow does not seem to have been long in use.

Camp Blossom, Clackamas County. Camp Blossom is about one-half mile west of Timberline Lodge at timberline on Mount Hood. Before the lodge and all weather access road were built in 1937, Camp Blossom was the usual staging point for climbs of the south side. Fred McNeil in *Wy'east* *"The Mountain"*, page 114, states that Lige Coalman insisted that the original Camp Blossom was some distance east at the head of the old timberline road and that Judge M. C. George selected a new site in 1907 when the original campsite was taken over by a USGS survey party making the first contour map of Mount Hood. The Camp Blossom cabin was built by Coalman in 1916 as a supply base for the summit lookout. It has since been torn down but the hearth and chimney base are still visible. Regardless of whether or not the cabin site was the original Camp Blossom, the location was used very early by climbers for tree carvings still readable in 1974 show names and dates back to 1890. While no definite proof is available, the writer believes that Camp Blossom, wherever it may have first been located, was named for James M. Blossom, a pioneer hardware merchant of Portland. Blossom was born in Maine in 1817 and came to Oregon in 1852. The *Oregonian* for August 6, 1859, has an account of the climb of Mount Hood on July 26, 1859 by T. J. Dryer and six others including J. M. Blossom. The account describes Blossom as the nimrod of the party and comments on the campsite at timberline. The description could apply to innumerable places but their route came within a mile of Timberline Lodge.

Camp Carson, Union County. The origin of the name Camp Carson, for a place near the headwaters of Grande Ronde River in the south part of the county, is a mystery as far as the writer is concerned. There seems to be no satisfactory explanation of the name nor of the exact location of the place. A War Department map of 1887 shows Camp Carson on Fly Creek in the west part of the county near the toll house on the road between Pilot Rock and Powder River Valley. The place is marked "Abandoned" and there is an implication that it had been a military establishment. However, a diligent search of military records fails to bring to light any mention of such a camp, and there is no mention of it in campaign reports. Modern maps show Camp Carson in quite a different location. It now appears to be about ten miles southeast of the location on the War Department map, and a little to the northeast of Chicken Hill. It is possible that it was named by gold seekers from the Carson City area of Nevada. There were many Nevadans in eastern Oregon in the early 1860s and they may have brought the name along with them. Camp Carson was well known in the mining days of the

1860s, which seems to set its naming at the time of the gold rush and prior to military activities.

Camp Castaway, Coos County. This appropriate descriptive name was applied to a military camp used by soldiers and sailors who got ashore from the wreck of the transport *Captain Lincoln* a couple of miles north of the entrance to Coos Bay. The *Captain Lincoln* sailed from San Francisco December 28, 1851, with C Troop of the First Dragoons under command of Lieutenant H. W. Stanton. A medical officer, Dr. Francis Sorrel, was also on board. Instead of making Port Orford, the ship got into difficulties and in very bad weather was wrecked on the morning of January 3, 1852. A report, dated at Benicia, March 24, 1852, is in the annual report of the Secretary of War, dated December 4, 1852, page 109, and gives many details. There are other reports and letters about Camp Castaway in the same volume. Stories of the wreck are in Dodge's *History of Coos and Curry Counties*, page 144, *et seq.* See also Victor's *Early Indian Wars of Oregon*, page 290. Camp Castaway was apparently used about four months, and was a tent town. The troopers finally reached Port Orford after some remarkable adventures.

Camp C. F. Smith, Harney County. This camp was established in June, 1866 by troops relocated from Camp Alvord which was abandoned at the same time. See under that heading. The new camp was on a low point of land just above Whitehorse Creek about a mile northeast of the Whitehorse Ranch. Lieutenant-Colonel M. A. Reno's Inspection Report dated October 14, 1867 gives details of several permanent buildings. Presumably it was named for Major-General Charles Ferguson Smith, a distinguished officer of the regular army. This camp was abandoned November 9, 1869.

Camp Colfax, Malheur County. This camp was used for a few months during the Indian wars of the 1860s and is mentioned in the Oregon Adjutant General's *Report,* 1865-66. It is described as being where the Canyon City-Boise road crossed Willow Creek. *A Webfoot Volunteer, The Diary of William M. Hilleary 1864-1866* has some amusing references to the post as well as some specific information. Hilleary's unit, F Company of the First Oregon Volunteer Infantry, established Camp Colfax about August 24, 1865, on South Willow Creek about six miles east of Ironside Mountain. It was apparent that temporary protection would not stand against the weather, so in late October logs were snaked and hauled in from Ironside Mountain and at least two and maybe three cabins were built, with common walls so as to save logs. The roofs were poles and willows, covered with earth and there were good fireplaces of stone. The camp seems to have been used as a way-station by outfits other than F Company. The detachment proceeded to Fort Boise at the end of the year and Hilleary says with satisfaction that the cabins were set fire on December 27, 1865, and the soldiers marched away. He does not say for whom the camp was named, but it was probably intended to honor Schuyler Colfax, popular member of Congress from Indiana and in 1865 speaker of the House of Representatives. Colfax visited Oregon in the summer of that year.

Camp Creek, Clackamas County. This stream rises near Government Camp, and flows westward into Zigzag River. Laurel Hill, the terror of the emigrant trains, lies between these two streams like a wedge, and over its brow travellers on the Barlow Road let their wagons down by ropes snubbed around trees. It seems probable that this stream was named for its connection with Government Camp. See under that heading. Joel Palmer of the Barlow party mentions Camp Creek under date of October 13, 1845, but the description in his journal shows this to be a tributary of White River some fifteen or twenty miles southeast of Government Camp. The name has not prevailed in the original location and the exact stream can no longer be identified.

Camp Creek, Douglas County. This stream flows into Mill Creek, north of Loon Lake. Camp Creek was named in 1853 by a party from Scottsburg headed by L. L. Williams which camped on the stream on the way to Loon Lake. See Walling's *History of Southern Oregon,* page 439.

Camp Creek, Lane County. Camp Creek is a prominent stream that flows into McKenzie River from the north between Thurston and Walterville. It was called Camp Creek in very early pioneer days. There are two stories about the origin of the name, both of which may be true. One is that pioneer settlers found an Indian camp near the stream, called *Chaston* by the Indians themselves. On the other hand Walling, in *Illustrated History of Lane County,* page 468, says that the stream was named because a party of pioneers chasing Indian stock thieves camped there. Walling gives several paragraphs of history of the little valley of Camp Creek. Camp Creek post office was established July 12, 1871, with William Pattison, Jr., first of seven postmasters. This office was closed to Springfield, September 15, 1922. It is apparent from an inspection of maps of various dates that Camp Creek office moved a good deal depending on the availability of postmasters.

Camp Creek, Lane County. The stream referred to in this heading rises south of Stony Point and flows south into Siuslaw River near Alma in the west part of the county. Writing of this stream, P. M. Morse, Lane County Engineer, under date of August 4, 1943, says ". . .has usually been called Camp Creek, as it has been a favorite camping spot during the summer and for hunters during the deer season."

Camp Creek, Wallowa County. This stream drains a considerable area in the vicinity of Zumwalt and flows into Sheep Creek a little above Imnaha. In early days stockmen going from Wallowa Valley into the Imnaha country found a good campground near the mouth of the stream, and as a result the name Camp Creek was applied. Also the Indians had a campsite on the stream which they used traveling from Chesnimnus south to other localities. The first homesteader on the stream was Waldo Chase. Trail Creek flows into Camp Creek.

Camp Currey, Harney County. According to the Oregon Adjutant General's *Report,* 1865-66, Camp Currey was established in the fall of 1865 at Indian Springs on what is now known as Silver Creek. In January, 1944, J. C. Cecil of Burns wrote the compiler that Camp Currey was at what is now known as the Cecil 71 Ranch, a pioneer landmark. "Pat" Cecil sent the following extract from a statement made by the Adjutant General's Office at Washington, April 23, 1930: "The camp was established in August, 1865, and was abandoned in May, 1866. No formally declared reservation existed at this point. It was occupied on September 30, 1865, by Companies D and I, 4th California Infantry, detachment of Company E, 1st Washington Territorial Infantry and a detachment of Company K, 1st Oregon Infantry. In November, 1865, the 2nd Battalion, 14th U. S. Infantry, was stationed at this post. Company K, 1st Oregon Infantry, was also at the post. It was commanded on September 30, 1865, by Captain L. S. Scott, Company D, 4th California Infantry, and on November 30, 1865, 1st Lieut. Frank W. Perry, Brevet Major, Company E, 2nd Battalion, 14th U. S. Infantry, assumed command of the post and remained until the post was abandoned in May, 1866." In addition "Pat" Cecil wrote the compiler: "Many years ago we removed the foundation stones of about forty cabins, measuring about 10 by 12 feet, and judging by the charred remains, I think they were built of hewed logs. There is an excavation on the hillside that may have been used as a cellar or storehouse. There were three graves back of the camp, apparently of soldiers." The camp was named for Colonel George B. Currey, who had been an officer in the First Oregon Volunteer Cavalry but who had succeeded to the command of the Columbia District when Brigadier-General George Wright was drowned. The spelling, Curry, is wrong.

Camp Dahlgren, Crook County. Camp Dahlgren was established August 22, 1864, by Captain John M. Drake of the First Oregon Volunteer Cavalry, and was named for Colonel Ulric Dahlgren who was killed March 2, 1864, in a cavalry engagement near Richmond, Virginia. Drake had already occupied Camps Maury and Gibbs, but had to move because of poor forage. Camp Gibbs was apparently on what is now known as Drake Creek near the north base of the Maury Mountains, and Camp Dahlgren is described as being twenty miles to the northeast on Beaver Creek. Drake's report says that Camp Dahlgren was abandoned September 20, 1864, but he gives no details about its location. It was probably not far from the present town of Paulina.

Camp Day, Klamath County. In the files of the Oregon Historical Society are family letters from Lieut. Lorenzo Lorain of the Third Artillery which give a few details of a march made by a detachment of two officers and sixty-six enlisted men of Company L, 3rd Artillery, under the command of 1st Lieutenant Alexander Piper, from Fort Umpqua to a point near Klamath River, where a post called Camp Day was established. Piper and his party left Fort Umpqua June 26, 1860, and proceeded by way of Scottsburg and Canyonville to the Rogue River Valley. The soldiers passed through Jacksonville, and from that point followed the Yreka road to the junction with the emigrant trail from the Klamath country. This trail was followed to the vicinity of Klamath River, where a camp was made July 16, 1860, apparently on Spencer Creek about half a mile from the river, although the identification is by no means certain. This establishment was called Camp Day, in honor of Lieutenant Edward Henry Day, also of the Third Artillery. Day was a native of Virginia and a classmate of Piper's at the Military Academy. He died January 2, 1860, and this circumstance undoubtedly impelled Piper to select his name for the camp. Piper left Camp Day with his troops October 6 and arrived at Fort Umpqua October 18, 1860. Lorain was interested in photography, which was a novelty in 1860. He took pictures of Camp Day and these along with Piper's journal are reproduced in an article in *OHQ*, volume LXIX, pp 223 *et seq*.

Camp Elliff, Douglas County. Preston's *Map of Oregon*, 1856, shows the

Elliff place in section 11, township 32 south, range 5 west. This is near where the Pacific Highway first reaches Cow Creek Valley after going south from Canyonville. A post called Camp Elliff was established in this locality in the Rogue River War of 1855-56, which was occupied by Captain Laban Buoy and a detachment of B Company, Second Oregon Mounted Volunteers, mostly from Lane County. It was Buoy's duty to keep the road open along Cow Creek. The compiler has found no record of any permanent structures at this camp. See Victor's *Early Indian Wars of Oregon,* page 368.

Camp Gibbs, Crook County. This camp at the north base of Maury Mountains was in use for a short time in the summer of 1864 during the Snake War and was probably named for Governor Addison C. Gibbs. Camp Maury was established on what is now Maury Creek on May 18, 1864, but because of poor forage, the post was moved west about five miles on July 21, 1864, and named Camp Gibbs. The compiler does not know the exact location, but it seems apparent that it was on or near what is now known as Drake Creek. Captain John M. Drake of the First Oregon Volunteer Cavalry was in command of the camp. The post was moved again August 22, on account of poor forage. The new post was called Camp Dahlgren.

Camp Gordon, Douglas County. Camp Gordon is one of the elusive military camps used in the Rogue River War of 1855-56. It is described by Mrs. F. F. Victor in *Early Indian Wars of Oregon,* page 368, as being eight miles above the mouth of Cow Creek. The compiler is of the opinion this means up the main route of travel, for there was no road up Cow Creek itself. Eight miles south along the route of travel would put Camp Gordon somewhere on Canyon Creek south of Canyonville. The camp was in command of Captain Samuel Gordon and was doubtless named for him.

Camp Grant, Douglas County. This trail shelter just southeast of Red Butte was named arbitrarily by USFS ranger Fred Asam.

Camp Ground, Multnomah County. Camp Ground post office was established on May 19, 1884, with Edward F. Wright postmaster, and remained in service only until June 9, 1884. In fact the office may never have been in actual operation. It was just at this time that Gresham post office was established. That event took place on May 15, 1884, and James F. Roberts was the first postmaster at Gresham. There was a good deal of rivalry between the proponents of the two offices, Camp Ground and Gresham, and not a little bad feeling developed among the partisans. William H. Stanley wrote from Gresham in July, 1947, that the proposed offices were within rock throwing distance of each other, at or near the intersection of Main Street and Powell Valley Road. Gresham beat Camp Ground to the draw. Mr. Stanley says that a campground was situated near Main Street and Powell Valley Road, with some small cabins used during camp meetings. Edward F. Wright had some connection with this campground, probably managed it at camp meetings.

Camp Hancock, Wheeler County. Camp Hancock is a memorial to Lon W. Hancock, an amateur paleontologist and geologist. Hancock was born in Harrison, Arkansas in 1884. He left school at an early age and spent most of his adult life as a Post Office employee in Portland. He had an abounding interest in fossil hunting and during the 1940s he began taking young boys on outings in the Clarno area. These became more complex and in 1951 Lon and his wife took fourteen boys and ten volunteer staff members for the first formal twelve day summer camp at Camp Hancock under the sponsorship of the Oregon Museum of Science and Industry. Interest grew apace and the early tent camp has grown to a modern, well-equipped facility. Hancock died in 1961 and left his collection of more than 10,000 fossils and artifacts to OMSI.

Camp Henderson, Malheur County. Camp Henderson was one of the establishments of the Indian wars of the 1860s. On May 26, 1864, Captain George B. Currey of the First Oregon Volunteer Cavalry camped on Crooked Creek about eight miles southwest of the mouth of Jordan Creek and called the place Camp Henderson in compliment to J. H. D. Henderson, representative in Congress from Oregon, 1865-67. The stream was called Gibbs Creek in honor of Governor A. C. Gibbs, but that name did not persist. Camp Henderson was not long in use and was a very simple establishment. See Bancroft's *History of Oregon,* volume II, page 499 and Oregon Adjutant General's *Report,* 1865-66, page 36. Preston E. Onstad in *OHQ,* volume LXV, pages 297 *et seq.,* has further details and pictures. He states that the location was on Crooked Creek just south of the present US95 highway bridge.

Camp Lincoln, Grant County. Camp Lincoln, named for Abraham Lincoln, was established by Lieutenant J. A. Waymire of the First Oregon Volunteer Cavalry March 15, 1864, and abandoned May 1, 1864. It was used during the Indian outbreaks, but was a temporary post. See Oregon Adjutant General's *Report,* 1865-66, page 67, *et seq.* It was on South Fork John Day River, but the compiler has been unable to get the exact location. Probably it was near the present community of Dayville.

Camp Logan, Grant County. Camp Logan was established September 2, 1865 by Captain A. B. Ingram, Company K, First Oregon Volunteer Infantry, during the Indian troubles. It was not a large camp and not long in use although according to Lieutenant-Colonel M. A. Reno's inspection report of October, 1867, it was then still occupied by regular army troops. William M. Hilleary, in *Recollections of a Linn County Volunteer* in the Oregon Historical Society Library says quarters were built for 40 men. This was in August or September, 1865. The place is mentioned in the Oregon Adjutant General's *Report,* 1865-66, but no details are given. In January, 1944, R. H. Sullens of Prairie City wrote the compiler that Camp Logan was on Strawberry Creek about six miles south of Prairie City near what is now the Roger Kent ranch. This information agrees with War Department maps, although the stream was apparently known in 1865 as Indian Creek and later as Logan Creek. In fact Strawberry Mountain was once called Logan Butte on account of the camp. The post was named for William Logan, Indian Agent at Warm Springs Reservation during the early 1860s. C. W. Brown of Canyon City has written the compiler confirming the location at the Kent ranch and says there were several log houses, the remains of some of them still in evidence in January, 1944. Formerly this was the J. J. Cozart ranch. An old box stove from Camp Logan is still in use at the Prairie City Grange Hall.

Camp Maury, Crook County. Camp Maury was about 30 miles airline southeast of Prineville, on the south side of Crooked River Valley near the base of Maury Mountains. It was named for Colonel R. F. Maury, who took a prominent part in the Snake War of 1864, and was at the time in command of the First Oregon Volunteer Cavalry. The camp was in the southeast quarter of section 20, township 17 south, range 21 east, on the southeast side of Maury Creek and just west of Rimrock Creek. It had been occupied previously by a command under Major Enoch Steen, and the site had been selected for a supply depot. A company of the Oregon Cavalry under command of Captain John M. Drake made camp at the place in the evening of May 18, 1864, and Drake, in his journal, says he named it for Colonel Maury. It was on May 18 that Lieutenant Stephen Watson and two men were killed by Indians. They were buried by the side of a small knoll south of the camp and at the edge of the timber. The bodies were later moved to Camp Watson, a more important establishment to the northeast. The account given by Bancroft in *History of Oregon,* volume II, page 498, is wrong in some particulars. Camp Maury was occupied until July 21, 1864, when the depot was moved five miles west to a place called Camp Gibbs. This was done to get better forage. In January, 1943, Mrs. Florence Knox of Post wrote about Camp Maury and said that a number of stone walls were still standing, three or four feet high, apparently built to protect sleeping soldiers. The site of the camp is on the J. T. Stewart homestead.

Camp McDowell, Umatilla County. Camp McDowell was established on Camas Prairie on May 31, 1865, by Captain Abner W. Waters and a detachment of Company F, First Oregon Volunteer Infantry. According to *A Webfoot Volunteer, The Diary of William M. Hilleary, 1864-66,* it was on what they called Humbug Fork John Day River and was called Camp Humbug. The stream is now known as Camas Creek. On June 11, 1865, the camp was moved a short distance and renamed Camp McDowell for Major-General Irvin McDowell, then commanding The Military Department of the Pacific. It was abandoned on July 11, 1865, when the troops returned to Fort Walla Walla. For information about McDowell see under McDowell Peak.

Camp McKinley, Multnomah County. The Spanish-American War broke out April 20-22, 1898, and no time was lost in mobilizing the Oregon National Guard. A camp was officially established April 29, 1898, on the racetrack grounds at Irvington Park, named Camp McKinley in honor of then President William McKinley and it was at this camp that the Second Oregon Infantry was mustered into the service of the United States. Camp McKinley was just east of what is now Northeast Seventh Avenue, between Northeast Brazee and Northeast Fremont streets in Portland. The locality no longer shows any traces of camp or racetrack. Between May 11 and May 16, 1898, the Second Oregon was moved to the Presidio of San Francisco, from which post it embarked for Manila on May 25, to be away from the United States for more than a year. Brigadier-General Raymond F. Olson of the Oregon Military Department, on October 8, 1947, sent the compiler a copy of part of General Orders No. 2, dated April 29, 1898, establishing Camp McKinley, but added that no orders of disestablishment could be found and it was assumed that the camp officially ceased its life on May 19, 1898, when the last of the state and federal property was removed. The compiler recalls visiting the camp several times, and has no recollection of anything more than the most temporary sort of facilities.

Camp Meriwether, Tillamook County. Camp Meriwether is the summer camp of the Boy Scouts, Portland area. It is on the ocean front about two miles south of Cape Lookout and not far from Sand Lake. It was named for Meriwether Lewis in 1925 by G. H. Oberteuffer, scout executive of the Boy Scouts of America, Portland area.

Camp Millard, Clackamas County. The ground for this camp was given to the Boy Scouts of America in 1925 by Mrs. Alvira Millard in memory of her son, Samuel Brown Millard.

Camp Namanu, Clackamas County. The Camp Fire Girls of Portland and vicinity have a summer camp a little northwest of Bull Run, on Sandy River just below the mouth of Bull Run River. The name of this place and its summer post office is Camp Namanu. *Namanu* is said to be an Indian word meaning beaver, and that animal was once plentiful in the locality. The compiler does not know from what Indian language *namanu* is taken. The Chinook jargon word for beaver is *ee-na.* Namanu may be a variation of the Chinook jargon word *ne-nam-ooks,* meaning land otter. A Camp Namanu post office was established January 7, 1939, by change of name from Bullrun. Elaine S. Gorman was the first postmaster.

Camp Polk, Deschutes County. Camp Polk is about three miles northeast of Sisters on the west bank of Squaw Creek, and there is now little to show that it was once a military post. The camp was established in 1865 at the time of Indian uprisings in eastern Oregon. Captain Charles LaFollette was commanding officer of Company A of the First Oregon Volunteer Infantry and a resident of Polk County. His company was stationed at this camp and he named the place in honor of his home county. Some cabins were built and the troops spent the winter of 1865-66. About 1870 Samuel M. W. Hindman settled near the camp and for a time ran the post office. Mrs. Nellie M. Miller, long a resident of Sisters, died in July, 1941, and left a substantial sum to be used in improving and maintaining the Camp Polk cemetery, also known as the Hindman cemetery. The locality of Camp Polk is shown on the USGS map of the Sisters quadrangle. A post office with the name Camp Polk was established in March, 1875, with Samuel M. W. Hindman postmaster. In July, 1888, the office was moved about three miles southwest to the community of Sisters and the name was changed to agree with the new locality.

Camp Rilea, Clatsop County. Camp Rilea was founded in 1927 as Camp Clatsop, a summer training area for the Oregon National Guard. Prior to this, places in southern Oregon had been used but the termination of land grant railroad military rates in 1926 made it desireable to have a location nearer the central Willamette Valley. Additional land was added during the 1930s and at the start of World War II the camp was operated as a federal post for troop training and staging. It is now wholly owned by the state of Oregon and in 1959 was renamed Camp Rilea in honor of Major-General Thomas E. Rilea, long time Adjutant General of Oregon. Rilea was born in Chicago, Illinois on May 5, 1895 and died in Portland on February 4, 1959. For obituary see *Oregonian*, February 4, 1959, page 1.

Camp Russell, Marion County. When the First Oregon Volunteer

Infantry was organized in 1864-65, at least four companies appear to have been mustered in at a place called Camp Russell, but the *Report* of the Adjutant General, 1865-66, fails to locate the camp. However, *Recollections of a Linn County Volunteer* by William M. Hilleary of F Company, on file at the Oregon Historical Society, say that the camp was on the Fair Grounds at Salem. Among other things, Hilleary says: "One wing of the old pavilion was fitted up for squad room, in which were our bunks. It was our sitting room, parlor, bedroom, hall, all in one. Another wing of the pavilion was occupied by the kitchen and culinary department, which was dubbed 'Hotel de Russle' for it was here that we, with an eye on the main chance, 'rustled' for our grub." This camp was named in honor of Major-General David Allen Russell, who was killed at the battle of Opequan, Virginia, September 19, 1864. Russell had served in Oregon and was a popular soldier and his death occurred about the time the camp was established. The order naming the camp is in the *Official Records of the Union and Confederate Armies*, volume L, part II, page 1086.

Camp Sherman, Jefferson County. This post office is on the Metolius River about two miles north of its source. It was named because of the fact that a number of families from Sherman County spent their summer vacations at this camp.

Camp Spencer, Josephine County. Camp Spencer was a place used in the Rogue River War of 1855-56, and is mentioned in Victor's *Early Indian Wars of Oregon,* page 366. It is described as being on the lower Applegate River. Mrs. Victor gives neither the exact location of the camp nor the reason for the name.

Camp Stuart, Jackson County. A list of military establishments in Oregon should include the name of Camp Stuart, although it is not mentioned in Heitman's *Historical Register.* In 1917, Princeton University Press published *Mexican War Diary of George B. McClellan,* edited by William Starr Myers. On page 14 is a note of an entry by McClellan on a page otherwise blank, of an event several years after the Mexican War. The note as printed is: "On the 18th June, 1851, at five in the afternoon died Jimmie Stuart, my best and oldest friend. He was mortally wounded the day before by an arrow, whilst gallantly leading a charge against a party of hostile Indians. He is buried at Camp Stuart —about twenty five miles south of Rogue's River [Oregon?], near the main road, and not far from the base of Cishion (?) Mountains. His grave is between two oaks, on the left side of the road, going south, with J. S. cut in the bark of the largest of the oaks." Captain James Stuart was graduated from West Point in 1846 and served with distinction in the Mexican War, gaining two brevets. Stuart was wounded in an engagement probably near Rogue River a little upstream from Upper Table Rock. Walling in *History of Southern Oregon,* page 197, gives an account of the incident and says that Stuart was buried near the present town of Phoenix, close to the site of the Colver house, but mentions no military establishment. There is additional information in Bancroft's *History of Oregon,* volume II, page 227. The camp was used intermittently at least as late as 1853. The stream flowing northward through the valley at this point was named Stuart Creek in honor of James Stuart, but settlers later changed the name to Bear Creek, which cannot be considered an improvement. The compiler is of the opinion that McClellan wrote *Ciskiou* (?) in his note and not *Cishion* (?).

Camp Warner, Lake County. Camp Warner occupied two places in the Warner Valley, some distance apart. In 1866 troops from Vancouver made a reconnaissance into southeast Oregon, and, among other things, selected a site for Camp Warner on the west side of the Warner Valley. Soldiers were sent from Boise, Idaho, with orders to build the camp, but the command reached the east side of the Warner Valley and concluded that it would be impractical to cross the string of lakes and swamps. Accordingly, the camp was built a little east of the valley on the north part of Hart Mountain and named for Brevet Captain William Horace Warner, who was killed by Indians in September, 1849, probably in Surprise Valley, just over the line in California. For information about the event, see under Warner Valley. The Camp Warner mentioned in this paragraph is now generally known as Old Camp Warner. The winter of 1866-67 was very severe and the troops at Old Camp Warner suffered great hardships. Major-General George Crook, then a lieutenant-colonel, took command at Boise in 1866, and in 1867 made an inspection of the Warner Valley. He disapproved of the camp and the locality and was provoked by the story that the troops could not cross the lakes. He caused a rock causeway to be built in a few days and relocated Camp Warner in the west part of the valley, at about the place originally selected by the troops from Vancouver. For additional information about Camp Warner, see *History of Central Oregon,* page 811, *et seq.* Therein it is stated that the troops were moved from the camp in October and November, 1873. Heitman's *Historical Register* lists Camp Warner but gives no details. There is also some information in Bancroft's *History of Oregon,* volume II, page 536. See also under Stone Bridge. In October, 1943, C. H. Langslet, county assessor at Lakeview, informed the compiler that the second location of Camp Warner was on Honey Creek in the southwest part of township 36 south, range 22 east, at what is now known as Fort Warner Ranch. The USGS Little Honey Creek quadrangle dated 1968 shows the site in section 33 on Dent Creek, a small tributary of Honey Creek.

Camp Watson, Wheeler County. All that is left of Camp Watson is on a little stream called Fort Creek about five miles west of Antone. The place is clearly shown on the USGS Derr Meadows quadrangle. Camp Watson was named in honor of Second Lieutenant Stephen Watson of the First Oregon Volunteer Cavalry who was killed in action with Snake Indians on the upper reaches of Crooked River May 18, 1864. According to the report of Captain H. C. Small of Company G of the Oregon Cavalry, he selected the site of Camp Watson October 1, 1864, and his command built huts for the winter. The name was applied by order of Brigadier-General Benjamin Alvord. It is apparent that there was a temporary Camp Watson a little earlier in the campaign four miles to the east. Late in 1866 the Oregon volunteers were recalled to Fort Vancouver and mustered out of service, but the camp was occupied by federal cavalry and infantry detachments for several more years. Local tradition says that a log stockade about fifteen feet high was the main defense, and there were several groups of log cabins and a blacksmith shop. In addition there was a building used for a stage station. A large meadow was used for a parade ground. In 1935 there were reported to be seven graves at Camp Watson, but it could not be determined if Watson's body was in any of them. A post office with the name Camp Watson was established to serve the locality on November 11, 1867, with Charles L. West first of four postmasters. This office was discontinued November 3, 1886, with papers to Caleb.

Camp White, Jackson County. George Ared White was born in Illinois July 18, 1881. When but a youth he became interested in military life and served in the Spanish-American War. He came to Oregon from the Rocky Mountain states in 1904 and joined the staff of the *Oregonian*. The compiler recalls many pleasant weeks spent with George White and Gene Howe in 1905 reporting the Lewis and Clark Fair for the *Oregonian*. In 1915 George White became adjutant general for Oregon and from that time on his rise in military rank was remarkable. He served with distinction in World War I. Successively he held more important positions and was major-general in command of the 41st Division when that organization was called into the federal service September 16, 1940. He served with that rank until his death November 23, 1941. He received many honors from both government and private agencies. Under the name Ared White he gained wide popularity as an author. Camp White, near Rogue River in southern Oregon, was north of Medford, and was named in honor of George A. White. It was a large installation for use in World War II. The camp was authorized in January, 1942, and the first concrete was poured March 11. The camp was officially dedicated September 15, 1942, with Mrs. White the guest of honor.

Camp Withycombe, Clackamas County. Camp Withycombe, which is just east of Clackamas station, is named for James Withycombe, governor of Oregon from 1915 to 1919. In February, 1944, Colonel Elmer V. Wooton, acting adjutant general of Oregon, wrote the compiler: "Camp Withycombe was established in 1909, under a lease arrangement with option to purchase. The United States Government was the lessee and the purchase option was exercised in 1910. Originally known as the Clackamas Rifle Range, it was redesignated Camp Withycombe during World War I and in 1934 was officially designated as Camp Withycombe. The original tract was added to several times, so that now the area embraced in the camp site totals 257 acres."

Camp Wright, Harney County. Camp Wright was used during the Indian troubles of the 1860s. According to the Oregon Adjutant General's *Report,* 1865-66, it was established October 3, 1865. It was occupied by Captain L. L. Williams and H Company of the First Oregon Volunteer Infantry, and it was situated on Silvies River close to the east end of Wright Point near what was later Island Ranch. It was named for Brigadier-General George Wright who was drowned in the wreck of the *Brother Jonathan.* See under Wright Point. The camp was not many months in use and was not substantially fortified. See Bancroft's *History of Oregon,* volume II, page 514 and page 490, footnote. *Recollections of a Linn County Volunteer* by William M. Hilleary on file at the Oregon Historical Society say that the soldiers protected themselves by building up sod walls with roofs of poles covered with earth.

Campbell Canyon, Morrow County. This canyon empties into Willow Creek five miles below Heppner. It was named for a well-known family that included Morrow County pioneer, Eugene F. Campbell, and County Judge William T. Campbell.

Campbell Falls, Douglas County. The USFS has adopted the name Campbell Falls for a drop in South Umpqua River, in section 13, township 29 south, range 1 west, just above the mouth of Boulder Creek. These falls were named to commemorate Robert G. Campbell, a former employee of the USFS who was killed in action in World War II, November 12, 1944.

Canary, Lane County. This place received its unusual name because local residents could find none other that would satisfy both postal authorities and railroad officials. Many names were suggested but to no avail. The writer is informed that Canary has no local significance and it is not known who suggested it.

Canby, Clackamas County. Canby was named for Major-General Edward R. S. Canby, commander of the Department of the Columbia, who was killed by Modoc Indians on April 11, 1873, at a peace parley not far from the California-Oregon line south of what is now Klamath Falls. For a short account of the Modoc War, see Scott's *History of the Oregon Country,* volume II, page 334. See also Jeff C. Riddle's *The Indian History of the Modoc War,* which gives detailed accounts of the war and subsequent happenings. Edward Richard Sprigg Canby was a veteran of the Seminole, Mexican and Civil wars. In 1874 Fort Canby, Washington, at the mouth of the Columbia River, was named for him. Stories to the effect that the community of Canby was once called Knighttown for Adam Knight, an early resident, could not be confirmed in June, 1943. Adam Knight, then still living, denied all knowledge of the matter. The general locality from Canby north to the Willamette River was called Baker Prairie.

Canemah, Clackamas County. Canemah was founded in 1845 by A. F. Hedges. During many years it was the loading and unloading point for the portage around Willamette Falls. Leslie M. Scott says that the name is supposed to have been that of an Indian chief.

Canfield Hill, Curry County. Canfield Hill is north of Rogue River five miles above Wedderburn. It was named for Jason W. Canfield who was born in Ohio in 1843 and homesteaded here on Rogue River before the turn of the century.

Cannery Hill, Tillamook County. Cannery Hill is the high ground projecting northward into Nestucca Bay. Before the bay was closed to commercial fishing, a cannery was located on the west side of the hill. When local roads were developed after World War I, fish were taken elsewhere for processing and now all that remains is the name.

Cannery Mountain, Lincoln County. Cannery Mountain, elevation 1065 feet, is on the south side of Siletz River about two miles southeast of the present site of Kernville. This mountain is about south of and across the river from the site of the former Kern fish cannery and it was named on that account. For information about the cannery, see under Kernville.

Cannibal Mountain, Lincoln County. Cannibal Mountain, elevation 1946 feet, in the Coast Range about five miles south of Tidewater, has one of those names that seems to defy efforts to find a reason for the application. The region is not noted for its cannibals, unless they be deer flies and mosquitos, and it seems hardly likely that anyone ever named the peak for such pests. The compiler has an old map with the name Cannonball Mountain for this peak, but in 1946, H. G. Hopkins, district ranger for the USFS at Waldport, tried to learn the history of the name of the mountain and could find no one in the locality that ever heard of Cannonball. The point was sometimes called Canniber Mountain, supposed to be an Indian name meaning saddle, but search so far has disclosed no such Indian word. Canniber was also said to be derived from the fact that oldtimers went to the place for canning berries, but this seems fanciful. Hopkins reports that stories that two well-known hunters went there to get venison to eat raw were denied as ridiculous by one of the hunters still surviving. Stories that a pioneer trapper, during a snowstorm ate his squaw rather than starve are of the guidebook type rather than for jury trial.

    Cannon Beach, Clatsop County. Lieutenant Neil M. Howison, U.S.N., arrived in the Columbia River July 1, 1846, in the schooner *Shark* for the purpose of making an investigation of part of the Oregon country for the government. For details of his visit see Carey's *History of Oregon,* page 451. For details of his report, see *OHQ,* volume XIV, page 59. The *Shark* was wrecked on attempting to leave the Columbia River on September 10, 1846, and part of her deck and a small iron cannon drifted ashore south of Tillamook Head, thus giving the name to Cannon Beach. The cannon is still there. For information about this disaster see *OHQ,* volume XIV, page 355. Cannon Beach is a well-known summer resort, and is of historic interest. In January, 1806, William Clark climbed over Tillamook Head and visited the locality. At the south end of Cannon Beach is Arch Cape, which blocks automobile travel on the beach itself. Hug Point, about two miles north of Arch Cape, formerly blocked beach traffic, but a narrow road has been cut around its face in the solid rock. Other important points are Humbug Point, Silver Point, and Chapman Point, which is at the north end and is a southern spur of Tillamook Head. Haystack Rock, 235 feet high, is one of the prominent sights on the beach itself. Ecola Creek flows into the ocean at the north end of Cannon Beach. The community has been known by various names including Elk Creek and Ecola, but the Post Office Department in 1922 changed the office name from Ecola to Cannon Beach to agree with the natural feature and to avoid confusion with Eola, where mail was frequently missent. The cannon and the capstan of the *Shark* are standing a little south of Hug Point, above high water line. Construction of Oregon Coast Highway just above the beach has made unnecessary the dangerous passage around Hug Point. Cannon Beach is about eight miles long. Cannon Beach post office was established May 29, 1891, with James P. Austin postmaster. This office was on or near the Kissling property at Hug Point, not far from the spot where the old cannon stands and several miles south of the present Cannon Beach community. The office was closed November 2, 1901. The office called Ecola was established November 25, 1910, with Lester E. Bill postmaster. This office was at the place called Elk Creek, now called Cannon Beach community. The name of the office was changed to Cannon Beach on May 25, 1922, when Eugene Lamphere was the postmaster.

Canoe Encampment Rapids, Morrow County. These rapids were in the Columbia River between Castle Rock and Blalock Island. The encampment at the foot of the rapids was a popular one with the fur traders and trappers. The name appears in early journals, but when first so used cannot be determined. It has been suggested that possibly the name was originally applied by traders because of an encampment of Indians with canoes at that point, as it seems strange that the traders themselves would single out those rapids as being particularly associated with their canoes, which they had with them at all rapids.

Canyon City, Grant County. This historic community is the county seat of Grant County, and derives its name because of the fact that it is situated in a canyon about two miles south of the John Day River. This part of the state was the scene of gold discoveries in the fall of 1861 and for some time there was a great influx of miners. Canyon City post office was established in what was then Wasco County on April 23, 1864. Grant County was formed from part of Wasco County on October 14, 1864. Canyon City suffered from a disastrous fire on April 18, 1937, a large part of the community being destroyed.

Canyon Road, Multnomah and Washington counties. Canyon Road, at the head of Southwest Jefferson Street, Portland, was a highly important factor in the development of the city. Rival communities such as Linnton, Milton and Saint Helens were at a disadvantage because they did not have as good access to the rich farm lands of the Tualatin Valley. The road was named because it traversed the canyon of Tanner Creek. See under that heading. Canyon Road was first opened in the fall of 1849 (letter of Joseph Smith in the *Oregonian,* July 13, 1884). Citizens of Portland formed, for the improvement of the road in 1850, the Portland and Valley Plank Road Company, which was chartered by the legislature and organized at Lafayette July 30, 1851. Subscription for funds opened March 10, 1851, at Portland, Hillsboro, Lafayette, Nesmiths Mills, Marysville (Corvallis), Albany and Salem. Grading began in 1851. Stephen Coffin took the contract for laying the planks. The first plank was laid September 27, 1851, amid ceremonies. In September, 1851, Thomas Stephens became superintendent. For further work, see advertisements in the *Oregonian* in 1851. The work soon lapsed for lack of funds (article by George H. Himes, *ibid.,* August 14, 1902). The first plank was laid near the present Art Museum. The route was surveyed by Daniel H. Lownsdale. The road was badly damaged by rains in the winter of 1851-52, *ibid.,* January 10, 1852. A statement of the work on the road appears, *ibid.,* April 3, 1852. The sum of $14,593.83 was expended up to that time. On May 10, 1852, the third and fourth installments to stock subscriptions were called for. In the summer of 1852 a scandal, or rupture, occured in the company, and the new directors were elected, *ibid.,* August 7, 1852. An earlier road, built by F. W. Pettygrove, passed through what is now Washington Park.

Canyonville, Douglas County. Canyonville is an historic community of Oregon, and is situated at the north end of Canyon Creek Canyon, where this defile opens into the valley of the South Umpqua River. It was in this canyon that the immigrants of 1846 had such great hardships on their way into the Willamette Valley. The canyon was known in pioneer days as

Umpqua Canyon. For a graphic description of the difficulties experienced
here by the pioneers of 1846 see Bancroft's *History of Oregon,* volume I,
page 563. For information concerning the proposed location of a railroad
in the canyon see Scott's *History of the Oregon Country,* volume IV, page 5.
The railroad route finally selected ascended Cow Creek from Riddle and
joined the old stage road not far from Glendale. The stage route for many
years continued up Canyon Creek and today travelers over the Pacific Highway may see where there have been earlier routes through the canyon. The
total descent from the pass at the head of Canyon Creek to Canyonville is
nearly 1300 feet, most of which occurs in the south part of the canyon.
Difficulties have continued here in modern times for on January 16, 1974
nine men working in a Pacific Northwest Bell Company relay station about
a mile south of Canyonville were killed when a massive earth slide swept
away the building. For details, see the *Oregonian,* January 18, 1974. Canyonville was for many years known as North Canyonville, the post office having
been established with that name July 6, 1852, with John T. Boyle, postmaster. There was a locality farther south known as South Canyonville, but this
was not a post office. The post office name was changed to Canyonville
June 1, 1892. Canyon Creek is erroneously supposed by many to be Cow
Creek. The Pacific Highway does not follow the canyon of Cow Creek
although it does traverse that stream through a wide valley east of Glendale. The pass at the head of Canyon Creek is about 2020 feet in elevation.
Canyonville has an elevation of 747 feet. Those who have visited this part
of the state will realize that Canyon Creek and Canyonville are appropriate
names.

Cape Arago, Coos County. Cape Arago is the western point of a large
headland just south of the mouth of Coos Bay. The northern point of this
headland is Coos Head. Captain James Cook sighted it on March 12, 1778,
and named it Cape Gregory for the saint of that day. Since 1850 this cape
has been called Cape Arago, and is officially so known by the USBGN.
Dominique Francois Jean Arago (1786-1853) was a great French physicist
and geographer. He was the intimate of Alexander von Humboldt, and his
friendship with Humboldt "lasted over forty years without a single cloud
ever having troubled it." The name Cape Arago first appeared on the
USC&GS chart prepared by William P. McArthur in 1850, and issued the
following year. It seems apparent that McArthur applied the name Arago
as the result of the naming of Humboldt Bay, California, which took place
about the same time. Humboldt Bay was named in 1850 during the visit of
a company of miners styled the Laura Virginia company or association. A.
J. Bledsoe, in *Indian Wars of the Northwest,* 1885, page 118, gives an account
of the exploration of the Laura Virginia expedition in the ship *Laura Virginia,* and he says that Humboldt Bay was named at the solicitation of a
member of the party who was an admirer of the great scientist. Elsewhere it
is reported that the name was selected by Lieutenant Douglass Ottinger,
captain of the *Laura Virginia,* but this does not agree with Bledsoe. McArthur visited Humboldt Bay and mapped it in 1850 and a few weeks later
charted Port Orford which he named Ewing Harbor for his Coast Survey
schooner *Ewing.* He charted the vicinity of Cape Arago shortly after leaving
Ewing Harbor. It seems obvious that the well-known friendship between

Arago and Humboldt suggested the name for the cape. Family tradition says that McArthur was greatly interested in mathematics and physics and it seems certain that he was familiar with the association of Arago and Humboldt. The compiler is of the opinion that Cape Arago was named on account of this friendship. H. R. Wagner, in *Cartography of the Northwest Coast of America*, volume II, page 373, says that Cape Arago is the same as Cabo Toledo of Bodega's and Heceta's larger map of 1775.

Cape Blanco, Curry County. Cape Blanco is in north latitude 42° 50' 14'' and is the most westward point in Oregon, but not, as some suppose, of continental United States. *Blanco* is a Spanish word meaning white. In 1602 Sebastian Vizcaino sailed from Acapulco at the head of an exploring expedition, and after one of his ships had turned back at Monterey, Vizcaino in his ship and Martin de Aguilar in a *fragata*, quitted Monterey on January 3, 1603, sailing northward. During a storm the two ships separated and Vizcaino sailed up the coast alone, reaching a point which he named Cape San Sebastian on January 20. He returned to Acapulco without meeting the *fragata*. In the meantime de Aguilar also sailed northward, and he records that on January 19 he reached the 43rd parallel, and found a point which he named Cape Blanco. North of the cape he reported a large river. Here he turned back. Most of the crew of the *fragata*, including de Aguilar, died on the way to Acapulco. H. R. Wagner in *Cartography of the Northwest Coast of America*, volume I, page 111, describes this voyage and calls attention to the fact that Cape Blanco was mentioned in the instructions, so that name was already in use before 1602. The recorded latitudes of this expedition are too great and there is nothing to show that the members ever reached the coast of Oregon or saw what is now Cape Blanco. The large Heceta-Bodega map prepared as a result of the 1775 expedition refers to this point as *Cabo Diligensias*. Bodega was off the cape September 27, 1775. See Wagner's *Cartography*, volume II, page 376. On March 12, 1778, Captain James Cook writes of his discovery of Cape Arago, which he called Cape Gregory, and stated that he thought he observed the Cape Blanco of de Aguilar in proximity. He was too far away to see the mouth of Coos Bay. On April 24, 1792, Captain George Vancouver sighted what we now know as Cape Blanco, and named it Cape Orford in honor of George, earl of Orford, his "much respected friend." Vancouver determined its latitude as 42° 52', very nearly its true position. There was some speculation on Vancouver's ship as to whether or not it was the Cape Blanco of de Auguilar, but the position and its dark color "did not seem to intitle it to the appellation of cape Blanco." Vancouver brings up the matter again in his *Voyage of Discovery* in the latter part of the entry for April 25. He passed and identified Cape Gregory (now Cape Arago) of Captain Cook, and made a reasonably accurate determination of its latitude, though he noted the difference between his figures and Cook's. There was no other important point and he said: "This induced me to consider the above point as the cape Gregory of Captain Cook, with a probability of its being also the cape Blanco of D'Aguilar, if land hereabouts the latter ever saw." Vancouver finished his observations for the day by expressing a doubt that Cook saw Cape Blanco or any other cape south of Cape Gregory on March 12, 1778, and stated that it was fair to presume that what Cook saw was an inland mountain.

Notwithstanding all these facts the name Cape Blanco has persisted for the most western cape of Oregon, even though it may not have originally been applied to it, and Vancouver's name Cape Orford has fallen into disuse and has been decided against by the USBGN. Part of the name is still in use in Port Orford, which is just south of the cape. Cape Alava, Clallam County, Washington, is the most westward point in continental United States, with a longitude of 124° 44'. It is in approximate latitude 48° 10'. It is more than 10' of longitude further west than Cape Blanco. Authorities are not unanimous as to the color of Cape Blanco, but George Davidson, whose opinion carries great weight, says in the *Coast Pilot* for 1869 that the rocks were of a dull white appearance but bright when the sun shone on them. However, this is probably more or less true of other capes in the neighborhood. For illustrated story about Cape Blanco and the lighthouse, by Alfred Powers, see the *Oregonian*, Sunday, September 15, 1915.

Cape Falcon, Tillamook County. Cape Falcon is the next cape south of Arch Cape, and has been known in the past as False Tillamook Head, which lies further north. On August 18, 1775, Captain Bruno Heceta, while cruising along the north Pacific Coast discovered a cape in latitude 45° 43' north and named it Cape Falcon. While this is not far from the correct latitude of what we now know as Cape Falcon, 45° 46', the records of Heceta are so meager as to make it impossible exactly to identify his discovery. Cape Falcon as we now know it derived its name from Heceta, irrespective of what point he originally discovered. The present application of the name was made by George Davidson of the USC&GS in 1853, as being preferable to a name with the "false" in it. Heceta speaks of Cape Falcon, but Fray Benito de la Sierra, one of his chaplains, uses the expression "a range of high hills, to which we gave the name *Sierra de Montefalcon*." See *California Historical Society Quarterly*, volume IX, page 235. The day of Santa Clara de Montefalco is August 18, and this name was obviously given in her honor. Cape Falcon has been the cause of considerable misunderstanding among students of Oregon history. Greenhow, in his *History of Oregon and California*, appears to have started the trouble by confusing Cape Falcon, or as it was sometimes known, False Tillamook Head, with Clarks Point of View. This he does in two places, one in chapter IV and another time in appendix E. This error has been perpetuated by both great authorities on the Lewis and Clark expedition, Coues and Thwaites. As a matter of fact Clarks Point of View was on Tillamook Head, as is clearly shown by Clark's description of the view he had from the point and also by two maps in *Original Journals of the Lewis and Clark Expedition*, atlas volume. Davidson perceived this error. See *Coast Pilot* for 1869. However, Davidson was of the opinion that the Cape Grenville of Meares was the same as Cape Falcon, but this seems improbable to the writer. At the time of his discovery of Cape Falcon, Heceta also named *La Mesa* or The Table, putting it some 15 minutes of latitude further south than the cape, with no indication as to whether it was an inland mountain or not. It seems to the compiler that *La Mesa* must have been what is now Cape Meares, or some flat-topped mountain inland. It is improbable that the name *La Mesa* had anything to do with Neahkahnie Mountain. The latitude given for *La Mesa* is much too far south, and the summit of Neahkahnie Mountain is not prominent and flat as seen from the sea. There are several more imposing and higher points in the immediate vicinity.

Cape Ferrelo, Curry County. Bartolome Ferrelo (Ferrer) was a pilot in the expedition of Juan Rodriguez Cabrillo, a Portuguese, who sailed from Mexico in June, 1542, for the purpose of exploring the coast of California. When near the 34th parallel of north latitude Cabrillo sank under the fatigue of the voyage and turned the command over to Ferrelo. The latter discovered a cape on the 41st parallel which he called *Cabo de Fortunas,* and on March 1, 1543, found himself to be as far north as the 44th parallel, but on the following day bad weather drove him south. It is now not easy to determine how far north Ferrelo came, nor what he actually discovered. H. R. Wagner in *Cartography of the Northwest Coast of America,* volume II, page 373, says that *Cabo de Fortunas* was probably the modern Point Arena, and apparently Ferrelo saw no more land north of that. His latitudes were considerably in error. There is nothing to connect the Cape Ferrelo with Bartolome Ferrelo the pilot, though it was named in his honor by George Davidson of the USC&GS, probably in 1869. Cape Ferrelo is but a short distance from the Oregon-California boundary line. It is the first prominent headland north of St. George Reef, and while not projecting seaward to any considerable extent, it is nevertheless noticeable on account of its bold rugged face.

Cape Foulweather, Lincoln County. Cape Foulweather was discovered and named by Captain James Cook, the English explorer, on March 7, 1778. This was the first geographic feature that Captain Cook named in his voyage to the north Pacific Ocean. On the day of his discovery the weather was particularly inclement. The *Coast Pilot* for 1869 gives a detailed account of this cape and incidents surrounding its discovery, compiled by George Davidson.

Cape Kiwanda, Tillamook County. This cape was once known as Sand Cape, but Kiwanda is the name in general use and the one adopted by the USBGN. Cape Kiwanda is a low, yellow, rocky point, much broken and eroded, projecting about one half mile from the general trend of the coast. Behind the cape are bright sand dunes, and it is probable that these rather than sand on the cape itself suggested the name Sand Cape. There is some uncertainty about the origin of the name Kiwanda, and it is said to mean "wind mountain." However, John W. Meldrum of Oregon City, former surveyor general of Oregon, said that Kiwanda was the name of a Nestucca Indian chief and local celebrity. This origin of the name seems much more probable, as the name Wind Mountain is not applicable to the cape.

Cape Lookout, Tillamook County. Cape Lookout is one of the most prominent on the Oregon coast. It projects into the ocean one and one-half miles and has a narrow promontory over 400 feet high on its seaward end. East of the cape the mountains rise to an elevation of over 2000 feet. Cape Lookout bears its present name in error which will doubtless never be corrected. The name was originally applied by John Meares to what is now known as Cape Meares, which he described fully and accurately, and his description was subsequently corroborated by Vancouver. The name was probably changed to the new position on the USC&GS charts of 1850 and 1853. Cape Lookout is about ten miles south of Cape Meares and is much more prominent, which is doubtless the reason for the change. Having once become attached to the new cape it was deemed inadvisable to attempt to restore the name to the old location and as a result George Davidson applied Meares' name to the feature that Meares called Cape Lookout. For further information on this point, see the entry for Cape Meares and also refer to United States *Coast Pilot* for 1869.

Cape Meares, Tillamook County. Cape Meares is just south of Tillamook Bay, and bears the name of the most interesting of all the early explorers of the north Pacific Coast. Meares is well described in the following words by Professor Edmond S. Meany in his *History of the State of Washington,* page 25: "John Meares, a retired lieutenant of the British Navy, was the most unconventional and interesting personality of all those figuring in these early marine annals. He sailed under double colors, he succeeded as fur hunter and geographer, he was the pioneer of two great industries, he sought to plant a colony of Chinese men with Kanaka wives, he wrote a book, he precipitated a quarrel between England and Spain which came near embroiling also the new republic of the United States in a serious war. There was nothing dull about John Meares. In 1786, he sailed from Bengal with two vessels, the *Nootka* and *Sea-otter,* names redolent of furs and adventure. Little is known of this voyage except that it was confined to the shores of Alaska. In 1787 English merchants in India fitted out two ships, the *Felice Adventurer* and the *Iphigenia Nubiana,* and placed them in command of John Meares and William Douglas. To avoid excessive port charges in China and to evade licenses from the South Sea and East Indian monopolies, a Portuguese partner was taken in, who procured from the governor at Macao, Portuguese flags, papers and captains. In case of need the real masters would appear as clerks or super-cargoes. While little use was made of this scheme, the trick of double colors is condemned as a cheat, closely akin to piracy. In May, 1788, Meares in the *Felice* arrived at Nootka, and for two pistols bought some land from Chief Maquina. He at once erected a little fort, and began an important enterprise. He had brought the framework of a schooner. His ship's company included fifty men, crew and artisans, part of each group being Chinamen. This little schooner, the *North West America,* was the first vessel built in this part of the world and this also was the first introduction of Chinese labor on the Pacific Coast." While Meares' organization was engaged in these activities, he himself set sail on an exploring expedition along the coast. He passed the mouth of the Columbia River on July 6, 1788, but he failed to identify it as a river. By nightfall of that same day he had discovered and named three important features, the first of which he referred to as Cape Grenville, and the next Quicksand Bay, the third feature he christened Cape Lookout, and the volume containing the story of his travels has a very fine plate showing this cape together with the remarkable rocks a little to the southwest. Having failed to discover the new river he was seeking, he returned to Nootka. For further information about the history of Nootka and the controversy between England and Spain over Meares' enterprise, see Meany's *History.* It is not easy at this time to identify Cape Grenville. George Davidson supposes it to be Cape Falcon. Quicksand Bay seems to be what is now known as Tillamook Bay. Meares' description and pictures of Cape Lookout, beyond all doubt, refer to what we now call

Cape Meares, and the rocks that Meares christened Three Brothers are now known as Three Arch Rocks and form a bird reservation that is frequently written about. George Davidson applied the name of Cape Meares to the feature herein described in 1857. Davidson was for many years connected with the USC&GS and is considered the authority on the early explorations of the Pacific Coast. It appears that through some misunderstanding the USC&GS adopted the name Cape Lookout on its charts of 1850 and 1853 for a point about ten miles south of Meares' original location. The name of Cape Lookout having become so well established in its new position and attaching to a point quite striking in appearance, it was apparently thought by Davidson best to leave the name where it was and honor Meares by applying his own name to the feature that he discovered. Professor Meany's remarks about Meares being the pioneer of two great industries refer to shipbuilding and timber exporting. When the *Felice* started for China she carried with her a deck load of spars, the first to be shipped from the Pacific Northwest. The spars were lost in rough weather, but this does not rob Meares of the glory of starting our lumber industry.

Cape Perpetua, Lincoln County. Cape Perpetua, which is in the extreme southwest corner of the county, is one of the historic geographic features of Oregon. It was discovered on March 7, 1778, by Captain James Cook, the famous English explorer, and it has been frequently asserted that he named the cape because the bad weather seemed to hold him perpetually in sight of it. It is apparent from a careful reading of his journals that this was not the case, but that he named the headland for St. Perpetua, who was murdered in Carthage on March 7, 203, for it was on St. Perpetua's Day that he made his discovery. A pious gentlemen informs the writer that Perpetua the Martyr was a noble lady of Carthage, and in the face of her father's pleading and tears, professed the faith and was thrown to the beasts and beheaded.

Cape Ridge, Lane and Lincoln counties. Cape Ridge gets its name because its western end forms Cape Perpetua. It lies between Yachats River on the north and Cummins Creek on the south, and Cape Creek, a short stream in between the two, bisects it unequally, with the larger part to the north, this terminating in the Cape. Cape Ridge rises rapidly from the cape and about a mile and a half from the ocean, it has an elevation of 1400 feet, and about three miles from the ocean there is a well defined summit 1947 feet high. This ridge together with others extending from the ocean finally blends itself into the Coast Range at higher elevations. For geography of this feature see USGS map of Waldport quadrangle.

Cape Sebastian, Curry County. Cape Sebastian gets its name from the fact that on January 20, 1603, Sebastian Vizcaino on an exploring expedition north from Mexico sighted a high white bluff near what he determined to be the 42nd parallel. He named it in honor of the saint of that day, San Sebastian. This point marked the northern limit of his voyage, but his recorded latitudes are much too high. What cape he saw and named it is not now possible to determine with accuracy, but the name Cape Sebastian is fixed on a cape in north latitude 42° 19′ 40″. The name was first applied to this feature by George Davidson in the USC&GS *Coast Pilot* for 1869, page 112. For more information about Vizcaino's voyage, see under Cape

Blanco. Cape Sebastian is prominent from north or south, and rises abruptly from the sea to a height of about 700 feet. The style Cape San Sebastian is wrong for this feature and is not in accord with the name given by Davidson.

Capes, The first exploration of the Oregon country by white people was by the sea, and on account of presumed ease of identification, capes and promontories were sought after and named by the early navigators. Cape Blanco was the first geographical feature of the state to be named by a white man, although it is not at all certain what feature was originally so identified. For a period of nearly 200 years explorers carried on the work of naming the headlands of Oregon before the interior was touched upon. The history of the naming of the Oregon capes is therefore worthy of study, particularly in view of the fact that much uncertainty exists as to what some of the early navigators saw and named on their charts. In order that the matter may be understood, it is necessary to have a table of latitudes, shown below. This table gives the positions north of the equator of the important capes of the state, such positions being taken from the publications of the USC&GS except for that marked (a) which is scaled from reliable maps, and is approximate. The positions marked (lt) are for the lighthouses on the capes, and all others are for some important triangulation point on the cape, though not necessarily in the exact center, or on its most westward point.

Cape	North Latitude
Point Adams	46° 12′ 38″
Tillamook Head	45° 57′ 54″
Arch Cape	45° 48′ 10″
Cape Falcon (a)	45° 46′ 04″
Neahkahnie Mountain	45° 44′ 38″
Cape Meares (lt)	45° 29′ 12″
Cape Lookout	45° 20′ 16″
Cape Kiwanda	45° 13′ 03″
Cascade Head	45° 03′ 41″
Cape Foulweather	44° 46′ 21″
Yaquina Head (lt)	44° 40′ 37″
Cape Perpetua	44° 17′ 15″
Heceta Head (lt)	44° 08′ 15″
Cape Arago (lt)	43° 20′ 29″
Cape Arago	43° 18′ 10″
Coquille Point (USGS)	43° 06′ 52″
Cape Blanco (lt)	42° 50′ 14″
Cape Sebastian	42° 19′ 40″
Crook Point	42° 15′ 07″
Cape Ferrelo	42° 06′ 08″

Cape Blanco is the most westward point in Oregon and its lighthouse is in west longitude 124° 33′ 45″. The most westward triangulation station on the cape is in longitude 124° 33′ 50.712″ and is close to the edge of the cliff of the middle point. For detailed information on the above points see

USC&GS Special Publication 175 and supplemental data. The table of latitudes given above will be of use in considering the discoveries on the Oregon coast, and will also indicate why it is impossible now to determine exactly what features each explorer recorded since in some instances the headlands are not unlike and are near together. The matter of fog and low lying clouds must also be taken into account. For instance it seems incredible that Heceta could so accurately describe the mouth of the Columbia River, then miss Tillamook Head completely and hit upon Cape Falcon.

Captain Cook Point, Lincoln and Lane counties. Captain Cook Point is the first prominent point south of Cape Perpetua, and Captain Cook Chasm is a well-known landmark at the end of the point. The Oregon Coast Highway crosses this chasm on a concrete viaduct. These features bear the name of Captain James Cook, R. N., one of the greatest explorers of all time. He sailed along this part of the Oregon coast in 1778, and on March 7 of that year discovered and named Cape Perpetua, just north of Captain Cook Point. James Cook was born in 1728 in Yorkshire, and joining the Royal Navy in 1755, he soon began to demonstrate his talents as a navigator. Before 1776 he had made two very important voyages and, above all, had made remarkable advances in the prevention of scurvy. He sailed from England in 1776 on his third and last voyage, during which he sighted the Oregon coast. After important discoveries in Alaska, he visited the Hawaiian Islands, where he met death at the hands of natives on February 14, 1779. Distinguished honors were paid to him by many countries. The compiler was unable to find that any geographic features had been named for him in continental United States and in 1931 recommended to the USBGN that the name Captain Cook Point be applied to the Oregon promontory. The board adopted the name in October of that year.

Captain Keeney Pass, Malheur County. Jonathan Keeney was born in Indiana on April 27, 1813. As a young man he was with Sublette in 1834 and then worked for the American Fur Company under Jim Bridger. He later spent several years in Missouri raising a family and made an uneventful trip to the Willamette Valley with the emigration of 1846. He arrived in Oregon in the early fall and is reported to been a member of the first party to bring wagons over the newly completed Barlow Road. Keeney settled in Linn County and in 1855 was elected Captain, Company C., Oregon Mounted Volunteers when that unit was mustered in for the Rogue River Indian War. About 1860 he moved to Walla Walla and thence to the Boise basin where he maintained a ferry and kept the travel near the mouth of Malheur River, dying near there on August 15, 1878. The emigrant road ran from south of Nyssa northwest to Vale and in 1975 the low divide between these two points was named Captain Keeney Pass to honor this Oregon pioneer.

Carberry Creek, Jackson County. This stream is formed by Steve and Sturgis forks, and flows into Applegate River. It was for a time also known as Steamboat Creek, but it is now universally known as Carberry Creek, in memory of an early resident of that section. It was called Carberry Creek in pioneer mining days, and that name seems to have antedated the form Steamboat Creek. See *OHQ*, volume XXIII, page 154.

Carcus Creek, Columbia County. Carcus Creek, west of Apiary, flows north into Clatskanie River. In 1941 Sinclair Wilson of Portland, who knew much of the early history of the county, told the compiler that many years ago this stream was called Carcass Creek because a local resident found a dead horse on its banks. However, the formal style of spelling soon gave way to the form now universally used throughout the county. Efforts to adopt the original spelling have been unavailing, and the name Carcus Creek seems to be here to stay.

Carey Bend, Marion County. This bend in Willamette River near Dayton is named for John and Ruth Carey whose donation land claim included the area. Carey was born in Philadelphia in 1802 and came to Oregon in 1847.

Carey Creek, Curry County. Government land records show that in 1897 Robert A. Carey applied for a homestead along this creek which flows into Chetco River east of Brookings.

Carey Stearns Ranch, Deschutes County. This ranch in the La Pine area was owned by one of the sons of Sidney Stearns, the early Deschutes and Crook County cattleman.

Carico, Columbia County. Carico was a post office in the woods about six miles west of Deer Island, but the place did not develop into a community. The office was established December 4, 1889, with Mrs. Lydia Pinckney first postmaster. Her husband, Nelson Pinckney, became postmaster on March 25, 1904, and the office was closed to Deer Island on May 15, 1913. In June, 1947, Mrs. Nellie C. Buss of Saint Helens, daughter of Mr. and Mrs. Pinckney, told the compiler that the office was named for one John Carico who had squatted on a claim in the locality prior to the arrival of the Pinckneys. John Carico moved away many years ago and the compiler knows nothing of his history.

Carll, Douglas County. Carll was a post office on the upper reaches of Cow Creek named for a local family. This office served the area later served by Binger and by Anchor. The office was established October 22, 1883 with George McCormick first of five postmasters. Carll office was closed July 16, 1894, and it seems probable on that date the name was changed to Binger, although the official record is not exactly precise on this point. As with many other offices of this type, it was doubtless moved from time to time.

Carlton, Yamhill County. A. E. Bones, postmaster at Carlton, wrote in October, 1925, that the place was named for John Carl, Sr., and that it was done at the request of R. R. Thompson of Portland at the time the west side railroad established a station there about 1874. Carl was an early settler in the neighborhood and Thompson owned a farm there. It has been stated elsewhere that the town was named for Wilson Carl, an ex-county commissioner. Possibly the two were members of the same family. Carlton post office was established July 21, 1874, with F. J. Fryer first postmaster.

Carmichael Canyon, Morrow County. Carmichael Canyon empties into Skinners Fork in the upper Willow Creek drainage. It was named for John A. Carmichael who was born in Pennsylvania in 1853 and came to Oregon in 1877.

Carnahan, Clatsop County. This community is on Clatsop Plains and was named for Hiram Carnahan, a pioneer of 1846. He was born in Tennessee in 1820. After arriving in Oregon he visited the California mines, but returned and settled in Clatsop County about 1849. He married Mary E. Morrison. For information about the Carnahan family, see editorial page of *Oregon Journal,* June 30, 1928. Hiram Carnahan died in January, 1896.

Carnation, Washington County. This post office just south of Forest Grove was established May 20, 1905, with Clarence L. Bump first postmaster. It was so named because the Carnation Milk Products Company formerly had a condensery nearby, and Bump's store where the post office was situated was the Carnation store. This post office was operated with the name South Forest Grove from April, 1906, until November, 1914, when the old name Carnation was restored.

Carney Butte, Umatilla County. Carney Butte has an elevation of 4813 feet and is about a mile east of Battle Mountain summit. It was named for an early day family. One member, Leonard S. Carney, took up government land in the area as early as 1876.

Carney Canyon, Umatilla County. This canyon five miles south of Vinson was named for Samuel J. Carney who settled near its mouth in the 1890s.

Carnine Canyon, Gilliam County. This canyon running to Sixmile Canyon east of Condon was named for J. M. Carnine, a veteran of the Civil War, who settled nearby in 1901. See *Illustrated History of Central Oregon,* page 586.

Carpenterville, Curry County. Carpenterville is on the old Oregon Coast Highway about sixteen miles north of Brookings. In 1921 D. W. Carpenter and his family settled at this locality and among other things operated a small mill for fence lumber. Carpenter later moved to California and then to Bandon, but his sons continued to run the mill. He returned to the place about the time the highway was built and started a store and tourist cabins. In April, 1932, a post office was established and named for the family.

Carpet Hill Creek, Lane County. A few miles below Westfir, Carpet Hill Creek flows into Middle Fork Willamette River from the north. Jess McAbee, a pioneer resident of Lowell, is authority for the story of this name. The old Middle Fork road crossed the toe of a hill near the creek, and a large, smooth, sloping rock caused the oxen to slip and lose their footing. One outfit overcame the difficulty by laying a large carpet over the rock, and as a result the creek soon had its present name.

Carroll Rim, Wheeler County. In 1971 at the suggestion of Phil Brogan this high ground facing Painted Hills State Park was named for Samuel Carroll. Carroll was born in Illinois in 1820 and came to Linn County in 1847 where he took a donation land claim. About 1870 he moved to the Painted Hills area and raised a substantial family. Carroll Creek near West Branch was named for a son, Samuel Carroll, Jr., and Carroll Butte on the headwaters of Marks Creek was named for another son, Charles.

Carson, Baker County. The postmaster of Carson in 1925 wrote that this community was apparently named for Tom Corson who settled about 1870 on a small stream flowing into Pine Creek. Neighbors pronounced his name Carson and applied it to the stream in question and subsequently to a small sawmill which was called the Carson Mill because it was situated on the creek. When the post office was established July 26, 1893, the name was applied to it as well. The office was discontinued in April, 1952. The area is served by rural route out of Halfway.

Carter, Lane County. This was a station on the Cascade line of the Southern Pacific Company east of Lowell. It was named for Joe Carter, an old settler of the neighborhood.

Carter, Malheur County. Carter post office was one of those establishments that did not last long. It appears on the Malheur County list as of July 15, 1898, and was discontinued November 2, 1901, with papers to Rockville. William C. Carlton was the only postmaster. The post office was named for an early settler, one Carter, whose initials are not available to the compiler. Carter post office was on Carter Creek eighteen or twenty miles eastward of the place known as Watson and something over twenty miles north of Sheaville. Carter Creek was also named for the pioneer settler. His home was near the junction of Carter Creek and Succor Creek.

Carter Branch, Linn County. This stream flows into Beaver Creek about seven miles northeast of Lebanon. It was named for a family of early settlers nearby.

Carter Lake, Douglas County. This is a long, narrow lake in the extreme northwest corner of Douglas County about one-half mile from the Pacific Ocean. It was named for an early settler who lived on its shore.

Carter Spring, Jefferson County. In 1888 Richard H. McCarter took up a homestead including this spring near Pony Butte. The Scotch prefix has vanished along with most of the small ranchers.

Cartney, Linn County. This is a station on the Oregon Electric Railway north of Harrisburg. It apparently was named for J. M. McCartney, an early settler in the neighborhood, as the station is on part of what was his land. The compiler does not know why his full name was not used.

Cartwright, Lane County. D. B. Cartwright was born in Syracuse, New York, in 1814 and came to Oregon in 1853. He settled in the upper reaches of Siuslaw River and established a hotel and stage station which he called Mountain House. After World War II the building was still standing about eight miles west of Cottage Grove and a picture of it was published in the *Sunday Journal,* December 9, 1945. It was torn down in the summer of 1973. Cartwright died in 1875. William Russell, a native of Ohio, came to Oregon in 1848, and in 1866 married Miss N. C. Cartwright. He took over the activities of the Mountain House and was instrumental in having a post office established with the name of his father-in-law. This occurred on August 7, 1871, and the office continued under Russell's direction until September 18, 1890. For biographies of Cartwright and Russell see *Illustrated History of Lane County,* page 482; for picture of the Mountain House, *ibid.,* page 232. In May, 1946, P. M. Morse, Lane County Engineer, informed the compiler that the Mountain House was situated on the east side of the Territorial road in the extreme west part of section 30, township 20 south, range 4 west.

Carus, Clackamas County. Carus is a locality on SH 213 about seven miles south of Oregon City and a little to the southwest of Beaver Creek.

Carus post office was established June 7, 1887, with David Hunter first postmaster, and was discontinued July 27, 1907. The origin of this name has long been a mystery, and some information dug up early in 1946 merely adds to the confusion. The compiler has been informed by two reliable persons that it was planned to name the place Carns, and that is the way the name was sent to the postal authorities at Washington. It was not unusual to misread an "n" for a "u" and the name was innocently converted into Carus when the office was established. It may have been intended to name the office for a Carns in another state, or what is more probable, for a family named Carns.

Carver, Clackamas County. Carver is a post office near Baker Bridge on Clackamas River. It is at the site of the former office of Stone, which was established a number of years ago, and was later discontinued. The old office was called Stone because of the number of large boulders in the locality. About 1915 Stephen S. Carver promoted an interurban line from Portland into this part of Clackamas County, and a townsite at Stone was surveyed and platted with his name, Carver. The post office of Carver was established about 1924. S. S. Carver was born in Iowa in 1866 and died at Carver November 25, 1933. For obituary, see the *Oregon Journal,* November 27, 1933.

Carver Glacier, Deschutes County. Jonathan Carver was the first person known to have used the name Oregon, which he did in his book published in 1778. The only place in Oregon where his name has been perpetuated is in Carver Glacier, which is on the north slope of the South Sister and is one of the sources of Squaw Creek. It was named by Professor Edwin T. Hodge of the University of Oregon in 1924. Carver was born at Weymouth, Massachusetts, April 3, 1710. He served in the French and Indian wars, and later became an adventurous traveler. He had difficulties in getting the story of his travels published, and soured and discontented, he went to England where he was in a measure successful. He died in want in London in 1780. For his travels Carver outfitted at Mackinac and went to Green Bay, on Lake Michigan, and from there, by portage and river, to the Mississippi at Prairie du Chien, and then up the Mississippi to the Saint Peter, to spend the winter of 1766-67. He returned by way of Lake Superior, in 1767. Carver's *Travels* have been criticised as to their originality, and questions of plagiarism have been discussed by historical and literary authorities for many years. He is alleged to have plagiarized the writings of Charlevoix, Lahontan and James Adair, and the parallels have been freely quoted. For narrative of Carver's travels and discussion of this "plagiarism," see *The American Historical Review,* volume XI, pages 287-302, by Edward Gaylord Bourne. See also *Bibliography of Carver's Travels,* 1910, and *Additional Data,* 1913, by John Thomas Lee, published by the Wisconsin Historical Society. For details of Carver's family and of his birth, see *The Wisconsin Magazine of History,* volume III, No. 3, page 229, by William Browning. While Jonathan Carver originated the form of the name Oregon, it now seems probable that he did not originate the name itself. That was apparently done by Major Robert Rogers, an English army officer who was commandant at the frontier military post at Mackinac, Michigan, during the time of Carver's journey into the upper valley of the Mississippi. For particulars of this matter see the *OHQ*, volume XXII, No. 2, for June, 1921, containing an article by T. C. Elliott. See under the heading Oregon. Rogers used the form Ourigan.

Cascade Head, Tillamook County. Cascade Head is a jagged, wooded cape with a cliff on the seaward side, about three miles long and in places over 100 feet high. It was named because of the fact its face is cut deep by gorges through which the waters of three creeks are discharged from cascades 60 to 80 feet high. The name was applied to it by George Davidson of the USC&GS in the *Coast Pilot* for 1869.

Cascade Locks, Hood River County. The federal government adopted a plan for permanent improvements at the Cascades of the Columbia in 1875, and began work in 1878. For the history of the construction of the Cascade locks see the *Oregonian*, January 1, 1895, page 8. The locks were completed November 5, 1896. The community was named for the locks. Scott's *History of the Oregon Country*, volume III, page 190, gives a detailed history of the various aids to transportation developed at this point. The locks were submerged early in 1938 as a result of the construction of Bonneville Dam, but the town was not disturbed.

Cascade Range. The Cascade Range is the great mountain backbone of Oregon and Washington, and divides both states into separate climatic and geographic provinces. Probably the first attempt at a name for the range was by the Spaniard, Manuel Quimper, 1790, who roughly mapped it as *Sierras Nevadas de S. Antonio*. In 1792 George Vancouver, the English explorer, gave names to a number of the most prominent peaks, but referred to the range as "snowy range," "ridge of snowy mountains," or "range of rugged mountains." Lewis and Clark, 1805-1806, mention the named peaks and frequently refer in general terms to the range of mountains. Lewis wrote: "The range of western mountains are covered with snow," while Clark wrote: "Western mountains covered with snow." (Thwaites' *Original Journals of the Lewis and Clark Expedition*, volume IV, pages 313 and 305-306.) "Western Mountains" is the nearest to a name for the range adopted by Lewis and Clark. John Work, of the Hudson's Bay Company, wrote in December, 1824: "A ridge of high mountains covered with snow." (*Washington Historical Quarterly*, volume III, pages 213, 215.) David Douglas, the botanist, in writing his journal had great need of a name for these mountains and he seems to have been the first one to use the name "Cascade." He refers again and again to the "Cascade Mountains" or "Cascade Range of Mountains." (*Journal Kept by David Douglas*, 1823-1827, pages 221-222, 252, 257, 342.) Douglas does not claim to have originated the name for the range, and earlier use of it may yet come to light. William A. Slacum's report, 1836-1837, says the mountains called "Klannet range, from the Indians of that name." (*OHQ*, volume XIII, page 201.) Hall J. Kelley, early enthusiast of the Oregon country, who is sometimes referred to as "The Boston Schoolmaster," sought in a memoir (1839), to change the names of the great peaks by calling them after former presidents of the United States and to christen the range "Presidents range." The Wilkes Expedition, 1841, charted the mountains as Cascade Range.

Kelley's memoir is in 25th Congress, 3rd Session, House Report 101, Supplemental Report, dated February 16, 1839, page 47. The original report, dated January 4, 1839, is generally referred to as the Cushing report and the supplement of February 16, 1839, is an addition. Kelley's memoir is listed as Appendix O, and is dated Boston, January 31, 1839. It was addressed to the Committee on Foreign Affairs of which Caleb Cushing of Massachusetts was chairman. On pages 53-54 Kelley says: "The eastern section of the district referred to is bordered by a mountain range running nearly parallel to the spine of the Rocky Mountains and to the coast, and which, from the number of its elevated peaks, I am inclined to call the Presidents' range." In a footnote Kelley adds: "These isolated and remarkable cones, which are now called among the hunters of the Hudson's Bay Company by other names, I have christened after our ex-Presidents, viz:

1. Washington, latitude 46 degrees, 15 minutes [Saint Helens or Adams];
2. Adams, latitude 45 degrees, 10 minutes [Hood];
3. Jefferson, latitude 44 degrees, 30 minutes [Jefferson];
4. Madison, 43 degrees, 50 minutes [Three Sisters];
5. Monroe, 43 degrees, 20 minutes [Diamond];
6. John Quincy Adams, 42 degrees, 10 minutes [McLoughlin];
7. Jackson, 41 degrees, 40 minutes [Shasta];"

Farnham's *Travels in the Great Western Prairies* was published in 1843. Page 96 (New York edition) describes the Presidents Range and its several peaks. Farnham mentions ten peaks south of the 49th parallel (Canadian boundary). "Five of these latter have received names from British navigators and traders. The other five have received from an American traveler, Mr. Kelley, the names of deceased Presidents of the Republic. Mr. Kelley, I believe, was the first individual who suggested a name for the whole range. For convenience in description I have adopted it. And although it is a matter in which no one can find reasons for being very much interested, yet if there is any propriety in adopting Mr. Kelley's name for the whole chain, there might seem to be as much in following his suggestion that all the principal peaks should bear the names of those distinguished men. . . I have adopted this course." Farnham's names and positions, together with modern names are:

1. Mount Tyler, 49 degrees [Baker]
2. Mount Harrison [Rainier]
3. Mount Van Buren [Olympus]
4. Mount Adams, 45 degrees [Adams]
5. Mount Washington [Hood]
6. Mount Jefferson, 41½ degrees [Jefferson]
7. Mount Madison [Three Sisters]
8. Mount Monroe, 43 degrees 20 minutes [Diamond]
9. Mount Quincy Adams, 42 degrees, 10 minutes [McLoughlin]
10. Mount Jackson, 41 degrees, 10 minutes [Shasta]

Some of Farnham's positions, as well as those of Kelley, are widely erroneous, yet it is surprising that they are as good as they are. Farnham's position for Mount Jefferson is obviously a typographical error for 44½ degrees, otherwise it does not fit the sequence. The latitudes of both authors are generally too low. These presidential names were started by Kelley, and were confused by later writers who adopted his names but not his locations. In this way, difference of names appears as to Mount Adams, Mount Saint Helens, Mount Hood and other peaks. The original names remain with Mounts Hood, Saint Helens, Rainier, Baker and Jefferson; otherwise with Adams, Three Sisters, McLoughlin and Shasta. John Work, in his journal (*OHQ*, volume X, pages 308-09, by T. C. Elliott), calls Mount Adams Mount Saint Helen, Mount Saint Helens Mount Rainier, and Mount Rainier Mount Baker. The name Cascades was first that of the narrows of the Columbia River, which yet bears the title. This name for the Columbia River narrows is used commonly by writers as far back as the Astor expedition. In the Cushing supplemental report, referred to above as containing the Kelley memoir, there is also a memoir of Nathaniel J. Wyeth, dated February 4, 1839, which uses the name Cascade mountains. In Greenhow's *History of Oregon and California,* the name Far-West mountains is suggested. See also Bancroft's *History of Oregon,* volume I, page 164, note. As far as the writer knows, but one tribe of Indians had a name for the Cascade Range as such. The Klamath Indians called it the *Yamakiasham Yaina,* literally "mountains of the northern people." Cascade Range is the official form of name adopted by the USBGN and the feature to which it applies extends from Canada to the gap south of Lassen Peak in California. The Cascade Range is primarily volcanic in character and particularly in Oregon and in northern California its crest is made up of the remains of a series of giant volcanoes. The Cascade Range differs essentially in construction and in origin from the Sierra Nevada of California and there is no connection between the two. The highest point in the Cascade Range in Oregon is Mount Hood, 11,235 feet, and the lowest pass is the gorge of the Columbia River. The important routes of travel through the Cascade Range in Oregon include the Columbia River Highway at water level, and the Mount Hood Loop Highway, which in certain sections follows closely the Barlow Road, and which has a maximum elevation of 4670 feet where it goes through Bennett Pass on a spur east from the main range. The elevation of the roadway at Barlow Pass is 4155 feet. The Wapinitia Highway goes through Wapinitia Pass at an elevation of 3949 feet, but this highway also crosses a higher spur east of the main divide, at Blue Box Pass, elevation 4024 feet. Santiam Highway goes through the north part of Santiam Pass, in the vicinity of what was once called Hogg Pass, at an elevation of 4817 feet. The old Santiam toll road goes through Santiam Pass about three miles south of Santiam Highway at an elevation of 4773 feet, but here again the road reaches higher ground two miles east of the main divide at an elevation of 4774 feet. McKenzie Highway takes the place of the McKenzie toll road. Its maximum elevation is 5324 feet. The next highway to the south is the Willamette, which goes through Willamette Pass at 5128 feet just west of Odell Lake. The old Oregon Central Military Road goes through Emigrant Pass west of Summit Lake at an elevation of about 5600 feet. The Diamond Lake Highway crosses through a pass north of Crater Lake at an elevation of about 5920 feet. Crater Lake Highway has a summit elevation of about 6016 feet, west of Annie Spring. The Lake of the Woods Highway crosses south of Mount McLoughlin at an elevation of 5105 feet. The highest point on the Green Springs Highway between Ashland and Klamath Falls is 4696 feet at Hayden Pass. The backbone of the Cascade Range and the foothills have been accurately mapped by the USGS fron the Columbia River to the California border. This work was started about 1900, with revisions during the past 15 years and as a result the table of peak elevations in Oregon printed below is probably not subject to much change:

Mount Hood	11,239	feet
Olallie Butte	7,215	''
Mount Jefferson	10,497	''
Three Fingered Jack	7,841	''
Mount Washington	7,794	''
Belknap Crater	6,872	''
Black Crater	7,251	''
North Sister	10,085	''
Middle Sister	10,047	''
South Sister	10,358	''
Broken Top	9,175	''
Bachelor Butte	9,065	''
Irish Mountain	6,893	''
Maiden Peak	7,818	''
Mount Yoran	7,100	''
Diamond Peak	8,744	''
Cowhorn Mountain	7,664	''
Howlock Mountain	8,351	''
Mount Thielsen	9,182	''
Mount Bailey	8,363	''
Mount Scott	8,926	''
Hillman Peak	8,156	''
Garfield Peak	8,060	''
Applegate Peak	8,135	''
Union Peak	7,698	''
Mount McLoughlin	9,495	''

In 1933 the USGS remapped the area surrounding Crater Lake National Park and determined new elevations for Mount Bailey and Mount Thielsen, which are shown above. The 1920 elevation for Mount McLoughlin is not used because it refers to the top of the lookout house and not the groundline. It should be noted that the Cascade Range extends well into California and includes both Mount Shasta and Lassen Peak.

Cascade Summit, Klamath County. Cascade Summit railroad station in the extreme northwest corner of the county, came into being with the completion of the Southern Pacific Cascade Line in 1925-26. The office is just east of the summit tunnel through the Cascade Range and got its name on that account. The elevation is 4841 feet. Cascade Summit post office was established September 8, 1927, with Oliver M. Shannon first postmaster.

Cascades, Hood River County. The Cascades of the Columbia River were caused by natural obstructions. According to carbon dating, there was a massive earth slippage north of the river about 1260 AD. This was certainly one of the largest in the United States in the last millennium and it is now referred to as the Cascade Landslide. The remains are largely in Washington and extend roughly from Bonneville Dam to Cascade Locks. It is estimated that more than four billion cubic yards of earth moved south off the Table Mountain massif and for a short period of time, perhaps only hours, completely blocked the Columbia River. Reslumped slide material can be seen one hundred feet or more above the river on the south bank near Ruckel Creek. Lewis and Clark, 1805-1806, the first white men to see this geographical feature, used the word "cascades," but not as a name. The Upper Cascades they called "Great Shute." Alexander Ross, in his *Adventures of the First Settlers on the Oregon,* writing as of 1810-1813, mentions the cascades a number of times, indicating the obstruction in the river. David Thompson, of the North West Company of Montreal, on July 13, 1811, referred to "Rapids and Falls" and on July 27 to "Grand Rapid." John Work, of the Hudson's Bay Company, on June 22, 1825, wrote: "Embarked at 3 o'clock and reached the Cascades at 1." (*Washington Historical Quarterly,* volume V, page 85.) David Douglas, the botanist, in his journal for 1826 uses the word often, but not always for the same locality. Rev. H. H. Spalding, writing from Fort Walla Walla on October 2, 1836, uses the words: "The Cascades or Rapids." For an account of the fight with the Indians at the Cascades see OPA *Transactions* for 1896. The Cascades were submerged early in 1938 as a result of the construction of the Bonneville Dam.

Cascadia, Linn County. This post office was so named because it was situated in the Cascade Range. It was established in 1898.

Case Creek, Marion County. Case Creek flows into Champoeg Creek near Champoeg. It is named for William M. Case, a pioneer of Oregon, who was born in Indiana in 1820 and came to Oregon in 1844. In the following year he took a donation land claim on this creek about three miles south of Champoeg. Case built a large home on the property in 1858 which was still standing in 1973. He died on his own farm on February 11, 1903, and the building eventually fell into disrepair. In the 1970s it was purchased by Wallace K. Huntington of Portland and completely restored under the supervision of architect Gilman Davis. The building is on the National Register of Historic Places.

Casey, Clatsop County. Casey post office was on Youngs River about ten miles south of Astoria. It was named for a local family. The office was established in August, 1903, with Catherine Quinn postmaster. Casey office operated until August, 1911, when it was closed out to Astoria.

Cason Canyon, Gilliam County. Cason Canyon is southwest of Condon. It was named for Pemberton F. Cason, a nearby resident. The next canyon to the east, Pemberton Canyon, bears Cason's first name. See under

Pemberton Canyon. For biography, see *History of Central Oregon,* page 618.

Cason Canyon, Morrow County. Cason Canyon empties into Rhea Creek at Ruggs. It was named for James P. and Mary Cason who settled there in the early days. Cason was a son of Fendel Cason of Clackamas County and came to Oregon with his family in 1843. Mary Ellen Marsh Cason came west in 1847. Her mother died enroute and Mary Ellen stopped at the Whitman Mission. She was there at the time of the massacre and was one of the women held captive by the Indians and rescued by Peter Skene Ogden in December, 1847.

Cassiday Butte, Curry County. This 1818 foot butte southeast of Carpenterville was named for William F. Cassiday, an early settler.

Casteel Spring, Umatilla County. The Casteel family is well known in the Pilot Rock area but Lloyd Waid of the USFS in Ukiah believes this spring was named specifically for Mick Casteel.

Castle Creek, Jackson and Klamath counties. The various branches of Castle Creek rise on the west slope of the rim of Crater Lake, and Castle Creek itself flows into Rogue River. It was named Castle Creek because of the many spires and pinnacles in the canyon.

Castle Rock, Clatsop County. Castle Rock stands in the Pacific Ocean about a mile northwest of Arch Cape and has an elevation of 157 feet. It has upward projections that simulate battlements with some degree of fidelity and as a whole looks not unlike a castle. The name is apposite.

Castle Rock, Morrow County. It does not seem to have taken much imagination on the part of early settlers to build rock castles in the air, for there are Castle rocks in most of the counties of the state. The one in Morrow County about a mile northwest of the present railroad station Castle was probably the best known. It was a low bluff said to actually resemble a castle from the river. This formation as well as the old railroad and highway grades were inundated by Lake Umatilla behind John Day Dam.

Catalpa Lake, Wasco County. This lake 1.3 miles east of Frog Lake Butte was named by a fish planting crew of the Oregon State Game Commission about 1950. The catalpa, *Bignoniaceae catalpa,* is not native to the Pacific Northwest and the compiler is unable to explain the application.

Catched Two Lake, Wallowa County. This is a small lake in township 4 south, range 43 east, on the divide between Lostine and North Minam rivers. J. H. Horner, an old time resident, reported that many years ago Lyle Shumway was herding sheep in the area. His camptender neglected to set up the tent and after a row he departed and Shumway spent the night under the stars. The camptender and a friend returned the next day and Shumway recounted that "he catched two damn fools today." He publicised his opinion by carving "Catched Two" on a board and posting it nearby.

Catching Creek, Coos County. Catching Creek is an important stream tributary to South Fork Coquille River. It was named for Ephraim C. Catching, an early settler in the vicinity of Myrtle Point. Other geographic features in Coos County are also named for E. C. Catching or for his family.

Catching Creek, Douglas County. James Catching was born in Tennessee in 1827 and came to Oregon in 1847 with his brother, Epnraim. He took part in the Cayuse War and then moved to California. In the 1850s he returned to Oregon and spent some time in the Coos Bay area where one brother, Epnraim Catching, was an early well-known settler. James Catching then moved to the lower Cow Creek Valley where he and another brother, John, took donation land claims southwest of the present town of Riddle. Gaston has a biography of James Catching in *Centennial History of Oregon,* Volume III, page 309.

Cathedral Ridge, Hood River County. This ridge is one of the northwest spurs from Mount Hood and it is notable for the impressive cathedral-like spires along its summit. It was named in 1922 by a party of explorers from Hood River, led by C. Edward Graves, who was living in Arcata, California, in 1943. This party also named Eden Park, Wy'east Basin and Vista Ridge.

Catherine Creek, Union County. Catherine Creek is an important tributary of Grande Ronde River southeast of La Grande. It was named for Catherine Godley, the daughter of Thomas and M. E. Godley, early settlers near Union. Information about the Godley family is sparse and the compiler is indebted to John W. Evans of Eastern Oregon State College for unearthing the above facts. The Godleys were among the earliest Union County settlers for Captain Seth Weldy, 23rd Infantry, in his report dated August 15, 1867, describing his march from Fort Dalles to establish an outpost on Willow Creek in Malheur County, says that the detachment camped by Catherine Creek on July 27, 1867. Little Creek near Union was originally named Julianna Creek for the Godley's other daughter.

Cathlamet Bay, Clatsop County. Cathlamet Bay is on the south side of the Columbia River east of Tongue Point. Like many other Indian names, its meaning is hard to trace. Myron Eells identified the term with the Indian word *Kalama,* which is a town in Washington. On November 11, 1805, Lewis and Clark passed near the Indian village of Cathlamet and referred to *Calt-har-mar* nation of Indians. Thwaites refers to this nation as an extinct Chinookan tribe. It was obviously a small unimportant group of natives, and there is a possibility that the tribe name was associated with the word *calamet,* meaning stone, indicating that the Indians lived in a stony place. The Indian village of *Caltharmar* was on the south bank of the Columbia River, possibly not far from the present site of Knappa. Thomas N. Strong of Portland is authority for the statement that after the visit of Lewis and Clark, the Caltharmar nation, much reduced by disease, crossed the Columbia River and settled near the present town of Cathlamet, Washington. Wilkes, in *U. S. Exploring Expedition,* volume XXIII, page 335, and in accompanying atlas refers to Cathlamet Bay as Swan Bay.

Catlow, Harney County. This place and several other geographic features nearby were named for John Catlow, who was born in Yorkshire in 1824, and who, after emigrating to the United States, engaged in mining and stock raising in several parts of the West. He had extensive holdings in Harney County. He died in 1901. For biography, see *History of Baker, Grant, Malheur and Harney Counties,* 1902, page 701.

Caulkins Creek, Tillamook County. Charles W. Calkins homesteaded in southern Tillamook County in 1902 and his son, David Calkins, ranched along Caulkins Creek near the new alignment of US 101 over Cascade

Head. Another son, Elmer Calkins, told the author in 1968 that this creek was called Shinglebolt in the early days because a small shingle and shake mill was located nearby. He could not explain why the spelling was changed from the family form but the name Calkins is preserved in the small creek emptying directly into Salmon River from the north about a mile west of the US 101 bridge.

Cave Junction, Josephine County. This is the name of a community and post office on the Redwood Highway about 30 miles southwest of Grants Pass where the branch highway goes east to the Oregon Caves. In 1935 traffic into the caves had resulted in a community developing at the junction and a post office was applied for, with the name Caves City. The name was not satisfactory to the authorities, partly because the use of the word City implied that the place was incorporated, which was not a fact. Other suggestions were made, but on May 29, 1936, the USBGN adopted the name Cave Junction, which seemed to be satisfactory to those concerned. The post office was established in 1936.

Cave Mountain, Klamath County. This mountain east of Chiloquin between Williamson and Sprague rivers is named for the prominent cave in its lower slopes.

Caverhill, Grant County. The post office of Caverhill was established through the efforts of W. S. Caverhill, a local resident, and it was accordingly named for him. The post office was established February 7, 1916, and Nellie Caverhill was first postmaster.

Caviness, Malheur County. Caviness is a locality about fifteen miles west of Brogan and about ten miles southeast of Ironside, both airline measurements, named for a prominent local family. It is in the stock country. Caviness post office was established January 24, 1908, and was closed December 15, 1910. William P. Caviness was the only postmaster.

Cavitt Creek, Douglas County. Cavitt Creek is a tributary of Little River. It flows about 20 miles east of Roseburg. It was named for Robert L. Cavitt, a bachelor who settled on its banks. He lived there alone for many years and was found dead in his cabin. The spelling Cavatt is wrong.

Cayuse, Umatilla County. Cayuse is a railroad station and post office about 11 miles east of Pendleton and is one of the few geographical features in the state named for the Cayuse Indians. In 1924 Professor Edwin T. Hodge of the University of Oregon applied the name Cayuse Crater to a vent in the south part of Broken Top Mountain in Deschutes County. The Cayuse Indians were a Waiilatpuan tribe, formerly living at the headwaters of Walla Walla, Umatilla and Grande Ronde rivers, and between the Blue Mountains and Deschutes River. The tribe was closely associated with the neighboring Walla Wallas and Nez Perces, but was linguistically independent. After 1855 the tribe lived at the Umatilla Reservation. Their language is practically extinct, and their members have been absorbed by other tribes. The Cayuses committed the Whitman massacre in November, 1847. Alexander Ross gives the name *Cajouse* in *Adventures of the First Settlers on the Oregon,* page 127; Townsend's *Narrative* gives *Kayouse;* Palmer gives *Caaguas* and *Kioose* in his *Journal,* 1847, page 53; Hale gives *Cailloux* in his *Ethnography and Philology,* page 214; Scouler gives *Cayoose;* Wyeth, *Cayouse* and

Skiuse; George Wilkes, *Kiuse;* Farnham, *Skyuse;* John Work, *Kyauses;* Washington Irving gives *Sciatogas.* The Cayuses had linguistic affinities with the Molallas of western Oregon. Indian horses have come to be called "cayuses" because the Indians of that name were large breeders of the animals. The name formerly had only local use, but later spread over the Pacific Northwest. Cayuse in Umatilla County was formerly a stage station, and was at the foot of what was known as Meacham Hill. Cayuse post office was established October 29, 1867, with John S. White first postmaster. There is a Cayuse Canyon opening onto Rock Creek northeast of Condon in Gilliam County. It was doubtless so named because cayuse ponies pastured there.

Cazadero, Clackamas County. This was a station on the Estacada line of the Portland Electric Power Company near which the Cazadero power plant of the company is located on the Clackamas River. For many years previous to the time the company made its additional development further up the river, Cazadero was the end of the interurban line. It was named by the original promoters of the line, and the word is Spanish, meaning a place for the pursuit of game. The name was doubtless suggested by Cazadero, California.

Cecil, Morrow County. This is a railroad station and post office in the western part of Morrow County, at an elevation of 619 feet. It derived its name from the Cecil family, large landowners in the neighborhood who gave land for the post office.

Cedar Camp, Marion County. Cedar Camp post office was established November 26, 1932, and operated until July 22, 1933. Mrs. Edith M. Filer was the only postmaster. This office was a little to the northeast of Hullt and in the same locality as the older Bridge Creek post office. Cedar Camp was so known because there were several cedar shingle camps in the vicinity. Cedar Camp appears to be a name synonymous with the Bridge Creek locality. The compiler has been told that Cedar Creek is another name for Bridge Creek, but he cannot find any official sanction for the name Cedar Creek as applied to the stream.

Cedar Mill, Washington County. This name was given by John Quincy Adams Young, who settled at the locality in 1862 and built a cabin. He ran a sawmill for a few years, then sold it to W. R. Everson. Young was the son of Dr. Elam Young, a well-known Oregon pioneer, who, with his family, came to Oregon from Ohio in 1847. Young who was working in the Whitman sawmill at the time of the massacre on November 29, 1847, escaped, but his son James was killed. The Young family arrived in Oregon City in 1848 and soon thereafter settled near the present site of Hillsboro. When J. Q. A. Young established Cedar Mill, he specialized in the cutting of cedar siding, shingles, shakes and other products, most of which were used in buildings in the town of Portland, which was then growing rapidly. He died in 1905, aged about 77 years. Cedar Mill may be reached from Portland by the Barnes and Cornell roads and has an elevation of 274 feet. The style Cedar Mills is wrong, although often seen in print.

Cedar Mountain, Malheur County. Cedar Mountain consists of several rounded summits the highest of which is 5564 feet. It is in township 26 south, range 41 east, about twelve miles southwest of the south end of Lake

Owyhee. It has been called both Cedar Mountain and Juniper Mountain in the past but in 1975 the USBGN in *Decision List 7502* settled on the former name. There are no cedars in this part of Oregon but the common juniper, *Juniperus occidentalis,* was often miscalled cedar by early settlers.

Celilo, Wasco County. On March 9, 1957 the final closure was made at The Dalles Dam and Lake Celilo, the impounded pool, began to form. This pool with a normal elevation of 160 feet contains 330,000 acre feet of water and powers the 1,806,800 kilowatt rated capacity of the 26 turbines. It also inundated The Dalles of the Columbia from Big Eddy to Celilo Falls. In addition to the lake, the name Celilo is perpetuated in Celilo Village built by the USCE to replace Indian facilities at their traditional fishing grounds. In bygone days the name was used for a railroad station, for the navigation canal along the south bank of the Columbia River, and for "the rather low but romantic horseshoe shaped falls at the rock reef composing the upper end of this obstruction (Dalles) below which the Indian was accustomed to stand with his spear to pierce the jumping salmon. Like all other river falls these were known to the fur traders as The Chutes, and where the name *Celilo* was first used or whence it came is not known." T. C. Elliott, *OHQ,* June, 1915. Gustavus Hines, in *Oregon: Its History, Conditions and Prospects,* Buffalo, 1851, page 14, says: "A boy whose Indian name was Ken-o-teesh, belonging to the Si-le-lah tribe, was received into the mission in April, and died on the 19th of the following August." Whether Si-le-lah is the same as Celilo is a matter of conjecture, although a study of Oregon tribe names gives no other solution. Early journals of fur traders and travelers do not mention Celilo. Celilo was used in 1859, according to Mr. Elliott, who said there are several suggested meanings, including "tumbling waters," "shifting sands," and the name of an Indian chief, etc. Dr. Leo Frachtenberg of the Smithsonian Institution, in the *Oregon Journal,* December 31, 1917, says Celilo is a Yakima word meaning "cleft in the bank." Mr. Elliott's article referred to above gives more theories about the name and much information about the Celilo Canal. Stories to the effect that Celilo is a name based on a remark of a steamboat captain, "I see, lie low," may be dismissed as fiction.

Cemetery Hill, Wallowa County. Cemetery Hill is in section 20, township 1 north, range 48 east, near Imnaha. In 1931 J. H. Horner told the compiler that it was named because more than a dozen Indian graves were found there in pioneer days by Jack Johnson and others. A. C. Smith talked to the Indians about the origin of these graves but could learn nothing. They told him the graves were very old.

Cemetery Ridge, Wallowa County. This ridge is in the northeast part of the county and extends from Buckhorn Springs northeast. It is in townships 3 and 4 north, range 48 east. According to J. H. Horner of Enterprise, it was named because in the vicinity were the remains of some Indians killed in a battle between Nez Perces Indians and a band of renegade Snakes. The circumstances of this fight were within the memories of the older Indians in the Wallowa Valley.

Centerville, Washington County. Centerville was the name of a small community on Dairy Creek at the road crossing about two miles north of

Cornelius. The principal activity of the place revolved around the Trullinger mills, but today there is little to show for it. The locality was probably named because it was about the center of the Tualatin Plains, although it may have been named because it was supposed to be near the center of the county. Centreville post office was established October 11, 1866, with Edward Jackson first postmaster. This office was closed March 30, 1874. Ingles post office was established at the same place or nearby on September 28, 1881, with William S. Ingles, postmaster. The name of this office was changed to Centerville on September 2, 1889, and the office was closed September 30, 1904. These three offices may not all have been in exactly the same place, but they were in the same general locality.

Central, Linn County. Central was one of the earliest post offices established in what is now Linn County. The office was established June 13, 1852, with Joel Ketchum postmaster, and it was discontinued April 19, 1861. Early maps show the place about nine miles east of Albany and a little south. The office bore a descriptive name, probably because it was in a central location between Albany and the early settlements to the east.

Central, Multnomah County. On June 13, 1900, a post office named Central was established on the Multnomah County list. The office was discontinued December 14, 1903. James Channing was the first and only postmaster. According to the Portland city directory of 1902 the post office was at the southeast corner of Claremont Avenue and the East Ankeny street carline. Due to the change of Portland street names the location of this post office should now be described as the southeast corner of Northeast Glisan Street and Northeast 53rd Avenue. This falls within the limits of Center Addition, a tract that was platted in 1890. A question arises as to why the name of the post office Central differed from the name of the addition Center. This discrepancy was doubtless caused by the fact that there was then a post office in Washington County called Centerville and postal authorities did not wish to run the risk of confusion. Also there was a community in Clackamas County called Center. This old Central post office had of course no connection with a later Portland office called Central station.

Central Point, Jackson County. This community received its name because two important pioneer wagon roads of the Rogue River Valley crossed at this point which was near the center of the valley. One of these roads was the north and south road from the Willamette Valley and the other was the road leading from Jacksonville, which was then the center of settlement, northeast to Table Rock, Sams Valley and other localities. Central Point was named by Isaac Constant who was a pioneer of 1852 and who lived near the crossroads. Magruder Brothers established a store at this point about 1870 and a post office was soon given the name of Central Point. The town is on the Siskiyou line of the Southern Pacific Company and on the Pacific Highway and has an elevation of 1272 feet.

Cerro Gordo, Lane County. Cerro Gordo is a point on the north side of Row River about five miles east of Cottage Grove. The words are Spanish and mean a rich hill in a mining district, otherwise a fat or round hill. *Gordo* also means obese. In 1945 John C. Veatch of the Portland bar told the writer that a number of veterans of the Mexican War settled in the vicinity of this butte and presumably displayed their knowledge of Spanish by naming the mountain. There is a notion that this hill resembles the one in Mexico where the battle of Cerro Gordo was fought but Mr. Veatch thinks this improbable and that the real reason for the name was that the slopes are of a golden brown in late summer, giving the appearance of a gold or rich mountain. Mr. Veatch is well acquainted with the locality because he was born there.

Chadwell, Clatsop County. Chadwell is a locality on Lewis and Clark River about four miles south of Miles Crossing and south of Astoria. It bears the name of a place in England. Mr. and Mrs. William True were early settlers in the Lewis and Clark Valley. They came from Chadwell, England, and when the local post office was established February 20, 1882, True was the first postmaster and he named the place for his former home. The Clatsop County office was closed July 27, 1898, with papers to Melville. See information in the Astoria Column in the *Astorian-Budget,* June 7, 14, 20, and 26, 1946.

Chadwick Canyon, Douglas County. This canyon running into South Umpqua River at Missouri Bottom was named for Jacob J. Chadwick who settled near its mouth in 1868.

Chain Canyon, Wasco County. J. A. Rooper, who was born on the old Rooper Ranch, told the compiler in 1969 that this canyon that empties into Ward Creek was named because in the early days someone found a piece of abandoned chain presumably left by emigrants who strayed into the rough defile.

Chamberlain Hill, Multnomah County. Chamberlain Hill is east of Sandy River and north of Springdale. It bears the name of Elijah D. and Sarah Ellen Chamberlain who came to Oregon from Kansas in 1881 and settled in the Springdale area.

Chamberlain Lake, Tillamook County. This lake on the Camp Meriwether property of the Boy Scouts of America was named for the former owner, E. A. Chamberlain. It is a pleasant fresh water swimming spot within a few hundred yards of the Pacific Ocean. Chamberlain's father, Ezra B. Chamberlain, took up a homestead north of the lake in 1886.

Chambers Lakes, Deschutes and Lane counties. These are a small group of moraine lakes on the crest of the Cascade Range between the Middle and South Sisters. They were named in 1924 by Professor Edwin T. Hodge for James Blair Chambers, an early merchant of Eugene. Chambers was born in Quincy, Ohio in 1833 and came to Oregon in 1884. He moved to Eugene in 1887 and founded Chambers & Son Hardware Company. His son, Frank L. Chambers, succeeded to the business in 1890 and lived to be an extremely prominent Eugene business man. James B. Chambers died in Eugene in 1902.

Chambers Spring, Wheeler County. Chambers Spring near the headwaters of Fry Creek south of Mountain Creek was named for Calvin Chambers who homesteaded nearby at the turn of the century.

Champagne Creek, Douglas County. This stream flows into Umpqua River from the south a few miles northwest of Roseburg. It is in a locality known as the French Settlement because it was here that a number of French-Canadians established a sort of colony in the 1850s. One of these settlers was Joseph Champagne and the creek bears his name. For data about the French Settlement, see Walling's *History of Southern Oregon,* page 428.

Champion Creek, Lane County. Champion Creek, in the Bohemia mining district, was named for the Champion mine, which is situated near its headwaters. Champion post office was in operation in this locality from September, 1909, until October, 1918.

Champlain, Multnomah County. A post office with the name Champlain was in service at Holbrook from January 27, 1892, to May 21, 1892, with Fred Gaskell postmaster. Information about the origin of the name is unsatisfactory. Holbrook post office had been in operation at or near this place from September, 1887, to October, 1888, when it was closed to Arthur. Millard C. Holbrook of Portland wrote the compiler in September, 1946, that Fred Gaskell was associated with his (Holbrook's) grandfather, Samuel Wilson, in a general merchandise store on the Holbrook farm. Gaskell applied for a post office to replace the discontinued office, and the name Champlain was suggested as being that of a nearby stream. The name Champlain was changed to Holbrook by postal authorities on May 21, 1892, and thus the old title was put back in service. Mr. Holbrook adds that the name Champlain is not known in the area and there does not seem to have been any stream called Champlain Creek. Just what Gaskell had in mind is a mystery.

Champoeg, Marion County. The name Champoeg (Champooick, in early official records of the provisional government) is variously explained. According to F. X. Matthieu, the name was derived from the French words *Campment du Sable,* "camp of sand" (*OHQ,* volume I, page 88). According to other testimony, the origin is from French *champ* ("field"), and an Indian word, probably *pooich* ("root"); or the word may be purely Indian, designating a root or weed. According to H. S. Lyman, the name is not of French, but of Indian origin; *Cham* (hard *ch*), as in *Chehalem, Chenamus, Chemeketa, Calapooya, OHQ,* volume I, page 176. Frederick V. Holman says *Champoeg* is an Indian word, *Champoo,* a weed, (*ibid.,* volume XI, pages 22-23). Wilkes' map of 1841 shows Champooing. Champoeg was the site of the first warehouse of the Hudson's Bay Company on the Willamette River, south of Oregon City, and the shipping place of wheat of the Willamette Valley. The accessibility of Champoeg by land and water caused it to be chosen as the meeting place to consider a provisional government. The site of the Champoeg meeting place and monument is on the south bank of the Willamette River about midway between Newberg and Butteville. The settlement of Champoeg is about a half mile to the south on Mission Creek. Events leading up to the Champoeg meeting of May 2, 1843, are set forth in Scott's *History of the Oregon Country,* volume II, page 3, where begins Harvey W. Scott's address on the occasion of the unveiling of the Champoeg Monument on May 2, 1901. On February 15, 1841, Ewing Young died at a point not far from the present site of Newberg and as he left considerable property and no heirs, the necessity of a civil government was manifest. Some little headway toward securing a government was made, but it was not until two years later that the movement acquired enough momentum to amount to anything. Two preliminary meetings were held in the spring of 1843, at the second of which a committee was appointed, and this committee was to report at a meeting to be held at Champoeg May 2, 1843. At the appointed time about an equal number of American and British citizens met, and by a narrow margin, the Americans gained control of the situation and started the organization that developed into the provisional government of Oregon, the first government by Americans on the Pacific Coast. The site of the Champoeg meeting is now owned by the state of Oregon, and is a public park. The state built a memorial building which was dedicated May 2, 1918. For further details of Champoeg Memorial Building see Scott's *History of the Oregon Country*, volume II, page 221. Champoeg post office was established April 9, 1850, with F. X. Matthieu first postmaster. The name was changed to Buteville on September 9, 1850. A post office named Champoag was then established on July 10, 1851, with Robert Newell postmaster. The name was changed to Newellsville on August 2, 1864, and to Champoeg on May 24, 1880. This office was discontinued in the summer of 1905.

Chandler, Polk County. Chandler post office was about five miles south-southwest of the present site of Valsetz, and a little north of the southwest corner of the county. It was in operation from April, 1895, until July, 1900, and bore the name of the first postmaster, Thomas C. Chandler. It was closed to Rocca. The office was on North Fork Rock Creek. Chandler Mountain nearby got its name from the same source as the post office.

Chanticleer Point, Multnomah County. Chanticleer Point is about one mile west of Crown Point on the Columbia River Scenic Highway. It was named by Mr. and Mrs. A. R. Morgan who purchased the property in 1912 and erected a popular resort called Chanticleer Inn after the cock in *Reynard the Fox*. The spot has a fine overlook of the lower Columbia Gorge and the name of the inn was soon attached to the viewpoint. In 1931 the building was destroyed by fire and the property subsequently passed to Julius L. Meier and was included in his country home. In 1956 the Portland Women's Forum resolved to purchase 3.7 acres including the main overlook to be donated to the State Park system. A large stone marker was dedicated in May 1960 but title was not passed to the state until October, 1962. The name Portland Women's Forum State Park was specified by the grantor but fortunately Chanticleer Point is preserved in the inscription on the marker.

Chaparral Creek, Wallowa County. This is a tributary of Minam River. Chaparral is a word that is often supposed to refer to a specific bush or shrub, but such is not the case in the western United States. Chaparral means any dense thicket of low shrubs, especially those that bear thorns. There is no such thing as a chaparral plant in this part of the world. In Spain and in other places *chaparral* refers frequently to dense growths of low evergreen oak trees, and it is from *chaparro*, an evergreen oak, that the word is derived.

Chapin Creek, Morrow County. Chapin Creek is in the south part of the county and flows into Rock Creek about six miles southeast of Hardman. It bears the name of George Chapin who homesteaded in the neighborhood in early days. The spellings Chopen and Chapen are wrong.

Chapman, Columbia County. Chapman took its name from Simcoe Chapman, who operated a logging enterprise in the eastern part of Columbia County. Simcoe Chapman was born in Ontario, Canada, in 1840. As a young man he engaged in lumbering and logging activities, a business which he followed all his life. He operated in Michigan and Minnesota, and came to Oregon in 1901. He founded both the Chapman Timber Company and the Chapman Lumber Company. He died in 1923.

Chapman Creek, Josephine County. This stream is about four miles southeast of Kerby. It bears the family name of William Chapman, a pioneer settler on its banks.

Chapman Hill, Polk County. Chapman Hill is in the southeast part of Eola Hills, about two miles northwest of Salem. It has an elevation of a little over 400 feet. It was named for a Captain Chapman, who lived near the hill. Chapman Corners just to the north is named for the same man. In other days Chapman Hill was known as Schindler Hill but that name seems to have fallen into disuse.

Chapman Point, Clatsop County. Chapman Point is the first important projection into the sea north of Elk Creek and the first outlying southern point of Tillamook Head. It received its name from W. S. Chapman, a civil engineer of Portland who owned the point and considerable property nearby.

Chapman Slough, Harney County. This slough is part of Silvies River south of Burns. It was named for a pioneer settler along its banks, John Chapman.

Chapman Spring, Wheeler County. This spring on the north end of Sutton Mountain was named for Archie Chapman who homesteaded there in 1900. Chapman was the son of George W. Chapman who settled near Richmond in 1869.

Charcoal Cave, Deschutes County. This cave just southwest of Arnold Ice Cave was named by Dr. L. S. Cressman, University of Oregon anthropologist, because of the large, inexplicable deposit of prehistoric charcoal found on its floor. Phil Brogan gives more details in an article in the *Oregonian*, March 25, 1973.

Charcoal Point, Douglas County. Charcoal Point on North Umpqua River about nine miles east of Steamboat was named by USFS ranger Fred Asam for a natural charcoal outcrop.

Charleston, Coos County. Charleston was named for Charles Haskell, who is said to have taken up a claim at the mouth of South Slough in 1853.

Charlotte, Lane County. Charlotte post office was in service so long ago that the compiler knows little about it except its location, and that information is none too reliable. Charlotte post office was established in June, 1880, and was discontinued in April, 1881. Edgar R. Hayfield was the only postmaster. There is no available information about the reason for the name although the chances are it was the given name of Mrs. Hayfield or some other relative. A map dated 1889 shows Charlotte near the southwest corner of township 16 south, range 1 west. This puts it east-southeast of Mohawk.

Charlton, Columbia County. This station on the west bank of the Columbia River south of Goble was named for A. D. Charlton of Portland, for many years general passenger agent for the Northern Pacific Railway.

Chase, Yamhill County. William O. Chase was the first of five postmasters at Chase, and the office was named in compliment to him. Chase was about seven or eight miles west of McMinnville, in the west part of township 4 south, range 5 west. The office was established March 24, 1896, and operated for about ten years. The exact closing date is not available to the writer.

Chase Mountain, Klamath County. Francis Landrum of Klamath Falls informed the writer that this mountain southwest of Keno was named for George Chase who in the 1890s built the stage station at the junction of the Agar and Applegate roads. This was near Klamath River in section 32, township 39 south, range 7 east.

Chaski Bay, Crater Lake National Park, Klamath County. This bay is on the south side of Crater Lake, and lies between Phantom Ship and Eagle Point. It was named by Will G. Steel for a minor deity of the Klamath Indians. A. S. Gatschet in his *Dictionary of the Klamath Language* gives the word as *Tchashkai,* meaning weasel. The "Weaslet" was a mythical being often alluded to by western Indians, and conjurers frequently mentioned weasels because of their curious freaks and jumps.

Chatfield, Wasco County. This siding is on the Union Pacific Railroad near Mosier. The station was named in 1920 for Roy D. Chatfield, a fruit grower in the neighborhood, who was at one time manager of the Mosier Fruit Growers Association. He was the donor of Memaloose Park, now owned by the state. It is east of Mosier.

Chatham Island, Multnomah County. In the last week of June, 1975, Admiral Sir Charles Madden, Bt. GCB, Chairman of the Board of Trustees of the National Maritime Museum and former Commander-in-Chief of the British Home Fleet and NATO came to Portland to attend the opening of the memorable Cook Exhibition put on by the Oregon Historical Society. To commemorate the part played by the Royal Navy in the exploration of Oregon, the OGNB, at the suggestion of the compiler, voted to call the unnamed island southwest of Flag Island, Chatham Island for the ship commanded by Lieutenant William R. Broughton of Vancouver's expedition, and Sir Charles participated in an appropriate ceremony. There have been a number of British ships of this name and Broughton's command was launched in 1758 and continued in service until 1814. She was a vessel of 135 tons and carried a crew of 55 officers and men. It is interesting to note that Broughton, who was in the Columbia River in October, 1792, had discovered the Chatham Islands near New Zealand the previous year and named them for his ship. For information about Broughton, see under Broughton Bluff. For information about Cook, see under Captain Cook Point.

Chautauqua Lake, Clackamas County. A partly filled lake between Gladstone and I 205 is all that is left to remind Oregonians of one of the social phenonema of the first quarter of the twentieth century. The Chautauqua Movement was started in the summer of 1874 by John H. Vincent and Lewis Miller as a training operation for Sunday School instructors, and took its name from its location on the shore of Chautauqua Lake, New York. During the balance of the nineteenth century it grew and gradually shifted emphasis to the general field of adult education utilizing both professional educators and popular luminaries such as William Jennings Bryan. Melvil Dewey taught library management while developing his Dewey Decimal classification system between 1900 and 1910. About 1900 the system was tremendously expanded by the establishment of travelling groups or Chautauquas which visited innumerable cities in the United States and a favorite operating spot would be a wooded area near a lake, similar to the founding location in New York. The subject has been well covered in *We Called it Culture,* by Victoria and Robert Ormand Case and *The Chautauqua Movement,* by John H. Vincent. Chautauqua Lake in Oregon was in Gladstone Park, part of the Fendel Cason claim and now a summer camp for the Seventh Day Adventist Church. The park featured a giant assembly hall with wood roof trusses carrying a clear span remarkably long for its day. The Oregon City *Enterprise-Courier,* July 23, 1954, has an excellent account of the Oregon Chautauqua. Gannett says Chautauqua is an Indian word that has been the subject of much controversy. Meanings are varied and range from "foggy place" through "where the fish was taken out" to "place of easy death".

Cheeney Creek, Clackamas County. Cheeney Creek is a tributary of Salmon River south of Welches. This stream was formerly called Sheeny Creek, a name applied by a survey party in the early 1870s because of some episode connected with the camp cook, who was a Jewish boy unfamiliar with the woods. Many years later the USFS changed the name to Cheeney.

Chehalem, Yamhill County. Joseph B. Rogers owned property where Newberg stands today. In 1848 he had the town of Chehalem platted but he died in 1853 and his original settlement passed into obscurity. Chehalem was one of the earliest post offices in Yamhill County. It was established March 14, 1851, the same day as Lafayette and North Yam Hill offices. The only earlier office in the county was Yam Hill Falls, established January 8, 1850. Chehalem post office was discontinued January 6, 1852. Daniel Dodge Bayley was the first postmaster at Chehalem. Bayley was born in Vermont in 1801. and he and his family were among those who came to Oregon in 1845 by the Meek Cutoff. The Bayleys arrived in the Chehalem Valley in September, 1845, and settled on a place near what is now Newberg. The Chehalem office was at the Bayley home. See under West Chehalem. Daniel Dodge Bayley later went to Tillamook Bay, where he named the town of Garibaldi, and served as first postmaster.

Chehalem Mountains, Washington and Yamhill counties. These are the highest mountains in the Willamette Valley, and that section of the valley north of them is generally known as the Tualatin Valley, drained by Tualatin River. The Chehalem Mountains and some more or less independent spurs extend from the Willamette River east of Newberg northwest to the foothills of the Coast Range south of Forest Grove. The highest known point at the southern end is due north of Newberg, and has an elevation of 1447 feet. At a point on the northern end east of Wapato is a summit of 1633 feet, called Bald Peak. It may be assumed that the modern word Chehalem comes from the Indian name *Chahelim,* listed under the heading

Atfalati (Tualatin), *Handbook of American Indians,* volume I, page 108. This name is given by Gatschet in 1877 to one of the bands of Atfalati, a division of the Kalapooian family of Indians. Gatschet lists more than twenty of these bands, all living in the general vicinity of the Chehalem Mountains. H. S. Lyman in *OHQ,* volume I, page 323, refers to a point near the mouth of what is now known as Chehalem Creek and calls it *Cham-ho-kuc,* but gives no meaning or explanation.

Chehulpum Creek, Marion County. This stream rises in the hills northeast of Jefferson and flows westward into a branch of Santiam River. It has also been known as Doty Creek, but in 1934 a number of local residents petitioned to have the Indian name adopted. The petition was approved by the Marion County Court and the OGNB. In February 1935 the USBGN adopted the name Chehulpum Creek for the stream, which flows under Pacific Highway East just south of Looney Butte. George H. Himes is authority for the statement that *Chehulpum* was an Indian word meaning Beaver Illahe, or land where beaver were plentiful.

Chemawa, Marion County. Chemawa is one of the Indian names in the state that has several fanciful meanings attributed to it, including "our old home," "true talk" and "gravelly soil." There is little on record to substantiate any of the meanings. Silas B. Smith, Clatsop County pioneer, is authority for the statement that *Chemay-way* was the Indian name for a point on the Willamette River about two and a half miles south of Fairfield where Joseph Gervais settled in 1827-28. The same name was applied to Wapato Lake. Indian names were bestowed generally on account of physical peculiarity, and not for sentimental reasons, and the name may mean "gravelly soil," but gravel is neither peculiar nor abundant at either one of the places mentioned. Many Indian names began with *Che* and *Cham,* particularly those applied to places in the Willamette Valley, such as *Chemawa, Chehalem, Chemeketa* and *Champoeg.* For information on this matter see article by H. S. Lyman, *OHQ,* volume I, page 316. Chemawa has an elevation of 165 feet.

Chemult, Klamath County. This community, elevation 4758 feet, is toward the north end of the county, on The Dalles-California Highway. It is also a station on the Southern Pacific Cascade line and the junction with that line and the Burlington Northern, Inc. The name is that of a Klamath Indian chief who was one of the twenty-six who signed the treaty of October 14, 1864. The geography of the locality is shown on the USGS map of the Chemult quadrangle.

Chenoweth Creek, Wasco County. Chenoweth Creek rises in the hills west of The Dalles, and after flowing across Chenoweth Flat reaches the Columbia River southeast of Crates Point. This stream was named for Justin Chenoweth who was a prominent pioneer of Oregon. He was born in Clark County, Illinois, November 17, 1825, and was educated as a surveyor. He started to California in 1849 by way of New Orleans and Panama, but on reaching New Orleans he changed his plans and proceeded up the Mississippi to Saint Louis and thence to Fort Leavenworth. At Fort Leavenworth he joined, as a civilian, the party of the First U. S. Mounted Rifles which reached The Dalles in the fall of 1849. Chenoweth lived for a short time in the Willamette Valley, taught school, was a clerk for the territorial legislature and was employed in the territorial library. He married Mary H.

Vickers, at Butteville, December 9, 1852. He settled on a claim west of The
Dalles, and carried the mail between The Dalles and the Cascades in a small
boat. He was actively engaged in surveying public lands, both as a private
surveyor and as United States surveyor at the Vancouver land office. His
cousin, Francis A. Chenoweth, was one of the promoters of the tramway at
the Cascades and it is a family tradition that Justin surveyed the line. He
left The Dalles about 1866. He died in Portland March 16, 1898, and his
obituary appears in the *Oregonian* March 20, 1898. Nathan Olney owned a
store near Crates Point before Chenoweth settled there, and Chenoweth
Creek was then known as Olney Creek, but that name did not persist. The
name of the geographic feature near The Dalles is frequently spelled Che-
nowith, but the USBGN has officially adopted the form Chenoweth. Dr.
William C. McKay is authority for the statement that the Wasco Indian
name for the locality of Chenoweth Creek was *Thlemit*, which means a cav-
ing or washing away of the banks.

Cherry Creek, Jefferson County. This creek was named on account of
the wild cherries growing along its banks. It flows into John Day River near
Burnt Ranch, and was one of several geographic features in central Oregon
named by the pack train party of Joseph H. Sherar on the way to the John
Day mines in 1862. See also Antelope, Bakeoven and Muddy Creek.
Cherry Creek post office was named for the nearby stream. The office was
established on the Crook County list on June 23, 1884, with Mrs. Harriet P.
Tucker first postmaster. The office was closed June 21, 1886. All the evi-
dence available to the compiler shows that this office was in what is now
Jefferson County, but that may not have been the fact.

Cherry Creek, Wallowa County. William Duncan, a pioneer stockman,
named this stream because of the many wild cherry trees that grew along its
banks. Cherry Creek flows into Snake River in township 5 north, range 48
east.

Cherry Grove, Washington County. Cherry Grove was founded in
1911 by August Lovegren. Lovegren came to this country from Sweden in
1883 and for many years operated a lumber mill at Preston, Washington.
Mr. Lovegren wanted a name connected with fruit for the new community
and thought of Appleton but there was already a place by that name in
Oregon. His cousin, Anna Ryberg, then suggested Cherry Grove after her
home in Goodhue County, Minnesota. Cherry Grove post office was established May 8, 1912 and operated until June 30, 1959.

Cherryville, Clackamas County. Cherryville is near the Mount Hood
Loop Highway. It is said to have been named because of the wild cherries
growing in the neighborhood.

Chesher, Lane County. The pioneer post office Chesher was named
for James P. Chesher, its first postmaster. The office was established April
1, 1875, and was closed August 21, 1890. It was reestablished December 27,
1892, the name was changed to Varien and it went with that name until
June 7, 1895, when it was closed again. For a short biography of J. P.
Chesher, see *Illustrated History of Lane County*, page 500. The post office was
a few miles west of what is now Veneta, not far from the present community of Noti, in the Coast Range on the upper drainage of Long Tom River.
The name should not be confused with Cheshire, later applied to a place

west of Junction City. The name Varien came from Paul Varien Bollman, son of John W. Bollman, the postmaster at the time the name was changed.

Cheshire, Lane County. Cheshire is a station on the line of the Southern Pacific Company south of Corvallis. It is near the Long Tom River. It was platted in 1913 as Hubert, but this caused confusion with another station on the same line, Huber, so the railroad company changed the name to Cheshire. The name Hubert was selected to compliment Hubert Cheshire, a favorite small boy of the neighborhood. Hubert post office was established March 20, 1914, with Henry C. Ball postmaster. The name of the office was changed to Cheshire on May 12, 1914. The Cheshire family has been prominent in the locality.

Chesnimnus Creek, Wallowa County. This stream flows into Joseph Creek, and for many years was shown on maps as Chesninimus Creek. Investigations by the USFS indicated that this spelling was in error, and the USBGN adopted the shorter form. The word is Indian in its origin and according to J. H. Horner of Enterprise means Thorn Butte, referring to a locality near the head of the stream where there were several thorn thickets. The Indians camped there and called the place *Sis-nim-mux,* accent on the second syllable. The suffix *mux* meant butte or mount.

Chestnut Spring, Wallowa County. Chestnut Spring is about ten miles southeast of Minam. It bears the name of Ed Chestnut, who had a homestead in the vicinity. He was an early settler on Cricket Flat.

Chetco River, Curry County. The name is applied to various features in southwest Oregon, and is derived from the name of a small Indian tribe that lived along the lower reaches of the river. Early day spelling was Chetko and Chitko. For information about the Chetco Indians, see *Pioneer History of Coos and Curry Counties,* edited by Orvil Dodge. Mt. Emily in the southwest part of Curry County is sometimes known as Chetco Peak, but the real Chetco Peak is in the east part of the county and has an elevation of 4660 feet. See USGS topographic map of the Chetco Peak quadrangle. The spelling Chetco has been adopted by the USBGN. For editorial about an Indian woman, Lucky Dick, the last of the Chetcos, see the *Oregonian,* January 23, 1940. A post office named Chetco was among the earliest in southwest Oregon. This office was established March 3, 1863, with Augustus Miller first postmaster. It was discontinued November 15, 1910. Old maps show this office at various places on the coast between the mouth of Chetco River and the Oregon-California state line. It was probably moved according to the availability of a postmaster.

Chewaucan Marsh, Lake County. This is a large marsh, fed principally by Chewaucan River and draining into Lake Abert. The elevation of the upper end of the marsh is 4311 feet and that of the lower end 4291, according to the Strahorn railroad survey. The name is derived from the Klamath Indian words *tchua,* meaning wild potato, and *keni,* a general suffix meaning locality or place. The wild potato is generally known in Oregon and Washington as the wapato, arrowhead or sagittaria. It was an article of food with many tribes. See *USGS WSP 220* and *363* for information about the marsh. See also the *Oregonian,* September 14, 1925, page 11, for information about the wapato.

Chicken Hill, Grant and Union counties. Chicken Hill is in the Blue

Mountains on the watershed between the Grande Ronde and North Fork John Day rivers. The local tradition about the origin of the name is to the effect that in the days of the mining fever a freighter was hauling in supplies from Columbia River points and on top of an otherwise bulky load were several crates of chickens for the mining camps. The load capsized before reaching the top of the hill and the chicken coops were so badly smashed that the fowls escaped into the brush, crowing and cackling. The locality has been called Chicken Hill ever since..

Chickenhouse Gulch, Grant County. This gulch was named for a sheepherder's cabin built there in the early days. The cabin was very rough and so were the herders when they referred to their abode.

Chico, Wallowa County. The town of Chico was named by George Harris, who had formerly lived in Chico, California, and when he took up a homestead in Wallowa County, he named it for his former home. *Chico* is a Spanish word meaning little. Chico, California, is laid out on the old Spanish land grant, *Rancho del Arroyo Chico*. This *rancho* was in 1854 certified to General John Bidwell, an early California pioneer, who laid out the town of Chico. Stories to the effect that Chico, California, was named for a governor, Chico, seem to have no foundation and the compiler can find no record of any such person.

Chief Joseph Mountain, Wallowa County. This mountain has been known at various times as Tunnel Mountain and Point Joseph, but in 1925 the USBGN officially named it Chief Joseph Mountain in honor of the famous Nez Perce Indian chief. Joseph, or Young Joseph as he was sometimes known, was born near the mouth of Imnaha River in June, 1837, and died at Nespelem, Colville Indian Reservation, September 21, 1904. He was the son of Old Joseph, who died about 1871, and the grandson of Ollicut, a Cayuse Chief. Old Joseph took his wife from a band living near the mouth of Asotin Creek. In May, 1877, Young Joseph and his band began to threaten the white settlers in the Wallowa Valley, claiming the valley as his ancestral home. After some skirmishing and encounters, the Indians finally began their famous journey to Montana, pursued by troops. Chief Joseph made his last stand at the Battle of the Big Hole, August 9, 1877, and on October 4, 1877, he surrendered to Colonel Nelson A. Miles at Bear Paw, Montana. For references to this matter see Scott's *History of the Oregon Country*, volume II, pages 104 and 332. For news story about launching of Liberty ship named for Chief Joseph, see *Oregon Journal*, March 28, 1943, main section, page 15.

Chilcoot Mountain, Douglas County. This mountain is in section 6, township 25 south, range 1 east, just south of the Lane County line. USFS ranger Fred Asam and Ed Lough named this after a trail locating cruise. They had considerable difficulty crossing this peak and felt it must be similar to Chilkoot Pass in the Klondike. The ridge and creek of the same name nearby were named sometime later. There is no explanation for the different spelling.

Chiloquin, Klamath County. Chiloquin is the whiteman's form of a Klamath Indian family name *Chaloquin*. Chaloquin was the village chief of the old Indian town of *Bosuck Siwas*, or Painted Rock, and his name was given as *Chaloquenas* in the treaty of 1864. Two sons, George and Mose Chaloquin, served with the state troops in the Modoc War.

Chilson Creek, Umatilla County. Sanford W. Chilson settled along this creek running through Bridge Creek Flats in the early part of the century.

China Cap, Union County. This peak is in the southwest part of Wallowa Mountains and has an elevation of 8638 feet as shown on the USGS map of the China Cap quadrangle. While the compiler has no written record of when it received its name, it is obvious from its picture that it bears a close similarity to the hats worn by Chinese laborers throughout the Pacific Northwest in the early days of development, and it must have been named on that account.

China Creek, Wallowa County. This is a small stream flowing into Snake River from China Gulch in township 4 north, range 49 east. In the days of placer mining in the Pacific Northwest and particularly near Lewiston there were a great many Chinese panning for gold, and there are China bars, China creeks and China flats in many parts of Oregon, Washington and Idaho. It was at these points that large colonies of Chinese carried on their mining operations.

China Hat, Deschutes County. China Hat is a butte east of Paulina Mountains. It received its name because, when viewed from Fort Rock, it resembled the style of hat worn by Chinese during early days of the Pacific Northwest.

Chinchalo, Klamath County. This is a station on the Cascade line of the Southern Pacific Company. It bears the name of a Klamath Indian chief and medicine man. According to Will G. Steel his domain was in the Klamath Marsh country. He was a signer of the treaty of 1864 as Makosas.

Chinidere Mountain, Hood River County. This mountain is just west of Wahtum Lake and has an elevation of 4674 feet. H. D. Langille, pioneer resident of Hood River Valley and an authority on the Mt. Hood region, said that Chinidere was the last reigning chief of the Wasco Indians, and that this mountain was named for him.

Chinook Bend, Lincoln County. Chinook Bend is about three miles upstream from Kernville, at a point where the Siletz River makes a pronounced bend first south, then north. The geography of the locality is shown on the USGS map of the Euchre Mountain quadrangle. In November, 1945, Andrew L. Porter of Newport wrote the compiler as follows: "Chinook Bend was so named because the early run of Chinook salmon would lie there and wait for the rain to make fresh water before going up to the spawning ground. It was a good place to troll for salmon."

Chinquapin Mountain, Jackson County. There are a number of geographic features in Oregon named for the western chinquapin, *Castanopsis chrysophylla;* of these Chinquapin Mountain, in the southeast part of Jackson County, is probably the best known. The western chinquapin is sometimes called the golden leaved chestnut. In the lower mountain altitudes it grows into a handsome tree, 75 feet high in some places. On the high mountains it is generally a shrub. It is found generally on the slopes of the southern Cascade Range and the Sierra Nevada.

Chisholm Canyon, Sherman County. Duncan P. Chisholm was born in

Glen Elg, Scotland in 1860. Along with many other Scots caught by the agrarian decline of the Highlands, he emigrated to the United States and in 1888 homesteaded above this canyon six miles east of Kent. Wool was a common cash crop of the small rancher in this area and Chisholm's fleece won a gold medal at the Lewis and Clark Fair in 1905. He was a man of remarkable physical strength and many stories are told of his ability to lift or move incredible weights.

Chitwood, Lincoln County. This is a station on the line of the Southern Pacific Company between Corvallis and Toledo. George T. Smith, postmaster at Chitwood, wrote in 1925 that the station and post office were named for Joshua Chitwood, who lived near the present site of the community when the railroad was built down the Yaquina River. This railroad was built between 1881 and 1885. For particulars of this construction see Scott's *History of the Oregon Country,* volume IV, page 334.

Chitwood Creek, Tillamook County. This creek rises on Cascade Head and spills into the Pacific Ocean. It was named for John D. Chitwood, the first postmaster at Emma.

Chloride, Baker County. Chloride post office was established in the Blue Mountains on June 18, 1901, with George B. Rogers first postmaster. The office was closed on May 28, 1904. It was installed to serve a mining development in the east part of township 8 south, range 37 east. In December, 1945, LeRoy A. Grettum of Baker wrote the compiler as follows: "This post office was at the Chloride Mine in the Blue Mountains near the headwaters of Rock Creek, west of Haines. According to people in Haines who were working there at the time, both the post office and the mine shut down in the spring of 1904 because a very bad snow slide carried away a lot of surface improvements and the resulting debris blocked the tunnel." According to F. W. Libbey of the State Department of Geology and Mineral Industries the name Chloride was doubtless applied because of the presence of silver chloride in the local outcrops. Mr. Libbey writes: "Chloride is not an uncommon name in western mining camps. In the early days in the West a lessee or prospector who followed a thin vein or small high-grade ore deposit was called a chlorider. According to Albert H. Fay in his *Glossary of the Mining and Mineral Industry* the term is said to have originated at Silver Reef in southwestern Utah when the rich silver chloride ores were being worked. The name was later extended to apply to similar workers in other fields and to other types of high-grade deposits."

Chocktoot Creek, Lake County. This creek flows into Sycan Marsh from the east, and was named for a well-known Indian chief of the Piute or Snake tribe.

Choptie Prairie, Klamath County. Choptie Prairie is between Saddle Mountain and Chiloquin Ridge. The name is derived from a Klamath Indian word meaning secluded, or hidden, which well describes the place.

Christensen Slough, Baker County. John C. Christensen came to Baker County in 1869 and settled near Haines. This slough bears his family name.

Christman, Lane County. Christman post office was established January 6, 1888, and discontinued September 6, 1893, with Mattie Kirk the only postmaster. It was on Row River southeast of Cottage Grove, probably in the northeast part of township 21 south, range 2 west. In 1947 John C. Veatch of Portland, reared in the Cottage Grove area, wrote the compiler as follows: "I think this office was on the ranch of Wes Christman who lived on Row River a few miles from the Star office. As I remember, Wes moved into Cottage Grove about 1893 and this was probably the reason for closing the office."

Christmas Creek, Wallowa County. This small stream flows into Snake River in section 32, township 4 north, range 50 east. It was named by James Tryon and Lu Knapper. They took their sheep to the canyon for winter range on Christmas Day, 1888, and built a cabin on the creek.

Christmas Lake, Lake County. Christmas Lake is a small body of water in township 26 south, range 18 east, about 25 miles east of Fort Rock. The name is one of the puzzles in Oregon nomenclature. It is frequently asserted that John C. Fremont discovered and named the lake in question, which is not a fact. A map of the Oregon territory accompanying Senator Lewis F. Linn's report, prepared under the direction of Col. J. J. Abert in 1838, shows a river flowing from a lake near what is now known as Drew Valley, the river being labeled Christmas River. It is not clear where this name was obtained, but it is possible that such a stream may have been named by Hudson's Bay Company men. Fur brigades visited central Oregon as early as 1825, and may have had something to do with the name of Christmas River. During the second exploring expedition of Captain Fremont, which left Kansas in May, 1843, its leader conducted the party through the Deschutes Valley, and after naming a number of geographic features, he arrived in the Warner Valley and on December 24, 1843, he reached and named Christmas Lake. This lake is much further southeast than the lake now known by that name, and there is but little doubt that it was what is now known as Hart Lake that Fremont christened. It is an important member of the Warner Lakes group, and near the central part of the valley. There is at present no information as to how the other Christmas Lake got its name, but it is some distance from Fremont's route, and there is no evidence that he ever knew of its existence. The surveyor general of Oregon issued a map of the state in 1863 which shows Christmas Lake in the Warner Valley in the place where Fremont discovered and named it. It has been called Hart Lake for many years.

Christy Creek, Lane County. This is the largest tributary of North Fork Willamette River. It was named for one "Doc" Christy, a veterinarian of Eugene, who located a mining claim near its mouth in the early days.

Chrome Ridge, Grant County. Chrome Ridge is south of John Day River and just west of Fields Creek. It is one of several geographic features in Oregon named for the mineral chromite. In July, 1945, Dr. F. W. Libbey, director of the State Department of Geology and Mineral Industries, wrote the compiler as follows: "The word chrome is used rather loosely to mean chrome ore or chromite. Chromite is found in lenticular deposits at various places in southwest Oregon and central Oregon, especially in Grant, Josephine and Curry counties. Thus there is the connection between chromite deposits and the word chrome which has been applied to some geographic features in Oregon. Chromite or chrome ore is usually considered to be a chemical mixture of ferrous oxide and chromic oxide. However, it never occurs in nature as this theoretical compound because it always contains impurities such as silica, alumina and magnesia. The chromite ore in Grant County is, generally speaking, lower grade than the chromite ore of southwest Oregon. The Grant County ore averages a lower percentage of chromic oxide." Chromite was not searched for in pioneer days and the use of the name for Oregon geographic features is relatively modern.

Chucksney Mountain, Lane County. This mountain, elevation 5756 feet, is about 12 miles north of Waldo Lake. It bears the name of a local Indian celebrity who made his home in the valley of Middle Fork Willamette River.

Cinnamon Butte, Douglas County. This butte is about five miles north of Diamond Lake, and has an elevation of 6400 feet. It was named by O. C. Houser of the USFS in 1908 because of the characteristic color of the brush and rock formation near its summit. The USBGN has adopted this name.

Cipole, Washington County. The name of this station on the Southern Pacific line west of Tualatin is pronounced *si-pole*. Cipole is near the large onion raising lands of the county and the name represents an imperfect representation of the Italian word for onion, *cipolla,* pronounced *chi-po-la.*

Circle Bar, Harney County. This railroad station was named for the Circle Bar Ranch which used that brand. It is about nine miles southeast of Crane.

Circle Creek, Clatsop County. Circle Creek and its tributaries drain a considerable part of Tillamook Head. The stream got its name because of its circular course, though it far from describes a complete circle. The Circle Creek bridge was a well-known structure on the Oregon Coast Highway southwest of Cannon Beach Junction. The relocation of US101 eliminated the horseshoe curve crossing.

Civil Bend, Douglas County. Civil Bend is one of the amusing place names of Douglas County because it was applied in derision—the locality was so uncivil. The Bend is a prominent reverse kink in South Umpqua River a little to the southwest of Roseburg. The name is said to refer to the boisterous activities of visitors who came to see the horse races in early days. According to Israel B. Nichols, an old timer in the locality, in the Roseburg *News-Review,* May 7, 1948, "there was always lots of drinking and lots of fights, so they called it Civil Bend." Civil Bend post office was in service from September, 1881, to October, 1888, with James M. Dillard first postmaster. When the office was reestablished in 1889, postal authorities objected to a name with two words. A new name, Brockway, was selected in honor of B. B. Brockway, a pioneer settler.

Clackamas, Clackamas County. The Indian word Clackamas has been used as the name for two post offices in Clackamas County, at different times and places. The first of these offices, established September 29, 1852, with the name Clackemas and John Foster postmaster, was put on the Marion County list, but was changed to the Clackamas County list with the revised spelling Clackamas on March 22, 1853. It was discontinued October 18, 1853. Preston's map of 1856 shows the site of the office about two miles northwest of what was later Logan. When the Oregon and California began railroad service from Portland south on September 5, 1870, to the place then called Waconda, a station between Milwaukie and Oregon City was called Marshville and it is shown that way on the first time card. See Scott's *History of the Oregon Country*, volume IV, page 30, for a facsimile of this time table. It is not clear just why the name Marshville was applied, as there is very good land drainage in the locality, though topographic maps show a small swampy area about a mile to the south. The name Marshville may have been named for a person, Marsh. There are references to the place by the name Marshfield, but that was not the railroad name. On December 8, 1873, a post office was established at the locality with the name Clackamas, and with Noah N. Matlock first postmaster. The railroad was not long in changing the station name from Marshville to Clackamas. All was then in harmony.

Clackamas County. This county, together with Clackamas River and other features in Oregon, received its name from the Clackamas Indians, a Chinookan tribe, living along the river. The remnants of the tribe were moved to the Grand Ronde Reservation. It was formerly a large tribe. Lewis and Clark use the form *Clackamus,* and other forms are *Klackamus,* in George Wilkes' *History of Oregon* and on Charles Wilkes' map of 1841; *Clackamus; Nekamus,* in *OHQ,* volume I, page 320; *Klackamas,* in Townsend's *Narrative: Akimmash, Clackamis, Clackamos, Clackemus, Clackemurs, Klackamat, Thlakeimas, Tlakimish,* and many others. Clackamas County was one of the original four districts of early Oregon, the other three being Twality, Yamhill and Champooick. It was created July 5, 1843, and at present has a land area of 1890 square miles. An excellent map of Clackamas County is published by the Bureau of Soils of the Department of Agriculture. For full information concerning the name and establishment of this county see *OHQ,* volume XI, No. 1, which contains an article by Frederick V. Holman on the origin of Oregon counties.

Clark Branch, Douglas County. Walling, in his *History of Southern Oregon,* page 441, says this stream north of Myrtle Creek was named for James A. Clark, whose land claim was near its mouth. William Hudson later owned the property.

Clark Butte, Lane County. A. J. Briem, in his notes on file at the OHS, says that both this butte and Clark Creek on the upper reaches of Fall Creek were named for early settler Austin Clark.

Clark Creek, Hood River County. This creek drains one of the lobes of Newton Clark Glacier, and is named Clark Creek on that account. The next large stream to the north is called Newton Creek for the same reason. Both are tributaries of East Fork Hood River.

Clark Creek, Union County. Clark Creek is the correct name of this stream, not Clarks. The creek was never owned by anyone named Clark, and the possessive of this and many other geographic names should be discarded.

Clark Glacier, Lane County. This is the westward of the two small glaciers on the south side of the South Sister, and was named for William Clark in 1924 by Professor Edwin T. Hodge of the University of Oregon. So far as known it is the only geographic feature in the state named for the great explorer except the Lewis and Clark River in Clatsop County. Thwaites' *Original Journals of the Lewis and Clark Expedition* gives a detailed account of the exploration, and on page xxvii of the first volume is a short biography of William Clark. He was born in Virginia on August 1, 1770, and was the younger brother of George Rogers Clark (1752-1818). At the age of 23 he was a first lieutenant in General Anthony Wayne's western army. He retired from the army in 1796 with brevet rank of captain, and lived quietly with his family, occupied chiefly in adjusting the affairs of his older brother until 1803 when he was invited by Meriwether Lewis to join Jefferson's proposed exploring expedition to the Pacific Ocean. After the expedition Jefferson appointed Clark brigadier-general of the militia of Louisiana, and also Indian agent for Louisiana. Subsequently Clark was surveyor general for Illinois, Missouri and Arkansas. He died on September 1, 1838. For details of Clark's life see Coues' *History of the Expedition of Lewis and Clark,* volume I. William Clark spelled his name without the final "e," though that form has been used in many places, especially in Clarke County, Washington, until 1926, when the state legislature cut off the "e." For editorial comment on this error see the *Oregonian* December 3, 1925.

Clark Spring, Umatilla County. This spring located three miles above the mouth of Bridge Creek was named for Ralph G. Clark, an early homesteader.

Clarke, Clackamas County. Clarke is a crossroads community in the Highland district about fifteen miles southeast of Oregon City. In pioneer days this was known as the Ringo Settlement. About 1870 one "Friday" Jones bought some property there for "1 yoke of oxen, a shotgun and $200." This he sold in 1876 to Irving L. Clarke, the latter transaction covering 320 acres. Clarke started a store and a little later got a post office. This office, called Clarkes, was established May 13, 1889, with Clarke first postmaster. The office was closed December 13, 1904. Raymond Caufield of Oregon City was good enough to gather these facts from George A. Clarke, a son of Irving L. Clarke, in September, 1945.

Clarke Springs, Jefferson County. These springs and the nearby orchard on the old Madras-Ashwood road were on the homestead of James G. Clarke who settled in eastern Jefferson County about 1900.

Clarks Canyon, Morrow County. This canyon runs northwest into Willow Creek just west of Lexington. It was named for Oscar Clark who settled near its mouth in 1864.

Clarks Creek, Baker County. This stream is a tributary of Burnt River. It is said to have been named for a miner who accidentally shot himself there in the early 1860s. There was at one time a post office known as Clarksville near this stream. This office was organized to serve a territory near placer diggings developed along Burnt River in 1861-63.

Clarnie, Multnomah County. The origin of the name Clarnie is obscure, but the following explanation is derived from trustworthy sources. Two locators of the Oregon Railway and Navigation Company decided to name the railroad station after their daughters, the name of one being Clara, and that of the other being Jennie. They combined syllables of the two names to make Clarnie. This station is five miles west of Fairview.

Clarno, Wheeler County. This post office was on John Day River near

Clarno Bridge, and when it was closed in 1949 happened to be in Wheeler County. Clarno was named for one of the earliest white settlers on John Day River, Andrew Clarno. The Clarno post office was generally situated not far from the bridge, depending upon who could be prevailed upon to take the postmastership. Sometimes it was in Wasco County, sometimes in Wheeler. Clarno has an elevation of 1304 feet. Clarno post office was established September 15, 1894, with Nannie Chichester postmaster. It was then in Gilliam County, as Wheeler County had not yet been formed. When Andrew Clarno settled on John Day River, he had no neighbors. Stockmen in those days did not feel the need of any. When he heard that a friend had settled on a homestead about 20 miles to the east, near the present site of Fossil, he rode over on horseback, and said: "Bill, don't you think you're crowding me a little?" Maps and postal records of the 1880s show a post office named Crown Rock in the present locality of Clarno, but the compiler has been unable to get information about it, except that it was named for a rock formation nearby.

Classic Ridge, Tillamook County. Classic Ridge is between Nehalem and Neahkahnie Mountain. Classic Lake is east of the ridge. These features were named by J. H. Edwards of Portland, who was interested in music, and had hopes of developing a community of persons devoted to the arts.

Clatskanie, Columbia County. Silas B. Smith, Clatsop County pioneer, is quoted in the *OHQ,* volume I, page 322, to the effect that *Tlatskani* was a point in the Nehalem Valley reached by the Indians from the Columbia River either by way of what we now know as Youngs River, or by way of Clatskanie River. The Indians used the word *Tlats-kani* by applying it to certain streams indicating the route they took to get to *Tlats-kani,* and not as the name of the streams for Indians were not in the habit of naming streams. White men carelessly applied the name to the stream. Clatskanie River in Columbia County, and Klaskanine River in Clatsop County were thus named, and Clatskanie, a town, developed near the point where the former joined the Columbia River. Clatskanie is the spelling adopted by the USBGN for the features in Columbia County. The locality *Tlats-kani* in the hills south of Clatskanie River was named for the Tlatskanai Indians, who lived along the river and in the Nehalem Valley to the south. See *Handbook of American Indians,* volume II, page 763. There are many variations in the spelling of the name. A news story in the Rainier *Review,* October 2, 1931, says that the town of Clatskanie was first known as Bryantville, which was platted early in 1884. A similar story is carried in an Historical Records Survey release printed in the *Review,* March 27, 1936. The compiler is unable to reconcile these statements with the fact that Clatskanie is shown on the official post office list as early as December, 1871.

Clatsop, Clatsop County. Clatsop post office was established near the south end of Clatsop Plains in July, 1894, with Alexander Tagg first postmaster. This office operated with one intermission until July 25, 1919, when the business was turned over to Warrenton. The office was of course named for the county and for the Clatsop Indians. It was doubtless moved from time to time. The Tagg place was about a half a mile east of Clatsop school.

Clatsop County. Clatsop District was created by the provisional legislature by an act passed June 22, 1844, and comprised parts of the northern and western parts of Twality District. F. V. Holman's article on the history of Oregon counties in *OHQ*, volume XI, page 24, gives detailed information about the formation and boundaries of the county. *Clatsop* is the name of an Indian tribe; mentioned in Lewis and Clark *Journals* and Gass' *Journal*. For description of Clatsop County in 1855, see the *Oregonian*, June 16, 1855. For history of Clatsop County, by Preston W. Gillette, *ibid.*, November 20, December 12, 1895; January 18, 1896. For narrative of the Clatsop Indians, by Preston W. Gillette, *ibid.*, October 23, 1899, page 6; his narrative of Mrs. Michel, last of the Clatsops, *ibid.*, March 10, 1903, page 3; his narrative of pioneers of Clatsop County, *ibid.*, November 20, 1895, page 6; January 18, 1896; description of Clatsop County in 1881, by Alfred Holman, *ibid.*, September 9, 1887; biography and portrait of Mrs. Michel, February 26, 1905, page 22. *Clatsop* is given as *Tlahsops* by Silas B. Smith, in the *OHQ*, volume I, page 320. Townsend's *Narrative* gives *Klatsop*. Hale, in *U. S. Exploring Expedition, Ethnography and Philology*, 1846, page 215, gives *Tlatsap*. In OPA *Transactions* for 1887, page 85, the name is *Tschlahtsoptchs*. Dart, in *Indian Affairs Report* for 1851, gives *Clatsops*. Lewis and Clark give *Clat Sops, Clatsops*, etc. Farnham, in *Travels*, New York, 1843, page 111, gives *Clatstops*. There are many other variations. The Clatsops were of the Chinookan family, formerly at the mouth of the Columbia River, on the south side, between Tongue Point and the ocean, and south to Tillamook Head. Lewis and Clark spent the winter of 1805-06 among them at Fort Clatsop. Clatsop County has a land area of 820 square miles, according to the U. S. Bureau of the Census. The name Clatsop has been applied to a number of geographic features in Oregon, including Clatsop Plains and Clatsop Spit.

Claxtar, Marion County. Claxtar is one form of the name of the Tlatskanai Indian tribe, generally known as Clatskanie. For information about this tribe see *Handbook of American Indians*, volume II, page 763. When the Oregon Electric Railway was built officials used this name for a station north of Salem, adopting the spelling employed by Lewis and Clark.

Claypool Bridge, Linn County. This bridge was about four miles north of Lebanon. C. H. Stewart of Albany wrote the compiler in 1927: "In early days the old Indian trail south through the Willamette Valley crossed the South Santiam near this point. The bridge is on the donation land claim of Samuel R. Claypool, a prominent pioneer citizen of that locality."

Clear Creek, Columbia County. Clear Creek flows into Nehalem River from the west in the extreme southwest corner of the county. Its name is of course descriptive. Many years ago there was a post office called Clear Creek, but it did not last long. Old maps show the place close to the mouth of the stream. Clear Creek post office was established January 11, 1878, with Henry D. Sluter (Sleeter?) postmaster. The office was discontinued January 22, 1879.

Cleawox Lake, Lane County. This lake is about a mile south of Siuslaw River and a mile east of the Pacific Ocean. It has an elevation of 82 feet. The name is obviously an Indian one but the writer has been unable to get its meaning. The USBGN has officially adopted the name Cleawox Lake instead of Cleawok Lake or Buck Lake.

Cleek, Jefferson County. Cleek post office was established on the Wasco County list May 19, 1881, with Harley A. Belknap first and only postmaster. The office was discontinued February 21, 1883, and the business turned over to Hay Creek. The best available information is to the effect that the office was at the Henry A. Cleek ranch two or three miles west of what was later Grizzly post office. Belknap rented the Cleek place while the Cleeks were at The Dalles for a time. The ranch was one of the points where stage coach horses were changed. The compiler has not been successful in getting the exact location of the place, but it seems to have been on or near Willow Creek.

Cleetwood Cove, Crater Lake National Park, Klamath County. This cove was named for the boat from which Will G. Steel sounded Crater Lake for the government in 1886. In a dream Steel fancied he heard the word applied to a golden arrow. The dream was so vivid that he christened his boat *Cleetwood*.

Clem, Gilliam County. Clem was named for a well-known Gilliam County character, Clemens Augustus Danneman, who owned a ranch where travelers could get accommodations. He was a native of Germany and a veteran of the Civil War. He was born October 13, 1835. He came to America about 1856, to Oregon 1879, and settled in Gilliam County. Clem is a station on the Condon branch of the Union Pacific Railroad.

Cleo, Coos County. Cleo is a station on the Southern Pacific Company line south of Coos Bay. This station was named by using, backward, the initials of the name of a lumbering concern, Oregon Export Lumber Company, which was then operating nearby.

Cleveland, Douglas County. F. M. Good came to Oregon from Kentucky in 1853 and was one of the early settlers near the present community of Cleveland, west of Winchester. He started a sawmill and flour mill, and named his brand of flour for the Cleveland flour mill in Ohio. Thus the place in Oregon received its name indirectly for the city in Ohio. Cleveland post office was established December 16, 1874, with Francis M. Good first postmaster, who was the F. M. Good just mentioned. The office was discontinued February 15, 1923.

Cleveland Cave, Deschutes County. Cleveland Cave is one of the numerous volcanic tube ice caves in the Bend area. It was named for George Cleveland who discovered it while working as a forester near Wanoga Butte. Phil Brogan reports on this in *Oregonian*, June 15, 1958.

Cliff, Lake County. Cliff post office is said to have been named for a nearby geographic feature, but the compiler has no further information about the name or the bluff. The office was in operation from January, 1906, until June, 1920, in the north part of the Christmas Lake Valley.

Clifford, Baker County. Clifford was a stage station near the upper reaches of North Fork Burnt River on the stage road from Baker to Canyon City. It was a popular stopping place operated by Mr. and Mrs. Marsh Young. The Youngs were warm personal and political friends of Judge Morton D. Clifford and they named the place in his honor. Clifford post office was established March 10, 1894, with Nellie Clark first postmaster. The office was discontinued effective September 15, 1901. Morton D. Clifford was born in Iowa in 1859 and with his widowed mother came to Grant

County in 1871. He attended school at Canyon City and read law under W. Lair Hill at The Dalles. He was a lifelong Democrat. He served as district attorney and also as circuit judge until 1904 when he moved with his family to Baker. He had an extensive law practice from which he retired a few years before his death, which occurred in Portland on his 82nd birthday, May 22, 1941. Judge Clifford married Edith Haseltine in 1885.

Clifton, Clatsop County. Clifton was a settlement on the south bank of the Columbia River long before the railroad was built and at one time J. W. and V. Cook, pioneer salmon packers, had a cannery there. The name is descriptive of the cliffs above the river. Clifton post office was established January 6, 1874, with Vincent Cook first postmaster. J. H. Middleton, who was living near Waldport in 1927, and who went to Clifton in the fall of 1873, told the compiler that Clifton was the name of the farm of Stephen G. Spear, and that he was of the opinion that Spear named the place Clifton before the property came into the possession of J. W. and V. Cook. Members of the Cook family are also of the belief that Spear named the place before the Cooks became established there.

Clifton, Hood River County. This name has been applied to the locality about three miles west of Hood River, where the Columbia River Highway begins to drop down from the top of the well defined cliffs that characterize the place. The highway has an elevation at this point of about 250 feet above the river.

Climax, Jackson County. Appeals for information about the name of this place brought an interesting letter from Mrs. Walter F. (Bertha B.) Charley of Central Point, who was postmaster at Climax from 1920 to 1933. In July, 1946, Mrs. Charley wrote in substance as follows: "The proposed post office at Climax was a popular project among the people of upper Antelope Creek valley, and the petition, circulated by John Wyland, was signed by every adult then living there. It seems that that word 'climax' was a favorite of this man, who stated that 'the climax of his efforts was a tee-total landslide.' He suggested that the post office, when established, be named Climax. The post office was first in the home of Jacob Worlow, Mrs. Worlow being the first postmistress. The office traveled about the community as new postmasters were appointed, and was in at least six different homes. Finally I was appointed in 1920, and was the last postmistress, serving until 1933, when the patrons dwindled to so few that the office was closed. The few people remaining in the settlement drive twenty-five miles to Medford for mail." According to postal records Climax office was established November 10, 1891, with Mary E. Worlow first postmaster. The office was closed August 11, 1933, with all papers to Eagle Point. The place is east of Medford.

Cline Falls, Deschutes County. Cline Falls are on the Deschutes River about four miles west of Redmond. The McKenzie Highway crosses the river just south of the falls. They were named for Dr. C. A. Cline (1850-1926), a well-known dentist of Redmond, who owned the falls. Cline Buttes just southwest of the falls received their name from the same source. Dr. Cline died July 19, 1926. For obituary see the *Oregonian* for July 22, 1926, page 20.

Cline Hill, Benton and Lincoln counties. Cline Hill is the summit where US 20 crosses the Coast Range between Newport and Corvallis. The name commemorates Walker F. Cline, a pioneer homesteader.

Cloud Cap, Crater Lake National Park, Klamath County. Cloud Cap is the highest point on the east rim of Crater Lake and has an elevation of 8070 feet above sea level and 1893 feet above the water of the lake. It received this somewhat fanciful name from J. S. Diller of the USGS, because of its high dome.

Clover, Malheur County. Clover post office was established as of April 3, 1882, and was closed January 9, 1883. Josephine M. Reeves was the first postmaster. The compiler has been told that this post office was named for Clover Creek, but no one has come up with a definite locality for the establishment. Clover Creek was named in pioneer days because of the growth of wild clover along its banks.

Clover Flat, Lake County. Clover Flat is a descriptive name for a locality about seven or eight miles airline west of Valley Falls. Clover Flat post office was established December 31, 1914, with Janie N. Bryan first and only postmaster. The office was closed out to Paisley on March 15, 1918.

Cloverdale, Tillamook County. Cloverdale was founded and named by Charles Ray (1851-1925), who settled in Tillamook County about 1884 on the farm that subsequently became the site of the community. He later established a store, hotel, bank and cheese factory at Cloverdale, and was a charter member of Cloverdale Grange. It is apparent that the name is descriptive of the surroundings, which constitute a fine dairy country. The name was suggested by Cloverdale, California, where Ray occasionally visited.

Clymer, Marion County. Clymer post office, which operated with one break from May, 1883, to May, 1901, served an area a little to the southeast of Macleay in the vicinity of McAlpin school. The office was named for the first postmaster, Mary Clymer.

Coal Creek, Columbia County. Coal Creek flows into Pebble Creek from the east at a point about three miles south of Vernonia. The stream got its name from small coal outcrops along its banks. In fact there have been mining operations in some of these outcrops but so far not on a large scale.

Coal Creek, Lincoln County. Coal Creek, which flows into Pacific Ocean a couple of miles north of Yaquina Head, was named in pioneer days because of supposed coal deposits along its course. In October, 1945, Andrew L. Porter of Newport told the writer that this coal-like mineral was just large pieces of shale. He tried to burn some without success. In earlier days this stream was on the Siletz Indian Reservation and could not be prospected. Some people thought they were being deprived of a good fuel supply until the true nature of the rock was determined.

Coal Point, Curry County. This point is about three miles south of Port Orford and just north of Humbug Mountain. It is immediately north of Brush Creek. It is believed that Coal Point is the one mentioned by George Davidson in the USC&GS *Coast Pilot* for 1869, which he says was named because of the reported existence of coal in the vicinity, but he could find none after careful examination.

Coalbank Slough, Coos County. This slough is a branch of Coos Bay.

It received its name in pioneer days. Upon its waters a great deal of coal was taken out of the coal mines in light craft and in sea-going boats.

Coalca, Clackamas County. Coalca is a station on the Southern Pacific Company railroad about a mile north of New Era. It was named for an Oregon Indian celebrity. East of the station, and up on the side hill above the highway, is a natural rock formation called Coalcas Pillar. This pillar is a rock spire with a peculiar knob or capstone at the top. In earlier days the railroad station at or near this point was called Rock Island for the natural feature in the Willamette River, but due to confusion with other places of the same name, the railroad company made a change in its official list.

Coaledo, Coos County. Coaledo was named because of a coal lead or vein. The place is on Beaver Slough a few miles northwest of Coquille. George Bennett, in *OHQ*, volume XXVIII, page 346, says a man named Vandenburg was the first settler in the locality. Postal records for 1875 show Coaledo post office, established in that year.

Coalman Glacier, Clackamas and Hood River counties. In the 1930s it became evident that the ice mass on the south face of Mount Hood above Crater Rock was not directly connected with Zigzag and White River glaciers. Thousands of people have toiled up this final pitch called either "The Chute" or "The Hogsback" depending upon the location of the route up the ever changing ice. In 1970 Elijah Coalman, the most famous of the Mount Hood guides, died and the OGNB promptly recommended that this be called Coalman Glacier. Lige Coalman was born near Sandy, Oregon on November 26, 1881. He first climbed Mount Hood at the age of fifteen and in the ensuing 31 years made a total of 586 ascents, a record not likely to be surpassed. He was instrumental in the design and construction of the USFS summit lookout on Mount Hood and spent three summers on top prior to World War I. Coalman was later very active in youth work with the YMCA and spent several years at Spirit Lake on Mount Saint Helens. In 1938 he moved to California where he spent his remaining years. For further information see *Mazama*, 1970 and editorial comment in the *Oregon Journal*, July 1, 1970.

Coalmine Creek, Douglas and Jackson counties. Coalmine Creek flows south across the county boundary in township 31 south, range 1 east, and drains into Sugarpine Creek. It got its name because of the discovery on its banks of some black rock that appeared to be coal. However, subsequent investigation showed that the substance was not coal. See also under Kettle Creek. A deer lick at the junction of Sugarpine and Coalmine creeks is called Coalmine Lick.

Coast Fork, Lane County. Coast Fork post office, named for Coast Fork Willamette River, was established December 28, 1867, with George W. Rinehart postmaster. The office was closed October 1, 1872. Gill's map of Oregon of 1874 shows the place on the railroad about four miles south of Creswell, but the railroad was not built when the office was established, so the legend on the map may be for a later railroad station and not for the post office as originally established. Local tradition is to the effect that the post office was a little east of the present site of Creswell.

Coast Fork Willamette River, Lane County. This is the smallest of the three streams that combine in the neighborhood of Eugene to form Willamette River. The other two are McKenzie River (formerly McKenzie Fork) and Middle Fork. Coast Fork was so named because it headed more nearly toward the coast than did the other two. It has been so called since pioneer days.

Coast Range. Mountains close to the sea are characteristic of almost the entire eastern shores of the Pacific Ocean. From Bering Sea to Cape Horn ranges of varying heights are constantly visible from the ocean, and Oregon is no exception to the rule. The entry made by Meriwether Lewis in his diary for April 1, 1806, shows that he perceived quite clearly that the mountains along the coast were separated from the Cascade Range by a valley drained by a large river. However, the term Coast Range does not seem to have been used by early explorers in the Oregon country, and the name was doubtless developed by the pioneer settlers. Between the Columbia River and the Siuslaw River the Coast Range is rather well defined, particularly west of the Willamette Valley, but from the Siuslaw south, the Coast Range gradually merges with spurs from the Cascade Range until finally both are consolidated with the Klamath Mountains, whose name is used by geologists in referring to the group near the Oregon-California line, part of which is popularly referred to as the Siskiyou Mountains. The Coast Range of Oregon is, however, geologically, quite independent both of the Cascade Range and of the Klamath Mountains and its dividing line with the latter is considered by geologists to be at or near Rogue River. However, government map makers use the name Coast Range continuously from Oregon into California, and do not employ the term Klamath Mountains. Interesting information about these mountain groups will be found in USGS Bulletins 196 and 546 by Dr. J. S. Diller. The style Coast Range has been officially adopted by the USBGN. The Coast Range is an irregular group of maturely dissected hills and peaks, and while the main divide is generally parallel to and about 30 miles from the coast, this divide is frequently not in line with the highest summits. From the Columbia River south to Rogue River there are several important peaks. The best available elevations for these peaks and authority therefore are as follows:

Peak	Altitude in feet
Saddle Mountain (USCE)	3283
Onion Peak (USCE)	3058
Neahkahnie Mountain (USC&GS)	1795
Mount Hebo (USC&GS)	3153
Euchre Mountain (USGS)	2446
Bald Mountain (USCE)	3246
Marys Peak (USC&GS)	4097
Table Mountain (USGS)	2804
Grass Mountain (USC&GS)	3612
Prairie Peak (USCE)	3392
Roman Nose Mountain (USGS)	2856
Kenyon Mountain (USC&GS)	3266
Mount Bolivar (USC&GS)	4297

Mount Bolivar is the highest peak in the Oregon Coast Range north of Rogue River. There are higher peaks in the Oregon Coast Range south of Rogue River. The Columbia River cuts the Coast Range to water level. The next stream to find its way through the Coast Range is the Nehalem, which pursues a winding course, first east, then north, and finally west and southwest until it reaches the ocean. In the north part of the range the highest summits lie in a well defined line beginning at Clatsop Crest on the Columbia River, passing through Saddle Mountain and Neahkahnie Mountain. South of the Nehalem and north of the Siuslaw there is a succession of peaks and mountains most of which are west of the drainage divide. The South Yamhill River cuts deeply into the Coast Range from the Willamette Valley with a resultant pass to the ocean of but little over 700 feet. Yaquina River does the same, except from the west. The Siuslaw River has also cut a pass below 500 feet, and the Umpqua River likewise.

Coburg, Lane County. Coburg is said to bear the name of a well-known Lane County stallion. A blacksmith named Thomas Kane operated a smithy where Coburg is now situated and because the horse was brought to his shop to be shod, Kane applied the name to the incipient community. This information was furnished to the writer by Lucien Ward, a prominent resident of the neighborhood.

Coburg Hills, Lane County. These hills are a spur of the Cascade Range. They lie between the Willamette Valley and the Mohawk River. McKenzie River swings around their southern end. They have an extreme elevation of over 3000 feet. Coburg Hills take their name from the town of Coburg just to the west.

Cochran, Washington County. Cochran post office and railroad station were named for Judge Joseph W. Cochran and J. Henry Cochran, brothers, of Ashland, Wisconsin, who owned a large tract of timber in the locality.

Cochran Creek, Linn County. Cochran Creek is a stream northwest of Brownsville. It flows into Butte Creek north of Saddle Butte. William Cochran was a pioneer landowner on the upper part of this stream, and it was named for him.

Coe Glacier, Hood River County. This is one of the important glaciers on the north slope of Mount Hood and has its source near the top of the mountain. It lies east of Pulpit Rock, and Coe Branch flows northeast from its base. It was named for Captain Henry Coe, a pioneer resident of the Hood River Valley, who with several others, operated a stage line to the mountain.

Coffee Creek, Douglas County. This stream flows into South Umpqua River from the north about 15 miles east of Myrtle Creek. Reinhart in *The Golden Frontier,* page 152, says a party of soldiers chasing hostile Indians camped by this creek about 1858. They were out of coffee and made fun of one of their companions who complained bitterly of this lack. The name Coffee Creek continued even after the discovery of gold.

Coffee Island, Marion County. Coffee Island is in the Willamette River southwest of St. Paul. It was named for the Coffee family, early settlers on the east bank of the river.

Coffeepot Creek, Lane County. This stream flows into Middle Fork

Willamette River south of Oakridge. According to C. B. McFarland of the USFS the creek was named in pioneer days. A coffeepot fell out of an immigrant's wagon and was run over by a wheel and ruined. John H. Hill, an early resident of the vicinity, vouched for the story.

Coffin Butte, Benton County. Coffin Butte lies about three miles southwest of Suver, and just west of the Pacific Highway West. It has an elevation of 732 feet. Viewed from the southwest, this hill has a remarkable resemblance to a coffin, hence the name applied.

Coffin Canyon, Gilliam County. Coffin Canyon emptying into Thirtymile Creek southwest of Condon is named for one of Gilliam County's earliest settlers. George Coffin settled near its mouth in 1877.

Coffin Mountain, Linn County. Coffin Mountain is a name that well describes this 5771 foot peak south of Idanha. When viewed up Blowout Creek from Detroit Lake it appears as a flat top box of awesome proportions. The name is very old.

Coffin Rock, Columbia County. Coffin Rock is in the Columbia River a little more than a mile north of Goble. It is so called because it was an Indian burial place. Broughton mentions it in his report on October 28, 1792. "Mr. Broughton continued to proceed against the stream, and soon passed a small rocky islet, about 20 feet above the surface of the water. Several canoes covered the top of the islet, in which dead bodies were deposited." The first use of the name Coffin Rock that the compiler has seen is in Coues' *Henry-Thompson Journals,* volume II, page 796, under date of January 11, 1814. This islet should not be confused with Mount Coffin, a point on the Washington shore west of Longview.

Cogswell Creek, Lake County. This stream flows westward into Goose Lake at a point about ten miles south of Lakeview. Members of the Cogswell family were pioneer settlers in Goose Lake Valley as early as 1869, and the stream was named for M. Cogswell or one of his relatives.

Colby Spring, Crook County. Charles Colby bought forty acres of school section lieu land including this spring southwest of Conant Basin. He also at one time owned the old Way Ranch on Crooked River west of Combs Flat Road. For information on the sale of "school sections" by the state after withdrawal, see under School Section Cabin.

Cold Camp Creek, Wasco County. In 1862 Joseph H. Sherar named Cold Camp near the headwaters of this creek on The Dalles-Canyon City road. The creek flows westerly to Antelope Creek.

Cold Springs, Umatilla County. Cold Springs railroad station, Cold Springs Wash, Cold Springs Reservoir and Cold Springs Canyon are all well-known geographic names in northwest Umatilla County. The station is on the Union Pacific Railroad on the south bank of Columbia River about ten miles east of Umatilla. The names are all descriptive. A post office named Arroyo was established in these parts on July 15, 1878, with Clinton V. B. Reeder postmaster. The name of the office was changed to Cold Springs on April 2, 1880, with Andrew C. Bryan postmaster. This office was short lived and was closed probably in 1883. *Arroyo* is a Spanish word meaning rivulet or small stream, and in western United States the term is frequently used for intermittent creeks or dry watercourses. The name Arroyo was doubtless suggested by Cold Springs Wash.

Colebrook Butte, Curry County. This butte has an elevation of 2046 feet and is about ten miles south of Port Orford and two miles east of the Pacific Ocean. Euchre Creek flows around its eastern and southern slopes. It was named for a pioneer settler, F. W. Colebrook, who located a homestead nearby about 1860. Colebrook was born in Scotland, October 13, 1816, and came to Oregon about 1858. He died May 21, 1889.

Colegrove Butte, Curry County. This butte southeast of Carpenterville was named for Delmar Colegrove who took over the Raleigh Scott holdings in this area in 1902.

Coleman Canyon, Jefferson County. Coleman Canyon is west of Hay Creek and north of Hay Creek Ranch. It was named for Henry Coleman, a partner in Teal & Coleman, the famous ranchers of Trout Creek in the 1870s. Phil Brogan tells of their history in *East of the Cascades.*

Coleman Creek, Jackson County. Coleman Creek drains an area south of Medford. It bears the name of M. H. Coleman, a pioneer of 1853, who was the first settler on the stream.

Coleman Mountain, Harney County. This mountain and a nearby creek were named for a stockman who lived in that vicinity. These features are about 35 miles east of Burns.

Coles Valley, Douglas County. This valley was named for Dr. James Cole, the first settler therein. It is along the Umpqua River northwest of Roseburg. Dr. Cole established his home in the valley in 1851. See University of Oregon *Extension Monitor* for September, 1924. For information about the Cole family, see story by Fred Lockley in the *Oregon Journal,* August 17, 1937.

Colestin, Jackson County. The Coles were pioneer settlers in the southern part of the county. Steel says that Colestin was named for Rufus Cole in 1885, the one who then owned the nearby springs.

Collard Lake, Lane County. This lake is about three miles north of Florence. It was named for Roy L. Collard who took up a homestead near the lake.

Collawash River, Clackamas and Marion counties. This important tributary of Clackamas River was first named Miners Fork because of the mining activity near its headwaters in northern Marion County. There is a Colowesh Basin in Washington just north of The Dalles and a local chief named Colwash lived nearby in the early days. Jacobs in *A Sketch of Northern Sahaptian Grammar,* says "tcalu-, kalu-, possibly means in origin—basket work" and "wac or wass—site" as in Wasco-pam. *Kalu-wass* seems to mean a place where awl baskets were made. This is appropriate for the site in Washington but does not indicate direct Indian application to the extensive, wooded watershed of the Oregon river. The compiler has been unable to learn when or under what circumstances the present name was first applied.

College Creek, Wallowa County. College Creek is a short tributary of Imnaha River in the eastern part of the county. A. N. Adams, better known as Sam, named this stream. He was a Civil War veteran, and pioneer of Wallowa Valley. He applied the name after a school had been established nearby. He was a rancher.

College Crest, Lane County. In the 1850s there was an educational institution in Lane County called Columbia College. It was situated in the south part of Eugene and the name of the institution has been perpetuated in a geographic name College Crest. This term is applied to an upland, most of which is in section 6, township 18 south, range 3 west. College Crest is not near the University of Oregon and was not named for that institution. In 1909 J. O. Story and Wesley Whitbeck filed a plat for College Crest but whether they originated the name the compiler does not know. About that time, Fred S. Williams, Jr., settled in the area and in 1913 applied for a post office to be called College Crest. This office was duly established June 13, 1913, and Williams was appointed postmaster, but he asserted that he had never received any notice from the Post Office Department and did not know that the office had been established. Williams operated a neighborhood store and he planned to run the post office in connection with this store. The little store which was to have been the post office was situated at the northwest corner of what is now Friendly Avenue and Lorane Highway in Eugene. At one time there was a street car waiting station at this point.

Collier Creek, Curry and Josephine counties. This stream, now part of the boundary line between the two counties, was named for an early resident, and old maps and records show it Cole Collier Creek. The first part of the name is now omitted.

Collier Glacier, Lane County. Collier Glacier heads on the west side of North Sister and drains into White Branch. It is the largest glacier in the Three Sisters region and was named for Professor George H. Collier of the University of Oregon, who made an ascent of the Three Sisters in 1880. Professor Collier was a prominent early-day instructor, and came to Oregon from Ohio in 1868. His son, Dr. Arthur J. Collier, was also an instructor at the University of Oregon and a well-known geologist.

Collings Mountain, Jackson County. This mountain is in the southwest part of the county, and has been shown at times as Collins Mountain. The USFS informs the compiler that it was named for a local resident named Collings, and that Collins is wrong.

Colorado Lake, Linn County. This lake which has an elevation of 195 feet, lies on the south bank of the Willamette River a few miles east of Corvallis. The compiler has been unable to obtain information as to why this lake is called Colorado Lake.

Colson, Klamath County. Colson post office was given the family name of the first and only postmaster, Mary E. Colson. The office operated from March to December, 1895. It was in the northwest corner, probably in section 7, of township 40 south, range 10 east. An old map shows this post office very close to the banks of Lost River, at a point seven or eight miles northwest of Merrill.

Colton, Clackamas County. Colton is situated on Milk Creek at an elevation of 706 feet. It was named about 1892. Two local residents, Joshua Gorbett and a man named Cole each wished to name it for the other, but the Post Office Department objected to Gorbett because it was too much like Corbett, in Multnomah County. As a result, Colton was selected.

Columbia City, Columbia County. This city, just north of St. Helens, was founded in 1867 by Jacob and Joseph Caples. Columbia City was ambitious to become the terminus of Ben Holladay's Willamette Valley railroad in 1870, at the time Portland became the terminus of the west side line with a bonus of $100,000. The prospective community was named for the Columbia River, but the expected growth has not materialized. Columbia City post office was established August 16, 1871.

Columbia County. This county was created January 16, 1854, by the territorial legislature. It comprised the northeast part of Washington (Twality) County as it was after Clatsop County had been created. It was named for the Columbia River, its northern and eastern boundary, and St. Helens is its county seat. The land area of Columbia County is 646 square miles (Bureau of the Census).

Columbia River, northern boundary of Oregon. Columbia is one of the most abundantly used geographic names in America. Aside from the beauty of the word, its history reflects efforts to honor the achievements of Christopher Columbus. Its greatest use in the Pacific Northwest is as the name of the great river. Captain Robert Gray, in the American vessel *Columbia,* on May 11, 1792, at 8 a.m. sailed through the breakers and at 1 p.m. anchored in the river ten miles from its mouth. On May 19, Gray gave his ship's name to the river. (*United States Public Documents,* Serial Number 351, House of Representatives Documents 101.) This was the American discovery and naming of the river. Prior to this, the river's existence had been suspected and other names had been suggested. In 1766-1767, Jonathan Carver, while exploring among the Indians of Minnesota, wrote about a great river of the West and called it Oregon, a word which he may have stolen. On August 17, 1775, Bruno Heceta, Spanish explorer, noted the indications of a river there. He called the entrance *Bahia de la Asuncion,* the northern point *Cabo San Roque* and the southern point *Cabo Frondoso.* Later Spanish charts showed the entrance as *Ensenada de Hecata* and the surmised river as *San Roque.* In 1788 John Meares, English explorer and fur trader, sought for and denied the existence of the Spanish river *Saint Roc.* He called the Spaniard's *San Roque* Cape Disappointment and the entrance he changed from *Bahia de la Asuncion* or *Ensenada de Heceta* to Deception Bay. That was the situation when Captain Gray made his discovery. In 1793, Alexander Mackenzie, of the North West Company of Montreal, made his memorable journey to the western coast. He came upon a large river which he said the Indians called *Tacootche-Tesse.* This afterwards turned out to be Fraser River, but for a time it was confused with the Columbia. Captain Meriwether Lewis mapped it as a northern branch of the Columbia, spelling it *Tacoutche.* Arrowsmith's 1798 map of the Columbia River was made from Broughton's survey. The name Columbia is not used but instead, the sheet is entitled *Plan of the River Oregan.* William Cullen Bryant in his great poem *Thanatopsis,* 1817, revived and gave wide circulation to Oregon as the name of the river. Another literary name was Great River of the West, which, of course, did not disturb Columbia as a geographic term. *Oregon Historical Quarterly,* volume XXII, December, 1921, contains the "Log of the Columbia" by John Boit. This furnishes many interesting details of the discovery of the mouth of the Columbia River by one who was there at the time. The first examination of the Columbia River for the USC&GS was made in 1850 by Lieut.-Commanding Wm. P. McArthur, U. S. N. For account of this survey and McArthur's comments on the Columbia River see *OHQ*, volume XVI, No. 3, September, 1915, which contains an article by Lewis A. McArthur. This article, among other things, contains the first hydrographic notice ever published by the Coast Survey for the Pacific Coast. It is entitled *No. 3 Columbia River, Oregon*, and gives sailing directions for entering the Columbia River as far as the harbor at Astoria by Lieut.-Commanding Wm. P. McArthur, U. S. N., assistant in the Coast Survey. For a more recent overview see article by Don Holm in *Sunday Oregonian*, Northwest Section, July 20, 1975.

Colvin Creek, Morrow and Wheeler counties. This stream heads in the extreme northeast of Wheeler County and flows northeast into Morrow County, where it joins Porter Creek. Its waters eventually find their way into North Fork John Day River. Colvin Creek bears the name of John Colvin, who had a homestead on the stream about a half mile east of what is now the Heppner-Spray Highway and about 18 miles south of Hardman. The spelling Colivin is wrong.

Combs Flat, Crook County. On October 18, 1947, Remey Cox of Prineville wrote as follows: "Combs Flat is a benchland area embracing most of sections 13 and 36, township 15 south, range 17 east. It was named because it was the home ranch of James Combs, whose lands extended north to the area now in the Ochoco Irrigation district reservoir. Norval Powell, scion of another pioneer Crook County family, now occupies the shrunken remnant of the Combs ranch, and there is a county road debouching from our well-known Ochoco Highway a few miles east of Prineville and connecting with the Crooked River Highway below Post." James Parker Combs was born in Indiana and was married to Jane Dyer of that state. The Combs came to Oregon in 1852 and settled first near Lebanon, moving in 1870 to what was later Crook County. For biographical information about several members of the family, see Crook County *News* of Prineville, August 4, 1930, and Prineville *Central Oregonian*, March 20, 1947. The name of the flat is sometimes spelled Coombs, which is wrong.

Comegys Lake, Harney County. Comegys Lake off the north end of Steens Mountain is named for Lloyd and Elmer Comegys who both homesteaded nearby. There appears to be no basis for the name Cummings Lake and the USBGN adopted Comegys in *Decision List 8201*.

Comer, Grant County. Comer post office was near the junction of Comer Gulch and Dixie Creek, about eight miles north of Prairie City. It was named for R. H. J. Comer, Grant County pioneer printer and mining man, who lived on Dixie Creek and in Prairie City for many years. According to a letter of Mrs. Louise King, printed in the Canyon City *Eagle*, March 7, 1947, Comer came from Canada. He was an old time printer and printed the seven scattering numbers of *The City Journal*, which appeared in Canyon City in 1868 and 1869. It is probable that he wrote most of the contents of the little sheets. Comer's main interest was in mining, and on September 6, 1869, he published the last issue of the *Journal*, which included the following paragraph: "With this issue we (i. e. the typo) withdraw from public life to more remunerative occupation of again swinging the pick and shovel. To a majority a newspaper is a very easy thing to run, but we cannot see it, so the outside world will remain in ignorance of the advantages of this section of Oregon." Comer is said to have been blown to bits many years ago in Prairie City by mine caps. Comer post office was established May 27, 1896, with Henry A. Hyde first postmaster. The compiler does not know when the office was closed.

Company Hollow, Wasco County. Company Hollow is a little vale in section 12, township 1 north, range 14 east, about three miles south of Fairbanks School. In February 1949, Judge Fred W. Wilson of The Dalles wrote the compiler as follows: "Company Hollow got that name because prior to 1863 when J. C. Ainsworth and the Oregon Steam Navigation Company completed the portage railroad from The Dalles to Celilo, passengers, mail and freight had to be hauled by teams and the company used this hollow and surrounding country for pasturing its horses." Company Hollow was well known for its fine stand of bunchgrass. Wasco County has a road in this locality officially called Company Hollow road. English post office was near this hollow.

Compass Creek, Hood River County. Compass Creek is the tributary of Coe Branch that flows from Langille Glacier on Mount Hood. Van Embree of Parkdale named it after he lost his compass while building the Timberline Trail crossing.

Comstock, Douglas County. This station on the Southern Pacific Company line in the north part of the county was named for James J. Comstock, an early day sawmill operator.

Conant Basin, Crook County. Conant Basin and Conant Creek are on the north slopes of Maury Mountains southeast of Prineville. They bear the name of Ed G. Conant, pioneer stockman of the locality. See the *Oregonian,* September 18, 1927, section V. page 1. Conant was born in Cuba, but not of Cuban blood. He settled in Crook County in November, 1869, and raised horses until his death in the 1890s.

Concomly, Marion County. This station on the Oregon Electric Railway about three miles southwest of Gervais was named for Chief Comcomly, head of the Chinook tribe, who is described in Irving's *Astoria,* and also in Alexander Henry's journal. He died in 1830, and his grave was visited by Wilkes in 1841. For references to Chief Comcomly see Scott's *History of the Oregon Country,* volume II, page 139. The spelling used by the railway company is a variation of the original name. Lewis and Clark met Comcomly on November 20, 1805, and gave him medals and a flag. Irving describes him in a decidedly humorous vein. His daughter married Archibald McDonald of the Hudson's Bay Company and their son Ranald McDonald is an interesting figure in northwest history. *Ranald MacDonald,* 1824-1894, edited by Lewis and Murakami, and published in 1923 by the Eastern Washington State Historical Society, contains much interesting information about Comcomly and his family, and also about McDonald's visit to Japan in 1848-49, which is of great historic interest. An editorial in the *Oregonian* for November 29, 1893, treats of McDonald's pretensions to the Chinook throne.

Condon, Gilliam County. Condon is the county seat of Gilliam County, and has an elevation of 2844 feet. It is an important trading center and is on the John Day Highway, and is also the southern terminus of the Condon branch of the Union Pacific Railroad. About 1883 a man named Potter owned a homestead just north of Thirtymile Creek, upon which there was a fine spring. He platted the land around the spring, but became involved in financial difficulties, and the land became the property of Condon and Cornish of Arlington. Condon and Cornish sold lots in the townsite, and in 1884 David B. Trimble took the necessary steps to secure a post office, and was appointed the first postmaster. Trimble suggested the name Condon, which was adopted by the department. The office was established July 10, 1884. Harvey C. Condon, for whom the place was named, was a practicing lawyer and located in Arlington, or as it was then known, Alkali, about 1882, and was a member of the firm of Condon and Cornish. He was the son of Judge J. B. Condon, a pioneer jurist of eastern Oregon, and the nephew of Dr. Thomas Condon, Oregon's great geologist. H. C. Condon lived in the state of Washington during the latter part of his life, and died at Vaughn, Washington, June 21, 1931.

Condon Butte, Lane County. This butte is about five miles northwest of North Sister and one mile east of the McKenzie Highway. It was named in 1924 by Professor Edwin T. Hodge of the University of Oregon in honor of Dr. Thomas Condon (1822-1907), distinguished geologist and scientist, and for many years a member of the faculty of the University of Oregon. Dr. Condon's discoveries of the prehistoric horse had a large influence on the conclusions of scientists and went far to establish evolutionary theories. The richest field of his discoveries was in the John Day Valley. For details concerning his life and work see Scott's *History of the Oregon Country,* volume III, page 169, and McCornack's *Thomas Condon.* Dr. John C. Merriam of the Carnegie Institution selected the John Day fossil bed as the scene of intensive investigations looking toward the development of Dr. Condon's discoveries.

Conley Creek, Douglas County. Conley Creek in North Umpqua River drainage three miles northeast of Rock Creek Guard Station was named for John A. Conley who homesteaded near its mouth in 1903.

Connley, Lake County. Connley post office and Connley Hills between Fort Rock and Silver Lake were named for a local family. The compiler has seen the name spelled in other ways, but Connley was the style used by postal officials. Connley post office was established April 18, 1912, with Warren B. Graham first of three postmasters. The office was closed out to Fort Rock on July 31, 1920.

Conser, Linn County. Conser is a station on the Oregon Electric Railway about four miles north of Albany. This station was named for John A. Conser, who owned land nearby. He was the son of Jacob Conser, a pioneer of 1848.

Contorta Point, Klamath County. This point is on the east shore of Crescent Lake. It was named in 1925 by F. W. Cleator of the USFS because of the abundance nearby of lodgepole pine, *Pinus contorta.*

Conyers Creek, Columbia County. Conyers Creek drains an area south of Clatskanie and flows into Clatskanie River at Clatskanie. It bears the name of the Conyers family, several members of which have been prominent residents of the area and have occupied important posts both in public affairs and in business.

Cook Creek, Tillamook County. S. M. Batterson, for many years a resident of the lower Nehalem Valley, informed George B. McLeod of Portland in August, 1927, that this stream was named for a local character, Indian Cook, who settled near the mouth of the creek in 1877 or 1878. Cook is said to have been a Cherokee, and there was some feeling against him on the part of the Tillamooks, although he married a Tillamook woman. Cook was a man of fine character, and was murdered by his enemies, not far from the present site of Nehalem.

Cook Slough, Clatsop County. This is a small tidal slough that joins Youngs Bay. It is situated a short distance east of Miles Crossing. Cook Slough takes its name from Geo. W. Cook, who was an early settler on land nearby. He was born in Vermont in 1818 and came to Oregon in 1850.

Coombs Canyon, Umatilla County. This canyon drains into Umatilla River from the south, just west of Rieth. According to James H. Raley of Pendleton, it bears the name of Calvin Coombs, who settled in the vicinity in the late 1870s. The name Comas Canyon as applied to this canyon is wrong.

Coon Town, Harney County. Coon Town is now nothing more than a flavorful place name in Oregon history. Even in full vigor before the turn of the century, it was only a tiny community in section 23, township 28 south, range 33 east, on the homestead of a well-known rancher, Sylvester "Coon" Smith. The name came from the nickname of its principal citizen and was without racial connotation.

Cooper Creek, Clackamas County. This creek runs from the vicinity of Fryingpan Lake south to the north end of Timothy Lake. When Oak Grove Fork was dammed to create Timothy Lake it flooded out Cooper Lake in the same basin and Cooper Creek was so called to perpetuate the name. T. H. Sherrard of the USFS informed the compiler that the lake was named for Warren Cooper, now deceased. Cooper, the son of David R. Cooper for whom Cooper Spur was named, was for several years district ranger for the USFS at Parkdale.

Cooper Mountain, Washington County. This is a prominent hill about four miles southwest of Beaverton and has an elevation of 794 feet. It was named for Perry Cooper who was born in Ohio in 1825 and was a pioneer of Oregon. He settled on the slopes of this mountain in March, 1853.

Cooper Spur, Hood River County. David Rose Cooper was an early settler in Hood River Valley, and lived not far from the present site of Mount Hood post office. He had a camping place on the east slope of Mount Hood and the spur was named for him. This was about 1886. Cooper Spur separates Eliot Glacier from Newton Clark Glacier.

Coopers Ridge, Linn County. Coopers Ridge is the high ground south of Idanha. Earl Stahlman of Detroit told the writer that it was named for Jack Cooper who ran a regular pack train to Breitenbush Hot Springs in the early days.

Coopey Falls, Multnomah County. Coopey Falls were named for Charles Coopey, for many years a well-known tailor in Portland. Coopey was a native of England. He owned land adjacent to the falls that bear his name.

Coos Bay, Coos County. As the result of votes at two city elections held November 7 and December 28, 1944, the name of the community Marshfield was changed to Coos Bay, thus doing away with a geographic title that had been in use for ninety years. On January 8, 1965, the city of Empire also voted to consolidate under the new name. For the history of the names Marshfield and Empire, see under the respective headings. The new name was of course taken from the natural feature, Coos Bay. For comments on the origin of the name Coos, see under Coos County.

Coos City, Coos County. Coos City was one of the early post offices of Coos County and it was named for the county or the bay. It was established June 25, 1873, with Henry A. Coston first postmaster. The office continued in service until March 18, 1884. It was situated on Isthmus Slough about five miles south of Marshfield as it was then known. There is little left of the community, but the name is retained by the Coos City bridge. An important road turned eastward at this point headed to Roseburg.

Coos County. Coos County was created December 22, 1853, by the territorial legislature. It was originally formed from the west parts of Umpqua and Jackson counties. *Coos* is an Indian name of a native tribe whose habitat was the vicinity of Coos Bay. The name is first mentioned by Lewis and Clark, who spell it *Cook-koo-oose* (Thwaites' *Original Journals*, volume VI, page 117). The explorers heard the name among the Clatsop Indians. Alexander R. McLeod in his journal of 1828 gives the name *Cahoose;* Slacum, in his report of 1837, gives the name of Coos River *Cowis;* Wilkes, in *Western America,* spells it *Cowes.* The spelling has been variously *Koo'as, Kowes, Koos, Coose,* and finally *Coos.* For description of Coos Bay, see the *Oregonian,* June 11, 1873, article signed "Northwest." For description of the Oregon coast south of Coos Bay, by the same writer, *ibid.,* July 9, 1873. One Indian meaning of Coos is "lake," another, "place of pines", *ibid.,* August 26, 1902, page 12. Perry B. Marple, who began exploiting Coos Bay in 1853, spelled the word *Coose,* and said it was an Indian perversion of the English word coast, meaning a place where ships can land. See his advertisement, *ibid.,* January 7, 1854. Another version is that the Indian word was made to resemble the name of a county in New Hampshire, (*ibid.,* December 9, 1890, page 6). The Coos Indians were of the *Kusan* family, formerly living at Coos Bay. Lewis and Clark estimated their population at 1500 in 1805. The name is often used as synonymous with the family name. Hale, in *U. S. Exploring Expedition, Ethnography and Philology,* 1846, page 221, gives the name as *Kwokwoos* and *Kaus;* Parrish, in Indian Affairs *Report* for 1854, page 495, gives *Co-ose.* Interesting details of the early history of southwest Oregon may be found in Orvil Dodge's *Pioneer History of Coos and Curry Counties,* published in Salem in 1898. Coos County has a land area of 1611 square miles. In 1844 Duflot de Mofras got off the prize pun in the history of Oregon geographic names when he published his work *Exploration du Territoire de l'Oregon.* He called Coos River *la riviere aux Vaches,* or Cows

River, apparently after talking to some of the Scots employed by the Hudson's Bay Company.

Coos Head, Coos County. Coos Head is the point on the south side of the entrance to Coos Bay. It extends northward from Cape Arago, but is much lower than the main part of the cape. Between Coos Head and the west point of Cape Arago is the Cape Arago Lighthouse, a well-known landmark. The locality of this lighthouse is sometimes called Gregory Point, perpetuating after a fashion the name Cape Gregory, which was originally applied by Captain James Cook in 1778. See under Cape Arago.

Coos River, Coos County. Coos River, named for the stream nearby, was the third post office in Coos County. It was established March 7, 1863, with Amos C. Rogers first postmaster. This office was closed September 20, 1864. The office was opened again February 10, 1873, with Frank W. Bridges postmaster and was closed September 24, 1875. Available maps show the location of this office on Coos River near the mouth of the Millicoma. It may have been in a different locality the first time, but probably not far away. Rogers and Bridges were well-known pioneer settlers in the locality.

Cooston, Coos County. Cooston is on the east shore of Coos Bay and the origin of the name is the same as that of Coos County. Cooston post office was established May 13, 1908, and the first postmaster was William E. Homme, who named the place.

Copeland Creek, Douglas County. Copeland Creek rises in township 27 south, range 2 east, and flows into North Umpqua River near Eagle Rock. It was named for Thomas Bent Copeland. who prospected along its banks. Copeland was born in St. Joseph, Missouri in 1850, and came to Oregon in 1864. He and his brother Matt homesteaded on Scott Mountain north of Glide.

Copeland Creek, Jackson and Klamath counties. Copeland Creek was named for Hiram Copeland of Fort Klamath. The stream rises west of Crater Lake and flows into Rogue River.

Copper, Jackson County. Copper is the name of a locality on Applegate River, near the mouth of Carberry Creek and about a mile north of the Oregon-California line. It got its name from the copper mining activity in the vicinity, especially at the Blue Ledge mine just over the line in California. The post office was established in November, 1924, with Mrs. Mamie Winningham first postmaster. The office was discontinued in May, 1932.

Copper, Wallowa County. A post office with the name Copper was established January 5, 1904, with Anna Bigham postmaster. It was in operation until May 3, 1907, at which time the office was closed and all papers sent to White Bird, Idaho, the most convenient nearby office. Copper post office was in section 14, township 3 north, range 50 east, and was established to serve some copper mine claims in the vicinity. There is a pinnacle called Copper Mountain in the locality and also a Copper Creek flowing into Snake River. The post office was about a half mile west of Snake River.

Copperfield, Baker County. Copperfield is on the west bank of Snake River. The place has had a meteoric career. About 1900 there were many prospectors in the place and it was called Copper Camp, because of the character of the nearby ore. Soon after this the community was definitely named Copperfield, and by 1910 there were about 1000 inhabitants, the increase in population being due to the digging of two tunnels by the railroad company and by the predecessor of the Idaho Power Company, near the Oxbow. In 1914 Copperfield became really famous when Governor Oswald West sent his secretary, Miss Fern Hobbs, double armed with determination and a signed declaration of martial law, to clean up the morals of the place. The community was trying to recover from the struggle between Miss Hobbs and the Power of Darkness, when fire swept away most of the buildings, so it was impossible to determine if Righteousness had prevailed. Two more fires have made Copperfield a thing of the past.

Copperfield Draw, Klamath County. This spot east of Chiloquin was named for early settlers David and Anna Copperfield.

Coquille, Coos County. This name is applied to a city, a point and a river in Coos County, south of Coos Bay. Coquille is a word of unknown origin, probably Indian, but with French spelling. The French word means a shell. *Scoquel* appears in the *Oregonian,* January 7, 1854, in an advertisement of the Coose Bay Company. The name is there said to be Indian for "eel." *Coquette* appears on a map of John B. Preston, surveyor-general of Oregon, 1851, probably intended for *Coquelle.* It appears *Coquille* in Preston's map of 1856. Canadian-French fur traders may have left the form of name among the Indians. See *OHQ,* volume XIX, pages 73-74, by Leslie M. Scott, and also the *Oregonian,* for September 3, 1907, where Harvey W. Scott makes some comments on the pronunciation of the name. Captain William Tichenor in *Pioneer History of Coos and Curry Counties,* page 29, says the Indian name of this stream was *Nes-sa-til-cut,* but gives no further information. In an article in the *Coos Bay Times,* November 29, 1943, Mary M. Randleman, Coos County pioneer, says the word is of Indian origin and cites a number of early uses of the style Coquelle and Coquel. The *Handbook of American Indians,* volume I, page 871, lists the Mishikhwutmetunne Indians, who lived along the Coquille, and says that the Chetco names for some of these Indians was *Ku-kwil-tunne,* and *Kiguel* is a form listed as being used as early as 1846. This seems to indicate an Indian origin of the name. On October 25, 1938, the *Oregonian* printed on its editorial page an interesting letter from Sam Van Pelt, an aged Indian living at Brookings, who recounted the difficulties of spelling Indian names with "English" letters. "Coquilth" was the result of his efforts to produce the correct sound, but no interpretation of the word was furnished. The letter and accompanying editorial are well worth reading. Interesting information about the founding of the town of Coquille is given in an article in the *Coquille Valley Sentinel* for November 20, 1941. In Coos County there have for many years been spirited differences of opinion about the pronunciation of the name Coquille. See editorial in the *Oregonian,* October 17, 1938, as well as editorial mentioned above.

Coquille Point, Lincoln County. Coquille Point is on the east shore of Yaquina Bay about a half mile north of Yaquina community. The place is said to have been named for some Indian families who lived there many years ago and were supposed to have been members of the Coquille tribe of

Coos County. The writer does not know how they became settled at Yaquina Bay.

Corbell Butte, Klamath County. Corbell Butte, the 5389 foot high point on the north end of Chiloquin Ridge, was named for an early day family. Corbell served in the army at Fort Klamath during the Modoc troubles.

Corbett, Multnomah County. This post office and station on the Union Pacific Railroad, as well as Corbett Heights upon the Columbia River Scenic Highway above, were named for Senator Henry Winslow Corbett, one of Oregon's prominent pioneer citizens, for many years a resident of Portland. Mr. Corbett owned a farm near the post office. For a concise biography of Mr. Corbett, see Carey's *History of Oregon,* volume II, page 305. Scott's *History of the Oregon Country* has biographical information about Senator Corbett in volume I, pages 108 and 280, and Harvey W. Scott's tribute, volume V, page 183.

Corbin, Curry County. Walter F. Riley wrote the compiler from San Jose, California, in March, 1947, that Corbin was named for a man interested in the operations of a sawmill in the locality. Corbin was on Mussel Creek, about fifteen miles south of Port Orford, and when the USGS map of the Port Orford quadrangle was made in 1897-98, the place was about a mile east of the old coast road between Port Orford and Gold Beach. Corbin post office was established May 8, 1901, with Richard D. Jones postmaster. The office was discontinued in January, 1910, and had four different postmasters, so that it may have been moved from time to time.

Cord, Malheur County. Cord was a rural office on Duck Creek on the west edge of the county about twenty-five miles southeast of Venator in Harney County. Cord post office was established April 13, 1897, with Thomas M. Seaweard first postmaster. The office, which was named in compliment to Mrs. Cordelia Seaweard, wife of the postmaster, was closed December 31, 1917, with papers to Mooreville.

Cordes, Coos County. For a number of years the Southern Pacific Company maintained a railroad station with the name Coos near the north shore of Coos Bay and about two and a half miles north of North Bend. In the latter part of 1944 the name of the city of Marshfield, also on the railroad, was changed to Coos Bay. The similarity of names of two stations so near together was unsatisfactory and as a result the company changed the name of Coos siding to Cordes. R. C. Cordes deeded part of the right of way at this point when the railroad was built.

Cornelius, Washington County. Cornelius was named for Colonel T. R. Cornelius, a pioneer of 1845. He was the son of Benjamin Cornelius, who with his family emigrated to Oregon during that year as a member of the Meek party. The family settled on Tualatin Plains. Colonel Cornelius served in the Cayuse War of 1847-48, and the Yakima War of 1855-56. He served twenty years in the Oregon legislature, and in 1861 raised a regiment of volunteer cavalry. He was a merchant and also for a time ran a sawmill. Colonel Cornelius was born in November, 1827, and died June 24, 1899. The town of Cornelius is between Hillsboro and Forest Grove and has an elevation of 175 feet. Cornelius post office was established December 18, 1871.

Cornett Lake, Klamath County. This small lake in section 23, township 24 south, range 5½ east, was named in 1949 by a fish planting crew of the Oregon State Game Commission for Marshall Cornett, president of the Oregon Senate, who was killed in a plane crash on October 28, 1947.

Cornucopia, Baker County. This name is derived from Latin words meaning "horn of plenty" and the word is frequently applied to mines and other enterprises where there are large hopes of success. In 1885 mines were discovered on the southern slopes of the Wallowa Mountains in Baker County, and among the prospectors were several who came from Cornucopia, Nevada, who suggested that name for the new camp.

Cornutt, Douglas County. George B. Abdill of Roseburg provided the following information about this station on the Southern Pacific Railroad five miles southwest of Riddle. In the early days the stop was called Glenbrook for the Glenbrook Farm of William H. Riddle but from time to time it was confused with the more important Glendale station to the south. In 1906 the name was changed to Cornutt to honor pioneer settler Noah Cornutt. The place was of minor importance until it became the shipping point for the Hanna Mining Company when they opened their nickel operation in 1954.

Corral Basin, Wallowa County. Corral Basin is in the northwest corner of township 3 south, range 43 east. It was named because Standley and Sturgill built some sheep corrals there, made of heavy poles and logs. This was in the late 1880s.

Corral Creek, Clackamas County. Corral Creek drains the east slope of Parrett Mountain and flows into the Willamette River one mile west of Wilsonville. There are many other Corral creeks in Oregon, especially east of the Cascade Range. The word was originally Spanish and meant an inclosure or pen for stock. It was possibly from the same source as the South African Dutch word *kraal*. There were two reasons for describing creeks with this word. The first was that stockmen built their corrals with streams running through them as a matter of convenience. In the second place there were many valleys, especially in eastern Oregon, where rock formations produced natural corrals, with water running through them.

Corral Creek, Jackson County. George F. Wright of Jackson County was the authority for the following facts concerning the naming of this Corral Creek near Pinehurst. His uncle, William A. Wright, said that in the middle 1860s a gang of rustlers built a set of corrals along the creek. They would round up cattle in the Rogue River valley, bring them to the corrals and obliterate the brands, then drive them to the Klamath basin for sale. Vigilantes apprehended three of the thieves and hanged them in thick brush where Lincoln Creek empties into Keene Creek. George Wright's father, Thomas J. Wright, told of seeing the bones and fragments of clothing still hanging in 1866, and many years later he showed George the rotting log remnants of the corrals.

Corral Creek, Wallowa County. Corral Creek flows into Imnaha River in township 3 north, range 48 east. J. H. Horner of Enterprise told the compiler that the stream was named for a corral built nearby in 1884. A trail follows down this creek from the locality called Indian Village. It was in this general locality that a fight took place between Nez Perces and a band of renegade Snake Indians. This fight is well remembered. See under Cemetery Ridge.

Corset Creek, Linn County. Corset Creek is tributary to Rainbow Creek two miles southeast of Idanha. George and Arly Dickie who were raised in the area told the writer in 1977 that they well remembered an old fashioned corset securely constraining a burgeoning tree trunk near this stream. The garment itself and the cause of its curious location are now both lost in antiquity.

Corvallis, Benton County. In the winter of 1847-48 Joseph C. Avery began to lay out the community now known as Corvallis. In 1846 Avery settled on property on the north side of Marys River where it flows into the Willamette, and in the same year William F. Dixon settled on land just to the north. Avery's building sites were known as the Little Fields. The first lots are said to have been sold in 1849. The place was first called Marysville, and while Avery probably selected this name, the evidence is not positive. He was using his own name for the post office in 1850. It is generally believed that the place was named because it was on Marys River, but there may have been additional reasons. The origin of the name Marys River is uncertain. See under that heading, where it will be seen that the river name was in use at least as early as 1846. In 1853 the legislature changed the name of the locality from Marysville to Corvallis. Information about the early history of Corvallis may be found in *History of Benton County*, page 422. E. A. Blake, in a letter printed in the Corvallis *Gazette-Times*, June 7, 1935, says that Marysville was named for Mrs. John Stewart, also known as Aunt Mary Stewart, one of the first settlers in Corvallis. On the same page is a reprint of an interview with Mrs. Stewart, giving incidents of the early history of the place. Mrs. Stewart is authority for the statement that J. C. Avery told her he would name the community Marysville for her because she was the first white woman to live there. Joseph C. Avery was the first owner of the site of Corvallis, and he was a pioneer of 1845. He died in 1876. Avery made up the name Corvallis by compounding Latin words meaning heart of the valley. It is said that the name Marysville was changed to prevent confusion with Marysville, California. Corvallis has an elevation of 224 feet and the geography of its immediate surroundings may be seen on the USGS map of the Corvallis quadrangle. Avery's post office was established January 8, 1850, with J. C. Avery postmaster. The name was then changed to Marysville September 9, 1850, with Alfred Rinehart postmaster. Avery became postmaster again on March 14, 1851; Wayman St. Clair on November 5, 1851; Geo. H. Murch on January 7, 1853, and Avery again on June 7, 1853. The name of the office was changed to Corvallis on February 18, 1854. The name Marysville was applied to another post office, Forks of Mary's River, for a few weeks in the summer of 1850. This was probably an error, the authorities at Washington applying the change to the wrong office. See *OHQ*, volume XLI, page 55 for records of these offices.

Coryell Pass, Lane County. This pass is on the narrow shelf of ground between the Willamette River and the hills about a mile south of Springfield Junction. It is occupied by the tracks of the Southern Pacific Company, with the Pacific Highway just above. It was named for Abraham H. Coryell, a pioneer of 1847, who lived nearby, and the pioneer routes of travel led through this gap. A memorial stands just east of the highway at this point bearing the following inscription: "Coryell Pass. Oregon Trail 1846. Erected by Oregon Lewis and Clark Chapter, D. A. R. 1917."

Cosper Creek, Polk and Yamhill counties. This stream is near Grand Ronde, and was named for a pioneer family. Casper Creek is wrong.

Cottage Grove, Lane County. Cottage Grove is an important community in the southern part of Lane County, on the line of the Southern Pacific Company and on the Pacific Highway. Its elevation is 641 feet and the Coast Fork Willamette River flows through it. The post office was first established east of the present site of Creswell, March 3, 1855, with G. C. Pearce as postmaster. Pearce had his home in an oak grove, and named the post office Cottage Grove. Andrew Hamilton became postmaster in September, 1861, and he moved the office to the present site of Saginaw. When Nathan Martin was postmaster in the latter 1860s the office was moved to a point on the west bank of Coast Fork Willamette River in the extreme southwest part of what is now the town of Cottage Grove. When the railroad was built through in the 1870s a station was established more than half a mile north and east of the post office. This was the start of a bitter neighborhood controversy that ran on for nearly two decades. The people living near the post office would not allow it to be moved to Cottage Grove railroad station, so a new post office was established at that point and named Lemati. *Lemati* is a Chinook jargon word meaning mountain, but why it was selected as a name for the new post office is not apparent. *Lemiti* is the generally accepted spelling of the word as used elsewhere in Oregon. Cottage Grove was incorporated in 1887, but in 1893 the eastsiders rebelled and secured a charter for East Cottage Grove. The name of this place was changed to Lemati by the legislature in 1895, and the railroad station sported two names on its signboard, although Lemati was in small letters. The differences were subsequently composed and an act was passed in 1899 to consolidate the places with the name Cottage Grove. Lemati post office, as a rival to Cottage Grove, was in operation from November 21, 1893, to September 5, 1894, with Laban F. Wooley postmaster. However, on March 28, 1898, the name of the Cottage Grove office was changed to Lemati and it operated that way until May 10, 1898, when the name Cottage Grove was restored. Perry P. Sherwood was postmaster at that time.

Cotton, Multnomah County. Cotton was a station on the line of the Portland Electric Power Company about a mile west of Gresham. It was named for William Wick Cotton (1859-1918), a well-known attorney of Portland, who owned a large farm near the station. Cotton was a native of Iowa, and studied law at Columbia University, New York City. He came to Portland in October, 1889, and practiced law continuously until his death, at which time he was counsel of the Oregon-Washington Railroad & Navigation Company and other important corporations.

Cottonwood, Lake County. Cottonwood post office was named for Cottonwood Creek which flowed nearby the office. The place was about ten miles southwest of Lakeview, and Rial T. Striplin was the only postmaster the office ever had. Cottonwood office was established May 1, 1897, and was discontinued November 1, 1897, with papers to Lakeview. The office was near the west quarter-corner of section 34, township 39 south, range 19 east. Cottonwood Creek flows very close to this land corner.

Cottonwood Creek, Lake County. This stream is northwest of Goose Lake and drains several townships. There are a score of Cottonwood creeks in Oregon, and all serve to testify to the popularity (no pun intended) of members of the *Populus* group, including *Populus angustifolia, Populus trichocarpa* and others. General H. M. Chittenden, in *The American Fur Trade of the Far West,* says that one of, if not the most important tree in the fur trade business was the cottonwood. Not only were cottonwoods beautiful trees, but lines of them were welcome sights to the trappers and travelers, indicating water courses and fuel supplies. They provided shelter in winter and summer and rather surprisingly, fairly good horse feed. Ponies ate and throve on cottonwood bark quite successfully. Most of the Cottonwood creeks in Oregon have borne their names so long that it is impossible to say who named them.

Cottrell, Clackamas County. Cottrell is a crossroads locality in the extreme north part of the county on the Bluff Road about five miles north-northwest of Sandy. The post office was established March 26, 1894, with Charles Andrews first of two postmasters. The office was closed June 29, 1904, probably because of the extension of rural free delivery. In addition to the locality Cottrell, there is a Cottrell School nearly a mile eastward, and at one time there was a station Cottrell on the Mount Hood electric railway about a mile north of the community. This station was in Multnomah County, but the electric railway and station have been abandoned. Cottrell was named for the family of Mrs. Charles Andrews, *nee* Cottrell.

Couch Lake, Multnomah County. It is not suprising that thousands of Portland residents have never heard of Couch Lake but in the flood of June, 1948, this pond made an effort to reestablish itself. Its success was short-lived. Couch Lake was in the vicinity of Portland Union Station. It was named for Captain John Couch, one of the founders of Portland. An account of Captain Couch and his activities will be found in Oregon Pioneer Association *Transactions* for 1886. Captain Couch built a home on the west bank of this lake according to an article in the Oregon *Sunday Journal* for October 20, 1946. The lake covered about twenty-two Portland city blocks and had a depth of about fifteen feet. The compiler has a dim recollection of this body of water of about 1890 and as he recalls it the lake had been reduced in size by that time. In the 1880s this lake and surrounding land was bought by the Northern Pacific Terminal Company which had been organized in 1881. The first contract for filling the lake was let in 1888. The material used was ballast from incoming ships and sand from the river bed. The Union Station was formally opened February 14, 1896, and the first train left it that evening. There was much delay between the time the property was purchased and the time the station was completed due to financial problems. The architects of the station were Van Brunt & Howe of Kansas City. If McKim, Mead and White of New York ever drew any plans for this station, as has been reported, they were not used.

Cougar Lake, Lane County. This six mile long artificial lake was formed by damming South Fork McKenzie River about three miles south of Rainbow. It is a combination flood control and hydro-electric project and is an excellent example of how names proliferate. Originally Cougar Reservoir, it was named by Congress in 1950 in conjunction with the legislation for Cougar Dam. This in turn was named because the preliminary surveys designated the site from its proximity to Cougar Creek, an insignificant nearby stream. In common with many other man-made objects, it is regrettable that a name of more distinction or historical significance was not selected. There are many features in Oregon named for the cougar or *Felis concolor.* Vernon Bailey in *Mammals and Life Zones of Oregon* has a good account of these animals.

Council Butte, Klamath County. This butte is near Sprague River about two miles from Yainax. The USBGN adopted the name Council Butte in 1927, thus bringing to an end a controversy of many years standing. Gatschet, in *Dictionary of the Klamath Language,* uses the name *Yainaga* for this butte. *Yainaga* is the diminutive of *yaina,* meaning hill or mountain. For many years now the butte has been officially known as Council Butte, and the name Yainax Butte became transferred to a mountain with an elevation of 7226 feet, about 12 miles to the southeast. The name Council Butte had its origin in the council held at the little butte when a treaty was signed between the whites and certain Snake Indians on August 12, 1865. Government surveyors used the name Council Butte in 1866 when they surveyed the township. During the past few years efforts have been made by some of the older residents of the county to have the name Yainax returned to the little butte near Yainax community, but it was not considered practicable to do so because the name Council Butte had been so long in use by some of the government bureaus. See under Yainax and Yainax Butte.

Council Creek, Douglas County. Council Creek runs north to Cow Creek about three miles southwest of Riddle. It takes its name from the council held near its mouth in 1853 when Joel Palmer, Superintendent of Indian Affairs, met with several bands of lower Cow Creek Indians. George Riddle tells of this meeting in *Early Days in Oregon,* page 78.

Council Crest, Multnomah County. This is the highest point on a range of hills south of Portland. Its elevation is 1073 feet. It was a part of the John B. Talbot donation land claim and was subsequently owned successively by C. A. Beal, James Steel, and Graham Glass, Sr. The hill was for a time known as Glass Hill and was later called Fairmount, which name is still retained by the boulevard which encircles it. On July 11, 1898, delegates to the National Council of Congregational Churches met on top of this hill. Some discussion was had concerning a good name for it. A delegate from Portland, Maine, suggested Council Crest. This name was at once approved by Geo H. Himes, who was present, and a report of this meeting was sent to newspapers. The Indians at one time may have used the crest as a meeting place and signal station because of its wide outlook, but there is no historic record of it. For additional information about the naming of this crest see the *Oregonian,* editorial page July 29, August 5, 1927. For denial that the crest was used by Indians as a signal point, see interview with Miss Ella Talbot, *Oregon Journal*, March 15, 1914. The wooden observation tower long in use on top of Council Crest was torn down late in 1941, and in 1942 a steel standpipe with a capacity of 500,000 gallons of water was built in its place.

Courthouse Rock, Grant County. This is a well-known landmark in the west part of the county. The name is quite descriptive. See under Courtrock.

Courthouse Rock, Wasco County. This prominent flat topped rock with vertical sides is two miles west of Antelope. Its descriptive name is very old.

Courtney Creek, Linn County. Courtney Creek, south of Brownsville, was named for John B. Courtney, who operated a pioneer sawmill near the point where the stream leaves the foothills. He settled in the vicinity in 1846.

Courtney Creek, Wallowa County. Courtney Creek was named for pioneer stockmen, Lins, Alex and Bent Courtney. It is in the north part of the county.

Courtrock, Grant County. Courthouse Rock is the name of a peculiar formation in the hills in the west part of the county. This rock may be seen for many miles in all directions. When the post office was established nearby in April, 1926, postal authorities selected the name Courtrock from among several that were suggested. Mrs. Viola A. Lauder was the first postmaster.

Couse Creek, Umatilla County. Couse is derived from the Nez Perce Indian word *kowish,* and is the name of an edible root used for making bread. Piper and Beattie in their *Flora of Southeastern Washington* give its botanical name as *Cogswellia cous.* It is a member of the natural order *Umbelliferae.* The stream in Umatilla County rises in the western slopes of the Blue Mountains and flows into Walla Walla River southeast of Milton. There are probably other geographic features in the state with the same name, due to the fact that the Indian found the roots plentiful in such localities.

Cove, Jefferson County. The place on Crooked River known as Cove is not inappropriately named. At this point, which is about two miles south of the old river mouth, the stream was in a canyon with an overall depth of some 900 feet. About half way down from the bluffs west of Culver, there is a bench or shelf, and this shelf is closed on the east by rock walls, forming a natural cove. Further down into the canyon there was another natural cove near the river. The county highway from Culver to Grandview crossed Crooked River at the Cove Bridge, and after passing over a rocky divide several hundred feet high, made a second descent this time to cross the Deschutes River. It then climbed a seven mile grade to the bench west of the Deschutes. In 1940 the OSHD acquired several thousand acres including the early farmsite at the Cove bridge. This was developed into The Cove Palisades State Park, one of the most popular units in the State Parks System, but with the completion of Round Butte Dam the site was flooded by Lake Billy Chinook. Portland General Electric Company financed the relocation of the park facilities to the present location on the pass between the Palisades and the Island where the old county highway crossed from Crooked River to Deschutes drainage.

Cove, Union County. Cove lies in a natural pocket where Mill Creek flows from the Wallowa Mountains, and it has an elevation of 2893 feet. It is on the east edge of the Grande Ronde Valley and at the west foot of Mount Fanny. The first family settled there on October 9, 1862, and on June 4, 1863, a post office was established which was given the name of Forest Cove, for descriptive reasons. Samuel G. French was the first postmaster and he probably suggested the name. On June 29, 1868, post office authorities eliminated the first part of the name because of the confusion with Forest Grove in Washington County. As a result of this simple action there arose in Union County a feud that lasted many years. In 1864 Union County was created, and as was frequent in pioneer days, there was contention over the location of the county seat. In 1872 a bill was passed putting the matter to a vote, and the two communities that received the highest vote in the preliminary balloting were to be eligible for the final election. Some votes were cast for Forest Cove by old timers to whom the new name did not mean much, and as a result an attempt was made to deprive Cove of its position in the contest. T. T. Geer's *Fifty Years in Oregon,* chapter XXXVI, gives an entertaining account of these matters.

Cove Orchard, Yamhill County. This is a descriptive name applied to a community in the northern part of the county. It was platted with this name by F. C. Graham of Portland.

Coverdale, Wallowa County. Coverdale is a locality in township 5 south, range 47 east, close to Imnaha River, but it is not a community. It is a campground and forest guard station. The place was named in 1909 by J. Fred McClain, a forest ranger, for Marion Coverdale, a hunter and trapper who lived on Prairie Creek in the early 1880s.

Cow Creek, Douglas County. This stream is one of the historic landmarks of southern Oregon. It is tributary to the South Umpqua River and for a large part of the way from Glendale to Riddle it occupies a narrow defile through rugged mountains. The Siskiyou line of the Southern Pacific Company shares Cow Creek Canyon with the creek. For many years very high water in the stream has been a menace to traffic. It is popularly supposed that the Pacific Highway passes through Cow Creek Canyon but this is not true. South of Canyonville the Pacific Highway follows Canyon Creek, which is also in a narrow defile. Some miles to the south the Pacific Highway crosses Cow Creek, but at this point the creek occupies a wide valley. Walling's *History of Southern Oregon,* page 424, says an immigrant recovered his cattle from thievish Indians in this valley, from which fact the creek derived its name.

Cow Gulch, Grant County. Cow Gulch drains into Murderers Creek from the north about a mile up from the mouth of the creek. It has been so called for a long time. The name was applied because the gulch was a natural collecting point for cattle.

Cowhorn Mountain, Douglas and Klamath counties. This mountain is at the summit of the Cascade Range, at the junction with the spur known as

Calapooya Mountains. In pioneer days it was known as Little Cowhorn to distinguish it from Big Cowhorn, farther south, now Mount Thielsen. It had a peculiar spire or rock pinnacle on its summit, making it resemble Mount Thielsen, and the two peaks were named because of resemblance to a cow's horns. Many years ago the pinnacle on Little Cowhorn fell off.

Cox Creek, Linn County. Cox Creek is a stream east of Albany that heads near Spicer and flows northwest to Willamette River. Between the new and the old locations of Pacific Highway East it forms Waverly Lake. Cox Creek was named in pioneer days for Anderson Cox, a prominent Linn County citizen and member of the Oregon constitutional convention. Cox took up a donation land claim on this stream. Willard Marks of Albany told the compiler in 1942 that when he was much younger, youthful cronies spent Sundays and holidays in the vicinity of this stream, doubtless fishing and otherwise obtaining physical refreshment. In 1911-13 the USGS mapped the area and applied the name Second Periwinkle Creek to the stream, apparently overlooking Cox Creek as having the first title. Thus the matter rested for three decades until local residents bestirred themselves to get the old name restored. This was done on February 26, 1942, by decision of the USBGN, and the official designation is now Cox Creek.

Cox Island, Lane County. This island in Siuslaw River is about two miles upstream from Florence. It is named for Captain William Cox, a prominent early day resident. The island was apparently acquired by Cox from one John Lyle in the 1890s. About 1902 Cox built a fine two story house to which were later added several ancillary buildings. In 1903 the Siuslaw Boom Company acquired the island and for many years used it as a headquarters for their log rafting operations on the river. In 1953 it passed to Champion International Company and in 1977 they in turn donated it to The Nature Conservancy for preservation as a natural area. In October, 1979, the two story house, the only remaining building, was listed in the National Register of Historic Places while The Nature Conservancy proceeded with plans to restore the structure so that it could be used as a base for their Cox Island preserve.

Coxcomb Hill, Clatsop County. This is the summit of the ridge south of Astoria, between the Columbia River and Youngs Bay. The compiler has been unable to learn who first applied the name. The spelling used is the customary form applied to court fools and jesters who wore an imitation coxcomb, and were frequently called coxcombs. The Astoria Column, given by Vincent Astor as the result of efforts made by Ralph Budd, then president of the Great Northern Railway Company, stands at the top of Coxcomb Hill. It depicts important events in the history of the Pacific Northwest. It was dedicated July 22, 1926, before a notable gathering. The bench mark in the base of the Astoria Column has an elevation of 595 feet, and the top of the tower dome, at the base of the finial, has an elevation of 720 feet.

Coyote Creek, Lane County. The word Coyote is used to describe a number of geographic features in Oregon, including a station in Morrow County, a butte in Baker County known as Coyote Point, and several streams. Coyote is derived from the Mexican or Aztec name *coyotl*, the word for the prairie wolf, or barking wolf of western North America, *Canis latrans*. Early settlers looked upon the coyote as a nuisance because of his noisy habits and his tendency to pay a midnight visit to the chicken roost, on which occasion he could be perfectly quiet. Creeks and points where coyotes were seen or heard had the name of the animal attached, and possibly some were named because of the fact that a coyote had been killed nearby. The Chinook jargon word for the coyote was *talapus*, with which was associated an idea of deity, or god of the plains.

Cozad Mountain, Douglas County. This prominent mountain northeast of Oakland was named for a pioneer of that neighborhood, Jonathan Cozad, who is said to have come to Oregon in the 1850s. The accent is on the second syllable.

Cozine Creek, Yamhill County. This stream rises in the eastern foothills of the Coast Range and flows through McMinnville where it joins South Yamhill River. It was named for Samuel Cozine, who was born in Kentucky in 1821 and was a pioneer of Oregon. He settled on land adjacent to the present site of McMinnville in 1849.

Crabtree Creek, Linn County. This creek rises in Crabtree Lake on the west slope of the Cascade Range and flows into South Santiam River just east of the forks of the Santiam. The lake has been known both as Wolf Lake and Crabtree but the OGNB approved the latter in the summer of 1966. The stream and lake, were named for John J. Crabtree, a native of Virginia, who crossed the plains in 1845. After wintering on the Tualatin Plains, Mr. and Mrs. Crabtree bought the William Packwood claim east of the forks of the Santiam in the spring of 1846. See editorial page *Oregon Journal*, December 3 and 4, 1924, and Carey's *History of Oregon*, volume II, page 203. The station on the Southern Pacific branch North of Lebanon was named for a cousin, Fletcher Crabtree.

Craggy Rock, Wheeler County. Named by the pioneer Maurice Fitzmaurice family who homesteaded in the Rowe Creek area in the early 1880s, Craggy Rock is a conspicuous remnant of a basaltic flow, slightly tilted, on the range skyline about ten miles south of Fossil. From the top, some 400 feet high at one point, can be obtained a grand panoramic view of the mountainous, deeply eroded lands just north of John Day River. The compiler cannot improve upon the preceeding text furnished by central Oregon author and amateur geologist Phil Brogan.

Craig Lake, Lane County. Craig Lake is near the summit of McKenzie Pass. It is a pond at the side of the McKenzie Highway. It was named for John T. Craig, one of the founders of the McKenzie toll road, who died of exposure in December, 1877, while in pursuance of his duties as a mail carrier across the pass. See article on editorial page of the Portland *Telegram*, September 17, 1925. A masonry tomb has been built over the remains of John Templeton Craig, close beside the highway, and on July 13, 1930, a bronze plaque on the headstone was dedicated in his honor. This was done by the Oregon Rural Letter Carriers Association. Robert W. Sawyer of Bend made a short talk about Craig, which is printed in *OHQ*, volume XXXI, page 261. Craig was born in Wooster, Ohio, in March, 1822, and came to Oregon in 1852. Much of his mature life was involved with the McKenzie road construction.

Craig Mountain, Union County. Dunham Wright of Medical Springs informed the compiler in 1927 that this mountain west of Union bears the name of "Pap" Craig, a pioneer resident of the county, former sheriff and also county judge.

Crale, Lane County. Crale is a station on the Southern Pacific Cascade Line southeast of Lowell. It is at the mouth of Crale Creek which in turn is named for John Crail who homesteaded there in the 1870s. A. J. Briem, a long time USFS ranger in the area, mentions several members of the Crail family in his notes on file at the OHS. Both he and the BLM records use the form Crail but it is not likely that the spelling will be corrected at this late date. C. B. McFarland of Oakridge told the compiler in the 1950s that one member of the family had a mellifluous voice and was much in demand for funerals.

Crane, Harney County. The community Crane was named because of its situation near Crane Creek and Crane Creek Gap, prominent geographic features in the Harney Valley. Crane post office was first established on June 10, 1895, with Henry C. Turner first postmaster. The office was discontinued June 30, 1903, but was reestablished October 11, 1916. It may have been moved a time or two.

Crane Creek, Harney County. Crane Creek is prominent because the valley of the stream and Crane Creek Gap to the west form a natural pass between the drainage area of South Fork Malheur River and Harney Valley. Crane Creek is doubtless named for the sandhill crane, *Grus canadensis tabida*, formerly a common summer resident of eastern Oregon. For information about this bird, see *Birds of Oregon*, Gabrielson and Jewett, page 229. A smaller bird, the little brown crane, has been known in Oregon. The California heron or blue crane is found generally in western Oregon.

Crane Creek, Lake County. Crane Creek flows into Goose Lake a few miles south of Lakeview. Crane Mountain, elevation 8447 feet, is a little to the southeast of the creek and about five miles south of the Oregon-California state line. These two features were named for an early settler. *History of Central Oregon*, page 816, says this man's name was Samuel Crane and that he settled on the creek in 1869. The compiler has a statement from John Venator of Lakeview, made in 1943, to the effect that his father bought land from a man who was called "Bill" Crane and that the creek and peak were named for him. The two Cranes may have been brothers or otherwise related. In any event, the geographic features do not seem to have been named for the bird, despite the popular notion.

Crane Prairie, Deschutes County. Crane Prairie, before the regulating dam for irrigation storage was built at its lower end, was a natural meadow, with several river channels cutting across it. The main stream flowing through the prairie is Deschutes River. When unregulated, the water stands on the prairie in the spring, but by midsummer the meadows are comparatively dry. The dam built at the south end of the prairie can be made to hold back sufficient water to flood the entire area several feet deep. This has been done to such an extent that the natural woods fringing the prairie have been water killed and present a desolate appearance. The prairie is so called because of the number of cranes that fish there. When full, the water surface of the reservoir has an elevation of about 4440 feet and covers an area of about seven square miles.

Cranston Ditch, Baker County. Cranston Ditch runs along Powder River near Keating. Edward P. Cranston came to Baker County in 1862 and was an early, prominent citizen. However, the ditch was probably named for his son, Herbert Cranston, who had a large ranch in the area and was at one time postmaster at Keating.

Crater Creek, Clackamas County. This creek runs south into Little Crater Meadows and eventually drains to Timothy Lake. It was named in the early days before the diminutive was added to Little Crater Lake.

Crater Lake, Crater Lake National Park, Klamath County. This is a mountain lake between five and six miles in diameter, with an area of about 21 square miles, situated in the caldera of the extinct volcano, Mount Mazama, on the summit of the Cascade Range. It is fed by small streams from melting snowbanks on the inner slopes of the rim, and has no visible outlet. Elevation 6177 feet. This lake is one of the deepest in the world, and soundings have been made of 1996 feet. The highest point on the rim is Hillman Peak, 8156 feet above the sea. The water is of an intense blue. Crater Lake was discovered on June 12, 1853, by John W. Hillman and a party of prospectors, and was christened Deep Blue Lake. It has been known at times as Mysterious Lake, Lake Majesty, Lake Mystery, and other similar names, but on August 4, 1869, it was named Crater Lake by a party of visitors from Jacksonville, Oregon. For information about the discovery of the lake and the various names, see *Mazama*, volume I, number 2. For information about Mount Mazama, see under that heading. For particulars about the unveiling of the tablet in memory of J. W. Hillman, see the *Oregonian*, September 21, 1925, page 1 and editorial. Crater Lake National Park was created by an act of Congress May 22, 1902, and embraces about 250 square miles of land and water. The lake may be reached by highway from Medford, Fort Klamath, or Bend. The USGS publishes a contoured map of the Crater Lake National Park, and the National Park Service issues maps and other valuable information. For many years the most comprehensive story of the park and its geology was that in USGS Professional Paper 3, *Geology and Petrography of Crater Lake National Park*, by Diller and Patton, Washington, 1902. In more recent years there has been a demand for an appraisal of the older theories about the origin of the lake and for a popular account of the business. The latter need has been met by the publication of *Crater Lake, the Story of its Origin*, by Howel Williams of the University of California, Berkeley, 1941. This volume, full of interest and well illustrated, has been followed by *Geology of Crater Lake National Park, Oregon*, also by Williams, published by the Carnegie Institution at Washington, 1942. This is a more formal publication of great scientific importance. Crater Lake is one of nature's marvels. It is more in the nature of a scenic wonder than anything else the writer has ever seen. Oddly enough it is not a real crater lake at all, because it occupies a caldera far larger than the crater of the original mountain. Crater Lake has been the subject of so

much writing and is so well known to the public that the writer does not feel
it necessary to elaborate. There are, however, two illusions about the lake
that should be dispelled. The lake does freeze over, contrary to popular
belief. Also many people discuss the possibility of underground outlets
from Crater Lake. It is doubtful if there are any. The lake receives almost
its entire supply direct from precipitation, as the drainage area is but a little
larger than the lake. It is fairly certain that evaporation accounts for all of
the outgo from the lake, without allowance for underground flow.

Crater Peak, Crater Lake National Park, Klamath County. This peak
was named by engineers of the USGS because of the extinct crater in its
summit. It has an elevation of 7265 feet.

Crater Rock, Clackamas and Hood River counties. Crater Rock is a
well-known point on the south slope of Mount Hood. It was so named
because of the smouldering crater on its north side, between the rock and
the slope of the mountain. Crater Rock was once near the central axis of the
mountain, but the preponderance of precipitation on the southwest slope
of Mount Hood has resulted in the slope wearing away more rapidly than
the other sides, which has caused the summit to be shifted gradually
northeast.

Crates Point, Wasco County. This is a conspicuous promontory west of
The Dalles, around the toe of which flows the Columbia River, changing
course from north to west. It is part of the east portal of Columbia River
Gorge. A nearby railroad station is known as Crates. These features were
named for Edward Crate, a French-Canadian who came to Oregon as an
employee of the Hudson's Bay Company in 1838. He was born in Canada
about 1821. He is reported to have been one of those who manned the boat
that brought down the river the survivors of the Whitman massacre, rescued from the Indians by Peter Skene Ogden. He served in Thomas
McKay's company in the Cayuse War of 1848. Crate stayed in Oregon City
until 1850 and in April of that year went to The Dalles to settle. The
records of the land office indicate that he made settlement on his claim on
April 1, 1851, at the place now called Crates Point, which he selected
because it was adapted to landing boats. The Crate claim was near the river
under the slope of the bluff. The name on the original application at the
land office is spelled Crete, but the family apparently abandoned this form
of spelling long ago. According to Dr. William McKay, the Indian name of
the locality of Crates Point was *Thleyap Kanoon,* which referred to a variety
of freshwater mussels. These were gathered and used for a great feast and
general good time. Crate was married to Sophia Boucher, a native of New
Caledonia, on June 24, 1844, at Vancouver. The marriage record is in St.
James parish register. She was born about 1830. The couple had 14 children, some of whom became well-known citizens of Oregon. Edward Crate
died in 1894. In a list of Indian names for localities near The Dalles, Dr.
McKay gives *Kat-ka Talth* for the mountain at Crates Point. This means
Flint Mountain.

Crawford, Yamhill County. This was a station between Lafayette and
Newberg, and was named for Medorem Crawford, who was born in
Orange County, New York, June 24, 1819. He came to Oregon in 1842

with Dr. Elijah White, and took a prominent part in the affairs of the state. He died December 27, 1891. For biographical information, see Scott's *History of the Oregon Country*. Medorem Crawford was esteemed by all who knew him and his narrative of the emigration of 1842 appeared in OPA *Transactions* for 1881.

Crawfordsville, Linn County. Crawfordsville is on Calapooia River about eight miles above Brownsville. It was named for Philemon V. Crawford, upon whose land the town was built. He was born in Madison, Indiana, in 1814, and crossed the plains in 1851. The town was founded in 1870 by Crawford and Robert Glass. Crawford died in Eugene February 1, 1901. His son, Jasper V. Crawford, was first postmaster at Crawfordsville. Information to the effect that the place was named for George F. Crawford is wrong.

Crazyman Creek, Wallowa County. Crazyman Creek follows a circuitous course through township 4 south, range 48 east, and drains into Imnaha River. In 1931 J. H. Horner of Enterprise told the compiler that the stream was named in the early 1880s because of an incident involving Jack Johnson, who was hunting. Johnson, looking down into the canyon, saw a man who acted as if demented, cavorting and jumping about. Johnson found the man to be Scotty McKinnel, who was camped nearby with John Williamson, William Ellis and Dock Fake. McKinnel's antics were caused by surprise at seeing another man in the neighborhood. The party named the stream Crazyman Creek because of this event.

Crescent, Crook County. Crescent post office was established on the Crook County list July 31, 1886, with Nettie M. Powell postmaster. The office was closed in September, 1888, but was reopened in December, 1888, and was finally closed October 1, 1890. At the first closing, the business was turned over to Prineville and at the second closing to Mitchell. The writer has been unable to get data about this office, why it was named, or where it was situated. A map of 1889 shows the place about 35 miles east of Prineville, but there are no details.

Crescent, Deschutes County. B. J. Pengra settled in the upper Deschutes Valley probably in the 1880s and undertook the development of some of his holdings. He was instrumental in having a post office established on April 10, 1893, with the name Crescent. This office was closed on April 6, 1895. Details about Crescent have been hard to gather. Pengra had a place on Little Deschutes River near the mouth of Paulina Creek and this may have been the location of Crescent post office. There is nothing to indicate that the office was at or even near the present community of Crescent. Pengra had named Crescent Lake in the Cascade Range in 1865 and the name may have stuck in his mind. There had already been a Crescent post office in eastern Crook County, but it had no connection with Pengra's office. See also under the headings Lava, Pengra and Rosland.

Crescent, Klamath County. This town, with an elevation of 4452 feet, is an important trading point on The Dalles-California Highway about 50 miles south of Bend. It was at this place that the proposed junction of the Harriman north-south and east-west railroads was to have been situated, with the name of Odell, for Odell Lake. There was another Odell in the state in the Hood River Valley, so the promoters of the townsite changed the name to Crescent for Crescent Lake, one of the large lakes of the Cascade Range located 15 miles to the west.

Crescent Lake, Klamath County. This is one of the impressive mountain lakes of Oregon, on the east slope of the Cascade Range just southeast of Diamond Peak. It is fed principally by Summit Creek, and its outlet is Crescent Creek, which flows into Little Deschutes River. Its south shore is skirted by the old Oregon Central Military Road, and the Southern Pacific Cascade line passes a little to the east of the lake. It is named because of its shape. The normal elevation is about 4837 feet, but there is some variation due to water storage. USGS Professional Paper 9 describes this lake in detail. The geography of the lake and its immediate surroundings are shown on the USGS maps of the Crescent Lake, Odell Lake and Summit Lake quadrangles. Crescent Lake was named in July, 1865, by B. J. Pengra and W. H. Odell, while making a reconnaissance for the Oregon Central Military Road. Pengra's report, dated November 29, 1865 is in part on file at the Oregon Historical Society.

Crescent Lake, Klamath County. When the Cascade line of the Southern Pacific Company was constructed, a station called Simax was established near the north end of Crescent Lake. See under Simax Bay. The railroad company later changed the name of the station Simax to Crescent Lake for the lake a half a mile to the south.

Crescent Mountain, Linn County. Crescent Mountain is about 20 miles east of Cascadia and four miles north of the South Santiam Highway. The name is descriptive and has been in use for a very long time. The mountain, as seen from the air, is a well-defined ridge, shaped like a horseshoe, open to the east. Crescent Creek, which flows eastward, drains the horseshoe. The highest point is on the southwest turn, elevation 5761 feet.

Creston, Malheur County. Creston is a descriptive name and was given because the post office was on a divide or crest east of South Fork Malheur River. The name was proposed by T. R. Beers in 1910.

Creswell, Lane County. Creswell was named by Ben Holladay for John A. Creswell, postmaster general from 1869-74. John A. Creswell was born in Maryland in 1828, and served as U. S. representative and as senator before joining the cabinet. In 1874 he was appointed counsel of the United States in the Alabama Claims matter and served until 1876. He died December 23, 1891. Creswell station was named by Holladay several years before the post office was established. The date of establishment of Creswell post office is uncertain, due to difficulty in reading postal records. It may have been on March 4, 1873 or possibly on March 4, 1876. Creswell has an elevation of 543 feet and is on the line of the Southern Pacific Company and the Pacific Highway. Creswell Butte, about a mile to the south, has an elevation of 982 feet.

Creswell Canyon, Marion County. This is a canyon in the hills north of Jefferson and its lower end is crossed by the Pacific Highway East just north of Steiwer Hill. It was named for Donald C. Creswell, a pioneer of Oregon. He was born in Tazewell County, Illinois, in 1830, and his land office certificate 4993 says that he arrived in Oregon on October 10, 1852. He cultivated his donation land claim near this canyon beginning October 31, 1853.

He was married to Mary Ann Rush on November 30, 1851, in Louise County, Iowa. He spelled his name without a "t."

Crews Creek, Baker County. Willis W. Crews came to Baker County in 1880 and settled at the mouth of this creek near Keating. Crews built the first lime kiln in the Baker area.

Cribbins Hill, Coos County. This is a small hill south of Myrtle Point. It was named for William Cribbins, a pioneer settler nearby.

Cricket Flat, Union County. J. H. Horner of Enterprise told the compiler in 1927 that this flat was named for the very large crickets which infested this place in the early 1870s. William Knight, whose parents settled at what is now Cove, Oregon, in the 1860s, informed Horner that his father drove hogs from Cove to Cricket Flat to feed on these crickets. Cricket Flat was considered to be a fine hog pasture. General O. O. Howard crossed this flat in the late summer of 1878 and camped about three-quarters of a mile west of the present site of Elgin.

Crims Island, Columbia County. Broughton discovered Crims Island and nearby islets in the Columbia River on October 26, 1792, and named them Bakers Islands for the second lieutenant of Vancouver's ship *Discovery*. This seems to be the same island that Lewis and Clark named Fannys Island, in honor of Frances, William Clark's youngest sister. Wilkes gives the name Gull Island in the atlas accompanying *U. S. Exploring Expedition,* volume XXIII, Hydrography. James F. Crim took up a homestead on the island and received his patent February 10, 1871. The USBGN adopted the name Crims Island on October 5, 1927, at the suggestion of the compiler of these notes. With the lapse of time Wilkes' name Gull Island has become transferred to a small isle north of the west end of Crims Island.

Cripple Creek, Clackamas County. This stream flows into the Clackamas River from the east in township 5 south, range 6 east. In 1927 W. C. Elliott, civil engineer of Portland, told the compiler that a surveyor in his employ cut his foot with an ax at this point in 1897.

Criterion, Wasco County. It is understood that a number of homesteaders suggested several names to the Post Office Department when the application was made for a post office at this point. The first preference was for Three Notches and the second was for Criterion. The Post Office Department objected to the first name because it was made of two words and adopted the second name. The writer has been unable to learn why this name was suggested. The word means a standard by which to judge of the character or excellence of an object or thing. Pioneer stockmen called the locality Three Notches because of three cuts in a prominent juniper tree, still standing in 1946, east of the highway. Criterion Summit is the highest point on The Dalles-California Highway between The Dalles and Redmond. The bench mark just west of the highway has an elevation of 3362 feet and the highway summit is a couple of feet lower. This was once known as Lakeview Summit, but why is a mystery. There are no lakes within miles of the place. Criterion post office was established in September, 1913, and closed in June, 1926.

Croisan Ridge, Marion County. Croisan Ridge and Croisan Gulch lie not far from the east bank of the Willamette River just southwest of Salem. These features were named for a prominent Marion County pioneer family. The first member of this family to live in Oregon was born in Bavaria in 1812 of Huguenot parents. He emigrated to the United States in 1839 and came to Oregon over the Applegate route in 1846. After various pioneer experiences, including a trip to California, he settled on a donation land claim southwest of Salem in March, 1850. See editorial page, *Oregon Journal*, December 18 and 19, 1925. He died September 14, 1875. The original application for the land claim shows the name spelled in various ways, including Croisant, Croisint and Crossint. The given names of this pioneer settler were John Henry. While the land office records seem to indicate that the spelling Croisint was the correct one, present members of the family state that the name was really Croisant. The second generation in Oregon found the name so frequently mispronounced that the final "t" was dropped and the name has become Croisan. The Croisan family tradition says the name originally meant growing, the French for which would be *croissant*. *Croissant* is also the French for crescent.

Cromwell, Union County. Old maps show Cromwell on the railroad at a point between Telocaset and North Powder. The post office was established July 24, 1882, and was closed December 2, 1884. Julius T. Cromwell was the only postmaster and the office was named for him. Polk's *Gazetteer* for 1886-87 says that Cromwell was also called Antelope Valley. The post office was close to Antelope Creek wagon bridge on the original homestead of Robert Brannan.

Crook, Crook County. Crook, a place on the headwaters of Bear Creek, was named for the county. Available maps show the office moved about a little, apparently depending on who would accept the postmastership. Crook post office was established June 16, 1886, with Nancy Hinton postmaster. The office was finally closed in November, 1908.

Crook County. Crook County was created October 24, 1882, from a part of Wasco County after Lake County had been taken off on the south. (*Special Laws* of 1882, page 178.) For many years it was one of the large counties of central Oregon, but is now diminished in size as the result of the creation of Deschutes and Jefferson counties. It has an area of 2980 square miles, according to the U. S. Bureau of the Census. Prineville is its county seat. Crook County was named for George Crook, major-general in the U. S. Army, who was born near Dayton, Ohio, September 8, 1829; died at Chicago March 21, 1890. He was graduated from West Point in 1852. Prior to the Civil War he served in the West and was wounded in 1857 in the Pit River country. He made a brilliant record in the Civil War, and afterwards in Indian wars of the West. See Scott's *History of the Oregon Country*, volume II, page 184, and volume V, pages 223-25.

Crook Peak, Lake County. Crook Peak was undoubtedly named for Major-General George Crook, who fought Indians throughout south central Oregon in several campaigns. See under Crook County. Crook was in the territory west of Warner Valley near what is known as Crook Peak in 1867. See Bancroft's *History of Oregon*, volume II, page 535, *et seq.* The USC&GS gives the elevation of Crook Peak as 7834 feet.

Crook Point, Curry County. This point is in approximate latitude 42° 15', and is within 20 miles of the Oregon-California boundary. It is also about five miles south of Cape Sebastian. The point is moderately low, but terminates seaward in a rock knoll 160 feet high, with lower ground immediately back of it. It was named for A. H. Crook, who for many years operated a large stock ranch nearby.

Crooked Creek, Klamath County. This is a stream near Klamath Agency, tributary to Wood River. It bears a descriptive name. The Klamath Indian name is *Yanaldi Koke,* literally "Stream bordered by the Yanaldi Ridge." *Koke* is the Klamath word for stream. For additional information see under Agency Hill.

Crooked Creek, Lake County. This stream drains Antelope Valley north of Lakeview and flows north into Lake Abert. The correct name is Crooked Creek and not Crook Creek. There is a story to the effect that it was named for Major-General George Crook but such is not the case. It owes its name entirely to its physical characteristics.

Crooked Creek, Malheur County. This stream has a descriptive name. It joins Owyhee River a few miles below the mouth of Jordan Creek in the vicinity of the place called Rome. Captain George B. Currey of the First Oregon Volunteer Cavalry calls the stream Gibbs Creek in the Oregon Adjutant General's *Report,* 1865-66, page 35, in compliment to Governor Addison C. Gibbs. Currey established Camp Henderson on Gibbs Creek May 26, 1864. The name Gibbs Creek has not prevailed.

Crooked Finger Prairie, Marion County. This prairie is southeast of Silverton. According to Down's *A History of the Silverton Country,* page 3, it bears the name of a Molalla chief. He is supposed to have died at Grand Ronde Agency, although there is another story to the effect that he was shot near the Clackamas River.

Crooked River, Crook, Deschutes and Jefferson counties. This stream was named during the fur trading period, and the name bestowed is unusually appropriate. Arrowsmith's map of North America, London, 1824, with pen corrections probably to 1832-33, shows Crooked River by name and in good detail. A map prepared under the direction of Col. J. J. Abert, dated 1838, shows the name Crooked River. This map is attached to the Cushing report, more properly described as 25th Congress, 3rd Session, House report 101, entitled *Territory of Oregon,* with supplemental report. USGS bulletin 252, by Dr. I. C. Russell, is the standard handbook of the geology of central Oregon and contains much valuable information about Crooked River. In 1925 the USGS made an extended survey of the topography and geology of Crooked River between its mouth and Trail Crossing, with particular reference to the remarkable springs that feed the stream in this section. The state of Oregon and the U. S. Reclamation Service published a bulletin in 1915 entitled *Ochoco Project* which contains much other information about Crooked River. For information about the highway bridge over Crooked River near Terrebonne, see *Oregonian,* August 1, 1926, section 7, page 1.

Crooks, Union County. Crooks is a station on the Union Pacific Railroad in the Blue Mountains. It was named for William Crooks, who was born in New York City in 1831, and died in Portland December 17, 1907. He was for some years an official of the railroad. For his biography, see the

Oregonian, December 18, 1907. Colonel William Crooks was the son of Ramsay Crooks, of the Astor overland party. For adventures of Ramsay Crooks, see Irving's *Astoria.* He was born in Scotland in 1787, and died in New York City June 6, 1859. He was credited with being "the strongest man, next to Mr. Astor himself, who at any time stood at the helm in the home office at New York." (Chittenden.)

Crooks Creek, Linn County. This stream is in the extreme north part of the county and is intermittent in character and its waters eventually find their way into Willamette River about eight miles north of Albany. This stream was named for John T. Crooks, who took up a donation land claim nearby.

Cross Hollows, Wasco County. Cross Hollows is just south of Shaniko and is named for the prominent right angle crossing of two canyons. It was the location of Sherar's station where John Ward kept the hotel. Cross Hollows post office was established May 23, 1879. For further information see under Shaniko.

Cross Keys, Jefferson County. Much research has been expended on the origin of the name of Cross Keys post office, first established on the Wasco County list, but applicable to a locality now in the extreme north part of Jefferson County. The locality is just south or southwest .of the mouth of Cow Canyon, and close to the banks of Trout Creek. The post office was doubtless moved from time to time. An office with the name Trout Creek was established July 3, 1878, with Jasper A. Friend postmaster. William Heisler became postmaster on October 17, 1878, and on February 13, 1879, Robert Ashby became postmaster. On this date the name of the office was changed to Cross Keys. Edward G. Bolter became postmaster on July 8, 1879, and ran the office until September 24, 1898, when it was closed to Ridgeway. It was reopened a few weeks later and ran until July 31, 1902. There is a notion in central Oregon that Cross Keys was named for the place in Wales, but so far the compiler has found no confirmation of the statement. It has been asserted that either Heisler, Ashby or Bolter applied the name, but these assertions are also without confirmation. Statements that Cross Keys was several miles south in the valley of Hay Creek are not confirmed by any maps in the possession of the compiler. A later office called Willowdale was not far from the original site of the Trout Creek office.

Croston, Marion County. Croston was the name of the post office on the east bank of Willamette River at the east landing of Halls Ferry. This landing was several miles down stream from Independence. The post office was established December 22, 1884, with Benjamin F. Hall first of three postmasters and continued in service until March 19, 1901. When it was established, Croston post office was put on the Polk County list, but this must have been in error, for there is nothing to indicate that it ever operated in Polk County. It is obvious that the name was intended to indicate a place where there was a crossing, in this case a ferry.

Crow, Lane County. The postmaster at Crow informed the writer that the community was named for one Andy Crow who was first postmaster, although this information does not agree with data furnished by the postal authorities, who state that the post office at Crow was established November 6, 1874, with Alexander Wood first postmaster. However, members of the Crow family were prominent pioneer settlers in that part of the county, and the community doubtless bears the name of one of them. Will G. Steel told the compiler that the word Crow was a literal translation of an Indian word *Andaig*, applying to the locality, but search failed to bring any confirmation of the statement.

Crow Creek, Wallowa County. Crow Creek is northeast of Enterprise and flows northward to join Joseph Creek. According to J. H. Horner of Enterprise, the stream was named by A. C. Smith and Jasper Matheny in the late 1870s because they found the birds so thick in the aspen groves along its banks.

Crow Ridge, Wallowa County. This ridge lies between Joseph and Deer creeks in the northeast part of the county. It was named for Bert Crow, first settler on the ridge in the early 1880s. He was the first man to take a wagon from this ridge down to Grande Ronde River.

Crowcamp Creek, Harney County. Crowcamp Creek rises on the west slope of Crowcamp Mountain, elevation 5887 feet. This high ground on the east side of Harney Valley has been known as the Crowcamp Hills. Second-Lieutenant John F. Noble, Company G, 1st Oregon Cavalry, a member of Captain John M. Drake's command, kept a diary of the expedition from Fort Dalles to the Harney Valley. They camped at "Smith's Camp" the nights of June 16 and 30, 1864. The spot is where Crowcamp Creek emerges from the hills into Harney Valley and Noble's diary, on file at the OHS Library, under the latter date calls the stream Crow Creek. See *OHQ*, volume LXV, page 56 *et seq*. Old timers in the area say that the hills and creek were named for Rankin Crow, a stock herder working for Todhunter & Devine, pioneer cattlemen. Crow discovered an excellent spring in the locality, and camped there. Later the Crowcamp Ranch was established nearby. However he could not have predated 1864.

Crowfoot, Linn County. Crowfoot is a crossroads community on the South Santiam Highway about two miles south of Lebanon. It has not had a separate post office, but has been served through Lebanon. All the available evidence says that the locality got the name Crowfoot because the roads intersecting there came together in a pattern that suggested the track left by a crow's foot. This is shown clearly by the USGS map of the Lebanon quadrangle. Katherine Harris, in a column headed "Off the Record," in the Lebanon *Express* for January 23, 1947, gives a good deal of history about the place called Crowfoot. It was named many years ago, apparently by Hester Sturdevant, an early resident of the locality. The Grange Hall, one of the important buildings at Crowfoot was formerly the old college hall at Sodaville. When the college was abandoned, the building was moved to Crowfoot.

Crowley, Polk County. This station is on the Southern Pacific Company line between Holmes Gap and Rickreall, and was named for Solomon K. Crowley, an early resident of the neighborhood. He was born in Missouri in 1833 and came to Oregon in 1852. See Hines' *Illustrated History of the State of Oregon*, page 1012.

Crowley Creek, Malheur County. Crowley Creek was named for G. B. Crowley who with his son James Crowley settled along its banks in 1874. In May, 1878, during the Bannock War, Indians burned their home but the family escaped injury. Crowley post office was established March 2, 1911 and closed January 29, 1935.

Crown Point, Multnomah County. In 1884 Lorens Lund, a native of Schleswig Holstein, took up a homestead on the high ground above and including Crown Point. His family farmed the homestead for many years and when the Columbia River Highway was built, Lund donated the land on which the Vista House was constructed. His daughter, Thora Lund, told the writer in 1973 that her father always referred to the top of the bluff as "The Point" and he would often walk down from the farmhouse on a summer evening to watch the sunset. Gertrude G. Jensen, an authority on the Columbia River Gorge, says that Marshall Dana of the *Oregon Journal* first used the present name when discussing plans for the Vista House. He said it would "put the crown on Crown Point". The compiler has been unable to find when this first use occured but Crown Point is used by Samuel Lancaster in *The Columbia*, and in numerous newspaper accounts of the construction and dedication of the highway prior to World War I. Crown Point was designated a National Natural Landmark in August 1971, and the Vista House, a remarkable example of Jugendstil architecture designed by Edgar M. Lazarus, was entered in the National Register of Historic Places on November 5, 1974.

Crown Rock, Wheeler County. Crown Rock was a post office not far from the present site of Clarno. Huntley post office was established February 28, 1876, with Joseph Broughton first postmaster. The compiler has not been able to get the history of the name. The name of the office was changed to Pine Creek on June 23, 1876. This name was of course for Pine Creek, a prominent stream flowing into John Day River from the east. On December 10, 1877, the name was changed again, this time to Crown Rock for a prominent geological formation in the vicinity, apparently a rimrock of basalt.

Crutcher, Malheur County. Crutcher post office was established on the Malheur County list March 20, 1900, with Elliott W. Crutcher first and only postmaster. The office bore his family name. It was in operation only until August 13, 1901, when it was closed to Jordan Valley. The compiler has not been able to learn the exact location of this office but obviously it was in the east part of the county and south of Vale.

Crutcher Bench, Clackamas County. This side hill bench lies just north of the junction of Sandy and Zigzag rivers. It was named for H. P. Crutcher, who filed a claim on the bench about 1890.

Cruzatte, Lane County. Cruzatte, a station on the Cascade line of the Southern Pacific Company, was named for a member of the Lewis and Clark party, Peter Cruzatte. Lewis and Clark spelled his name in several ways, and named a stream in Washington for him, now known as Wind River.

Cryder Butte, Klamath County. Cryder Butte is south of Davis Lake in the extreme north part of the county. It was named for W. W. Cryder, the first and only supervisor of the short lived Paulina National Forest prior to World War I.

Crystal, Klamath County. This name was originally applied to a fine stream flowing into Upper Klamath Lake near Pelican Bay. In 1925, Postmaster S. A. Brown reported that he thought the stream was named in 1891 by G. W. Malone and John Young. Crystal, as the name of the office, was proposed by the first postmaster, D. G. Brown, in 1894, when it was established through his efforts.

Cucamonga Creek, Harney County. This stream rises on the northwest slopes of Steens Mountain, and enters Kiger Creek, a tributary of Donner und Blitzen River. The name is derived from Cucamonga Creek, San Bernardino County, California, and was applied to the Harney County stream by Mrs. Dolly Kiger. Cucamonga is an Indian name and according to Mrs. Nellie Van de Grift Sanchez, in *Spanish and Indian Place Names of California,* was originally applied to a native village about 42 miles east of Los Angeles, and later to a land grant. Mrs. Kiger wrote the compiler in 1927 that she lived in the Harney Valley from 1874 to 1878 and that one of her neighbors, Mace McCoy, had formerly lived in California and frequently spoke of Cucamonga wine, a variety made in the southern part of the state. Mrs. Kiger named Cucamonga Creek because she liked the sound of the word.

Cullaby Lake, Clatsop County. A lake on Clatsop Plains, about two miles long, fed by small streams. The present outlet is through a ditch into Skipanon River. Many years ago this lake drained through Neacoxie Creek, which first flowed northward and then turned south and emptied into the estuary of Necanicum River. Shifting sands have from time to time interfered with the flow of Neacoxie Creek and thus changed the drainage from Cullaby Lake. In recent times extensive cranberry culture has developed along the shores of the lake. Its elevation is near sea level. Silas B. Smith is authority for the statement that the Indian name for this lake was *Ya-se-yama-na-la-tslas-tie*. See *OHQ,* volume I, page 322. It was later named for Cullaby, a well-known Indian character on Clatsop Plains. Cullaby had a peculiar light complexion, and was a son of the Indian whom Lewis and Clark saw on the last day of the year 1805, and whom they described as "freckled with long dusky red hair, about 25 years of age, and must certainly be half white at least."

Culp Creek, Lane County. Culp Creek is a post office as well as stream tributary to Row River southeast of Cottage Grove. Culp Creek was named for John Culp, who settled in this neighborhood a few years prior to 1900. A logging company established a camp there and called it the Culp Creek camp, and when the post office was established February 24, 1925, the name naturally attached itself to the new office. Geo. E. Potter, a local merchant, was the first postmaster. For additional information, see Cottage Grove *Sentinel,* March 28, 1929.

Cultus Creek, Douglas County. Cultus Creek heads on the South Myrtle Creek divide and flows north into Cavitt Creek. Former USFS ranger Fred Asam informed the compiler in 1968 that the name was applied by a U. S. Land Office surveyor called Sturdevant who had considerable trouble finding his way about in the rough terrain and who considered the whole area very troublesome. For the Indian meaning see under Cultus Lake.

Cultus Lake, Deschutes County. *Cultus* is a Chinook jargon word, quite expressive, meaning bad or wholly worthless. It is used in many places in the Pacific Northwest, generally because of the lack of one or more of the pioneer traveler's greatest needs, "wood, water and grass." Cultus Prairie meant that the horse feed was poor. The word found its way into the jargon from the Chinook Indian word *kaltas*. In addition to Cultus Lake in Deschutes County, there is also a Little Cultus Lake and Cultus Mountain. The latter was doubtless named for the lakes. Cultus has been spelled in many ways, including Kultus, Cultos and Cultis, but the USBGN has adopted the form Cultus.

Culver, Jefferson County. In the latter part of 1900 at a dinner party of old settlers living in the Haystack country O. G. Collver was requested to make an application for a post office and to act as postmaster. A number of names of old settlers were submitted to the department, and Culver was adopted, this being the ancestral name of Mr. Collver. O. G. Collver was born at Roseburg February 10, 1854, and went into central Oregon in June, 1877. He was appointed postmaster of Culver October 31, 1900. The site of Culver post office as first established was about five miles east of the present town. O. G. Collver died in Portland November 14, 1939. For a short biography, see Madras *Pioneer*, November 23, 1939.

Cumley Creek, Linn County. This stream is west of Detroit. Charles C. Giebeler of Detroit, wrote the compiler in 1927 that the creek was named for a nearby resident, but that he could secure no detailed information about the man.

Cummings Creek, Grant County. Cummings Creek is a tributary, from the north, of John Day River, 13 miles east of Dayville. J. E. Snow, of Dayville, informed the compiler in October, 1927, that James Cummings settled on this stream in pioneer days. He came from Maine and was a bachelor. Members of his brother's family still live in the neighborhood. James Cummings' house was one of those burned by the Indians in 1878. The stream was named for him.

Cummins Creek, Lane County. This creek and Cummins Ridge to the south are in the extreme northwest corner of the county. They were named for F. L. Cummins, an early homesteader. The form Cummings is wrong.

Cunningham Canyon, Morrow County. This canyon empties into Butter Creek at the Umatilla County line. It was named for Charles Cunningham, the founder of the Cunningham Sheep and Land Company, who was born in County Galway, Ireland in 1846. Cunningham came to the United States in 1864 and after service in the navy took a land claim at the mouth of the canyon in 1878. He was a prominent person in the livestock industry and at one time was president of the *Woolgrowers Stock Journal*.

Cunningham Creek, Coos County. This stream is north of the town of Coquille. It was named for Evan C. Cunningham, a pioneer settler on its banks.

Cupids Knoll, Polk County. In November 1972, the voters of Colorado disapproved a measure to complete the financing for the 1976 Winter

Olympics which had been awarded to Denver. This necessitated choosing a new location. Amid the well organized and advertised appeals from the world's great winter sports areas one tiny voice from the Willamette Valley was audible. The good burghers of Monmouth with pardonable pride and commendable financial acumen made one last, desperate effort to save these events for the western United States. However, the International Olympic Committee felt the proposal to hold all alpine events on 321 foot high Cupids Knoll with a total budget of $2.25 did not quite come up to their august standards. A full account of these proceedings can be found in Section 2, *Oregon Journal*, December 18, 1972. Cupids Knoll was named in the days when automobiles were less plentiful and students at the then Oregon Normal School were wont to seek seclusion within walking distance. The compiler's unrelated namesake, Scott McArthur of Monmouth, was kind enough to pass on this information before the knoll lapsed back into obscurity. He added that the city had terminated the romantic activity by installing a chain link fence.

Cupit Mary Mountain, Lane County. Cupit Mary Mountain, elevation 6175 feet, is a prominent point just west of Waldo Lake. In March 1943, C. B. McFarland, for many years a ranger with the USFS at Oakridge, furnished the compiler with information about Cupit Mary. She was the youngest daughter of an Indian known as Old Moses, who lived at an Indian village near what is now Oakridge. She was not well thought of by other Indians. Her name, Cupit, is reported to be an Indian word meaning last, indicating her position among Old Moses' children. It is doubtless the same as the Chinook jargon word which Gibbs gives as *ko-pet*, meaning stop, the end or enough. Old Moses was probably discouraged. *Ko-pet* is accented on the second syllable.

Cupper Creek, Grant County. Cupper Creek is in the northwest corner of the county and flows south into North Fork John Day River a few miles west of Monument. The name of this stream perpetuates a type of story that is full of human interest, but perhaps not romantic enough to get the attention it deserves. The history of the immigration of the Cupper family illustrates what it took to develop that part of Oregon that produces livestock. Henry Adams Cupper and his wife, Cordelia Harriet Cupper, together with three small children, left England in January, 1877, and after a stormy voyage across the Atlantic, reached the end of rail travel at Redding, California. They took stage to Linkville, now Klamath Falls, and Cupper got a job of sorts in the Poe Valley. They spent the winter in Ashland and in the spring started with wagon and team looking for a location to settle. They journeyed near what is now La Pine, and got lost, but finally reached Farewell Bend where they "loaded up with water and crossed the desert to Prineville." From Prineville they continued northward, crossing John Day River at McDonald Ferry and then turned southeast through Lone Rock to Heppner. At Heppner they undertook to freight a load of provisions in to Bill Welch. Dodging the Indians, they delivered the cargo, and were so impressed with the Welch Ranch, the natural meadows and the abundance of game that they arranged to buy the squatters' right. Welch is said to have assumed that they would not stay, and he would get the place back. In the meantime the Indians had "broken out" and had attacked Long Creek, and so many settlers returned to Heppner that they swept the Cuppers along with them. The Cuppers remained at Heppner six weeks and then returned to the ranch and braved the rest of the Indian troubles. Cupper brought sheep into the cattle country, which did not endear him to his neighbors. They raised a large family and lived on the ranch until 1918. They moved to Salem and celebrated their golden wedding anniversary on October 1, 1922. Mr. Cupper died in January, 1923, and Mrs. Cupper in 1938, when she was 90 years old. Cupper Creek is still fifty miles from a railroad and some seven miles from a post office.

Curiosity Creek, Wallowa County. Curiosity Creek flows into Imnaha River in section 32, township 2 north, range 48 east. It was named in 1883 by Hugh Conahar for a curious limb of an alder tree. The branch grew back into the tree like a jug handle.

Currant Creek, Jefferson and Wasco counties. The old road from The Dalles to Canyon City passed along Currant Creek before reaching John Day River. The creek was named in early days for the profusion of wild currants that grew along its banks and *The History of Central Oregon,* page 637, describes a pack train ambush in 1862 when Indians secreted themselves behind these bushes.

Currin Creek, Clackamas County. Currin Creek is a tributary of Eagle Creek near Estacada. It was named for the Currin brothers mentioned under Currinsville.

Currinsville, Clackamas County. This was a station on the now abandoned line of the Portland Electric Power Company two miles north of Estacada. It was named for George and Hugh Currin, who were pioneer settlers in Clackamas County and took up donation land claims near this point. For editorial comment about the members of the Currin family, see the *Oregonian,* November 19, 1943. See also editorial page *Oregon Journal,* September 25, 1928. A post office named Zion was established in this general locality on June 24, 1874, with William H. H. Wade first postmaster. The name of the office was changed to Currinsville on January 8, 1884, with George J. Currin postmaster. The office was closed February 16, 1906. Zion post office was obviously named by a biblical enthusiast.

Curry County. Curry County was created December 18, 1855, and was taken from the south part of Coos County. It was named for George Law Curry, who was born at Philadelphia July 2, 1820; died Portland July 28, 1878. On arrival at Oregon City he acted as editor of the *Oregon Spectator* from October 1, 1846, until the end of 1847, and in April, 1848, published the *Oregon Free Press.* He represented Clackamas County in the provisional legislature of 1848-49, served as chief clerk of the territorial council of 1850-51, and represented Clackamas in the house of the territorial legislature in 1851. In 1853, President Pierce appointed Curry secretary of the territory of Oregon. A few days after taking that office, he became acting governor through the resignation of Governor Joseph Lane. In December, 1853, Governor John W. Davis arrived, but in August, 1854, Davis resigned, and Curry was acting governor until appointed governor a few months later. He served as governor until the territory became a state, in

1859. "He was of singularly amiable disposition, honorable, and gifted with a versatility of such degree that whatever he undertook was well performed." (OPA *Transactions* for 1878, page 80.) He was editor of the Portland *Advertiser,* the third daily newspaper at Portland, first published January 1, 1861, and the *Evening Journal,* January 25 to April 25, 1876. For biography of himself and his wife, Chloe Boone Curry, see the *Oregonian,* February 12, 1899. For his narrative of early history of Oregon, *ibid.,* March 15, 1872, page 3; February 28, 1872, page 3. Curry was territorial governor when Curry County was created. For early history of Curry County, see the *Oregonian* for February 14, 1886, by O. W. Olney. See also Scott's *History of the Oregon Country,* volume V, page 222, for a tribute to Curry. *The Pioneer History of Coos and Curry Counties,* edited by Orvil Dodge, contains much interesting material about early days in Curry County. Bancroft, in *History of Oregon,* volume II, page 415, says it was first proposed to name this county Tichenor, for Captain William Tichenor of Port Orford, a member of the legislative council from Coos County. Tichenor declined this honor saying that his constituents wanted the new county named for Governor Curry.

Curtin, Douglas County. This place was named for Daniel Curtin, who operated a sawmill there in the early 1890s. Curtin is on the Southern Pacific railroad about seven miles northeast of Drain.

Cushing Falls, Wasco County. Cushing Falls are on Fifteenmile Creek a short distance above its mouth. They carry the name of Milo M. Cushing who came to The Dalles in 1852 with the Fourth United States Infantry Regiment. Cushing is credited with erecting the first hotel and commercial building in The Dalles and for many years he lived near the falls that now bear his name. He was born in Truxton, New York in January 1820, and died in The Dalles in 1906. In 1854 he married Mary Piggott, the first marriage in Wasco County after its formation.

Cushman, Lane County. Cushman is a station on the Coos Bay line of the Southern Pacific Company on the north bank of the Siuslaw River. It is about a mile east of Cushman community, which was formerly Acme. It was named by the railroad company for C. C. and I. B. Cushman, local residents. The company already had an Acme on its lines and did not wish to duplicate that name, and after the station was changed, the post office authorities followed suit. The name Acme was originally applied by Mrs. W. A. Cox, an early settler. It is said that Mrs. Cox dreamed she was to live in a place called Acme, so when her husband platted a townsite in Lane County, the place was called Acme. Cushman post office was established July 3, 1916 by change of name from Acme. The office was closed in 1961 with papers to Florence.

Cusick Mountain, Wallowa County. Cusick Mountain is some three miles southeast of Eagle Cap and forms the south buttress of Hawkins Pass. It is named for William C. Cusick, the pioneer botanist of eastern Oregon. Cusick came to Oregon in 1853 as a small boy and spent much of his adult life near Union where he amassed a substantial botanical collection. He died in 1922. For further information see Corning's *Dictionary of Oregon History,* page 68.

Custer, Coos County. Custer post office in the south part of the county was named for Custer M. Hermann, son of Cass M. Hermann, a prominent Coos County pioneer. The office was at the Cass Hermann stock ranch on the mail road south from Myrtle Point to Eckley, Curry County, and was in the hills just north of the head of Rowland Creek. Custer Hermann did not live to maturity. Custer post office was established July 19, 1893, with Cass M. Hermann first and only postmaster. The office was closed May 17, 1901. A. H. Bender of Myrtle Point, a nephew of Cass M. Hermann, sent in the information about this name.

Cutler City, Lincoln County. Cutler City, just south of Taft and on the east shore of Siletz Bay, has had a remarkable development as a resort town. It was started by Mr. and Mrs. George Cutler, who are said to have acquired the property from "Uncle Charley" DePoe, a Siletz Indian. The Cutlers formerly lived near Dallas. Mr. Cutler died in 1913 and Mrs. Cutler in 1939. For obituary of Mrs. Cutler, see *Oregon Journal* for June 19, 1939. On December 8, 1964, Cutler City voted to become part of a new community to be called Lincoln City.

Cutsforth Corner, Morrow County. This spot three miles north of Lexington is named for a well-known local resident, Orville Cutsforth.

D River, Lincoln County. D River connects Devils Lake with the Pacific Ocean at Lincoln City. It is the shortest river in the world, about 200 yards long, although it is difficult to define exactly where the lake ends and the river begins. U S 101 crosses D River and the entire course of the stream may be seen from a viewpoint adjacent to the bridge.

Dad Spring, Wallowa County. Dad Spring is in section 19, township 2 north, range 50 east. It was named for Elbert B. Wilson, who was generally known as Dad or Snake River Wilson. He came to Wallowa County in July, 1900, and ranged cattle near this spring in the summers. This spring was at one time known as Brigham Spring because it was on Mormon Flat.

Dairy, Klamath County. This place was named by William Roberts, pioneer settler. He is said to have lived in the Rogue River country and also in the Klamath country as early as 1865. He selected the word Dairy because he had previously lived in a community by that name in an eastern state. The post office of Dairy was first established May 8, 1876, with Roberts postmaster. The valley in which Dairy is situated was at one time known as Alkali Valley, but now bears its Klamath Indian name, Yonna Valley. See under that name.

Dairy Creek, Multnomah County. Dairy Creek is on the east part of Sauvie Island. It drains Marquam Lake into Columbia River. It was named for a small dairy operated nearby by a French-Canadian employee of the Hudson's Bay Company. This was in pioneer days. For additional data see under Marquam Lake.

Dairy Creek, Washington County. Dairy Creek and its tributaries are an important part of the Tualatin River drainage. The main stream is formed by two long branches which join a few miles northeast of Forest Grove. West Fork Dairy Creek rises near Buxton and East Fork Dairy Creek rises in the extreme south part of Columbia County north of Mountaindale. Dairy Creek has been so called for a long time. While the evidence is not positive, it is probable that the stream was named by employees of the Hudson's Bay Company during the fur trading period. The company operated a dairy on what is now Dairy Creek, but the compiler does not know the exact location. On July 5, 1882, George B. Roberts, retired Hudson's Bay Company employee, wrote to Mrs. Frances Fuller Victor: "Wyeth's Fort William. . . was located with the view to easy communication with the Tualatin plains. Our people used that road over the hills and we had a dairy there on what is now called Dairy creek." Roberts is referring to the Logie Trail. The date the dairy was established is uncertain, but by inference it must have been prior to 1840.

Daley Creek, Jackson County. In September, 1947, Miss Venita Daley of Medford sent the compiler data about her grandfather, William Carter Daley, and the geographic features in the east part of Jackson County named for him. These features include Daley Creek and Daley Prairie. The creek, which is about four miles long, starts at a spring in the south part of the prairie, and flows west to join Deadwood Creek. Daley Creek is in township 37 south, range 4 east. The creek and the prairie were named many years ago in memory of an elk hunting expedition organized by Daley, an Ashland pioneer of 1864, and his brother-in-law, Samuel B. Hamilton, a Jacksonville miner of 1856. These two built a hunting cabin near Daley Creek about 1873, and for several years packed in from Ashland. Daley shipped a considerable number of beaver and other pelts from Ashland to San Francisco, where there was a ready sale. Daley abandoned the campsite and cabin after game laws became effective and bought a ranch about a mile above Lakecreek post office, where he farmed for nearly 35 years. He died at his home in Eagle Point in 1930, aged 84. He was a well-known resident of the Little Butte Creek area.

Daley Lake, Tillamook County. This lake is near the ocean about two miles southwest of Oretown. It is known as Fletcher Lake and also Daley Lake. D. R. S. Daley was an Oregon pioneer. He came to Tillamook County in the 1870s and took up a homestead near the south end of the lake. Fletcher Lake is a modern name and in the opinion of the writer is not the correct one.

Dallas, Polk County. Dallas is said to have been called Cynthia Ann originally. It was settled in the 1840s on the north side of Rickreall Creek, but was moved more than a mile south in 1856 because of inadequate water supply. It was named for George Mifflin Dallas (1792-1864), vice-president of the United States from 1845 to 1849. Dallas was vice-president during Polk's administration, and when a name was needed for the county seat of Polk County, it was but natural that Dallas was chosen. A narrow gauge railroad was built into Dallas in 1878-80 as a result of a county seat fight with Independence. Independence was after the county seat honor, but citizens of Dallas raised $17,000 and secured the branch line, and this settled the contest for the seat of government. Dallas post office was established October 22, 1852, with John E. Lyle postmaster. Attention is called to discrepancies in the available information about the early name Dallas. It appears both as Cynthian and Cynthia Ann. An article in the *Oregon Spectator,* February 10, 1852, makes sarcastic reference to Cynthian. It is reported that this name was chosen by a Mrs. Lovelady in memory of a place in Kentucky, but the name in Kentucky is Cythiana. Mrs. Harriet McArthur and Judge C. H. Carey of Portland and Captain O. C. Applegate of Klamath Falls informed the compiler in 1927 that the place was named for Mrs. Jesse Applegate, whose given name was Cynthia Ann. The Applegates lived in Polk County at the time the place was named.

Dalreed Butte, Morrow County. Dalreed Butte is in the extreme west part of the county about two miles north of Willow Creek. Roy Scott, postmaster at Cecil, Oregon, wrote the compiler in 1927 that this butte received its name about 50 years previously. It was named for Dal Reed, who lived near the butte at that time.

Daly Creek, Baker County. Daly Creek is south of Richland. The stream was named for an early settler. Dunham Wright of Medical Springs told the compiler that Daly came to Oregon in 1862. See also letter from H. E. Daly on editorial page, the *Oregonian,* October 7, 1927.

Daly Spring, Crook County. This spring on Williamson Creek in the Bear Creek Buttes was named for the Dealy family who settled there about the time of World War I.

Damascus, Clackamas County. Mrs. John C. Elliott of Clackamas, Clackamas County, wrote the compiler in September, 1945, that Damascus was named by Henry Pedigo, who did so because of a verse in the Bible. The compiler has not been able to identify the verse. Damascus post office was established August 26, 1867, with John S. Fisher first postmaster. It was closed in August, 1904.

Damon Creek, Grant County. This stream flows into John Day River from the north, west of Mount Vernon. Patsy Daly of Prairie City told the compiler it was named for Robert Damon, who settled nearby in the 1860s.

DaMotta Branch, Douglas County. In the early days this tributary of Deer Creek just east of Roseburg was known as Goose Creek. Phil DaMotta came to Roseburg before the turn of the century where he was a barber by profession and a horse breeder by hobby. His farm was on this fork of Deer Creek and the name soon changed to DaMotta Branch. George B. Abdill of Roseburg furnished this information and added that the form DeMonty was incorrect.

Danebo, Lane County. Edward F. Bailey of Eugene told the writer that this area west of Eugene was named in the early 1900s for the large number of Danish settlers.

Danger Bay, Crater Lake National Park, Klamath County. Will G. Steel, the authority on Crater Lake, told the compiler that this name was ill chosen, as he never saw the time that danger befell anyone boating on Crater Lake. However, it is an old name, and will doubtless remain.

Daniels Creek, Coos County. This stream flows into South Fork Coos River about seven miles east of Coos Bay. It bears the name of an early settler, William Daniels, who lived near the mouth of the creek. S. B. Cathcart wrote in 1929 that Daniels left the locality many years ago.

Danner, Malheur County. It is reported that this town was originally known as Ruby, but the postal authorities would not accept the name for a post office. Several other names were submitted including Danner, which was suggested in honor of J. H. Danner, one of the pioneer settlers in the community. Robert E. Danner, his son, was the first postmaster. The office was established April 3, 1920.

Dans Creek, Curry County. M. S. Brainard of Brookings told the writer that this creek near Illahe was named for a well-known character named Indian Dan who homesteaded nearby in the 1860s.

Dant, Wasco County. In 1950 Dant & Russell, Inc. established a perlite mine near Frieda on the Oregon Trunk Railway in Deschutes Canyon. Frieda was renamed for Thomas Dant, president of Dant & Russell, Inc. The mine has since been abandoned and according to reliable reports from a visiting fisherman little commercial activity remains.

Dardanelles, Jackson County. Dardanelles was a place of importance in pioneer days in the Rogue River Valley, but the community passed into discard. Dardanelles post office was established October 19, 1852, with William G. T'Vault postmaster. T'Vault was a prominent pioneer of southwest Oregon and started this settlement south of and across Rogue River from the present town of Gold Hill. At this point the river passes from a wider valley into a much more constricted section, with hills close on each hand. Apparently this natural setting suggested the Strait of the Dardanelles to T'Vault, although it could hardly be more than a suggestion. T'Vault was a newspaper editor of prominence and had a wide range of interests. The original Dardanelles gets its name from the city of Dardanus. It is said that the first quartz mill in southern Oregon was installed near Dardanelles in 1860. There are interesting references to this event in Walling's *History of Southern Oregon,* pages 329 and 379.

Darling Canyon, Gilliam County. Darling Canyon empties into Thirtymile Creek halfway between Condon and Lonerock. Linus W. Darling built one of the first buildings in Condon in 1887 where he operated a drug store and later served as postmaster. Darling also patented a Timber Culture claim and owned land near the head of Darling Canyon.

Darrow Rocks, Polk County. These rocks are in the Willamette River about five miles downstream from Salem, and Darrow Chute is just below the rocks. The name is spelled Darrough on some maps, but this does not seem to be correct. Hedda S. Swart of Salem kindly investigated the history of the name in 1943 and found that William and Marion Darrow conveyed some property at this locality to William McGee in 1874. This record is found in the deeds in volume 8, page 481, at the Polk County courthouse, Dallas. Swart had this spelling confirmed by Mr. and Mrs. John Schindler, local residents of long standing. Army engineers, in their work along the river, use the spelling Darrow and not Darrough.

David Hill, Washington County. David Hill, about three miles northwest of Forest Grove, was named for Frederick W. David who homesteaded there in 1876. His daughter, Mary, married the son of Harmon Thatcher for whom nearby Thatcher is named.

Davidson, Josephine County. Davidson post office was near Applegate River in the extreme east part of the county, about five miles southeast of Murphy. The office was named for J. E. Davidson, whose place was next door to the post office. Davidson, a younger brother of Elijah J. Davidson the discoverer of the Oregon Caves, was born in Independence, Polk County, September 6, 1866, and in March, 1947, was living in Grants Pass. Davidson post office was established June 12, 1900, with Alice R. Bailey first and only postmaster. The office was closed to Murphy October 11, 1907. Mr. Davidson has informed the compiler that the office was kept in the country store of W. S. Bailey, and Mrs. Bailey was the official postmaster. The office was closed by the advent of rural free delivery.

Davidson, Morrow County. On April 26, 1893, Davidson post office was established on the Morrow County list with Gamaliel Davidson first and only postmaster. The office was named for the postmaster, and after a relatively short life, it was closed August 27, 1897, with all papers to Eightmile. The post office was about ten miles west-northwest of Hardman and just north of Rock Creek.

Davidson Hill, Hood River County. This is the hill on the west side of Hood River Valley north of Tucker Bridge. It was named for William Davidson, who settled at this point about 1880.

Davidson Hill, Polk County. Davidson Hill is two miles west of Buena Vista. It was named for Carter T. Davidson, born in 1802, a pioneer of Oregon of 1852, who settled on a donation land claim nearby in the fall of the year he came to Oregon. It has an elevation of about 425 feet.

Davin Spring, Crook County. This spring is about six miles east of Paulina, and was named for John Davin, a Frenchman who came to Paulina from Nevada about 1890. The name is not connected in any way with that of John Devine, pioneer stockman of southeast Oregon.

Davis Canyon, Morrow County. Davis Canyon empties into Eightmile Canyon. It takes its name from Charles N. Davis who ranched there in the first part of the century.

Davis Creek, Deschutes County. Davis Creek is the official name given by USBGN to the outlet of Davis Lake. The stream flows underground beneath a superficial lava flow nearly two miles before coming to the surface. It is joined by the flow of other large springs, apparently not fed by the lake and is tributary to Deschutes River. Davis Creek is below the water surface of Wickiup Reservoir at higher stages and resumes its flow only as the reservoir is drained.

Davis Creek, Grant County. This stream is just west of Austin. Patsy Daly of Prairie City wrote the compiler in 1927 that it was named for Jim Davis, an early day miner.

Davis Creek, Wallowa County. Davis Creek flows into Snake River in township 2 north, range 51 east. It was named for Ben Davis, who had a squatter's claim on its banks.

Davis Creek, Wallowa County. This stream, which is about ten miles long, flows northward and joins Swamp Creek in the extreme southwest corner of township 4 north, range 45 east. It was named in the 1870s for James Davis, hunter, trapper and Indian interpreter.

Davis Creek, Wasco County. Davis Creek is a small tributary of Standard Hollow near Emerson on Fifteenmile Creek. It was named for D. O. Davis who took up land along it in the 1880s. Davis was a businessman in The Dalles who, in common with others, availed himself of the Homestead Act to increase his land holdings.

Davis Lake, Deschutes and Klamath counties. This is one of Oregon's important mountain lakes and has an area of a little over four square miles. It is fed principally by Odell and Moore creeks and the USGS gives its normal elevation as 4389 feet. The south shore of the lake is a grassy flat, but the north end is dammed by a rough flow of jagged lava. The outlet, Davis Creek, is subterranean for nearly two miles. After it comes to the surface, it is joined by streams from other large springs, apparently not fed from the lake, and makes its way to Deschutes River. Davis Lake was named for one "Button" Davis, a stockman of Prineville, who was formerly from Shedd in Linn County. He ran stock in the vicinity of the lake, according to information furnished in 1927 by W. P. Vandevert of Bend. Davis Mountain, just east of the lake, was named for the same man. The names were applied probably before 1880.

Davis Spring, Wallowa County. This spring is in section 29, township 3 north, range 47 east. It was named for Frank Davis, who ranged sheep there.

Day, Sherman County. Day was a station on the line of the Union Pacific Railroad near the mouth of John Day River. It was originally known as John Day, but this name was confused with the station John Day in Clatsop County, and also with the post office John Day in Grant County, so the railroad cut the words in half. For the origin of the name see John Day River. The name of the station in Clatsop County was changed to Van Dusen.

Day Creek, Douglas County. William P. and George W. Day both took up donation land claims in Camas Valley in 1853. The brothers were prominent early settlers and William was the first man to plant and raise a garden in the valley. The creek was undoubtedly named for the family rather than either of the individuals.

Day Ridge, Wallowa County. Day Ridge is a well-known divide between Mud and Courtney creeks, southwest of Flora. It bears the name of Len and Foster Day, who homesteaded there in the early 1890s. William Fornier was the first white settler on the ridge.

Days Creek, Douglas County. Walling, in his *History of Southern Oregon,* page 441, says this stream was named for Patrick and George Day who settled near the mouth of the creek in 1851. It is an important tributary of South Umpqua River northeast of Canyonville. The post office near the mouth of Days Creek was for some years called Day's Creek, but the name was changed to Days Creek about 1890.

Dayton, Yamhill County. Dayton was settled in the winter of 1848-49 by Joel Palmer and Andrew Smith, and was named for Dayton, Ohio, the former home of Smith. Dayton post office was established on June 5, 1851, with Christopher Taylor postmaster. Edward L. Bill became postmaster on May 25, 1852; Joel Palmer on August 2, 1852; and Cyrus Jacobs on August 16, 1853. The principal landmark at Dayton is the Grand Ronde Blockhouse in the northwest corner of the City Park. This structure was built by Willamette Valley settlers on Fort Hill in the Grand Ronde Valley in 1855 and 1856. In 1856 federal troops established Fort Yamhill adjacent to Fort Hill. Among the famous officers stationed at this military establishment were P. H. Sheridan, A. J. Smith, D. A. Russell, and W. B. Hazen. Fort

Yamhill was abandoned as a military post in the 1860s and the blockhouse was moved to Grand Ronde Agency. After Grand Ronde Agency was abandoned by the government the blockhouse fell into disrepair. John G. Lewis, a patriotic citizen of Dayton, fearing that the building would disappear, secured permission from authorities to move the logs to Dayton, which was done in 1911. The structure was rebuilt and dedicated to Joel Palmer, a founder of Dayton and donor of the City Park. General Palmer was one of Oregon's outstanding pioneer citizens and was superintendent of Indian affairs, 1853-57. See under Palmer Peak.

Dayville, Grant County. The original site of the Dayville post office was some three miles west of the present location. The first office was established December 8, 1868, with James N. Brackett first postmaster. The place was named for John Day River, which was named for John Day, a member of the Astor expedition. It is of interest to note that during a period of 50 years there were but three postmasters at Dayville, the second being John W. Lewis and the third J. E. Snow. The present site of the community is at the mouth of South Fork John Day River.

Dead Indian Creek, Jackson County. This creek and Dead Indian Mountain are in Jackson County, and the Dead Indian Road extends from near Ashland past these two geographic features to Upper Klamath Lake in Klamath County. It is said that about 1854 some settlers from Rogue River Valley found two dead Rogue River Indians in some deserted wigwams near the creek, and supposed that Klamath Indians had killed them in a fight. They named the stream for their discovery. For many years the road did not extend over the Cascade Range, but in 1870 Captain O. C. Applegate and a band of Klamath Indians opened the road all the way to Pelican Bay on Upper Klamath Lake.

Dead Mountain, Lane County. Dead Mountain is the high ground north of Salmon Creek east of Oakridge. C. B. McFarland of the USFS said that this was formerly known as Green Mountain but took its present name after the forest fires of 1883, 1898 and 1910.

Dead Point Creek, Hood River County. This stream is a tributary of West Fork Hood River, not far from Dee. Various maps have shown it as Dry Point Creek and Burnt Creek. Ross Winans, an early resident of the vicinity, informed the compiler that the pioneer name of this stream was Dead Point Creek, and in his opinion that was the correct name. Winans never heard it called Burnt Creek. The stream was named in contradistinction to Green Point Creek nearby, as one creek rises on a point covered with green timber and the other on a point covered with dead timber.

Deadhorse Canyon, Clackamas County. This canyon drains into North Fork Molalla River. Dee Wright, a native of Molalla, told the compiler that in pioneer days several stray horses were lost in this canyon and perished, hence the name. Deadhorse Butte nearby took its name from the canyon.

Deadhorse Ridge, Wallowa County. Deadhorse Ridge is a prominent divide between Bear Gulch and Sheep Creek, and the northeast end is in township 1 south, range 48 east. Deadhorse Lake is on the ridge. According to J. H. Horner of Enterprise this lake was named by George A. Wilson and James Simmons in the late 1880s. They turned out a blooded stallion to range and the horse ran himself until too warm and was found dead in the lake.

Deadman Canyon, Wasco County. Deadman Canyon was named because when the area was first settled in the 1880s a body was found in a cave near the mouth of the canyon where it empties into Ward Creek north of Willowdale.

Deadman Creek, Wallowa County. This creek in township 5 south, range 46 east, does not seem to have been named for a corpse. The stream drains into Imnaha River, and according to J. H. Horner of Enterprise, it was named by James Dale in the early 1890s, because he said he might just as well be dead as to be in such a lonesome place. He was a sheepherder for Aaron Wade.

Deadman Pass, Umatilla County. Deadman Pass is a gap on Emigrant Hill southeast of Pendleton and its formation is shown at the east edge of the USGS map of the Cabbage Hill quadrangle. This is not a pass for east-west travel on the Oregon Trail but is a transverse pass across the ridge, hence a dip on the highway. It gets its name as the result of an incident of the Bannock War, in July 1878, recounted by Fred Lockley on the editorial page of the *Oregon Journal,* August 8, 1931. George Coggans, a traveler en route from La Grande to Pendleton and four teamsters, James Myres, Olney P. McCoy, Charles McLoughlin and Thomas Smith, were killed by Indians in the vicinity of what is now known as Deadman Pass.

Deadman Spring, Wasco County. This spring, in the northwest part of Warm Springs Indian Reservation, was named because an outlaw Indian was killed there many years ago by a posse.

Deadwood Creek, Lane County. Deadwood Creek, which drains a considerable area in the western part of the county, flows into Lake Creek which in turn flows into Siuslaw River. Deadwood Creek got its name in early days because of the dead timber snags adjacent to its banks, the result of extensive forest fires in the Coast Range. Deadwood post office, named for the stream, was established April 15, 1884, with Thomas Pope first postmaster. The office was near the mouth of Deadwood Creek, It was discontinued to Greenleaf June 15, 1914, but reopened February 15, 1950.

Deady, Douglas County. Until World War II a flag station on the Southern Pacific line north of Roseburg and located on his donation land claim was the only geographic feature in Oregon to bear the name of one of the state's most distinguished citizens, Judge Matthew P. Deady, 1824-93. This station is now long abandoned leaving nothing to honor Deady, a pioneer of 1849, and for more than a half century a member of the bench and bar of his adopted state. He was president of the constitutional convention in 1857, and later prepared codes of civil and criminal procedures. He was for more than 30 years United States district judge for Oregon. For an estimate of his life by Harvey W. Scott, see Scott's *History of the Oregon Country,* volume V, page 188. Deady Hall at the University of Oregon, now a National Historic Landmark, bears his name. He was president of the board of regents of the university for many years.

Dean Creek, Curry County. This creek flowing through Gold Beach was named for George Dean, an early settler and county clerk in the 1860s.

Dean Creek, Grant County. Dean Creek, east of Canyon City, was named for a man who operated a small sawmill there during the mining excitement of the 1860s.

Dean Point, Tillamook County. Dean Point projects southward along the west side of Nehalem River just south of the town of Nehalem. It bears the name of George Dean, a well-known settler in the Nehalem area, who at one time owned land on the point.

Deardorff Mountain, Baker and Grant counties. Fleming Byars Deardorff settled in this part of eastern Oregon about 1870 and this mountain was named for him. It is 7207 feet high. There is a Deardorff Creek just southwest of the mountain, flowing into John Day River. The creek is in Grant County. Deardorff was a son of Joseph M. Deardorff, a pioneer of 1853, who settled near Oakland, Douglas County, where members of the family still reside.

Deathball Rock, Lane County. This rock is southeast of Blue River. It received its name because of an attempt made by a surveying party cook to bake some biscuits. It appears that he was not entirely successful. Deathball Mountain is a little southwest of Deathball Rock and seems to have been named after the rock was named.

Dedman Ranch, Wheeler County. Robert H. Dedman owned this ranch at the head of Dedman Canyon southeast of Fossil. The style Deadman is wrong.

Dee, Hood River County. Dee was named for Thomas D. Dee, a business associate of the late David C. Eccles and a stockholder in the Oregon Lumber Company. The name was used when the lumber company mill was built at Dee in 1906.

Deer Creek, Douglas County. This stream rises in the hills east of Roseburg and joins South Umpqua River at Roseburg. Its name dates back to pioneer days and the community of Roseburg was known as Deer Creek as late as 1854. The name of the place was subsequently changed to Roseburg because of the settlement of Aaron Rose, who settled at the site of the present city of Roseburg on September 23, 1851. He crossed the plains to Oregon from Michigan in that year. See under Roseburg.

Deer Island, Columbia County. Deer Island, in the Columbia River, was named by Lewis and Clark. They first visited the island on November 5, 1805, on their way down the Columbia, and again on March 28, 1806, on their return. It was on the second visit that the party had good luck getting venison. Captain Lewis noted in his diary that the Indian name for the island was *E-lal-lar,* or Deer Island. The compiler is unable to identify this Indian word. The town of Deer Island, which is on the mainland, was named for the island.

Deer Meadows, Clackamas County. R. S. Shelley and Ralph Lewis of the USFS named this meadow about 1906 when they watched a doe and fawn feed and play one Sunday morning.

Deering, Josephine County. In June, 1948, Fred Ahlberg was kind enough to write the compiler that Deering post office was situated in the southeast quarter of section 11, township 41 south, range 9 west, in the extreme southwest part of Josephine County and about a mile and a half north of the California state line. This location is about a quarter-mile east of the Redwood Highway. The post office was established in November, 1902, and was discontinued in December, 1908. David S. Webb was the only postmaster. The compiler is of the opinion that Deering post office was named for the Deering school nearby and the school was named for a family of early settlers. In July, 1948, L. C. Moffitt, Josephine County school superintendent, wrote that he got this information from Lincoln Savage, who was superintendent about 1900.

Degner Canyon, Jefferson County. Trout Creek flows through this canyon near its headwaters. Ernest and Jonathan Degner both homesteaded nearby about the time of World War I.

Del Norte, Harney County. *Del Norte* is a Spanish expression meaning of or from the north. On July 12, 1888, a post office named Del Norte was established in Harney County, with Francis M. Jordan first and only postmaster. The office was discontinued July 20, 1889, with papers to Burns. In September, 1946, Archie McGowan of Burns told the compiler that Del Norte post office was in the vicinity of Saddle Butte a few miles northwest of Crane. The Jordan family lived at a place generally called the Crossing, on Malheur Slough, and moved away many years ago. No one in the locality appears to know just why the post office name was selected.

Delaine, Lake County. Delaine post office was established August 5, 1912, with Walter S. Lyon first and only postmaster. The office was closed to Plush on August 15, 1913. The place was in section 9, township 35 south, range 26 east, and east of the Warner Valley. It is now in the Hart Mountain Antelope Refuge. This post office was named for the Delaine sheep, as Lyon ran sheep of that breed in the area. Dr. John Leonard Lyon of Lakeview was a partner in the enterprise and a brother of the postmaster. Delaine is a word that has been used to describe a number of things. It refers to a fine dress goods, and also to a superior type of soft wool. Delaine Merino sheep were developed in southwest Pennsylvania and in areas in the neighboring states of West Virginia and Ohio.

Delake, Lincoln County. A. C. Deuel, postmaster at Delake in 1925, told the writer that Delake was the name agreed upon by himself and Judge Frank L. Mann, a Lincoln County resident, because it was the way many local Finnish people pronounced Devils Lake. Delake post office was near Devils Lake. It was established in January, 1924. On December 8, 1964 Delake voted to become part of a new community to be called Lincoln City.

Delco Creek, Wasco County. This stream heads on the ridge west of Cow Canyon and runs westward towards Deschutes River. It is named for Johnny Delco who herded sheep for Hinton and Ward in the late 1800s. The family is one of Oregon's oldest and descends from Jean Baptiste Delcour who came from Montreal as a fur hunter for the Hudson's Bay Company and later took a donation land claim on French Prairie.

Delena, Columbia County. Delena is on the Columbia River Highway east of Clatskanie. Postal records show that Delena post office was established April 22, 1892, with Lincoln J. Meserve first of nine postmasters. The office was discontinued March 15, 1922, although its operation was not continuous for the three decades indicated. In November, 1947, W. N.

Meserve of Grays River, Washington, wrote the compiler that Lincoln J. Meserve, his brother, named the post office. W. N. Meserve says that his brother found the name in a classical dictionary or in a book on mythology. Stories that the place was named for a town in Nebraska are wrong, says Mr. Meserve. Also it has been reported that Delena was the name of a girl in the Meserve family, but Mr. Meserve says that this is not a fact. The compiler has been unable to find any trace of a place called Delena in Nebraska.

Dell, Malheur County. An army map of 1887 shows a place called Dell about 10 miles northwest up Willow Creek from Vale. Dell post office was established in June, 1881, with George W. Perkins first postmaster. The office continued in operation until February, 1911. The compiler does not know why it was named unless the title was descriptive of some locality on Willow Creek. The difficulty in getting localized information about a place like Dell is shown in the following quotation from the *Illustrated History of Baker, Grant, Malheur and Harney Counties,* page 553, written as of about 1902: "Dell is located at Cole's ranch. . . on Willow Creek. It is simply a post office, which shifts from one ranch to another as the postmasters die or resign, or the national administration changes. In this portion of Willow Creek Valley are located some of the best hay and grain ranches in the county." To add to the difficulty about the history of the post office Dell is the fact that old postal records indicate the existence of an office called Snake that may have been a predecessor of Dell. Snake office was established April 5, 1881, with James S. Stark first postmaster. The records seem to show that the name was changed to Dell within a couple of months, but the date and nature of the change are not clear. The name Snake seems to indicate that the office was on or near Snake River. The office may have been moved from Snake River not far away to Willow Creek when the name was changed.

Dellmoor, Clatsop County. Dellmoor was a station and locality about three miles north of Gearhart and just east of the Oregon Coast Highway. It was named for the late J. S. Dellinger of Astoria, editor of the *Astorian.* Dellinger, among other things, was interested in cranberry culture on Clatsop Plains, and it is probable that he devised the name Dellmoor himself. The style Delmoor is wrong and not in accord with the original spelling.

Dellwood, Coos County. Dellwood is a place on South Fork Coos River about 12 miles airline east of Coos Bay. The locality was formerly called Idlewood, but when the post office was established November 2, 1940, postal officials would not approve of that name because of possible confusion with Idleyld in Douglas County. Several new names were suggested, but the form Dellwood was chosen because it was not unlike the old name. Leo A. Lindros was the first postmaster and kindly sent the compiler the above information.

Delmar, Coos County. Delmar is a well-known name for a place on Isthmus Slough a few miles south of Coos Bay and a little to the north of Coaledo. It is on the Oregon Coast Highway and is near the mouth of a drain coming in from the west that is sometimes called Delmar Creek or Delmar Gulch. The best available information is to the effect that Delmar was named for Delmar Hennessey. The Hennessey family was interested in a coal mine project near the head of the gulch. Delmar post office was established March 16, 1914, with Lemuel V. Cole first of five postmasters. The office was discontinued July 15, 1918, but there was still a store at Delmar in 1947 and a little commercial activity in the vicinity.

Delp Creek, Lane County. This is a tributary of Fall Creek. It was named for a mining prospector, George Delp.

Dement Creek, Coos County. This stream is a tributary from the west of South Fork Coquille River. It was named for Samuel M. Dement, who was said to have been the first white man who actually settled with his family in South Fork Valley. He was born in Ohio, October 5, 1822. He came to California in 1852, and settled in Oregon in 1853. He died in December, 1885.

Democrat Gulch, Josephine County. This is an historic place southeast of Kerby. It was named during the pioneer gold mining days of the Illinois Valley because of the political views of some of the prospectors.

De Moss, Sherman County. De Moss was a station on the Union Pacific Railroad. There was at one time a post office there by the name of De Moss Springs. The station was named for a celebrated pioneer family of the county, members of which styled themselves the "Lyric Bards." They were musical entertainers, and made extended tours when wheat growing did not require their labors at home. They also operated a recreation park in connection with the springs. Professor James M. De Moss was the leader of the "Lyric Bards." He was born in Indiana May 15, 1837. He was reared in Iowa and in 1862 moved to Powder Valley, Oregon. He located in Sherman County in 1883. He is said to have been the founder of the town of North Powder, Baker County, where he kept the stage station.

Dencer, Marion County. Dencer post office was in operation for a few years in the Jacob Dencer home at a point about a mile or so southwest of the community called Liberty, and was named for the first postmaster. The office was established February 12, 1889, with Dencer postmaster and was continued until April 20, 1892, when the name was changed to Rosedale. When the name was changed the office was moved two miles southeast to the Rosedale community on Battle Creek.

Denio, Harney County. Aaron Denio settled in this locality in 1885 and the place was named for him. The post office was established in September, 1888. The community was located within a few yards of the Nevada border and after World War II, a number of business establishments relocated to the south in Nevada to avail themselves of more liberal liquor and gambling laws. The post office was also moved and opened on the Nevada list on December 31, 1950. Aaron Denio was born in Illinois in 1824 and after various rovings, emigrated to California in 1860. For twenty five years he engaged in milling, mining and farming in California and Nevada, then settled in the extreme south edge of Oregon. He died at Denio in 1907. For additional information about his ancestry and life see *OHQ*, June, 1946, pages 200-201. For more recent information on Denio see a story by Mark Kirchmeier in the *Oregonian*, June 16, 1979, page D3.

Denmark, Curry County. The writer was informed by the postmaster

of this community in 1925 that the first settlers were natives of Denmark,
hence the name adopted. He must refer to Captain N. C. Lorentzen, who
settled there in 1878, according to Dodge's *Pioneer History of Coos and Curry
Counties.* Lorentzen and his daughter Lena were drowned near Humboldt
Bay in December, 1892, at the time of the wreck of the barge *Majestic.*

Denning Spring, Umatilla County. This spring on the upper reaches
of Pearson Creek was named for Dick Denning, a contract logger who built
the road up the creek.

Dennis Creek, Lane County. Dennis Creek is named for W. B. Dennis
who opened the nearby Black Butte Mine in 1898. The mine produced
mercury from what was once described as the largest low grade cinnabar
deposit in the world but operations were sporadic and ceased many years
ago.

Denson Canyon, Umatilla County. Forest H. Denson settled along this
canyon near McKay Creek before World War I.

Dent, Columbia County. Dent was the name used for a post office
from June, 1892, to October, 1898. Frances M. Fuller was the only postmaster. This office was a few miles west of Rainier and close to Beaver Creek. It
was closed out to Delena. W. N. Meserve wrote in November, 1947, that the
place was apparently given the family name of Mrs. U. S. Grant, but Mr.
Meserve could give no reason except that the name Dent was terse. Members of the Meserve family were reared at Delena on Beaver Creek and
their opinions about the history of the area are doubtless reliable.

Denver, Clatsop County. Denver, a locality in the Nehalem Valley, was
not named for the Colorado city of the Plains, but for William J. Denver,
the postmaster. The post office was established May 26, 1884, and discontinued October 31, 1888. The business was turned over to the Jewell office,
and little remains in the place.

Denzer, Lincoln County. This post office was named for its first postmaster, Frederick C. Denzer. It was established April 10, 1909.

Depoe Bay, Lincoln County. Depoe Bay is a popular place on the Oregon Coast Highway. The exact origin of the name has been obscured by
time, although there is a general knowledge of the matter. The bay and
other geographic features in Lincoln County, including a creek flowing
into Yaquina River near Toledo, appear to have been named for an Indian
who was associated in some way with an early-day army or Indian supply
depot in the Siletz territory. He assumed or was given the name Depot, but
it appears to have been entered on the records as Depoe, and that is the
form now generally used. The spelling Depoe has been adopted by the
USBGN for the community, bay and two streams, while Depot is correct for
the stream near Toledo. The name is generally pronounced without stress
on either syllable. For editorial comment about the name Depoe Bay, see
the *Oregonian,* September 9, 1936, where it is said that the bay was named
for Willie DePoe, a Siletz Indian. He was also known as "Old Charley" and
his wife's name was Matilda. An interesting item about the bay appears
under a Pendleton dateline in the *Oregon Journal* for November 8, 1935,
and recounts the fact that Dr. F. W. Vincent of Pendleton and his grandfather cruised up the Oregon coast north from Newport in 1878 and

observed a break in the shoreline. Lowering the sails of their 40-foot boat, they finally rowed it into the little harbor. "We found there the anchor chains of a sea-going craft, two headlights and the letters 'U.S.,' so we named the little spot 'Wreckers Cove'," said Dr. Vincent. That name has not prevailed.

Depot Slough, Lincoln County. This slough forms the tidal end of Depot Creek and empties into Yaquina River near Toledo. At one time the slough was spelled Depoe and the creek Depot but the OGNB decision of June, 1961, and USBGN *Decision List 6203* eliminated this inconsistency. Both features were named for William DePoe who is discussed under Depoe Bay. The spelling Depot may have been selected originally to avoid confusion with North and South Depoe Bay Creeks that empty into Depoe Bay.

Derby, Jackson County. Derby, a locality northeast of Eagle Point, was named for William H. Derby, a well-known local settler. The post office was established January 23, 1892, with Derby first of a series of five postmasters. The office was closed May 15, 1919, with papers to Eagle Point. The locality name continues in use, even though the post office has been closed.

Derby Creek, Tillamook County. Derby Creek rises on Giveout Mountain and flows southeast to Nehalem River east of Cochran. In 1977 the OGNB voted to name this stream for Captain George Horatio Derby, U.S. Topographical Engineers. Derby was stationed in Oregon as a lieutenant in 1855 when he reconnoitred the military road from Astoria to the vicinity of Forest Grove. Part of the alignment followed or came near to this creek. Derby graduated from West Point in 1846. He was wounded in the Mexican War but his military career was undistinguished and he died in 1861 prematurely at age 38. However, his memory is preserved through his alternate career as a humorist. His writings under the pen name John Phoenix, Esq., appeared in the *Knickerbocker* magazine and the *Atlantic*, often accompanied by his own illustrations. For further information see article by Robert Frazier in the Eugene *Register-Guard*, June 26, 1977, page 17A, and *The Veritable Squibob* by George R. Stewart.

Derr Meadows, Wheeler County. Derr Meadows west of Antone and the creek running through them were named for Martin Derr, a rancher from Caleb, who had summer range in the area.

Derry, Polk County. This station on the line of the Southern Pacific Company just east of Rickreall, was named by James W. Nesmith shortly after the railroad was built, for Derry, New Hampshire, where his family had resided. In 1912 an effort was made to change the name of Derry to Loganberry. For editorial on the subject, see the *Oregonian*, August 12, 1912. See also news items and letters, *ibid.*, August 13, 14, 1912.

Deschutes, Deschutes, Sherman and Wasco counties. There have been several post offices and localities in Oregon named Deschutes, in compliment to Deschutes River. In 1943 the name was used for a place between Redmond and Bend, no longer a post office. A post office named Deschutes Bridge was in operation from March 3, 1860, to December 6, 1860, with John Moran postmaster. It was on the Wasco County list, but Fred W. Wilson of The Dalles informed the writer that the office was doubtless at the east end of the old toll bridge over Deschutes River, near the mouth, and therefore in what is now Sherman County. A post office named Deschutes was established in July, 1868, with Ezra L. Hemingway postmaster. Hemingway owned land at what is now known as Sherars Bridge and at one time owned the bridge itself. This post office was in that place. Joseph H. Sherar became postmaster on January 11, 1872, and the name was changed to Sherars Bridge January 4, 1883. An office called Deschutes was established February 20, 1888, with Rosa Burrell postmaster. This office operated until October 14, 1893, and according to Judge Wilson was probably at the east end of the bridge at the mouth of the river, in the same location as the Deschutes Bridge office first mentioned above. In later years a railroad station named Deschutes was established at the mouth of Deschutes River and when the railroad was built up the Deschutes Canyon a station called Deschutes Junction was established about a mile and a half east of Deschutes. When the railroad reached central Oregon, Fred S. Stanley asked that the name Deschutes be given a station between Redmond and Bend. Stanley was accommodated and the two older stations at the mouth of the river were changed. Deschutes was named Miller and Deschutes Junction was named Sherman, which was changed to Ainsworth in October, 1930. In the meantime Bend post office was established January 18, 1886 with John Sisemore postmaster. This office was probably in the Sisemore cabin in the south part of what is now Bend. Sisemore asked for the name Farewell Bend, but the postal authorities objected to two words. After some other incumbents, William H. Staats became postmaster of the Bend office on April 18, 1899. The records are not quite clear from this point. Staats apparently tried to change the name of the office to Pilot Butte, and this was ordered May 13, 1901, but for some reason the new name was not actually used. Staats' next move was to get the name of the Bend office changed to Deschutes on December 30, 1902. It is reported that Staats took the office away from the Sisemore place to his own locality further downstream, but the date of this move cannot be determined from the records. On March 7, 1904, a new Bend office was established near the former Pilot Butte Inn and began to compete with Staats' Deschutes office. The Deschutes office operated until June, 1906, when it was discontinued. The name Deschutes was given to the office between Redmond and Bend in July, 1911.

Deschutes County. This county was created December 13, 1916, out of a part of Crook County. Bend is the county seat. Deschutes County was named for Deschutes River which was known during the period of fur trading as *Riviere des Chutes* or River of the Falls. For derivation of the name see under Deschutes River. The County has a land area of 3041 square miles.

Deschutes River, Deschutes, Jefferson, Klamath, Sherman and Wasco counties. Lewis and Clark discovered the Deschutes River on Tuesday, October 22, 1805, and referred to it by an Indian name *Towornehiooks*. See Thwaites' *Original Journals of the Lewis and Clark Expedition*, volume III, page 147. However, on their return journey the explorers called the stream Clarks River, presumably for William Clark. (*Ibid.*, volume IV, page 292, and also atlas volume, map 32, part I, and map 40.) Neither of these names prevailed. The Klamath Indians apparently referred to the Deschutes as *Kolamkeni Koke*. *Koke* was a general name for stream, while *kolam* referred to a wild root used for food, possibly a species of *Aralia*. *Keni* was a suffix meaning place. A literal translation would be stream of the place where the kolam grew. In the fur trading period the stream was known as *Riviere des Chutes* or *Riviere aux Chutes*, meaning River of the Falls. As a result of the modern tendency to simplify geographic names, the expression is now universally written Deschutes. The trappers applied their name because the river flowed into the Columbia near the falls of that river and not because of any falls in the Deschutes itself. The following two quotations show this very clearly: ". . . I lost no time in joining Mr. Finan McDonalds party who I found encamped on the River of the Falls of the Columbia, about four days march from the Main stream." Peter Skene Ogden under date of October 10, 1826, in *Fur Trade and Empire*, page 281. . . . "3. Mr. Ogden Hunted last winter in the Space of country Bounded on the north by the Head waters of the River of the Columbia falls, on the west by the Umqua, from thence East to the River Malheur in the Snake Country." John McLoughlin, August 11, 1827, in *The Letters of John McLoughlin, First Series*, page 49. F. N. Blanchet, in *Historic Notes*, 1883, page 14, has a paragraph about the name *La Riviere des Chutes* and says that it was for the *Chutes* in the Columbia River and not for the falls in the stream itself. The Rev. A. F. Waller, in his diary under date of May 8, 1845, refers to the Deschutes River by an Indian name, *Wanawont*. The diary gives no explanation of the name.

Desert, Jefferson County. Desert post office was established June 21, 1890, with William G. Rogers first postmaster. It was named for the surroundings. The office was closed in April, 1892. The record shows that an effort was made to revive the office in May, 1904, with James O. Colb postmaster, but apparently the revival was not completed. It is possible that the 1904 office was in a different location from the earlier office. According to information sent by Devere Helfrich of Klamath Falls, Desert post office was in the northwest part of township 13 south, range 14 east, near Gray Butte School. According to Mr. Helfrich it is probable that Desert post office was at different times in sections 5 and 6 of the township mentioned above, and very close to the first location of Lamonta post office. Mr. Helfrich was born in the immediate neighborhood. Desert and Lamonta post offices were between ten and twelve miles airline southward of Madras.

Desert Cone, Crater Lake National Park, Klamath County. Desert Cone is north of Crater Lake, and has an elevation of 6651 feet. It is at the west edge of Pumice Desert, and is named on that account.

Desert Ridge, Crater Lake National Park, Douglas and Klamath counties. This ridge is north of Crater Lake, and has an elevation of 6941 feet at its highest point. It is about a mile long. It gets its name because it is just west of Pumice Desert.

Despain Gulch, Umatilla County. Despain Gulch is east of Hermiston, and the intermittent stream therein flows into Cold Springs Reservoir. This gulch was named for Jerry DeSpain, a prominent Umatilla County pioneer.

Deter, Jackson County. Deter post office was named for the David M. Deter family. This family owned a cattle ranch near the present site of the post office. Deter was a flag station on the Southern Pacific Company line in the Siskiyou Mountains south of Ashland. The post office was established July 15, 1920.

Detroit, Marion County. Charles C. Giebeler, the well-known postmaster and packer of Detroit, wrote the compiler in 1925 that the first name suggested for this community was Coe, but the post office authorities disapproved of the name because it was too much like Cove in eastern Oregon. Detroit was the name then selected because of the presence in the community of a number of Michigan people. Detroit post office was established October 16, 1891, with Vanness G. Danforth first postmaster. The original townsite was inundated in the summer of 1952 when the USCE finished Detroit Dam, a 463 foot high concrete gravity structure that impounds 340,000 acre feet of water and has an installed generating capacity of 100,000 kilowatts. Detroit community was relocated about half a mile northwest of the original site on slightly higher ground. It is now a popular headquarters for water sports.

Devils Backbone, Clackamas County. This is a narrow divide between Sandy and Bull Run rivers. It was named in pioneer days because of the great difficulty emigrants experienced in getting their wagons past the place.

Devils Backbone, Crater Lake National Park, Klamath County. Well named. This is a gigantic series of serrated rocks forming a vertical backbone on the inside rim of Crater Lake. Its name is imaginative.

Devils Canyon, Gilliam County. There are a number of canyons of this name in the state, at least two of which are in Gilliam County, opening into the canyon of John Day River. They are so called on account of the unusual rock formations suggestive of satanic influences, and also because they are so difficult to get through.

Devils Garden, Lake County. Devils Garden is northeast of Fort Rock. It is an irregular area of several square miles, with a growth of juniper trees, and it is surrounded by extensive lava flows, which form a striking contrast to the enclosed tract which is mostly of ordinary soil. The surrounding lava has given the place its name.

Devils Horn, Deschutes County. This butte of peculiar color is in the south part of Paulina Mountains. It is composed of lava of a reddish hue, and its shape is suggestive of the name that has been given it. It is several hundred feet high.

Devils Lake, Lincoln County. Devils Lake is near the Pacific Ocean in the northwest part of the county. It was named because of an Indian legend which is to the effect that a giant fish or marine monster lived in the lake and occasionally came to the surface to attack some hapless native. There are several versions of the story but this one is sufficient to indicate the origin of the name. The post office was called Delake, a corruption of Devils Lake. See also under Neotsu.

Devils Lake Fork, Tillamook and Washington counties. Devils Lake

Fork, one of the larger tributaries to Wilson River, heads in the extreme west edge of Washington County and flows northwest to join the main stream near Wilson River Highway. The fork has become well known in recent years because of the conspicuous steel viaduct that carries the highway over the stream. Devils Lake Fork takes its name from the fact that it drains a small body of water called Devils Lake, so called as a result of Indian nomenclature. The Indians, particularly of the Coast Range region, were fearful of a number of lakes and localities that were supposed to be inhabited by skookums, or evil wood-spirits. Some of the lakes are still called Skookum lakes, others are called Devils lakes. The general run of Indians avoided these places, and considered them haunted.

Devils Pulpit, Hood River County. This is a prominent shelf or bench on the east slope of Preachers Peak, at the summit of the Cascade Range, south of Lost Lake. It was named when R. S. Shelley of the USFS named Preachers Peak for his father. The remark was made that if the preacher were there, the Devil wouldn't be far away. See also under Preachers Peak.

Devils Run, Wallowa County. Devils Run is a stream flowing into Chesnimnus Creek in the southwest corner of township 4 north, range 47 east. It was named because of the roughness and swiftness of the water.

Devils Stairway, Douglas County. This series of rocky ridges is in section 26, township 25 south, range 2 east. Before the USFS trail was developed, it was difficult to traverse and Perry Wright, an early settler, named it Devils Ladder. This was later changed to the present form.

Devine Canyon, Harney County. Devine Canyon is north of Burns, and is traversed by the Canyon City-Burns Highway. The canyon bears the name of John Devine, noted Harney County pioneer. John S. Devine was born in Richmond, Virginia, in November, 1839, and settled in Harney County in 1868, where he made his home until his death in Burns, September, 1901. The firm of Todhunter & Devine established the famous Whitehorse Ranch in the south end of the county, and the partners were among the so-called cattle barons, around whom gathered so much controversy. The John Devine monument in Devine Canyon was dedicated on July 22, 1928. For description of exercises and address by John W. Biggs of Burns, see *OHQ*, volume XXIX, page 236.

Devitt, Benton County. This community got its name from the two Devitt brothers who operated a sawmill nearby for a number of years.

Dewey, Yamhill County. Dewey is a crossroads locality about five miles northeast of Yamhill and near the north end of Ribbon Ridge. The Lakeview School is in the same general locality. Dewey post office was established on June 21, 1898, with P. W. Watkins postmaster. The country was ringing with praise for Admiral George Dewey at the time because of his victory at the battle of Manila Bay, and the office was named in his honor. The office was discontinued on September 30, 1904. Lakeview School was so named because it overlooks Wapato Lake to the north.

Dewies Canyon, Jefferson County. This canyon rises in the Baldwin Hills and empties into Mud Springs Creek. It was named for Frank L. Dewies who applied for a homestead near its head in 1914.

Dexter, Lane County. Dexter post office was established in May, 1872, and was first called Butte Disappointment. This name was derived from a local landmark which was so named by pioneers in 1848. On July 19, 1875, the post office name was changed to Dexter. Samuel Handsaker, was then postmaster. His son, John Handsaker, in an interview with Myron Tinker, Eugene *Register-Guard*, June 3, 1951, stated that the family had a "Dexter" brand cook stove with the name emblazoned on the front. He always understood that this was the source of the place-name.

Deyoe Creek, Tillamook County. Deyoe Creek is a tributary of Devils Lake Fork Wilson River near its headwaters. It is named for Daniel and Jacob Deyoe who took up adjacent government land about 1900. The form Deo is incorrect.

Diablo Mountain, Lake County. *Diablo* is the Spanish word for devil. Diablo Mountain is east of the north end of Summer Lake, and has an elevation of 6145 feet, according to the USC&GS. Diablo Canyon is nearby. It is said that the canyon was named first, because it was rough and difficult to travel, and the name, Diablo Mountain, came later. The name, Mount Diablo, appears to be wrong.

Diamond Craters, Harney County. Diamond Craters and the old Diamond post office both got their names from the Diamond Ranch, which was established in pioneer days by Mace McCoy. This ranch used a diamond shaped brand. Mrs. Dolly Kiger applied the name of the ranch to the community about 1874, according to information given the writer by C. H. Smyth, postmaster at Diamond in 1925. In 1927 Mrs. Minerva J. Kiger, of Corvallis, wrote the compiler that she was the Dolly Kiger referred to above. She confirmed the history of the name Diamond as given herein. Diamond Craters are about six miles northwest of Diamond post office site. There are about 20 of them occupying an area of some five square miles, described in USGS Bulletin 217. In the 1970s the craters were in the news because stone dealers were removing the *pahoehoe* or sheet lava to sell for veneer stone. The variety of craters and other examples of volcanism within such a small space makes the area unique and the BLM has made various plans to protect it. There is an excellent illustrated article by Connie Hofferber in the *Oregonian*, August 3, 1979, page E1.

Diamond Hill, Linn County. Diamond Hill is on the east edge of the Willamette Valley about six miles north of the south line of Linn County, and about ten miles north of Coburg, Lane County. The compiler is of the opinion that Diamond Hill was named for John Diamond, prominent Lane County pioneer, whose home was near Coburg. Diamond Peak and Diamond Lake in the Cascade Range were named for the same man. John Diamond was born in Londonderry, Ireland, in 1815, and emigrated to New York in 1833. He lived at times in the states of New York, Michigan, Illinois, and emigrated to Oregon in 1847. He took up a claim where the town of Coburg now stands. He sold the property in 1858, and after three years of traveling, settled just east of Coburg. For additional biographical information, see Walling's *History of Lane County*, page 488. Along with other pioneers, he made explorations into the Cascade Range, which accounts for the application of his name to geographical features in that area. The compiler does not know the circumstances of the naming of Dia-

mond Hill. It seems certain that Diamond did not live in the locality, which
was about ten miles north of his homestead. He may have had some business interests there, or possibly pastured stock there. John Diamond was a
sturdy citizen and neighbors may have complimented him on that account.
Diamond Hill post office was established on the Linn County list on September 16, 1858, with James H. Pierce first postmaster. This office was closed
September 28, 1869. An office with the name Diamond was in service from
April 23, 1887, to October 4, 1887, with David H. Pierce postmaster. It was
doubtless in the same community.

Diamond Lake, Douglas County. This is one of the important mountain lakes of Oregon, and lies in the southeast part of the county between
Mt. Thielsen and Mt. Bailey. It has an elevation of 5182 feet. About 1927
George H. Kelly of Portland and Wm. P. Vandevert of Bend, both of whom
were familiar with the history of the middle Cascade Range, informed the
compiler that Diamond Lake was named for John Diamond. This was the
same man for whom Diamond Peak was named. Diamond discovered the
lake from the summit of Diamond Peak in 1852. The name has nothing to
do with the shape of the lake. See under Diamond Hill.

Diamond Lake, Klamath County. Diamond Lake is a station on the
Cascade line of the Southern Pacific just northeast of Beaver Marsh. It was
named for the large lake about twenty miles westward. When the railroad
was built, the station was named Lonroth for Elias Lonnrot, 1802-1884,
Finnish philologist and discoverer of the *Kalevala,* the great epic of Finland.
Shortly after the Cascade line was built, the railroad changed the name
from Lonroth to Diamond Lake. This was about 1926.

Diamond Lake, Union County. Diamond Lake is in township 5 south,
range 43 east, and drains into Elk Creek, a tributary of Minam River. Diamond Lake was not named because of its shape. The lake is inaccessible and
a sheep herder named Diamond agreed to stock it with fish, which was a
difficult task, owing to the rugged character of the surrounding country.
The lake was named for him.

Diamond Peak, Klamath and Lane counties. This is a fine peak of the
Cascade Range, and has an elevation of 8750 feet according to the USGS.
For the geography of the region surrounding the mountain see the USGS
map of the Waldo Lake quadrangle. The writer has been told that there is a
small living glacier on Diamond Peak, but he has no direct knowledge of it.
Diamond Peak was named in 1852 for John Diamond, a pioneer settler
near Coburg, Oregon, who was a member of a party of road viewers opening a road between Middle Fork Willamette River and Idaho for an immigration route. The report is contained in the *Journal* of the Oregon
territorial council, 1852-53. *Appendix,* pages 13-15. Other viewers were:
William M. Macy, W. T. Walker, William Tandy, Alexander King, Joseph
Meadows and J. Clarke. For additional references see Scott's *History of the
Oregon Country,* volume IV, page 8. For information about John Diamond,
see editorial page of the *Oregon Journal,* June 4, 1931.

Diamond Prairie, Wallowa County. This little prairie is west of the
town of Wallowa. It is said to be named because of its shape.

Diamond Rockpile, Lane County. This point is in the southeast corner of the county south of Diamond Peak and has an elevation of 6437 feet. It received its name because of its peculiar formation and its nearness to Diamond Peak.

Dick Point, Tillamook County. John A. Biggs, who was born nearby, told the writer in 1971 that when he was a very small boy, an Indian called Indian Dick lived at this spot near the mouth of the Tillamook River.

Dickey Prairie, Clackamas County. Dickey Prairie is about four miles east-southeast of Molalla. The prairie was an old Molalla Indian campground. The property was homesteaded by one of the Dickey family and it was given his name by general usage.

Diffin, Grant County. Jimmy Diffin is said to have been the last surviving resident of the old mining town of Robisonville in the Blue Mountains south of Granite, and Diffin post office was probably named for him. Former County Judge R. R. McHaley of Prairie City has an interesting paragraph about Jimmy Diffin in a letter published in the Canyon City *Eagle* for March 7, 1947. Diffin preserved his independence till the very end and refused to be sent to the county farm as a public charge. He was frequently called "49 Jimmy." Diffin post office was established March 19, 1890, with John H. Mitchell the first and only postmaster. The office was discontinued April 10, 1891.

Dillard, Douglas County. John Dillard, for whom the town of Dillard was named, was born in Missouri in 1813 and came to Oregon by ox team in 1850. In 1852 he settled on a donation land claim about 11 miles south of Roseburg and when the railroad was built through that part of the state about 1882 a station was established and named for Dillard. He continued to live on his claim until his death in 1892. See Down's *A History of the Silverton Country,* page 132, note 19.

Diller Glacier, Deschutes County. This is a large important glacier on the east slope of Middle Sister. It was named for Dr. Joseph Silas Diller, for many years connected with the USGS and the authority on the geology of western Oregon. He was the author of a number of important bulletins of the USGS and several geologic folios. His most popular work was the Geological Survey's *Guidebook of the Western United States,* Part D., *The Shasta Route.* The name Diller Glacier seems to have been applied by Dr. I. C. Russell of the USGS in August, 1903. See USGS Bulletin 252, page 125. Dr. Diller was born in Pennsylvania in 1850 and graduated from Harvard (Lawrence) in 1879. He joined the USGS in 1883 and was a valued member of the organization until his retirement in 1923. Most of his field-work was in southwest Oregon and northern California. His knowledge of the geology of those areas was profound. He died at Washington, D. C., November 13, 1928.

Dilley, Washington County. Dilley was named for Milton E. Dilley, a pioneer resident. Dilley post office was established December 31, 1873 and continued until May 1, 1961. For a recent description see the *Oregonian,* February 22, 1977, page B3W.

Dillon, Wasco County. This was a station on the railroad near the Celilo Canal. It was named for an army officer, Captain Theo. H. Dillon, who was a member of the engineer corps and assisted in the construction of the canal. One of the construction camps was known as Dillon's Camp, which the railroad company called Dillon.

Dillon Falls, Deschutes County. This white water cataract on Deschutes River some nine miles southwest of Bend is well known to anglers. The name is derived from Leander Dillon who homesteaded nearby about 1890 and later figured in the timber claim contests of 1906. Dillon moved to Prineville and died there in a fire on January 25, 1907.

Dinger Lake, Clackamas County. Forest ranger Joe Graham of Clackamas Lake is authority for the statement that this lake was named because Mack Holloman caught fine trout therein, calling them "humdingers." Only the last part of the word was applied to the lake.

Dinner Creek, Clackamas County. Dinner Creek is a small stream tributary to Clackamas River about two miles above Roaring River. W. C. Elliott, a well-known civil engineer of Portland, told the writer that he named the stream in 1897 because his surveying party stopped there for dinner.

Dinwiddie Valley, Linn County. C. H. Stewart of Albany wrote the compiler in 1927 as follows: "This valley, in the hills southwest of Brownsville, I am told was named for a little old bowlegged Scotchman named Hugh Dinwiddie, who for many years was secretary of the Brownsville Woolen Mills."

Dipping Vat Creek, Wheeler County. This creek rises south of Little Summit Prairie and flows to Paulina Basin. There are Dipping Vat creeks and springs also in Grant, Harney and Malheur counties and numerous similar names elsewhere in eastern Oregon. They originated with an act of the 1907 Legislature "To suppress and avoid contagious and infectious diseases among sheep". Prior to that time, scab and other afflictions had wiped out the native rimrock sheep. Serious infection of domestic sheep prompted the legislation which included provision for a State Sheep Inspector and an annual dip to U S Department of Agriculture specifications. The animals were totally immersed and where flocks ran into the thousands, a large water supply was needed. Consequently many streams and springs bear the name of this early, odoriferous adjunct of the large bands of range sheep.

Discovery Point, Crater Lake National Park, Klamath County. Crater Lake was discovered on June 12, 1853, by John W. Hillman and a party of prospectors. The party first came on the lake at a point on the southwest rim. This place has since been called Discovery Point to commemorate the event.

Disston, Lane County. Disston post office was established October 25, 1906, with Crampton Jones first postmaster. The early records show his name as Cranston Jones, but this apparently is in error as Mrs. R. L. Gawley informed the compiler in 1967 that she knew Jones well and was present when he received notice of the appointment. Her husband was one of the organizers of the first saw mill at Disston and she stated that the name of the mill and town both came from the well-known Disston saws.

Divers Creek, Hood River County. L. M. Baldwin of Hood River gave the compiler the following interesting facts about this name. Davis Divers came to Oregon City in 1852 and moved to Hood River Valley in 1862 where he took up a homestead not far from Odell. While raising a large family, he would frequently travel afoot over the mountains to Oregon City by way of what came to be known as the Divers trail. Baldwin's uncle told him that he had been over the trail many years ago and thought it had originally been an Indian route. It is not clear whether the creek was named to honor Divers or because the Divers trail crossed it.

Divide, Douglas and Lane counties. Divide is a natural name for a station on the Southern Pacific a few miles southwest of Cottage Grove on the watershed between the Willamette and the Umpqua rivers. Eastward the drainage is toward Coast Fork Willamette River and to the west is Pass Creek, a tributary to Elk Creek. Divide station is in Lane County and it has an elevation of about 625 feet. This is east and somewhat lower than the actual divide which has an elevation of 751 feet according to railroad records. Divide post office was established to serve this neighborhood on May 31, 1900, with Edna Hedrick first postmaster. This office was on the Douglas County post office list. The office is shown on the Lane County list as of May 10, 1909, and it was discontinued January 15, 1921. The office may have actually been moved from one county to the other, the writer thinks it probable that a relocation of the county boundary brought about the change.

Divide, Wallowa County. Divide was the name of a post office that operated in Wallowa County from January, 1891, until November, 1893, with Annie E. Shaw first postmaster. This office was situated in what is called the Divide country between Sheep Creek on the east and Little Sheep Creek on the west. When Annie E. Shaw had the office it was in section 11, township 3 south, range 46 east, and during the rest of its existence it was not far away. When the office was first asked for, it was suggested by Joe Wasson that it be named Threebuck because it was near the headwaters of that stream, but it was decided that the name was too cumbersome.

Dixie, Baker County. Dixie, a locality on Burnt River about five miles north of Lime, was named because it was near the confluence of Burnt River and Dixie Creek, which flows in from the west. Dixie Creek was named in the mining days because of the prevalence of southerners on its upper reaches. Dixie post office was established March 21, 1913, and was discontinued April 30, 1924. The post office was not in the mining area, but close to the railroad along Burnt River.

Dixie, Washington County. Dixie post office was established in the extreme northeast corner of Washington County on November 21, 1887, with John Dix first of four postmasters. It seems obvious that the office was named for the family of the postmaster and not for Dixie, the land of the magnolia and the mocking bird. The office was five or six miles southwest of Scappoose, and when it was closed May 4, 1905, it was closed to that office. The name Dixie Mountain is still used for a prominent ridge in that part of the state. The fact that the office was named for the family was confirmed by a letter dated February 2, 1948, signed by W. D. Moreland of the Skyland Land Company, which operates in Multnomah and Washington counties. Mr. Moreland says that when real estate in this area was put on the market in 1933 it became desirable to adopt a locality name. The property was near Wallace school, but that name was considered rather unsatisfactory. A community picnic was held about 1936-37 at the John Tannock picnic grounds. There was a good deal of discussion about a place name. When a formal vote was taken nearly eighty percent of those present were in favor of Dixie to commemorate the old Dixie post office and John Dix, its postmaster.

Dixie Creek, Grant County. This stream flows into John Day River near Prairie City. Patsy Daly of Prairie City told the compiler in 1927 that the stream was named during the mining excitement of the early 1860s because there were so many southerners mining along its banks.

Dixie Jett Gulch, Wallowa County. Dixie Jett Gulch drains into Sheep Creek in township 2 south, range 47 east. The name is an odd one, and was applied to commemorate a settler who built a cabin in the canyon. The compiler has been furnished with several spellings of this man's name, all purporting to be the veritable form. These include: Dick Se Jett, Dixie Jett and Dick Surjett. The man himself, a prospector and hunter, went his way many years ago. The USFS uses the spelling Dixie Jett because it is the simplest and is in general use.

Dixon, Wasco County. Dixon is a station on the Burlington Northern, Inc. line in Deschutes Canyon. It was named for T. F. Dixon, former Vice President and General Manager of the Spokane Portland & Seattle Railway.

Dixon Creek, Benton County. Dixon Creek, north of Corvallis, was named for William F. Dixon, a pioneer of Oregon, who took up a donation land claim nearby. For information about him see land office certificate 903.

Dixonville, Douglas County. Dixonville is about five miles east of Roseburg. The post office was established September 16, 1901, and named for R. B. Dixon who owned the land where the post office and other buildings were situated.

Do Little Flat, Wheeler County. Grover C. Blake told the compiler that this flat south of Lawson Mountain was named because the local homesteaders had little or nothing to do. In the peak of the homestead activity after the turn of the century, many settlers would eke out a minimum existence until they were able to patent their land and then would immediately sell to one of the large and well organized local ranchers.

Doane Lake, Multnomah County. Doane Lake is an overflow lake on the west bank of the Willamette River near the Burlington Northern, Inc. bridge. Doane Point is in the same neighborhood. These two features were named for Milton Doane, who took up a donation land claim there, his certificate being numbered 1392. Doane's name has been spelled several ways, and it appears as Done on land office plats, but he could not read and write, hence the variety of styles. Doane is the form in general use, and is the name adopted by the USBGN. The lake has been filled with material dredged from the river.

Dobry Point, Wasco County. This point above Lost Creek north of the Barlow Road was named for Jack Dobry, an employee of the USFS before World War II.

Doc Canyon, Wallowa County. This canyon drains into Bear Creek, south of Wallowa. It was named for one "Doc" Cussins who herded sheep and prospected there.

Dodge, Clackamas County. Dodge, a place about four miles southeast of Springwater, was named for a local family. The post office was established March 25, 1896, with Almon T. Dodge first of five postmasters. The office was closed May 31, 1914.

Dodge Canyon, Douglas County. Dodge Canyon, west of Oakland, was named for J. R. Dodge, who took up a donation land claim near its mouth.

Dodge Island, Multnomah County. Dodge Island is in Bull Run Lake. It was named in honor of Frank T. Dodge, superintendent of Portland Water Works, 1889-1913. A metal tablet was installed on a rock on this small islet in September, 1918. For a photograph of the tablet, see the *Oregonian,* May 12, 1918. For article about the dedication of the tablet, *ibid.,* September 15, 1918.

Dodson, Multnomah County. Dodson is a railroad station just west of the post office of Warrendale. The name of the station comes from Ira Dodson, an early settler in that part of the county. Dodson station has been moved several times and was once near the present location of Warrendale.

Dodson Mountain, Douglas County. Dodson Mountain is an important peak east of Dillard, with an elevation of about 3200 feet. It was named for Samuel Dodson, a pioneer stockman who settled nearby. His land was still owned in 1926 intact by his son, Samuel Dodson, Jr.

Dog Creek, Douglas County. This creek rises south of Dog Mountain and flows into North Umpqua River just west of Horseshoe Bend. It was named in 1916 by Perry Wright, an early settler. Wright with two dogs was crossing the creek on a partly submerged log near very turbulent water. The dogs both slipped off and were only rescued with considerable difficulty. This again goes to show that man is a dog's best friend.

Dog Lake, Lake County. Dog Lake is west of Goose Lake and was formerly called Dogleg Lake because its outline on a map is strongly suggestive of a dog's hind leg. The name has become contracted as a matter of convenience. Dog Mountain to the north takes its name from the lake.

Dog River, Hood River County. In pioneer days Hood River was known as Dog River because a party of travelers ate dog meat there in preference to starving. Mrs. Nathaniel Coe of Hood River Valley objected to the name, and secured a change to Hood River, on account of Mount Hood. The name Dog River is now applied to a stream heading in Brooks Meadows southeast of Parkdale, and flowing into East Fork Hood River. It is the source of The Dalles water supply. See under Hood River.

Dog Thief Point, Clatsop County. Dog Thief Point overlooks the Sunset Highway about seven miles east of Elsie. It is near the old Astoria-Tualatin Plains Military Road of 1855, and there has been a supposition that the name is a corruption of "Dog Robber", the military slang for an officer's orderly. In early 1980 after some lengthy investigation by a number of people, J. W. Forrester, Jr., of Astoria forwarded the following facts provided by Henry Rierson, a lifelong resident of the area. Rierson stated that about 1900 two men from Astoria were walking east over the military road.

They stopped for the night at Joe Lynch's place near Elsie and after they left the following morning, Lynch found that his shepherd dog was missing. He gave chase and later found the men with his dog camped in a lean to on the mountain. The animal returned to Elsie with his master, Lynch proclaimed that the hill should be called Dog Thief Mountain and another strange place name entered the Oregon rolls.

Doghouse Gulch, Grant County. Doghouse Gulch, which drains into South Fork John Day River about 15 miles south of Dayville, got its name as a result of a sarcastic reference to a shanty occupied by a sheepherder. The structure apparently was short of some of the modern conveniences.

Dogwood Creek, Clatsop County. This stream is about 18 miles east of Astoria. It was at one time known as Hall Creek, after an early settler, but the name did not persist. There are few trees of the forest that are held in such affectionate esteem as the dogwood, and yet the name of the tree is almost never used for a geographic feature. At least that is the situation in Oregon, where hundreds of place-names have been applied for firs, cedars, pines, oaks, willows and cottonwoods. The Pacific dogwood, *Cornus nuttallii*, is a lovely tree and should not be neglected.

Dollar Lake, Hood River County. This lake is near the north end of Barrett Spur, north of Mount Hood. The name is descriptive. Richard J. Grace of Portland wrote the compiler: "Dollar Lake is apt, as the lake is very small for a permanent one and is almost perfectly round."

Dollar Lake, Wallowa County. Dollar Lake is in the Wallowa Mountains in township 4 south, range 45 east, and was named by J. Fred McClain because it was so nearly circular.

Dolph, Tillamook County. This community was named for Joseph N. Dolph, who came to Portland in 1862. He served as city attorney and as United States attorney and also in the state legislature. He served as United States senator from Oregon in 1883-95, and had large influence in the Senate and was a close friend of President Harrison. He was born in New York in 1835 and died in Portland in 1897. See the *Oregonian* for March 11 and March 19, 1897. Dolph was named for him while he was in the Senate. It was for a time a post office.

Dominic, Marion County. This was a station northeast of Mount Angel. It was named for Father P. Dominic, O. S. B., for many years a moving spirit in the activities of Mount Angel College.

Dompier Creek, Douglas County. Dompier Creek flows into South Umpqua River two and one half miles northeast of Tiller. It was named for a family of early settlers.

Don Lake, Linn County. This small lake in township 12 south, range 6 east, was named for Don Carlos Stahlman, son of Fred Stahlman the early USFS district ranger at Detroit.

Donaca Lake, Linn County. Donaca Lake is south of Detroit, and drains through Donaca Creek into Middle Santiam River. W. B. Donaca came to Oregon in 1852 and settled in Linn County in 1861. For a good many years he was a merchant in Lebanon. This lake and the creek were named for him or for some member of his family.

Donahue Creek, Multnomah County. This small tributary of Bridal

Veil Creek is the only feature on the map today that remains to commemorate the Bridal Veil Lumber Company operation on the slopes of Larch Mountain. Certain of their logging was contracted to Donahue & Kelley with M. C. Donahue supervising. The lumber company operated a railroad from their mill at Palmer south along the slopes of Larch Mountain and there was a station named Donahue where the railroad crossed this creek not far from the present Larch Mountain Road.

Donald, Marion County. Donald is a station on the Oregon Electric Railway, on French Prairie, northwest of Woodburn, and was named for the late R. L. Donald, of Portland, who was an official of the construction company that built the railway.

Donaldson Canyon, Morrow County. This canyon south of Heppner was named for Samuel C. Donaldson who was born in Pennsylvania and came to Morrow County in 1871. He was a large landowner and sheepman before the turn of the century. The proper name for the stream in the lower end of the canyon is Shobe Creek.

Donnelly Butte, Harney County. Donnelly Butte is about 30 miles northwest of Burns and has an elevation of 6033 feet. At one time it was called Black Butte but was renamed to honor Edgar W. Donnelly, USFS district ranger in the area for many years.

Donnelly Creek, Crook County. This creek flows into North Fork Crooked River in township 15 south, range 22 east. The stream and nearby spring were named for R. N. Donnelly, a prominent sheepman. Donnelly was born in Tennessee and came to Oregon in the early days. He was at one time a member of the Oregon Legislature. He died near Richmond in 1936.

Donner und Blitzen River, Harney County. This stream was named during the Snake War of 1864, when troops under the command of Colonel George B. Currey crossed it during a thunder storm, and gave it the German name for thunder and lightning. The river is frequently called simply Blitzen.

Donnybrook, Jefferson County. This name is now applied to a school in the east end of the county, but some years ago Donnybrook referred to the whole community. Phil Brogan, in the Bend *Bulletin,* April 20, 1943, discusses the name with sympathetic understanding as follows: "It was in the community's range epoch that a group of Celts, celebrating some undetermined occasion at a sheep cabin in Calf gulch, just over the ridge from Axehandle, did the thing in true Donnybrook style. There was no fair, but one fine fight. Joe Brannon heard of the party and with typical Irish wit, called the locality Donnybrook. And gradually that name spread to the community, and the county school, below Axehandle spring, was named the Donnybrook school. For many years the community was known as Donnybrook far and wide. Then came the homesteading era. Across Currant Creek and near the shadow of Coyote mountain, Jesse Kilts homesteaded. Eventually, as homesteaders moved in, a postoffice was obtained, and postal officials named the community after the postmaster. Since then the community, Axehandle of pioneer days and Donnybrook of the ranch era, has been known, at least to Uncle Sam, as Kilts." The original Donnybrook is a suburb in the southeast part of Dublin, famous for a fair held under license from King John in 1204. The entertainment furnished at the fair reached such specialized disorder that the institution was abolished in 1855. Phil Brogan reports that he has seen the name of the Oregon school called Donnybrooke. If this is true, and it probably is, the compiler thinks the authorities in Jefferson County better put a stop to such nonsense.

Dooley Mountain, Baker County. This is a prominent point south of Baker, near the Baker-Unity Highway. It bears the name of a well-known eastern Oregon pioneer, John J. Dooley, who came to the vicinity of Baker in 1862. For many years he was connected with various mining and construction enterprises in Oregon and Idaho, and built a toll road near the mountain which bears his name. A letter by J. C. Bowen is printed on the editorial page of the *Oregon Journal,* June 7, 1929, and it recounts some of the history of John J. Dooley and his kindly wife. At that time the Dooleys were 92 and 89 years of age, respectively, and lived in Baker.

Dora, Coos County. Dora post office was established August 10, 1874, with John H. Roach postmaster. It has been reported that the place was named for Dora Roach, apparently the small daughter of the first postmaster.

Dorena, Lane County. This post office was established in 1899 with Alfred H. Bigelow first postmaster. The place was named for Dora Burnette and Rena Martin, by consolidating parts of their first names. In 1949 the USCE completed Dorena Dam and Reservoir about seven miles downstream on Row River. This is an earth fill flood control project with about 70,000 acre feet of usable water storage. The recreation facilities are operated by Lane County.

Doris Creek, Lane County. Mrs. R. L. Gawley who lived in Disston many years ago told the compiler in 1967 that this tributary of Layng Creek was named for the daughter of Elza Holderman, an early USFS ranger.

Dorman, Umatilla County. Dorman post office was in the south part of the county, probably not far from Ukiah. It was established October 3, 1887, and named for James W. Dorman, the first postmaster. The subsequent history of this post office is not clear. The name was changed to Dale on November 11, 1891, but whether the office was moved at that time is not certain. In any event, the office was shown on the Grant County list in 1903 with the name Dale. The compiler has been to Dale several times and finds it hard to fit the name to the geography, although the man who selected the word may not have had the same difficulty. This part of Oregon is deeply cut by canyons. It does not seem that the name Dale describes them very accurately. The name Dale as applied to this locality may have had a significance other than topographic.

Dorrance Meadow, Deschutes County. This meadow five miles west of La Pine was named for early day homesteader Samuel H. Dorrance. Dorrance was later killed by J. L. Melvin of Melvin Butte.

Dosch Road, Multnomah County. Few Oregon pioneers have been so greatly respected as Colonel Henry E. Dosch. His contributions to the development of the state were substantial, and his character such as to win him a host of friends. He was born in Germany June 17, 1841. He emigrated to

St. Louis, Missouri, in January, 1860, and had been in the United States but little more than a year when he enlisted in the northern army, and finally reached the rank of acting colonel of volunteers. In 1863 he crossed the plains, and after visiting California arrived in The Dalles in 1864. After various mercantile experiences in eastern Oregon and elsewhere, he retired in 1890, and devoted the remainder of his life to horticulture. His knowledge of the state and its products was profound. He represented Oregon at every important exposition beginning at the World's Columbian Exposition held at Chicago in 1893. For many years he resided near Hillsdale, and the country road between Green Hills and Hillsdale was named for him. There was also a station on the Southern Pacific west of Bertha called Dosch. Colonel Dosch died at Portland in 1925.

Dothan, Douglas County. Dothan post office was established in March, 1896, to serve the locality of West Fork station on the Southern Pacific Company railroad in Cow Creek Canyon. It is said that the station agent, one Hudson, thought that the name of the post office should be different from the station name in order to avoid confusion in accounts. He suggested the name Dothan which he found in biblical history. Dothan was a place near Samaria in Palestine. Dothan post office in Oregon was closed in 1942. The post office list for Douglas County shows an office named Herman, established April 15, 1886, with James W. Gilmore postmaster. The office was discontinued December 13, 1887. The compiler has been told that this office served the locality of West Fork railroad station. It is possible that the office was named in compliment to Binger Hermann, then Oregon's representative in Congress, who may have assisted in getting it established. It will be noted that there is a discrepancy in the spelling.

Dotyville, Linn County. The early-day post office called Dotyville in Linn County was named in compliment to the Doty family, local residents. Dotyville was near the south line of township 10 south, range 1 west, and just a little to the southeast of Scio. The office was established October 3, 1884, with J. A. Richardson first postmaster. The office continued in operation until October 6, 1890. The place is not shown on modern maps.

Double Corral Creek, Wheeler County. This creek is in the south part of the county west of Derr Meadows. Early sheepmen built counting and separating corrals at its headwaters near Blevins Spring. These have been rebuilt several times and relocated slightly but are still in use.

Dougherty Slough, Tillamook County. This slough flows westward under the Oregon Coast Highway about a half mile north of Tillamook and empties into Hoquarten Slough. It bears the name of Nathaniel Dougherty, one of the first white settlers in the vicinity of Tillamook Bay and an esteemed and prominent pioneer of the county.

Dougherty Spring, Wallowa County. This spring, in the northeast part of township 4 north, range 46 east, was named for William Dougherty, who herded sheep there and established a camp for Hayes and Kernan about 1902.

Doughty Creek, Tillamook County. This stream was named for William Thomas Doughty, who settled in Tillamook County in 1870. It rises about two miles east of Bay City and flows south, thence west into Tillamook Bay. Its mouth is just north of Kilchis Point.

Douglas County. On January 24, 1851, the territorial legislature created Umpqua County and named it for the Umpqua River. It is said that the short life of Umpqua County was due to political troubles. In any event, on January 7, 1852, the territorial legislature created Douglas County out of the eastern part of Umpqua County. Another part of Umpqua County was added to Coos County in December, 1853, and the remainder was given to Douglas County in 1862. Douglas County was named for Stephen Arnold Douglas (1813-1861), distinguished American politician and Democratic candidate for the presidency in 1860. He was a strong supporter of Oregon in the Congress, and at the time Douglas County was named for him, he was in the United States Senate from Illinois. According to the Bureau of the Census, Douglas County has a land area of 5062 square miles.

Douglas Hollow, Wasco County. Douglas Hollow drains into Fifteenmile Creek about a mile north of Emerson. It was named for John Douglas, a very early Wasco County settler, who brought land near its mouth in 1864.

Dougren, Lane County. Dougren is a station on the Southern Pacific Cascade Line west of Dexter. When the railroad was relocated around Lookout Point Dam, land for this station was purchased from a man named Green who stipulated that his name be used. The railroad already had a station named Green just south of Roseburg so Dougren was coined from the names Douglas Green.

Douthit Springs, Crook County. These springs and the creek in section 10, township 14 south, range 19 east, near Ochoco Creek were named for one Douthit, an early homesteader. The spelling Drouthit is incorrect.

Douty, Tillamook County. Douty post office was in the extreme northeast part of the county, established to serve the Douty Lumber Company. This enterprise was situated just a little northeast and over the county line from Cochran, Washington County. The Douty Lumber Company was named for one of its owners, F. A. Douty. There was a Southern Pacific Company railroad station called Douty but it did not have an agent. Douty post office was established January 19, 1921, and was ordered discontinued August 7, 1924. James M. White was the only postmaster.

Dover, Clackamas County. Dover post office was established June 16, 1890, with Frederick R. French first of a series of nine postmasters. The office was closed August 31, 1911, so that the number of postmasters was large for a total service of twenty-one years. Dover was a few miles southeast of Sandy. The first location is said to have been in section 32, township 2 south, range 5 east, but the USGS map of the Cherryville quadrangle shows it a mile or so further south, toward the end of its service. In July, 1947, William H. Stanley of Gresham, sent in some of the early history of Dover, secured from Mrs. Joel Jarl, daughter of Mrs. Ethel Roberts, third postmaster at Dover. According to Mrs. Jarl the first postmaster, Frederick French, was either a native of England, or of English descent and named the office for the locality in England where he himself or his forebears came from. In 1917 the old Dover area in Clackamas County was served by a rural carrier from Eagle Creek.

Doves Bar, Marion County. This bar is near the east bank of Willamette River southwest of Salem. It was named for Bethuel Dove, who owned a nearby donation land claim on the west bank of the river in Polk County. Dove lived on what is known as Hayden Island.

Dovre Peak, Tillamook County. This point is in the northeast part of township 3 south, range 7 west, in the east part of the county. It bears the name of geographic features in the Province of Christiansand, Norway. It was named by USBGN about 1930 at the suggestion of F. E. Berg, a homesteader who lived in the vicinity of the peak.

Downey Gulch, Wallowa County. This gulch is in township 5 north, range 47 east, and is in the extreme northeast corner of the county. It was named for R. M. Downey, a pioneer resident and at one time county assessor. Downey Gulch is tributary to Cook Creek. Downey Saddle in the same township was also named for R. M. Downey. There is a much smaller Downey Gulch in the north part of township 2 south, range 47 east, named for the same man.

Downing, Umatilla County. Downing is a station on the Union Pacific Railroad north of Weston. It was named for J. A. Downing who farmed the land through which the railroad was built.

Downing Creek, Linn County. Downing Creek enters North Santiam River from the east about four miles south of Marion Forks. While there is no specific evidence, the writer feels confident that this stream was named by John Minto for George S. Downing, a member of both Minto's 1874 survey party and the 1881 party which located the route to the present Santiam Pass.

Downs, Marion County. This was a station about two miles north of Silverton. It was named for James Down, a native of Saltash, Devonshire, England. He was born in 1835, came to the United States during the Civil War, and settled in Oregon in 1864. He engaged in the hop and grain business. He died May 28, 1898. See Down's *A History of the Silverton Country,* chapter XXII.

Drain, Douglas County. This place was named for Charles Drain, a pioneer settler in the locality. The donation land claim on which the town of Drain is situated was taken up by Warren Goodell. He sold it to Jesse Applegate who in turn sold the property to Charles Drain in 1861. In 1872 the Oregon and California Railroad reached northern Douglas County. Drain and his son, John, had sold sixty acres of their land to the railroad for one dollar "in consideration of establishing a station. . .and laying out a town to be called 'Drain' ". Drain postoffice was established on April 25, 1872. Charles Drain, Sr. was once a member of the legislature, and his son, J. C. Drain, was also in the legislature and was speaker of the house. The town's most imposing residence, a Queen Anne style house built in 1893 for Charles Drain, Jr., is still standing and in 1978 was entered on the National Register of Historic Places. For additional information about the Drain family, see article by Fred Lockley on editorial page of the *Oregon Journal,* August 8, 1927.

Drake Peak, Lake County. Drake Peak, with an elevation of 8407 feet, is a prominent point in the mountains northeast of Lakeview. It was named for John M. Drake, a well-known officer in several campaigns against the

Snake Indians in south central Oregon. He reached the rank of colonel toward the conclusion of the Snake War. For information about his activities in this territory see Bancroft's *History of Oregon,* volume II, page 488, *et seq.* Drake Butte and Drake Peak, in the Maury Mountains in Crook County, are also named for Colonel Drake.

Draper, Jackson County. This place, southwest of Gold Hill, was named for Silas Draper, a miner. Draper post office was established February 9, 1882, with Draper first postmaster. The office was closed in October, 1912.

Dread and Terror Ridge, Douglas County. This ridge is on the south side of North Umpqua River in the northeast part of the county. It is about four miles long and has an elevation of 4896 feet. The name was applied by district ranger C. V. Oden of the USFS in 1908 because of the dense thickets of thorns and other brush which made the prospects of fire fighting in that section extremely disagreeable.

Dreadnought Island, Klamath County. This island, in the west end of Crescent Lake, was named by F. W. Cleator of the USFS in 1925 because it resembled a dreadnought battleship.

Drew, Douglas County. This place is said to have been named for a local resident, Robert Drew.

Drew Creek, Lake County. This stream drains into Goose Lake. It was named for Lieutenant-Colonel C. S. Drew, in command of the Owyhee Reconnaissance of the First Oregon Cavalry in 1864. The stream has been dammed for irrigation storage.

Drewsey, Harney County. Abner Robbins started a store at this place in the summer of 1883 and called it Gouge Eye, apparently to commemorate the frontier method of settling disputes. About a year later Robbins applied for a post office but postal authorities were reluctant to accept the original name, so he substituted a new name, Drusy. Eventually the office was named Drewsey. *Oregon, End of the Trail (Oregon Guide),* page 468, says the new name was in compliment to Drewsey Miller, the daughter of a rancher. In 1926 the compiler was told that the name submitted to Washington was Drusy, which authorities changed to Drewsey. Drusy seems more like a girl's name. The *Oregon Guide* calls the name Gouge Eye unpleasant, but the compiler thinks it a stout, picturesque bit of nomenclature, much better than some of the gutless expressions of today.

Drift Creek, Lincoln County. Drift Creek post office was one of the very first in the southwest part of what is now Lincoln County, then Benton. It was established August 6, 1874, with Matthew Brand postmaster, and was named for the stream flowing into Alsea Bay. The creek was named for the accumulations of driftwood on its banks. There is also a Drift Creek in Lincoln County flowing into Siletz Bay. The name of the office was changed to Collins in January, 1876, in honor of a local family. The name of this office was changed to Waldport in June, 1881, and back to Collins in February, 1882. This post office called Waldport may have been on the north side of Alsea Bay, not on the south side. Collins was changed to Lutgens in May, 1890, and Lutgens was changed to Stanford in July, 1893. Stanford it remained until June, 1897, when it became Lutgens again. The name of the office was changed to Nice in April, 1917, and was closed in November, 1919. This post office had eight names during its forty-five years of service, a record in the opinion of the compiler. No other Oregon office seems to have approached this mark. It is obvious that the office was moved a number of times. However, the offices mentioned above were all in the general vicinity of Alsea Bay. Lutgens was named for Albert H. Lutgens, also spelled Lutjens, and Nice was named for Harry Nice. Both of these men were local residents. The compiler has been unable to learn why Stanford post office was so named.

Drift Creek, Marion County. This stream was named Drift Creek in early days because of the accumulation of driftwood along its banks. Its upper reaches were in heavily wooded country.

Drift Fence Campground, Umatilla County. This USFS campground northeast of Dale was named because of its proximity to a drift fence used to control open range livestock.

Drury Creek, Lane County. This stream, a tributary to Mohawk River from the northwest, and Drury Butte south of Marcola were named for a family of early settlers. The post office and community Mabel, situated a little to the south of the mouth of the stream was named for Miss Mabel Drury.

Dry River, Crook and Deschutes counties. This is the bed of an ancient river that once drained the High Desert. The course of the channel is well marked from the west end of the desert to Crooked River, a distance of more than 50 miles. In some places the dry bed is in a canyon, and in other places in a narrow defile between abrupt basalt walls. The Ochoco highway between Redmond and Prineville crosses this defile at a point where an excellent view may be had of it. In many places water may be uncovered by digging in the gravel bed.

Dryden, Josephine County. Dryden, in the Deer Creek Valley east of Selma, was named for John Dryden, famous English poet, playwright and critic, who lived from 1631 to 1700. Mrs. Alma Harmon Kiphart of Eugene, a native of the Deer Creek country, sent this information, which has been confirmed by other sources. A paragraph from Mrs. Kiphart's letter of March 20, 1947, is as follows: "Dryden post office was named by J. P. (Perry) Mills, a Deer Creek Valley pioneer, for John Dryden the poet. Mr. Mills was a great reader and had in his possession many good books. It was through his influence that the post office was established. Early in 1900 he went to the Soldiers' Home at Roseburg, where he spent his last days. The establishment of this office is one of my fondest recollections." Dryden post office was established February 8, 1892, with Mary E. Tolin first of a long line of postmasters. In the summer of 1946 the compiler drove up Deer Creek to satisfy his curiosity about this isolated office and found it still in service and in good order, but in 1979 it was no larger in operation.

Drylake, Crook County. This post office was in the south part of Crook County. There is a small lake nearby which fills with water in the early spring, but is generally dry during the late summer. For many years the stockmen have referred to this as Dry Lake or Dry Lake Flat. When the post office was established in September, 1913, the name Dry Lake was selected by local residents, but the post office authorities telescoped this name into one word and it has been so known ever since. The office was closed in January, 1937.

Duckworth, Lane County. Duckworth was apparently named for a local family, but the compiler does not know for which one. Isaac W. Duckworth was postmaster at Long Tom office as early as 1859, and there may have been others of the name. Duckworth post office was established March 4, 1884, with Gilbert D. Chamberlain first postmaster. Byron Ellmaker was appointed November 25, 1884, and lost no time in getting the name changed to Elmira on December 22, 1884. See also under Elmira.

Dudley, Jackson County. Dudley was a post office in the mountains about six miles north of Butte Falls. It was established April 2, 1909, with Theresa E. Spencer first and only postmaster. The office was closed October 31, 1912, with papers to Butte Falls. In February, 1947, Judge J. B. Coleman of Medford wrote the compiler that Dudley post office was named for a Mr. Dudley who at one time owned or controlled what was known as the Dudley timber tract north of Butte Falls. Dudley post office was in the home of Mr. and Mrs. Spencer in section 12, township 34 south, range 2 east. A few years ago the old Spencer cabin was still standing with the mail boxes still in place therein, according to Judge Coleman.

Dufur, Wasco County. According to the *History of Central Oregon,* the first settler in the neighborhood of Dufur was Lewis P. Henderson, who established a home about four miles from the present site of the community in 1852. During the next three years Messrs. Reynolds, Marsh and Brown, stockmen, established ranches nearby. In 1863 David Imbler built a farmhouse where the town of Dufur now stands. In 1872 Andrew J. and E. Burnham Dufur bought a farm where Dufur is now situated. These two men were members of a well-known Wasco County pioneer family which came from New England by way of Panama to Oregon in 1859. On January 11, 1878, the post office was established and named for the Dufur family. Chauncey A. Williams was first postmaster, and is said to have selected the name of the office.

Dukes Valley, Hood River County. This is a sort of natural cove on the north slope of Booth Hill between the Mount Hood Loop Highway and Hood River. There seem to be plenty of legends as to how the valley got its name. The compiler is of the belief that it was named for a man named Duke who lived in the valley in the 1860s. There is a story, however, to the effect that it was named for a well-known ox, used by Peter Neal in logging operations, which much preferred wandering off into the secluded pastures of Dukes Valley to hauling logs. In 1886 Captain J. H. Dukes, a veteran of the Civil War, came to the Hood River Valley, and the compiler has been told that Dukes Valley was named for him, although there is nothing to indicate that he actually lived in Dukes Valley, but in the town of Hood River, except for a short time when he lived near Oak Grove.

Duley Creek, Curry County. Duley Creek flows into Lone Ranch Creek east of Cape Ferrelo. It was named for Winfield S. Duley who lived on its banks before the turn of the century.

Dumbbell Lake, Lane County. Dumbbell Lake is in the Cascade Range about two miles south of Horse Mountain. According to USFS records it was named by Dee Wright because of its shape.

Dumont Creek, Douglas County. This tributary of South Umpqua River northeast of Tiller was named for James and Frank Dumont who maintained a hunting camp nearby many years ago. This information was provided by Ira Poole of Canyonville.

Duncan, Umatilla County. Ida M. Wilbur, postmaster at Duncan in 1925, told the writer that the community was named for Isaac Duncan, a veteran of the Civil War. He lived in the neighborhood for many years, and the name of Duncan was proposed for the place in 1899. The post office was established October 28, 1899.

Duncan Creek, Lake County. Duncan Creek is near Silver Lake. It was named for George C. Duncan who first settled on the land where the stream emptied into Silver Lake. The Duncan family arrived in the Silver Lake Valley about 1873.

Duncan Ditch, Baker County. This ditch was named for the family of Charles H. Duncan who settled near Keating in the 1890s.

Duncanville, Grant County. Duncanville was a post office in the west or upper end of Bear Valley, southwest of Canyon City. Postal records show that the office was established September 27, 1897, with Wesley P. Duncan postmaster. The office was discontinued May 15, 1902, with all mail to Canyon City. It was named for the postmaster.

Dundee, Yamhill County. William Reid came to Oregon in 1874 from Dundee, Scotland. Among other things he became interested in Willamette Valley railroad construction, and he assisted in organizing the Oregonian Railway Company, Limited, a corporation of Dundee, Scotland, which succeeded to the interest of The Oregon Railway Company in 1880. The Oregon Company had previously taken over property of the Willamette Valley Railroad Company, which had gotten into financial difficulties. The Oregonian Railway Company made several narrow gauge extensions on the west side of the Willamette Valley, and an east side extension from Dundee. The town of Dundee was established and named for Reid's home in Scotland. For details of Reid's history and of the construction of the railroad mentioned above, see Scott's *History of the Oregon Country*. The post office history of Dundee is a little more complicated than ordinary. An office named Ekins was established there in 1881 which ran until the summer of 1882 when the name was changed to Dundee in commemoration of Reid's birthplace. The name Dundee was used for the post office name from July 25, 1882, until June 30, 1885, when the postal business was turned over to Lafayette. On April 16, 1887, a new post office with the name Dundee Junction was established with Frank D. McCain, first postmaster. The name Dundee Junction was used because there had been a good deal of talk about building a railroad bridge over Willamette River from Fulquartz Landing on the Yamhill County side to Rays Landing on the Marion County side. The east side narrow gauge line would thus be brought to Dundee where a junction would be made with the west side line and also a connection to Portland. The writer is of the opinion that the name Dundee Junction was in use by the railroad company prior to the time that Dundee

Junction post office was established. In any event, the name Dundee Junction for the post office prevailed until February 13, 1897, when it was changed to Dundee, the present style. The bridge has not been built.

Dundon Bridge, Lincoln County. Dundon Bridge is just west of Toledo, and the name is frequently misspelled. Alonzo T. M. Dundon was born in Peoria, Illinois, in 1852, and came to Oregon with his parents in 1864 in the train of Captain Frank Shedd. In 1866 the Dundon family settled near what is now Toledo. Alonzo Dundon ran a brickyard and also a freight line from Corvallis to the coast. He died December 27, 1940. For obituary, see Toledo *Leader,* January 2, 1941.

Dunes City, Lane County. In the early 1960s there was a movement to establish a Dunes National Park in the Siltcoos Lake area. The local residents including Westlake and North Beach wished to avoid being included in the proposed park so in 1962 they voted to incorporate as Dunes City. Westlake post office, established in 1915, continues to serve the area and North Beach is retained as the name of the neighborhood near the mouth of Woahink Creek.

Dunlap Lake, Marion County. This lake, northeast of Detroit, was named for Harry Dunlap, a prospector, who located a prospect nearby. The name was first applied about 1906, according to information furnished by Charles C. Giebeler of Detroit.

Dunning Creek, Yamhill County. Dunning Creek west of Carlton Lake was named for Alexander Dunning whose donation land claim was along its banks. He settled there in 1853 but left Yamhill County in 1858.

Durbin, Marion County. Durbin was a railroad station east of Salem. It was named for F. W. Durbin of Salem, who had a switch put in so that he could load cordwood at this point. For information about the Durbin family, see the *Oregonian* August 1, 1926, section 1, page 12.

Durham, Washington County. Albert Alonzo Durham came to Oregon in 1847. He built a sawmill below Oregon City, which he sold. Then he built a sawmill at Oswego, where he did a large business until 1869. See advertisement of his sawmill at Oswego in the *Oregonian* in 1850-1851. He named Oswego for Oswego, New York. After operating at Oswego, he moved into Washington County and built a sawmill and a flour mill on Fanno Creek. These mills were operated by water power, and for a number of years the place was known as Durhams Mills. When the Oregon Electric Railway was built the station at this point was called Durham. A. A. Durham was born in Genesee County, New York, March 15, 1814; died in Washington County, Oregon, April 4, 1898.

Durkee, Baker County. The community Durkee was named for a family of early settlers. The first post office in the locality was called Express Ranch, with C. W. Durkee first postmaster. It was established April 21, 1865, but was later moved to Weatherby. See under Express Ranch for the history of this office. The existing post office Durkee was established February 26, 1902, probably by change of name from another office called Express.

Dusty, Benton County. In February, 1946, Robert Johnson of Corvallis wrote the compiler as follows: "Frank Elgin opened a country store five miles northwest of Monroe, and a post office was established therein with Helen Elgin, his daughter, postmaster. The storekeeper suggested the name Elgin for the new office but as many residents of the community came from Bellefontaine, Ohio, they wanted it named for their native heath. No agreement could be reached and as the store was located on dusty crossroads, the name Dusty was adopted. But the people of the community were not satisfied until the name was changed to Bellfountain and Bellfountain today is surrounded by a prosperous community." The post office at Dusty was established December 6, 1895, with Helen Elgin first postmaster. Whatever the local argument may have been about the name of the office, the real reason why Elgin was not selected was because there was already an Elgin in Oregon and duplications were not allowed. Postal records are not entirely clear, but it seems probable that the name of the office Dusty was changed to Bellfountain on July 31, 1902.

Dutch Flat, Wasco County. In the early 1870s a German settled on the plateau east of and above Mill Creek. His home was known as Dutchman's Cabin and the flat has been called Dutch Flat ever since.

Dutch Oven Camp, Lane County. Dutch Oven Camp is on South Fork McKenzie River. S. L. Taylor of McKenzie Bridge is authority for the story of origin of the name. A burro, packed for a fishing party, fell over a cliff at this point and was killed. About the only part of the pack that was undamaged was a demijohn of whisky, but an iron Dutch oven was badly broken and the rest of the pack ruined. The remains of the oven lay in the vicinity for several years and caused the application of the name.

Dutcher Creek, Josephine County. Dutcher Creek flows into Rogue River from the southwest nine miles downstream from Grants Pass. It takes its name from John Dutcher whose donation land claim was near its mouth.

Dutchman Butte, Douglas County. Before the turn of the century a German named Chris Swagerman lived in Elk Valley just west of this 3907 foot summit. Swagerman was a solitary individual who disliked visitors and the butte was given the vernacular name so often applied to his stubborn compatriots.

Dutchman Flat, Deschutes County. The late Judge H. C. Ellis of Bend was responsible for the story that a German sheepherder and party discovered the flat years ago when they were blocked by snow near Sparks Lake and forced to winter nearby. An editorial in the Bend *Bulletin,* November 21, 1958, gives a more reasonable origin. After noting that snows on 6200 foot Dutchman Flat or even 5500 foot Sparks Lake are often fifteen feet deep, they properly conclude that neither man nor sheep could have survived an ordinary winter. This comment is followed by the opinion of the Vandevert brothers that the flat was named for "Dutch John" Felderwerd who ranched near the present location of Bend in the 1880s. Felderwerd ranged sheep and cattle as far west as Sparks Lake and built and maintained cabins for his herders in many locations.

Dutton Canyon, Morrow County. This canyon just west of Heppner was named for William P. Dutton, an early homesteader. He was born in Vermont in 1852 and came to Rhea Creek about 1875.

Dutton Cliff, Crater Lake National Park, Klamath County. This cliff is t the southeast corner of Crater Lake at an elevation of 8150 feet. It was named by Will G. Steel in 1886 for Captain Clarence E. Dutton, U. S. A.

Duwee Canyon, Crater Lake National Park, Klamath County. This canon lies to the south of Crater Lake, and is remarkable for its unusual spires and pinnacles. The name is from the Klamath Indian word *ti-wi*, indicating the rushing noise made by a cascade. A waterfall in the canyon has the same name. The spelling Duwee has been adopted by USBGN, and the style Dewie is obsolete.

Dwyer Creek, Curry County. This stream flows into South Fork Floras Creek near Edson Butte. It was named for P. F. Dwyer, an early settler.

Dyar Rock, Crater Lake National Park, Klamath County. This rock is on the south rim of Crater Lake, and has an elevation of 7880 feet. It was named in 1872 by Captain O. C. Applegate for Leroy S. Dyar, of Ontario, California, then Indian agent on the Klamath Indian Reservation, and later a member of the Modoc Peace Commission. Dyar was the only member of the commission who escaped uninjured when attacked by Captain Jack and his band of Indians in the Lava Beds April 11, 1873, at which time General E. R. S. Canby and Dr. E. Thomas were killed and chairman A. B. Meacham was wounded and left for dead.

Dyer Well, Deschutes County. This well was on the property of Howard F. Dyer who homesteaded near Horse Ridge in 1912.

Eagle Butte, Hood River and Multnomah counties. This butte was formerly called Eagle Creek Butte, because it was near the headwaters of the creek, but the name was cumbersome and the USFS has adopted the shorter form.

Eagle Cap, Wallowa County. This peak was for many years thought to be the highest mountain in eastern Oregon. In early days the Wallowa Mountains had a variety of names, including Eagle Mountains, and Eagle Cap was supposed to be the top of them all, hence the name. According to the USGS it has an elevation of 9595 feet so there are other peaks in the Wallowa Mountains that are higher.

Eagle Creek, Baker and Union counties. There are a good many geographic features in Oregon named for the eagle including mountains, streams and places. One of the most important is Eagle Creek which rises on the south slopes of the Wallowa mountains and flows southeastward into Powder River. This stream has played a prominent part both in the mining and in the irrigation history of northeast Oregon. An account of the naming of this stream is given by Isaac Hiatt in his book *Thirty-one Years in Baker County*, page 30. Knight and Abbott were herding cattle in the Powder River Valley in 1861, and coming to a considerable tributary, they shot an eagle. That circumstance gave the name Eagle Creek to the stream.

Eagle Creek, Clackamas County. Eagle Creek is the name of a post office as well as of a stream. There are many streams of the same name in the state. A. C. Cogswell, postmaster at Eagle Creek in 1925, wrote the compiler that the place was called Eagle Creek as early as 1844, and that the name originated with Indians because there were so many eagles along the stream.

Eagle Point, Jackson County. Just east of the town of Eagle Point is a prominent rocky cliff, surmounted by pine trees, and in pioneer days this was a favorite nesting place for eagles. It was called Eagle Point. It is said that John Mathews suggested the name of this point for the post office, which was established about 1872, with Andrew McNeil first postmaster. By 1981 there was only one water-powered, stone ground gristmill still operating in Oregon. For a story about the Butte Creek Mill in Eagle Point, see the *Oregonian*, January 8, 1982, page E1. The mill, built in 1872, was placed on the National Register of Historic Places in 1976.

Eagleton, Baker County. Eagleton post office was in the extreme north part of the county a little to the northeast of Sanger. It was on one of the forks of Eagle Creek and took its name on that account. When established the office was in Union County, but a change of boundaries brought it into Baker County. Eagleton post office was established April 22, 1896, with Frank McGee first postmaster. It was closed in February, 1902. The compiler was told that the place was established in connection with mining activity.

Earl, Lane County. Earl post office was established April 26, 1898, with Arthur J. Johnson first postmaster, and was named for Earl R. Johnson, the small son of the postmaster. It is reported that several names were sent in and postal authorities selected Earl from the lot. The office was then in Douglas County, on the headwaters of Sweet Creek southeast of Point Terrace. About 1913 the Douglas-Lane county boundary line was changed and the office was then in Lane County. It was discontinued June 15, 1925. In March 1947, Earl R. Johnson, then living on Crow Stage Route, wrote the compiler in part as follows: "At that time all the mail was carried on horseback over steep mountain trails, and though the mail came only once a week, mail day was really an event to the people in that out of the way station. The route led from Point Terrace at the mouth of Sweet Creek on the Siuslaw River up the creek to Earl, a distance of nine miles. I helped circulate the petition which led to the change of the county boundary. About the time Earl post office was established, an office was also established at Ord, which was about seven miles east over the mountains on the headwaters of Smith River. Horace Fisk was the first postmaster at Ord."

Early, Sherman County. Early post office was established in the northeast part of Sherman County on January 9, 1902, with Herbert K. Porter first of three postmasters. Members of the Wall family later ran the office, which was discontinued August 30, 1919. On September 10, 1946, Giles French wrote the compiler as follows: "Early was a post office on the north line of township two north just west of John Day River. At Early there was a flour mill where early-day farmers obtained their bread-stuff, and I am told the name was given the place because garden sass became edible early when grown there. The elevation is low and the sun shines brightly in the John Day Valley when it is cold and windy on the hills above. The Walls built a dam a short way above the mill and James Fox now grows alfalfa there. It would be a quiet and peaceful spot in which to retire from the cares of the world, the telephones, the Russians, bureaucracy, radio, UNRRA, the whips and scorns of time, the unworthy spurns that patient merit takes."

East Lake, Deschutes County. This is a landlocked lake about two miles in diameter, occupying what was probably once part of the crater of a volcanic peak known to geologists as Mount Newberry. It is in the Paulina Mountains southeast of Bend. It is in the eastern part of the crater, opposite Paulina Lake, and is called East Lake on that account.

East Morrison Street, Multnomah County. In the summer of 1909 the Southern Pacific Company opened a new station to serve the east part of Portland and the official name was East Morrison Street. In the days of more frequent local train service, this station did a good business and the regular patrons were augmented by travelers who found they could not make the time to the Union Station but could catch their trains at East Morrison Street by judicious use of taxicabs or family automobiles. Station attendants and train crews saw the finish of many a close race. The East Morrison Street station was demolished in the winter of 1945-46. For news story and pictures of the event, see the *Oregonian,* January 13, 1946. The reference to the East Side station is incorrect. The railroad name-board read East Morrison Street, and at one time the lettering was gilt on a black background. The station served little or no passenger business in later years. The original Oregon & California Railroad station established about 1879 was on what was known as L Street in East Portland, later East Washington Street. The building was generally called the L-Street station but the official name was East Portland. Later there was another station near the mouth of Sullivan Gulch which was called the East Side station, but still later East Portland, serving two railroads. See under East Portland. After the station name East Portland was moved from East Washington Street to the new East Portland station near the mouth of Sullivan Gulch, it was necessary to adopt a new name for the old station. The railroad company decided on the style East Washington Street and that name was used up to the time that the new East Morrison Street establishment was put in service.

East Portland, Multnomah County. East Portland existed as a separate community from pioneer days until June 1, 1891, when an election was held on the proposal to consolidate the three communities Portland, East Portland and Albina. The proposal carried and the program became effective July 5, 1891. James B. Stephens was the founder of East Portland. In 1845 Stephens bought for $200 property previously owned by a French-Canadian, one Porier. Stephens laid out a town in 1850-51 and filed the East Portland plat in 1865. The selection of the name seemed to have been natural, but not imaginative, and in this respect followed the pattern of much other Oregon nomenclature. For the early history of Stephens and East Portland by Leslie M. Scott, see *OHQ,* volume XXXI, page 351. East Portland post office was established May 15, 1866, with Milton Hosford first postmaster. The office continued in service until March 4, 1892, when it was consolidated with Portland. John M. Lewis was then postmaster of East Portland. When the Oregon & California Railroad began to operate about 1870, it had a station called East Portland. This station was near the foot of what was then L Street, now known as Southeast Washington Street. This station was popularly known as the L-Street station, although East Portland was its official name. This was not the same station as East Morrison Street, a later structure that served many years and was demolished in the winter of 1945-46. The railroad had a terminus farther north near the mouth of Sullivan Gulch, which was called the East Side Station. Later the Southern Pacific and the Union Pacific had a station near this point called East Portland, but it was a separate operating point from either the original East Portland or East Morrison Street.

Eastside, Coos County. This is a descriptive name, because the community is on the east side of Coos Bay. This place was at one time the terminal of the old Coos Bay Military Wagon Road. It was originally called East Marshfield, but about 1908 the name was changed to the present style.

Ebell Creek, Baker County. This creek where the Union Pacific Railroad leaves Sutton Creek was named for August Ebell who homesteaded along its banks. Ebell was a brother of George Ebell who came to Baker County in 1865.

Ebell Picnic Area, Baker County. This park in the narrow neck between Mill and Marble creeks was named for George Ebell, an early settler. He was the brother of August Ebell who settled near Encina.

Echo, Umatilla County. This place was named for Echo Koontz, daughter of Mr. and Mrs. J. H. Koontz. The community was started about 1880, and the Koontz family was among the first to settle there. Echo is near the site of Fort Henrietta, so called for Mrs. Henrietta Haller, wife of Major Granville O. Haller, U. S. A., who commanded troops in early Indian campaigns. When the post office at Echo was established, Major Lee Moorehouse, of Pendleton, tried to have the name Henrietta adopted, but as Koontz was interested in the town, his daughter's name was selected. James H. Koontz was born in Ohio in 1830 and came to Oregon in 1862, settling at Umatilla in 1863. Echo Koontz was born at Umatilla Landing and later was Mrs. Charles H. Miller. Koontz died in 1912. For additional information about the locality of Echo, once known as Brasfield Ferry, see story by Fred Lockley in *Oregon Journal*, August 30, 1931. In 1861-62 Thomas A. Brasfield ran a stage station called The Crossing along with the ferry and kept the travel.

Eckley, Curry County. Eckley is a place at the east edge of the county near North Fork Sixes River on the old mountain road from Myrtle Point southwest to Port Orford. The post office has had three different names. A post office called New Castle was established in this locality on December 19, 1879, with Mrs. Charlotte Guerin first postmaster. The name was changed to Tell Tale on May 21, 1883 and to Eckley on June 29, 1883. This office was in operation until December 15, 1916, when it was closed out to Myrtle Point. A study of the Guerin family history as printed in Dodge's *Pioneer History of Coos and Curry Counties,* indicated that Mrs. Guerin's daughter-in-law, Mrs. George H. Guerin, was a native of Wingate, a place near Newcastle-on-Tyne in the north of England. It seems more than probable to the compiler that the name New Castle for the Curry County post office was suggested by Mrs. George Guerin, or by somebody in the family in her compliment. That there was a difference in the spelling is not a great objection to this theory. So much for New Castle. The name Eckley for this post office came from Mrs. Guerin's grandson, Eckley Guerin, son of Mr. and

Mrs. George H. Guerin. Eckley Guerin was born in August, 1882, and the name Eckley was applied to the post office June 29, 1883.

Eckman Slough, Lincoln County. Eckman Slough and Eckman Creek are south of Alsea Bay. The postmaster at Waldport wrote the compiler in 1927 that these two streams were named many years ago for a Scandinavian settler who lived nearby.

Ecola Creek, Clatsop County. Captain William Clark was the first white man of record to visit the vicinity of this stream, which he did on Wednesday, January 8, 1806. He called the stream *Ecola* or Whale Creek. From pioneer days until 1974 the stream was called Elk Creek but then at the instigation of the Oregon Lewis and Clark Trail Committee the original name was restored. The village near its mouth at the north end of Cannon Beach was first called Elk Creek, then Ecola, but for many years its postal name has been Cannon Beach. See under Ecola and Cannon Beach for additional information. Thwaites on page 324 of volume III of his *Original Journals of the Lewis and Clark Expedition,* is confused about Whale Creek and mistakes it for Nehalem River, the more important stream to the south. He has done the same with other features visited by Captain Clark during the first days in January, and identifies them with points too far south. See under Tillamook Head.

Ecola Point, Clatsop County. Some time prior to 1900 J. Couch Flanders of Portland was attracted by the name Ecola and he applied it to a group of cottages owned by the Couch family on the south flank of Tillamook Head about two miles north of what was then known as Elk Creek. The name was attractive, and people living near the mouth of Elk Creek asked for a post office to be named Ecola, which was established November 25, 1910. To avoid confusion R. L. Glisan and L. Allen Lewis then changed the name of the Couch family cottages to Ecola Point, because of the prominent projection nearby. Ecola Point is between Chapman Point and the main promontory of Tillamook Head. The name Ecola is no longer used for the post office, which is now Cannon Beach. George Gibbs, in his *Dictionary of the Chinook Jargon* gives the word *ehkoli,* a whale, and indicates that it came from the Chinook Indian word *ekoli,* with the accent on the first letter. The modern spelling with the accent on the middle syllable is, however, firmly established.

Eddeeleo Lakes, Lane County. These three lakes north of Waldo Lake were first stocked and fished by three early USFS employees. The name is a combination of the first names of Ed Clark, Dee Wright and Leo McMahon.

Eddyville, Lincoln County. This post office seems to have had more than the usual number of moves. It was first called Little Elk, because it was near the mouth of Little Elk Creek. About 1888 Israel F. Eddy, the postmaster, moved the office about a mile west and had the name changed to Eddyville. Some four years later the office was brought back to its original location and the name changed to Little Elk. About 1893 it was moved again to Eddy's place and was continued under the name of Eddyville until 1900 when it was moved back to the mouth of Little Elk Creek, but this time the name was not changed and the office still goes by the name Eddyville.

Eden, Coos County. Eden was the name used for a post office in the extreme southeast part of Coos County, in the very rough, mountainous country on West Fork Cow Creek. Eden post office was established July 21, 1914, with Edward A. Zimmerman first of three postmasters. The office was discontinued January 14, 1922, with mail to Dothan on Cow Creek. The compiler has been told that transportation to this post office was very primitive and he puts great faith in the report. The name for the post office was doubtless suggested by that of Eden Ridge to the southwest. Eden Ridge has been so called for many years. The ridge and the post office apparently were named by people fond of isolation and pioneer living.

Eden, Wallowa County. Wallowa County has had more than its share of post offices with names showing that its settlers seemed to be pleased with the prospects. Among these names have been: Paradise, Promise, Joy, Arcadia, Utopia, Eureka and Enterprise. There was also a post office called Lovely but that was the family name of the postmaster. A post office with the name Eden was established October 2, 1907, with B. E. Puller, postmaster. Apparently the office never operated because the appointment was rescinded on April 29, 1908. It was planned to put the office at the Puller ranch on the breaks of the Grande Ronde River a few miles southwest of Troy. The locality is generally known as Eden Ridge.

Eden Park, Hood River County. Eden Park, on the northwest slope of Mount Hood, was named in the summer of 1922 by a camping party led by C. Edward Graves, then of Hood River, but living in Arcata, California, in 1943. At the same time the party applied the names Cathedral Ridge, Vista Ridge and Wy'east Basin. These names were all adopted by the USBGN.

Edenbower, Douglas County. Edenbower is a locality about two miles north of Roseburg. It was named as long ago as 1888 by a family that moved from the rigorous climate of Winnipeg, Manitoba, to the Umpqua Valley. This family was impressed by the warm sunshine of that part of Douglas County and coined the name Edenbower. In April, 1948, Mrs. John Ferguson wrote from Days Creek, Oregon, that Mr. and Mrs. Donald Ferguson and three children came to Roseburg from Winnipeg in 1888 and after living in town a short while bought a ten-acre tract, and proceeded to make it their home. Mrs. Ferguson was so much impressed by the climate and the surroundings that she wrote a poem in November, 1888, extolling the locality and referring to it as Edenbower. It was not long after this, perhaps in 1890, that a school was organized and Mr. Ferguson suggested that it be called Edenbower. The name was adopted. Edenbower community did not have a post office until August 1, 1908. John Botcher was the first postmaster. This office was discontinued January 31, 1919. The area is served now by a rural route. Mrs. Ferguson's poem, "Winter— A Contrast", will be found in the Roseburg *News-Review* for May 21, 1948. It appears in the column by Charles V. Stanton and along with it are some other items about Edenbower.

Edison Ice Cave, Deschutes County. On June 6, 1910, a large fire blazed some 30 miles southwest of Bend. One of the firefighters was Jack Edison, who, when returning to camp with George Vandevert, discovered a cool opening in the earth, entered and found an ice cave. Not only was

Edison's name given the cave but also the fire. A butte nearby is named for the same man, apparently a member of a transient crew. Edison Ice Cave is about four miles west of Wanoga Butte.

Edson Butte, Curry County. Edson Butte is a prominent landmark about seven miles east of Langlois. Both it and the creek that flows into Sixes River were named for Avery J. Edson who came from New York with the Applegate train of 1846. Edson operated the Pacific Hotel at Port Orford in 1854 and later took as his second wife Christina Geisel, a survivor of the massacre north of Gold Beach.

Edwards Creek, Tillamook County. Edwards Creek rises on 3168 foot Edwards Butte and is tributary to South Fork Trask River. Both were named for John D. Edwards, an early day timber cruiser, who took up a timber claim near the creek in 1889.

Egg Creek, Linn County. Roy Elliott, who was district ranger for the USFS at Detroit for many years, told the writer in 1978 that around 1915 a trail crew camped on this creek near the headwaters of Middle Santiam River. Roy Talbert was insulted by one Anderson, another member of the party, and Talbert retaliated by hitting Anderson with a hard boiled egg.

Eight Dollar Mountain, Josephine County. Eight Dollar Mountain, elevation 3992 feet, is one of the prominent features in the Illinois Valley. There are several stories as to how it got its name, the most probable being that it came about as a result of the discovery nearby of a gold nugget worth $8.00. Another version is that a man wore out a pair of shoes worth $8.00 walking around its base. Its sides are excessively rough and inasmuch as the distance is about 12 miles it is quite possible that the latter story may be true. The battle of Eight Dollar Mountain, a skirmish in the Rogue River Indian War, was fought in this locality March 25, 1856. See Victor's *Early Indian Wars of Oregon,* pages 391-92.

Eightmile, Morrow County. The post office at Eightmile took its name from Eightmile Canyon, which was so named because its mouth was about eight miles up Willow Creek from the Columbia River. The name was first used by pioneer stockmen.

Eightmile Creek, Wasco County. This stream was so called because the pioneer wagon road from The Dalles into central Oregon crossed it about eight miles from town. Eightmile Creek and Fivemile Creek join, and the combined stream, called Eightmile Creek, flows into Fifteenmile Creek. For information about the names of this group of streams see under Fifteenmile Creek.

Eilertson Meadow, Baker County. Herbert Ensminger of Haines was authority for the information that this meadow west of Hunt Mountain was named for Eilert Eilertson who had a cabin and fish pond near its lower end. Eilertson lived there in the summer and in Haines the rest of the year. He died in 1919.

Ekins, Yamhill County. The first post office to serve the locality now known as Dundee was named Ekins for the postmaster, Claudius Ekins, who was appointed June 7, 1881. The name of this office was changed to Dundee on July 25, 1882. For the further history of this office see under Dundee. Ekins post office was established about the time that the narrow gauge railroad was being extended from Dayton northeast through what is now Dundee to Fulquartz Landing on the Willamette River. See Scott's *History of the Oregon Country*, volume IV, page 305, *et seq.*

Ekoms, Curry County. The order establishing Ekoms post office was dated June 20, 1899. George W. Billings was to be the first postmaster. However, for some reason, the office never went into service and the order was rescinded September 15, 1902. In April, 1948, Mr. Billings wrote that the name Ekoms was made by spelling Smoke backward. The office was to be in the Rogue River area, and the method of getting a name may have been suggested by the method used to make the name Ragic for a post office further down stream. Ragic, or Cigar spelled backward, was the name of a post office on Rogue River near the mouth of Lobster Creek.

Elam, Benton County. Elam is the post office name for a small community known as Harris, near Philomath. Postal authorities would not accept the name Harris for the post office because of similarity to Harrisburg in Linn County. Accordingly the office was named for Mrs. Gladys Elam, the first postmaster. See under Harris.

Elbow Lake, Douglas County. This little lake is about a mile east of the Pacific Ocean, just west of Tahkenitch Lake. It is known as Elbow Lake on account of its shape. See the USGS map of the Siltcoos Lake quadrangle.

Elder Creek, Josephine County. Elder Creek is about two miles east of Waldo. It was named for John Elder, a pioneer rancher.

Eldriedge Bar, Marion County. Eldriedge Bar is on the Willamette River about three miles downstream from Wheatland. It got its name from Freeman E. Eldriedge, a pioneer settler on French Prairie. Eldriedge School, north of Waconda, was named for the same man. He was born in Pennsylvania in 1826 and came to Oregon by way of California in 1846-47. For a time during the 1850s Eldriedge rented his farm near the Willamette River and operated a grist mill at Parkersville about ten miles eastward. He was instrumental in having the Parkersville post office established and was the first postmaster.

Eldorado, Malheur County. Eldorado, as a geographic name, is taken from the Spanish expression *el dorado,* meaning the gilded, and by analogy a golden or otherwise valuable object. It also means a legendary land abounding in gold. Its principal use in the West is in the Sierra Nevada of California, where it is applied to the county in which gold was discovered in 1848. The name has been used in many localities and may be found spelled El Dorado and also ElDorado. Modern usage tends toward Eldorado. The place called Eldorado in Shasta Gulch in what is now the extreme north part of Malheur County was a few miles northwest of the community of Malheur. It was named in the days of the eastern Oregon gold rush of the 1860s, doubtless by some of the many Californians who took part in the excitement. Miners began to work the placers of Eldorado as early as 1865, and about 1868 a town was started. A writer in the *Oregonian* of about that time says that the embryo town rejoiced in the name El Dorado City and was indifferently supplied with everything but whisky. The place thrived for a few years, but when Eldorado ditch began to bring in the waters from upper Burnt River many miles away, it missed the town of Eldorado, which

was abandoned in consequence. Early in the 1870s many of the movable
structures were taken to a new locality called Malheur City. El Dorado post
office was established September 1, 1869, with Samuel B. Reeves first postmaster. The office was finally closed in November, 1879. Building Eldorado ditch was one of Oregon's remarkable construction enterprises.
William H. Packwood was a moving spirit in the business. The ditch
gathered the waters of a number of tributaries on the south side of Burnt
River and conveyed them eastward to a pass in the ridge south of Burnt
River called Shasta Gap. It went through this pass toward Shasta Gulch and
the Willow Creek drainage, where it was extensively used in mining. The
ditch was originally about 135 miles long. In recent years it has been used
for irrigation.

Elephant Mountain, Douglas County. This is in the northeast part of
the county northwest of Diamond Lake, and has an elevation of 5950 feet.
The name was applied by V. V. Harpham and O. C. Houser, of the USFS
in 1908, because the mountain when viewed from the west is suggestive
both in shape and size, of the animal whose name it bears.

Elephant Mountain, Lane County. Mrs. R. L. Gawley who lived for
many years in Disston told the compiler in 1968 that this mountain in the
Bohemia district bore a singularly appropriate descriptive name.

Elgarose, Douglas County. Elgarose, a post office in the southeast part
of township 26 south, range 7 west, a couple of miles northwest of Melrose
was named by the first postmaster, John E. Carlson, for Algaros in Sweden.
The Reverend Mr. Carlson was born in the place in Sweden, and thought
to perpetuate its name in Douglas County when the opportunity presented
itself. Elgarose post office was established January 28, 1916, with Carlson
postmaster. The office was closed November 27, 1924, and the business
turned over to Melrose.

Elgin, Union County. In early days the locality of Elgin was called both
Indian Valley and Fishtrap, because of the presence of Indian fishing gear.
Elgin post office was established on September 28, 1885, with W. B. Hamilton postmaster. A news story in the Elgin *Recorder* for Feb. 18, 1932, is
authority for the statement that when the application for a post office was
being prepared, Hamilton heard his niece and nephew, Lottie and Charlie
Hamilton, singing about the wreck of the steamer *Lady Elgin,* and he was so
impressed by the name that he suggested the title Elgin for the post office.
The news item in the *Recorder* is based on a statement from C. W. Hamilton,
then 88 years old and living on Lower Cove market road. Presumably he
was the nephew, Charlie Hamilton. The compiler has been unable to learn
that the community was named for Elgin, Illinois. The wreck of the *Lady
Elgin* was one of the worst lacustrine disasters in the history of the United
States. This steamer was loaded with a group called the Union Guard, composed of Third Ward boys of Milwaukee, who formed an excursion to
attend a mass meeting in the presidential campaign of 1860. The Union
Guard went to Chicago to hear their favorite, Stephen A. Douglas, on September 7. The excursion and the political rally were highly successful, and
the happy crowd started back for Milwaukee, Irish lads and lassies dancing
as the boat ploughed through a Lake Michigan fog. About midnight the

Lady Elgin was hit by a lumber schooner, the *Augusta,* which proceeded on her way after being assured that the *Lady Elgin* was not seriously damaged. This was a mistake, because the steamer sank in a short time, with a loss of nearly 300 lives. This disaster was the subject of a lugubrious ballad that was popular for a couple of decades, and the community of Elgin, Oregon, appears to have been named for the melancholy song, "Lost on the *Lady Elgin.*"

Eliot Glacier, Hood River County. Eliot Glacier is one of the larger glaciers on Mount Hood and occupies the northeast part of the mountain north of Cooper Spur. It is the source of Eliot Branch, and its lower end is not far from Cloud Cap Inn. It was named for Dr. Thomas Lamb Eliot, for many years one of Portland's most revered citizens. Dr. Eliot was born in St. Louis, Missouri, on October 13, 1841, and graduated with the first class from Washington University in St. Louis, of which his father was chancellor. He came to Portland December 24, 1867, and took over the pastorate of the Unitarian Church. For a short biography of Dr. Eliot see the *Oregonian,* October 13, 1925, page 5. Dr. Eliot was at one time greatly interested in mountaineering and the glacier on Mount Hood was named for him on that account. He died in Portland April 26, 1936. In 1925 the Mazamas research committee made a number of investigations as to the rate of flow of Eliot Glacier. These observations were carried on at an elevation of approximately 7800 feet, and notes were taken for 14 weeks. The investigations indicated that the stakes which were set in the glacier traveled about four feet a week. The maximum movement was near the center of the glacier and the movement near the side walls was somewhat less, and during part of the season the sides of the glacier moved eight inches a week. Additional observations at an elevation of 7200 feet indicated a movement of about two feet a week for the central part of the glacier. See *Mazama* for December, 1925. *Mazama,* monthly edition, for August, 1926, gives additional information about the flow of this glacier. The greatest record for a year of any of the marks was made by one on the upper line, which moved 183.7 feet.

Elk Butte, Lake County. Elk Butte is near the southwest corner of section 12, township 27 south, range 22 east, a little to the southwest of Wagontire Mountain. This is in an area where elk have not frequently been found because of the lack of water. In May, 1947, Archie McGowan of Burns informed the writer that Elk Butte was named in the early 1890s by members of the Hutton, Egli and other local families who discovered the track of a lone elk which took them to what they called Elk Butte. They were positive they were on the trail of a stray elk, which was very unusual for the desert country of Lake County.

Elk City, Lincoln County. Elk City is at the junction of Elk Creek and Yaquina River, and was named for the creek. It is said to have been the first settlement in what is now Lincoln County. Postal records show that Newton post office was established in July, 1868, with E. A. Abbey first postmaster. Marshall Simpson became postmaster in November, 1869. He was out of the office for a few years, but held the position again on November 23, 1888, when the name was changed from Newton to Elk City. It is said that he instigated the change. Statements to the effect that Elk City was named by pioneer settlers about 1865 do not agree with the records unless the locality and the post office went by different names. This has happened at a number of places in Oregon.

Elk Creek, Benton and Lincoln counties. Jerry E. Henkle, Benton County pioneer, is authority for the statement that Elk Creek was named in 1856 by a party of explorers who went westward into the Coast Range looking for grazing land. The name was given because a fine bull elk was shot near one of the camps on the stream. Elk Creek rises on the west slope of Marys Peak and flows westward into Yaquina River.

Elk Creek, Douglas County. Elk Creek joins Umpqua River near the town of Elkton. The stream has borne the name of Elk Creek since the period of the fur traders. The writer does not know when the stream was first named, but John Work mentions it as Elk River in his diary on June 7, 1834. See *OHQ*, September, 1923. Elk appear to have been plentiful in the Willamette Valley and in the Umpqua country, and there are many features named for them in those parts of the state.

Elk Creek, Douglas County. Judging by the number of geographic names in Oregon commemorating elk, that animal must have been both plentiful and popular in the days of the fur traders and the pioneers. Elk furnished more than their share of early-day provisions. A recent count by the State Engineer shows about thirty Elk creeks in the state. An important stream named Elk Creek flows into South Umpqua River at Tiller, in the southeast part of the county. It was named in pioneer times. There was an Elk Creek post office near the mouth of the stream, established December 18, 1877, with S. C. Cramer first postmaster. This office operated with the name Elk Creek until August 22, 1884, when the name was changed to Perdue, in compliment to John Perdue, Sr., then postmaster. Perdue took office June 11, 1884. About this time the office was moved west and down South Umpqua River about six miles below the mouth of Elk Creek, and the new locality became known as Perdue. It is not clear from available records just when this move was made. Tiller post office was established near the mouth of Elk Creek October 15, 1902, with Alfred B. Marquam first postmaster, and was still in operation in 1972. Tiller was named for Aaron Tiller, a local settler. The locality has become of importance in the news because of its place on the Tiller-Trail highway.

Elk Flat, Union County. Elk Flat is east of Elgin. It is an extension, to the south, from Cricket Flat. In January, 1947, Geo. T. Cochran of La Grande wrote the compiler: "Elk Flat joins Cricket Flat on the south. There is probably no dividing line between the two areas. In pioneer days there were many elk that grazed along the south part of Cricket Flat, and from that fact the locality became known as Elk Flat. I can remember going there many times with my father to get our winter's meat in the form of Elk." Elk Flat post office was established April 17, 1878, with Joseph M. Tucker first postmaster. The office was discontinued November 11, 1886. Tucker took up a homestead and built a house and blacksmith shop in section 17, township 1 north, range 40 east. According to Mr. Cochran he later found that his improvements had been installed on the wrong land. This was such an irritation that he gave up the post office and returned to his old home in Iowa. However, he came back to Oregon later. The Elk Flat post office was continued at various locations, and during the time James S. Brayton had it (1881-1886), it was at the Brayton place on Owenby Hill in section 10 of the township mentioned above, about five or six miles northeast of Elgin.

Elk Horn, Polk County. Elk Horn was one of the pioneer post offices of the county and as with many others it was not always in the same place. Without a doubt it was named for some incident connected with an elk's horn. Probably a pair was nailed over the door of the Buell home. Elk Horn post office was established November 16, 1869, with Cyrus Buell postmaster. Buell was a prominent settler on Mill Creek and was interested in the grist mill that gave the stream its name. For about five years the post office was at the Buell place about two miles south or upstream from the highway bridge and present location of the community called Buell. On May 18, 1874, Thomas R. Blair was appointed postmaster of Elk Horn and during his incumbency the office was about two miles north or down Mill Creek from what is now Buell. The office was closed October 4, 1882, but the locality, which is a little over four miles southwest of Sheridan by road, is still called Elk Horn.

Elk Lake, Deschutes County. Elk Lake is a fine body of water southwest of Bend, and Elk Lake post office is nearby. The lake was named in 1906 by USFS ranger Roy Harvey of Eugene. The post office was established because the lake was and is extensively used for recreation purposes.

Elk Mountain, Deschutes and Lane counties. This prominent peak of the Cascade Range is south of South Sister and west of Elk Lake. The mountain and Elk Lake were named about 1906 by Roy Harvey. A band of elk came across the summit of the range every year from the west and spent most of the summer on the side of a butte, which Harvey called Elk Mountain. This is said to be the only place where elk range on the east slopes of the Cascade Range.

Elk Point, Washington County. This is a prominent hill about 960 feet high, just west of the community of Sylvan. The Pointer family settled near this hill in pioneer days, and called it Elk Point because the animals browsed on the sides of the point in question. In later years this feature has been called Pointers Point, but this was not its original name and on June 3, 1925, the USBGN officially adopted the name Elk Point.

Elk River, Curry County. This is a well-known stream that flows into the Pacific Ocean between Cape Blanco and Port Orford. It has been known as Elk River since territorial days and was probably named during the gold rush to the beach placers in southwest Oregon. There were many elk in those parts. The style Elk River is used in an article by William V. Wells in *Harper's Magazine,* October, 1856, page 591, describing experiences in southwest Oregon in October, 1855.

Elkhead, Douglas County. The community and post office were named because they were near the head or source of Elk Creek in the western slopes of the Calapooya Mountains. A post office with the name Elk Head was established here on May 28, 1877, with R. J. Hendricks postmaster. On February 27, 1895, the name was changed to Elkhead, and the office was discontinued March 31, 1926. The best available maps show the name in one word. Elkhead was sometimes called Shoestring.

Elkhorn, Marion County. This is a community on Little North Santiam River a few miles northeast of Mill City. While the origin of the name is obvious, the writer does not know the circumstances in which it was applied. The USGS map of the Mill City quadrangle shows Elkhorn and Elkhorn School to be several miles apart in the valley. Elkhorn post office was established in March, 1892, with William D. Morehouse postmaster. The office was finally closed in June, 1917. Its principal business doubtless had to do with mining activity along the upper reaches of Little North Santiam River. There was an earlier post office in this neighborhood called Ivie, established in June, 1890, with Martha J. Heath postmaster. The name of this office was changed to Elkhorn in March, 1892, but the writer does not know if the offices were at the same place.

Elkhorn Spring, Wallowa County. This spring is in township 5 north, range 42 east. It was named by William Adams and Hector McDonald because of a pair of elk horns that lay nearby for a number of years.

Elkton, Douglas County. Elkton was laid out and named in August, 1850. See *OHQ,* volume XVII, page 356. However, it did not have a post office until September 26, 1851. David B. Wells was first postmaster. Elkton received its name because it was at the junction of Elk Creek and the Umpqua River. At one time the Hudson's Bay Company maintained an establishment known as Fort Umpqua very close to the present site of Elkton. For further information see Leslie M. Scott's article on John Work in *OHQ,* September, 1923. John Work visited the Umpqua River in 1834 and Fort Umpqua, which was on the south side of the Umpqua River at the mouth of Elk Creek, apparently did not exist at the time of Work's visit. He mentions "umpqua old fort" which appears to have been established in 1832 near Calapooya Creek. There was of course, later on, Fort Umpqua, near the mouth of the river, which had nothing to do with the Hudson's Bay Company forts.

Ella, Morrow County. Ella post office was established April 24, 1882, with Frank Oviatt first postmaster. The office was discontinued on September 30, 1910. The place is about seven miles east of Cecil. Four miles south of Ella is Ella Butte. Roy Scott of Cecil wrote the compiler in 1927 that at the time the matter of establishing a post office was considered, a meeting was held in a blacksmith shop owned by Oviatt. It was decided that the office should be established in Oviatt's house, as that seemed to be the best location, but a name could not be agreed upon. Oviatt's little daughter, Ella, was playing around the blacksmith shop and having hurt herself, began to cry. One of the men told her that they would name the office for her if she would stop crying, which she did. Ella Butte was formerly known as Well Spring Butte. Well Spring was a prominent point on the immigrant road about five miles east of the location of Ella post office. The spring is mentioned in many emigrant journals.

Ellendale, Polk County. This pioneer community was about two miles west of Dallas, on Rickreall Creek. In 1845 James A. O'Neal built the first grist mill in Polk County, a few hundred feet west of what was later Ellendale. About 1849 O'Neal sold the mill to James W. Nesmith and Henry Owen, who operated it until 1854, and then sold it to Hudson & Company. The post office O'Neals Mills was established January 8, 1850, with O'Neal postmaster. The name was changed to Nesmiths on August 21, 1850, with J. W. Nesmith postmaster. The office was discontinued October 22, 1852. Due to the length of time necessary to communicate with Washington, D. C., O'Neal's appointment may have been made after he had sold the mill. Reuben P. Boise came to Oregon in 1850, and took up a donation land claim at Nesmiths Mills in 1852. He named the place Ellendale for his wife, Ellen Lyon, a native of Massachusetts, who sailed from New York to San Francisco in the record time of 89 days on the *Flying Cloud*. The mill flume took water from the creek on the south side and crossed to the north side near the present county bridge. One of Oregon's pioneer woolen mills was started in Ellendale in 1860. See Lomax, *Pioneer Woolen Mills in Oregon*.

Elliott, Coos County. Elliott post office was on the property of James K. Polk Elliott near Catching Creek a few miles southwest of Myrtle Point. Elliott post office was established September 24, 1883, and was discontinued September 11, 1897. J. K. P. Elliott was the only postmaster. He was a prominent pioneer of the county.

Elliott Creek, Coos County. Elliott Creek flows into South Slough from the east. It bears the family name of Hiram Elliott, a pioneer of 1849, who was born in Ohio in 1812 and settled in Coos County in 1865. He was a farmer and logger who raised a large family in the South Slough area. Elliott died in 1888.

Elliott Prairie, Clackamas County. This prairie lies east of Pudding River and Butte Creek. It was named for William Elliott, who came to Oregon in 1846. He was born in Indiana in 1815 and served in the Florida War in 1836. He married Nancy Sconce in 1838. He died at Park Place February 27, 1905. His wife died in 1888. Elliott served in the Cayuse and Yakima wars.

Elliott State Forest, Coos and Douglas counties. Elliott State Forest, consisting of 71,105 acres, was established through an exchange of state school grant lands which were widely scattered throughout the national forests for a solid block of federal forest lands, formerly known as the Millicoma Tract. The first move to establish a state forest by this means was made in 1913 by Governor Oswald West and State Forester F. A. Elliott. The exchange was not completed until 1929. Elliott died in 1930 and the forest was named to commemorate his work. This forest lay in the path of the historic Coos Bay fire of 1868, which left the land denuded for years. A study made in 1923 showed that only about half the area was stocked. Twelve years later a survey showed that more than 90 percent was stocked with western conifers, while most of the rest of the tract was producing maple, alder, myrtle, madrona, and cascara.

Elmira, Lane County. Amos F. Ellmaker, in 1925, informed the writer that Elmira was named by his brother, Byron Ellmaker, for Elmira, California, a place that he greatly admired. About 1884 Byron Ellmaker bought a location for a wood and iron smithy near the present site of Elmira, which was then called Duckworth. Ellmaker did not like this name and persuaded postal authorities to change it to Elmira.

Elmonica, Washington County. So named for Eleanor and Monica Stoy, daughters of Sam B. Stoy, who lived there in 1909. Stoy was an insurance man of Portland at the time and coined the name from the names of his two daughters.

Elowah Falls, Multnomah County. These falls on McCord Creek were named by a committee representing the Mazamas and other organizations in 1915. The name is obviously Indian, but the writer has not been able to determine its meaning.

Elrus, Lane County. This station, on the Coos Bay branch of the Southern Pacific Company, was named for Elmer Russell, owner of a lumber mill nearby.

Elsie, Clatsop County. Elsie was named for Elsie Foster, a relative of the first postmaster, George Gragg, about 1892. The compiler is informed that an effort was made to name the office Clover, but the name was not accepted.

Elwood, Clackamas County. Elwood is a locality between Colton and Springwater southeast of Highland Butte, probably named for Elwood Sylvanus, son of a Presbyterian minister of the neighborhood. The Rev. Mr. Sylvanus bestirred himself about getting a post office in the early 1890s, and the office was established with the name Ellwood on April 28, 1892, with Eunice T. Sylvanus postmaster. There seems to have been an error in the procedure, because the name of the office was changed to Elwood on September 12, 1892. The office was closed June 30, 1914.

Ely, Clackamas County. Ely, also called Elyville, is a suburb on the Cascade Highway in the extreme south part of Oregon City. The locality is sometimes called Mountain View, probably because it is near the cemetery of that name. The place was named in honor of Fred and George Ely, who settled there in early days. They were well-known public spirited citizens. George Ely later went to Inglewood, California. Ely post office was in operation from early 1891 until late 1894, with George C. Ely postmaster. The office was in operation again from July, 1895, to December, 1904.

Ely Canyon, Morrow County. John and George Ely homesteaded in this canyon in the 1880s. It empties into Willow Creek near Morgan.

Embody, Lake County. In March, 1947, Mrs. Delbert Cloud, New Pine Creek, Oregon, wrote the compiler that Embody was named for Charles Embody, who at one time operated a sawmill there. Embody was about sixteen miles northwest of the town of Silver Lake, on the old Military Road. Mrs. Cloud's father, S. L. Porter, took up a homestead in the locality in 1903 and proved up on it in 1908. He operated a small mill, which he sold to Charles Embody of Portland. Embody post office was established August 3, 1908, with Stephen S. Lowing first and only postmaster. The office was discontinued February 15, 1910, with mail to Silver Lake.

Embree Slough, Harney County. Earl H. Conser of Burns, who knew the facts of such matters, wrote the compiler as follows: "Embree Slough, near Burns, was named for one 'Doc' Embree, through whose land the slough followed an irregular course. He had several initials, but I am unable to find anyone who knows them exactly. He was a doctor of sorts." This was Thomas Van Buren Embree, son of Cary Embree. Cary Embree was a pioneer of 1844 and a resident of Polk County.

Emele Ditch, Baker County. This ditch was named for the family of William D. Emele who settled near Keating in the 1880s.

Emerson, Wasco County. Emerson was a community and station on the Great Southern Railroad on Fifteenmile Creek about eighteen miles southeast of The Dalles. It was named for Chester W. Emerson who settled there in 1884. The railroad was torn up in the 1930s and little now remains except a local crossroads.

Emerson Creek, Douglas County. This tributary of South Umpqua River was named for Lemuel N. Emerson who homesteaded the nearby ranch in 1915.

Emery, Jefferson County. The Post Route map of 1900 shows Emery at a point seventeen miles by road northeast of Sisters and a little to the west of Squaw Creek. In July, 1946, Sterling J. May, acting postmaster at Sisters, informed the compiler that the office was at the Trahan homestead, and that it was named for Emery Trahan. The office operated from September, 1899, to July, 1901, with Antoine G. Trahan postmaster. The Trahan place was about three miles southwest of Geneva, in sections 8 and 17 of township 13 south, range 11 east.

Emigrant Butte, Klamath and Lane counties. Emigrant Butte lies west of Summit Lake, in the southeast corner of Lane County, at the summit of the Cascade Range. It has an elevation of 6535 feet. It was named because of the emigrants that traveled over the emigrant route nearby.

Emigrant Buttes, Umatilla County. These buttes are west of Stanfield, and have an elevation of 759 feet. They are close to the route of the Oregon Trail, and were named for the emigrants.

Emigrant Creek, Jackson County. Emigrant Creek is southeast of Ashland and is supposed to be so named because emigrants who crossed the Cascade Range over the southern route came down this stream into Rogue River Valley. Emigrant Lake was formed in 1926 when the creek was dammed for irrigation. The dam was raised and the lake enlarged with work completed in 1960. When full the lake totals 790 acres and is a popular recreation spot as well as important for flood control.

Emigrant Hill, Umatilla County. Emigrant Hill is a very prominent ridge of the Blue Mountains, southeast of Pendleton. The Oregon Trail traverses this hill as it proceeds westward, then descends to the northwest to Umatilla River. Emigrant Hill is sometimes referred to as Cabbage Hill, but Cabbage Hill is a spur south from the main hill and the Oregon Trail does not touch Cabbage Hill. Geography of this locality may be found on the USGS map of the Cabbage Hill quadrangle. Emigrant Hill was of course named in pioneer days because the emigrant trains traveled over it.

Emigrant Pass. Klamath and Lane counties. This pass is about one half mile west of Summit Lake in township 24 south, range 5½ east. It was originally called Willamette Pass as the emigrant road through it followed Middle Fork Willamette River to within a few miles of the summit. In 1960 the crossing of SH 58 just north of Odell Lake was named Willamette Pass and this redesignated Emigrant Pass. The primitive road is rarely travelled and care must be taken to avoid confusing this early Willamette Road with the present highway.

Emigrant Springs, Sherman County. Giles L. French of Moro was good enough to dig up some facts about this place in December, 1945. Emigrant Springs are of good size and situated in section 27, township 2 north, range 18 east, in the northeast corner of Sherman County. The Oregon Trail passed through the area about a half mile south of these springs, but many wagons pulled down the canyon and camped at the springs where the water was good. Some emigrants camped there several days to refresh their stock. A post office called Emigrant was established in this vicinity on January 20, 1887, with William J. Peddicord first postmaster. The name was changed to Emigrant Springs on June 29, 1889, and the office was closed June 12, 1895. The record indicates that the office was at or near the springs after the name was changed, but before that it may have been at the springs or in fact on the Oregon Trail. It should be added that the office was on the Wasco County list when first established.

Emile Creek, Douglas County. Emile Creek rises north of Taft Mountain and flows westward into Little River about ten miles southeast of Glide. It was named for Emile Shivigny, a native of France, who settled nearby about 1875.

Emma, Tillamook County. Emma post office was in service for about six years at a point on Neskowin Creek about five miles southeast of the present community of Neskowin. The office was named for Emma Chitwood, a local resident, and the name Emma Trail was applied to a route of travel from what is now Otis over the mountain to Emma, where settlers on lower Salmon River got their mail until they had their own post office at Otis, in April, 1900. Emma post office was established December 16, 1896, with John D. Chitwood first postmaster. The office was closed February 26, 1903, and the business was turned over to Neskowin.

Empire, Coos County. Empire City, as it was first known, was founded in 1853 by men from Jacksonville, called the Coos Bay Company, headed by Perry B. Marple. For a list of members of this company, see Scott's *History of the Oregon Country*, volume III, page 161. The name Empire City was suggested by the expectation that the town would be the center of a large region. Discovery of gold in northern California and southwestern Oregon led to the formation of the project, and stock in the company was offered for sale in the *Oregonian*, January 7, 1854. Empire City was formerly county seat of Coos County. A custom house was established at Empire City in 1853 for the southern collection district of Oregon, with David Bushing collector. Empire City post office was established in April, 1858. It operated with that name until October, 1894, when the title was changed to Empire. On January 8, 1965, the city voted to consolidate with Coos Bay and the name Empire, in use for over a century, like Marshfield, became a thing of the past.

Enchanted Prairie, Coos County. This little prairie of about a hundred acres is an open spot alongside the Coos Bay-Roseburg Highway approximately four miles east of Bridge and about 25 miles east of Myrtle Point. In the summer of 1943 Mrs. Alice B. Maloney of Berkeley, California, wrote the compiler that the place had a special significance for the Indians, who buried their dead there in a sort of cavern. John Yoakam investigated it as a boy and local Indians threatened him with violence. Enchanted Prairie post office was established January 9, 1871, with Rufus P. King first postmaster. The name of the office was changed to Angora August 3, 1883. Angora post office, which was apparently named by a goat fancier, was closed May 5, 1894.

Encina, Baker County. *Encina* is Spanish for evergreen oak. J. C. Mayo, of Stayton, wrote that he named this station. During the time of railroad construction the siding was called Oak Cut, but this name was cumbersome, and Mayo, who had lived in Mexico, changed it to the form now used.

Endersby, Wasco County. This place was named for W. E. Endersby, a local settler. Endersby School is about three miles north-northwest of Dufur and the spelling is that used in 1946 by the county school authorities. It is also reported to be correct by members of the family. A post office called Endersly was in operation in this vicinity from April, 1892, to October, 1906, with George W. Fligg postmaster. All postal records available to the writer spell the name Endersly. No explanation has been found for the discrepancy in spelling.

Endicott Creek, Coos County. Endicott Creek is a tributary of Middle Fork Coquille River. This stream was named for J. J. Endicott, a pioneer settler near its mouth.

Engels Creek, Douglas County. This creek which flows into Little River at Peel was named for Abraham A. Engels who crossed the plains in 1852 and settled in the Glide-Peel area sometime in the 1860s. He later filed several land claims but although the various entries in BLM records all use the form Engles, members of the family still living in the area state this is incorrect. The OGNB adopted the above form in June 1968.

English, Wasco County. English post office got its name from the fact that it was situated on the English farm near Company Hollow about eight miles southeast of The Dalles. The office was established July 2, 1896, with Christopher C. English postmaster and was in operation until August 12, 1898. Judge Fred W. Wilson wrote the compiler in February, 1946, as follows: "The roads were bad then, and the farmers in that vicinity did not want to travel through the mud for their mail. When the roads were made better the need no longer existed. There were a very few farmers served by the office."

English Mountain, Lane County. This mountain lies southeast of McKenzie Bridge. It was named during World War I in honor of the English people. French Mountain lies just to the west and was named at the same time.

Enola Hill, Clackamas County. Enola Hill lies just north of Zigzag River and west of Devil Canyon. The name Enola was made by spelling Alone backward. It was applied by a homesteader who had a home that was quite isolated.

Enright, Tillamook County. Enright is a station on the Southern Pacific Company branch line to Tillamook. It is in the east part of the county near Salmonberry River and is about midway between Timber and Wheeler. Enright post office was established May 27, 1932 and closed February 28, 1943. Enright is said to have been named for Mrs. E. E. Lytle. Before her marriage she was Miss May Enright and was well known in Oregon railroad circles. E. E. Lytle was a prominent railroad builder and was instrumental in extending railroad service to Shaniko, in north central Oregon, and from Hillsboro west to Tillamook. Lake Lytle, on one of the Tillamook beaches, bears his name.

Enterprise, Wallowa County. Ben Weather, postmaster of Enterprise in 1925, informed the writer that the community was named in 1887. A meeting was held in a tent owned by a mercantile company and several names were suggested, including Bennett Flat, Wallowa City, Franklin and Fairfield. Finally R. F. Stubblefield suggested Enterprise, and that name was selected by a majority vote. The post office was established November 9, 1887, with Catherine Akin first postmaster.

Eola, Polk County. The village of Eola was formerly known as Cincinnati, and so appears when the post office was established on June 5, 1851. It is said to have been named by A. C. R. Shaw because of the fancied resemblance of the site to that of Cincinnati, Ohio. The place was incorporated with the name of Eola by the territorial legislature on January 17, 1856. Miss A. J. Scott, later Mrs. A. S. Duniway, taught school in Cincinnati in 1853, and during pioneer days an effort was made to establish the state capital there. The name Eola comes from *Aeolus,* god of the winds in Greek mythology. There seems to be good authority for the belief that the name Eola was suggested by a local musical enthusiast named Lindsay Robbins, who disliked the name Cincinnati, and offered the new name because he was fond of the Aeolian harp. However, Geo. H. Himes thought that Shaw suggested Eola as well as the original name, so there you are.

Eola Hills, Polk and Yamhill counties. These hills, which have an extreme altitude of 1170 feet, extend from Eola on the south to a point near Amity on the north, a distance of about 15 miles. They constitute one of the important groups of isolated hills in the Willamette Valley. They have had various names, including Bethel Hills and Yamhill Mountains, but Eola Hills seems firmly established, except for the northern extension, which is separated from the main ridge by the pass east of Amity. This northern extension is known as Amity Hills. Eola Hills got their name from the village at their southern end. Bethel Academy, Bethel Institute and Bethel College were prominent pioneer establishments situated in Eola Hills. See under Bethel.

Erickson Ranch, Wheeler County. Erickson Ranch south of Antone is near the site of the 1889 homestead of John C. Erickson.

Erk Hill, Hood River County. This high ground north of Odell was named for William Ehrck, a native of Germany and a stonemason by trade, who settled on the hill in early days. Ehrck did the stone work on Cloud Cap Inn in 1888. This information was provided by L. M. Baldwin of Hood River.

Erma Bell Lakes, Lane County. These three mountain lakes are just west of the summit of the Cascade Range and about five miles north of Waldo Lake. They are shown on the USGS map of the Chucksney Mountain quadrangle. They were named for Miss Erma Bell, for a number of years employed as a computer in the Portland office of the USFS. She died April 27, 1918, as a result of an automobile accident near Troutdale, and it was thought proper to perpetuate her memory by naming these lakes for her.

Errol, Clackamas County. Errol station received its name from Joseph A. Strowbridge, Jr. His father came to this country from England many years ago on a four-masted vessel named *Errol*. The post office at Errol station was installed about January 1, 1922.

Erskine, Sherman County. This place is between Moro and Grass Valley, and has also been known as Millra, Erskineville and Erskine Springs. About 1882 C. A. Williams opened a store there and Erskineville post office was established Dec. 19, 1882, with Abiel Erskine postmaster. When the railroad was built through, the shorter name Erskine was used for the station. Erskineville post office was closed April 20, 1907, but the locality still goes by the name Erskine.

Erwin, Baker County. The place called Erwin was named for a well-known stockman, John Erwin, who was born in New York state in 1839 and settled in Oregon in 1868. He served in the Civil War and was wounded. He developed a stock ranch in Lower Powder Valley northeast of Baker. His biography is in the *History of Baker, Malheur, and Harney Counties,* page 304. Erwin post office was established July 13, 1892, with Mrs. Elizabeth A. Pierce first postmaster. The office was closed as of November 15, 1910. Gill's map of Oregon, 1911, shows Erwin in section 17, township 8 south, range 42 east, a little northwest of Keating. The name of Erwin post office was not changed to Keating as is sometimes reported.

Estacada, Clackamas County. *Estacada* is a Spanish word and means staked out, or marked with stakes, and the principal use of the name in the United States is in northwestern Texas where the form *Llano Estacado* is employed to describe a tract of land that would be called in English Staked Plain. The Spanish name refers to the trunks of an upright desert plant that remain standing like stakes or poles over an area of many hundred square miles. The name was used in Oregon because it had a pleasing sound, with no thought of its original significance. In the summer of 1927 a number of letters were written to the *Oregonian* asserting that Estacada was named for a girl whose name was first given as Esther Keady or Esther Cady, and by later correspondents as Esther Williams. These letters were printed on the editorial page of the *Oregonian* for July 16, 25 and 27. Other letters denying this version and supporting the *Llano Estacado* version were printed on July 18, 23 and 29. W. P. Keady was a right of way agent for the railroad company that built into that section of Clackamas County, and on April 7, 1909, he wrote from Spokane, Washington, to L. E. Belfils, Estacada, and gave his story of the application of the name. The letter is too long to quote in full, but the substance is that on December 27, 1903, a meeting was held at the office of the Oregon Water Power Townsite Company, First and Alder streets, Portland. Townsite and railroad company officials suggested various names, as follows: G. W. Morrow suggested Rochester; W. H. Hurlburt suggested Lowell; W. P. Keady suggested Lynn and George J. Kelly suggested Estacado. Kelly's suggested name, Estacado, was drawn from a hat, and adopted for the townsite, but through an error in drafting was filed as Estacada. One of Keady's sons was named Lynn, which was probably the reason for the suggestion of the name Lynn mentioned above. George J. Kelly, in a letter on the editorial page of the *Oregonian*, July 23, 1927, gives his version of the matter, which is substantially the same as Keady's, except that he says he was responsible for the change from Estacado to Estacada. He was chief clerk in the office, and selected the name at random from a map of the United States which showed *Llano Estacado*, in Texas. The compiler of these notes spent several weeks in Estacada shortly after the town was established and was informed by a number of persons at the time that the *Llano Estacado* of Texas was the origin of the name.

Estes, Baker County. This small suburb on the northwest edge of Baker carries the name of Hardin W. Estes who was born in Mississippi in 1828 and came to Baker County with the White Horse company in 1862.

Estes Creek, Douglas County. This creek is near the headwaters of Middle Fork Coquille River above Camas Valley. It was named for Jesse Estes who homesteaded there in 1888. His family first went from Missouri to Colorado in 1859 where they settled in the Rocky Mountain valley that is now Estes Park.

Estrup, Lane County. Estrup post office was established on the Lane County list as of March 31, 1898, with Peter E. Peterson postmaster. This office was west of Junction City, probably not far from the place that was later called Horton. According to information which is believed to be reliable Peterson named the post office with a Danish name, but the compiler has been unable to learn the exact significance of the word Estrup. According to J. J. Winn, an old timer in Lane County, the name Estrup may have been derived from the name of a Danish queen, but reference books do not mention such a sovereign. Estrup is or was a family name in Denmark but the compiler can find no record of its being a given name. Jacob B. S. Estrup was a prominent member of the Danish government at various times in the latter half of the nineteenth century. It is reported that there is a village called Estrup in SchleswigHolstein and in 1905 there was an Estruplund parish in Denmark. It seems obvious that the name of the Lane County post office had its origin in Denmark. According to post office records Samuel M. Horton was appointed postmaster of Estrup post office on September 27, 1901. The office was discontinued April 4, 1902. Mr. Winn says that Horton never actually served as postmaster.

Etelka, Coos County. Etelka post office, which was established September 23, 1891, was named for a famous Hungarian opera singer, Etelka Gerster, 1855-1920. Mlle. Gerster, whose married name was Gardini, had a distinguished career both on the continent and in the British Isles. She also sang in America. For additional information see Grove's *Dictionary of Music and Musicians*, volume II. Etelka post office remained in service until March 30, 1909, with Julia A. Carman the only postmaster. It was about ten miles south of Myrtle Point, near South Fork Coquille River. In July, 1948, Mrs. Mary E. Coke of San Diego wrote the compiler that she was a daughter of Mrs. Carman and that she selected the name Etelka from a magazine or catalogue. She was then a young girl. The compiler has been told that in recent years Etelka has been referred to as Etalka but that certainly was not the name of the post office.

Etna, Jackson County. Etna was an early-day post office and located on upper Rogue River, and for a time at least the office was about four miles below the present site of Trail. Doubtless it moved around, but it was always close to Rogue River. The post office was established July 5, 1882, with William P. Knighten first of five postmasters, and was discontinued June 26, 1896, when Louis J. Marck was postmaster. In the summer of 1946 the compiler had some correspondence about this office with D. W. Pence of Eagle Point. It was Mr. Pence's recollection that Etna post office was named for the niece of one of the postmasters, possibly of Mr. Marck. Mr. Pence was of the opinion that Marck was the first postmaster, but this is not in accord with government records. The compiler thinks that the girl was probably the niece of one of the earlier postmasters, probably of the first, William P. Knighten.

Etna, Polk County. Etna was a post office at the Riggs place a few miles north of Rickreall, but the reason for the name seems to have eluded historical records. The office was established September 4, 1856, with Thomas J. Riggs first and only postmaster. It was discontinued May 8, 1868. Rickreall post office was out of service from 1857 to 1866, so there was need of another office in the locality. Despite help from various Polk County people, including Cecil L. Riggs of Dallas, the compiler has been unable to get the reason for the name Etna. There does not seem to have been any member of the Riggs family named Etna. Cecil Riggs wrote in January, 1947, that he had always thought the office was named for the mountain on the east coast of Sicily, but perhaps without any definite reason. Mount Etna had a violent eruption in 1852, which may have been news in the Willamette Valley soon enough to produce a post office name in 1856. This is no more than a theory.

Euchre Butte, Lake County. This is a prominent mountain north of Lake Abert. It is said to have been so named because of an historic card game played nearby by cowboys in pioneer days.

Euchre Creek, Curry County. This stream apparently takes its name from the Tututni Indian band *Yukichetunne*. The name indicates "people at the mouth of the river." The *Handbook of American Indians,* among others, gives the following forms of the name: *Euchees, Eucher, Euchre, Eu-qua-chee, Uchres* and *Yoquichacs.* George Davidson, in the *Coast Pilot,* 1889, page 373, refers to the stream as Ukah Creek for the *U-kahtan-nae* Indians. Miners applied the style Euchre Creek in the early 1850s, apparently influenced by the name of the popular card game. Davidson says that the stream was also called Savage Creek, but that name is not explained and has not persisted.

Euchre Mountain, Lincoln County. Accurate information about the name of Euchre Mountain seems hard to obtain, but it is generally believed that the word Euchre was used by pioneer surveyors as an approximation of the Indian name of the mountain. The correct pronunciation and meaning of the Indian name are not now available. The USGS gives the height of Euchre Mountain as 2446 feet.

Eugene, Lane County. Eugene F. Skinner took his land claim at

Eugene at the foot of Skinner Butte in 1846, and built his cabin, and in 1847 moved his family into it. His wife, Mary Cook Skinner, was the first white woman to dwell in Lane County. Skinner came to Oregon in 1846, and first settled at Dallas. He was born September 13, 1809, in Essex County, New York; died at Eugene December 15, 1864. His wife was born February 7, 1816; died June 4, 1881. Eugene City in 1855 is described by Thomas J. Dryer in the *Oregonian*, June 23, 1855. The first steamboat to ascend the Willamette River to Eugene was the *James Clinton*, March 3, 1857, (*ibid.*, March 21, 1857). The Indian name of Skinner Butte was *Ya-po-ah* (*ibid.*, April 23, 1897, page 3), or *Ya-po-oh* (*ibid.*, November 17, 1890). For notes on Eugene in 1885, *ibid.*, January 31, 1885. This post office was established with the name Skinner's on January 8, 1850, with Eugene F. Skinner postmaster. The name was changed to Eugene City on September 3, 1853, and to Eugene on May 29, 1889.

Eugene Glacier, Lane County. Eugene Glacier is on the north slope of South Sister, between Skinner and Lost Creek glaciers. It was named for the city of Eugene in 1924 by Professor Edwin T. Hodge of the University of Oregon.

Eula, Lane County. Eula post office was named for Eula Blakely, daughter of Joe Blakely, an early resident. The post office was established about the time the railroad was built, with the name Blakelyville, but the railroad company adopted a shorter name, Eula. To avoid confusion, postal officials changed the name of the office to Eula, and both station and office operated with this name until about 1925 when the railroad changed the station name to Armet because Eula was too much like Eola, Polk County. Armet was selected arbitrarily by the company. It is the name of a form of head armor used in the middle ages. Properly the word is accented on the first syllable, but not so at Armet.

Eureka, Wallowa County. Eureka post office was established in August, 1903, and operated until July, 1906. Thos. E. Alyea was the first postmaster. The office was near the southwest bank of Snake River in township 4 north, range 48 east, and was established to serve the Eureka mines which were being developed in the vicinity. There was mining activity at various points between the Imnaha River and the stream called Eureka Creek which flows into Snake River about three quarters of a mile farther down stream. The office and presumably the creek were named for the Eureka mines. The writer does not know the exact location of the office, possibly it was on the river between the two tributaries. Eureka is a Greek expression meaning "I have found it," and the word is frequently applied to mines and other enterprises where there are high hopes of success. There is a bar in Snake River just below the mouth of the Imnaha, and this is known as Eureka Bar. In 1945 it was reported that mining activity in the locality appeared to have ceased many years before.

Eustis, Wallowa County. This post office was named for Harry R. Eustis, a nearby homesteader. It was situated in section 15, township 3 north, range 41 east. The office was established February 29, 1904, with Charles H. Campbell first postmaster and it was in operation until May, 1907, at a point about ten miles north of Minam.

Evans, Wallowa County. R. L. Forsythe of Enterprise wrote the compiler in 1927 as follows: "When the branch line railroad was built from Elgin to Joseph in about the year 1909, the railroad people agreed to run the railroad through Lostine if that city would pay a bonus of $1500, the cost of the additional construction by reason of a cut that would have to be made through a small hill east of Lostine. One man, Mr. James Haun, prominent citizen of Lostine, was strongly in favor of paying the sum but a majority was against him and the proposition was lost. As a result the railroad missed Lostine by about one mile and a depot was established a mile away and named Lostine by the railroad company. Mr. Haun had said that he would leave the town if it failed to land the railroad. This he did by moving two good residence buildings out of Lostine and onto land that he owned near the depot. He, together with John McDonald and S. W. Miles, laid out a new townsite at this point, and the name of Evans was selected (in honor of Mrs. Sam Wade). The settlement soon grew to include ten or twelve houses, a couple of store buildings, three wheat warehouses, a church and school house, as well as a few smaller buildings. Later a post office was established at the new townsite with the name of Evans. The last few years has shown a decline in the place, one store building having recently been torn down and hauled away and a number of the residences and buildings stand vacant. Locally the place has always been known as Jim Town, Jim being Mr. Haun's first name. There is, of course, a post office at the original town of Lostine and also one at Evans. The railroad has never recognized the name of Evans and it is still called Lostine on its map even though the station is actually at Evans." Post office records show Evans post office was established June 3, 1913 and closed January 31, 1940. In 1980 Lostine and Lostine Station were still a mile apart and Evans remained in decline.

Evans Creek, Hood River County. This prominent tributary of East Fork Hood River rises on the slopes of Mount Hood below Cloud Cap Inn. Captain H. C. Coe in an article in the Hood River *News*, March 6, 1918, says that it was named for R. O. Evans, an early resident of Hood River who took a homestead along the creek.

Evans Creek, Jackson County. Evans Creek was named for a pioneer settler on Rogue River, who operated a ferry about three miles west of Evans Creek, and was also first postmaster for the office of Gold River. This office was near the site of the ferry. Davis Evans was generally known as Coyote Evans, but why, the compiler does not know. Gold River post office was established April 18, 1855. The territorial legislature changed the name of Rogue River to Gold River in 1854, and reversed itself in 1855. The post office name Gold River was doubtless the result of this action. The battle of Evans Creek, an important encounter in the Rogue River Indian War, was fought on the headwaters of this stream August 24, 1853.

Evans Well, Deschutes County. This well south of Millican Valley was on the 1911 homestead of Clifton L. Evans.

Evarts, Umatilla County. Evarts post office in the south part of the county was named for one Squire Evarts, at one time a lawyer in Pendleton, later a storekeeper at Evarts and probably also justice of the peace. The compiler has been unable to learn if the name Squire was Evart's given name, or an honorary title. The post office at Evarts was established Novem-

ber 11, 1885, with William Roberts first postmaster. The office was closed
to Ridge November 11, 1886. It is reported that Evarts had probably
moved away from the locality before the post office was established. Sam E.
Darr of Adams has written the compiler that Evarts' establishment consisted of a store, hotel and feed stable all under one roof, on the old mail
route from Nye to Alba. It was on the west side of the road, on a ridge, and
about four miles north of the old post office Ridge on the same mail route.
Mr. Darr says that Evarts also owned the store at Ridge. The site of Evarts
post office is now on the Pendleton-John Day Highway about five miles
south of the junction with the highway to Heppner.

Evergreen, Harney County. Evergreen post office was established on
June 30, 1882, with Miss Mary E. Bedell first postmaster. The office was
finally closed January 21, 1887, and the business turned over to the Riley
office. The history of the office is contained in the Grant County records,
because Harney County had not yet been organized, but the office was in
what is now Harney County. Old maps show Evergreen on Silver Creek a
little below Camp Currey. Evergreen was about 300 yards down Silver
Creek from the Military road crossing, on the A. O. Bedell land, later the
Cecil ranch. There was a small green meadow at this point, and the Bedell
children named the office on that account.

Ewe Creek, Josephine County. Edith A. Keyte in *Josephine County Historic Highlights,* page 63, says that Ewe Creek is only correct phonetically.
She was born and raised in nearby Merlin and says that the correct form
should be Yew Creek for the many trees of that species that line its banks.

Ewing Young Historical Marker, Yamhill County. Ewing Young came
to Oregon in 1834 and at the time of his death in 1841 lived in his cabin in
Chehalem Valley near this marker. His nearby grave is beneath an oak tree
that was planted as an acorn in 1846. Young's death and the necessity of
probating his estate, created the need for a provisional government, which
was organized in 1843. It is curious that the name of one of the most indus-
trious and prosperous early settlers who posthumously gave the impetus to
organized government lies overlooked amid a welter of names of little
distinction.

Express Ranch, Baker County. The post office called Express Ranch
was very prominent in Baker County during the days of the mining excitement. The office was established April 21, 1865, with C. W. Durkee first
postmaster. It was situated at or near the place later called Durkee and was
named because it was a stopping place for stage coaches or expresses as
they were frequently called. The name of this office was changed to Weatherby on July 2, 1879, and it was apparently moved at that time to the Weatherby place about ten miles to the southeast, down Burnt River. Andrew J.
Weatherby was postmaster at the time the name was changed. The Weatherby office continued in operation until February, 1920. The removal of
the post office to Weatherby left the Express Ranch without a post office,
and a new office named Express was established November 26, 1884, with
Joseph McKay postmaster. The name of this office was changed, probably
on February 26, 1902, to Durkee, in compliment to the early settler of the
locality. This change was doubtless made because the name Express was

unsuited to an office situated on a railroad. Such a name would cause confusion in express shipments.

Face Rock, Coos County. Face Rock is in the ocean, just a little off shore and about a mile south of the mouth of Coquille River at Bandon. The rock looks like a human head, with a lifelike face peering up from the ocean and gazing toward the North Star. There are a number of Indian legends about Face Rock. The rock is sometimes called Graystone, but Face Rock is the name in general use.

Fair Grounds, Marion County. The first of the long series of Oregon State Fairs was held in the first week of October, 1861, at grounds a little to the north of Oregon City. While the facilities were good, they were not entirely satisfactory, and it was decided to move the fair to the Marion County Fair Grounds in the northeast part of Salem. The fair was held there on four days beginning September 30, 1862, and the place has since continued as the State Fair Grounds. For historical notes, see *OHQ*, volume VIII, page 317, *et seq.* A post office with the name Fair Grounds was established in December, 1871, and was discontinued in March, 1874. The office was reestablished with the name Fair Grounds in April, 1892, and was continued until September, 1914, when the business was turned over to Salem. It should be noted that the post office established in April, 1892, was officially called Fair Grounds. The name was reduced to one word, Fairgrounds, sometime about 1895 and it remained that way until the office was discontinued in 1914. However, the railroad station was called two words, Fair Grounds, for many years.

Fair Oaks, Douglas County. Fair Oaks was an early-day office near Calapooya Creek a few miles eastward of Oakland, which received its name because of the surrounding tree growth. The post office was established April 5, 1878, with William R. Smith first of three postmasters. It was discontinued May 25, 1882, with mail to Oakland. Available maps are not in agreement as to its exact location, and it probably moved around a little to suit the postmasters.

Fairbanks, Wasco County. Fairbanks is a locality on Fifteenmile Creek near the mouth of Company Hollow. When the Great Southern Railroad was built along the creek in 1905, a station named Fairbanks was established. W. H. McNeal in *History of Wasco County*, page 276, says that it was named for Charles W. Fairbanks who had just taken office as vice-president under Theodore Roosevelt. There is another story that it was named by Daniel Farrington for his old home in Maine. In 1891 Farrington had filed on a homestead some distance to the south near Wrentham so the latter explanation appears improbable. Fairbanks post office was established October 31, 1905 with Cyrus Cooper postmaster. It was discontinued July 31, 1909 with papers to Freebridge.

Fairchild Spring, Wallowa County. Fairchild Spring, in township 4 north, range 47 east, was named by George Mitchell, Dr. C. T. Hockett, S. L. Burnaugh and F. I. Vergere for Henry Fairchild, who directed them to the spring for a hunting camp. It is in the northeast corner of the county.

Fairfield, Marion County. Postal authorities have informed the compiler that this post office was established March 24, 1852, with John C. Peebles first postmaster. Fairfield is not now a post office. The name is apparently descriptive and belongs to a locality about six miles south of St. Paul, on the east bank of Willamette River. For short history of Fairfield, see Salem *Statesman,* October 28, 1931. John C. Davidson is reported to have built the first store in 1856. Before the days of the railroads Fairfield was an important shipping point for river freight.

Fairmount, Lane County. Fairmount post office was established June 10, 1891, with Lavinna E. Yeager first postmaster. John Lyndon Marsh became postmaster February 15, 1902, and the office was closed to Eugene February 20, 1904. Fairmount is one of those pleasant and popular descriptive names that can be and have been used without overworking the imagination. It has been applied to almost any sort of rise in ground, sometimes but a few feet higher than the surrounding land. The popularity of the name is attested by the fact that in 1945 there were well over a dozen post offices in the United States with the word Fairmount in some form. The Fairmount in Lane County was just east of Eugene, and during the time that John L. Marsh had the office it was what was in 1947, 1873 Franklin Boulevard, at the intersection of Villard (extended), within the present city limits of Eugene and a short distance east of the University of Oregon. By 1980 the building had gone in favor of a parking lot sandwiched between two of the currently ubiquitous fast food stores.

Fairview, Coos County. Fairview is a locality or community on North Fork Coquille River about six miles northeast of Coquille. It does not now have a post office. The name is said to be descriptive. Fairview post office was established for the first time on May 7, 1873, with Francis Braden first postmaster. It was closed August 15, 1913. It was because of the Fairview post office in Coos County that an office of the same name could not be established in Multnomah County to handle the mail at Fairview railroad station just west of Troutdale. A distinct name was necessary for the Multnomah County situation, and Cleone was chosen, though the railroad continued to use the name Fairview for its station. After Fairview office in Coos County was closed, the name of Cleone office in Multnomah County was changed to Fairview in 1914.

Fairview, Multnomah County. The locality, Fairview, west of Troutdale, on the Columbia River, has also been known as Cleone. Fairview was adopted, in 1855, as the name of a Methodist Sunday school, organized in 1853. The late Stephen Roberts proposed the name, and it was adopted in preference to Mount Pisgah and Mount Pleasant. After the Oregon Railroad & Navigation Company's line was built, about 1882, and a station was established, named Fairview, a confusion in mail matters ensued because an older Fairview existed in Coos County, Oregon. Milton Hosford proposed Cleone, which was accepted as the name of the post office, but the railroad adhered to the old station name Fairview. Cleone post office was established March 27, 1883, with Hosford postmaster. Differences over the name of the place were composed, probably due to the abandonment of the Coos County office of Fairview, and on January 14, 1914, the name of the office of Cleone was changed to Fairview. In 1927 Milton W. Smith of Portland told the compiler that it was his opinion that the community of

Fairview was named in the early 1880s by Mrs. Hannah M. Smith, who platted the townsite. Mrs. Smith was the widow of Hiram (Redshirt) Smith. This does not agree with the data given above, which is from Scott's *History of the Oregon Country*, volume II, page 313. A news item in the *Oregonian*, September 10, 1901, page 9, says the name Fairview had been in use about 45 years, and this seems to substantiate the Scott version. It is probable that Mrs. Smith merely adopted the old name for her town.

Fairview Peak, Lane County. Fairview Peak is the highest point in the Bohemia district with an elevation of 5933 feet. According to Fred Asam, an early USFS ranger, it was originally South Lookout Mountain but this was changed to Fairview to eliminate duplication.

Falcon Rock, Tillamook County. Falcon Rock, elevation 15 feet, is in the Pacific Ocean a little less than a mile westward of Cape Falcon. The rock got its name from Cape Falcon. For the origin of the name of the cape, see under Cape Falcon. The rock is sometimes called Cape Falcon, but that form does not reflect the best usage, and is not the style used on the charts of the USC&GS.

Fall Creek, Deschutes County. Fall Creek heads in Green Lake east of South Sister, and flows south about four miles into Sparks Lake. It has a succession of falls and rapids, culminating in a fine drop of about 30 feet at a point about a half a mile north of Century drive. It gets its name from this fall, which is most attractive. Professor E. T. Hodge, in *Mount Multnomah*, pages 61 and 62, gives a good description of this stream and adjacent points of interest.

Fall Creek, Lane County. Fall Creek is a post office on the stream of the same name, which is tributary to Middle Fork Willamette River. Fall Creek post office is near the junction of Little Fall Creek and the main stream. The writer is told that many years ago the community was called Tay for the River Tay in Scotland, apparently by the Stuarts and other Scotch settlers in the neighborhood. James Stuart located there as early as 1853. Postal authorities inform the compiler that Tay post office was established August 9, 1880, with A. R. Randall, first postmaster. The name of the office was changed to Fall Creek on August 3, 1885, apparently at the request of T. C. Randall, then postmaster. The stream has been known in the past as Big Fall Creek in contradistinction to Little Fall Creek, a tributary, but federal mapping agencies nearly always drop the word *Big* from pairs of names of this sort, and consider the larger stream the main stem, with *Little* applied to the tributary. In 1965 Fall Creek Reservoir was completed by the USCE. It is a 1820 acre pool retained by a 195 foot high rockfill dam operated for flood control and water conservation. The pool stores approximately 115,000 acre feet of water at a normal elevation of 830 feet and provides a popular lake for water sports.

Fall River, Deschutes County. Fall River heads in giant springs, and after flowing through pine woods for some eight or ten miles joins Deschutes River from the west, north of Pringle Falls. About half way between the source of the river and its mouth, it descends a series of small falls and cascades with a total drop of about a hundred feet. It was from these falls that it received its name.

Falls City, Polk County. This town was named for the falls in Little Luckiamute River, which are near the west edge of the community. The name was proposed at the meeting which was held to initiate proceedings for incorporation. This place was originally served from a post office called Syracuse, situated between Dallas and the present site of Falls City. Syracuse post office was established in February, 1885, with Frank K. Hubbard first postmaster. The name of the office was changed to Falls City in October, 1889, and the office was doubtless moved at that time. It is said that the name Falls City was suggested by a family that had previously lived in Falls City, Nebraska.

Faloma, Multnomah County. This post office was north of Portland and served a community which was at one time known as Bridgeton. About 1921 the post office authorities were requested to establish an office there, but they objected to the name Bridgeton because of the duplication of other similar names in the United States. A meeting of local citizens was held and it was decided to ask to have the place named Faloma. This name was made up by using the initials of three original landowners in the neighborhood, to-wit: Messrs. Force, Love and Moore.

Fandango Canyon, Lake County. This canyon east of Silver Lake is named with the Spanish word for dance. The compiler has been unable to learn why.

Fangollano, Malheur County. Charles J. Bush, postmaster of the nearby office of Harper, wrote the compiler in December, 1925, as follows: "Fangollano is the Spanish translation *(fango llano)* of Mud Flat, the name the locality bore before the post office was established. Those responsible for the later christening no doubt got their inspiration from hearing Spanish spoken by the Spanish and Basque sheepmen who are wont to graze their flocks nearby; and wishing to retain, I presume, something of the significance of the old name without advertising what they considered a certain obloquy that attached to it, they compromised on Fangollano. The post office at Fangollano is now discontinued." It should be noted that the Fangollano post office was at Little Mud Flat, which is six miles west of Mud Flat.

Fanno Creek, Washington County. Fanno Creek takes its rise north of Garden Home, and after flowing westward turns sharp to the south and enters Tualatin River just north of Tualatin. It was named for Augustus Fanno, who settled on its bank in pioneer days. Augustus Fanno was born in Maine in 1804. He came to Oregon in 1846, with his wife and little son. Mrs. Fanno died on the arrival of the family at Oregon City, and after casting around for a home, Fanno selected a spot in Tualatin Valley on the trail from Oregon City to Tillamook Bay. This claim was about 12 miles from Oregon City, on what is now called Fanno Creek. He was married a second time, and died on his farm June 30, 1884.

Faraday, Clackamas County. This was the station for the Cazadero power plant of the Portland General Electric Company, on Clackamas River. It was named by O. B. Coldwell, vice-president of the company, for Michael Faraday, the great British scientist, who discovered the induction of electric currents.

Farewell Bend, Baker and Malheur counties. Farewell Bend on Snake River is where westbound immigrants turned northwestward from the river and took a pass through the hills to the present site of Huntington on Burnt River. Farewell Bend was named in the days of the pioneers. Today I 84 leaves Snake River at the same point and passes through the gap in the hills to Huntington. The geographic situation is the same as it was a century ago. Farewell Bend post office was in service from March 19, 1867, until November 19, 1867, with William H. Packwood postmaster. This post office is listed in the list for Baker County, but it was in operation before Malheur County was formed, and in fact its location may have been in what is now Malheur County, very close to the Baker County line. The location of Farewell Bend, was also known as Olds Ferry, although the modern place of that name is on the Idaho side of Snake River. R. P. Olds began to operate a ferry at Farewell Bend as early as 1862, having obtained a license from authorities in what is now Idaho. His license to operate in Oregon was granted in March, 1865, although he had actually been in business for three years prior. See Hiatt's *Thirty-one Years in Baker County*, page 94. Packwood was also interested in the ferry at Farewell Bend and in the Burnt River toll road.

Fargher, Sherman County. Fargher was a station not far from the east end of Sherars Bridge. It was named for Arthur W. Fargher, a nearby landowner. He was born on the Isle of Man in 1855. He came to the United States in 1870 and to Oregon in 1878. He was at one time employed by the predecessors of the Oregon-Washington Railroad & Navigation Company.

Farley, Hood River County. This station, east of Cascade Locks, was formerly known as Herman for Herman Creek nearby. See under that heading. The name caused confusion with Sherman, a station east of The Dalles, and Farley was substituted in honor of a local resident.

Farm Creek, Clackamas County. Farm Creek lies in township 7 south, range 6 east. It was named by Joe Davis, Jim Russell, Andy Wyland and Joe Dickey, who prospected and mined in that part of the county in the 1880s. They found good horse feed at the head of Farm Creek and left their stock there to pasture, calling the place The Farm.

Farmer Creek, Curry County. M. S. Brainard of Brookings told the compiler in 1967 that this creek two miles east of Carpenterville was named for Henry Farmer, a homesteader. Farmer was well known locally for his beautiful handmade rugs and enormous feet. He died at Gold Beach March 7, 1945.

Farmer Creek, Tillamook County. This creek flows into Nestucca River two miles above Hebo. It was named for A. D. Farmer who homesteaded along it in 1879.

Farmington, Washington County. Farmington, a place near Tualatin River eight or nine miles southwest of Beaverton, bears a descriptive name. The post office was established November 24, 1884, with Isaac B. Everson first of five postmasters. The office was closed December 23, 1904, with papers to Hillsboro. The locality is a well-known point on a secondary highway extending from Beaverton.

Farrell Lake, Klamath County. This small lake just east of Snell Lake was named in 1948 by a fish planting crew of the Oregon State Game Commission for Robert S. Farrell Jr., Oregon Secretary of State, who was killed in a plane crash October 28, 1947.

Fashion Reef, Multnomah County. Fashion Reef is in the Columbia River a little downstream from Multnomah Falls. It was probably named for the river steamer *Fashion*. This boat, the first on the middle river, was built with the name *James P. Flint* in 1851 by the Bradfords and Van Bergen at the Cascades. She was sunk in September, 1852, apparently on what is now known as Fashion Reef. She was raised in 1853 and taken to Vancouver, where she was renamed the *Fashion* and put back in service. See Wright's *Marine History of the Pacific Northwest,* pages 35 and 45. Whether the reef was named as the result of the grounding in 1852, or some later trouble, the compiler does not know, but thinks the first alternative the more probable.

Fate Creek, Douglas County. David and Mary Ann Fate came to Oregon in 1852 and the following year settled east of Roseburg. They later moved to the Days Creek area and bought land including Fate Creek. David Fate was the chairman of the first Republican Convention in Roseburg.

Faubion, Clackamas County. This post office was established late in 1925 and was named for a local family. W. J. Faubion was the first postmaster and the office was half a mile southeast of Zigzag ranger station, on the old Mount Hood Loop Highway. The post office was closed on September 30, 1937 with mail to Zigzag and W. J. Faubion died the following year.

Fawcett Creek, Tillamook County. This stream southeast of Tillamook was named for W. H. Fawcett, who took up a homestead nearby. His land office number is 997.

Feasters Rocks, Marion County. This spot on Willamette River near Lambert Bend bears the name of Daniel Fiester who with his wife, Rachel Anne, took up a donation land claim nearby. Fiester arrived in Oregon in 1847 and worked as a miller for John McLoughlin in Oregon City. His large family became well known in Marion County and several members used the form Feaster at one time or another.

Fellers, Marion County. This station south of Donald was named for the family of a pioneer settler on French Prairie, Francis Feller.

Fence Creek, Wallowa County. Fence Creek flows from the west into Imnaha River about six miles north of Imnaha. The stream takes its name from some stone fences built in the vicinity in very early days by A. C. Smith, one of the first white settlers in the Wallowa Valley. A news story about the activities of A. C. Smith appears in the Enterprise *Chieftain* for October 3, 1940. For biography of A. C. Smith see *History of Union and Wallowa Counties,* page 577.

Fennell Lake, Linn County. This small intermittent pond southeast of Jefferson was named for J. Fennell, an early settler. The spelling Fennel is wrong.

Ferguson Creek, Crook County. Ferguson Creek rises in the Maury Mountains and flows south to Bear Creek. Thomas J. Ferguson took up land along its banks in 1911. According to an article by Charles Hutchinson in the Prineville *Central Oregonian,* January 22, 1970, this creek was once known as Belknap Creek, possibly for Doctor Horace Belknap, the pioneer central Oregon doctor. However, in the early 1930s the USFS renamed the creek for Ferguson.

Ferguson Creek, Lane County. This stream flows into Long Tom River south of Monroe. It was named for a pioneer family. See *OHQ,* volume V, page 136.

Fern, Benton County. Fern post office was in operation from October, 1899, until September, 1903, with Edward L. Davis postmaster. The office was on the Davis farm on the road between Philomath and Bellfountain, and got its name because of the fern-covered hill nearby. The Davis place was about four miles west of Greenberry.

Fern Hill, Clatsop County. Fern Hill has been used as a locality name in Clatsop County for many decades. The place is about eight miles east of Astoria, close both to railroad and highway. Fern Hill post office was established October 24, 1879, with Mrs. Mary A. Dennis postmaster. This office was closed April 1, 1881. An office called Fernhill was established November 16, 1901, with Margaret Lewis first postmaster. This office was closed May 12, 1922, with papers to Svensen. The fern growth is heavy in that part of the state, especially on cleared land, and the name of the plant has been used frequently in geographic nomenclature. The most prolific fern in the locality of Fern Hill is the eagle brake or bracken.

Fernvale, Douglas County. Fernvale post office was about four miles northeast of Glendale on Windy Creek. The office was established October 9, 1906, with Helma Nelson first postmaster, and operated until May 31, 1924. The locality has a descriptive name with a mildly sentimental touch.

Ferry, Curry County. The post office Ferry took its name from the early-day means of getting across Chetco River at a point about a mile up from the stream's mouth. The ferry was not far from the present Oregon Coast Highway bridge but the writer does not know the exact location. Ferry post office was established March 5, 1888, with Sarah E. Cooley, first postmaster. The office was discontinued September 22, 1898, and the business turned over to Harbor post office.

Ferry, Wasco County. Ferry post office was named for the postmaster, William T. Ferry. The office was established October 26, 1912, and was at or near a place called Dillon, close to the Celilo Canal. The name of the office was changed to Dillon on April 8, 1914, and to Celilo on May 20, 1915. For information about the name Dillon, see under that heading. According to Judge Fred W. Wilson of The Dalles, Ferry at one time worked for the railroad and may have been employed on the construction of Celilo Canal. He was a man of considerable clerical ability.

Ferry Creek, Coos County. Ferry Creek is south of the town of Coos Bay and east of Delmar. In August, 1943, Mrs. Mary M. Randleman of Coquille wrote the compiler that the stream was named for the Ferry family, pioneer settlers, and not for a ferryboat.

Ferry Creek, Coos County. This stream flows into Coquille River near Bandon. According to information from Mrs. Emma Drane, a pioneer resident of the locality, John Lewis operated a ferry on Coquille River near the mouth of this stream in 1870, and the creek took its name from the ferry.

The style Fairy Creek is wrong according to Mrs. Drane. There was, however, an earlier ferry at this locality, mentioned by William V. Wells in a story of experience in southwest Oregon in *Harper's Magazine*, October, 1856, page 595, describing conditions in October, 1855. Wells says the scow ferry was operated by a Yankee and an Englishman and was "for man and beast." There is nothing to indicate that Ferry Creek was named for the first ferry.

Fiddle Creek, Lane and Douglas counties. Fiddle Creek heads in the Coast Range and flows westward into Siltcoos Lake. The origin of the name is unusual, but certainly not improbable. In December, 1942, Millard Martin, postmaster at Ada, wrote the compiler that about 1894 two men passed through the neighborhood on the way from North Fork Smith River to the Siuslaw country with the intention of buying cattle. One of the men had the misfortune of breaking his leg, and the two were forced to retire to a cabin about a half mile from the present site of Ada post office and wait for the injury to heal. This made a long and tiresome wait and the injured man wished repeatedly for his fiddle to help him pass the time. This expressed desire caused the nearby stream to be called Fiddle Creek.

Fielder Creek, Jackson County. This creek and Fielder Mountain west of Evans Creek, were named for Thomas Fielder, a pioneer settler.

Fields, Lane County. Fields, a station on the Cascade line of the Southern Pacific Company, was named for two members of the Lewis and Clark party, Joseph and Reuben Fields. It is sometimes said that Fields station was named for L. R. Fields, for many years an operating official of the railroad company in Oregon, but such is not the case, as is shown by the company records.

Fields, Harney County. Charles Fields took up a homestead where Fields post office is now situated. He established a "station and kept the travel and freight haulers." He sold out to John Smyth in 1911, and when the post office was established in 1913, Smyth had it named for Fields.

Fields Peak, Grant County. This peak, elevation 7360 feet, and Fields Creek nearby were named for Harvey Fields, a pioneer stockman. Fields Peak is about eight miles southwest of Mount Vernon.

Fife, Crook County. Fife is in the southeast part of the county. The compiler is informed that the place was named for the county of Fife, Scotland, former home of the first postmaster. This postmaster was Thomas Balfour. The office was established May 17, 1890.

Fifteenmile Creek, Lake County. Fifteenmile Creek was so named because the old road crossed it about that distance northeast of Fort Bidwell, California. The stream heads east of Goose Lake and flows southeast nearly to the California state line, where it empties into Twelvemile Creek. It in turn flows east and north and into Twentymile Creek. The flow from these streams eventually reaches the Warner Valley.

Fifteenmile Creek, Wasco County. This is the stream that flows through Dufur, and it received its name in pioneer days because the road from The Dalles crossed it about 15 miles from The Dalles. The road also crossed Fivemile Creek and Eightmile Creek before it reached Fifteenmile Creek. The Dalles-California Highway extends along all of these streams between The Dalles and Dufur. The three streams combine before they flow into the Columbia, and the name Fifteenmile Creek follows through to the Columbia, even though at its mouth it is only about four miles from The Dalles. The mouth of Fifteenmile Creek is at Seufert, and there was a substantial concrete bridge carrying the old Columbia River Highway over the creek at that point, known as Seufert Viaduct. All highway traffic now moves over I84 immediately to the north although the old viaduct was still standing in 1981. Old maps show Fifteenmile Creek as Nansene Creek, and there was once a community of that name in Wasco County, but the compiler has been unable to secure information about the word Nansene. This is probably the same stream mentioned by Fremont on November 25, 1843, as Tinanens Creek. Nansene post office was established May 17, 1880, with William C. Adams first postmaster. The office has been discontinued.

Fin Roberts Creek, Lane County. This is a tributary of Salt Creek east of Oakridge. It was named for one Fin Roberts, who it is said, resembled the creek in that he was always dry.

Final Falls, Clackamas County. This forty five foot high falls on the Salmon River is about seven and three quarters miles downstream from the mouth of Linney Creek. It is the final of six falls between Linney Creek and Welches. For details of this group see under Stein Falls.

Findley Buttes, Wallowa County. The Findley Buttes are in the Wallowa Valley between Enterprise and Imnaha. They are named for Florence Findley who took up a homestead there in the 1880s. These buttes are sometimes known as Brumback Buttes for N. W. Brumback, a nearby settler, but Findley Buttes is the older name and in the opinion of the writer, the correct one. Florence Findley married J. J. Johnson, an old settler. There was an early day post office near the Findley Buttes called Joy, because nearby settlers were so happy to get mail service.

Findley Creek, Wallowa County. Findley Creek flows west into Imnaha River near Imnaha. It was named for the Findley family. See under Findley Buttes.

Fingerboard Gulch, Wallowa County. This gulch and Fingerboard Saddle where it heads are in the southeast part of township 3 north, range 49 east. The gulch drains into Cow Creek, and it is named for a wooden fingerboard that was nailed to a tree at the beginning of the trail up the stream. This trail was used to go eastward to the James Tryon place in the early 1880s, according to J. H. Horner of Enterprise.

Fingerboard Prairie, Lane County. This prairie owes its name to the fact that for many years there was a signboard nearby cut in the shape of a pointing finger. Fingerboard Prairie is about six miles northeast of Belknap Springs.

Finley, Wallowa County. Finley post office was established September 11, 1913, with Virgil T. Floch postmaster, but the office was short lived and was closed November 30, 1914, at which time John E. Jackson was postmaster. The office was in section 36, township 1 north, range 46 east, about 15 miles northeast of Enterprise. It was intended that the office should be named for the Findley Buttes nearby but somewhere along the line the letter "d" was dropped, presumably in error.

Finley Butte, Deschutes County. Finley Butte just east of La Pine is a source of ballast cinders for the Burlington Northern Inc. It was named for

David Alex Findley, an early settler and first postmaster at Lava. The form Finley has been in universal use for many years.

Finley Buttes, Morrow County. These buttes are in township 3 north, range 26 east, about fifteen miles south of Irrigon. They are named for William B. and Hannah Finley who homesteaded in the area about 1880.

Finn Rock, Lane County. Finn Rock is a peculiar formation on McKenzie River not far from the mouth of Finn Creek. The rock resembles a shark's fin but was not named on that account but instead for Benjamin F. Finn, an early settler. Finn Creek was named for the same reason. Finn Rock post office, established January 6, 1947, is no longer an independent station but operates as a community post office of Eugene.

Finney and Egan Lake, Marion County. Old plats show James Finney and W. H. Egan as nearby landowners, and the lake was apparently named for them. It is southwest of Waconda.

Finzer, Marion County. Finzer was a station on the Oregon Electric Railway about five miles southwest of Salem. It was named for William E. Finzer, at one time adjutant general of the Oregon National Guard. The state had a rifle range at this station, which was named Finzer on that account.

Fir, Hood River County. Information about Fir post office is not contained in the available records of Hood River County, yet the office is known to have been in service about 1915. It was in section 6, township 1 north, range 11 east, approximately four miles southeast of Odell near Neal Creek, and was named for the fir forests in the locality.

Fir, Washington County. Fir was the name of a post office in the valley of Gales Creek not far south from the 1945 location of the Glenwood office. In other words it was about four miles northwest of the town of Gales Creek. The office of Fir was established with the name Bateman on June 30, 1890, with Clara J. Collins postmaster. It was named in compliment to an early settler of the locality, whose name has been perpetuated in the Bateman store which is also about four miles northwest of Gales Creek office. On April 27, 1891, the name of the office Bateman was changed to Fir and it operated with that name until October 9, 1900. Clara J. Collins continued as postmaster through the life of Fir post office. The compiler does not know the exact origin of the name of Fir post office. It may have been named for the trees which grow vigorously in the locality, or it may have been suggested by the name of Fir Creek, a small stream flowing east from the Coast Range to join Gales Creek just southeast of the Bateman store. Fir Creek School is situated on the creek at the toe of the foothills on a side road about two miles northwest of the town of Gales Creek. For information about the varieties of firs growing in Oregon, see under Firwood.

Fire Spring, Klamath County. On July 29, 1938, the men fighting a forest fire in the Cascade Range west of Chemult found this spring in the southwest quarter of section 26, township 27 south, range 6½ east. This was the only available water supply except that carried in by airplane, and in the circumstances, it was called Fire Spring. The name has been approved by the USBGN.

Firholm, Polk County. Firholm post office was very close to the place called Elk Horn. Elk Horn office, with Thomas R. Blair postmaster, was closed October 4, 1882. Nathan Blair, son of Thomas, decided to petition for the reestablishment of postal facilities in the locality. It was planned to use a small shop near the Blair home, and as there were some prominent fir trees close by, the name Firholm was suggested for the new office. Firholm was established April 8, 1883, with Nathan Blair postmaster. This office was closed July 9, 1883.

First Creek, Linn County. This stream is the first tributary of South Santiam River from the north, east of Lebanon, and is named on that account. It has also been known as Calloway Creek, but federal mapping agencies use the style First Creek.

First Lake, Linn County. First Lake is one of a series of four on the east bank of the Willamette River north of Albany. These lakes are named in order from Albany north. First Lake is the one nearest the city.

Firwood, Clackamas County. Firwood is a community near the Mount Hood Loop Highway southeast of Sandy. It has been so called for many years. It is a nice descriptive name and, considering the enormous quantity of firs in Oregon, some people have thought it remarkable that there are not more geographic names with "fir" in them. There are many Pine creeks and Cedar creeks but few Fir creeks. George R. Stewart in *Names on the Globe*, page 75, states that "the namer is more likely to use the uncommon term than the common one." but in Oregon's case "fir" was the uncommon term. The great firs of the Pacific Northwest were far better timber than the eastern firs that were held in low esteem by people familiar with eastern hardwoods and Michigan white pine. Mills and dealers avoided this opprobrium by using various pseudonyms, the most popular of which was "Oregon Pine", a term used by the Hudson's Bay Company in the manifest of the first shipment of lumber from the Columbia River. By 1900 "Douglas Fir" was well established in the northwest but "Oregon Pine" was still a familiar designation in other parts of the United States until after World War I. The fir is Oregon's most important forest growth. These trees may be divided into two classes, the Douglas fir, and the Balsam firs. The Douglas fir is also known as the Douglas spruce, and its botanical name is *Pseudotsuga menziesii*. It is not of the fir family, but is a false hemlock. It was first classified in 1792 as *Pinus taxifolia* by Archibald Menzies of Vancouver's command at Nootka Sound. Menzies' notes were mislaid and not published until many years after a second discovery in 1827 by David Douglas, the great botanist, who gave the name *Pseudotsuga taxifolia*. It is fitting that these two naturalists are both commemorated, Menzies by the botanical and Douglas by the common name. There are but two species of this *genera*, the Douglas Fir and a near relative, the Bigcone Fir or *Pseudotsuga macrocarpa*. The Douglas fir is of great commercial importance in Oregon. The Balsam firs are the true firs, and there are six that are of interest to Oregonians. They are much alike, and are frequently confused even by people familiar with the woods. Their names are often mixed, and colloquial expressions such as red fir, yellow fir and Oregon fir are employed in attempts to describe them to the uninitiated. Probably the most important of the six Oregon species are the noble fir, *Abies nobilis* and silver fir, *Abies* *amabalis*. These two trees, particularly the former, are generally called larch by lumbermen. They are very important commercially. *Abies lasiocarpa*, or alpine fir, is small and not so important. The lowland white fir, *Abies grandis*, and the white fir, *Abies concolor* are important lumber producers, and are generally known as the white fir. The red fir of California, *Abies magnifica* also grows in Oregon, together with its variety *shastensis*. With the exception of the California sequoias, the firs of Oregon are the most magnificent of our forest trees, and attain heights of over 300 feet. Diameters of ten feet are not uncommon. For detailed descriptions of the species mentioned above, together with their ranges, see Sudworth's *Forest Trees of the Pacific Slope*, and Mathews' *Field Book of American Trees*.

Firwood, Columbia County. Firwood was named for its natural, rustic surroundings. The post office was on or near Clatskanie River about ten miles southeast and upstream from Clatskanie. A contemporary map shows the office in the extreme south part of township 7 north, range 4 west, but a recent army map shows Fir Wood school in the next township to the east. The post office may have been moved from time to time, and in fact been in both locations in its career. The post office with the name Firwood was established February 14, 1917, with Percy A. Frazer first of three postmasters. The office was discontinued May 31, 1918, with mail to Clatskanie.

Fischer Island, Benton County. Fischer Island is the lower part of a land-area in Willamette River upstream from Corvallis. The upper part is Stahlbusch Island. Fischer is the correct spelling and not Fisher. The Fischer Flouring Mill Company owned the land.

Fisher, Lincoln County. Fisher post office is named for a small fur bearing animal, colloquially known as the fisher, but more properly the marten. There are three important members of the *Musteline carnivores*, to-wit: beech marten, pine marten and American marten or sable. Fisher post office was established March 19, 1892. It has not always been in its present location. It is reported that Bennett Olsen suggested the name. Martin Johanson was the first postmaster, and J. W. Mink later held the office. Remarkable nomenclature.

Fisher Creek, Lane County. Fisher Creek is a tributary of North Fork Willamette River and was named for a pioneer cattleman who grazed stock nearby.

Fishhawk Creek, Clatsop and Columbia counties. There are two streams called Fishhawk Creek tributary to Nehalem River from the north. One of these streams flows into the river in the extreme west part of Columbia County. The other flows into Beneke Creek at Jewell. These streams were named because of incidents connected with the many fishhawks in Oregon and it is surprising that more streams have not been named for them. Ernest E. Hogberg was appointed postmaster at Fishhawk, Columbia County, on January 17, 1890, and he held the office until it was discontinued August 15, 1910. It was at, or very close to, the mouth of this stream near the extreme west edge of Columbia County. The area is now served by Birkenfeld post office. On February 14, 1917, another post office, this time called Fish Hawk in two words, was established in the east part of Clatsop County. Florence M. Bennett was the postmaster but her tenure was short.

The office was ordered discontinued September 22, 1917. This office was doubtless on a short section of Fishhawk Creek that loops into eastern Clatsop County.

Fishtrap Creek, Coos County. This is a tributary of Coquille River between Coquille and Myrtle Point. It was named because Indians had many traps for catching salmon here in pioneer days.

Fisks, Grant County. According to R. R. McHaley in a letter published in the Canyon City *Eagle,* March 7, 1947, Fisks was about a half mile north of the present site of Austin. The place was named for D. Walter Fisk, who owned a station there. Fisks post office was established November 29, 1905, with Sarah P. Cecil first and only postmaster. The office was closed July 14, 1906, with mail to Austin.

Fitzgerald Ranch, Wheeler County. Thomas Fitzgerald started this ranch on Bear Creek in the 1890s. He was a well-known sheep man who, in 1904, had 1000 head slaughtered by the "Sheepshooters". Phil Brogan in *East of the Cascades,* chapter 13, describes the range wars between cattle and sheep ranchers including the activities of the self styled Crook County Sheepshooters Association. He estimates that more than 10,000 sheep were destroyed between 1902 and 1906.

Fivemile Creek, Coos County. Fivemile Creek is a little south of Cape Arago and flows into Pacific Ocean. The stream was named during the Coos County gold rush of 1853-55 because it was thought to be about five miles north of the mining town of Randolph on Whisky Run. The distance is in fact about four miles, but it doubtless seemed more to the tired gold seekers.

Fivemile Creek, Douglas County. This creek flows into Tahkenitch Lake. It was so named because it is about five miles long.

Fivemile Creek, Wasco County. This stream was so named because the pioneer road from The Dalles into central Oregon crossed it about five miles from town. Fivemile Creek and Eightmile Creek join, and about a mile and a half from the junction the combined stream, Eightmile Creek, flows into Fifteenmile Creek. For information about the names of this group of streams see under Fifteenmile Creek.

Fivemile Point, Coos County. This point was named by George Davidson of the USC&GS because it was thought to be about five miles south of Cape Arago. It was suggested to navigators as a range point from Cape Arago. See *Coast Pilot* for 1889.

Fivemile Rapids, Wasco County. These great rapids of the Columbia River were named by USCE because of their distance east from the boat landing at The Dalles. They formed a part of The Dalles of the Columbia, and were formerly known as the Long Narrows, The Dalles and The Great Dalles. See under The Dalles in this book and article in *OHQ,* March, 1926, page 115. Fivemile Rapids was inundated by Lake Celilo when The Dalles Dam was completed in 1957.

Flag Island, Multnomah County. This little island is on the south side of the Columbia River about midway between Troutdale and Corbett station, just upstream from Gary Island. It has been named Flag Island by USBGN because it was in this vicinity that Lieutenant W. R. Broughton of the Royal Navy raised the British flag on October 30, 1792. The name was suggested by J. Neilson Barry of Portland, in 1929.

Flagg, Lane County. Flagg was a station west of Eugene on the Southern Pacific Company line to Coos Bay. It was named for L. Randolph Flagg, who was a member of the contracting firm that built the railroad.

Flagstone Rock, Douglas County. In 1939 field officers of the USFS recommended that a prominent unnamed rocky, barren point in section 23, township 28 south, range 1 east, be named Flagstone Rock because of its appearance. The name was approved by the USBGN. Flagstone Creek is named because it heads near the rock.

Flagtail Mountain, Grant County. This mountain was named because of the large number of flagtail deer that formerly grazed in the vicinity. It is about 20 miles southwest of Canyon City.

Flanagan, Wasco County. Flanagan, a community and post office on the east side of Deschutes River six or seven miles east of Maupin, was named for a local family. Flanagan post office was established in October, 1905, with John Flanagan first postmaster, and operated until March, 1912.

Flatiron Point, Douglas County. Flatiron Point is a descriptive name used by the USFS to describe a very prominent pointed plateau that lies just south of the junction of North Umpqua River and Fish Creek. The point is about 20 miles northwest of Diamond Lake and is remarkable for its flat top and steep sides. The point is toward the north.

Flavel, Clatsop County. Named for Captain George Flavel, who once owned the land on which the community is situated. In 1892 ambitious schemes were put on foot to build a railroad from Salem to Flavel, and the townsite concern, the Flavel Land and Development Company, laid plans for a big terminal to rival Astoria. In 1897, a fine hotel was built, which enjoyed a short season of social gaiety, but Astoria was too strongly entrenched for the rival community, which so far has not made the expected development. Silas B. Smith says that the name of the Clatsop Indian village at what is now Flavel was *Konapee*.

Fleetwood, Lake County. Fleetwood, a post office in the north part of Fort Rock Valley, came as a result of the homesteading movement into that part of Oregon. The office was established September 25, 1913 with Helen A. Fleet postmaster. The name was coined from the family name. The office was closed in June, 1928.

Fleming Spring, Baker County. Boyd Fleming filed on land at this spring southeast of Pleasant Valley in 1919.

Fletts, Gilliam County. George W. Flett was an early settler on Rock Creek on the east edge of what is now Gilliam County at a point a few miles northeast of Gwendolen. He had a post office established with the name Flettville on November 4, 1881, which was operated until February 25, 1884, with Flett postmaster. Another office called Fletts was established May 5, 1884, with Orlando Rowland postmaster. D. F. Stricklin and Henry M. Pitman were later postmasters. The office was closed on April 12, 1888. Charles E. Stricklin, Oregon State Engineer, was reared in these parts and on December 24, 1945, he wrote the compiler as follows: "Apparently the post office was moved around. When my father was postmaster, a bedroom in the residence was used. During Mr. Flett's tenure as postmaster, he erected a small building in front of his residence which was used as a post office. When Mr. Flett was postmaster, the post office was located in the vicinity of the Flett School, but at that time there was no school there and the post office was across Rock Creek from where the school is now situated."

Flickbar, Baker County. Flickbar post office was established on the Baker County list on May 3, 1897, with James Grant first postmaster. The office was discontinued in April, 1899. Flickbar sounds like the name of a five-cent slab of candy, but an investigation made by LeRoy A. Grettum of Baker in December, 1945, indicates that was not the source of the title. According to Mr. Grettum, Flickbar was about ten miles up Snake River from Robinette, just north of Quicksand Creek and between the old stations Titus and Park. A man named Flick owned a ranch there and did some placer mining on a bar in Snake River. When the post office was established, it was named in compliment to Flick and his gravel bar. Irving L. Rand of Portland informs the compiler that it is his understanding that the geographic feature called Flicks Bar was on the Idaho side of Snake River and not in Oregon.

Flock Mountain, Wheeler County. John and Charles Flock settled in Mitchell near the turn of the century. John served a term as city recorder but Charles' wife, Sally, took up government land on the west side of Flock Mountain so the name probably comes from this side of the family.

Flora, Wallowa County. Flora was a post office in the extreme north part of Wallowa County. It was named for the daughter of the first postmaster in that district, A. D. Buzzard. This information was given the compiler by N. J. Hansen, postmaster at Flora in 1925. The office was opened October 6, 1890 and closed December 27, 1966. The little of Flora that remains is described by Phil Adamsak in the *Oregon Journal*, July 31, 1981, page 19.

Floras Creek, Curry County. Floras Creek is a well-known stream in the north end of the county, flowing into the Pacific Ocean north of Cape Blanco. About 1910 William H. Packwood told the compiler that in the summer of 1852 he was a member of Lieutenant H. W. Stanton's command which was ordered to cut a trail from Fort Orford up Rogue River to the Rogue River Valley. They had with them a civilian named Fred Flora, who had been engaged in mining near the coast and Floras Creek was named for him. An editorial in the *Curry County Reporter,* printed in 1939, mentions this man, but spells his name Fred Florey. It says that Florey had opened up a trail along Floras Creek before 1855. It seems possible that miners from California, who were familiar with Spanish, changed the spelling from Floreys Creek to Floras Creek. The compiler has never seen any evidence that Floras Creek was named for the pilot of a Spanish expedition along the coast. Martin de Aguilar is said to have had a pilot named Flores, but there is nothing to show that his expedition ever saw Oregon.

Florence, Lane county. Florence is on the north bank of Siuslaw River near the mouth. The town is said to have been named for A. B. Florence, who was a member of the state senate at the sessions of 1858, 1859 and

1860, representing Lane County. According to another story (*Oregonian*, October 7, 1903, by Lionel Johnson), the town was named for a French vessel, wrecked about 1873, at the mouth of Siuslaw River. Alfred L. Lomax discusses the wreck of the Florence in *OHQ*, volume XXXVI, page 222. The actual date was February 17, 1875. Lewis & Dryden have further information in *Marine History of the Pacific Northwest* including the comment that the ship was "a veritable floating coffin".

Flounce Rock, Jackson County. Flounce Rock is a peculiar geological formation north of Rogue River between Trail and Prospect. It bears a fancied resemblance to the flounces on a woman's dress. It was so named at a time when flounces were worn, by Hiram Abbott, a pioneer resident of the neighborhood.

Flournoy Valley, Douglas County. Flournoy Valley, a couple of miles west of Lookingglass, was named for H. B. Flournoy, who settled there in 1850. Fort Flournoy blockhouse was built in the valley in 1855. See Walling's *History of Southern Oregon*, page 419.

Foland Creek, Tillamook County. Foland Creek flows into Nestucca River near Beaver. It was named for Merriman Foland who settled nearby in the 1880s.

Foley, Tillamook County. A post office with the name Folley was established near Foley Creek on June 7, 1888, with Frank Worthington first postmaster. This office was out of service for a short time in the latter part of 1893. The name of the office was changed to Foley on December 27, 1894, and that is the way it remained until it was closed by an order dated July 13, 1906, and effective July 31, 1906.

Foley Creek, Crook and Jefferson counties. In 1878 Elijah T. Foley homesteaded along this creek in township 11 south, range 17 east. Foley Butte to the southwest takes its name from the creek.

Foley Creek, Tillamook County. This stream is east of Nehalem Bay. Miss Lucy E. Doughty of Bay City wrote the compiler in 1927 that the search for the origin of this name had led to a story to the effect that when the first white people settled in that part of the country they found a cabin that had evidently been built by a white man. When the Indians were asked about it, the whites were informed that it had been constructed by a man named Foley. Who Foley was, whence he came, whither he went, is apparently unknown.

Foley Slough, Harney County. This is a part of Silvies River east of Burns. It was named for an early settler, J. C. Foley.

Foley Spring, Baker County. E. W. Coles who was born in Haines in 1878 told the compiler in 1973 that this spring northeast of Haines was named for an early settler.

Foley Springs, Lane County. Walling, in *History of Lane County*, page 466, says that Foley Springs were first discovered by William Hanley and William Vick. In 1865 a man named Alexander settled on the premises and in 1870 a Dr. Foley purchased the springs and opened them to the public under the name Bethesda Hot Springs. Lane County records seem to show that what Dr. Foley bought from Alexander was not more than a squatter's rights, for Abram A. Foley received a patent from the government for the property. It was dated March 30, 1882, and filed for record November 30, 1889. Dr. Foley operated the springs for nine years, when they passed into the hands of Henry Hill, who sold out to Peter Runey in 1882. Runey made extensive improvements and got a post office, which was called Foley-springs in compliment to Dr. Foley. Postal authorities spelled the name as one word, but ordinary mortals used the style Foley Springs. The water is hot, about 188 degrees, rendering the baths very agreeable when adequately tempered. The building Runey constructed about 1916 was destroyed by fire in March 1981. See article in Eugene *Register-Guard,* March 6, 1981.

Follyfarm, Malheur County. This post office was formerly on the extreme east edge of Harney County, and received its name because of the farming operations of J. H. Neal, who attempted to irrigate land in adverse conditions. Neal, unlike many persons in similar circumstances, possessed a sense of humor, and called his place Neal's Folly, which subsequently became Folly Farm. The post office was established about 1909, and Neal suggested the name of his farm for the name of the office, and the authorities promptly accepted it, as being distinctive and non-duplicating, but coupled it into one word. Dorcas N. Neal was first postmaster. The office was later moved a short distance eastward to a road junction on the west edge of Malheur Counry. John Scharf informed the compiler in 1981 that J. H. Neal was the first homesteader on Smyth Creek and that he surveyed the early meander line of Malheur Lake.

Foots Creek, Jackson County. Walling, in *History of Southern Oregon,* page 379, says this stream was named for O. G. Foot, a miner who prospected along the creek in early days. Foots Creek flows into Rogue River from the south a few miles west of Gold Hill. The community at the mouth of Foots Creek has been known as Bolt since pioneer days. A post office called Foots Creek was in operation near this stream from April, 1878, until July, 1879, with Silas Draper postmaster. The writer does not know the exact location of the office, but Draper was interested in mining on the upper reaches of the creek and the office may have been near what was later known as Draper. See under that heading.

Fopiano Creek, Wheeler County. Fopiano Creek rises west of Waterman and flows to Mountain Creek. John Fopiano located along this creek in 1875 after mining near Canyon City. After he died in 1891, his wife's brother, James Wilson, moved from California to manage the ranch.

Force Lake, Multnomah County. This overflow lake on the south bank of the Columbia River south of the east end of Hayden Island was named for George W. Force, a pioneer settler.

Foreman Point, Wasco County. This prominent nose about six miles east of Bear Springs is the site of a state forest lookout. It was named for a well-known Wapinitia family. Benjamin L. Foreman settled on Juniper Flat in 1889 and married Eliza Abbott, sister of sheepmen James and Joe Abbott.

Forest, Klamath County. This post office is said to have been named for the fine stand of timber adjacent. The compiler is quite prepared to believe the statement. In 1902 the pine forests of the vicinity must have been magnificent. Forest post office was about seven miles west of Keno on the old Ashland road. It was just east of Spencer Creek. Forest post office was established May 20, 1902, with Nathan S. High first postmaster. The office was discontinued to Keno, March 4, 1908. Forest post office was about three miles northeast of a later office called Wampus. Both places were on the old Pokegama-Klamath Falls freight and stage road as well as on the road to Ashland. Both probably owed a good share of their existence to the business between Klamath Falls and Pokegama.

Forest Crossing, Crook County. Forest Crossing of Crooked River is at the south end of Lone Pine Flat just north of O'Neil, in the extreme north-west corner of the county. The locality was named for Francis Forest, who was born in Polk County, Oregon, in 1857, and settled in Crook County in 1876. For biography, see *Illustrated History of Central Oregon,* page 784.

Forest Grove, Washington County. At a meeting of the trustees of Tualatin Academy (Pacific University), January 10, 1851, the name Forest Grove was adopted for the community. The name Vernon was first proposed and rejected. J. Quinn Thornton moved to adopt the name Forest Grove and the motion was passed. Previously that part of the county was known as West Tualatin Plain. It seems probable that the name Forest Grove was the idea of Thornton himself. Thornton arrived at his home-stead in the Willamette Valley in November, 1846, and he named his claim Forest Grove. See Thornton's *Oregon and California in 1848,* volume I, page 239. The words Forest Grove seem to have stuck in his mind. Postal authorities inform the compiler that Tualatin post office was established February 1, 1850, with David Hill first postmaster. The name was changed to Forest Grove on December 31, 1858. David Hill was the founder of Hillsboro, and information about him will be found under that heading. The compiler has been unable to learn why Hill was postmaster of a community apparently situated several miles away. However, post offices were frequently moved considerable distances in pioneer days. Tualatin post office was just south of the present site of Forest Grove. For early history of Forest Grove by Fred Lockley, see *Oregon Sunday Journal,* March 22, 1931.

Forman Canyon, Jefferson County. Roy and Frank Forman operated a wheat ranch immediately north of this canyon near Trout Creek before World War I.

Fort Bailey, Josephine County. This was one of the camps or so-called forts used in the campaign against the Rogue River Indians in 1855-56. Data about its location are conflicting, but the statement by Victor, in *Early Indian Wars of Oregon,* page 368, is probably correct. It is to the effect that the fort was five miles south of Cow Creek. That means that it was on Wolf Creek, at or close to the present community of Wolf Creek. It was apparently named for Captain Joseph Bailey of the Oregon Mounted Volunteers. Bailey was from Eugene. Fort Bailey is sometimes described as at Grave Creek, but Fort Leland is known to have been the post at that place.

Fort Birdseye, Jackson County. Fort Birdseye was one of the stockades used by the settlers during the Rogue River Indian uprising of 1855-56. It was on the south bank of Rogue River near the mouth of Birdseye Creek, at the David Birdseye place. In 1856 some of the logs from the stockade were used to build the Birdseye cabin. A D.A.R. marker has been placed on the south side of the Pacific Highway at the site of the stockade. When Rogue River Valley settlers gathered in one of these stockades, they called it "forting up."

Fort Briggs, Josephine County. In January, 1944, James T. Chinnock of Grants Pass wrote the compiler as follows: "Fort Briggs was on the George E. Briggs donation land claim in section 35, township 39 south, range 8 west, near Sucker Creek. This was a log house in the Illinois Valley at which settlers gathered during the Rogue River War of 1855-56. Briggs was a pioneer settler."

Fort Clatsop, Clatsop County. This was the first military establishment to be built in Oregon, and it served as the Lewis and Clark winter-quarters for 1805-06. The various factors which influenced the selection of a locality for winter-quarters are mentioned in Thwaites' *Original Journal of the Lewis and Clark Expedition,* volume III, page 246, *et seq.* The men were allowed to vote on the location. Lewis made a reconnaissance and on December 5, 1805, rejoined Clark, reporting that he had found a good situation. Construction of a stockade about 50 feet square was started at once. This was built around seven cabins. On January 1, 1806, Captain Lewis recorded in his orderly book that the fort was completed, and the first orders for its operation and security were officially issued on that date. The name Fort Clatsop is not given in the orders, but appears later in the journals. The party left the fort on the return trip at 1 P.M., Sunday, March 23, 1806. On March 20, Lewis wrote: "we have lived quite as comfortable as we had any reason to expect we should." The site of Fort Clatsop, three acres of land, is now owned by the Oregon Historical Society and is marked. It is about three-quarters of a mile south of the Oregon Coast Highway, just west of Lewis and Clark River and is easily accessible by road. Postal records show that Fort Clatsop post office was established November 10, 1852, with Thos. W. Shane first postmaster. Carlos W. Shane was a prominent pioneer of this locality and it is possible that the authorities misread his name and put it down Thos. Franklin Shane became postmaster on February 18, 1854. The office was discontinued on February 15, 1855. The office was in service again with other postmasters from March, 1876, to September, 1881. The name of the office established in 1852 is very indistinct in early postal records, and may in fact be Port Clatsop. In view of the fact that the Shanes lived at Fort Clatsop and also in view of the name used for the office in 1876, the compiler thinks that the style Fort Clatsop is correct. The locality could hardly be called a port.

A restoration project was begun in 1958 under the National Park Service. The Fort Clatsop National Monument consists of a replica of the log stockade and cabins along with modern visitor facilities. See the *Oregon Journal,* August 22, 1963.

Fort Dalles, Wasco County. Fort Dalles was a regular military post used during various Indian disturbances from 1850 to 1866. It was situated on Mill Creek, in the west part of the community of The Dalles, and before it was abandoned, it had developed into a commodious post. Fort Lee was established at The Dalles in the fall of 1847 at the time of the Cayuse War, but it had nothing to do with Fort Dalles. In May of 1850 Colonel W. W. Loring, then stationed at Vancouver, sent two companies of the Mounted Rifles to The Dalles to establish a supply depot. Heitman, in the *Historical Register,* says the post was first called Camp Drum. This was apparently to commemorate Captain Simon Henry Drum, who was killed in the assault on the City of Mexico, September 13, 1847. For information about Fort Dalles, see *Illustrated History of Central Oregon,* pages 102-105. The first buildings were of logs, but some of them burned, and the post was reconstructed in 1856-57, rather elaborately. A Captain Thomas Jordan had charge of the new construction. There is no record of any fortifications or defenses, either before or after the reconstruction. The reservation at first very large, was finally reduced to 640 acres, with the northeast corner at the mouth of Mill Creek. In 1905 the Old Fort Dalles Historical Society secured possession of the only remaining building, the Surgeon's quarters. This building is now used by the society as a museum and is visited by a great many people each year. It was built in 1858 and its design gives a good idea of Fort Dalles after the development of 1856-57.

Fort Flournoy, Douglas County. Fort Flournoy was a settlers defense blockhouse built in the Flournoy Valley in 1855. It was never actually used. Walling, in his *History of Southern Oregon,* page 419, says the structure was built of hewn logs, about 18 feet square, with the superstructure about 28 feet square. This was a typical method of blockhouse construction. The building was still standing in 1883 a couple of miles west of Lookingglass.

Fort George, Clatsop County. The North West Company took over Astoria and the Astor enterprise in October, 1813, and the Astor post was named Fort George, presumably in compliment to King George III. Franchere says that the bargain for the transfer was signed on October 23, 1813, but he does not say that the name was changed on that date. Captain William Black of the British sloop of war *Raccoon* was in the Columbia River in December and pulled down the American flag on December 12 or 13. In his report to the Admiralty Black says that he named the post Fort George. Fort George was technically returned to the United States October 6, 1818, but continued as a British post. Americans revived Astoria many years later. The compiler has been unable to find any contemporaneous record that the Astorians used the expression Fort Astor. They referred to the post as Astoria. Franchere says the Northwesters planned to move the factory to Tongue Point, but this was not done. A diagram of Fort George as of 1818 is on file at the Oregon Historical Society and shows it to be a substantial installation, more than 150 by 200 feet, with a stockade and other defenses. A note on the diagram shows that the original Astoria establishment was about 75 by 110 feet, apparently not fortified. In 1930 workmen excavating in Astoria found remains of the stockade, probably the north wall, running from Fifteenth to Sixteenth streets, between Duane and Exchange streets. A plan of the fort has been painted on the sidewalks and pavements in this vicinity.

Fort Harney, Harney County. During the Indian outbreaks of the 1860s, there were a number of army camps in southeast Oregon, but most of them were temporary. It seems to have been the plan of the authorities to make Fort Harney something more permanent. However, the place was a fort in name only if evidence can be relied on. Fort Harney was established August 16, 1867, and was first called Camp Steele. On August 28, 1867, Major-General H. W. Halleck, commanding the Military Division of the Pacific wrote to Brevet Major-General George Crook at Camp Warner regarding the naming of military posts. His thoughts on name selection are concise. "As a general rule, I think military posts should not be named after civilians, but after military officers as a compliment for military services. In most cases, it would be most appropriate to adopt the names of those who have served in the country where the post is established. I, therefore, cannot approve the name of Camp Wood, but think the new post should be called Camp Warner, or if you prefer, New Camp Warner. There is already one Camp Steele in the Department of the Columbia, and it would, therefore, be improper to give the same name to another. The present name of Camp Wright would also be objectionable, as there is now a Camp Wright in California. As the new post is in Harney Lake Valley, I suggest the name of Camp Harney, after General Harney." On September 14, 1867, the name was changed in compliment to Major-General W. S. Harney but the record is not clear whether it was first "camp" or if it proceeded directly to "fort". See under Harney County. The post was near the mouth of Rattlesnake Creek and about two miles east or north of what was later the community of Harney. In 1864 troops had been in this vicinity at a place called Rattlesnake Camp. In January, 1944 Archie McGowan of Burns wrote the compiler: "A portable sawmill was established in the timber north of the fort and extra good pine lumber was cut and practically all of the buildings were built of this lumber. There never were many of them, probably two small houses for officers, a barracks, some sheds or barns with log corrals for the horses. I can remember as a boy seeing some of those logs still lying around the corral, but the houses were all torn down and moved away by the settlers just as soon as the fort was abandoned. I have been told there was really no stockade." The *Illustrated History of Baker, Grant, Malheur and Harney Counties*, page 633, says Fort Harney was abandoned June 14, 1880. It seems to have been used in the Indian disturbances of 1878. By order of the president, the Fort Harney military reserve of 640 acres was created January 28, 1876, but on September 13, 1882, this was reduced to 320 acres. The compiler has a statement from the late J. J. Donegan of Burns to the effect that the rest of the reserve was restored to public entry March 2, 1889, "and the fort was abandoned." War Department records say that the soldiers marched out June 13, 1880, and Donegan's statement means that the land was abandoned as military property in 1889. A post office with the name Camp Harney was established August 10, 1874, with William T. Stevens first postmaster. The writer has been unable to learn why postal authorities did not use the official name as adopted by the War Department. The name of the office was changed to Harney September 16, 1885, with Robert J. Ives postmaster. The office was doubtless moved to the new community at that time.

Fort Hayes, Josephine County. Fort Hayes was a gathering place for settlers during the Rogue River War of 1855-56 and was close to what is now the Redwood Highway southwest of Grants Pass. Walling, in his *History of Southern Oregon*, page 452, says that Fort Hayes was at the Thornton place, about nine miles north of Kerby. James T. Chinnock of Grants Pass is of the opinion that the fort was near the south end of Hayes Hill, probably at what is also known as Anderson Station. The compiler has not been able to get more definite information. Members of the Hayes family were early settlers in the Illinois Valley and the fort was named for them.

Fort Henrietta, Umatilla County. Fort Henrietta was built by a detachment of the First Oregon Mounted Rifles under the command of Major Mark A. Chinn in November, 1855, in the Yakima War. Chinn named the fortified post Fort Henrietta, in compliment to the wife of Major Granville O. Haller of the United States Army. The fort was a stockade one hundred feet square, built of large split timbers, with two bastions of round logs, and an outside stock corral enclosed with rails found on the ground. See Victor's *Early Indian Wars of Oregon*, page 439. Fort Henrietta was near the west bank of Umatilla River not far from the present (1942) site of the Catholic Church in the town of Echo. Statements that the fort was near Well Spring do not seem to be substantiated by the records.

Fort Hill, Polk County. Fort Hill, just northeast of Valley Junction, was named because Willamette Valley settlers built a blockhouse on its summit in 1855-56. The federal government sent troops to this place and established Fort Yamhill on August 30, 1856. See under Fort Yamhill for additional information. The blockhouse was later moved to Grand Ronde Agency and still later to Dayton and set up in a public park.

Fort Hoskins, Benton County. Data about most of the early military establishments in Oregon are neither plentiful nor accurate, but fortunately there is a good account of the history and physical facts of Fort Hoskins. This information is in an article by Colonel Oscar W. Hoop, U.S.A., with the title "History of Fort Hoskins, 1856-65," in *OHQ*, volume XXX, page 346. Fort Hoskins was established as the result of the concentration of Indians at Siletz Agency and was named in honor of Lieutenant Charles Hoskins who was killed in the battle of Monterrey, Mexico, September 21, 1846. Captain Christopher C. Augur, Fourth Infantry, and his command reached Kings Valley July 25, 1856, and according to army records printed in *OHQ*, volume XXXVI, page 59, Fort Hoskins was established the next day. It was on Luckiamute River near the mouth of what is now known as Bonner Creek, probably on land owned by Rowland Chambers, later by Franz. Later in the year Lieutenant P. H. Sheridan began to build a road or trail from the fort over the Coast Range to the Siletz country. Augur's selection of the site for the fort was not approved by Brigadier-General John E. Wool, his superior, and there was a good deal of controversy. Augur stuck to his guns and the fort stayed where it was until it was evacuated April 13, 1865. A blockhouse was built in the Siletz country, but there was also a squabble about this, and it had to be moved. Colonel Hoop has written entertainingly of the establishment of Fort Hoskins and the life there. The present community and post office of Hoskins are close to the site of the fort, but there is nothing left of the establishment. Colonel Hoop says that Sheridan left Fort Hoskins for Fort Jones, Califor-

nia, May 19, 1857, and "this is the last we hear of Sheridan in the valley of
the Willamette." The implication is wrong for Sheridan was at Fort Yamhill
in 1861 and was not ordered east until September of that year. Heitman's
Historical Register says Fort Hoskins was on Siletz River and Old Fort Hoskins was on the Willamette River six miles north of Corvallis. Neither of
these statements, apparently based on official records, is correct. Fort Hoskins was actually about 15 miles airline northwest of Corvallis. Heitman's
Fort Hoskins on Siletz River seems to have been the Siletz blockhouse. The
official records of two forts may have been based on the notion that General Wool had the post moved, but as a matter of fact Captain Augur refused to budge.

Fort Kitchen, Coos County. Fort Kitchen was a stockade where settlers
"forted up" under command of an elected captain, William H. Packwood.
It was about a mile south of the present town of Myrtle Point, on South
Fork Coquille River near the mouth of Catching Creek. An account of the
establishment of this fort in November, 1855, is contained in Dodge's *Pioneer History of Coos and Curry Counties,* page 96, *et seq.,* where it is said the
post was named for the creek. See also Victor's *Early Indian Wars of Oregon,*
page 373, *et seq.* It seems probable that the firm stand taken by Captain
Packwood in dealing with local Indians was successful in avoiding
bloodshed in the Coquille Valley. According to Dodge, *supra,* page 211, the
stream was named for E. C. Catching, a pioneer settler. The Catching place
became a rendezvous at an early date. It is the opinion of the compiler that
the name Fort Kitchen came as the result of the mispronunciation of the
family name.

Fort Klamath, Klamath County. For the origin of the word Klamath,
see under Klamath County. The Klamath Indian name for the locality of
Fort Klamath was *Iukak,* meaning within, or in the midst, and referred to
the location close to or between mountains. The fort was established with
two companies of soldiers in 1863. It was an important post during the
Modoc, Snake and Piute wars, and was at a point about a mile southeast of
the present community. The troops were removed in 1889. For story about
Fort Klamath, see *Oregon Journal,* October 24, 1937.

Fort Lamerick, Curry County. The locality of Big Meadows was important during the Rogue River War of 1855-56. It is in the extreme northeast
part of Curry County, about two miles north of Rogue River and near the
southeast corner of township 32 south, range 10 west. It is mentioned
several times in Victor's *Early Indian Wars of Oregon* and also in Walling's
History of Southern Oregon. On account of their strategic position, the Oregon Volunteers decided to establish a post at the Big Meadows, and a site
was selected May 1, 1856. This post was called Fort Lamerick in compliment to Brigadier-General John K. Lamerick of the Oregon troops. Since
hostilities were over in the summer of 1856, Fort Lamerick was short lived.
In February, 1944, forest ranger L. J. Cooper of Galice kindly sent some
information about Fort Lamerick. The post was very close to the quartercorner between sections 1 and 2, township 33 south, range 10 west, and was
about 300 feet above the present (1944) site of the Frye barn. In 1896 there
were remains of the fort, some rotting logs and what appeared to be a

dugout. These remains were cleared off by C. J. Frye when he took up a homestead. Local tradition is to the effect that the fort was a crude affair, hardly more than low log breastworks enclosing a camping place. Despite that, Fort Lamerick was important as a rendezvous and merits recording.

Fort Lane, Jackson County. Fort Lane was built for service in the Rogue River War. It was established September 28, 1853, and evacuated in September, 1856. See *OHQ,* volume XXXVI, page 59. In the files of the Oregon Historical Society is a letter from Captain A. J. Smith of the U. S. Dragoons, dated December 18, 1853, and addressed to General Lane, saying that the fort had been completed and that the detachment of three companies of dragoons and one company of infantry was quite comfortable. The fort was named in compliment to General Joseph Lane, whose career is described under Lane County. Walling, in *History of Southern Oregon,* page 231, says: "Appropriately named Fort Lane, it was commodiously and even handsomely built, and in a manner well adapted to the uses of such a post. A stockade enclosed quite a spacious area in which was a parade ground, together with barracks for private soldiers, houses for officers, an armory, hospital, and other necessary buildings, all built of logs." The D.A.R. marker for Fort Lane is about a quarter of a mile north of Tolo on the road to Gold Ray, near the Southern Pacific tracks. Stones for the marker were taken from the remains of the fort.

Fort Lee, Wasco County. Fort Lee was the stockade or post established at The Dalles by the Oregon Volunteers during the Cayuse War in the fall of 1847. It was named for Major H. A. G. Lee of the expeditionary force. According to Bancroft, *History of Oregon,* volume I, page 703, the only piece of ordinance at the governor's command was a ninepounder belonging to Oregon City. This was sent to The Dalles, which place was designated as army headquarters. The compiler does not know the exact location or the details of construction of Fort Lee.

Fort Leland, Josephine County. Fort Leland was one of the posts used by the Oregon volunteers during the Rogue River Indian uprising of 1855-56. It was just north of where the Pacific Highway crosses Grave Creek north of Grants Pass. For the history of the name Leland see under Grave Creek and Leland. Fort Leland was established in the fall of 1855 by the Oregon volunteers, and the name is mentioned several times by Victor in *Early Indian Wars of Oregon* and also in Walling's *History of Southern Oregon.* There are some ambiguities about the location, but the consensus is that it was at the Grave Creek House and that is the local tradition. Walling, page 255, says that after the battle of Hungry Hill, Harkness and Twogood, proprietors of the Grave Creek House built a stout stockade of timbers and prepared for a siege. This stockade appears to be what was called Fort Leland. Troops had their headquarters there for several months.

Fort Miner, Curry County. This fort was not a military establishment, but a log structure built by settlers and miners about a mile and a half north of the mouth of Rogue River, on an open prairie near the ocean. The fort was used during the Indian fighting in 1855-56 as a place of refuge. Rodney Glisan in *Journal of Army Life,* page 290, uses the name Fort Miner under date of March 8, 1856, and mentions the fort in several places. In one place, on March 25, 1856, he refers to it as Citizen Fort, and it is apparent that the establishment was built some time in 1855. Dodge, in *Pioneer History of Coos and Curry Counties*, gives a good deal of information about the place and on page 83 refers to it as "Miner's Fort." On page 347 is the name "Fort Miners." Fort Miner seems to have been a semi-official name for the establishment. Glisan says it consisted of two log houses, surrounded by a high earth embankment. Dodge, on page 361 of his history, gives some reminiscences of Judge Michael Riley, which include a statement that the Rogue River miners and settlers built their stockade at first on the south side of the river near the present site of Gold Beach. Riley was absent at San Francisco at the time and on his return in January, 1856, objected to the location because there was not enough open space around. Riley was responsible for building a new Fort Miner north of the river where there was no cover for attacking indians.

Fort Orford, Curry County. Fort Orford was established September 14, 1851, and evacuated in October, 1856. See *OHQ*, volume XXXVI, page 59. According to R. C. Clark, the first troops were sent from Astoria. On October 18, 1851, 135 soldiers sailed from the Depot of the Military Division of the Pacific, Benicia, California, to garrison Fort Orford. The detachment was in command of Lt. Colonel Silas Casey, See annual report of the Secretary of War, dated November 29, 1851. The soldiers built the fort with cedar logs and with lumber shipped from San Francisco. The buildings were at the community of Port Orford and the post was named on that account. Dr. Rodney Glisan was stationed at Fort Orford from June 21, 1855, to August 21, 1856, and has written an interesting account of activities there in his *Journal of Army Life*. In addition to the military post, there was an earlier civilian stockade with blockhouses, also called Fort Orford. Captain William Tichenor's second expedition landed at Port Orford July 14, 1851, and immediately built the first Fort Orford. See under Fort Point. For Tichenor's account of the establishment of the civilian fort, see Dodge's *Pioneer History of Coos and Curry Counties*, chapter II. The army post was a few hundred feet northwest of the civilian Fort Orford. The civilian fort was destroyed by the Port Orford fire of October 10, 1868.

Fort Point, Curry County. Fort Point is at the south edge of the town of Port Orford, overlooking the ocean. It is just northwest of the famous Battle Rock. On July 14, 1851, Captain William Tichenor's second expedition landed at Port Orford and built two blockhouses on Fort Point, with log defenses. This establishment was built as a place of refuge for local settlers. The government, on September 14, 1851, established the military post of Fort Orford, but this was in addiiton to the original blockhouses. The blockhouse fort was destroyed in the fire that burned Port Orford October 10, 1868.

Fort Rock, Lake County. This is a rocky landmark. There is a post office of the same name nearby. The rock is an isolated mass, imperfectly crescent shaped, nearly one-third of a mile across, and its highest point is about 325 feet above the floor of the plain on which it stands. It has perpendicular cliffs 200 feet high in places. It is not surprising that it has been likened to a fort. An item in the Bend *Bulletin*, June 20, 1925, says that

William Sullivan, an early resident, named Fort Rock. Sullivan settled in what is now Lake County in 1873. In 1938 prehistoric artifacts were discovered in a large cave at the base of Fort Rock. Dr. L. S. Cressman of the University of Oregon supervised extensive excavations that uncovered weapons, tools and even sandals, and subsequent carbon dating showed some items 9000 years old. Phil Brogan has a full description including pictures in chapter 4, *East of the Cascades.*

Fort Rowland, Coos County. William Rowland settled on South Fork Coquille River in 1853, on what is now known as Rowland Prairie, and his place was used as a settlers defense headquarters against the Indians in the fall of 1855. The stockade was called Fort Rowland. For information about Fort Rowland and William Rowland, see Dodge's *Pioneer History of Coos and Curry Counties,* pages 97-100 and 187. See also Victor's *Early Indian Wars of Oregon,* page 374. Mr. and Mrs. Albert Powers, well-known residents of Coos County, owned the Rowland property in 1945. According to Mrs. Powers the Rowland home was on the Rowland donation land claim in the southwest quarter of section 27, township 30 south, range 12 west, close to the line of the Robert Y. Phillips claim.

Fort Smith, Douglas County. Fort Smith was a post used by the Oregon Volunteers during the Rogue River War of 1855-56. See Victor's *Early Indian Wars of Oregon,* page 368. It was at the place of William Henry Smith on Cow Creek. It was near the southwest corner of section 25, township 32 south, range 6 west, and about four miles up Cow Creek from the present town of Glendale, close to the Pacific Highway. Available records do not describe any defenses, although there may have been a stockade.

Fort Stevens, Clatsop County. Isaac Ingalls Stevens was governor of Washington Territory, 1853-57, and delegate to Congress, 1857-61. He was killed while leading the Seventy-ninth Regiment New York Volunteers, at Chantilly, Virginia, against the Confederates, September 1, 1862. He was major-general, and had seized the colors of the regiment after the color-sergeant had fallen. Governor Stevens was highly energetic and constantly active, and was very popular with the people of the territory. He was born at Andover, Massachusetts, March 18, 1818. In 1839 he was graduated from West Point. He served with distinction in the war with Mexico. The route of his journey to the territory in 1853, laid out and surveyed, by him, as one for a railroad, was largely followed by the Northern Pacific. A biography, by his son, Hazard Stevens, is a meritorious book: *Life of Isaac Ingalls Stevens,* Houghton Mifflin & Company, 1900. For a prospectus of Stevens' railroad surveys, see the *Oregonian,* July 16, 1853; progress of the surveys, *ibid.,* October 1, 22, 1853. Stevens visited the eastern states in 1854. He left Portland March 29, 1854. His report on his council with the Blackfeet, dated June 8, 1854, appears, *ibid.,* July 29, 1854. Fort Stevens, in Oregon, was named for him by Captain George H. Elliott, USCE, who built the fortifications there and at Cape Disappointment in 1864, *ibid.,* September 21, 1864.

In 1955 Clatsop County gave a large parcel of land immediately south of Fort Stevens to the state for inclusion in the State Parks system. In 1968 the parks system obtained control of the military reservation via long term lease from the USCE and most of the area is now Fort Stevens State Park. It is not only one of the more popular camping areas but also attracts large numbers of visitors to Battery Russell and the other historic gun emplacements. In 1980, *Fort Stevens: Oregon's Defender at the River of the West,* a detailed history of the post by Marshall Hanft, was published by the State Parks and Recreation Division. See also Hanft's article "The Cape Forts: Guardians of the Columbia", *OHQ,* volume LXV, pages 325 through 361.

Fort Umpqua, Douglas County. This was a United States military establishment, not to be confused with Hudson's Bay Company forts of the same name. Fort Umpqua was established July 28, 1856. See *OHQ,* volume XXXVI, page 59. It was one of three forts set up to watch over the Indians at Grand Ronde and Siletz agencies. The other two were Fort Yamhill and Fort Hoskins. A letter in the Bancroft Library, University of California, dated Umpqua City, March 20, 1862, with a signature that seems to be J. V. Cately, says that the post was built to accommodate two companies of soldiers, but on that date had but one lieutenant and 22 men. The post was at the same place as the community and post office of Umpqua City, about two miles north of the mouth of the river, on the west bank, not far from what is now known as Army Hill. Walling, in *History of Southern Oregon,* page 438, says that in the summer of 1862 a paymaster visited the fort and found all the officers, commissioned and non-commissioned, away on a hunting trip. As the result of this episode, the post was abandoned.

Fort Vannoy, Josephine County. Fort Vannoy was one of the more important posts used by Oregon volunteer troops during the Rogue River War of 1855-56. James T. Chinnock of Grants Pass has furnished the compiler with the following information: "Fort Vannoy was on the north bank of Rogue River about four miles west of what is now Grants Pass, near the northwest corner of section 21, township 36 south, range 6 west, on the Margaret Vannoy donation land claim adjoining the James N. Vannoy claim. Vannoy was a pioneer of 1851 and established a ferry in that year. A man named Long operated a ferry a little below this point in 1850. Fort Vannoy was in no sense a fortification, but a headquarters camp for the volunteers of the 1855-56 Indian War. It was probably established in late October or November, 1855. The exact location cannot be determined, because there are no marks remaining. There was a group of log houses, and possibly some defense, such as log breastworks or a low stockade hastily constructed. The word fort seems to have been used for any place where the settlers gathered for mutual protection rather than for a place fortified. Fort Vannoy was important because it was used for headquarters as well as for settlers' refuge. The land is now owned by C. H. Eismann." A good article about Fort Vannoy, written by James T. Chinnock, is in Grants Pass *Courier,* August 8, 1942.

Fort William, Columbia and Multnomah counties. Fort William was established on Sauvie Island by Nathaniel J. Wyeth, and occupied two sites. The first was near Warrior Point, where the fort was established temporarily in the autumn of 1834. Wyeth wrote on October 6, 1834: "We are near the mouth of the Multnomah." About May 1, 1835, the establishment was moved south opposite the Logie Trail, which was a route of travel into

Tualatin Valley. This was to be the permanent location. It was on the west side of the island, in section 7, township 2 north, range 1 west. Owing to the commercial rivalry of the Hudson's Bay Company, Wyeth was forced to abandon Fort William. Carey, in *History of Oregon*, page 302, says that Fort William was named for one of Wyeth's partners but does not say which one. The site is shown as Fort William Bend on the USGS Sauvie Island quadrangle.

Fort Yamhill, Yamhill County. In 1855-56 Willamette Valley settlers built a blockhouse on Fort Hill, near the present community of Valley Junction, as a protection against Indians who had been moved onto the reservation. The federal government sent troops to this place and established Fort Yamhill on August 30, 1856. See *OHQ*, volume XXXVI, page 59. The fort was named for the Yamhill River. For the origin of the name Yamhill, see under Yamhill County. There is a good general account of the activities at Fort Yamhill in Glisan's *Journal of Army Life*. Dr. Glisan arrived at Fort Yamhill early in September, 1856, and his journal runs through February 10, 1859. It is well worth reading. The compiler does not know when Fort Yamhill was evacuated as a military establishment, but it was subsequent to June 30, 1865. Official records do not seem to warrant the use of the name Fort Sheridan for this establishment. The D. A. R. marker for Fort Yamhill is about a half a mile north of Valley Junction on the Three Rivers Highway and it says that the fort was about 300 yards east of the monument, which would place it close to Fort Hill east of Cosper Creek. In a general way this agrees with Glisan's description. After the army authorities abandoned Fort Yamhill as a military post, the Fort Yamhill blockhouse was moved from the top of Fort Hill to Grand Ronde Agency and used for a jail. It stood about where the Agency Community Hall stood in 1944. Later it was moved again, this time to Dayton and set up in a public park. After the blockhouse was moved to Dayton, dedication ceremonies were held August 23, 1912, and an address was given by Judge M. C. George. It contains historical information about Fort Yamhill. See *OHQ*, volume XV, page 64.

Foss, Tillamook County. Foss is a place on Nehalem River about four miles east of Mohler. The post office was in operation from 1928 to 1943. The office was named for Herbert Foss who had timber holdings in the locality. He was living in Mohler in 1943.

Fossback Marsh, Lane County. This is a swampy area not far from the mouth of North Fork Siuslaw River. It was named for a pioneer family of the vicinity.

Fossil, Wheeler County. The compiler is informed that this post office was established February 28, 1876, at the ranch of Thomas B. Hoover, who was the first postmaster. He had discovered and was removing some fossil remains on his ranch at the time, and this suggested the name of the new office.

Foster, Linn County. The post office was established February 8, 1892, with Aaron H. Yost first postmaster. C. H. Stewart of Albany told the compiler in 1927 that the place was named for P. J. Foster, who operated a grist mill in the neighborhood.

Foster Butte, Douglas County. This butte near the headwaters of Black

Creek east of Red Butte was named for Roy Foster, a nearby resident and part time USFS employee. This information was furnished by Fred Asam of Canyonville.

Foster Creek, Curry County. Foster Creek rises on Ophir Mountain and flows into Rogue River near Illahe. According to M. S. Brainard of Brookings it was named for Charles Foster who was born in New York about 1820. He came to Port Orford about 1851 and was a captain in the Gold Beach Guards during the Indian wars. He homesteaded near the mouth of Foster Creek where he died April 21, 1883.

Foster Road, Multnomah County. Philip Foster came to Oregon in 1842, by sea. His wife was Mary Charlotte Pettygrove, sister of F. W. Pettygrove, one of the founders of Portland. Foster was born at Augusta, Maine, January 29, 1805. During his first four years in Oregon, Foster engaged in the mercantile business at Oregon City. His farm, at Eagle Creek, was the first on the Oregon Trail in the Willamette Valley. This made the Foster farm the most widely known in Oregon. The Foster place was, during many years, a depot of supplies for new settlers. He was preceded there by Samuel McSwain, a pioneer probably of 1842. Foster died March 17, 1884. Mrs. Foster died in 1879. For his biography, see the *Oregonian*, March 28, 1884, page 1. Foster Road bears his name. For detailed information about him and his early experiences in Oregon, see the *Oregonian*, December 18, 1927, section 1, page 10.

Fourbit Creek, Jackson County. Fourbit Creek is tributary to South Fork Big Butte Creek northwest of Mount McLoughlin. Anne Weatherford in *Real West*, September 1967, has an interesting account of the naming of this stream. It appears that in the spring of 1859 Eli Ledford and four companions attempted to cross from Jacksonville to the Klamath country. Because of deep snow, they were unable to get through and they made camp at Rancheria Prairie. Here all the party were murdered but whether by Indians or renegade whites is unknown. Ledford's four companions were found first in a common grave but his body was finally located about a half mile away. Ledford habitually carried a money belt filled with 50 cent pieces, and while trying to escape the fate of his companions, he scattered the coins. For many years the fourbit pieces would occasionally be found in the prairie or along the banks of Fourbit Creek.

Fourmile Canyon, Gilliam and Morrow counties. This canyon opens into Eightmile Canyon, and is so called on the assumption that its mouth is about four miles up Eightmile Canyon from the point where that canyon opens onto Willow Creek.

Fourmile Creek, Coos County. A stream called Fourmile Creek flows into Pacific Ocean a little more than seven miles south of Bandon, and the origin of the name of the stream is somewhat of a puzzle. It is said that it was so called because it was about four miles south of Coquille River, but it is nearly twice that far. Whoever did the original measuring greatly underestimated the distance. It is of interest to note that the Oregon Coast Highway crosses the main branch of Twomile Creek at a point three miles north of Fourmile Creek, and something like five miles south of Bandon. Fourmile post office was established near Fourmile Creek on March 3, 1906, with Harlan P. Dunning first and only postmaster. The office was closed to Langlois June 15, 1907. It was reestablished as Four Mile in 1947 and finally closed May 24, 1963.

Fourmile Lake, Klamath County. So called because it was assumed that the lake was four miles long. This lake is just northeast of Mount McLoughlin in the heart of the Cascade Range.

Fourth Lake, Linn County. This lake is the fourth of a series of four lakes, beginning at Albany and extending north along the east bank of the Willamette River. They are named in order from Albany.

Fox, Grant County. Fox takes its name from Fox Creek, an important tributary of North Fork John Day River. The name was applied to the stream in pioneer days on account of some incident that occurred on a hunting or prospecting trip that had to do with a fox. The post office was established about 1883.

Fox Butte, Lake County. Fox Butte is in the extreme north end of Lake County and southeast of the Paulina Mountains. In December, 1945, Avon D. Derrick of Fort Rock wrote the Bend *Bulletin* that the butte was named for a black fox seen there by his father, H. E. Derrick, in the summer of 1909. Stories to the effect that the feature was named for a nearby settler, one Fox, do not seem to be true.

Fox Creek, Marion County. Charles C. Giebeler of Detroit, informed the compiler that this stream, which flows into Breitenbush River, was named for one Fox, a camp cook for a party of trail builders. While camped near this stream Fox fell into a fire as the result of an epileptic fit, and was burned so badly that he died.

Fox Hollow, Lane County. Fox Hollow drains a considerable area southwest of Spencer Butte and also southwest of Eugene and adds the water to Coyote Creek. It has been called Fox Hollow since pioneer days and while the natural assumption is that it was named for some incident connected with a fox, Cal M. Young, long a resident of Lane County, wrote the compiler in 1947 expressing his doubts. Mr. Young says that he was told many years ago that the hollow was named for the many fox squirrels that lived therein. These fox squirrels, also called Oregon gray squirrels, were so named because of their bushy tails. There was at one time a Fox Hollow post office near the road junction in section 5, township 19 south, range 4 west, with Mrs. Aslaug I. Knox postmaster. This office was in service from November 27, 1922, to September 1, 1924, in the Fred G. Knox farm home, and was closed by the extension of rural route 3 from Eugene.

Fox Valley, Linn County. Fox Valley is a cove on the south side of North Santiam River about two miles east of Lyons. It has been so called since pioneer days and was named for John Fox, one of the first settlers. He had an Indian wife. Fox Valley post office was established July 21, 1874, with Abner D. Gardner first postmaster. The office operated on and off until May 6, 1907, when it was supplanted by rural free delivery.

Francis Creek, Douglas County. Francis Creek flows into South Umpqua River nine miles northeast of Tiller. It was named for Francis Rondeau, a member of a pioneer Douglas County family and a sister of USFS employee John Rondeau.

Francisville, Wheeler County. Information about this early-day post office is very meagre. It was established January 4, 1883 and closed June 28, 1883. John F. Jordan was the first postmaster. Old maps show the office situated on Pine Creek a few miles east of what was later Clarno. The compiler has not been able to learn the origin of the name, or anything else about the place for that matter.

Franklin Butte, Linn County. This butte is just southeast of Scio. Its greatest elevation is 911 feet. Riley Shelton, of Scio, informed the compiler in 1927 that the butte was named for Franklin M. Rice, who took up a donation land claim at the west and southwest part of the butte. It was at first called Paynes Butte, but the name was changed to the present form about 1860. Rice operated a blacksmith shop near the southeast corner of his claim, and some of the cinders remained there in the road for many years. Mrs. Rebecca Morris, a pioneer of 1845 from Missouri, furnished these data to Shelton. Shelton was born near the butte in 1853, and was well acquainted with Rice.

Franklin Hill, Morrow County. This hill near Matlock Canyon on the east edge of the county was named for early settler James C. Franklin.

Franklin-Smithfield, Lane County. The Franklin-Smithfield controversy has been outstanding in Lane County for many years, and up to 1942 the difference of opinion had not been composed. The locality is on the Territorial road a few miles north of Elmira. There have been many news stories about the squabble. The most comprehensive that the compiler has seen are in Eugene *Register-Guard,* March 1, 1931, and by Professor John B. Horner in the *Oregonian,* May 14, 1933. It is not easy to follow all the arguments. About 1852-53 Daniel Smith made his homestead at what is now Franklin-Smithfield and in 1857 R. V. Howard established a store in the vicinity. In the meantime Franklin post office was established on March 3, 1855, with Enos Elmaker postmaster. The compiler does not know if the office was at that time near the Smith home, or some distance away, as it seems to have been in several nearby localities. Howard attempted to have a post office called Smithfield, but this name ran afoul of Smithfield in Polk County, and the authorities would not allow duplication. It is not clear whether Howard wanted to change the name of the Franklin post office or establish a new one. In 1891 Daniel Smith laid out a townsite and filed the plat for Smithfield. In the meantime Franklin post office was in operation and it appears on the 1900 postal map. In 1909 the USGS mapped the locality as Smithfield. It was shortly after this that there began to be marked differences of opinion as to the name of the village. The controversy was acute in 1931 and in 1934 an effort was made to have the county commissioners adopt one of the names. The commission however passed a resolution calling for double-barrelled direction signs on roads and highways, reading both Smithfield and Franklin. This arrangement did not satisfy the partisans of the two names, but it represented the situation in 1943. By 1966 the Franklin contingent appeared to have triumphed for maps no longer included Smithfield.

Frankton, Hood River County. This is a community on the west side of the Hood River Valley, and is said to have been named for one Frank

Backus, who platted a tract of land with the hope of developing a town. E. L. Smith, a well-known pioneer of Hood River, was interested in this enterprise.

Fraser Canyon, Wasco County. Hugh Fraser homesteaded near the head of this canyon north of Antelope in 1883.

Frazer Creek, Lincoln County. This creek flows into Salmon River two miles from the Pacific Ocean. It was named for Alec F. Frazer, an early settler.

Frazier, Lane County. Frazier, a station on the Cascade line of the Southern Pacific Company, was named for Robert Frazier, a member of the Lewis and Clark party. See also Fields, Cruzatte and Pryor.

Frazier Mountain, Clackamas County. Frazier Mountain, elevation 5110 feet, was named for Donald Frazier, who died in 1918 in military service during World War I. He was a forest guard on the Mount Hood National Forest. The mountain was formerly called Shellrock Mountain, one of several in the state, and it was believed the new name would be more suitable than the duplication, as well as honor a man who died for his country. Frazier Mountain is in township 5 south, range 7 east.

Frazier Mountain, Union County. Dunham Wright of Medical Springs, wrote the compiler in 1927 that this mountain was named for an old hunter named Frazier, a pioneer settler in Antelope Valley near Telocaset.

Freebridge, Wasco County. Freebridge was a station on the Great Southern Railroad about four miles north of Emerson on Fifteenmile Creek. It was so called because here the old stage road to what is now Sherman County left Fifteenmile Creek to cross over the ridge to the Deschutes canyon where it in turn crossed the river at Free Bridge. The Free Bridge was the result of a plan by Wasco County to provide free going between The Dalles and Sherman County communities, so that the toll bridge at the mouth of Deschutes River could be avoided. The project was undertaken in September, 1885, and in October of that year a contract for the bridge was awarded to Hoffman and Bates of San Francisco and Portland. When railroad construction was started in the Deschutes canyon in 1909, advance camps of both lines were established in this area and supplied in part by wagon over the Free Bridge Road from the railroad along Fifteenmile Creek. The Deschutes Railroad, the Union Pacific line up Deschutes River, called their camp station Freebridge. It was located on the Sherman County side of the Deschutes River near the Free Bridge and about opposite the present Burlington Northern station called Kloan. Freebridge post office was established at the Fifteenmile Creek location on January 29, 1908 with Frederick L. Petersen first postmaster. Ida Carlisle succeeded him on November 24, 1908 and after the completion of the construction in the northern part of the Deschutes canyon, the post office was closed on July 30, 1910 with papers to Wrentham. W. H. McNeal, who devotes an entire page of *History of Wasco County* to this tangled toponomy, says the situation was clarified about 1920 when the Great Southern changed the name of their Freebridge station to Daneville. This name was apparently a compliment to Petersen who was a native of Denmark.

Freedom, Coos County. Freedom post office was established May 21, 1878, with Yelverton M. Lowe first postmaster. This office was closed January 8, 1883. In September, 1946, Mrs. Mary M. Randleman of Coquille wrote the compiler that the office, which was at the mouth of Beaver Slough, was named for patriotic reasons. When the post office was closed the mail was handled through Coquille.

Freedom, Lane County. Post office records show that Freedom post office was established February 17, 1858, with Thomas M. Awbrey first postmaster. The name of the office was changed to Lancaster on May 7, 1866, when Joseph S. Lyman was postmaster. It seems probable that this office was at or near the place called Lancaster, which is just southwest of Harrisburg. Walling in his *Illustrated History of Lane County*, page 458, says that in the early 1850s a man named Woody started a house of entertainment in this locality and called it Woodyville. The term house of entertainment seems to have been a fancy name for a roadhouse. Walling also says that Johnson Mulkey bought the property, changed the name to Lancaster and built a sawmill. The writer has no information about the origins of the names Freedom or Lancaster. It is interesting to note that Lancaster, a city in Pennsylvania, is not far east of Harrisburg. The associations of names in Pennsylvania may have had something to do with naming a place Lancaster in Oregon because it was close to a town called Harrisburg. The author has no evidence to support this theory, but it is appealing. On January 23, 1872, the name of Lancaster post office was changed to Junction City. It is probable that at that time the office was moved south so as to be on the recently constructed railroad. The first postmaster of the Junction City office was David McAlpine.

Freeman Dry Camp, Lake County. R. A. Long of Fort Rock said that this spot south of Oatman Flat was a camp site used by early day sheepman Roy Freeman. The form Feeman is incorrect.

Freewater, Umatilla County. Freewater was established as a rival community to Milton, just to the south, and hoped to get settlers by the device of offering free water for irrigation purposes. The original plat of the town was filed as New Walla Walla, on account of proximity to Walla Walla, Washington. This filing was made November 30, 1889, but a note in Umatilla County records says the plat was later withdrawn. There is nothing now on file to show its nature. The plat for Freewater was filed August 16, 1890. The rivalry between Freewater and Milton continued unabated until 1951 when the two communities merged. Milton-Freewater post office was established September 1, 1951 and for further information see under that name.

Freezeout Creek, Wallowa County. This stream is in the eastern part of the county. It was named by one Jack Johnson because he nearly froze there one night. Johnson was a prominent pioneer character of the Wallowa country.

Freezeout Ridge, Morrow County. This long north and south ridge about thirteen miles east of Heppner divides the headwaters of Willow and Butter creeks. It was named in 1899 when John Kilkenny and James Carty lost 1000 head of sheep in a spring blizzard after shearing.

Fremont, Lake County. For some years, beginning about 1909, Fremont was a post office. It was about six miles west of Fort Rock. The name was probably suggested by the name Fremont National Forest, which was named for Captain John C. Fremont, who explored central Oregon in 1843. Regardless of the fact that Fremont made an accurate and valuable record of his trip through Oregon, he is frequently spoken of lightly, as a general who never commanded an army and an explorer who never made a discovery. He was born in Georgia in 1813. At the age of 25 he was appointed a second lieutenant in the topographical engineers of the army. He made several explorations in the West, and these, coupled with his experiences in California, led to his nomination by the Republicans in 1856 for the presidency. He served in the Civil War, and attained the rank of major-general. He died in 1890. While his geographical work was of good character, too many claims were made in his behalf. See editorial in the *Oregonian*, April 2, 1926.

Fremont Canyon, Deschutes and Jefferson counties. This canyon is northeast of Sisters. It is popularly supposed to be the canyon ascended by Captain John C. Fremont early in December, 1843, while he was on his way south through Deschutes Valley.

Fremont Highway, Deschutes, Klamath and Lake counties. This highway was named in honor of Captain J. C. Fremont, who explored central Oregon in the fall of 1843. For data about Captain Fremont, see under Fremont. The name Fremont Highway was suggested by Robert W. Sawyer of Bend, and it was adopted by the Oregon State Highway Commission August 30, 1927. For article about Captain Fremont and Fremont Highway, by John W. Kelly, see magazine section, *Oregonian*, March 18, 1928.

Fremont Meadow, Deschutes County. This little natural meadow is on Tumalo Creek in section 34, township 17 south, range 11 east, and lies within Shevlin Park, property of the city of Bend. Captain John C. Fremont and his exploring party camped in this vicinity on the night of December 4, 1843, and mentioned following an Indian trail southward to a meadow, obviously on Tumalo Creek. In September, 1855, the officers of the Pacific Railroad Surveys, Williamson and Sheridan, followed a trail southward to the same locality and met Abbot who was traveling north. The position given is that of the meadow in question and the description is accurate enough for a check. This indicates that the Indian trail crossed Tumalo Creek at this meadow, sometimes called Upper Meadow, the same place used by Fremont in 1843. In January, 1943, the city of Bend and some interested residents asked to have the name Fremont Meadow adopted, which was done by the USBGN later in the year.

French Creek, Douglas County. This tributary of North Umpqua River near Glide was presumedly named for John H. French who took up a donation land claim nearby in 1852.

French Gulch, Baker County. French Gulch is in the vicinity of Auburn and it was an important place at the time of the eastern Oregon gold rush of the early 1860s. Some French miners operated in this gulch and it got its name on their account.

French Mountain, Lane County. This mountain lies southeast of

McKenzie Bridge. It was named during World War I in honor of the French people. Just east is English Mountain, named at the same time.

French Pete Creek, Lane County. This stream is an important tributary of South Fork McKenzie River. Smith Taylor told the compiler that it was named for French Pete, an early day sheepherder, who ranged his band along the stream. The compiler has been unable to get the rest of French Pete's name, but the omission may not matter. In the 1970s the creek became the point of a major confrontation between environmentalists and timber interests. The environmentalists were trying to preserve a substantial stand of young timber with a high potential value at maturity. Their efforts were eventually successful and the bulk of French Pete Valley was added to the Three Sisters Wilderness on February 28, 1978. This section has one of the lowest elevations of any of the Oregon wilderness areas.

French Prairie, Marion County. French Prairie lies in the Willamette Valley, between the Willamette River and Pudding River, north of Salem. Its general elevation is less than 200 feet and it is well shown on the USGS map of St Paul quadrangle. The prairie was named for the early French-Canadian settlers, most of whom were former employees of the Hudson's Bay Company. Early days on French Prairie are described by H. S. Lyman, in reminiscences of Louis Labonte in *OHQ*, volume I, page 169. For similar article by Lyman, reminiscences of F. X. Matthieu, including list of French-Canadian settlers, *ibid.*, page 73. For article about settlement of French Prairie, by Oswald West, *ibid.*, volume XLIII, page 198.

French Settlement, Douglas County. This locality is mentioned under the heading Champagne Creek. It was a few miles northwest of Roseburg. A post office with the name French Settlement was in operation from August 10, 1874, until December 14, 1874, with John M. Wright postmaster. The place was named for a number of French-Canadians who established a colony there in the 1850s.

Frenchglen, Harney County. Dr. Hugh James Glenn was born in Virginia in 1824 and spent his youth in Missouri, where he was married in March, 1849. In that year he emigrated to California, and after working in the mines, in 1853 he settled temporarily in what is now Glenn County, California. After several trips across the plains, he brought his family to California in 1868 and settled there permanently. In 1867 he began to buy land on a large scale and in 1874 he was reported to own 55,000 acres in the Sacramento Valley. He was known as the Wheat King. He was killed by one Miller on February 17, 1883, on his Jacinto Ranch only 17 days after his oldest daughter Ella had become the bride of Peter French. French was born John William French in Missouri in 1849 and came to California as a child. During his teens he took the Christian name Peter and worked for Glenn on the Jacinto Ranch. In 1872 Dr. Glenn sent Peter French to southeastern Oregon as a scout and landbuyer. French bought large holdings for the Glenn account and became a partner in the French-Glenn business. He was impressed with the valley of the Donner und Blitzen River for cattle raising and among other properties, bought a small ranch from a local cattleman and prospector who was using a P branding iron. This place was a favorite of Pete French and became his headquarters, with the name P Ranch. The P Ranch became one of the most famous properties of the West and was the center of very large holdings. Pete French was shot and killed near Sodhouse on December 26, 1897, by Edward L. Oliver. This tragedy was the result of an altercation over some land, and Oliver was acquitted by a jury. For many decades the P Ranch and the French-Glenn holdings were landmarks in Harney County. Frenchglen post office was near the P Ranch, and the name of the office perpetuates the name of the owners of the enterprise, with a single modification in spelling. A large part of the property is now in the Malheur Migratory Bird Refuge. For further details, see under Malheur Lake and P Ranch. See also news stories in the *Oregonian,* December 29, 30, 1897. Frenchglen post office was established by change of name from Somerange October 1, 1930, with Jesse L. Bradeen postmaster. For the history of this office, see under Somerange.

Frickey Canyon, Wheeler County. This tributary to Amine Canyon was named for William Frickey who homesteaded there in 1920.

Friend, Wasco County. Friend was named for George J. Friend, as the post office established February 28, 1903, was on his homestead. The name was proposed by Theo. H. Buskuhl, first postmaster.

Friendly Reach, Multnomah County. This is part of the Columbia River, about 8 miles long, from the mouth of the Willamette River eastward. It was named by Lieutenant W. R. Broughton on October 31, 1792, in commemoration of the friendly behavior of an old Indian chief, who acted as a guide. The name was adopted by the government in 1926 at the request of the Camp Fire Girls.

Friends Peak, Jefferson County. In 1881, Jasper Friend homesteaded on Trout Creek near the mouth of Cow Canyon and this peak to the south bears the name of his well-known family. Friend was first postmaster at Cross Keys near present Willowdale and was a brother of Columbus Friend who settled north of Antelope.

Frissell Point, Lane County. This point, which is northeast of McKenzie Bridge, together with Frissell Creek to the north, and Frissell Crossing on South Fork McKenzie River, were named for "Uncle" George Frissell, a pioneer settler on the upper McKenzie River.

Frizzell Ranch, Wheeler County. Joseph Frizzell came to Wheeler County in the 1870s. He settled first east of Fossil and then moved to this ranch on upper Girds Creek.

Frog Hollow, Wheeler County. Frog Hollow is five miles southwest of Waterman on the road to Mitchell. George W. Nelson who was raised in the area told the writer in 1969 that the place couldn't have been better named. On a spring evening, the constant, blatant croaking compared favorably with the radio born rock and roll music of two generations later.

Froman, Linn County. This was a railroad station southeast of Albany, named for Thomas Froman, a pioneer resident of the neighborhood.

Fruita, Wallowa County. Fruita is situated in a park on Imnaha River near the mouth of Grouse Creek. When the post office was established, various names, including Imnaha Park and Grouse Creek were suggested, but postal authorities rejected them all, mostly because of duplication.

Finally the department sent a *Postal Guide* and requested that a name of one word be selected that did not duplicate any other name in Oregon. A local resident by the name of T. F. Rich, had lived at Fruita, Colorado, and he suggested that name.

Fruitland, Marion County. Fruitland is the name of a locality about five miles east of Salem and a mile north of the Penitentiary road, applied because of the excellence of the soil. Fruitland post office was established September 5, 1892, with George H. Nichols postmaster. The office was closed March 19, 1901, and the locality, which is thickly settled, is served from Salem.

Frustration Falls, Clackamas County. This fifty-five foot high falls on Salmon River is about six and three quarters miles downstream from the mouth of Linney Creek. It is the fifth of six falls between Linney Creek and Welches and was named because it is so difficult to reach. For details of this group see under Stein Falls.

Fry, Linn County. Fry is a railroad station between Albany and Lebanon, named for Olney Fry, Sr., a pioneer settler of the vicinity.

Fryingpan Lake, Clackamas County. This lake is south of Salmon River in the eastern part of the county. It is supposed to simulate the shape of a fryingpan, hence the name.

Fryrear Butte, Deschutes County. This butte is east of Sisters, and was named for an early settler nearby, John B. Fryrear.

Fuego, Klamath County. This station on the Cascade line of the Southern Pacific Company is named for Fuego Mountain to the east. See under that name.

Fuego Mountain, Klamath County. Fuego Mountain is in the east central part of what was the Klamath Indian Reservation. *Fuego* is Spanish for fire. Captain O. C. Applegate told the writer that in early days there were several bad forest fires on this butte, and owing to remoteness, they were hard to control. He thinks this was the reason for the name.

Fuller Canyon, Morrow County. James S. Fuller homesteaded in this canyon five miles west of Heppner about 1880.

Fulton Canyon, Sherman County. Fulton Canyon is in the northwest part of the county. It was named for the Fulton family, pioneer settlers in Wasco and Sherman counties. Colonel James Fulton was born in Missouri and came to Oregon in 1847. He served in the Indian wars and subsequently settled in Wasco County. Later he lived with other members of his family in Fulton Canyon. He was the postmaster at the post office of Fultonville, now discontinued. He died in 1896. In 1976 Giles French, the sage of Sherman County, was kind enough to provide the following details of Fulton's three sons and the geographic features connected with each of them. Fulton Canyon was named for John Fulton who took up a claim there in 1878 and later built an impressive home. He was for many years county judge of Sherman County. Frank Fulton Canyon, which comes into Fulton Canyon from the east about a mile south of the Columbia River, was named for another son. His home was near the center of section 20, township 2 north, range 15 east, about where the county road leaves the canyon to head north to Biggs Junction. Frank Fulton Canyon extends south only to the forks where the east branch becomes Locust Grove Canyon and the west branch Neece Canyon. Frank had a son named Charles who was occasionally inclined to the local tipple and some older residents referred to this feature as Whiskey Canyon. A third son of Colonel Fulton was named Dave and he lived in Mud Hollow, the next canyon to the east. At one time this was called Dave Fulton Canyon but this name has not survived. In 1977 the USGS prepared new maps of the area and the nomenclature was adjusted to fit the above facts.

Fulton Ridge, Wasco County. This is the high ground overlooking the south bank of Columbia River and the west bank of the Deschutes. R. E. Newcomb of the USGS proposed the name in 1965 as descendants of the Fulton family still farm in the area. For information on the source see under Fulton Canyon.

Furnish Creek, Lane County. This is a tributary of Salmon Creek east of Oakridge. It was named for James Furnish, a forest ranger. Furnish was of the opinion that there was no such stream in the neighborhood and when it was finally discovered it was named for him as a reminder of his error.

Fuzztail Butte, Deschutes County. Fuzztail Butte is ten miles north of East Lake. Phil Brogan of Bend informed the writer that a fuzztail was a wild or escaped horse whose unkempt tail was a sure sign of a lack of human attention.

Gage Creek, Wheeler County. Gage Creek flows into West Branch Bridge Creek from the east. It was named for Isaac Gage who took up a homestead along its banks in 1876. He was not related to the Gage family who lived in West Branch about the turn of the century.

Gale, Klamath County. On April 10, 1890, the name of Tule Lake post office in the south part of Klamath County was changed to Gale. It seems probable that the office was moved, although the compiler does not have exact information. Williston D. Woodcock was the postmaster at the time the name was changed from Tule Lake. He continued to operate the Gale post office until March 6, 1891, when the name was changed back to Tule Lake. In September, 1948, R. H. Anderson of Klamath Falls wrote that he had talked to a Mrs. Johnson, daughter of Woodcock, and in 1948 living at Lakeview. She said she remembered the circumstances of the post office very clearly. The family had difficulty in selecting a name for the new office and finally someone suggested that it be called Gale because of the severe winds and sand storms that then prevailed. This name was in use only about a year.

Galena, Grant County. Galena was a post office in the valley of Middle Fork John Day River, at a place once the site of Susanville post office. It is alleged to the writer that about 1901 a mine and its employees about two miles away up Elk Creek, secured the removal of the Susanville office to a point near the mine. This left the abandoned post office site without an office. A new office with a new name was petitioned for, and, due to the fact that there was a body of ore in the vicinity, Galena was suggested. Galena is a common ore of lead, chemically known as lead sulphite. A news story in the *Oregonian*, September 7, 1943, announced the closing of Galena

304 OREGON GEOGRAPHIC NAMES

post office in August, 1943. Mrs. Genevieve Saling was the last postmaster. For editorial comment, *ibid.*, September 9, 1943.

Gales Creek, Washington County. Gales Creek and Gales Peak nearby were named for Joseph Gale who came to Oregon in 1834, with Ewing Young, from California. He was born April 27, 1801, near Washington, D. C. He settled on East Tualatin Plain and afterwards at the foot of Gales Peak, on a tributary of Tualatin River, and later in Eagle Valley, Union County. Gale, in his younger days, followed the sea; afterwards, he became a trapper in the Rocky Mountains. Gale was master of the *Star of Oregon*, the first ship to be built in Oregon, which was launched in the Willamette River in 1841 and finished in 1842. Lieutenant Charles Wilkes gave him papers for sailing the *Star of Oregon*. He sailed the schooner to San Francisco Bay. For story of this enterprise, see magazine section of the *Oregonian*, May 18, 1941, and OPA *Transactions* for 1891. Together with Alanson Beers and David Hill, Gale constituted the executive committee of the provisional government, elected July 5, 1843. He died in Eagle Valley, Union County, Oregon, December 13, 1881. For his biography see the *Oregonian*, December 29, 1881, page 4; February 12, 1882, page 4; October 12, 1883, page 1; May 9, 1877, page 4. "Captain Gale has always been a man of great energy, brave, fearless and honest." (J. W. Nesmith, in an address before OPA on page 12 of *Transactions* for 1880.) Gales Creek post office, named for the stream nearby, was established September 10, 1874, with Lester Ray first postmaster. The place was sometimes called Gales City.

Galesville, Douglas County. Galesville was a pioneer post office in the Cow Creek Valley, established October 14, 1854, with George F. Hall first postmaster. The office was closed January 31, 1916, and the business turned over to Azalea. In August, 1946, Miss Bess A. Clough of Canyonville informed the compiler that two men, Gale and Goshen first settled on the place later purchased by Daniel Levens, and when the post office was established, it was named for Gale, whose first name is not known to the compiler.

Galice, Josephine County. The postmaster at Galice, in 1926, wrote the compiler that the place took its name from a French doctor, Louis Galice, who came as early as 1852, and discovered placer gold. It is said that this Frenchman is buried close to Galice Creek nearby. For additional details about the discovery of gold at Galice, and the history of the community, see Walling's *History of Southern Oregon*, page 460.

Gallagher Canyon, Wasco County. This canyon in the extreme southeast corner of the county is on the old The Dalles-Canyon City road. Grover C. Blake in *Blazing Oregon Trails*, page 14, says that in 1863 one Gallagher, a packer, was camped along the trail at the mouth of this gulch. During the night his helper named Berry Way did him in, disposed of his body and departed with the pack train with a disputedly large amount of gold dust. Way was apprehended and later hanged in Canyon City but the gold was never recovered. The canyon has since carried the name of the ill fated Gallagher. See also under Bearway Meadow.

Galloway, Morrow County. Galloway is in the Butter Creek drainage northeast of Heppner. It is about two miles south of the locality called Pine

City, and bears the name of an early settler. Galloway post office was first established July 31, 1886, with John J. Galloway postmaster. The office served intermittently until September 30, 1915, when it was closed out to Echo.

Galls Creek, Jackson County. Named for Jacob Gall, who settled on this stream on September 7, 1852. The spelling Galls is in general use. The form Gauls is wrong.

Garden Creek, Wallowa County. This stream is in township 6 north, range 47 east, and is in the very northeast corner of the state. It flows into Snake River, and according to J. H. Horner of Enterprise was named because an early settler had a fine garden on a bar at the mouth of the creek.

Garden Home, Washington County. This name is mildly sentimental, and may be classified with Sweet Home, Pleasant Valley and others of that class. The community of Garden Home has existed for many years, and became prominent when the Oregon Electric Railway was built. The site of Garden Home station was somewhere east of the older settlement.

Garden Valley, Douglas County. This valley, at the junction of North and South Umpqua rivers gets its name from the character of the soil, which is well adapted to vegetable and garden products. See Walling's *History of Southern Oregon,* page 432.

Gardiner, Douglas County. Gardiner is on the north bank of the Umpqua River near its mouth. It is an historic community of Oregon, and bears the name of a Boston merchant who sought to trade on Umpqua River. His vessel, *Bostonian,* was wrecked at the mouth of the river October 1, 1850. Most of the goods on the vessel were saved and moved to the location of what was subsequently the town of Gardiner. The place became the headquarters of the Umpqua customs district in 1851, with Colin Wilson as collector. See advertisement in the *Oregonian,* December 6, 1851. The community is described in the *Oregonian* for June 23, 1855. The post office of Gardiner's City was established on June 30, 1851, with Geo. L. Snelling first postmaster. The form Gardiner City was used on October 20, 1853, which was the date that Harrison Spicer became postmaster. The official name is now Gardiner.

Gardner Creek, Tillamook County. Gardner Creek flows into Deer Creek on the south slope of Cascade Head immediately adjacent to the headquarters of the Cascade Head Experimental Forest. Gayton Phelps wrote the compiler that it was named for Jesse N. Gardner who came to the Salmon River country before World War I. On March 11, 1911, Gardner patented a land claim in section 21, township 6 south, range 10 west, and in 1935 the land was sold to the USFS.

Gardner Ridge, Curry County. Johnson Gardner came to Curry County in 1877 and settled on this ground near the mouth of North Fork Chetco River where he raised a large family. This information was provided by M. S. Brainard of Brookings.

Garfield, Clackamas County. Garfield is about three miles east of Estacada. It is not now a post office. It was named for James A. Garfield, twentieth president of the United States. A post office with the name Leon was established in this locality May 1, 1893. The name was changed to Garfield May 26, 1897, and the office was closed February 15, 1906.

Garfield Peak, Crater Lake National Park, Klamath County. This peak is on the south rim of Crater Lake and has an elevation of 8060 feet. It was named by Will G. Steel for James R. Garfield, then Secretary of the Interior, on July 15, 1907. Garfield was the first cabinet officer to visit Crater Lake.

Garibaldi, Tillamook County. T. B. Handley, an attorney of Portland, wrote the compiler on October 1, 1927, that his grandfather, Daniel Bayley, was one of the first white settlers in Tillamook County, and in the 1860s named the community of Garibaldi for the Italian patriot. D. D. Bayley was an ardent admirer of Garibaldi, and wanted his name perpetuated in Oregon. Giuseppe Garibaldi was born in Italy July 4, 1807. His life was at all times eventful, and he had been condemned to death before he was 27 years of age. He was a revolutionist in South America for several years, then returned to Italy in 1848 to join the revolution in that country. Then for more than 15 years he was for the most part engaged in military activities connected with the establishment and early period of the kingdom of Italy. He died in 1882. The compiler has been unable to associate Joseph C. Champion with the naming of Garibaldi in 1848. In 1848 Garibaldi was just starting the most active part of his career, and it is doubtful if anyone in Oregon knew much about him at that time. Champion was the first white settler in what is now Tillamook County, having come from Astoria by boat in 1851. Champion lived in Garibaldi, but not, however, until he had lived at other places in the county. Garibaldi post office was established August 9, 1870, with Daniel D. Bayley first postmaster. This was apparently the third post office in Tillamook County, although the office at Nehalem may have been established the same day. The Nehalem record is not clear. William Ralston became postmaster on September 17, 1873, and the office is shown as closed on February 29, 1876. Garibaldi office was opened again on February 2, 1880. The name was changed to Hobsonville February 6, 1883. It may be assumed that the office was moved to a new location at Hobsonville, although these early post office records do not contain information about moving of offices. The office at Hobsonville was closed October 26, 1887, and the business was transferred back to Garibaldi, where an office had been reopened September, 1886. Except for a couple of interruptions, the Garibaldi office has been in operation ever since.

Garlinghouse Lake, Benton County. This is a small slough lake northeast of Monroe. Its elevation is 265 feet. It was named for William Garlinghouse, a pioneer settler nearby.

Garner, Klamath County. Garner Lundy, a young man living on the east edge of Klamath County, had his first name perpetuated at Garner post office, which was established June 7, 1902, at a point about four miles airline north of Bly. This post office was across the creek from the George Boyd home ranch, in section 14, township 36 south, range 14 east. Jessie M. Boyd was the only postmaster. She ran the office until June 3, 1903. Garner Lundy is said to have been the first student in the local school.

Garoutte Creek, Lane County. Garoutte Creek rises south of Black

Butte and flows north to Coast Fork Willamette River. It was named for S. P. Garoutte who discovered the cinnabar deposits at Black Butte in the 1890s. The form Saroute Creek is incorrect. Bill Lynch has an interesting article in Eugene *Register-Guard*, March 10, 1980, giving a good deal of history of the Garoutte family and the creek name.

Garrison, Linn County. Garrison post office was in the locality later known as Upper Soda, and was established August 9, 1892, with Charles H. Foster first of five postmasters. The office was closed November 30, 1904. In September, 1946, William R. Mealey of Foster was kind enough to supply some history of various post offices in the vicinity of the South Santiam River, and said that Foster was the prime mover in getting the post route established as far as his home. He was given the privilege of naming his office, which he did with the family name of his mother-in-law, a Mrs. Garrison.

Garrison Butte, Deschutes County. This small butte is about seven miles north of Sisters and just south of the Jefferson-Deschutes county line. While the evidence is not conclusive, it is probable that the butte was named because of its proximity to Camp Polk, an establishment built in the Indian wars, 1865-66. The site of the camp is about five miles south of the butte. The compiler has been unable to learn of any local resident named Garrison.

Garrison Lake, Curry County. This lake is shown on some maps as Garrison Lagoon, but the generally accepted name is Garrison Lake, and that style has been adopted by the USBGN. In 1931 Louis L. Knapp of Port Orford wrote the compiler that the lake was named for a pioneer settler, John B. Garrison, who was a member of the Tichenor party. Statements to the effect that the lake was named because U. S. troops were stationed nearby in 1851-56 do not appear to be correct.

Garwood Butte, Douglas County. Garwood Butte bears the name of Leroy E. Garwood, one-time administrative officer of the Umpqua National Forest, who died in March, 1944. The butte, which has an elevation of 7027 feet, is about seven miles west of Diamond Lake. It was formerly called Bear Butte, a name of no distinction. The name was changed in honor of Garwood by the USBGN early in 1946.

Gasco, Multnomah County. This is a station between Portland and Linnton. It was named for the Portland Gas & Coke Company whose plant was nearby.

Gaston, Washington County. Joseph Gaston emigrated to Oregon from Ohio in 1862 and actively promoted the west side railroad southwest of Portland, which was built by Holladay and Villard. He built the narrow gauge line from Dayton to Sheridan in 1878. He wrote and published histories of Portland and of Oregon. He died July 20, 1913, aged 79 years. Gaston was named for him.

Gatch Falls, Linn County. In 1874 the original Gatch Falls some three miles northwest of Marion Lake was named by John Minto and the Marion Road party to honor Professor Thomas M. Gatch, a well-known pioneer educator afterward president of what was then known as Oregon Agricultural College. Trouble started almost at once as in the 1880s Nathan Gooch

took a squatter's claim just above the falls and his name was firmly fixed by
the local residents. In 1970 the OGNB recognized this fact and decided in
favor of Gooch Falls while a sub-committee under Tom McAllister was
instructed to locate a suitable substitute so that the name Gatch could be
continued. Mr. and Mrs. McAllister, William Wessinger and the writer
spent a delightful day inspecting the back reaches of Marion Creek and
suggested that the lower of the double Marion Falls be renamed Gatch.
Marion Falls are about one half mile downstream from Marion Lake and
were originally named Orla Falls by the Minto party for Orla Davenport,
the daughter of their surveyor, T. W. Davenport. The name did not prevail
and later Marion Falls was applied to the upper and the lower was known as
Linn Falls. This latter name has also passed into disuse so the lower falls
appeared a most acceptable substitute. The OGNB accepted the name
Gatch Falls in December 1972. For further information, see under Gooch
Falls.

Gate Creek, Lane County. This creek is tributary to McKenzie River
near Vida. An article in the Eugene *Guard,* July 12, 1893, says that Mr.
Stormant applied the name because near its mouth there was a foot log
crossing where the creek passed between two immense rocks. The arrangement had the appearance of a gate and gateposts. Gate Creek post office
was established December 30, 1874, with Thomas M. Martin postmaster. It
was discontinued on September 30, 1880, and reestablished May 29, 1891,
with Benjamin F. Finn postmaster. The office was discontinued on July 22,
1895, and again reestablished January 22, 1897. On December 3 of that
year the name of the office was changed to Elliston. Elliston post office was
discontinued in March, 1900.

Gate Creek, Wasco County. Gate Creek is a tributary of White River. It
was named because one of the Barlow Road tollgates was built near the
stream. See *OHQ,* volume XXV, page 167.

Gates, Marion County. The post office which serves Gates was originally on the south side of North Santiam River and was therefore in Linn
County. The office was established in February, 1882, with the name Henness and with Mrs. Jane Henness first postmaster. The name was changed
to Rock Creek on August 23, 1883. About 1892, W. R. Robertson, then
postmaster, moved the post office across the river to a place called Gates-
ville and the name of the office was changed to Gates. This was in honor of
Mrs. Mary Gates, one of the oldest settlers in the vicinity. The name Gates-
ville was first applied to the place about 1888. Mrs. J. P. McCurdy, postmaster at Gates in 1925, wrote the compiler as follows: "There was much
opposition to the adoption of the new name of Gates by the older settlers
who wished to retain the name of Rock Creek. A petition was signed to
keep the old name. The party circulating the petition got drunk and lost it,
and therefore the name of Gates remained." Page Mr. Volstead.

Gateway, Jefferson County. Gateway is named for a natural depression in the terrain north of Madras, caused by erosion by Trout Creek and
its tributaries. It is in effect a natural gate for the railroad and vehicular
traffic north and south through central Oregon. The name was applied to
the post office in 1913, possibly by George McFarland. The post office was

originally known as Youngs, but it was not at the present site of Gateway. Youngs was named for Louis A. Young, a local resident, and was about three miles from where Gateway office is now situated.

Gatton Creek, Multnomah County. This small stream flows into Ramsey Lake just north of St. Johns. It was named for William Gatton, a pioneer of 1852, who settled near the present site of St. Johns. He was born in 1831, and died March 24, 1924. For information about Gatton property see Portland *Telegram*, August 10, 1925, where the name is spelled Gratton, and letter from J. N. Pearcy, on editorial page, *ibid.*, September 1, 1925. Drainage projects are changing and eliminating geographic features in the vicinity of Ramsey Lake.

Gawley Creek, Clackamas County. This stream is in the south part of the county and flows into Molalla River. A man by the name of Gawley prospected on the creek in early days, and it was named for him.

Gazley, Douglas County. Gazley is a locality just north of South Umpqua River a little to the north-northeast of Canyonville. It bears the name of James F. Gazley, who came to Oregon in the early 1850s and took up land in the valley of the South Umpqua River. For further information, see OPA *Transactions,* 1919, page 170. Gazley post office was established September 16, 1915, with Belle Butcher first postmaster. The office was discontinued January 29, 1935.

Gearhart, Clatsop County. Philip Gearhart was a pioneer settler on Clatsop Plains, and on part of his donation land claim is now located the summer resort of Gearhart. The record of Philip Gearhart is shown on land office certificate 3109. He was born in Pennyslvania in 1810, arrived in Oregon in 1848, and settled on his claim in 1850. He died in September, 1881.

Gearhart Mountain, Lake County. Gearhart Mountain is about ten miles northeast of Bly, very close to the Klamath-Lake county line. It has an elevation of 8364 feet, and according to the USFS was named for some incident connected with one Gearhart, a pioneer cattleman. James P. Gearhart and his brother, William H. Gearhart, were in the stock business in this part of Oregon from about 1873 to 1882 and traded into California, and the mountain was probably named for one or both of the brothers. They were born in Howard County, Missouri, and came to Oregon in 1852, living in Benton County and later in Josephine County and also in California. The latter part of their lives was spent near Drewsey, Harney County. For biographies of the two brothers, see *Illustrated History of Baker, Grant, Malheur and Harney Counties,* pages 687 and 703.

Geer, Marion County. Geer is a railroad station east of Salem. It was named for the family of T. T. Geer. His parents were pioneers of Oregon and he himself was once governor of the state. His book *Fifty Years in Oregon,* is one of the most interesting contributions to the intimate history of early days in Oregon.

Geisel Monument, Curry County. In a small state park just west of the Oregon Coast Highway about seven miles north of Gold Beach stands the Geisel Monument, marking the graves of John Geisel and his family. A granite shaft is inscribed: "Sacred to the memory of John Geisel, also his three sons, John, Henry, and Andrew, who were massacred by the Indians, February 22, A.D. 1856, ages respectively 45, 9, 7, and 5 years. Also wife and mother died September 20, 1899, age 75 years." There are individual grave stones and the plot is surrounded by an ornamental iron fence. The Geisel massacre was the outstanding tragedy in the early history of Curry County. It is described in Dodge's *Pioneer History of Coos and Curry Counties*, pages 346-48.

Geiser, Baker County. This mining camp was named for Albert Geiser, owner of the Bonanza mine. Geiser post office was established July 15, 1898, with Ed. Geiser first postmaster. The office was discontinued May 18, 1909.

Gem, Baker County. Gem was the name applied to the post office later called Sparta. Gem was named for a mine but the compiler does not know its exact location. William Lynn White served as postmaster from August 7, 1871, to October 29, 1872, when the name of the office was changed to Sparta. White did not continue as postmaster, which may mean that the office was moved at the time the name was changed. This is just assumption, however. When Gem post office was established it was in Union County in what was known as the Panhandle. The Panhandle was later attached to Baker County.

General Patch Bridge, Deschutes County. This bridge over Deschutes River south of Sunriver was named for Lieutenant-General Alexander M. Patch USA. General Patch commanded the IV Army Corps during training manoeuvres near Camp Abbot in the fall of 1943 and later led the 7th Army in Europe.

Geneva, Jefferson County. This post office was established about 1914 through the efforts of John T. Monical. His wife's name was Geneva Monical, and the office is said to have been named for her, as she was the first postmaster.

George, Clackamas County. This community was named for Melvin C. George, of Portland, former representative in Congress from Oregon. Judge George was born in Ohio in 1849. He came to Oregon when he was two years old. He was a practicing lawyer for many years and occupied various political positions, including that of circuit judge. He was representative in Congress from 1881 to 1885, and while he was in that position a petition was received at Washington for a post office in Clackamas County. Walter Q. Gresham was postmaster general at that time and suggested Judge George's name for the new office, which was accordingly adopted. The place is not now a post office. Judge George died February 22, 1933.

George Creek, Tillamook County. F. E. Kellow of Cloverdale told the writer in 1971 that this creek north of Hebo was named in the early days for George Bodyfelt who homesteaded the surrounding land. Kellow said that his grandfather, George Kellow, specified the creek was not named for him but for Bodyfelt.

Gerber Reservoir, Klamath County. Gerber Reservoir, in southeast Klamath County, stores water for irrigation. It was named for Louis C. Gerber, an early settler in the locality, who owned a considerable part of the reservoir site.

Gerdine Butte, Deschutes County. Gerdine Butte, elevation 6600 feet, is in the extreme southwest corner of the county, about seven miles north of Maiden Peak and just east of the summit of the Cascade Range. It was named in compliment to Thomas Golding Gerdine, for many years a topographic engineer in the USGS. Major Gerdine was born at West Point, Mississippi, on June 2, 1872, and graduated from the University of Georgia in 1891. He joined the Geological Survey in 1893 and with the exception of short services for the General Land Office and for the War Department, he remained with the Survey until his death. He spent nearly ten years in difficult field work in Alaska, and in 1908 was appointed division geographer for the USGS in charge of operations in the Pacific Coast states and Hawaii. During the first World War he was in charge of War Department mapping in various strategic areas, but returned to the USGS early in 1919 and continued in charge of Pacific Coast work, with headquarters in Sacramento. He died in that city on October 31, 1930. His knowledge of Oregon geography and topography was profound. The last piece of mapping carried on in Oregon under his supervision was that of the Maiden Peak quadrangle. The OGNB suggested that an unnamed butte in this area be called Gerdine Butte, which was done. Mount Gerdine, elevation 12,000 feet, an important peak in central Alaska, was also named in honor of Major Gerdine.

Gerking Canyon, Sherman County. The USGS Wasco quadrangle dated 1957 shows this canyon near Rufus as Girkling. This apparently was not satisfactory and the USBGN in *Decision List 5904* changed to Gherkin. The original homesteader and namesake was William Gerking who settled in section 20, township 2 north, range 17 east, in 1880. When the new USGS map of the Rufus quadrangle was published in 1971, the spelling was finally brought into accord.

Gerlinger, Polk County. Louis Gerlinger, a well-known Oregon lumberman and railroad builder, promoted The Salem, Falls City and Western Railway, later purchased by the Southern Pacific Company. The crossing of this line and the original west side line a mile south of Derry was named in honor of Mr. Gerlinger.

Germantown Road, Multnomah and Washington counties. Germantown Road was named when the thoroughfare was built westward from the Willamette River to serve settlements on the North Plains of the Tualatin Valley. Many of the settlers were Germans and Swiss and the road got its name on that account.

Gervais, Marion County. Named for Joseph Gervais, a pioneer citizen of Oregon, and an early resident on French Prairie. Gervais came to Oregon with the Hunt party of the Astor enterprise in 1811, and for a number of years was engaged as a trapper for the various companies. He settled on French Prairie, but his claim was not at the present site of Gervais. Gervais is on the Peter Depot claim. Neill Johnson is said to have given the name to the town of Gervais. Gervais and Etienne Lucier may have named Pudding River in 1813. Both of these men voted at Champoeg in 1843 for a provisional government. Gervais died on French Prairie July 13, 1861, aged 84 years.

Gesner, Marion County. Gesner was a railroad station east of Salem. It was named for the Gesner family, early settlers. Alonzo Gesner was at one time county surveyor, a fact which may have had to do with the selection of the name.

Getchel Meadows, Wallowa County. Getchel Meadows are in township 4 north, range 46 east, and were named for William Getchel who built a cabin in the locality and wintered there. He was for a time in the railroad service between La Grande and Enterprise.

Gettings Creek, Lane County. This stream flows into Coast Fork Willamette River a few miles northeast of Cottage Grove. It was named for Samuel A. Gettings who lived in the vicinity in 1888. The spellings Gittings and Giddings are incorrect. The USBGN has adopted the spelling Gettings for this name and also for North Fork Gettings Creek, the name of a tributary.

Ghost Creek, Clackamas County. This small stream heads on the west side of Bird Butte and flows into Salmon River. The Wapinitia Highway crosses it 1.5 miles north of Frog Lake. Ghost Creek was named because of ghost-like white tree trunks standing on the hillside nearby.

Ghost Ridge, Hood River County. This ridge lies immediately east of Eliot Branch and runs from Cloud Cap down towards Inspiration Point. It takes its name from the whitened snags left after a series of early day fires. The first of these in 1886 was supposedly set by sheepman Johnny O'Leary who was trying to improve the grazing range. A series of natural fires came afterward but since World War II new growth has gradually covered the ethereal remains.

Gibbon, Umatilla County. This is a station on the Union Pacific Railroad 20 miles east of Pendleton just west of the junction of Umatilla River and Meacham Creek. It bears the name of John Gibbon, 1827-96, a distinguished American army officer, who gained the rank of brevet major-general. In 1885-86 he was in command of the Department of the Columbia at Vancouver, Washington. For references to General Gibbon, see Scott's *History of the Oregon Country,* volume II, pages 104 and 283. During the railroad construction there was a station at or near the present site of Gibbon known as Mikecha. See under Kamela. About the turn of the century the name of Gibbon railroad station was changed to Bingham Springs, because it served Bingham Springs resort about eight miles east up Umatilla River, but the name of the post office remained Gibbon. The name of the station was later changed back to Gibbon. Bingham Springs were named for Dr. John E. Bingham of Walla Walla, Washington.

Gibraltar Mountain, Lane County. USFS ranger A. J. Briem stated that this peak southeast of Vida was named Gibraltar Rock in the 1870s by Thomas Warner because of its resemblance to the original.

Gibson Creek, Crook County. This small tributary of Newsome Creek near its headwaters in the Maury Mountains was named for early settlers John and Molly Gibson who moved there in the 1880s.

Gibson Gulch, Polk County. Gibson Gulch is in the southeast part of the Eola Hills. Daviess Gibson was a pioneer settler in the Eola Hills, and the gulch was named for him. He was an Oregon pioneer of 1849, and after returning to Illinois by Panama, came to Oregon again in 1852. He died prior to 1900, and was buried in Spring Valley.

Gibson Gulch, Umatilla County. Gibson Gulch empties into Stewart Creek about five miles east of Pilot Rock. It was named for Thomas S. Gibson who bought up numerous small homesteads to form a substantial ranch. One of these belonged to Milton E. Pomeroy who took up his claim in 1895. At that time the draw was called Pomeroy Gulch but the name did not prevail.

Gilbert River, Columbia and Multnomah counties. Gilbert River pursues a meandering course on Sauvie Island, draining a number of lakes, and finally emptying into Multnomah Channel. W. H. H. Morgan, a pioneer resident of Sauvie Island, told the compiler in 1926 that the stream was named in fur trading days because a trapper, supposed to be in the employ of the Hudson's Bay Company, was drowned in it. He was a French-Canadian called Gilbert, and his name has been attached to the stream ever since.

Gilchrist, Klamath County. Gilchrist is a mill town and post office on The Dalles-California Highway in the north end of the county. The community was developed in 1938 and the post office was established on November 14, 1938. The town was named for Frank W. Gilchrist, vice president and general manager of the Gilchrist Timber Company.

Gilchrist Butte, Wheeler County. This butte is north of the old community of West Branch. It was named for James C. Gilchrist, an early resident and one of the first USFS rangers.

Gilchrist Valley, Crook and Deschutes counties. Gilchrist Valley is drained by one of the tributaries of Crooked River, and lies east of Hampton Butte. It is about 20 miles long, north and south, and ten miles wide, and its physical characteristics are well described by Dr. I. C. Russell in USGS Bulletin 252. Dr. Russell named the valley for Charles Adams Gilchrist, its first settler, as a tribute to his enterprise and hospitality. C. A. Gilchrist was born in Indiana November 5, 1855. He lived in Missouri, California and New Mexico, and finally came to Oregon, and began ranching in what is now known as Gilchrist Valley. He married Miss Mabel F. Johnstone of Indiana in 1899. He died March 3, 1926. See Portland *Telegram* March-5, 1926. During the latter part of his life he lived in Portland.

Gillespie Butte, Lane County. Gillespie Butte is in the north part of Eugene and has an elevation of 605 feet. It was named for Jacob Gillespie who came to Oregon from Missouri in 1851 and took up a donation land claim near the butte in 1852. He was in charge of building the Cumberland Presbyterian church in Eugene and held a negro slave in this state. After the death of his wife, Amelia, in 1867, he married the widow of Alexander Goodpasture. See under Goodpasture Island.

Gilliam County. Gilliam County was created February 25, 1885, by the state legislature. It has a land area of 1211 square miles, according to the Bureau of the Census, and its county seat is Condon. The county was named for Colonel Cornelius Gilliam, who commanded the forces of the provisional government in 1847-48, after the Whitman Massacre, in the campaign against the Cayuses. He was killed toward the end of the campaign, March 24, 1848, while drawing from a wagon a rope for his horse; the rope caught the hammer of a gun and discharged it. Gilliam was born in North Carolina in 1798. He came to Oregon in 1844. "He was brave, obstinate, impetuous and generous, with goodnatured abilities but little education. Thus died an honest and patriotic and popular man, whose chief fault as an officer was too much zeal and impetuosity in the performance of his duties." (Bancroft's *History of Oregon*, vol. I, page 725.) For narrative of his death, see the *Oregonian*, June 29, 1888, page 2, letter by William A. Jack, and *ibid.*, January 24, 1926, section 1, page 20, article by Opal Clark of Heppner.

Gilman Canyon, Morrow County. This canyon on the upper reaches of Balm Fork was named for David E. Gilman who settled along Balm Fork just after the turn of the century. The spelling Gillman is wrong.

Ginkgo Creek, Jackson County. This creek rises east of Rogue River and flows into Mill Creek north of Prospect. Apparently in the early days a group of Chinese miners planted a ginkgo tree near one of their camps and when the tree was later discovered, the name was attached to the nearby creek. The ginkgo or *Salisburia adiantifolia* is native to China and Japan where it is a popular garden tree although there are now no known natural stands. The species is very old and at one time widespread as fossil ginkgo leaves have been found in the Eagle Creek Gravels in the Columbia River Gorge.

Girds Creek, Wheeler County. This stream was apparently named for William Gird of Corvallis. Gird was a well-known horse fancier and breeder in Benton County in the 1860s. He was also a close friend of T. B. Hoover and when this gentleman and his companions came to Butte Creek near Fossil in 1869 to raise horses in eastern Oregon, Gird probably accompanied or visited them. Old timers in Wheeler County say that the creek was named for a settler prior to 1872 and Oswald West in *OHQ*, volume XLVI, page 148, says the creek in the John Day Valley was likely named for him. For further information on Gird see *OHQ*, volume XLVIII, page 141.

Gist, Deschutes County. A post office called Gist was established on the Crook County list on February 14, 1907, and named for the first postmaster, Charles L. Gist. The office was a few miles southeast of Sisters on the old road, a little southwest of the new highway from Sisters to Tumalo. When Deschutes County was formed in 1916, the office was put on the list for that county. It was closed on June 25, 1920, and the business was turned over to Tumalo.

Glacier Creek, Lane County. This creek rises east of Sunshine Shelter. Ray Engels of the USFS named it because of its proximity to Collier and Renfrew Glaciers although it does not flow directly from either.

Glad Tidings, Clackamas County. Glad Tidings is a puzzle among Oregon geographic names. The place is about three miles northeast of Marquam on the Cascade Highway. The compiler has been quite unable to learn the character of the cheering news that produced the name. Glad Tidings post office was established August 30, 1860, with George W. Jackson first postmaster. The office was closed to Butte Creek on September 2, 1887. During this operation of twenty-seven years no one seems to have made a record of the origin of the unusual name. It has been suggested that the good news had to do with the admission of Oregon as a state, but that event was about a year and a half earlier than the date of the post office, during which time the news must have become quite stale, and if the old stories can be believed, the news was none too well received when the event took place.

Gladstone, Clackamas County. The community of Gladstone was platted in 1893 and named for William Ewart Gladstone, the British statesman. However, The Gladstone Real Estate Association was incorporated in 1889, so that the name was really chosen at this earlier date. Harvey Cross of Oregon City was one of the incorporators of the association and was actively interested in developing the townsite, and is credited with selecting the name Gladstone. He was a great admirer of the prime minister. Gladstone post office was established June 30, 1890.

Glasgow, Coos County. Glasgow is a small community on the north side of Coos Bay. It was started by speculators in the 1890s and, after an initial burst of enthusiasm, it languished for thirty years until the construction of US 101 when it became the northern terminus of the Coos Bay ferry. It is supposed to have been named by a Scot because it reminded him of Glasgow in Scotland, but the compiler has been unable to verify this. The promoters were the Pacific Coal & Transportation Company whose principals included Henry L. Pittock, Phil Metschan, Admiral Schley and several other well-known citizens.

Glass Buttes, Lake County. Glass Buttes are in the northeast corner of Lake County. They have an elevation of 6390 feet according to the USC&GS. There are two prominent rounded domes, and several lesser hills, and the whole group makes an important landmark. The buttes take their name from the obsidian or volcanic glass scattered over their slopes. They stand about 2000 feet above the surrounding plain, just south of Central Oregon Highway.

Glaze Lake, Lane County. Prince Glaze was USFS guard at Frog Camp after World War I. This lake and nearby Prince Lake were both named for him.

Glaze Meadow, Deschutes County. This meadow is just south of Black Butte. It bears the name of Tilman Glaze, an early settler in this part of what was then Crook County. Frances Juris has an account of Glaze Meadow with pictures in *Old Crook County,* pp 8 and 9.

Glen, Lincoln County. Glen post office was in the west part of township 12 south, range 9 west, a few miles south of Salado. It was on upper Drift Creek or one of its tributaries. Glen post office was established January 17, 1894, with Simeon J. Wilhoit first of three postmasters. The office was closed to Elk City on June 30, 1912. The name Glen is said to have been applied by Jerry Banks in honor of some town where he had lived previously, but the compiler has been unable to identify the place.

Glenada, Lane County. Glenada townsite was platted by Geo. H. Colter about 1890. The writer is informed that since the place was in a circle of the Siuslaw River, it was called "Glen-Ada," the Ada being for Mrs. Colter. Why the circle of the river suggested Glen has not been explained. Postal

authorities played havoc with Colter's name by condensing it into Glenada.
The office was established about 1890 with Margaret I. Grant first postmaster. She was a sister of Mrs. Colter. Colter was born in Nova Scotia in 1846
and died on May 8, 1934.

Glenbrook, Benton County. The descriptive name Glenbrook was
given a post office that operated in the foothills of the Coast Range a few
miles west of Monroe. The office was established May 4, 1898, with Ella
Atkins first postmaster. It was discontinued January 17, 1905, about the
time many other offices were closed because of the establishment of rural
free delivery. The locality called Glenbrook is on Hammer Creek about
three miles southwest of Alpine.

Glencoe, Washington County. The community called Glencoe has
been absorbed by the village of North Plains, of which it constitutes the
northeast part. In October, 1945, the writer was told by J. M. Brown of
Hillsboro that Glencoe was named by Charles McKay for the place in Scotland with the melancholy history. McKay was a Scot, although available
records indicate that he was born at sea in 1808. The naming of Glencoe,
Oregon, must have been for sentimental reasons because physically the
location does not resemble the place in Scotland by any stretch of the imagination. The post office at Glencoe was established January 9, 1871, with
William H. Silvers postmaster. The office was discontinued in December,
1904.

Glencullen, Multnomah County. Glencullen is a community in the
extreme southwest part of Portland. It was named in compliment to Captain John Winchell Cullen, a prominent pioneer citizen of Oregon. Cullen
was born at La Porte, Indiana, June 18, 1838, and came to Oregon in 1847.
He fought in the Indian wars of 1855-56 and also in the Civil War. He took
part in many affairs of importance in developing the state. He died in Portland December 14, 1939, and is buried in Lone Fir Cemetery. For information about Captain Cullen, see editorial page of the *Oregon Journal* for
November 30, 1937.

Glendale, Douglas County. When the railroad was extended south
from Roseburg in 1881-83, Solomon Abraham acted as right-of-way agent,
and platted several communities, including the present site of Glendale.
This site he named Julia, for Mrs. Abraham. The chief engineer of the
railroad, Charles A. F. Morris, and Abraham got into a controversy about
the townsites, and Morris changed the name of the station from Julia to
Glendale, although the post office and townsite remained as before. This
resulted in confusion, and the post office was subsequently changed from
Julia to Glendale. There are several stories as to why the name Glendale
was selected. Will G. Steel says it was suggested by G. Wingate, for the
Scottish glens. Albert Abraham of Roseburg, son of Solomon Abraham,
told the writer that Morris was a native of Glendale, Massachusetts, or Glendale, Scotland, and suggested the name himself. A large part of the Glendale business district was burned on July 11, 1928. Walling in his *History of
Southern Oregon,* page 426, says that it was first planned to name this place
Montgomery because it was laid out on the L. D. Montgomery land claim,
but that name did not prevail. L. D. Montgomery was the first postmaster at

Julia office, which was established in February, 1883, and continued in office after the name was changed to Glendale in August, 1883.

Gleneden Beach, Lincoln County. Gleneden Beach is a type of descriptive name frequently found in seashore areas where there are high hopes of real estate sales. The place is about a mile south of the south end of Siletz Bay. Gleneden Beach post office was established November 1, 1927, with William F. Cary first postmaster.

Glenn, Malheur County. Glenn post office was established on the Baker County list on April 5, 1881, with William S. Glenn postmaster. The office was doubtless named for the postmaster. The office was moved to the Malheur County list when that county was organized in February, 1887, and it was discontinued in December, 1888. The office was situated near Willow Creek about nine miles northwest of Vale.

Glenn Creek, Polk County. This stream flows through the south part of Eola Hills, just northwest of Salem. The writer is informed that it was named by C. A. Park, who lived nearby. Park is said to have named the stream because it ran through a glen or narrow valley, but in this event the name should be spelled Glen Creek. However, the style Glenn Creek has become well established through long use, and is the form used on government maps.

Glenora, Tillamook County. The name Glenora was applied about 1898 to a weather station near the old Wilson River wagon road. The name of this weather station has an interesting history. As far as the writer can determine the first use of this name in the Pacific Northwest was for a place on Stikine River in northern British Columbia. This area was called Cassiar district and there was a good deal of gold excitement there in 1873-75. A river landing was named Glenoraville but this was shortened to Glenora almost immediately. Glenora is said to mean vale or glen of gold. One of the first residents was Walter J. Smith, a former member of the Union army. After his discharge from the armed forces he engaged in mining and is said to have built the first house at Glenora, British Columbia. Mr. Smith later came to Oregon and in the spring of 1885 settled near the upper Wilson River. He liked the name Glenora and eventually tried to have it adopted for a post office, but the authorities objected because of the similarity to the name Glenwood used for an office in nearby Washington County. Mr. Smith had to be content with a post office named Wilson. Whether this office was named for Wilson River or for William L. Wilson of West Virginia, the postmaster general, is a matter of argument. About 1898 a weather station was established at the James F. Reeher place with Mrs. Jennie A. Reeher in charge. The writer has been informed that Mrs. Reeher adopted the name Glenora for the weather station.

Glentena, Lane County. In June, 1947, Mrs. B. W. Inman of Noti wrote the compiler that Glentena post office was at or near the place later called Linslaw. Glentena office was established July 26, 1888, with Aaron C. Barbour first postmaster, and was discontinued August 26, 1902. It was named for Mrs. Glentena Barbour, the wife of the first postmaster.

Glenwood, Washington County. This name is said to have been originated about 1880, and was adopted because the natural surroundings suggested a glen in the woods. It is not inappropriate, differing in this respect from many similar names in the state. The post office was established in August, 1886, with Nira E. Catching postmaster. The office has not always been in the same location.

Glide, Douglas County. The post office at Glide was established in 1890, and Virginia C. Laird was the first postmaster. According to information furnished the compiler, Mrs. Laird had considerable difficulty thinking of a suitable name for the new office until one day she observed her small son playing about and singing "The River Goes Gliding Along." Without more ado Mrs. Laird christened the place "Glide," and it has been gliding along ever since.

Glisan Glacier, Hood River County. In the summer of 1937, Kenneth N. Phillips, chairman, and other members of the Mazamas' Research Committee made a study of the ice fields on the northwest slope of Mount Hood, and among other things recommended that the name Glisan Glacier be applied to an ice stream lying between Sandy and Ladd glaciers and just east of Cathedral Ridge. The name was approved by USBGN in 1938. The name Glisan Glacier is in honor of Rodney Lawrence Glisan, well-known citizen of Portland, prominent because of his high character and his long devotion to the study of many phases of natural history and mountaineering and exploring and to outdoor photography. Rodney L. Glisan was born in Portland April 3, 1869. He was educated at Bishop Scott Academy, and after studies in Paris, attended Yale, where he was graduated in 1890. He was admitted to the Oregon bar in 1892. He served in the Portland city council and also in the Oregon legislature and was on the Portland charter revision committee. He was much interested in sports and played on the first football team of the Multnomah Athletic Club and was a member of the Portland Rowing Club. He was president of the Mazamas in 1903. He died in Portland May 6, 1934.

Goat Island, Curry County. Goat Island is in the Pacific Ocean west of Brookings. In 1935 it was declared a migratory bird refuge and is under special access restrictions to protect the great numbers and varieties of birds that nest there. For an interesting account of the island see Brookings *Pilot,* June 15, 1967. The name Goat Island is very old and the compiler has been unable to learn the circumstances connected with its application.

Goble, Columbia County. This place was first settled by Daniel B. Goble, in April, 1853. He took up a donation land claim, and later sold it to George S. Foster, who laid out the town and named it for the previous owner. Goble was born in Ohio in 1815 and arrived in Oregon in August, 1852. His land office certificate was numbered 4157.

Gods Valley, Clatsop and Tillamook counties. Gods Valley lies east and south of North Fork Nehalem River, and drains into that stream by means of Gods Valley Creek, the mouth of which is in the extreme south part of Clatsop County. It was named many years ago. In December, 1945, J. H. Scott of Nehalem wrote the compiler in part as follows: "The valley was discovered by John Hunt and E. K. Scovell, who were hunting elk on the North Fork and followed a trail east over the ridge and down into an unknown valley where they found and shot several elk. It is reported that they were badly in need of meat, and when they shot the elk, one of them said, 'What shall we call this valley?' The other replied 'We needed meat and God led us here, so let's call it Gods Valley.' The largest spruce tree in Oregon or Washington is said to be in the northern part of this valley, although the tree has been dead for many years."

Goff, Sherman County. Goff is a station on the Union Pacific Railroad just east of John Day Dam. It was established about the time of World War I and while the compiler has no positive proof, he assumes it was named for Theodore H. Goffe. Goffe, who died in 1916, was the engineer who tested and ran the Oregon Pony over the portage railroad at the Cascades in the spring of 1862. He also appeared at the Lewis and Clark Exposition where the locomotive was on display. Frank B. Gill gives many details of these matters in *OHQ*, volume XXV, page 172 *et seq.*

Gold Beach, Curry County. Gold was discovered in the sands of Curry County in the early 1850s and the beaches were named on that account. They were the scene of operations of hundreds of placer miners in pioneer days. This particular beach was at the mouth of Rogue River, and the settlement there was for some years known as Ellensburg, but it is said that there was confusion with Ellensburg, in Washington Territory, and the name was changed to Gold Beach. The name Ellensburg was derived from Sarah Ellen Tichenor, daughter of Captain William Tichenor. See under Tichenor Rock. Bancroft and Mrs. Victor both refer to the fact that the settlement at the mouth of Rogue River was once known as Whaleshead, but Orvil Dodge says that is a mistake. What is now known as Whalehead Island is some distance south of Gold Beach. For information about early history of Gold Beach see Port Orford *News*, December 14, 1926, where it is said that Sebastopol was one of the early names for the place. For additional history of Gold Beach, see editorial page *Oregon Journal*, July 20, 21, 1927, and under Fort Miner.

Gold Creek, Clackamas and Marion counties. Gold Creek and a tributary East Gold Creek drain a large basin that is traversed by the Clackamas-Marion county line. Gold Creek flows into Little North Santiam River from the north just east of the west line of township 8 south, range 5 east. Gold Creek is in the very heart of the North Santiam mining area, and from time to time there has been a good deal of activity in that region. The stream was named for the gold ore that was uncovered. There were also silver, copper, iron, galena and other minerals. For an account of these discoveries, see Down's *History of the Silverton Country*, pages 85 and 86. Down does not give the date of the discovery of minerals in the North Santiam area, but it seems probable that it was in the middle 1860s.

Gold Creek, Polk County. Gold Creek flows into South Yamhill River from the south a little west of Willamina. It is sometimes shown on maps as Cold Creek but various county authorities have informed the compiler that Gold Creek is the correct name, not Cold Creek. The local school is officially known as Gold Creek School. The compiler has not been able to get the origin of the name; its history seems to be as closely guarded as the metal itself.

Gold Hill, Jackson County. Gold Hill was the scene of an early gold discovery in southern Oregon. There is now some controversy as to the exact location of the hill so known, but from what evidence the writer has seen it is quite certain that the original Gold Hill was on the south bank of Rogue River opposite the present community of Gold Hill. There seems to be no historic reason to believe that it was north of the town, even though so shown on some maps. The hill to the north is somewhat more imposing than the original Gold Hill to the south, and this may be the reason that some local residents tried to move the name. The town is of course named for the hill. In pioneer days the main settlement in this neighborhood was that of W. G. T'Vault at Dardanelles, on the south side of Rogue River.

Gold Ray, Jackson County. Colonel Frank Ray of New York was interested in the power development at the falls of Rogue River at Lower Table Rock, and named the place Gold Ray. This name caused confusion on the line of the Southern Pacific Company, because of the close proximity of Gold Hill, the next station to the west. The railroad name for Gold Ray is Ray Gold. The California Oregon Power Company used the original arrangement of the words.

Golden, Josephine County. Golden post office was named for the mining activity of a locality a few miles southeast of Wolf Creek. The office was established January 10, 1896, with Schuyler C. Ruble first postmaster, and continued in operation until March 31, 1920. The place was on Coyote Creek and had quartz and stamp mills.

Golden Falls, Coos County. These falls are in Glen Creek Valley northeast of Allegany. In March, 1929, S. B. Cathcart of Marshfield wrote the compiler that they were discovered by Frank Ross and soon thereafter they were visited by Dr. C. B. Golden, first Grand Chancellor of the Knights of Pythias of Oregon, E. A. Anderson and Thomas Hirst. At that time they were named Golden Falls in compliment to Dr. Golden. Some time later other falls were found on a stream nearby, and the names Silver Falls and Silver Creek were applied in contradistinction to Golden Falls in the belief that the first falls were named for the metal, which is not a fact, according to Cathcart.

Goldson, Lane County. According to information received by the writer from Seth W. Harpole, postmaster at Goldson in January, 1926, the place was named for the first postmaster, J. M. Goldson. The post office was established about 1891.

Goltra, Linn County. Goltra was a station between Albany and Lebanon named for W. H. Goltra, a pioneer settler of the vicinity.

Gone Creek, Clackamas County. Gone Creek is a curious example of *ex post facto* naming. When Portland General Electric Company cleared the reservoir site at Timothy Lake, they picked a location for a forest camp near a small un-named stream. When the lake was filled, the creek was inundated leaving only the intermittent upper reaches. Ralph H. Millsap of the power company suggested this name for a creek that was of little importance until it was gone.

Gooch, Linn County. This station, about two miles west of Mill City, was named for Fred Gooch, who once ran a sawmill there.

Gooch Falls, Linn County. These falls on Marion Creek about three

miles below Marion Lake have been the subject of more than usual controversy. They were originally named Gatch Falls by John Minto in 1874 to
honor Thomas M. Gatch, a well-known pioneer educator. However, in the
1880s Nathan W. Gooch took a squatter's claim that included the falls and
built a small cabin immediately above. His name was soon applied to the
falls and as his family continued in the area, it has been so known locally for
many years. The similiarity of the two names compounded the confusion as
the map makers and purists used Gatch while the residents used Gooch.
After some study, the OGNB in December 1970 decided on Gooch Falls
and this was confirmed by the USBGN in *Decision List 7102*. Concurrently
steps were taken to apply the name Gatch to another falls on Marion Creek.
See under Gatch Falls.

Goodfellow Lakes, Clackamas County. These lakes are in township 2
south, range 7 east. They were named for one Goodfellow, a clothing manu-
facturer in Minneapolis, who owned land in this part of the county.

Goodman Creek, Lane County. This creek empties into Lookout Point
Lake. A. J. Briem, in his notes on file at the OHS, says that it was named for
William Goodman, an early settler.

Goodpasture Island, Lane County. This piece of land is off the east
bank of Willamette River in the north part of Eugene. There has been
considerable shifting of the main river channel to the west and the original
island is now bounded on the east by intermittent and disconnected
sloughs. It was not named for the succulent forage but for Alexander Goodpasture who took up a donation land claim in the area in 1853. After Goodpasture's death in 1862 his widow married Jacob Gillespie who lived near
Gillespie Butte. To further cement the new family ties, Marcellus M. Gillespie, the son of Jacob and his first wife Amelia, married Alexander and
Elizabeth Goodpasture's daughter, Rachel. Two Goodpasture sons, William and Thomas, farmed the original land well into the twentieth century.

Goodrich Creek, Baker County. Goodrich Creek rises on the east
slopes of Elkhorn Peak in the Blue Mountains west of Baker and flows
eastward to join Pine Creek near the locality called Wingville. The stream
was named in the mining days for A. C. Goodrich, who came into eastern
Oregon from the mining regions of the Sierra Nevada with experience as a
surveyor and in ditch construction. He made a survey for the Auburn Ditch
and had much to do with the construction of the conduit. For details see
Hiatt's *Thirty-one Years in Baker County,* chapter IV. The Auburn Ditch
reached the headwaters of Goodrich Creek.

Goose Creek, Lane County. This little stream flows into McKenzie
River from the north, just west of McKenzie Bridge. Scott Taylor of
McKenzie Bridge has furnished the compiler with the history of the name.
About 1870, Mr. and Mrs. John Sims were traveling eastward along the
road on their way to have Thanksgiving dinner with Uncle George Frissell.
Mrs. Sims had her baby in one arm and a dressed goose in the other. When
her horse reached the creek, he jumped suddenly, and the goose fell into
the water. Ever since that event, the brook has been known as Goose Creek.

Goose Lake, Lake County. The Klamath Indian name for Goose Lake
was *Newapkshi.* Goose Lake seems to have been named during pioneer days

rather than in exploratory times. The compiler has no record as to who named it, but there was good reason to call it Goose Lake. Wild geese frequented central Oregon in large numbers in early days. In his diary for October 21, 1832, John Work of the Hudson's Bay Company fur brigade, mentions "pit lake." On the next day the party camped near the lake itself. See *California Historical Society Quarterly*, September, 1943, page 205. This is clearly Goose Lake and the text of the diary implies that the trappers had been in those parts before. Pit River in this locality is shown on Arrowsmith's map of North America corrected to 1832-33. The map of the Territory of Oregon, prepared by direction of Colonel J. J. Abert of the U. S. Topographical Engineers, 1838, shows Pit Lake and the hot springs to the north. The name Pit Lake went out of use long ago.

Gooseberry, Morrow County. Gooseberry is a locality west of Heppner near the west edge of the county. The place was known as Gooseberry Spring at least as early as 1872 and was well known to cattlemen. It was named for a large wild gooseberry bush just above the spring. Gooseberry post office is shown on the 1884 post office list, but it has been out of service for a good many years. There are many places in eastern Oregon named for wild gooseberry bushes.

Gooseberry Creek, Wallowa County. This stream flows into Chesnimnus Creek in township 3 north, range 46 east. In 1931 J. H. Horner of Enterprise told the compiler that it was named by Jack Johnson, George Vail and William Duncan because they found some very good wild gooseberries nearby, which they cooked and ate.

Gooseneck Creek, Polk County. Gooseneck Creek flows into Mill Creek, southeast of Willamina. It is said to have received its name in early days because its course is curved like a goose neck.

Gopher Valley, Yamhill County. Vernon Bailey in *Mammals and Life Zones of Oregon* lists no less than fifteen varieties of pocket gophers in the state, surely enough for all requirements. It is not surprising that a pleasant vale in the east foothills of the Coast Range was called Gopher Valley. This valley is north of Sheridan and drains south through Deer Creek into South Yamhill River. Gopher post office was established April 6, 1899, with Edward H. Taylor postmaster. The office was discontinued September 14, 1905. The office was on the east side of Gopher Valley about a mile south of Gopher School.

Gordon, Sherman County. Gordon post office, Gordon Butte, and Gordon Ridge, all near Deschutes River in the west part of Sherman County, were named for Tom Gordon, an Irish homesteader who settled nearby in the middle 1860s. Giles French in the *Golden Land*, page 61, relates how William Hand, editor of The Dalles *Mountaineer*, accompanied Governor George Woods' party of inspection over The Dalles Military Road in 1869. They stopped at Gordon's place and Hand mentions his well established orchard. In 1965 an effort was made, due to a cartographic error, to rename Gordon Butte McDermid Cone. This was thwarted by the timely intervention of Mr. French. Gordon Butte is in section 13, township 1 north, range 15 east, and is not the high ground four miles southeast at the end of Gordon Ridge. Gordon post office was established July 7, 1896, with

Joseph P. Walker first and only postmaster. The office was closed December 18, 1896.

Gordon Butte, Wasco County. Gordon Butte is 4821 feet high and lies north of Badger Creek. It was named for Eric Gordon, USFS District Ranger at Dufur from 1923 to 1945.

Gordon Creek, Union County. William Gordon, a rancher, had a place on this stream in the early 1870s and it bears his name. Gordon Creek flows into Grande Ronde River a little below Elgin.

Gore Creek, Jackson County. Gore Creek is a tributary to Bear Creek at a point about three miles southeast of Medford. It flows in from the south and passes under the Pacific Highway. It was named in compliment to Elijah Emerson and Mary Elizabeth Gore, who came to Oregon from Lee County, Iowa, in 1852. The Gores settled in the Rogue River Valley on September 27 of that year. The first winter was spent at Jacksonville, and then the family moved to a donation land claim near what is now Voorhies station, and adjacent to the stream. The name has been approved by USBGN.

Gorman, Sherman County. Gorman post office was established August 25, 1892, and was discontinued on October 5, 1900. John E. Morrow was the first of three postmasters. In June, 1948, Giles L. French of Moro wrote the compiler that the Morrow family homesteaded in section 30, township 1 north, range 19 east. It is believed that the name Gorman perhaps came from a local resident but that is not certain. There was a Gorman school district in this locality on what is known as Starvation Point. Mr. French says that name was given for obvious reasons.

Gorton Creek, Hood River County. This creek near Wyeth was named because Edwin Gorton had his homestead along its banks in the 1890s.

Goshen, Lane County. In biblical geography, Goshen was a pastoral region in lower Egypt, occupied and colonized by the Israelites before the Exodus. The compiler does not know who applied the name to the Lane County community. Goshen post office was first established September 6, 1874, with John Handsaker, first postmaster.

Gourlay Creek, Columbia and Washington counties. This little stream is a tributary to South Scappoose Creek. It was named for Alexander Gourlay, a pioneer homesteader nearby.

Government Camp, Clackamas County. The First U. S. Mounted Rifles crossed the plains in 1849, and reached The Dalles in the fall of that year. Most of the soldiers were taken down the river to Vancouver by boat, but a small command was left behind with the wagons and animals. Before the horses and mules could recuperate from the overland journey, the command was ordered to Oregon City by way of the Barlow Road. Nearly two-thirds of the animals were lost in trying to travel around Mount Hood, and 45 of the wagons were abandoned. There was much controversy both before and after the trip about the advisability of attempting it with the stock in such poor condition. The name Government Camp came from the fact that some of the wagons were abandoned nearby and remained as evidence of military activity. Government Camp is on the Mount Hood Loop Highway and has an elevation of 3888 feet. Official reports about the

First U. S. Mounted Rifles are to be found in 31st Congress, 2nd Session, Senate Executive Document 1, part II, page 126, *et seq.* There are many interesting illustrations. The journals have been edited by Raymond W. Settle with the title *March of the Mounted Riflemen,* Clark Company, Glendale, 1940. See also Bancroft's *History of Oregon,* volume II, page 82, and Portland *Telegram* editorial page, March 1, 1926.

Government Cove, Hood River County. Government Cove, formed when the pool was raised behind Bonneville Dam, is two and one half miles east of Cascade Locks. A substantial rocky hillock left above high water was quarried for jetty rock but this venture was abandoned. The slack water cove has also been used for the storage of log rafts. Either of these uses could have been the reason for the name which is now well established and shown on current maps.

Government Island, Multnomah County. Government Island is in the Columbia River. Broughton spent the night of October 29, 1792, in the vicinity of this island. In fact, he may have camped on the island itself, or possibly on Lemon Island. Broughton spent the day of October 30 exploring the Columbia River to a point above Sandy River, and returning in the evening, camping not far from his position of the previous night. The next white men to visit the island were Lewis and Clark, on November 3, 1805. They called it Diamond Island, because of its shape. The Lewis and Clark maps indicate that what is now known as Government Island was then divided into two large islands, besides smaller ones, and it was the upper of the two larger islands that was named Diamond. The lower island is not named in the text, but the maps show it and another islet to the west as White Goose Island. This western islet is probably the Lemon Island of today. The two larger islands are now consolidated, though part of the dividing channel still exists. At the time of Lewis and Clark the western of the two larger islands was nearly consolidated with the islet to the west mentioned above. In February, 1850, the government reserved this island for military purposes, and raised hay on it. It was then called Miller's Island. The name, Government Island, came into use after government occupation. See Bancroft's *History of Oregon,* volume II, page 89, and the Secretary of War's annual report, dated December 4, 1852, page 123.

Gowdy Ranch, Lake County. This ranch on Silver Creek south of Silver Lake was started prior to World War I by James Gowdy.

Grabenhorst Corners, Marion County. Grabenhorst Corners are about four miles south of Salem, on the Pacific Highway East. These corners were named for G. H. Grabenhorst, who owned land nearby.

Grade, Wheeler County. Grade post office was established June 28, 1880, with George M. Wasson first postmaster. This office was named for a short section of the old stage road from Antelope to Mitchell. This section was known as The Grade, and it had been cut out of the side hill on the southwest side of John Day River just south of the mouth of Cherry Creek, at the very west edge of what is now Wheeler County. The post office and toll house were in the southeast corner of township 9 south, range 20 east. In the summer of 1947 Mrs. Goldie Van Bibber (Mrs. Charles F.) Putnam of Inchelium, Washington, sent the compiler some very entertaining reminiscences of youthful experiences at The Grade. According to Mrs. Putnam

the original stage and freight road in this locality was difficult and dangerous and it was improved by a man called "Monty," the improvements being
made by hand labor over a period of several years. Monty did not live long
to enjoy the fruits of his labor. Monty was another name for the postmaster,
George Montgomery Wasson. Addie S. Masterson was appointed postmaster on October 24, 1882, and the name of the office was changed to Burnt
Ranch on January 15, 1883. About this time the office was doubtless moved
from its original location to the site of Burnt Ranch about four miles east,
near the mouth of Bridge Creek. Grade office was reestablished in May,
1896, by change from Burnt Ranch, and it was in the period of 1897-98
that Hattie Van Bibber, Mrs. Putnam's mother, was postmaster. The office
was closed July 31, 1901. Grade post office and toll house was a natural
stopping place for the freighters, and Mr. Van Bibber operated a smithy to
take care of the trade. Among other matters Mrs. Putnam writes of the
following: "Mother was postmistress; served meals to freighters at twenty-
five cents and collected the toll for "Mac" Cornett,who was interested in the
road. The toll was twenty-five cents for each horse, regardless of the number of wagons or their weight. We could not charge Indians and preachers,
and naturally there was no charge to the neighbors. In good weather there
were often ten, twelve or even twenty freighters camping along the road
from the house far up past the blacksmith shop. It was a sight to remember
to see the Grade at starting time, lined with freight teams pulling out
toward The Dalles, loaded with huge sacks of wool. Not a few outfits had as
many as three wagons and ten or twelve horses. Most drivers sat on a high
seat and deftly manipulated a line for each horse. Many rode the left wheel
horse and drove the leaders. At least one team in each outfit had warning
bells on an arch fastened to the hames. Some horses were sleek and strong,
well harnessed, others were pitiable creatures, victims of cruelty and ignorance. You could almost read a man's character by his team and wagon.
One of the best outfits on the road belonged to Jack McCauley who had a
family of ten children on a little homestead near the town of John Day.
After I was grown I stayed one night with them when the stage broke down
and was struck with the splendid discipline and high moral tone of the
family."

Graeme, Clackamas County. The name of Graeme post office in the
extreme west part of the county came from the Scottish family name Graham. There was a Graham's Ferry in this vicinity in early days and it was
situated two or three miles upstream from Wilsonville. The compiler has
been told that when an application was made for the establishment of Graham post office postal authorities objected to the name Graham because of
possible confusion with Gresham post office in nearby Multnomah County.
The name Graeme was used as a compromise. Graeme is an alternative
form of the Scotch word Graham. The Graham family was well known in
the locality and one member, Robert Graham, was living in Oregon City in
1948. Graeme post office was established February 1, 1896, with T. Howard Baker first postmaster. It was discontinued August 12, 1903. The compiler has been told that Baker bought the Graham house about the time
Graeme post office was established.

Graham Butte, Deschutes County. Graham Butte is about five miles southwest of Black Butte and Graham Corral is nearby. According to Phil Brogan of Bend, Mr. and Mrs. E. A. Graham arrived from California on October 20, 1880 and soon settled on a homestead near Graham Corral. The location alongside the road to the Willamette Valley was a busy place in the summer and the Grahams kept the travel for the sheep and herders moving to the high pasture.

Graham Creek, Jackson County. This small creek north of Prospect was named for Edwin Graham who came from Texas prior to 1904 and endeavored to raise ginseng along this stretch of Rogue River. Mr. Graham's operation is not included in the history of Oregon's more successful business ventures.

Graham Pass, Clackamas County. This pass is on the divide between Clackamas and Collawash rivers near the Marion County line. It was named for Joe Graham, a former USFS ranger.

Grand Island, Yamhill County. This is one of the largest islands in the Willamette River, and is so named on that account. It is separated from the rest of Yamhill County on the west by Lambert Slough, over which there is a bridge. In pioneer days it was known as Deer Island, which caused some confusion with Deer Island in Columbia County. Later it was called simply the Island. Island settlers organized a community club about 1913, and the name Grand Island was adopted by popular vote. For short history of Grand Island by Mrs. C. A. Ferguson, see Salem *Statesman,* October 2, 1931. The island contains about 4000 acres of tillable land, mostly rich river soil. Statements that it is only 46 feet above sea level are not substantiated by government maps, which show that much of the area is about 100 feet above sea level, with one point 107 feet in elevation.

Grand Prairie, Lane County. In pioneer days that part of the Willamette Valley floor northwest of Eugene and southwest of Harrisburg was generally referred to as Grand Prairie, but the name has sunk into disuse. Grand Prairie post office was established June 22, 1854, with Jonathan Butler first postmaster. E. Blachley became postmaster on September 3, 1858, and Jonathan Butler, Jr., on March 18, 1859. The office was closed March 30, 1860. The office was of course named for the natural feature. In February, 1947, J. M. Nighswander of Eugene wrote the compiler that this office was probably near the "center, the school, or the thickest of the settlement." This center was near the northeast corner of the Andrew Jackson Simmons donation land claim, at the place later called Meadow View and also Grand Prairie School. Mr. Nighswander's mother was a daughter of Simmons, and his father, Francis Marion Nighswander taught school at Grand Prairie in 1873. Modern maps show Meadow View as a Burlington Northern Inc., siding about five miles south of Junction City, and also on the Pacific Highway.

Grand Rapids, Clatsop County. In August, 1892, articles of incorporation were filed in the Clatsop County records at Astoria for the Grand Rapids Improvement and Development Company. The compiler has been told that the enterprise was named for Grand Rapids, Michigan, and a program of lumbering and furniture manufacturing was planned. The community was to be at the bend of Nehalem River about four miles south of Jewell and Grand Rapids post office was established December 28, 1892, with Horace M. Spencer first postmaster. The compiler has not found any record of a platted townsite with the name Grand Rapids and knows of no rapids in the river at that point that might warrant the name. However, the post office continued to operate until July 7, 1897, when it was closed out to Vinemaple. It seems apparent that Grand Rapids office was reestablished May 12, 1902, with Fred Springer postmaster, but available records give no postal history. At one time the Tidepost Timber Company maintained an office, machine shop and roadhouse in the neighborhood.

Grand Ronde, Polk and Yamhill counties. This name, as applied to a valley and two communities in western Oregon, is universally misspelled, but the style is so firmly fixed in the public mind that there seems little chance to change it. The USBGN tried to secure the use of Grande Ronde but without avail. The French word *ronde,* meaning circle or roundness, requires the adjective agreement *grande,* and the two words together may be taken as describing a fine large valley of excellent appearance, more or less hemmed in by hills. This valley and the one in Union County were named by French-Canadian trappers because of their aspect, but the valley in eastern Oregon is always called Grande Ronde. For many years there was a Grand Ronde Indian Reservation in Polk and Yamhill counties. There were 1064 Indians on this reservation in the census of 1867. The Grand Ronde Agency, which was in Yamhill County, was closed in the fall of 1925, but a community remains. See editorial in the *Oregonian,* November 18, 1925. In the 1920s the railroad was extended from Willamina and the present Salmon River Highway was started along South Yamhill River. These both bypassed Grand Ronde Agency about a mile and a half south in Polk County and the present community of Grand Ronde grew up just west of the mouth of Rock Creek. Grand Ronde post office was established February 16, 1861, with Benjamin Simpson first postmaster. The office was first at the site of Fort Yamhill, about a half mile north of what is now Valley Junction. About 1894 the office was moved to Grand Ronde Agency in Yamhill County, and in the early 1920s it was moved to the present site in Polk County. The post office has always been called Grand Ronde. In 1895 Butler post office was established at the locality of Fort Yamhill.

Granddad Butte, Douglas County. This butte in section 10, township 25 south, range 2 east, was named by USFS ranger Fred Asam for an aged prospector known only as "Grandad".

Grande Ronde Valley, Union County. This imposing valley has given its name to Grande Ronde River and also to La Grande. In this part of Oregon, the French name has retained both final "e"s. Grande Ronde, in eastern Oregon, is mentioned as early as 1827 by Peter Skene Ogden. In the copy of his journal at the Oregon Historical Society he says: "Saturday [September] 14th at 7 A.M. we started advanced one mile and reached Clay River or commonly Called Riviere deGrande Ronde. This river discharges in the South branch of the Columbia, about two days march across land from Fort Nez Percy. . ." The name Clay River may have been applied because where the Grande Ronde River leaves the valley it is frequently very slightly yellow in appearance, or putty colored, doubtless due to valley drainage. Robert Stuart uses the name Glaise River several times in his journal early in August, 1812. See *Discovery of the Oregon Trail*, edited by P. A. Rollins, page 76 *et seq. Glaise* is a French term for clay. Washington Irving quotes Bonneville as calling this stream *Fourche de glace*, or Ice River. Rollins suggests that *glace* is a misunderstanding of *glaise*, which seems likely, as the river where Bonneville saw it, hardly merits the name Ice. There are good descriptions of the Grande Ronde Valley in *Astoria* and in Stuart's narrative. It is obvious that Grande Ronde River was named after the valley.

Grandview, Jefferson County. The name of Grandview suggests an hyperbole, but the compiler is of the opinion that the view justifies the name. Residents of the community enjoyed a view of the eastern slopes of the Cascade Range that was certainly inspiring. However, an inspiring view was not enough and by 1960 nothing was left except the remnants of a few homesteads.

Granger, Benton County. The Oregon Pacific railroad was put in service between Albany and Corvallis early in 1887. Granger was one of the early stations on this line about midway between the two cities mentioned. Granger post office was established February 25, 1888, and it was in service until September 30, 1903. Levi Joy was the only postmaster. The compiler has been informed that the place was named because of the well-known Granger movement which was prominent about that time. It is not known whether the station was established and named before the post office but the compiler thinks that was probably the case.

Granite, Grant County. Details of the early history of many Oregon mining communities are either non-existent or hard to come by. Granite is no exception and the reader will have to reconcile the following facts as best he can. Albert G. Tabor discovered gold along Granite Creek on July 4, 1862. He named his claim the Independence to commemorate the date and the area was promptly designated the Granite Creek Mines. By 1863 Granite City had been established and was so called on Alonzo Leland's *New Map of the Mining Regions of Oregon & Washington Territory* as well as the map prepared by Lieutenant John Bowen of Currey's command during the 1864 campaign against the Snake Indians. Some historians claim that the community was known as Independence and it was so shown on Foster's *Mining Map of Eastern Oregon* dated 1888 but the post office established March 26, 1878 was named Granite and this persisted until the final closure in 1957. The USGS Granite quadrangle dated 1972 shows Tabor Diggings about three miles down Granite Creek from Granite and the Independence Mine about the same distance upstream. The compiler does not know which of these two spots, if either, was the site of the original discovery nor if the community called Independence was the same settlement now called Granite. A paragraph in the *Oregonian*, October 9, 1862 under a Granite Creek Mines dateline states that a town called Pleasant City had been laid out on Granite Creek but this name did not survive and the *Oregonian*, June 10, 1863 uses the name Granite City Mines. In a more recent vein, an article in the *Oregon Journal*, May 8, 1974 describes the revival of municipal government in Granite, a necessity caused by the resurgence of the population from one in 1958 to eight in 1974. Granite Creek was named for the granite rocks prevalent in the area.

Granite, Josephine County. Granite, a Southern Pacific Company industrial station a couple of miles northwest of Grants Pass, was named for the immense quantities of decomposed granite in the locality, granite that the railroad used for ballasting hundreds of miles of tracks. This granite was of fine texture, packed well and was practically dustless, qualities of great value to a railroad. There was a good deal of railroad business at this point at the time when the Oregon lines were reballasted and a post office was found necessary. It could not be called Granite because of duplication with Granite in Grant County, then an operating post office. The office in Josephine County was therefore named Granite Hill. It was established June 12, 1905, and closed June 3, 1908. Lloyd B. Wickersham was the only postmaster. The railroad station was discontinued some years later.

Granny Creek, Wallowa County. Granny Creek is a short stream that flows into Freezeout Creek in township 2 south, range 48 east. The creek was named for a favorite old mare owned by James Wilson and called Granny, which ranged along the stream in the late 1880s. She was killed by cougars and her body was found near the creek. At the head of the stream is a well-known natural lookout, Granny View Point. It commands a wide territory.

Grant, Grant County. Grant post office was established June 13, 1870, with William N. Bonham first postmaster. W. W. Stone became postmaster on October 9, 1871, and the office was closed April 14, 1873. This office appears to have been the third in what is now Grant County, preceded only by Canyon City and John Day City. The office was of course named for the county and for General U. S. Grant. In a letter printed in the *Blue Mountain Eagle*, Canyon City, March 7, 1947, R. R. McHaley, former county judge, says: "William N. Bonham owned a ranch about a half mile northward from the present town of Mount Vernon, and W. W. Stone lived in the same neighborhood, so that this must have been the location of Grant post office. There was no town of Mount Vernon when Grant post office was created. I stayed all night at the Bonham residence in 1875, and there was no town of Mount Vernon then. The Bonhams kept a public stopping place at their ranch home." The compiler thinks that Mr. McHaley has solved the problem of the location of Grant post office. There was of course another Grant post office much later on in what is now Sherman County.

Grant, Sherman County. Grant was a station on the railroad in the north part of Sherman County. It is not now a post office although it was at one time. The place came into being when the railroad was built in the early 1880s and it was known at that time as Villard in honor of Henry Villard, the great railroad man. The name was later changed to Grant for William Grant of The Dalles. In 1883 the community was burned. The townsite was platted in November, 1883, by William Murray and W. Lair Hill. The Columbia River flood in 1894 practically wiped out the town and citizens were forced to seek hillsides for safety.

Grant County. Grant County was created October 14, 1864, and was named for General U. S. Grant, who at the time was at the height of his fame as a military leader for the northern armies. Grant County was carved out of parts of Wasco and Umatilla counties. Grant County has a land area of 4532 square miles.

Grant Creek, Crook County. Grover Blake, one of the first USFS rangers in the area, told the writer in 1971 that the creek, spring, butte and meadows in the north part of the county were all named for one Grant, a very early sheep man from Antelope who used the area for summer graze.

Grants Pass, Josephine County. Many stories have been circulated as to how this community got its name. Grants Pass citizens for the most part are inclined to the belief that the name was applied as a result of the capture of Vicksburg by General U. S. Grant. About the time the news arrived in southern Oregon, men were engaged in improving the road over the low hills north of the point where the city is now situated, and they celebrated General Grant's victory by naming the summit Grants Pass. This name was later applied to a nearby stage station and then to a post office, and on completion of the railroad the post office was moved from the stage station near the geographic feature called Grants Pass to a point near the railroad station and the present community took its name from the post office. On October 12, 1921, Geo. H. Parker wrote Geo. H. Himes that the post office at Grants Pass was established in 1865 and the first postmaster was Thomas Croxton. Croxton desired to perpetuate the name of General Grant because of Grant's record in the Civil War, and asked the postal authorities to name the new office Grant. According to Parker the petition was refused because there was another Grant in Oregon. Government records indicate that the office was established March 22, 1865, with the name Grants Pass, and with Croxton postmaster. This substantiates Parker's statement, although it does not prove that Croxton originated the idea of the name. The fact that he substituted Grants Pass for his original proposal indicates that the form Grants Pass was already in use. Wm. M. Colvig of Medford says E. B. Dimmick probably named the pass itself. Versions of the story ascribing the name to a visit of General Grant appear erroneous, because there is no evidence that General Grant was ever in that part of Oregon. He was stationed at Fort Vancouver from September, 1852, to September, 1853. The death of Colonel Bliss, of the adjutant-general's department, on August 5, 1853, caused the promotion of Grant to the rank of captain of a company then stationed at Humboldt Bay, California. Grant made the journey from Fort Vancouver to Humboldt Bay by sea to San Francisco, and thence north to the place of his destination. He went to Fort Vancouver in 1852 by sea, from San Francisco. Stories to the effect that General Grant "passed" in a card game at Grants Pass may be dismissed as pure fiction. For additional information about the naming of Grants Pass see editorial page *Oregon Journal,* August 30, 1927. For editorial about Grant's experiences in the Pacific Northwest, see the *Oregonian,* March 7, 1943.

Grass Valley, Sherman County. Pioneer settlers, without ever changing countenance, tell newcomers that in early days the rye-grass was so tall in this part of Oregon that it was well over a man's head. They even state that this was so when the man was on horseback. This accounts for the name. Grass Valley was incorporated as a result of a popular vote held September 10, 1900.

Grass Valley Canyon, Sherman County. Grass Valley Canyon heads in Grass Valley, hence the name. The canyon wanders northward through Sherman County, and finally joins the canyon of John Day River. This name is one of that class that is cumbersome, due to the fact that the name of one feature is used to describe another. Salmon River Glacier is another example. Grass Valley Canyon is an old name, however, and will probably persist.

Grater Butte, Jefferson County. One of the earliest settlers on upper Trout Creek was James M. Grater who came to the Ashwood country in 1869. The 3643 foot butte was named for him although his two nephews, H. C. and L. G. Grater, were also well-known early settlers.

Grave Creek, Jackson and Josephine counties. This stream rises in the northwest corner of Jackson County and flows into Josephine County. It receives Wolf Creek near Leland. In 1846 a girl named Martha Leland Crowley, died on what is now Grave Creek, and her burial there gave rise to the name. James W. Nesmith, in a letter published in the *Oregonian*, November 23, 1883, wrote that in the late summer of 1848 he started for California with a party of gold seekers, and they found Miss Crowley's grave had been desecrated by Indians. They reinterred the remains, and called the stream Grave Creek. In January, 1854, the legislature passed an act changing the name of Grave Creek to Leland Creek, in honor of Miss Crowley, but the public did not accept the new name and it remains Grave Creek. Statements that Miss Crowley's name was Josephine and that the county may have been named for her cannot be substantiated by the compiler. See also under Leland. Martha Leland Crowley was the daughter of Thomas and Catherine Linville Crowley, who came to Oregon from Missouri in 1846. Thomas Crowley and Martha Leland Crowley died in Oregon, but before the family reached the Willamette Valley. Thomas Crowley's daughter Matilda and a son Calvin also died on the trip out from Missouri, as well as Calvin's wife and child. In 1848 Mrs. Thomas Crowley was married to James M. Fulkerson in Polk County. See Grants Pass *Courier,* January 23, 24, 26, 1934.

Gravelford, Coos County. Gravelford is a place on North Fork Coquille River a few miles northeast of Myrtle Point. The name came from the natural ford in the stream. Gravel Ford post office was established in April, 1878, with Solomon J. McCloskey first postmaster. It was finally discontinued April 30, 1934, with mail to Myrtle Point. The name in two words is the style used in post office records available to the writer, but the form Gravelford is used on the post route map of 1900 and on the USGS atlas sheet for the Bridge quadrangle.

Graveyard Point, Curry County. This point is a high headland southwest of the town of Port Orford extending southeastward into the harbor. In February, 1944, Louis L. Knapp of Port Orford wrote the compiler: "During the time the military garrison was maintained at Port Orford, two soldiers were buried on this point. Thereafter the oldtimers always spoke of the headland as Graveyard Point and it is generally known and referred to as such. No other burials have ever been made there."

Gray, Curry County. Gray post office was in service from November, 1884, to November, 1887, with Loftin Gray first and only postmaster. The office was obviously named for him. In May, 1948, Douglas Cooley of Brookings wrote that this office was situated on Gray Flat, two miles north of Brookings.

Gray, Linn County. This was a station on the Oregon Electric Railway southwest of Albany. It was named for Carl R. Gray, formerly president of the Oregon Electric and other roads, and later president of the Union Pacific Railroad Company at Omaha.

Gray Butte, Jefferson County. There is a story, unconfirmed, that this butte was named for Dr. Asa Gray, the botanist, but residents nearby all say that the name is due to the characteristic color.

Gray Eagle Bar, Marion County. Gray Eagle Bar is on the east bank of Willamette River about three miles southwest of Salem. It received its name from the fact that the river steamer, *Gray Eagle*, was once stuck on this gravel bar for several days.

Green, Douglas County. This community three miles south of Roseburg was named for Jeptha Green who settled nearby in 1853. The station on the Southern Pacific Railroad was originally called Green's but the railroad has dropped the possessive.

Green Basin, Marion County. The post office Green Basin, situated on North Santiam River about two miles east of Niagara, was named for a fine stand of green timber north of the office and in the vicinity of Rocky Top. A saw mill was operated near the post office. Green Basin post office was established October 3, 1890, with John D. Montgomery first of four postmasters. The office was closed May 1, 1896, with papers to Niagara.

Green Hills, Multnomah County. Green Hills, the name of a residence district in the southwest part of Portland, was suggested by Henry Hewett when his own and neighboring property was platted in 1913. The style Greenhills is not that of the official plat and was not the form suggested by Mr. Hewett. The name Green Hills has extended its growth eastward until it now includes the Green Hills crossroads. The locality of the crossroads was known as Mount Zion in early days. According to Mrs. Hildegarde Plummer Wither, for many years a resident on Dosch Road, the name Mount Zion was applied by her grandfather, Albert Kelly, a son of Samuel Kelly of Kentucky, and brother of Oregon's well-known pioneer, Clinton Kelly. The Kelly family lived near the Mount Zion meeting house in Pulaski County, Kentucky, and had a sentimental attachment to the biblical name. In 1854 the Rev. Clinton Kelly suggested the name Mount Zion for what is now known as Mount Tabor in east Portland but his son Plympton Kelly was in favor of Mount Tabor and that name was adopted. It was about 1860-61 that Albert Kelly suggested the name Mount Zion for what is now called Green Hills. About the time mentioned Patton road was opened up to the pass in the hills and a small school was built at the southeast corner of what became the main intersection. This little school was just about the same location as the Green Hills service station in operation at this writing 1972. The school house provided a meeting place for local residents and it was on this account that Kelly called the locality Mount Zion because of his sentimental interest in the Mount Zion meeting house in Kentucky. The selection was a little odd from a geographic point of view because Kelly gave the name Mount Zion to a pass in the hills and not to one of the summits. For many years the locality now called Sylvan was known as Zion Town. This name was originated by Nathan B. Jones. It is possible that the name Zion Town was applied because the place was so near Mount Zion School and crossroads. There was no town at Mount Zion.

Green Lakes, Deschutes County. These are a group of one large and several small lakes directly between the South Sister and Broken Top. They are one of the sources of Fall Creek and the large lake has an elevation of 6505 feet. The name is descriptive, especially when viewed from above.

Green Mountain, Lane County. This Green Mountain is three miles north of Disston and has an approximate elevation of 3450 feet. Loren W. Hunt of Cove, who lived nearby for many years, told the compiler that this peak was named for Claud Green, an early trapper.

Green Peter, Linn County. For the meaning of the word peter when used to describe a rocky summit, see under Bald Peter. Green Peter is situated northeast of Sweet Home and is the site of a forest lookout. Some maps and records refer to this point as Bald Peter, but the Linn County Fire Patrol has informed the writer that Bald Peter is about a mile north-north-east of Green Peter. In 1967 the USCE completed Green Peter Dam, a concrete gravity structure 380 feet high, on Middle Santiam River about one mile west of the mouth of Green Peter Creek.

Green Point, Columbia County. Broughton, of Vancouver's expedition, camped at Green Point on October 26, 1792, and called it Point Sheriff, presumably after John Sheriff, master's mate of the *Chatham*.

Green Springs Mountain, Jackson County. Named because of the perennial verdure around the springs near the summit of this mountain on the highway between Ashland and Klamath Falls. The highway was for many years known as the Green Springs Mountain Road. The form Green Spring is wrong.

Green Valley, Douglas County. This valley is northwest of Oakland. It seems to have been named because of its appearance. For the early history of the valley see Walling's *History of Southern Oregon,* page 439.

Greenback, Josephine County. The locality called Greenback in the northeast part of the county was named for the Greenback mine, but the writer does not know the reason the mine was named unless it was expected that it would produce plenty of money. Generally miners were more interested in metallic money than that of the folding type. Greenback post office was established in August, 1902, with Carey W. Thompson first postmaster. The office operated until June, 1908. The place is a couple of miles north of Grave Creek and about four miles airline east of the Pacific Highway.

Greenberry, Benton County. Greenberry is a station south of Corvallis. It bears the given names of Green Berry Smith, a pioneer of 1845, who settled in Benton County in 1846, and who for a time lived on his farm near this station. Smith was generally called Greenberry, despite the fact that he had two given names. For further information, see under Smith Hill in this book.

Greenburg, Washington County. This was a station north of Tigard named by the officials of the Oregon Electric Railway Company for a local resident, and not because of any remarkable verdure. His family name was Greenburg.

Greenhorn, Baker County. Miles F. Potter in *Oregon's Golden Years,* page 77, gives the following interesting account of this name. On the east slope of Vinegar Hill in section 7, township 10 south, range 35 east, there is a prominent rock or horn of green serpentine. The USGS Bates quadrangle shows this point with an elevation of 7780 feet. It is highly visible and was known in the early days as the Green Horn. When the mining excitment developed during the 1860s, the name was corrupted to Greenhorn and applied to both the district and a creek near the headwaters of North Fork Burnt River. An early community grew in the 1870s but Greenhorn post office was not established until May 24, 1902 with Burton Miller postmaster. The office was closed December 15, 1919. Apparently the early postal needs of the area had been met by the Robisonville office, less than a mile to the northeast.

Greenleaf, Lane County. The name Greenleaf was first applied to this community about 1885, and when the post office was established about 1892, the same name was used for the office. It also was used for Greenleaf Creek, a stream flowing into Lake Creek where Greenleaf post office was first situated. The name is said to have been used because of the abundance of green maple trees in the vicinity. About 1908 the post office was moved some three miles down Lake Creek.

Greenman Creek, Douglas County. In 1908 John W. Greenman settled on Little River west of Wolf Creek along this creek which bears his name.

Greens Bridge, Linn and Marion counties. Greens Bridge is over North Santiam River about two miles east of Jefferson. It bears the name of Thomas Green, an early settler in the vicinity.

Greenville, Washington County. Greenville, a crossroads community about two miles south of Banks, at one time had a post office, but commercially the place has dried up. The office was established January 9, 1871, with E. W. Dixon first postmaster. The office operated under various postmasters until April, 1907, when it was moved north to the locality of the old Banks office and the name Banks restored. Greenville was apparently a descriptive name, given because the locality was so verdant. The writer has found no evidence that the place was named for a person.

Gregory Point, Coos County. Gregory Point is the northwest promontory of Cape Arago. The Cape Arago Lighthouse is on this point. The name perpetuates the name Cape Gregory, originally applied by Captain James Cook on March 12, 1778, to what is now called Cape Arago.

Greiner Canyon, Gilliam County. This canyon south of Condon was named for an early settler, Andrew Greiner, who homesteaded there in 1885. Members of the Greiner family still live in the Condon area after almost 100 years.

Gresham, Multnomah County. Gresham was named for Walter Quinton Gresham, (1832-1895), soldier and statesman. He made an enviable record in the Civil War, displaying gallantry in action, and in 1865 was brevetted major-general of volunteers. After the war he practiced law and became a member of the federal judiciary. He was postmaster general in Arthur's cabinet from April 3, 1883, to September 24, 1884, when he became secretary of the treasury, and served about a month in that position. He was a candidate for the Republican nomination for president in 1884 and 1888, but eventually drifted away from the Republican party, and was secretary of state in Cleveland's cabinet from March 7, 1893, until his death on May 28, 1895. Gresham post office was established in May, 1884, and the name was suggested by Benjamin F. Rollins because W. Q. Gresham was then postmaster general. Gresham named the post office of George, in Clackamas County, for Judge M. C. George of Portland. See under that heading.

Gribble Prairie, Clackamas County. This prairie is a well-known locality about four miles southeast of Aurora. It was named for John G. Gribble, who was born on the line between North and South Carolina in 1799 and after migrating to Missouri, came to Oregon in 1846. He settled near Macksburg in 1847 on a donation land claim, and his name was applied to the prairie in consequence. He died June 3, 1869. For additional information, see *Portrait and Biographical Record of Portland and Vicinity,* pages 393 and 853.

Grice Hill, Polk County. Grice Hill is in the Eola Hills about three miles northwest of Salem. It has an elevation of about 550 feet. It was named for L. Grice, a nearby landowner. There was a pioneer quarry on the east part of this hill from which a good deal of building stone was taken for construction in Salem. This was before the days of concrete.

Griffin Canyon, Wheeler County. This gulch is tributary to Dry Hollow, south of Fossil. Sometimes it is shown as Griffith Canyon, but in 1931 a correspondent in Fossil wrote the compiler that Griffin was correct. This was confirmed by W. H. Steiwer of Fossil in February, 1944, who said that the canyon was named for Tom Griffin.

Griffin Creek, Baker County. The locality of Griffin Creek just southwest of Baker was one of the most prominent places in the early history of northeastern Oregon. It was close to this stream that Henry Griffin and others struck pay dirt on the evening of October 23, 1861. This may be considered the beginning of placer mining in that section of the state and there was a good deal of subsequent activity, including the rise and fall of the town of Auburn. For the history of the discovery, see *History of Baker, Grant, Malheur and Harney Counties,* page 142. The stream was of course named for the prospector. Griffin is buried with other members of his family in the Auburn cemetery. Sometime in the 1920s the Baker Chamber of Commerce erected an antique headstone with the name spelled Griffen. This is apparently in error since the many early records and references all use "in".

Griffin Creek, Jackson County. This stream rises in the mountains south of Medford and flows northward to join Bear Creek not far from Central Point. It was named for Captain B. B. Griffin, a pioneer of 1848, who settled in the Rogue River Valley in 1852. Griffin is the correct spelling.

Grindstone Ridge, Washington County. Grindstone Ridge runs southward from South Saddle Mountain about four miles and terminates in Windy Point. It was named because an early settler with a timber claim on the ridge had a grindstone by his cabin. During the 1890s a surveying party sharpened their axes on the stone and its disappearance a short time later caused much local comment.

Grizzly, Jefferson County. This post office was established about 1890, with Elsie Edmund first postmaster. It was named for Grizzly Mountain, a prominent butte about four miles to the southeast. The office was closed June 30, 1948.

Grizzly Mountain, Crook County. W. P. Vandevert of Bend in 1926 told the compiler that Grizzly Mountain received its name in the 1870s because of its grizzled color, and not because of any adventure with a grizzly bear.

Grizzly Mountain, Curry County. This mountain is three miles east of Gold Beach. There is a story to the effect that an early citizen nicknamed "Grizzly" lived on its slopes and hunted meat for the Gold Beach miners in the early days.

Grossman, Wallowa County. Grossman post office got its name from Grossman Creek. It was situated about four miles southwest of Promise. The office was established in December, 1904, with Rhoda A. Pool, postmaster, and was closed in March, 1921.

Grossman Creek, Wallowa County. Grossman Creek was named for a pioneer trapper. He died many years ago near what is now Rondowa. Grossman Creek is about ten miles north of Minam.

Grouse, Wallowa County. This community is in the extreme north part of the county. It was at one time a post office. The place has also been known as Grouse Flat. In earlier days there were many grouse in the neighborhood. Grouse post office was established January 28, 1896, with Samuel M. Silver first postmaster.

Grouse Hill, Crater Lake National Park, Klamath County. Grouse Hill is a prominent feature north of Crater Lake, and has an elevation of 7401 feet. It was so called because of the abundance of grouse found there.

Grouslous Mountain, Curry County. This mountain was named for John and Peter Groslouis who settled near Port Orford about 1853. Herman Reinhart, in *The Golden Frontier,* refers to them several times both when they lived in Curry County and later when they had moved back to their family home on French Prairie. Reinhart spells the name Grosluis and F. F. Victor, in *The Early Indian Wars of Oregon,* page 324, speaks of John Grolouise. The correct spelling of this French family name is Groslouis and there were several of the family in Oregon in very early days.

Grove City, Malheur County. On April 3, 1888, a post office with the impressive name Grove City was established near Malheur River at a point about ten miles west of Vale. John F. Tilson was the first postmaster. This office was discontinued September 19, 1899, with papers to Vale. The office was apparently named in consequence of Osborn Grove, a well-known place in the neighborhood.

Guano Lake. Lake County. This is a mud lake or playa about five miles long situated in township 39 south, range 27 east. It is fed by Guano Creek, an intermittent stream heading on Hart Mountain. Guano Lake has no outlet. The lake and creek were so named because of the guano deposits along their banks. The lake was named first, in the summer of 1864, during the Owyhee Reconnoissance of the First Oregon Cavalry under Lieutenant-Colonel C. S. Drew. See Drew's *Official Report,* page 15. For a number of years the stream feeding the lake was called Warner Creek, but is now generally known as Guano Creek.

Guild Lake, Multnomah County. This was a shallow lake within the city limits of Portland, on the west bank of Willamette River. It was gradually filled with material sluiced down from the nearby hills and dredged from the river. It was named for Peter Guild, a pioneer of 1847.

Gull Island, Columbia County. This is a small island in the Columbia River north of Crims Island. Wilkes shows it as Weaqus Island in the Atlas accompanying *U. S. Exploring Expedition,* volume XXIII, Hydrography, but does not explain the name. Wilkes shows Crims Island as Gull Island, and it seems obvious that the name Gull later became attached to the smaller island to the north.

Gulliford Spring, Umatilla County. This spring on East Fork Butter Creek four miles south of Gurdane was named for the Gulliford family who in the early 1900s settled near Ukiah.

Gumbo, Gilliam County. A post office with the name Gumbo was established on the Gilliam County list on October 18, 1892, with Zachariah J. Martin postmaster. The appointment was rescinded November 15, 1892, and the office was never in service. The compiler has not been able to find the site for this proposed establishment, but supposes it to have been in a locality of gumbo, or sticky soil. Gumbo is the English form of the Louisiana-French *gombo,* meaning the okra plant, used to thicken soups. The word is derived from the African Congo expression *quingombo,* or okra. Not only is gumbo used to refer to thick soups, but also to the Negro-French patois of Louisiana and also to certain heavy, sticky soils. See Read's *Louisiana-French,* page 122, published by the Louisiana State University Press.

Gumboot Creek, Wallowa County. This stream is in the southeast part of the county. It was named because Jack Johnson, a prominent pioneer stockman, once found an old gumboot in it. Gumboot Butte took its name from the stream. Johnson was one of the earliest settlers on Imnaha River.

Gumjuwac Saddle, Hood River County. This pass is a mile southwest of Lookout Mountain, on the watershed between Hood River and Badger Creek. It is about 5200 feet in elevation. The name is not of Indian origin but a phonetic or illiterate rendition of Gum Shoe Jack, an early day sheepherder with an affinity for rubber boots, who resided nearby. Jack Springs is presumably named for the same man.

Gunaldo Falls, Yamhill County. Gunaldo Falls are well known to those who traverse the Three Rivers Highway between Hebo and Grand Ronde. They are just northeast of the highway, on Sourgrass Creek, at a point about a mile east of Dolph. The compiler has been informed that these falls were given a synthetic name when a county road was built through in 1915-19. This name is said to have been made by taking the first letters of the last names of two county commissioners and a county judge. In May, 1948, County Clerk A. R. McLaughlin wrote the compiler that William Gunning and W. S. Allan were county commissioners at that time and J. B. Dodson was county judge. Parts of their names have been handed to posterity in this scrambled form.

Gunter, Douglas County. Gunter post office was established in the fall of 1905, with J. O. Gunter first postmaster. Gunter petitioned for the office and suggested the name of his father-in-law, Craig. Other petitioners sent in Gunter's name, which was adopted by the authorities. Gunter was born in Indiana August 7, 1852, and came to Oregon in November, 1885.

Gurdane, Umatilla County. The post office of Gurdane was named for John S. Gurdane, a pioneer settler of south Umatilla County. He was one time a member of the state legislature. The post office was established in 1890.

Guy W. Talbot State Park, Multnomah County. For a description and history of this park see under Latourell Falls. Guy W. Talbot was born in Centerville, Michigan in 1873 and died in Portland on December 1, 1961. He was employed by various railroad enterprises and became president of the Oregon Electric Railroad in 1907. In 1910 he helped organize and became the first president of the Pacific Power & Light Company. For further information see the *Oregonian* for December 2, 1961.

Gwendolen, Gilliam County. Walter H. Guild, superintendent of the Oregon-Washington Railroad & Navigation Company at La Grande, informed the compiler in 1927 that Gwendolen was named for Miss Gwendolen Worthington, daughter of B. A. Worthington formerly vice-president and general manager of the railroad company. Information to the effect that the station was named for the daughter of a railroad conductor is wrong. The Condon branch line was built shortly before 1900 and the post office was established a few years later.

Gwinn, Malheur County. This station about six miles east of Juntura, on the Union Pacific Railroad was named for Monte Gwinn, a stockman of Boise, Idaho. In 1943 it was reported that the station was no longer in service.

Gwynn Knoll, Lane County. This is a knoll on the Pacific Coast in the northwest part of the county. It is south óf Cape Perpetua. It was named for an early settler.

Gypsum, Baker County. According to information received by the writer from the postmaster at Gypsum in January, 1926, the place was named in the fall of 1907 on account of the gypsum deposit that is situated about a mile northwest of the station. General Charles F. Beebe of Portland was interested in the development of this deposit and probably suggested the name for the station. The post office was established about 1913, with J. C. McNaught as first postmaster.

Haas Ridge, Wallowa County. Haas Ridge lies just west of Lightning Creek in the northeast part of the county. It was named for the Haas family, pioneer sheepmen.

Hackett Creek, Clackamas County. Hackett Creek flows west into Sandy River near Brightwood. It was named for John C. Hackett who settled near its mouth in the 1890s.

Hackleman Creek, Linn County. This stream is near the South Santiam Highway. It rises in Tombstone Prairie just east of Tombstone Summit and flows eastward into Fish Lake. It bears the name of Abram Hackleman, one of the first settlers in Albany and one of the organizers of the Willamette Valley and Cascade Mountain Wagon-Road Company. Hackleman was born in 1831 and came to Oregon in 1847. He moved to Crook County about 1880. His name is often spelled Abraham, which is wrong, according to a letter from Willard L. Marks of Albany, dated February 26, 1943.

Hadleyville, Lane County. Hadleyville is the name of a locality on Coyote Creek about four miles southeast of Crow. Recent maps show a Hadleyville school in the area. Hadleyville was named for a local family. For biography of H. G. Hadley, an Oregon pioneer who settled in Lane County in the early 1850s, see *Illustrated History of Lane County*, page 486. Hadleyville post office was established October 3, 1890, with Frank Hadley the first of four postmasters. The office was closed to Crow on October 31, 1903.

Haflinger Creek, Lane County. Haflinger Creek empties into Horse Creek four miles above Foley Springs. It was named for Mrs. Ella Haflinger who operated the resort at the springs for many years. Mrs. Haflinger's first husband was Peter Runey who purchased the property at the springs in the 1880s.

Hager Mountain, Lake County. Hager Mountain, about ten miles south of the town of Silver Lake, was at one time known as Hagerhorst Mountain for a pioneer settler in Silver Lake Valley. For many years it has been called by its modern name, which seems well established. The Klamath Indian name for Hager Mountain was *Chock-chock-lisk-se.* Some old maps call it Bald Butte.

Haig, Multnomah County. About 1889 a real estate addition was laid out in the southeast part of what is now Portland by Louis and Maria Feurer. This addition lies a little to the south-southeast of Powell Boulevard. Most of the streets were given German names, presumably by the Feurers. These German street names became subject to criticism in World War I and some of them were changed. As is natural with an activity of this sort there was a good deal of confusion. The name Karl Street was changed to Haig in honor of the great British field marshal. At the time of World War II so much traffic developed north of the Brooklyn yards that it was necessary for the Southern Pacific Company to extend its double track southward through east Portland. The railroad adopted the name Haig for the end of this section of double track and a station with this name was established for operating purposes.

Haines, Baker County. F. W. Castor, postmaster at Haines in 1926, informed the writer that the community was named for "Judge" I. D. Haines, of Baker, who owned land on which the town was situated. The community was started in 1883, the year before the railroad was constructed through Baker Valley. The post office was established in November, 1884, with Florence A. Dorsett first postmaster. For story about the early history of Haines, see Baker *Record Courier,* July 2, 1936.

Hale, Lane County. Hale post office was near Elk City about five miles northwest of the place now called Noti, and was given the family name of the postmaster, George H. Hale. The office was established August 4, 1886, and was closed out to Elmira on May 23, 1907. Lumbering was the chief industry.

Hale Butte, Linn County. Hale Butte is about two miles west of Jefferson and has an elevation of 427 feet. It was named for Milton Hale, whose donation land claim took in part of the butte. Hale established Hale Ferry and the city of Syracuse on the Santiam River near the butte in pioneer days, but his town did not grow to maturity. Hale Butte has been shown on maps as Gale Butte, a typographical error. For information about Hale and Syracuse, see *OHQ*, volume XXXII, page 195.

Haley, Clackamas County. Haley was a station about one mile northwest of Boring. It was named for P. W. Haley, a nearby resident.

Halfway, Baker County. An article printed in the Baker *Democrat-Herald* on August 29, 1935, which seems to be authoritative, says that the post office was established about 1887 on the Alexander Stalker ranch, now Canaday farm, and the office was named Halfway because it was about midway between Pine and Cornucopia. This appears to be correct. Later the office was moved and it is now much nearer Pine. The original significance of the name has been lost. The compiler has received several letters about this name, in which it is stated as a matter of historical fact that the place was named because it was halfway between the following points: Pine and Carson, Baker and Cornucopia, Baker and Brownlee and Brownlee and Cornucopia. Halfway is not midway between any of these places, as may be seen from an inspection of the map. C. A. Moore, in the *Oregonian*, December 13, 1926, editorial page, says Halfway is midway between Pine and Carson. This is not a fact. The compiler believes that the first paragraph printed above contains the most reliable information. In January, 1906, it was planned to change the name of Halfway post office to Bellevue, and an order was entered on January 8, 1906, establishing the post office with the new name, and with George S. Gillett postmaster. For some reason the order was not put into effect and was rescinded January 13, 1906. On January 17 Gillett was appointed postmaster at Halfway and the business of that office appears to have been carried on without any ripples. Bellevue is a descriptive name that has been used in many places in the United States. The compiler has been unable to learn the reason for the proposal to change the name of Halfway post office to Bellevue.

Hall Creek, Coos County. This stream joins Coquille River at Arago. It was named for David Hall, who took up a donation land claim near its mouth.

Hall Ridge, Marion County. Earl Stahlman of Detroit told the writer that this high ground northeast of Detroit Dam was named for Bruce Hall who logged it many years ago.

Halls Ferry, Marion County. Halls Ferry was a station on the Oregon Electric Railway not far from the site of Halls Ferry which crossed the Willamette River north of Independence. This ferry was first established about 1868 by Noah Leabo. He sold it to J. A. Colby about 1874 and B. F. Hall bought it about 1882 and after that it was known as Halls Ferry. B. F. Hall was the younger son of Reason B. Hall, who founded the town of Buena Vista. For information about the Hall family see under Buena Vista.

Halo Creek, Lane County. *Halo* is the Chinook jargon word meaning none, and the name Halo Creek means that very little water flows in the stream, perhaps none at all at certain seasons. Halo Creek flows into Salmon Creek from the north about twelve miles east of Oakridge.

Halsey, Linn County. This place was named for William L. Halsey, vice-president of the Willamette Valley Railway Company during the construction period. Halsey was one of the Holladay organization. The railroad was built through what is now Halsey in 1871, and the name was doubtless applied at that time. Halsey was not named for the man of that name connected with the Astor enterprise. For biography of William L. Halsey, see the *Oregonian*, February 22, 1884, page 3.

Hamaker Mountain, Klamath County. Hamaker Mountain is a prominent point 6596 feet high southwest of Keno. It was named for John Wesley Hamaker who was a land law specialist and surveyor of Klamath County in the 1880s. He was later United States Land Commissioner in Klamath Falls. Both he and his brother, Joseph O. Hamaker, were involved in the land frauds at the turn of the century. One of the points of controversy was the use of assumed names and this may account for the numerous variant spellings.

Hambone Butte, Clackamas County. This butte is between Salmon and Roaring rivers. Its elevation is about 4900 feet. It was named by T. H. Sherrard of the USFS who said that the selection of the name was arbitrary, and that it had no peculiar significance.

Hamilton, Grant County. Hamilton was named for J. H. Hamilton, a pioneer stockman of the neighborhood and also the first settler where the town is now situated. Hamilton located there some time in 1874 and lived there until his death in 1909. The first store was built by Anson C. Frink who was the first postmaster. The Hamilton ranch was headquarters where settlers met to try the speed of their favorite horses, as Hamilton was a fancier of horseflesh.

Hamilton Creek, Curry County. Adam Hamilton homesteaded near this creek three miles east of Brookings in the 1880s.

Hamilton Creek, Linn County. C. H. Stewart of Albany wrote the compiler in 1927 as follows: "Hamilton Creek is one of the foothill streams of Linn County east of Lebanon. I have been told it was named for a family that settled in that locality at an early date and only resided there a short time."

Hamlet, Clatsop County. Hamlet post office was established about 1905, with Albert Hill as first postmaster. The story of the name is printed in the Seaside *Signal* for January 10, 1929. Herman Ahlers, an old settler on the Necanicum River, is authority for the statement that when he was postmaster at Necanicum, a petition was brought in by a man named Hutinen, living in the valley of North Fork Nehalem River, asking for a post office to be called Hamlet. Ahlers said he asked if the place was named for Shakespeare's play or because it was just a small community. Hutinen told him the latter. The same story contains a statement by A. W. Utzinger, also an old resident, that Hamlet was once called Push in honor of the Astoria Push Club and the name was changed to Hamlet in compliment to Harry Hamlet, member of the club, which was interested in the development of the locality. In a subsequent letter Ahlers denies all this and points to the fact that it was Necanicum post office that was called Push, not the Hamlet post office, and that the Astoria club had no interest in the locality. Government records confirm Ahlers' statement that Push was used at Necanicum and not at Hamlet.

Hamlin Prairie, Douglas County. Hamlin Prairie is on the divide between Elk Creek and Jackson Creek about seven miles southeast of Tiller. It was named for Edmund T. Hamlin who settled there in 1916.

Hammer Creek, Benton County. Hammer Creek bears the name of Jacob Hammer, a pioneer settler on its banks. The stream is west of Monroe. For biography of Jacob Hammer, see *History of Benton County,* Portland, 1885, page 514.

Hammersley, Josephine County. A post office with the name Hammersley was established June 7, 1894, with M. Hammersley postmaster. For some reason it was never placed in service and the appointment was rescinded October 8, 1894. The compiler is informed that the office was intended to serve the locality of the Hammersley mine on the extreme east edge of the county northeast of Grants Pass.

Hammond, Clatsop County. Named for Andrew B. Hammond, a pioneer of the Pacific Northwest. He was born in New Brunswick July 22, 1848, and in 1866-67 came to Washington and then settled in Montana, where he lived about 30 years, successfully engaged in mercantile and railroad affairs. From 1895 to 1898 he built the Astoria and Columbia River Railroad, later acquired by the Spokane, Portland and Seattle Railway Company. In later years he lived in San Francisco, where he died January 15, 1934. He was one of the foremost business men of the Pacific Coast and was interested in timber, lumber, shipping, fishing and various mercantile enterprises. Silas B. Smith says that the Clatsop name of the Indian village near the present site of Hammond was *Ne-ahk-stow.* See *OHQ,* volume I, page 321.

Hamner Butte, Klamath County. Hamner Butte is a prominent mountain southeast of Davis Lake. It was named for Frank Hamner, a homesteader near Black Rock south of the butte.

Hampton, Lane County. This station on the Southern Pacific Cascade Line was established when the railroad was relocated around Lookout Point Lake. It was named for Harry A. Hampton, railroad division engineer from 1922 to 1943.

Hampton Butte, Deschutes County. Hampton Butte is really a group of dissected hills, part of which is in Crook County. The summit, with an elevation of 6333 feet, is apparently in Deschutes County. W. P. Vandevert of Bend told the compiler in 1926 that the butte was named for one Joe Hampton, who moved into Hampton Valley in the 1870s from near Eugene. There is a description of the butte in USGS Bulletin 252, which says that it was the result of explosive volcanic eruptions, which discharged acid lavas and probably furnished most of the material for the extended tuff sheets forming the surface of much of the adjacent country. The butte is of importance geologically and is well described in detail by Dr. I. C. Russell in the bulletin mentioned above. Hampton post office was established in 1911. A. S. Fogg, the first postmaster, suggested naming the office for the butte.

Hancock Creek, Clackamas County. Hancock Creek drains a small area east of Molalla. Its waters find their way into Molalla River. Isaac V. Trullinger is authority for the statement that a man named Hancock operated a small sawmill on the stream and the creek was named in compliment to him.

Handy, Marion and Clackamas counties. The post office called Handy had an interesting history from two distinct aspects. It was given a descriptive name by its enthusiastic promoters who did not wish to travel miles for their mail. Also, it was moved bodily from one county to another though the distance was not great. There have been several Oregon post offices that have appeared on the lists for two different counties but these situations have generally been the result of moving the county boundaries. In the case of Handy the office was moved. Handy post office was established April 18, 1896, on the Marion County list. Samuel Sweaney was the first postmaster. This office was moved to the Clackamas County list probably some time in September, 1898, and the new postmaster was Pearliette Killin. After this change the office went in service on the east side of Butte Creek near the Killin bridge. A little later Pearliette Killin became Mrs. Pearliette K. Pendleton. The office was discontinued in June, 1903, apparently as a result of the extension of rural delivery. The following quotation is from the editorial of the Canby *Herald* for June 17, 1948: "The post office was established in 1896 by Samuel Sweaney on the Marion County side of Butte Creek serving Union community. The Sweaneys named it Handy for the simple and logical reason that it was handy to have a post office there instead of having to traipse all the way to Woodburn to get the mail."

Haner Butte, Deschutes County. Haner Butte, west of Wickiup Reservoir, was named for Joseph H. Haner. He came to central Oregon in 1901 from Minnesota and was active for many years as a timber cruiser and fire patrol supervisor. When Deschutes County was formed in 1916 , Haner was the first county clerk. He died in 1953 at age 81.

Hanks Marsh, Klamath County. Hanks Marsh is on the east side of Upper Klamath Lake between Klamath Falls and Algoma. It was named for James L. Hanks, a second cousin of Abraham Lincoln, who was born in Illinois in 1820 and came west in 1853. He settled alongside Upper Klamath Lake in 1873 where he became a successful rancher and stockman.

Hanover, Baker County. Some of the place names in the early mining areas present problems that so far have been unsolved by the compiler. Such a case is that of Hanover post office, established November 3, 1888, with George L. Howard postmaster. The name of the office was changed to Cracker, February 2, 1889, and it may have been moved at that time. Hanover has been widely used as a place name in the United States, and the 1945 *Postal Guide* contains a list of more than twenty post offices with the title Hanover or some adaptation of it. It is not surprising that a place in Baker County was named Hanover but it is more than likely that the name was brought from some other state rather than directly from Germany. Hanover in Baker County was near the mouth of Silver Creek, where that stream flows into Cracker Creek, nearly two miles southwest of Bourne. This office was operated with the name Cracker until it was discontinued September 28, 1891. Cracker post office was obviously named for Cracker Creek, but the origin of that name is also a mystery to the writer.

Hansen Creek, Marion County. Hansen Creek is east of Detroit. It was named for Elijah S. Hansen who took up government land near its mouth in 1900.

Happy, Harney County. In the fall of 1916 plans were made to establish a post office called Happy, apparently in the hills just south of Happy Valley. Matilda McCrudden was appointed postmaster on November 16, 1916, but the office was never operated and there is no further record.

Happy Valley, Harney County. Mrs. Minerva J. Kiger, better known as Mrs. Dolly Kiger, of Corvallis, wrote in 1927: "George McCoy named Happy Valley. He said the settlers were so hospitable and happy." Mrs. Kiger lived near Steens Mountain from 1874 to 1878.

Harbor, Curry County. Harbor post office is where the old office of Chetco was once situated. The Chetco office was in operation from 1863 until 1910, in various places, and at one time was near the mouth of Chetco River at the present site of Harbor. Later it was moved southward several miles. When Harbor post office was established on November 24, 1894, the name Chetco could not be used because the Chetco office was then serving the locality near the Winchuck River. It is reported that the new name was taken from the title of the Chetco Harbor Land and Townsite Company. For the history of the name Chetco, see under Chetco River.

Hardesty Mountain, Lane County. This peak, elevation 4270 feet, is in township 20 south, range 1 east. The notes of A. J. Briem, early USFS ranger, on file at the Oregon Historical Society, state that it was named for Charles Hardesty who was elected Judge in 1854. Hardesty settled near Eugene in the early 1850s.

Hardin, Crook County. In June, 1946, John W. Biggs of Burns told the writer that this post office was named for Colonel Hardin, a stockman who operated extensively in central Oregon in partnership with Amos Riley. Riley post office in Harney County was named for the other partner. These two did not live in Oregon, according to Judge Biggs, who said they had headquarters at Santa Rosa, California. However, they spent a great deal of time in Oregon and had many friends in the cattle country. The history of Hardin post office is slightly perplexing. All old maps available to the writer show the office in the extreme east part of Crook County near Grindstone Creek, in the locality later known as Angell Ranch. However, the office was first established on the Grant County list on May 23, 1882, with Seth Bixby first postmaster. It was transferred to the Crook County list without date. William McLagan became postmaster July 6, 1887, and the office was closed July 31, 1890. The significance of the original listing in Grant County is not clear. If it was an error, that is an end to the business.

However, if the office was actually in what was then Grant County, the question arises as to whether it was in what is now Grant or what is now Harney. Grant, Harney and Crook counties come together in this locality. In early days the locality of Hardin was also called Twelvemile, probably because it was that distance from Paulina.

Harding, Clackamas County. George A. Harding, for more than half a century a much-respected resident of Oregon City, was born in Sydney, Australia, in 1843, and after a short visit in California, arrived in Oregon in 1857. He was a director of the Willamette Valley Southern Railway Company, and this station on that line was named for him on that account. He died September 23, 1926.

Harding Butte, Douglas County. Harding Butte is north of North Umpqua River near Illahee Rock. It was named in 1920 by USFS ranger Fred Asam for President-elect Warren G. Harding.

Hardman, Morrow County. Hardman is an old community. The post office was established in 1881. The place was named for a pioneer family engaged in the stock business. Dave Hardman was first postmaster.

Hardscrabble Hill, Linn County. Hardscrabble Hill is the northeast part of a butte about two miles southwest of Jefferson. Hardscrabble Hill itself has an elevation of 369 feet and is close to the west bank of Santiam River. This hill and other features in the state bearing the same name are so called because of the poor character of the soil and the difficulty of cultivating it. See also Hungry Hill and Needy.

Hardtack Island, Multnomah County. Hardtack Island is just southeast of Ross Island in Willamette River in the south part of Portland. It was once part of Ross Island, and probably still is at low water. It was known as Hardhack Island about 1905 on account of the *Spiraea douglasii* which grew there, but the influence of boating and yachting visitors overcame the botanical name and substituted one of nautical significance. Hardtack Island has been adopted as the official name by USBGN. See also under Ross Island. Riverward from the south end of Ross Island is a gravel bar which was platted in 1868-69 as Toe Island, because of its shape. The three islands of the Ross Island group were charted as Oak Islands by Wilkes in 1841. Henry E. Reed, who had a wide knowledge of Portland history, was of the opinion that the name Hardtack Island was probably originally applied to Toe Island because of the well-known difficulty in tacking or bringing a sail-boat about at that point on the river. Wind and currents were unobliging. There is not much of Toe Island left today. Whatever may have been the original application of the name Hardtack Island, it is now universally applied to the island southeast of Ross Island and east of what is left of Toe Island. The compiler remembers very well that about the beginning of the century the name Hardhack Island was used, but that name has not prevailed. The early plats show the name Ross Island covering both of the larger islands, Ross and Hardtack.

Hardy Creek, Lane County. Hardy Creek is a tributary of South Fork McKenzie River. It was named for Charles A. Hardy, an attorney of Eugene, who built a hunting and fishing lodge near the mouth of the stream. Hardy Ridge nearby derives its name from the same source.

Charles Albert Hardy was born in Michigan in 1874, graduated from the University of Wisconsin in 1896 and died at Portland on November 29, 1937.

Hare, Clatsop County. In the early 1890s Levi Knapp, well-known pioneer settler of Clatsop County, operated a country store in the woods east of Astoria at or near the place later called Svensen. For convenience of local residents, James W. Hare, then postmaster at Astoria, arranged for a post office in the Knapp store and also for a supply route from Astoria. The new office was given the name Hare in compliment to the man who was so helpful to the little community. It was established April 25, 1891, with Levi Knapp first postmaster. Victor H. Coffey carried the pouches from the river landing about a half mile to the store. Coffey became postmaster at Hare on May 8, 1893, about the time he took over the interest in the store. The office was either closed out to Svensen in 1895 or had its name changed to Svensen at that time, the compiler cannot tell which from the available records. The Svensen office records show that it was established August 15, 1895, with A. B. Coe first postmaster, but Coffey became postmaster on November 7, 1895, so to all intents the history of the two offices merged at that date. For additional information, see Astoria Column in Astoria *Astorian-Budget,* June 14, 1946.

Hare, Curry County. Hare post office was established April 21, 1898, in the extreme north part of the county about six miles east of Langlois on the road to Myrtle Point. The office was given the family name of the first postmaster, Joseph Hare. It was finally closed August 15, 1913. For short biography of Joseph Hare, see Dodge, *Pioneer History of Coos and Curry Counties,* appendix, page 47.

Harkens Lake, Benton County. This lake is about three miles northeast of Monroe. Its outlet is an intermittent stream flowing into Willamette River. Its elevation is 260 feet. It was named for a nearby settler.

Harl Butte, Wallowa County. Harl Butte is in the extreme northwest corner of township 3 south, range 48 east. It was named for John Harl who had a homestead near the foot of the butte.

Harlan, Lincoln County. James R. Harlan was one of the originators of the plan to secure a post office, and the office, when established about 1890, was named for him. He was first postmaster, according to information by the postmaster in 1926.

Harlow Crater, Lane County. This is one of the small craters southwest of Black Crater and north of the North Sister. Professor E. T. Hodge of the University of Oregon named it for M. H. Harlow, one time president of the McKenzie toll road project. See *Mount Multnomah,* page 112.

Harney County. Harney County has a land area of 10,132 square miles, and is the largest county in Oregon. It was created February 25, 1889, and was named for William Selby Harney who was appointed to the command of the Department of Oregon of the United States Army, in 1858, and was recalled in 1859, for his summary seizure of San Juan Island, from the British, in July, 1859. He served in the Black Hawk War, and the Mexican War, and was in command of Union forces in Missouri in the early part of the Civil War. He was breveted major-general in 1865. He was a noted Indian fighter, and was popular in the Pacific Northwest. He died

May 9, 1889. For obituary, see Scott's *History of the Oregon Country,* volume
V, page 212. Harney County was not named until after Harney Lake and
Harney Valley had been so called for a number of years, and the name of
the county was undoubtedly suggested by the name of those features.

Harney Lake, Harney County. The first written information about
Harney Lake is in Peter Skene Ogden's journal of his third Snake expedition, published in *OHQ* for June, 1910. On October 29, 1826, when the
expedition was not far from what is now known as Harney Valley, Ogden
wrote that Thomas McKay, who had been sent on in advance, rejoined the
party and reported the discovery of "a country of rivers and lakes, one of
the latter the water is salt." The entry for Tuesday, November 1, is: "At
sunset we reached the lakes. A small ridge of land an acre in width divides
the fresh water from the salt lakes. The two lakes have no intercourse. The
fresh water has an unpleasant taste 1 mile wide 9 long. In this [Malheur]
lake discharges Sylvailles River and 2 small forks; but it has no discharge.
Salt Lake at its south end is 3 miles wide. Its length at present unknown to
us but appears to be a large body of saltish water. All hands give it a trial but
none could drink it. . . . ." Subsequent entries give more information
about the lakes. There is no doubt in the mind of the writer that what
Ogden called Salt Lake is the Harney Lake of today, and the fresh water
lake is Malheur Lake. During certain stages Malheur Lake discharges into
Harney Lake, with the result that Harney Lake gradually tends to get more
alkaline. T. C. Elliott who edited the journals is slightly confused about the
lakes, and in a footnote states that Harney is not salt, which is incorrect. J. J.
Donegan of Burns told the writer that in the days of emigrations Harney
and Malheur were known as Bitter lakes. The Indian name for Harney
Lake is said to have been *Tonowama.* Harney Lake received its present name
on July 7, 1859. Captain H. D. Wallen of the Fourth Infantry, in charge of
a military expedition from The Dalles to Great Salt Lake, reached a body of
water which he described as measuring about twenty by nine miles, unfit to
drink. He applied the name Lake Harney in compliment to then Brigadier-
General W. S. Harney in charge of the Department of Oregon. Details of
this event are in 36th Congress, 1st Session, Senate Executive Document
34, which contains Wallen's report in full. Wallen mentions the sand ridge
or dike east of Harney Lake and recounts the discovery of "Lake Stampede," now Malheur Lake or its arm, Mud Lake. This water was potable
and he applied the name because his stock became unmanageable. Time
has brought a change in the name of the alkali lake from Lake Harney to
Harney Lake.

Harney Valley, Harney County. Harney Valley was named for Major-
General W. S. Harney. The valley is quite well defined, and has an average
elevation of about 4100 feet. The south part of the valley is occupied by
Harney and Malheur lakes and their surrounding marshes and meadows.
The main valley and adjoining tributary valleys have an area of about 750
square miles, for the most part quite level. The name was applied as the
result of the naming of Harney Lake or of the establishment of Fort Harney during the Snake War. See Bancroft's *History of Oregon,* volume II, page
488, *et seq.*

Harper, Malheur County. Harper is on the Malheur River and it has been a post office since 1913. Harper was named for the Harper Ranch of the Pacific Livestock Company on which it is situated. The ranch, in turn, took its name from one of the early settlers near the Malheur River.

Harper Bridge, Deschutes County. H. J. Overturf told the compiler in 1969 that this bridge over Deschutes River just below the mouth of Little Deschutes River was named for one Harper, an early homesteader.

Harper Creek, Lane County. This creek flows into Lookout Point Lake. It is named for John Harper who took up land near its mouth in the 1880s.

Harriet Lake, Clackamas County. Harriet Lake was named for the daughter of Franklin P. Griffith, the first president of Portland General Electric Company. It was formed when a predecessor company dammed Oak Grove Fork Clackamas River for hydro-electric power.

Harriman, Harney County. This place is just between Malheur Lake and Crane Creek Gap. H. Denman owned the land where this community developed, and when the Oregon Short Line Railroad Company began to build from Ontario into the Harney Valley, Denman named his place for Edward H. Harriman, the railroad magnate.

Harriman, Klamath County. Effective October 1, 1947, the name of the post office Rocky Point on the west shore of Upper Klamath Lake was changed to Harriman in compliment to the memory of Edward H. Harriman, the railroad man. For several years Mr. Harriman maintained a summer camp near this place and he was very much interested in the development of that part of Oregon. The post office at Rocky Point had several names. It was called Lawrentz, Recreation, Pelican Bay and Rocky Point and later Harriman until finally closed on February 15, 1954. The Harriman lodge was in this same locality but the compiler does not know if the various post offices and the lodge were in the same spot.

Harrington Creek, Douglas County. This creek in North Umpqua River drainage five miles northwest of Mace Mountain was named for Lee G. Herrington who took up timber claims in the vicinity just after the turn of the century.

Harris, Benton County. Harris was the name of the station served by Elam post office, not far from Philomath. The place has been a community since about 1890, and bears the name of a pioneer landowner. When the post office was petitioned for, residents asked that it be named Harris but postal authorities were afraid of confusion with Harrisburg, Linn County. For additional information see under Elam.

Harris Creek, Curry County. Harris Creek and Harris Beach State Park are both named for George S. Harris who was born in Perth, Scotland in 1836. After travelling to India and New Zealand, he came to the Pacific Coast in 1860 and settled in the Chetco country in 1871 where he bought several hundred acres along Harris Creek to run sheep. Harris died near Brookings on January 4, 1925.

Harris Creek, Josephine County. This is a small tributary of Jumpoff Joe Creek near Merlin. It bears the name of George W. Harris who took a donation land claim along its banks. Harris was killed by Indians on October 9, 1855, at the beginning of the Rogue River uprising.

Harrisburg, Linn County. Harrisburg was incorporated in 1866. Presumably it was named for Harrisburg, Pennsylvania. Some persons say the name was proposed by Hiram Smith, pioneer of 1853; others, by Asa A. McCully, pioneer of 1852. The locality was called Prairie Precinct in 1852. In that year D. and A. A. McCully started a store there. W. A. Forgey surveyed the site in 1853. At that time the place was named Thurston, and soon afterwards, Harrisburg. Thurston post office was established on December 31, 1853, with Gamaliel Parrish postmaster. Harrisburgh post office was established in November, 1855, but records show that Thurston post office was not closed until December 3, 1856. This inconsistency can not be explained nor do the records show clearly when the name was changed to Harrisburg.

Hart Mountain, Lake County. Hart Mountain is a prominent landmark on the east side of Warner Valley. It has an elevation according to the USC&GS of 8020 feet. Its western face is abrupt and impressive and the bold escarpment stands over 3,000 feet above the floor of Warner Valley. Near the foot of Hart Mountain is Hart Lake. Hart Mountain was at one time known as Warner Mountain. Wilson and Alexander established a ranch near the foot of the mountain and used a heart as a cattle brand. The vaqueros were not noted scholars and the ranch was immediately known as the Hart Ranch and has been so known ever since and Hart Mountain and Hart Lake derived their name from this source. It is not likely that the spelling will ever be changed, as the incorrect form is universally used.

Hartshorn Butte, Wallowa County. Hartshorn Butte is in sections 17 and 18, township 1 north, range 48 east. It was named for L. C. Hartshorn who ranged stock there in the 1890s. The butte was at one time called Masterson Butte for R. H. Masterson, but that name has fallen into disuse according to J. H. Horner of Enterprise.

Harvey Creek, Lane County. Mrs. R. L. Gawley who lived in Disston many years ago told the compiler in 1967 that this tributary of Layng Creek was named for the son of Elza Holderman, an early USFS ranger.

Harvey Creek, Yamhill County. Harvey Creek flows through the donation land claim of Andrew E. Hervey into Chehalem Creek at Newberg. Hervey was born in Pennsylvania and came to Oregon in 1852. He left Yamhill County prior to the Civil War and the present spelling came into general use.

Harvey Mountain, Lane County. This mountain was named for J. Roy Harvey, who was a pioneer forest officer in the Pacific Northwest. He served in many positions with the USFS. Harvey Mountain is about six miles southeast of Blue River.

Hascall Spring, Umatilla County. This spring is on upper Birch Creek drainage north of Granite Meadows. Charles Hascall was a well-known early settler and cattleman on Birch Creek.

Hash Rock, Crook County. Allan Hash was an early settler in central Oregon. See article by A. L. Veazie, *OHQ*, volume XXXIX, page 380. It may be assumed that Hash Rock, about 20 miles airline northeast of Prineville, was named for this man or one of his family.

Haskell Reservoir, Baker County. Haskell Reservoir is in Blue Canyon. It takes its name from Monroe Haskell who settled on the land before the turn of the century.

Haskin Butte, Wallowa County. Haskin Butte is in the south part of township 3 north, range 46 east. It bears the name of Robert J. Haskin, who took up a homestead in the neighborhood and ranged his stock there. The butte has also been called McKibbin and also Greenwood, but the style Haskin Butte has superseded the other forms. The name Haskins Butte is wrong.

Hastings Peak, Wasco County. Hastings Peak is six miles east of Antelope. It was named for James A. Hastings who took up a homestead near its base in 1915.

Hat Creek, Wallowa County. Hat Creek is in the southeast part of the county and flows into Snake River. It was named many years ago when Alex Warnock was riding an unruly pony and had his hat bucked off near this stream. That hat hung on a bush for some time and the stream was named on that account. Hat Point, a prominent peak near the headwaters of Hat Creek, was named for the stream.

Hat Rock, Crook County. Hat Rock is a descriptive name applied to a formation on the southeast slopes of Powell Buttes in the southwest corner of the county. This rock is near the middle of township 16 south, range 15 east. Hat Rock post office was named for this formation. The office was established September 6, 1910, with Louisa E. Becker postmaster. The office was closed November 18, 1911.

Hat Rock, Umatilla County. Hat Rock is a prominent monolith on the south shore of Lake Wallula nine miles east of Umatilla. Lewis and Clark mention a rock which resembled a hat in its shape under date of October 19, 1805. This is the earliest description but it reappears in many subsequent journals. In 1951 the property was aquired by the state and incorporated into Hat Rock State Park.

Hatfield Spring, Jefferson County. Hatfield Spring north of Teller Butte was named for the man who homesteaded the area in 1913, Ira J. Hatfield.

Hauser, Coos County. Hauser is a station on the line of the Southern Pacific Company north of Coos Bay. It was named for Eric V. Hauser of Portland. About 1914 Eric Hauser and his sons had a construction contract on the railroad. The community now known as Hauser was then called North Slough, but the name was changed to Hauser because the old name suggested miasmatic surroundings.

Hawkins Pass, Wallowa County. Albert Hawkins was for many years on the staff of the *Oregonian* before he died May 8, 1930. He was profoundly interested in Pacific Northwest history and geography and was a tireless pedestrian and climber in the most difficult circumstances. His enthusiasm for the Wallowa Mountains was immense, and on July 27, 1929, he was a member of a small party that climbed over a pass on the divide between Imnaha and the Wallowa drainage about three miles southeast of Eagle Cap. Shortly after his death a petition signed by various public officials and private citizens asked to have the pass named in his honor, which was done by USBGN. The compiler lists the pass in Wallowa County, but it is very close to the county line and in fact may be in Union County. For biography of Albert Hawkins, see the *Oregonian*, May 9, 1930.

Hawley Canyon, Jefferson County. Hawley Canyon was named for Henry Hawley who homesteaded east of Axehandle in 1912.

Hawley Creek, Lane County. William W. Hawley homesteaded near the present town of Dorena in 1883. He was a freighter to the Bohemia mines and the creek and butte near Dorena both bear his name.

Hawn Creek, Yamhill County. Hawn Creek flows into Yamhill River west of Lafayette. It was named for Jacob Hawn who settled near the present townsite in 1846. He operated a hotel and tavern and was first postmaster at Yam Hill Falls in 1850. The falls of Yamhill River are near the town of Lafayette and not downstream at Yamhill Locks.

Hawthorne, Douglas County. According to an article by Charles V. Stanton in the Roseburg *News-Review*, February 14, 1947, Hawthorne post office was on Calapooya Creek about fifteen miles east of Oakland, and was given the middle name of the postmaster, Erastus Hawthorne Cooper. The Hawthorne school was situated nearby. Hawthorne post office was established February 10, 1905, with Cooper first and only postmaster. It was closed July 20, 1911, with mail to Oakland. In February, 1947, Margaret Smith of Sutherlin wrote about the difficulties of mail service in the days before good roads. "The mail was delivered to Hawthorne each Tuesday and Saturday by Edgar L. Rone. He was assisted by the various youngsters of the neighborhood, who considered the trip to town and back a real privilege. Often the roads were impassable for wagons or hacks and the mail followed devious trails over hills and through fields on horseback. The boys were not afraid of fractious cayuses or roads of bottomless mud."

Hay Creek, Jefferson County. There are a number of Hay creeks in Oregon but the most important historically is the stream that drains a considerable area east of Madras and flows northward to Trout Creek. This Hay Creek was named in pioneer days in central Oregon on account of the fine natural forage that grew in its valley. It had a natural attraction for stockmen, many of whom had come into the area from Linn County and from other parts of the Willamette Valley. There are many references to the early history of Hay Creek in the *Illustrated History of Central Oregon,* page 699, *et seq.* Hay Creek post office was established on the Wasco County list in December, 1875, with Lafayette Tirrill postmaster. With one intermission this office continued in operation until July, 1920. It was east of Madras, though it may have been moved from time to time. For many years the famous Baldwin Sheep and Land Company had its headquarters at Hay Creek.

Hayden Creek, Wallowa County. This stream is tributary to Little Sheep Creek in township 2 south, range 46 east. B. T. Hayden settled near the mouth of the stream in the early 1880s and ranged stock on its banks and as a result, the creek bears his name.

Hayden Glacier, Deschutes County. This glacier is on the northeast slope of Middle Sister, and southeast of North Sister. It was named for Lieutenant E. E. Hayden, U.S.N., by Dr. I. C. Russell of the USGS. See USGS Bulletin 252, page 125. Edward Everett Hayden, born in Massachusetts April 14, 1858, was a member of the class of 1879 at the Naval Academy. He was ordered for special duty with the Smithsonian Institution and was attached to field parties of the Geological Survey in Nevada and Arizona in 1882, and visited the Cascade Range with J. S. Diller in 1883. The party fitted out for this trip at Red Bluff, California, and made a detailed inspection of many important localities, including Lassen Peak, Mount Shasta, Crater Lake and Mount Thielsen. While attempting to climb the Three Sisters, Ensign Hayden suffered a serious fall of some 200 feet. Diller got two men from camp and they started to carry the injured scientist to a place of safety. While this was being done a rock fell from the mountainside and struck Diller senseless. The packers took Diller to camp and Hayden had to lie out all night. After other adventures Hayden was finally landed at Prineville, where he was put on the stage and reached the hospital at Portland on September 22, 1883, fourteen days after the accident. On November 11 his left leg was amputated at the thigh and he was able to proceed to his home in the East on January 15, 1884. E. E. Hayden eventually became a rear admiral on the retired list and lived in Washington, D. C. He took part in much scientific work carried on by the Navy Department. He died in Baltimore on November 17, 1932, and was buried at Arlington National Cemetery.

Hayden Island, Multnomah County. Hayden Island was discovered on October 29, 1792, by W. R. Broughton, who reported the fact in the following language: "From Belle Vue point they proceeded . . ., passed a small wooded island, about three miles in extent, situated in the middle of the stream. Their route was between this island and the southern shore, which is low. . . . This obtained the name of *Menzies Island;* near the east end of which is a small, sandy woody island that was covered with wild geese." Broughton named this Goose Island on October 31. It is indeed unfortunate that the name of Archibald Menzies has not been perpetuated in Oregon geography. Memoir No. V of the Archives of British Columbia, entitled *Menzies' Journal of Vancouver's Voyage,* gives an excellent account of the great botanist and his work in the Pacific Northwest. Lewis and Clark reached Hayden Island on November 4, 1805, and named it Image Canoe Island, because of the presence of a canoe with carved images at the bow. It is perhaps not surprising that Thwaites confused Image Canoe Island with Wapato, now Sauvie Island, when he edited the Lewis and Clark journals, for while Lewis and Clark maps are quite clear, the text is somewhat perplexing. Gay Hayden, a pioneer of 1850, owned all of or part of this island in pioneer days, and it has borne his name ever since. He was for many years a resident of Clark County, Washington. Some maps show the names of Shaw Island and Vancouver Island, but the USBGN has decided against these forms. Dr. John Scouler used the name Menzies Island on May 2, 1825, when he and David Douglas made a short excursion from Fort Vancouver and found a number of interesting plants. See *OHQ,* volume VI, page 173.

Hayden Lake, Polk County. Hayden Lake is near the west bank of the Willamette River, two miles southwest of Eola. It was named for Benjamin Hayden, a picturesque pioneer lawyer of Oregon, who also achieved fame as a rustic raconteur. West of Hayden Lake is Hayden Slough and nearby in the Willamette River is Hayden Island, both of which were named for the same man.

Hayes Hill, Josephine County. Hayes Hill was in pioneer days a place that travelers had to reckon with, between Rogue River and Kerby. The road was steep and hard to negotiate. Hayes Hill was named for Jarvis Hayes, a pioneer settler nearby. For additional information about this locality and Fort Hayes, see Walling's *History of Southern Oregon,* page 452.

Hayesville, Marion County. Homer Simmons of Tillamook wrote the compiler in 1970 to give the following information regarding this community on old Portland Road just north of Salem. He stated that his wife's great grandfather, Adam Stephens, bought the surrounding property in 1849 for a rifle, a pony and $30.00. During the Hayes-Tilden campaign of 1876 the local residents voted to name the area in honor of Rutherford B. Hayes.

Hayland, Tillamook County. The compiler is of the opinion that Hayland was a natural, descriptive name, selected by Mr. and Mrs. Mulligan, local landowners, because of the low grassy meadows of several acres. Hayland post office was established April 16, 1888, with Mary J. Mulligan first and only postmaster. The office was discontinued September 26, 1888, with papers to Dolph. This office was at the place now known as Boyer, very close to the John Boyer monument on the Salmon River Highway. It is possible that John Boyer purchased the property from the Mulligans, although that is not certain.

Haynes Inlet, Coos County. Haynes Inlet is the large north arm of Coos Bay and is fed principally by Larson Slough and Palouse Creek on the east, and on the west it is joined but not exactly fed by North Slough. The mouth of the inlet is about a mile wide. The east shore of Haynes Inlet is traversed by the Oregon Coast Highway. Dodge, in his *Pioneer History of Coos and Curry Counties,* page 134, says that the inlet was named for Henry Haines, an early day settler who discovered coal near the present site of Glasgow, just south of the inlet. However, on page 16, Dodge spells the name Haynes. Whatever the facts are about the way that this pioneer spelled his name, the geographic feature has been called Haynes Inlet for many years and that is the style used on government maps.

Haypress Creek, Wheeler County. This creek flows into Double Corral Creek west of Derr Meadows. "*A History of the Ochoco National Forest,*" says that the stream flows through Haypress Meadows where soldiers from Camp Watson cut hay in the 1860s. Remains of an old haypress were still visible until the time of World War I.

Haystack, Jefferson County. Haystack post office was established on the Crook County list June 21, 1890, with Elijah McClenahan first postmaster. The office was a little to the north of Haystack Butte and was named for that mountain. This happened before Jefferson County was formed. Haystack office was finally closed out to Culver February 28, 1907. Culver post office had been established in 1900, only a little distance away, but apparently in a more strategic location. There was not enough business to support two offices.

Haystack Butte, Jefferson County. Haystack Butte bears a descriptive name, due to its shape. It has been so known for many years, and the territory near its base is known as Haystack country. The butte lies east of Juniper Butte, and The Dalles-California Highway passes through a saddle between them.

Haystack Creek, Wheeler County. Haystack Creek is not far from Spray. W. F. White, in a letter on the editorial page of the *Oregonian*, November 8, 1927, says this stream was named for a mound in a field at the Fleming and Wagner ranch. This mound resembled a haystack, both in size and form. Stories to the effect that the stream was named because it washed away a haystack do not seem to be substantiated.

Haystack Rock, Clatsop County. Haystack Rock is a prominent monolith on Cannon Beach which has done far more than its share to advertise Oregon. It is 235 feet high and for many years it has been a popular and favorite landmark on the Oregon coast. It very much resembles a haystack, hence its name. The compiler has no idea when it was named or who named it.

Haystack Rock, Tillamook County. About a mile southwest of Cape Kiwanda is a very prominent pinnacle known as Haystack Rock. It has an elevation of 327 feet and is considerably higher than the Haystack Rock on Cannon Beach. It bears a descriptive name. Davidson, in the *Coast Pilot*, 1889, says that Cape Kiwanda was once called Haystack Point because of its proximity to Haystack Rock.

Haystack Rock, Wallowa County. Haystack Rock is a prominent point in township 4 north, range 45 east. It was named because of its resemblance to a haystack.

Hayward, Washington County. The locality called Hayward is in sections 19 and 20 of township 2 north, range 4 west. It is northeast of Gales Creek and northwest of the Thatcher district. In the summer of 1948 Paul L. Patterson of Hillsboro was able to gather some interesting information about the name of this place. The story came from Nicklaus Bothman who homesteaded at what is now Hayward. There were several settlers and they got their mail at Greenville which was very inconvenient. An appeal was made to Binger Hermann, then representative in Congress from Oregon. Mr. Hermann was able to get the post office established and apparently suggested the name Hayward. It is said that Mr. Hermann called attention to the fact that there was a place called Hayward in almost every state of the Union and Oregon should have one too. The difficulty about this story is that there do not seem to have been many places called Hayward but that difficulty is not an objection to the theory that Mr. Hermann named the place. Mr. Bothman was willing to accept Mr. Hermann's suggestion, concluding that it would be better than to try to dig up a better name. A school district was formed and that was also named Hayward and later Mr. Bothman applied the name to the Hayward Cemetery where his little son was buried. As far as the compiler knows these names are still in use. Hayward post office was established December 19, 1891. Katie Bothman was the first postmaster. It was discontinued November 25, 1904, and the business turned over to Greenville.

Hayward Peak, Curry and Josephine counties. Hayward Peak bears the name of Stanton B. Hayward, a forester who served several years in the Siskiyou National Forest prior to his death on November 29, 1939. The peak is about 20 miles northwest of Kerby on the high divide south of Illinois River. It has an elevation of about 4300 feet. The name was adopted by the USBGN on December 4, 1941.

Hazel Mountain, Wallowa County. Hazel Mountain is in the northwest part of township 4 south, range 43 east. It was named for Hazel Taylor of Milton, Oregon, who at that time was camping nearby. The name was applied in August, 1913, by N. Jay Billings of the USFS.

Hazelau, Marion County. Hazelau was a station on the Oregon Electric Railway about two miles southeast of Salem. It was named by R. G. Halberg, a landowner nearby. The compiler is informed that Halberg was born in Hazelau, Germany, and he wished to perpetuate the name of his native town. Atlases do not give a Hazelau in Germany, but do show a Haslau in Bohemia.

Heather, Lane County. Heather is a station on the Cascade line of the Southern Pacific Company, named for the small plants that grow in the higher altitudes of Oregon. They are not true heather, although they are members of the *Ericaceae*, or heath family. These Oregon plants are *Phyllodoce*, and are low growing, with small, leathery evergreen leaves.

Hebo, Tillamook County. Hebo was named for Mount Hebo, an important peak in the Coast Range nearby. See under that name.

Heceta Head, Lane County. The following editorial by Harvey W. Scott, in the *Oregonian*, August 20, 1895, effectively sums up Heceta's claim to fame: "The Columbia River was first seen by civilized man August 17, 1775. Captain Bruno Heceta, commanding the Spanish corvette *Santiago*, in a voyage along the coast from Mexico, noticed an opening in the coast from which rushed a current so strong that he could not enter. His nautical observations, published with his report, show that the position of his ship was within one minute of the latitude of Cape Disappointment, which he called Cape San Roque. The smoke from forest fires then was not so thick as now, though it was the same time of year; for Heceta saw clearly the distant mountains. Heceta Head, further down the coast, perpetuates his name." There are several accounts of the voyage of Bruno de Hezeta (Anglicized spelling Heceta). The best summary is that of H. R. Wagner in *Cartography of the Northwest Coast of America*, volume I, page 175. *California Historical Quarterly*, volume IX, page 201, *et seq.*, contains Fr. Sierra's account. See also under Cape Falcon and Columbia River. Heceta commented on shallow water some distance off-shore from what is now known as Heceta Head. Soundings by the USC&GS confirmed this discovery, and as a result, in 1862, George Davidson of the Coast Survey named Heceta Head and also suggested the name Heceta Bank. Both of these names were adopted by the government and have come into universal use, thus complimenting the Spanish navigator. The name Heceta is frightfully mispronounced on some parts of the Oregon coast, where it is called Heketa, with a strong accent on the first syllable. In Castillian the pronunciation would be *Ay-thay-tah,* with the accent on the second syllable. This sound is a little difficult for Oregonians, most of whom seem to have Anglicized the word into *Heseta,* with the accent on the second syllable. Doubtless that style will prevail. There was a post office called Heceta but it has been discontinued.

Heckletooth Mountain, Lane County. Mrs. Lina A. Flock of Oakridge, member of a pioneer family of the neighborhood, wrote the compiler in 1927 that this mountain, four miles east of Oakridge, was named by her grandmother, Mrs. Elizabeth Stuart Warner, about 1872, because of the tall rocks with which it is surrounded near the summit. These resemble the teeth of a heckle, an instrument for handling flax.

Heflin Creek, Crook and Wheeler counties. This creek bears the name of Miles Heflin who homesteaded west of West Branch in 1900.

Hehe Butte, Wasco County. There are a number of geographic features in Oregon named *Hehe,* the Chinook jargon for laughter or fun. The name is applied to a creek, trail and mountain in Lane County, and doubtless elsewhere. Indians used the name for places, not in the sense of funny, but because of the presence of good spirits, Hehes, in contrast to the Skookums, which were powerful and evil wood-gods. Hehe localities were considered good places to visit, and they were especially used for religious festivities, games and horseracing. The compiler has been informed by Indians that the locality of Hehe Butte on Warm Springs Indian Reservation was a place of good spirits and was used for contests of various sorts.

Heisler, Jefferson County. William Heisler was one of the prominent pioneer operators in central Oregon and Heisler post office on Hay Creek northeast of Madras was named for him. This office was established in May, 1905, with Alfred R. Lyle first postmaster. The office operated, but not continuously, until May, 1910. William Heisler opened a store in Prineville in 1871, and was a contemporary of Barney Prine. He was appointed first postmaster at Prineville, then called Prine, in April, 1871. In October, 1878, he was appointed postmaster at Trout Creek, an office whose name was changed to Cross Keys in February, 1879. He was active in various enterprises in what are now Crook and Jefferson counties, and later in Wasco County. For a detailed biography, see *Illustrated History of Central Oregon,* page 255.

Held, Crook County. Held post office was on the upper reaches of Bear Creek and south of Maury Mountains. It was named for Paul Held, the first postmaster, and had a relatively short life during the homesteaders' era. The office was established May 1, 1909, and was discontinued May 15, 1919.

Helix, Umatilla County. Helix post office was established on May 6, 1880, with Mary Ann Simpson postmaster. The name first selected was Oxford, but postal authorities objected because of possible confusion with similar names elsewhere. In 1927 the writer was told that W. B. Henderson selected the name Helix, but the reason given was not plausible. Since then additional information has come to light that indicates that the place was named because a local resident had a painful experience with an infection in the helix of his ear. The testimony is not as conclusive as it might be, but is probably true. In July, 1942, W. H. Morrison of Pendleton, who lived in Helix when he was a boy, informed the compiler that in early days Dr. John

Griswold was a prominent resident of Helix, and at a community meeting told the audience that about the time the post office was established, one of his patients developed a very sore ear and had to be taken to Pendleton for treatment. The patient was either Henderson or Peter Hjelseng. During a consultation with another doctor in Pendleton, the word helix was mentioned, and the sick man thought it would be a fine name for the proposed office. In November, 1927, H. V. Christensen of Helix, wrote the compiler and described the event. In April, 1942, Dr. F. W. Vincent of Pendleton visited Helix at the request of the compiler and made inquiries about the matter. He was told the story of the infected ear and was informed that Henderson was the patient. Dr. F. A. Kiehle of Portland told the compiler that he heard this story after he came to Oregon in 1908 from the secretary of one of the medical societies. Reports that Henderson's first name was Helix have not been substantiated.

Hellgate Canyon, Josephine County. Because of inadequate communications, the physical characteristics of Hades are unknown. However, this appears to act as a stimulant to the use of "hell" as part of the name of many rough terrain features. Hellgate Canyon is a typical tortuous constriction of Rogue River five miles west of Merlin. The form Hellsgate is wrong.

Helloff Creek, Tillamook County. Helloff Creek flows into Nehalem River from the north near Rector, and got its odd name because the rough area along the banks of the stream presented such difficulties to cruisers and loggers. There is a little flat near the mouth of the creek, which was said to be just off hell. When a logging camp was established on the flat, it was called Helloff, and that name was used for the post office, which was established January 17, 1920, with Francis E. Hays first of four postmasters. The office was closed March 31, 1924, and little evidence remains of the place.

Hells Canyon, Baker and Wallowa counties. Prior to 1950 this name was applied to a rough, deep canyon that empties into Snake River in township 3 south, range 49 east. In the 1950s Wallowa County and the Snake River gorge were popular topics and the subject of several Sunday Supplement promotions. A touch of sensationalism was necessary and the publicists applied the name Hells Canyon to the valley of Snake River from about the present site of Oxbow Dam to the mouth of Grande Ronde River. Regardless of accuracy, the name is now in general use and the OGNB recognized this in December, 1970, when they voted to change the name of the original Hells Canyon to Hells Canyon Creek. The compiler of the fourth edition has a substantial file by the late Lewis A. McArthur protesting this name transfer, but feels that only a token objection can be taken to this *fait accompli*. It is doubtful that this will contribute much to the peace of mind of the departed.

Helmick Hill, Polk County. Helmick Hill is just west of the point where the Pacific Highway West crosses Luckiamute River. It was named for Henry Helmick, a pioneer of 1845, who with his wife Sarah took up a donation land claim on the Luckiamute in 1846. Their home was at the base of the hill. Helmick died in 1877. In 1924 Mrs. Helmick presented to the state land adjacent to the highway for a park which was dedicated with appropriate honors, and named Helmick Park. She celebrated her 100th birthday on July 4, 1923. For information about the Helmick family and the park see *OHQ*, December, 1925.

Helms Canyon, Sherman County. Helms Canyon is three miles east of Rufus. It was named for C. I. Helms who had a horse ranch there in the early days. When the homesteaders began to arrive in the 1880s, Helms picked up and left for the Grand Coulee country. The compiler thinks he must have wanted his solitude in monumental doses if he left Sherman County in 1880 because of overpopulation.

Helvetia, Washington County. Helvetia is a community on North Plains. Several Swiss families settled in the neighborhood and gave the place the Latin or Roman name of their mother country. For story of the early history of the community, see the Hillsboro *Argus*, December 31, 1931. It is said that David Tschabold moved to adopt the name Helvetia at a meeting of the local school board in 1892.

Hembree, Tillamook County. The post office serving the Sand Lake section was first called Hembree, in compliment to a local resident. Hembree post office was established July 10, 1890, with Absalom J. Hembree first postmaster. The name of the office was changed to Sandlake on January 18, 1898. The writer does not know to what extent it may have been moved around the neighborhood.

Hemlock, Tillamook County. There are a number of geographic features in Oregon named for the hemlock tree, which is an important part of our forests. The place in Tillamook County, which has been discontinued as a post office, was named for the western hemlock, *Tsuga heterophylla,* which grows in great abundance in the Coast Range. It is a fine large tree, growing 160 feet high, and even taller, and is characteristic of the middle, moist, forest zone, on western slopes, but is not common east of the Cascade Range. The other variety of hemlock in Oregon is known as mountain or black hemlock, *Tsuga mertensiana,* and is an alpine tree with little resemblance to the western hemlock. It has drooping slender branches, and its height is not often more than 60 feet. It grows near the timber line, and is not often found below 4000 feet in the Cascade Range, and in other mountains in eastern Oregon. It prefers a north exposure, and will endure dense shade. It grows in Oregon above 8000 feet. See Sudworth's *Forest Trees of the Pacific Slope*. The mountain hemlock has a rather larger cone than the western hemlock. Its leaves are rounded and plump looking, differing in this respect from other hemlocks. The leaves of the western hemlock are flat and grooved.

Hemstad, Deschutes County. According to Robert W. Sawyer of Bend, Hemstad post office was named for a local homesteader, Olaf Hemstad. The office was near the middle of the northeast quarter of township 22 south, range 16 east, near the south boundary of Deschutes County, east of the Paulina Mountains and about fifteen miles southeast of Millican. The post office was established December 8, 1917, with Frank P. Drake first and only postmaster. It was discontinued November 15, 1918.

Henderson Creek, Lincoln County. Henderson Creek flows into the Pacific Ocean about two miles south of Yaquina Bay. The Oregon Coast

Highway crosses the creek a little to the northeast of the old Lifesaving Station which is near the beach. In 1945 Mr. Andrew L. Porter of Newport told the writer that the stream was named for a nearby landowner who had moved away some years before.

Henkle Butte, Deschutes County. Jeremiah E. Henkle was born in 1843 and came to Oregon when he was ten years old. He spent most of his life in Benton County, where he was well known. He enlisted in Company A of the First Volunteer Infantry in December, 1864, and served at Vancouver Barracks and at Fort Yamhill. The company left Fort Yamhill on September 4, 1865, and arrived at Camp Polk near what is now the town of Sisters, on September 23, 1865. Henkle spent the winter at the camp and was mustered out on June 30, 1866. See Oregon Adjutant General's *Report,* 1865-66, and also story by Fred Lockley, editorial page, *Oregon Journal,* June 25, 1935, which contains more data about Henkle. Henkle Butte, elevation 3390 feet, is on the north side of Squaw Creek about two miles northeast of the site of Camp Polk. In February, 1943, Billy Wilson of Sisters, then 86 years old and in good health, recalled the story of the naming of the butte. Wilson said the commanding officer at the camp put up a prize for the soldier who made the round trip from camp to the butte in the shortest time and Jerry Henkle won the race. The point has borne his name since that time. The spelling Hinkle is wrong.

Henline Mountain, Marion County. Henline Mountain is about 12 miles northeast of Mill City, near Little North Santiam River. It was named for an early settler who was interested in a mining enterprise nearby.

Henry Creek, Wallowa County. Henry Creek drains into Imnaha River in township 4 south, range 48 east, opposite the mouth of Crazyman Creek. It was named for an Indian who camped near its mouth.

Henry Creek, Yamhill County. Henry Creek flows into Yamhill River just east of Lafayette. It was named for Anson B. Henry who owned much of the land along its banks. Henry was born in New York about 1830 and came to Oregon in 1852 with Anson G. Henry who was probably his uncle.

Henryville, Coos County. In 1874 coal mining operations were undertaken on the east side of Isthmus Slough on or near the Charley Wheeler place about midway between what are now known as the Coos City bridge and Delmar. A Dr. Henry was one of the main promoters of this mining activity, and at first the mine held considerable promise of success. However, the success was not achieved. For a short history of the enterprise, see Dodge's *Pioneer History of Coos and Curry Counties,* page 425. The mining activity called for a post office, and one was established with the name Henryville on January 28, 1875, with Stephen D. Megeath first and only postmaster. The office was closed April 7, 1876. The office was apparently named for the Dr. Henry mentioned above.

Heppner, Morrow County. Named for Henry Heppner. He and Jackson L. Morrow opened the first merchandise store there, in 1873. The county was created and named in 1885. The town of Heppner was founded in 1873 (*Oregonian,* September 15, 1877, page 2). Morrow settled at Scott Prairie, near Shelton, Washington, in 1853, and was one of the founders of Tumwater. In 1855-56 he served in Captain Swindall's company in the

Indian war. Heppner died at Portland February 16, 1905, aged seventy-six years (biography and portrait, *ibid.,* February 18, 1905). Destruction of a large part of the town of Heppner June 14, 1903, by flood, was one of the great tragedies of Oregon. Heppner post office was established February 3, 1873, with George H. Stansbury first postmaster. The post office has been in continuous operation. The earlier history of this office is confusing. It was first established on the Wasco County list with the name Butter Creek and with Stansbury postmaster. That was on June 3, 1872. It was later put on the Umatilla County list, and was on that list when the name was changed to Heppner. How the name Butter Creek happened to be applied to the office now called Heppner is hard to understand, as Heppner is a long way from Butter Creek. It is possible that Stansbury's office was actually on Butter Creek and he moved it bodily to a new location. Another office was established on Butter Creek on July 28, 1873, with John S. Vinson postmaster. That was at the place later known as Vinson, in Umatilla County. The new Butter Creek office may have followed the desertion by Stansbury.

Hereford, Baker County. At the time this community was being formed, it is said a Hereford bull was led through the settlement, and as the local residents were mostly interested in stock, someone suggested Hereford as the best name for the place.

Herlihy Canyon, Klamath County. Herlihy Canyon is just east of Algoma. It was named for Stephen Herlihy who had a ranch and kept a hotel and stable on the old Fort Klamath road just after the turn of the century.

Herling, Jackson County. A post office with the name Herling was established on the Jackson County list on July 26, 1888, with Henry A. Bauten postmaster. It was discontinued on July 9, 1895, with papers to Jacksonville. Herling was the family name of people who lived about four miles southwest of Jacksonville on the road to Ruch, and the office was at the Herling place. The Ruch office had not yet been established. The Herling house was burned about the time the office was closed, and the Ruch office was established a couple of years later to take care of local postal needs.

Herman Creek, Hood River County. Investigations by H. H. Riddle of Portland indicate that the spelling Herman is correct, Hermann is wrong. The stream was named for an early settler, James H. Herman.

Herman Creek, Lane County. Herman Creek flows southward near the east line of township 16 south, range 10 west, into Indian Creek, a little to the northwest of Reed. It was named in compliment to Binger Hermann, prominent Oregon pioneer and for many years a representative in Congress from this state. The name was applied by Stephen Milledge, a local resident. There is a minor discrepancy in the spelling, but the form Herman has been so long in use that it will probably not be changed.

Hermann, Lane County. Hermann was a post office in western Lane county north of Mapleton and always at or near the main fork of Indian Creek. The office was named for Binger Hermann, Coos County pioneer, and for many years a representative in Congress from Oregon. He was in

Congress at the time the office was established and doubtless was of some assistance in getting the installation. Hermann post office was established June 26, 1889, with Mrs. Laura J. Dickey first of four postmasters. The office was closed March 16, 1900, with papers to Mapleton. There is still a Herman School at the forks of Indian Creek, but the spelling has been slightly changed. In 1906 a post office called Belle was established to serve the area, but it was closed in 1908.

Hermansville, Coos County. Hermansville post office was situated about seven miles south of Myrtle Point on South Fork Coquille River and was named in compliment to Dr. Henry H. Hermann, one of the most prominent of the Coos County pioneers. Dr. Hermann was the prime mover in the Baltimore Company, an organization that came to Oregon by Panama in 1859. See Dodge's *Pioneer History of Coos and Curry Counties,* page 390. For biography of Dr. Hermann, *ibid.,* Biographical Appendix, page 41. It will be noticed that there is a slight discrepancy in the spelling of Dr. Hermann's name and the name of the post office, Hermansville. The compiler has been unable to get satisfactory early history of this post office. Levi Gant was the first postmaster, but the year of establishment is uncertain, apparently prior to 1872. With one intermission the office operated until October 17, 1881. A. H. Bender of Myrtle Point, a grandson of Dr. Hermann, has been kind enough to furnish the compiler with information about several Coos County geographic names.

Hermiston, Umatilla County. Hermiston was named by Colonel J. F. McNaught, a pioneer settler in the community. The name was suggested by Robert Louis Stevenson's unfinished novel, *Weir of Hermiston.* Colonel McNaught liked the sound of the name, and found that it did not duplicate any other post office name in the United States. The railroad station at Hermiston was originally called Maxwell probably after A. L. Maxwell, who was at one time a passenger traffic official of the railroad company. Postal authorities would not accept the name Maxwell as a post office name because of duplication, and it was for this reason that Colonel McNaught picked out a new name.

Hershal, Baker County. A. C. Moore wrote in the *Oregonian,* December 13, 1926, editorial page, that this place was named for Dr. Herschel E. Currey, a physician of Baker. It was at one time known as Currey, but the post office was later called Hershal. The office was discontinued in 1928. For biography of Dr. Herschel Eugene Currey, see Gaston's *Centennial History of Oregon,* volume II, page 12. The compiler does not know why the post office name was spelled differently from the doctor's name.

Hess Creek, Yamhill County. This stream is at Newberg. It was named for a pioneer settler, who operated a mill nearby. The forms Hess Branch, Hess Mill Creek, Joseph Hess Mill Branch and Mill Creek are incorrect. The government has officially adopted the name Hess Creek as reflecting the general local use. Alexander Henry visited the vicinity of Hess Creek on January 24, 1814. See *OHQ,* volume XXV, pages 308-11.

Hewett Boulevard, Multnomah County. Hewett Boulevard is west of Council Crest, and connects Green Hills with Sylvan. It was named for Henry Hewett, a pioneer grain merchant and insurance man of Portland.

Mr. Hewett was born at Hunters Hill, near Gateshead, County Durham, England, January 15, 1847. He came to the Pacific Coast about 1864, and settled in Portland in 1870, and in the following year shipped the first cargo of wheat that ever went from Portland to the United Kingdom. He later extended his activities to include marine insurance, and was for many years Lloyd's agent in Portland. He lived for a time at Twentieth and Glisan streets in Portland, where the Couch School now stands, and personally planted many of the shrubs now standing in the school yard. In 1888 he moved to the hills west of Council Crest and developed a country place, setting out many shrubs and trees brought from abroad. In the later years of his life he devoted himself entirely to the insurance business. He possessed a great fund of information about the marine history of the Pacific Coast. He died at his home on Green Hills February 16, 1915.

Hibbard Gulch, Baker County. Hiatt in *Thirty One Years in Baker County,* page 19, says that Mr. Hibbard arrived in 1863 and took up a claim near Morrison. This was southeast of Pocahontas and obviously near the gulch which bears his name.

Hickman Lake, Clackamas County. This lake and other geographic features in the northeast corner of the county were named for Orre Hickman, a guard in the early days of the USFS.

Hiddensprings, Harney County. Hiddensprings post office was established June 21, 1916, with Mary E. O'Malley postmaster. The name is descriptive of a spring near what is known as Clover Swale, a range district on the desert about twenty miles south of Harney Lake.

Hideaway Falls, Clackamas County. This one hundred foot high falls on Tumbling Creek is about two thirds of a mile above Salmon River. It is one of a group of seven falls in the area and was named because it is so difficult to see even when one is directly in front. For details of this group see under Stein Falls.

High Camp, Clackamas County. This point is near North Fork Molalla River. Dee Wright, a native of Molalla, told the compiler that the camp was originally established by the Ogle family, pioneers of the Molalla Valley, and they gave the camp its descriptive name.

High Desert, Deschutes and Lake counties. Early maps bear such names as Great Sandy Desert and Rolling Sage Plains, descriptive of that part of Oregon which is traversed by the Central Oregon Highway near the southeast corner of Deschutes County. Today the name High Desert is universally used, in contradiction to the Low Desert further south. The line of demarcation of the two deserts is not well defined, and the difference in elevation does not amount to a thousand feet.

Highland, Clackamas County. The Highland district is about eight or ten miles southeast of Oregon City, and Highland Butte, elevation 1728 feet, is within the area. Godfried Wallace, the first postmaster at Highland, is said to have originated the name, but whether first applied to the butte or the area, is unknown to the writer. Highland post office was established February 21, 1870, with Wallace first postmaster. The office was in service until after the turn of the century, but the compiler has not been able to learn the exact date it was closed. The name Highland for the district is in general use.

Hildebrand, Klamath County. This post office was first established with the name Edgewood in August, 1890, and with Newton F. Hildebrand first postmaster. The name of the office was changed to Hildebrand in December of the same year. From October, 1919, until May, 1923, the name of the office was Hilderbrand, but the error was corrected. This office has not operated continuously and as with other early-day post offices, it may not always have been in the same place.

Hilgard, Union County. Hilgard was apparently named for Eugene W. Hilgard, Dean of the College of Agriculture at the University of California. He was a cousin of Henry Villard who built the railroad over the Blue Mountains and was engaged by Villard in the early eighties to make an agricultural survey of the area. A post office with the name Dan was established in this locality July 9, 1883, with George A. Steel postmaster. The name of the office was changed to Hilgard August 23, 1883, when Hilgard, a well-known individual, was in the Northwest. For information on Villard see under Villard Glacier.

Hilliker Gulch, Wallowa County. This gulch in township 4 north, range 48 east, was probably named for some early day miner. J. W. McClaren stated in 1965 that he purchased the Hilliker claim from the Eureka Mining Co. and that Hilliker was gone prior to 1918.

Hillman Peak, Crater Lake National Park, Klamath County. This peak is at the west edge of Crater Lake, and is the highest point on the rim above the lake, with an elevation of 8156 feet. It was at one time known as Maxwell Peak, for Sir William F. Maxwell, of Edinburgh, Scotland, who explored the Crater Lake region in 1871. It was later called Glacier Peak because on its slopes were found the first evidences of glacial scratchings, indicating the occurence of glacial action on Mount Mazama. Finally the USBGN adopted the name Hillman Peak, in honor of John W. Hillman, who was one of the party that discovered Crater Lake on June 12, 1853.

Hills Creek, Lane County. This stream flows into Middle Fork Willamette River at Jasper. It bears the name of Cornelius J. Hills, who came to Oregon from Herkimer County, New York. He is reported as having crossed the plains three times. He was the father of Jasper Hills. See Walling's *History of Lane County*, page 490.

Hills Creek, Lane County. This stream is an important tributary of Middle Fork Willamette River, which it joins about four miles southeast of Oakridge. It drains a large area south of Salt Creek. It was named for John H. Hill, who settled near its mouth about 1870. At that time he was about 38 years old. His wife was generally known as Aunt Phoebe. The Hills had a ranch and kept the travel, and John Hill spent a substantial part of his time hunting and fishing. This stream should not be confused with Hills Creek, near Jasper, which was named for Cornelius J. Hills. A post office called Hill was in operation from June, 1882, to December, 1885, with John H. Hill postmaster. Hills Creek Dam and Reservoir on Middle Fork Willamette River were named because the damsite is just downstream from the former creek mouth. The earth fill dam is 304 feet high, stores 250,000 acre feet of water and has two 15,000 kilowatt generators.

Hillsboro, Washington County. Hillsboro was named for David Hill who was born in Connecticut in 1809 and came to Oregon in 1842. He was at the Champoeg meeting on May 2, 1843. He settled at the site of Hillsboro at least as early as 1845 and represented Twality in the provisional legislature in 1847. He died May 9, 1850. Hillsboro was formerly spelled Hillsborough. Prior to 1849 the place was called Columbia and Columbus. The *Oregon Spectator,* on January 10, 1849, mentions Hillsborough, and Abraham Sulger as having a store there. On January 10, 1850, the place was still referred to as Hillsborough. An early name of the locality was East Tualatin Plain; that of the Forest Grove locality, West Tualatin Plain. Postal authorities inform the compiler that Hillsborough post office was established August 5, 1850, with Abraham Sulger first postmaster. The early abbreviation of the name of the place seems to have been Hillsboro', rather than Hillsboro. Hillsborough post office was discontinued March 30, 1855, reestablished October 3, 1855, and changed to Hillsboro on April 20, 1892.

Hillsdale, Multnomah County. Hillsdale is a suburban community in southwest Portland. When the Southern Pacific Company West Side branch railroad was operated through Hillsdale, the company found it inadvisable to use the name Hillsdale for the station because of possible confusion with Hillsboro on the same line. The station was named Bertha for Mrs. Richard Koehler, wife of the railroad manager. The track has been torn up and Bertha station is no more. The name Hillsdale has been in use since pioneer days, and is quite suitable for the place. Hill is from the old Anglo-Saxon *hyl,* and Norse *holl.* Dale means a small valley. It comes from the same source as dell, and the German *thal* and Slavonic *dol.*

Hillside, Douglas County. Hillside post office was established March 20, 1891, with George N. Elliot postmaster. The office was closed on August 26 of the same year. An editorial in the Roseburg *News-Review* of February 14, 1947, says that the office was situated on the Oakland-Elkton road in the Kellogg district. The editorial goes on to say that the Ross Hutchinson home was either on or near the site of the Hillside post office.

Hillside, Washington County. Hillside is a community seven miles northwest of Forest Grove. The school district was organized in 1869 and the Congregational Church in 1884. The first pastor of the church was the Reverend Horace Lyman who was also first Superintendent of Schools in Washington County in 1850. The name comes, of course, from the local topography. This information was supplied by L. E. Bamford of Forest Grove.

Hilton Ridge, Wallowa County. Hilton Ridge is in the extreme northwest part of township 3 north, range 47 east. Hilton Creek is nearby. These two features were named for James Hilton, a little Englishman who ranged his horses in the vicinity. He had a homestead on Pine Creek.

Hines, Harney County. Fred Herrick, a sawmill operator, founded the Fred Herrick Lumber Company and promoted the railroad north of Burns. The mill was just southwest of Burns, and a community was established with the name Herrick. In 1928 Edward Hines of Chicago bought the railroad and lumber business and in 1940 it was operated with the name Edward Hines Lumber Company. A post office called Hines serves the mill and the nearby community.

Hinkle, Umatilla County. Hinkle Freight Classification Yard is the principal northwest switching point for the Union Pacific Railroad. When the Oregon Railway & Navigation Company line was completed to Huntington in 1884 it branched off the Spokane line at Umatilla, Oregon and followed the Umatilla River to Pendleton. About 1915 a cutoff was built from Boardman that rejoined the main line at Hinkle. A station was needed and Joseph T. Hinkle, an early day Umatilla County attorney, sold the railroad .05 acres of land. He thus unknowingly assured himself a prominent place in local geography for while Hinkle languished in obscurity for a third of a century, it sprang into prominence when the completion of McNary Dam in 1951 required relocation of the tracks along the Columbia River. The Union Pacific then located a major yard at this junction and in 1976 began the expansion to its present importance. The Portland *Daily Journal of Commerce* for June 27, 1978, has a feature article including pictures. Joseph Hinkle died about 1933.

Hinkle Butte, Jefferson County. This butte near Horse Heaven Mine has an elevation of 3832 feet. It bears the name of William S. Hinkle who bought government land there in 1879.

Hinton Creek, Lane County. Ray Engels of McKenzie Bridge told the writer in 1971 that this stream in the upper Separation Creek drainage was named for Jim Hinton, an early sheep man.

Hinton Creek, Morrow County. Hinton Creek flows into Willow Creek at Heppner. It was named for John T. Hinton who settled five miles east of Heppner in 1864.

Hipower Creek, Douglas County. This creek rises south of Chilcoot Mountain and flows south into Canton Creek. In the early 1920s USFS rangers Fred Asam and Ed Lough were locating trail. They found themselves in this steep, rugged area and one remarked to the other: "It would take a high-powered man to get through this." At the end of their journey the name seemed even more appropriate so the stream was called Highpower Creek. It was subsequently shortened to the present form.

Hipp, Benton County. Hipp was the name of the post office that served the community of Alder. Postal authorities would not accept the name of Alder for a post office because of confusion with many other offices of that name. The name Hipp was suggested by L. M. Roser who was office manager of the Climax Lumber Company mill nearby. The compiler is informed that the name Hipp was made up from the initials of the given names of members of the families owning the mill. Hipp post office was established April 18, 1922, with Efrann Anderson first postmaster. Roser was the second postmaster, and Rufus E. Wood held the position when the office was closed January 15, 1930.

Hirsch Reservoir, Deschutes County. This reservoir northeast of Millican near West Butte was apparently named for Max Hirsch who homesteaded nearby.

Hiyu Mountain, Clackamas and Hood River counties. This mountain is just south of Bull Run Lake. Its name is the Chinook jargon word for much, or plenty, and is used to indicate that the mountain is large. There is a Hiyu Ridge in Lane County south of South Fork McKenzie River.

Hoaglin, Douglas County. The name Hoaglin is said to be of Indian origin. The writer was informed by the postmaster at Hoaglin in 1926 that the name had been used for the post office since about 1898. A nearby Indian told the postmaster that the word meant some sort of medicine. There is a community Hoaglin in Van Wert County, Ohio, and it is quite possible that the name of the place in Oregon came from that source. The name of the Oregon post office was changed to Idleyld Park on December 1, 1932.

Hobo Lake, Wallowa County. Hobo Lake is in township 3 south, range 43 east. In early days Robert B. Bowman and others found a hobo camped at this lake, apparently living quite happily. They were not able to learn his identity. The lake has been known as Hobo Lake ever since.

Hobsonville, Tillamook County. In 1927 Miss Lucy Doughty of Bay City wrote the compiler as follows: "John Hobson and family were among the pioneers of Clatsop Plains. About the year 1885 Messrs. Hobson and Leinenweber of Astoria, erected a salmon cannery at the place since called Hobsonville. Frank Hobson, son of the Mr. Hobson mentioned above, came here about the time the cannery was built, and still lives at Garibaldi."

Hoevet, Tillamook County. Hoevet was a post office serving the extreme west part of Wheeler. This was the location of the original Wheeler post office but about 1931 the Wheeler office was moved eastward to the business district of the community at the request of local residents. This was done with the provision that an office would be provided to serve the Wheeler lumber mill and its employees, all in the west part of town. The new office was named Hoevet for C. R. Hoevet, at that time manager of the mill.

Hoffman Dam, Crook County. According to Phil Brogan of Bend, this irrigation diversion dam on Crooked River four miles below Prineville Reservoir was built by Jim Hoffman, an early day rancher.

Hog Hollow, Umatilla County. Judge John F. Kilkenny told the author the early legend regarding the name of this canyon just south of Vinson. An emigrant train strayed from the Oregon Trail and during their wanderings a band of hogs escaped near this canyon. In time they turned wild and provided both food and sport for the chase.

Hogan, Douglas County. Hogan post office was established May 18, 1887, with James McKinney first postmaster. Hogan post office is reported to have been named for a local landowner who later moved to Roseburg and opened a store. Hogan post office was close to the banks of South Umpqua River, northwest of Roseburg. The name of the office was changed to Melrose on October, 10, 1890.

Hogg Rock, Linn County. Hogg Rock is a prominent point about a mile west of the summit of the Cascade Range. The Santiam Highway skirts its western and southern slopes. This rock was named for Colonel T. Egenton Hogg, promoter of the Yaquina railroad project. For a history of this project, see Scott's *History of the Oregon Country,* volume IV, page 328. Among other things, Hogg proposed to extend his railroad through the Cascade Range into eastern Oregon. The style Hogg Butte is sometimes applied to this feature, but the compiler thinks it is wrong. For many years the name Hogg Pass was applied to the locality now used by the Santiam

Highway in crossing the summit of the Cascade Range and the name Santiam Pass was used for the low point traversed by the Santiam toll road
about three miles to the south. In 1929 there developed an agitation to
apply the name Santiam Pass to both these localities on the theory that they
constituted but one main geographic feature and also because the Santiam
Highway would eventually draw the name Santiam Pass, to the elimination
of Hogg Pass. The USBGN, in 1929, adopted the name Santiam Pass for
the pass as a whole, rejecting the style Hogg Pass. John Minto, in *OHQ*,
volume IV, page 248, says that Hogg's name was probably applied by J. I.
Blair of New York, who was connected with the Hogg enterprises. Minto
also says that John B. Waldo first noted the apparent lowness of Santiam
Pass. However, Andrew Wiley crossed the pass as early as 1859 and recognized its importance. See under Wiley Creek.

Holbrook, Multnomah County. Philo Holbrook was a pioneer of Oregon, and owned a farm at the present site of Holbrook. When the post
office was established, it was named for him.

Holcomb Creek, Washington County. Holcomb Creek rises in the hills
north of Helvetia and flows into Rock Creek about a mile north of the
Sunset Highway. It was named for Stephen A. Holcomb, a pioneer settler,
who took up a donation land claim nearby. Originally there was a small lake
with the same name near where the two streams joined but this has been
drained.

Holderman Mountain, Lane County. This mountain on the headwaters of Mosby Creek near the Douglas County line was named for Elza
Holderman, an early USFS ranger.

Holdman, Umatilla County. Holdman brothers were early settlers in
this community, and when the post office was established in 1900, it was
named for them.

Hole in the Ground, Douglas County. Perry Wright gave this descriptive name to a natural depression east of Calf Creek about two miles south
of North Umpqua River. Wright homesteaded near Cap's Illahee in 1909
and made his living farming and hunting in the area until his death in
1966.

Hole-in-the-Ground, Lake County. This very remarkable place is well
described by its name. It covers an area of about a quarter of a mile, and its
floor is over three hundred feet below the surrounding land level. It is
about eight miles northwest of Fort Rock.

Holladay, Clatsop County. Holladay was the station a mile or so south
of Seaside at the end of the railroad line from Portland. The line was aban-
donded and the rails taken up prior to 1980 and nothing exists in Oregon
today of a geographic nature to call to mind one of Oregon's most important pioneer citizens. Ben Holladay came to Oregon in August, 1868, with
what was considered immense wealth and plunged into the Willamette Valley railroad fight that was then raging. Holladay was a native of Kentucky
and came west in 1856, and having made money in the overland stage
business, he sold out to Wells Fargo & Company about 1866 and turned his
attentions to Oregon. He allied himself with the east side, or Salem interests, and built in all about 240 miles of railroad. In 1873 his railroad

defaulted, and today is part of the Southern Pacific system. Holladay's ventures and extravagances scattered his wealth. He died July 8, 1887, aged 68 years. For references to his activities and controversies see Scott's *History of the Oregon Country*, volume III, page 172. His name was applied to the station in Clatsop County because for some years he was interested in the Seaside House, a famous pioneer resort south of the present site of Seaside. A post office called Ben Holladay was established in Clatsop County on June 13, 1890, with C. C. Cooper postmaster. The office was closed April 9, 1891.

Holland, Josephine County. Holland post office was established in April, 1899, and the first postmaster was John M. Smock. The post office was named after a pioneer settler in the neighborhood, James E. Holland.

Holley, Linn County. The post office at Holley was established about 1890 and George W. Pugh, an early settler and first postmaster, named the place after his home in Wisconsin. There is no record of a Wisconsin post office or major community of this name, but Lamar Newkirk, a grandson of Mr. Pugh, told the author in 1968 that this was the correct origin and that the name had nothing to do with holly trees or the shrub Oregon grape.

Holman Guard Station, Lane County. This USFS installation west of Nimrod was named for L. G. Holman, a well-known state fire warden in the World War II era.

Holmes Creek, Douglas County. Holmes Creek on the west side of Camas Valley was named for Manasseh B. Holmes who came to Douglas County in 1854 and raised stock along this stream. Combs in *God Made A Valley* says that he was titled "General" by all who knew him.

Holmes Gap, Polk County. Holmes Gap and Holmes Hill are five miles north of Rickreall, the former being a natural pass used by the Southern Pacific Company and by the Pacific Highway West. The gap has an elevation of 166 feet and the hill just to the east 567 feet. These features were named for Horatio Nelson Viscount Holmes, a pioneer of Oregon, who took a donation land claim at this point.

Holton Creek, Josephine County. Holton Creek flows into the Illinois River just south of Kerby. It was named for Dr. D. S. Holton, a pioneer physician of the neighborhood. For biography of Dr. Holton, see Walling's *History of Southern Oregon,* page 508. See also under Kerby.

Home, Baker County. Home, a community on Snake River at the mouth of Conner Creek, was inundated in 1959 by the pool behind Brownlee Dam. Information about the origin of the name is unsatisfactory. The post office was established August 1, 1918 and closed February 28, 1946 with papers to Huntington. John W. Flick is said to have been the first postmaster. He asked for the name Marble but the department refused that name and called the place Home instead. This seems to have been satisfactory to the local residents. The writer has not been able to learn why the name of Home was selected. This office should not be confused with an earlier office called Home, established on the Baker County list in June, 1878. This earlier office was in what is now Malheur County.

Home, Malheur County. Home post office was established on the Baker County list in June, 1878, with Alvin R. Roberts postmaster. The office was situated in what is now Malheur County near Willow Creek a few miles northwest of Vale. The history of the office is a little confusing. The office was discontinued in November, 1878, but was put in service again within a few weeks. There was another short interruption in 1879. At the time of these interruptions William S. Glenn was postmaster. The writer can find no record of this office after June, 1880, and it may have stopped functioning in that month. It should be noted that Glenn was postmaster at the new office of Glenn, in the same general locality, in April, 1881. It is possible that when Glenn was postmaster at Home, he may have had the office at the place later called Glenn. There was not much formality about moving post offices in those days.

Home Creek, Harney County. Home Creek flows westward from Steens Mountain into Catlow Valley, and the Home Creek Ranch near the stream is a prominent landmark. In his memoirs, *The Cattle Drives of David Shirk*, page 115, Shirk says that he moved to the Catlow Valley on May 10, 1877 and built his house on a stream which he called Home Creek. This was immediately after his marriage to Frances Crow, the niece of Rankin Crow. Other members of the Shirk family settled nearby.

Homer, Grant County. Homer post office was established September 20, 1889, with Wells W. Stone first postmaster. The office was in Bear Valley, in the same locality as the later offices Duncanville and Logdell. The second postmaster at Homer was B. S. Duncan, who was living at Mount Vernon in March, 1947. Mr. Duncan has recorded that he was postmaster at Homer for considerably more than a year, and that his salary amounted to twenty-five cents. He resigned, and the office was closed November 4, 1895. Homer post office is said to have been named for Homer Stone, son of the first postmaster W. W. Stone. At least that is the opinion of Mr. Duncan. See also under Logdell.

Homestead, Baker County. It is reported to the writer that Frank E. Pearce took up a homestead at this point in connection with his operations with the Iron Dyke Mine, and that the office was named on account of the homestead claim. This was about 1900. J. H. Pearson was the first postmaster, and he suggested the name.

Homestead Creek, Lane County. This creek is part of Steamboat Creek drainage just north of the Douglas County line. It was named by USFS ranger Fred Asam because he thought it a very desirable homestead site. His opinion was not shared as no one ever filed upon this location.

Hominy Creek, Wallowa County. Hominy Creek flows into Snake River in township 1 north, range 50 east. It was named because Alex Warnock spilled a kettle of hominy when camping there.

Homly, Umatilla County. In 1928 the Union Pacific Railroad established an additional station east of Cayuse and named it Homly. The name was supposedly taken from a tombstone in the nearby Indian graveyard. If so, it was appropriate for Homly or Homily was a Walla Walla chief who remained friendly during the Bannock War of 1878. The *Private Journal* of C. E. S. Wood, *OHQ*, volume LXX, page 34, states that Homily was present at the council at Umatilla on August 26, 1878 and Wood later tells of his visit to Homily's camp on February 22, 1879, *ibid*, page 167.

Honey Creek, Lake County. Honey Creek, one of the largest streams of the Warner Valley, was named in 1864, according to Judge William M. Colvig of Medford who wrote the compiler in April, 1927, as follows: "I was a cavalry soldier under Col. C. S. Drew in 1864, in what is known as the Colonel Drew Expedition, from Fort Klamath to Fort Boise, Idaho. I was one of sixty members of Company C, 1st Oregon Cavalry who went with Drew. In the fore part of August, 1864, we struck the Warner Lakes country, and scouted over the entire valley. I was with a small party that went up the west side to what is now known as Honey Creek. We camped on the creek bottom and noted that the leaves of the willows were heavily laden with a white substance that was as sweet as honey. It would scale off in flakes, often the size of a twenty-five cent coin. It only happens in hot, dry weather, and is the product of the drying up of honey dew, which falls during the night. We named it in our camp record Honey Creek. We gave Drew Valley, Crockett Springs, Beatys Butte, Sprague River and a great many other names now on the map. I know for I was company clerk and kept the records."

Honeyman, Columbia County. Honeyman was a station between Scappoose and St. Helens. It was established to serve a farm owned by William Honeyman, a prominent pioneer hardware dealer of Portland, and was named for him.

Hood Mountain, Coos County. This mountain which has an elevation of about 1700 feet is in the valley of South Fork Coquille River. It was named for William L. Hood, a prominent stockman who owned land nearby.

Hood River, Hood River County. This stream was discovered by Lewis and Clark on Tuesday, October 29, 1805, and called Labeasche River, an improvised method of spelling the name of Francis Labiche, one of the French-Canadian watermen. *La biche* is French for female deer or doe, but in French-Canadian, it frequently was used to mean elk. There is nothing in the journals to indicate that game was seen at this point, and the river was named for the man. In pioneer days some travelers, being in a starving condition, ate dog meat near Hood River, and the unpopular name Dog River was the result, but not because of any suggestiveness of the French name. Later on, Mrs. Nathaniel Coe, a well-known pioneer resident of the valley, objected to the name Dog River and succeeded in changing local usage to Hood River on account of Mount Hood, its source. For narrative of settlement, in 1852, see the *Oregonian*, June 11, 1889, page 3; May 9, 1881, page 3; description, *ibid.*, May 14, 1903; October 4, 1914, page 4. Hood River Valley is famed for apples and pears which producers there ship in large quantities. The name Dog River is now attached only to a small stream that heads in Brooks Meadows about eight miles southeast of Parkdale and flows into East Fork Hood River. In October, 1852, an advertisement in the *Oregonian* says that a road had been cleared from "Dog River to the ferry" which was one of the first on the Columbia. The name Hood River appears on a map as early as 1856.

Hood River, Hood River County. The city of Hood River was named for the stream nearby. Hood River post office was established on the Clackamas County list on September 30, 1858, with Nathan Benson, first postmaster. Charles C. Coe became postmaster May 16, 1860.

Hood River County. This county was created June 23, 1908, and was taken from Wasco County. Since most of the new county was drained by Hood River, it was appropriate to name it Hood River County. According to the Bureau of Census, it has a land area of 529 square miles.

Hoodoo Butte, Linn County. Hoodoo Butte, elevation 5721 feet, is a prominent point just south of Santiam Highway very near the summit of the Cascade Range. The place has become well known because it is a fine locality for skiing. The origin of the name is uncertain. Hoodoo may come from the word that indicates a run of bad luck or a Jonah. On the other hand, throughout the western part of the United States the word is used to refer to natural rockpiles or pinnacles of fantastic shape. The name Hoodoo Butte may have been applied during the days of the Santiam toll road because of difficulties in construction or travel, although the second reason given above is just as likely.

Hoodoo Spring, Wallowa County. This spring is in township 6 north, range 42 east. In earlier days, the place was hard to get to because of poor trails and in 1907 Roy Smith, a forest ranger, applied the name Hoodoo Spring.

Hoods Bar Light, Multnomah County. This navigation aid is on the north side of Government Island, in the Columbia River. It is sometimes suggested that Hoods Bar was named because of the excellent view to be had there of Mount Hood, but such is not the case. The Hood family has for many years been landowners on Government Island, and the bar was named for the family. Frederick W. Hood and James Hood purchased a farm on Government Island in the early 1880s. The obituary of Frederick W. Hood was published in the *Oregonian,* November 30, 1927, page 8.

Hook, Gilliam County. Hook was the last name of the railroad station formerly called Squally Hook because it was at this point on the south bank of the Columbia River that rough weather was frequently experienced by steamboat men. In the interest of simplicity the railroad company eliminated the word Squally. A nearby post office was once known as Quinook, which was a name made up by taking parts of the station names of Quinton and Squally Hook. The present station name is Quinton.

Hooskanaden Creek, Curry County. This creek enters the Pacific Ocean northwest of Carpenterville. Dodge's *Pioneer History of Coos and Curry Counties,* page 106, says that this name comes from the *Wish-to-na-tan* Indians who lived along the creek. The early settlers had great difficulty with this Indian name and Hooskanaden was about as close as they could come. There have been numerous variants including Houstenader but the matter was resolved in *Decision List 8003.*

Hoover, Marion County. Hoover post office, named for the first postmaster, was on North Santiam River two or three miles upstream from Detroit. The office was established in May, 1907, with R. N. Hoover, first postmaster. It was discontinued in October, 1916, and the business turned over to the Detroit office. The name has been retained in Hoover Ridge, the high ground between North Santiam and Breitenbush Rivers.

Hoover Creek, Wheeler County. Hoover Creek is a tributary of Thirtymile Creek. It flows north of Black Butte about three miles from Fossil. T. B. Hoover settled nearby many years ago and the stream bears his name.

Hope, Malheur County. Hope station near Malheur River was named for M. G. Hope, a landowner nearby. It is just west of Vale.

Hope Creek, Wallowa County. Hope Creek is tributary to Freezeout Creek just west of Freezeout Saddle in township 2 south, range 48 east. It was named in compliment to Harry Hope, who ranged stock there.

Hopewell, Yamhill County. Hopewell was named in optimism. It is at the east base of the Eola Hills at a point ten miles south of Dayton and a couple of miles west of Wheatland. Hopes of growth have not been ful- filled. Hopewell post office was established June 21, 1897, with John W. Spencer first postmaster in a series of four. The office was closed out to Amity on January 9, 1903, doubtless as a result of the extension of rural free delivery. Hopewell does not appear in gazetteers of the middle 1880s.

Hopkins, Clatsop County. Hopkins post office was near Nehalem River at a point six or seven miles northeast of Jewell. It was named for the first postmaster, Thomas Hopkins. This post office was established Febru- ary 24, 1890, and was discontinued to Jewell November 15, 1892. The office was reestablished April 10, 1894, and continued in operation until July 14, 1902. There is little left of the community.

Hopmere, Marion County. Officials of the Oregon Electric Railway named this station Chemeketa when the line was built, hoping to perpetu- ate the original Indian name of the locality of Salem. However, local enthu- siasts were not satisfied, and succeeded in changing the name to Hopmere, a silly mongrel.

Hoquarten Slough, Tillamook County. This slough is at Tillamook. Miss Lucy E. Doughty, of Bay City, wrote the compiler in 1927, as follows: "I do not know the meaning of this name. It is thought to be of Indian origin. It has been in use since the first settlers came, as Mr. W. N. Vaughn used it in a memorial that he compiled. He always spelled the word 'Ho- quarton.' Now the name is applied only to the slough and to a voting pre- cinct in the city, but for a long time after we came here, Hoquarton Prairie was the name used for the neighborhood now known as Fairview. When a town was first laid out on the bank of this slough, it was named Lincoln, but as there was already a post office of that name in Polk County, the post office had to be Tillamook. The site had been called Hoquarton, the Land- ing, or Tillamook Landing. I think it was usually called Hoquarton by the settlers in the bay neighborhood and it was not until 1885 that I began to hear the town called Tillamook. Before that, when we said 'Tillamook' we meant the county." The government now uses the spelling Hoquarten for the slough. This style is well established.

Horn Creek, Linn County. Horn Creek flows into North Santiam River just south of Marion Forks. William Horn was an early homesteader on the adjoining flats and Scott and Nan Young named this creek in his memory when they settled at Marion Forks in 1932.

Horning Gap, Lake County. Horning Gap is a pass in the hills north of Silver Lake, named for a homesteader.

Horse Canyon, Umatilla County. Lloyd Waid of Ukiah said that this canyon four miles east of Dale was named because its south facing slopes provided an excellent winter range for horses.

Horse Creek, Lane County. This stream joins McKenzie River from the south, not far from McKenzie Bridge. George Frissell, an early settler on McKenzie River, is authority for the story that the stream was named because in pioneer days some emigrants succeeded in getting a wagon over the summit of the Cascade Range near the head of Horse Creek and got their wagon down on the west slope a considerable distance. They lost their horses, and the stream was named on that account. Many years ago the remains of the wagon were found near the bank of the stream which tends to substantiate the story.

Horse Creek, Wallowa County. Horse Creek is an important tributary to Imnaha River from the east. It was so named because Jack Johnson wintered his horses there in 1878-79.

Horse Heaven, Jefferson County. In August, 1946, Frank E. Lewis, postmaster at Horse Heaven, wrote an interesting letter about the place, from which the following information has been condensed: "The name Horse Heaven for this area was given perhaps sixty odd years ago. At that time the springs were accessible to wandering herds and the grass was better. Then followed a period of overgrazing, fencing off the better springs and more line fences. The climate became drier. There is some open country in the area and at times one sees small bands of range horses. The grass seems to have come back. Here at Horse Heaven cinnabar was discovered about 1933. Active production of mercury began in 1934 and the Horse Heaven Mines, Inc., assumed control in 1936. The mine is now closed down after about ten years operation. The entire area was homesteaded in the 1920s I believe, but practically all the homesteaders have left. Horse Heaven is forty-six miles eastward of Madras and about eighteen miles east of Ashwood. The country is on the John Day side of the divide." Horse Heaven post office was established April 23, 1938, with Mrs. Mary E. Finnell first postmaster. Mail went in twice a week from Ashwood. The office was closed in the summer of 1946.

Horse Heaven Creek, Lane County. This stream rises in the Calapooya Mountains and flows southward into Steamboat Creek. Near the head of the creek, which is close to the Bohemia mining district, there was a natural pasture, where miners and prospectors fed their stock. The name Horse Heaven is used in a great many places in the West, indicating natural pastures along streams, where horses could be turned loose without fear that they would stray away, or good forage on ranges where large numbers of wild horses congregated.

Horsepasture Mountain, Lane County. Ray Engels of McKenzie Bridge told the writer in 1971 that this 5660 foot summit south of Horse Creek was named because of the excellent pasture on the south slopes. This was important in the early days when the lookout was supplied by pack animals.

Horseshoe Lake, Jefferson County. This lake is near the summit of the Cascade Range south of Olallie Butte. It drains to the north into Monon Lake. It was not named because of its shape, but because a horseshoe was found near its shore.

Horsetail Falls, Multnomah County. This name is supposed to be descriptive of the falls and has been in use since pioneer days. The lower falls, visible from the highway, are 176 feet high.

Horton, Lane County. Three brothers by the name of Horton settled near the present Horton post office in 1903. They were E. J. Horton, Sam M. Horton, and J. C. Horton. They established a sawmill called Horton Mill. The post office was established the latter part of 1913 with the name of Horton. Sam M. Horton was the first postmaster and was still in office in January, 1926. Horton is the center of the dairying and lumbering community.

Hoskins, Benton County. In 1856 the federal government established a fort in Benton County known as Fort Hoskins. It was named for Lieutenant Charles Hoskins, who was killed in the battle of Monterrey, Mexico, September 21, 1846. He was appointed to the army from North Carolina. Fort Hoskins in Benton County was not a large military establishment. The post office of Hoskins was named in memory of the fort. Although Fort Hoskins is now nothing more than a memory, there was a time when it was an important post. Several officers who later achieved prominence in the military establishment were at one time in command at Fort Hoskins or were stationed there. Captain C. C. Augur was there in the late 1850s. He was later a major-general. Captain Frederick T. Dent, later a brigadier-general, was commandant at Fort Hoskins in 1861. He was a brother of Mrs. U. S. Grant. General P. H. Sheridan in his *Personal Memoirs,* volume I, page 97, says "I spent many happy months at Fort Hoskins." For additional information, see under Fort Hoskins.

Hosmer Lake, Deschutes County. This lake is about one mile due east of Elk Lake on the Cascade Lakes Highway west of Bend. It was originally named Mud Lake, possibly because the large population of trash fish would rile the fine pumice silt bottom. In 1962 the OGNB approved the change to Hosmer Lake in memory of Paul Hosmer, a long time resident of Bend and a well-known amateur naturalist. For further information on Hosmer see the Bend *Bulletin,* January 19, 1962. By 1962 the trash fish had been eliminated and the lake restocked experimentally with Atlantic Salmon or *Salmo salar.*

Hospital Creek, Lane County. Hospital Creek flows into Lookout Point Lake near Hampton. When the original railroad was built up the Middle Fork Willamette River in 1909, it was on the north side of the river. A construction camp hospital was established at the mouth of this creek.

Hot Lake, Union County. This is a steaming mineral lake at Hot Lake station near Union. The name is quite descriptive, although the compiler does not know when it was first used. On August 7, 1812, Robert Stuart and companions traveling from Astoria to St. Louis, visited Hot Lake. As far as known this was the first time it was seen by white men. Washington Irving's *Astoria* describes the event in the following words: "In traversing this (Grande Ronde) plain, they passed, close to the skirts of the hills, a great pool of water, three hundred yards in circumference, fed by a sulphur spring, about ten feet in diameter, boiling up in one corner. The vapor from this pool was extremely noisome, and tainted the air for a considerable distance. The place was much frequented by elk, which were ound in considerable numbers in the adjacent mountains, and their horns, hed in the springtime, were strewed in every direction around the pond." See also *Discovery of the Oregon Trail, Robert Stuart's Narrative,* edited by P. A. Rollins, page 78.

Hot Springs, Lake County. Hot Springs was one of the earliest post offices in what is now Lake County, and it was established in December, 1871, with William Greenman first postmaster. According to J. O. Jewett of he *Lake County Examiner-Tribune,* who gathered some data for the compiler n October, 1945, the office was at or near the Abram Tenbrook ranch about five or six miles south of Lakeview, approximately at the present site of the Ned Sherlock ranch. The office was named for the numerous hot springs on the east side of Goose Lake in the vicinity of the Tenbrook ranch. Abram Tenbrook became postmaster in December, 1872, and Robert H. Dunlap took the office in April, 1873. Charles Hagerhorst was postmaster at two different times. On September 24, 1875, the name of the office was changed to Goose Lake, and the establishment was closed on August 28, 1877. This was probably due to the fact that offices had been established at Lakeview and at New Pine Creek in December, 1876. Both of these places drew business from the older office. John Work in *Fur Brigade o the Bonaventura* mentions these springs under date of October 22, 1832.

Houghton Creek, Baker County. This creek empties into Powder River at Keating. Philip Houghton took up government land just above its mouth in 1878.

Houlton, Columbia County. Houlton post office was situated at Saint Helens railroad station. The main town of Saint Helens is about a mile from the station. Houlton was originally called Milton. For information about this see under Milton Creek. The post office was established about 1890, and inasmuch as there was already a post office in Umatilla County by the name of Milton, it was necessary to find a new name for the Columbia County community. B. W. Plummer was the first postmaster, and he recommended the name Houlton for Houlton, Maine, his former home. The scheme of having post offices with different names serving the same community has never been satisfactory and it never worked well at Saint Helens. As a result the name of Houlton office was changed in the summer of 1946 to Saint Helens, Station A.

House Rock, Deschutes and Lane counties. This House Rock is on the summit of the Cascade Range, a few miles south of the Three Sisters, and has an elevation of 6737 feet. It is named because of its shape. It has also been called McArthur Hill in compliment to Judge Lewis L. McArthur, 1843-97, Oregon attorney and jurist, but that name has not prevailed.

Houston Butte, Crook County. This butte in the Bear Creek drainage north of Brothers was named for John W. Houston, a member of a well-known Crook County family, who homesteaded the area in 1910.

Howard, Crook County. The community of Howard was in at least two different places in the Ochoco Valley, but the post office was abandoned about 1918 and now Howard is a ghost town. The original Howard was what is now known as the Ochoco Mines on Ochoco Creek near the mouth of Scissors Creek. It was named for a rancher and prospector who found gold there in 1872. Mining became active in the place, but the boom petered out in the early 1890s. It revived and with its resumption came a post office. It was about 28 miles northeast of Prineville. In 1909 the post office was moved to a point in the Ochoco Valley about 18 miles east of Prineville on the Ochoco Highway. The office was discontinued about 1918.

Howard Canyon, Morrow County. This tributary of Little Butter Creek northeast of Freezeout Ridge was named for James L. Howard who established a sheep ranch at its mouth in 1885.

Howard Canyon, Multnomah County. Howard Canyon is southeast of Corbett. It was named for James Howard who settled nearby in the 1880s.

Howard Meadows, Wallowa County. These meadows are in township 3 north, range 41 east. They drain through Howard Creek into Wallowa River. They bear the name of Abe Howard who took up a homestead in the vicinity about 1885. Howard was killed when a horse fell on him, and his sons buried him on the north edge of the meadows named for him.

Howard Spring, Wallowa County. This spring, in township 4 north, range 47 east, was named for General O. O. Howard, who camped in the vicinity in the summer of 1878 when he was leaving the Grande Ronde Valley. For information about General Howard, see under the heading Mount Howard.

Howe, Yamhill County. Howe station near Carlton was named for William Addison Howe, a resident of Carlton and Portland for many years. He was born in Massachusetts, graduated from Harvard in 1881, and came to Oregon the following year. While a student at St. Mark's School in Massachusetts Mr. Howe made and used the first baseball mask, by reinforcing a fencing mask with stronger wire. Mr. Howe died in Portland, February 2, 1934.

Howell Prairie, Marion County. Howell Prairie is west of Silverton, between the branches of Pudding River. It was named for a pioneer settler, John Howell, who came to Oregon in 1843. For information about Howell Prairie and the Howell family, see Down's *History of the Silverton Country*.

Howlock Mountain, Douglas and Klamath counties. This is an important peak in the Cascade Range north of Mount Thielsen, and has an elevation of 8351 feet. It was at one time known as Walker Mountain, possibly for W. T. Walker of the road-viewing party that explored Middle Fork Willamette River in 1852. See under Walker Mountain for additional information. About 1916, at the suggestion of the compiler hereof, the USBGN changed the name of the peak to Howlock Mountain, for a well-known Piute Indian chief who ranged central Oregon. The reason for this change was that the name Walker Mountain was applied to a more important mountain southeast of Crescent, a comparatively short distance away, and it was thought advisable to avoid duplication.

Howluk Butte, Harney County. Howluk Butte is 4780 feet high and is two miles east of Alvord Lake. It was named in 1860 by Enoch Steen during his campaign against the Snake Indians. Howluk or Howlock was a Piute chief of some fame whose activities apparently reached as far west as Klamath Lake. The USBGN adopted the spelling Howluk in *Decision List 6601*. Howlock Mountain north of Mount Thielsen is named for the same man.

Hubbard, Marion County. Hubbard was named for Charles Hubbard, who was born in Kentucky February 14, 1800, and came to Oregon in 1847. A few months after his arrival in Oregon City with his family, he was visited by Thomas Hunt, a squatter not far from Pudding River, and induced to rent Hunt's land while Hunt went gold seeking in California. Hunt was never heard from again, and Hubbard bought the right in the claim from Hunt's widow, and settled there. He built a cabin in 1849 about where Hubbard High School stood in 1926. The railroad was built through that part of the Willamette Valley in 1870 and Charles Hubbard gave land for a station, and laid out a townsite, which was named for him. He died on Mission Bottom in 1884.

Hubbard Creek, Curry County. In February, 1944, Louis L. Knapp of Port Orford wrote the compiler as follows: "Hubbard Creek empties into the ocean one mile southeast of Port Orford. Captain William Tichenor, in founding the town of Port Orford in 1851, had as one of his partners Isaac M. Hubbard, who was also purser in the steamship *Sea Gull.* Mr. Hubbard was to have a land claim on the east side of the town through which runs this large stream. Thereafter people generally referred to it as Hubbard Creek." It is a coincidence that Dr. Alonzo Hubbard of Scituate, Massachusetts, made at least two trips to Curry County in very early days. An account of one of these trips is in a story with the title "Wild Life in Oregon," by William V. Wells, *Harper's Magazine,* October, 1856, but the compiler has found no evidence that connects Dr. Hubbard's name with the stream.

Hubbard Lake, Marion County. Hubbard Lake, northwest of Waconda, was named for W. C. Hubbard, who owned land on its banks. He was an early settler.

Huber, Washington County. Huber was a station west of Beaverton. It bore the name of Jacob Huber, an early resident. The community was established about 1910 and the post office in 1916. The post office was closed December 31, 1953.

Huckleberry Mountain, Wallowa County. This point is a very prominent peak in the Wallowa Mountains and has an elevation of about 7550 feet. It is in the extreme northwest corner of township 2 south, range 43 east. It was named in early days by Sam Wade and William Masterson, who ran stock on the mountain. Their families camped on the mountain for many years.

Hudson, Columbia County. Hudson is a locality about five miles west of Rainier and close to Beaver Creek. It was named for a local family. Hudson post office was established June 20, 1892, and was discontinued October 31, 1913. Susan A. Hudson was the first of five postmasters.

Hudson Bay, Umatilla County. This name is attached peculiarly to a tract of land, or a flat, and not to a body of water. Hudson Bay is west of Milton-Freewater and is so named because many years ago the Hudson's Bay Company operated a farm and grazed stock on the plain. The name is definitely established and is in universal use, notwithstanding its oddity. Isaac I. Stevens visited the Hudson's Bay Company farm on November 4, 1853, and the visit is mentioned on page 152 of the Pacific Railroad Surveys *Reports,* volume XII, book I.

Hug Point, Clatsop County. Hug Point is on Cannon Beach. It is so called because it was necessary to hug the rocks to get around the point without getting wet. A makeshift automobile road had been cut in the face of the point, but the writer felt that he would just as soon be drowned as scared to death.

Hughey Creek, Tillamook County. Mrs. Sylvester Siskey told the compiler in 1971 that this creek east of Tillamook was named for her grandfather, James Hughey. Mrs. Siskey at that date was still living on the family farm.

Hugo, Josephine County. Hugo post office was established in 1896, and was named for Hugo Garber, an early settler who was instrumental in securing the office.

Hulbert Lake, Lane County. This is a long narrow lake fed by intermittent streams and surface drainage. It is four miles west of Harrisburg and has an elevation of 295 feet. It was named for Joseph Hulbert, a pioneer settler nearby.

Hullt, Marion County. Hullt post office was first established about 1891 on the Hullt homestead and was named for that family, which settled there many years ago. C. J. Hullt was the first postmaster. The office was near the famous Silver Creek Falls, of which there are ten cascades in all, the highest of which is about 178 feet. The post office was discontinued in the summer of 1943.

Humboldt Basin, Malheur County. A post office named Humboldt Basin was established June 29, 1869, with Marcus F. Colt postmaster, to serve a locality in what was then called Humboldt Basin and also Mormon Basin. The name Humboldt Basin for the geographic feature gradually gave way to the name Mormon Basin and Mormon Basin is the style now generally used. See under Mormon Basin. Humboldt Basin post office was established on the Baker County list, but according to the best information available to the compiler it was actually in what is now Malheur County. This office was closed May 23, 1883. A new post office with the name Basin was established in the same general locality in November, 1894, with Andrew M. Johnson postmaster. This office was discontinued in August, 1895.

Humbug Creek, Jackson County. This stream, near Applegate, was named as the result of a quarrel over the value of a mining claim.

Humbug Mountain, Curry County. This prominent landmark, elevation 1748 feet, is on the shore of the Pacific Ocean, about six miles southeast of Port Orford. It was once known as Sugarloaf Mountain, but its name was changed to Tichenors Humbug as the result of a mistake made by one of the exploring parties sent out by Captain William Tichenor. This party lost its way and went to the north of Port Orford instead of to the south. See *Pioneer History of Coos and Curry Counties*, page 25. This was in 1851. Since that time Tichenors Humbug has become known as Humbug Mountain. George Davidson in the *Coast Pilot*, 1889, page 373, says that in 1853 the mountain was called Mount Franklin and that the Indian name was *Me-tus*. Davidson does not explain these names, which have not prevailed.

Humbug Point, Clatsop County. This point is on Cannon Beach north of Hug Point. It has long been known as Humbug Point because travelers going along the beach flattered themselves that they had reached Hug

Point only to find that they had been humbugged, and had a mile yet to go. The two points look much alike.

Hungry Hill, Josephine County. Hungry Hill is a place in the mountains about seven miles west of Kerby in the Illinois Valley. Various points called Hungry Hill were generally named in the mining days because miners who worked at them went hungry because of poor diggings. There is another Hungry Hill in the north part of the county and also others in the state.

Hungry Hill, Josephine County. This hill is an historic point in the south part of section 17, township 33 south, range 7 west, a few miles southwest of Glendale. Important engagements in the Rogue River Indian War were fought hereabouts on October 31 and November 1, 1855, called the battle of Hungry Hill and also the battle of Bloody Spring. See Victor's *Early Indian Wars of Oregon*, pages 352-55. This Hungry Hill should not be confused with the point in the Illinois Valley west of Kerby.

Hungry Hill, Linn County. This hill is southwest of the town of Scio, and has an elevation of 665 feet. Jefferson Myers was authority for the statement that it was named because the soil on its slopes was so poor and rocky that farmers who tried to till it were driven out by starvation.

Hunt Butte, Jefferson County. Hunt Butte, on the headwaters of Muddy Creek, is 4115 feet high. It was named for Edgar O. Hunt who homesteaded the land in 1914.

Hunt Creek, Clatsop County. This stream is about 25 miles east of Astoria. It was named for Henry H. Hunt, a pioneer sawmill operator, whose mill began operations at Hunts Mill Point in 1844.

Hunt Creek, Lane County. This stream flows into Row River east of Culp Creek. James T. Hunt settled near its mouth about 1883 and he and his family lived there many years. In 1967 his son, Loren W. Hunt, gave the compiler this information but added that when he was a boy the creek had no formal name.

Hunt Mountain, Baker County. Hunt Mountain bears an historic name, but the name was applied in modern times. It was at the request of J. Neilson Barry and other Oregonians that the USBGN attached the name of Wilson P. Hunt, leader of the Astor overland expedition, to the summit of the northeastern spur of Elkhorn Ridge, northwest of Baker. For details concerning Hunt and the overland expedition see Irving's *Astoria*. Hunt is mentioned as having seen the range northwest of Baker, on December 28, 1811. Wilson Price Hunt was chief partner in the Pacific Fur Company after Astor. He was born at Ashbury, New Jersey, about 1782. He went to Saint Louis in 1804, and engaged in the fur trade there. After the Astor enterprise at Astoria, he returned to Saint Louis, and was appointed postmaster there in 1822. He died in April, 1842. He was a man of remarkable energy, strong purpose and fidelity, and was highly respected.

Hunt Rock, Curry County. F. S. Moore, in *Curry County Reporter,* December 16, 1926, says this is the correct name of the rock at Wedderburn, and not Hume Rock. Hunt Rock was named for James M. Hunt, a gold seeker of 1853, and a prominent pioneer settler at the mouth of Rogue River.

Hunter Spring, Umatilla County. Lloyd Waid of the USFS told the compiler that this spring south of Hidaway Creek in the east part of the county was named by the USFS in the 1960s as it was a favorite camping spot for the Nimrods.

Hunter Spring, Wallowa County. Hunter Spring is in the southeast part of township 3 north, range 43 east. It was named for Charles Hunter, who ran stock in the locality. Tom Willet, one of his men, found the spring, cleaned it out and carved Hunter's name on a nearby alder tree to commemorate the event.

Hunters, Columbia County. Hunters post office was established May 29, 1888, to serve a settlement a mile or so south of Goble. Stephen H. Walker was the first postmaster. Hunters was named for the Hunter family, local residents. The office was closed to Reuben in October, 1893.

Hunters Cove, Curry County. Hunters Cove is just southeast of Cape Sebastian, and Hunters Island is south of the cove. F. S. Moore, of Gold Beach, wrote the compiler that in the early days sea otter hunting was an important industry, and those engaged in the business used small boats for cruising along the coast, and in heavy weather sought protection in the cove. This cove finally took its name from these sea otter hunters. Hunters Island took its name from the cove.

Hunters Hot Springs, Lake County. These springs are just north of Lakeview and are named for the late Harry A. Hunter who had large holdings in Lake County. The springs are mentioned by John Work in his journals under the date of October 21, 1832. See *California Historical Society Quarterly,* September, 1943, pages 205 and 215. Indians of northern California and Nevada used hot springs as places to deposit their dead.

Huntington, Baker County. This place was named for J. B. and J. M. Huntington, brothers, who settled there in 1882. The place was originally Miller stage station. J. B. Huntington bought out Miller. J. M. Huntington was the first postmaster.

Huntley Spring, Curry County. This spring west of Collier Butte was supposedly the favorite campsite of Nathaniel Huntley, a member of a well-known early Curry County family.

Hunts, Jackson County. Hunts was the name of a post office in the extreme east part of the county on the old mail route from Ashland northeast to Pelican Bay. The office operated from April, 1898, until June, 1902, with Arthur F. Hunt postmaster, and it was named with his family name. The place was about twenty miles eastward of Ashland.

Hunts Mill Point, Clatsop County. This point is between Clifton and Wauna. It was named for Hunts Mill, a pioneer sawmill owned by Henry H. Hunt and Ben Wood. This mill was built during the winter of 1843-44, and began operations in 1844. Edward Otey, a pioneer of 1843, was the millwright. Hunt Creek, nearby, was named for the same reason. Hunts Mill was the first sawmill in Clatsop County.

Hurlburt, Multnomah County. Mr. and Mrs. John Quincy Adams Hurlburt made settlement in the east part of Multnomah County about 1877 or 1878 at a point about three miles southeast of Springdale. The Hurlburt home was on a bench about a half mile northeast of Sandy River and about 800 feet west of what was later Hurlburt School. Hurlburt post office was established in the Hurlburt home on June 20, 1899, with John A.

Hurlburt postmaster. By this time Mr. Hurlburt had discarded the Quincy part of his name. The office was closed November 14, 1903, apparently because of the extension of rural free delivery.

Huron, Umatilla County. Huron is a station on the Union Pacific Railroad about eight miles northeast of Meacham. The station is also on Meacham Creek. Huron was apparently named for one Jake Huron, who in company with Eph Johnson, operated a pioneer sawmill in this locality. The mill was later purchased by Wilbur and Son. It produced much of the ties and timber used to build the railroad. It is said that Huron station was originally called Reardon for a track laying foreman. This name was later changed to Laka and still later to Huron, but the compiler does not know the dates. Huron post office was in operation from May, 1905, to June, 1913.

Hurricane Creek, Wallowa County. Named by C. A. Smith in the early 1880s. He explored the creek after a big storm and found a great many trees blown down. In 1931 J. H. Horner of Enterprise told the compiler that the first sawmill in the Wallowa Valley was built on this creek about 1878 by E. V. Cohorn.

Hurt Cabin, Curry County. This cabin on the upper reaches of Collier Creek in the east part of the county was named for E. G. Hurt who lived there in the early days.

Huston Canyon, Morrow County. Huston Canyon northeast of Eightmile was named for Luther Huston who settled there in the 1890s.

Hutchcroft Creek, Yamhill County. Mrs. Harvey Stoller of Dayton supplied the following information regarding this tributary of North Yamhill River. The creek was named for John and Margaret Hutchcroft who came to Yamhill County in 1874 and bought part of the Elisha Bedwell donation land claim. They were well-known citizens of the area for many years. Hutchcroft was born in England and came to Oregon via Canada and Wisconsin.

Hutchinson, Baker County. Hutchinson was a station on the Union Pacific Railroad about five miles northwest of Haines. It was named for a local family. The post office was established August 3, 1900, with James H. Hutchinson first postmaster. The office was discontinued August 5, 1902.

Hymes Creek, Benton and Lincoln counties. In 1969 this tributary of Tumtum River near Summit was named in honor of Alva D. Hymes. Hymes settled along its banks in 1906 and died there in 1942.

Ibex Butte, Crook County. Ibex Butte is in the south part of the county, in the northwest quarter of township 20 south, range 23 east. There is also a Little Ibex Butte nearby, and the two features are about 25 miles airline northwest of Suntex. These buttes bear the popular name of the rimrock or lava bed sheep. This wild sheep resembles the Rocky Mountain bighorn, but the two varieties are not identical. The lava bed bighorn ranged over a large part of eastern Oregon. There is a good deal about both varieties in *Mammals and Life Zones of Oregon,* by Vernon Bailey. There is a popular notion that there was at one time a post office called Ibex in the vicinity of the buttes, but the compiler has not been able to find any trace of it in post office records.

Idaho Point, Lincoln County. This is a prominent landmark on the south side of Yaquina Bay about two miles southeast of Newport. In times past it has been known both as Point Virtue and Hinton Point. Andrew L. Porter, a resident of the Yaquina Bay district since the 1860s, told the compiler in 1945 that the point was named for one Hinton who settled there in the early days. This was apparently Columbus Hinton who filed on a homestead some two miles upstream in 1873. The name Idaho Point appears to have been the result of a real estate venture but after World War II it became well established. The USBGN made this offical in *Decision List 7602*.

Idanha, Marion County. Idanha is a place on North Santiam River about four miles upstream from Detroit. John Minto in *OHQ,* volume IV, page 248, says the original name was Muskrat Camp but that it was renamed by the proprietor of the resort hotel. T. Egenton Hogg's Oregon Pacific Railroad Company built east up the North Santiam River and reached the vicinity of Idanha in 1889. All construction ceased at the end of that year and there was little activity in the area until 1895 when Idanha post office was established with Alma Kriesel postmaster amid a rash of land entries. The origin of the name is apparent but the reason baffling. In 1887 Fred J. Kiesel of Ogden, Utah, was the principal incorporator of The Natural Mineral Water Company which bottled Idan-Ha water from the Ninety Percent Spring in Soda Springs, Idaho. The company went on to build the Idanha Hotel in Soda Springs and both the water and the hostelry became known throughout the northwest. Alma Kriesel had two brothers who were active in Idanha, Oregon, possibly in the resort hotel, and the compiler is certain that some member of the family was familiar with the Soda Springs operation. Extensive research has shown that both the Kiesel and Kriesel families came originally from Germany but no connection can be established. There is an Idaho legend to the effect that Idan-Ha, as the name was used on the bottle labels, was the Indian name for the legend or spot of the Spirit of the Healing Waters. More than this the reader must find or deduce for himself.

Idaville, Tillamook County. Idaville was platted about 1870 by Warren N. Vaughn, and the land was part of his donation land claim. He named the place for his oldest daughter, Ida Vaughn.

Idea, Gilliam County. Idea is obviously an odd name for a post office, but that is the record. This office was established February 5, 1886, in section 10, township 4 south, range 23 east. This locality is on West Fork Dry Creek about twelve miles east of Condon. Earlier information placed the office much closer to Condon and confused the names of the people involved. In January 1977, Mrs. Raymond Bennett of Bend wrote and clarified the matter giving the following facts. James Washington Hiatt was the first postmaster and he intended to name the office Ida for his sister-in-law, Ida Chance Keizur, the wife of Manly Keizur, a local rancher. Somewhere along the line the name was misspelled with this odd result. Hiatt was succeeded as postmaster by James Royse whose tenure was very short. The post office was closed July 26, 1889, and what little business there was, was turned over to Gooseberry.

Idiot Creek, Tillamook County. Idiot Creek flows into Devils Lake

Fork Wilson River from the north about two miles west of the summit of the Coast Range on SH 6. The compiler has pondered this name ever since it was officially applied in USBGN *Decision List 6503*. After some publicity in November 1977 by Jim Jordan in the Portland *Daily Journal of Commerce*, Calvin Clayton who had worked the truck lines along Wilson River since World War II called to confirm the suspected origin. About one half mile up Idiot Creek was the site of Ryan's Camp, a logging operation in the Tillamook Burn. This was such an out of the way spot that supposedly only an idiot would go there to work, and the camp was popularly known as Idiotville. The name was applied to the stream in due course.

Idleyld Park, Douglas County. Idleyld Park is one of Oregon's mystery names. The place is on North Umpqua River near the mouth of Rock Creek, a locality formerly served by Tioga post office, later by the Hoaglin office. In January, 1946, K. D. Lytle of Roseburg, division engineer of the Oregon State Highway Commission, wrote the writer that about 1918-19 an amusement hall was built in the place and the owner named it Idleyld Park for a similar place he had heard of in California. There is a post office in California named Idyllwild. If that name is the genesis of the Oregon name, there has been some fancy confusion along the line. As nearly as the writer can determine, the post office at Idleyld Park was established December 1, 1932, by change of name from Hoaglin. Earl D. Vosburgh was postmaster at the time.

Idol, Harney County. A post office with the name Idol was established on the Harney County list as of March 25, 1892, with Joseph Morris first and only postmaster. The office was closed to Harney on August 9, 1893. In 1947 Archie McGowan of Burns wrote the compiler that in the early 1890s gold was discovered on the head of Trout Creek north of Harney. There was a mild stampede to the diggings, but the gold petered out. Even to this day after the spring freshets small grubstakes of very fine gold are recovered. Joseph Morris, better known as Joe, moved his store from Harney to the new camp, which was called Idol City. No one seems to remember why this name was selected, unless it was because gold was the idol of miners the world over.

Igo, Gilliam County. In July, 1946, J. D. Weed, then district attorney at Condon, sent the following information about Igo: "Igo was a post office in the Ferry Canyon country and it was named for John Igo, an early settler. There is a Grange hall there at the present time known as the Igo Grange." Igo post office was established in February, 1891, with James J. Fix postmaster. The office was closed in December, 1892, with papers to Condon. Old maps show Igo in the south part of township 3 south, range 20 east.

Ikt Butte, Deschutes County. *Ikt* is the Chinook jargon word for one. The name was applied by the USFS to a butte northwest of Paulina Mountains, at a time when several buttes were named with the Indian series of numbers.

Illahe, Curry County. This is the Chinook jargon word meaning land or earth and is also used to connote country. George Gibbs states that it is derived from the Chinook Indian word *ilahekh*. There are of course, various spellings, but the government has adopted Illahe as a standard. Besides the post office in Curry County, there are other features bearing the name, including a place on North Umpqua River, Illahe Hill about four miles southwest of Salem, and Tenasillahe Island in the Columbia River.

Illingworth, Tillamook County. Illingworth post office was on Wilson River about fourteen miles northeast of Tillamook, and was named in compliment to members of a local family. The office was established in June, 1896, with James R. Harris first postmaster. The office was closed in December, 1899.

Illinois River, Josephine County. C. H. Stewart, of Albany, wrote the compiler in 1927 that Illinois River was named as the result of the early discovery of gold thereon by the Althouse brothers of Albany. These brothers, Samuel, John and Phillip, were pioneers of 1847, emigrating from Peoria, Illinois, and settling in Albany, where they made their homes. They mined on Althouse Creek and Illinois River in southern Oregon in the early days of the placer diggings.

Illumination Rock, Clackamas County. On this rock occurred the first successful illumination of Mount Hood. This illumination was part of the Independence Day celebration in Portland on July 4, 1887. Will G. Steel organized a party that carried one hundred pounds of red fire to this rock and the light was seen as far as the mountain was visible.

Imbler, Union County. This place was named for the Imbler family, pioneer settlers. The post office was established April 27, 1891, with Albert E. Imbler first postmaster.

Imnaha River, Wallowa County. Imnaha is a beautiful name for a stream that rises in the Wallowa Mountains, and flows to Snake River through one of the deepest river gorges on the continent. The word was used by William Clark, on a map issued with the original Lewis and Clark journals in 1814, in the form *Innahar.* As far as the writer knows, Captain Bonneville was the first white man to go into the Wallowa country. For information about this exploration, see under Bonneville. He was in the vicinity of Imnaha River in January and February, 1834. It is difficult to follow Bonneville's march as described by Irving, for the geography of the country is obviously confused, but the general character of the landscape is very well described, and Irving's somewhat extravagant style is quite suitable to the remarkable rock formations and almost bottomless canyons the traveler encountered. Besides the river, there is a post office named Imnaha. J. H. Horner of Enterprise, the authority on Wallowa County history, told the writer in 1927 that *Imna* was the name of a sub-chief and that it was the custom among the Indians to sound *ha* to indicate the territory ruled over by a chief. Thus Imnaha was the land ruled over by *Imna.* See also Wenaha River.

Imperial, Deschutes County. This place is said to have been named by someone who had formerly lived in Imperial Valley, California.

Inavale, Benton County. Inavale post office was established July 2, 1896, with John Mitchell first postmaster and operated until May 4, 1905. The place was about eight miles southwest of Corvallis and about three miles west of Greenberry. The office was in a productive little valley and was given the descriptive name "In a vale" on that account.

Ince Camp, Wasco County. Ince Camp is on the old road from Antelope to John Day River about two miles north of Currant Creek. It was named for the Ince brothers, Arthur and Elby, who homesteaded there in 1913.

Inch Creek, Clackamas County. This stream is in the east part of the county near Salmon River. It was named by W. B. Osborne of the USFS because it was about an inch long on a map on the scale of 1-62,500.

Independence, Polk County. Independence was named by Elvin A. Thorp, who founded the community. The name was in compliment to Independence, Missouri. Thorp was born in Howard County, Missouri, in 1820. He came to Oregon in 1844, took up a donation land claim at the present site of Independence, Oregon, in June, 1845. Independence post office was established April 3, 1852, with Leonard Williams first postmaster.

Independence Prairie, Linn County. This small prairie is at the junction of Marion Creek and North Santiam River. It was named by the Marion County road viewing party on Independence Day, July 4, 1874. John Minto was in charge of the party. Independence Rock, a little to the southeast, was named for the prairie.

Indian Beach, Clatsop County. This fine little beach, well hidden from general observation, is on the southwest front of Tillamook Head and about two miles airline northwest of the mouth of Ecola Creek. Indian Point is at the north end of the beach and Bald Point at the south end, and Canyon Creek flows over the beach just south of Indian Point. The compiler is of the opinion that this is the beach referred to by Captain William Clark on January 8, 1806, in the following words: ".   . .I proceeded on down a Steep decent to a Single house the remains of an old *Kil a mox* Town in a nitch immediately on the Sea Coast, at which place a great No. of eregular rocks are out and the waves comes in with great force." Clark adds that the Indians used the place to deposit their dead in canoes. His description is remarkably accurate and in addition, old Indians told Rodney L. Glisan about 1895 that Indian Beach had a village in ancient days and later was a *memaloose illahe,* or place of the dead. They also said that it was the place where Captain Clark first came down to the sea and brought the Indian woman. Clark's map of Tillamook Head (Point of Clark's View) is also remarkably accurate and shows Indian Beach with fidelity.

Indian Creek, Hood River County. In pioneer days there was a permanent Indian town or camp in the flat where the main west side road crosses this creek, and the name was applied on that account.

Indian Creek, Wasco County. This Indian Creek rises south of Shaniko and flows to Antelope Creek. In the early days the flats above Cross Hollows south of Shaniko were a gathering spot for Indians to trade and compete in tribal games. Dolph Kimsey who was raised in the area told the compiler that the Indian Creek valley was marked by innumerable Indian campsites.

Indian Ridge, Lane County. In 1927 Smith Taylor of McKenzie Bridge told the compiler that Indian Ridge was named for an old Indian hunting trail that extended along its summit. The ridge is west of South Fork McKenzie River. The elevation of Indian Ridge Lookout is 5426 feet.

Indian Mountain, Hood River County. Before World War I the springs on this mountain were a favorite camping spot for Indians on huckleberry and hunting trips. Ralph Lewis told the compiler that he had seen numbers of their camps and that they took many deer from the upper Eagle Creek valley.

Indian Valley, Union County. Indian Valley is the flat land along Grande Ronde River just north of the mouth of Indian Creek, now largely occupied by the City of Elgin. It was named in the late 1860s because the first settlers found numerous Indian artifacts in the valley of Indian Creek. The Indians found the stretch of Grande Ronde River near Elgin excellent for fish traps and were frequent visitors. Prior to 1885 even the present community of Elgin was called Indian Valley. However, Indian Valley post office was about three miles up Indian Creek from its mouth near where the pioneer road from Summerville to Cricket Flat crossed the stream. It was established April 10, 1873, with John W. White postmaster, and was discontinued January 13, 1874. Indian Valley post office was reestablished June 11, 1877, with Joel Weaver postmaster. This office operated until October 26, 1881. There were also three other postmasters.

Indianhead Rock, Hood River County. This rock is about one half mile north of the intersection of Indian Creek with Lake Branch of West Fork Hood River. When the area was logged about 1960, this prominent rock became visible from the road and the USFS named it to help local area identification. The resemblance to an Indianhead is fanciful but the location near Indian Creek and Indian Mountain makes the name appropriate.

Inglis, Columbia County. Inglis post office, which was established September 30, 1902, was given the family name of the first postmaster, John E. Inglis. Inglis post office and railroad station lay about midway between Clatskanie and Quincy. The office was out of service from 1910 to 1914, and was discontinued again in 1918.

Ingram Point, Crook County. This mountain is northeast of Prineville and bears the name of Douglas C. Ingram of the USFS. The name was applied on May 3, 1933, to honor Ingram, who lost his life in August, 1929, in a fire in Chelan National Forest. He was born in Scotland, November, 1882, and joined the USFS in 1909. He served in the field and in the Portland office, and was an authority on range management. He had an important collection of forest plants. He first used Ingram Point, then known as Tamarack Point, as a lookout and it is quite fitting that the place should bear his name. Ingram Butte, elevation 4333 feet, about sixteen miles airline northeast of Oakridge and near the headwaters of Christy Creek, was named for the same man.

Inlow, Lane County. In January, 1947, Elwin A. McCornack of Eugene wrote the compiler as follows: "The first wagon road from Eugene to Mapleton left the present route at Hale or Elk Prairie west of Noti and by following Chickahominy and Nelson creeks intersected the Lake Creek road near Greenleaf. For years this route was followed by Whisman Brothers four and six in hand stage coaches. On the Chickahominy end of this section there lived a pioneer settler by the name of Igo Inlow. His place was well known and it may be there was a post office established there at one time." Well, the post office actually was established on June 20, 1899, with

Clemons E. Carlisle first postmaster. The office was closed to Hale on January 16, 1901. In April, 1948, McCornack wrote that the office was named for "Doc" Inlow, father of Igo Inlow. The office was said to have been in "Doc's" house. His given name has not been recalled.

Ione, Morrow County. The name of this small community in eastern Oregon furnished Harvey W. Scott with ammunition for a characteristic editorial which appeared in the *Oregonian* for June 22, 1903, after the Willow Creek flood of June 14 had brought into prominence various geographic names in that part of the state. He said: "Let us take advantage of the present occasion to correct the current pronunciation of 'Ione,' the town on Willow Creek, below Heppner. In current use they call it I-one, with accent on the last syllable, almost universally. But Ione is a name of three syllables, the accent properly on the second. So, many of our people say I-rene, two syllables, with accent on the last. But Irene is a name of three syllables, with accent on the second. We have a steamboat that most persons call Cal-li-ope, with accent on the final syllable. But Calliope is a name of four syllables with accent on the second. Again, in the name Arion, the accent is commonly placed on the first syllable. But the correct pronunciation places it on the second syllable making the 'i' long. Our schools and academies should insist on right pronunciation of these and other names. In Idaho, on the Oregon Short Line, they call a town Sho-shone—two syllables, with accent on the ultimate. Now, Shoshone is not a classical Greek name, as the foregoing are, but an Indian one. Nevertheless, the Indians called it Sho-sho-ne, accenting the final syllable, as emigrants who came across the plains perfectly remember." The town of Ione was named by E. G. Sperry, who owned the land, in 1883, for Ione Arthur, a girl from Brownsville who was visiting the Sperry family. She was with her father, John Arthur, and others of her family. The post office was established in 1884, with Aaron Royse first postmaster. He ran the first store in the community.

Iowa Hill, Washington County. Iowa Hill is a prominent point about three miles airline east of Gaston and just north of Laurelwood. It has an extreme elevation of about 1165 feet at its north end. This hill has been called Iowa Hill for many years because of the fact that several families of settlers came to the locality from Iowa.

Iowa Slough, Coos County. Iowa Slough flows into Coquille River from the north just west of Riverton. Walling, in his *History of Southern Oregon*, page 488, says the stream was once called Deadman Slough because of the murder of two white men, Venable and Barton, upon its banks in 1854. Five Indians were thought to be guilty of the crime and three were hanged. A post office named Iowa Slough was established in March, 1872, with Harrison E. Nosler postmaster. The office was discontinued in November, 1878.

Ipsoot Butte, Klamath County. This butte, in the extreme northeast corner of the county, is named with the Chinook jargon word for hidden, or secluded. The word *ipsoot* should not be confused with *itswoot,* meaning bear.

Irish Bend, Benton County. Irish Bend is a land area with limits not exactly defined lying west of Willamette River and east of Long Tom River, a few miles northeast of Monroe. The name of the locality comes from a prominent eastward bend in Willamette River in township 14 south. Several Irish families settled in this vicinity about 1860, and gave the name to the river bend and to the bottom land west of the Willamette. The families of James Martin, James Herron and Robert Herron have been among the leading contributors to the development of the area.

Irma, Curry County. Irma was a post office on the old road about midway between Gold Beach and Harbor. It was very close to the north line of township 39 south, range 14 west. The office was established February 11, 1895, with Clara A. Clarke first postmaster. This office was discontinued July 23, 1902. Dodge's *Pioneer History of Coos and Curry Counties* lists N. D. and Clara A. Clark as having settled in that part of Oregon in 1891. Clark appears to have been interested in a variety of things and was an inventor of sorts. Among the children of Mr. and Mrs. Clark was Irma, born in 1879, and it is reasonable to suppose that the post office was named for this sixteen year old girl. Post office records use the spelling Clarke but Dodge has simplified it. The compiler does not know which is correct but past experience has shown post office records in respect of the spelling of proper names are generally reliable. Emma Hardenbrook was appointed postmaster of Irma post office on June 20, 1898, and it is reported that the office was moved about five miles south at that time.

Iron Mountain, Clackamas County. Iron Mountain is the name applied to the area west of Oswego and north of Oswego Lake. In recent years the principal application of the title has been in the expression Iron Mountain Boulevard. An iron ore called limonite was mined extensively in this locality from 1867 to about 1894. F. W. Libbey of the Department of Geology and Mineral Industries has sent the compiler a short statement about this activity which was carried on at first by a company known as the Oregon Iron Company. A small blast furnace was built close to the town of Oswego in 1867, probably the first of such furnaces on the Pacific Coast. The furnace was used fairly continuously to 1886, when a new furnace of modern type was built and put into operation in 1888. Record of iron production ceased after 1894. The new furnace produced nearly 11,000 long tons in 1890 and the industry was of great importance to the Pacific Northwest.

Iron Mountain, Coos and Curry counties. This mountain is a north-south ridge about 15 miles east of Port Orford and has a maximum elevation of about 4000 feet. The compiler does not know by whom the name was applied, but the style Iron Mountain was in use as early as March, 1856. See Glisan's *Journal of Army Life,* page 295. In December, 1943, Earl K. Nixon, director of the State Department of Geology and Mineral Industries, wrote the compiler that the mountain was probably named because of the reddish-brown color of the rock mass and not because of the presence of iron ore as such. The rock outcrops are prominently stained with ferric oxide and there is a lot of manganese stain but no commercial ore deposits.

Iron Mountain, Harney County. This is about ten miles west of Harney Lake and has an elevation of 5380 feet, according to the USGS. It is known as Iron Mountain because of the hard metallic appearance of the rock of which it is composed. During the Indian disturbances of the 1860s, this point was called Pleasanton Butte, apparently in compliment to a well-known officer in the regular army, Alfred Pleasanton, who had been stationed in the Pacific Northwest.

Iron Mountain, Lincoln County. Iron Mountain, elevation 654 feet, a conspicuous point near the Pacific Ocean about four miles north of Newport, is remarkable for its conical symmetry. The upper part is red brown and has a sort of burned, metallic appearance, hence the name. The mountain is just east of the Oregon Coast Highway.

Ironside, Malheur County. The name Ironside was first applied in 1891. It is said that J. M. Young, who was the first postmaster, suggested the name of the post office. The name was chosen because of the proximity of Ironside Mountain, the most prominent geographical feature nearby.

Ironside Mountain, Malheur County. This is the most important landmark in the north part of the county. The highest point is 7804 feet above the sea. It is so called because of its iron-like appearance.

Irrigon, Morrow County. Irrigon is near the site of Grande Ronde Landing, a former rival of Umatilla. For information about these places see under Umatilla. Later the place was called Stokes, and it was a station on the railroad with that name even after Irrigon post office was established. Irrigon post office was established November 16, 1903, with Frank B. Holbrook first postmaster. Addison Bennett made up the name of the place from the words Oregon and Irrigation. Irrigon was the scene of a promising irrigation enterprise, hence Bennett's style of name. He was editor of the first newspaper in the place, called the *Oregon Irrigator*, later the *Irrigon Irrigator*, its initial number appearing January 27, 1904. After various ventures in the newspaper business, he served for many years as a staff writer on the *Oregonian* and died in Portland, September 30, 1924. Stokes post office was in operation from May 26, 1897, until April 25, 1899, with Douglas W. Bailey postmaster.

Irving Glacier, Lane County. Dr. E. T. Hodge of the University of Oregon gave the name Irving Glacier to a small glacier between Middle Sister and South Sister. This was in commemoration of Washington Irving, the author of *Astoria* and *The Adventures of Captain Bonneville*.

Irwin Rocks, Douglas County. These rocks near Reston are named for William Irwin who settled nearby before the turn of the century.

Island City, Union County. Island City got its name because it is on an island formed by a slough which leaves Grande Ronde River west of the town and rejoins the river several miles to the east. The slough is south of the main stream.

Isolate, Douglas County. Isolate was named because of its isolation, and apparently well-named at that. The office was near Days Creek (stream) about ten or twelve miles northeast of Canyonville, near the northwest corner of township 30 south, range 3 west. Isolate post office was established April 17, 1917, with Thomas F. Epping first postmaster. The office was closed to Days Creek office on April 30, 1919.

Israel Well, Deschutes County. This well was on the 1912 homestead of John H. Israel five miles northwest of Brothers.

Isthmus Slough, Coos County. Isthmus Slough was known as Wapello Slough in pioneer days, but the name was changed because the slough led to the isthmus over which there was a trail to Beaver Slough, a tributary of Coquille River. The isthmus lies east of Isthmus Slough. East of the isthmus are Ross Slough, Catching Slough and the mouth of Coos River. A post office named Isthmus was established in the vicinity of Isthmus Slough December 11, 1871, with Gilbert Hall postmaster. The name of the office was changed to Utter City February 11, 1875. The office was closed June 22, 1880. Utter City was named for the Utter brothers, who operated a coal mine.

Ivan, Klamath County. Ivan, once a station on the Southern Pacific Company railroad between Klamath Falls and the California state line, is said to have been named shortly after the railroad was built. The compiler has been unable to get confirmed information, but several sources, generally reliable, are of the opinion that the station was named for Ivan Daniels. Daniels was a railroad employee, probably a pump expert, who is said to have been killed in a tunnel accident not far from the state line. Statements to the effect that the station may have been named for Ivan Kesterson, connected with a local sawmill enterprise, are wrong. In June, 1948, Irving E. Kesterson wrote from Atherton, California, ruling out any connection between the station name and that of his brother Ivan. The two Kestersons were at one time associated in the operation of a sawmill near Ivan station. Irving Kesterson says that he bought the mill in 1917 and his brother Ivan joined the enterprise in 1918. The station had been named some years before. Ivan post office was established November 18, 1926, with Andrew J. Hanan postmaster. The name of the office was changed to Worden in March, 1930. The office was doubtless moved several miles to Worden at that time. There had been a post office at Worden some years previously.

Ivison, Lane County. Ivison was a post office on Wildcat Creek west of Eugene and a few miles east of Walton. The office was established March 3, 1893, with Isaac S. Day first postmaster. Thomas T. McGlynn was appointed postmaster May 11, 1909. The office was discontinued September 15, 1909, with mail to Elmira. In February, 1947, Mrs. C. A. Stephens of Eugene wrote the compiler that she was the daughter of Isaac Day, the first postmaster, and at the time the office was established, Day was asked to submit a name for the place. There was a schoolteacher boarding at the Day home, and the teacher was given the selection of the name, and she chose Ivison. She was with the impression that Day's given name was Ivison and not Isaac, and she selected Ivison in supposed compliment to Day. By the time the error became apparent, postal authorities had established the office with the name Ivison.

Ivy, Clatsop County. This railroad station east of Astoria was so named because of a heavy growth of ivy over the remains of a building south of the track.

Izee, Grant County. In 1927 J. E. Snow of Dayville told the compiler that this post office was so oddly named because a local stockman, M. N. Bonham, used the letters I Z for his cattle brand. Postal authorities inform the compiler that Izee post office was established November 6, 1889, with Carlos W. Bonham first postmaster and was discontinued July 31, 1954.

Jack Creek, Klamath County. Jack Creek is in the northeast part of the county. It heads east of Walker Mountain and flows generally southward to Klamath Marsh and Williamson River. It was originally Jackass Creek, but the passage of time has shortened the name. Dr. Thomas Condon on July 31, 1877, wrote while on a trip to Fossil Lake: "Finally we reached water (at Jackass Gulch), where we camped." See *Thomas Condon,* by Ellen Condon McCornack, page 199. Despite the fact that there are more than a dozen Jack Creeks in Oregon, it is improbable that the original name of Jack Creek will be revived.

Jackknife Canyon, Sherman County. Mrs. Lulu D. Crandall of The Dalles told the compiler that her father, Z. Donnell, named Jackknife Canyon because of the circumstances connected with losing a jack knife near the canyon in the fall of a year in the late 1860s. He found the knife the following spring and named the canyon on that account.

Jackpot Meadow, Clackamas County. Jackpot Meadow is about ten miles south of Mount Hood and drains into Salmon River. It was named because after periods of wet weather it was easy to get into and hard to get out of.

Jacks Bridge, Clackamas and Marion counties. Jacks Bridge is on Butte Creek about a mile southwest of Marquam. The name commemorates that of Jeremiah J. Jack, a native of Tennessee, a pioneer of 1847, and an early settler near Butte Creek. For biography, see *History of the Silverton Country,* page 44. Bute Creek post office was established January 24, 1851, with Jack postmaster. The office was discontinued November 3, 1851. It was on the Marion County list. This office was reestablished in 1867 in Clackamas County with the name Butte Creek and in November, 1889, the name was changed to Marquam. For a time during the 1870s the office may have been in Marion County, although the records are conflicting.

Jackson County. The discovery of gold in southern Oregon in the early 1850s made it desirable to provide a county government for that part of the state and accordingly on January 12, 1852, Jackson County was created and named for Andrew Jackson, seventh president of the United States. As then constituted the county comprised all that part of Oregon west of the Cascade Range and between the south boundary of Umpqua County and the north boundary of California. The county has been reduced in size considerably since its original establishment. Large areas have been taken to form most of Curry and Josephine counties to the west. According to the Bureau of the Census the present area of the county is 2817 square miles.

Jackson Creek, Douglas County. This stream was for many years called South Fork South Umpqua River, a name sufficiently cumbersome to call for a change. It was renamed by the USBGN for Clarence W. Jackson, who was killed by a truck in the state of Washington while in the employ of the USFS. He had formerly been a ranger on the Umpqua National Forest in Oregon.

Jackson Creek, Multnomah and Washington counties. This stream is a tributary of McKay Creek and is about eight miles north of Hillsboro. The falls of this stream are known as Jackson Falls. These features were named for John B. Jackson, a pioneer settler who took up a donation land claim nearby.

Jackson Creek, Tillamook County. Jackson Creek flows through Cape Lookout State Park and empties into the south end of Netarts Bay. It was named for J. H. Jackson, an early settler at Netarts and road supervisor in the 1880s. The creek originally flowed into Pacific Ocean but was diverted into Netarts Bay after World War II.

Jackson Hill, Marion County. Jackson Hill is about eight miles south of Salem. For many years one of the main county highways went over this hill. When the Pacific Highway East was built south of Salem, a new route was followed which eliminated the bad grade over Jackson Hill. Jackson Hill is about one-half mile south of Sunnyside school. It was named for L. A. Jackson, a pioneer resident.

Jackson Lake, Wallowa County. Jackson Lake was named for J. H. Jackson, formerly a resident of Lostine, who first stocked it with trout. It is in the Wallowa Mountains about twenty miles south of Lostine, in the northwest quarter of section 2, township 4 south, range 43 east, and its waters drain into Lostine River.

Jacksonville, Jackson County. The development of Jacksonville began with the placer gold discoveries there in 1851-52. Leslie M. Scott told the writer in 1927 that Jacksonville was named for Jackson Creek, upon which it is situated and Jackson Creek was named for one of the men who discovered gold on its banks. For information about Jacksonville see the *Oregonian,* August 1, 1926, section 1, page 12. Jacksonville post office was established on February 18, 1854, with R. Dugan first postmaster. Sylvester H. Taylor was appointed postmaster on December 19, 1854.

Jacques Creek, Douglas County. This tributary of Elk Creek three miles southeast of Drew was named for Lott M. Jacques who homesteaded nearby in 1901.

Jakey Ridge, Wallowa County. This ridge is the high ground west of Sleepy Creek about eight miles north of Hat Point. It was named for Jakey Wilson whose family owned the Wilson ranch on the Idaho side of Snake River south of Pittsburg Landing. The form Jackey is incorrect.

Jalland Creek, Hood River County. This creek is tributary to Badger Creek near Badger Lake. It was named by USFS ranger Eric Gordon for his mother whose maiden name was Jalland.

James, Clackamas County. James post office operated from November, 1904, to March, 1906, and was obviously named for Dudly (or Dudley) James its first postmaster. In May, 1948, Isaac V. Trullinger, formerly a resident of Clackamas County, wrote that the James post office was situated near Milk Creek between Meadowbrook and Colton. Thomas W. Gerber has written from Canby confirming Mr. Trullinger's statement and adding that James post office was in the north part of section 5, township 5 south, range 3 east. The James family came into that part of Clackamas County about the turn of the century according to Mr. Gerber. There were nine sons and the old gentleman used to brag that he had sired a baseball team, although there is nothing to indicate that the sons ever played after they came to Oregon. Mr. Gerber contributes another morsel to the effect that about the time Dudly James, the oldest son, put up a little store building at the location mentioned above, it burned down and postal activities were transferred to the James house where they were continued until the post office was discontinued in 1906.

Jamestown, Baker County. Jamestown post office was established on the Union County list on June 5, 1882, with James B. Sams first postmaster. The office was apparently named in compliment to the postmaster. It was finally closed on June 21, 1886. Jamestown was near Big Creek, in the extreme north part of Baker County, northeast of Baker. The locality was once in Union County, but a subsequent boundary change brought it into Baker County. Jamestown was also called Big Creek, for the stream.

Jamieson, Malheur County. Oregon Short Line Railroad Company officials named Jamieson for a Dr. William Jamieson, who was an early settler on Willow Creek. The post office was established in 1911, with J. L. Pope first postmaster.

Jamison Meadow, Klamath County. This meadow west of Tea Table Mountain was part of the Jamison Ranch started by William J. Jamison at the turn of the century.

Japanese Hollow, Wasco County. In 1908 three Japanese, S. Nishizasi, H. Okita and M. Yasui incorporated the Columbia Land and Produce Company. They purchased a sizeable tract of land in what soon became known as Jap Hollow where they raised produce for shipment to The Dalles. In the early 1970s as the United States became more sensitive about the feelings of our minorities, the form was changed to Japanese Hollow.

Jarboe Meadow, Union County. This meadow is about 15 miles north of Elgin, in the extreme north end of the county. It drains southward through Jarboe Creek into Lookingglass Creek and bears the name of William H. Jarboe, a local homesteader who was a well-known character of the vicinity. The compiler has seen Jarboe's original signature attached to a letter dated December 29, 1898, written to Fay S. LeGrow, then of Walla Walla, spelled as indicated. The styles Jarbeau and Jarbo are wrong.

Jasper, Lane County. This is a siding on the Southern Pacific Company's Cascade line southeast of Springfield. It was named for Jasper B. Hills who was born in the locality in 1859. He was the son of Cornelius Joel Hills, who settled at the present site of Jasper in 1846. The place was named about 1880.

Jaynes Ridge, Wallowa County. This ridge is in the southeast part of the county. It was named for Barren Jaynes, a pioneer rancher.

Jean Lake, Hood River County. This lake just northwest of Badger Lake was named by USFS ranger Eric Gordon for his eldest daughter Jean.

Jeff Davis Creek, Grant County. This stream, which is just east of Prairie City, was named during the Civil War because there were southern sympathizers mining and prospecting on its banks.

Jeffers Slough, Clatsop County. Jeffers Slough drains an area west of Miles Crossing and flows into Lewis and Clark River. It was named for a landowner. The spelling Jeffries is wrong.

Jefferson, Marion County. Apparently the earliest name for the locality of Jefferson was Conser's Ferry, named for Jacob Conser, the owner. Conser, a pioneer of 1848, was a prominent settler in the Santiam Valley who was mixed up with various business enterprises at several places, including Syracuse and Santiam City, about two miles downstream from Jefferson. He left Santiam City and took up a claim upstream and started his own community. He built his ferry in 1851, but it appears that he was still serving as postmaster at Santiam City in the summer of 1852. Jefferson Institute was established in the vicinity of the ferry, and the name of the institute was eventually adopted by the community, probably on account of the strength of the Democratic party in the neighborhood. The institute was of course named for Thomas Jefferson, third president of the United States. For early history of Conser and the community of Jefferson, see article by Jesse Steiwer Douglas in *OHQ*, volume XXXII, number 4. Milton Hale, a pioneer of 1845, was apparently first to sense the strategic importance of this general locality. He established Hale Ferry on the Santiam River, below the present site of Jefferson. He also established Syracuse on his claim on the south bank. Santiam City sprang up on Samuel S. Miller's claim on the north bank. Conser seem to have been ubiquitous. Moving from the vicinity of Scio, he became first postmaster at Syracuse when that office was established on October 4, 1850. Jacob L. Miller became postmaster on March 14, 1851. On July 27, 1852, the name was changed to Santiam City with Jacob Corson postmaster, an obvious misprint in the postal records for Jacob Conser. Samuel S. Miller became postmaster on October 16, 1852. Postal records of this office are confusing because Syracuse office is listed in Marion County, but the community was of course in Linn County. Santiam City office was listed in Linn County on October 16, 1852, and the community is supposed to have been in Marion County. Douglas, in *OHQ*, volume XXXII, number 3, mentions the complex history of these two places and Conser's activities. Conser's new community gradually drew business up river and Syracuse and Santiam City faded from the picture. The post office was changed to Jefferson on June 13, 1861.

Jefferson County. Jefferson County was created December 12, 1914, and the territory comprising it was taken from Crook County. It was named for Mount Jefferson, which is one of the principal geographic features in the district, and stands at the west end of Jefferson County. For details concerning the name of Mount Jefferson see under that name. Jefferson County has a land area of 1794 square miles.

Jefferson Park, Jefferson and Marion counties. Jefferson Park is a place of peculiar beauty, wedged in across the Cascade Range by Mount Jefferson on the south and by the almost perpendicular walls of a great rock barrier to the north. The floor of the park is about a mile wide north and south, and probably three miles long from east to west. It was formerly known as the Hanging Valley, a name lacking in descriptive quality and appropriateness. The present name of Jefferson Park is much more suitable and is now well established. It was of course suggested by the mountain. The park is about 5900 feet above the sea, and the views to be had from it of the glaciers on the north slope of Mount Jefferson and of the great canyon of the Whitewater to the east must be seen to be appreciated. For excellent pictures of the park and other information see *Mineral Resources of Oregon*, volume II, No. 1, and *Mazama* for December 1925.

Jeffries Creek, Lincoln County. This stream, which flows into Big Creek just north of Newport, was named for a homesteader who settled in the northeast quarter of section 5, township 11 south, range 11 west.

Jennies Peak, Wheeler County. This point, elevation about 4000 feet, is about 12 miles south of Fossil. It was named for Jennie Clarno in the early 1870s. The Clarno family were pioneer settlers in that part of John Day Valley.

Jennings Lodge, Clackamas County. Jennings Lodge was platted as a townsite about 1905 and became a post office in 1910. It was named by Judge B. F. Bonham for Berryman Jennings, an Oregon pioneer of 1847. He was receiver of the Oregon City land office under President Buchanan and helped build the *Lot Whitcomb*, the first steamer built on the Willamette River, at Milwaukie in 1850. In 1927 his house was still occupied by one of his several children, W. B. Jennings. Jennings post office was established November 3, 1910, with Lenora D. Miller postmaster. The name of the office was changed to Jennings Lodge on January 6, 1911.

Jenny Creek, Jackson County. Jenny Creek is formed about one and one half miles southeast of Howard Prairie Lake by the junction of Soda and Grizzly creeks. George F. Wright of Jackson County says the name was applied by U. S. soldiers in the 1850s. They were fording the creek in midwinter and a jenny, or female mule, slipped and drowned in the high water.

Jennyopolis, Benton County. This was an early day post office south of the present site of Corvallis. It was established March 24, 1852, with Richard Irwin first postmaster. It was discontinued April 18, 1857. Such a name would be a handicap to any community.

Jensen Spring, Wallowa County. Jensen Spring is on Summit Ridge at the headwaters of Freezeout Creek. It was named for Mart Jensen, an early settler, who died in 1901. This name has been incorrectly applied to Coyote Springs about three quarters of a mile northeast.

Jerome Prairie, Josephine County. Jerome Prairie is about six miles southwest of Grants Pass. It was named for Jerome Dyer, one of the very early Josephine County settlers. Dyer along with Daniel McKew, was killed by Rogue River Indians on June 1, 1855.

Jessie Flat, Wasco County. This flat in Sorefoot Creek drainage northwest of Clarno was named for Jessie McLennan who took a Stock-Raising Homestead there in 1922. The Stock-Raising Homestead Act of 1916 increased the maximum homestead area to 640 acres when the lands were suitable only for grazing livestock, and required only certain range improvements before patenting. It was repealed in 1934 by the Taylor Grazing Act.

Jessie M. Honeyman Memorial State Park, Lane County. This park which includes parts of Cleawox and Woahink lakes is one of the most popular overnight facilities in the Oregon State Parks system. It was named to honor Mrs. Walter J. Honeyman who was a long time resident of Portland and active in the early conservation movement. For many years she was president of the Oregon Roadside Council whose primary concerns were the beautification of highway roadsides and the preservation of existing natural environment. The park was dedicated July 12, 1941 with Mrs. Honeyman the honored guest. Jessie Honeyman was born in Glasgow, Scotland on June 2, 1852 and died in Portland on July 3, 1948. For obituary see *Oregonian,* July 5, 1948.

Jett, Baker County. Jett was a station on the Union Pacific Railroad about eight miles northwest up Burnt River from Huntington. It bore the name of a family of early settlers. A post office called Jett was at one time in operation in this locality. It was established July 13, 1895, with Mary F. Jett, postmaster and was closed March 15, 1901.

Jewell, Clatsop County. This place was named after Marshall Jewell, postmaster general from 1874 to 1876. The name was given by W. H. Kirkpatrick, first postmaster at Jewell in 1874.

Jim Creek, Jefferson County. Jim Creek is tributary to Awbrey Creek near Hay Creek Ranch. It was named because Jim Scates, Jim Connelly and Jim Howell all settled along its banks. The name Calivan Creek is wrong.

Jim Creek, Wallowa County. This stream enters Snake River in the northeast part of the county, about seven miles south of the Oregon-Washington state line. J. H. Horner informed the compiler that it bears the name of James Wright, who attempted to cross the creek on a small footlog, lost his balance and fell in. This was in the late 1870s. He squatted on a claim near the creek, ranged cattle there and started to build a log cabin on the place.

Jim Hunt Creek, Curry County. James M. Hunt was a gold seeker of 1853 and prominent pioneer settler near the mouth of Rogue River. He is mentioned in *Pioneer History of Coos and Curry Counties.* Jim Hunt Creek bears the name of this pioneer. It flows into Rogue River from the south about six miles northeast of Gold Beach. Hunt Rock at Wedderburn is named for the same man.

Jobs Garden, Douglas County. USFS ranger Fred Asam named this spot on the north bank of North Umpqua River west of Steamboat because the jumble of rocks and boulders was reminiscent of the Bible story.

Jockey Cap, Clatsop County. The name Jockey Cap has been applied to a prominent monolith standing close to the shore at a point a little south of Silver Point. The rock is plainly visible both from the beach and from the Oregon Coast Highway, and should be viewed from the southeast to get the characteristic appearance. The visor of the cap points to the southwest.

Joe Ney Slough, Coos County. This slough is a tributary of South Slough of Coos Bay. S. B. Cathcart of Marshfield informed the compiler in 1929 that Joe Ney settled on the slough in pioneer days. He later went to Elk River in Curry County and bred horses. He died many years prior to 1929.

Joes Point, Wasco County. This promontory three miles northeast of Fivemile Butte was named for Joe White, a very early USFS employee.

John Day, Grant County. The town of John Day in Grant County took its name from John Day River. The post office, with the name John Day City, was established January 20, 1865, with Abraham Himes first postmas-

ter. This office was discontinued in March, 1871. The office was reestablished in July, 1879, with the name John Day. For a good many years there
was a station on the railroad just west of the mouth of John Day River in
Sherman County called John Day, but due to confusion in shipments, the
name was changed to Day. Similar difficulties with John Day station at the
mouth of John Day River in Clatsop County resulted in a change to Van
Dusen, for a well-known county family.

John Day River, Clatsop County. This stream, like the other of the
same name, in eastern Oregon, was named for John Day of the Astor-Hunt
overland party of 1811-12. For information about him, see under the other
heading, John Day River. John Day Point, just east of the river, takes its
name from the stream. Lewis and Clark mention the river in their journals
for November 27, 1805, and give an Indian name *Kekemarke.* Wilkes, in
U. S. Exploring Expedition, volume XXIII, Hydrography, atlas, shows this as
Swan Creek. There was formerly a railroad station near this river, originally called John Day, but some years later changed to Van Dusen, in honor
of the pioneer family of Astoria.

John Day River, Gilliam, Grant, Sherman, Jefferson, Umatilla, Wasco
and Wheeler counties. John Day River is one of the important rivers of
Oregon, but due to the fact that it drains an area with little rainfall, the
stream does not deliver much water. If it is remarkable in this respect, it is
still more so for the great amount of suspended material it carries from its
drainage basin. Measured in tons per square mile, the John Day carries off
198 a year, or practically double that of any other important stream in the
state. (This calculation is at Dayville.) Its total delivery at the Columbia is
more than 750,000 tons of suspended matter a year. It bears the name of
John Day (1771-1819) of the Astor overland party. John Day was a Virginia
backwoodsman. He was a member of the Astor-Hunt overland party, and
he and Ramsay Crooks fell behind the main party in the Snake River country in the winter of 1811-12. They had several terrible experiences, but
eventually got through the snow of the Blue Mountains and fell in with
friendly Walla Walla Indians. These Indians aided the wanderers and sent
them on their way down the Columbia River. In the vicinity of the mouth of
John Day River Crooks and Day met hostile Indians who robbed them,
even of their clothes. The two naked men started back to the Walla Walla
country, but fortunately were rescued by Robert Stuart's party which was
descending the Columbia. John Day's name was applied to the Oregon
river apparently because it was near the mouth of the stream that the two
men were attacked. According to one account John Day went insane in
Astoria in 1814 and was buried there, but T. C. Elliott cites McKenzie's
statement that Day died in the Snake River country in 1820. See *OHQ,*
volume XVII, page 373. Lewis and Clark named this stream Lepages River
on October 21, 1805, after one of their party. John Work uses the name
Day's River in his journal for June 25, 1825. (*Washington Historical Quarterly,*
volume V, page 86.) Peter Skene Ogden mentions John Day's river by that
name November 29, 1825. (*OHQ,* volume X, page 337.) For editorial by
Harvey W. Scott showing impossibilities of Mrs. S. A. Weeks of Sherwood
being daughter of John Day, see the *Oregonian,* January 10, 1910. The

fossil beds of the John Day country are among the most important in America. John Day Dam on the Columbia River just downstream from the mouth of John Day River was completed in 1968. It is a 105 foot high concrete gravity structure impounding Lake Umatilla. The powerhouse generating capacity in 1979 was 2,160,000 KW.

John Henry Lake, Wallowa County. This lake was named for John Henry Wilson of Wallowa, who had mining interests nearby. It is in township 3 south, range 43 east.

John Smith Island, Benton County. This is an island in the Willamette River south of Corvallis. It was named for a prominent citizen of Benton County, who lived in Corvallis for many years. He owned the island and other land in the vicinity.

Johnnie Spring, Douglas County. This spring near the headwaters of Cavitt Creek was named for John Rondeau, an early USFS employee. Rondeau Butte was named for the same man.

Johnny Kirk Spring, Grant County. This spring is on John Day Highway, north of Dayville. It bears the name of an eccentric pioneer character who settled in the John Day Valley, after having been a participant in the '49 gold rush to California. He came to Oregon probably about 1870. In the winter he lived in his bachelor's cabin near the spring that now bears his name; during the summer he mined and prospected in the Blue Mountains. He was popular because of his inveterate story-telling.

Johnson, Lincoln County. Johnson post office was at the Parmele place about half a mile up Drift Creek from the mouth of that stream on the east side of Siletz Bay. The office was established March 11, 1899, with George S. Parmele first and only postmaster. The office was closed May 23, 1903, and what business there was was turned over to Kernville. Parmele operated a general store. The office was named in compliment to Jakie and Sissy Johnson, a local Indian couple, well and favorably known. Jakie is said to have been a Siletz Indian, but his wife was from California. The Johnsons held land by patent and part of the town of Taft is on property owned by the pair.

Johnson Canyon, Morrow County. This canyon runs north into Little Butter Creek northwest of Lena. It was named for Felix Johnson, Sr., who settled near its mouth. Both he and his son, Felix, Jr., were well-known sheep men.

Johnson City, Clackamas County. Johnson City near Gladstone was incorporated by a 49 to 10 vote on June 16, 1970. At the time of the election it had the distinction to be owned entirely by one man, Delbert Johnson. Johnson started the development as a trailer court in 1959 and tried unsuccessfully to have the 45 acre area annexed to Gladstone in 1968. The 1969 Oregon Legislature established a boundary review board to prevent a proliferation of small incorporated cities but the proponents had filed for an election before the effective date of the law. For more details see *Oregon Journal,* June 11, 1970, and *Oregonian,* June 17, 1970.

Johnson Creek, Clackamas and Multnomah counties. U. S. land surveyors named this stream for William Johnson, a pioneer of 1846, who settled near what is now Lents, and there built a sawmill in the 1850s. Scott's *His-*

tory of the Oregon Country gives some additional facts and also has information about Johnson's sons Jacob and Jasper W. Johnson. See also *Oregon Journal*, August 20, 1934, editorial page.

Johnson Creek, Grant and Wheeler counties. This stream flows into John Day River about 10 miles southeast of Spray. It was named for Henry Johnson, a pioneer stock man who settled near the mouth of the stream in the 1870s.

Johnson Creek, Morrow County. This stream in the Butter Creek drainage south of Vinson was named for the well-known family of Felix Johnson, a native of Ireland. Johnson arrived in Morrow County in the 1870s with his two sons, Felix and James. They were well-known local stockmen and the creek was probably named for James whose own holdings were near its mouth.

Johnson Creek, Multnomah County. This stream, which formerly flowed from the neighborhood of Barnes Road across the northern part of Portland, has been partly confined to a drainage sewer and is no longer visible outside of the canyon west of Washington Park. It was named for Arthur Harrison Johnson, a leading meat dealer of Portland for many years. He arrived in Portland in 1852 and soon formed a partnership with Richard S. Perkins in the butcher business. In 1862 Perkins retired but Johnson continued and enlarged the business. His slaughterhouses were in the neighborhood of Twenty-third and Flanders streets, Portland. For information about Johnson, see Scott's *History of the Oregon Country*, volume II, pages 82 and 273, and for his obituary, see the *Oregonian*, April 30, 1902.

Johnson Creek, Umatilla County. James Johnson took up property along this creek on upper McKay Creek drainage in 1917.

Johnson Creek, Wallowa County. This is a small tributary of Imnaha River from the east at a point about 25 miles east of Wallowa Lake. It was named for one Tom Johnson, who took up a homestead along the stream and ranged cattle there.

Johnson Heights, Wheeler County. Hugh S. Johnson homesteaded in 1900 about eight miles north of Waterman at the north end of this prominent ridge.

Johnson Meadows, Lane County. These meadows in the Bohemia district were named for James Johnson, the discoverer of the Bohemia Mine. For further information see under Bohemia Mountain.

Johnson Mountain, Coos County. Johnson Mountain is in the southwest part of the county and Johnson Creek flows around it on the south. These two geographic features were named for a pioneer miner, "Coarse Gold" Johnson, who discovered gold nearby in rich nuggets in 1854. The *Coos Bay News*, August 31, 1887, contains an item to the effect that George Bailey had recently found the remains of a man in the woods south of Sixes River. The remains were identified as those of "Coarse Gold" Johnson, who discovered gold on what was later called Johnson Creek.

Johnson Prairie, Jackson and Klamath counties. This prairie and the creek of the same name on the county line east of Howard Prairie Lake were named for Cal Johnson who settled there in early days.

Jones Butte, Union County. Jones Butte is 3295 feet high and is about two miles north of Elgin. It is named for John E. Jones who was born in Wales in 1818 and emigrated first to the United States and then to the Pacific Northwest. In 1875 he brought his family across the Blue Mountains from Walla Walla and settled by the butte near Elgin or as it was then called, Indian Valley. Jones died in 1889. This information was provided in 1975 by his granddaughter, Ethel M. Chandler.

Jones Creek, Josephine County. Jones Creek is a tributary of Rogue River, about two miles east of Grants Pass. John K. Jones was a pioneer settler near the banks of this stream and it was named in his honor. He and his wife were killed by Indians, and their heirs subsequently owned the claim.

Jones Creek, Lane County. According to A. J. Briem, long time USFS ranger, this small tributary of upper Fall Creek was named for early settler Allison W. Jones.

Jones Hill, Morrow County. Henry Jones who was born in England in 1834 settled southwest of Lena in the 1870s and this hill and nearby canyon both carry his name.

Jonesboro, Malheur County. This station was named for William Jones, a local cattleman. The place is between Juntura and Harper, on the Union Pacific Railroad.

Jont Creek, Polk County. Jont Creek is a small stream that rises in the extreme south border of the county and flows northeastward through Airlie. It was named for one Jont Williams, an early day homesteader in the vicinity.

Joppa, Washington County. The *Pacific Monthly and Official Gazette,* date uncertain, but probably about 1880, contains the following: "Joppa is not the celebrated place where the timber was floated to build King Solomon's Temple, but a discontinued post office eight miles northwest of Forest Grove. A migratory peddler was the postmaster. The authorities in Washington City having learned that he carried the post office in his pocket, concluded it was rather an inaccessible place for the numerous population of Joppa to obtain their mail, and discontinued the office." The compiler has not been able to get much additional information about this post office except that it was established March 13, 1874, with Alvin C. Brown the first of three postmasters. The office was closed July 5, 1876. It has been impossible to get the exact location of the office. It seems probable that the office was named by a biblical enthusiast. The original Joppa was one of the most ancient seaports of the world, on the coast of the Holy Land about 35 miles northwest of Jerusalem. The spelling of the more modern community on the coast of Israel is generally given as Jaffa.

Jordan Butte, Morrow County. Jordan Butte just south of Ione was named for John Jordan who settled near the mouth of Rhea Creek in 1865. Jordan Canyon takes its name from the butte.

Jordan Creek, Curry County. This creek east of Brookings was named for Robert Jordan who homesteaded nearby in the 1870s.

Jordan Creek, Lane County. Jordan Creek flows into Coyote Creek about four miles upstream from Crow. Some maps show this stream with the name Jorden Creek, but in December, 1945, Merle Nighswander, an old timer of the vicinity, wrote the compiler that the correct spelling was Jordan. Mr. Nighswander added that the name was that of an early-day squatter on the banks of the creek.

Jordan Point, Coos County. When the USGS mapped the Coos Bay quadrangle in 1895-96, it applied the name Jordan Point to a feature on the east side of Coos Bay just north of the mouth of Kentuck Slough. This name was supposed to be derived from James Jordan, an early settler who ranged Kentuck Slough as a hunter for the North Bend mill. See Dodge's *Pioneer History of Coos and Curry Counties,* page 358. When the area was remapped nearly a half century later it was found that the name Jordan Point had wandered off to a low promontory on the north side of the bay just west of the Southern Pacific Company railroad. In 1866 Jordan had taken up government land near this point and what is now the adjacent Jordan Cove while four years later he bought property at the first mentioned location on the east side of the bay. It appears he may be entitled to have his name on both sides but in the 1970s the western position was firmly established and prominently identified by one of the largest wood chip loading facilities in Oregon. The eastern feature is now known as Glasgow Point. For further information, see under Glasgow.

Jordan Valley, Linn County. Jordan Valley is just south of North Santiam River, but it does not drain to that stream. Jordan Creek carries the waters of the valley southward into Thomas Creek, which flows into South Santiam River west of Scio. Local tradition says that Jordan Valley was named by Linn County's famous pioneer circuit rider, Joab Powell, in compliment to the Valley of the Jordan in the Holy Land. Many years ago there was a post office called Jordan on the lower reaches of Jordan Creek. This office was established August 10, 1874, with Elias Forgey first of six postmasters. The office was closed out to Scio October 21, 1905. This was due to the extension of rural free delivery. Most maps show this office close to the mouth of Jordan Creek, but it may have wandered around a little.

Jordan Valley, Malheur County. Jordan Valley is the name of a post office in Jordan Valley on the banks of Jordan Creek, which is a tributary of Owyhee River. The stream was named for Michael M. Jordan who was the leader of a party that discovered gold on its banks in May, 1863. He was killed in an Indian fight in the Owyhee country in 1864. See Bancroft's *History of Washington, Idaho, and Montana.*

Jory Basin, Jefferson County. Jory Basin west of Ashwood was the location of the 1888 pre-emption claim of Lorinda P. Jory. Mrs. Jory was the daughter of A. H. Crooks and the wife of Stephen J. Jory. Crooks and Jory were murdered by Lucius Langdon near Grizzly in March 1882 as the aftermath of a property dispute. Langdon was apprehended and a day or so later shot by a lynch mob in Prineville who also hanged a supposed accomplice named W. H. Harrison.

Jory Hill, Marion County. Jory Hill, with an elevation of 737 feet, is southwest of Salem. Several members of the Jory family settled in this neighborhood in pioneer days on donation land claims, and the hill was named for them.

Joseph, Wallowa County. Joseph is a town in the Wallowa Valley and is named for Chief Joseph, (1837-1904), who claimed the valley as his ancestral home, thus bringing on a war with the whites, which resulted in Joseph's retreat to Montana. For details of his life see under Chief Joseph Mountain. Joseph Creek in Wallowa County also bears his name. In January, 1944, J. H. Horner of Enterprise told the compiler that the community of Joseph was first called Silver Lake and also Lake City. When the post office was established about 1880 these two names were suggested but authorities would not accept them because of duplication with other Oregon places. Matt Johnson then suggested the name Joseph, which was accepted.

Josephine County. Josephine County was created January 22, 1856, from a western part of Jackson County. It now has a land area of 1625 square miles. It was probably named for Josephine Rollins, who was the daughter of the discoverer of gold in the Josephine Creek that bears her name, according to H. H. Bancroft, (*History of Oregon*, volume II, pages 415 and 713). This is confirmed by Walling, on page 447 of his *History of Southern Oregon*, who says that Josephine County received its name from Josephine Creek, which was named for Josephine Rollins. Further confirmation is contained in a letter from the woman herself, dated February 19, 1909, a copy of which is in possession of the Oregon Historical Society. She signs herself Virginia Josephine Rollins Ort, and says she was born in Morgan County, Illinois, in 1833. In 1850 the family started for California from Missouri, but finally landed in Oregon. The family again started for California in 1851, and several members, including Miss Rollins, went into the valley of the Illinois River near the stream that bears her name. Mrs. Ort says as far as she knew she was the first white woman in that part of Oregon, and that the county was named for her. She was married in 1854 to Julius Ort, in Colusa County, California, and in 1863 moved to Sonora County, where she was living at the time she wrote the letter. Walling's statement that Miss Rollins' married name was O'Kelly does not seem to be correct. According to Geo. H. Parker (letter to the *Oregonian*, November 2, 1913), Josephine Rollins was then (1913) living at Sonoma, California; Parker wrote that he had received a photograph of her taken when she was forty-five years of age; that she was the sister of the wife of Jacob Thompson, of Ashland; that she came with her father, in 1851, to the county now bearing her name. In 1846 a girl named Martha Leland Crowley died on what has since been called Grave Creek. The legislature, by act of January 6, 1854, tried to change the name to Leland Creek, in honor of Miss Crowley (see *Special Laws* of legislature, page 19). The general public never adopted the new name and the stream is still called Grave Creek. Assertions that Miss Crowley's first name was Josephine and that the county may have been named for her do not seem to be substantiated by the available records. Josephine Rollins was the first white woman who made her abode there, so that the name of the county is probably hers. For history of the grave of Martha Leland Crowley, by C. P. Fullerton, *Oregonian*, November 23, 1883; by James W. Nesmith, *ibid.*, November 23, 1883; page 2; by Matthew P. Deady, *ibid.*, December 5, 1883.

Josephine Creek, Josephine County. This is a tributary of Illinois River west of Kerby. According to Bancroft's *History of Oregon,* volume II, page 713, it was named for Josephine Rollins, who was a daughter of the man who discovered gold in the creek. In another place, volume II, page 227, note 38, Bancroft makes the conflicting statement that Josephine Creek was named for Josephine Kirby whose father discovered gold nearby. The compiler has been unable to reconcile these statements, and in view of what is known about Josephine Rollins, suspects that the story of Josephine Kirby is wrong or possibly a typographical error. For further information, see under Josephine County.

Joy, Wallowa County. Joy was a pioneer post office near the Findley Buttes, about fifteen miles airline northeast of Enterprise. J. H. Horner told the compiler in 1931 that the office was named because of the joy settlers expressed at the possibility of mail service. These people did not then know about circular letters and advertising by mail. Newton W. Brumback was the first postmaster at Joy, in 1888.

Judkins Point, Lane County. Judkins Point, in the east part of Eugene, was named for Thomas H. Judkins, who settled on a farm just east of the promontory in 1853. Judkins was born in New York in 1803 and came to Oregon in 1851. He settled first near Monroe. He died in 1878.

Judson Rocks, Marion County. These rocks are in Willamette River about two miles northwest of Sidney. They were named for L. H. Judson, a nearby landowner of pioneer days.

Jumpoff Joe Creek, Josephine County. Jumpoff Joe Creek is in the extreme northeast corner of the county. The Pacific Highway crosses it in Pleasant Valley. James W. Nesmith, in a letter printed in the *Oregonian* for November 23, 1883, says the stream was named for an exploit of Joe McLoughlin, in 1837 or 1839, but does not state the nature of the exploit. McLoughlin died December 14, 1848. Data in possession of Oregon Historical Society indicate the naming of the stream probably took place in 1828 rather than at the time mentioned by Colonel Nesmith. Joe McLoughlin, son of Dr. John McLoughlin, was in southern Oregon in a trapping party under the leadership of Alexander R. McLeod. The trappers camped one night on this stream and McLoughlin, who came in after dark, fell over the edge of the bluff and received very severe injuries, which, it is said, subsequently caused his death. Myron Eells gives this as the correct origin of the name, and practically the same facts are printed in *West Shore,* October 1883, page 26. Other stories about this name do not seem to be substantiated by historical records.

Junction City, Lane County. About 1870 when the railroad construction war was being waged in the Willamette Valley, Ben Holladay had a scheme to build a west side railroad. It was to join his east side line at a point in the Willamette Valley, not further south than Eugene. Junction City was selected to be the place where the two roads were to come together. The west side road was not built according to plans and as a result the city never became a junction for railroad traffic, but fifty years later it did become a junction of the two main branches of the Pacific Highway through the Willamette Valley. The name, therefore, is now quite appropriate.

June, Lane County. June post office, which was situated on the upper reaches of Lost Creek south of Dexter, was established January 3, 1899, with Malinda Mathews first postmaster. The office was discontinued September 18, 1907, and the business was turned over to Zion, which was a few miles north down Lost Creek. June post office was named for Mount June, a prominent point to the southeast. Mount June was named because snow generally lies on its summit and slopes until that month of the year.

Juniper, Umatilla County. Juniper is a station on the Union Pacific Railroad, in the extreme north part of the county, close to the Columbia River. It is just north of the mouth of Juniper Canyon, which drains a considerable area north of Holdman. These features were named for the scattering juniper trees of the locality. Juniper post office was established June 26, 1884, with John B. Davis first postmaster. Except for a period from June, 1894, to March, 1898, this office was in service until January 31, 1912, though it appears to have been in several different places, never very far from Juniper Canyon.

Juniper Butte, Jefferson County. Juniper Butte is just south of Culver. It is a prominent feature on the landscape, and has a rather peculiar concavity on the north, like a natural amphitheater on a large scale. The compiler is unable to determine why it should have been called for the juniper tree any more than several other buttes in the neighborhood which have as many of these trees growing on their slopes. The juniper of Oregon is *Juniperus occidentalis,* or western juniper.

Juniper Mountain, Lane County. Juniper Mountain is the high point on the west end of Juniper Ridge fifteen miles southeast of Oakridge. It is not named for the eastern Oregon *Juniperus occidentalis* but for an entirely different tree, the dwarf *Juniperus communis* which grows in most sub-alpine areas of western Oregon. This tree is distinguished from other junipers by its dark, lustrous green, keenly pointed leaves or needles as opposed to the scaly gray green leaves of *Juniperus occidentalis.* See Sudworth, *Forest Trees of the Pacific Slope,* page 176 *et seq.*

Junkins Cemetery, Morrow County. William E. Junkins homesteaded southeast of Valby in 1883. When he died in 1887, his family donated this plot of land for a cemetery which now has 15 or 16 graves.

Juntura, Malheur County. *Juntura* is the Spanish word for juncture. It was applied to a community in Malheur County because it was near the junction of the North Fork with the main Malheur River. The name is said to have been selected by B. L. Milligan who settled in the locality in the early 1880s and was later county school superintendent. Juntura post office was established May 5, 1890 with Edw. Ashley first postmaster. After World War II development flagged and on November 2, 1976, the town voted 29 to 1 to unincorporate.

Kah-Nee-Ta, Jefferson County. Kah-Nee-Ta Vacation Resort is north of Warm Springs on Warm Springs River. Once privately owned, it was acquired in the early 1960s by the Warm Springs Tribal Council and developed as one of their self-governed activities. The compiler does not know the time or circumstances of the naming but Kah-Nee-Ta was in use prior to World War II. In 1966, Vern Jackson, Tribal Secretary, said the name meant "gift of the Gods" in Warm Springs dialect but the writer believes his is modern paraphrase.

Kaleetan Butte, Deschutes County. This butte near Devils Lake is named with the Chinook jargon word for arrow.

Kamela, Union County. The compiler has been furnished with several explanations as to how this community got its name, and there is much discrepancy in the various stories that are told. Several early residents of northeastern Oregon say that the word was made up by combining the initials of civil engineers during railroad construction but this is not agreed to by other equally reliable pioneers who say that the word is Cayuse Indian for a tree. Kamela was, during the stagecoach period, known as Summit station. This was unsatisfactory to the railroad company and J. C. Mayo of Stayton informed the compiler in 1927 that Dr. W. C. McKay was asked to furnish a number of names of Indian origin which could be used at various points on the line. From this list Kamela was selected. Mr. Mayo said it meant black pine, although as far as the compiler knows there are not many of these trees in the neighborhood. The official interpreter at Umatilla Agency said in 1927 that Kamela was a Nez Perce word meaning tamarack, and this ought to settle the matter. Miss L. C. McKay, daughter of Dr. McKay, was certain that the word means summit. There was at one time a station on the railroad known as Mikecha, which was made up from the names of three civil engineers, Mink, Kennedy and Chalk, and the writer is of the opinion that this name has been confused with Kamela by those who think that Kamela was a compiled name. Mikecha was at or near the station now known as Gibbon.

Kane Creek, Jackson County. According to Walling, in *History of Southern Oregon,* page 377, the stream near Gold Hill was named for a Doctor Kane who settled nearby in 1853. It was at one time known as T'Vault Creek for W. G. T'Vault, Oregon's pioneer editor, who lived at Dardanelles, near what is now Gold Hill.

Kane Springs, Hood River County. Kane Springs just east of Bonney Meadows was named by USFS ranger Eric Gordon for his wife whose maiden name was Marion Kane.

Kansas City, Washington County. Kansas City is the name of a crossroads community about six miles north-northwest of Forest Grove. It is said that the name was applied because some settlers from Kansas City, Missouri, established themselves there. The writer has not been able to find the name Kansas City on the Washington County post office list and apparently the locality never had a post office called Kansas City.

Kapka Butte, Deschutes County. This butte near Tumalo Mountain was named with the Klamath Indian word for lodgepole pine.

Karlson Island, Clatsop County. Karlson Island is in the south part of Columbia River near Knappa. It has been variously known as Carlson, Carlsen and Karlson. Arthur Dempsie of Astoria informed the compiler that the United States issued a patent on the land on the island in December, 1892, running to the name of Karl Karlson. The property was apparently a homestead. The transaction is filed in Clatsop County Transfer Records, volume 26, page 84, Government certificate 2576. In 1941 Mrs.

Karlson was still alive and vigorous. The USBGN has adopted the spelling Karlson, although some of the younger members of the family spell the name Carlson.

Kaser Butte, Jefferson County. This butte was named for Jake Kaser who settled east of Axehandle in the 1900s. His brother, Julius Kaser, also took up land nearby.

Kaser Ridge, Wasco County. In 1913 Julius Kaser moved onto this high ground on the south bank of Columbia River about five miles east of The Dalles. The USC&GS established a triangulation station named Kaser on the ridge in 1930, but the name Kaser Ridge was first officially applied by the USGS in 1960 when they needed a designation for a water survey.

Kaskela, Wasco County. This is a railway station on the east side of Deschutes River in the south part of the county. The name was suggested by Malcolm A. Moody. Kaskela was the first Warm Springs Indian chief after the establishment of the agency.

Katsuk Butte, Deschutes County. This butte, west of Sparks Lake in the Cascade Range, was named with the Chinook jargon word for middle, presumably because of its location. There is another Katsuk Butte in Lane County five miles southeast of Blue River.

Kawak Butte, Deschutes County. This butte in Paulina Mountains was named with the Chinook jargon word meaning to fly. The name was selected arbitrarily by the USFS.

Keasey, Columbia County. Keasey was named for a local settler, Eden W. Keasey, who was instrumental in securing the post office. This office was established on August 5, 1890, with Keasey the first postmaster. In 1924 the writer was informed that Keasey had moved from the community some years before.

Keating, Baker County. "Uncle Tom" Keating, a jovial British sailor, was one of the first settlers in this community, and owned much of the adjacent land, although he lost most of it in subsequent financial reverses. The office was established about 1880.

Keck Canyon, Morrow County. Keck Canyon was apparently named for Edward Keck who settled near where it empties into Rhea Creek before World War I.

Keen, Wasco County. A post office with the name Keen was established April 14, 1911, with Owen Jones postmaster. The office was closed March 31, 1912. The compiler has tried unsuccessfully to get the significance of the name. Judge Fred W. Wilson has informed the compiler that Owen Jones, who was later murdered, lived near the intersection of the Tygh Ridge road and the old road leading from The Dalles southeast to Sherars Bridge.

Keene Creek, Jackson County. This stream was named for Granville Keene, who was killed nearby by Rogue River Indians about September 1, 1855. The spellings Keen, Kean and Keane are incorrect.

Keener Gulch, Wallowa County. This canyon running south into Imnaha River in township 4 south, range 48 east, takes its name from the G. W. Keener homestead near its mouth.

Keeps Mill, Wasco County. Keeps Mill Camp of the USFS commemorates Joseph R. Keep who just after the turn of the century had a sawmill where Clear Creek flows into White River.

Keeton Creek, Wheeler County. Keeton Creek is tributary to Mountain Creek south of Waterman. It was apparently named for James L. Keeton who took up a homestead in 1887 about two miles above its mouth. Keeton was mayor of Mitchell in 1898.

Keizer Bottom, Marion County. Keizer Bottom is on the east bank of Willamette River north of Salem. It was named for J. B. and T. D. Keizer, pioneers of Oregon, who took up donation land claims nearby in early days. Thomas D. Keizer (Kaizur) was born in Buncombe County, North Carolina, in 1793. In 1828 he moved to Giles County, Tennessee; in 1833 to Van Buren County, Arkansas. He died in 1871. He was an active leader of the 1843 party. He was a member of the legislative committee of 1844, of the provisional government.

Kelleher, Douglas County. Kelleher post office, a few miles west of Yoncalla, was named for William J. Kelleher, a native of County Cork, Ireland, who was an early settler in Douglas County, Oregon. He acquired a number of holdings, including a sawmill at a place he named for himself. The post office was established April 5, 1904, with William H. Sykes first postmaster. Kelleher sold to an eastern lumbering concern, headed by one Skelley, and the name of the office was changed to Skelley, December 21, 1904. The office was discontinued October 31, 1910.

Kelley Point, Multnomah County. On January 6, 1926, the USBGN, at the request of several citizens of Portland bestowed the name Kelley Point on the projection of land between the Columbia River and the Willamette River. This projection is the north point of Pearcy Island, and up to 1926 had no name. It once was the site of a small lighthouse. This action on the part of the Board was taken in honor of Hall J. Kelley, a prominent character in the early exploration of Oregon. About 1817, Kelley, who was a Boston school teacher, began to work on behalf of the development of the Oregon country. He was an enthusiastic eccentric and as early as 1820 began to publish pamphlets on Oregon. He addressed memorials to Congress on Oregon, worked up schemes for colonizing the country, talked Oregon and wrote Oregon, in season and out, until he succeeded in drawing the attention of "many persons in public and private life." In 1830 he issued *A Geographical Sketch of Oregon,* which contained 80 pages and a map. Space does not permit a full discussion of Kelley and his difficulty in reaching Oregon, which he did in 1834. Five years before, in 1829, he drew up a plan for a city in Oregon on the peninsula between the Columbia and Willamette rivers. Real estate men note with interest the prescience of this gentleman one hundred years ago. He even got out a "prospectus." He left Oregon in 1835 and died in Massachusetts in 1874, still writing about Oregon at the age of 85 years. It is appropriate to attach Hall J. Kelley's name to the point where he predicted there would be a great city. The development of Portland is ample vindication of Kelley's judgment and nationally known docks and shipyards are within a few miles of the spot he chose for his metropolis. For information about Kelley's proposal to name mountain peaks in Oregon after various presidents, see under Cascade Range. For information about Kelley and his influence on N. J. Wyeth, see Scott's *History of the Oregon Country*, volume I, page 199. Broughton visited the mouth of the Willamette River on October 29, 1792, and named the southeastern point Belle Vue Point. However it seems apparent that at that time there was a different arrangement of channels and islands in this vicinity from that which exists today. Federal mapping agencies have applied the name Belle Vue Point to a locality on the east shore of Sauvie Island just northwest of the mouth of Willamette River. See under Belle Vue Point for additional information.

Kellogg, Douglas County. S. D. Evans of Roseburg wrote the compiler in July, 1927, as follows: "The above name was given to a place kept by two brothers, Lyman and Adna Barnes "Barney" Kellogg, on the Umpqua River, where freighters hauling from Scottsburg to the mines in southern Oregon found accommodations. A post office was established in early days and may be there yet, but I think it was discontinued a few years ago." This post office is no longer in operation. For additional information about Kellogg see the *Oregonian*, June 21, 1927, editorial page.

Kellogg Creek, Clackamas County. This stream flows into Willamette River at Milwaukie. It was named for Joseph Kellogg, a pioneer of 1848. The widened part of the stream at Milwaukie is known as Kellogg Lake.

Kellow Creek, Tillamook County. This tributary of Little Nestucca River above Meda was named for Thomas Kellow who settled there in 1896. Clarence Dunn of Meda told the compiler in 1967 that it was first called Norton Creek after Seba Norton who homesteaded there in 1891.

Kelly Butte, Lane County. Kelly Butte, near Springfield, was named for John Kelly, a native of County Wexford, Ireland, who came to Oregon from Milwaukee, Wisconsin, about 1843, in the employ of the Hudson's Bay Company. He returned to the United States and took part in the Mexican War, and came to Oregon again with the U. S. Mounted Rifles in 1849 as wagonmaster. He traded in stock between Oregon and California, and finally took a donation land claim near Roseburg. Later he became engaged in milling and other enterprises near Springfield. He married Elizabeth Parker. He was one time collector of customs in Portland, and also receiver or registrar of the land office at Roseburg.

Kelly Butte, Multnomah County. Kelly Butte bears the name of Plympton Kelly, a son of pioneer Clinton Kelly. Clinton Kelly, a Methodist preacher, was born in Kentucky, June 15, 1808, and came to Oregon in 1848. He took up a donation land claim east of the Willamette River, in what is now the east part of Portland. He platted Kelly's Addition to Portland. See the *Oregonian*, January 6, 1872, page 3. He died at Portland June 19, 1875. See OPA *Transactions*, 1887. His biography appears in the *Oregonian*, June 21, 1875, page 3. See also editorial in Portland *Telegram*, June 22, 1926. Kelly Butte is just north of Powell Valley Road and has an elevation of 577 feet.

Kelly Creek, Multnomah County. Kelly Creek, which rises southeast of Gresham and flows northward to join Beaver Creek, bears an old family name, sometimes incorrectly spelled Kelley. Kelly Creek was named for Gilmore Kelly, who had a donation land claim through which the stream flowed. Gilmore Kelly was the brother of Clinton Kelly, one of Oregon's well-known pioneers.

Kelly Gulch, Wasco County. Kelly Gulch runs north towards Pine Grove west of Wapinitia. It was named well before the turn of the century for Hampton Kelly, the son of Portland pioneer Clinton Kelly, who settled near Pine Grove about 1880. Hampton's son, Lucern B. Kelly, was also a well-known resident of Juniper Flat.

Kelsay Valley, Douglas County. This valley is along North Umpqua River north of Diamond Lake. It was named for an early day stockman, "Ves" Kelsay, who ran sheep in that part of the Cascade Range, according to information furnished the compiler by George H. Kelly of Portland.

Kelso, Clackamas County. Kelso is a cross-roads community near the Mount Hood Loop Highway about three miles northwest of Sandy. According to information furnished by William H. Stanley of Gresham, in July, 1947, the place was named for Kelso, Washington. Mr. Stanley got this information from Joel Jarl, the only postmaster the Clackamas County office ever had. In the 1890s Jarl built a little store on his mother's property at this location. The first name proposed for the place was Martinville, but this was rejected by postal officials. The next name to be selected was High Forest for the local High Forest School which had been named for the tall fir trees of the vicinity. This name was also rejected, probably because it was in two words. Jarlson was then suggested, with another veto. T. G. Jonsrud suggested Kelso in compliment to Kelso, Washington, and with the help of Captain Robert Smith of Orient, Kelso post office was established May 31, 1894. The office was closed May 26, 1904, due to the extension of rural delivery.

Kennedy, Harney County. Kennedy post office was west of Harney Lake and in the westward half of the county, several miles northeast of the OO ranchhouse. It was in service from March 10, 1906, to September 15, 1908, with Julius E. Chandler postmaster. It was closed out to Narrows. The office bore the family name of Mrs. Chandler, *nee* Kennedy. Mrs. Chandler's mother, Mrs. Kennedy, was living with the Chandlers at the time the office was established, and the name was doubtless applied on that account.

Keno, Klamath County. This place has had several names, and their history is confusing. Post office records are not as complete as they might be. A post office called Whittles Ferry was established at or near what is now Keno on September 22, 1876, with Robert Marple first postmaster. Apparently the ferry was operated by Robert Whittle and the office was named for him. There was some objection to the name of the office, possibly because it was in two words. Captain O. C. Applegate told the writer that he suggested the name Klamath River, but postal officials also objected to this, for some undisclosed reason. Captain Applegate then suggested the name Plevna, a word then prominent in the news from the Russo-Turkish War. Accordingly the name Whittles Ferry was changed to Plevna on January 9, 1878, but later the office was moved northeast a couple of miles to Juniper Ridge, along with the name. This incensed local patrons and they secured a new office in August, 1887, and named it Keno for Captain D. J.

Ferree's dog. Nellie Doten, postmaster at Keno in January, 1926, informed the writer that her father surveyed and platted the townsite, and called it Doten. This name was objected to for a post office because of the similarity to Dayton. According to her version, the name Keno was then adopted for the office on account of Captain Ferree's bird-dog. Keno, the dog, was named after the popular card game of earlier days.

Kent, Sherman County. J. E. Norton, postmaster at Kent in 1926, wrote the compiler that a petition was circulated in January, 1887, for a post office where the community of Kent is now situated. In order to select a name a number of persons wrote their preferences on slips of paper, which were subsequently stirred in a hat. The name, Kent, was drawn and was the one suggested by R. C. Bennett. M. H. Bennett was the first postmaster. The only reason R. C. Bennett gave for the selection of the word Kent was that it was "nice and short." However, Giles French of Moro told the writer in 1975 that R. C. Bennett was not involved and that Milton H. Bennett was alone in the Kent venture and named the post office on his own.

Kent Station, Douglas County. Kent Station was a military establishment of sorts during the Indian disturbances of 1855-56. It was at the L. D. Kent place on Tenmile Prairie, and was for the protection of the settlers between Roseburg and Coos Bay. Captain W. W. Chapman stationed thirty men there. See Victor's *Early Indian Wars of Oregon*, pages 368-69.

Kenton, Multnomah County. This post office is now a branch of the Portland main post office. Kenton community was established by Geo. F. Heusner. Heusner platted this addition to the city of Portland for an industrial section in 1905. He originally intended to name the addition Kenwood, but found he could not do this because there had been an addition to the city dedicated with that name. He then selected the name Kenton. He told the writer that the name had no particular significance.

Kentuck Slough, Coos County. Kentuck Slough is fed by Kentuck Creek, and flows into Coos Bay from the east. It was named for George W. Thomas, a native of Kentucky, who settled on the slough in pioneer days. He was generally called Kentuck. About 1860 he had a contract to furnish elk meat to Charles Merchant for the North Bend mill. See *Pioneer History of Coos and Curry Counties*, page 358.

Kerby, Josephine County. Kerby is a very old community in Oregon, and was established in the days of gold mining in the southwest part of the state. It was named for James Kerby or Kerbey, who was not consistent in the way he spelled his last name. The name of the community has had even more variations. Josephine County was established by an act passed January 22, 1856, and it was provided that the county seat was to be selected at the next county election. Among the polling places was listed Kirbey's Ranch. Kerby and Samuel Hicks were in the general mercantile and supply business, and according to James T. Chinnock of Grants Pass, in a letter in the Grants Pass *Courier,* December 21, 1928, probably founded a town for the county seat race. The election was held in June, 1857, and Kerbyville was selected. In 1857-58 Dr. D. S. Holton got a large interest in the town of Kerbyville. He was probably responsible for an act of the legislature December 18, 1856, changing the name from Kirbeyville to Napoleon. This was either because of the association of the name of the county and the Empress Josephine, or because Holton was an admirer of Napoleon III. The new name was not popular, and an effort was made to get a bill through the next legislature to adopt the old name. In the fall of 1860 the house passed a bill to change the name from Napoleon to Kirbeyville, but on October 10, Holton succeeded in getting the bill referred to the senate judiciary committee, where it is still embalmed. The county commissioners used the name Napoleon for a short time, but seem to have dropped it in favor of Kerbyville about April, 1860. A list of county seats in the Oregon *Statesman*, February 11, 1861, includes Kerbyville, and that is the name that was used for a good many years, despite the fact that the legislature declined to restore it. Later still the name was changed to Kerby in the interest of simplicity, and Kerby it now is. The name of the first post office has had a much simpler history. Kerby office was established in September, 1856, with James Kerbey postmaster. It is still operating with the original name. It is said that in the mining days one of the founders of the original town brought a pool table on his pack train from Crescent City. The table was intended for another mining camp, but on arrival near the site of the present town of Kerby, the mule packing the principal part of the table strayed away one night, loaded, and the weight of his load was so great that he died before morning. The packer concluded that the location was as good a place for a pool hall as any, and after burying the mule, set up shop on the spot. On December 4, 1937, the Grants Pass *Courier* printed an interview with B. Kerbey Short of Auburn, Washington, in which Short said he was a grandson of the man for whom Kerby was named and that the family spelling was Kerbey. It seems improbable that the name of the community will be changed.

Kernan Point, Wallowa County. Kernan Point is in the northeast part of the county in township 2 north, range 50 east. It was named for John Kernan, due to the circumstance that he and one Nate Tryon killed a deer nearby. He ranged sheep in the vicinity of the point. Kernan and Wilkes Jennings were drowned in Snake River on March 4, 1894, while attempting to cross in an Indian boat or canoe.

Kernville, Lincoln County. In April, 1943, Miss Grace Kern of Portland wrote the compiler about the beginnings of this community. Kernville was named by the late Daniel Kern of Portland, who with his brother, John H. Kern, operated a salmon cannery on Siletz River not far from its mouth. The business was known as Kern Brothers Packing Company and was started in 1896. The locality was isolated and could be reached only by water. The cannery was sold in 1898 to Mat P. Kiernan and J. W. Cook of Portland. Later it passed to the hands of Sam Elmore of Astoria. Kernville is now on the Oregon Coast Highway, a great change from 1896. The cannery was on the north bank of Siletz River about two miles up stream from the Oregon Coast Highway bridge and the location of Kernville in 1945. The sawmill, post office and original community of Kernville were on the southwest bank about a mile up stream from the present site of Kernville. See also story by Ben Maxwell in *Sunday Oregon Journal,* magazine section,

November 4, 1945. Kernville post office was established July 6, 1896, with John H. Kern first postmaster. Matthew P. Kiernan became postmaster August 7, 1899. The office has been out of service at times.

Kerr Notch, Crater Lake National Park, Klamath County. This is the lowest part of the rim above Crater Lake and is about 500 feet from the surface of the water. It was named for Mark B. Kerr, USGS engineer in charge of the party that surveyed the lake in 1886. He pronounced his name as though spelled *Kar.* Kerr Valley is just southeast of Kerr Notch.

Kerry, Columbia County. Kerry is at the junction of what was the Columbia and Nehalem River Railroad and the Spokane, Portland and Seattle Railway. It was named for A. S. Kerry, who started the community in 1912, when he was interested in the development of the first named railroad, extending it into his extensive timber holdings in the Nehalem Valley. Kerry was for many years a prominent business man of Portland and Seattle. He died at Seattle on April 27, 1939. The Columbia and Nehalem River Railroad has been dismantled, and Kerry is no longer a railroad station, but it is a community on the Columbia River Highway.

Ketchketch Butte, Deschutes County. This butte is southwest of Crane Prairie. The name comes from the Klamath Indian word *Ketchkitchli,* meaning rough. A derivative of the same word is *ketchkatch,* the rough-furred little gray fox. The USFS applied the name because of its distinctive sound and with the desire of perpetuating Indian words.

Ketchum Ranch, Hood River and Wasco counties. William K. Ketchum came to The Dalles as a boy in 1883 and homesteaded this ranch on Mosier Creek in 1900.

Kettle Creek, Jackson County. Kettle Creek is in the north part of the county and flows south to join Sugarpine Creek on the north line of township 32 south, range 1 east. In May, 1946, Howard L. Ash of Trail, an old-timer in that part of Oregon, wrote the compiler that the stream was named because Andy Pool and Sam Gray found a kettle on its banks in 1905. They were on a hunting trip. This old iron kettle held a few lumps of what appeared to be coal, and the hunters turned prospectors. They searched the stream and also the rock point just to the west, but found no coal. This rock point is now called Kettle Rock. Later what appeared to be coal was found a few miles to the northwest, but the compiler has been told that it is just a black rock. See under Coalmine Creek.

Kettle Creek, Wallowa County. According to J. H. Horner of Enterprise this stream was named in 1883 because a broken camp kettle lay in the creek. A packhorse belonging to Enoch G. Vaughan and David M. Dennis bucked his pack off and jammed the kettle beyond use. The kettle lay in the water for many years. The creek flows into Imnaha River in section 10, township 2 north, range 48 east.

Keyes Creek, Wheeler County. Keyes Creek was named for James E. Keyes who settled near Mitchell, and nearby Keyes Mountain was probably named for his cousin Zachary Keyes. The two drove 600 cotswold ewes from Philomath to the Bridge Creek area in 1873 to start the local sheep industry. Judge Henry D. Keyes, the well-known rancher and County Judge, was the son of Zachary.

Kiger Creek, Harney County. The name of this stream is frequently misspelled Kieger and Keiger. It was named for the Kiger family, well-known pioneers near Malheur Lake. For information about the Kiger family, see under Kiger Island, also *OHQ,* volume XXXII, page 125, and Lockley article on editorial page of the *Oregon Journal,* June 25, 1927.

Kiger Island, Benton County. Kiger Island is southeast of Corvallis between the main channel of the Willamette River and the Booneville Channel. It was named for Reuben C. Kiger, a pioneer resident of Benton County. He was born in 1828 and died in 1907. In 1874 the Kiger family moved to Harney County and settled near Steens Mountain, but Kiger moved back to western Oregon in 1878 because of Indian troubles. Kiger Creek in Harney County was named by his wife Minerva J. (Morgan) Kiger, better known as Dolly Kiger. She also named McCoy Creek and Cucamonga Creek in the Steens Mountain country. She was born July 28, 1850, and was married to Reuben C. Kiger on November 18, 1866. She died at Corvallis on January 8, 1928.

Kilbride, Grant County. Kilbride was a post office near Middle Fork John Day River about six or eight miles northwest of and down stream from Galena. The office was established March 22, 1901, with Margaret Hamilton first of four postmasters. It was discontinued May 31, 1908, with mail to Susanville. Margaret Hamilton was Mrs. Robert Hamilton. Mrs. Hamilton named the office for Kilbride, Scotland, which was at or near the place of her birth.

Kilchis Point, Tillamook County. Kilchis Point is on the east shore of Tillamook Bay, and Kilchis River is close by. These features were named for Kilchis, a chief of the Indians of the Tillamook Bay region. He was friendly to the whites. Kilchis post office was established about 1872 with W. D. Stillwell first postmaster. The office was closed about 1890, because the community of Bay City had been established nearby, with a post office, and there was no longer a need for an office at Kilchis. The locality of Kilchis Point was called Jawbone in pioneer days, it is said, because a sawmill enterprise was built on "jawbone" when no cash was available.

Kilkenny Fork, Morrow County. Kilkenny Fork is a tributary of Hinton Creek about eight miles east of Heppner. It was named for John S. Kilkenny, a native of Ireland, who came to Morrow county in 1890 and settled along the creek in 1914.

Killam Creek, Tillamook County. Killam Creek is a pleasing stream that finds its way into Tillamook River southeast of the town of Tillamook. It bears the name of Leonard Killam who took up a claim in 1879, his land bordering on the stream. Various other spellings such as Kilham, Killum and Killiam are wrong according to county authorities.

Killamacue Creek, Baker County. This stream drains Killamacue Lake and flows into Rock Creek. Old maps show a variety of spellings, but the USBGN has adopted this as best representing the pronunciation of the name. The compiler has been unable to learn the meaning of the name.

Killgaver, Multnomah County. Killgaver post office was in operation from August 5, 1886, to October 9, 1899, with John Howard the only postmaster. This office was in the Howard home on the Section Line road, now Southeast Division Street in the vicinity of what is now Southeast 112th Avenue. In July, 1947, the compiler was informed that the Howards were either born in Ireland or were of Irish descent and named the Oregon post office for a place in the Emerald Isle. Modern atlases do not show such a place in Ireland, but Killgaver may have been used as an Irish place name in the early 1880s.

Kilts, Jefferson County. Kilts post office was named for Jesse Kilts, an early resident of the place and once postmaster. The office was discontinued June 29, 1940. While Kilts was the post office name, the local residents called the locality Donnybrook. An earlier name was Axehandle, but Donnybrook was adopted as the result of a gathering in Calf Gulch at which there was considerable disorder and some blood was shed. An editorial in the Bend *Bulletin,* April 20, 1943, says that Kilts was a homesteader and relatively a newcomer. The editorial contains the following paragraph: "But old timers have long resented a community name which honors a newcomer, a member of the homesteading fraternity whom elderly stockmen referred to as 'scissorbills.' To Dan Crowley, one of the few old time survivors of the olden days, Kilts is still Donnybrook. And if you stop in Ashwood on your way east to the Horse Heaven mines to ask about the country beyond Ash Butte and the Red Jacket mine, folks of the Trout Creek village will tell you that the community up on the highlands is known as Donnybrook. Only postal inspectors are told that the region is known as Kilts." Another editorial in the Bend *Bulletin,* September 18, 1937, says that Kilts post office was originally on the John Day side of the divide, but when Dan Crowley became postmaster he had the office moved to the locality of Donnybrook in the Deschutes drainage.

Kimball Hill, Curry County. Kimball Hill is near the south bank of Rogue River about seven miles east of the Pacific Ocean. It was named for Ira Kimball who, with his wife, Amanda, located on the small river bottom near the western base of the hill. Kimball Creek nearby received its name from the same source.

Kimberly, Grant County. The name of this post office was suggested by Elizabeth C. Murphy. She chose the name because the Kimberly family was well known thereabouts.

Kime, Malheur County. Kime station was named for William Kime, a former resident of the vicinity. It was just west of Harper.

Kincaid Canyon, Morrow County. This canyon is in the Eightmile drainage north of Utts Butte. John L. Kincaid patented the adjacent land in 1890.

Kincheloe Point, Tillamook County. This is the south point at the entrance of Tillamook Bay. It bears the name of Sub-Assistant Julius Kincheloe, of the USC&GS who was drowned at the mouth of the bay on May 20, 1867. An account of this tragedy appears on page 11 of the *Report of the Superintendent* of the Coast Survey for 1867. Kincheloe joined the Coast Survey in 1854, and from the remarks of the superintendent, appears to have been an efficient and experienced officer, and was held in high esteem by his associates. At the time of his death Kincheloe was attempting to complete a line of soundings across the bar, and when his boat was capsized, five of his crew of six were drowned with him. Miss Lucy E. Doughty of Bay City, an early resident of the community, wrote the compiler that Mrs. Kincheloe was on the shore at the time of the accident and saw her husband swept into the sea. Later, she completed her husband's report, copied all the necessary notes and sent them to Washington with an account of the tragedy.

Kindred, Clatsop County. A post office named Kindred was established on the Clatsop County list May 19, 1894, with Mabel N. Ford postmaster. The National Archives says that the office was discontinued August 14, 1894. It seems apparent that the establishment was never in actual operation as a post office. The office was doubtless named for Bartholomew C. Kindred who lived at what was known as New Astoria or Kindred Park on the Kindred donation claim near what is at present known as Flavel. The office may have been intended to serve the community now known as Hammond, which is on the original Kindred property. Mr. and Mrs. Bartholomew C. Kindred came to Oregon in 1844.

King, Marion County. King post office was in the west part of township 8 south, range 1 east, probably near Drift Creek. A map of 1911 shows it near the south line of section 17. This office was established August 21, 1890, with William H. King first of four postmasters. With one intermission the office operated until September, 1903, when it was closed to Jefferson. This move seems strange to the compiler as there were other operating offices much nearer than Jefferson. It is apparent that the office was named for the first postmaster.

King Canyon, Morrow County. Albert T. King was one of the earliest Morrow County settlers and he took a homestead near this canyon south of Ione in 1882. His daughter Dollie's marriage to Bert Haney in March, 1885, was the first recorded in Morrow County. King had three sons, Benjamin, John and William, who also took up land nearby.

King Canyon, Wasco County. Cold Camp Creek flows through King Canyon just before it empties into Antelope Creek. It was named for Zachary T. King who homesteaded there in 1903.

King City, Washington County. King City is a planned adult community organized by the Tualatin Development Company, Inc., and incorporated in March 1966. The name was an arbitrary selection by R. B. Sorensen, the president of the development company, who also used the royalty theme in naming streets and certain other facilities.

King Creek, Coos County. King Creek is a tributary of Middle Fork Coquille River. It was named for a Dr. King, who settled nearby in pioneer days.

King Creek, Lane County. This creek rises on the high ground south of McKenzie Bridge and flows north. It was named for Andy King who lived on its upper reaches after World War I. The compiler has been told that King found the solitude particularly suitable for the manufacture of a certain type of refreshment at that time not available through regular commercial channels.

King Mountain, Harney County. King Mountain is about 20 miles north of Harney. It was named for E. H. King, who established a mountain sawmill nearby about 1880. He came to Oregon from Red Bluff, California. The name Trout as applied to this mountain is an error, and is caused because the point is near the head of Trout Creek. The name King Mountain is now generally accepted by the public.

King Slough, Lincoln County. King Slough is a fairly large inlet on the south side of Yaquina Bay. In the 1880s one Jack King had a homestead near the head of this slough and the feature took his name. King also ran a small camp in the locality. In earlier days the inlet was called Hinton Slough, but that name did not persist.

King Well, Deschutes County. This well was on the property of Orlea O. King who settled four miles west of Brothers before World War I.

Kingman, Malheur County. Kingman was a station on the Union Pacific Railroad south of Nyssa. It was named for A. G. Kingman, a resident and founder of the small community. The only use of the name on maps of the 1970s is Kingman Road.

Kings Landing, Coos County. Kings Landing was the name of a locality about nine miles south of Coos Bay, on the west side of Isthmus Slough, at or about the same place that in recent years has been called Delmar. It was named for one King, who lived there. Kings Landing was the transfer point where passengers and goods were set ashore at the head of navigation from Coos Bay. At Kings Landing a narrow gauge railroad took off and extended south to Coaledo, at which point there was a transfer back to boats again. There was no post office with the name Kings Landing.

Kings Valley, Benton County. Kings Valley was named for Nahum King, the first settler, who was an Oregon pioneer of 1845. The flour mill was built by Rowland Chambers in 1853. Kings Valley post office was established on April 13, 1855, with Chambers first postmaster.

Kingsley, Wasco County. Judge Fred W. Wilson informed the compiler in 1927 that Kingsley was named by his mother, Mrs. E. M. Wilson, about 1878 when she was postmaster at The Dalles. A delegation from Kingsley called on Mrs. Wilson at The Dalles post office with a petition for a new post office to serve a part of the county south of Dufur. The petition suggested a commonplace name. Mrs. Wilson had been reading Charles Kingsley's *Westward Ho!* and the book lay in her lap. She immediately suggested the name of the great English clergyman and writer for the new office and the suggestion was accepted on the spot. The town plat was filed on May 16, 1893. Kingsley was not a post office in April, 1927.

Kingsley Field, Klamath County. Kingsley Field is a USAF Base and Klamath Falls Municipal Airport. During World War II the field was a U. S. Naval Air Station. This was deactivated in 1946 and replaced in 1956 by the present USAF installation. It was named for Lieutenant David R. Kingsley of Portland, Oregon, who was killed in action over Ploesti, Rumania, on June 23, 1944. Kingsley was posthumously awarded the Medal of Honor for heroic action when he sacrificed his own life to save a wounded companion.

Kingsley Guard Station, Hood River County. This USFS Guard Station and Forest Camp east of Mount Defiance are at the site of an early summer home of Edward D. Kingsley, president of the West Oregon Lumber Company. Kingsley was active in lumber circles in the Northwest. He died in Portland September 4, 1940.

Kingston, Linn County. This was a station near the North Santiam River, not far from Stayton. It is said to have been named for Samuel King, who lived there many years before the railroad was built.

Kingston Creek, Tillamook County. This tributary of Neskowin Creek was named for Paul Kingston, an early settler who lived near the site of the old Neskowin Forest Camp.

Kinton, Washington County. Kinton is a place on the Scholls Ferry Road south of Cooper Mountain. It was named for Peter Kindt, who took up a donation land claim nearby in pioneer days. For information about Kindt and Kinton, see the Hillsboro *Argus,* January 21, 1932.

Kinzel Creek, Clackamas County. This stream, which flows into Salmon River south of Rhododendron, is near a mining prospect owned by Tom Kinzel, and was named on that account. Kinzel was a prospector and packer in this part of the Cascade Range. The small lake or pond drained by Kinzel Creek is known as Kinzel Lake.

Kinzua, Wheeler County. Kinzua lumber town and post office was established in 1928. The place was named by the Kinzua Pine Mills Company for Kinzua, Warren County, Pennsylvania, a community on Allegheny River. At the time, it was said that Kinzua meant a place of many fishes. On October 16, 1930, the postmaster at Kinzua, Pennsylvania, told the compiler that highway signs in that community said Kinzua was an Indian name meaning waters of many and big fish. However, an inquiry to an old Indian in the vicinity brought the information that he believed that the word actually meant that there were always fish for the spear rather than for other methods of catching.

Kirby Creek, Baker County. Kirby Creek, in Eagle Valley, was originally called Little Eagle Creek, because it was a separate channel of Eagle Creek. This caused confusion with another Little Eagle Creek, tributary to the main stream, about eight miles further north. Local residents recommended that the creek in Eagle Valley be called Kirby, for a local resident, which was done by the USBGN.

Kirk, Klamath County. Kirk is the name of the family upon whose allotment the community is situated. Jesse Kirk was a prominent and respected Indian, an ordained Methodist minister. The name was first chosen by the Southern Pacific Company for a station name at a point that was for several years the end of the line north of Klamath Falls. The post office was established in 1920, with the name Kirkford; why the additional syllable no one seems to know, although it is true there is a ford in Williamson River nearby. The scheme of different names for station and for post office has always been unsatisfactory, and it was so in this case, and in 1925 the postal authorities changed the office name to Kirk to agree with the station name.

Kirkbride Canyon, Jefferson County. J. A. Rooper of Antelope told the writer in 1969 that this canyon near upper Trout Creek was named for Al Kirkbride who ranched there with his brother about the time of World War I.

Kirkendall Branch, Douglas County. James A. Kirkendall homesteaded near this creek in Camas Valley in 1877.

Kirkland Spring, Wallowa County. This spring in section 13, township 4 north, range 45 east, was named for Wright Kirkland, a pioneer stockman of the locality.

Kishwalks, Wasco County. Kishwalks is a locality on the Warm Springs

Indian Reservation, north of the agency. It bears the name of an old Indian, very lame, who lived there. It is possible that the word in some way referred to his infirmity and that it was a mixture of the Wasco and English languages, but in January, 1944, Indians at the agency were not definite about the origin.

Kist, Columbia County. Kist post office was in the southwest part of the county near Nehalem River, several miles upstream from the mouth of Clear Creek. The office, which was established January 21, 1899, is said to have been named for a local homesteader who had the misfortune of being frozen to death a short time before the office was established. Kist post office was discontinued May 31, 1912, and the business was turned over to Timber. Nearby Kist Creek retains the name.

Kitson Hot Springs, Lane County. Dave Kitson of Springfield, a left-handed English carpenter, took up these springs many years ago and established a summer resort there. The springs and Kitson Ridge just to the north bear his name.

Kittredge Lake, Multnomah County. This was the correct name of the small overflow lake on the west banks of the Willamette River east of Oilton, not Kittridge. It was named for George Kittredge, a pioneer settler who was born in Vermont in 1808. The lake was filled in in the 1940s, but since then the Kittredge Viaduct has been an important overpass over the Burlington Northern tracks.

Kiwa Butte, Deschutes County. This butte southwest of Bend was named by the USFS with the Chinook jargon word for crooked or bent. The name is descriptive.

Kizer Creek, Lane County. Kizer Creek is a tributary of Mosby Creek about five miles southeast of Cottage Grove. It was apparently named for Thomas C. Keizur who took up a donation land claim along its banks in 1863.

Klak Butte, Deschutes County. This butte southwest of Bend, was named by the USFS with the Chinook jargon word for cut off, indicating its shape.

Klamath Agency, Klamath County. Klamath Agency was established May 12, 1866, on the shore of what is known as Agency Lake, about three miles south of the present site of the agency. It is now on Crooked Creek. The Klamath Indian Reservation was abolished in 1961 but the community of Klamath Agency continues. For the origin of the name Klamath see under Klamath County.

Klamath County. Klamath County was created October 17, 1882, by the state legislature. It was taken from Lake County as it existed at that time. It was named for the tribe of Indians called Klamath by the white travelers. The first appearance of the name as far as the compiler knows is in a letter from Peter Skene Ogden, dated Burnt River, July 1, 1826, which refers to the "Claminitt Country." See Merk's *Fur Trade and Empire,* page 274. On October 5, 1826, David Douglas wrote of looking into the country called "Clamite" by the natives who inhabited it. Ogden, who used the form "Clammitte" on November 5, 1826, reached the headwaters of the Klamath drainage on November 27 of that year, but indicates in his diary that McKay and McDonald, of his party had been there before. The theory has been advanced that the name originated with the French words *clair metis,* meaning light mist, which frequently lies above Upper Klamath Lake. The trouble with this notion is that the French style would be *metis clair,* and if these words mean anything, they mean a light colored halfbreed. However that may be, both Indians and white men used the name at an early day, the former for the lakes, and the latter for the Indians. The name may be a corruption of *Mak-laks.* See under that heading. Among the spellings used by early writers are: *Clemmat, Clam-ath, Klamet, Clemet, Tlamath* and many others. For references, see *OGN,* 1928 edition, page 186. The Klamath Indians are classed as a Lutuamian tribe, living about Upper Klamath Lake, also on Williamson and Sprague rivers. They call themselves *Euksh-ikni,* or *Auksni,* "the people of the lake." For information about the lakes, see under Lower Klamath Lake and Upper Klamath Lake. According to the Bureau of the Census, Klamath County has a land area of 5973 square miles.

Klamath Falls, Klamath County. The community of Klamath Falls is situated at the falls of Link River, where that stream flows into Lake Ewauna. The place was originally known as Linkville and was named for Link River. The Klamath Indian name for the place was *Yulalona,* or *Iuauna,* which referred to the peculiar blowing backward of the waters of Link River during strong south winds. For information about these Indian names see under Lake Ewauna and Link River. The Klamath name for the falls in Link River was *Tiwishkeni,* or rush of falling waters place. George Nurse founded the town of Linkville in 1867, and a memorial tablet commemorating the event is installed in one of the concrete columns of the Link River bridge, in the west part of Klamath Falls. The name was changed to Klamath Falls in 1892-93.

Klamath Marsh, Klamath County. This marsh is fed principally by Williamson River, of which it is an enlargement, and by small streams flowing from the Cascade Range. Its main outlet is Williamson River. Its elevation is just about 4500 feet. It was named for the Klamath Indians. These Indian called the marsh *Eukshi,* and used the same word to indicate the whole of the Klamath territory from Modoc Point up along the east shore of Upper Klamath Lake to the marsh. By slight differences in intonation, they indicated different localities with the same word, *Eukshi.* At the southern part of the marsh are Wocus Bay and Little Wocus Bay. For information about these features, see under the respective headings. In the fall of 1826 Peter Skene Ogden took a trapping and exploring party into the Klamath country. Apparently on November 30, 1826, the party reached the neighborhood of Klamath Marsh, although at just what point the compiler is not certain. On December 6 of that same year Ogden mentions in his diary that Finnan McDonald, one of the Hudson's Bay Company men, had been that far the year before. At that date Ogden was further south than Klamath Marsh, so in all probability McDonald was the first white man to reach Klamath Marsh. For additional data, see under Klamath County. John C. Fremont reached and very accurately described Klamath Marsh on December 10, 1843, although at that time he thought he was at "Tlamath lake." Much of the marsh has been drained.

Klamath Mountains, Curry, Douglas, Jackson and Josephine counties.

This is the name used by Dr. J. S. Diller in USGS Bulletin 196, *Topographical Development of the Klamath Mountains,* to describe part of the Coast Range of Oregon and California between the 40th and 43rd parallels of latitude. The name is used by geologists rather than by geographers and map makers. The Klamath Mountains are made up of subordinate systems, including the Siskiyous. Geologically they resemble to a considerable extent the Sierra Nevada. The bulletin mentioned gives a detailed account of the development of these mountains, and explains why they are considered a separate group.

Klamath River, Klamath County. Klamath River receives the drainage of Upper Klamath Lake through Link River and Lake Ewauna. See under these headings for information about their Indian names. The Klamath Indian name for Klamath River was *Koke,* the general name for river, and the hearer had to judge from the context which river was meant, Williamson, Lost, Sprague or Klamath. For information about the name Klamath, see under Klamath County. Klamath River has a total drainage area of 11,850 square miles in Oregon and California, and has a total length of 180 miles between Lake Ewauna and the Pacific Ocean. About five miles above Keno the river is connected to Lower Klamath Lake by a stream, now under dike control, known as Klamath Strait. Water formerly flowed through Klamath Strait either way, depending on the relative stages of Klamath River and Lower Klamath Lake.

Klamath Strait, Klamath County. Klamath Strait is the correct name of the outlet of Lower Klamath Lake, not Klamath River. Klamath River flows from Lake Ewauna, and the river is connected with Lower Klamath Lake by Klamath Strait. This strait formerly flowed either way, but its course has been interfered with by the Southern Pacific Company railroad grade.

Klaskanine River, Clatsop County. For information about this name see under Clatskanie. The Klaskanine River affords a route of travel from the mouth of the Columbia River to the place in the Nehalem Valley where part of the Tlatskani Indian tribe lived. The name of the stream in Clatsop County is spelled differently from the name of the Columbia County stream. In recent years, and as a result of more accurate mapping, the names of the branches of this stream have become established. South Fork Klaskanine River presents no problem. North Fork Klaskanine River heads south of Wickiup Ridge and joins the South Fork about two miles east of Youngs River, the two forks forming Klaskanine River. North Fork North Fork Klaskanine River flows into the North Fork at Klaskanine Hatchery. It heads west of Wickiup Ridge. Southeast of this branch is Middle Fork North Fork Klaskanine River which also heads west of Wickiup Ridge and flows into North Fork about five miles upstream from the hatchery.

Klawhop Butte, Deschutes County. *Klawhop* is the Chinook jargon word for hole, and this butte southeast of Bend presumably was named because it had a crater in the top.

Klickitat Mountain, Lane County. This is a prominent peak near the east end of Klickitat Ridge, in the Coast Range in the extreme north part of Lane County. It is unusual that the name of an Indian tribe, whose dwelling place was near The Dalles of the Columbia River, should be attached to a mountain so far away, and yet there is good evidence to verify the story that the Klickitat Indians traveled over a wide area. In pioneer days there was a trail near Rickreall Creek known as the Klickitat Trail, and there was a definite Klickitat camping place near the Boyle Lakes, northwest of the present community of Rickreall. J. W. Nesmith, in a letter in the *Oregonian*, February 7, 1877, says that in September, 1849, he and General Joseph Lane went from the Willamette Valley to the Siletz River over a trail used by Klickitat Indians at that time living in Kings Valley. For description of the origin of the name Klickitat see Meany's *Origin of Washington Geographic Names*. Early writers spelled the word in a variety of ways. General Hazard Stevens says that the word meant robber and tradition in the Willamette Valley in Oregon favors this meaning. The writer has been told by a number of Indians that the correct definition of the word was robber or marauder. General Stevens had first hand information, and the writer is inclined toward his opinion in the matter. David Douglas mentioned the tribe as *Clickitats* on June 20, 1825, which is as far as the writer knows the first use of the word by early explorers.

Klingers Camp, Wasco County. Louis J. Klinger was born in Missouri in 1837 and came to Oregon ten years later. He settled in the Eightmile area in 1863 where he ranched and freighted on the Barlow and Canyon City roads. At one time he maintained a supply camp on the Barlow Road near the present USFS marker above White River. In 1889 he retired to Dufur and later served a term as mayor. He was an indefatigable supporter of the then proposed road from Dufur west to the Mount Hood area. Clinger Spring near Brooks Meadows above East Fork Hood River was probably named for him as it was on the early alignment.

Kloan, Wasco County. This station on the Oregon Trunk Railway was named with the Chinook jargon word for three, since it was the third station from the north end of the line up Deschutes River.

Klondike, Sherman County. The post office at Klondike was established January 11, 1899 with A. B. Potter first postmaster. Due and French in *Rails to the Mid Columbia Wheatlands*, page 49, says that when the Columbia Southern Railway was being built to Shaniko it reached Klondike in the summer of 1898. Most of the construction crew deserted the job and headed for the northern gold mines so it was decided to so name the station. For many years the railway used the form Klondyke but the compiler has been unable to find out why. Klondike post office was closed November 30, 1951.

Klone Butte, Deschutes County. Klone Butte, in the north part of the Paulina Mountains, was named with the Chinook jargon word for three, it being the third of a series of buttes named at one time by the USFS. This is a variation of the spelling Kloan. See under that heading.

Kloochman Creek, Crook County. Kloochman Creek flows south from the Maury Mountains into Bear Creek. *Kloochman* is the Chinook jargon word for woman, and Kloochman Creek is just another way of saying Squaw Creek.

Klovdahl Bay, Lane County. This bay on Waldo Lake and Klovdahl Lake to the north were named for Simon Klovdahl, an engineer connected with the development of the Waldo Lake irrigation and power project. Klovdahl died at Eugene November 26, 1932.

Klumb, Marion County. A half century ago Klumb post office served a small area about three miles northwest of Mehama, not far from Fern Ridge School. It was named for Mrs. Jacob Siegmund, whose maiden name was Mary Margarethe Klumb. The Siegmunds were early day settlers in the locality. The writer has had an interesting letter from Mrs. Matilda S. Jones, *nee* Siegmund, of Amity, who was reared in the vicinity of Klumb post office. When Jacob Siegmund became interested in getting an office established, he submitted the name Klumb for his wife's family, and Cope, in compliment to Mrs. Lucy A. Pugsley, a neighbor and wife of Walter Pugsley. Mrs. Pugsley's maiden name was Cope. Mr. Siegmund was active in local civic and improvement matters, which may have influenced postal officials to select Mrs. Siegmund's maiden name, but it is also probable that the authorities thought that the name Cope was too much like that of Cove in Union County. The department was anxious to steer clear of names that might be confused. In any event Klumb post office was established January 4, 1893, with Mrs. Pugsley first postmaster. Her husband Walter Pugsley was the first mail carrier, and he made the regular round trip to Mehama on horseback. The Pugsley family soon moved away, and on June 10, 1893, Jacob Siegmund was made postmaster and the office was moved to the Siegmund home where it remained until it was closed February 15, 1910, because of the extension of rural free delivery from Stayton.

Knappa, Clatsop County. Knappa was named for Aaron Knapp, Jr. He was a pioneer settler who resided in the community many years. According to Silas B. Smith, the Indian name for the locality was *Tle-las-qua*. See *OHQ*, volume I, page 321. For information about the Indian village found by Lewis and Clark nearby, see under Big Creek and Cathlamet Bay.

Knieriem Canyon, Multnomah County. Knieriem Canyon heads southwest of Crown Point and runs southwest to Big Creek and Sandy River. It bears the family name of George Knieriem who was born in Germany in 1844 and came to the United States as a boy. He came west in the 1890s and located in the Corbett area in 1896.

Knight, Marion County. Knight post office was near Silver Creek at a point near the north line of township 8 south, range 1 east, about ten or twelve miles upstream from Silverton. The office was named for Daniel E. Knight, a local resident and the first postmaster. Knight post office was established February 16, 1880, and was in service until July 27, 1895, when it was closed to Argenti.

Knight Creek, Wallowa County. Knight Creek flows into Snake River in township 4 north, range 48 east. It was named by the USFS for M. V. Knight who had some mining claims along the stream. In early days it was known as Bear Creek because R. M. Downey and Jerard Cohorn killed a bear there in 1881. The name was changed because there were too many Bear creeks in the county.

Knox Butte, Linn County. This butte has an elevation of 634 feet, and is situated about six miles east of Albany. It was named for James Knox, a pioneer of 1845, and a cousin of James Knox Polk, president of the United

States. James Knox was a native of Pennsylvania and lived in Ohio and Iowa before he came to Oregon.

Knox Ranch, Wheeler County. This ranch on the headwaters of Cove Creek northeast of Clarno was homesteaded by Frank A. Knox in 1884.

Knutson Saddle, Marion County. This saddle between Sardine Mountain and Dome Rock bears the name of Carl Knutson, an early day logger.

Koch Mountain, Lane County. Koch Mountain is west of Waldo Lake. It was named for an early day trapper who is reported to have died nearby.

Kokostick Butte, Deschutes County. This butte near Devils Lake is named with the Chinook jargon word for woodpecker.

Kolb Reservoir, Baker County. This reservoir on the southwest edge of Baker is named for the family of Franz H. Kolb who homesteaded the property prior to the turn of the century.

Koler, Douglas County. For many years there was a station on the Southern Pacific Company railroad about four miles west of Glendale bearing the name Reuben, probably derived from Mount Reuben not far away. When residents at Reuben station wanted a post office a little after the beginning of the century they were not allowed to use the name Reuben because of duplication with the name Reuben post office in Columbia County. Accordingly, the name Koler was selected apparently in compliment to Richard Koehler, for many years manager of the Southern Pacific Company lines in Oregon. Mr. Koehler was a native of Germany and was brought to Oregon by Henry Villard. He had an outstanding career as a railroad administrator. He died in Portland in 1932. Along the line of the Southern Pacific he was always called by the Americanized form of his name which accounts for the style used by postal authorities. Koler post office was established September 17, 1907, with Alonzo W. Moon first postmaster. The office was closed to Glendale November 15, 1923.

Koosah Falls, Linn County. These falls are immediately above Carmen Reservoir on McKenzie River. Before the development of the Clear Lake recreation area, they were known as Middle Falls but the USBGN confirmed the present name in *Decision List 6103. Koosah* is the Chinook jargon word for sky.

Koosah Mountain, Deschutes and Lane counties. This mountain at the summit of the Cascade Range west of Sparks Lake is named with the Chinook jargon word for sky.

Kotan, Klamath County. Kotan was a station on the Cascade line of the Southern Pacific. Railroad officials say the name is an Indian word for horse. It is probably an adaptation of the Chinook jargon word cuitin, from the Chinook *ikiuatan,* a horse. There does not seem to be a Klamath Indian word of this sound.

Kotzman Basin, Deschutes County. This basin southeast of Pine Mountain was apparently named for Charles V. Kotzman who settled there about the time of World War I.

Kramer Canyon, Umatilla County. Jacob Kramer ranched near the head of this canyon east of Vinson in the 1890s.

Kroll, Douglas County. Kroll is a station on the Southern Pacific Company railroad on the east side of Tahkenitch Lake in the extreme west part of the county. The station was named for a member of the firm of Sparrow and Kroll who owned a large tract of timber nearby. There was a post office at Kroll from November 2, 1920, to September 30, 1921, with William L. Forsythe postmaster.

Kronenberg, Multnomah County. In July, 1947, William H. Stanley of Gresham wrote the compiler in part as follows: "Kronenberg post office was named for Joseph Kronenberg, the only postmaster. It was at the present site of Meadowland dairy at 162nd (Barker Road) and Powell Valley Road. The old Kronenberg house is still standing and occupied by the Andregg family which owns the premises and dairy. I did not know that the Kronenbergs had a post office, but I knew the entire family. One son is still living somewhere in California." Kronenberg post office was established April 10, 1893, with Joseph Kronenberg first and only postmaster. The office was closed February 8, 1897, with papers to Rockwood.

Krumbo Creek, Harney County. Krumbo Creek flows off Krumbo Mountain, a foothill of Steens Mountain. It was named for a pioneer settler in the neighborhood. The spelling given here, Krumbo, is in accordance with official plats and with the best local use. Krumbe and Crumbo are incorrect.

Kuamaksi Butte, Deschutes County. This butte, southwest of Bend, was named by the USFS with the Klamath Indian name of a locality near Sprague River, literally "at the cave." Gatschet gives the spelling *Kumakshi.* The word is derived from *kumme* or *kume,* meaning cave or cavern. The USFS used the word in order to perpetuate an Indian name, even though the butte is a long way from Sprague River.

Kubli, Jackson County. Kaspar Kubli came to Oregon from Switzerland in 1852, and his brother Jacob came some years later. Both settled in Jackson County, where they became prominent citizens. Jacob Kubli bought the Barnes claim near Applegate River in the extreme west part of the county in the locality called Missouri Flat. His son, Kaspar J. Kubli was born on this place, and in June, 1891, was appointed postmaster at Kubli post office, which was but a few hundred feet east of the Jackson-Josephine county line. The office was closed November 30, 1907, due to the establishment of rural delivery. Kaspar J. Kubli died July 2, 1942. He was postmaster at Kubli during the entire existence of the office.

Kuckup Park, Jefferson County. This is a natural park just east of the summit of the Cascade Range and slightly south of Breitenbush Lake. Kuck-up and Kuck-ups were sub-chiefs among the signers of the 1865 Treaty with the Middle Oregon Tribes. The compiler does not know why this name was applied to this specific area although it is on the extreme west side of the Warm Springs Indian Reservation.

Kuder Creek, Washington County. Kuder Creek flows east into West Fork Diary Creek near Manning. It bears the name of David E. Kuder, a pioneer sawmill operator. There have been numerous spellings of the name including Cueter but the present form was established in *Decision List 7801.*

Kuhn Ridge, Wallowa County. Kuhn Ridge is a well-known divide between Mud and Buck creeks in township 4 north, range 43 east. It was named for Henry and Dave Kuhn who ranged stock there in early days. Henry Kuhn took up the first homestead on this ridge.

Kweo Butte, Deschutes County. This butte in Paulina Mountains was named by the USFS with the Chinook jargon word for ring or circle, which well describes it.

Kwinnum Butte, Deschutes County. Kwinnum Butte, in the Paulina Mountains, is named with the Chinook jargon word for five, it being the fifth in a series of buttes all named at the same time by the USFS.

Kwolh Butte, Deschutes County. Kwolh Butte, elevation 7349 feet, is about two miles south of Bachelor Butte. *Kwolh* or *kwalh* is the Chinook jargon word for aunt, and the name was applied to this butte arbitrarily as a means of identification in fire fighting. Tot Mountain, a point between Kwolh Butte and Bachelor Butte, is named with the Chinook jargon word for uncle. These two names of relationship appear to have been suggested because of the proximity of such features as the Three Sisters, Bachelor Butte, The Husband and The Wife, all prominent points in the Cascade Range. See also under Wanoga Butte.

Kyser, Columbia County. Kyser was a locality on the Lost Creek drainage south of Delena, and near the center of the southwest quarter of township 7 north, range 3 west. It was named for a local resident. Kyser post office was established June 20, 1892, with William H. Kyser postmaster. Ella M. Kyser became postmaster May 8, 1908, and the office was closed to Rainier on May 30, 1918.

La Butte, Marion County. This hill, elevation 427 feet, is between Butteville and Champoeg. It was named in pioneer days by the French-Canadian settlers on French Prairie. Butteville was named for the hill.

Lachmund, Marion County. This railroad station east of Salem was named for Louis Lachmund, a prominent resident of Salem, who owned a farm nearby.

Lacomb, Linn County. J. E. Turnidge, a pioneer settler in this community, liked the name Tacoma and tried to have postal authorities adopt it, but they did not do so on account of duplication. W. J. Turnidge, a son, finally compromised the matter by suggesting the name Lacomb, which was chosen. This was in 1889.

Lacy, Clackamas County. In May, 1948, Isaac V. Trullinger wrote from 217 N. E. Skidmore Street, Portland, that the old Lacy post office was named for a local family. Mr. Trullinger was a pioneer of Clackamas County and should have known the facts. Lacy post office was established in March, 1892, with John R. Lewis first and only postmaster. It ran four or five years but the compiler does not know the exact date it was discontinued. Mr. Trullinger said that the office was in the north part of the county on a mail route that served such places as Eagle Creek, Viola, Clarkes and other offices.

Ladd Canyon, Union County. This canyon was named for John R. Ladd who ran a hotel at the foot of the hill where the immigrant road came into the Grande Ronde Valley. For information about Mr. and Mrs. Ladd and their activities in the days of the eastern Oregon and the Idaho gold rush, see Lockley's article on editorial page of the *Sunday Journal,* January

13, 1946. W. W. Curtis, who was familiar with eastern Oregon history, wrote the compiler in 1927 that in early days pioneer wagons were let down the slopes of Ladd Hill, near the canyon, with log drags attached to the wheels. In early days there were hundreds of pine logs at the bottom of the hill.

Ladd Glacier, Hood River County. Ladd Glacier was named for William Mead Ladd of Portland who, with C. E. S. Wood, built Cloud Cap Inn. It is on the northwest slope of Mount Hood west of Pulpit Rock above Barrett Spur and is the source of Ladd Creek which flows into West Fork Hood River. Although the name Ladd Glacier has been in general use for many years, Captain Henry Coe in an article in the Hood River *News*, March 6, 1918 says that in 1886 he named it Stranahan Glacier in honor of Oscar Stranahan, a close friend and associate.

Lafayette, Yamhill County. Lafayette was founded in 1846 by Joel Perkins, and named after Lafayette, Indiana. It was the county seat of Yamhill County until 1889, when that designation was transferred to McMinnville. The post office was established March 14, 1851, with Hardin D. Martin first postmaster.

LaFollette Butte, Deschutes County. Jerome B. LaFollette made his camp at this butte in early days and let his horses run at large nearby. Later he was killed in central Oregon when he fell off a load of hay. The butte is near Lower Bridge.

La Grande, Union County. It is said that at one time an effort was made to call this place Brownsville for one Ben Brown, who settled there in 1861. A meeting was held for a discussion of the matter, and instead, the name La Grande was adopted, doubtless suggested by the name of Grande Ronde Valley and its impressive scenery. La Grande post office was established May 28, 1863, with Benjamin P. Patterson first postmaster.

Laidlaw Butte, Deschutes County. Laidlaw Butte is about a mile west of Tumalo. It was named in compliment to W. A. Laidlaw, one of the promoters of the town now called Tumalo, but originally called Laidlaw. See under Tumalo.

Lake, Coos County. Lake post office was named for the Tenmile lakes. The office was established February 8, 1892, with Jane E. Fox first postmaster, and was discontinued October 12, 1903, with all mail to Templeton, which was about five miles eastward. Lake post office is shown on the post route map of 1900 as being on the peninsula between Tenmile Lake and North Tenmile Lake, but the scale of the map is small and this location may not be exact. In any event it was not far from the community later called Lakeside.

Lake, Lake County. Lake post office was formerly near Christmas Lake, about four miles from its present location. Christmas Lake as a name for the office was not acceptable to the authorities. A name of one word was wanted, so Christmas was dropped. The office was established in 1906 and closed July 31, 1943.

Lake Abert, Lake County. Lake Abert is one of the large lakes of Oregon with a normal area of about 60 square miles. It is fed principally by the outlets of Chewaucan Marsh and by Crooked Creek. The water is highly impregnated with sodium carbonates and other salts. The elevation of high water is about 4250 feet, and the lowest part of the bed is about 4244 feet, according to surveys of the Oregon State Highway Commission. John Work and his brigade of 1832-33 reached the north end of this lake on October 16, 1832, and called it Salt Lake. See *California Historical Society Quarterly*, September, 1943, page 204. Work does not say so, but his diary implies that this was not a new discovery and that trappers had been there before. Arrowsmith's map of North America, corrected to 1832-33, shows this Salt Lake with reasonable accuracy. The lake was visited on December 20, 1843, by then Captain John C. Fremont, and named for his chief, Colonel J. J. Abert of the U. S. Topographical Engineers. The lake was reported entirely dry in 1924, but has contained water since that year. Very complete descriptions of the lake and its surroundings including the Abert Rim, the imposing fault scarp on the eastern shore, are in USGS Water-Supply Papers 220 and 363.

Lake Billy Chinook, Jefferson County. The water impounded by Round Butte Dam on Deschutes River was named Lake Billy Chinook in honor of a Wasco Indian born about 1827. Chinook joined Fremont in 1843 and accompanied him to California and thence to Washington D.C., in 1844. He returned west with the emigration of 1845 and settled near The Dalles in 1851. In 1856 he moved to the Warm Springs Indian Reservation where he resided until his death. In 1866-67 during the Shoshone Indian War he served a year as acting first sergeant of Captain John Darragh's Indian Scouts. Billy Chinook was one of the nominal chiefs of The Dalles band of Wascos and as such was a signer of the "Treaty With the Tribes of Middle Oregon, 1855". He died December 9, 1890 and was buried in the Warm Springs cemetery.

Lake Charline, Douglas County. This lake four miles southwest of Cowhorn Mountain was named for Charline Thurston, daughter of USFS ranger Charles Thurston.

Lake Chetlo, Lane County. Lake Chetlo is northwest of Waldo Lake. *Chetlo* is a Chinook jargon word meaning oyster. It was applied to this lake because of its shape.

Lake County. Lake County was created October 24, 1874, by the state legislature, and received its name because of the number of large lakes within or partly within its borders, including the Klamath lakes, Lake Abert, Summer Lake, Goose Lake, Silver Lake and the lakes of the Warner Valley. The territory comprising Lake County was taken from Wasco and Jackson counties. Lake County in 1940 had a land area of 8270 square miles, according to the Bureau of the Census. Klamath County was formed from the west part of Lake County in 1882, and the Klamath lakes are not now in Lake County. In 1876 there was a lively squabble about the selection of a county seat for Lake County. For details, see under Bullard Creek.

Lake Creek, Deschutes County. Lake Creek is the outfall of Suttle Lake. It flows toward Metolius River, but about two miles from its source it splits and partly disappears later to form three forks which rejoin prior to entering Metolius River south of Camp Sherman.

Lake Ewauna, Klamath County. This is an enlargement or elbow in the outlet of Upper Klamath Lake. The connection to the north from Upper Klamath Lake is Link River. The outlet of Lake Ewauna is Klamath River. The name of the lake is from the Klamath Indian Iuauna, a condensed form of *Yulalona*, the name of a place below the falls of Link River.

Lake Kiwa, Lane County. Lake Kiwa is north of Waldo Lake. The name is from the Chinook jargon word meaning crooked, and was applied to this lake because it was elbow shaped. The word is said to have come originally from the Wasco Indian language.

Lake Labish, Marion County. This is a marshy area east of Brooks and Chemawa, now almost completely drained and in cultivation. Lake Labish ditch, which flows into Little Pudding River, is practically all that is left of the original lake. The lake was named by early settlers on French Prairie for *la biche*, the female deer, although French-Canadians frequently used the word to mean elk. In the evening of November 12, 1890, a Southern Pacific train, bound for California, plunged through the Lake Labish trestle. Five persons were killed and many injured.

Lake Lytle, Tillamook County. This is a seashore lake about five miles north of the entrance to Tillamook Bay. It has an intermittent outlet. There was once a post office nearby of the same name. These features were named for E. E. Lytle, a prominent Oregon railroad builder, who, among other things, constructed the Pacific Railway and Navigation Company line from Hillsboro to Tillamook, now owned by the Southern Pacific Company.

Lake Marr, Lane County. This small pond is about a mile from the Pacific Ocean and five miles north of the Siuslaw River. It was named for Ezra E. Marr, who at one time owned a ranch adjoining the lake. In 1925 it was reported that he was a lighthouse keeper in the state of Washington.

Lake Merritt, Coos County. Lake Merritt is the former Lower Pony Creek Reservoir constructed by the Coos Bay-North Bend Water Board. On November 6, 1967 the board voted to name this body of water Lake Merritt to honor Byron W. "Barney" Merritt who went to work for them in 1929 and continued until his death in March 1967.

Lake Miller, Klamath County. Lake Miller is the large drained meadow that US 97 crosses just north of the California line. It was named for a very early ranching family in Klamath County. *History of Central Oregon*, page 940, mentions a Mr. Miller and his three sons, John H., William and Warren, settling here in 1868. John H. and W. Y. Miller both took up government land in 1873 but the compiler can only assume the lake was named for the family in general.

Lake of the Woods, Klamath County. This is a descriptive name, given because of the dense stand of timber nearby. The lake is about three and a half miles long on the east slope of the Cascade Range, partly fed by a stream rising southeast of Mount McLoughlin. Its elevation is about 4950 feet, and SH 140 between Medford and Klamath Falls skirts its northern end. In a letter to Will G. Steel, dated October 28, 1925, Captain Oliver C. Applegate of Klamath Falls says that he named Lake of the Woods in 1870 when he was building a road by the lake. He built a cabin at the south end of the lake in that year. A post office called Lake of the Woods was established to serve the area on May 17, 1930, with Fred E. Wahl postmaster. This office was closed August 15, 1931. It was near the north end of the lake. In the late 1930s an effort was made to establish the mongrel form Lake O' Woods and a post office using that style was established July 19, 1941. The USBGN in *Decision List 6103* adopted the original form, Lake of the Woods, for the lake and the community. The post office soon followed. suit and in 1981 was operating as a community post office under Klamath Falls.

Lake Oswego, Clackamas County. The original community of Oswego was named for Oswego, New York, by A. A. Durham, a pioneer of Oregon of 1847. At one time he operated a sawmill in the Oregon community which he named for his former home in the East. For information about his activities in Oregon see under Durham. Oswego post office was established on December 31, 1853, with Wesley C. Hull postmaster. On May 1, 1959, the residents of Oswego and those of Lake Grove at the west end of Oswego Lake voted to merge into a single city called Lake Oswego.

Lake Simtustus, Jefferson County. When Pelton Dam on Deschutes River was built in 1958 by Portland General Electric Company, the Warm Springs Indians chose this name for the impounded waters to honor Kyuslute Simtustus, a warrior of the tribe, who served as a scout for the U. S. Army in the 1867-68 campaign against the Piutes. After his discharge, he returned to the the Warm Springs Reservation and lived there until his death in 1926. Simtustus was equally well known by his nickname, Pipsher.

Lake Umatilla, Gilliam, Morrow, Sherman and Umatilla counties. This lake was formed in 1968 when the Columbia River was impounded by John Day Dam. It is the final link providing slack water for navigation from Bonneville Dam, just above tidewater, to the Washington State line passing through Lake Wallula. The name comes from the town of Umatilla at the east end of the pool. For a discussion of the name see under Umatilla River.

Lake Wallula, Umatilla County. Lake Wallula is formed by the Columbia River impounded at McNary Dam near the town of Umatilla. The lake was named for the town of the same name at the confluence of Columbia and Snake rivers in Washington. *Walla* is an Indian word for "running water" in several languages and Wallula is a variant in a manner similar to Walla Walla meaning "fall after fall" or "small, rapid river." For additional information see Scott's *History of the Oregon Country,* volume II, page 314.

Lakecreek, Jackson County. Lakecreek post office takes its name from Lake Creek, an important stream that flows into Little Butte Creek. Lake Creek post office was established December 10, 1886, with Joseph T. Delk first of a long list of postmasters. In the 1890s the Post Office Department had an attack of efficiency, and consolidated the names of a great number of offices made up of two words, though for some reason names like New York, San Francisco, and Niagara Falls were overlooked. In any event, the name of the office in Jackson County was changed to Lakecreek on April 24, 1894, and that was the official style until the office was closed after World War II.

Lakeport, Curry County. Lakeport was the name of a locality in the northwest part of the county, so called because it was established on Floras

Lake about three miles southeast of Langlois. It was hoped that some form of ocean transportation might become available, but there was no such development. Lakeport post office was established June 22, 1910, with Emil Burg first postmaster. The post office was closed June 30, 1915. In June, 1946, Louis L. Knapp of Port Orford told the compiler that the project at Lakeport included a plan to cut a channel from the lake to the ocean to accommodate ocean vessels of sorts. This scheme turned out to be impracticable. The locality was sometimes called Pacific City, but that name could not be used for a post office because of duplication with an office in Tillamook County.

Lakeside, Coos County. Lakeside is situated near the shores of Tenmile and North Tenmile lakes, and was named on that account.

Lakeview, Lake County. Lakeview is said to have been named at a citizens' meeting held in 1876. John A. Moon suggested the name. A post office was established late in 1876. Goose Lake was larger in those days and the water was nearer the town, hence the selection. Lakeview is one of the highest towns in Oregon. The bench mark in the county courthouse has an elevation of 4800 feet. M. W. Bullard was one of the first settlers arriving in 1869, and in the first county seat election, offered 20 acres of land should his place be chosen. This choice was made at an election in 1876, and Bullard gave land for the courthouse. He sold 300 acres to Moon, who filed the plat for the town on May 26, 1877. In May, 1900, every business house in town but two was burned, and by October reconstruction was nearly complete. For story of the county seat fight of 1876, see under Bullard Creek.

Lamberson Butte, Hood River County. This is a well-known point east of Mount Hood, with an elevation of about 6600 feet. It was named for Lewis H. Lamberson of Portland, an early day member of Mazamas. He spent several summers at Cloud Cap Inn, and members of the Langille family named the butte for him because he made a trip to its top. This was about 1895.

Lamonta, Jefferson County. Harold Baldwin of Prineville informed the compiler in 1927 that this place was named by Miss Kate Helfrich, the name referring to Grizzly Mountain nearby. *History of Central Oregon,* page 734, says the townsite was platted in April, 1905, by John C. Rush. While the intent of the name is obvious, the words *la monta* are not part of any language with which the compiler is familiar. Lamonta post office was established September 7, 1898, with Miss Helfrich first postmaster. The office was closed in April, 1918.

La Mu, Harney County. A post office with the odd name La Mu was established in Harney County November 6, 1889, and discontinued March 19, 1890. Elizabeth Newman operated the office for this short period, and when it was closed, what little business there was was turned over to Harney. It was in Crane Creek Gap, near what was later the site of Crane.

Lampa Creek, Coos County. Lampa Creek is tributary to Coquille River a few miles east of Bandon. The name has been spelled several ways. It was originally called Lamper or Lampa Creek, for an old settler. The name of this settler is given as Seth Lampa in *Pioneer History of Coos and Curry Counties,* page 395. The stream was later called Lampy Creek by a local property owner, and the style Lamprey was used on some government maps. Local usage finally crystallized on Lampa, and that style has been employed for a good many years. A post office called Lampa was established near this stream on May 9, 1905, with James L. Bean first and only postmaster. This office was closed to Bandon on October 15, 1918. Highway signs use the style Lampa.

Lancaster, Malheur County. This station was named for Lancaster, Pennsylvania, by D. M. Brogan, who was born in the Pennsylvania town. Lancaster was between Vale and Brogan.

Lancaster Falls, Hood River County. Lancaster Falls is a fine cascade on the first stream west of Warren Creek about a mile west of Starvation Creek State Park. In 1970 at the suggestion of Gertrude G. Jensen and Donald J. Sterling, Jr., the OGNB applied the name of Samuel C. Lancaster, the engineer who designed the scenic Columbia River Highway prior to World War I. Lancaster was born in Magnolia, Mississippi, January 11, 1864. After attending college in Tennessee, he worked on the Tennessee highway program, one of the first hard surfaced networks in the United States. He came to Oregon in 1908 and first designed the campus at Linfield College in McMinnville. He then proceeded to his best-known work, the Columbia River Highway, which was opened to traffic in 1915. Lancaster died on March 4, 1941 and in 1963 a bronze plaque was dedicated to him at the Vista House on Crown Point. For editorial comment see *Oregon Journal,* November 11, 1970. An interesting letter from Mrs. Jensen is printed adjacent to the editorial.

Lancelot Lake, Lane County. Ray Engels of the USFS named this lake along with nearby Camelot Lake because of a fancied resemblance to the terrain of an old time jousting field. See also under Camelot Lake.

Landax, Lane County. The name Landax was first used by the Southern Pacific Company for a siding but the compiler has been unable to determine why the selection was made. When the post office was established in December, 1914, the name was used for the office. Wilbur H. Hyland was the first postmaster. The name of the office was changed to Signal on June 16, 1927, and this office was discontinued in November, 1938. The writer does not know if Landax and Signal were in exactly the same place.

Landes Creek, Lane County. Landes Creek flows into Hills Creek southeast of Oakridge. It was named for Joe Landess, an early USFS employee. The final "s" has been lost for many years.

Landrith Bridge, Coos County. This bridge is over South Fork Coos River east of the town of Coos Bay. In May, 1943, Mrs. S. B. Cathcart, formerly Dora Landrith, of Coos Bay, wrote the compiler that the correct spelling of this pioneer family name is Landrith and not Landreth. The bridge was named for a member of the family who owned land nearby.

Lane County. Lane County was created January 28, 1851, by the territorial legislature. It has a land area of 4594 square miles. It was named for Joseph Lane, who came to Oregon in 1849, as first territorial governor. In 1851 and 1853 he led the campaigns against the Rogue River Indians. In 1859 he was elected United States Senator. He supported the contentions of the seceding states in 1860-61, and when his term as senator expired in 1861, he retired to private life. In 1860 he was nominee for vice-president with Breckenridge. His death occurred April 19, 1881, at Roseburg. Joseph

Lane was born in North Carolina, December 14, 1801. Prior to coming to Oregon, he had distinguished himself in the Mexican War, and had been a member of the Indiana legislature. His attitude on secession wholly changed his political standing in Oregon. For references to Lane, see *OGN*, 1928 edition, pages 193-194. For history of early boundaries of Lane County, by F. V. Holman, see *OHQ*, volume XI, page 33.

Lane Creek, Jackson County. Lane Creek is a short stream that flows into Willow Creek from the west about three miles west of Central Point. Walling, in *History of Southern Oregon*, page 377, says the stream was named for an old man named Lane, who was murdered on its banks in very early days. There was active gold mining along Lane Creek in the early 1850s. The community of Willow Springs, one of the first settlements in Jackson County, was situated near the junction of Lane and Willow creeks.

Lane Mountain, Douglas County. This mountain, about 12 miles east of Roseburg, was named in honor of General Joseph Lane, who was an early settler in the Umpqua Valley. For data concerning him, see under Lane County.

Lang Canyon, Gilliam County. Lang Canyon drains into the Columbia River from the south at a point about five miles west of Arlington. The canyon was named for Thomas Stackpole Lang, 1826-1896, a native of Maine, who came to Oregon in 1875 and for a time engaged in the sheep business in the vicinity of Heppner. He loaded wool on the Columbia River boats by means of a chute or tram in the canyon that now bears his name. Thomas Lang held a number of prominent positions in Maine, both in business and in politics. The latter years of his life were spent at The Dalles and for four years he was receiver of the U. S. Land Office at that place. For biography see *Illustrated History of Central Oregon*, page 261. See also under Rockville.

Langdon Lake, Umatilla County. This lake is near the summit of the Blue Mountains and is skirted by the highway between Weston and Elgin. It is an artifical lake made by damming one of the sources of Lookingglass Creek. The elevation of the lake is about 4875 feet. It was named for John W. Langdon of Walla Walla, who furnished a substantial part of the money necessary for surveying the ground and building the dam. Langdon did this from public spirit, to provide a camp ground.

Langell Valley, Klamath County. Langell Valley is a natural geographic feature, and a post office bears the same name. Both were named for Arthur Langell, an early settler, who took part in the Modoc War. He was afterward killed in an altercation with a neighbor named Swingle. The post office was established about 1871 and has been moved about to several locations. It is now near the Oregon-California boundary line.

Langille Crags, Hood River County. These crags were named for the Langille family, early settlers in the Hood River Valley and for many years associated with the development of transportation and hotel facilities on Mount Hood. William Langille was a pioneer guide on the mountain.

Langlois, Curry County. This post office is near Floras Creek. It was named for the Langlois family which has for many years been prominent in Curry County. William V. Langlois was born on the Island of Guernsey, English Channel, and came to Curry County in 1854. His wife was Mary A.

King. A number of their children have been prominent in Curry County affairs. For additional information about the Langlois family, see editorial page, *Oregon Journal*, June 28, July 1, 1927.

Langrell Gulch, Baker and Union counties. This gulch runs northwest and empties into Big Creek valley at the Union County line southwest of Medical Springs. It was named for Richard T. Langrell, an early Baker County settler, who operated a local sawmill.

La Pine, Deschutes County. La Pine was named by Alfred A. Aya. The name was suggested by the abundance of pine trees in the neighborhood. When the post office was established the postal authorities consolidated the two parts of the name into Lapine. The original form continued in some popularity and on April 1, 1951 the Post Office Department changed to La Pine. This temporarily compounded the confusion as certain progressive elements had previously conformed with the Post Office. At this writing, La Pine prevails uncontested, but if this form is supposed to indicate a French origin, it is of course incorrect, as the French word would be *Le Pin*. Lapine post office was established in September, 1910, by change of name from Rosland.

Lapover Lake, Wallowa County. Lapover Lake, which is in section 27, township 3 south, range 43 east, is named for Lapover Cabin on Lostine River. The cabin was named because an addition to the original structure lapped over the main part of the building.

Laraut, Douglas County. Postal records show that Laraut post office was established June 16, 1890, with Narcisse LaRaut postmaster, and was closed March 19, 1891, with all papers to Wilbur. The LaRaut home was about eight or ten miles west of Wilbur and near the Umpqua River. In February, 1946, Kenneth F. Barneburg of Wilbur dug up some history of the office, which was apparently never in actual operation. Mr. Barneburg located Narcisse LaRaut, Jr., then living in Salem, who reported that the elder LaRaut received a supply of stamps and other equipment but for some reason the office was not operated.

Larch, Yamhill County. This office named for the forest tree was established at the Summit House station on the Trask toll road seventeen miles west of Yamhill. Miss Clara Rhude was the only postmaster the place ever had. She was the daughter of Mr. and Mrs. Oliver Rhude, who operated the Summit House. In addition to post office duties Miss Rhude helped cook and in general housekeeping and in making a dozen beds for travelers and residents. It is reported that the post office was established to provide a legal but fictitious and temporary address for persons proving up their homesteads. The Summit House was built in 1889 by Martin T. Record and was in use for many years after the post office was closed. See McMinnville *Telephone-Register,* September 5, 1946, page 1, for news story and picture. Postal records show that Larch post office was established September 9, 1891, and was closed February 10, 1894, with papers to Byersville. It is more than probable that the name Larch was used because of the presence of the noble fir rather than of any of the true larches.

Larch Mountain, Multnomah County. Larch trees probably do not grow on Larch Mountain. Forest experts assert that the tree grows only in that part of the state east of the Cascade Range. The tree on Larch Mountain known by lumbermen as the larch is really the noble fir, *Abies nobilis,* and is not related to the larch in any way. The name Larch Mountain is, however, well established for an important and beautiful geographic feature, and there it will doubtless remain. Larch Mountain has an elevation of 4058 feet.

Larison Rock, Lane County. This rock and the creek nearby were named for George Larison, a resident of the valley of Middle Fork Willamette River. He was a son-in-law of B. J. Pengra, a pioneer of Oregon. The spelling Lairson is wrong.

Larson Creek, Jackson County. Lawson Creek flows into Rogue River about three miles north of Prospect. Mrs. Frances Pearson, who was born in the area, told the compiler in 1979 that this creek was named for an early homesteader and BLM records show that John A. Larson filed for a homestead nearby in 1902.

Larwood, Linn County. Larwood post office was in operation from July 25, 1893, until August 12, 1903, and was named for the postmaster, William T. Larwood. This office was about ten miles east of Crabtree and in the foothills of the Cascade Range.

Last Chance Creek, Wallowa County. This stream flows into Minam River in township 4 south, range 42 east. It was named by George Miller in the fall of 1890. Miller was a sheep man and the last chance he had to make camp before getting out of the mountains was on this creek.

Latham, Lane County. Latham is a station on the Southern Pacific Company railroad a little more than a mile south of Cottage Grove. It is more than probable that it was named for Senator Milton S. Latham of California. Latham post office was established September 16, 1878, with James J. Comstock first postmaster. The office was closed February 14, 1888. Comstock, who was an associate of Ben Holladay, was interested in the lumber business both at Latham and at Comstock, a station a little to the southwest in Douglas County. Holladay named several stations for public characters and it seems apparent that Latham station was named for Senator Latham, either by Holladay or by Comstock or both of them.

Lathrop Creek, Josephine County. This creek rises in Grants Pass and flows west about four miles to join Vannoy Creek. It was originally called Dutcher Creek, but there is another Dutcher Creek emptying into Rogue River at Finley Bend about nine miles west of Grants Pass. The Josephine County Planning Commission voted in 1965 to change the name to Lathrop Creek to honor the late Judge Raymond Lathrop who resided near the creek for many years and was County Judge of Josephine County when he died in 1961. This was duly approved by the USBGN in *Decision List 6602.*

Lathrop Glacier, Douglas County. In 1966 Dr. Theodore G. Lathrop discovered a small glacier on the north side of Mount Thielsen, apparently the southernmost glacier in Oregon. Studies were made of the glacier and these were reported in *Mazama,* 1968, 1971 and 1976. Dr. Lathrop, who was also an authority on hypothermia, died in 1979 and, at the instigation of the mountaineering community, the OGNB named this glacier in his honor.

Latigo Creek, Grant and Harney counties. This creek rises on the south slopes of Snow Mountain and flows southeast into Whiskey Creek about thirty miles northwest of Burns. *Latigo* is the Spanish word for whip that in western America has come to mean saddle strap. There is also a Latigo Lake appropriately near Cincha Lake near the headwaters of North Santiam River in Linn County.

Latourell Falls, Multnomah County. Latourell Falls is the name of a beautiful feature adjacent to the Columbia River Highway, and also the post office name of the early community. The railroad station name was Latourell. Joseph Latourell was a prominent settler in the locality and it was named for him. The name Latourell frequently appears in print with a final "e," which is wrong. The falls are on property formerly owned by Guy W. Talbot of Portland, who had them accurately measured and found their height to be 249 feet. Latourell Prairie, on the bluffs above the Columbia River east of Latourell Falls received its name from the same source. For information about Joseph Latourell and the dedication of the falls to the state, see *OHQ*, volume XIX, page 78. Early in 1929 Mr. and Mrs. Talbot gave the state of Oregon about 220 acres of land adjoining the Columbia River Highway and Latourell Falls. This property is known as Guy W. Talbot State Park. In 1934 the heirs of George W. Joseph also gave property for a park on the upper part of the stream and this is known as the George W. Joseph State Park. Rooster Rock was the name of the first post office in this vicinity. It was established in May, 1876, with John Gilstrap postmaster, and was named for the natural feature nearby. Joseph Latourell became postmaster in August, 1876, and the name was changed to Latourell Falls in August, 1887. The compiler does not know if the office was moved when the name was changed.

Latta Crater, Deschutes County. This crater is on the northwest slope of Black Crater. Professor Edwin T. Hodge in *Mount Multnomah*, page 112, names it Lotta Crater for the discoverer of Lost Creek Canyon, but he misspells the name. John Latta was an early settler in Lane County and went to the Prineville area in the 1860s. At one time he was interested in the McKenzie toll road and was an associate of John T. Craig. See *OHQ*, volume XXXI, page 261.

Laughlin Hills, Wasco County. These hills lie south of SH 216 between Bear Springs and Wapinitia. They are named for Robert A. Laughlin who settled on Juniper Flat in 1872.

Laughlin Hollow, Wasco County. Laughlin Hollow north of Antelope was named for Benjamin Franklin Laughlin who homesteaded near Antelope in the 1870s. Laughlin was the son of William O. Laughlin, one of the founding settlers of The Dalles.

Laurance, Marion County. On July 7, 1898, Ellsworth Benjamin Fletcher was appointed postmaster at Laurance by Charles Emory Smith, then postmaster general. The post office was established in Mr. Fletcher's home at the North Howell crossroads. M. Louetta Carwood was appointed postmaster November 23, 1900, and the office was discontinued December 22, 1902, with papers to Gervais.

Laurance Lake, Hood River County. Laurance Lake was formed in

1969 when the Middle Fork Irrigation District completed their dam on
Clear Fork southwest of Parkdale. It is named in honor of Sheldon Laurance who was chairman of the district during the planning and construction period. Laurance died in Hood River on December 23, 1968 just
before the completion of the project.

Laurel, Washington County. Laurel was named early in 1879 at a meeting held at a school about a quarter of a mile east of the present site of the
community. C. W. (Cooney) Williams suggested the name because there
were so many laurel trees in the vicinity. The post office was established
March 14, 1879, with Alfred Mulloy postmaster. The office was at his
home, about a mile south of the present site of Laurel. It was moved to the
present location about 1890. For additional information about the community, see Hillsboro *Argus,* November 26, 1931. Laurel community should
not be confused with Laurelwood, about five miles due west. This is the site
of Laurelwood Academy, a Seventh Day Adventist school founded in 1904
and named for a fine stand of what were supposed to be laurel trees. The
compiler was told in 1981 that one of the original trees was still standing
but that it was a madrone or *Arbutus menziesii,* a pleasing and common tree
in western Oregon.

Laurel Hill, Clackamas County. Laurel Hill lies between Zigzag River
and Camp Creek and is traversed by the Mount Hood Highway over a fine
grade. It was one of the terrors of the emigrants who traveled the Barlow
Road. Wagons had to be let down the slopes of this hill with ropes. The
name Laurel Hill was applied in the earliest pioneer days. For comments on
this name and Zigzag River, see under Barlow Creek and Zigzag River. It is
probable that the pioneers named Laurel Hill for the rhododendrons that
grew thereon rather than true laurels.

Lava, Deschutes County. Lava was the name once applied to a post
office near the Deschutes River south of Bend in what was then Crook
County. The name was derived from Lava Butte and its remarkable lava
flows, which were a little to the northeast. The locality was from time to
time served by offices with other names. Crater post office was established
February 18, 1888, with David A. Findley first postmaster. This office,
which was discontinued May 21, 1890, is shown on a map of 1889 as being
just a little north of the Vandevert ranch. It was obviously named for Lava
Butte and the nearby lava flows. A post office named Carlisle was established at the Vandevert ranch on May 10, 1893, with William P. Vandevert
postmaster. Vandevert family tradition says that Mrs. Vandevert, who was
from Kentucky, was an admirer of John G. Carlisle of that state who
became secretary of the treasury in 1893. She named the office in compliment to Carlisle. This office was closed April 6, 1895. It was planned to
reestablish the office with a new name Lava, and this was done on June 11,
1895, with Sarah J. Potter postmaster. However, this order was rescinded
and Lava post office was not actively established until April 8, 1896, when
David W. Aldridge was appointed postmaster. Lava office was on the
Aldridge ranch a few miles north of the Vandevert place. On December 29,
1899, Mrs. Sadie Vandevert was appointed postmaster of Lava and the
office was moved to the W. P. Vandevert ranch. The office operated until
November, 1908.

Lava Butte, Deschutes County. Lava Butte is a conspicuous lapilli cone with a deep crater in its summit. From the south base of this butte a stream of basaltic lava was poured out, which flowed to the northwest and dammed Deschutes River which resulted in Benham Falls. For detailed information about Lava Butte and its flow, see USGS Bulletin 252, by I. C. Russell, page 110. The butte is composed of cinders and scoriaceous fragments and volcanic bombs. The name Lava described the flow at the base of the butte rather than the butte itself. Russell gives the opinion that in 1903 the flow was more than 150 years old. There was once a post office called Lava not far from the butte, but it has been discontinued.

Lava Cast Forest, Deschutes County. In 1970 Phil Brogan of Bend provided the following information regarding this region. "This interesting feature, recently set aside by the USFS as a place of special geologic interest, is midway up the north slope of Newberry Crater. Here some 5000 years ago a massive flood of lava spilled through a forest of pines, congealing around bases of trees and enveloping toppled conifers." The USFS has designated Lava Cast Forest a Special Interest Area and built a special trail with interpretive signs.

Lava Lake, Deschutes County. This is the source of Deschutes River and it takes its name from the surrounding lava flows. Lava Lake ordinarily has no surface outlet, but during high water flows through an open channel to Little Lava Lake nearby, from which flows Deschutes River. The name Big Lava Lake is wrong.

Lava River Cave, Deschutes County. Lava River Cave is really a lava tunnel about two miles long, caused by the outflow of the molten lava after the top had hardened. It is near Lava Butte. It is open at one place for a distance of about 400 feet, and is 30 to 40 feet deep and 50 feet wide. In this section the roof has fallen in. The floor of the cave is covered with fine sand, apparently deposited by a stream. Land along the course of the Lava River was given by The Shevlin-Hixon Company to the state for a park adjacent to The Dalles-California Highway. The lava flow forming the river came at an earlier date than the outflow from the base of Lava Butte. For additional information see editorial page of the *Oregonian,* December 9, 1925, and USGS Bulletin 252.

Lavacicle Cave, Deschutes County. This cave is located about thirty-five miles southeast of Bend and about two miles northwest of Antelope Butte. It was discovered in 1959 by Dan Beougher, Max Stenkamp and Lester Martin and contains some remarkable lava drip formations. The name Lavacicle was coined by Phil Brogan of Bend.

Lavadoure Creek, Douglas County. Lavadoure Creek flows into South Umpqua River about five miles above Days Creek and nearby is Lavadoure Community Hall. Lavola Bakken of the Douglas County Museum informed the compiler in 1976 that Joseph Lavadoure was a fur trader who may have been in western Oregon as early as 1825. He spent many years as a resident of the South Umpqua River region although he is buried near Pendleton. She adds that the dates on his tombstone are 1791-1892.

Laverty Lake, Wallowa County. Laverty Lake is in the Wallowa Mountains in township 3 south, range 43 east. It was named for Frank Laverty by J. H. Jackson who stocked the lake with fish in 1914. This information came from J. H. Horner and R. L. Forsythe of Enterprise. Laverty lived at Lostine for a number of years.

Lawen, Harney County. This place, according to one writer, was named after Henry Lauen, who settled in the neighborhood about 1887. No explanation is given as to the difference in spelling. Another correspondent informs the compiler that the place was named because of the green lawn-like appearance of the neighboring shore of Malheur Lake. This version of the story says that the local applicant for the post office misspelled Lawn into Lawen. It seems to the writer that the first version is the more probable.

Lawler Canyon, Umatilla County. Milton P. Lawler settled along this canyon near McKay Creek shortly after the turn of the century.

Lawrentz, Klamath County. Lawrentz post office was established January 31, 1894, and was discontinued April 17, 1895. It was named for Martha A. Lawrentz, the first and only postmaster. In January, 1947, Mrs. Fred G. Brown wrote that Lawrentz post office was situated where Pelican Bay Lodge resort was later established. It was at the site of Rocky Point post office, which was later called Harriman. Mrs. Brown adds an interesting paragraph to the effect that Lawrentz post office may have been discontinued because of a letter sent by Mrs. Lawrentz, the postmaster, to officials in Washington in reply to an inquiry about an alleged irregularity. She told her superiors "If you will attend to your affairs in Washington, we shall run the post office here." Mrs. Brown adds that the mail was carried on horseback from Klamath Falls to Lawrentz.

Lawson Creek, Curry County. This stream, which heads near Fairview Mountain, was named for a pioneer prospector.

Lawson Creek, Lane County. Lawson Creek is tributary to Siuslaw River east of Cushman. In December, 1942, Earl H. Hill wrote the compiler that the stream was named for John Lawson, a homesteader who lived near its mouth. He had a large family and has been dead many years.

Lawson Mountain, Wheeler County. Gilbert Lawson settled near West Branch after the turn of the century and applied for a homestead on the slopes of this mountain in 1911.

Lawton, Grant County. Lawton was a mining camp in the northeast part of the county in the Blue Mountains. This camp was a couple of miles down stream from Granite. The place was named for Major-General Henry Ware Lawton, who was born in Ohio in 1843. General Lawton had a distinguished career in the United States Army. He was killed in the battle of San Mateo, Philippine Islands, on December 19, 1899. Lawton post office was established on the Grant County list on May 14, 1900, with Frank G. Hull first of three postmasters. The office was discontinued to Granite, June 15, 1905. The country was ringing with the praises of General Lawton at the time the post office was petitioned.

Layng Creek, Lane County. Layng Creek is southeast of Cottage Grove. It was named for George Layng, a nearby resident.

Layton Point, Harney County. This is the correct name of the point on the east side of Harney Valley, not Laton. It was named for a pioneer resident.

Lazarus Island, Tillamook County. Lazarus Island, in the Nehalem River opposite Wheeler, was named for one Lazarus, a homesteader who tried to develop the land but had little success.

Leaburg, Lane County. Leaburgh post office was established January 29, 1877, with Leander Cruzan as first postmaster. The name of the office was adapted from Cruzan's first name. Later the spelling was changed to Leaburg, but the compiler cannot tell when. The name was changed to Deerhorn on May 25, 1907, and that style was used until the office was closed in September, 1913. The change to Deerhorn also included a change of location about two miles west and a new Leaburg office was established September 20, 1907. As of 1981 it is a CPO out of Eugene.

Leander, Linn County. This station was just east of Albany on the Oregon Electric Railway. C. H. Stewart of Albany told the compiler in 1927 that it was on the donation land claim of Leander C. Burkhart, a pioneer of 1846, and was named for him. The facilities were incorporated into the railway's Albany Yard in the early 1940s.

Leap, Wallowa County. Leap is a place north of Enterprise in section 8, township 1 north, range 44 east. According to J. H. Horner of Enterprise it was first planned to call this community Fairview, but postal authorities would not accept that name because of duplication. Mrs. F. W. Heskett suggested that the office be named Leap because it was leap year. That name was accepted, and the office was established at the Heskett house in April, 1892. Ben Weathers carried the mail in from Wallowa to Leap on horseback. Leap has not been a post office for some years prior to 1944.

Lebanon, Linn County. Lebanon was first called Kees Precinct for Morgan and Jacob Kees, who came there in 1848. Jeremiah Ralston had the site surveyed and recorded in 1851 and adopted the name Lebanon after his birthplace, Lebanon, Tennessee. The first post office in the vicinity, Santyam, was established March 14, 1851, with Russel T. Hill postmaster. The name was changed to Washington Butte July 30, 1852, with John W. Bell as the new postmaster. At the time the change was made, the old name was put down as Santiam and not Santyam. Leland H. Wakefield became postmaster on March 29, 1855. Later the post office name was changed to Lebanon to agree with the townsite. Early post office lists show that a Lebanon post office was established on June 5, 1851, with Jno. S. Hunt postmaster. The place was about twelve miles east of Salem, in Marion County, and had nothing to do with Lebanon in Linn County. The Marion County office Lebanon was discontinued in June, 1858.

Le Conte Crater, Deschutes and Lane counties. This crater is on the summit of the Cascade Range south of the South Sister. Dr. E. T. Hodge of the University of Oregon named it for Professor Joseph Le Conte, of the University of California, famous Pacific Coast scientist. Le Conte Crater is just southwest of Rock Mesa and has an elevation of 6574 feet.

Lee, Coos County. Lee post office was established in 1888. William P. Mast was the first postmaster and was a native of North Carolina. He named the office for the great Confederate leader General Robert E. Lee. Lee was not a post office in 1929.

Lee Wood Spring, Jefferson County. This spring was on the property of Lee Wood, the son of Whitfield Wood of Ashwood.

Leeds, Jackson County. Leeds post office, about ten miles up Rogue River from Trail, was named for W. H. Leeds, a newspaper publisher of Ashland and onetime state printer for Oregon, by A. J. Florey, for many years postmaster at Eagle Point. Florey was postmaster at Eagle Point in April, 1890, when Leeds post office was established with Frank M. Manning first postmaster. For information about W. H. Leeds, see Turnbull's *History of Oregon Newspapers,* page 260. The post office apparently did not operate continuously and was finally closed February 28, 1913. See also under Peyton.

Leeds Island, Douglas County. Leeds Island is in the Umpqua River northwest of Reedsport, and was named for Captain Josiah B. Leeds, a pioneer of Gardiner. Captain Leeds was born in New Jersey, December 1, 1829, and went to sea with his father when he was eight years old. He sailed into San Francisco Bay in June, 1851, as mate of the schooner *Frances Helen.* He was made master of the schooner and sailed her in the coastwise trade. He crossed the bar into Umpqua River May 10, 1853. He gave up seafaring and settled in Gardiner in 1865. He operated a boat on Umpqua River and went into the sawmill business with G. S. Hinsdale and Edward Breen. This enterprise later became the Gardiner Mill Company. He sold his interest in 1882 and after four years in the stock business, sold out in 1886 and moved to San Francisco with his family. He died there in 1889. For additional data, see Walling's *History of Southern Oregon,* page 532.

Lees Camp, Tillamook County. About 1939 Rex Lee bought approximately sixteen acres of the Reeher property on Wilson River near the mouth of North Fork and the place was later developed into a tourist and sportsmen's camp with the name Lee's Wilson River Camp. In 1947 it was reported that H. M. Slauson was associated in the establishment, which is about twenty-five miles upstream from Tillamook on the Wilson River Highway and not far from the summit of the Coast Range. The post office, established in 1947 with the name Lee's Camp and with Mrs. Slauson postmaster, is very nearly in the same location as the much earlier office called Wilson. It now operates as a CPO out of Tillamook.

Leggins Spring, Wheeler County. Grover Blake, an early USFS ranger, told the writer that this spring north of Spanish Peak was named for Frank Leggins, a miner in the early days.

Lehman, Umatilla County. Lehman, which is the site of Lehman Springs, was named for a pioneer settler, James Lehman, probably about 1873. The springs were discovered by Dr. John Teel, an old time physician. Lehman post office operated from September 8, 1899, to February 29, 1928.

Leland, Josephine County. Leland is an historic name in southern Oregon, used for a railroad station and for a post office about four miles west of the original location, which was known in early days as Twogood's, Leland, Fort Leland and the Grave Creek House. The old location is just north of where the Pacific Highway crosses Grave Creek north of Grants Pass. Miss Martha Leland Crowley, a member of the emigration of 1846, died on what is called Grave Creek, and was buried there under a prominent oak tree. For the history of this event, see under Grave Creek. See also Grants Pass *Courier,* January 23, 24, 26, 1934. In January, 1854, the legislature passed an act to change the name of Grave Creek to Leland Creek in honor of Miss Crowley, but the public never accepted the name. About 1852 Bates and Twogood operated a ranch on Grave Creek and packed into the mines. Preston's map of 1856 shows Twogood's place approximately in the southeast corner of section 3, township 34 south, range 6 west, although the real point may have been in section 2 or 11. About 1853 McDonough Harkness bought out Bates, and continued with James H. Twogood, operating the packing business and keeping the travel. The place was called the Grave Creek House, and also Leland Creek House. Leland post office was established March 28, 1855, with Harkness postmaster. He was killed by Indians near lower Rogue River April 27, 1856, and apparently Twogood took his place as postmaster at Leland. About 1860 Twogood sold out to the Harkness family. During the Rogue River Indian War of 1855-56 a military post called Fort Leland was established at this point, where Twogood and Harkness had already built a stockade for the protection of local settlers. In the early 1880s the railroad was built about four miles west of the old locality of Leland. A station named Leland was established on the railroad and it has been in service for almost a century. Leland post office was closed April 30, 1943.

Lemish Butte, Deschutes County. This butte, west of Crane Prairie, is named with the Klamath Indian word for thunder, or the mythical genii of the Thunder, five in number, and their parents, Old Thunders.

Lemiti Meadow, Clackamas County. Lemiti Meadow is near the summit of the Cascade Range north of Olallie Butte. It drains into Clackamas River through Lemiti Creek. This name presents the curious but not infrequent application of a descriptive geographic name that does not describe the feature to which it is attached, but something entirely different. *Lemiti* is the Chinook jargon word for mountain, and is a corruption of the French *la montagne.* The compiler has been told that Ephraim Henness, pioneer resident in the valley of North Santiam River and one of the first forest rangers in the north Cascade Range, established and named Lemiti Ranger Station. The word *lemiti,* or mountain, was later applied to a nearby point, Lemiti Butte, and also to Lemiti Meadow and Lemiti Creek by someone who did not understand its exact significance.

Lemolo Falls, Douglas County. These falls are on North Umpqua River below Kelsay Valley. They were named by the USFS. *Lemolo* is a Chinook jargon word meaning wild or untamed. It is from the French-Canadian *le moron,* a corruption of *marron,* a runaway negro. The spelling Lemolo has been approved by the USBGN.

Lemolo Lake, Douglas County. This reservoir was formed by damming North Umpqua River at the lower end of Kelsay Valley about two miles upstream from Lemolo Falls from whence came the name. The lake is primarily for hydro-electric power but is also a popular recreation area and campsite. Normal elevation is 4148 ft.

Lemon Island, Multnomah County. Lemon Island is a low body of land west of Government Island in the Columbia River. It is occasionally spelled Lemmon Island. Investigations by George S. Shepherd, attorney at law, Portland, Oregon, indicated that this island once belonged to Peter Lemon who was unable to sign his name and used a cross on legal documents. His name was variously spelled Lemmons and Lemons, but later use is invariably Lemon, and deeds given by Lemon to correct title to the island were apparently made for the purpose of eliminating the uncertainty caused by the spelling Lemmons, Lemons, etc. As a result of Shepherd's investigation it may be assumed that Lemon spelled his name as indicated herein.

Lena, Morrow County. The postmaster at Lena in 1926 wrote the compiler that this post office was named by J. S. Vinson and C. E. Hinton, local residents. It was understood that the name was selected because it had a pleasing sound. This is all the information the writer has been able to get. Lena post office was established June 11, 1873, with Hinton postmaster and closed August 31, 1942.

Leneve, Coos County. Leneve post office was established about 1917. The name Conlogue was suggested to postal authorities but it was considered too difficult. Leneve is the name of a pioneer family of Coos County. Leneve was not a post office in 1935.

Lenhart Butte, Clackamas County. Lenhart Butte, south of Cherryville, was named for Joe Linhart who homesteaded there in 1888. His son, Frank, was still living on the old homestead in 1970 and he told the compiler that the family name had been misspelled on an early map. The form Lenhart is firmly established.

Lenox, Washington County. David T. Lenox, a pioneer of 1843, was one of the most prominent early settlers in Washington County. His land claim was about three miles east of the present community of North Plains. Lenox post office, named in compliment to this pioneer, was established in March, 1895, with Peter Jossy postmaster. This office was about a mile south of what is now Helvetia and about a half a mile north of Germantown road. It was a little south of the center of section 10, township 1 north, range 2 west. The office operated until August 4, 1903.

Lent Canyon, Wallowa County. Lent Canyon empties into Cottonwood Creek in the northeast part of the county in township 5 north, range 46 east. It bears the name of one Joe Lent, who squatted on a claim in the canyon and built a cabin near the canyon mouth.

Lents, Multnomah County. Oliver P. Lent settled where the town of Lents stands in 1866, on a tract of 190 acres. He was born near Marietta, Ohio, August 31, 1830; died at Mount Tabor, Portland, April 22, 1899. His wife, Martha A. Buckley, was born at Parkersburg, Virginia, March 19, 1833; died April 5, 1905. Soon after arriving in Oregon, about 1852, Lent settled on the site of Sycamore, east of Lents. During many years he engaged in the sawmill business. He was a prominent and resourceful man, and served as school director, road supervisor and justice of the peace.

Lenz, Klamath County. Lenz, a station on the Cascade Line of the Southern Pacific Company, was named for Carl C. Lenz who settled nearby before the turn of the century. His wife, Anna Corbell Lenz, lived in Klamath County for over 100 years.

Lenz Butte, Hood River County. This butte near Odell was named for John Lenz, an early settler.

Leona, Douglas County. The town of Leona was named for a young girl, Leona Perkins. This was about 1900. In earlier years the place was called Hudson, and a post office with that name was in operation from June, 1889, until October, 1890. Leonard M. Perkins was the first postmaster. When it was planned to revive this office, it was found that the old name, Hudson, could not be used because of duplication. Leona post office was established February 14, 1901, with Thomas E. Bledsoe first postmaster. Miss Leona Perkins was the granddaughter of Newt Mulvaney, a prominent local resident.

Leonard Creek, Douglas County. Leonard Creek flows into Umpqua River near Tyee in section 33, township 24 south, range 7 west. It was named in 1973 at the request of the local residents to honor Bessie Leonard who was born in New York in 1878 and moved to Tyee in 1914. Mrs. Leonard served many years as postmaster as well as clerk of the Tyee School. She died in April, 1968.

Lepage Park, Sherman County. This park at the mouth of John Day River was one of several constructed along the borders of Lake Umatilla after John Day Dam was placed in service in 1968. Lewis and Clark passed the mouth of John Day River on October 21, 1805, and named it LePage's River for Baptiste LePage, one of their boatmen. It is most fitting that the park should recall the original name.

Leslie Gulch, Malheur County. The Rev. Melville T. Wire, in the *Oregonian,* December 5, 1926, section 5, page 5, gives the story of the name of this feature. The gulch originally drained into Owyhee River from the east not far from the old post office called Watson, but now drains into Owyhee Reservoir. It bears the name of a cattleman, one Leslie, who was killed there by lightning about 1880. For illustrated story about Mazama expedition to Leslie Gulch, see magazine section, *Sunday Oregonian,* August 17, 1947.

Leuthold Couloir, Clackamas County. Joseph R. Leuthold was born in Switzerland in 1906 and came to this country as a small boy. He was an ardent skier and one of the founders of the Mount Hood Ski Patrol as well as an accomplished mountain climber with numerous first ascents of northwest peaks. Leuthold died on December 12, 1965, and in 1970 at the instigation of representatives of the American Alpine Club, Mazamas, Wy'East Climbers and Crag Rats, the "Hourglass" gully climbing route above Reid Glacier on Mount Hood was named Leuthold Couloir in his honor. For his obituary see *Mazama,* 1965.

Lewis, Wallowa County. Postal authorities inform the compiler that this post office was established September 11, 1913, with Alta E. Lewis first postmaster. She was the wife of Frank Lewis, and the post office was apparently named for the family. J. H. Horner of Enterprise told the compiler that the name was suggested by a neighbor, Herbert L. Dunbar.

Lewis and Clark River, Clatsop County. Lewis and Clark mentioned this stream as Netul River. This was on December 7, 1805. Their winter quarters for 1805-06 were on this river, and were called by them Fort Clat-

444

sop. Since that time the Indian name has been abandoned, and the form Lewis and Clark River is universally accepted. It was named in honor of the explorers. The earliest use of the modern name that has come to the compiler's attention is in Lee and Frost, *Ten Years in Oregon,* 1844, page 15. Silas B. Smith, the authority on Clatsop County history, says that the name *Netul* referred to a point on the bank of the river rather than to the stream itself. It seems not to have been the custom of many Oregon tribes to name streams, but places along streams. The Klamath Indians were an exception to this rule. The site of Fort Clatsop was acquired by the Oregon Historical Society in 1901. It comprises three acres of land, two miles from Youngs Bay, on Lewis and Clark River. For description of the place, see the *Oregonian,* June 27, 1885, page 3. For details of Fort Clatsop and its restoration see under that heading.

Lewis Rock, Wheeler County. This high point south of Mitchell was named for Charles G. Lewis who settled there in 1887. Lewis later moved to West Branch where nearby Lewis Butte also carries his name.

Lewis Glacier, Deschutes County. This small glacier is on the southeast slope of South Sister and was named for Meriwether Lewis by Professor Edwin T. Hodge of the University of Oregon in 1924. The most comprehensive information about Meriwether Lewis is to be found in Elliott Coues *History of the Expedition of Lewis and Clark,* volume I. Lewis was born August 18, 1774, near Charlottesville, Virginia, of distinguished family. At the age of 20 he enlisted in the militia to suppress the Whisky Insurrection, and three years later had reached the rank of captain. In 1801 he became private secretary to President Thomas Jefferson. Jefferson accepted, in 1803, Lewis' offer to become a member of the expedition to explore the West. On April 30, 1803, the treaty concluding the Louisiana purchase was signed at Paris, and in the summer of that year the party under the joint command of Meriwether Lewis and William Clark set out for the Pacific Ocean. The expedition was successful, and the leaders were in Washington again in February, 1807. Lewis was rewarded by being made governor of Louisiana. His death occurred October 11, 1809, in the exact center of what is now Lewis County, Tennessee, this county having been created in his honor. The manner of his end is a mystery. There is some belief that he committed suicide during a fit of mental derangement, but the weight of evidence seems to indicate that he was murdered for his money. Coues discusses this at some length. For other information about Lewis and the expedition see Thwaites, *Original Journals of the Lewis and Clark Expedition.*

Lewisburg, Benton County. Haman C. Lewis, a pioneer of 1845, settled near this place on a donation land claim, and the station bears his name. Lewis was a member of the Oregon constitutional convention.

Lewisburg, Marion County. Lewisburg post office was named for a family of pioneer settlers, information about which will be found in Down's *History of the Silverton Country,* page 92. Daniel P. Lewis came to Oregon in 1851 and settled near Drift Creek in the Waldo Hills. Lewisburg post office was established in April, 1889, with Samuel Lewis first of seven postmasters. The office was closed in April, 1904. The office was probably moved around, but was generally about eight miles south-southeast of Silverton. In later years the locality was called Victor Point but the writer has not been able to learn why.

Lewisville, Polk County. John T. Ford of Dallas wrote the compiler on October 3, 1927, that Lewisville was named for David R. Lewis, a pioneer of 1845. The community is on the Lewis donation land claim. David R. Lewis' certificate was numbered 2995.

Lexington, Morrow County. The town of Lexington was named by William Penland, a prominent and successful pioneer resident of that part of Morrow County. He was a native of Lexington, Kentucky, and when he founded the new town he called it for his birthplace. Lexington post office was established November 11, 1885, with Nathaniel A. Yeats first postmaster.

Libby, Coos County. Libby is a place in the Coalbank Slough area two or three miles south of Coos Bay, named for a well-known Indian woman, Libby, who was kind to white settlers. The locality was once called Eastport and was the location of coal mining activity. Libby post office was established June 11, 1890, with Enoch Gore postmaster. This office was closed July 5, 1892, but the locality still goes by the name Libby. The historic named Eastport could not be used for the post office in 1890 because of possible confusion with East Portland, then an incorporated community with its own post office. For additional information about Libby Tinilon and the mines at Libby see Beckham, *Coos Bay, The Pioneer Period,* pages 18 through 26.

Liberal, Clackamas County. Liberal is a community about four miles north of Molalla. It is said to be named for Liberal, Missouri. The late Dee Wright told the compiler that Liberal, Missouri, was named because of liberal credit terms by a pioneer storekeeper in the community. However reference works say that the Missouri town was named because of the liberal views of its citizens. Harrison Wright, a pioneer of 1844, settled near the present site of Liberal, Oregon, and was instrumental in securing a pioneer post office with the name Molalla, established April 9, 1850, with Wright first postmaster. This office was not at the present site of Molalla, but was moved to that place in the 1870s. Liberal post office was established March 25, 1893, with Katie Willett postmaster. The office was discontinued April 30, 1918.

Liberty, Benton County. Gill's map of Oregon, 1874, shows a place called Liberty to the northeast of Corvallis and about a mile south of what is now Wells. The post office was established in April, 1856, with James Gingles first postmaster. The office was finally discontinued in May, 1867. The compiler does not know the reason for the name unless it was a patriotic one.

Liberty, Marion County. Liberty is a well-known community situated about four miles south of Salem on the old highway south to Albany. It is about a mile west of the Pacific Highway East. It is the center of a very productive fruit section. Liberty post office was established January 24, 1895, with J. R. Willard postmaster. The office was closed March 19, 1901, and the community is now served through the Salem office. The community took its name from Liberty School, which was probably established prior to 1875. H. R. Crawford of Salem wrote the compiler in November, 1945, that Liberty School apparently was named because it was on the Liberty road running south from Salem, and the road got its name because it was an extension from Liberty Street in Salem itself.

Liberty, Wheeler County. Liberty post office was on West Branch Bridge Creek about twelve miles southwest of Mitchell on the old road to Prineville, now the Ochoco Highway. It was near the foot of the hill where the road started up grade over the Ochoco Mountains. Liberty post office was established January 2, 1889 with James M. Mansfield postmaster. The office was closed July 24, 1894. G. C. Blake of Roseburg wrote the compiler in January, 1966 that Mrs. Mansfield's mother was Sarah Ann Ross, not Liberty Ann Ross, and that the post office and church were named for Liberty, Missouri, the former home of Caleb and Coanza Woodward, early settlers in the area.

Lick Creek, Wallowa County. Lick Creek was named in early days by hunters and stockmen because of the alkali and salt licks which attracted elk and deer. Lick Creek flows into Little Sheep Creek in township 4 south, range 46 east.

Lightning, Wallowa County. In April, 1907, Lightning post office was established with Eva P. Johnston postmaster. The office operated until July, 1909. Lightning post office was near the mouth of Lightning Creek where that stream flows into the Imnaha River about twenty miles north of and downstream from Imnaha, and was named for the creek.

Lightning Creek, Wallowa County. Lightning Creek was so named because of the frequent storms in the neighborhood. The stream flows into Little Sheep Creek east of Enterprise.

Lightning Creek, Wallowa County. This is an important tributary to Imnaha River, into which it flows in township 3 north, range 49 east. According to J. H. Horner of Enterprise, it was named because of an incident connected with Abe Tharp who later homesteaded on the creek. Tharp and James Wilson once had great difficulty working their way down the creek and when they met Jack Johnson on the Imnaha, they told him they had had a "lightning" time making the trip because it was so rough. Johnson told Horner this was the origin of the name.

Lillard Ditch, Baker County. Several members of the Lillard family homesteaded east of Haines in the first decade of the present century. Shortly thereafter they banded together and formed the Lillard Ditch Company to handle irrigation water.

Lilly Lake, Wallowa County. This lake in township 4 south, range 43 east, was named for Samuel W. Lilly, a resident of Wallowa Valley. The name was applied by J. H. Jackson, who stocked the lake with fish about 1914.

Lilyglen, Jackson County. Lilyglen is a locality on the Dead Indian road northeast of Ashland, at the Lindsay ranch, owned by Charles and William Lindsay. The name was suggested by Mrs. Lindsay, mother of the two ranchers, on account of the wild mountain lilies that grew in the surrounding meadows. Lilyglen post office was established August 13, 1904, with William Lindsay postmaster. The office was closed May 31, 1909, but the locality is still called Lilyglen. It is in the east part of township 38 south, range 3 east.

Lime, Baker County. The post office at Lime was established on September 4, 1899 to serve the community that grew around the lime manufacturing business. The large deposits of limestone provided lime for a considerable area of eastern Oregon and western Idaho. In 1925 the Sun Portland Cement Company built a plant at Lime to provide cement for the Owyhee Dam. After the dam was completed in 1928, the operation was sold to the Oregon Portland Cement Company who are still, in 1981, running a large facility. The post office has been closed for some years.

Limpy Prairie, Douglas County. There are several features that include the name Limpy in township 27 south, range 1 east. G. C. Blake of Roseburg informed the compiler in 1966 that they were all named for an aged Indian who made his home on Little River or East Fork as it was then known. He took his nickname from an injured leg and a halting gait.

Lincoln, Jackson County. Lincoln is a community on the Green Springs Highway a little west of Pinehurst. A story about this lumbering town in Medford *Mail-Tribune,* September 29, 1929, says that it was named for Lincoln, New Hampshire, by the Henry family, which owned the Oregon mill and formerly operated in New England.

Lincoln, Polk County. This community, which is on the west bank of Willamette River north of Salem, is said to have been named for Abraham Lincoln. The post office was established May 31, 1867, with Daniel J. Cooper postmaster. There had previously been an office at or near this location, called Valfontis. See under that heading. For story about Lincoln community, see Salem *Capital Journal,* June 17, 1941. Lincoln post office was discontinued about 1901 and patrons have been served by a rural route from Salem.

Lincoln Beach, Lincoln County. Lincoln Beach is a summer resort area about three miles north of Depoe Bay on the Oregon Coast Highway. It was so named because it was in Lincoln County. The post office was established May 22, 1933, with George W. Betts postmaster.

Lincoln City, Lincoln County. On December 8, 1964 the cities of Oceanlake, Delake and Taft and the unincorporated communities of Cutler City and Nelscott voted to combine to form a new single community. The name Lincoln City was of course derived from the county and was a non-controversial solution to the often thorny surviving name problem. For information on the components see under the individual headings.

Lincoln County. Lincoln County was created February 20, 1893, by the state legislature and was named for Abraham Lincoln, the sixteenth president of the United States. The county has a land area of 1006 square miles.

Lincton Mountain, Umatilla County. In 1862 a group headed by Samuel Linkton and Dorsey Baker of Walla Walla formed a company to build a road across the Blue Mountains to the Grande Ronde Valley to compete with the road from Umatilla Landing on the Columbia River. The route ran generally south from Walla Walla and crossed this high ground between Walla Walla River and Couse Creek where Linkton had previously built a steam powered saw mill. Advertisements and news accounts in the *Washington Statesman* in the 1860s show that Linkton probably spelled his name with a "k" but the form Lincton has been in general use for many years.

Lindsey Creek, Hood River County. This stream is reported to have been named for one John Lindsey, who took up a claim near the creek afterwards known as Lindsey Creek. Lindsey is said to have taken part in the battle at Cascades in 1856 and was wounded therein. He was at one time a fireman on one of the river steamers. The stream is now well known by the name of Lindsey Creek.

Line Creek, Umatilla County. Charles Kopp of Ukiah stated in 1969 that this tributary of Hidaway Creek was so named because it was at one time the dividing line between two sheep grazing allotments.

Link River, Klamath County. This short stream connects Upper Klamath Lake with Lake Ewauna, and is named on that account. It is within the limits of the city of Klamath Falls, formerly known as Linkville. The Klamath Indian name for this stream was *Yulalona,* which meant to move back and forth, referring to the fact that during strong south winds the waters of Link River were blown back above the falls, leaving the bed of the stream, including the falls, partly dry. The name *Yulalona* was also used to refer to the settlement of Linkville near the falls. A condensed form of the name was *Iuauna,* which white people have adopted in the name Lake Ewauna. The Indian name for the falls in Link River was *Tiwishkeni,* literally rush of falling waters place. See under Duwee Canyon, and also under Lake Ewauna. The name Link River has been adopted by the USBGN.

Linn County. Linn County was created December 28, 1847, by the provisional legislature. It was named for Senator L. F. Linn of Missouri, who nearly a decade before had been urging the American occupation of Oregon. Linn County was the first county to be taken from the original Champooick District, and comprised all of Oregon between the Willamette River and the Rocky Mountains, and between Santiam River and North Santiam River and the northern boundary of California. It was subsequently much reduced in size, but is still a large county, with a land area of 2294 square miles. Lewis Fields Linn was born near the site of the city of Louisville, Kentucky, November 5, 1795. He was the author of the donation land law, which gave free land to settlers in the West, and which was the forerunner of the homestead law. He was appointed United States senator for Missouri in 1833, elected in 1836 and re-elected in 1842, and served until his death. His work in the Senate was highly important to western settlement and acquisition of Oregon. His activity in the Senate, in support of his bill to occupy Oregon and granting land to actual settlers, was his last of importance, for he died October 3, 1843. Calhoun, McDuffie and Dayton led the fight against the Linn bill. They contended the bill would make a breach of faith with Great Britain, and cause international complications. The donation land act, based on Linn's idea, passed Congress September 27, 1850. For history of his work for Oregon, see the *Oregonian,* April 8, 1901, page 6: May 8, 1887; *OHQ,* volume XIX, pages 283-305, by Lester

Burrell Shippee. Senator Linn was a surgeon and lived at Ste. Genevieve, Missouri. His nephew, Lt.-Commanding William Pope McArthur, U.S.N., made the first survey of the Pacific Coast for the U.S. Coast Survey, 1849-50. His grand-nephew, Lewis Linn McArthur (1843-97) came to Oregon in 1864 to practice law, and was at one time a member of the supreme court of the state.

Linnemann, Multnomah County. This station on the Portland Traction Company line is two miles west of Gresham. It was named for Mr. and Mrs. John G. D. Linnemann, pioneers of 1852, who owned land nearby. Linnemann died in 1892, and Mrs. Linnemann November 15, 1926, at the age of 98. For information about the family see the *Oregonian,* November 17, 1926, page 4. The name is persistently misspelled. A. C. Giese, in a letter in the *Oregonian,* September 22, 1927, calls attention to the fact that the platted name of the community is Cedarville, part of the Giese donation land claim. Apparently the railroad company and the Giese family were unable to agree on a name for the station.

Linney Creek, Clackamas County. This stream flows into Salmon River from the south, east of Linney Butte. The two features were named for an engineer connected with the Mount Hood Railway and Power Company project.

Linnton, Multnomah County. Peter H. Burnett and M. M. McCarver, pioneers of 1843, laid out the town of Linnton soon after their arrival in Oregon. They named it for Senator Lewis Fields Linn of Missouri. See under Linn County. Burnett said of his town: "I have no doubt that this place will be the great commercial town of the territory." Burnett was afterwards first governor of the state of California. Linnton is now within the city of Portland.

Linslaw, Lane County. In 1917 a petition was sent to Washington for a post office, and in due season it was established and named Linslaw. Local residents are at a loss to explain the name, and say that they had nothing to do with its selection. The writer has a theory that the postal authorities had the name Siuslaw on file and the handwriting was not clear, with the result that the name Linslaw was applied to the office. This confusion could occur very easily. Linslaw is near the Siuslaw River.

Lint Slough, Lincoln County. Lint Creek flows into Lint Slough and Lint Slough empties into Alsea Bay at Waldport. These streams were named for one Lint Starr, reported to have been the first white man to claim land in the vicinity of the creek. The name Indian Slough is no longer applicable by decision of USBGN.

Linville, Lincoln County. Linville post office was named for the first postmaster, Robert W. Linville. The office was near Drift Creek a few miles east of Bayview. It was established May 26, 1896, and continued in operation until April 15, 1915. Recent government maps do not show the place.

Little Applegate River, Jackson County. This is the correct name of an important tributary of Applegate River, not North Fork Applegate River. See decision of the USBGN, which agrees with local use. For origin of the name, see Applegate River.

Little Brother, Lane County. Little Brother is a small butte northwest of the North Sister. It was so named because of its position in respect to the Three Sisters.

Little Crater Lake, Clackamas County. For many years this lake, some four miles north of Clackamas Lake, was called Crater Lake because of a peculiar crater or sink hole in the grassy marsh surrounding it. There was a notion that the name was not particularly apposite, especially on account of the much more important Crater Lake in Oregon and after World War II, the name was altered by the addition of the diminutive. The name Turquoise Lake had been suggested and when the matter was brought to the OGNB in 1967 others were also brought forward. However, past usage prevailed and the USBGN approved the present form in *Decision List 6802.*

Little Deschutes River, Klamath and Deschutes counties. This stream heads on the east slopes of the Cascade Range north of Mount Thielsen. It joins Deschutes River between La Pine and Bend. For several years federal authorities called the stream East Fork, but it was locally known as Little River. In 1926, at the suggestion of the writer, the USBGN officially named the stream Little Deschutes River, and this name has come into general use.

Little Eagle Creek, Baker County. This stream joins Eagle Creek on the range line between ranges 44 and 45 east. The name Little Fork is incorrect. See decision of USBGN.

Little Luckiamute River, Polk County. This stream rises in the Coast Range southwest of Dallas. It joins Luckiamute River south of Independence. In the interest of simplicity government mapping agencies have dropped the word "Big" from the main branch. *Luckiamute* is an Indian word the meaning of which is unknown. Stories to the effect that it is based on an incident having to do with a deaf mute may be dismissed as fiction.

Little Nestucca River, Polk, Tillamook and Yamhill counties. As far as the writer knows, there is no translation into English of this Indian name. S. H. Rock, postmaster at Oretown, is authority for the statement that the real name of Little Nestucca River as given by the Indians was Nestachee. This probably referred to the lower part of the stream or to a point on its banks. See under Nestucca River. Little Nestucca River flows into Nestucca Bay.

Little Niagara Falls, Clackamas County. This fifteen foot high falls on Salmon River is about six miles downstream from the mouth of Linney Creek. It is the third of six falls between Linney Creek and Welches and was named because it resembles its eastern namesake. For details of this group see under Stein Falls.

Little North Santiam River, Marion County. This is the correct name of the main tributary of North Santiam River, which it joins at Mehama. Little North Fork is incorrect, and has been ruled against by the USBGN.

Little Santiam River, Marion County. This stream is a by-pass from the main Santiam River into Willamette River, and is about two miles long.

Little Wocus Bay, Klamath County. This bay is at the south end of Klamath Marsh. Wocus is the English form of the name given by the Klamath Indians for the seed of the yellow pond lily, *Nuphar advena.* This plant grows in immense numbers in the marshes of Klamath County. The seeds were roasted by the Indians and ground for food.

Littlefield Spring, Baker County. This spring in Blue Canyon near the site of Auburn was on the ranch of David Littlefield, one of Henry Griffin's three companions when he discovered gold nearby in 1861.

Live Oak Mountain, Douglas County. Live Oak Mountain was applied to a prominent geographic feature, elevation 3429 feet, near the head of Olalla Creek, and in the extreme northwest corner of section 26, township 30 south, range 8 west. The history of the name is unknown to the writer, but it was obviously applied because of a patch of canyon live oak trees on its slopes. Live oaks are not numerous in Oregon, although they constitute a prominent part of scattered forests in California. This live oak is known botanically as *Quercus chrysolepis* Liebman. Live oaks are sufficiently scarce in Oregon that a good sized grove is immediately conspicuous. Information about this patch of live oaks was secured from the supervisor of the Siskiyou National Forest and from District Assistant Edwin Frye. Mr. Frye visited this grove some years ago.

Liverpool, Linn County. Liverpool post office was in operation in Linn County from August 6, 1877, to February 19, 1879, with Frank Sutter postmaster. The only reference to the place that the compiler can find is in the *Historical Atlas Map of Marion & Linn Counties,* 1878, page 55, in the biography of Thomas Alford, where it is stated that the village of Liverpool was on his property about four miles northeast of Harrisburg. See under Muddy Station. The locality is now known as Alford.

Llano, Malheur County. *Llano* is a Spanish word meaning flat or plain. A post office was established with this name on June 5, 1888. It was closed to Vale September 18, 1894. Francis O'Neill was the only postmaster. The compiler has not been able to get the exact location of Llano post office, but it was probably at or near the location of a later post office Fangollano in the central part of the county. Fangollano is a Spanish name meaning mud flat.

Llao Rock, Crater Lake National Park, Klamath County. This is a great bluff on the northwest rim of Crater Lake. Its top is 8046 feet above sea level, and 1869 feet above lake level. A bay at its foot is called Llao Bay. These two features were named by Will G. Steel on August 15, 1885, for a Klamath Indian deity supposed to be associated with the lake. The rock was once called Mount Jackson for Colonel James Jackson, U. S. A., veteran of Indian wars and a well-known resident of Portland for many years. He was at one time in command at Fort Klamath.

Llewellyn, Lane County. Llewellyn was about eleven miles west of Eugene on the old Crow stage road, where it crossed Coyote Creek. The post office was established February 18, 1886, with Mrs. Lilias Llewellyn Perkins first of three postmasters. The office was discontinued September 17, 1904, due to the extension of rural free delivery. The name was of course taken from Mrs. Perkins' middle name. Henry Clay Perkins, her husband, was a prominent pioneer farmer and nurseryman, who had a place on Coyote Creek.

Loafer Creek, Douglas County. This creek forms the south border of Thorn Prairie on the upper reaches of North Umpqua River. It was named by the USFS for the intermittent sections of running water and dry creek bed. The creek just "loafs" along.

Lobert Draw, Klamath County. Lobert Draw south of Chiloquin was named for a well-known early family. There were several Loberts in the general area but the draw was probably named for Hager Lobert who took up an Indian Allotment near its mouth.

Lobster Creek, Curry County. This stream is tributary to Rogue River a few miles above Wedderburn. It was doubtless named for the native crawfish or crayfish, as there are no real lobsters in Oregon waters, although there are many on land. The name was applied in very early days. Glisan, in *Journal of Army Life,* mentions the name several times when he was stationed at Fort Orford in 1855-56 and indicates that the expression Lobster Creek was already established and well known. There is another Lobster Creek in Lincoln, Benton and Lane counties, apparently named for the crawfish, but the compiler does not know the circumstances. A post office called Lobster was established on the Benton County list in March, 1883. It was in operation until July, 1896. Old maps show the place in Lobster Creek valley about a mile east of the west boundary of Benton County.

Lockhart Creek, Coos County. This tributary of South Fork Coquille River east of Eden Ridge was apparently named for Herbert Lockhart who took up property at its mouth in 1907.

Lockit, Wasco County. Lockit is a station on the Oregon Trunk Railway named with the Chinook jargon word for four, since it was the fourth station from the north end of the line up Deschutes River.

Lockit Butte, Deschutes County. Lockit Butte, in the north part of Paulina Mountains, is named with the Chinook jargon word for four, it being the fourth butte of a series named all at the same time by the USFS.

Locoda, Columbia County. Locoda was a station on Spokane, Portland and Seattle Railway northeast of Clatskanie. It was once called Bradbury. The name Locoda was made by taking letters from the corporate title of the Lower Columbia Co-operative Dairy Ass'n and telescoping them into one word.

Locust Grove, Douglas County. A pioneer post office with the name Locust Grove was established on the Umpqua County list on February 9, 1858, with Richard Smith first and only postmaster. The office was discontinued September 10, 1863. Locust Grove, which was obviously given a descriptive name, was in one of the parts of Umpqua County that was annexed to Douglas County. Locust Grove was on the route of travel about six miles south of Yoncalla on the road to Oakland, but the compiler does not know its exact location. Old maps show it near what is now known as Rice Hill.

Log Cabin, Klamath County. Log Cabin post office was short lived. It was situated at the Log Cabin service station and lunch rooms on The Dalles-California Highway about five and a half miles south of the north boundary of Klamath County. The post office operated from June 13, 1930, until December 31, 1930, when it was closed and the business transferred to Crescent. George H. Davis was postmaster. The main structure was of rustic construction, hence the name. The last time the compiler saw this establishment, the name had been changed to The Timbers.

Log Creek, Wallowa County. Log Creek was named for an accumulation of old logs lying across the trail along the stream. Log Creek flows into Imnaha River in township 2 north, range 48 east.

Logan, Clackamas County. Logan community and post office were named for Major-General John A. Logan of Civil War and political fame. The post office was established June 13, 1884, with Lafayette Hunniston, first postmaster. This office was on the flat or table land west of Clackamas River and east of Clear Creek. The locality is well known although the post office was closed October 12, 1903, doubtless as the result of the extension of rural delivery. General John A. Logan was Republican candidate for vice-president in 1884 when the post office was established. His name had been frequently in the news which may have been the reason that the post office was named for him.

Logan Butte, Crook County. Logan Butte is a well-known landmark in the south part of township 18 south, range 20 east. Some of the butte may overlap into the township adjoining on the south. In February, 1948, Fisher C. Logan of Bend wrote that the butte was named for his uncle, Thomas Logan, who acquired nearby property in the early 1870s. An interesting feature of this area is the extensive deposit of bones of extinct animals.

Logdell, Grant County. Logdell post office was established August 7, 1916, with Ella Sproul first postmaster. The locality is southwest of Canyon City, and was once served by an office called Homer. The history of the name Logdell is not as clear as it might be, but it is said that the word Logdale was included on a list submitted to postal authorities. The spelling Logdell was officially adopted, but whether due to poor writing on the original list the compiler does not know. In any event it was intended to be a name descriptive of logging activity in the vicinity and either Logdell or Logdale is apposite.

Logie Trail Road, Multnomah County. James Logie was one of the earliest settlers on Sauvie Island. He was a Hudson's Bay Company employee, and was sent to the island about 1840 to take charge of butter making in one of the company's dairies. He worked on the old Indian trail over the hills into the Tualatin Valley, and made a better route out of it. It was named for him on that account. James Logie was born in the Orkney Islands. He died March 24, 1854, and his widow, Isabella, also from the Orkneys, married Jonathan Moar. See letter by George B. Roberts in Oregon Historical Society files.

Logsden, Lincoln County. Mrs. Hazel Schaffer, postmaster at Logsden in April, 1927, informed the writer that this place was named for an old Indian of the community, a Mr. Logsden. This is an unusual Indian name and may be a corruption of some other form. Logsden was a very old resident on the Siletz Indian Reservation. The post office was established in June, 1914, with the name Orton, in compliment to a local family. The name of the office was changed to Logsden in June, 1921.

Lolah Butte, Deschutes County. This butte is northeast of Crane Prairie and the compiler is told that the name is from the Chinook jargon. If that is the case, the name is probably a form of *lo-lo*, meaning round, whole or complete. The accent is on the second syllable. This word is not the same as *lolo,* meaning to pack, or carry, which has the accent on the first syllable. There is a Lolo Butte not far from Lolah Butte.

Lolo Butte, Deschutes County. This butte southwest of Bend was named by the USFS with the Chinook jargon word for pack or carry, apparently because supplies had to be carried to it.

Lolo Pass, Clackamas and Hood River counties. Lolo Pass lies at the summit of the Cascade Range about two miles south of Bull Run Lake. From the west it is reached by way of Clear Fork Sandy River. Its elevation is about 3400 feet. It was named by Thomas H. Sherrard of the USFS for Lolo Pass in the Bitterroot Range in Idaho-Montana. John E. Rees, in his pamphlet *Idaho,* says that Lolo Pass in the Bitterroot Range received its name from a hunter and trapper named Lawrence who was buried on the banks of a stream on the Montana side. The Indians called the creek Lolo Creek because that was the best they could do with the name. They pronounced the name Loulou Creek. This stream heads northeast of the pass. It was called Travelers Rest Creek by Lewis and Clark. The attention of the compiler has been called to the fact that the Chinook jargon word for carrying and back-packing is *lolo,* and it is said that the pass in the Bitterroot Range was named from this source. Pioneers familiar with the Lolo Pass do not seem to have considered this to be the origin of the name. Gannett has yet another theory about *lolo,* and says that it is Nez Perce for muddy water.

Loma, Harney County. *Loma* is a Spanish word meaning rising ground, or slope, frequently used for a locality from which there is a good view. Loma post office in Harney County was about eight miles north of the place called Narrows, in what was known as Sunset Valley. At one time there were thirty-five or forty homesteaders in Sunset Valley, who later moved from the area. Loma post office was established January 20, 1911, with Nathaniel Henney postmaster. The office was closed to Burns November 27, 1912. Henney had made a previous effort to get postal service. An office named Henney, with Henney as the postmaster, was established June 4, 1908, but was never put in active service. The order was rescinded as of January 31, 1909. The Loma post office was in the Henney home, just about south of the east end of Wright Point, near the center of the Henney homestead. This homestead claim was at the southeast corner of the intersection of the road east to Lawen and the road south to Narrows.

Loma Vista, Lake County. The name Loma Vista was made up of Spanish words meaning rising ground where a view was to be had. It is the same sort of a name as Viewpoint. Loma Vista post office was established in the Fort Rock Valley on September 6, 1913, and was closed May 31, 1918.

London Peak, Josephine County. Up to recent times this peak seems to have had no name, but in 1939 Mrs. Helen Paul of Wolf Creek requested that it be named London Peak in honor of Jack London, the writer. Mrs. Paul is authority for the statement that Jack London spent several months in the vicinity when he was writing *Valley of the Moon,* and the peak was one of his favorites. London Peak is about a mile and a half southwest of the town of Wolf Creek and a mile west of Pacific Highway and has an elevation of about 3000 feet. The USBGN adopted Mrs. Paul's suggestion.

Lone Grave Butte, Lake County. Lone Grave Butte is in the southeast corner of Lake County and has an elevation of 6582 feet. It takes its name from a solitary grave near its east base. The eroded inscription on the headstone apparently reads "W. Kilbey NOV 28129", but the date could also be NOV 28/29. The grave is on BLM property and they report that the marker was stolen in the fall of 1980. See *Oregon Journal*, December 1, 1980.

Lone Ranch Creek, Curry County. Lone Ranch Creek flows into Pacific Ocean south of Cape Ferrelo. The name comes from Lone Ranch, the 1860 homestead of John Cresswell. In 1872 Cresswell discovered borate of lime, now known as priceite, and in 1890 one Fleming took an option on the property with the intent to open the deposit. He allowed the option to lapse and Walter Gray purchased the land for the Pacific Coast Borax Company. After two years of desultory mining, operations ceased and the area returned to obscurity until 1961 when the new route of US 101 was opened for traffic. Part of the original ranch lying between the highway and the ocean was donated to the state in 1950 by Borax Consolidated Limited, parent company of Pacific Coast Borax Company. A second parcel was donated in 1960 by United States Borax & Chemical Corporation, successor to Pacific Coast Borax Company. Both parcels are now part of Samuel H. Boardman State Park.

Lonely, Lake County. Lonely post office with a descriptive name was established in the Warner Valley June 11, 1891, with Coelia Lemberger first and only postmaster. The office was closed June 10, 1895. The best available information is to the effect that Lonely was at or near the place later called Adel. Adel office was established in April, 1896, with Erastus C. Sessions first postmaster. Mrs. Lemberger was postmaster at Adel from December, 1896, to August, 1901. In July, 1947, Mrs. Orvilla Stein, daughter of Mrs. Lemberger, wrote from Lakeview that she had never heard of Lonely post office, and there was a doubt in her mind that the office ever was in actual operation. In any event little is known about the place called Lonely with its appropriate name.

Lonerock, Gilliam County. Lonerock has been so called for many years. The place gets its name from a rock about 100 feet high and some 60 feet in diameter. It is a prominent landmark not far from the central part of the community. The post office was established in November, 1875. Lone Rock Creek takes its name from the same source. The town of Lonerock was founded by R. G. Robinson and Albert Henshaw in 1881 and was platted in 1882 by Robinson. The name used by the platters was Lone Rock, but the post office is Lonerock.

Lonesomehurst, Harney County. Lonesomehurst post office was established January 16, 1917, and discontinued February 28, 1918. Henry K. Hardisty was the only postmaster. In the summer of 1946 Archie McGowan of Burns interviewed Mrs. Hardisty, widow of the postmaster, and among other things she reported as follows: "This post office was in our ranch home on Trout Creek about twenty miles south of Silvies post office, on the main road at that time. The mail was picked up at Silvies. I sent in several suggested names and they were rejected. In reading the 'funny' pages in the paper I found the name Lonesomehurst, which I submitted." Mrs. Hardisty appears to have had a keen sense of humor, and her selection of a name was certainly appropriate.

Long, Malheur County. This station was named because of the length of the siding. It is on the Union Pacific Railroad between Riverside and Juntura.

Long Creek, Grant County. Long Creek is an important stream in Grant County and is said to have been so called because it is the longest creek in that part of the state. An inspection of the map indicates that this is probably not founded on fact although it may be the longest in the John Day River drainage. The name of the community Long Creek was suggested to postal authorities because it was near the stream.

Long Tom, Lane County. Long Tom post office was established September 3, 1853, with Augustus L. Humphrey first postmaster. It was out of service for about six months in 1884, but was reestablished. The name was changed to Madison on September 19, 1904. The office was west of Eugene in the general vicinity of Elmira or Veneta, but it was doubtless moved around to suit the convenience of the various postmasters. It was never very far from Long Tom River. The change to Madison was doubtless in compliment to Madison Canaday, a local resident, and for many years postmaster at Long Tom office. For information about the history of the name see under Long Tom River.

Long Tom River, Benton and Lane counties. Geo. H. Himes said this stream bears an imitation of an Indian tribal name, *Lung-tum-ler.* While on his way to Umpqua River in 1834, John Work called it Sam Tomeleaf River. On his return trip, Work used the name Lamitambuff on July 1, 1834. David Douglas used the form Longtabuff River. Wilkes spelled it Lumtumbuff in 1841. See *OHQ* for September, 1923, page 264.

Lookingglass, Douglas County. Lookingglass Valley was visited in 1846, according to local stories, by Hoy Flournoy, and he is said to have named the valley because of the beautiful appearance of the green grass in the valley, which reflected the light almost as well as a mirror.

Lookingglass Creek, Umatilla and Union counties. This stream flows into Grande Ronde River from the west. It bears the name of Lookingglass, a chief of the Nez Perce, who was so called by the whites because he carried with him a small looking-glass. His Indian name was *Apash-wa-hay-ikt.* For information about him see *The Life of Isaac Ingalls Stevens,* by Hazard Stevens. There is also a Lookingglass Lake, presumably named for the same man, in townships 5 and 6 south, range 44 east, on the boundary between Baker and Union counties.

Lookout Creek, Baker County. This stream is in township 14 south, ranges 35½ and 36 east. It was at one time known as Sheep Creek, but the USBGN was prevailed upon to rename it Lookout Creek because there were already too many Sheep creeks in that part of the state.

Lookout Creek, Wallowa County. Lookout Creek flows into Snake River in the southeast part of township 3 north, range 50 east. The stream was named because of the difficulty in operating pack trains on the ridge above. Packers had to be on the lookout to see that their horses did not roll off the trail. It is said that the name was given by James and Nate Tryon.

Lookout Rock, Curry County. This is a well-known and peculiar landmark on the Oregon coast about four miles south of Humbug Mountain. It is just west of the Oregon Coast Highway, and rises almost vertically several hundred feet above the ocean. This descriptive name was given in the 1850s, probably during the mining excitement. George Davidson in the *Coast Pilot,* 1889, page 373, says the Indian name for the rock was *Nog-gi-sa,* but gives no explanation.

Loon Lake, Douglas County. Walling, in *History of Southern Oregon,* page 439, says that in 1852 L. L. Williams, Joseph Peters and Job Hatfield, while on an exploring expedition from Scottsburg, found this lake. In the center was a floating log with a loon's nest containing two eggs. Two loons were observed at some distance in the water. The eggs were packed in moss and taken to Wilbur Academy. In view of these facts the lake was named Loon Lake. Gabrielson and Jewett in *Birds of Oregon,* page 64, *et seq.,* describe three loons that are found in Oregon.

Looney Butte, Marion County. Looney Butte is a few miles north of Jefferson and is skirted on its east slope by the Pacific Highway East. It has an elevation of 630 feet. It was named for Jesse Looney, who came to Oregon in 1843. He was one of the leaders of the migration that year. He died March 25, 1869, aged eighty-eight years. His home was near Looney Butte, where his descendants still reside. His wife, Ruby Crawford Bond, died there May 7, 1900, aged ninety-two years. For biography of Jesse Looney, see the *Oregonian,* March 27, 1869, page 2. For information about the Looney family, see the *Oregonian,* August 1, 1926, section I, page 11.

Looney Spring, Wheeler County. This spring near US 26 above Keyes Creek was named for Eugene Looney. Looney was an early day rancher and businessman of Mitchell.

Lorane, Lane County. This post office was established May 27, 1887, with William N. Crow postmaster. In February, 1947, Mrs. L. H. Johnson of Eugene, a niece of Crow, wrote that postal authorities asked Crow to submit several names for the proposed office. The name Loraine was suggested by Mrs. Crow because it was the name of a favorite niece. Officials accepted this suggestion but changed the spelling to Lorane as a matter of simplicity and also because there were already several Loraines in the country.

Lord Flat, Wallowa County. This flat is near Snake River. It is sometimes known as Buckaroo Flat. It was named for James Lord, who hunted and ranged stock there.

Lorella, Klamath County. Lorella was first known as Haynesville, and the post office was established August 3, 1887, with Joseph K. Haynes postmaster. It is said that the place was confused with Haines, Baker County, and as a result the name was changed to Lorella on December 13, 1894. Captain O. C. Applegate of Klamath Falls told the compiler that this was in honor of Mrs. Lorella Wisner, a local resident.

Lost Cabin Creek, Baker County. This is a tributary of Paddy Creek in township 7 south, range 44 east. In early days a miner had a cabin on this creek and after the diggings were abandoned the brush grew so profusely that it was passed unnoticed by travellers on the trail a few feet away.

Lost Creek, Lane County. This stream flows north into Middle Fork

Willamette River near Dexter and it drains a north-south valley several miles long. In earlier days the vale was generally called Lost Valley, and the valley may have been named before the creek. Walling in *Illustrated History of Lane County* says that Elijah Bristow named the valley, but the exact reason is uncertain. It is probable that the name was applied because the valley was quite secluded.

Lost Lake, Hood River County. This lake is said to have been originally known as Blue Lake, and it is stated that the Walk Up Trail from The Dalles to Sandy River passed by it. This does not agree with information printed in *Mazama* for December, 1920, which is to the effect that the lake was discovered by Joe and John Divers. Acting on information gathered from these two men by E. L. Smith of Hood River, a party of twelve was organized in 1880 for the purpose of locating the lake. It is of course possible that the Divers brothers called it Blue Lake. The searching party started to look for the lake on August 18, 1880. Dr. T. L. Eliot wrote an account of this search which appeared in the *Oregonian* on August 27, 1880. The party found the lake and christened it Lost Lake. Owing to the smoke and some misunderstanding of routes the party did not find the search any too easy, and the old story: "Indian not lost — wigwam lost," furnished the basis for the name. Dr. Eliot made several efforts to learn the Indian name of this lake, but was unsuccessful.

Lost Prairie, Wallowa County. Lost Prairie is an area not well defined, lying southeast of Grande Ronde River, north of Courtney Creek and west of East Bear Creek. It is not exactly a prairie, but a series of benches separated by canyons. The locality was named by A. C. Smith in the late 1870s. He and a party of settlers were following a band of renegade Indians who had run off with some stock. Smith and his party got to a place where the trail ran out on them, and they named the locality Lost Prairie. There was a post office called Lost Prairie, established about 1887. R. H. Bacon was postmaster. The postal map of 1900 shows this office a little south of the Oregon-Washington state line and close to Grande Ronde River. It was in the south part of section 19, township 6 north, range 44 east.

Lost River, Klamath County. This stream rises in California and flows into Oregon. It formerly debouched into Tule Lake, but it is now controlled for irrigation, and as a result Tule Lake is being dried up and reclaimed for farm land. During its course through Langell Valley Lost River disappears for several miles, hence its name. The famous natural stone bridge, by which the Applegate party crossed Lost River on July 6, 1846, may be seen near Merrill. The rocks were submerged when seen by the compiler, and seem more like a series of stepping stones than a natural bridge. See Bancroft's *History of Oregon*, volume I, page 548, and *OHQ*, volume XXII, page 24. A dam of the U. S. Bureau of Reclamation has been built at the natural bridge and the stones are covered. Lost River was discovered by Fremont early in May, 1846, and named McCrady River for a boyhood friend, but that name did not prevail. There was a pioneer post office called Lost River on or near this stream, probably at the Horton ranch above Olene. It was in service from February, 1875, to April, 1876, with W. H. Horton postmaster.

Lost Valley, Wheeler County. The compiler has not been able to get definite information about the origin of the name Lost Valley other than it is supposed that the valley was named because some soldiers lost their way in it during the early Indian wars in eastern Oregon. Many years ago the *Oregonian* contained the following news item: "Lost Valley, Gilliam County, is looking forward with unmitigated delight to a grand ball next Friday night at which time William D. Johnson, of Lost Valley, will be united in marriage to Miss Edith Waddle, of Thirty-mile. Tickets to the ball, including the wedding supper and horse feed, are going freely at $1.50 per couple." This social affair apparently took place before Wheeler County was established in 1899. The community was always located in what is now Wheeler County but Vere A. McCarty of Salem in 1981 called attention to the fact that the Lost Valley School was always a little to the north in Gillian County.

Lostine, Wallowa County. Lostine is a town on Lostine River in the Wallowa Valley. Local authorities wrote the compiler in 1927 that the place was named by a pioneer settler for Lostine, Kansas. The meaning of the name Lostine is unknown to the compiler. Lostine was a place in Lowell Township, Cherokee County, Kansas. The census of 1870 gives it as a post office for farmers. The post office was discontinued before 1880 and the name does not appear in modern gazetteers. Lostine, Oregon, is an important trading center and does not seem to be headed for the fate that met Lostine, Kansas. The post office at Lostine, Oregon, was established August 6, 1878, with W. R. Laughlin first postmaster.

Lostine River, Wallowa County. This stream has been called South Fork, and also Middle Fork Wallowa River, but local use is in favor of Lostine River, and the USBGN has adopted that name. See under Lostine.

Loughs Mine, Douglas County. Loughs Mine is on North Umpqua River about two miles northwest of Horseshoe Bend. Ed Lough was a packer for the USFS in early days and worked this claim when not employed elsewhere.

Louse Canyon, Malheur County. Louse Canyon heads just north of the Nevada line a few miles east of McDermitt. It runs east and north into the Owyhee River south of Three Forks. The story is that in the early 1900s a cow camp in the canyon became infested with the ubiquitous vermin. During the 1960s the OGNB received a plausible and earnest plea to change the name to La Rosa, supposedly given by Basque sheepherders for the profusion of wild roses therein. In due course this change was effected in *Decision List 6402*. The canyon is in an out of the way area and little more was heard of the matter until the late 1970s when the USGS started a major mapping project and the change of name received some attention. The locals took umbrage, declaring vehemently that the graybacks had been there in force while roses were conspicuous by their absence. After due progression through channels, Louse Canyon was restored in *Decision List 8004*.

Louse Creek, Josephine County. This creek north of Grants Pass was originally so called because of an Indian camp on its banks that was infested with vermin. Sporadic efforts have been made to change the name to something more romantic, such as Grouse Creek, but there does not appear to be much steam behind such movements.

Lousignont Lake, Washington County. Lousignont Lake, now almost entirely drained, is about five miles northwest of Forest Grove. It bears the name of a pioneer family of the county. Lousignont Creek northwest of Timber was named for the same family.

Love Lake, Lane County. This small body of water east of Junction City was named for Hugh Love who took up a donation land claim there in 1852. In the early days this lake drained north to Long Tom River but by the 1950s it had become intermittent.

Love Reservoir, Baker County. Love Reservoir in Ritter Creek drainage south of Keating was named for Walter S. Love. Love was the son of early Baker County settlers and was one of the first proponents of irrigation and water diversion. His brother, Avon Love, was equally well known.

Lovely, Wallowa County. Lovely post office was established May 10, 1902, with Sarah A. Lovely postmaster. It was situated about three miles northeast of Minam and operated until June, 1907. The place was named for Walter Lovely who homesteaded there.

Low Gap Creek, Josephine County. This stream is in the extreme southeast corner of the county. It was named because it heads in a low pass between Lake and Whisky peaks. The name Whisky Creek is incorrect.

Lowell, Lane County. Amos D. Hyland, who came from Lowell, Maine, in the fifties, established the community and helped secure a post office, of which he was once postmaster. He named the place for his former home. He was a successful stock-raiser, and, the writer is informed, was an energetic and hard-working man. He brought up a family of fourteen children! The first post office in this locality was called Cannon. It was established August 9, 1880, with C. E. Byers postmaster. The name was changed to Lowell February 19, 1883.

Lowell Creek, Lane County. This stream flows into Christy Creek northeast of Oakridge. According to Mrs. Lina A. Flock of Oakridge, the creek was named for E. D. Lowell, who at one time pastured his stock in the neighborhood.

Lower Bridge, Deschutes County. This name is purely descriptive and originated at the time when the bridge was down stream from Tetherow bridge, which was the other important bridge in the upper Deschutes country. There was a post office of the same name not far from the bridge. This bridge is six miles west of Terrebonne, and near its western end is the well-known diatomite deposit.

Lower Klamath Lake, Klamath County. This is the correct name of the smaller of the two Klamath lakes, not Little Klamath Lake. Lower Klamath Lake is on the boundary between Oregon and California, and part of it is in California. Its outlet is Klamath Strait, which connects it with Klamath River. Klamath Strait formerly flowed either way, depending on the stage of water in Lower Klamath Lake, but this characteristic has apparently been interfered with by the construction of a railroad embankment. For information about the origin of the name, see under Klamath County. The Klamath Indian name for Lower Klamath Lake is *Aka-ushkni E-ush*, the latter word meaning lake. Attempts at reclamation have caused much variation in the size of Lower Klamath Lake in recent years.

Lower Land Creek, Coos County. This creek, together with Upper Land Creek nearby, was named for T. C. Land, a pioneer settler on South Fork Coquille River.

Lowersoda, Linn County. A post office with the name Lower Soda was established in the vicinity of what is now Cascadia on August 27, 1892, with John Atkinson postmaster. The office was discontinued May 21, 1894, but was reestablished in about two weeks with the name Lowersoda and with Atkinson continuing as postmaster. The office was finally closed April 21, 1899, and the business transferred to Cascadia office which had been established on May 12, 1898. Lowersoda which was very close to Cascadia was at the old roadhouse of William R. Finley. According to William R. Mealey, of Foster, who wrote in September, 1946, this old roadhouse was built in the late 1860s or early 1870s. The soda springs at Cascadia were at one time known as Lower Soda springs in contradistinction to the Upper Soda springs about ten or twelve miles further east.

Lowullo Butte, Deschutes County. *Lowullo* is the Chinook jargon word for round. The name was applied to this butte three miles north of East Lake by USFS officials when they gave Indian names to a number of features.

Lubbing Flat, Wasco County. W. D. Ketchum of The Dalles told the writer in 1967 that this flat between Mosier Creek and Mill Creek was named for an early settler. A check of BLM records in Portland showed that Heinrich Lubbing filed for a homestead in section 17, township 1 north, range 12 east, on August 24, 1893. For a number of years this feature was shown on maps as Lugan Flat but this error was corrected by the USBGN in *Decision List 7701.*

Luckiamute, Polk County. The Luckiamute River has given its name to two places in the Willamette Valley, a post office and a railroad station, neither of which survived the march of time. The meaning of the name, which is of Indian origin, is unknown. A post office with the name Lackemute was established March 14, 1851, and was therefore one of the earliest in the county. Harrison Linville was the first postmaster. The compiler has been unable to find this place on a map, but it is apparent from the list of postmasters that the office was close to the Luckiamute River, probably a little west of the present Pacific Highway West, and in the extreme south part of the county. It also seems apparent that the office was moved to suit the postmasters. It was finally closed on November 23, 1874. In later years there was a railroad station Luckiamute on the Oregonian Railway narrow gauge line a little north of the Luckiamute River and about four miles northeast of Pedee. This place did not have a post office, and time has done much to obliterate the community.

Luckiamute River, Benton and Polk counties. This is an Indian tribal name, the meaning of which is unknown. Bancroft says the Lakmiut tribe was of the Kalapooian nation. The name Luckiamute is an old one, and has nothing to do with a deaf mute who is said to have operated a ferry on the stream. This derivation is purely fanciful. The southern stream is the main fork and is officially known as Luckiamute River, not Big Luckiamute River. The northern branch is officially called Little Luckiamute River.

Luckman Canyon, Morrow County. Luckman Canyon south of Lena was named for Joseph Luckman, an early settler, who took up land there in 1896.

Lucky Creek, Curry County. Lucky Creek is in the Siskiyou Mountains, at the extreme east edge of the county and southeast of Mount Billingslea. It flows into Tincup Creek. Along it was started the backfire used to stop the Chetco 30,000 acre fire in 1938. The fire was held at this creek, which became known as Lucky Creek by the firefighters.

Lucky Queen, Josephine County. The Lucky Queen mine is one of the best known in southwest Oregon and bears a name redolent of high hopes. The property is in the north part of Josephine County, just southeast of Sexton Mountain. This mine is described briefly in Walling's *History of Southern Oregon,* page 463. Little or no work has been done at this mine for many years. Lucky Queen post office was established December 13, 1876, with David H. Sexton postmaster. The office was closed July 24, 1896, and local commercial activity is at a standstill.

Luckyboy, Lane County. Luckyboy post office was established February 16, 1901, with George A. Dyson first postmaster, to serve the Lucky Boy mine four or five miles north of Blue River community. The mine was of course named in a spirit of optimism. The office was closed November 26, 1906, with papers to Blue River.

Luda, Coos County. Luda post office was named for Luda Krantz, the daughter of the postmaster, David C. Krantz. The office was on East Fork Coquille River a few miles upstream from Gravelford. The locality was on the main road between Myrtle Point and Brewster Valley. Luda post office was established June 3, 1901, with Krantz first and only postmaster. The office was closed August 28, 1902.

Ludwick Cabin, Wheeler County. Ludwick Cabin northeast of Stephenson Mountain was the location of the homesteads of Walter and Elmer Ludwick just prior to World War I.

Lumrum Butte, Deschutes County. *Lumrum* is a Chinook jargon word meaning whisky or rum, although the form *lum* is more generally used. The name has been applied to a butte northeast of Crane Prairie by the USFS, possibly because of some incident connected with the making or using of whisky in the vicinity.

Lund Park, Lane County. Loren W. Hunt of Cove told the compiler that this spot was a stopping place for travellers to the Bohemia mines. The name is a combination of the original residents Alex Lundberg and Tom Parker.

Lundell Canyon, Morrow County. Frank Lundell came to Morrow County in 1887 and took up a homestead at the mouth of this canyon near Gooseberry. Lundell was born in Sweden in 1848 and died at Ione, April 4, 1932.

Luper, Lane County. Luper was a station on the Southern Pacific line north of Eugene. Rhea Luper, state engineer, wrote the compiler on July 1, 1927, as follows: "This station was located on property owned by my father, James N. Luper, and his brother Lewis (Bud) Luper. My father when 19, and his brother about 21, bought this property about 1869 or 1870. When the railroad came through, my father had a spur constructed and built a warehouse, and this was at one time quite a wheat shipping point. The warehouse burned and was never rebuilt. The spur track was taken up, but it is still a whistling post. Incidentally, this is the place on which I was born."

Lurley, Douglas County. In February, 1947, Charles V. Stanton of the Roseburg *News-Review* started a systematic program to harvest information about old Douglas County post offices, with some very commendable results. The following paragraph from the issue for February 14, 1947, slightly condensed, refers to Lurley post office: Lurley post office was on the Buckhorn road about twelve miles east of Roseburg. It was established by the late James J. Webb, father of Percy Webb, Roseburg, the latter having served for a number of years as sheriff of Douglas County. The office was named for Blanche Lurley Webb, a granddaughter of the postmaster and daughter of Percy Webb. She died at Lurley when she was but seven years of age. The site was later occupied by the Justin Eifert home. According to official records the post office was established December 18, 1897, with James J. Webb first and only postmaster. It was discontinued February 28, 1901, with mail to Roseburg.

Luse, Malheur County. This place was named for F. N. Luse, formerly a dispatcher on the Oregon Short Line Railroad. The station is between Ontario and Vale.

Lyle Gap, Jefferson County. The Dalles-California Highway traverses Lyle Gap at a point about thirteen miles northeast of Madras, where it goes through the ridge just west of Hay Creek. The gap was named for Alfred R. Lyle, a prominent settler on Hay Creek, in Wasco County as it was in 1877. Lyle went to central Oregon from Polk County to take charge of the cattle ranch of his brother-in-law, Edmund F. Veazie, who died in mysterious circumstances in John Day River in 1877. Lyle prospered in the business, added to the holdings, and became a prominent citizen of Crook County, which was established in 1882. He represented the county in the state legislature and died in 1906.

Lyman, Wallowa County. According to J. H. Horner of Enterprise the post office at Lyman in the north part of Wallowa County was named for Harry Lyman Murdock, the first postmaster. The office was established in May, 1910, and operated until the following May. Lyman was in section 21, township 5 north, range 43 east, about three miles northeast of Powwatka. Local settlers who wrote the petition for the office selected Murdock's middle name.

Lyman Mountain, Jackson County. Lyman Mountain has an elevation of 2730 feet and overlooks Rogue River near the mouth of Sams Creek about three miles northeast of Gold Hill. It was named for George S. Lyman, a pioneer apple grower, who discovered gold on its slopes in 1894.

Lyons, Linn County. Lyons was named for the family that established the community. They were early settlers. Lyons is in the valley of North Santiam River.

Lyons Ridge, Jefferson County. James Lyons homesteaded near this ridge south of Currant Creek in 1923.

Lytle Creek, Crook County. Lytle Creek is in the northwestern corner of the county. It was named for a pioneer settler, Andrew Lytle.

Mabel, Lane County. This post office was named for Miss Maud Mabel

Drury, second daughter of the first postmaster, Alfred Drury. The post office has not always been in its present location. It was established about 1878.

Macduff Peak, Lane County. This peak lies in the Cascade Range about four miles airline south of McKenzie Bridge. It bears the name of the late Nelson F. Macduff, for many years supervisor of the Cascade National Forest. The suggestion which led to the naming of the peak was made by Smith Taylor, formerly forest ranger at McKenzie Bridge. The name has been officially adopted by the USBGN.

Mace Mountain, Douglas County. Mace Mountain is on North Umpqua River about six miles west of Steamboat. G. C. Blake of Roseburg told the writer the mountain was named for Mace, an Indian born about 1860, who was raised by the Meshach Tipton family near Lone Rock. Mace, known as Indian Mace or Mace Tipton, in the summers hearded sheep on the mountain for Tipton.

Macey Cove, Douglas County. Mrs. R. W. Williams of Reedsport wrote the compiler about 1925 that the name of the little cove on the east side of Umpqua River about two miles northeast of Winchester Bay is Macey Cove and not Macy Cove. She said the cove was named for a Colonel Charles Macey who was at one time at Fort Umpqua, Umpqua City. Macey's descendants are still living in the neighborhood. Heitman's *Historical Register* lists no officer with the name Charles Macey. Possibly Macey was a civilian attached to the post or resident of Umpqua City.

Mack Arch, Curry County. The name Mack is applied to the prominent natural rock arch about one mile offshore as well as a reef, point and cove nearby, all thirteen miles south of Gold Beach on US 101. The name is very old as the USC&GS chart of 1854 not only uses the name Mack's but also has a fine pictorial engraving of the landfall. The form Max's in honor of Maxime Langevin who later homesteaded nearby, while logical, is incorrect, and the story that the name comes from Mack Anderson, a transient of indifferent reputation, also completely fails the chronological test.

Mack Hall Creek, Clackamas County. This is a small tributary of South Fork Salmon River above Welches. It was named to honor Mack Henry Hall, a part time USFS employee. Hall attended school in Eugene and graduated from the University of Oregon in 1931 where he had been active in college journalism. He was killed in an automobile accident near Eugene in 1933.

Macklyn Cove, Curry County. This cove near the mouth of Mill Creek in Brookings was the best protected anchorage in the area. Elza J. Macklin homesteaded on the shore in 1864. In 1901, a wharf was built and borax brought by scows from Lone Ranch was transferred to ocean going vessels. Following current usage the USBGN decided on the present spelling in 1960 but the early records indicate that Macklin used this form.

Macksburg, Clackamas County. Macksburg is about five miles east of Canby. The little community was named for the Mack family, well known in the locality. Macksburg post office was established March 6, 1884, with Geo. H. McPherson first postmaster and was discontinued in September, 1903.

Macleay, Marion County. Donald Macleay, a prominent merchant of Portland, was interested with William Reid in the Oregonian Railway Company, Limited. This company built the narrow gauge railroad in the east part of the Willamette Valley, subsequently a branch of the Southern Pacific Company. Mr. Macleay gave several hundred dollars to build a school house at a station in Marion County which was forthwith given his name. For a short history of the community, see Salem *Statesman*, December 20, 1931.

Mad Creek, Linn County. This stream just east of Gates, was named by Thomas J. Henness in 1863 because of the turbulent waters. See the Salem *Capital Journal*, June 18, 1927, page 1. There is no truth in the story that the creek was named for an insane woman. Some maps show the stream as Mud Creek, which is wrong.

Madden Butte, Curry County. Cyrus Madden came to Curry County in 1865 from Ohio and settled north of Sixes near the butte which bears his name. He was of contentious nature and always acted as his own attorney. There is a story to the effect that once, when incarcerated, he prepared his own *habeas corpus* and procured his release by serving it himself on the dumbfounded sheriff. He obviously was an early advocate of the rights of the accused.

Madras, Jefferson County. Madras is in a more or less circular valley, and in earlier days the place was known as The Basin. When the community became established, and the post office was applied for, the name Palmain was suggested to postal authorities in Washington, in honor of John Palmehn, a well-known resident. Palmehn platted part of the town now called Madras with the name Palmain, which he thought would be easier spelled than Palmehn. However, the authorities objected, fearing confusion with a post office called Palmer. On February 10, 1944, the Madras *Pioneer* published a letter from Bert Doze, a newspaperman in Wichita, Kansas, saying that he was sent to the new community about 1903 by his uncle, Joshua Hahn, to open a store. The name of the place was still undetermined. Willow Creek was suggested but was thought to be too cumbersome. Finally Hahn or Doze suggested the name Madras, which was taken from a bolt of cloth in the store. Madras is a well-known cotton fabric named for the city in India. Howard W. Turner, a long-time resident of Madras, did not accept the Doze story and thought that the Post Office Department named the place. However the compiler queried postal authorities on this point some years ago and was told the department had no record of suggesting the name Madras. The name of the Oregon town is generally pronounced with the accent on the first syllable, but the name of the place in India is pronounced with the accent on the second syllable.

Magone Lake, Grant County. Patsy Daly of Prairie City informed the compiler in 1927 that this lake was named for Major Joseph W. Magone, a resident of Canyon City. Magone stocked the lake with fish, and it was named for him on that account. The spelling Magoon is wrong. Magone was born in New York in 1821 and came to Oregon in 1847. He was a miller by occupation. He served in the Cayuse War with the rank of major. He lived in the Willamette Valley until 1872, when he went to eastern Oregon. He served in the Bannock War under General O. O. Howard as a guide and express messenger. When he was over 70 years old, Major Magone walked all the way from Canyon City to Chicago to see the World's Columbian Exposition and won a wager for the feat. He died at Ogdensburg, New York, February 15, 1902. For additional information, see *OHQ*, volume III, page 276, *et seq.,* and volume IX, page 309. See also several references in Down's *History of the Silverton Country.*

Magpie Peak, Baker County. This butte is near Haines. J. Neilson Barry told the writer that during early days in Baker County this was a convenient place for cattle round-ups. As a result of stock being driven to the peak for sorting, a great many magpies flew in with the cattle, and the country around the place became covered with them.

Mahogany Creek, Wallowa County. This stream, in township 4 south, ranges 47 and 48 east, as well as several other geographic features in eastern Oregon, is named for the curlleaf mountain mahogany, *Cercocarpus ledifolius.*

Maiden Gulch, Baker County. This gulch is near Sparta. For the history of this locality during the mining days, see editorial page, the *Oregonian,* October 7, 1927, and the Baker *Morning Democrat* of October 19, 1927. Dunham Wright, of Medical Springs, told the compiler that the prospects in Maiden Gulch were discovered by a bachelor who was of a romantic turn of mind and decided to compliment the opposite sex.

Maiden Peak, Deschutes and Lane counties. Explanations of this name are not satisfactory. One is to the effect that the mountain, which is at the summit of the Cascade Range, was named in contradistinction to the Three Sisters and Bachelor Butte to the north. Another is that the shape of the mountain resembles a reclining female figure, while a third is that the shape is like a woman's breast. The compiler thinks the first named reason is most likely the correct one. Maiden Peak has an elevation of 7811 feet.

Maidu Lake, Douglas County. Maidu Lake is the source of North Umpqua River. The name is that of an Indian family or tribe of the Sierra Nevada region of California. The writer does not know how it got transferred to Oregon.

Majors Prairie, Lane County. Dee Wright told the compiler that Majors Prairie and Majors Creek nearby, both in the valley of North Fork northeast of Oakridge, were named for one Majors, a stockman. The form Major is wrong.

Makin Creek, Wallowa County. Makin Creek drains into Cherry Creek in township 4 north, range 48 east. It bears the name of Elzie O. Makin who bought a squatter's right from George Cusker, built a cabin near the stream and moved his family into it. He was a sheep man.

Maklaks Pass, Crater Lake National Park, Klamath County. This pass is in a spur running southeast from the rim of Crater Lake. It divides Dutton Ridge to the north from Grayback Ridge to the south. *Maklaks* is a Klamath Indian word meaning literally the encamped, hence a body of Indians encamped, or a community, or tribe. It is also a generic term for Indian. The USFS has named a mountain in northwestern Klamath County between Davis and Odell lakes Maklaks Mountain.

Malheur, Malheur County. This post office is in the valley of Willow Creek in the extreme north part of the county. There seems no doubt in the mind of the writer that the post office name came from the same source as the name of Malheur River. See under that heading. The community of Malheur was a center in the gold excitement in the late 1860s, and there is a story to the effect that the place was named Malheur (French for evil hour or misfortune) because a tunnel caved in and killed a French miner. The compiler has no evidence that this event did not happen, but thinks it highly improbable that the name of the town originated in such a manner, and places no credence in the story.

Malheur County. Malheur County was created February 17, 1887, and was taken from Baker County as that county was then constituted. Subsequently there were several readjustments in the Malheur County boundary. The county was named Malheur because Malheur River flowed through it. For the origin of the name Malheur, see under Malheur River. The county has a land area of 9870 square miles, according to the Bureau of the Census. It is the second largest county in Oregon. In February, 1931, a bill was introduced in the Oregon legislature to change the name of Malheur County to Sinnott County, in honor of Nicholas J. Sinnott, representative in congress from the second Oregon district, 1913-28, who died July 20, 1929. The bill passed the house, but died in the senate. Despite the high esteem in which Mr. Sinnott was held, it appeared to be the sentiment of the citizens of the county to leave the name alone.

Malheur Lake, Harney County. Peter Skene Ogden's party discovered this lake in October, 1826. Details of the discovery are given under the heading Harney Lake. Ogden did not name the lake, and referred to it simply as a freshwater lake. He described the ridge or dike that separated the fresh lake from the salt water, to the west, now known as Harney Lake. On July 7, 1859, Captain H. D. Wallen of the Fourth Infantry, while on an expedition from The Dalles to Great Salt Lake, reached the salt water and named it Lake Harney. He found and described the dike between the two lakes. His stock would not drink the alkaline water and stampeded over the dike eastward to what is now Malheur Lake. Wallen thereupon named the fresh water Lake Stampede. That name has not prevailed. Later Malheur Lake was named for Malheur River. For the origin of the name, see under that heading. The compiler does not know who gave the lake its present name, which has been used for many years. Wallen's name Lake Stampede may actually have been applied to a part of Malheur Lake frequently called Mud Lake, which is west of the Narrows. At high stages Malheur Lake flowed over the dike and into Harney Lake, with the result that the latter lake tended to become more alkaline. In 1882 water was so high in Malheur Lake that it cut a wide passage through the dike. See *OHQ*, volume XXXII, page 129. Malheur Lake is always relatively shallow and substantial changes in precipitation have produced wide variations in the size of the lake. There has been a good deal of litigation about the ownership of the lake bed. The Malheur Lake region has been one of the most productive of the waterfowl breeding places in western North America. It was formerly a mecca for plume hunters, market hunters and fur trappers. In 1908 President Theo-

dore Roosevelt dedicated the area as a bird refuge. In 1935 the federal
government purchased a large part of the old P Ranch in the Blitzen Valley
and thus assured the lake of a permanent water supply. The Malheur
Migratory Bird Refuge now comprises nearly 160,000 acres of open water,
vast tule swamps, wild meadows and wooded areas. Stanley G. Jewett of the
Fish and Wildlife Service says: "It ranks first in the number of breeding
waterfowl, upland gamebirds, big game and fur bearers. During the fall
and spring migrations hundreds of thousands of ducks and geese stop to
feed and rest within the refuge. Among the abundant nesting waterfowl to
be found are mallards, pintails, redheads, gadwalls, shovelers, cinnamon
teal, bluewinged teal and canvasbacks. Canada geese nest abundantly in the
meadows and even lay eggs and rear their young on the basaltic rimrocks
along the edge of the Blitzen Valley. Here, too, are found nesting each year
numbers of sandhill cranes, great colonies of ring-billed and California
gulls, Foster's and black terns and white-faced glossy ibis. Malheur Lake
marks the northern limit for breeding colonies of American egrets and the
black-necked stilts. Long-billed curlews, western willets, avocets and Wilson's snipes are found nesting abundantly in the meadow lands. The heron
family is also well represented." Jewett says that about 220 species of birds
have been found on and adjacent to the Malheur Refuge. The compiler is
prepared to believe the statement, and without reservation can say that the
bird colonies of this area are among the most remarkable things he has ever
seen.

Malheur River, Baker, Grant, Harney and Malheur counties. This
stream rises on the southern slopes of the Blue Mountains. The name Malheur River is attached to the main stream which has in the past been known
as Middle Fork but which the USBGN recognizes as Malheur River. There
is also a North Fork Malheur River which joins the main stream at Juntura
and a South Fork which joins the main stream at Riverside. The South Fork
and its tributaries undoubtedly at one time drained the Harney Valley, but
at the present time there is a low divide between the head waters of South
Fork and Malheur Lake. The name Malheur was used by Peter Skene
Ogden, a Hudson's Bay Company trader, who made an expedition into the
Snake River country in 1825-26. In Ogden's journal, in Hudson's Bay
House, appears the following entry: "Tuesday, February 14, 1826—We
encamped on *River au Malheur* (unfortunate river) so called on account of
property and furs having been hid here formerly, discovered and stolen by
the natives." Ogden was accompanied by French-Canadian hunters. See
Ogden's Snake Country Journal, Hudson's Bay Record Society, volume XIII,
also article of T. C. Elliott, *OHQ,* volume X, page 353; volume XI, page
364.

Malin, Klamath County. Malin is a rapidly growing community on
land that was formerly at the bottom of Tule or Rhett Lake. Tule Lake bed
has been almost entirely reclaimed. On September 30, 1909, 65 Bohemian
families settled at the present site of Malin and named the place for a town
in Bohemia, Czechoslovakia, their former home. For information about
fossil remains near Malin, see the *Oregonian,* December 3, 1925, editorial
page.

Mallett, Malheur County. Mallett was named for C. W. Mallett, a pioneer rancher and nearby landowner. The station was just east of Vale.

Manhattan Beach, Tillamook County. This is a summer resort in Tillamook County. The name strongly savors of real estate activity. In 1926 the postmaster wrote that the town was named Manhattan Beach by its promoters because it was a watering place. There seems to be something peculiarly inappropriate about the name being used for a watering place because Gannett (USGS *Bulletin 258*) says the name *Manhattan,* as applied to the island in New York, was an Indian word, probably meaning place of drunkenness. The Indian name may well describe the locality of New York City, but it is generally understood that no one gets drunk in Oregon, certainly not at watering places. No indeed.

Manila, Yamhill County. Manila was a post office with a very short life. It was about five miles airline west of McMinnville or about eight miles by road, on the headwaters of Muddy Creek. It was named because the name Manila was so prominent in the news of the Spanish-American War in the Philippines in the summer of 1898. Manila post office was established June 27, 1898, with Moses Morgan first of two postmasters. The office was closed to McMinnville on November 30, 1898.

Mann Lake, Harney County. This small lake is in the north end of Alvord Valley. It is fed by small streams from Steens Mountain. It was named for a nearby rancher, Phillip Mann.

Manning, Washington County. This community has been known as Manning for many years, and was named for Martin Manning, a local landholder.

Manzanita, Tillamook County. Manzanita is a beach resort and was surveyed and platted in 1912. The post office was established in 1914, with Emil G. Kardell first postmaster. *Manzanita* is Spanish for little apple, and the name is used on the Pacific Coast to designate shrubs of the *Arctostaphylos* group. They bear little fruits like miniature apples. Sweetser states that the shrub growing in Oregon is *Arctostaphylos tomentosa.* It grows at various places along the coast.

Maple Grove, Polk County. Maple Grove is a prominent highway intersection about four miles northeast of Pedee, characterized by some fine Oregon maple trees. There was a post office called Maple Grove in operation in this locality from July 27, 1903, to January 19, 1904, with William S. Bristow postmaster. The place is just north of Luckiamute River.

Mapleton, Lane County. The consensus of western Lane County is that Mapleton was named by "Grandma" Bean because of the presence of so many maple trees. These are the *Acer macrophyllum,* or bigleaf maple, also called the Oregon maple. "Grandma" Bean was born at Cadiz, Ohio, February 25, 1838, and her maiden name was Julia Ann Sharp. She was married to Obediah Roberts Bean on October 24, 1853, at the Nelson ranch north of Newberg, and the couple lived in the Chehalem Mountains until 1855, when they moved to Lane County. They were outstanding citizens and were the parents of eleven children, the eldest of whom was Oregon's famous judge, Robert Sharp Bean. The Beans moved to Mapleton about 1886 and the place was named shortly thereafter. Obediah R. Bean died in

1890, but Mrs. Bean continued to live in Mapleton until about 1906, when she moved to Eugene, where she died on February 19, 1908. The Beans were both pioneers of 1852. A post office called Seaton was established near this locality in November, 1885, with William W. Neely postmaster. Mrs. Bean became postmaster in April, 1889, and the name of the office was changed to Mapleton March 26, 1896.

Maplewood, Multnomah County. When the Oregon Electric Railway was built this station was called Kusa for the Kusan family of Oregon Indians. Some objection arose to the name Kusa and the name was changed to Maplewood because of the trees in the vicinity.

Marble Creek, Baker County. Marble Creek rises on Elkhorn Ridge of the Blue Mountains west of Baker and flows northward toward the ghost town Pocahontas. The stream drains Marble Gulch, which received its name in the 1860s because of the large marble deposits near its headwaters. See Hiatt's *Thirty-one Years in Baker County*, page 33. Marble Point on Elkhorn Ridge has been a controversial feature. The USGS Sumpter quadrangle of 1939 showed a Marble Point but the small scale made the exact spot difficult to pinpoint. When the new 7½' Elkhorn Peak quadrangle was made in 1972, both the OGNB and the USBGN agreed on a subsidiary peak with an elevation of 7791 feet in section 15, township 9 south, range 38 east. This was approved in *Decision List 7504* and so appears on the map. However, the USFS objected on the grounds that peak 7931 in adjoining section 22, while originally named in error, was now the accepted summit. This alteration was made in *Decision List 7603* and now all reigns serene. According to Norman Wagner of Baker, a geologist well informed on such matters, this area does have limestone deposits and is also in line above both the original east side quarry of the Chemical Lime Company on Marble Creek and the newer west side quarry on Baboon Creek above Sumpter.

Marcola, Lane County. The post office of this community was once known as Isabel. About 1885 the railroad was built through the Mohawk Valley and a station known as Marcola was established near the post office. As a result of this the post office name was changed to agree with the station name. The wife of the founder of the town was Mary Cole and the name Marcola was made up in her honor.

Margaret, Grant County. Margaret post office was established May 23, 1898, with Walton H. Wilcox first and only postmaster. The office was discontinued December 31, 1900, with papers to Prairie City. The post route map of 1900 shows the office about eleven miles southeast of Prairie City. In a letter printed in the John Day *Ranger,* March 7, 1947, R. R. McHaley, long a resident of Grant County, says that Margaret post office was situated at Blue Mountain Hot Springs, and was probably named for the foster mother of Postmaster Wilcox.

Marial, Curry County. Marial was named for Marial Billings, daughter of the first postmaster, Thomas W. Billings. The office was established January 29, 1903.

Marion, Marion County. This station was named because it was situated in Marion County. A. N. Bush of Salem was authority for the statement that when the railroad was built the officials decided to build a station near

Mill Creek, at the present site of Turner. This proposed station was to be called Marion. Material for a station and warehouse was sent out from Portland, but the man in charge of the shipment made a mistake and threw it off at the present site of Marion. When the officials found this had been done they concluded to finish the building and retain the name of Marion for the present community of that name. They subsequently had an additional shipment sent to the place they first had in mind and built a station there and called it Turner, for a prominent pioneer resident of the neighborhood, Henry L. Turner.

Marion County. Champooick District, as originally created and named, comprised all that part of Oregon south and east of the mouth of Pudding River. The eastern boundary was the Rocky Mountains, and the southern boundary was the 42nd parallel. The district was created July 5, 1843. In 1847 Linn County was created, and the new boundary between the two counties was put on Santiam River and North Santiam River, thence to the Rocky Mountains. This was the situation when on September 3, 1849, the territorial legislature changed the name of Champoeg County, as it was then called, to Marion County. The name was in honor of General Francis Marion of Revolutionary War fame. The Weems-Hory *Life of General Francis Marion* was then largely read in Oregon and other frontier settlements, and the praise of Marion in this book greatly appealed to the settlers. Marion County had a land area of 1173 square miles in 1940, according to the Bureau of the Census.

Marion Creek, Wasco County. This small creek is tributary to Fifteenmile Creek just east of the Hood River County line. It and the nearby point were both named for Marion Gordon, wife of USFS ranger Eric Gordon.

Marion Lake, Linn County. This lake was named in 1874 by the Marion County road viewing party under the leadership of John Minto. See *OHQ*, volume IV, page 249. The outlet of this lake is now known as Marion Creek, and not Marion Fork Santiam River.

Marks Creek, Crook County. Marks Creek is northeast of Prineville and US 26 follows it eastbound into the Ochoco Mountains. It was named for William H. Marks who was born in Indiana in 1826 and came to Oregon in 1853. He settled in Linn County with Bluford and William Marks, apparently a brother and a cousin. In 1868 he went to Crook County along with Bluford Marks and settled along Marks Creek. There is no evidence that the other William Marks ever lived in Crook County but two of his daughters and one son did settle there presumably at the instigation of their uncles or cousins. William H. Marks' donation land claim in Linn County was two miles north of Sweet Home on Marks Ridge which is also named for him.

Marley Creek, Union County. Leonard Marley came to the Starkey area about 1885 and took up government land in 1890 where Marley Creek flows into Meadow Creek. The creek bears his name.

Marmot, Clackamas County. Adolf Aschoff, for many years a forester and guide about Mount Hood, settled at the present site of Marmot on March 16, 1883. He found an abundance of peculiar burrowings, especially in the fern growth near the borders of the timber. Local residents told him that these holes were dug by marmots, but Aschoff determined otherwise, and found that they were made by the so-called mountain beaver, or *Aplodontia rufa*. When the post office was established Aschoff and two cronies decided to call the place Marmot on account of this error. One of these friends of Aschoff's was an old miner, Fauntleroy S. Peake, who became first postmaster about 1886. Aschoff became postmaster in 1891. For information about him see under Aschoff Buttes.

Marquam, Clackamas County. Marquam post office was established in 1889, by change of name from Butte Creek. It was named for Alfred Marquam, a pioneer settler.

Marquam Hill, Multnomah County. Marquam Hill in southwest Portland bears the name of Philip A. Marquam, who was born near Baltimore, February 28, 1823, and came to Portland in 1851. In 1862-70 he was county judge of Multnomah County. He was elected to the legislature in 1882. In the late 1880s Judge Marquam financed and built the Marquam Grand Opera House, one of Portland's historic landmarks. The opening performance, *Faust,* was given February 10, 1890. The building was on the north side of Morrison Street, between what were then Sixth and Seventh. Marquam died in Portland, May 8, 1912. For additional biographical data, see Scott's *History of the Oregon Country,* volume II, page 273.

Marquam Lake, Multnomah County. Marquam Lake is on the east part of Sauvie Island. W. H. H. Morgan, one of the pioneer settlers on the island, told the compiler that in pioneer days, a French-Canadian employee of the Hudson's Bay Company operated a dairy near this lake. He was called Marquam, and the Morgan family named the lake for him. Marquam Lake drains into Columbia River through Dairy Creek. This stream was also named by the Morgan family, because of the dairy mentioned above.

Marr Creek, Wallowa County. This stream is in the southeast part of the county and flows into Sheep Creek. It heads near Marr Flat. These features were named for William Marr, who settled near the head of the stream in the early 1880s.

Marshall Butte, Wheeler County. Marshall Butte is two miles northeast of Mitchell and has an elevation of 4538 feet. It was named for Alfred Marshall who settled in Mitchell in 1874.

Marshfield, Coos County. G. A. Bennett, a pioneer of Coos County, is authority for the statement that the land upon which the city of Marshfield was built was once a part of a claim taken up by Wilkins Warwick in 1855, and that it was the general understanding of Oregon pioneers that Warwick named part of his claim for Marshfield, Massachusetts. The records of Coos County show that Warwick sold part of his claim on March 11, 1856, to Andrew J. Davis for $3000, and the description of this property states that the land is particularly "known and designated as the Marshfield claim at the mouth of Wapello Slough." Wapello Slough is now known as Isthmus Slough as it leads to the isthmus over which there was a trail to Beaver Slough on the Coquille River side of the county. There is another version of the history of the name, according to S. B. Cathcart, also a pioneer resident of Coos County. Cathcart wrote that the name was applied by J. C.

Tolman, who settled on the claim prior to Warwick, and inasmuch as he was a great admirer of Daniel Webster, Tolman named the Marshfield claim after Webster's home in Massachusetts. While the details of these two stories differ somewhat, it is apparent that Marshfield, Oregon, was named about 1854 for the Massachusetts community. Tolman later was surveyor-general of Oregon. Marshfield did not make progress until John Pershbaker started lumber and shipbuilding industries there in 1867. In that year there were but two buildings at the place. (Dodge's *Pioneer History of Coos and Curry Counties,* page 154.) For description of the town in 1902, see the *Oregonian,* December 25, 1902; description in 1903, *ibid.,* September 3, 1903, page 14; description in 1890, *ibid.,* January 1, 1891. On November 16, 1943, an election was held on a proposal to consolidate Marshfield, North Bend and an unincorporated area between the two places with the name Coos Bay for the new municipality. The proposal carried in Marshfield but lost elsewhere, hence did not go into effect. However, at the general election a year later, November 7, 1944, the people of Marshfield adopted a new charter and a new name, City of Coos Bay. The change in name was confirmed at a special election held December 28, 1944, and the name Marshfield, in use nearly a century, became a thing of the past. This change did not affect the community of North Bend.

Marshland, Columbia County. When Z. B. Bryant settled on the marshy prairie west of Clatskanie about 1862, the place was known as Skunk Cabbage Flat. The post office of Marshland was established about 1873, and it is understood that Bryant selected the name as being more suitable than Skunk Cabbage Flat. It is quite descriptive.

Mart Davis Creek, Coos County. Mart Davis Creek is a small tributary of Millicoma River. It was named for an early settler on its banks, J. M. Davis, better known as Mart. The name Mark Davis Creek is wrong.

Marten Buttes, Marion County. These buttes, north of Detroit, were so named because some trappers caught a number of martens there. Charles C. Giebeler of Detroit furnished the compiler with this information, adding that the name is not an old one.

Marx, Tillamook County. Marx post office was established April 9, 1904, with Franklin C. Varner first of two postmasters. The office was about two miles southeast on Neskowin Creek from the place called Neskowin, on the Varner ranch. Varner was a great admirer of Karl Marx the German Socialist and named the office for him. Maps showing the name Mary and Marks are wrong. The Marx office was later moved northwest toward Neskowin, and finally to a point near the mouth of Neskowin Creek. The Neskowin post office had been discontinued in October, 1905, and that locality was without an office. The name of Marx office was changed to Neskowin on March 30, 1910, and thus the old name of Neskowin was revived.

Marylhurst, Clackamas County. The compiler remembers when this locality was called Villa Maria. That was about 1910. In April, 1943, Father Leo J. Linahen was kind enough to look into the history of the name Marylhurst, and he reported as follows: "Since a modest count showed that there were altogether too many Villa Marias in the country, a more distinctive name was sought. A Sister Mary Claudia (MacIntosh) is credited with the choice of Marylhurst, or at least with the suggestion of the insertion of the *l*, for euphony. This was in 1913. The Mary part is easily explained. The Sisters of the Holy Names of Jesus and Mary try always to put some reference to the Virgin in the names of their schools—witness their many St. Mary's Academies. The hurst part is not too mysterious, either. When the property was acquired, the Sisters thought, as did everyone else, that the proposed highway would be below their holdings, along the river. This would have put their buildings among the trees on the heights above the river, on the hurst. The front of the College faces upward toward the new highway, but the older buildings, Christie Home and the Provincial House, face downward toward the river and toward the place where the Sisters thought the highway was going to be built. From the new road, they seem to be not on a height but in a hollow; they thought they were going to be precisely on a hurst."

Marys Creek, Clatsop County. This stream is about ten miles east of Astoria. It was named for Mary Burnside, whose husband was a settler at the place known as Burnside station.

Marys Peak, Benton County. Marys Peak, elevation 4097 feet, is one of the best-known points in western Oregon. It is just southwest of Corvallis. It is the highest peak in the Oregon Coast Range north of Coquille River, but there are a number of mountains in the Coast Range south of Coquille River that are higher. The Indian name is said to have been *Chintimini*, with the accent on the second syllable, but the compiler does not know the meaning of the word. An editorial in the Corvallis *Gazette-Times*, September 20, 1935, says that the Indian name *Chintimini* was not used in earliest pioneer days, but the peak was called Mouse Mountain, a translation of an Indian name. This statement is attributed to Cal Thrasher, a well-known pioneer resident. Some color is given to this story by the fact that in the days of the fur traders, Marys River was called Mouse River or Mice River. See under Marys River. The compiler has not found the name *Chintimini* in early records nor is there any contemporary evidence that the fur traders used the style Saint Marys Peak. It is probable that the name Marys Peak came as the result of the naming of Marys River, a stream which heads north of the mountain. The name Marys River was in use in 1846 and possibly earlier.

Marys River, Benton County. In the early days of the fur traders Marys River, which heads north of Marys Peak, was known as Mouse River. In his journal for October 17, 1833, John Work refers to this stream as River *de Souris*, or Mouse River, and the context seems to show that the name Souris was already established. Duflot de Mofras used the name *Riviere des Souris*, Mice River, in 1841, and Joel Palmer called the stream Mouse River in 1845-46. Cal Thrasher, a Benton County pioneer, is authority for the statement that Marys Peak in early days was called Mouse Mountain, a translation of an Indian name. See editorial page of the Corvallis *Gazette-Times*, September 20, 1935. The name Marys River appears in an act passed by the Oregon legislature December 12, 1846, and it was apparently in public use at that time. There are at least two stories about the origin of the name Marys River. One is to the effect that it was applied by Adam E.

Wimple, an early settler from Oneida County, New York, for his sister, who had never been in Oregon. Wimple murdered his girl wife, Mary, August 1, 1852, whom he had married the year before, and he was hanged at Dallas October 8, 1852. She had attacked him with a pistol. For narrative of the murder, see the *Oregonian*, August 8, September 11, 25, 1852. The other story is that the stream was named by Wayman St. Clair for Mary Lloyd, daughter of John Lloyd, who came to Oregon from Clay County, Missouri, in 1845, and in 1846 settled near the present town of Monroe in Benton County. She was said to be the first white woman to cross Marys River, in 1846 (George H. Himes). She married John Foster in Benton County, June 20, 1846; died in August, 1854. Lloyd was born in Buncombe County, North Carolina; died in Benton County, Oregon, January 6, 1880. His house is said to have been the farthest south in the Willamette Valley at one time. Wayman St. Clair was a member of the territorial legislature in 1850-51, representing Benton County in the lower house; also in 1854. He was an immigrant of 1845. He and John Lloyd were alternate captains of the last party that followed the Meek Cutoff. In the winter of 1847 Joseph C. Avery began to lay out a town at the mouth of Marys River, and the place was called Marysville. In 1853 the name was changed to Corvallis. See under that heading. Marysville was probably named for the stream, although there may have been additional reasons. Mrs. John (Mary) Stewart, one of the first settlers, said that Avery told her he would apply the name Marysville in her honor. See Corvallis *Gazette-Times*, June 7, 1935. It has been suggested that French-Canadian employees of the Hudson's Bay Company may have named the stream Saint Marys River, but there seems to be no contemporary record of the event.

Mascall Ranch, Grant County. In the early 1870s the Mascall family settled in the John Day Valley near Dayville. The ranch was the headquarters for the first fossil hunters, and the name Mascall formation is now widely used by geologists.

Mast Creek, Coos County. Mast Creek is tributary to Middle Creek about two miles north of McKinley. William P. Mast was born in Watauga County, North Carolina in 1834. He came to Oregon in 1872 with a group of about sixty people from that state including several other members of his family. Mast settled in Lee Valley where he named the post office and was first postmaster. The creek was named for him or some other member of his family.

Masten Butte, Deschutes County. This butte, elevation 4881 feet, is about eight miles southwest of La Pine. It bears the name of John N. Masten who at one time ran a sawmill on Little Deschutes River about two miles east of the butte.

Matheny Creek, Coos County. Matheny Creek is just west of Myrtle Point. It was named for James H. Matheny, who took up a land claim on its banks in pioneer days.

Matlock Canyon, Morrow County. Matlock Canyon drains into Butter Creek in township 1 north, range 28 east, on the extreme east edge of the county. The canyon was named for three Matlock brothers who settled and lived in the canyon. The spelling Mattlock is wrong.

Matney, Wasco County. Matney post office was established June 12, 1895, with Isaac C. Matney postmaster. The office was closed April 23, 1896, with all papers to The Dalles. This record implies that Matney post office was near The Dalles.

Matney Flat, Gilliam County. Matney Flat southeast of Condon takes its name from H. C. Matney who settled there in 1872. Matney post office was established on December 4, 1886 with Godfrey Schilling postmaster and was closed on April 20, 1892. Matney School was located at the extreme northeast corner of section 20, township 4 south, range 22 east, and the post office was probably nearby.

Matoles, Jefferson County. Matoles, an early spelling for Metolius, was the style used for a post office established March 17, 1888, with Isaac Blanton first postmaster. According to O. D. Allingham of Bend, this office was in the southwest corner of what is now Jefferson County, north of Black Butte. It was on Lake Creek, west of what was later called the Hansen Resort. Blanton sold his holdings to E. R. Carey of Prineville, who did not care to operate the post office. Benjamin Hoover was then appointed, May 27, 1889, and moved the office half to three quarters of a mile east. The office was closed September 12, 1890. Matoles post office was reestablished June 2, 1893, with Mrs. Margaret J. Allingham postmaster on the Allingham ranch, about two miles north of and downstream from its original location. The office was discontinued August 29, 1896. All this information was gathered from Allingham by Robert W. Sawyer of Bend in September, 1946. For information about the name Metolius see under that heading. The later post office Metolius, is a good many miles northeast of the place once called Matoles.

Matterhorn, Wallowa County. The Matterhorn, named because of a fancied likeness to the great mountain of Switzerland and Italy, is one of the highest peaks in the Wallowa Mountains, and is situated southwest of Wallowa Lake. *Matterhorn* means a peak or horn with green meadows at its base. The village of Zermatt in Switzerland, at the foot of the Matterhorn, is so named because it is on a meadow.

Matthieu Lakes, Deschutes County. The name Matthieu Lakes was bestowed in 1924 by Professor Edwin T. Hodge of the University of Oregon on two small lakes on the southern part of Black Crater, near the summit of the Cascade Range. Professor Hodge thus honored Francis Xavier Matthieu, a pioneer of the Oregon country, who was born near Montreal, April 2, 1818, and died near Butteville, Oregon, February 4, 1919. He came to Oregon in 1842 with the Hastings company. He settled in the Willamette Valley not far from Butteville and was present at the meeting held at Champoeg May 2, 1843, to consider a provisional government. He was one of those who favored a provisional government and his name is one of the most honored in pioneer history. See memorial address of Charles B. Moores, published in *OHQ,* June 1914.

Maud, Jefferson County. Maud post office was situated at the Samuel A. Sandvig homestead about ten miles west of Ashwood. The office was established May 9, 1912, with Sandvig postmaster, and was in operation until March 31, 1914. The office was named for Maud Sandvig, wife of the postmaster. It was near Pony Butte.

Maupin, Wasco County. Maupin bears the name of one of the most celebrated of Oregon pioneers. Beside being applied to the post office, the name is also used for several geographic features in the central part of the state. Howard Maupin was born in Kentucky in 1815, and when he was about 15 years old moved to Missouri. He came to Oregon in 1863 and after spending a short time in the Willamette Valley, went to central Oregon. He first settled in Antelope Valley. The famous central Oregon Chief Paulina and his renegade Indians stole all of Maupin's stock shortly after he settled in Antelope Valley. Maupin established a stopping place for travelers and in 1871 was the first postmaster of the town of Antelope. Maupin also lived and operated at other points in central Oregon. He had a farm at the forks of Trout Creek and it was near that location that Paulina stole more of his stock. Maupin pursued the Indians and surprised them near Paulina Basin, where he killed the old chief, who had been the terror of settlers for several years. Maupin was a veteran of the Mexican War and was said to be a crack shot. Later he had a ferry on Deschutes River near the mouth of Bakeoven Creek, which was subsequently owned by W. E. Hunt. The place was then called Hunts Ferry. W. H. Staats bought the townsite when the railroads were built up Deschutes Canyon and named the place Maupin Ferry, but the postal authorities cut off the last word and since about 1909 the place has been called Maupin.

Maury Mountains, Crook County. Maury Mountains are south of Crooked River, near the central part of Crook County. They form an isolated group of dissected hills drained by various tributaries of Crooked River. They were named for Colonel R. F. Maury, who was prominent during the various Indian wars fought in central Oregon in the 1860s. For information about Colonel Maury and his participation in these Indian wars, see Bancroft's *History of Oregon,* volume II, page 488, *et seq.* In 1887 a post office was established near Maury Mountains and it was intended that it should be named in Colonel Maury's honor, but in the petition the name was incorrectly spelled Mowry. This post office was discontinued about 1899. See also under Camp Maury.

Maxville, Wallowa County. Maxville was a logging camp owned by the Bowman-Hicks Lumber Company. At the time the town was started the lumber company superintendent's name was J. D. McMillan, and the first part of his name was used to form the name of the community Maxville. The name was suggested by H. N. Ashby, of La Grande, general manager of the lumber company. The post office was discontinued about 1933, but the community was still in existence in April, 1943.

Maxwell, Coos County. Maxwell community and post office were situated six or seven miles south of what is now the city of Coos Bay, on the right or east of Isthmus Slough. William A. Maxwell came to the place about the turn of the century and started to develop a coal property. Bunkers and housing were built, but the mines failed to become a paying proposition. Maxwell post office was established January 29, 1902, with Fred Ward first postmaster. The office was closed May 15, 1907, and the place has become quite deserted.

Maxwell Point, Tillamook County. John W. Maxwell was one of the early Tillamook County settlers. He homesteaded at Oceanside in 1883.

Maxwell Pond, Baker County. This is a small impoundment on Favorite Slough. E. W. Coles of Haines told the compiler in 1973 that James O. Maxwell was an early settler in the area and the pond bears his name. He added that Maxwell did his bit to populate the west by fathering ten children.

Maxwell Spring, Wheeler County. This spring near the Wheeler Monument east of Mitchell was named for William T. Maxwell who homesteaded there in 1882. Maxwell married the sister of the well-known Nelson brothers.

May, Coos County. May post office, which was near the shore of Haynes Inlet north of Coos Bay, was named for May Peterson, daughter of the first postmaster. The office was established June 21, 1898, with Peter Peterson first postmaster in a series of two. The office was closed November 15, 1904.

Mayflower Creek, Marion County. This stream flows into North Santiam River west of Detroit. It was sometimes known as Watertank Creek, because of a railroad water tank nearby. C. C. Giebeler of Detroit told the compiler in 1920 that Mayflower was the older name and in his opinion the one in general use. He was not able to explain the origin of the name.

Mayger, Columbia County. C. W. Mayger, a native of France, came to Oak Point, Washington, about 1865, and later settled at what is now Mayger. The post office, established in 1889, was named for him, and he was first postmaster.

Mays Canyon Creek, Wasco County. This creek east of Dufur commemorates one of the earliest stockmen in central Oregon. Robert Mays came to Oregon with the emigration of 1852 and settled near Dufur in 1858. In 1862 he moved to the Tygh area and also bought an interest in Sherars Bridge. He subsequently enlarged his operation to several ranches in Wasco and Wheeler counties. Mays Rock near the headwaters of Muddy Creek and May Basin near Amine Peak were both named for his ranges.

Mayville, Gilliam County. Mayville is said to have been named for an incident connected with the establishment of the post office in 1884, possibly for the month in which the petition was sent in. The office was put in operation in October, 1884, with Sam Thornton postmaster. William McConnell platted the townsite with the name Clyde, but the place is commonly called Mayville.

Maywood Park, Multnomah County. The city of Maywood Park was incorporated by vote of the residents August 1, 1967. The triangular area northeast of Rocky Butte was opened as a subdivision in 1926 and by 1940 was a fully developed suburb. In the 1960s the OSHD located I 205 through the edge of Maywood Park and this sparked a movement to incorporate as some opponents of freeway construction felt city status could prevent the highway encroachment or minimize its effect. Arthur M. Taylor, son of F. E. Taylor, the developer, wrote the compiler in 1968 to say that the name was selected by his mother one wintry evening when they were remembering what a lovely spot the woods were in May.

Mazama Creek, Douglas County. Mazama Creek is a small stream in the extreme southeast part of the county. It flows into Rogue River. It was named because of its proximity to Mount Mazama in Crater Lake National

Park. See under Mount Mazama for origin of the name. Several other features in Oregon are named Mazama.

McAlister Creek, Wallowa County. This creek was named for James W. McAlister, a stockman. It is in township 3 north, range 43 east. McAlister Ridge and McAlister Spring in the same locality are named for the same man.

McBee Island, Benton County. J. W. McBee, a pioneer of Oregon, took up a donation land claim in early days northeast of Peoria, and this island in the Willamette River was named for him. See land office certificate 3958. McBee Slough nearby was named for the same man.

McBride, Columbia County. This station was named for Judge Thomas A. McBride, for many years a distinguished member of the judiciary of Oregon, and chief justice of the state supreme court. He had a farm near the station that bears his name.

McCaffery Slough, Lincoln County. McCaffery was the name of a pioneer settler who lived near this slough and tonged for oysters in the waters of Yaquina Bay. The slough flows into the bay on the south side, about a mile west of the locality called Oysterville. It is shown as Johnson Slough on some maps but the best authorities favor the name McCaffery Slough. Andrew L. Porter, who settled in Lincoln County in the 1860s, was one of those who said that McCaffery is the correct name.

McCarty Spring, Union County. McCarty Spring, two miles southwest of Starkey, was on the property of John McCarty who settled in the area at the turn of the century.

McClellan Meadow, Union County. This meadow and spring near the headwaters of McCoy Creek in the extreme west part of the county were named for an old couple who settled in the meadow and were later killed by Indians.

McCord Creek, Multnomah County. This creek has had several names, including Pierce Creek and Kelly Creek. A committee representing various historical organizations recommended that it be named McCord Creek, and that name was adopted by the USBGN. This was in honor of W. R. McCord, a pioneer of Oregon, who built the first fish wheels near the mouth of the stream. The falls near the highway are named Elowah, and the creek runs through John B. Yeon State Park.

McCorkle Spring, Jefferson County. This spring was named for Chester L. McCorkle who had a homestead south of Ashwood in the 1880s.

McCornack Point, Klamath County. This point on the southwest corner of Upper Klamath Lake was near the site of the McCornack Brothers Ranch operated by Frank H. and Eugene P. McCornack.

McCoy, Polk County. E. T. Hatch of Vancouver, Washington, informed the compiler in December, 1926, that McCoy was named for Isaac McCoy, who owned the land on which the town was built. He gave right-of-way for the railroad and wanted the station named McCoyville, but the railroad officials clipped off the last syllable.

McCoy Creek, Harney County. The writer is informed that this stream, which drains the northwest slope of Steens Mountain, was named by Mrs. Dolly Kiger for a local resident, Mace McCoy.

McCoy Creek, Umatilla and Union counties. McCoy Creek rises in the

Blue Mountains and runs southeast to Meadow Creek and Grande Ronde
River. It was named for James G. McCoy, an early settler who came to
Umatilla County prior to 1870. He filed on government land near the
mouth of the creek in 1883 but he had probably lived in the area for some
years previously. His son, Olney P. McCoy, was one of the four freighters
killed at Deadman Pass in July, 1878. In earlier days some maps showed
this stream as Ensign Creek but this name has not prevailed.

McCredie Springs, Lane County. McCredie Springs on Salt Creek
were named for Judge William Wallace McCredie, well-known Portland
baseball enthusiast. They are on the Southern Pacific Cascade line and on
the Willamette Highway about ten miles southeast of Oakridge. Mrs. Paul
Sims of McCredie Springs wrote the compiler that Judge McCredie bought
an interest in the springs about 1916. They were then known as Winino
Springs. For additional information, see under that heading. There was
once a post office on Salt Creek called Winino. There are several hot
springs of varying temperatures, and a resort development. McCredie
Springs post office was established September 14, 1926, with Mrs. Vivian
Cartwright postmaster. This office was out of service for a time, reestablished and finally closed October 2, 1953. Judge McCredie used the resort
as a training quarters for the Portland baseball players. His nephew, Walter
McCredie, was also interested in the activities of the Portland team.

McCubbin Basin, Wallowa County. This basin, in township 2 south,
range 43 east, was named for Leander McCubbin, who ranged sheep
thereabouts.

McCubbins Gulch, Wasco County. This gulch starts two miles east of
Bear Springs and runs towards Wapinitia. William H. McNeal in *History of
Wasco County,* page 255, says it was named for an early day sheep man who
had been gone so long that even old timers had forgotten his given name. It
obviously was named for the same family as McCubbin Basin since *History of
Union and Wallowa Counties,* page 537, states that Abraham McCubbin settled in Wasco County in the 1880s and his son, Leander, was raised there
before he moved to Wallowa County in 1889. The USBGN *Decision List
6604* adopted the form McCubbins.

McCully Creek, Wallowa County. McCully Creek was named for
Frank D. McCully, who ranged sheep there with Charles Christy. He was
the second merchant in Joseph, Oregon.

McCurdy, Klamath County. A post office named McCurdy was established on the Klamath County list in February, 1882, and ran for a little
over a year when it was closed to Linkville. Martin V. McCurdy was the first
postmaster. The following quotation from the editorial column of the Klamath Falls *Herald and News,* June 4, 1948, contains useful information: "Yes-
terday, Jesse Drew was in from Hildebrand with the story of McCurdy post
office. He said this post office, located about three miles from the present
Lakeview-Hildebrand intersection at the Bliss store, was run for just about
one year." Drew went on to say that he was living in the former McCurdy
house, which he had remodeled. This house is situated about a quarter of a
mile south of the northeast corner of section 10, township 38 south, range
11½ east. It is about four miles north and a half mile east of Dairy.

McDaid Springs, Morrow County. These springs on the upper reaches of Juniper Canyon were named for Ed McDaid, an early homesteader. The spelling McDade is incorrect. When they mapped the area in 1968, the USGS reported the springs had filled up and little evidence remained.

McDermitt, Malheur County. A post office with the name McDermitt was in service in the extreme south end of Malheur County from May 20, 1904, to May 26, 1908, when it was changed to the list for Humboldt County, Nevada. As far as the compiler can determine, the office has been in operation in Nevada ever since it was moved from the Oregon list. What there is of the community is very close to the state line. The writer has been unable to get the early history of this office, which was apparently established in Nevada. It was named for the military establishment Fort Dermit, and the fort was named for Lieutenant-Colonel Charles McDermit of the Second Cavalry, California Volunteers, who was killed by Indians August 7, 1865, while scouting along a creek westward of what was later the post office. The name McDermitt is used for a voting precinct in southern Malheur County. The compiler does not know what brought about the discrepancy in the spelling of the name. McDermitt for the post office is a style well established, and it is the official name of the voting precinct. Maps show the stream with the name spelled either way.

McDevitt Springs, Morrow County. McDevitt Springs in Juniper Canyon near Strawberry were named for Bernard McDevitt who took up land nearby in 1896.

McDonald, Sherman County. McDonald post office was established near the John Day River on the east border of the county on March 15, 1904, with William G. McDonald postmaster, and remained in service until October 14, 1922, when it was closed to Klondike. It was of course named with the family name of the postmaster. This office was at the McDonald Ferry on John Day River at the mouth of Grass Valley Canyon. The Oregon Trail crossed the river at this point. For the history of earlier post offices in this locality, especially on the Gilliam County side, see under Rockville.

McDonald Canyon, Umatilla County. McDonald Canyon enters McKay Creek south of Table Rock. Angus McDonald was born in Canada in 1855 and came to Umatilla County in 1881. In 1891 he purchased land along McKay Creek where he was one of the first to farm and raise sheep. The family was numerous, and it is possible that the canyon may have been named for Charles McDonald who took up land near its mouth in 1910.

McDowell Creek, Linn County. This stream flows into South Santiam River not far southeast of Waterloo. It was named for James McDowell, an early settler of the vicinity.

McDowell Peak, Lake County. McDowell Peak and McDowell Creek which rises on its east slope were named for Major-General Irvin McDowell. McDowell Peak is between Drake and Crook peaks about two and one half miles south of the site of New Camp Warner. McDowell was commanding The Military Department of the Pacific in 1866 when troops were using the military road along Honey Creek but the features probably were not named until Camp Warner was relocated to the west side of Warner Valley in 1867. Irvin McDowell was born in Ohio and graduated from West Point in 1838. He served in the Mexican War and as a brigadier-general was in command at the first battle of Bull Run at the start of the Civil War. After involvement in the disasterous Union operations of 1862, he was relieved of command in the field and sent to the Pacific Coast in 1864. During a second tour as commander of The Military Department of the Pacific, he was General Howard's superior during the Nez Perce War.

McElligott Canyon, Morrow County. In the 1890s Richard McElligott homesteaded near the head of this canyon and Jeremiah, his brother, settled near its mouth. Richard's family is still living in the area and stated in 1969 that while Jeremiah left Morrow County in 1903, the canyon was probably named for him.

McEwen, Baker County. This community was named for Thomas McEwen, a pioneer settler.

McFarland Butte, Lane County. This butte is just northwest of Cottage Grove and lies between Bennett Creek and Silk Creek. It was named for James McFarland, who came to Oregon in 1850 and settled near what is now Cottage Grove in 1853. His brother, John W. McFarland, was also an early settler in the vicinity. Several descendants have been prominent in the community.

McGlynn, Lane County. McGlynn was the post office name for the railroad station of Penn. Postal authorities were unwilling to accept the name Penn as a post office name because of possible confusion. McGlynn was suggested because Thomas McGlynn owned the land on which the post office was established. This was in 1923. McGlynn post office was closed November 21, 1938.

McGraw Creek, Wallowa County. McGraw Creek was named for an early day hunter and trapper. It flows into Snake River in township 5 south, range 49 east, in the extreme southeast corner of the county.

McGribble Guard Station, Curry County. This guard cabin three miles northeast of Humbug Mountain was built in 1906 by two USFS employees who combined their names, Macduff and Gribble. In 1975 Mrs. Ivan F. Duff of Ann Arbor, Michigan, wrote to say that she was certain the Macduff was her father, Nelson F. Macduff, for whom Macduff Peak was named. He had just graduated in the first class of the new Forestry School at the University of Michigan and had moved to Oregon to start a long career with the USFS.

McKay, Umatilla County. This post office was named McKay because of its proximity to McKay Creek and because of a desire to honor Dr. William C. McKay. See under McKay Creek, Umatilla County.

McKay Creek, Crook County. This stream is in the northwest part of the county. It was named for Donald McKay, a well-known scout in the Indian troubles in central Oregon, who took a conspicuous part in the Modoc War. He was a son of Thomas McKay and a grandson of Alexander McKay, who was blown up with the Astor ship *Tonquin* at Clayoquot Sound in June, 1811. Thomas McKay came to Oregon with his father in 1811. Alexander McKay's widow married Dr. John McLoughlin and came to Oregon. Thomas McKay was married twice. Dr. William C. McKay was a child of the first marriage, and Donald McKay of the second.

McKay Creek, Umatilla County. This stream rises on the west slopes of the Blue Mountains and flows into the Umatilla River just west of Pendleton. It was named for Dr. William C. McKay, who was born at Astoria in 1824 and died in Pendleton in 1893. He settled near the mouth of McKay Creek in 1851-52, and called the place Houtama. Dr. McKay was the son of Thomas McKay. For biography of Dr. McKay, see Pendleton *East Oregonian,* January 2, 1889.

McKay Creek, Washington County. This stream drains a considerable area north of Hillsboro. It was named for Charles McKay, a pioneer settler, who took up a donation land claim nearby. The stream has also been known as Johnson Creek and Davis Creek, because it passes through land once owned by early settlers with these names. The USGS, however, used the form McKay Creek when it mapped the Hillsboro quadrangle, and C. G. Reiter, city manager of Hillsboro, informed the compiler in October, 1927, that McKay Creek was the name generally used in the county.

McKay Dam, Umatilla County. McKay Dam is so called because it dams McKay Creek. For the origin of the name McKay Creek, see under that heading. McKay Dam is part of the Umatilla reclamation project and is situated about seven miles south of Pendleton. The dam was built for the purpose of storing water in McKay Creek and the reservoir created by the dam has a capacity of about 73,000 acre feet. This water is used to supplement the natural flow of Umatilla River for irrigating 38,000 acres of land near Echo, Stanfield and Hermiston. The post office of McKay Dam was established about 1923, and was discontinued in the summer of 1925. For additional details about this dam see *New Reclamation Era* for September, 1925.

McKee, Marion County. McKee station north of Mount Angel was named for a pioneer family of the neighborhood.

McKenzie Bridge, Lane County. McKenzie Bridge has long been an important crossing of McKenzie River, and was named for the stream. For many years the post office was called McKinzie Bridge, and after much protesting, postal authorities agreed to correct the spelling, which was done in November, 1918. One of the enthusiastic supporters of the McKenzie road project was John Templeton Craig who is buried in McKenzie Pass. In the 1860s Craig lived like a hermit near what is now McKenzie Bridge, and the location was called Craigs or Craigs Pasture. See under Craig Lake, and also *OHQ,* volume XXXI, page 261. It is said that the location of McKenzie Bridge was once called Strawberry Prairie.

McKenzie Canyon, Deschutes County. This canyon lies between Sisters and Lower Bridge. It is said to have received its name, not because of any local settler named McKenzie, but because the cattle trail from Lower Bridge up this canyon led to McKenzie Pass.

McKenzie Pass, Lane, Linn and Deschutes counties. Authorities who are presumed to know about such matters have informed the writer that nowhere are there such remarkable evidences of comparatively recent volcanism as in central Oregon. The writer is prepared to believe this, and is of the opinion that the lava fields and flows of McKenzie Pass present the most unusual aspect of nature that he has ever seen. Fortunately the development of an excellent highway over McKenzie Pass brought these lava flows within view of many people who knew little of them. McKenzie Pass is named for McKenzie River, and beside being well known for its unusual lavas, is also historically interesting by reason of the construction by pioneer citizens of Oregon of a toll road over the Cascade Range at this point. After toll collecting was abandoned, the road over the summit languished until active reconstruction was taken up about 1920. The road was relocated and widened, and on September 21, 1925, the highway project was completed between Biue River and Sisters, a distance of about 50 miles. See Bend *Bulletin* of that date. The highest point on the highway through the pass is 5325 feet, according to computations made by the writer.

McKenzie River, Lane County. As a fine mountain river the McKenzie may be equalled in Oregon, but it is surely not surpassed. It was named for Donald McKenzie, a member of Astor's Pacific Fur Company. In 1812 he explored the Willamette Valley, and it was doubtless this expedition that caused his name to be attached to what is now McKenzie River. It was called McKenzie's Fork by John Work in 1834, and during pioneer days the name was shortened to McKenzie Fork. This term was used in contradistinction to Middle Fork and Coast Fork Willamette River. The name is now universally McKenzie River. A South Fork heads southwest of the Three Sisters. Donald McKenzie, a kinsman of Alexander Mackenzie, was an old "North Wester," before he joined the Astor enterprise. He came west with the overland party and arrived at Astoria January 18, 1812. He went east to Fort William in 1814. He returned to the Columbia River with the North West Company in 1816, and thereafter made notable expeditions in the Snake River country. He accumulated a fortune in the fur trade and retired to New York, where he died at Mayville, Chautauqua County, in 1851. McKenzie was a remarkable rifle shot, skilled in woodcraft and Indian warfare, and was an able trader with the Indians. Ross Cox describes him favorably; "To the most cautious prudence he united the most dauntless intrepidity; in fact, no hardships could fatigue, no dangers intimidate him." Franchere calls him "a very selfish man, who cared for no one but himself." However, Alexander Ross, in *Fur Hunters of the Far West,* volume I, pages 281-83, presents a much more agreeable picture of McKenzie, credits him with some excellent qualities and winds up by calling him "Perpetual Motion." For data about McKenzie's activities in the Pacific Northwest, see article "Snake River Fur Trade," by W. T. Atkin, *OHQ,* volume XXXV, page 295. For short biography, see *Colin Robertson's Correspondence Book,* Hudson's Bay Record Society, 1939, page 233.

McKinley, Coos County. McKinley post office was established in July, 1897, and was named in honor of William McKinley, president of the United States, by Homer Shepherd, who took the necessary steps to have the office established. Shepherd was the first postmaster.

McKinley Ranch, Klamath County. Hartley B. McKinley settled on this ranch west of Antelope Flat prior to World War I.

McKinney Bottom, Marion County. McKinney Bottom, east of Jefferson, was named for a pioneer landowner, William McKinney.

McKinney Butte, Deschutes County. McKinney Butte is about a mile northeast of Sisters. In November, 1943, George E. Aitken of Sisters told the compiler that it was named for Jesse O. McKinney, who at one time owned a ranch near the base of the butte. McKinney died about 1942 at Stevenson, Washington.

McKinney Creek, Linn County. This stream is a tributary of North Santiam River and was named by Thomas J. Henness because William McKinney, a pioneer settler of the Santiam Valley, found a gold nugget worth $5 at the mouth of the stream in 1861. See the Salem *Capital Journal,* June 18, 1927, page 1.

McKinney Creek, Morrow County. Willis E. McKinney settled on this creek near Ruggs in the 1870s.

McLean Point, Lincoln County. McLean Point is a well-known place on the north shore of Yaquina Bay about a mile and a half east of Newport. It was named for Rufus McLean, who settled there in the late 1860s and had a house on a small bench above the bay. He used to haul freight to the Siletz Agency.

McMahan Branch, Polk County. This stream rises on the west slopes of the Eola Hills and flows into Mud Slough, a tributary of Rickreall Creek. It was named for Richard McMahan, who was born in Kentucky in 1812 and who settled on a donation land claim nearby in March, 1851.

McMillan Canyon, Morrow County. John F. and George L. McMillan were brothers who settled along this canyon just east of Ione. The family came from Tennessee to Morrow County in 1886.

McMinnville, Yamhill County. McMinnville was named by William T. Newby, who was born in McMinnville, Warren County, Tennessee, in 1820, and came to Oregon in 1843. He settled near the present site of McMinnville early in 1844, and in 1853 built a grist mill and founded the town. In 1854 he started a store. He was county assessor in 1848 and state senator in 1870. McMinville post office was established on May 29, 1855, with Elbridge G. Edson postmaster. The name was later changed to the present spelling. McMinnville is on the land claim of Thomas Owens.

McMullin Creek, Josephine County. This is a tributary of Deer Creek near Selma. It bears the name of William McMullin, a pioneer of the Illinois Valley. See Walling's *History of Southern Oregon,* page 452.

McNab, Morrow County. This station west of Ione was named for Wesley T. McNab, who came to Pendleton from Iowa, and subsequently settled in Morrow County. He was a stockman and later a grain buyer.

McNary, Polk County. McNary was a station on the Southern Pacific railroad about one and one-half miles west of Eola. It was named for the McNary family, pioneer settlers in Polk County.

McNary Dam, Umatilla County. This dam on the Columbia River near Umatilla was built by the USCE for flood control and hydroelectric power. It was named for Charles Linza McNary, United States senator from Oregon from 1917 to 1944. McNary was born of a pioneer family near Salem on June 12, 1874. He practiced law and from 1913 to 1915 was a member of the Oregon Supreme Court. He died in Miami, Florida, on February 25, 1944. For additional information see the *Oregon Journal* for February 25, 1944. McNary post office was established September 1, 1949.

McNeece Flat, Wheeler County. This flat near West Branch was the site of the 1910 homestead of Flora McNeece.

McNeil Point, Clackamas and Hood River counties. This prominent point is at timberline on Bald Mountain ridge of Mount Hood. It lies on the Cascade divide at an approximate elevation of 6000 feet between McGee Creek and Muddy Fork Sandy River. The nearly level promontory is about a quarter mile above the "Round the Mountain " trail and is marked by one of the stone shelters constructed during the 1930s. The point as well as the forest camp on Sandy River were named for Fred H. McNeil, a long time mountain and outdoor enthusiast. McNeil was born in Illinois in 1893 and moved to Oregon in 1912. His newspaper career, principally with the *Oregon Journal*, lasted more than forty-five years until a few months before his death on December 28, 1958. He was an active Mazama and was instrumental in organizing the Pacific Northwest Ski Association. During World War II he trained and directed the volunteer fire lookout and guard station personnel that formed the USFS Reserves. For additional information see the *Oregon Journal*, December 29, 1958, and July 13, 1959.

McNulty Creek, Columbia County. This stream and a railroad station were named for John McNulty, a pioneer of Oregon, who took up a claim not far from the present site of Saint Helens.

McTimmonds Valley, Polk County. This valley, about three miles west of Lewisville and draining into Luckiamute River, was named for Lambert McTimmonds, who received a patent for land in the vicinity in 1875.

McVay Rock, Curry County. William R. McVay came to Curry County in 1861 and settled near this rock south of Brookings.

McVey Spring, Wasco County. This spring west of Mosier Creek was named for the McVey family who homesteaded nearby just after the turn of the century.

Meacham, Umatilla County. Meacham is a station on the Union Pacific Railroad near the summit of the Blue Mountains. It is where H. A. G. Lee established Lees Encampment in the 1840s. Meacham was named for Harvey J. and Alfred B. Meacham, brothers, who operated Meacham Station in the 1860s and early 1870s. See interview with Mrs. Nellie Frances Meacham Reddington, editorial page of the *Oregon Journal*, November 9, 1935. She was the daughter of A. B. Meacham. Harvey J. Meacham, already in Oregon, urged his brother to come here from California, which he did in February-March, 1863, and the two started a small stage station at Lees Encampment. A larger station was built in the spring of 1865 and called Meacham Station. Harvey Meacham was killed at the station May 29, 1872, when a tree fell on him. Alfred B. Meacham was born in Orange County, Indiana, April 29, 1826. He joined the gold rush to California in 1850, and came to Oregon in 1863. On May 1, 1869, he was appointed Superintendent of Indian Affairs by President U. S. Grant. For his activities in trying to bring about peace with the Modocs, see his book, *Wigwam and Warpath*, and also *The Indian History of the Modoc War*, by Jeff C. Riddle. In the Modoc Lava Beds attack on April 11, 1873, General E. R. S. Canby and the Reverend Eleazar Thomas, D. D., were killed, and Meacham was badly wounded and left for dead. See under Canby in this book. After the Modoc War Meacham interested himself in Indian affairs in various parts of the United States. He died February 16, 1882, at Washington, D. C. After the railroad began operating over the Blue Mountains it built an eating house at Meacham, which later became famous under the management of "Grandma"

Munra. Encampment post office was established May 8, 1882, with Mary M. Strickland first postmaster. The name of the office was changed to Meacham March 26, 1890.

Meadow, Crook County. Meadow was the name of a post office established on the Crook County list on December 21, 1910, with Emma J. Merritt first postmaster. This office was operated until July 9, 1919, when the name was changed to Ochoco. The office is said to have been moved to a new location at that time. The compiler has not been able to learn the location of Ochoco post office of which Claud W. Martin was the only postmaster. Meadow post office was given a descriptive name because of its proximity to Big Summit Prairie. Many parts of this big prairie simulate a meadow. The prairie covers a large part of township 14 south, range 21 east, and Meadow post office was in section 13 of this township. At least that is where it is shown on a map of Ochoco National Forest dated 1915.

Meadow, Lane County. Meadow was a place in the west part of the county on Siuslaw River about a mile south of the north line of township 18 south, range 8 west. Meadow Creek flows into the river nearby. In January, 1947, Elwin A. McCornack of Eugene wrote the compiler as follows: "After a road had been cut through over Badger Mountain, down Wildcat Creek to the Siuslaw and to Swisshome, the mail and stage coaches from Eugene followed this new route. Stage stations were established every twenty or thirty miles where horses were changed and passengers fed or put up for the night. One of these stations on the Siuslaw was known as Meadow and was owned and operated by a Mr. Tallman. I always assumed this place was called Meadow because of the fact that in a very restricted valley the Tallman ranch had a good expanse of hay meadow." Meadow post office was established August 30, 1887, with Levi P. Tallman first postmaster. The office was closed August 31, 1908, with papers to Walton.

Meadow Creek, Umatilla and Union counties. Meadow Creek is a good size stream flowing eastward in the Blue Mountains and draining into Grande Ronde River near Starkey. Some old maps show this as Starkey Creek, but letters from the postmaster at Starkey in 1933 and from the USFS say that Meadow Creek is the correct name and the one in general use.

Meadowbrook, Clackamas County. The name Meadowbrook, as applied to a locality a few miles northeast of Molalla, is mildly sentimental and certainly not very original. The place may have been named for Milk Creek which flows nearby, but that stream hardly merits the name "brook." Meadow Brook post office was established May 13, 1889, with Charles Holman postmaster. The name was changed to Meadowbrook September 5, 1895, and the office was closed May 20, 1905.

Meadows, Umatilla County. In pioneer days that part of the county in the vicinity of what is now Hermiston was called the Meadows because of its characteristic appearance and in contradistinction to the canyon of Umatilla River west of Pendleton. There was an early post office on or near the Meadows called Meadowville. It was closed in 1874 and on May 10, 1880, a new office was established called Meadows. The office was closed to Echo December 19, 1882.

Meadowville, Umatilla County. One of the pioneer post offices of

Umatilla County was called Meadowville. It was situated near what is now Stanfield, but it passed from the picture many years ago. Meadowville post office was established February 2, 1867, with Hawkins Shelton first postmaster. The office was closed October 26, 1874.

Mealey, Linn County. The place called Mealey was near the foot of Moss Butte about seven miles southeast of Foster on the military road. It was named in compliment to Charles Mealey and his wife Mary Jane, *nee* Settlemier, who came to Oregon in separate wagon trains in 1852. After marriage, the Mealeys lived in Brownsville and also in Albany, before homesteading near the South Santiam River in 1874. This homestead was near the middle of section 4, township 14 south, range 2 east. Mealey post office was established August 19, 1892, with Orange J. Mealey first and only postmaster. The office was discontinued March 1, 1898, with papers to Foster. Information about the Mealey family was sent the compiler in September, 1946, by William R. Mealey of Foster, son of Mr. and Mrs. Charles Mealey and brother of Orange J. Mealey. William Mealey was born in Albany in September, 1870, and was brought up on the Mealey place described above.

Mecca, Jefferson County. Mecca is a place on the east bank of Deschutes River a few miles east of Warm Springs Agency and in days gone by it sported not only a post office but it was a station on the Oregon Trunk railway line. The old wagon road from Madras to Warm Springs Agency came down from Agency Plains on a hair raising grade, and crossed the Deschutes at Mecca. There is some uncertainty about the origin of the name Mecca as applied to the railroad station, but it is generally believed that the name was used because when the railroad was built to this point it was out of the worst part of Deschutes Canyon and one of its main objectives had been reached. Mecca post office was established September 18, 1911, with Edward Chaoupka first postmaster. The office was discontinued May 31, 1924. A new highway has been built from Madras to Warm Springs and a new bridge has been installed more than a mile upstream from Mecca. The railroad has been torn out. Mecca, Oregon, is not now a focal point for tourists and pilgrims.

Meda, Tillamook County. Meda post office was on Little Nestucca River about midway of Oretown and Dolph. This post office was established May 11, 1887, with Wallace Yates first postmaster. In May, 1948, Mrs. Affolter of Hebo told the compiler that Meda was the name of Yates' sweetheart in England. The sentimental side of this story is tinctured with melancholy because Meda is reported to have died just before or just after Yates left England. In any event it was in her memory that he named the post office. This office was out of service from 1892 to 1915. It was discontinued again in September, 1920. The Meda schoolhouse is still in service. Meda post office had seven different postmasters and it seems probable that it moved around a little as time went on.

Medford, Jackson County. Richard Koehler, a resident of Oregon for more than half a century and for many years operating head of Southern Pacific Company lines in this state, told the compiler that the town of Medford was named by David Loring who was at the time of construction a civil engineer connected with the right-of-way operations for the Oregon and California Railroad Company. The railroad was opened to traffic from Grants Pass to Phoenix in 1884. The name was apparently applied shortly before that date. In August, 1927, David Loring was living in Portland, and in conversation with the compiler confirmed Mr. Koehler's statement. Mr. Loring said that while the form of the name was suggested by Medford, Massachusetts, he really named the new community in Oregon because it was situated at the middle ford on Bear Creek. Mr. Loring was a native of Massachusetts. People in Jacksonville were not enthusiastic about the new rival community of Medford and referred to it as Chaparral City. The best authorities seem to agree that the name of Medford, Massachusetts, comes from the old English words mead and ford, meaning a ford at a meadow. Mr. Loring may have had in mind a combination of mede and ford, in which mede is an obsolete abbreviation for medium, hence middle.

Medical Springs, Union County. Medical Springs is a descriptive name applied to the hot sulphur springs at that place.

Medicine Creek, Wallowa County. Jake Sheets got sick on this stream, and his companions, Charles and James Rice, mixed up all the medicine they had and forced him to take it. The mixture nearly killed him. The stream was named to commemorate the dose.

Medicine Rock, Lincoln County. Medicine Rock is a well-known point on the north or left bank of Siletz River about five miles upstream from the mouth. In this locality the river flows eastward. The geography of the location is shown on the USGS map of the Euchre Mountain quadrangle. The rock was named because of an Indian custom of leaving offerings at its base. The rock was supposed to be the abode of a Skookum, or bad medicine man, whom the Indians propitiated by giving articles of food, pieces of cloth and sometimes native tools and fishhooks.

Medley, Clatsop County. Medley post office was established early in 1890 with William Medley first and only postmaster. It was named in his compliment. The office was nearly three miles west of and up Fishhawk Creek from Jewell, and was therefore not far from an earlier post office called Denver, which had been closed in 1888. Medley post office was closed January 2, 1904, with papers to Jewell.

Meek Lake, Klamath County. This small lake is west of Crescent Lake and near the summit of the Cascade Range. It is said to have been named because of some incident connected with a party of immigrants traveling over the Meek Cutoff through central Oregon. However, the Meek Cutoff was not in the vicinity of the lake, although a party of immigrants may have left the cutoff and passed by the lake.

Meengs Canyon, Grant and Umatilla counties. This canyon and the springs by North Fork John Day River about three miles east of Dale were named for Dr. Peter C. Meengs who homesteaded there in 1905. The spelling Mings is incorrect.

Mehama, Marion County. This town was named for Mehama Smith, wife of James X. Smith, who laid out the townsite and who operated a ferry on North Santiam River in pioneer days. A post office with the name of Mehamah was established March 12, 1877, with John J. Blair first postmaster. The error was corrected and the name of the office changed to Mehama on March 30, 1881. Lewis Stout ran a ferry at this place before Smith Ferry was put in operation. Mehama Smith died April 8, 1895.

Mehl Creek, Douglas County. Mehl Creek, near Elkton was named for Gottlieb Mehl, an early settler in Douglas County who took a donation land claim including the mouth of the creek. The military road built along the Umpqua River in the late 1850s went along Mehl Creek while cutting off one of the numerous oxbow bends in the river. After an unsuccessful venture with a combination grist mill and saw mill, Mehl sold out in 1864 and moved to Roseburg where he operated a brewery.

Melrose, Douglas County. Melrose was named for Melrose Abbey in Scotland, by Henry Scott. Scott was a native of Scotland and came from near Melrose Abbey. A post office named Hogan was established at or near the place in Douglas County on May 18, 1887, with James McKinney first postmaster. Henry Scott became postmaster on November 10, 1887. He was not satisfied with the name of the office and had it changed to Melrose on October 10, 1890. Hogan was the name of a nearby resident.

Melville, Clatsop County. This place is said to have been named for the oldest son of D. J. Ingalls, who resided there. It is on Lewis and Clark River.

Melvin Butte, Deschutes County. This butte is in the foothills of the Cascade Range about ten miles southeast of Sisters. It was named for J. L. Melvin, who took up a timber claim nearby about 1902. Melvin got into a controversy with S. H. Dorrance, which is said to have started because Dorrance put sawdust in Melvin's irrigation ditch. As a result of this altercation Melvin killed Dorrance on the side of the butte now known as Melvin Butte. Melvin was cleared by a jury which considered that he was not to blame for the difficulty.

Memaloose Island, Wasco County. There are a number of geographic features in Oregon bearing the Chinook jargon word for death or dead. They were so named because they were Indian burial places. Several islands in the Columbia River are named Memaloose. The most important is near the south bank of the river between The Dalles and Mosier directly opposite the rest area on I84. On it is buried Vic Trevitt, a prominent pioneer citizen and for many years a resident of The Dalles. His monument is easily seen from the mainland. Memaloose is given by Gibbs as *memaloost,* who says it is from the Chinook Indian word *memalust,* meaning to die. Memaloose is the spelling adopted by the USBGN and is in general use.

Meno, Hood River County. This station, west of Hood River, was originally named Menominee, for the place in Michigan. The naming was at the request of J. E. Cameron, who had formerly lived in the Michigan town, and when he established a sawmill in Oregon, he desired to perpetuate the name of his old home. After the mill was abandoned, the railroad company shortened the name of the station because the long form of the name was awkward in telegraphing. For obituary of J. E. Cameron, see *Oregon Journal,* Sunday, May 22, 1927, section I, page 2. A post office with the name Nicolai was established in this locality on November 13, 1900, with George H. Nicolai first postmaster. The name was changed to Menominee on October 13, 1903. The office was discontinued March 31, 1909.

Mercer, Lane County. This post office was named Mercer because of its proximity to Mercer Lake. It was established in June, 1904. For the origin of the name see Mercer Lake.

Mercer Lake, Lane County. This lake is about five miles north of Florence and was named for a government surveyor, George Mercer. Mercer surveyed the line between township 17 south of ranges 11 and 12 west in 1879, and his name became applied to the lake on that account. The line passed through the lake. The name Mercer Lake is shown on maps prepared in 1883. The compiler is informed that the Indian name for Mercer Lake was *Kow-y-ich*, meaning the place of the lake.

Merganser, Klamath County. Merganser was the name of a town that lived for a decade then passed into limbo. The place was established about 1870 by J. P. Roberts and Albert Handy to compete with the nearby village of Linkville, now Klamath Falls. It was situated about two miles below Klamath Falls, on the west bank of Klamath River not far from the bridge for The Dalles-California Highway. The first post office was called Klamath. It was in service from June, 1872, to April, 1873, with Albert Handy postmaster. On April 9, 1873, the name of the office was changed to Lakeport, and Handy continued in office. On May 19, 1875, the name of the office was changed to Merganser. John P. Roberts was postmaster at the time. Merganser office was closed May 12, 1879. The name Merganser was selected because of some incident connected with the shooting of a merganser duck in the vicinity. The town petered out about 1880. For short history of this place, see *Illustrated History of Central Oregon*, page 983.

Meridian, Marion County. Meridian is a crossroads locality about two miles south of Monitor, named because of its position on the Willamette Meridian. Meridian post office was established in October, 1900, with B. W. Otto first postmaster. The office was discontinued in October, 1903.

Meriwether, Clatsop County. Meriwether was a station east of Warrenton, and was platted with that title in 1896 by S. D. and Mary R. Adair. It was named for Captain Meriwether Lewis, because it was near the bay called Meriwether Bay by Lewis and Clark but now known as Youngs Bay. For additional information see under Youngs Bay and Lewis and Clark River.

Merlin, Josephine County. David Loring, of Portland, for many years engaged in civil engineering in Oregon, and at one time in the employ of the railroad company building from Roseburg to Grants Pass, informed the compiler in August, 1927, that he named the community of Merlin for the merlins that he saw in the neighborhood about 1882. These birds were probably what are locally known as pigeon hawks. John G. Lanterman was the first postmaster.

Merrill, Klamath County. Merrill was named for Nathan S. Merrill, who was born in New Hampshire in 1836, and moved to California in 1869. He moved to Chehalis County, Washington, in 1881, and in 1890 settled at the present site of Merrill. He bought a ranch in the spring of 1894 and laid out part of the town of Merrill, which was named for him.

Merrill Creek, Columbia County. George Merrill, for whom this stream was named, was born in Ohio September 11, 1826, and came to Oregon with his parents in 1847. His father died on the overland journey.

Merrill went to the California mines but returned to Oregon in 1850. In 1851 he married Ann Martin and settled on a donation land claim on Deer Island where he lived the rest of his life. Merrill was once assessor of Columbia County and served three terms as county clerk. He was an amateur geologist, naturalist, and botanist. He died at his home on Deer Island November 8, 1912, aged 86. His obituary is in the *Oregonian*, November 24, 1912. Merrill Creek rises in the hills west of Deer Island and drains eastward to the Columbia River.

Merritt Spring, Klamath County. This spring southwest of Kirk was named for an Indian family who took up land nearby.

Mesa Creek, Lane County. So named because it heads near Rock Mesa, south of the Three Sisters. *Mesa* is Spanish for table.

Metlako Falls, Hood River County. These falls are on Eagle Creek. They were named for an Indian legendary goddess of the salmon.

Metolius River, Deschutes and Jefferson counties. Three of the western tributaries of the Deschutes have their sources in giant springs, Metolius, Spring and Fall rivers, and of these three the Metolius is the largest and longest. It flows from the north base of Black Butte, fullbodied and icy cold, and after winding northward through beautiful pine forests, swings around the north end of Green Ridge through a canyon of great depth and majestic grandeur, joining the Deschutes just north of the mouth of Crooked River. The gorge of the Metolius is more than 1500 feet deep in places, with sides sufficiently precipitous to make a descent a real problem. The source of the water from Metolius Springs was a matter of conjecture for many years. In the spring of 1972, N. V. Peterson and E. A. Groh published *Geology and Origin of the Metolius Springs* in the *Ore Bin,* volume 34, number 3, pages 41-51. Their investigation shows that the water comes from the south and west sides of Black Butte. Dry Creek and Cache Creek lose most of their water to underground seepage west of Black Butte and other streams to the south drain into Black Butte Swanp. These waters follow the prehistoric course of Metolius River under the geologically more recent Black Butte to emerge at the springs at a relatively constant rate of 50,000 gallons per minute. As far as the writer knows, the first mention of Metolius is in the Pacific Railroad Surveys *Reports,* volume VI, where the name is given Mpto-ly-as. The army officers who compiled these reports visited the valley of the Deschutes in the latter part of 1855, and apparently heard the name from Indians at that time. Other early forms were Metoluis and Matoles, but modern use has standardized on Metolius. Around Bend there is a story to the effect that *metolius* is a Warm Springs Indian word meaning spawning salmon, but Warm Springs Indians have informed the writer that *metolius* means white fish, indicating by that expression that they meant a light colored salmon rather than a whitefish. The two translations may both be correct. There was a post office in Jefferson County named Metolius, for the river. Fremont forded what we now call the Metolius River on December 1, 1843, but gave it no name. His Indian guides told him it was a salmon-water.

Metzger, Washington County. Metzger townsite was laid out by Herman Metzger, a prominent pioneer merchant of Portland, who was born in

Bavaria, and was in business in Portland for many years. The property was actively marketed in 1908-09. The post office was established in 1912, with C. C. Taylor first postmaster, and closed February 28, 1954.

Meyers Canyon, Wheeler County. In 1863 Christian W. Meyer settled beside The Dalles-Canyon City Road where this canyon joins Bridge Creek. Phil Brogan in *East of the Cascades,* page 85, describes his activities as an inn keeper and early irrigationist. F. A. Shaver in *History of Central Oregon,* page 638, describes the Indian attack on H. H. Wheeler and states that this occurred three miles east of Mitchell. He adds that the survivors fled two miles further east to Meyer's establishment which he later notes as five miles east of Mitchell. The compiler has checked BLM records and talked to people who knew Meyer's son and had visited the original acreage. The location was five miles west of Mitchell and as no one has ever questioned the place of the attack, one must assume that Shaver was incorrect in his directions.

Miami River, Tillamook County. Miami River empties into Tillamook Bay at the lower end, that is, toward the ocean. In pioneer days the stream was referred to as *Mi-me Chuck,* a Chinook jargon expression meaning a tributary creek or river coming in downstream. George Gibbs in *Dictionary of the Chinook Jargon,* 1863, gives *mi-mie,* meaning downstream, with accent on the first syllable. In 1927, T. B. Handley of the Portland bar wrote the compiler that Tillamook Indians and others used the expression Mime Chuck for the locality of the river down the bay, but the name has been corrupted into the style used in Ohio, Florida and elsewhere.

Middle Fork Willamette River, Douglas and Lane counties. This is the main tributary of Willamette River, and it has been known as Middle Fork since early pioneer days. It heads in Timpanogas Lake. The name is well established. It was named in contradistinction to Coast Fork and to McKenzie Fork, now McKenzie River. From time to time there have been efforts to change the name of Middle Fork Willamette River to that of the main stream, Willamette River. Popular sentiment has always been against the proposal.

Middle Mountain, Hood River County. This mountain is the high ground east of Hood River and west of Neal Creek that marks the north end of the Upper Hood River Valley. Its name comes from its position in the center of the Hood River drainage. In early days it was called Gilhouly or Gilhooley and today old timers protest the prosaic modern term. The compiler has been told that Gilhouly is of Indian origin. This appears fanciful but the name does have a firm base in local slang and legend.

Middle Santiam River, Linn County. This is the name given this stream by the USBGN, not Middle Fork. The largest tributary is Quartzville Creek, from the north. See under Santiam River.

Middleton, Washington County. Will G. Steel is authority for the statement that this place was once known as Stringtown. When the railroad was built the name was changed to Middleton because the station was about half way between Portland and Lafayette.

Midland, Klamath County. Messrs. Campbell and Reams platted this townsite about 1908, and named it Midland. It is said that the name was chosen because the place was about half way between Portland and San Francisco on the new Cascade line of the Southern Pacific. However, the station is not half way between the two cities, and could not have been named on that account. Midland was on land partly surrounded by marshes, and was probably named for that reason.

Midnight Spring, Douglas County. Midnight Spring is about a mile east of Steamboat Creek and just south of the Lane County line. It was named because USFS ranger Fred Asam and packer Jack Illeg were benighted on the trail and it was very late before they found this suitable camping spot.

Midway, Morrow County. The pioneer post office Midway was about twelve miles south-southwest of Heppner. It was obviously named because it was approximately midway between Heppner and some other place. Early maps indicate that this other place may have been Adamsville, Dairyville or Hardman. These three places were all in the same general locality. Dairyville is not on the county post office list and it is believed the name referred to the place now known as Hardman. Midway post office was established October 27, 1874, with Henry C. Myers first postmaster. Except for one lapse the office operated continuously until February 1, 1881.

Mikkalo, Gilliam County. Mikkalo was named in 1905, for John Mikkalo, an early settler in the community. This was at the time the railroad was built from Arlington to Condon. The post office was established a few years later.

Milbury Mountain, Curry County. Milbury Mountain was named for William Milbury who was a USFS ranger in the Siskiyou Mountains for many years. The mountain is about ten miles southeast of Port Orford in township 33 south, range 13 west, south of Elk River. It has an elevation of about 2600 feet.

Miles, Baker County. Miles was a locality name for a place near the upper or northwest end of Lower Powder Valley northeast of Baker. The post office, which was established May 22, 1901, was named for the first postmaster, William Miles, and it was in service a little over eleven years. It was near Powder River in the south part of township 7 south, range 41 east.

Miles Lake, Tillamook County. This lake and nearby mountain northeast of Cape Kiwanda were named for Heman A. Miles who settled on the lake about 1890. His daughter, Mrs. Clarence Dunn, told the compiler in 1967 that when she was a little girl, the lake was known as Kiwanda Lake.

Milk Canyon, Morrow County. Rachel Harnett of Heppner wrote the compiler in 1970 to say that John A. Williams had a dairy farm in this canyon south of Sand Hollow in the 1880s and he delivered milk and butter to Heppner. Williams later purchased land near Williams Canyon by Utts Butte.

Milk Creek, Clackamas County. This stream, a tributary of Molalla River, flows over a deposit of rock resembling soapstone, and receives a milky color therefrom. This deposit is near Colton.

Milk Creek, Jefferson County. This stream drains one of the glaciers on the east slope of Mount Jefferson, and flows into Whitewater River. It carries a considerable quantity of glacial silt of a light color, and received its

name on that account. There is another Milk Creek on the west part of
Mount Jefferson, in Linn County, that is so called for the same reason.

Mill City, Marion County. Mill City is on the North Santiam River.
The post office is in Marion County. Part of the community is on the south
side of the river in Linn County. John Shaw and others moved the sawmill
from Stayton to this place in 1887 and in the following year had a post
office established with the name Mill City. Shaw was a son of Angus Shaw,
who established the town of Shaw in Marion County. For story about Mill
City by Fred Lockley, see the *Oregon Journal,* editorial page, July 9, 1932.
Just west of the highway bridge across North Santiam River is the old railroad bridge. This interesting structure is largely made of wrought iron
although some steel reinforcement was added in 1919 when it was relocated to its present position. It was made by Phoenix Bridge Company in
1888 for the crossing of Cienega Creek south of San Jose, California on the
Southern Pacific Company Coast Line. The compression members are seg-
mented wrought iron sections rivetted together to form tubes. These sections are similar to the iron framework of the Washington Monument and
the columns used to support the first elevated railways in New York City.
When the Southern Pacific Company abandoned the Mill City branch, they
gave the bridge to the city. It is now decked over for a foot path.

Mill Creek, Crook County. Old residents of Prineville say that the first
sawmill of the county was built on this stream, hence the name. The creek
flows into Ochoco Creek east of Prineville.

Mill Creek, Marion County. This stream joins the Willamette River in
the north part of Salem. It was named for the pioneer sawmill established
on its banks as part of the operations of Jason Lee's Methodist mission,
which was begun on Mission Bottom in 1834. The sawmill was probably
built in 1840-41. The canal from North Santiam River, augmenting the
flow of Mill Creek, was finished in 1857. The stream in the south part of
town, sometimes called South Mill Creek, is largely artificial and is not the
original Mill Creek.

Mill Creek, Umatilla County. Mill Creek is for the most part a stream
of the state of Washington, but not far from its source in the Blue Mountains it flows through Oregon for several miles. The Rev. Myron Eells is
authority for the statement that Dr. Marcus Whitman rebuilt his flour mill
in the Walla Walla Valley in 1844, and the next year went up the stream
about 20 miles into the Blue Mountains and built a sawmill, which caused
the stream to be called Mill Creek. Eells' *Marcus Whitman,* page 135.

Mill Creek, Union County. Mill Creek, near Cove, is so called because
one of the pioneer sawmills of Grande Ronde Valley was built on the
stream by James M. De Moss. See under De Moss and North Powder.

Mill Creek, Wasco County. The neighborhood of Mill Creek, which
flows into the Columbia River at The Dalles, was called *Quenett* by the local
Indians, which was a name for salmon trout. When the government
decided to establish Fort Dalles, an officer was sent to build a sawmill to be
operated by mule power. Upon his arrival he found a small waterpower site
and built a mill on this stream, now known as Mill Creek, just north of the
present site of the bridge on Ninth Street. The writer is informed that the

officer was court-martialed and discharged from the service for disobeying orders and not using mule power. Dr. William C. McKay is authority for the statement that the mouth of Mill Creek was called *Will-look-it* by the Indians. This meant looking through an opening or gap.

Mill Slough, Lane County. This slough through the outskirts of Coburg originally carried water for the old Booth-Kelly sawmill. It emptied into Canterbury Creek, a tributary of McKenzie River. Both Mill Slough and Canterbury Creek are now dry and hardly discernible after years of farming.

Miller, Malheur County. Miller was a mining community about eighteen miles north of Brogan. Miller post office was established July 18, 1913, with William Miller first and only postmaster, and the office was given his name. The office was closed March 31, 1917, with papers to Rye Valley. Miller was in the extreme north end of the county, and a change of county lines between Baker and Malheur counties may have put the locality in what is now Baker County.

Miller, Sherman County. Miller is the railroad station and community on the south bank of the Columbia River just east of Deschutes River. It was named for a pioneer family of the vicinity. There is a Miller Island in the Columbia River, but it is in Klickitat County, Washington. The locality of Miller has had several names at various times. It was once called Deschutesville and later Fultonville in compliment to Colonel James Fulton of Sherman County. For a time the railroad station now known as Miller was called Deschutes. For the history of the name Deschutes as applied to places in Oregon, see under the heading Deschutes and also under Ainsworth.

Miller Butte, Marion County. This butte, elevation 556 feet, is about two miles west of Marion. It was named for a family of pioneer settlers. The head of the family was Charles Miller. At the exposition at Philadelphia in 1876, a sample of flax sent by "Uncle Charley," beat the whole world.

Miller Creek, Marion County. Miller Creek drains the hills east of Ankeny Bottom, in the southwest part of the county. It was named for W. F. Miller, a pioneer settler on its banks.

Miller Hill, Klamath County. Miller Hill and Miller Island on the southern outskirts of Klamath Falls were named for Colonel J. N. T. Miller, Commissary General of Oregon Volunteers during the Modoc War. His ranch was near the base of the hill. Colonel Miller should not be confused with the Miller family of Lake Miller.

Millers, Linn County. Millers post office was established a few miles northeast of Albany on February 7, 1873, with Henry Newman first postmaster. The office was in operation for more than twenty years with several different postmasters. The office was named in compliment to Isaac Miller, a prominent pioneer resident of the vicinity. Millersburg is the name of the railroad station that still serves this locality. It seems possible that the post office may have moved with the various postmasters and in that event the railroad company used a different form of name for the station so as to avoid confusion.

Millersburg, Linn County. This is a station on the Southern Pacific a few miles north of Albany. Members of the Miller family have lived there nearly a century. Isaac Miller took up a donation land claim nearby in pioneer days.

Millican, Deschutes County. George Millican was a prominent stockman of central Oregon. He was born near Otsego, New York, November 22, 1834, and came to the Pacific Coast when he was a young man. He visited mining camps from California to Idaho, and finally settled on the McKenzie River east of Eugene in 1862. He made a trip into the Ochoco country as early as 1863, and subsequently became interested in developing the toll road over McKenzie Pass. He took a band of cattle into the Crooked River country in 1868 and settled there. A few years later he located a ranch near the present site of Millican in Millican Valley, about 27 miles southeast of Bend. He carried on the business of raising high grade stock, and finally sold out in 1916. He died on November 25, 1919. See Carey's *History of Oregon,* volume III, page 714. Millican was at one time postmaster at Walterville, Lane County, which he named for his son, Walter Millican. Walter Millican was born in 1870, and is said to have been the first male white child born in central Oregon. Millican Crater, just south of Black Crater, in northwest Deschutes County, was named for George Millican. The old Millican store was on the P. B. Johnson homestead on the Bend-Burns road a little over a half a mile south of the 1942 location and the post office was established in 1913, with Johnson postmaster. Johnson proposed the name Mount Pine, and Mrs. George Millican suggested her husband's name, which was adopted. There was some objection to Mount Pine because of possible confusion with La Pine. Johnson later sold out to J. A. Smith and a man named Moore became postmaster. William A. Rahn was made postmaster about 1920 and the community became a one-man affair. In October, 1930, the Central Oregon Highway was opened on a new location to the north and Rahn found it necessary to move his one-man town, which was done to the accompaniment of suitable publicity. Nearly everything was shifted but the well. In 1941 and 1942 Millican and "Billy" Rahn received nation-wide publicity as a one-man town and its sole citizen. In the fall of 1942 Rahn reached the age of retirement for postmasters, and it was necessary to close the office as no one was available to take it. For illustrated story about Millican and Billy Rahn by Phil Brogan, see magazine section of the *Sunday Oregonian,* September 1, 1940.

Millican Creek, Yamhill County. Millican Creek rises in the Red Hills of Dundee and flows south to Yamhill River at Lafayette. It was named for Elijah and Lucinda Millican whose donation land claim was along the creek near the present town of Lafayette.

Millicoma River, Coos County. Millicoma River is the main north branch of Coos River and is sometimes called North Fork Coos River, although the USBGN has adopted the style Millicoma. In 1929 S. B. Cathcart, pioneer surveyor of Coos County, told the compiler that Millicoma was the original Coos Indian name for the stream and not North Fork. The meaning of the word is not known.

Millwood, Douglas County. Will G. Steel told the writer that this place was named by W. B. Clarke, who built a sawmill nearby. Millwood post office was established on the Umpqua River just west of Coles Valley on

June 7, 1886 with Clarke as first p_stmaster. It was closed on July 31, 1931 with papers to Oakland.

Milo, Douglas County. Milo was established as a post office on March 13, 1923, with Cora E. Buker first postmaster. Amos O. Buker, the husband of the postmaster, was born in Milo, Maine, and suggested the name. Milo post office is at the site of a former post office called Perdue. The Perdue office was closed in 1920, because no one could be found to accept the position of postmaster after Amos O. Buker had been removed from office for acting as a census enumerator when he was postmaster at Perdue, contrary to the rules of the postal authorities. Milo, Maine, was named for the Grecian island of Milo.

Milton-Freewater, Umatilla County. This place is said to have been called Freeport originally. The compiler has been told that the name was changed to Milton about 1873, but an article in the *Oregon Journal,* August 3, 1926, page 8, implies that the name Milton was selected shortly after 1868 by William S. Frazier, a pioneer resident, because a mill was projected for the community. The form Milltown was rejected, according to the article mentioned. The discrepancy in dates may not be important, as it may have taken some time for the new name to come into use. The article says that the first postmaster was Isom Quinn, but this does not agree with postal authorities, who inform the compiler that the post office at Milton was established February 3, 1873, with William A. Cowl postmaster. The compiler can find no confirmation for the statement that the place was named for the great poet, John Milton. The long time rivalry between Milton and neighboring Freewater was terminated in 1951 by the merger of the two communities. Milton-Freewater post office was established September 1, 1951. For additional information see under Freewater.

Milton Creek, Columbia County. The town of Milton in Columbia County was one of the early rivals of Portland. It was laid out as a town in 1851 and was founded by Captain Nathaniel Crosby and Thomas H. Smith. It was once swept away by a flood. Crosby and Smith ran advertisements in the *Oregonian* in 1851 offering to give two lots to each married man and one lot to each single man who would make his home there and build a house. A district school advertisement for the town is in the *Oregonian,* September 13, 1851. About 1890 efforts were made to secure a post office, and it was necessary to change the name of the community because there was already a post office named ˆMilton in Umatilla County. Milton in Columbia County was accordingly renamed Houlton. See under that heading. Houlton post office was near Saint Helens railroad station. The name of Milton is still attached to a creek that flows near the post office and railway station. The name Milton was adopted for the town because of the location nearby of a pioneer sawmill. The original townsite of Milton was near the mouth of Milton Creek, and not where Houlton was situated.

Milwaukie, Clackamas County. Lot Whitcomb founded Milwaukie in 1847, as a rival to Oregon City. It was named probably for the Wisconsin city, the spelling of which, in its early days, was varied. Milwaukie had a population of 500 in 1850 (Bancroft's *History of Oregon,* volume II, page 251). For narrative of pioneer episodes, see the *Oregonian,* June 7, 1903, page 15; April 3, 1884, page 3. For information about various spellings of

Milwaukee, Wisconsin, see *Steel Points*, by Will G. Steel, issue for March, 1917. The derivation of the name is Indian, but its meaning is in dispute. It is said to mean council place, and also good land. Postal authorities inform the compiler that Milwaukie post office was established February 1, 1850, with Lot Whitcomb first postmaster.

Minam, Wallowa County. Minam is the name of a community which is situated at the junction of the Wallowa and Minam rivers. The name of the town was taken from the Minam River. For the origin of the name Minam see under that entry. Minam post office was established June 25, 1890, with Elizabeth Richard first postmaster. The office was closed February 4, 1891, and was not reestablished until June, 1910. The opening of the railroad branch through to Joseph in 1908 was doubtless the reason for the revival of the Minam post office.

Minam River, Union and Wallowa counties. J. H. Horner of Enterprise told the compiler that the Indian name for the locality of this stream was *E-mi-ne-mah,* with the accent on the second syllable. This name described a valley or canyon where a certain sort of plant was abundant. This plant, which the compiler has been unable to identify, is said to have resembled a small sunflower, and the root, growing in loose rocks, was used for food. The suffix *mah* was the Indian word for valley or canyon. The form Minam River was used as early as 1864. There is a town named Minam on Wallowa River at the mouth of Minam River. Minam Lake, in southwestern Wallowa County, is remarkable because of the fact that it has an outlet at either end. Minam River flows from the south end, and Lostine River from the north.

Mineral, Baker County. So named because prospectors struck ore on the opposite side of Snake River, and named their prospect Mineral.

Mineral, Lane County. Mineral post office was in a mining area in the west part of township 23 south, range 1 east, a few miles west of Bohemia. It was named for the mineral prospects of the region. The office was established July 31, 1903, and was discontinued July 31, 1908. Ulysses C. LeRoy was the first postmaster.

Minerva, Lane County. When the post office at Minerva was petitioned for in the early nineties the name of Bays Landing was suggested to the department out of respect to James E. Bay, a local resident. The authorities suggested that a name of one word would be more convenient, and L. C. Akerly, who had framed the petition, decided to name the office Minerva, which was Mrs. Bay's first name.

Minnie Scott Spring, Lane County. In 1971 Ray Engels, the retired USFS ranger at McKenzie Bridge, told the compiler that he named this spring four miles south of McKenzie Pass at the suggestion of Dee Wright. Engels understood Wright to say that Minnie was the wife of Felix Scott, Jr., but this is incorrect as she was his niece, the daughter of his brother Rodney. Felix Scott the younger died in Nevada in 1876 unmarried. For additional information about him, see under Scott Mountain.

Minniece Point, Linn County. This 4432 high point nine miles south of Detroit Dam was named for John Minniece, an early USFS employee in the Detroit District.

Minor Gulch, Wallowa County. This gulch drains into Tope Creek in township 3 north, range 43 east. It was named for William Minor, who came into the Wallowa Valley in 1878 and ranged his stock near the gulch.

Minthorn, Umatilla County. This station east of Pendleton bears the name of a prominent family nearby.

Minto, Marion County. Minto, a locality on North Santiam River two miles east of Gates, was named for Douglas Minto, a son of John Minto. He was interested in lumbering in the North Santiam Valley. Minto post office was in service near this station from January 29, 1892, to April, 1904. Thomas S. Ball was the first postmaster.

Minto Mountain, Linn County. John Minto was for many years champion of the plan to develop transportation facilities up the North Santiam River and over the Cascade Range by what he considered an especially favorable route. For a description of the investigations of this route made by Marion County see *OHQ,* volume IV, page 241. As a result of Minto's interest in this matter a number of geographic features in that section of the state were named for him about 1879. These include Minto Mountain. John Minto is a leading authority, among early pioneers, on subjects of Oregon history and his contributions are of high value. He was born October 10, 1822, at Wylam, Northumberland, England; came to the United States in 1840, with his father's family and came to Oregon in 1844. In 1867 he purchased a 250 acre island in the Willamette River just south of Salem. The land soon took the name of Minto Island and today, though no longer a true island, is part of Minto-Brown Island Park. John Minto died at Salem February 25, 1915. For biography and portrait, see the *Oregonian,* April 27, 1901, page 10. Minto wrote frequently for the *Oregon Historical Quarterly.* His narration of the migration of 1844 appears in OPA *Transactions,* 1876, pages 35-50. For references to other writings, see Scott's *History of the Oregon Country,* volume I, page 307.

Mishawaka, Clatsop County. Mishawaka post office was established March 26, 1878, with James F. Kimberlin first postmaster. It was near Nehalem River a little eastward of the location now called Elsie. The office is said to have been named for Mishawaka, the well-known manufacturing town of Indiana, but the compiler has been unable to learn the circumstances. The place in Indiana is said to have been named for an Indian chief. The Clatsop County office was closed May 15, 1901, with papers to Vinemaple. The list of county precincts of 1940 contains Mishawaka precinct.

Mission Bottom, Marion County. Mission Bottom is on the east side of Willamette River south of Wheatland. It was here that Jason Lee established his Methodist Mission in the fall of 1834, and the bottom was named on that account.

Mission Creek, Marion County. Mission Creek flows through St. Paul, and was named for the pioneer Catholic mission of that place. Mission Landing on Willamette River, about a mile and a half northwest of St. Paul, is named for the same reason.

Mission Creek, Umatilla County. Mission Creek is about six miles east of Pendleton and slightly east of the Umatilla Indian Agency Headquarters. Professor Theodore Stern of the University of Oregon has spent considerable time investigating the history and location of the Catholic mission church of St. Anne. The original building was destroyed during the Cayuse War but was replaced by a new structure with the same name. There has been controversy as to its exact site with Clifford Drury even placing it as far east as Thorn Hollow. However, Professor Stern's studies show the church was near the present agency headquarters about a mile and a half west of the mouth of Mission Creek. The name was in use at the turn of the century for the 1892 Oregon Railroad & Navigation Company timetable shows the station Mission, where it is today, near the agency.

Missouri Bottom, Douglas County. This bottom, along South Umpqua River south of Myrtle Creek, took its name from the fact that a number of Missourians were pioneer settlers thereon. See Walling's *History of Southern Oregon,* page 423.

Missouri Flat, Baker County. A substantial number of early Oregon emigrants literally were from Missouri. E. W. Coles of Haines told the compiler that this section of Baker Valley was settled by a number of Missourians including his future wife, Ollie Ann Taylor who was born in Monroe County.

Mist, Columbia County. There was a post office called Riverside not far from this community, established about 1874. This caused confusion with another place in Oregon with the same name, and in April, 1888, the office was moved and the name changed to Mist, describing the atmospheric condition prevailing in the Nehalem Valley. The townsite of Mist was surveyed and platted with the name of Esto. It has never been so called.

Mitchell, Wheeler County. Mitchell was named for John Hipple Mitchell, former U. S. senator from Oregon, and for many years prominent in the political history of the state. The name was suggested by W. W. (Brawdie) Johnson, the first postmaster, and the post office was established in April, 1873. J. H. Mitchell was senator from Oregon in 1873-79, 1885-97 and 1901-05. He was born in Pennsylvania in 1835, came to Oregon in 1860, and died in Portland December 8, 1905. In 1884 the town of Mitchell experienced its first catastrophe. Water rushed over the bluff above the community, carrying boulders and mud. In March, 1885, I. N. Sargent platted the townsite of Mitchell. It was incorporated in 1893. About half the town was consumed by fire in August, 1899. It was rebuilt. On July 11, 1904, it was almost destroyed by a cloudburst; two lives were lost. September 25, 1904, it was visited by another flood, but the damage was slight.

Mitchell Point, Hood River County. Beyond the fact that a man named Mitchell lived and died near this point, little information is available. He is reported to have been a trapper. Efforts have been made to change the name to Storm Crest, but the public has not looked with favor on the plan, and prefers the old name.

Mixup Spring, Klamath County. This spring is in the southeast corner of township 37 south, range 15 east, very close to the Lake County line. In April, 1944, Ida M. Odell of Klamath Falls told the compiler that it was named because two bands of sheep once got mixed up nearby.

M & M Creek, Linn County. This creek was named for M & M Woodworking Company who logged its watershed above the southwest finger of Detroit Reservoir.

Moccasin Lake, Wallowa County. Moccasin Lake is in the Lake Basin north of Eagle Cap. The lake, when seen from the north side of Eagle Cap, looks like a moccasin, hence the name.

Modoc Point, Klamath County. This is a prominent point on the east shore of Upper Klamath Lake, about fifteen miles north of Klamath Falls. It bears this name because the Modoc Indians, under Captain Jack, lived there from December 31, 1869, to April 26, 1870, and then escaped and went to their old habitat further south. Modoc Point is a well-known locality in Klamath Indian folklore, where it is spoken of as *Kiuti* and also *Muyant.* Will G. Steel is authority for the statement that the mountain is also known as *Nilakla,* which is the Klamath Indian name for dawn or sunrise. The Indian name *Modoc* is derived from the Klamath words *moa,* meaning south, and *takni,* meaning a native of that place or country, hence from the point of view of the Klamath Indians, natives of the country just to the south. The term Modoc Lake was formerly used in the Klamath country to refer to Tule Lake, because Modoc Indians lived nearby.

Moffat, Washington County. This station on the Oregon Electric Railway was near the east city limit of Hillsboro. It was named for George Barclay Moffat, a prominent New York banker and president of the railway company. While on a visit, George B. Moffat died in Portland December 4, 1911.

Moffett Creek, Multnomah County. Investigation by H. H. Riddell of Portland indicated that the family for which this stream is named spelled its name Moffett and not Moffatt. The original Columbia River Highway crossed Moffett Creek on a remarkable concrete arch. At the time it was built it was said to have been the longest flat arch bridge in America. See S. C. Lancaster's *The Columbia, America's Great Highway.* This bridge, now unused, is still standing just north of I 84.

Moffitt Butte, Klamath County. This 4900 foot butte is just east of SH 31 about ten miles south of the junction with US 97. It was named for James A. Moffitt who took up government land nearby in 1888. After World War II this name appeared on maps as Moffit but the proper spelling was restored in USBGN *Decision List 7101.*

Mohawk River, Lane County. According to Gustavus Hines, Mohawk River was named for the stream in the state of New York. The Oregon stream was probably named by Jacob C. Spores, a pioneer of 1847 and a native of Montgomery County, New York, a county drained in part by the original Mohawk River. For short biography of Spores, see *Illustrated History of Lane County* by Walling, page 481. Darrel Spores, great-grandson of Jacob Spores, and a resident of the Mohawk Valley in Oregon, says that Jacob Spores and a few other whites chased a band of Indians into the valley in 1849 and that Spores, viewing the locality from a high bluff, said that it reminded him of the valley of his birthplace in New York state. The name Mohawk River came into use as a result of this incident. Jacob Spores was one of the earliest settlers in Lane County and operated a pioneer ferry on McKenzie River not far from the present site of Coburg. A post office named Mohawk was established on the banks of the Oregon stream on December 20, 1862, with Robert M. Robertson first postmaster. This office did not operate continuously and was converted to a Rural Station on January 1, 1958. This, in turn, was terminated December 31, 1961. Gannett in *The Origin of Certain Place Names*, says that the name of the eastern Mohawk tribe signifies an eater of live meat.

Mohler, Tillamook County. Mohler post office was originally established as Balm in May, 1897, with Everett R. Bales postmaster. The office was on Foley Creek, a little above the mouth, and about two miles southeast of the present site of Mohler. In December, 1911, the name of the office was changed to Mohler and it was moved to the new location. The change is said to have been made at the request of E. E. Lytle, who built the Pacific Railway and Navigation Company line into that part of Tillamook County. The station and post office were named in compliment to A. L. Mohler, a prominent railroad official and one-time president of the Union Pacific.

Mokst Butte, Deschutes County. This butte in the Paulina Mountains was named by the USFS with the Chinook jargon word for two, as it was the second of a series all named at the same time.

Molalla, Clackamas County. This is an important community that takes its name from Molalla River nearby. See under that name. Molalla post office was established April 9, 1850. It was at or near the present site of Liberal and was discontinued August 25, 1851. Harrison Wright was the postmaster. The office was reestablished December 2, 1868, with Wright postmaster, but available records do not give its location. It operated until March, 1874. It was reestablished again in January, 1875, and it seems probable that this was the date it was placed at the present community of Molalla.

Molalla River, Clackamas County. Molalla was the name of the tribe of Indians that inhabited much of the territory now in Marion and Clackamas counties. The Molallas were a Waiilatpuan tribe akin to the Cayuses, forming the western division of the family. The Cayuses have a tradition that the Molallas were detached and driven west in wars with hostile tribes. The Molalla dialect shows that the separation from the Cayuses took place in remote times. Whether the Indians took their name from what is called Molalla River, or *vice versa,* is not known. For a short account of the Molalla Indians see *Handbook of American Indians,* volume I, page 930. Many methods of spelling the name by a variety of authors are listed. By decision of the USBGN, the name Molalla River extends to the headwaters of the main south branch of the stream. The style South Fork is wrong. The middle branch is Table Rock Fork.

Monitor, Marion County. Robert H. Down says that local residents have a story to the effect that this place was named for a certain type of flour mill known as a Monitor mill, which was in use at Monitor in early days. This sounds reasonable, and is probably the origin of the name.

Monkland, Sherman County. N. W. Thompson of Moro told the compiler that his father named the community of Monkland, presumably for Monkland, Ontario, because several nearby residents had formerly lived in the Canadian town.

Monmouth, Polk County. The town of Monmouth was named for Monmouth, Illinois. In 1852 a group of citizens of the Illinois community crossed the plains to Oregon, and after spending the first winter at Crowley, five miles north of Rickreall, settled in 1853 near the present site of Monmouth. Members of the party gave 640 acres of land on which to establish the town and a college under the auspices of the Christian Church. The place was surveyed in 1855 by T. H. Hutchinson. The money secured from the sale of lots was devoted to the building of the Christian college, which was known as Monmouth University. At a mass meeting the people selected Monmouth as the name of the new community, in honor of their old home. In 1856 mercantile buildings were erected. The first house was built in 1857. The post office was established February 25, 1859, with Joseph B. V. Butler first postmaster. In 1871, due to the influence of the church, the name of Monmouth University was changed to Christian College. The college underwent vicissitudes due to lack of funds, and was once offered to the state for a state university. In 1882 the Oregon legislature passed a bill creating the Oregon State Normal School at Monmouth, which absorbed the Christian College. The name of the school was later changed to the Oregon College of Education. For information about the names of Monmouth pioneers, see the *Oregonian*, August 13, 1916.

Monon Lake, Jefferson County. This lake south of Olallie Butte was named by forest ranger Joe Graham. The name was selected because it had a pleasing sound.

Monroe, Benton County. The town Monroe was started in 1853 on the land of Joseph White, who had built a small sawmill in the neighborhood about 1850. The first post office in the vicinity was Starrs Point. Starrs Point was established April 22, 1852, and was a little north of the present site of Monroe. Starrs Point was named for George Starr who had a store nearby. The name Starrs Point was changed to Monroe on February 2, 1874, for James Monroe, fifth president of the United States. The first postmaster of Starrs Point was Samuel F. Starr.

Monroe Roughs, Wheeler County. Monroe Roughs is a piece of mountainous terrain cut by steep canyons filled with mountain mahogany and other brush. The roughs lie between Girds Creek and Flock Mountain and form the headwaters of Monroe Creek. Thomas J. Monroe, one of the earliest settlers in the Mitchell area, was born in Ohio in 1837 and came to Oregon in 1865. He moved to Wheeler County in the early 1870s and settled where Monroe Creek joins Girds Creek.

Montague, Gilliam County. Montague, the name of a locality in Eightmile Canyon about eight miles southeast of Arlington, came from a local family. Montague was at the place where the Oregon Trail crossed this canyon three miles east of Shutler. Montague post office was established April 1, 1911, and was discontinued January 15, 1915. L. C. Montague was the postmaster.

Montavilla, Multnomah County. Montavilla post office was established September 21, 1891 but for many years operated as a station of the Portland office. The name Montavilla is a contraction of Mount Tabor Villa. Mount Tabor Villa addition to the city of Portland was platted June 11, 1889. The name was cumbersome and the place was immediately known as Montavilla, and has been ever since. Besides being cumbersome the original name was more or less meaningless. Mount Tabor was taken from the nearby geographic feature. *Villa* is a Latin word, meaning a county-seat, or sometimes farm buildings. It is also used to refer to a detached suburban residence. The addition of Montavilla, platted July 13, 1904, was named long after the name Montavilla was applied to that part of Portland.

Monte Rico Ridge, Lane County. This ridge is in the southeast part of the Bohemia mining district. *Monte Rico* is Spanish for rich mountain, and in this case the name probably refers to the ore prospects.

Montgomery Ranch, Deschutes County. This ranch on Little Deschutes River south of Vandevert Ranch was the headquarters of James and Charles Montgomery who homesteaded land to the west in 1899.

Monument, Grant County. This post office was established October 27, 1874, with Prior S. Wilson postmaster. It was named for a peculiar rock or mountain nearby which resembles a pulpit or rostrum. This peak is called Monument Mountain.

Moody, Wasco County. Moody is a station on the Oregon Trunk Line near the mouth of Deschutes River. It was named for Malcolm A. Moody of The Dalles, who was a member of a prominent pioneer family, and at one time U. S. representative in Congress from eastern Oregon. He owned a power site near the mouth of the Deschutes River. When the Oregon Trunk Railway was built there was a large material yard at Moody, and a post office was established to take care of mail for construction camps along the line in Deschutes Canyon. When the work was completed the town of Moody faded away, and is now only a station. Moody post office was established December 7, 1911, with Ida Carlisle postmaster. Available records of its history are not clear. It may have been moved to Sherman County and renamed Miller, or it may have been consolidated with the Miller office, already in operation. The move and change in name of Moody post office has not affected the name of Moody station in Wasco County, which remains as originally established.

Moolack Creek, Lincoln County. Moolack Creek, named with the Chinook jargon word for elk, is a couple of miles north of Agate Beach. The style Moloch Creek, commemorating the bull-headed idol of the Canaanites, is wrong, and is due to a mishearing of the real name.

Moolack Mountain, Lane County. This mountain was formerly known as Elk Mountain because of the local abundance of that animal. Of late years it has been called Moolack Mountain, which is the Chinook jargon word for elk. The name was changed because there were a number of other Elk mountains in the state. Moolack Mountain has an elevation of 5500 feet, and is north of Waldo Lake.

Moon Creek, Tillamook County. There were several members of the Moon family who settled along this creek which flows into Nestucca River at Blaine. Mr. Frank Kumm of Blaine stated in 1968 that he believed the creek was named for John Moon as the others left at an early date.

Mooney Mountain, Josephine County. Walling, in *History of Southern Oregon*, page 452, says that one Mooney was the first settler in the Illinois Valley to avail himself of the privilege of the donation land law. Samuel Mooney's claim was in the valley just south of Mooney Mountain. His certificate was number 57.

Moore Park, Klamath County. This City Park in Klamath Falls was donated by members of the Moore family as a memorial to early pioneers Charles S. and Rufus Moore.

Mooreville, Malheur County. The locality called Mooreville is in the high country about twenty-five miles south-southeast of Riverside, airline. It bears the name of a local family. Mooreville post office was established September 23, 1912, and was closed June 30, 1919, with mail to Crowley. Esther M. Moore was the only postmaster.

Moorhouse, Umatilla County. Moorhouse post office was established with the name Morehouse on January 5, 1880, and with Thomas L. Moorhouse postmaster. The name should have been spelled Moorhouse, and accordingly the Post Office Department changed the record to Moorhouse with Thomas L. Moorhouse postmaster on March 25, 1880, and it remained that way until it was discontinued June 6, 1883. Thomas L. Moorhouse was the same man as Thomas Leander Moorhouse, but far better known as Major Lee Moorhouse. Major Moorhouse was one of eastern Oregon's most prominent characters and in later years became famous for the remarkable Indian pictures that came from his camera. Moorhouse post office was situated at the Prospect Ranch of the John R. Foster Company, about five or six miles northeast of what is now the town of Stanfield. It was on the old stage road northwest of Pendleton. It was on what were called the Meadows, a considerable area near the Umatilla River in the northern part of the county, not exactly defined.

Moosmoos Creek, Clatsop County. This stream flows into Youngs River about a mile north of Youngs River Falls. *Moosmoos* is the Chinook jargon word for cattle, which have been plentiful in the locality for many years.

Morgan, Morrow County. The original name of this post office was Saddle for Saddle Butte about three miles to the south. Saddle post office was established November 20, 1882, with Ozwell T. Douglas postmaster. The name of the post office was changed to Douglas on December 31, 1890. About 1906 the name was changed to Morgan, apparently in compliment to Alfred C. Morgan, a local resident who had been postmaster. For a time there was a discrepancy between the names of the post office and the railroad station, but it is probable that one of the changes listed above composed the difficulty.

Morgan Butte, Wallowa County. This butte is in the southeast part of the county. It was named for Albert Morgan, a sheepman.

Mormon Basin, Baker and Malheur counties. Mormon Basin was named in 1862 at the time of the eastern Oregon gold rush. A party of prospectors from Salt Lake City found pay dirt and the basin was named either by or for these miners. About the same time a group of miners from the Humboldt River region found gold in another part of the basin, and the name Humboldt Basin was at once applied in compliment to this group. The Nevada miners had been working at Auburn with poor results and were on their way back home when they made a strike in Humboldt Basin. See Fred Lockley's article in *Oregon Journal*, April 29, 1932. The two names, Mormon Basin and Humboldt Basin were used concurrently for a time, but the style Humboldt gradually gave way to Mormon Basin and modern usage is well crystallized in favor of the latter name. The stream draining the area is generally called Mormon Basin Creek. For postal history of the locality, see under Humboldt Basin.

Mormon Flat, Wallowa County. This flat is in the east part of the county. It was named for W. H. Winters, an early settler, who was of the Mormon faith. He was drowned in Snake River.

Moro, Sherman County. Moro is the county seat of Sherman County, and has an elevation of 1807 feet. It is generally believed that Henry Barnum was the first resident of the place, settling there in 1868, and establishing a trading post some eleven years later. There are several stories as to how the town got its name. One version is that it was named for Moro, Illinois, by Judge O. M. Scott, who formerly lived in that place. Another version is that it was named for Moore Brothers, who were interested in the townsite. Still another story is that it was named Moro for the Moors, which seems unlikely to the compiler. The reader may take his choice.

Morris Canyon, Morrow County. Frederick M. Morris settled where this canyon empties into Butter Creek in 1876.

Morrison, Clatsop County. This station was named for Robert W. Morrison, an early settler. It was on Clatsop Plains. Robert W. Morrison was born in Kentucky in 1811, came to Oregon in 1844 and died in May, 1894.

Morrow County. Morrow County was created February 16, 1885, by the state legislature and was taken from the western part of Umatilla County. For data about the boundaries of Morrow and Umatilla counties at the time Morrow County was created, see *OHQ,* volume XI, number 1, which contains an article, "Oregon Counties," by Frederick V. Holman. The following editorial from the *Oregonian* for November 5, 1909, gives details concerning the naming of this county: "A letter to the *Oregonian* asserts that Morrow County, Oregon, was named for Colonel H. A. Morrow, a soldier of the Civil War, stationed later at Vancouver; and the writer desires to correct the *Oregonian's* statement that it was named for an early pioneer. But the *Oregonian's* statement was correct. The county was named for Jackson L. Morrow, one of the very earliest settlers there. He first settled on Puget Sound, and Shelton Bay, in 1853; a few years later went to eastern Oregon, and was a member of the legislature from Umatilla when Morrow was formed out of a part of that county. In the debate about what the name of the new county should be, some one said: 'Let's call it for Jack Morrow; he is entitled to the honor.' " For Morrow's biography, see the *Oregonian,* April 18, 1898. Morrow County has an area of 2059 square miles.

Morrow Well, Jefferson County. This well northwest of Grizzly bears the name of Andrew Morrow who homesteaded along Willow Creek in 1880.

Morton Butte, Curry County. William Morton homesteaded on the north edge of this butte in 1903. It is located about six miles north of Brookings.

Mosby Creek, Lane County. This stream has its source on the western slopes of the Cascade Range, and has a length of approximately twenty miles. It flows into Row River, about two miles southwest of Cottage Grove, at an elevation of about 665 feet. It was named for David Mosby, who settled on its banks near its mouth in pioneer days. The creek was once known as Brumbaugh Creek, but that name did not prevail.

Mosier, Wasco County. Mosier is a pioneer settlement on the Columbia River. J. H. Mosier started the community about 1853-54 by settling on a claim near the mouth of Mosier Creek. Mr. and Mrs. Mosier ran an impromptu stage station, a stopping place for travelers. Jonah H. Mosier was born March 10, 1821, in Maryland, and moved to Missouri in 1839, and learned cabinet making. He went to California in 1849, but returned to the eastern states. He came to Oregon in 1853, and soon settled on his homestead. He served in the Oregon legislature and died in 1894. Pierce Mays, prominent Wasco County resident, told the writer that Mosier's large collection of artificial books in a handsome cabinet was one of the best of its kind in Oregon. He once tried to read one of the wooden books.

Mosquite, Malheur County. Mosquite was a locality in the northeast corner of the county, on the west bank of Snake River ten or a dozen miles north of Ontario. Mosquite post office was established April 18, 1893, with one Shepherd first postmaster, but with what given name and of what sex cannot be determined from available records. The office was finally closed May 31, 1911. The name was perhaps intended to be that of a shrub, the mesquite, but as far as the compiler can determine no variety of the mesquite grows in Oregon. However, in November, 1979, Beth Magrini of Ontario wrote to say that the place may have been named for the familiar pesky insect. She added that there were many Italian emigrants brought in to work on the railroad when it was built in the 1880s and that a common Italian pronunciation was "mosquit" without the "o". The compiler has also heard older Italians use the same pronunciation and must agree that this is an equally probable origin.

Moss Butte, Linn County. Moss Butte, elevation about 2600 feet, is a prominent cone standing near the middle of section 3, township 14 south, range 2 east, just south of South Santiam River at a point about ten miles eastward of Sweet Home. In September, 1946, W. R. Mealey of Foster wrote the compiler that the butte was named for Mack Moss, a very early settler of the Sweet Home area, who roamed the South Santiam hunting and exploring.

Moss Lakes, Clackamas County. These two small lakes are between Oregon City and Park Place. They were originally one lake, but have been much reduced in size by draining. They were named for Sidney Walter Moss, who was born in Benton County, Kentucky, March 17, 1810, and who came to Oregon in 1842. He organized the Falls Debating Society at Oregon City in 1843, and built the first hotel in Oregon City in 1844. He also engaged in the merchandise business. He died September 24, 1901, and his biography is in the *Oregonian* for September 25, 1901, and March 6, 1898, page 19. Moss claimed to have written the original tale of the *Prairie Flower,* which he gave to William Johnson for publication and which was expanded by Emerson Bennett of Cincinnati. This became a popular sketch of border life. Moss wrote many articles about pioneer life in Oregon. He carried an advertisement in the *Oregonian* in 1852, of his "Main

Street House" at Oregon City, signed by himself and "The Widow,"
announcing that, "owing to pressing necessities and our cheap rate of fare,
we are compelled to say:

To *all,* high or low,
Please down with your dust,
For he's no friend of ours,
That would ask us to trust."

"The Widow" was Mrs. Richardson, before she married Moss. For reminiscences of Sidney W. Moss, see the *Oregonian,* September 29, 1901, page 22.

Mother Lode Mountain, Marion County. This mountain was named
for the Mother Lode mine nearby. It is about 12 miles north of Detroit.

Mound, Lane County. For nearly two decades a post office with the
name Mound served an area close to Siuslaw River in western Lane County.
The place was about a mile and a half east of Alma, in section 30, township
19 south, range 6 west. Postal records indicate the office was established
June 1, 1892, with Joseph B. Beebe first of three postmasters. The office
was closed September 30, 1910, and the business turned over to Alma post
office, but the name Mound was not changed to Alma as is sometimes
reported. Alma post office was already in service in 1910. As a matter of
fact Alma post office was established in 1888. In the summer of 1946 P. M.
Morse, Lane County engineer, gathered some data about Mound post
office from Hazen Johnson, who reported that his grandfather, Bowker
Beebe, moved to the Siuslaw Valley from Mound, Nebraska, in 1890, and
when the new post office was established, Beebe asked to have it named for
his former home. Mound, Nebraska, was an office in Howard County,
about twenty miles from Saint Paul. Mr. Johnson reported that Bowker
Beebe had formerly been postmaster at Mound, Nebraska. It is probable
that Joseph B. Beebe and Bowker Beebe were the same person.

Mount Angel, Marion County. The community of Mount Angel was
named in 1883 by the Reverend Father Adelhelm Odermatt, O.S.B., in
compliment to Engelberg, Switzerland. Mount Angel is the anglicized version of the German name Engelberg. Benjamin Cleaver came to Oregon in
1848 and in 1850 settled at the present site of Mount Angel. Some years
later he planned a townsite to be named Roy, and his adjoining neighbor,
George Settlemier, actually platted a place in 1881 with the name Frankfort. Cleaver bought the Settlemier townsite in 1882 and changed the name
to Roy. A post office was established in 1882 with the name Roy. The compiler does not know the reason for selecting either of the names Frankfort or
Roy. In 1880 a narrow gauge railroad was built through the locality and in
the following year a station was established with the name Fillmore, in compliment to James M. Fillmore, an official of the railroad company. Father
Adelhelm Odermatt had received his theological training at Engelberg in
Switzerland, came to Oregon in 1881, and was soon in charge of the par-
ishes at Gervais, Fillmore and Sublimity. After overcoming many difficulties, Father Odermatt succeeded in establishing a Benedictine community
in Gervais in 1882-83. In 1883 a pilgrimage chapel was built on the summit

of Lone Butte or *Tapalamaho*, and in the same year Father Odermatt
applied the name Mount Angel to the butte and the community. He had
the name Mount Angel adopted both for the railroad station and for the
post office and the old designations Fillmore and Roy were discarded. The
City of Mt. Angel was incorporated April 3, 1893 and the railroad station
also uses the abreviation although the post office is Mount Angel. In 1884
the Benedictine establishment was moved from Gervais to Mount Angel.
See under Saint Benedict. For history of Mount Angel and its Benedictine
institutions, see *Mt. Angel, Oregon, 1848-1912*, by Sister Ursula Hodes, University of Oregon Thesis Series, No. 20. T. W. Davenport, in *OHQ*, volume
V, page 36, says the Indian name for the butte southeast of Mount Angel
was *Tap-a-lam-a-ho*, indicating a mountain used by the Indians for commun-
ion with the Great Spirit. Early settlers called it Lone Butte, Lone Tree
Butte, and also Graves Butte for John P. Graves, a nearby resident. The
new name Mount Angel quickly superseded the old forms.

Mount Ashland, Jackson County. This mountain lies about eight miles
due south of Ashland and was named for that community. In the past it has
been known as Ashland Peak and sometimes Siskiyou Peak. It is now universally known as Mount Ashland and that form is shown on the USGS map of
the Ashland quadrangle, published in 1954. The elevation is now accepted
as 7533 feet. Accurate mapping indicates that Siskiyou Peak, elevation 7147
feet, is about three miles to the southwest. The two points were formerly
confused one for the other.

Mount Avery, Curry County. This mountain is near the headwaters of
Sixes River. It was named for Frederick S. Avery, who owned a small ranch
just west of the mountain and lived there for many years. Mount Avery has
an elevation of 2613 feet.

Mount Bailey, Douglas County. This is an important peak in the Cascade Range and has an elevation of 8363 feet. It lies west of Diamond Lake.
The writer has been unable to get much information as to the origin of the
name. Older maps show the mountain as Old Baldy and Old Bailey. It is
possible that Old Bailey is the result of a draftsman's error. The summit of
the mountain has a bald, burnt-over appearance. The compiler has found
no record of any person named Bailey connected with the peak, but it has
been known as Mount Bailey for many years. Will G. Steel wrote in 1927
that the Klamath Indian name for the mountain was *Youxlokes*, which
meant Medicine Mountain. According to Indian tradition, the medicine
men and priests often feasted on the summit of this mountain and com-
muned with the upper world.

Mount Billingslea, Curry and Josephine counties. This peak, elevation
4181 feet, is about 20 miles northwest of Kerby on the high divide south of
Illinois River. It was named for James H. Billingslea, who served in the
USFS for more than fifteen years, including six years as supervisor of Siskiyou National Forest. He died November 7, 1939.

Mount Bolivar, Coos and Curry counties. Mount Bolivar, elevation
4297 feet, is at the extreme southeast corner of Coos County, and as far as
the writer knows, is the highest peak in the Oregon Coast Range north of
Rogue River, although there are higher peaks to the south. The elevation

given above was determined by the USC&GS in 1907 and may be superseded. Mount Bolivar was named by a well-known Coos County surveyor, Simon Bolivar Cathcart, during a township survey carried on about 1900. While the name was his own, it was applied to the mountain in honor of the South American patriot, Simon Bolivar, 1783-1830, who was born in Caracas, Venezuela, and who spent his mature years and a large part of his fortune in securing the independence of Columbia, Peru and Ecuador. The name is frequently misspelled Boliver and generally mispronounced. The correct accent is on the second syllable of each word. For information about Simon Bolivar Cathcart, see under Mount Cathcart.

Mount Bonneville, Wallowa County. This mountain was formerly known as Middle Mountain, but in 1925 the USBGN, at the suggestion of J. Neilson Barry of Portland, changed the name to Mount Bonneville, in honor of Captain Benjamin L. E. Bonneville, U. S. A., who was possibly the first white man to visit the Wallowa Valley. For additional information see under Bonneville. Mount Bonneville is just south of Wallowa Lake.

Mount Cathcart, Coos County. This point is in the Coast Range east of Coos Bay, and bears the name of Simon Bolivar Cathcart, prominent civil engineer and surveyor of Coos County. S. B. Cathcart was born in Indiana in 1842, came to Oregon in 1853, and in the 1860s served in the First Oregon Cavalry. He engaged in the stock business at various places, and studied surveying. In 1872 he settled at the head of tide on Millicoma River. In 1929 he informed the compiler that Mount Cathcart was named for him by R. U. Goode and W. T. Griswold of the USGS. This was apparently about the time the Survey was mapping the Coos Bay area in 1895-96. Mr. Cathcart served as mineral surveyor and also as Coos County surveyor, and was a prominent citizen of southwest Oregon. He died on May 13, 1932.

Mount David Douglas, Lane County. The USBGN, at the suggestion of the writer, adopted on November 2, 1927, the name Mount David Douglas for a conspicuous, angular peak on the north side of Salt Creek Valley, opposite the Cascade line of the Southern Pacific Company. This peak has an elevation of 6253 feet. David Douglas was the great pioneer botanist of Oregon, and his discoveries in this state were of the first order. Douglas was born in Scotland in 1798. He served his apprenticeship as gardener to the Earl of Mansfield, and later received an appointment in the Glasgow botanical gardens. The Royal Horticultural Society became interested in the country of the Hudson's Bay Company, and asked to have an exploring botanist recommended for American research. Douglas received the appointment and sailed for America the first time in 1823. He worked along the Atlantic Coast and returned to England in the fall of the same year. Douglas came to the Columbia River on April 8, 1825. In the Oregon country he made extensive explorations. An interesting account of his activities appears in *The Scientific Monthly,* July, 1926, page 81, by Major John D. Guthrie of Portland. See also *OHQ,* from September, 1904, to December, 1905. The Royal Horticultural Society published a *Journal Kept by David Douglas,* in London in 1914. After two years' activities in the Oregon territory and Canada, Douglas returned to England in September, 1827. Douglas later made some additional explorations in the Oregon country, and then went to the Hawaiian Islands, where he met a tragic death in August, 1834. He fell into a cattle pit and was gored to death by a wild bull. For editorial comment on David Douglas and peak in Oregon named for him, see the *Oregonian*, December 11, 1927. Douglas may have been the first white man to climb Mount Hood. See *OHQ*, volume VI, bottom of page 309. The Douglas fir, Oregon's most important forest tree, was noted by David Douglas and he bestowed its early botanical name, *Pseudotsuga taxifolia*. It is most fitting that Douglas is remembered by the common name of this great tree although it is not a true fir but a false hemlock. For further information on the Douglas fir, see under Firwood.

Mount Defiance, Hood River County. This is a well-known landmark west of Hood River Valley and has an elevation of 4960 feet. It was named by Dr. P. G. Barrett, an early settler in the Hood River Valley, because the mountain was the last to hold its snow in spring, thus defying the elements.

Mount Elijah, Josephine County. Mount Elijah, elevation approximately 6400 feet, is in township 40 south, range 6 west, and is about a half a mile southwest of Lake Peak. The Oregon Caves are under its northwestern slopes. The name Mount Elijah was adopted by the USBGN in 1930-31 in honor of Elijah J. Davidson, a prominent pioneer of southern Oregon, who discovered the caves in 1874. Previously the mountain was known as Cave Mountain and Sand Mountain, but these names were not well established.

Mount Emily, Curry County. F. S. Moore, a pioneer of the county, says this name is the white man's version of the Indian name *Emney*. See *Curry County Reporter*, December 16, 1926. The meaning of the Indian name is not known. Maps show this mountain with various names including Mount Emery and Chetco Peak, but the real Chetco Peak is farther east. The government has officially adopted the form Mount Emily, even though it does not exactly conform to the reported Indian pronunciation. Mount Emily became famous in 1942 as the result of an attack, apparently by a small airplane based on a Japanese submarine. In September bombs and incendiary material were dropped near the lookout, with negligible damage.

Mount Emily, Union County. There is a story to the effect that a family named Leasy lived at the foot of this mountain in pioneer days. Leasy weighed about 100 pounds and his wife nearly 300, and it is said that he named the mountain for his wife, Emily, because of her great size. There is another history of the name to the effect that a very popular young lady named Emily lived on the slopes of the mountain in early times, and she was often visited by the young men of La Grande, who christened the mountain because they so frequently went up to Mount Emily.

Mount Fanny, Union County. "The beautiful peak on the summit of the mountain range east of the Cove is called 'Mt Fanny' in honor of Mrs. Fanny McDaniels, one of the first women to settle in the Cove—in 1862— and the first white woman to reach its summit, which she did in June, 1863." This quotation is from Geer's *Fifty Years in Oregon*. The statement is incorrect, for the name should be Mrs. Fannie McDaniel. Her sons were well-known physicians in Portland. However the form Mount Fanny is too well established to change. Mount Fanny is a prominent peak to the east of Grande Ronde Valley and has an elevation of 7132 feet.

Mount Gauldy, Tillamook County. Mount Gauldy is a point south of Hebo and east of the Oregon Coast Highway. It is said to have been named for the Gauldy trail and the Gauldy trail was named because it was so steep and hard on men and horses. Packers and animals sustained pack-strap and saddle galls so frequently that the trace became known as the Galldy trail which was transformed into Gauldy trail.

Mount Gurney, Douglas County. Mount Gurney is west of Reston. It was named for Robert M. Gurney who took up a donation land claim near its base in 1853.

Mount Harriman, Klamath County. This prominent peak is west of Upper Klamath Lake. It was named to compliment Edward H. Harriman, financier and railroad magnate, who for a time had a summer camp on Pelican Bay nearby.

Mount Harris, Union County. Mount Harris, northeast of La Grande, was named for Joseph Harris, a pioneer resident nearby.

Mount Hebo, Tillamook and Yamhill counties. The compiler of these notes spent six years as a small boy on a farm in Polk County, and the most important landmark visible from his home was Mount Hebo. He speculated about Mount Hebo considerably, both then and later, and always had a notion that its name was corrupted from Mount Nebo. This does not seem to be a fact. On January 7, 1919, Miss Lucy E. Doughty of Bay City wrote the compiler sending information about Mount Hebo that came from Warren N. Vaughn, a Tillamook County pioneer. Vaughn relates that the mountain was named by a viewing party to find a new route to the Willamette Valley. The party climbed the mountain to get a better understanding of the country. One of the party, Cadiler, was impressed by the fine view and said, "We are very high up, so I will call this mountain Hevo." Miss Doughty explains this peculiar name by saying that Isaac Alderman, a member of the party, told her parents that the name was intended to be Heave Ho, because from their position the mountain seemed to have been heaved up above the surroundings. However that may be, it is apparent that the name became distorted somewhere along the line, and the present form is Mount Hebo. In 1926 the postmaster at Hebo wrote the compiler that the name Hebo was a misunderstanding of the name Heave Ho, and attributed the original form to the Indians. This seems improbable to the compiler. Vaughn was a reliable citizen and his story plus Alderman's explanation is probably nearer the truth. A determination made some years ago by the USC&GS gives the elevation of Mount Hebo as 3153 feet.

Mount Hood, Hood River County. This post office was in the upper Hood River Valley about three miles northeast of Parkdale. It is reported that the community developed on land owned by a man named Tieman, and when the post office was applied for, it was named Mount Hood for the reason that the mountain was the most important object in the landscape. In 1976 the Post Office Department consolidated the offices of Parkdale and Mount Hood. The former was the much larger community but the latter had the name preferred by the local residents so on October 9,

1976 the Mount Hood office was relocated to the community of Parkdale and the Parkdale office closed.

Mount Hood, Hood River and Clackamas counties. On October 29, 1792, Lieutenant William Robert Broughton, of Vancouver's command, discovered Mount Hood and in his *Voyage of Discovery,* Vancouver makes the following comment: "A very distant high snowy mountain now appeared rising beautifully conspicuous in the midst of an extensive tract of low, or moderately elevated, land, lying S. 67 E., and seemed to announce a termination of the river." Broughton was somewhere near the mouth of the Willamette River when he had this view of Mount Hood, and the description which he gave Vancouver would be difficult to improve upon. The next day, while near Point Vancouver, Broughton saw the mountain again, and Vancouver wrote as follows: "The same remarkable mountain that had been seen from Belle Vue point, again presented itself, bearing at this station S. 67 E., and though the party were now nearer to it by 7 leagues, yet its lofty summit was scarcely more distinct across the intervening land which was more than moderately elevated. Mr. Broughton honored it with Lord Hood's name; its appearance was magnificent; and it was clothed with snow from its summit, as low down as the high land, by which it was intercepted, rendered it visible." Here Broughton's report shows him to be a keen observer and a judge of natural beauty. Professor Edmond S. Meany, in his *Vancouver's Discovery of Puget Sound,* has taken pains to present a suitable picture of Lord Hood, and the compiler hereof cannot do better than to paraphrase from Professor Meany's notes. The Lord Hood, to whom Vancouver referred, was Samuel Hood, born December 12, 1724, and entered the Royal Navy as a captain's servant in 1741. As the result of his own efforts coupled with the fact that he served under splendid officers he rose to the rank of lieutenant in 1746, and after experiencing considerable service in America and elsewhere, reached post rank on the *Lively* on July 22, 1756, but just at his promotion, he was returned to England and paid off. He was forced to resort to temporary commands for a time, but was so successful in these that he was reinstated in regular line, and served in a number of places with no remarkable distinction, but always satisfactorily, until he was practically retired in 1778 as Commissioner at Portsmouth and Governor of the Naval Academy. The king visited Portsmouth and created him a baronet, and Hood lived quietly enough when to the surprise of everybody in 1780, he was promoted to the rank of rear-admiral of the blue, and was sent with a squadron to reinforce Rodney in the West Indies. Hood remained second in command in American waters until the peace of 1783, and took part in nearly all the stirring engagements that marked the close of the War for Independence. As a reward for his services he was on September 12, 1782, raised to the Irish peerage as Baron Hood of Catherington, Hampshire. This was before his return to England. On his return he was given other honors, and made vice-admiral of the blue. In 1788 he was made a member of the Board of Admiralty under the Earl of Chatham, and while in this position signed the original instructions for Vancouver's voyage. But Hood's career did not end here. He served in the Mediterranean during the French Revolution. Nelson was a captain under him, and praised his vigor of mind and judgment. Sir William Hotham wrote that he never saw an officer of more intrepid courage or warmer zeal. Before his recall he was elected an Elder Brother of Trinity House in March, 1795, and a little later was made an admiral. In 1796 he was appointed governor of Greenwich Hospital and created Viscount Hood in the peerage of Great Britain. His remarkable mind and body made him a noted man, and shortly before he died, on January 27, 1816, at the great age of 92, he received the Grand Cross of the Bath. Mount Hood is an unusual mountain, and none can say but that it was named for an unusual man. Occasional statements to the effect that Mount Hood was named for other members of the Hood family, cannot be substantiated. It is certain that the mountain was named for Samuel Hood. He was Lord Hood, a baron, when he signed the original instructions for Vancouver's voyage. The mountain could not possibly have been named in honor of Alexander Hood, Lord Bridport, younger brother of Lord Hood and also an admiral. Alexander Hood was not raised to the peerage until after 1793, and never had the title Lord Hood, but instead that of Lord Bridport. He was a viscount when he died in 1814, after a long and distinguished life. Lord Hood and Lord Bridport had two famous cousins, also named Samuel and Alexander Hood, but in reverse order. Alexander was the elder of this pair and died in action at sea in 1798, but never received a title. His younger brother, Sir Samuel Hood, had a remarkably successful naval career, but was not a peer. It will be seen from the above that there was but one Lord Hood in 1792, when the mountain was named, and that was the first Samuel. It will also be seen that the statement that Mount Hood and the famous British warship *Hood* were named for the same man is difficult to prove. There have been several ships named *Hood*. In 1935 the compiler secured a copy of the picture hanging in the wardroom of H.M.S. *Hood,* and it turned out to be of Vice-Admiral Sir Samuel Hood and not that of Lord Hood. Alexander Hood, Lord Bridport, seems, from his biography, to have done more sea fighting than the other three, and was raised to the peerage even though his brother was already a peer. The *Oregonian* had an editorial on the name Hood on June 1, 1941, which says that the ships and the mountain are named for the same man, but offers no definite evidence and in fact fails to mention Admiral Alexander Hood, Viscount Bridport, who is obviously one of the most important men of the family group.

Lewis and Clark saw Mount Hood for the first time on Friday, October 18, 1805, and wrote: "saw a mountain S. W. conical form Covered with Snow." On October 25 Clark wrote at a point near The Dalles, "The Pinical of the round toped mountain which we Saw a Short distance below the forks of this river is S. 43° W. of us and abt 37 miles, it is at this time toped with Snow we called this the *falls mountain* or *Timm* mountain. [*this the Mount Hood or Vancouver.*]" Timm was a name given to a point at The Dalles of the Columbia, said to have been applied because the word sounded like the noise of falling water. It is obvious that Clark meant to write *this the Mount Hood of Vancouver,* and it is also obvious that he and Lewis must have had a reasonably accurate knowledge of Vancouver's discoveries, though it seems they did not have Vancouver's engraved charts. See Coues' *History of the Expedition of Lewis and Clark,* volume I, page xxiv. The fur traders had many other things to occupy their attention, and did not go in for mountaineer-

ing, and for the most part, neither did the pioneers. There are many references to Mount Hood in early day journals and diaries, but nothing of
importance, except Hall J. Kelley's plan to change the name to Mount
Adams (see under Cascade Range), until Joel Palmer made one of the earliest attempts by a white man to climb the mountain, on October 12, 1845.
See the volume containing Palmer's journals in *Thwaites' Early Western Travels*, page 132, and also under Camp Creek and Palmer Peak in this book.
David Douglas, the botanist, is said to have attempted to climb the mountain in 1833. See *OHQ*, volume VI, page 309. Possibly the first ascent of
Mount Hood was in August, 1854. See the *Oregonian*, August 19, 1854. Joel
Palmer is said to have been a member of the first party to make the complete ascent. For information about early ascents and references to interesting articles about the mountain, see Scott's *History of the Oregon Country*,
volume II, page 302. The first reasonably accurate determination of the
height of Mount Hood, 11,225 feet, was made on August 23, 1867, by a
party under direction of Lieutenant-Colonel Robert S. Williamson. See the
Oregonian, September 24, 1867, and Scott's *History of the Oregon Country*,
volume V, page 119. For information about Williamson see under Williamson River. The Mazamas were organized on the summit of Mount Hood
July 19, 1894. See *Mazama*, volume I, number 1. For additional information about Mount Hood, see the booklet *Mount Hood*, issued by Mazamas. It
will be noted in this booklet that doubts are cast on the reliability of the
reports on the ascent of August, 1854. For information on the movement
of glaciers on Mount Hood, see under Eliot Glacier. The best general books
about Mount Hood are Fred H. McNeil's *Wy'east "THE Mountain,"* and
MOUNT HOOD, A COMPLETE HISTORY, by Jack Grauer. For many years
there was a mild controversy about the elevation of Mount Hood, the USGS
and the USC&GS using different values in their publications. These differences were composed in 1939 when a USC&GS party under Lieutenant
William M. Scaife established a triangulation station on the summit and
fixed its elevation by means of vertical angles measured with great accuracy. The measurement was based on the elevation of a first-order bench
mark near Warrendale, and produced an elevation of 11,245 feet. In 1958,
the USGS field survey crew working on the Mount Hood remapping project made a revised determination of 11,235 feet. This reduction of ten feet
is explained by the fact that vertical angles were taken from six control
spots of known elevation instead of the two used in 1938. Improvements in
instruments and techniques also contributed to more accurate results. The
development of orbital measuring and surveying during the 1970s could
possibly result in further revisions in the height of Mount Hood and other
peaks of the Cascade Range but with minor exceptions, these would be
computation differences and not physical change of the summits themselves. The official height of Mount Hood in 1981 was 11,237 feet.

Mount Hood, Wasco County. A post office with this name was established May 27, 1872, with William Hollandsworth first postmaster. Other
postmasters were named McAtee, Shannon, Paquet, Hinkle and Steers.
The office was discontinued January 11, 1878. The writer has not been
able to associate this office with the place called Mount Hood in Hood River
County. Old maps show a community called Mount Hood in the general

vicinity of Tygh Valley, Wasco County, but not always in the same place. It is obvious that such a place was named because of the fine view of Mount Hood that is obtained in that part of the country.

Mount Hood, Yamhill County. John Richardson was a pioneer settler in Yamhill County and his claim was at the east foot of the Amity Hills about two miles north of the present site of Hopewell. A post office named Mount Hood was established October 14, 1854, with Richardson postmaster and it may be assumed that it was on or near this claim. Richardson probably named the office because of the view of the top of Mount Hood, although the mountain was a long way from the locality. This office was closed in January, 1862. Other postmasters included James M. Belcher and Daniel C. Doherty.

Mount Horeb, Marion County. This butte, with an elevation of nearly 4500 feet, lies about eight miles northeast of Mill City. An article published in the Salem *Capital Journal,* June 18, 1927, page 1, says that it was named in 1873 by David Smith, a local Bible enthusiast.

Mount Howard, Wallowa County. This was formerly Signal Peak, and lies southeast of Wallowa Lake. The name was changed in 1925 by the USBGN at the suggestion of J. Neilson Barry, of Portland, to honor Major-General Oliver Otis Howard (1830-1909), who graduated from West Point in 1850 and served with great distinction in the Civil War and throughout the Indian uprisings. He was not only brevetted for gallantry at the battle of Ezra Church, but received a vote of thanks of the Congress for heroic valor at the battle of Gettysburg, and the coveted Congressional Medal of Honor for distinguished bravery at the battle of Fair Oaks, where he lost his right arm. He was in command of the Department of the Columbia at the time of Chief Joseph's uprising in the Wallowa Valley, and took the field in person against that famous Indian, driving him into Montana. He was accused of dilatory tactics, but time has had the effect of establishing General Howard's reputation as a soldier. See Howard's *My Life and Experiences,* and Scott's *History of the Oregon Country,* volume II, page 332.

Mount Ireland, Baker and Grant Counties. This peak, which is on the summit of the Blue Mountains, has an elevation of 8330 feet. It was known for some years as Bald Mountain, but the name was changed to Ireland Mountain by the USBGN at the request of the USFS and eastern Oregon citizens. This was in honor of Henry Ireland who was for many years supervisor of the Whitman National Forest, and who died May 31, 1916. Before being connected with the USFS he was with the Department of the Interior. The form Mount Ireland was set in *Decision List 7502.*

Mount Isaac, Douglas County. Mount Isaac is about a mile west of Riddle. George W. Riddle of Roseburg informed the compiler that the mountain was named for Isaac Flint, a nearby pioneer settler of 1852.

Mount Isabelle, Jackson County. Mount Isabelle, elevation about 4500 feet, is ten miles south-southwest of Gold Hill. The peak was named for Isabelle Smith, daughter of a pioneer settler, Jakey Smith. He was an old squawman, who had squatted on a little ground on the east side of the mountain. In 1946 it was reported that there were some remains of the old Smith cabin and possibly a few apple trees in the clearing.

Mount Jefferson, Jefferson, Linn and Marion counties. This is the second highest peak in Oregon and has an elevation of 10,495 feet, according to the USGS. It was seen by Lewis and Clark on Sunday, March 30, 1806, from a point near the mouth of the Willamette, and it was named by them in honor of Thomas Jefferson, president of the United States. Since it was already named for a president, Hall J. Kelley did not attach a new name to it when he rechristened the Cascade Range Presidents Range and tried to change the names of the individual peaks. Kelley's geographic position of Mount Jefferson was in error, and so was Farnham's in his *Travels in the Great Western Prairies,* but the latter mistake in text is possibly due to a typographical error in notes, "44½" being misprinted "41½." See under Cascade Range for details of Kelley's scheme. Mount Jefferson is really in north latitude 44° 40' 28''. While the mountain has rarely been referred to by any other name, Thornton in *Oregon and California* mentions the fact that the British used the name Mount Vancouver but gives no reference. He may have seen either Arrowsmith's map of *British North America,* 1834, or the *Territory of Oregon* map drawn by Washington Hood for the Bureau of Topographical Engineers under Colonel J. J. Abert, dated 1838. On both maps Mount Jefferson is clearly shown as Mount Vancouver. However, Wheat in *Mapping the American West,* pp 87-88 states that Captain Hood apparently disregarded then recent North American sources and relied heavily on the 1834 Arrowsmith. It is important to note that David Douglas uses the name Mount Jefferson in his *Journal Kept by David Douglas* under date of April 19, 1825, and again on October 5, 1826, thus indicating that he, at least, did not know the mountain by the name Mount Vancouver. Douglas does, however, use the name Mount Vancouver in his journal on October 13, 1826, referring to a snowy peak south of Mount Hood, but it seems obvious from his text that he never saw such a mountain and mentions it only by hearsay. It is not clear just what mountain he refers to.

Mount Jefferson by any route is considered by mountaineers to be the most difficult of the major Oregon peaks. While there are some questions, the first ascent is generally credited to E. C. Cross and Ray L. Farmer via the south ridge on August 12, 1888. There were a limited number of other successful climbers until after the turn of the century when, on August 9, 1903, S. S. Mohler climbed from Jefferson Park alone. It is not clear whether he climbed the true north ridge or ascended alongside Jefferson Park Glacier which at that time was much larger. By either route it was a remarkable achievment. The best available information about Mount Jefferson is contained in the following publications: USGS Bulletin 252, *Geology and Water Resources of Central Oregon,* by Israel C. Russell; *Mineral Resources of Oregon,* volume II, number 1, and *Mazama,* volume II, number 3, for July, 1903; volume III, number 1, for March, 1907; volume IV, number 3, for December, 1914; volume V, number 2, for December, 1917, and volume VII, number 2, for December 1925. More recently, Don A. Hall in *On Top of Oregon,* 1975, gives a good layman's account of the geology along with the climbing history.

Mount June, Lane County. Mount June is about 15 miles due east of Cottage Grove and has an elevation of 4616 feet, according to the USGS. Mount June was named by Elijah Bristow because he saw snow on its summit in that month when he was making an early exploring trip.

Mount Mazama, Crater Lake National Park, Klamath County. Mount Mazama is the name of a prehistoric mountain, the caldera of which is now occupied by Crater Lake. For information about the discovery and naming of Crater Lake, see under that heading. The rim enclosing the lake formed part of the base of Mount Mazama. It was named for the Mazamas, the mountaineering organization of the Pacific Northwest, at the annual outing August 21, 1896. *Mazama* is the Spanish name of the mountain goat. See the publication *Mazama*, volume I, numbers 1 and 2. For information about Mount Mazama, *ibid.*, volume I, number 2, and the booklet on Crater Lake issued in 1922 by Mazamas. For geography of Crater Lake and picture of Mount Mazama restored, see USGS map of Crater Lake National Park. The highest points on the rim of Crater Lake are Hillman Peak, 8156 feet; Applegate Peak, 8135 feet; Garfield Peak, 8060 feet; Llao Rock, 8046 feet, and The Watchman, 8025 feet.

Mount McLoughlin, Jackson County. This mountain is called Mount McLoughlin on a map issued in 1838, accompanying the *Journal of an Exploring Tour Beyond the Rocky Mountains, in* 1835, '36 *and* '37, by the Reverend Samuel Parker. It was later called Mount Pit, for Pit or Pitt River, which was named for the pits dug by Indians to trap game. Peter Skene Ogden mentions the name Pit River in his journal for May 21, 1829, and spells it Pitts River. See *OHQ*, volume XI, page 394. Sir George Simpson in *Narrative of a Journey Round the World*, London, 1847, volume I, page 351, refers to Pit Mountain in this locality, "so called from the number of pitfalls dug by the neighbouring savages for the wild animals." T. J. Farnham in *Travels in the Great Western Prairies*, New York, 1843, page 96, refers to Mount McLaughlin, but is inaccurate as to location. Mount McLaughlin is shown on Wilkes' map in the *U. S. Exploring Expedition*, 1841. The name Mount Pitt appears for the first time on a map made by Charles Preuss, Fremont's cartographer, in 1843, but no mention is made of it by Fremont in his report. The compiler has never found any evidence that associates this name with that of William Pitt, British statesman. Lieutenant R. S. Williamson of the corps of topographical engineers explored the region of Pit River in 1855, and the report of this expedition, prepared by Lieutenant Henry L. Abbot, was published by the government in volume VI, of the Pacific Railroad Surveys *Reports.* Under date of August 8, 1855, the journal says: "We passed many pits six feet deep and lightly covered with twigs and grass. The river derives its name from these pits, which are dug by the Indians to entrap game. On this account Williamson always spelled the name with a single t, although on most maps it is written with two." Early settlers in the Rogue River Valley called the mountain Snowy Butte and Big Butte. As early as 1839 Hall J. Kelley tried to have the name John Quincy Adams applied to this mountain, but his plan for a Presidents Range fizzled out. See under Cascade Range. The name Mount Pitt came into common use about 1864, supposedly due to George H. Belden, a civil engineer in the employ of the United States surveyor general of Oregon. Klamath Indians called the mountain *M'laiksini Yaina,* or mountain with steep sides.

The name Mount McLoughlin was restored by the legislature in 1905, to honor Dr. John McLoughlin, and was recognized by the USBGN in 1912 through the efforts of Will G. Steel and George H. Himes. The spelling

McLaughlin is wrong. Dr. John McLoughlin, as chief factor of the Hudson's Bay Company, at Fort Vancouver, in 1824-46, possessed almost autocratic power in affairs in the Oregon country up to the time of the provisional government, and has therefore been called the first governor of Oregon. He was a man of broad views and ideas, generous and kind instincts and of large physical proportions. He was born in parish La Riviere du Loup, Canada, about 120 miles below Quebec, on the Saint Lawrence River, October 19, 1784. Young McLoughlin was educated in Canada and became a physician. He joined the North West Company, and became a partner and was one of the factors in charge of Fort William, the chief depot and factory of the North West Company, at the time of the consolidation with the Hudson's Bay Company. His wife was the widow of Alexander McKay, who had been killed in the *Tonquin* disaster at Clayoquot Sound, Vancouver Island, in June 1811. Dr. McLoughlin built Fort Vancouver in 1824-25, and there he created a farm of 3000 acres and established a sawmill and a flour mill. His district of the Hudson's Bay Company (the Columbia) grew to be profitable. There were numerous forts and posts tributary to Fort Vancouver, there being, in 1839, about twenty of these forts besides Fort Vancouver. In the development of the fur business, of agriculture and commerce, and in the government of the country, Dr. McLoughlin displayed rare powers of organization. He met the American traders with kindness, but with severe competition, and the American missionaries and settlers, with benevolence. He left the service of the Hudson's Bay Company in 1846, and became an American citizen at Oregon City May 30, 1849. After his resignation he carried on a milling and merchandise business at Oregon City, where he died September 3, 1857. Dr. McLoughlin's house at Oregon City, built in 1845-46, and occupied by him until his death, was moved, by the McLoughlin Memorial Association, to the bluff overlooking Willamette River, and restored to its first condition. It was dedicated as a permanent memorial September 5, 1909. For narrative, "Dr. John McLoughlin and His Guests," by T. C. Elliott, see *Washington Historical Quarterly*, volume II, pages 63-77; for biography, see F. V. Holman's *Dr. John McLoughlin; John McLoughlin: Patriarch of the Northwest*, by Robert C. Johnson, and Richard G. Montgomery's *The White-Headed Eagle*. For long list of references to published material about Dr. McLoughlin, see Scott's *History of the Oregon Country*, volume I, pages 295-96. McLoughlin's *Fort Vancouver Letters* have been published by the Hudson's Bay Record Society in three volumes. See also *Letters of Dr. John McLoughlin*, edited by Dr. Burt Brown Barker, 1948.

Mount Mitchell, Clackamas County. This mountain, elevation 5110 feet, was named for Roy Mitchell, a veteran of World War I, who was killed while fighting a forest fire August 20, 1919. The mountain was formerly called Oak Grove Mountain, an unsatisfactory name because there were no oak trees on the mountain, and also the name caused confusion with Oak Grove Butte, seven miles to the south. Oak Grove Mountain had been applied because the feature was near Oak Grove Fork Clackamas River.

Mount Moriah, Union County. This mountain is in township 1 south, range 41 east, and has an elevation of about 5500 feet. It is flat on top. In

early days it was called Stubblefield Mountain in compliment to Jasper Stubblefield who had a homestead west of the mountain in about 1878. Later
some Bible enthusiast named it for the place in Palestine, about which a
great deal seems to be unknown.

Mount Nebo, Douglas County. Moses viewed the Promised Land from
the summit of biblical Mount Nebo. The name was applied by pioneers to
the high ground in the bend of South Umpqua River that has a commanding view of the entire Roseburg area but affords an especial overlook of
fertile Garden Valley to the northwest.

Mount Pisgah, Lane County. Mount Pisgah is the prominent high nose
just southeast of the confluence of Coast and Middle forks Willamette
River. The Paul Bristow notes in the Lane County Pioneer Museum state
that Elijah Bristow bestowed this name because of the overview of the fertile upper Willamette Valley. Moses' view of the Promised Land was from
Mount Nebo, a summit of Biblical Mount Pisgah.

Mount Pisgah, Polk County. J. L. Ford, many years a resident of Dallas, wrote the compiler in August, 1927, as follows: "I find that Colonel
Cornelius Gilliam named the little butte southeast of Dallas 'Mt. Pisgah' for
a butte so named near his old home in Missouri, and probably also because
of his veneration for biblical names." Pisgah was a mountain of Abarim,
Moab, northeast of the Dead Sea. Mount Nebo was one of its summits.

Mount Pleasant, Linn County. Mount Pleasant is a descriptive name
for a nice viewpoint mostly in section 30, township 9 south, range 1 east.
This hill rises about 200 feet above the surrounding land but it pleased the
early settlers to call it a mount. The compiler does not know who was
responsible for this but probably members of the Irvine family who took up
property there in the early fifties. The locality was once known as the Irvine
District and it was called The Hill. There is a cemetery on the top of Mount
Pleasant and there are also nearby school grounds probably set aside by
Robert Irvine. The church property was set aside by Washington Crabtree
and it is reported that Ben Irvine raised the money for the various necessary buildings. A post office called Mount Pleasant was established in
August, 1874, with Elijah Richardson first of several postmasters. This
office was discontinued October 10, 1887. Mount Pleasant is about seven
miles northeast of Scio.

Mount Popocatepetl, Lane County. This mountain, elevation 1020
feet, is a well-known point in the Oregon Coast Range, but not one of the
highest. The peak was named about 1888 by R. O. Collier, a government
surveyor, because it was so hard to climb. The crew was smoking hot when
it reached the top. The original Mount Popocatepetl is the second highest
mountain in Mexico and is named with the Aztec word for smoking mountain. This information was furnished by E. A. Collier of Salem.

Mount Reuben, Douglas and Josephine counties. Mount Reuben is a
prominent peak about ten miles west of Glendale on the divide between the
waters of Cow Creek and those of Rogue River. It was named for Reuben
Field of Linn County, who was a member of Captain Jonathan Keeney's
company who fought Indians in this part of Oregon in 1855. While the
company was trying to cross Rogue River not far from this mountain Field

made a jocular prediction that the Indians would make an attack. The prediction was soon fulfilled and Mount Reuben and Reuben Creek nearby have since borne his name.

Mount Scott, Clackamas County. This well-known butte is in the southeast outskirts of Portland and is 1083 feet above sea level. It was named for Harvey Scott, editor of the *Oregonian,* by W. P. Keady, in 1889. In that year, and in 1890, Mr. Scott bought 335 acres of land on the north and west slopes of the hill. From that time until November, 1909, when he sold the land to Mount Scott Park Cemetery Corporation, the editor continually kept men working the soil and clearing away the forest and stumps. In this effort Mr. Scott expended considerable money, but he was determined to "tame that wild land," as he frequently expressed it. For a detailed description of Mr. Scott's life, see Scott's *History of the Oregon Country.* For W. P. Keady's part in the development and naming of Mount Scott, see editorial page of the *Oregon Journal,* September 24, 1928. There it is said that the butte was once called Mount Zion.

Mount Scott, Douglas County. Mount Scott post office was established October 14, 1854, and discontinued October 5, 1857. Andrew J. Chapman was postmaster. It was reestablished May 8, 1879, with Matilda Blakely postmaster and finally closed September 14, 1886. An army map of December, 1887, shows the place at a point on North Umpqua River a few miles west of what is now Glide. The office was of course named for Scott Mountain, a prominent point a little to the northeast, which was in turn named for Captain Levi Scott.

Mount Scott, Crater Lake National Park, Klamath County. This mountain lies east of Crater Lake and is one of the important peaks of the Cascade Range. It was named for Levi Scott, a pioneer of 1844, and the founder of Scottsburg, in Douglas County. For additional information see under that heading. Mount Scott has an elevation of 8938 feet. The Klamath Indian name for Mount Scott was *Tum-sum-ne,* according to the treaty of 1864.

Mount Sylvania, Multnomah County. Mount Sylvania is in the extreme southwest part of the county. It has an elevation of about 950 feet. The Pacific Highway West skirts its northwest shoulder. The name is derived from *Silvanus,* the deity or spirit of the Italian woodlands. Silvanus is not wholly associated with the wild woodlands, but those near civilization, and partly cleared, so to speak, or the bordering and fringing woodlands. Silvanus' name came from *silva,* Latin name for wood. His name is generally misspelled, Sylvanus, and from this we have the name Sylvan and Sylvania. The post office list of 1853 shows Mountsylvania, an office not far from the present site of Metzger, and a short distance from the mountain now known by the same name. The writer has been unable to learn who established the name, either for the post office or for the mountain, but he was told by the late Colonel Henry E. Dosch of Hillsdale that the mountain had been so called since pioneer days. Information furnished the compiler by postal authorities in Washington in 1927 does not agree with that printed in the list of post offices in the *Oregonian,* March 26, 1853. The records in Washington indicate that the name of the office was in two words, Mount Sylvania. This office was established August 6, 1852, and was discontinued November 14, 1854. It operated again for a short time in 1856. Israel Mitchell was the only postmaster. John B. Preston's *Map of Oregon and Washington* of 1856 shows the name in still another style, Montsylvania. The compiler has been unable to reconcile these discrepancies.

Mount Tabor, Multnomah County. Mount Tabor was named by Plympton Kelly, son of Clinton Kelly, pioneer resident of Portland. He had been reading *Napoleon and His Marshals,* by Joel T. Headley, and was impressed among other things by the battle fought by the French against the Moslems on the Plain of Esdraelon not far from the base of Mount Tabor in Palestine. He therefore named the hill near his home Mount Tabor for the mount in the Holy Land. It was first planned to call Mount Tabor in Oregon Mount Zion. See OPA *Transactions,* 1887, page 60. Mount Tabor post office was in operation many years.

Mount Talapus, Multnomah County. This peak is between the headwaters of Tanner Creek and north branches of Bull Run River. It bears the Indian name for coyote, or barking wolf of the plains. The coyote was a sort of deity or supernatural being in Indian mythology. Chinook jargon, *Talapus;* Chinook Indian, *Italipas;* Yakima Indian, *Telipa.* This peak was once called Shellrock Mountain, but the USBGN was prevailed upon to change the name because there were more than enough Shellrocks already. See under Coyote Creek.

Mount Thielsen, Douglas and Klamath counties. This mountain is one of the most remarkable in the state because of a great pinnacle or spire that forms its summit. Its elevation is 9173 feet. In early days it was known as the Big Cowhorn in contradistinction to Little Cowhorn farther north, now called Cowhorn. It is also said to have been called Diamond Peak, but the compiler has seen no written evidence of this. About 1872 it was named Mount Thielsen by John A. Hurlburt of Portland, in honor of Hans Thielsen, prominent pioneer railroad engineer and builder. For references to Thielsen, see Scott's *History of the Oregon Country.* For information about the mountain, see article by Ira A. Williams in *Mazama,* December, 1921. The Indian name of the mountain was *His-chok-wol-as.* See also under Cascade Range.

Mount Vernon, Grant County. Herman Oliver of John Day stated that David W. Jenkins, an early settler, owned a prize black stallion named Mt. Vernon. Both the town and the rocky eminence just to the north were named for the horse and the animal was stabled in a small stone building constructed especially for him as protection against Indians and thieves. During the Indian War of 1878 neighbors crowded into the stout little fortress along with the horse. In 1971 the building was still standing, unfazed by ninety years, just north of US 26 about one and one half miles east of Mount Vernon. The post office was established May 14, 1877 with Wm. J. Gray postmaster.

Mount Washington, Deschutes and Linn counties. In elevation, Mount Washington may be counted as one of the lesser peaks of the Cascade Range, but its unusual appearance and the fact that it is difficult to climb make it an important mountain. It has an elevation of 7802 feet. It doubtless received its name because of the proximity of Mount Jefferson, but who applied the name, and when, is apparently unknown. It was of course named for George Washington. It was not mentioned by any early explorers, or shown on early maps. The top part of Mount Washington is a rocky spire that defied all attempts at climbing until August 26, 1923, when six boys from Bend managed to reach the summit. In recent years it has become one of the popular ascents as varying routes on all three main ridges and faces range from moderate to extremely difficult. The first attempts to climb the peak are covered in *Mazama* for 1922 and 1923. Don A. Hall in *On Top of Oregon,* 1975, has an excellent summary of the geology and climbing history.

Mount Wilson, Clackamas and Wasco counties. This mountain, with an elevation 5595 feet, is an important lookout station on the summit of the Cascade Range. It was named for Bruce Wilson of Portland, when he was supervisor of forest areas in the northern part of the Cascade Range in Oregon. Older maps show the mountain as Tamarack Mountain. This name was unsatisfactory because of duplication, and USFS map makers changed it to Mount Wilson. At that time there was no rule against naming geographic features for living members of the Forest Service. However, Wilson protested against the change, but without result. Dee Wright of Eugene, formerly a member of the USFS, informed the compiler that there was no doubt that the mountain was named for Bruce Wilson, because Wilson told him of the circumstances. Robert Bruce Wilson, son of Dr. and Mrs. R. B. Wilson, was born in Portland on June 2, 1877. He graduated from Yale in 1901, and received a degree from the Yale Forest School in 1904. He entered the USFS and before he resigned, in 1908, he was supervisor of the forests of the Cascade Range between Columbia and McKenzie rivers. He died near Medford on June 19, 1919. He was not married.

Mount Yoran, Lane County. The top of Mount Yoran, elevation 7132 feet, is just west of the summit of the Cascade Range north of Diamond Lake. It was named for Louise C. Yoran of Eugene, who was at the time employed by the USFS. She married C. A. E. Whitton of Eugene.

Mount Zion, Lane County. According to the Paul Bristow notes in the Lane County Pioneer Museum collection, Mount Zion was named by his grandfather, Elijah Bristow, at the same time that he named Lost Creek just to the west.

Mountain, Josephine County. The place called Mountain, obviously for the surroundings, was a few miles north of Grants Pass in the southwest part of township 34 south, range 5 west. It was at or near the location of the Lucky Queen mine. The *Oregon Almanac,* 1915, says it was a lumbering community. Mountain post office was established November 30, 1908, with Allison Burnham first postmaster. The office was closed to Threepines on March 31, 1913, apparently having served its usefulness. Mountain was just southeast of Sexton Mountain.

Mountain Home, Washington County. Mountain Home is a locality or neighborhood about three miles south of Scholls. There is a Mountain Home School. The place was named for the Mountain Home farm of the Schmeltzer family, well known in that part of the country. Mountain Home

School is on the northwest slopes of the Chehalem Mountains. It was formerly called Schmeltzer School and the place where it stands was known as Fir Clearing. For a history of these matters, see Hillsboro *Argus,* December 24, 1931.

Mountain House, Yamhill County. Mountain House appears to have been an institution that moved westward as better transportation became available. According to available information it was first the home of Wilson Carl, two miles west of Carlton, but later there was another locality called Mountain House about seven miles northwest of Carlton and the same distance southwest of Yamhill. The compiler has not been able to learn the exact relationship, if any, between these various establishments. According to post office records Mountain House post office was established October 19, 1866, with Charles W. Cogle first postmaster. Wilson Carl became postmaster November 9, 1868, and Lewis C. Thompson took over the office in January, 1874. Mountain House post office was closed in November, 1874, but the use of the place name continued a good many years after that. It is assumed that the Mountain House was named because it was where travelers stopped before climbing westward over the Coast Range toward Tillamook.

Mountain Sheep Creek, Wallowa County. This creek flows into Snake River in township 4 north, range 48 east. It was named by Charles Holmes and R. F. Stubblefield who were looking for winter range and saw mountain sheep on the range above the stream.

Mountaindale, Washington County. Mountaindale is a descriptive name applied to a locality where East Fork Dairy Creek emerges from the hills at the north border of the Tualatin Valley. Mountain Dale post office was established June 11, 1873, with David O. Quick postmaster. The name was changed to Mountaindale probably in 1895, as the *Postal Guide* issued at the end of that year is the first to contain the name in one word. The office was discontinued in July, 1935.

Mouse Island Lake, Columbia and Multnomah counties. This lake is on Sauvie Island. It received its peculiar name because there was an island in the lake infested with field mice.

Mouth of the Willamette, Multnomah County. This pioneer post office was established on Sauvie Island, close to the south end, June 30, 1851, with Ellis Walker postmaster. It was first put on the list for Clark County, Washington, but it never was actually in that county. The name of the office was changed to Sauvies Island on March 5, 1852, and on May 19, 1853, it was moved to the Washington County, Oregon, list with Benjamin Howell postmaster. The locality is now in Multnomah County. See under Post Office Bar.

Mowich, Klamath County. *Mowich* is a Chinook jargon word meaning deer and it has been applied to a number of geographic features in Oregon. The word is used for a station name on the Southern Pacific Cascade line about twelve miles north of Chemult, and while there are doubtless deer in the locality many of these station names are Indian words selected because of their pleasing sound. Mowich post office was established January 3, 1936, with R. J. Watt postmaster. It was closed March 15, 1948.

Moyina Hill, Klamath County. Moyina Hill is a prominent landmark about midway between Klamath Falls and Dairy and north of Olene. Many years ago Will G. Steel told the compiler that the name was a Klamath Indian word meaning big mountain. The spelling Moyina is that used on maps of the USFS. Apparently it comes from the Indian word *yaini*, meaning mountain, with the prefix *muni* for big or bulky.

Mud Creek, Wallowa County. Mud Creek flows into Grande Ronde River in township 5 north, range 43 east. It was named for the mud springs and mud flats at its head. It has been known as Mud Creek for a long time.

Muddy Creek, Jefferson and Wasco counties. This stream rises in Jefferson County east of Ashwood and flows into Currant Creek, a tributary of John Day River. Its occasional turbidity caused its name. H. H. Bancroft in his *History of Oregon,* volume I, page 787, says that when in 1862 Joseph H. Sherar and his party were packing into the John Day mines, they named this as well as a number of other features.

Muddy Creek, Lane and Linn counties. This stream drains the eastern floor of the Willamette Valley. It rises in the hills east of Coburg and flows generally to the Willamette River, finally joining it east of Corvallis. It is a sluggish stream, and it is no surprise that the pioneers named it as they did. The name Muddy Creek appears in the *Oregonian* as early as November 7, 1857. Muddy Creek has two main tributaries, Dry Muddy Creek and Little Muddy Creek. There was a railroad station called Muddy, where the stream crossed the main line of the Southern Pacific, but that station is now Alford. There is another Muddy Creek, of similar characteristics, draining the western part of the Willamette Valley and flowing into Marys River south of Corvallis.

Muddy Station, Linn County. A post office with the name Muddy Station was established February 24, 1874, with William Landreth postmaster. Thomas Alford, Sr., became postmaster on November 5, 1874, and the office was closed February 19, 1875. Muddy Station was a place on the Oregon & California Railroad about four miles northeast of Harrisburg at the place where the railroad crossed Muddy Creek. Most old maps show the place as Muddy, but the official post office name was Muddy Station. Some time after the turn of the century the name of the station was changed to Alford in compliment to Thomas Alford mentioned above. Alford was a pioneer of 1850 and a well-known resident of Linn County. For a biography of Alford, see *Historical Atlas Map of Marion & Linn Counties,* 1878, page 55, wherein it is stated that the village of Liverpool was situated on Alford property. See under the heading Liverpool.

Mudjekeewis Mountain, Klamath County. Mudjekeewis Mountain, maximum elevation 6616 feet, is in the Cascade Range, on the west border of Klamath County, about four miles south of the southwest corner of Crater Lake National Park. It was named for the Indian deity, Mudjekeewis, spirit of the four winds, made famous by Henry W. Longfellow as the father of Hiawatha. As applied to the feature in Klamath County, the name is relatively modern. It may have been used because the mountain is in an unusually windy situation or because some forest ranger landed in the clutches of poetical romance.

Mugwump Lake, Lake County. One of the Warner Lakes. Will G. Steel told the compiler it was named Mugwump because it was so changeable from wet to dry and back again.

Muir Creek, Wallowa County. Muir Creek is a small stream in a canyon draining into Snake River in township 1 north, range 51 east. It was named for a Scottish prospector, one Muir, who worked in the canyon with a fellow countryman.

Mule, Harney County. Mule post office was established February 11, 1895, with James F. Mahon postmaster. It was in operation until February 14, 1901. It was reestablished May 13, 1903, with Lucy R. Mahon postmaster, and continued until January 14, 1906. In December, 1945, Archie McGowan wrote the compiler in substance as follows: "Mule post office was at the ranch home of James F. Mahon, early pioneer and noted mule breeder at his famous Anderson Valley ranch 55 miles southeast of Burns. The office was likely discontinued in 1901 because of lack of patrons. Its reinstatement in 1903 with Lucy R. Mahon, wife of James F. Mahon, was justified by the last wave of homesteaders that spread over the West. Mahon was a prominent Democrat and the appointment of his wife as postmaster by Theodore Roosevelt in 1903 was likely political. During the last years of the post office, Mahon had one John Hoss working on the ranch, who of course was a patron of the office. It was quite common to note letters and other mail addressed to John Hoss, Mule, Oregon. I think Ripley has used this item in his pictures."

Mule Creek, Curry County. Mule Creek is in the extreme northeast corner of the county and flows into Rogue River. Many years ago William H. Packwood told the compiler that the stream was named in the summer of 1852 when a company of soldiers from Fort Orford was trying to open a trail along Rogue River. Packwood was a soldier in the party. Lieutenant R. S. Williamson rode a mule named John, and when it was turned loose to graze near this stream, it wandered off and despite a search, the animal was not recovered. The stream was named John Mule Creek because of this incident. Old maps show the name in full, but in recent years the name has been reduced to Mule Creek. There is a Mule Mountain nearby. Packwood also said that a few years later he found the mule at Siletz in the possesion of an Indian, who had apparently salvaged it. Stories to the effect that the stream was named for a prospector John Mule cannot be substantiated.

Muleshoe Ridge, Wheeler County. Muleshoe Ridge is east of Service Creek, and Muleshoe Creek is just east of the ridge. J. H. Tilley of Service Creek told the compiler that there was a story in the neighborhood to the effect that someone found a muleshoe near the head of this creek, which accounts for the name. On the other hand it is also said that the ridge itself is shaped something like a muleshoe with the toe to the north. The reader may take his choice of the explanations.

Mulino, Clackamas County. Mulino was named by C. T. Howard in 1882, and the name was a corruption of the Spanish word, *molino,* which means mill. Postal authorities would not accept the name Molino because it was too much like the nearby Molalla. There was a flour mill at Mulino in pioneer days, and the place was known as Howards Mill. The mill building, still standing in 1981 although enlarged and altered, is probably the oldest surviving industrial building in Oregon. Mulino post office was established March 21, 1882, with James G. Foster first postmaster.

Multnomah, Multnomah County. The community of Multnomah took its name from Multnomah County. The Oregon Electric Railway was built from Portland south to Salem in 1907 and began operation in 1908 and it was the policy of the officials to apply Indian names, wherever possible, to the stations as they were established. For the origin of Multnomah, see under Multnomah County. The post office at Multnomah was established February 7, 1912, with Nelson Thomas first postmaster. It was closed April 15, 1940 but has operated since as a Portland station.

Multnomah Channel, Columbia and Multnomah counties. For many years the channel between Sauvie Island and the mainland to the west was known as Willamette Slough, probably because its southern entrance was close to the mouth of Willamette River. Commercial interests and citizens interested in historical matters prevailed upon the USBGN to adopt the name Multnomah Channel for this stream. Multnomah Channel was discovered on October 28, 1792, by W. R. Broughton, and named Calls River, apparently for Sir John Call. See Meany's *Vancouver's Discovery of Puget Sound,* page 261. Lewis and Clark called this channel Wappato Inlet because it lay to the west of what they called Wappato Island, now Sauvie Island. Wilkes used the name Warrior Branch because the stream joined the Columbia at Warrior Point. Sauvie Island was referred to as Multnomah Island by Wilkes.

Multnomah County. Multnomah County was created December 22, 1854, and was taken from Washington and Clackamas counties as they then existed. Multnomah County has a land area, according to the Bureau of the Census, of 424 square miles and is the smallest county in the state. Multnomah is an Indian name. The word is first used by Lewis and Clark in their journals for November 3, 1805, with the style Mulknomah, referring to the stream now known as the Willamette. On the following day the explorers record a village of *Mulknomans* on the east side of what is now known as Sauvie Island. On April 2, 1806, the stream is mentioned again in the spelling Multnomah, and this form is used on the maps prepared by the party, not only for the stream but also for the village on the east side of Sauvie Island. Coues thinks that the name as applied to the stream meant only that part of the Willamette below the falls, and says the word is a corruption of *nematlnomaq,* meaning down river. The Multnomah Indians were of the Chinookan tribe. The map of Lewis and Clark indicated that Multnomah River headed about where Great Salt Lake is now known to be. The map is said to have established the 42nd parallel as the boundary with Spain.

Multnomah Falls, Multnomah County. The compiler has been unable to learn who named these falls on Multnomah Creek, but Geo. H. Himes said that they were called Multnomah Falls in the 1860s, and he was of the opinion that S. G. Reed may have named them with the idea of trying to popularize points along the river for steamboat excursions. Lewis and Clark, Wilkes, and many others mentioned the falls on the south bank of the Columbia between the mouth of the Sandy and the Cascades, but no individual names seem to have been applied. Pioneer estimates of the height of Multnomah Falls, amounting to as much as 1000 feet, were grossly in error. In 1916 the USGS made detailed computations of the height of the falls and found the following elevations above standard sea level:

Top of upper falls, 659.8 feet.
Base of upper falls, 117.5 feet.
Top of lower falls, 103.1 feet.
Base of lower falls, 39.8 feet.
Total drop of two falls, 620.0 feet.
Floor of concrete bridge, above lower falls, 134.7 feet.

Multorpor Butte, Clackamas County. This prominent butte, elevation 4657 feet, lies just south of Government Camp, and is easily seen from the Mount Hood Loop Highway. It was named for the Multorpor Republican Club of Portland. The name Multorpor was made by combining the first parts of Multnomah, Oregon and Portland. The name Multiple for this mountain is wrong.

Munkers, Linn County. This station west of Scio was named for the Munkers family, prominent early-day settlers of Linn County. One of the family owned the land where the station was established.

Munra Point, Multnomah County. Munra Point was named in 1915 in honor of "Grandma" Munra, who for many years kept a railroad eating house at Bonneville, and later at Meacham. She was a widely known pioneer woman, and her name was attached to the point in question by a committee representing various Oregon historical organizations. Munra Point is just south of Bonneville, between Tanner Creek and Moffett Creek. The name has been approved by the USBGN. In 1928 the Union Pacific Railroad named a station (siding) east of Pendleton for "Grandma" Munra.

Munsel Lake, Lane County. This lake is about two miles north of Florence. It was named for David L. Munsel, who operated a small furniture factory and repair shop on Munsel Creek. Munsel, who was a French cabinet maker, also spelled his name Munselle, but Munsel is now the well established style for the name of the lake and creek.

Munson Creek, Tillamook County. Munson Creek and Munson Falls about six miles south of Tillamook were both named for Goran Munson who came from Michigan and settled along the creek in 1889. This information was provided by Mr. Munson's daughter, Mrs. D. H. Near of Tillamook.

Munson Point, Crater Lake National Park, Klamath County. This point and the valley just to the east were named by Captain Oliver C. Applegate for a Doctor Munson, physician at Klamath Indian Agency, who died from over-exertion while climbing near the point in 1871. See article in Klamath *Record*, March 22, 1918.

Murder Creek, Linn County. This stream is just northeast of Albany. It owes its name to the fact that on February 8, 1862, Andrew J. Pate killed

George Lamb near its banks, and Pate was hanged at Albany on May 17, 1862. Pate was the first man to be hanged in Linn County. Additional details about this murder are contained in a very rare pamphlet in the files of the Oregon Historical Society, which gives Pate's confession. The stream has been called Fisher Creek and also Powell Creek for nearby settlers, but Murder Creek seems well established and is used on government maps.

Murderers Creek, Grant County. Colonel William Thompson, in *Reminiscences of a Pioneer,* page 62, says this stream was named in the 1860s because Indians killed a party of eight prospectors who were exploring its banks. For additional information about the naming of this stream see news article by Martha Stewart in Canyon City *Blue Mountain Eagle,* October 21, 1927.

Murphy, Josephine County. B. O. R. Murphy settled on Applegate River May 7, 1854, and took up a donation land claim. The stream running through the claim became known as Murphy Creek. On January 7, 1875, Jacob O. C. Wimer had a post office established called Murphy in honor of the early settler.

Murphy Bar, Polk County. Murphy Bar is on the south bank of the Willamette River about three miles southeast of Independence. It was named for William Murphy who lived nearby many years ago.

Murphy Creek, Wallowa County. This creek was named for one Murphy, a pioneer trapper and hunter, who built a cabin on the creek. In 1926 part of this cabin was still standing. The stream flows into Minam River.

Mussel Creek, Curry County. This stream empties into the Pacific about two miles north of Sisters Rocks. Reinhart, in *The Golden Frontier,* page 80, says it was named after a small band of Indians. They apparently were part of the Takelma tribe.

Mutton Mountains, Wasco County. These mountains are in the northeast part of the Warm Springs Indian Reservation and have an extreme elevation of about 4500 feet. The eastern slopes are excessively steep down to the Deschutes River, and the group is so cut off from the routes of travel that it is little visited. Pierce Mays, a well-known resident of Wasco County, said that the Mutton Mountains were named for the large number of mountain sheep that formerly lived thereon. That eastern Oregon had at one time plenty of mountain sheep is attested by J. E. Snow, whose statement to that effect appears on the editorial page of the *Oregonian* for December 10, 1925. The use of the name Mutton Mountains began before 1855. There is a good deal of information about the mountain sheep in Vernon Bailey's *Mammals and Life Zones of Oregon,* beginning on page 63. The principal variety in Oregon is known as the rimrock or lava bed sheep, credited to David Douglas as of 1829, but mentioned by Ogden as early as 1825.

Muttonchop Butte, Klamath County. Muttonchop Butte, elevation 5489 feet, is about ten miles north of Chemult and west of the Southern Pacific Cascade line. The first explanation of the name that the compiler can find is that when the area was mapped by the USFS about 1930, the contour lines of this butte made a very fair representation of a mutton chop. This may be seen by inspecting the USGS map of the Muttonchop Butte quadrangle. In June, 1944, R. W. Crawford, supervisor of the Deschutes National Forest at Bend, wrote the compiler that he had been told that about 1913 a German took up a timber claim on Spruce Creek near this butte. This man grew some rather natty side whiskers and was generally called Old Muttonchops because of the hirsute adornment. Muttonchop Butte is said to have been named for this local settler. This story sounds reasonable.

Myers Creek, Curry County. Myers Creek is just south of Cape Sebastian and is a well-known stream flowing into Pacific Ocean. The name is variously spelled, but the form Myers has been adopted by USBGN. This was done on the recommendation of F. S. Moore, formerly county assessor of Curry County. In a letter to the compiler, dated March 29, 1932, Mr. Moore says that the stream bears the name of one Myers who settled nearby in the late 1850s and mined the beach sands. Myers abandoned his cabin. When F. S. Moore was about seven years old his father moved the family into the Myers cabin, and used the building while he built a new house on the Moore property about a mile to the north.

Myrick, Umatilla County. Myrick is a station on the Northern Pacific Railway northeast of Pendleton. The place was originally known as Warren, but was changed to Myrick because of confusion with Warren in Columbia County. Samuel Jackson Myrick came to Oregon from Missouri in the spring of 1884 and settled near the station now known as Myrick. When it was found necessary to abandon the name of Warren it was decided to name the place for Myrick.

Myrtle Creek, Douglas County. Myrtle Creek was named for the groves of Oregon myrtle in the vicinity. The site was first settled upon by James B. Weaver, in 1851, who sold it to J. Bailey for a yoke of oxen. Bailey sold to Lazarus Wright in 1852, who sold it to John Hall in 1862. Hall laid out the town in 1865. Myrtle Creek post office was established on February 18, 1854, with Lazarus Wright first postmaster. In the late 1860s a movement was on foot to divide Douglas County, and Myrtle Creek had hopes of becoming county seat for the south part. This county division was not made. For information about Oregon myrtle, see under Myrtle Point.

Myrtle Park, Grant and Harney counties. In 1942, Archie McGowan of Burns became interested in the problem of the origin of this name for the natural park southwest of Canyon City. There were no myrtle trees in that part of Oregon and a botanical significance seemed improbable. Mr. McGowan concluded that the locality might have been named for Minnie Myrtle Miller, wife of Joaquin Miller. He wrote an interesting letter on the subject in Canyon City *Eagle* for April 10, 1942. As to whether or not Mrs. Minnie Myrtle Miller ever lived in Grant County, the evidence seems positive that she did. Wagner's *Joaquin Miller* indicates that Mrs. Miller lived with the poet in Canyon City and the two youngest children were born there. In 1943 Mr. McGowan verified his theory. He found living near the park one Andy Pierce, aged 90, sound of mind and body, who joined the Canyon City gold rush in 1864. Pierce had lived in that vicinity ever since and was well acquainted with the Miller family. He made the positive statement that the Millers spent some time in an old cabin in the park and that Joaquin Miller named the place in honor of his wife.

Myrtle Point, Coos County. The early history of this place is given by Dodge in his *History of Coos and Curry Counties,* chapter XIV. It was a natural rendezvous of the Indians. Henry Meyers laid out the town about 1861 and named it Meyersville. It remained a paper community until 1866 when Chris Lehnherr bought the property and built a small flour mill. He named the place Ott in compliment to an old friend and his son. Lehnherr became the first postmaster in August, 1872. Binger Hermann and Edward Bender became interested in the townsite and suggested that the name be changed to Myrtle Point. Postal records show that the name of the post office Ott was changed to Myrtle Point in December, 1876. The name was due to the geographical location and also to the fact that the community was started where there was an abundance of myrtle. This Oregon or Coos Bay myrtle is the same as California laurel, *Umbellularia californica.* It is an evergreen tree, distinguished by a strong camphor odor. In favorable conditions it grows 80 feet high and four feet in diameter. In the dense forest it grows with a clean straight trunk, but elsewhere and more commonly it has a thick trunk and large low limbs. Its range in Oregon is in the Coast Range and Siskiyou Mountains. It has a beautiful grain and excels as a cabinet and finishing wood. It grows extensively in southwest Oregon.

Namorf, Malheur County. Namorf station west of Harper was named for George Froman, a local resident, by spelling his name backward.

Nansene, Wasco County. The name Nansene seems to have been derived from an Indian word used to describe Fifteenmile Creek. Fremont gives the style Tinanens Creek, but it is doubtless the same as Nansene. Nansene post office was established May 17, 1880, with William C. Adams postmaster. It was on the ridge southeast of Dufur and the name has been perpetuated by Nansene School. Nansene post office was closed in February, 1894.

Nan-Scott Lake, Linn County. This lake near Marion Forks was named for Nan and Scott Young, long time local residents.

Napton, Malheur County. This station was named for J. S. Napton, a local resident. The place is on the Union Pacific Railroad 17 miles south of Nyssa.

Narrows, Harney County. Narrows is a descriptive name suggested by the narrow channel connecting Malheur and Harney lakes. When these lakes are full this is the only point for a considerable distance where they may be crossed. There has been a bridge over the Narrows for many years. There was a post office nearby called Narrows. C. A. Haines started the community about 1892. A post office named Springer was established in this area in August, 1889, with Lewis B. Springer postmaster. The name was changed to Narrows in April, 1892.

Nash Crater, Linn County. This crater in the Cascade Range was named for Wallis Nash. See under Nashville. The railroad enterprise in which Nash was interested, projected a line into eastern Oregon, and several geographic features near the survey were named for the promoters. Nash Crater is just south of the junction of the North and South Santiam highways and has an elevation of 4770 feet. Little Nash Crater, elevation 4101 feet, is just west of the junction.

Nashville, Lincoln County. Nashville was named for Wallis Nash, a native of England, who visited Oregon in 1877, and came to this state to settle in 1879. He was prominently identified with various enterprises in Benton and Lincoln counties, including the construction of the railroad between Corvallis and Yaquina Bay. He lived at Nashville for many years. For interesting notes on his career, see his *A Lawyer's Life on Two Continents.* Nash was born near London August 16, 1837, and died at Nashville in 1926.

Nasoma, Washington County. Nasoma was a station on the Oregon Electric Railway southwest of Tualatin. When the railroad was built many Indian names were applied to the stations. The word Nasoma was apparently derived from one of the bands of Indians that originally lived near Port Orford in Curry County. The name was used by the railway company because it had a pleasing sound and not for any local reason.

Natal, Columbia County. The name Natal was once applied to a post office situated on Nehalem River between Pittsburg and Mist. This post office was established October 2, 1889, with Roderick D. Cole first and only postmaster. The office was discontinued to Mist January 26, 1891. Omar C. Spencer had a chance to dig up some evidence about the name Natal and on March 2, 1949, reported, among other things, that it was Mr. Cole's notion that the name of the office should honor N. C. Dale, who had owned land in the locality in the early 1870s and had accommodated his neighbors by fetching their mail from Mist to his own home. He served as county clerk for Columbia County from July, 1884, until July, 1888. Dale's first name was Nathaniel and the best available information is that the name Natal was an arbitrary contraction of his first name. The locality is still called Natal and the name is used by Natal Grange.

Natron, Lane County. Natron is the name of the native carbonate of sodium, or mineral alkali. Natrolite is a hydrous silicate of aluminum and sodium common in cavities in basalt and other igneous rock. It is generally of a white color and transparent or translucent. Natron station, east of Eugene, is said to owe its name to a confusion of the two substances described above. Richard Koehler, of Portland, for many years an official of the Southern Pacific Company and its predecessors, told the compiler that some natrolite was found near the station, and it was planned to name the place on that account, but owing to a mistake, the name Natron was selected.

Naylox, Klamath County. Naylox was the name of a pioneer stage station or roadhouse on the east shore of Upper Klamath Lake about midway of Klamath Falls and Modoc Point. It was not far from the well-known Barkley Spring. For story about this old stopping place by Mary W. Case, see magazine section of the *Oregon Journal,* March 17, 1946. Naylox took its name from Naylox Ridge, a prominent geographic feature that stands just east of the highway. The Klamath Indian word *Nilaksh* or *Nilaks* was the basis of the name Naylox, meaning Daylight Mountain, or mountain over which the sun rose. White settlers also used the style Nailix, but the form Naylox has been in general use for the locality for many decades. For additional information, see Gatschet's *Dictionary of the Klamath Language,* page

243. Naylox post office was established February 7, 1882, with Leroy S. Dyar first postmaster. The office was finally closed June 30, 1896.

Neacoxie Creek, Clatsop County. This is a stream on Clatsop Plains. Its course has undergone several changes since pioneer days, largely because of drifting sands. Part of the stream flows north from Cullaby Lake, then around a hairpin bend near Camp Rilea. During recent years the south part of the stream has drained Neacoxie Lake southward into the estuary of Necanicum River. If the long sand ridges shift positions, the course of the stream may be interfered with still further. The name is derived from *Neahcoxie,* the Clatsop Indian name of the village at the mouth of the creek. The form *Neacoxie* has been adopted by the USBGN, and is in general use. George Gibbs, in *Alphabetical Vocabulary of the Chinook Language,* New York, 1863, says this name, which he spells *Ni-a-kok-si,* is said to refer to the small pine trees near the mouth of the stream. Neacoxie Lake is sometimes called Sunset Lake, but that is not the historic name. Sunset Lake is a style that has resulted from real estate activity.

Neahkahnie Mountain, Tillamook County. There has at times been some controversy about the meaning of the Indian name of this bold headland north of Nehalem River. Neahkahnie is a place of romance and mystery. Tales of buried treasure, marooned Spaniards, galleons laden with beeswax candles and suchlike, have drawn the attention of the white man for three-quarters of a century. Chunks of engraved wax and curious letters on half-buried stones have been all the more mysterious. Joseph H. Frost's diary of 1841 in *OHQ,* volume XXXV, page 242, says: "This mountain is called Ne-a-karny—after one of the deities of these natives, who, it is said by them, a long time since, while sitting on this mountain, turned into a stone, which stone, it is said, presents a colossal figure of Ne-akarny to this day. And in our passage over the mountain, which is a prairie on the side next the ocean, we discovered a stone which presented a figure of this kind." Silas B. Smith says in *OHQ,* volume I, page 321, that *Ne-kah-ni* meant the precipice overlooking the ocean, the abode of *Ekahni,* the supreme god. Lee and Frost in *Ten Years in Oregon,* 1844, page 343, give the Clatsop word *Acarna,* meaning chief deity. Mrs. Ed Gervais, a Nehalem Indian, is authority for the statement that the name *Neahkahnie* had its origin in the word used by the supposed Spanish wreck survivors when they saw elk on the side of the mountain, and exclaimed: "Carne," meaning meat. This is probably fanciful. *Neahkahnie* is one of a number of Indian names beginning with the prefix *Ne-,* which had to do with villages or places where certain tribes lived. These names include also Necanicum, Nehalem, Neskowin, Netarts, Nestucca and Neacoxie. John Gill informed the writer that a Clatsop Indian told him *ne* meant a place. Neahkahnie Mountain presents a bold front to the Pacific, and stands 1795 feet above the water, an imposing sight. The best collection of romances and facts about the place is in the book by S. J. Cotton, *Stories of Nehalem.* Thomas H. Rogers' *Nehalem* should be read by all interested in Neahkahnie. It contains an excellent picture of the glyphic rock. For additional references see under Nehalem.

Neal Camp Burn, Jackson County. This spot in the northeast part of the county was named for Carl B. Neal, an early USFS supervisor of Umpqua National Forest.

Neal Creek, Hood River County. Peter Neal ran a saw mill on what is now known as Neal Creek in the early 1880s, and the stream was named for him. He built a dam near what was later the Wilson Fike farm and the mill pond was a favorite fishing place.

Neawanna Creek, Clatsop County. This stream flows into the estuary of Necanicum River just north of Seaside. In earlier days it was generally called Wahanna Creek, although some people called it Ohannah or Wahannah in the belief that it was named for a member of the R. W. Morrison family whose name was Hannah. This etymology always seemed dubious to the compiler, and was without substantial confirmation. The result of this variety of names was confusion. In 1930 Miss Clara C. Munson of Warrenton interested herself in the business of getting a better form of name for this little stream, and proposed Neawanna Creek, in the belief that the spelling more nearly expressed the original name. This style closely approximates the word *Newanah* which came to the compiler on the authority of the late John Gill of Portland, who was a reliable student of Chinook place names. Various official and civic organizations sponsored the change, and as a result, the USBGN on February 4, 1931, adopted the style Neawanna Creek and apparently everyone in the vicinity is happy. The meaning of this Indian word is unknown, although it is probable that it referred to a location along the bank of this stream near a rapid, or a waterfall. A large number of Indian place names in northwestern Oregon began with the syllable *Ne*. See under Neahkahnie Mountain.

Necanicum, Clatsop County. This community no longer has a post office. It was originally called Ahlers, for Herman Ahlers, a local resident. The name was changed to Push on April 13, 1899. The post office was subsequently known as Necanicum on account of Necanicum River which flowed nearby. For the origin of the name of Necanicum River see under that heading. Necanicum post office was at the Sly place about twelve miles southeast of Seaside on the Wolf Creek Highway. Ahlers selected the name Push because he expected the place to turn into an enterprising community. The name was changed from Push to Necanicum on May 27, 1907. Ahlers was postmaster at all three offices mentioned.

Necanicum River, Clatsop County. Necanicum is one of the many Indian names in northwest Oregon beginning with *Ne*, which was apparently a prefix indicating place. This stream flows into the Pacific Ocean at Seaside. William Clark named it Clatsop River on January 7, 1806, but that name did not prevail. *Necanicum* is derived from *Ne-hay-ne-hum*, the name of an Indian lodge up the stream, according to H. S. Lyman, *OHQ*, volume I, page 321. The name is given as *Nekonikon* in OPA *Transactions*, 1887, page 86. In 1929 Herman Ahlers, for some years postmaster at Necanicum post office, wrote that the name meant a gap in the mountains, apparently referring to the valley. In pioneer days the stream was known as Latty Creek, for William Latty, who took up a land claim in what is now the south part of Seaside. Necanicum is the form of spelling in general use and has been adopted by the USBGN.

Neece Canyon, Sherman County. Neece Canyon is the west fork of Frank Fulton Canyon starting near Locust Grove. It was named for the Neece family several of whom took up government land there in the 1880s.

Giles French in the *Golden Land* refers to T. Clay Neece as a part time preacher and music teacher.

Needy, Clackamas County. Geo. H. Himes told the compiler that this place was named, not because of the character of the soil, which was excellent, but because of the unfortunate condition of some pioneer settlers who lived there. Leslie M. Scott in *History of the Oregon Country,* says that the place was also known as Hardscrabble. Inquiries made by the compiler in 1943 failed to confirm stories of poor soil in the locality. Needy post office was established February 16, 1855, with John M. Bacon postmaster. John S. Vinson in an article on the *Oregonian* editorial page, March 17, 1928, says that James H. Brents originated the names Needy and Hardscrabble, and gives additional history of the place.

Neer City, Columbia County. Neer City is a ghost town on the Columbia River Highway at a county road junction about a half a mile north of Goble. This place was laid out by Abe Neer and the plat filed for record on August 31, 1883. It was a point on the Columbia River where boats found it convenient to get cordwood for their boilers and a little settlement of woodcutters developed at Neer City. An account of the activity, by Mrs. Abe Neer, is in the Saint Helens *Sentinel-Mist,* March 24, 1942. The *Postal Guide* for January, 1888, lists Neer post office, with that style.

Neet, Douglas County. Neet post office was near the middle of township 31 south, range 2 west, about five miles south of the place now called Tiller. The office was established October 11, 1899, with Charles W. Neet first and only postmaster. The office was closed February 28, 1901. The office was named in compliment to the postmaster. Charles Neet was a homesteader. In March, 1947, Mrs. Bertha B. Pennell of Tiller wrote the compiler that the office was in the log home of Neet, standing on the side hill west of Drew Creek, a little over a mile from the place now called Drew. This old building, apparently still standing in 1947, was a couple of miles up stream from the mouth of Drew Creek. Drew post office was not established until about a year after Neet was discontinued.

Negro Ben Mountain, Jackson County. For many years this 4500 foot peak in the Siskiyou Mountains, a little to the southwest of Ruch and Applegate River, was called Nigger Ben Mountain. The name was very old, and appears to have been derived from a Negro named Ben who operated a small blacksmith shop near the river and accommodated miners by sharpening picks and other tools. In his spare time Ben worked a tunnel on a small prospect he had developed. There are a number of stories about Ben, most of them probably apocryphal. Ben's last name appears to have been lost to posterity. In 1964, when integration was the watchword, the USBGN in *Decision List 6402* changed the name to its present form. There is no evidence the original name was derogatory, and if every name that might now or in the future offend some ethnic group must be altered to suit the changing times, the authorities might just as well resort to a simple numerical designation.

Nehalem, Tillamook County. The Nehalem Indians were a Salish tribe, formerly living on Nehalem River. Duflot de Mofras gives the name as *Nahelem* in *Exploration,* 1844, volume II, page 104. The name is *Naalem* in Senate Executive Document 39, Thirty-second Congress, first session, page

2, 1852; *Ne-ay-lem* in *OHQ*, volume I, page 320, by Silas B. Smith. The name is used for the town of Nehalem and Nehalem River. The latter flows in all four of the northwest counties of the state and cuts completely through the Coast Range. The first bold point extending to the sea north of Nehalem Bay is Neahkahnie Mountain. There is no little romance about Nehalem and Neahkahnie, having to do with treasure and marooned Spanish sailors. See under Neahkahnie. In addition to references given thereunder, see Scott's *History of the Oregon Country*, volume III, page 125, for data on the Nehalem beeswax controversy. USGS Bulletin 590, *Geology of Northwestern Oregon*, goes into the geology of the Nehalem region and strongly supports the beeswax theory of the Nehalem wax as against the natural mineral theory. John Gill told the compiler in 1927 that many years ago he had discussed the origin of Clatsop County names with a Clatsop Indian, Mrs. Jenny Williams, the widow of Bill Williams, who lived near Seaside. Mrs. Williams informed Mr. Gill that the Indian word *Nehalem* meant "place where people live" and indicated that the prefix *Ne* used frequently in the Indian names of northwestern Oregon, meant a place or locality. Nehalem post office was established in August, 1870 or 1871, with Samuel Corwin first postmaster. This office was probably about two miles north of the present community at the locality sometimes called Upper Nehalem, which is not now organized. The post office was moved to suit the convenience of the available postmasters and was from time to time at the Hunt, Scovell and Alley places. When John M. Alley was postmaster the name of the office was changed on February 6, 1884, to Onion Peak. By this time the office was some miles north up the valley of North Fork Nehalem River and it was of course named for the nearby mountain, Onion Peak, a conspicuous landmark. This office was closed April 7, 1893. While all this was going on a new post office with the name Nehalem was established May 12, 1884, with Henry Ober postmaster. This office was at or near the present community and has been in continuous operation since it was established.

Neil Creek, Jackson County. Neil Creek is tributary to Bear Creek south of Ashland. It was named for Claiborne Neil, a pioneer settler who was born in Tennessee in 1821 and came to Oregon in 1853. He settled in Jackson County the following year and took a donation land claim that included the stream. Neil installed one of the earliest irrigation projects in the area when he diverted the creek through his large orchard.

Nellies Cove, Curry County. Nellies Cove is the middle of three coves just west of the bay at Port Orford and just southwest of the town of Port Orford. Nellies Point is the promontory on the east of Nellies Cove. These features were named for Sarah Ellen Tichenor, youngest daughter of Captain William Tichenor, the famous pioneer of the locality. She was known as Nellie and the cove and point were her favorite spots on the old Tichenor property. The cove to the east of Nellies Cove is Tichenor Cove. Sarah Ellen Tichenor was born in Illinois in 1848. She was brought to Port Orford probably in May, 1852, and spent her girlhood there. Later she married E. W. McGraw and lived in San Francisco. In early days the town of Gold Beach in Curry County was called Ellensburg, in compliment to Ellen Tichenor.

Nelscott, Lincoln County. This has become an important summer resort on Oregon Coast Highway. A letter by Mrs. Alma Anderson, published in North Lincoln *Coast Guard* for May 4, 1939, indicates that the name was formed by combining parts of the names of Charles P. Nelson and Dr. W. G. Scott, who opened the townsite in April, 1926. Nelson died in December, 1946. For editorial comment about his activities, see *Sunday Oregonian,* December 25, 1946. On December 8, 1964, Nelscott voted to become part of a new community to be called Lincoln City.

Nelson Canyon, Morrow and Umatilla counties. James Nelson settled along Butter Creek south of Vinson in the 1880s and later took up several parcels of land near the head of this canyon.

Nelson Creek, Wheeler County. Rufus K. Nelson was a native of Kentucky who settled near Mitchell in 1877 along the creek which bears his name. His large family included three sons who later ranched nearby, and Nelson Reservoir was built by a grandson, George W. Nelson. R. K. Nelson was killed in a horse drive accident in 1889.

Nena Creek, Wasco County. Nena Creek rises in Mutton Mountains in the northeast corner of the Warm Springs Indian Reservation. It flows into Deschutes River. Indians inform the writer that the word means tall white cottonwood trees that grow near the stream. The style *Nee-nee* was used in the Pacific Railroad Surveys *Reports* in 1855. The form Nena Creek does not reflect the real Indian pronunciation, but it appears on government maps and is the name of a railroad station, and seems to be here to stay.

Nenamusa, Tillamook County. Nenamusa Falls are on the east border of the county in the west part of township 4 south, range 7 west, in the Nestucca River drainage. Nenamusa post office was established nearby January 16, 1912, with Peter N. Forsyth first and only postmaster. The office was closed August 31, 1917. It was about eight miles east of Blaine. Information about the origin of the name of the falls is unsatisfactory. The word is said to be Indian, meaning sweetheart, or love, but the writer has not been able to trace any such word or meaning in available Indian dictionaries. It is reported that the word may have been brought to Oregon from an eastern state. Indians known by the writer had no knowledge of the sentiment of love as known to white people, or of the word sweetheart, either. The prefix *ne* in the northwest Oregon area was used by Indians as a locative, and may be translated, roughly, as a place. The nearest approach to Nenamusa offered by the Chinook jargon is the expression *ne moosum,* which may be translated as place to sleep. It might refer to a place for a temporary camp. It has been suggested that Nenamusa means a place for a honeymoon, but all this is conjectural.

Neotsu, Lincoln County. Neotsu is a post office on the Oregon Coast Highway near the north end of Devils Lake, and the name is said to be an Indian word referring to the lake. The compiler has been unable to get a satisfactory translation. There are a number of Indian legends about Devils Lake, some of which are doubtless apocryphal. Apparently it was a place where evil skookums flourished. Davidson, in the *Coast Pilot,* 1889, uses the spelling *Na-ah-so,* but does not explain the word. The compiler has heard Devils Lake referred to as a *me-sah'-chie chuck,* which is Chinook jargon for evil water.

Neskowin, Tillamook County. Mrs. Sarah H. Page in a letter to the *Oregonian* published June 30, 1925, says that the name Neskowin is an Indian word, meaning plenty fish. Mrs. Page was appointed postmaster of this office in 1887 and the locality was then known as Slab Creek. Years before a ship had been wrecked on the coast and a quantity of slabwood washed up on the beach. One day she heard an Indian say as he pointed to the nearby stream, "Neskowin, Neskowin." She asked him what Neskowin meant and he said "plenty fish, plenty fish." In 1925 the USBGN was asked to change the name of the stream from Slab Creek to Neskowin Creek, and this was done, on October 7 of that year. Neskowin post office was established December 4, 1886, with Weston Burdick first postmaster. The office has not been in continuous service, and not always in the same place. When a small boy, the compiler always heard this locality referred to as Neskowin, with the accent on the second syllable, rhyming with how. Tillamook County pioneers have confirmed this pronunciation.

Nesmith Point, Multnomah County. Nesmith Point, elevation 3878 feet, is the highest point on the cliffs overlooking the Columbia River in the gorge through the Cascade Range. It is just south of Warrendale and east of Yeon Mountain. The point was named as the result of a suggestion made in 1915 by a committee of the Mazamas who selected a number of place names for un-named geographic features adjacent to the Columbia River Highway. James Willis Nesmith was born in New Brunswick July 23, 1820, while his parents, residents of Maine, were on a short visit. The Nesmith family was of Scottish ancestry, and came to New England from the north of Ireland in 1718. James W. Nesmith, as the result of his father's financial reverses, had no early advantages, and was forced to lead a more or less roving life eventually reaching the state of Ohio. He attempted to emigrate to Oregon in 1842, but was too late to join Dr. White's party that year. He was a member of the emigration of 1843, and was elected orderly sergeant. For his diary of events during the emigration see *OHQ*, volume VII, page 329. For his reminiscences of the emigration see OPA *Transactions* for 1875. The diary describes a severe windstorm on the Columbia River below the Cascades, which compelled him to put ashore and finish the day reading *The Merry Wives of Windsor.* It was this incident that suggested his name to the committee for Nesmith Point. Nesmith was a judge under the provisional government, representative from Polk County, captain in the Cayuse and other Indian wars, colonel of volunteers in the Yakima War, United States marshal, and superintendent of Indian affairs. He served in the United States Senate from 1861 to 1867, and although a Democrat, served on the military committee, and upheld the cause of the Union in every possible way. He served as representative in Congress from 1873 to 1875, and spent the rest of his life on his farm at Rickreall, where he died June 17, 1885. For Harvey W. Scott's estimate of Colonel Nesmith, see the *Oregonian,* June 18, 1885, and also Scott's *History of the Oregon Country,* volume V, page 172, *et seq.* For description of Nesmith's grave and epitaph, see the *Oregonian,* May 8, 1895, page 3; for tribute from U. S. Grant, *ibid.,* March 13, 1901, page 8; for episodes of Nesmith's life, *ibid.,* July 18, 1897, page 6. For other references see Scott's *History of the Oregon Country,* volume I, page

308. There was a railroad station Nesmith, in Polk County, south of Rickreall, but a short distance from the Nesmith farm. There was also a railroad station Nesmith on the Oregon Electric in Washington County.

Nestocton, Tillamook County. The Nestocton post office was one of the oldest in Tillamook County. It was established February 7, 1867, with Leonard Killam first postmaster. This post office remained in service until June 13, 1904, when it was discontinued, probably because of the extension of rural delivery which brought about the closing of so many post offices about that time. The locality of Nestocton was settled in the sixties. It is about eight or nine miles south along the Oregon Coast Highway from Tillamook. It is obvious from the names of its ten postmasters that the office was moved to fit their availability. Nestocton was the second post office in Tillamook County. The first post office was Tillamook, established March 12, 1866. The name is obviously an Indian word, but the compiler has been unable to learn its meaning.

Nestucca River, Tillamook and Yamhill counties. Nestucca is an Indian name for a part of this stream or a point on its banks, or for a tribe living nearby. As far as the writer knows there is no English translation of the word *Nestucca*. This stream is frequently called Big Nestucca River in contradistinction to Little Nestucca River nearby, but federal map makers leave off the word Big from such names, and it is apparent that the Indian name of the stream was not Big Nestucca. As a matter of fact the stream called Little Nestucca River was known to the Indians as Nestachee, so there would be no occasion for them to call the other river Big Nestucca. Little Nestucca River does not flow into Nestucca River but into Nestucca Bay. The spelling Nestugga is wrong. The *Handbook of American Indians* says the Nestucca Indians took their name from the country in which they lived, but that their real tribe name was *Staga-ush*. J. H. Frost in his journal of 1841, published in *OHQ*, volume XXXV, pages 253 and 254, used the name *Nea-Stocka* in referring to a place on Nestucca River.

Netarts, Tillamook County. Netarts community is on Netarts Bay south of Tillamook Bay. *Netarts* is an Indian name, and the writer has been unable to get its English meaning, although it is presumed to refer to the home of a small family, or tribe that lived on the bay. *Netarts* is one of the number of Indian names beginning with *Ne* which were probably used to indicate localities or the homes of certain tribes. See under Neahkahnie Mountain and also *OHQ*, volume I, page 321. George Davidson, in the *Coast Pilot* of 1889, page 433, refers to this bay as *Na-ta-at* or Oyster Bay. He does not explain the meaning of the Indian name and does not imply that it is the same as oyster.

Neubert Spring, Klamath County. Neubert Spring on the east slope of Naylox Mountain was named for the family of Will Neubert, an early settler in Swan Lake Valley.

Neverstil, Columbia County. On February 3, 1946, the *Oregonian* printed an editorial about Neverstil, inviting information. The place was described with some fidelity, and while it was referred to as a logging community, it was in fact the location of the repair shops for A. S. Kerry's logging railroad. A lively correspondence resulted from this editorial and letters were printed on February 5, 6, 10, 12 and 13. A number of stories were furnished about the origin of the word Neverstil, some based apparently on high-geared imagination. An impartial review of the evidence indicates to the compiler that the name was coined by Mr. Kerry of the Kerry Timber Company to describe the bustle and noise attendant upon the timber company railroad shops. The place was at the old Harvey ranch about two miles south of Birkenfeld where Deep Creek flows into Nehalem River. Neverstil post office was established June 10, 1916, with Florence M. Bennett first postmaster. The office was closed December 31, 1919. The logging railroad was in operation as early as about 1913 and it is said that the place was first called Evergreen, but that name could not be used for a post office because of duplication with another Evergreen, Oregon. There must have been some other reason for not continuing the name Evergreen, as there was no other post office with that name in Oregon during the period in question.

New Bridge, Baker County. New Bridge post office was originally on the banks of Eagle Creek near where an important pioneer bridge was built across the stream. The post office was established on July 22, 1878. Joseph Gale was the first postmaster. For information about him see under Gales Creek. New Bridge post office was burned about 1880. The post office is no longer in service.

New Era, Clackamas County. There are two stories about how this community got its name. Several persons have told the writer that the naming came about as the result of the construction of the railroad as far as the mouth of Parrott Creek, which made it possible for Willamette River boats to stop there and deliver produce. This was hailed as a new era in river transportation as boats then would not have to go to the falls below at Oregon City. This story has the earmarks of truth, but on the other hand it should be said that one correspondent has informed the compiler that a local family were spiritualists and devoted to a publication called the *New Era,* and named the place on that account.

New Pine Creek, Lake County. This is said to be the oldest town in Lake County. It was originally intended to name the place Pine Creek because of a nearby stream, but postal authorities objected to this because of duplication, so the name New Pine Creek was adopted. The post office was established December 8, 1876, with S. A. Hamersley first postmaster.

Newberg, Yamhill County. C. B. Wilson, postmaster at Newberg, Oregon, in 1926, informed the writer that Newberg was named November 5, 1869, by Sebastian Brutscher who was the first postmaster. Brutscher formerly lived in Germany at a place called Neuberg and adopted for the new office the English translation of the name of his former home. Modern atlases show a Neuberg in Styria, Austria, but none in Germany.

Newbern, Linn County. Newbern was the name of a short-lived post office established June 18, 1874, and closed September 1 of the same year. The General Land Office map of Oregon of 1876 shows the place near the west edge of township 11 south, range 2 west, on the old road from Albany southeast toward Lebanon. The office was about six miles southeast of Albany and a mile or so north-northwest of what was later known as Tall-

man. The compiler has not been able to get the significance of the name
Newbern, which is spelled Newburn on the map mentioned above. Benjamin N. Hardman was postmaster at the place. Newbern sounds like a family name and it may be represented by the postmaster's middle initial,
though this is no more than a surmise.

Newberry Crater, Deschutes County. Nature narrowly missed giving
Oregon two crater lakes almost equal in size and beauty, but like many
other attempts to improve upon a masterpiece, this one failed. Twenty-five
miles south of Bend lies Newberry Crater, a result of volcanism much more
recent than the caldera occupied by Crater Lake. Newberry Crater is situated in the summit of the isolated Paulina Mountains and in this crater are
two lakes, Paulina Lake and East Lake, at an elevation of about 6350 feet or
several hundred feet higher than Crater Lake. It is apparent that the caldera was at one time occupied by one lake, but subsequent volcanic action
has built up a series of small craters running north and south across the
middle which divides the depression and leaves East Lake with neither inlet
nor outlet. Paulina Lake overflows to the west down Paulina Creek, a tributary of Little Deschutes River. Paulina Creek is blessed with several pretty
waterfalls. Newberry Crater broke down its western side and if it had not
been for this break it is apparent that the water level would be much higher
in the crater, and the surroundings would have more nearly resembled
Crater Lake itself. At some points around the two lakes the walls are precipitous and high and Paulina Peak, which is just south of Paulina Lake,
affords one of the finest views in Oregon. It stands 7985 feet high, or 1600
feet above the lake, and its sides to the north are rough and jagged. From
the USFS lookout on top the writer has seen the great snow peaks of the
Cascade Range spread out like a fan in magnificent panorama, extending
from Mount Adams on the north to Mount McLoughlin on the south. In
1903 Dr. I. C. Russell examined this part of Oregon for the USGS and
attempted to name the Paulina Mountains and Paulina Peak Mount Newberry, for Dr. John Strong Newberry, who explored central Oregon for the
Pacific Railroad Surveys in 1855. Dr. Russell's proposal has never been
adopted in local practice, but instead the great caldera is now generally
known as Newberry Crater, and Dr. Newberry is well honored, though not
in the manner intended by Dr. Russell. Additional information may be
found under Paulina Peak.

Newbill Creek, Crook and Jefferson counties. Newbill Creek rises
northeast of Grizzly Mountain and flows into Willow Creek. It was named
for Jesse Newbill who homesteaded along its banks in 1873. The form New-
hill is incorrect.

Newell Creek, Clackamas County. Newell Creek is a small stream east
of Oregon City, flowing north into Abernethy Creek. This little creek was
named for one of the most prominent and picturesque pioneer citizens of
the Oregon country. "Doctor" Robert Newell rated his title by affectionate
courtesy rather than by professional training. He was a mountain man
when he was scarcely out of his 'teens, and it was in the mountains that he
learned to plug bullet wounds, set broken bones and prepare natural remedies for sick dogs, horses, Indians and fellow trappers. His companions

held him in esteem for his timely help and doubtless the dogs licked his hands. Robert Newell was born in Ohio, probably in 1807. He started trapping out of St. Louis when he was 22. T. C. Elliott has written entertainingly of his career in *OHQ*, volume IX, page 103. Not much is known of his life in the Rocky Mountains, but in December, 1840, he was in Oregon City. He played a conspicuous part in the formation of the provisional government; he was a member of the Legislative Committee and twice speaker of the House of Representatives. He took an active part in Indian problems. He moved to Lapwai, Idaho, in the 1860s and died at Lewiston in November, 1869.

Newell Spring, Jefferson County. Newell Spring is on the old Madras-Ashwood road near Hay Creek. It was named for Roy Newell who took up a homestead there in 1906.

Newman Canyon, Morrow County. Newman Canyon northwest of Lena was named for William R. Newman who settled near Heppner about 1890.

Newport, Lincoln County. This post office was established July 2, 1868, with Samuel Case postmaster. The compiler has not succeeded in learning who christened the community, although the name is obviously intended to be descriptive, and was doubtless suggested by Newport, Rhode Island.

Newsome Creek, Crook County. Newsome Creek east of Post was named for Samuel J. Newsom who was born in Springfield, Illinois on March 13, 1834 and came to Oregon with his parents, David and Mary Newsom, in 1851. Newsom lived in Marion County then moved to eastern Oregon in the 1870s. He was a prominent rancher in the vicinity of Post and later developed Newsom's Addition to the City of Prineville. The superfluous terminal "e" is fixed by current usage. For a short biography, see *Illustrated History of Central Oregon,* page 786.

Newton Clark Glacier, Hood River County. This glacier is on the southeast part of Mount Hood. Newton Clark was a native of Illinois, and after living for a time in Wisconsin, he served in the Civil War, and then settled in what is now South Dakota. It is said that Clark County in that state was named for him. Clark came to Hood River Valley in September, 1877 and was both a teacher and land surveyor. He was interested in nature and spent considerable time around Mount Hood. Captain Henry Coe and Oscar Stranahan reportedly named Newton Clark Glacier for him in 1886. Clark died June 21, 1918.

Newton Creek, Hood River County. This stream, together with Clark Creek to the south, drains Newton Clark Glacier. The two creeks were named by splitting the name of the glacier. See under that heading.

Niagara, Marion County. Niagara, a place on North Santiam River about eight miles east of Mill City, was named for the adjacent constriction in the river. After the railroad was built through here in 1889, it was believed that the narrow gorge, only five feet wide in one spot, would be an excellent waterpower site. A masonry dam was constructed and a paper mill planned but not completed. Electric power was generated but variations in stream flow coupled with maintenance problems on the dam caused the operation to be abandoned in 1912. Niagara post office was established as Niagora on October 3, 1890 with William H. Burns first postmaster. The spelling was corrected to Niagara in July 1893 and the office operated intermittently until June 14, 1934. In 1977 there is a pleasant Marion County Park there with a good flight of steps down to the narrow gorge and the remains of the original masonry. Maynard Drawson has an interesting history of the dam in *OHQ*, volume LXXI, pp 349 *et seq.*

Nibley, Union County. This place was named for C. W. Nibley, a well-known member of the Mormon church and prominent in various industrial enterprises in the Pacific Northwest.

Nice, Lincoln County. Nice was a community on the north side of Alsea Bay. J. H. Middleton, who lived there, informed the compiler in 1927 that the place was named for Harry Nice, who was born in New Brunswick about 1828 and came to California about 1867 and to Oregon about 1869. He fished for salmon and built boats on the Columbia River, and after having spent a short time in British Columbia, returned to the United States and was employed by the government in the construction of jetties near Newport. He later became interested in salmon packing on Alsea Bay. He died about 1922. The post office situated near the present site of Nice was established with the name Drift Creek on August 6, 1874, with Matthew Brand first postmaster. The name was changed to Collins on January 31, 1876, with Brand postmaster. On June 17, 1881, the name was changed to Waldport with David Ruble postmaster. The name was changed back to Collins on February 23, 1882. Collins was the name of a local family. The name of the office was changed to Lutgens on May 17, 1890, and Albert H. Lutgens was appointed postmaster on the same day. On July 29, 1893, the name of the office was changed to Stanford and W. C. Shepard was appointed postmaster. The name was changed again to Lutgens on June 21, 1897, and Albert H. Lutgens was appointed postmaster. The name was changed to Nice on April 24, 1917, with Nona L. Strake postmaster. The office was discontinued on November 15, 1919.

Nichols, Douglas County. Nichols was a railroad station in Cow Creek Canyon for many years. It is southwest of Riddle, and was named for a well-known Douglas County family. Nichols post office was established December 31, 1914, with Mrs. Viola B. Nichols postmaster. It was discontinued December 31, 1929. The railroad station Nichols was established when the railroad was built in the early 1880s.

Nichols Canyon, Umatilla County. Nichols Canyon is just south of Milton-Freewater. It was named for William Nichols who settled near its mouth in 1871 and later platted Nichol's 1st. and 2nd. additions to what was then Milton City. The OHS in *Scrapbook #270*, page 163, has an unidentified newspaper clipping giving an interesting interview with Nichols and his comments on the early days. The form Nicolis used on the USGS Milton-Freewater quadrangle dated 1964 is a typographical error.

Nichols Creek, Douglas County. This creek is a tributary of Jackson Creek about eight miles east of Tiller. Benjamin F. Nichols, who had a ranch along its banks, was the son of I. B. Nichols and grandson of William H. Riddle.

Nicholson Spring, Wheeler County. This spring in section 12, township 9 south, range 20 east, was named for a family of early settlers.

Nick Eaton Ridge, Hood River County. This ridge runs south from the Columbia River just east of Herman Creek. Mrs. Clifford L. Gorton of Cascade Locks stated that the ridge was named for Nick Eaton who had a farm between Wyeth and Cascade Locks about 1905.

Nickel Mountain, Douglas County. This mountain is four miles west of Riddle and has the only known major deposit of green silicate of nickel (garnierite) in the United States. Commercial production was started in 1954 by a subsidiary of the M. A. Hanna Company.

Nish, Sherman County. Nish was a railroad station near Moro. It was named for Alexander Nish who was born in Scotland February 15, 1847, and came to the United States in 1852. He served during the Civil War and later settled in Sherman County. It is said that his name was originally McNish or MacNish, but he changed his name at the time he entered the army.

Nixon, Linn County. This was a station on the Oregon Electric Railway southwest of Halsey. C. H. Stewart of Albany told the compiler that it was named for a pioneer resident, Samuel Nixon.

No Name Creek, Hood River County. Stanley Walters, USFS ranger, named this tributary of Lake Branch when the area was logged about 1950. He said that everything else was named so "No Name" would have to suffice.

Noah Butte, Coos County. Noah Butte is east across Coos Bay from the town of Coos Bay and north of Coos River. Members of the Noah family were early settlers in the county and the butte was named for one, but the compiler does not know which.

Noble School, Marion County. Noble School and the Noble district, about three miles southeast of Scotts Mills, were named for William Noble, who settled on the Abiqua some time prior to 1848. He sold out to Samuel Allen in the spring of that year, and went to Oregon City, where he soon died. See Down's *History of the Silverton Country,* page 41. Noble post office served this section from February, 1893, to May, 1908. Charles W. Roberts was the first postmaster of a series of six.

Noel Creek, Douglas County. Noel Creek flows into Smith River from the north a few miles northeast of Gardiner. It bears the name of Stephenson C. Noel who came to Oregon from Missouri. In pioneer days he and some companions left Eugene on a prospecting expedition and finally reached lower Smith River. Noel settled on the stream that now bears his name. See Reedsport *Courier,* April 10, 1936.

Nofog, Douglas County. Nofog post office bore a strictly descriptive name. It was on the upper reaches of Cavitt Creek about due east of Roseburg. Nofog post office was established June 7, 1915, and Hezekiah J. Robinett, the first and only postmaster, named the place because of the clear atmosphere. The office was discontinued February 28, 1918. The compiler has an interesting letter by Victor Boyd of Roseburg, written in February, 1948, about his experiences teaching school in 1903-04 in a log building on the Cavitt place. Except for the window sash, floor, desks and seats, the whole school building was hand split from cedar logs. Mr. Boyd writes that at one time eight of the seventeen pupils were from the family of S. W. Furnell. Robinett later bought the Furnell home.

Nohorn Creek, Clackamas County. This stream is in the southern part of the county and flows into the Hot Springs Fork of Clackamas River. Nohorn is the popularized version of the name Nachand. John Nachand was a pioneer prospector of eastern Clackamas County, with James Russell and Joe Davis. It is said that Nachand had formerly mined in the Cariboo district in British Columbia. Little is known of his history except that during the later years of his life he lived at Park Place, north of Oregon City. He died about 1905. He was universally called Nohorn, and the name Nohorn is well established for the stream.

Nonpareil, Douglas County. A locality on Calapooya Creek six or seven miles airline east of Oakland is called Nonpareil, a word meaning unrivaled or unique. Whoever named the place thought well of it. Nonpareil post office was established in December 19, 1882, with Elizabeth C. Sacry postmaster. The office was discontinued July 10, 1884. The name was derived from the nearby Nonpareil quicksilver mine, which at one time produced a considerable quantity of the mineral. The Nonpareil mine has not been worked in recent years.

Norfolk, Douglas County. Norfolk was a pioneer post office on Smith River in the west part of the county. It was near the mouth of North Fork Smith River. A report from Reedsport says that the post office was to have been called Norfork for the stream. However that may be, the spelling Norfolk was adopted by postal authorities and that is the way it appears on all records available to the compiler.

Norris, Clackamas County. This station near Barton was named for G. Norris who took up a homestead nearby. His land office certificate was number 3012.

North Bend, Coos County. The original settlement of North Bend was on the peninsula around which Coos Bay bends between the town of Coos Bay and the ocean. It is said that the name North Bend was originally applied in 1856 by Captain A. M. Simpson, the founder of the city. The post office was established February 27, 1872, with C. H. Merchant first postmaster.

North Fork Smith River, Curry County. This is the principal Oregon tributary of a river in California, which is named for Jedediah Strong Smith, explorer and fur trader. Smith discovered the river in California on Thursday, June 19, 1828. See *The Ashley-Smith Exploration* by Professor Harrison C. Dale. For information about Smith's exploration along the Oregon coast, see under Smith River, in this volume. Smith River in Oregon and Smith River in California are so far apart that they are not confused. The California stream is shown as Smiths River on a map accompanying Senator Lewis F. Linn's report dated June 6, 1838. The Reverend Samuel Parker uses the same name on his map of Oregon Territory published the same year. North Fork Smith River heads just west of Chetco Peak. The important tributary that heads southeast of Chetco Peak is Chrome Creek.

North Fork Smith River, Douglas and Lane counties. This is the largest tributary of the main stream. The name West Fork is wrong. West Branch is a small stream tributary to North Fork Smith River. For origin of the name Smith River, see under that heading. This refers to the Oregon river.

North Junction, Wasco County. North Junction station was established on the east bank of Deschutes River when the two railroads were built upstream from the mouth. From North Junction to South Junction, a distance of about twelve miles, but one track was provided. Later the Union Pacific track was torn up north of North Junction, so that the station name is no longer descriptive. The post office was established in June, 1927, some years after the railroads were built in the canyon. J. C. McCurdy was the first postmaster. The place was not listed in the *Postal Guide* in the fall of 1933.

North Minam River, Union and Wallowa counties. This important tributary of Minam River heads in Steamboat Lake. The name North Fork River is incorrect.

North Plains, Washington County. The name North Plains is used for a post office in the northern part of Tualatin Valley. This locality was known in pioneer times as North Plains, and the office gets its name from that source. Stories to the effect that a farmer named Nord lived hereabouts and gave his name to the plains do not appear to be founded on fact, for the plains were known as North Plains long before any settler of that name lived thereon.

North Pole Ridge, Wasco County. Dolph Kimsey who was raised near Antelope told the writer that a Scot named Finlayson had a sheep spread near Black Rock and he claimed that in the winter this cold, desolate ridge compared favorably with its namesake. Since Finlayson presumably had had experience with the rigours of winter in Scotland, the compiler feels his opinion must be given considerable weight.

North Portland, Multnomah County. This post office was established March 24, 1910, and was named because of its position in respect to Portland. The first postmaster was Vaughn D. Crosby. It is said that the name was suggested by a representative of Swift & Company, which concern operated a large meat packing plant in the community. The area is now served by Kenton Station out of Portland.

North Portland Harbor, Multnomah County. North Portland Harbor lies between Hayden Island and the flats north of St. Johns. The harbor is really a branch of the Columbia River. For many years it was known as Oregon Slough but at the request of Portland commercial interests the name was changed to North Portland Harbor because of rapidly developing activity in that part of Portland. The USBGN approved the change.

North Powder, Union County. North Powder took its name from North Powder River, a tributary of Powder River. For the origin of the name of Powder River see under that heading. North Powder was a pioneer station. James M. De Moss is said to have been the founder of the stage station. See under De Moss. Maps of Lewis and Clark show North Powder River as *Ta-kin-par.* North Powder post office was established December 2, 1866, with Joseph Austin first postmaster.

North Santiam River, Linn and Marion counties. This is the correct name of the main tributary of Santiam River, and not North Fork. South Santiam River is the correct name of the other important branch that combines with North Santiam River near Jefferson to form the main stream. See under Santiam River. The principal tributary of North Santiam River is Little North Santiam River, not Little North Fork.

North Scappoose Creek, Columbia County. This is the correct name of the main north tributary of Scappoose Creek, not North Fork. See under Scappoose Creek.

North Sister, Deschutes and Lane counties. This is the fourth highest mountain in Oregon, and has an elevation of 10,094 feet. The Three Sisters have been so known since pioneer days, but the compiler has been unable to find out who first used the name. There is an old story to the effect that in early days the three peaks were known as Faith, Hope and Charity, the North Sister being Mount Faith. These names have not prevailed. See under Three Sisters.

North Tenmile Lake, Coos and Douglas counties. This lake is known by the name given, and also by the name North Lake. The USBGN has officially declared in favor of North Tenmile Lake. Its outlet is into Tenmile Lake, which in turn drains into the ocean through Tenmile Creek. The two lakes and other nearby features doubtless received their names from Tenmile Creek, which flows into the Pacific Ocean about ten miles south of Winchester Bay. See under Tenmile Creek and also Tenmile Lake.

North Umpqua River, Douglas County. This is the correct name of the north branch of Umpqua River, not North Fork. It rises on the west slopes of the Cascade Range, north of Diamond Lake, and joins South Umpqua River near Winchester, forming Umpqua River. For origin of the name Umpqua, see under Umpqua River.

North Yamhill River, Yamhill County. This is the correct name of the main north tributary of Yamhill River, not North Fork. See under Yamhill River.

Norton, Clackamas County. A pioneer post office, named Norton for a local family, was established December 1, 1871, with Benjamin C. Lewis first postmaster. Zach C. Norton was the second postmaster. The office was closed June 9, 1881. The place is shown on old maps at a point about four or five miles northwest of Springwater, close to or actually on the Clackamas River, probably not far from the place known as Feldheimer Ferry. In response to an inquiry, the Oregon City *Banner-Courier* on January 1, 1946, published a statement by R. B. Holcomb, a pioneer resident of the county who was in the late 1880s a mail carrier. Mr. Holcomb avers that he recalled a building known as Norton's Hall at a point about four miles north of Springwater, although it does not appear from his statement that the building was on the river. Norton's Hall was apparently a meeting place of sorts, and bore insignia, possibly of the Masonic fraternity.

Nortons, Lincoln County. This railroad station was in the extreme east part of the county. It was named for the Norton family, who owned a ranch nearby. The place was originally called Norton but postal authorities did not accept this name as there was another post office in Oregon of the same name, so the "s" was added. The post office was established in 1895.

Norway, Coos County. Norway station and post office got its name from the fact that in early days the community was settled by Norwegians. The post office has been moved a few miles since it was first established in May, 1876.

Norwegian Creek, Lane County. Ray Engels of McKenzie Bridge told the writer in 1971 that this creek north of Belknap Springs was named about the turn of the century after a Norwegian committed suicide nearby.

Noti, Lane County. Postmaster H. G. Suttle told the writer in February, 1926, of the unusual origin of this name in the following words: "In the early days an Indian and a white man were traveling together from a point on the coast into the Willamette Valley with one horse between them. In order to make as rapid progress as possible they were doing what was known as 'riding and tying.' One would take the horse and ride ahead a distance, tie the horse and proceed on foot. When his companion reached the point where the horse was tied, he in turn mounted and rode a given distance beyond his partner and tied the horse again. It is said that the white man had agreed to tie the horse at about the point where the Noti Creek joins Long Tom River, where the present town of Noti is now located, but instead double-crossed the Indian and rode on to Eugene and left the Indian to walk. When the Indian discovered that he had been jobbed, he is said to have exclaimed, 'Him no tie,' and therefrom the place received its name."

Noyer Creek, Clackamas County. This creek north of Barton was named for Peter Noyer, who took up a donation land claim nearby in pioneer days. His land office certificate was number 3876.

Nugget, Douglas County. This post office was named Nugget because of gold mines in the vicinity.

Numbers Creek, Lane County. Numbers Creek flows into Coast Fork Willamette River south of Cottage Grove Reservoir. It bears the name of Phillip Numbers who in 1872 purchased the sawmill built nearby by William Payne in 1867.

Nye, Umatilla County. Nye post office was about eight miles southwest of Pilot Rock near the present three-way highway junction. This junction is still referred to as Nye and the general impression is that the locality was named for A. W. Nye, a well-known early resident of Umatilla County. The post office was established March 9, 1887, with Henry C. Wright first postmaster. The office was discontinued June 30, 1917.

Nyssa, Malheur County. This post office was established June 15, 1889. The name was first applied to a station when the railroad was built, but the town was not incorporated until about 1903. Accurate information about the application of the name is not available. It is said that a Greek section hand named the place for a town in Greece, but the compiler has been unable to find such a place in any modern atlas. However, in 1973 Professor William G. Loy of the University of Oregon provided the interesting information that the town Messene in Messenia was once known as Nissi. The geographical situation is remarkably similar. Both are situated on slight rises of land with a substantial river to the east and a ditch or small stream to the west. He adds that the word *nissi* meant island. As Loy has done extensive work on Greek geography, the the compiler feels this explanation should be given considerable weight. There are numerous other versions including an acronym for New York Sheep Shippers Association and that it is an Indian name for sage-brush. In botany, Nyssa is the name of the tupelo tree commemorating one of the so-called water nymphs for in Greek mythology Jove charged the Nysaean nymphs with rearing the infant Bacchus. The locale was not specified but Alexander the Great found at the foot of Mount Koh-i-nor west of Peshawar the ancient city of Nysa that tradition says was founded by Bacchus.

Oak, Coos County. On February 28, 1901, a post office named Oak was established about eight miles by road southeast of Myrtle Point near the banks of Middle Fork Coquille River, probably very close to Endicott Creek which flows in from the north. Solomon S. Endicott was the first and only postmaster. The office was closed August 22, 1902. It was named for the forest growth of the locality.

Oak Creek, Benton County. Oak Creek is near Corvallis. There are many geographic features in Oregon named for oak trees. Sudworth, in *Check List of Forest Trees of the United States,* page 105, lists but one oak in northern Oregon, *Quercus garryanna,* Oregon white oak, and most of the features named for the oak are named because of the nearby existence of this species. *Quercus kelloggii,* California black oak, is listed as growing as far north as McKenzie River, and *Quercus chrysolepis,* canyon live oak, is listed as far north as Cow Creek.

Oak Creek, Douglas County. Oak Creek, a locality about ten miles northeast of Roseburg, took its name from the stream on which it is situated. The stream name is very old and came of course from the oak trees which are so prominent in that part of the county. Oak Creek post office was established October 18, 1878, with Jeptha Thornton first postmaster. In 1896, when postal officials were in the throes of efficiency, the name was consolidated to Oakcreek, but the general public continued to use the style Oak Creek. The writer does not know when the post office was closed, but apparently it was some time between 1910 and 1912.

Oak Grove, Clackamas County. Harvey G. Starkweather, a resident of this neighborhood, is authority for the statement that the name of Oak Grove was suggested by Edward W. Cornell, a member of the surveying party that platted the townsite in the early 1890s. The company developing the property had not been able to secure a satisfactory name and Cornell's suggestion came as a result of a crew eating lunch in a fine grove of oak trees in the northwest part of the tract. The townsite was originally served from Milwaukie post office. About 1904 Creighton post office was established to serve the community. This name was adopted in honor of Susan Creighton who took up a donation land claim where the post office then stood. Postal authorities did not use the name Oak Grove because of duplication. The first postmaster was Thomas Howell, Oregon's great botanist. What was known as Oak Grove station was originally called Center station and what was St. Theresa was originally known as Oak Grove station. In order to prevent the confusion created by this state of affairs, postal authorities were prevailed upon in 1907 to change the post office name to Oak Grove and the name of Center station was changed to Oak Grove station, so that peace and happiness reigned insofar as the name was concerned. As of 1980 the tracks were gone and the station only a dim memory. The post office is a branch of Portland.

Oak Grove, Hood River County. This was originally part of the Barrett district on the west side of Hood River Valley. The first school was called Crapper School, but when the church was constructed it was called Oak Grove Church. About 1904 when the present school was constructed, residents changed the name of Crapper district to Oak Grove district.

Oak Grove Butte, Clackamas County. This butte, elevation 4626 feet, was named for Oak Grove Fork Clackamas River to the north and not because of any grove of oaks on its slopes.

Oak Grove Fork Clackamas River, Clackamas County. This is a principal tributary of the Clackamas. In early days Wapinitia, on the east side of the Cascade Range, was known as Oak Grove, and because this fork headed in that general direction it was known as Oak Grove Fork. For other information see under Wapinitia.

Oak Hill, Lane County. This hill west of Eugene was named by John Bailey for a fine grove of oak trees that grew thereon. Bailey, who took a donation land claim there in 1850, later moved five miles southeast to the hill which now bears his name. The record is filed under Roseburg Land Office #1770 with the spelling Baily. Edward F. Bailey, a grandson, told the compiler in 1968 that other family records used both spellings.

Oak Point, Columbia County. On June 1, 1810, Nathan Winship, William Smith and others of the Winship expedition on the ship *Albatross* came upon a grove of oak trees on the south bank of the Columbia River. These were the first oaks the party had found since entering the river on May 26 and the locality was named Oak Point. This point is west of and across Bradbury Slough from the west end of Crims Island where the Beaver ammunition shipping depot was located during World War II and the Portland General Electric Company auxiliary generating plant was built in the 1970s. Bancroft, in *History of the Northwest Coast,* volume II, pages 129 *et seq.,* gives an account of the settlement and the difficulties experienced. Later the name Oak Point emigrated across the Columbia River to the Washington side where it is now the name of a community. Lewis and Clark passed this locality on March 26, 1806, and named what is now Crims Island Fannys Island in compliment to Frances Clark, sister of William Clark. The extensive flat or prairie on the south bank of the river was named Fannys Bottom. It is perhaps just as well that Miss Clark was unable to foresee modern English usage. The explorers mention the prominent grove of oak trees at the point at the north corner of Fannys Bottom. Oak Point and vicinity are described in Coues' *Henry-Thompson Journals,* volume II, pages 794-95, under date of January 11, 1814, and the name seems to have been well established. Wilkes charted Oak Point on his maps and charts as of 1841. A few years later the Abernathy mill drew the name across the river to the Washington shore and there it has remained. In 1792 Broughton applied the name Oak Point to a place on the Washington side of the Columbia River a little below the present community of St. Helens. This Oak Point seems to have been in the same locality as Caples Landing.

Oakerman Ranch, Harney County. The name of this ranch is frequently misspelled. It bears the name of J. Fred Oakerman, who received his land patent from the United States. The ranch was a little north of Central Oregon Highway and is well known in central Oregon.

Oakland, Douglas County. Oakland post office was established February 21, 1852. In 1856 the office was on a prairie surrounded by oak trees, about three miles north of the present town. At that time the office, which was in charge of a preacher named Hull Tower, was the terminus of four mail routes, one to Jacksonville, one to Scottsburg, one via the pass to the Coast Fork and Eugene, and the other through Yoncalla to Corvallis. All mail was carried on saddle and pack horses. The office received its name on account of the oak trees that are so plentiful in the vicinity. See University of Oregon *Extension Monitor* for September, 1924. The first postmaster at Oakland was David C. Underwood.

Oakley, Harney County. Oakley was a post office in the east part of the county, in Crane Creek Gap, a little more than a mile east of the town now known as Crane. The significance of the name Oakley has not been determined. Oakley post office was established November 4, 1889, with Philander H. Gray postmaster, who served until the office was discontinued July 29, 1895. When the office was established in 1889, Mrs. Gray suggested the name Fairview, which was well suited to the locality, but this turned out to be a duplicate of another Fairview, in Coos County, and postal officials would not approve it. Mrs. Gray then suggested Oakley, a name apparently selected at random.

Oakridge, Lane County. This name was suggested by Major R. L. Edwards, a right-of-way agent of the Southern Pacific Company. It accurately describes a topography and surrounding timber cover. Oakridge post office was established in 1912. In earlier days the community was known as Hazeldell.

Oakville, Linn County. Oakville is a locality about six miles airline southeast of Albany, but it is not now classed as a commercial community. The prominent Oakville church has long been a landmark. The name was of course derived from the Oregon white oak trees native to the land. Oakville post office was established May 16, 1878, with James B. Coney first postmaster. This office served the area for nearly a quarter of a century and was not closed until August 15, 1902. Its demise was doubtless due to the extension of rural free delivery.

Oar Creek, Douglas County. Oar Creek flows into Scholfield Creek southeast of Reedsport. Despite the adjacent marine activity, the name has no nautical significance as it was so called for Alfred R. Oar who took up land there in 1896.

Oasis, Gilliam County. Oasis post office was given a descriptive name. It was established May 5, 1884, with Thomas Fairhurst first and only postmaster. The office was closed to Arlington November 3, 1886. On August 6, 1948, J. D. Weed, an early settler in Gilliam County, wrote the compiler from Condon as follows: "Oasis post office was in what is known as Eight-mile Canyon, about four miles south of and up the canyon from the site of a later post office called Montague, which was established in 1911. I was well acquainted with the son of Thomas Fairhurst and visited at the old Fairhurst home where the Oasis post office was situated. There was a large spring that broke out in this canyon and when I was a boy, there were about twenty-five acres of irrigated alfalfa land. On all sides of this place there was dry, arid bunchgrass land." It seems apparent that Oasis post office was well named.

Oatfield Road, Clackamas County. This road extends southeast from Milwaukie. It bears the name of a well-known pioneer family of the vicinity. For additional information, see obituary of Mrs. Minerva Thessing Oatfield, *Oregon Journal,* April 9, 1943.

Oatman Flat, Lake County. Burton R. Oatman settled on this flat west of Silver Lake just after the turn of the century.

O'Brien, Josephine County. O'Brien is a community and post office on the Redwood Highway about ten miles south of Kerby, at the junction with the old stage road to the southwest up West Fork Illinois River. The place bears the name of John O'Brien, one of the first settlers of the locality. The spelling O'Bryan is wrong.

Obsidian Cliff, Lane County. Dr. E. T. Hodge, in his *Mount Multnomah,* page 103, *et seq.,* describes Obsidian Cliff quite fully. Obsidian is black volcanic glass composed of acid lava which cooled so rapidly that it did not have time to crystallize. Obsidian Cliff is a prominent point west of the Three Sisters. See under Glass Buttes.

Oceanside, Tillamook County. Nothing could be simpler than this.

Oceola, Washington County. Oceola was a post office of pioneer days established June 24, 1854, with Laurence Hall postmaster. Preston's *Map of Oregon,* 1856, shows the place near the present site of Beaverton, but spelled Oseola. It passed from the picture many years ago. There are many places in the United States named for the Seminole Indian chief, and the spelling generally used is Osceola.

Ochoco Creek, Crook and Wheeler counties. Ochoco Creek and other geographic features in central Oregon are said to have been named for Ochoco or Ocheco, a Snake or Piute chief, and a contemporary of Paulina and Howlock. However, this is disputed by old-timers in Crook County, who say the chief was named for the stream because he lived nearby. It is also said that the word *ochoco* was a local Indian word for willows and the stream was named on that account. The compiler knows no way to compose these differences in legend.

O'Conner Meadow, Klamath County. O'Conner Meadow is south of Tea Table Mountain. Denis O'Conner settled there at the time of World War I.

Odell, Hood River County. This is a well-known community in the middle Hood River Valley. It was named for William Odell, who settled nearby as early as 1861, and whose son, Milton D. Odell, was the first white child born in the valley. Roswell Shelley started a store at Odell and applied the present name. William Odell was a native of Tennessee. Milton Odell was born in 1863. A news item in the Hood River *Glacier,* October 14, 1932, cites Mrs. Troy Shelley as authority for the statement that the name of the town was originally suggested by S. F. Blythe, the pioneer editor of the *Glacier.* Post office records show that when the post office was established in June, 1910, it was first called Newtown. The name was changed to Odell in March, 1911. The name Newtown did not refer to Hood River's famous apple, but to the new settlement that sprang up at the railroad station about three-quarters of a mile southeast of the old Crossroads.

Odell Creek, Klamath County. Odell Creek is the name applied to the outlet of Odell Lake. The stream flows into Davis Lake. For many years there was considerable confusion about the names of the streams in the upper Deschutes River drainage basin. A committee of USFS officials codified the names, and the term Odell Creek was chosen to indicate the stream described above. It has come into universal use.

Odell Lake, Klamath County. William Holman Odell was born in Indiana in 1830. He came to Oregon in 1852, and engaged in farming and teaching, and later in surveying and was connected with the construction of the military wagon road up the Middle Fork Willamette River. He was appointed surveyor general for Oregon in 1871, and was a presidential elector in 1876, and later engaged in the newspaper business. He died in Portland, April 27, 1922. Odell Lake, one of the finest mountain bodies of water in the state, was named for him. The name was applied in 1865, by B. J. Pengra. In July, 1865, Pengra and Odell made a reconnaissance in the vicinity of Diamond Peak for the Oregon Central Military Road, and part of Pengra's report is on file at the Oregon Historical Society. The report says that Pengra and Odell visited what is now known as Odell Butte, apparently on July 22, 1865. On July 26 Odell climbed to the top of the butte and discovered a fine lake to the northwest. On July 27 the two explorers visited the lake and Pengra named it for Odell. The report contains a very good description of Odell Lake. Odell Lake has an elevation of 4792 feet, and the Cascade line of the Southern Pacific Company skirts its southern shore. Willamette Highway is on the north bank of the lake. Other features in the neighborhood named for W. H. Odell include Odell Butte and Odell Creek, the outlet of Odell Lake. Odell Lake is fed from melting snows on Diamond Peak and Maiden Peak, and is about six miles long. Its western end is but a few minutes walk from the summit of the Cascade Range over the tunnel of the Southern Pacific. This lake occupies a depression cut by a glacier, and the terminal moraine makes the dam that impounds the water. Odell Creek connects this lake with Davis Lake to the northeast.

Odell Spring, Crook County. This spring on the south edge of the county near West Butte was on the early day ranch of Clint Odell.

Odessa, Klamath County. Odessa post office was established northwest of Klamath Falls and near Upper Klamath Lake May 16, 1902. Mrs. Blanche Griffith was one of a long string of postmasters. The office operated with one intermission, until July 31, 1919, when it was closed to Recreation. The compiler is not satisfied with the available information about the origin of the name of this office. In 1948 Mrs. Griffith, then living in San Diego, wrote the compiler that the place was named by the wife of her

husband's brother. This Mrs. Griffith had lived in France and it is said that
the name Odessa came to her attention in that country, but the compiler
knows of no Odessa in France. It seems more probable that the name came
from the important city in the southwest part of Russia.

Odin Falls, Deschutes County. These falls are said to have been named
by Joe Houston, a nearby resident. Odin was the name, in Norse mythology, of the chief god corresponding to the Anglo-Saxon Woden. He was
considered to be the patron of wisdom and heroes.

Offatt Spring, Jefferson County. Offatt Spring is on Blizzard Ridge
south of Ashwood. It was named for Z. B. Offatt who settled in the area in
1869.

Ogle Creek, Marion and Clackamas counties. Ogle Creek was named
for Bob Ogle, of Molalla, who prospected on this stream and located some
claims thereon. The stream flows into Molalla River in the south part of the
county.

O'Hara Creek, Tillamook County. This creek was named for William
C. O'Hara who settled at Netarts in 1876.

Ojalla Creek, Lincoln County. Ojalla Creek is tributary to Siletz River
near Ojalla Bridge. Ojalla is a Finnish name, apparently that of a local
settler. It should not be confused with the Indian word *olalla* or *olallie,*
meaning berries.

O K Butte, Douglas County. Shortly after World War I, Theo and
Leroy Bond, USFS employees, cut a way trail near this butte on Calf Creek
south of North Umpqua River. Upon completion they asked approval of
ranger Fred Asam. He replied "It's O K" and the name was fixed from then
on.

O K Gulch, Wallowa County. This is a dry gulch about a mile and a
half long. Its mouth is in section 1, township 2 south, range 45 east. J. H.
Horner of Enterprise told the compiler that the gulch was named for John
Creighton, who built a corral in the gulch and rounded up his cattle there
and branded them with the letters O K, connected. Creighton served with
John W. Cullen in the Bannock War.

Olalla, Douglas County. This was formerly a post office on Lookingglass Creek, but the community is now served through other offices. For
origin of the name see under Olallie Butte.

Olalla Slough, Lincoln County. This is the tidal reach of Olalla Creek
where it enters Yaquina River east of Toledo. The original spelling of both
slough and creek was Olallie but the USBGN adopted the present form in
Decision List 6202. For origin of the name see under Olallie Butte.

Olallie Butte, Jefferson and Marion counties. The most important geographic feature in Oregon bearing the name Olallie is Olallie Butte at the
summit of the Cascade Range between Mount Hood and Mount Jefferson.
The USGS gives it an elevation of 7210 feet. The name is used in a number
of other places, particularly along the Cascade Range. The word is from
the Chinook jargon and means berries in general, or salmon berries. Gibbs
gives it as a derivative of the Chinook word *klalelli,* meaning berries. Its use
along the Cascade Range generally meant huckleberries. The USBGN has
adopted this form of spelling.

Old Maids Canyon, Jefferson County. This canyon runs to Mud

Springs Creek north of Gateway. Cecily Beasley homesteaded there in 1911 and Turner in *Reminiscences of Jefferson County*, page 193, tells how this canyon was named for Miss Beasley, a maiden lady of strong religious bent.

Olene, Klamath County. Steel says this name is an Indian word meaning eddy place, or place of drift, and that it was applied by Captain O. C. Applegate in 1884. The original location of the post office was up Lost River from the present site.

Oler Spring, Wheeler County. Oler Spring is on the upper reaches of Cherry Creek. It takes its name from Andrew A. Oller who homesteaded there after World War I. The compiler cannot reconcile the two spellings.

Olete, Klamath County. About 1890 Mr. and Mrs. William T. Wilson of Sacramento moved into eastern Klamath County for the purpose of developing a stock ranch. They settled in or near what was known as the Horsefly Valley. The locality was so named because of the prevalence of the insect pests. Wilson was conspicuous because of his fine red beard and to distinguish him from other Wilsons in Klamath County he was familiarly known as "Horsefly" Wilson. In due season there came to be a demand for a post office which is said to have been based to some extent on Mrs. Wilson's desire to get the home papers from Sacramento. In any event a petition was sent in and also a list of suggested post office names. Accordingly Olete post office was established March 25, 1892, with Wilson first postmaster. Wilson suggested the name Olete by coining the word from the names of his daughter, Ora Letetia Wilson. That the name Olete was selected by postal authorities where there was an office not far away in the same county with the name Olene is remarkable. The post office was about twelve miles northeast of Lorella, on the road to Vistillas. Olete post office was closed to Lorella in January, 1904.

Olex, Gilliam County. When this post office was established it was intended to honor one Alex Smith, a local resident, but the enthusiasm of the petition writer was better than his handwriting, and the authorities at Washington misread Alex into Olex, and so it has been for many decades. The office was established October 27, 1874, with James H. Butler first postmaster.

Olney, Clatsop County. Cyrus Olney was a native of Ohio. He was appointed supreme court justice of Oregon Territory in 1853, and resigned in 1857. He was a member of the constitutional convention of 1857. He died at Astoria December 21, 1870, aged fifty-five years. The town of Olney bears his name. See Scott's *History of the Oregon Country*, volume V, pages 220-21.

Ona, Lincoln County. Ona is a place on Beaver Creek about three miles east of Seal Rock. It is shown as a post office in 1890, and did not have an office in 1944 nor for some years prior. Ona may have been named with a Chinook jargon word. The jargon word *ona* generally refers to the razor clam. The community is not on the seashore and not near the clam beds, but someone may have imported the name. However, the compiler has a notion that the jargon word *ee-na* is the basis for the name. *Ee-na* means beaver and is appropriate to the location of the place on Beaver Creek.

Oneatta, Lincoln County. Oneatta is a ghost town on the northeast side of Yaquina River and about a mile and a half upstream from Yaquina. The place was first settled and named by Ben Simpson in 1871. See *History of Benton County*, page 490. A sawmill was operated there for a time and a post office was established in May, 1876. The community appears to have been named for an Indian princess, who was, as usual, beautiful, accomplished and virtuous. A. B. Meacham, in *Wigwam and War-path*, chapter V, gives a lugubrious story about her, but it is hard to tell whether it is fiction or fact.

O'Neals Mills, Polk County. Apparently the first post office in Polk County was O'Neals Mills, established January 8, 1850, with James A. O'Neal postmaster. The name was changed to Nesmiths on August 21, 1850, with James W. Nesmith postmaster, and the office was discontinued October 22, 1852. It was about two miles west of the present site of Dallas. For the history of the locality, see under Ellendale.

O'Neil, Crook County. William G. O'Neil and family immigrated from Illinois to a place near the present site of Bend about 1881. Members of the family lived at various places in central Oregon and three of the sons at one time owned a store at the place now called O'Neil, which is west of Prineville. Philip Grinder Carmical settled in this general locality and built a cabin in the spring of 1872. He brought his family in July, 1873, and the place became known as Carmical Station, as it was on a main route of travel. Carmical was born in Illinois on August 27, 1821, and died at London, near Cottage Grove, Oregon, February 18, 1909. Carmical Station was apparently a little north of O'Neil. Francis Forest established himself in the vicinity in 1876. His first place was near Carmical Station but he later moved his store to the present site of O'Neil. Forest Crossing on Crooked River nearby bears his name.

O'Neil Creek, Crook County. This creek is tributary to Eagle Creek just south of Eagle Rock. George W. O'Neil took up government land there in 1888.

Oneonta Gorge, Multnomah County. The origin of this name is obviously the place in New York. The compiler has not been able to find out why the name was applied to the gorge in Oregon. Oneonta is said by Gannett to mean "place of peace." A handsome steamboat of the Mississippi River side-wheel type was built at Cascades in 1863 and named the *Oneonta*. She was operated by the Oregon Steam Navigation Company on the Columbia River until 1877, both above and below the Cascades. While the evidence is by no means conclusive, it seems probable that Oneonta Creek and Gorge were named after the steamboat was built, and it is possible that the geographic features were named because of some incident connected with the boat.

Onion Peak, Clatsop County. Onion Peak, elevation 3064 feet, is one of the highest points in Clatsop County, and its rugged summit makes it an outstanding landmark. The peak is east-northeast of Arch Cape and about two miles north of the south line of the county. In December, 1945, Mrs. H. V. Alley of Nehalem informed the compiler that the peak was named for the wild onions growing near the summit. Mrs. Alley came to the Nehalem settlements as a girl in 1879 and said the name was used in early days. There are a number of varieties of wild onion growing in Oregon and the compiler does not know what sort grows on Onion Peak.

Onion Springs Mountain, Jackson and Josephine counties. Onion

Springs Mountain is an important geographic feature at the north joint corner of the two counties. It is a main triangulation point of the USC&GS, and has an elevation of 5240 feet, according to that survey. The name comes from the presence of the wild onion, *Allium acuminatum,* which grows near the springs. This mountain is sometimes called King Mountain, but that is not its official name. There are a number of geographic features in western Oregon named for the wild onion.

Ontario, Malheur County. The following quotation is from the *History of Baker, Grant, Malheur and Harney Counties,* page 545: "Ontario was so named at the request of James W. Virtue, one of the founders, who wished thus to honor the place of his nativity — Ontario, Canada. In 1883, William Morfitt, Daniel Smith, James W. Virtue and Mrs. Mary Richardson, all of Baker City, exercised desert land rights under United States laws and took up four adjoining sections of desert land." In 1927 Robert E. Strahorn told the compiler that he laid out the town in the early 1880s, presumably in connection with the construction of the Oregon Short Line Railroad, and that the name Ontario had been selected by a landowner before he got there. James W. Virtue was a prominent citizen of Baker and one-time sheriff. Inquiries made at Baker in April, 1943, to members of his family, elicited the fact that he was born in Ontario, Canada, and came to Oregon in the 1860s. Family tradition is to the effect that he spent some time at what is now Ontario, Oregon, and named the townsite.

Ooskan Butte, Lake County. This butte southeast of the Paulina Mountains was named by the USFS with the Chinook jargon word for cup or bowl, indicative of the crater in the top.

Opal City, Jefferson County. Opal City was named for Opal Springs in the Crooked River Canyon not far away.

Opal Lake, Marion County. This lake and creek of the same name north of Detroit Dam were named for Opal Elliot, the wife of early USFS ranger Roy Elliot.

Opal Springs, Jefferson County. Opal Springs are the largest of the remarkable springs on the lower reaches of Crooked River. They issue in a sand-lined basin that contains small opal-like pebbles, and from this they have received their name. They discharge over 80 million gallons of water a day.

Ophir, Curry County. The name Ophir occurs in the Bible, and refers to a region celebrated for its proverbially fine gold. Efforts to localize the place have not been successful. The compiler has been unable to learn who named the place on Euchre Creek in Curry County, or when the name was applied, but the word is said to have been chosen because of fine gold in the black beach sands nearby. Ophir post office was established on the Curry County list on June 5, 1891, with Elizabeth J. Burrow first postmaster. It has not been in continuous service, but was operating in 1980.

Opie Dilldock Pass, Lane County. This spot on the Skyline Trail about five miles south of McKenzie Pass is where the route leaves the lava fields and begins the descent to White Branch and the Sunshine Shelter. It was named in 1932 by Dee Wright and Ralph Engels, then USFS district ranger at McKenzie Bridge. They had had difficulty finding a good way down into

White Branch canyon but finally found one small, practical passage. They were both reminded of a comic strip character of the early 1900s named Opie Dilldock who always found some way out of impossible situations so they decided to honor the pass with his name. The compiler spent many hours trying to locate a copy of this comic strip to give credit to the cartoonist and verify the spelling. Donald J. Sterling, Jr., of the *Oregon Journal* and Robert Frazier of the Eugene *Register-Guard* also gave generously of their time and in the fall of 1974, the former of these two came upon the true facts of the matter. *The Comics* by Jerry Robinson, New York, 1974, lists the strip *Old Opie Dilldock* by Frank M. Howarth. In December, 1974, the OGNB, backed by such an authority, voted unanimously to correct the spelling from the earlier form, Oppie Dildock. Only one other small nugget can be added to this gold mine of historical information. The name is a variant spelling of Knight's Opedildock, a well-known camphor and soap linament of bygone days.

Orcal, Jackson County. Orcal was a station on the Southern Pacific, near the Oregon-California line. The name was coined by railway officials who took the first parts of the names of the two states. The station was not in service in 1945.

Ord, Lane County. Ord post office was named in compliment to Ord, Nebraska. Horace N. Fiske was first postmaster of Ord in Oregon, and he had formerly lived in Ord, Nebraska. When it came to naming the place in the Coast Range in Lane County, he selected the name of his old home. Ord post office in Oregon was established May 18, 1898, with Fiske postmaster. The office was in service, with one intermission, until October 31, 1912, when it was closed to Earl. It was six or seven miles northeast of Earl, on the extreme south edge of Lane County, and on the very headwaters of North Fork Smith River. Ord, Nebraska, was named for Major-General Edward O. C. Ord, U. S. A., who made a distinguished military record in the Civil War.

Ordnance, Umatilla County. In the fall of 1941 the War Department put into commission an establishment in the north part of Umatilla County, with the name Umatilla Ordnance Depot. On December 6, 1943, Ordnance post office was established to serve this depot with Lorena Lane Bounds first postmaster.

Oregon. But one important contribution to our knowledge of the origin of the word Oregon has been made in the last hundred years. That was the discovery, not unexpected, that Jonathan Carver may have appropriated the name, but not the spelling, from a Major Robert Rogers, an English army officer who was commandant at the frontier military post at Mackinac during the time of Carver's journey into the upper valley of the Mississippi. Elliott has written on this point in the *OHQ*, volume XXII, page 91. Major Rogers used the form Ouragon or Ourigan in a petition or proposal for an exploring expedition into the country west of the Great Lakes. This was in London in 1765. His petition was not granted, but he was sent to Mackinac as commandant. Carver is the first person to have used the form Oregon in referring to the River of the West. For a short account of Carver see under Carver Glacier. His *Travels Through the Interior Parts of*

North America was first published in 1778 and in the introduction occurs the following passage purporting to list the names of the four great rivers of the continent: "The River Bourbon, which empties itself into Hudson's Bay; the Waters of Saint Lawrence, the Mississippi and the River Oregon, or the River of the West, that falls into the Pacific Ocean at the Straits of Annian." It is well to get clearly in mind the chronological sequence of Carver's book and the petition prepared by Major Rogers. Carver's *Travels* was first published in London in 1778 from manuscript finally prepared just previous to its publication, but to use Carver's own words, was based upon "journals and charts" claimed to have been made during his journey to the west in 1766-67, and while at Mackinac in the fall of 1767. Kenneth Roberts' historical novel *Northwest Passage*, 1937, has a good deal to say about Carver and his relations with Rogers. Rogers' petition containing the name Ouragon was dated August, 1765, and his second petition containing the spelling Ourigan was dated February, 1772. A petition by Carver to the King's Privy Council showing the original association of Carver with Rogers for the purpose of the western exploration was acted on in May, 1769, and another petition by Carver showing that the journals and charts previously mentioned had been and were still deposited with the Board of Trade in London is dated November, 1773. Not only did Major Rogers put into writing the name Ouragon during the year before he engaged Carver, but also none of Carver's petitions, so far examined, contain the name Oregon as we spell it, although he mentions other localities. Malcolm H. Clark, Jr., in *OHQ*, volume LXI, page 211 discusses the foregoing chronology in considerable depth and gives details of the respective travels of Rogers and Carver and the relationship of the two men.

The subsequent history of the word Oregon, and some of the theories of its origin were favorite themes of the late Harvey W. Scott, editor of the *Oregonian*. The compiler cannot do better than to reprint some of Mr. Scott's editorial comments on the subject, but it must be borne in mind that these comments were not originally printed together as they are here reproduced.

"But the name Oregon came very slowly into notice. It was long after the publication of Carver's book when it again made its appearance. The name seems not to have been known either to Vancouver or to Gray, since neither uses it. The latter, entering the river as a discoverer, called the river, not the Oregon, but the Columbia, for his ship — a fact which shows that the name Oregon was quite unknown. The name was not used by Lewis and Clark in the report of their travels; in Astor's petition to Congress, presented in 1812, setting forth his claim to national assistance for his undertaking, on the ground that his efforts to establish trade here, under the sovereignty of the United States, would redound to the public security and advantage, the name Oregon is not used to designate or describe the country; nor is it used in the act of Congress passed in response to his petition, by which the American Fur Company was permitted to introduce here goods for the Indian trade. At this time, indeed, the name appears to have been quite unknown, and perhaps would have perished but for the poet Bryant, who evidently had happened, in his reading, upon the volume of Carver's travels. The word suited the sonorous movement and solemn majesty of his verse, and he embalmed it in "Thanatopsis' published in 1817. The journal of Lewis and Clark had been published in 1814-17, and the description therein of the distant solitudes and 'continuous woods' touched Bryant's poetic spirit and recalled the name he had seen in Carver's book. There are men whose susceptibility to literary excellence, whose skill and power in producing literary effects, give us results of this kind.

"The textbooks in the hands of our children in the public schools continue to furnish them with erroneous information that the name of the state of Oregon was derived from the word *oregano*, the Spanish name for the plant we call 'marjoram.' This is a mere conjecture absolutely without support. More than this, it is completely disproved by all that is known of the history of the name. There is nothing in the records of the Spanish navigators, nothing in the history of Spanish exploration or discovery, that indicates, even in the faintest way, that this was the origin of the name, or that the Spaniards called this country, or any part of it, by that name. There is marjoram here, indeed; and at a long time after the Spaniards had discontinued their northern coast voyages, it was suggested that the presence of marjoram *(oregano)* here had led the Spaniards to call the country Oregon. From the year 1535 the Spaniards, from Mexico, made frequent voyages of exploration along the Pacific Coast toward the north. The main object was the discovery of a passage connecting the Pacific and Atlantic oceans. Consequently, the explorers paid little attention to the country itself. After a time, finding the effort to discover a passage fruitless, they desisted for a long period. But, after the lapse of two centuries, they began settlements on the coast of California; and then voyages toward the north were resumed by some of their navigators. In 1775 the mouth of the Columbia River was seen by Heceta, but, owing to the force of the current, he was unable to enter. The fact here to be noted is that the Spaniards of that day did not call the country Oregon, or, if they did, they have left no record of it. Others have professed or proposed to derive the name Oregon from the Spanish word *oreja* (the ear), supposing that the Spaniards noted the big ears of the native Indians and named the country from the circumstance. But the Spaniards themselves have left no record of the kind; nor has it been noted, so far as we are aware, that the ears of our Indians were remarkably large. The word *orejon* is nearer our form; it signifies 'slice of dried apple,' we may suppose, from its resemblance to the form of the ear. Many years ago Archbishop F. N. Blanchet, of Oregon, while in Peru, noted a peculiar use of the word *orejon* in that country, which he ingeniously conjectured might throw some light on the origin of the name Oregon. We believe it probable that the name Oregon arose out of some circumstances connected with western explorations of the French. Earlier than the English the French had pressed on westward from the Great Lakes to the Red River, to the Saskatchewan and to the foot of the Rocky Mountains. They were ranging the country of the upper Mississippi in search of furs and for trade with the natives; they were full of curiosity and active in inquiry about the great distant West and the unknown western sea. Of this sea they possessed Span-

ish charts and perhaps used among the natives the word *Aragon* as a homo-
nym of Spain. When Jonathan Carver, of Connecticut was on his
expedition to the upper Mississippi country, in 1767-68, he made all possible inquiries, he tells us, about the country toward the west, the western
river, and the sea and the word Oregon. Recent writers have shown that
much of Carver's book is made up of unacknowledged extracts from
French explorers before him, particularly from Hennepin, Lahontan and
Charlevoix; and, as Carver had no scholarship, it is believed the book was
compiled in London, partly from Carver's own story and partly from the
records of French and English exploration." Scott's quoted comment that
the name appears to have been quite unknown at the time of Astor's expedition cannot be accepted as correct. Arrowsmith's 1798 map of the river
made from Broughton's reconnaisance is plainly titled *Plan of the River Oregan, made from an Actual Survey.*

The most plausible present explanation of the name Oregon is given
by George R. Stewart. In an article in *American Speech,* April 1944, and
Names on the Land, 1967, he propounds that the origin was an engraver's
error naming the Ouisconsink (Wisconsin) River on certain French editions
of Lahontan's map published in the early 1700s. In early editions the name
was not only misspelled Ouariconsint but also hyphenated after Ouaricon
—with the final syllable oddly offset. Stewart feels that Rogers heard sec-
ondhand of the River Ouaricon that flowed west somewhere beyond the
Great Lakes and that he mistakenly or carelessly transformed the word first
to Ouragon and then to Ourigan. The odd nomenclature did not occur in
the English editions of the map so if Rogers had seen one, he would have
had no reason to suspect the Ouaricon was merely the Wisconsin by
another name. Previously for more than fifty years, the best opinion has
been that the name originated from one of three sources, French, Indian
or Spanish. T. C. Elliott, in the *OHQ,* mentioned in the first paragraph
under this heading, associated the names used by Major Rogers with the
French word for storm, *ouragan.* William H. Galvani wrote of the possible
Spanish origin of Oregon in the *OHQ,* volume XXI, page 332. Joaquin
Miller suggested the Spanish *oye agua,* hear the water, as a source of Oregon in the *Oregonian,* October 21, 1907, but this seems fanciful to the compiler. Thus the matter rests.

Oregon Caves, Josephine County. This is the name of a summer post
office established to serve visitors to Oregon Caves. Oregon Caves post
office was established July 10, 1924. The caves were formerly known as
Josephine Caves.

Oregon Caves, Josephine County. For information about the discovery of Oregon Caves, see *OHQ,* September, 1922, pages 271 and 274. The
caves were discovered about 1874 by Elijah J. Davidson, a well-known pioneer citizen of southern Oregon. The caves were first known as Elijah
Caves and later as the Marble Halls and Josephine Caves. President Taft by
proclamation dated July 12, 1909, set the caves aside as a national monument with the name Oregon Caves. See *OHQ,* December, 1909, page 400.
For obituary of Elijah Davidson, see the *Oregonian,* September 11, 1927,
section 1, page 21.

Oregon City, Clackamas County. Oregon City was laid out and named in 1842, by Dr. John McLoughlin, chief factor of the Hudson's Bay Company, who located his land claim there in 1829. A Methodist church was built there in 1843. For narrative of the early settlement, see the *Oregonian*, January 1, 1895, page 15; description and location of pioneer buildings, *ibid.*, June 16, 1893, page 9; history of Oregon City, *ibid.*, March 11, 1900, page 13; description in 1872, *ibid.*, July 8, 1872, page 3. The paper mill at Oregon City was first operated in 1867. *OHQ*, volume XXXI page 276. The first name of the locality was Willamette, or Willamette Falls. It is referred to by that name in correspondence of the Methodist mission, established there in 1840 on the arrival of the "great reinforcement" in the *Lausanne*. After 1840 the place grew as a political and trade center. According to Mrs. Mary Waller Hall, daughter of the Reverend Alvin F. Waller, who was one of the missionary party which came to Oregon on the *Lausanne* and settled at Oregon City in June, 1840, the first apple tree in that place grew in the lot where the Methodist church was first built, from seed that her mother threw outdoors after she had been preparing dried apples for cooking. Oregon City post office was established March 29, 1847, with David Hill first postmaster.

Oregon Coast Highway, Clatsop, Coos, Curry, Douglas, Lane, Lincoln and Tillamook counties. A short sketch of early highway projects along the Oregon coast, by Leslie M. Scott, appears in *OHQ*, volume XXXIII, page 268. On June 3, 1919, partly as a result of feeling aroused by World War I, a measure was passed at a special election approving a bond issue of $2,500,000 to be used in cooperation with the federal government to build the Roosevelt Coast Military Highway. The name was in honor of Theodore Roosevelt. Later it became apparent that this name was not strictly suitable. In the fall of 1928 the compiler of these notes suggested to Robert W. Sawyer, then state highway commissioner, that the name Oregon Coast Highway be adopted. This change was made by the legislature in 1931. It is now known as US101.

Oregon Trail. Nearly a hundred years ago Francis Parkman coined a geographic name of ideal simplicity, the Oregon Trail. These two words captured the interest of millions of Americans and visitors from abroad. For almost a century the name Oregon Trail stood every test. However, in recent years efforts have been made to call this great route of travel the Old Oregon Trail, which is just a touch of overripe sentimentality. It is unfortunate that the name Oregon lends itself to alliteration with the adjective Old. The possibilities of this sort of thing are very great. We may have the Pure Pacific Ocean, the Cute Cascade Range, Perpetual Portland. Perhaps the worst feature of the business is the official use of the name Old Oregon Trail for a modern high-speed highway, many parts of which are not close to the routes used by the great immigrations to the Pacific Northwest.

Orejana Canyon, Harney County. Orejana is a name applied to a canyon in the southwest part of Harney County near the outside corner of Lake County. Orejana is a word used in the cattle country to indicate a young, unbranded calf and sometimes a colt. These animals are also referred to as "slick-ears" and are liable to be branded by the first finder. The canyon was named because the young animals were frequently found therein. The spelling Oreana originally used in Harney County for this and some other geographic features followed that used for a post office in Idaho, named in the 1880s. However, the present form was adopted in *Decision List 7304*. There is no doubt that the word is derived from the Spanish or from the Basque, but its exact origin is a little uncertain. In some places it is spelled *Orijana* and even *orina*. *Orijana* does not appear in any Spanish dictionary available to the compiler and *orina* is a little impolite. It seems probable that there is some connection between the word orejana meaning a "slick-ear" and the Spanish word *oreja* meaning ear.

Orenco, Washington County. Orenco is a community about four miles east of Hillsboro. Oregon Electric Railway officials made up the name in 1908 by taking parts of the title of the Oregon Nursery Company, which operated several large plantations in the locality.

Oretown, Tillamook County. James B. Upton and S. H. Rock settled in this part of the state in 1875-76 and in 1877 sent a petition to Senator John H. Mitchell asking for a mail route to Grand Ronde and a post office. Upton had a seal with Oregon City cut in the die, and he suggested that the proposed post office be named Ore City, for he had an idea that he could alter the seal in such a way that it could be used for the new community. Senator Mitchell knew that confusion would result with Oregon City and suggested to the postal authorities that Oretown would be a better name, which was adopted. C. C. Christensen was the first postmaster. The subsequent history of the seal has not transpired.

Orient, Multnomah County. There are two stories about the origin of the name of this well-known place southeast of Gresham. While they do give conflicting sources for the name, together they tell the early history of Orient community and Orient School, names in use long before the post office was established. In August, 1946, Mrs. Louise M. Nelson wrote to say that her father moved into the community in 1872. A new school building was built in 1875 and the ground was dedicated by her father to school purposes. She added that she was a pioneer in that part of the country and the name Orient was given to the school because it was the most eastward in Multnomah and Clackamas counties. This explanation appears unlikely to the compiler because here, due to our location on the shore of the Pacific Ocean, we tend to look west to the Orient rather than east. A more reasonable explanation is given by Barbara Yasui in *OHQ,* volume LXXVI, page 228, where she tells how Andrew McKinnon brought Miyo Iwakoshi to Oregon as his bride in 1880. Miyo along with her younger brother Rikichi and her five year old adopted daughter were the first Japanese to settle permanently in Oregon. After their arrival in Portland, McKinnon with his new family and an old friend, Captain Robert Smith, established a sawmill near Gresham which was named Orient Mill in honor of the bride. The community which grew around the mill thus received its name. Orient post office was established in March, 1896, with James N. Campbell first postmaster. The office was discontinued November 30, 1908, and the business was turned over to Gresham. It is probable that the post office had previously operated with the name Pleasant Home. The Pleasant Home office was moved several times and while it was located at Orient the name was changed.

Orleans, Linn County. The compiler has been unable to get much information about this pioneer community, in fact none at all about the origin of the name. The place was established a little before 1850 on the Moore donation land claim, just east of and across the river from what is now Corvallis. Floods in the 1860s eliminated the settlement but not the name, which is now used for an important voting precinct in Linn County. There is also an Orleans school. The name Orleans does not appear on any of the Oregon post office lists.

Orodell, Union County. Orodell is a locality, a ghost town, on Grande Ronde River just northwest of La Grande. It is where the river leaves the canyon and enters the valley. Paul Van Scoy of La Grande wrote the compiler in January, 1944, that a man named Fox started a sawmill at this point in the early 1860s, the first mill in Grande Ronde Valley. A store and a post office followed in due time. The post office was named Orodell, and the name was apparently originated by a Captain Harlow, who worked for W. J. Snodgrass, storekeeper and for a time the postmaster. The name was coined by taking part of the Greek word *oros*, meaning a mountain, and adding the English word dell as a suffix. The place is still known as Orodell, but there has been no community there for many years.

Oroville, Harney County. Oroville is a synthetic name derived from the Spanish word *oro* meaning gold. The word has been applied in many places by miners and prospectors. In March, 1947, Archie McGowan of Burns wrote the compiler as follows: "Oroville post office was situated at the Melvin Doan ranch near the base of Pueblo Mountain, in the south part of the county, about five miles south of the place now known as Fields. The locality was long known for its various minerals and float quartz. Messrs. Catlow and Doan were always interested in this mineral showing and gathered more or less quartz for exhibition. Presumably they named the post office for this rock." Oroville post office was established July 19, 1911, with Byron T. Tiscal first postmaster. Edwin J. Catlow was appointed postmaster January 8, 1914, and the office was closed to Fields on June 30, 1915.

Orphan Butte, Deschutes County. Orphan Butte, which is northeast of Paulina Mountains, received its name because it stands alone.

Ortley, Wasco County. Ortley was named for the Ortley apple, a variety that was planted there in considerable numbers. About 1911 it was planned to develop Ortley as a model orchard or fruit growing community and the growers were to live in the town and operate their orchards from there. The place is on the heights above Rowena and is about seven miles southeast of Mosier. The post office was established about 1911, with L. D. Firebaugh first postmaster. It was discontinued November 30, 1922, and many of the apple trees have been taken out.

Orville, Clackamas County. Orville post office was established April 29, 1892, with Lawrence J. Perdue first postmaster. The compiler does not have the date on which this office was closed but it was subsequent to June 1, 1895. Orville post office was about eight miles south of Barlow where the road from Barlow to Monitor crosses the road east to Yoder. The Perdue family were among the early settlers in this part of Clackamas County and a close friend was Orville Byland who taught the Oak Lawn school. Mr. Byland later moved to Oregon City and became county school superintendent. There is an interesting editorial about this part of the county in the

Canby *Herald,* June 17, 1948. The compiler is indebted to Mr. Alvin Perdue, Route 1, Hubbard, for much of this history. He lives on part of the old Perdue farm where the post office was situated. It is a little to the north of Oak Lawn school.

Orville, Marion County. Orville is a station on the Oregon Electric Railway about two miles east of Independence. It was named for Orville Butler who owned land nearby.

Oswego Creek, Clackamas County. This is the outlet of Oswego Lake. The stream was once known as Sucker Creek, and Oswego Lake was called Sucker Lake. A number of years ago the USBGN changed the name of the lake, but the name of the creek was not disturbed. In 1927 local residents asked to have the name Sucker Creek changed to Oswego Creek to agree with the lake, and the board took the necessary action on February 2, 1927.

Oswego Lake, Clackamas County. Oswego Lake was known as Sucker Lake during pioneer times because of the fish of that name. Local residents objected to the name and it was subsequently changed to Oswego Lake for the town of Oswego nearby, and it is now universally so known. It is said that the Indian name was *Waluga* which meant wild swan.

Othello, Lane County. This post office was in service from March 28, 1855, to July 8, 1859, with Jerome B. Zumwalt the only postmaster. Early maps do not show the place but in 1968 Jax Zumwalt told the compiler that the office was on the Andrew Zumwalt donation land claim along US99W just south of the Benton County line.

Otis, Lincoln County. This post office was established April 24, 1900, with Archibald S. Thompson, postmaster. While definite information about the naming of the community is not available, it is the local belief that it was in honor of Major-General Elwell Stephen Otis, 1838-1909, who was placed in command of the Department of the Pacific in 1898 and was also military governor of the Philippines.

Otter Rock, Lincoln County. Otter Rock is a post office near the ocean. The name originated from a rock situated about a half mile offshore and three and a quarter miles north of Yaquina Head. The rock is 36 feet above low water. About a mile to the north is a larger rock. Sea otter formerly inhabited these rocks. The writer has been unable to learn who suggested the name either for the rock or for the post office.

Ottertail Lake, Hood River County. This lake about one mile east of Wahtum Lake was named in 1955 by the Oregon State Game Commission. The name was arbitrary and selected to avoid duplication.

Outerson Mountain, Marion County. Outerson Mountain, near Detroit, was formerly called Bald Mountain, but because of much duplication the USFS changed the name to Outerson Mountain in honor of the late John Outerson, a pioneer of the North Santiam Valley.

Ouxy, Klamath County. Ouxy, once a railroad station north of Klamath Falls, bore a name derived from the Klamath Indian word *E-ukshi,* meaning Klamath Lake. Ouxy Spring remains nearby.

Overstreet, Malheur County. This station was named for Robert R. Overstreet, a resident of the vicinity. It is on the Union Pacific south of Nyssa.

Overtime Spring, Umatilla County. Overtime Spring near where

Texas Bar Creek enters North Fork John Day River was named in the 1960s by the USFS. Lloyd Waid of Ukiah said that truck drivers for Georgia Pacific Company stopped nearby for their coffee breaks and thus were often forced to exceed the eight hour straight time limitations of the Federal Wage and Hour Act.

Owens, Tillamook County. Owens post office was situated in Gods Valley and was named for a nearby landowner. The office was established January 16, 1912, with William Schultz first postmaster. The office was closed January 15, 1917.

Owings Creek, Umatilla County. In 1885, John A. Owings took up property near the mouth of this creek about five miles south of Nye. At one time Owens Creek southeast of Battle Mountain was erroneously shown on some maps as Owing Creek.

Owyhee, Malheur County. A post office called Owyhee Ferry was established on the Baker County list as of March 19, 1867, with William Hill postmaster. This office, which was in what is now Malheur County, was closed September 16, 1868. The writer is informed that the ferry was on Snake River near the mouth of the Owyhee, and was not on Owyhee River itself. It was not far from the site of Fort Boise, Idaho. A post office with the name Owyhee was established on January 4, 1886, with William Grimes postmaster. This office was closed September 8, 1887, with papers to Jordan Valley. This seems to indicate that the office was farther south than the mouth of Owyhee River. An office with the same name was established July 11, 1890, with Belle Dryden postmaster. This office was on the lower reaches of Owyhee River, not far from Owyhee Ferry, and was closed in 1932. An army map of 1887 gives the name Kinney's Ferry for the establishment on Snake River near Fort Boise.

Owyhee Rapids, Gilliam County. Judge Fred W. Wilson of The Dalles informs the compiler that these rapids in the Columbia River just west of Arlington were named for some event in the history of the steamer *Owyhee*. It is said that the boat grounded in the rapids. For the history of the *Owyhee*, see Lewis & Dryden's *Marine History of the Pacific Northwest*. The *Owyhee* was built at Celilo about 1864, and operated for about 12 years. These rapids were inundated in 1968 when John Day Dam was completed.

Owyhee River, Malheur County. On Saturday, February 18, 1826, Peter Skene Ogden, then on his second expedition into the Snake River country, "reached Sandwich Island River, so called, owing to 2 of them murdered by Snake Indians in 1819." There seems to be no doubt that the Owyhee River was named for these Hawaiians, for on June 15 of the same year Ogden uses the word *Owyhee*. The name *Owyhee* was used a century ago for Hawaii. Owyhee River drains a large area in Oregon and western Idaho, and there are other geographic features bearing the name, derived from the name of the river. There is a community of Owyhee near the mouth of Owyhee River and also an Owyhee Ridge in Malheur County.

Ox Bow, Baker County. Western pioneers were so familiar with ox bows that the descriptive name was often used for geographic features. The best-known ox bow in Oregon is that of Snake River near Ox Bow station. The neck of land in the bow has been pierced by railroad and water tunnels.

Oxman, Baker County. This station on the Union Pacific Railroad between Pleasant Valley and Durkee was originally called Unity. Because of confusion with the more important Unity west of Bridgeport, a movement was started by the Durkee Grange to change the name to Oxman in honor of Frank C. Oxman, a local rancher. This was accomplished in 1935. Oxman was an important prosecution witness at the trial of Thomas J. Mooney for bombing the San Francisco preparedness day parade in 1916.

P Ranch, Harney County. The P Ranch is one of the historic and romantic landmarks of eastern Oregon. It is in the valley of the Donner und Blitzen River south of Burns and west of Steens Mountain. For many years it was the headquarters of Peter French, one of the West's great cattle kings. For information about him, see under the heading Frenchglen. It is frequently said that the P Ranch was named for a brand based on Pete French's first name, but in September, 1943, Archie McGowan of Burns, wrote the compiler that this is not a fact. French came to Oregon in the early 1870s as a scout for Dr. Hugh James Glenn, the great landowner of the Sacramento Valley. Among others, French bought out an old prospector and trapper who had a small ranch in the place that French wanted for headquarters. This man was already using a P iron, according to McGowan. French bought him out, iron and all, and made the brand famous throughout the West. It was a coincidence that it was the initial of Pete French's first name.

Pacific City, Tillamook County. Pacific City was named because of its proximity to the Pacific Ocean. The post office was established July 31, 1909, with Peter Murray postmaster.

Pacific Ocean, western boundary of Oregon. After crossing the Isthmus of Panama in September, 1513, Vasco Nunez de Balboa discovered the ocean which he called *Mar del Sur* or Sea of the South. In November, 1520, Fernando Magellan, also under the Spanish flag, sailed through the straits which have since borne his name. On sailing into the great sea, he found it calm and bestowed the name of Pacific Ocean. Both names were used for many years. The Lewis and Clark expedition, 1803-1806, used these names: "Entrance of the Columbia River into the Great South Sea or Pacific Ocean" and again, "The Great Western Ocian, I can't say Pacific, as since I have seen it, it has been the reverse." (Thwaites *Original Journals of the Lewis and Clark Expedition,* volume III, pages 235 and 162.)

Packard Creek, Lane County. This stream is six miles south of Oakridge. It was named for a logger who took a contract for getting out some sugarpine logs. He used ox carts for hauling logs from the woods to the river. This took place in the early 1870s.

Packsaddle Creek, Baker County. This short tributary of Gold Creek in section 3, township 7 south, range 44 east, was named because in early days a burro packsaddle was abandoned on a deer skinning pole near the creek. It was a familiar sight for many years and a reminder that trailside litter started before the twentieth century.

Packsaddle Mountain, Wheeler County. This high ground west of Girds Creek near John Day River has two rock walls that simulate a packsaddle.

Pacquet Gulch, Wasco County. Frank X. Pacquet came to the Wapinitia area in 1876 and opened the first store. He settled southwest of the community near the gulch which bears his name.

Paddys Valley, Douglas and Lane counties. This is the valley of Middle Fork Willamette River where that stream crosses the county line west of Emigrant Butte. George H. Kelly of Portland told the compiler that the name was very old, and that he had been unable to learn its origin. When he was a young man the place was called Paddys Marsh.

Padgett Canyon, Morrow County. This tributary of Butter Creek south of Vinson was named for Elisha H. Padgett who took up government land there in 1886.

Paisley, Lake County. There is conflicting information about the reason for the name Paisley. The compiler has been informed that the place was named by Charles Mitchell Innes, a Scot, for Paisley in his native land. This was about 1873. The writer was told that Innes bestowed the name because the Oregon townsite reminded him of Paisley in Scotland. Whatever the reason may have been, it certainly could not have been this. A letter from E. J. McDonald printed on the editorial page of the *Oregonian* July 21, 1927, says that the place was named by a Mr. Steele, also a native of Scotland. The reader will have to make his own choice. The post office was established May 12, 1879, with Samuel G. Steele first postmaster. Presumably he is the man referred to by McDonald.

Palanush Butte, Deschutes County. This butte, southeast of Crane Prairie, is named with the Klamath Indian word indicating a place that is dried up.

Palatine Hill, Multnomah County. Since the 1880s the hill or ridge just west of the west bank of the Willamette River and east of Tryon Creek has been called Palatine Hill. The Palatine Hill road traverses the summit of this hill, which has a maximum elevation of 506 feet. The Romans used the word palatine in referring to something pertaining to the emperor or king. The only clue that suggests itself about the name in Multnomah County is the fact that the plat of Palatine Hill was filed by A. N. and Melinda King February 24, 1886. It may be possible that the Kings selected the name Palatine Hill because of the historic significance.

Palestine, Multnomah County. Palestine post office was established June 30, 1891, with James Howe first postmaster. Later postmasters were Henry S. Lewis and Albert Vail. The office was closed February 16, 1903, with all papers to Lents. Palestine post office was situated in a store operated by Henry S. Lewis at 39th and Division streets. The name Palestine was given by James Howe, an Englishman, who is said to have visited the Holy Land and liked the name. The store and post office were later moved to the vicinity of the South Mount Tabor school, near the old cemetery.

Palmer, Multnomah County. Palmer post office was in service near Bridal Veil Creek in the hills about three miles east of Bridal Veil, from February 21, 1898, to December 15, 1919. Idona A. Pulley was the first postmaster. The office was near a logging railroad and was named for L. C. Palmer, president of the Bridal Veil Lumber Company.

Palmer Butte, Curry County. This butte five miles northeast of Brookings was named for D. H. Palmer who homesteaded on its slopes before the turn of the century.

Palmer Creek, Jackson County. Palmer Creek is tributary to Applegate River in the southwest part of the county. It rises on the southeast slopes of Palmer Peak, elevation about 4700 feet. The creek was named for one Palmer, an early-day miner who was the first to discover gold on the stream. The peak was named for the creek.

Palmer Glacier, Clackamas County. There was an unusually light snowfall in the winter of 1923-24 and as a result of this a new glacier was discovered on Mount Hood in the summer of 1924. This glacier is west of White River Glacier. Because it drained into Salmon River it was decided to name it Salmon River Glacier. The name was not satisfactory but was eventually adopted by the USBGN. At the suggestion of the compiler of these notes and with the approval of the Mazamas and other interested organizations the USBGN changed the name on February 3, 1926, to Palmer Glacier, in honor of General Joel Palmer, who may have been the first white man to attempt to climb Mount Hood. That was in 1845. For information about General Palmer and his activities in Oregon, see under Palmer Peak. In a letter printed in *OHQ* volume VI, page 309, Archibald McDonald says that David Douglas attempted to climb Mount Hood in 1833. The compiler has been unable to get any facts about this attempt.

Palmer Junction, Union County. Palmer Junction was the name given to the junction of the Palmer Lumber Company's railroad and the line now operated by the Union Pacific Railroad Company which extends into Wallowa Valley. The post office was established in 1909.

Palmer Peak, Multnomah County. Palmer Peak is a high point in the northeastern part of Multnomah County not far from the cliffs above the Columbia River. It has an elevation of 4010 feet and was named for General Joel Palmer, a pioneer of 1845, and a noted character in Oregon history. He was born of American parents in Canada in 1810. He came to Oregon from Indiana, and helped Samuel K. Barlow build the Barlow Road. He made an attempt to climb Mount Hood on October 12, 1845, and while he did not reach the top, his diary indicates that he climbed well up on the mountain, and assured himself that the summit could be reached. The next day he named Camp Creek. Palmer settled in the Willamette Valley and was one of the founders of Dayton, Yamhill County. He became superintendent of Indian affairs for Oregon in 1853, and later was president of the Columbia River Road Company that opened a toll road from Sandy River to the Cascades in 1863. It operated ferries at Sandy River and at Dog (Hood) River. He occupied important political positions, and was once a candidate for governor. He died at Dayton June 9, 1881. Palmer Peak was at one time called Cub Peak, a name without significance. Palmer Creek in Yamhill County, was also named for Joel Palmer.

Palos, Linn County. Palos post office was established March 4, 1856, and was closed October 30, 1857. Samuel G. Thompson was the first postmaster. The compiler does not know why this pioneer post office was named with the Spanish word meaning sticks or stones and sometimes timbers, but he has come to the conclusion that Thompson was a student of history and was familiar with the name of the port near the southwest corner of Spain from which Columbus sailed on Friday, August 3, 1492, on his eventful first voyage of discovery. The Spanish place-name Palos was doubtless the origin of the name of the Linn County post office.

Palouse Creek, Coos County. How this stream tributary to Haynes Inlet on the north part of Coos Bay got the name of Palouse River in eastern Washington is a problem that the writer has been unable to solve. Lewis and Clark called the stream in Washington Drewyers River after a member of the expedition, and referred to the Indians as *Palloat-pallah.* Canadian members of the Astor party in 1812 used the name Pavion for the river and *Pallatapalla* for the tribe. David Douglas called the tribe *Pelusbpa.* For other forms of the name, see *Handbook of American Indians,* volume II, page 195. Palouse is the style now used in referring to a large area of rolling country and to other geographic features in eastern Washington. The French word *pelouse* is used to describe terrain covered with fine grasses, a characteristic of the Palouse country before it was cultivated. Whether the name Palouse came from the French-Canadian trappers or from the Indians, or both, is a matter of conjecture.

Pamelia Creek, Linn County. Pamelia Creek, at the southwestern base of Mount Jefferson, was named for Pamelia Ann Berry, a girl cook in the Marion County road locating party described by John Minto in *OHQ,* volume IV, page 249. Minto named the stream in 1879, and gave as his reason, the unfailing cheerfulness of Miss Berry. It may be added that the wording of the article is ambiguous, and Miss Berry may have been with the party that opened the trail to Black Butte in 1879. Pamelia Lake was named for the creek, probably by Judge John B. Waldo.

Panky Spring, Klamath County. Panky Spring and Panky Lake are west of Gerber Reservoir and east of Bonanza. They were named for the family of Lewis Panky, ranchers in the vicinity.

Pansy Mountain, Marion County. This mountain is in the extreme north part of the county, north of Detroit. It was named for the Pansy Blossom copper mine, which was operated by Joe Davis and Robert Bagby. The ore at this mine was peacock colored, and the mine was named on that account.

Panther, Lane County. More than fifty Oregon streams have been named for the cougar or the panther, not because of the popularity of these animals but because early settlers disliked them so. Ordinarily panthers did not attack human beings, but they killed such an abundance of deer and livestock that they were held in great aversion. Most of the Panther creeks in the state were named because they were the scenes of the visits of the giant cats, or the scenes of their exterminations. An important Panther Creek in western Oregon is that in Lane County, southwest of Eugene. This stream rises southwest of Crow and flows southwest to join Wolf Creek. Panther Creek was named in very early days. Panther post office was established near the mouth of this creek on February 5, 1894, with Demetrius D. Hooker first postmaster. The office was closed May 15, 1909, but the locality retained the name Panther, despite the fact that what local business there was for the place eventually evaporated. There are two varieties of panthers or mountain lions in Oregon, the one in the west part of the state called the Oregon cougar and the Rocky Mountain cougar in the east part of Oregon. Vernon Bailey in *Mammals and Life Zones of Oregon* has a good account of these animals.

Paradise, Wallowa County. This place was named by Sam Wade, Pres Halley and William Masterson, who went from Wallowa Valley about October, 1878, to look for winter range. On returning to the valley, they informed the settlers that they had found a regular paradise, with fine grass. Settlers with about a thousand cattle went to the new range in November, 1878. Notwithstanding the appearance of the country the winter was severe and many cattle were lost.

Paris, Lane County. Paris, Oregon, is justly famous for two things. It was not named for Paris, France, or "Pah-is," Kentucky. George E. Parris asked to have the place made a post office, and was the first postmaster. The office was named for him with one "r" eliminated.

Park Place, Clackamas County. The plat for Park Place, written as two words, was filed for record August 10, 1889, and the post office was established the following year. Postal authorities soon consolidated the name into one word. Park Place was originally called Clackamas, but that name was subsequently moved to a station about three miles to the north and the former station of Clackamas was called Paper Mill. Remains of the old paper mills were in evidence about 1910. The name Park Place was chosen for the townsite because of the park in a nearby oak grove, and Paper Mill was no longer appropriate. The post office name was later changed from Parkplace to Park Place.

Parkdale, Hood River County. Parkdale is a descriptive name rather accurately describing the community and its surroundings. The name is said to have been selected by Ralph Davies about 1910, when the post office was established. In 1976, after much public discussion, the name of the post office was changed to Mount Hood. Simultaneously, the Mount Hood office, three miles to the northeast, was closed. The community retains the name Parkdale.

Parker, Polk County. This place was named for one "Lon" Parker, a pioneer landowner. Bloomington post office was established on May 25, 1852, near the present site of Parker, with Eli W. Foster first postmaster. The office was closed in 1863. The railroad was built through this area in the late 1870s and Parker's station was then established. Many years later the name of the station was changed to Parker. Parker post office was established in September, 1880, and was closed in March, 1882. From 1884 to 1907 it was operated with the name Parkers. In 1914 it was reestablished as Parker and was closed in 1927.

Parkers Mill, Morrow County. "Uncle Ben" Parker established himself in this community many years ago, after crossing the plains by ox team, and started a small sawmill known as Parkers Mill. "Uncle Ben" was also a stockman, and well known in central Oregon.

Parkersburg, Coos County. This place got its name from Captain Judah Parker, who built a sawmill in the community about 1876. For history of Captain Parker by Fred Lockley, see *Sunday Journal,* March 3, 1946.

Parkersville, Baker County. In March, 1917, R. R. McHaley of Prairie City, Oregon, wrote as follows: "Parkersville was on the old mail stage road leading from Austin to McEwen and Auburn near the headwaters of Burnt River and about three miles west of Whitney. Mr. and Mrs. Parker kept a stage station for years until the railroad bypassed the station, and the town of Whitney was established. Parkersville is in Baker County about four miles from the Grant County line." The history of Parkersville post office is remarkably obscure. The compiler has been unable to get the date of its establishment, believed to be 1874, or the names of the postmasters. It was discontinued June 29, 1876, on the Grant County list. By all reports, it was never in Grant County, always in Baker. This is a set of puzzles the reader will have to solve.

Parkersville, Marion County. This place was about three miles west of the present site of Mount Angel. Parkersville post office was established September 29, 1852, with Freeman E. Eldriedge first postmaster. The office was discontinued on December 2, 1861. The community was named for William Parker, a pioneer of 1846. See Down's *A History of the Silverton Country,* pages 31, 36, 224 and 226. The name is now used for Parkersville school.

Parkrose, Multnomah County. Parkrose is a branch post office of Portland serving an area northeast of the city. Prior to the incorporation of Maywood Park in 1967, the whole area was considered Parkrose and the name in 1981 is still in general use although a sizeable part is within the corporate limits of the new community. The plat of Parkrose was filed on October 5, 1911, and the name was doubtless suggested because of the proximity of Rose City Park, the plat of which was filed in March 1907. It is said that a Portland business man, Frank E. Beach, was the originator of the name Rose City as applied to Portland.

Parkwood, Multnomah County. Parkwood post office was established about 1913 with J. W. Spencer first postmaster. The name has a pleasant rustic suggestion which seems to be about the only reason it was selected. The post office was closed in 1928.

Parrett Mountain, Yamhill County. This well-known landmark lies about four miles east of Newberg. Its lower slopes extend into Clackamas and Washington counties. It is crescent shaped and the highest point is near its northern end, with an elevation of 1243 feet. It is easily seen from the hills southwest of Portland and has become a point of interest since it serves to locate Newberg and the Pacific Highway West. Parrett Mountain is a spur of the Chehalem Mountains from which it is separated by Chehalem Gap. It was named for the Parrott brothers, who were born in England and who settled in this vicinity in 1853. The three brothers spelled their name as indicated, but members of the present generation who have investigated the matter in England, use the form Parrett, which they say is correct.

Parrish Gap, Marion County. This gap is in the hills about a mile northeast of Marion. It was named for E. E. Parrish on whose donation land claim the gap is situated.

Parrott Creek, Clackamas County. The stream flowing through New Era was named for Joseph Parrott, a pioneer of 1844.

Parrott Creek, Douglas County. This creek in the south part of Roseburg was named for Moses Parrott, a pioneer settler from Tennessee who owned a large acreage in the area. His large, Queen Anne house, built in 1891, was still standing in 1980 and was entered on the National Register of Historic Places.

Pass Creek, Douglas County. This creek bears a descriptive name because of the fact that it heads in a comparatively low divide between the waters flowing into Willamette River and those flowing into the Umpqua River. In early days William Ward built a corduroy road through the canyon of Pass Creek and operated a toll gate. See under Wards Butte. J. J. Comstock built a sawmill on Pass Creek about the time the railroad was built and was given the privilege of using cut timber along the right of way. He had previously been in business with Ben Holladay, and Holladay favored him on that account. The name of the creek was used for an early day post office, Pass Creek, established May 31, 1867, with William A. Mulvaney first and only postmaster. The office was closed to Yoncalla on January 7, 1869. Drain post office had not yet been established. The compiler has been unable to get the location of Pass Creek post office, except that it was near the stream Pass Creek somewhere between Divide and Drain.

Pataha Creek, Lane County. Pataha Creek, which flows into Wildcat Creek east of Austa, is one of several features in the Oregon Coast Range that have Indian names imported from the state of Washington. The compiler does not know the reason for the application of the name Pataha to the stream in Lane County unless it was by someone who had once lived in southeastern Washington or who liked the name because he saw it on a map. Pataha is the name of a village near Pomeroy, Washington, on a creek bearing the same name. *Pataha* is said to be a Nez Perce word meaning brush. See Meany's *Origin of Washington Geographic Names,* page 208.

Patawa Creek, Umatilla County. Patawa Creek and its tributary, South Patawa Creek, rise on the west slopes of Emigrant Hill and flow northwestward to join Tutuilla Creek near Pendleton. Patawa is the name of a large and well-known Indian family of Umatilla County, members of which have lived on the banks of Patawa Creek for many years. The spelling Parawa is wrong.

Patjens Lakes, Linn County. These lakes are one and one-half miles southwest of Big Lake and the 45 minute walk on a pleasant forest trail is a popular summer hike for young and old. They were named for Henry Patjens, a member of a Sherman County sheep family, who had summer range near Mount Washington at the turn of the century.

Pattersons Mills, Douglas County. Pattersons Mills were a very well-known Douglas County commercial enterprise that began operations in pioneer days. The mills were near North Umpqua River not far from the place called Glide. The post office Pattersons Mills was established in August, 1878, with William Patterson postmaster. The office was closed in June, 1886, and the business turned over to Mount Scott post office a few miles to the west.

Patton Valley, Washington and Yamhill counties. Patton Valley was named for a family of early settlers. William and Mary Patton came from Missouri in 1850 and later settled in the valley. Their son Robert owned land therein and lived nearby for many years. The valley lies along Tualatin River from a point near Gaston westward to Cherry Grove.

Paulina, Crook County. In the opinion of the writer there are more than enough geographic features in Oregon named for this belligerent Snake Indian. We have Paulina town, Paulina Mountains, Paulina Peak, Paulina Marsh, Paulina Creek, Paulina Prairie and Paulina Lake. The Southern Pacific Company also had Paunina station in the early days of the Cascade line. There may be honest sentimental differences of opinion about naming these features for the Oregon chief, but practically confusion is the sure result of such a process, especially when the various features are not in the same locality, but yet are not widely separated. For an account of Paulina and his activities, see Bancroft's *History of Oregon,* volume II, page 504 *et seq.* The name is spelled in a variety of ways, but Paulina is generally accepted. Paulina was a skillful antagonist and his activities covered a large territory. Bancroft's pages are full of Indian atrocities in central and eastern Oregon during the years 1866-68 and scores of miners, trappers and settlers were exterminated, and it is generally believed that Paulina was to a large extent responsible, though of course we have only the white man's side of the story. In the summer of 1867 Paulina raided several ranches in the John Day country. He was pursued by J. N. Clark, Howard Maupin and William Ragan, and was shot down while he was feasting on a roasted ox. Bancroft says that Clark killed him, but in central Oregon it is generally believed that Maupin fired the shot. For additional information see under Maupin. Col. William Thompson of Alturas, California, published a book entitled *Reminiscences of a Pioneer.* He gives a geographic description of the activities of Paulina, and confirms the generally accepted belief that Maupin killed him in Paulina Basin. Paulina Basin is near the junction of Trout Creek and Little Trout Creek north of Ashwood in the northeast part of Jefferson County.

Paulina Creek, Deschutes County. According to Captain O. C. Applegate, the Piute Indian name for this stream and the vicinity of Paulina Prairie was *Mil-ka-ke.* Captain Applegate told the compiler in November, 1927, that he did not know the translation of the name.

Paulina Peak, Deschutes County. Paulina Peak, elevation 7985 feet, is a high point on the south edge of Paulina Lake in the Paulina Mountains. For information about this part of Oregon, see under Newberry Crater. Paulina Peak, shown on older maps as Pauline Peak, is one of a number of central Oregon geographic features named for Paulina, the famous Snake Indian chief. There are several spellings, including Paunina, Panina, Panaina and Palihi. He was of the Walpapi tribe of Snakes. For information about his activities see under Paulina. For a description of the neighborhood of Paulina Peak, see the *Oregonian,* January 16, 1916.

Paunina, Klamath County. Paunina was a station on the Southern Pacific railroad named for the famous central Oregon Indian chief. See under Paulina. During the construction period. Paunina was called Skookum.

Pawn, Lane County. The name of Pawn post office was composed by taking the first letter in the names of four local residents who were instrumental in getting the post office established. These four men were named

Poole, Akerley, Worthington and Nolen. Willis Nolen suggested manufacturing the name in this manner. Monroe Poole was the first postmaster.

Paxton, Jefferson County. Paxton is a station on the Burlington Northern north of Madras named for G. L. Paxton, a nearby landowner.

Payn, Clackamas County. Payn post office was on the extreme north edge of Clackamas County just about south of Lents and close to the west base of Mount Scott. It was named for the postmaster, William S. Payn. This office was established April 6, 1898, and was closed January 12, 1904. As with so many other small offices, its death was caused by the advent of rural free delivery.

Payne Creek, Wheeler County. Payne Creek is tributary to Girds Creek. George Nelson of Mitchell told the compiler that James Payne was a well-known early homesteader with a family of ten daughters.

Paynesville, Clackamas County. Paynesville was about three miles north of Sandy and a little to the west of the Bluff Road. The post office was established December 31, 1885, with John G. P. Lawlor first and only postmaster. The office was closed June 6, 1888. Paynesville was named for a local landowner who owned property adjacent to Lawlor. Later Lewis Hoaglum acquired some or all of this property. The site of the post office was said to be owned by a man named Pratt in 1947.

Peach, Malheur County. This Union Pacific Railroad station was named for a peach orchard nearby. The place was about nine miles east of Juntura, and in 1943 it was reported that the station was no longer in service.

Peak, Benton County. Peak post office was a few miles northwest of Marys Peak and was named for the mountain. It was on the extreme west edge of Benton County in the Coast Range and was relatively isolated. The office was established October 11, 1899, with Virgie Davidson postmaster. Peak post office was discontinued October 15, 1917.

Peak, Washington County. A post office with the name Peak was established in Washington County on March 13, 1874, with Bentley George postmaster. It was discontinued June 9, 1876. Peak post office was two or three miles northwest of Forest Grove and near Gales Creek. It was named for Gales Peak, a prominent feature a little to the northwest.

Pearcy Island, Multnomah County. This island is in the angle formed by the junction of the Columbia and Willamette rivers. South of the island is Pearcy Slough. These features bear the name of Nathan Pearcy, a pioneer of Oregon, who took up a donation land claim on the island in 1850. Drainage and reclamation projects are changing the character of islands and sloughs in this locality.

Pearse Peak, Curry County. Pearse Peak is four miles east of Humbug Mountain. Charles H. Pearse took up a homestead on its west slope in 1906 but probably did not personally prove it up as he was born in 1826 in Boston. He came to Oregon in 1871 and a short time later was lighthouse keeper at Cape Blanco. His son, Stoner P. Pearse,was at one time in the state legislature and reportedly had mining claims on the mountain so the homestead could have been a family enterprise.

Pebble Creek, Columbia and Washington counties. Pebble Creek, which bears a descriptive name, rises in the extreme north part of Washington County, and after crossing the Columbia County line flows northward to join the Nehalem River in the east part of Vernonia. It has been called Pebble Creek since pioneer times. Pebble post office was established January 31, 1891, with Richard J. Tyacke postmaster. It was on the Pebble Creek road about three miles south of Vernonia, on the Tyacke property. The office was in operation until December, 1895, when its affairs were turned over to the Vernonia office. The Pebble Creek road or trail was one of the first routes of travel into the upper Nehalem Valley, and many pioneer settlers went in that way from the Willamette Valley. See Fred Lockley's interview with Mrs. Sarah Spencer on editorial page of the *Oregon Journal*, August 18, 1928.

Pebble Springs, Gilliam County. Pebble Springs, three miles southeast of Arlington, is the site of the proposed controversial nuclear generating station planned by Portland General Electric Company in the late 1970s. The name comes from Pebble Springs Camp and not because nature provided a constant and bountiful supply of cold, crystal clear water at this location. Rather, according to information provided by long-time Arlington resident Alfred "Buzz" Clough, Pebble Springs Camp was part of Krebs Brothers Sheep Ranch. When they put in a cistern and other facilities, they needed a name. An observant worker noticed an abandoned (and empty) bottle of Pebble Springs Whiskey and all agreed that that name would serve admirably.

Peck, Douglas County. When the Oregon and California Railroad was built south of Roseburg in the early eighties a station called Nichols was established thirteen miles southwest of Riddle. This station was named for a well-known family of the vicinity. It did not have a post office however until December 31, 1914, when Nichols post office was established with Viola B. Nichols first and only postmaster. This office operated until December 31, 1929. The railroad company had difficulty with the station named Nichols due to the fact that there were other places on the line with the same name. Shipments went astray. As a result, the company changed the name of Nichols station to Peck. The origin of the name Peck is a mystery to the compiler and it is not certain just when the railroad made the change. In any event, a post office was named Peck and established December 29, 1931, with Homer V. Cook postmaster. This was just two years after the Nichols office had been closed. For some reason Mr. Cook never got the Peck office into operation and his appointment was rescinded June 2, 1932. As far as the compiler knows there has been no post office at this point since that date while the railroad station Peck has also succumbed to the paucity of travelers and shippers in the Cow Creek Canyon.

Pedee, Polk County. Pedee owes its name to Colonel Cornelius Gilliam who was born in North Carolina in 1798 and came to Oregon in 1844. See under Gilliam County. He was killed in 1848. Either he, or members of his family, named Pedee Creek, a tributary to Luckiamute River. Pedee community is near the mouth of this creek. The name is, of course, from the famous river of North and South Carolina which was doubtless frequently in the minds of the Gilliams. The stream in the South is officially Peedee, but the place in Oregon is spelled Pedee.

Pedro Mountain, Baker County. Pedro Mountain is west of Rye Valley in the southeast part of the county. In December, 1945, LeRoy Grettum of Baker wrote the compiler that old mining men of that area reported that the mountain was named by a group of Portuguese miners who operated there during the eastern Oregon gold rush of the 1860s. There was a Pedro Mine on the mountain, and it seems probable that the mountain took its name from the mine. Pedro post office was in operation for a few months in the early summer of 1879 with Lyman S. Brown postmaster. Doubtless it was connected with some work at the mining claim.

Peel, Douglas County. Peel post office was on Little River, a branch of North Umpqua River, about twenty-five miles east of Roseburg, and a few miles up Little River from Glide. The office was established January 18, 1888, with Robert McKure first postmaster. According to a story in the Roseburg *News-Review,* February 21, 1947, the office was named for Samuel West Peel, of Bentonville, Arkansas, by Hiram L. Engels, who became second postmaster at Peel on February 15, 1888. Peel and A. A. Engels, father of H. L. Engels, had been schoolmates many years before. Peel post office was closed December 15, 1921. S. W. Peel, 1831-1924, was a well-known citizen of Arkansas, of which state he was a native. He served in the Confederate army in the Civil War and reached the rank of colonel. He studied law, and held several political offices, including that of prosecuting attorney on one of the circuits. He was elected representative in Congress and served from 1883 to 1893.

Peepover Saddle, Wallowa County. This saddle, in the southeast part of the county, is very narrow, and its summit is sharp. It is called Peepover on that account, and the name is usually written P. O. Saddle. The initials conveniently suggest other forms of the name.

Peg Gulch, Jefferson County. This tributary of Little Muddy Creek east of Axehandle bears the name of a local homesteader, Daniel W. "Peg Leg" Morissey. Time has obliterated the details concerning the loss of Mr. Morissey's leg.

Peggy Butte, Wheeler County. Peggy Butte northeast of Mitchell was named for Margaret Reynolds whose family came from Tennessee and raised stock in the area.

Pelican, Klamath County. For the history of the post offices called Pelican and Pelican Bay, see under the heading Rocky Point.

Pelican Bay, Klamath County. Pelicans are much in evidence about the Klamath lakes, and this name was appropriately applied to an arm of Upper Klamath Lake. A few other geographic features in the state are also named for the pelican. The Oregon bird is *Pelecanus erythrorhynchos,* the American white pelican. The habits of this pelican, particularly in Oregon, are well described in Bulletin 121 of the United States National Museum, *Life Histories of North American Petrels and Pelicans,* page 285. The Klamath Indian name for these birds was *kumal* or *yamal.* Pelican Bay was named by Captain O. C. Applegate in 1866. There was at one time a post office called Pelican near the west shore of Pelican Bay and later another office named Recreation. For the most part these offices served summer patrons.

Pelican Butte, Klamath County. This butte was named for Pelican Bay nearby. One of the Indian names for the butte was *Mongina.* The USC&GS formerly listed it under the name Lost Peak, elevation 8026 feet.

Pelican City, Klamath County. Pelican City is the suburb of Klamath Falls north of Link River along the shore of Upper Klamath Lake. It is so called because it waś the site of the mill that belonged to the Pelican Bay Lumber Company. Pelican Bay itself is in the extreme northwest corner of the lake.

Pelican Creek, Umatilla and Union counties. Pelican Creek, prominent in the history of northeastern Oregon, rises in the Blue Mountains east of Kamela and flows southeast to join Dry Creek just northwest of Hilgard. In November, 1945, C. C. Fisher of the U. S. Bureau of Reclamation, then stationed at Salem, wrote the compiler as follows: "When I was a small boy my parents ran the old Pelican stage station on Pelican Creek a few miles above Hilgard. A short distance above the stage station is Pelican Prairie on the old stage road. It was reported that Pelican Creek and Pelican Prairie were named because someone saw a flock of pelicans flying over that area. This was quite an unusual event, as I never saw any pelicans during my young life in the Blue Mountains." The compiler has seen this stream shown as Tillicum Creek on some maps, but that name is wrong.

Pelton Dam, Jefferson County. Pelton Dam is a 203 foot high structure on Deschutes River five miles south of Warm Springs built by Portland General Electric Company for hydro-electric power. It takes its name from the one time Oregon Trunk Railway station of this name on Willow Creek just east of Deschutes River. When this line was built, James J. Hill, president of the railway, had several stations named for local residents. John Sisemore, the first postmaster at Bend, married the widow of Enoch C. Pelton of Jackson County. She had three sons by her first marriage and two of them, John and James Pelton, settled in central Oregon where they were well-known citizens at the turn of the century. *Pelton* is also the Chinook jargon word for crazy, but it is only coincidence that it described the emotions of some ardent anglers. Feeling ran high and old friends faced off on this issue of the first high dam on Deschutes River.

Pemberton Canyon, Gilliam County. This canyon is southwest of Condon. It was named for Pemberton Cason, a nearby resident. Pemberton F. Cason was born in Missouri in 1843 and came to Oregon in 1864. After experiences in the mines and elsewhere, he settled in what was later Gilliam County in 1881. Cason Canyon, west of Pemberton Canyon, was named for the same man.

Pendleton, Umatilla County. George Hunt Pendleton, of Ohio (1825-89), was Democratic candidate for vice-president in 1864. Pendleton was named in his honor, in 1868, by the commissioners of Umatilla County, J. S. Vinson, James Thompson and Samuel Johnson, on suggestion of G. W. Bailey, then county judge. In that year the Oregon Democratic state convention instructed its delegates for Pendleton for president. The town of Pendleton was designated the county seat against the rivalry of Umatilla Landing, which was just east of the mouth of Umatilla River. The Pendleton townsite was owned chiefly by M. E. Goodwin and G. W. Bailey. For progress of the town until 1890, see the *Oregonian*, January 1, 1890. Efforts to establish a trading center in what is now the locality of Pendleton began as early as 1851, when Dr. William C. McKay started a post at the mouth of McKay Creek and called it Houtama. Later one Marshall established Marshall Station about a half mile to the east, on the north bank of Umatilla River. This was also known as Swift Station. Marshall is said to have been a "White Collared Man," a euphemism for gentleman gambler. Marshall Station was about two miles west of the present business district of Pendleton. About 1863 Marshall Station was known as Middleton because it was believed to be about half way between Umatilla Landing and the Grande Ronde Valley. When Umatilla County was created in 1862, the temporary seat of government was put at Marshall Station. See under Umatilla County, and also Fred Lockley's article in *Sunday Journal*, June 3, 1945. Marshall post office was established April 21, 1865, with Jonathan Swift postmaster. The name of the office was changed to Pendleton on October 8, 1869.

Pengra, Deschutes County. Pengra post office was established on the Crook County list January 18, 1886, with Walter O'Neil postmaster. The office was closed December 22, 1888, with papers to Crater. Crater was an office a little to the southwest of Lava Butte and just north of the Vandevert ranch, close to Deschutes River. According to the Polk *Gazetteer* of 1889-90, Pengra was ten miles south of Crater, at or close to the present site of La Pine. B. J. Pengra had some interests in that locality and the office was obviously named for him.

Pengra, Lane County. Pengra was a station on the Cascade line of the Southern Pacific Company. It was named for B. J. Pengra, a pioneer of 1853, who was for a time a newspaper publisher, and in 1862 surveyor general for Oregon. He was an advocate of the Humboldt or Winnemucca railroad route from the Willamette Valley. Pengra had charge of the construction of the military road up Middle Fork Willamette River. He died at Coburg September 18, 1903. For many references to his activities, see Scott's *History of the Oregon Country*.

Pengra Pass, Klamath and Lane counties. The USBGN, at the suggestion of the compiler of this book, adopted on November 2, 1927, the name Pengra Pass for the pass in the Cascade Range just west of Odell Lake used by the Cascade line of the Southern Pacific Company. This action was taken in honor of B. J. Pengra, one of Oregon's pioneer railroad enthusiasts and an early advocate of a railroad from the Willamette Valley across the Cascade Range to Nevada. It was therefore thought proper that an important strategic point in the Cascade Range should be named in his honor. The proposal made by the compiler was approved by the government bureau concerned. At the time the compiler suggested the name Pengra Pass for this feature, he did not know that B. J. Pengra was its actual discoverer. The Oregon Historical Society has been provided with part of a report by Pengra, who, with W. H. Odell, made a reconnaissance of the Diamond Peak region for the Oregon Central Military Road in July, 1865. Writing as of July 21, 1865, Pengra mentions the probability of a good pass to the north of Diamond Peak. On July 27 Pengra and Odell visited Odell Lake and Pengra confirmed his belief that there was a good pass through the Cascade Range at this point. He gives the elevation of the pass as 5000 feet, or 600 feet lower than Willamette Pass, now Emigrant Pass, west of Summit Lake. Both of these observations are remarkably correct. For editorial comment on B. J. Pengra and pass in Oregon named for him, see the *Oregonian,* December 11, 1927. For the crossing of SH 58 just north of Odell Lake, see Willamette Pass.

Peninsular, Multnomah County. Peninsular post office was established April 25, 1890, with Anna B. Lyman first postmaster, to serve a growing suburban area that was later taken into Portland. The name was descriptive and had its origin in the Peninsular Addition and some additions to that addition. The writer does not know when Peninsular post office was closed, but it is shown as active on the post route map of 1900. The addition was named because it was on the peninsula between Columbia and Willamette rivers. The plat was filed in March, 1889.

Penn, Lane County. Penn was a railroad station for McGlynn post office. See under that name. The name Penn was used for the railroad station because of the Penn Timber Company, which was operating nearby.

Penola, Grant County. A post route map dated 1880 shows a post office with the name Penola at a point sixteen miles northeast of Prairie City on the road to Sumpter. Other postal records show that the Penola post office was established January 27, 1876, and was discontinued April 19, 1878. John R. Roy was the only postmaster. The compiler has been quite unable to get information about the origin of the name or word Penola. It does not appear in any available reference works except that it is used for a post office in Virginia. Correspondence with the postmaster in Virginia has failed to produce any explanations of the name.

Peoria, Linn County. This name came from Peoria, Illinois. The village of Peoria is below the mouth of Lake Creek, on Willamette River, 15 miles southwest of Albany and eight miles northwest of Halsey. The first settlement was by H. A. McCartney, in 1851. In 1875 the place contained four grain warehouses on the river bank, having a capacity of 60,000 bushels of wheat. There were 30,000 bushels in the warehouses. The school contained 60 pupils. The village was a shipping point for considerable business until the Oregon and California Railroad drew the business to Halsey and Shedd. See *Material Resources of Linn County,* A. S. Mercer, 1875, page 53. A post office called Burlington was established in this locality on November 17, 1855, with William M. McCorkle postmaster. The name of the office was changed to Peoria on November 7, 1857.

Perdue, Douglas County. Perdue post office was named for John Perdue, Sr., its first postmaster. The office was first situated on South Umpqua River at the mouth of Elk Creek, and was called Elk Creek. John Perdue, Sr., became postmaster of the Elk Creek office on June 11, 1884, and on the following August 22, the name of the office was changed to Perdue. About this time the office was moved down South Umpqua River about six miles, but the writer cannot determine just when this move was made. For nearly forty years Perdue post office continued to serve the territory, until it was closed rather abruptly on August 31, 1920, because Amos O. Buker, then postmaster, ran afoul of postal regulations prohibiting dual government employment. Buker took on the job of local census enumerator and the government quickly put a stop to his postal activities. The locality was without a post office for three years, until Milo post office was established

May 13, 1923, with Mrs. Cora E. Buker first postmaster. See under Milo. Perdue was about half way between Days Creek and Tiller.

Perham, Crook County. On August 9, 1946, Remey M. Cox, editor of the Prineville *Central Oregonian,* wrote the compiler: "Gardner Perry, for many years stage driver on the Prineville-Paulina run, reports he lived near Bear Creek buttes while Perham post office was open. The place was named for Ad Perham, who ran sheep on Bear Creek buttes. The post office was operated by Sadie E. Moore, wife of one of Perham's hands. Moore was carrying the mails from Prineville to Silver Lake at the time while his wife ran the post office in their home. There wasn't much of a settlement there, Perry reports. The Perrys lived about two miles north of the Perham post office. When the Moores moved to Prineville, the post office was closed. Moore ran a harness shop in Prineville." According to postal records, Perham post office was established December 26, 1888, with Sadie E. Moore postmaster. The office was closed November 1, 1890.

Perham Creek, Hood River County. This stream flows under the Columbia River Highway and into the Columbia River about seven miles west of Hood River. It was named to commemorate Eugene L. Perham who emigrated from Indiana to Oregon in 1850. After living at various places in Oregon he married the daughter of the Reverend Edward R. Geary, who came to Oregon in 1851. The newly married couple settled at The Dalles about 1857 or 1858, where Perham was connected with river navigation interests that became part of the Oregon Steam Navigation Company in 1860. The family remained in The Dalles for about 25 years and Perham took an interest in public affairs. He then moved to the vicinity of what is now Perham Creek, but later disposed of his holdings. He died in 1891 and Mrs. Perham died in 1926. The Perhams were a much respected family.

Periwinkle Creek, Linn County. Periwinkle Creek heads near Midway School southeast of Albany and flows northwest through the east part of town and into Willamette River. In earlier days this stream was known as Periwinkle Creek on account of the presence of a small mollusc, well known to fishermen. The name of this little mollusc has many forms, including the popular variation pennywinkle. About 1911 USGS map makers used the name First Periwinkle Creek for the stream in contradistinction to Second Periwinkle Creek to the northeast, but applied the title to the wrong fork. In 1942 the USBGN changed the name of Second Periwinkle Creek to its pioneer style, Cox Creek, and adopted the name Periwinkle for the creek that flows through Albany. The name should be used for the longer branch and not for the shorter fork to the northeast. The business now seems to be adjusted to the satisfaction of local citizens.

Perkins Creek, Lane County. This tributary of Mosby Creek was named for Joseph Perkins who settled on its banks in 1883.

Perkins Ditch, Baker County. This ditch in the Lower Powder River Valley was named for Edmond P. Perkins whose ranch at Keating was a stop on the stage line from Baker to Sparta. This information was supplied by Catherine Tyler of Baker, a descendant.

Perkins Flat, Malheur County. Perkins Flat is an area on the west shore of Lake Owyhee about ten miles south of Owyhee Dam where the

BLM has leased sites for recreation cabins. It is named for Fred Perkins who farmed the land before it was inundated by the lake.

Pernot Mountain, Lane County. This mountain was named for John F. Pernot, who was in charge of forest insect studies in the Pacific Northwest, for the USFS. He was killed by a runaway horse in the Ochoco National Forest, and this peak in the Cascade Range was named for him. It is in the northwest part of township 18 south, range 3 east.

Perrin Canyon, Wheeler County. Perrin Canyon opens into Pine Creek six miles south of Fossil. It was named for John P. Perrin who homesteaded there in 1887.

Perry, Union County. G. Earl Stoddard, postmaster at Perry in 1926, informed the writer that the name of that place was selected arbitrarily by postal authorities. Perry was first known as Stumptown, and later Stanley after the man who owned the sawmill, but the authorities would not approve the name Stanley because of duplication with some other Stanley in Oregon. The compiler has no data about any other Stanley in this state, but there may have been such a place.

Perry Butte, Douglas County. Perry Butte is north of North Umpqua River and four miles north of Toketee Falls. USFS ranger Fred Asam named it for Perry Wright of Cap's Illahee who grazed cattle nearby.

Perrydale, Polk County. Perrydale was named by William Perry, a pioneer landowner. The post office was established in 1870.

Persist, Jackson County. William W. Willits came to Oregon from Iowa in 1875, and his wife was born at Talent, Oregon, of pioneer parents, in 1858. They settled on a homestead at the present site of Persist post office in 1884, and after 18 years of persistent effort, secured an office to serve their immediate neighborhood in 1902 with Willits first postmaster. The name Persist means all it implies to those who for many years pioneered in this part of Oregon with road work, school development and other problems. Mail was first had at Trail post office, 22 miles away by trail, or ten miles by trail to Prospect. The Willits' suggested the name Persist on account of their pioneering.

Peter Paul Prairie, Douglas County. This prairie is near Red Butte south of Little River. In the early 1920s USFS supervisor Carl Neal and ranger Fred Asam were on a pack trip in the area. They camped one night in this nearly alpine meadow and since it was covered with fine grass for the animals, named it in honor of Neal's saddle and pack horses, Peter and Paul.

Peter Skene Ogden Park, Jefferson County. Peter Skene Ogden was the explorer of central Oregon during the period of the fur traders. He was born in Quebec in 1794 and entered the service of North West Company in 1811. He entered the Oregon country in 1818 at the head of a trapping party with headquarters at Fort George, now Astoria. He discovered and named Mount Shasta, California, February 14, 1827. He was one of the first to describe and name geographic features in eastern Oregon. He discovered the Humboldt River in Nevada in 1828, and the city of Ogden, Utah, is named in his honor. He was a chief factor of the Hudson's Bay Company at Fort Vancouver; he rescued the survivors of the Whitman massacre in December, 1847; and died in Oregon City on September 27, 1854. He is buried in Mountain View cemetery in Oregon City, where a monument was erected by pioneer and historical organizations, and dedicated to his memory on October 27, 1923. Summaries of Peter Skene Ogden's Journals, edited by T. C. Elliott, appear in the *OHQ*, volume X, page 331; volume XI, pages 201, 229 and 355. The complete Ogden journals of 1824-25 and 1825-26 were published in 1950 by the Hudson's Bay Record Society. The Oregon State Highway Commission has given the name Peter Skene Ogden Park to land adjacent to the Crooked River bridge on The Dalles-California highway in the south part of Jefferson County, to commemorate Ogden's explorations into central Oregon. For article by John W. Kelly about Peter Skene Ogden, see the *Oregonian*, magazine section, June 26, 1927, and for information about the dedication of Peter Skene Ogden Park, *ibid.*, July 16, 1927. The name Peter Skene Ogden Park was suggested by Robert W. Sawyer of Bend.

Petersburg, Wasco County. Petersburg was established in 1905 as a station on the Great Southern Railroad. W. H. McNeal in *History of Wasco County,* page 275, states it was named for Peter Strohler who homesteaded along Fifteenmile Creek about 1900. The *Illustrated History of Central Oregon* has a short biography of this man using the spelling Stoller and the reader is free to make his own choice. After the railroad was taken up in the 1930s, the population diminished but the name is retained by Petersburg School.

Peterson Butte, Linn County. Peterson Butte is southwest of Lebanon and has an elevation of 1430 feet. It was originally called Washington Butte, but in the course of time local custom changed the name to Peterson. It was named in honor of Asa H. Peterson, who crossed the plains in 1845, and settled in that locality. He was one of the party that was piloted from Fort Hall westward by Stephen Meek.

Peterson Ridge, Umatilla County. This ridge north of Blalock Mountain was named for Nels Peterson who had extensive land holdings north of North Fork Walla Walla River.

Petes Mountain, Clackamas County. Petes Mountain, maximum elevation 830 feet, is a well-known ridge south of Tualatin River and west of the town of Willamette. In July, 1945, Raymond P. Caufield of Oregon City informed the compiler that Peter A. Weiss received a patent for land on the slopes of this mountain in June, 1868, and that as far as could be learned the ridge was named for him. Weiss had a donation land claim, certificate number 3034, including the south part of the mountain.

Petes Point, Wallowa County. Petes Point is south of Wallowa Lake. This point was named for Peter Beaudoin, a Frenchman who was at one time one of the largest sheep owners in eastern Oregon. He started in the sheep business in the Wallowa Valley about 1884.

Petteys, Morrow County. A post office with the name Pettysville was closed in 1887. Postal records show that a new office with the name Petteys was opened November 9, 1900, with S. Pearl Jones postmaster. This office was in service until May 15, 1901. It was named for Amanuel C. Petteys, who came to Oregon about 1854 and for a time lived near Salem. He was interested in livestock and moved to the Willow Creek country probably before the 1870s. The name of the old post office Pettysville represented a misspelling of the family name and produced some irritation. Petteys operated the stage station until the railroad came about 1888. See also under Pettysville.

Pettysville, Morrow County. Pettysville was an important stopping point for early day travel. It was near the present site of Ione, perhaps a little to the east at the point where Rhea Creek flows into Willow Creek. A post office with the name Willow Forks was established in this locality on June 3, 1872, with Amanuel C. Petty postmaster. The name of the office seems to be descriptive of the juncture of the two streams at this point. The name Willow Forks was changed to Pettysville on December 24, 1878. The office was closed May 19, 1887, and the business turned over to Ione. The family says the name of the man was Amanuel C. Petteys. See under Petteys.

Peyton, Jackson County. Peyton is a locality on upper Rogue River about midway between Trail and Prospect, named for a local family. The post office was established August 30, 1900, with Anna B. Jones first of four postmasters. The name of the office was changed to Leeds January 16, 1912, and the office may have been moved a couple of miles west and downstream at that time. Leeds had already been a post office, operating from 1890 to 1906. Available records do not give a clear history of the movements of some of these old post offices.

Phantom Ship, Crater Lake National Park, Klamath County. This peculiar, spired island in Crater Lake bears an appropriately descriptive name.

Phelps Creek, Hood River County. This stream is named for A. C. Phelps who conducted a small cooperage business near Frankton. On May 14, 1864, Phelps, James Laughlin of The Dalles and William Jenkins with his young son Walter were ferrying a load of oak kegs out to the freight steamer. Young Jenkins fell into the Columbia and his father and Laughlin were both drowned in a vain rescue effort.

Philippi Canyon, Gilliam County. This canyon debouches into the Columbia River east of John Day Dam. Roy Philippi wrote the compiler in 1970 that his father, Albert, homesteaded this land in the 1880s and that four generations of the family have lived on the ranch. In 1970 the USCE developed Albert Philippi Park at slack water on John Day River on land that was part of the Philippi Ranch.

Phillips, Washington County. Phillips post office was established June 20, 1895, with Charles Hanson first postmaster. The office was in operation until December 23, 1904, when it was closed because of the advance of rural free delivery. Phillips was on the west side of the Cornelius Pass road a few hundred feet north of the 1945 location of Rock Creek School. The office was named in compliment to Phillip Pezoldt, a prominent local resident.

Phillips Lake, Baker County. This artificial lake on Powder River about seventeen miles west of Baker was formed when Mason Dam was built by the USBR in 1965. It was named for Fred Phillips, a prominent Baker resident and long time advocate of the project. For editorial comment on Phillips see the Baker *Record-Courier,* May 21, 1964.

Philomath, Benton County. *Philomath* is a Greek word meaning a lover of learning, an astrologer or prognosticator. Philomath College was opened in 1867, founded by the United Brethren Church. About the time the college was started, a post office was applied for, and named for the college.

Phoca Rock, Multnomah County. This rock, sometimes known as Lone Rock, is in the middle of the Columbia River north of Bridal Veil. It is conspicuous from Crown Point. It was named for the harbor seal, *Phoca vitulina*. Lewis and Clark passed this rock on November 2, 1805, and described it accurately but did not refer to it by name. However, it may be definitely attributed to Captain Clark as it appears in "Clarks Summary Statement of Rivers, Creeks, and Most Remarkable Places", Thwaites, *Original Journals of the Lewis and Clark Expedition,* volume VI, page 67. Wilkes, in *U. S. Exploring Expedition,* volume XXIII, Hydrography, refers to the rock as Hermit Islet.

Phoenix, Jackson County. Phoenix was settled in the early 1850s. Samuel Colver took a land claim there in 1851. In 1852 his brother, Hiram, settled adjoining him. In 1854 Samuel Colver laid out the town. Phoenix reached the height of its prosperity in 1864. Ten years later the town had greatly dwindled. For several months, in 1884, it was the terminus of the Oregon and California Railroad. During the Indian troubles in the fall of 1855 Milton Lindley's sawmill was running wide open providing timbers for a blockhouse as well as for a new flouring mill belonging to Sylvester M. Wait, A young lady named Kate Clayton was employed by Mrs. Wait to help with the cooking for the mill hands and for many years the place was known as Gasburg because of the loquacity of this fluent and attractive woman. The town was named by Wait (*Oregonian,* January 3, 1892), after whom later was named Waitsburg, Washington. Wait not only owned the flouring mill but was also the agent for the Phoenix Insurance Company of Hartford, Connecticut and he took that name for the post office which opened January 3, 1857. The Phoenix was a fabulous sacred bird of the Egyptians. There are many legends about the phoenix, which was described as a bird of the size and shape of an eagle, but with red and gold plumage. There was but one phoenix at a time, and it came to Egypt every 500 years from Arabia. The bird played a part in the mystic religion of Egypt, and the most popular legend about it is that it flew to Heliopolis every 500 years, and was burned on the altar of the temple. The next day there was a new phoenix on the altar.

Phys Point, Union County. This was named for John Phy, whose farm was nearby. It is about two miles west of Cove.

Pickett Butte, Douglas County. This prominent peak five miles east of Tiller is the site of a USFS lookout. It was named for William T. Pickett who homesteaded nearby in 1898.

Picture Gorge, Grant County. This is an imposing canyon, through which flows John Day River, a few miles northwest of Dayville. On its western walls are several Indian drawings or pictures, hence the name. The USGS has issued a splendid map of this gorge and its surroundings. See editorial page the *Oregonian,* December 10, 1925.

Picture Rock Pass, Lake County. Between Silver Lake and Summer Lake the Fremont Highway goes through a pass at an elevation of about

4830 feet, and the gap is known as Picture Rock Pass. The name comes from some strange desïgns or pictures on the rocks about a hundred feet south of the highway. These peculiar marks, made by Indians, are strongly suggestive of a WPA style painting project operated by the aborigines.

Pieper Canyon, Morrow County. This canyon was named for John and Ernest Pieper who settled near its upper end on Swaggart Buttes in the 1890s.

Pierce Creek, Linn County. This stream flows into Little Muddy Creek east of Harrisburg. It was named for James A. Pierce, a pioneer settler.

Piety Knob, Marion County. Piety Knob is now an island in Detroit Reservoir but before the dam was built it was prominent high ground north of North Santiam River. Earl Stahlman of Detroit told the compiler in 1968 that this was originally known as Mayborn Hill after an early homesteader but that it was renamed by Roy Elliot, a USFS ranger. He was unable to explain the religious significance.

Pike, Yamhill County. Considering the large number of persons who emigrated to Oregon from Pike County, Missouri, it is not suprising that the name was used here, but it is remarkable that some effort was not made to name a county for the famous middle western soldier and explorer. Zebulon Montgomery Pike was born in 1779 in New Jersey. He entered the army before he was of age, and was a lieutenant when he was 20. He explored the Mississippi River, and later went to the Rocky Mountains in what is now Colorado. Pikes Peak bears his name. He was killed at York, Upper Canada, April 27, 1813, in an engagement with the British. He was then a brigadier-general. Pike, in Oregon, is a small community northwest of Yamhill.

Pike Creek, Tillamook County. Pike Creek heads in the hills east of Bay City and flows south and west into Hathaway Slough, which joins Tillamook Bay just south of Kilchis Point. The stream flows through the homestead of Dan Pike, a pioneer settler, and was named on that account. It is the next stream east of Doughty Creek.

Pikes Camp, Lincoln County. Pikes Camp is on the northeast or right bank of Siletz River about a mile upstream from the mouth of the river and the location of Kernville in 1945. It is near the old ferry landing and about opposite the former Kernville post office, which was on the southwest bank. The camp was named for a fisherman who camped there while he fished for the Kern cannery.

Pilot Butte, Deschutes County. Pilot Butte, which is at the east city limits of Bend, has been a prominent landmark for travelers for many years. Farewell Bend on Deschutes River was the objective of emigrant trains because it afforded a suitable place to cross the river and was a convenient camp ground. Pilot Butte was an excellent signal to this stopping place. Some early maps refer to it as Red Butte because of its characteristic color, but the name has not prevailed. For information about the importance of this locality to pioneer travelers see under the name Bend. There is an automobile road to the top of the butte from which an impressive panorama may be seen. Pilot Butte has an elevation of 4139 feet according to the USGS. On September 30, 1928, Pilot Butte and Pilot Butte Park on its summit were given to the state of Oregon by F. R. Welles, Kempster B. Miller and Charles A. Brown, as a memorial to their former business associate, Terrence Hardington Foley. T. H. Foley was a prominent resident of Bend who died in 1925 as a result of an automobile accident.

Pilot Knob, Curry County. Preston's *Map of Oregon and Washington,* 1856, shows a prominent peak about ten miles southeast of Port Orford which is lettered Pilot Knob. This was a well-known landmark for mariners, and while the name may have been used to some extent on land, people on shore generally called this point Bald Mountain. For additional information, see under Bald Mountain.

Pilot Rock, Jackson County. Pilot Rock is an outstanding landmark in the Siskiyou Mountains south of Ashland, and east of the Pacific Highway. It has been so known since pioneer days because it served as a guide for travelers crossing the pass between Oregon and California. It has an elevation according to the USGS of 5914 feet. This rock is mentioned in Wilkes' *Narrative,* volume V, page 236. Wilkes named it Emmons Peak after Lieutenant George F. Emmons, U. S. N., of his expedition. Emmons saw the rock on September 28, 1841. The name Emmons Peak did not come into use.

Pilot Rock, Umatilla County. Pilot Rock was named for a large bluff of basalt near the community. The post office was established in December, 1868, but the town was not platted until about 1876. Andrew Sturtevant was the first postmaster.

Pilpil Butte, Deschutes County. Pilpil Butte is in the northern part of Paulina Mountains. It is composed of red cinders, characteristic of the area, and bears the Chinook jargon word for red.

Pine, Baker County. Pine post office was first established on June 27, 1878, with the name Pine Valley and with Reese W. Pindell postmaster. The office was on the Union County list and the compiler does not know its exact location. Andrew P. Greener became postmaster on April 3, 1879, and the office was then at the Greener farm about two and a half miles from where Pine is now situated. The name was changed to Pine June 1, 1892. The office was so named because it was in the Pine Creek Valley. There are many geographic features in Oregon named for pine trees. The timbered area of Oregon east of the Cascade Range is largely covered with species of pine. The pines have needle-like leaves and are distinguished from larches, spruces, hemlocks and firs by the length of the needles and the arrangement of the bundles. The only other tree which has its needles in bundles is the larch, but larch needles are short and have as many as thirty needles in a bundle. Pines do not shed all of their needles, and larches do, in the winter. Western white pine, sugar pine and white-bark pine all have five needles in a bundle. Western yellow pine has three needles in a bundle. Lodgepole pine has two needles in a bundle. The three pines of Oregon which have five needles in a bundle can be distinguished from each other by the cones and by the locality in which they occur. Western white pine, *Pinus monticola,* has a slender cone usually five or six inches in length and is made up of very thin scales. It is scattered through the Cascade Range. It is not considered a common tree and is found generally at altitudes above 2000 feet. Sugar pine, *Pinus lambertiana,* is the largest and most magnificent of the Pacific Coast members of the white pine family. It attains a diameter of from four to seven feet. It has a slender cone generally more than a foot in length made up of thin scales. Sugar pine does not occur in Oregon much further north than Mount Jefferson. The white-bark pine, *Pinus albicaulis,* has a short cone about three inches in length and made up of thick scales. It occurs on both sides of the Cascade Range at high altitudes generally near the timber line. Western yellow pine, *Pinus ponderosa,* is the only three-needle pine in Oregon. It has dark bark in its youth and yellow bark when it becomes older. Its needles are long. It is the most common of all forest trees east of the Cascade Range and even west of the range it occurs occasionally in small groups scattered through the Willamette Valley. It is of great commercial importance. Lodgepole pine, *Pinus contorta,* is a two-needle pine and is very common east of the Cascade Range. West of the Cascade Range it is found mostly along the seacoast. Owing to the dark color of its bark it is frequently called black pine and is also known as bull pine and jack pine. The cones are small and have a tendency to remain attached to the tree, sometimes for many years. These cones may break open during a forest fire and scatter the seeds in all directions. In central Oregon and on the east slopes of the Cascade Range there are in many places dense thickets of small lodgepole pine. This tree is not yet of great commercial importance but experiments are being made to develop new uses for its wood.

Pine, Linn County. Pine post office was situated about ten miles east-southeast of Harrisburg near the Lane County line. It was named for the yellowpine trees growing in the foothills. The office was established August 19, 1853, with the name Lat Shaw's Mill, and with William H. Latshaw postmaster. The name of the office was changed to Pine on January 3, 1855, with Thomas M. Weger postmaster. When the name was changed it was noted that the old name was Latshaw's Mill and not with the peculiar arrangement shown above. Pine office continued in operation until October 7, 1887, when the business was turned over to Coburg. It was doubtless moved from time to time but was always in the same general neighborhood.

Pine Creek, Baker County. Pine Creek heads on the northeast slopes of Elkhorn Ridge of the Blue Mountains and flows generally eastward and northeastward to join Powder River near Haines. This stream was named in the gold excitement of the 1860s because of the prominent yellowpine trees near its banks. In 1862 John McLain laid out a town called Pine City on or near this stream with the intention of providing facilities for traveling miners. Before it was well established, Pine City was moved to and consolidated with Pocahontas. See under that heading. See also Hiatt's *Thirty-one Years in Baker County,* pages 34 and 35.

Pine Creek, Umatilla County. This stream rises in the western slopes of the Blue Mountains and flows northward through Weston and thence into Walla Walla County, Washington. N. W. Durham says it is probably the *Te-hoto-nim-me* of Steptoe. (*Spokane and the Inland Empire,* page 222.)

Pine Grove, Umatilla County. It is not surprising that many geographic names in Oregon include references to the pine tree, generally by implication to the western yellow pine, *Pinus ponderosa,* or to use its trade name, Pondosa pine. Pine Grove in Umatilla County was a post office ten or a dozen miles south of Pilot Rock on one of the branches of Birch Creek. Pine Grove post office was established January 20, 1911, with Maud Warner first postmaster. The office was discontinued August 9, 1934.

Pine Mountain, Deschutes County. Named in pioneer days because its high slopes are covered with conifers, Pine Mountain is a prominent landmark at the edge of the High Desert six miles south of US 20 and thirty-five miles southeast of Bend. From its 6405 foot top is had a sweeping view of much of Oregon's interior plateau and the USFS established a permanent lookout there in 1921. Phil Brogan of Bend supplied this information to the compiler in 1967 when Pine Mountain was in the news spotlight as a site for a proposed University of Oregon astronomical observatory. The observatory was placed in service in the 1970s.

Pine Ridge, Klamath County. A descriptive name. The place was first known as Aspgrove, presumably for a grove of quaking aspen trees nearby.

Pinehurst, Jackson County. Pinehurst is a place on the Green Springs Highway in the east part of the county between Ashland and Klamath Falls. The name is a combination of the word pine with the old English word hurst, referring to a wooded eminence or just woods. The name is appropriate to the locality. Old maps show an early post office in this vicinity with the name Pioneer. This office was established March 26, 1878, with James Purvis postmaster. John Van Horn became postmaster December 29, 1880, and the office was closed December 19, 1882. The compiler does not know its exact location. The next post office to serve this area was called Shake. It was established in August, 1886, with George W. Bailey first postmaster. This office operated until November, 1911, when the name was changed to Pinehurst. Pinehurst office is said to be about a mile southwest of the old locality Shake. The name Shake was applied to this locality in early days because it was a place where shakes were riven from sugar pine bolts. These shakes were used extensively by early settlers in the Rogue River Valley for various types of buildings.

Pinewan Lake, Klamath County. This lake about one mile south of Crescent Lake was named by the Campfire Girls about 1953 when they began using it in connection with their summer camp. Pinewan is Campfire Girl jargon for "among the pines".

Piney, Lane County. Piney post office was established July 6, 1852, with Benjamin Richardson postmaster. The office was discontinued November 18, 1852. The place was a little northeast of Elmira and was apparently named by someone interested in trees.

Pinto Mountain, Lane County. Pinto Mountain, elevation 6355 feet, is in the Cascade Range near the headwaters of South Fork Salt Creek. Dee Wright of Eugene told the compiler that the mountain was named for a pinto pony that strayed away from his owner and ranged near the mountain.

Pioneer, Lincoln County. Pioneer was a post office near Yaquina River. The post office was for some years known as Morrison, but the name was changed in 1900 because of confusion with Morrison Street in Portland. Barney Morrison was the first postmaster. The name Pioneer was selected because of the operations in that section of the Pioneer Sandstone Company. Barney Morrison continued to act as postmaster at Pioneer after the name was changed.

Pioneer City, Lincoln County. The post office at Pioneer City, which was established July 2, 1868, with George Kellogg first postmaster, was one of the first in what is now Lincoln County. Newport office was established the same day, Newton was established July 12, 1868, and Little Elk, Toledo and Yaquina were established on July 14 of the same year. These six offices took care of the postal needs of that part of Oregon for several years. Pioneer City was named in honor of the steamer *Pioneer,* owned by Kellogg and engaged in general transportation from the mouth of Yaquina Bay to the new community at tidewater. It was about two and one quarter miles up Yaquina River from the place later known as Elk City and about three quarters of a mile downstream from the place later known as Morrison and still later Pioneer. Pioneer City and Pioneer were not in the same place, though they were not more than a mile apart. Pioneer Mountain and Pioneer Summit are west of these old post office locations, and the compiler has been told that the mountain was so named before the Pioneer City post office was established in 1868. Pioneer City post office was closed August 10, 1868, so it was in operation but little more than a month. It was in the southeast quarter of section 2, township 11 south, range 10 west.

Pioneer Gulch, Lane County. This gulch northwest of Emigrant Pass was named because the ill-fated wagon train of 1853 followed it down to Middle Fork Willamette River. According to C. B. McFarland of the USFS the wagon tracks were clearly visible for many years.

Pirtle, Linn County. Pirtle was a station on the Oregon Electric Railway south of Albany. It was named for Grant Pirtle, at one time proprietor of a hotel in Albany, and owner of land in the vicinity of the station.

Pistol River, Curry County. James Mace lost a pistol in this stream in 1853 and it has been known as Pistol River since that time.

Pitcher Creek, Lane County. The Pitcher Creek which flows into Row River near Dorena was named for Miles Pitcher who homesteaded near its mouth in 1888. Loren Hunt told the compiler in 1967 that the Pitcher Creek which flows into Layng Creek near Disston was named for Miles Pitcher's son, Ben Pitcher.

Pitcher Point, Tillamook County. Pitcher Point is the northernmost point on the road around the southwest side of Tillamook Bay to Cape Meares. John A. Biggs of Portland told the compiler in 1971 that his grandfather, Webley Hauxhurst, named the place because of a prominent rock that resembled a milk jug. The Biggs family at that time lived at nearby Biggs Cove. The rock was covered or destroyed when the present road was built in the 1930s.

Pitner, Tillamook County. Pitner post office in the extreme southeast corner of the county was named in honor of the postmaster, Mrs. Sarah Paul, *nee* Pitner. The office was established in August, 1901, and was discontinued April 30, 1910. This office was on or very close to what is now the Salmon River Highway at a point two or three miles southwest of the locality now known as Boyer. However, in those days Boyer post office was a mile or so southwest of Pitner, in what is now Lincoln County.

Pitsua Butte, Deschutes County. This butte, southwest of Bend, is named with the word used by Klamath Indians to describe an eminence about two miles southwest of the old site of Klamath Agency. Its use near Bend is to perpetuate a pleasant Indian name. The compiler has been unable to learn the meaning of the name of the butte near the old Klamath Agency. In 1939 Fred M. White of Portland called attention to the fact that the Piute Indian name for the Columbia five-toed kangaroo rat is *wapota pitsua*. Inquiries to authorities about the name of the butte on the Klamath Indian Reservation have not been wholly successful. In 1944, Indians professed to know very little about the word *pitsua*, although a few of them said they thought it referred to a rodent of some sort.

Pittsburg, Columbia County. Pittsburg is on Nehalem River at the mouth of East Fork and at the junction of Nehalem Highway and the highway east to Saint Helens. The place was named by Peter Brous, who made settlement there in 1879 and built a sawmill and a gristmill operated by waterpower. Brous had formerly lived in Pennsylvania and named the new settlement for the city in that state. The post office at Pittsburgh, Oregon, was established April 17, 1879, and Peter Brous was the first postmaster. The name was changed to Pittsburg April 26, 1892, and the office was discontinued November 30, 1908. There is now not much left at Pittsburg except a substantial highway bridge and a popular cafe. Omar C. Spencer was kind enough to dredge up the facts given above. The place was within his field of activities when he was a small boy in the 1880s.

Pix, Baker County. Pix post office was apparently established to serve the Pyx mine. The word can be spelled either way but probably Pyx is the more modern form. Pix office was established August 27, 1890, with William Parker postmaster. It was discontinued June 11, 1895. There is no doubt as to the spelling of the post office name Pix, and the office is said to have been in the extreme west part of Baker County. It may actually have been over the line in Grant County but officials in Washington did not know it. The Pyx mine was close to the divide but all the records say it was in Grant County. It was in section 2, township 10 south, range 35 east. Whether the post office was actually at the mine or over the hill in Baker County the compiler does not know. The Pyx mine was in what was called the Greenhorn district. The word pyx has several meanings. One, of course, is ecclesiastical. There is also an important meaning associated with metallurgy. It refers to the box used at the Royal Mint in London, in which are deposited sample coins struck off in the mint. These are examined annually in the "trial of the pyx" by a committee of the Goldsmiths' Company under direction of the King's Remembrancer. This trial is well known to metallurgists and may have been the reason for naming the Pyx mine.

Placedor Gulch, Grant County. Placedor Gulch drains into South Fork John Day River just south of the mouth of Murderers Creek. It is about a dozen miles south of Dayville and drains a small area east of the river. It is said to bear the name of a Mexican, Placedor Bravo, well known in that part of the state. Bravo came into central Oregon probably about 1890 and was much interested in horses and horseraces. He died at Mount Vernon Hot Springs about 1940.

Placer, Josephine County. Placer was named for the placer mining in the vicinity. The place is on Grave Creek a few miles east of the Pacific Highway. The Placer post office was established August 10, 1894, with N. F. Inman first postmaster. The writer does not know the date the office was closed, but it was about 1924.

Placer Lake, Lincoln County. Placer Lake is on Reynolds Creek about four miles south of Waldport. It was named by the USFS in 1966 as this part of the Siuslaw National Forest was developed for recreation. Sometime in the 1870s a promoter staked mining claims in the area and constructed an elaborate system of ditches and flumes to fool prospective purchasers. The scheme fell through but later Chinese miners moved in and reportedly recovered a sizeable quantity of gold by placer mining with water from the creek and lake. Evidence of the old ditches could still be seen in 1966.

Placidia Butte, Harney County. Placidia Butte, elevation 5513 feet, is at the west edge of the county, about ten miles west of Riley and a little to the south of the Central Oregon Highway. The name has long been a puzzle and its origin uncertain, but in the summer of 1946 Alphene Venator, pioneer resident of the Harney Valley, told the compiler the butte was named for a Mexican horse trader many years ago. This man is said to have moved north from the Harney Valley into Grant County. For a good many years there lived in the John Day Valley a Mexican named Placedor Bravo, an experienced character with horses. He died at Mount Vernon Hot Springs about 1940. For additional information, see under Placedor Gulch. While the evidence is certainly not conclusive, it seems probable that Placidia Butte was named for Placedor Bravo. The difference in spelling would be of little consequence to Senor Bravo.

Plainview, Linn County. This station is on the Springfield branch of the Southern Pacific Company north of Brownsville. The name is purely descriptive.

Plank Hill, Marion County. Plank Hill is a point on Croisan Ridge about five miles southwest of Salem. It has an elevation of about 850 feet. It was named for E. C. Plank who owned a farm nearby.

Plano, Baker County. A post office with the name Plano was established on the Baker County list July 28, 1897, with Frances Smith first postmaster. The office was discontinued October 12, 1899. Plano was in Burnt River Valley between Durkee and Weatherby. The reason for the name is not on record, but the compiler is of the opinion that the word Plano was intended to be in compliment to some local farm equipment. The Plano line of farm vehicles and harvesting machinery was well known in the 1890s and for some years thereafter.

Plaza Guard Station, Clackamas County. This station is near South Fork Salmon River. It was named by T. H. Sherrard of the USFS because of a natural plaza or clearing, which afforded a fine view of Mount Hood.

Pleasant Hill, Lane County. Pleasant Hill is east of Goshen. In earlier days there was a nearby post office of the same name. The origin of the name is given in *OHQ*, volume V, page 135. Elijah Bristow and several companions made a trip into the valley of the Middle Fork Willamette River in 1846. Bristow was struck with the beauties of the locality now known as Pleasant Hill, and said: "What a pleasant hill. This is my claim." He finished his house in the fall of that year, and it is said to have been one of the first built in Lane County. The name Pleasant Hill was given to his claim by an act of the legislature passed December 27, 1847. Pleasant Hill post office was established April 9, 1850, with Elijah Bristow postmaster.

Pleasant Home, Multnomah County. Pleasant Home, a locality on the headwaters of Johnson Creek about a mile east of Orient, had a post office in pioneer days. Pleasant Home office was established on the Clackamas County list on July 10, 1876, and was given a descriptive name. Orlando S. Murray was the first postmaster. The office was soon changed to the Multnomah County list, but the record does not show just when. This office operated until December 14, 1918, when it was closed out to Gresham. Wm. H. Stanley of Gresham says that Pleasant Home post office never was in Clackamas County, but the fact that it was less than a quarter of a mile from the county line may be the reason that postal officials placed the office on the Clackamas County list in error. See also under Orient.

Pleasant Valley, Baker County. Pleasant Valley post office was established September 28, 1868, with Jared Lockwood first and only postmaster. The office was in service for two months. A later office with the name Pleasant Valley was established March 21, 1890, with Thomas B. Moore postmaster.

Pleasant Valley, Jackson County. Pleasant Valley, which is on the extreme west edge of the county north of Rogue River, is drained by Evans Creek and by a tributary, Pleasant Creek. The valley and creek got their names in pioneer days as a result of the battle of Evans Creek in the Rogue River Indian War, fought on August 24, 1853, on which day Pleasant Armstrong of Yamhill County was killed. Armstrong was a prominent citizen and was acting as an aid to General Joseph Lane, in command of the white troops. See Walling's *History of Southern Oregon*, page 219 and also page 380. The valley has always lived up to its name, although the title was not applied descriptively.

Pleasant Valley, Tillamook County. Homer Simmons of Tillamook who was born and raised nearby sent the compiler the following interesting comment on this community. "Pleasant Valley on US 101 about seven miles south of Tillamook was probably named because of the pleasant surroundings. My father jokingly said it should have been called Wrangletown because of the disputes and feuds among the residents."

Plum Hills, Klamath County. These hills are north of Klamath Falls. They have been so called since pioneer days on account of wild plums that grew there. Stock have grazed on these hills for so long that the plum trees have practically disappeared. See editorial in the *Oregonian*, July 1, 1927, about the wild Pacific plum, *Prunus subcordata*.

Plum Valley, Polk County. Plum Valley is a little vale in the west part of Eola Hills. It is just south of Bethel and east of McCoy, and it drains westward into Ash Swale. Its name came from the wild plums that grew in the vicinity, and according to John E. Smith in his booklet, *Bethel*, the name was probably selected by Amos Harvey. Plum Valley post office was established November 30, 1854, on the Absalom H. Frier claim, a little to the south of the valley and about on the south line of section 20. Frier was the first postmaster. In 1856 Plum Valley post office was moved into Plum Valley proper. It was moved several times later but never far from Bethel. It was discontinued August 13, 1863.

Plush, Lake County. The town of Plush was named for a local Indian celebrity who was a member of the Piute tribe. The name was suggested by Dr. H. Wright who was for a time postmaster at Lakeview. A letter of C. A. Moore, published in the *Oregonian*, February 16, 1926, tells how the Indian received the name Plush. This was the result of a card game that he got into. The game was a frame-up. The Indian was dealt a flush by another member of the party, who held a better one. He could not pronounce the word "flush" and called it "plush," and that was the name he subsequently went by.

Plympton Creek, Clatsop County. Plympton Creek is at Westport. It was named for Silas B. Plympton who took up a land claim nearby in 1861, and who was the first postmaster at Westport, 1863.

Pocahontas, Baker County. Pocahontas is a ghost town at the base of the Blue Mountains a few miles northwest of Baker. It was established in the mining days of the 1860s, but so far the compiler has not had any success in getting the origin of the name or even much of value about the history of the place. Beyond the fact that it was named for the famous Indian princess of Virginia, little has transpired. Hiatt in his *Thirty-one Years in Baker County,* pages 34 and 35, says that a number of persons went up into the timber near the foot of the Blue Mountains and laid out a town called Pine City. It may be assumed from the text that this took place in 1862 and the place was on Pine Creek west of what was later Pocahontas. The community was laid out for the purpose of accommodating travel, which was forced to go close to the mountains to avoid spring waters. One John McLain had taken up a ranch at or near what was later Pocahontas and he persuaded the Pine City people to move to Pocahontas, which soon boasted a hotel, express office and blacksmith shop. Pocahontas was not primarily a mining town, but for the accommodation of travel through Baker Valley. One Morrison had a rival place a couple of miles to the south and Hiatt has some amusing comments about this rivalry. Pocahontas post office was established August 4, 1863, with Thomas McMurran postmaster. Available records about the closing date are inconclusive. In one place the date is given as June 24, 1864, and in another place the year is 1872.

Poe Valley, Klamath County. This valley which is southeast of Olene, was named for James M. Poe, who lived there a few years at the time of the Modoc War. Later he moved to Chehalis, Washington, where he spent the rest of his life. In 1945 his Poe Valley homestead was owned by members of the Liskey family. The Poes were the parents of Mrs. William H. Horton, wife of a prominent and long-time stockman of the Poe Valley-Bonanza area.

Point Adams, Clatsop County. This is on the Oregon side at the mouth of the Columbia River. The name was given by Captain Robert Gray on

May 18, 1792, in honor of John Adams. ("Boit's Log of the Columbia" in *Washington Historical Quarterly*, volume XII, January, 1921, page 35.) Later in the same year Vancouver recognized the name, saying: "Point Adams is a low, narrow, sandy, spit of land, projecting northerly into the ocean, and lies from cape Disappointment, S. 44 E. about four miles distant." (*Voyage of Discovery*, 1798 edition, volume II, page 53.) Point Adams was first described by Captain Bruno Heceta on August 17, 1775, and was named by him *Cabo Frondoso*, or Leafy Cape, "from the great number of trees which covered it." See *California Historical Society Quarterly*, volume IX, page 235. Heceta was at the mouth of the Columbia River but he did not know it. See Greenhow's *History of Oregon and California*, page 430, *et seq*.

Point Terrace, Lane County. Point Terrace was named by Mrs. Josephine R. Styles, the first postmaster. This was about 1890. The name is descriptive and refers to the three steps or beaches nearby. This was a popular Indian hunting ground in early days and a great deal of game was dried and smoked in this neighborhood.

Poison Creek, Harney County. This stream is on the northwest slopes of Steens Mountain and is tributary to Kiger Creek. It was so called in early days because a number of cattle were poisoned nearby by eating wild parsnips.

Poison Creek, Harney County. This stream is east of Burns. Like many others in eastern Oregon it was named because cattle were poisoned nearby when they ate wild parsnips.

Pokegama, Klamath County. In the early part of the century there was excitement in Klamath County because of prospects of a railroad. This line was surveyed from Thrall, a station on the Southern Pacific near Klamath River, in California, northeastward to the southwest corner of Klamath County, Oregon. Construction started in November, 1901, and in May, 1903, the line was completed to Pokegama, the Oregon terminus. The Pokegama Lumber Company was responsible for the project, and the name of the line was the Klamath Lake Railroad. It was about 24 miles long. Pokegama post office was established by change of name from Snow on September 2, 1899. The office was in operation until October 31, 1911. Snow post office was established in June, 1894, with Adelbert B. Smith postmaster. The writer does not know its location in respect of Pokegama. The lumber company got its name from the place in Pine County, Minnesota. Pokegama, Oregon, ceased to exist many years ago.

Poker Jim Ridge, Lake County. This ridge is the high ground east of Warner Valley above Campbell and Bluejoint lakes. The local tradition is that it was named for Poker Jim, an Indian Scout during the Bannock War of 1878. The compiler has been unable to find any mention of such a man in the available campaign accounts but the *Sunday Oregonian*, December 7, 1952 has a long article telling of Poker Jim, a well-known Pendleton Indian who was born about 1854 near Wallula and died in 1936 at Cayuse. His Indian name was *Sap-At-Kloni* and he is reported to have been a scout under Collier in the Bannock War. Collier is not identifiable and may be Captain Patrick Collins, 21st. Infantry. There is nothing to connect any of this with the east side of Warner Valley but some activity could have occured during or after 1878 to fix the name. In view of Poker Jim's well documented affinity for the gambling game, he may be responsible as well for the naming of nearby Plush.

Polallie Creek, Hood River County. This tributary of East Fork Hood River rises southwest of Cooper Spur. Over the centuries it has cut a deep canyon in the powdery soil. In the early days it was called Sand Creek and Sand Canyon but in the 1920s the USFS started a program to replace repetitious or mundane names. Sand Creek fits both these qualifications as "Sand" carries far more than its share of the place name burden. *Polallie* is a Chinook jargon word meaning sandy or powdery. George Gibbs says that *polallie* was undoubtedly from the French *poudre,* and was not originally a Chehalis or Chinook word.

Pole Bridge Creek, Crater Lake National Park, Klamath County. Soldiers from Fort Klamath built a bridge over this stream in the 1860s, using small lodgepole pine trees, and the name arose on that account.

Pole Creek, Wasco County. J. A. Rooper of Antelope told the compiler that this tributary of Ward Creek was named because of the excellent supply of juniper fence posts available in the canyon.

Pole Gulch, Baker County. Pole Gulch is the correct name of a drain in townships 12 and 13 south, range 36 east, not Sawmill Creek. See USBGN decision.

Polk, Polk County. The name Polk has been used for two different post offices in Polk County, both named in compliment to the county. An office called Polk was established March 9, 1885, with Lycurgus Hill first and only postmaster. This office was closed December 7, 1885. Lycurgus Hill lived in the locality called Bridgeport, and since Bridgeport post office had been abandoned in 1874, it is possible that Polk office was organized to fill the local need. However, the record of this Polk post office is far from clear. Members of the Hill family are of the opinion that the office never functioned, and some color is lent to the statement by the fact that the compiler has not been able to find the office on any contemporary maps. There have been a number of cases in Oregon postal history where post offices have been established, only to have local sponsors lose interest in the prospects. The other Polk office was about three miles northeast of Dallas. The name Polk for this locality was in use in the 1880s as a station on the Oregonian Railway narrow gauge line, and confusion between the two places may have been the reason that Hill's post office did not actively furnish service. Polk railroad station northeast of Dallas did not get a post office until April 12, 1899, when Peter R. Graber was appointed postmaster. This office was closed February 15, 1902. The locality is still called Polk Station, though both post office and railroad service are things of the past as far as the locality is concerned.

Polk County. Polk District, or County was created by the provisional legislature, December 22, 1845. It was named for James Knox Polk, then president of the United States. It comprised all that part of the original Yamhill District south of the south line of that district, which had been reestablished by an act of December 19, 1845, and the California line. Information about the establishment of Polk County will be found in the article on Oregon counties by Frederick V. Holman, in *OHQ*, volume XI, page 28. In his notes on Polk County Mr. Holman calls attention to the fact that he was unable to find the act of the legislature establishing the south boundary of the county immediatly prior to the creation of Benton County. However, the act was printed in the *Oregon Spectator,* February 10, 1848. This act was passed on December 9, 1847, and was approved December 23, 1847.

Pollard Creek, Tillamook County. This creek flows into Three Rivers about five miles above Hebo. It was named for an early homesteader near Sears Lake, Aaron B. Pollard, who was postman at Woods around 1900.

Pollman Dam, Baker County. This dam on Baldock Slough was named for William Pollman.

Poly Top Butte, Deschutes and Lake counties. This butte southeast of Paulina Mountains has several tops, hence the name.

Pompadour Bluff, Jackson County. This bluff is a peculiar, basaltic rock formation in the valley east of Ashland. It resembles, in a general way, the style of haircut made famous by the Marquise de Pompadour and by Jim Corbett. It was probably named about the time Corbett was the world's heavyweight boxing champion.

Pompeii, Clackamas County. Pompeii post office came as the result of the activities of Oliver C. Yocum, for many years a guide at Mount Hood. He started a community near the present site of Government Camp and chose the name Pompeii because of the volcanic soil in the vicinity. The office was established October 15, 1902, but available records do not give the closing date. It probably was never in service.

Pondosa, Union County. Pondosa is a lumber town not far from Medical Springs. It was named with the word Pondosa, the trade name for lumber from the western yellow pine tree, *Pinus ponderosa*. The post office was established September 28, 1927, with Holger M. Larsen first postmaster, to serve the Grande Ronde Pine Company, millers of western yellow pine. The office was not in service in 1973.

Pony Butte, Jefferson County. Pony Butte is a landmark in the eastern part of the county. Mrs. Chester Kennedy, the daughter of early settler Bidwell Cram, told the writer in 1971 that the butte was named because of an Indian drawing or petroglyph resembling a pony. She recalls as a small girl riding with her mother to view this rock near the top of the butte but said she had not been able to find the spot in later years. Pony Creek rises on the north slopes of the butte.

Pony Slough, Coos County. Pony Creek runs directly through North Bend into Pony Slough. The name is very old and supposedly was applied in the early days when a pony belonging to an Indian boy mired and drowned in the tidal marsh.

Poole Lake, Douglas County. Poole Lake is in section 29, township 29 south, range 3 east, on the upper reaches of Jackson Creek. It was named for Andrew T. Poole who was a forest ranger in the area for many years. The name Toad Lake is incorrect as this is about a mile north.

Pooles Slough, Lincoln County. According to information received from Andrew L. Porter of Newport in 1945, Pooles Slough was named for a homesteader who settled on the west bank, near the mouth. He was an oysterman at times.

Poore Creek, Douglas County. Fred Asam of Canyonville told the compiler that this tributary of Little River west of Taft Mountain was named by logger Harold Church. Church had so much difficulty logging in the rugged terrain that he called the job a "poor set-up" and subsequently Poor Creek. The terminal *e* is an affectation reflecting an attempt to change a poor situation.

Popcorn School, Polk County. Popcorn School in the Eola Hills about five miles northwest of Salem has borne its unusual name for a great many years. The only explanation that the writer has been able to get about the name is to the effect that in early days a group of rebellious children locked their teacher in the schoolhouse. Fortunately he had some popcorn with him and this he proceeded to pop. The youngsters opened the building to share the treat and thus liberated the resourceful pedagogue. How the teacher happened to have the popping corn and why he did not climb out a window have not been explained to the satisfaction of the writer. However, there are so many strange stories about geographic names that this one seems quite credible.

Poplar, Wheeler County. Poplar post office was established April 10, 1894, with Zachariah J. Martin first postmaster, and was discontinued September 22, 1899. A map of 1897 shows the office on Haystack Creek about a mile north of and upstream from John Day River. The office is said to have been named for some poplar trees on a nearby ranch.

Port Orford, Curry County. On April 24, 1792, Captain George Vancouver sighted what we now know as Cape Blanco, and named it Cape Orford in honor of George, Earl of Orford, his "much respected friend." For history of the name Cape Blanco, see under that heading. Cape Blanco is about seven miles north of Port Orford. McArthur's chart of the Pacific Coast, issued by the USC&GS in 1851, shows the name Ewing Harbor attached to what is now called Port Orford. He apparently named the harbor for his ship, the *Ewing,* which was used in the survey in 1850. The name Ewing did not prevail, and the place has been known since the early 1850s as Port Orford because of its proximity to the cape named by Vancouver. Tebenkoff's chart shows the name Indian Bay. George, third Earl of Orford (1720-1791) was the grandson of Sir Robert Walpole, first Earl of Orford and was the nephew of the fourth Earl of Orford, the famous Horace Walpole. Port Orford has given its name to a valuable lumber, Port Orford cedar, botanically known as Lawson cypress, *Chamaecyparis lawsoniana.* It is considered one of the most beautiful cedars in cultivation. Port Orford post office was established March 27, 1855, with Reginald H. Smith first postmaster.

Porter Hill, Umatilla County. Porter Hill is a spur of Rocky Ridge north of East Birch Creek. It was named for a prominent early settler, William T. Porter, who took up property along its slopes in 1895.

Porter Spring, Union County. Porter Spring is three miles north of the confluence of Meadow Creek and Grande Ronde River. It was named for William Porter who took a land claim there in 1900.

Porterville, Lake County. Porterville was a homesteaders' post office situated a few miles southwest of Silver Lake town, in the north part of section 7, township 29 south, range 13 east. This is on the Buck Creek drainage. The post office was established February 3, 1898, with James C. Porter first and only postmaster, and was discontinued June 15, 1899, with papers to Silver Lake. The office was named for the Porter family, several members of which had homesteads in the vicinity.

Portland, Multnomah County. Portland was named for Portland, Maine, in 1845, by Francis W. Pettygrove. Whether the name should be Portland or Boston was decided by Pettygrove and A. L. Lovejoy by the toss of a copper coin. Pettygrove was born at Calais, Maine, in 1812, and came to Oregon by sea in 1843 with a stock of merchandise. He built a warehouse at Champoeg, had a store in a log house at the southwest corner of Front and Washington streets, Portland, and a store called the Red House in Oregon City. There is uncertainty about the exact date that Portland was established. William Johnson and his Indian wife had a cabin as early as 1842 near what is now Southwest Macadam Avenue and Curry Street, but Johnson apparently had no notion of starting a town and his house was some distance south of the locality that became Portland in 1845. Etienne Lucier may have settled in what was later East Portland as early as 1829, but this was not in the original Portland townsite. A. L. Lovejoy and William Overton landed at the site of Portland in November, 1843, on the way from Fort Vancouver to Oregon City. That winter they returned and took a land claim of 640 acres. Lovejoy was the first proprietor, and Overton, his hired man. Overton took a share of land for his services, and in 1844 sold it to Pettygrove for fifty dollars. The subsequent history of Overton is unknown. In the winter of 1844, the first building was erected at the foot of Washington Street. In 1845, Lovejoy and Pettygrove laid off sixteen blocks of the townsite and named the place Portland by the process mentioned above.

Captain John Couch of Newburyport, Massachusetts, had been in the Columbia River trade and soon recognized the strategic importance of the locality of Portland. He made settlement in the place in 1845-46, and became an important addition to the community. In the fall of 1845, Lovejoy sold his interest to Benjamin Stark and moved to Oregon City. Daniel H. Lownsdale located on what later was called the King claim, and built a tannery. In September, 1848, Lownsdale bought out Pettygrove, then in sole possession of the 640 acres, for $5000 in tanned leather. The sale included a wharf at the foot of Washington Street, which was built in 1846. In 1851 Pettygrove became one of the founders of Port Townsend, Washington, where he died October 5, 1887. Lovejoy was born in Massachusetts in 1808 and came to Oregon first in 1842, went to Bents Fort on the Arkansas with Dr. Marcus Whitman and came to Oregon again in 1843. He died in Portland September 10, 1882. For references to Pettygrove and Lovejoy, see Scott's *History of the Oregon Country*, volume II, pages 266 and 319. For references to Captain Couch, *ibid.,* volume I, page 301. For synopsis of first hundred years of Portland history by the compiler, see the *Oregon Sunday Journal*, August 15, 1943. Portland post office was established November 8,

1849, with Thomas Smith first postmaster. At that time Astoria and Oregon City already had post offices and the Salem office was established the same day. For an interesting account of its first years see *Early Portland: Stump-town Triumphant* by Eugene E. Snyder.

Portola, Lane County. The plat for Portola townsite was filed in January, 1912, to provide for a community at the mouth of Noti Creek, where that stream flows into Long Tom River. The name Portola had been much in the news during the preceding few years of the Portola Festival held at San Francisco in October, 1909. This was in honor of Don Gaspar de Portola, commander of the expedition sent from Mexico to found the first European settlement in what is now the state of California. Portola reached San Diego about July 1, 1769, and continued northward to search for the famous Monterey Bay, which theretofore had been reached only by sea. Portola did not recognize Monterey, went far beyond it and on November 1, 1769, discovered San Francisco Bay. It is believed that the celebration of 1909 inspired the selection of the name Portola for the Lane County townsite. Portola post office was established March 19, 1912, with Herbert G. Suttle, postmaster. The name Portola for the new community did not prove satisfactory. Mail, freight and express were missent to Portland, in error. In addition, there was a Portola station in California on the recently completed Western Pacific Railroad, and this caused confusion. Residents of Portola, Oregon, petitioned to have a new name, and Noti was selected because of Noti Creek nearby. The name of the post office was changed to Noti on March 29, 1913. For information about the name Noti see under that heading.

Post, Crook County. Post, southeast of Prineville, was named for the postmaster, Walter H. Post. The office was established June 6, 1889.

Post Canyon, Hood River County. David Cooper told the compiler in 1967 that this canyon southeast of Mitchell Point was named because it was an abundant source of fence post stock in the early days.

Post Office Bar, Multnomah County. This is a bar in the Willamette River, about a mile above the mouth. W. H. H. Morgan of Sauvie Island told the compiler that it was named because the former Sauvie Island post office was once on the island, opposite the bar. This office was established with the name Mouth of Willamette, June 30, 1851, with Ellis Walker postmaster. It was listed in Clark County, Washington, in error, and never actually was in that county. The name was changed to Sauvies Island March 5, 1852, and was moved to the Washington County, Oregon, list May 19, 1853, with Benjamin Howell postmaster.

Postage Stamp Butte, Wasco County. Postage Stamp Butte is at the extreme west end of Tygh Ridge, about two miles west of The Dalles-California Highway, and has an elevation of 2902 feet. There once was a USFS lookout on the summit. The name was applied in 1925 by James Frankland, during observations for USFS triangulation. When seen from a distance, an arrangement of ground colors on the slopes of the butte simulated a letter with a postage stamp stuck in one corner.

Potato Hill, Linn County. This hill, elevation about 2000 feet, is five miles east of Mill City. It was named in 1863 by Thomas J. Henness on account of its shape. See Salem *Capital Journal,* June 18, 1927, page 1. This hill is locally known as Tater Hill.

Pounder Creek, Multnomah County. James Pounder was born in 1870 and came to Corbett in 1891. For many years he farmed about a mile south of Corbett along Pounder Creek. He died in August, 1951.

Powder River, Baker County. The name Powder River is probably first recorded by Peter Skene Ogden, in his journals, but he does not give any circumstances or history of its origin. See his journals in the *OHQ,* volume XI, pages 361 and 362. The river was probably named by Donald McKenzie. Dr. William C. McKay, born at Astoria in 1824, grandson of Alexander McKay, a partner of John Jacob Astor, says that the name Powder River came from the Chinook jargon words *polallie illahe,* meaning a sandy or powdery ground used to describe the soil along the stream. The first white people to visit the vicinity of Powder River were the Astorians in 1811. Lewis and Clark show Powder River on their map as *Port-pel-lah* River.

Powder Springs, Hood River County. David Cooper told the writer in 1967 that these springs on Brooks Meadows road were named because the powder house was located nearby when the road was built in the 1920s.

Powell Butte, Crook County. Powell Butte is the name of the post office near the northwest foot of Powell Buttes. It was named, of course, on account of the buttes, but the writer has not been able to ascertain why the singular form was used rather than the plural. Powell Butte post office was established March 12, 1909, with Moses Niswonger first postmaster.

Powell Buttes, Crook County. Powell Buttes form a well-known landmark between Bend and Prineville. These buttes are much dissected and there are a number of summits, the highest of which has an elevation of about 5100 feet. They were named for some member of the family of Jacob Powell of Linn County, probably for Daniel or John Powell. Several of the Powells crossed the Cascade Range into central Oregon in the early days to range stock.

Powell Creek, Douglas County. Powell Creek empties into Umpqua River in section 32, township 24 south, range 7 west. It was named in 1973 to honor William Powell, one of the first mail carriers to operate out of Tyee. The proponents of the name informed the OGNB that the mail was first carried on horseback and that twenty seven gates had to be opened and closed twice during each round trip. They also added the curious fact that it was a "backward" route where all mail was carried to the end of the line and delivered on the return trip. No explanation was given but one cannot help but imagine that even then officials were experimenting with new ways to prolong the arrival and heighten the suspense of the waiting patrons. William Powell died in Roseburg on May 15, 1970, just a few days short of his 101st birthday.

Powell Creek, Josephine County. Powell Creek was named for John L. Powell who settled on a donation land claim near the stream in 1855.

Powell Hills, Linn County. Powell Hills are northwest of Brownsville and have a maximum elevation of 516 feet. They were named for Silas Powell, a nearby resident. Silas Powell was a member of the family of Linn County's famous preacher, Joab Powell.

Powell Valley, Multnomah County. Powell Valley was named for three pioneer settlers, James Powell and Jackson Powell, of 1852, and Dr. J. P. Powell, of 1853. They were not related. See the *Oregonian,* July 19, 1899, page 9; November 5, 7, 1909. Powell Valley is east of Gresham. A post office with the name Powell's Valley was established February 13, 1873, with William H. Bond first postmaster. Theodore K. Williams was appointed postmaster December 16, 1874, and ran the office for nearly twenty years. On April 5, 1894, Albion B. Elliott was appointed postmaster and the name of the office was changed to Powell Valley. It was closed to Gresham February 28, 1903. For most of its life the office was near Powell Valley School No. 26.

Powers, Coos County. Powers was named for A. H. Powers in 1914. Powers was then superintendent of the Smith-Powers Logging Company. Powers post office was established July 24, 1915, with Gustaveous A. Brown first postmaster. Albert H. Powers was born of American parents in Ontario, Canada, November 6, 1862, and followed the logging and lumber business all his life, in several places. He was with the Smith-Powers Logging Company in Coos County from 1907 to 1922, and later with other organizations. He died at Indio, California, January 2, 1930, as the result of an automobile accident. Powers was an ardent sports enthusiast. For obituary, see the *Oregonian,* January 5, 1930.

Powwatka Ridge, Wallowa County. J. H. Horner of Enterprise told the compiler that the name Powwatka is the modern spelling of the Indian name *Paw-wa-ka,* meaning high, cleared ground, from where a view could be had. The form Powatka has been discarded by the USBGN. Powwatka post office was near the north end of Powwatka Ridge. It was established August 15, 1900, with Amanda F. Harris first of four postmasters. The office was discontinued November 30, 1920.

Prahl, Clackamas County. This was a station on the Oregon Electric Railway at the south end of the bridge over the Willamette River at Wilsonville. It was named for Fred Prahl, roadmaster for the railway, who had charge of the construction of the bridge. He died in 1908.

Prairie Channel, Clatsop County. This is the south channel of the Columbia River east of Tongue Point. It has been called Prairie Channel since pioneer days because of the prairie-like islands on either side. Wilkes, in *U. S. Exploring Expedition,* volume XXIII, Hydrography and accompanying atlas, refers to this channel as Dicks Run, but gives no explanation of the origin of that name. The name Dicks Run has not persisted.

Prairie City, Grant County. Prairie City is purely a descriptive name and quite accurately describes the community. *The History of Baker, Grant, Malheur and Harney Counties,* page 447, says that the first community was Dixie, started in 1862 about three miles up the stream of the same name. By 1870 much of the area had been destroyed by placer operations but a new townsite had already been selected at the mouth of the creek near John Day River. The name Prairie City is reported to have been chosen by J. W. King. Prairie City post office was established August 8, 1870, with Jules Le Bret first postmaster.

Prairie Creek, Wallowa County. Prairie Creek and Prairie Basin are east and southeast of Joseph. These features were named in early days by

Robert M. Downey, a pioneer settler of the Wallowa Valley who came from Missouri. He applied the names because of the fine stands of bunchgrass on the nearby prairies. Prairie Creek post office was established in January, 1876, with Downey the first postmaster. The office was closed in July, 1893. Prairie Creek was the second post office in what is now Wallowa County. Wallowa, established April 10, 1873, was the first. When first established the Prairie Creek office was in section 11, township 3 south, range 45 east, about two miles east of Wallowa Lake.

Prather Creek, Harney County. Prather Creek is about six miles east of Burns. It was named for Thomas Prather who was born in Clermont, Ohio on December 21, 1843 and came to Douglas County, Oregon in 1859. In 1872 he settled in the Burns area, then part of Grant County, where he stayed until 1882 when he moved to Montana. The name is pronounced Prater to rhyme with crater so *Decision List 6201* established that spelling. The correct form Prather was restored in 1981.

Prattville, Wasco County. Prattville post office is listed on the Wasco County list with Mrs. Mary J. Mackie postmaster, and operating from November, 1879, to September, 1880. The place was near the locality later called Wamic. The Pratt family settled there in the 1870s and even after Wamic post office was established in 1884, the name Prattville was continued for some years.

Pratum, Marion County. *Pratum* is a Latin word meaning meadow. The name is said to have been applied to the place by a group of the Mennonite Church established in the community. The railroad was built through this locality about 1880, and it is said a Mr. Larson opened the first store and called the place Enger, for a friend. This name was confused with Eugene, hence the change to Pratum. Postal authorities inform the compiler that Pratum post office was established with the name Switzerland on February 28, 1887, and with John Green first postmaster. The name of the office was changed to Enger on August 21, 1897, and to Pratum October 1, 1898. There is a community named Switzerland nearby, and the office may have been moved in addition to having its name changed.

Preachers Peak, Hood River and Multnomah counties. This name, sometimes misprinted Preachers Rock, refers to a point on the summit of the Cascade Range at the extreme southeast corner of Multnomah County. R. S. Shelley of the USFS named the peak for his father, Troy Shelley, a well-known minister of upper Hood River Valley. Shelley senior had a crippled foot. About the turn of the century he rode a horse to the summit and his son named it in his honor. According to Ralph Lewis of Parkdale who supplied this information Devils Pulpit nearby was named because the remark was made that if the preacher was there, the devil wouldn't be far away.

Prescott, Columbia County. Prescott was named about 1905 for owners of the sawmill. Prescott post office was established May 21, 1907, with Anna Barker first postmaster.

Preston, Lane County. Government records show that Preston post office was established October 11, 1853, and discontinued March 30, 1855. Henry Small was postmaster. The compiler has been unable to get the location of the place, but it was probably on Small's donation land claim now in the southwest part of Cottage Grove.

Preuss, Coos County. Preuss post office was established April 17, 1917, and was at the Beaver Hill coal mines of the Southern Pacific Company. The mines are now closed and the post office has been discontinued. It was named for Rosa Preuss, a school teacher, who helped to have the post office established.

Prevost, Baker County. This station on the railroad along Snake River was named for Jean Baptiste Prevost, a member of the Astoria overland party under Wilson Price Hunt. Prevost was drowned in Snake River in December, 1811. See Irving's *Astoria,* first edition, volume II, page 52.

Price, Crook County. Price post office was established November 16, 1886, with Mrs. Elmira Logan first postmaster. With one short intermission the office was in operation until July 11, 1902. The office was named for T. B. Price, one of the signers of the petition. It was in Camp Creek area, in section 15, township 19 south, range 20 east, about 47 miles southeast of Prineville. Although the office was established on November 16, Mrs. Logan's commission was not actually dated until December 9, 1886. The office was first in the living room of the log home of the Samuel Allen Logan family. Later the office was moved to other homesteads, but never very far from Camp Creek.

Prichard, Baker County. Prichard post office was named for a local resident. It was situated about fifteen miles airline east-northeast of Baker, in the Lower Powder Valley, about four miles north of Prichard Flat. Modern maps are lettered Middle Bridge at this point. Prichard post office was established May 24, 1872, with Royal A. Pierce first postmaster. The office was later on the Union County list, but it was when Union County included that part of what is now Baker County. Prichard post office was closed February 23, 1876. Postal records use the spelling Prichard for this office, but the name appears as Pritchard in other places. The writer does not know which style was used by the family in question.

Priday Agate Beds, Jefferson County. East of Hay Creek is the site of the old Priday Ranch. This was part of the Teal & Coleman holdings purchased by Albert James Priday who came to this country in 1880 from Westbury, England. Phil Brogan has been kind enough to provide the following facts about the rock deposits. "These beds, world known for the fine material, especially plume agates, which they produce, have been known since early days, and were among the first agate localities to bring fame to Oregon for its fine quality gem stones. The beds are in ancient formations near Trout Creek which slashes through a land of tilted mountains. The bedrock, dipping to the John Day formations and Clarno rocks, are mostly in rhyolite. Nearby on Pony Creek are the well-known Polka Dot Agate beds." Priday Reservoir in Warner Valley is on property that belonged to a son, Ernest Priday.

Prill Lake, Linn County. This is a small mountain lake near the summit of the Cascade Range, about eight miles south of Mount Jefferson. The lake was discovered by Dr. A. G. Prill of Scio, and about 1912 was named by representatives of the State Board of Fish and Game Commissioners, who stocked the lake with fish that year. Dr. Prill, long an enthusiastic amateur naturalist, conveyed his extensive bird and egg collection to the University of Oregon in 1945. See news story in *Sunday Journal,* September 23, 1945.

Prince Lake, Lane County. This lake southwest of Scott Mountain was named for Prince Glaze who was USFS guard at Frog Camp during the 1920s. Nearby Glaze Lake was named for the same man.

Princeton, Harney County. Archie McGowan wrote the compiler in August, 1927, as follows: "Princeton originated as a small rural post office in about 1912. C. B. Smith, a Bostonian and professional musician, settled on a homestead there about three years prior to the birth of the post office, and named the place for Princeton, Massachusetts, which was a town of his childhood." Postal authorities inform the compiler that Princeton post office was established October 15, 1910, with David Williams first postmaster. The compiler has been unable to reconcile the discrepancy in dates.

Prineville, Crook County. Prineville was named after the first merchant of the place, Barney Prine. His stock consisted of a barrel of first rate whisky in the front room of his establishment and some blacksmithing equipment in the back room. The prevailing opinion around Prineville is to the effect that most of the business was done in the front room. For article about Barney Prine by Fred Lockley, see *Oregon Journal,* March 31, 1927, editorial page. Prineville post office was established with the name Prine on April 13, 1871, and with William Heisler first postmaster. The name of the office was changed to Prineville on December 23, 1872.

Pringle Creek, Marion County. This stream rises in the hills south of Salem, and flows through the southern part of the town. Virgil K. Pringle, who arrived at Salem on December 25, 1846, took up a donation land claim near the stream, which was accordingly named for him. The Pringles left Missouri on April 15, 1846, and Octavius M. Pringle, son of Virgil K. Pringle, wrote an account of the trip under the heading *Experiences of an Emigrant Boy of 1846.* Octavius M. Pringle subsequently moved to central Oregon. See under Pringle Falls.

Pringle Falls, Deschutes County. Pringle Falls on Deschutes River were named for O. M. Pringle who, in 1902, bought from the government 160 acres of land near the site of the falls, under the Timber and Stone Act. Pringle came into central Oregon about 1874, from Salem, and for some years lived near Prineville. The locality of Pringle Falls is also known as the Fish Trap. Indians guddled salmon at this point, lying on the bank and grasping the fish in the gills as they swam up through the shallow channels.

Progress, Washington County. When Progress was named, optimism was fairly singing in the air. Progress post office was established August 28, 1889, with Joseph Hingley postmaster. The office was closed July 11, 1904, but Progress continued as a county crossroads, about three miles southeast of Beaverton. It is at the crossing of the Scholls Ferry Road and Hall Boulevard.

Promise, Wallowa County. John C. Phillips and W. Mann settled near the present site of Promise about 1891 and took up homesteads. Mann called the place "Promised Land" and "Land of Promise," and when the post office was established, December 22, 1896, it was called Promise on that account. Thomas C. Miller was first postmaster.

Prospect, Jackson County. In 1979 Mrs. Frances Aiken Pearson of Medford gave the compiler some interesting history of this small community on the Rogue River north of Medford. It was first established as Deskins and a post office with this name was opened on July 5, 1882 with Harvey P. Deskins postmaster. In the fall of 1883 Deskins, after a misguided business venture, fell on hard times and sold all his holdings to Squire Stanford Aiken, Mrs. Peason's father. Eventually Aiken became postmaster and on November 9, 1889, had the name changed to Prospect because some preliminary plans had been run for a railroad up the Rogue River.

Prospect Creek, Tillamook County. Prospect Creek flows into Neskowin Creek. Ralph Sutton, a long time resident, said that the name was given many years ago by a cowboy who claimed to have discovered gold along its banks, and in due course a company was organized, stock sold, furnace built and company bankrupted in that sequence. At least the promoters picked an original area for their operation.

Prosper, Coos County. Prosper post office was established August 8, 1893, with Adam Pershbaker postmaster. The name was apparently selected because of hopes that the locality would be prosperous. The office was discontinued in June, 1928.

Prouty Glacier, Deschutes County. Prouty Glacier was named for Harley H. Prouty who was born in Vermont June 26, 1857, of a distinguished New England family. He was engaged for a time in the lumbering business after he came to Oregon. Later he retired from active business and devoted much time to mountaineering, and was president of the Mazamas. He died September 11, 1916, and it was his wish that his remains be buried in the Cascade Range. As a result of this a party of Mazamas took his ashes to Obsidian Cliff, near the Three Sisters, and placed them in a cairn. Nearby is placed a bronze tablet bearing a suitable inscription. Prouty may have been the first man to climb the North Sister and one of the spires or pinnacles at the top of the mountain is known as Prouty Pinnacle. A short biography appears in the *Mazama* of 1916, and information about the bronze plate is in *Mazama* for 1917.

Providence Creek, Douglas County. Providence Creek flows into Umpqua River west of Reedsport. The name perpetuates a settlement called Providence, established in the early 1850s, but gone long ago. The compiler has been unable to get the history of the place, by whom it was settled and why it was named. In June, 1944, Mrs. Alice B. Maloney told the compiler that she had found an interview with C. C. Mann in the Bancroft Library at the University of California, Berkeley. Mann was a member of the *Samuel Roberts* party visiting Umpqua River in July, 1850. He stressed the fact that he was a graduate of Brown University, Providence, Rhode Island. It is possible this is the genesis of the name, but the evidence is of course rather tenuous.

Provolt, Jackson County. This post office was named for a pioneer family of the community. The office was established April 29, 1895, with Mary E. Provolt postmaster. It was then in Josephine County.

Proxy Point, Lane County. Proxy Point is just west of the Three Sisters. It was named by USGS surveyors during the time when the triangulation net was being extended along the Cascade Range. This point and Substitute Point were both selected for possible stations, where but one was to be occupied.

Pryor, Lane County. Pryor, a station on the Cascade line of the Southern Pacific Company, was named for a member of the Lewis and Clark expedition, Nathaniel Pryor.

Pucci Glade, Clackamas County. In 1936 Emilio Paola Pucci dei Marchese di Barsento came from Italy to pursue graduate studies at Reed College. He also undertook to coach the then fledgling Reed College ski team. Pucci picked for a practice slope this open glade immediately south and west of the present site of Timberline Lodge. Reed College was one of the early local entrants in Alpine downhill skiing competition and by the time the lodge was opened in 1937, the name was firmly entrenched. Emilio Pucci completed his studies and returned to Italy where he achieved considerable fame as a fashion designer and was also active in politics. He maintained his friendships with members of the Mount Hood skiing community and on March 10, 1978 the Friends of Timberline arranged a reunion of the ski team and a testimonial dinner at Timberline Lodge. The name of the glade was formally recognized and Pucci was able to demonstrate that he still retained his skiing dexterity. At the evening banquet he was presented with a handsome engraved replica of the present wood descriptive marker.

Pudding River, Clackamas and Marion counties. This stream rises in the Waldo Hills, east of Salem, and joins Molalla River just before that stream flows into the Willamette. Little Pudding River drains an area to the west of Pudding River, and joins that stream just west of Mount Angel. Pudding River is a name that originated in the days of the fur trade. W. H. Rees, in an address in OPA *Transactions,* 1879, page 23, gives the story of the name. The substance is that about 1821-22 Joseph Gervais and Etienne Lucier and their families were camped on the stream, which was called *Hons-u-cha-chac,* and in a period of severe weather had the good fortune to shoot some elk. The squaws immediately made a favorite French dish, known as a blood pudding, which went a long way toward overcoming the discomfort of rain and snow. While this feast was being enjoyed, Gervais and Lucier christened the stream *Riviere au Boudin,* or Pudding River. See also *Ten Years in Oregon,* of Dr. Elijah White, page 70, by Miss A. J. Allen. Rees is doubtless right in his account of the origin of the name, but wrong about the date, for Alexander Henry mentions Pudding River in his diary on January 23, 1814. The river was probably named in 1812-13. See under Gervais. Pudding River appears on the Wilkes map of 1841. Another form of the Indian name was Anchiyoke River, which was used in the act of July 5, 1843, creating Champooick District. Early writings show different spellings. See *Handbook of American Indians* under the heading "Ahantchuyuk."

Pueblo Mountain, Harney County. Pueblo Mountain is in the extreme south end of the county, south of Steens Mountain. It is named with the Spanish word for city or village. The name was applied in the early 1860s by prospectors and miners from Nevada, and a news item in the *Humboldt Register,* Unionville, Nevada, December 5, 1863, copied from the Virginia City *Union,* attributes the discovery of the "Puebla" district to Major M. D.

Harmon of Carson City. The form Puebla is the wrong gender for the Spanish word, and has been supplanted by Pueblo. In May, 1946, James F. Abel, then at the Bancroft Library in Berkeley, sent the compiler a transcript of the item about Harmon, which will be found in *OHQ*, June 1946, page 210. Mr. Abel concludes: "Puebla Mining District was in existence as early, at least, as the summer of 1863. It may have been established in 1862 but that is not probable. The district was believed to be in Nevada and is shown on Milleson's Map of the Reese River and Humboldt Silver Mines dated 1864. In reality the Territorial line ran south of or through it and all or most of it was in Oregon. Mentions of Puebla Mining District are numerous in 1864. Pueblo Mountain, Butte, Valley and City are shown with considerable accuracy on Lieutenant Colonel R. S. Williamson's map published in 1866."

Puget Bar, Clatsop County. Puget Bar lies in the Columbia River east of Tenasillahe Island and west of Puget Island. Broughton discovered Puget Island on October 26, 1792, and named it for Lieutenant Peter Puget, and the name Puget has by custom become attached to the bar. Puget Island is in Washington. Tenasillahe Island is in Oregon. Lieutenant Peter Puget was a member of the Vancouver expedition and it was for him that Puget Sound in Washington was named. Not a great deal is known about Peter Puget, though diligent search has been made, particularly by Professor Edmond S. Meany of the University of Washington. He was lieutenant on Vancouver's sloop *Discovery* at the time Vancouver visited the Pacific Northwest. What is known about Puget is printed in Meany's *Vancouver's Discovery of Puget Sound*. See also *British Columbia Coast Names*, by John T. Walbran.

Pulpit Rock, Hood River County. Pulpit Rock is the prominent buttress on Mount Hood dividing Coe and Ladd glaciers at the 9000 foot level. The earliest reference to this rock is in a letter from Dr. T. L. Eliot written in the summer of 1887 describing what must be assumed to be the first ascent of Cathedral Ridge. Dr. Eliot calls it "The Cockscomb" but this form has not prevailed. The present descriptive name, Pulpit Rock, is now in general use.

Pulpit Rock, Wasco County. Pulpit Rock is a peculiar formation of stone within the city limits of The Dalles. It is a pillar about 20 feet high, cleft at the top in such a way as to make it a natural pulpit, with a seat attached. Missionaries of the Methodist mission in The Dalles used this pulpit when they preached to the Indians. On the seventieth anniversary of the founding of the mission, a bronze tablet was unveiled and Pulpit Rock was dedicated in the presence of about five hundred persons. For information about the mission and Pulpit Rock, see Lulu D. Crandall's article in the *Oregonian*, October 24, 1927, editorial page.

Puma Creek, Lane County. A. J. Briem, in his notes on file at the OHS, says that this creek was named because the small daughter of a road camp cook saw a cougar on its banks.

Pumpkin Creek, Wallowa County. This stream is east of Imnaha and was named because Ike Bare camped on its banks while hunting, and cooked some pumpkins, of which he was fond.

Pursel, Jackson County. Pursel post office and community were named in compliment to the postmaster, C. C. Pursel. The office, which was in the Applegate Valley about ten miles north of Watkins, operated from February, 1898, until January, 1904, and was then closed out to Buncom.

Pyburn Hollow, Sherman County. Jacob Pyburn homesteaded in this canyon west of John Day River in the 1890s.

Pyle Canyon, Union County. This canyon, south of Union, was named for James M. Pyle, a pioneer settler of that part of Oregon, and one of the first members of the legislature from Baker County as it then existed.

Pyramid, Columbia County. This station on the south bank of the Columbia River west of Rainier was named for a peculiar pyramidal rock standing above the railroad track.

Quail Creek, Curry County. This stream, a tributary of Rogue River, was named for Peter Quail, a pioneer prospector.

Quaking Aspen Swamp, Lane County. This is a feature of the Quaking Aspen Swamp Botanical Area between French Mountain and South Fork McKenzie River in township 17 south, range 6 east. The swamp itself is a prime example of mountain sphagnum bog and is named because a small grove of aspen or *Populus tremuloides* grows at the upper end. The name Quaking Asp Swamp is incorrect. For further information on aspen see under Aspen Lake.

Quartz Creek, Wasco County. Quartz is not a rare mineral in the Cascade Range, nevertheless it is not plentiful as compared with other rocks. As a result, when it occurs, it attracts attention. Quartz Creek in the north part of the Warm Springs Indian Reservation was named for the mineral in very early days. Captain H. D. Wallen of the Fourth Infantry conducted a military expedition from Fort Dalles to Great Salt Lake in 1859, and on the night of June 10 of that year camped at a place about 50 miles south of The Dalles which he named Quartz Spring because of the first quartz seen on the march. This was after passing Tygh Valley and Oak Grove (Wapinitia). However, in the table of distances given for the trip Wallen uses the name Quartz Creek. See 36th Congress, 1st Session, Senate Executive Document 34, pages 7 and 46.

Quartz Mountain, Lake County. Quartz Mountain is a ridge about thirty miles northwest of Lakeview, crossed by the Klamath Falls-Lakeview Highway. The mountain got its name from a narrow but rather prominent ledge of quartz, something out of the ordinary for the locality. The name of the mountain has spread to other nearby geographic features. Quartz Pass is the highest point on the highway, and Quartz Creek heads just east of the pass and flows southeast into Quartz Valley. On November 24, 1930, a post office with the name Quartz Mountain was established on the highway a little to the southeast of the pass. Mrs. Vera A. Real was the only postmaster. The office was closed to Lakeview August 31, 1943.

Quartzville, Linn County. Quartzville was once an important locality, due to gold discoveries in Dry Gulch in the early 1860s. The place was laid off as a town in 1864, and a stamp-mill was erected in the same year. For information about routes to the Santiam mines see the *Oregonian*, July 9, 1864. For other information *ibid.,* June 9, 16, 30; September 1 and 8, 1860;

October 14 and 22, 1863; June 30 and November 12, 1864, and October 29, 1869, page 3. See also Down's *History of the Silverton Country,* page 85. The excitement of the times is well expressed by the following text of a broadside described in detail in item 739 of *Oregon Imprints 1845-1870,* by George N. Belknap. "Ho! For Quartzville. All persons who want to go to Quartzville, will meet at the court-house, armed and equipped, at 3 o'clock this (Thursday) evening. Every man must furnish his own rations (say for 4 days) horse, and other necessaries gratis. Salem Aug. 25, 1864." For further information see *Sunday Oregonian,* August 14, 1960, section 1, page 22. When mining activity was resumed in the 1890s, the place was called Anidem, see under that heading. One of the largest tributaries of Middle Santiam River is Quartzville Creek, named for the town.

Quinaby, Marion County. Quinaby was a station on the Oregon Electric Railway named for a self-appointed chief of a small group of Calapooia Indians who lived north of Salem in the early days of statehood. Os West in an article in the magazine section, *Sunday Oregonian,* October 22, 1950, tells of old Quinaby and how he wintered in a camp about one half mile north of the Capitol and just west of Capitol Street in what were then the environs of Salem. Quinaby died in 1883.

Quincy, Columbia County. Quincy was settled about 1882, and named for Quincy, Illinois, by J. W. Barnes, who came from that place. The post office was established October 8, 1892.

Quines Creek, Douglas County. Quines Creek flows north into Cow Creek near where I 5 leaves Upper Cow Creek Valley to ascend to Canyon Creek Pass. There is a small roadside community which takes its name from the stream. Henry and Elizabeth Quine came to Oregon from Missouri in 1853. They first located in Benton County but in 1854 took a donation land claim including the mouth of the creek.

Quinn, Columbia County. The locality and post office called Quinn was near the south bank of the Columbia River on the low land northwest of Quincy. The post office was named for James Quinn, the first postmaster. He was appointed May 4, 1876, and served until June 30, 1909, at least that is the date the office was discontinued. There was never any other postmaster there.

Quinn Lakes, Lane County. These lakes north of Waldo Lake were named for a pioneer sheep man, William E. Quinn of Grizzly. He was fatally injured in 1894 while hunting in the Cascade Range near Waldo Lake, and died near Crane Prairie while being packed out toward Deschutes River. He was buried on the banks of the stream known as Quinn River, which is in Deschutes County.

Quinton, Gilliam County. Quinton is a railroad station that derives its name from an early settler named Quinn. The place was formerly called Quinn. For a few years there was a post office called Quinook, and this name was made up by taking part of the name Quinton and part of the name Squally Hook, which was the name of a railroad station to the west. For information about Squally Hook see under Hook. Quinook post office was discontinued in the fall of 1925.

Quitters Point, Marion County. Quitters Point is south of Firecamp

Lakes above South Fork Breitenbush River. It is a long, steep trail from the river at the 3000 foot level up to this 5000 foot high nose near the lakes. It was named by USFS personnel who found their enthusiasm for the outdoors momentarily dimmed by the ascent.

Quosatana Creek, Curry County. This name is said to come from an Indian word *Quosaten.* F. S. Moore of Gold Beach wrote the compiler that George W. Meservey, a half-blood Indian, told him that the Indian word meant a beautiful or fine creek. Quosatana Butte near the headwaters of the creek, got its name from the stream. J. Neilson Barry calls attention to the entry under Tututni, *Handbook of American Indians,* volume II, page 857, which lists among the bands of that tribe the Cosuttheutun, and other similar forms. The name is translated as "people who eat mussels," *ibid.,* volume 1, page 749. Possibly Quosatana is derived from it.

Rabbit Ears, Douglas County. These two peculiar rocks are in the mountains west of Rogue River opposite Crater Lake. The higher has an elevation of 6031 feet. The Indian name was *Kalistopox,* according to Will G. Steel. Two forest rangers, William E. White and Melvin E. Layton climbed one of them in 1912 and built a cairn on its summit. A stream nearby is Rabbitear Creek.

Rachel, Linn County. Rachel post office was situated on what is known as Middle Ridge at a point about five miles southeast of Sodaville. It was at the home of James W. Pierpoint, the first and only postmaster, and was named for his mother, Rachel Pierpoint. Rachel post office was established February 16, 1915, and discontinued June 15, 1916, with papers to Sodaville.

Rackheap Creek, Tillamook County. This stream is in the extreme north part of the county and flows into North Fork Nehalem River from the east. Little Rackheap Creek is just to the north and flows into Rackheap Creek. In January, 1944, J. H. Scott of Nehalem wrote the compiler that the term rackheap was used by loggers to indicate a heap or pile of logs to be driven down stream by splash dam operations. It also means an accumulation of waste and scrap logs and debris. An eddy in the North Fork Nehalem River piles up a collection of debris and brush at the mouth of Rackheap Creek, which is the reason for the odd name of the stream.

Rader Creek, Douglas County. William Rader came to Douglas County in the 1880s with a large family. He eventually settled near the headwaters of this creek that bears his name northwest of Tyee.

Ragged Ridge, Douglas County. Ragged Ridge is the high ground forming the divide between North Umpqua River and Steamboat Creek. This descriptive name was applied by USFS ranger Fred Asam in the 1920s.

Ragic, Curry County. Ragic is Cigar spelled backward. G. W. Meservey wrote from Illahe saying that a distinctive name was wanted, and Ragic was the result! Ragic post office was established September 10, 1898, with John H. McElhaney first postmaster. The office was closed October 5, 1900, and mail sent to Wedderburn. Ragic was about nine miles up Rogue River from Wedderburn, apparently on the McElhaney place about a mile west of the mouth of Lobster Creek.

Railroad Creek, Douglas County. This stream is in the west part of the county and is tributary from the east to North Fork Smith River at a point about a mile and a half up stream from the mouth of North Fork. In May, 1948, William Wroe, a local resident, wrote that the name Railroad was applied because there was once a logging railroad near the creek. Wroe added: "That was way over fifty years ago and there is no trace of the railroad left."

Railroad Gap, Jackson County. The name Railroad Gap has been used in the upper Evans Creek area for many years. It is applied to a natural pass and also to a USFS shelter, both of which are situated in the southwest corner of township 32 south, range 2 west. When the Oregon and California Railroad was being projected south from Roseburg in the 1870s, a survey was run through this section in hope of finding a practicable route from the drainage of Cow Creek into the Rogue River. This location was not used but the fact of the survey gave rise to the name Railroad Gap. For the geography of the locality, see USGS map of the Trail quadrangle, issued in 1945.

Rainbow, Lane County. The name of this post office was suggested by Mrs. L. Quimby, whose husband bought the property where the office is situated in May, 1922. The office was established July 1, 1924, and closed August 31, 1937 with mail to Blue River. Mrs. Quimby selected the name because McKenzie River nearby is the home of the popular rainbow trout, *Salmo gairdneri.*

Rainbow Point, Klamath County. This point is on the south shore of Crescent Lake. It was named by F. W. Cleator of the USFS in 1925 because of the presence of many rainbow trout in the water nearby.

Rainier, Columbia County. The town of Rainier was founded by Charles E. Fox, who settled there in 1851, and was the first postmaster. The name of the town was taken from Mount Rainier. The earlier name was Eminence. Mount Rainier, in Washington, has been the center of one of the most acute geographic name controversies in the history of the country. It was named by George Vancouver on May 8, 1792, for Rear-Admiral Peter Rainier, of the Royal Navy. For facts about the discovery and Admiral Rainier, see Meany's *Vancouver's Discovery of Puget Sound,* page 99. For additional information about the mountain and the name Tacoma as applied thereto, see *Mount Rainier,* by the same author. Eminence post office was established June 5, 1851, with Charles E. Fox first postmaster. The name of the office was changed to Rainier on January 6, 1852.

Rainrock, Lane County. This station was west of Eugene. The name was applied by H. L. Walter of the operating department of Southern Pacific Company. Walter told the compiler he selected this name arbitrarily and it had no particular significance.

Raker Point, Hood River County. This point on the west end of Sawtooth Mountain was named for its similarity to a raker tooth in a cross cut saw. Raker teeth clean out chips cut by the other teeth.

Raleigh, Washington County. The name Raleigh was derived from an old-time resident of the neighborhood, Raleigh Robinson. The place was on the Scholls Ferry road at a point about a mile southwest of the Hillsdale-

Beaverton Highway crossing, and just northeast of the Portland Golf Club. Raleigh post office was established April 26, 1892, with Frank T. Berry first postmaster. The office was closed April 29, 1904, with papers to Beaverton. In recent years the locality has been called Raleigh Hills, which sounds like a name coined by real estate operators.

Ramo Flat, Union County. This flat is southeast of Union. Dunham Wright of Medical Springs informed the compiler in 1927 that it was named for a Frenchman, one Raymou, who lived thereon.

Ramsey Lake, Multnomah County. This lake south of the mouth of the Willamette River was filled in by the Rivergate development during the 1970s. It was named for F. H. Ramsey, who was a pioneer settler of the neighborhood.

Rancheria Creek, Jackson County. Rancheria Creek rises on the west slopes of the Cascade Range south of Rustler Peak and flows southwestward to join South Fork Big Butte Creek east of Butte Falls. This name has been shown on maps since pioneer days. *Rancheria* is a Spanish word used to refer to an Indian village or frequently for creeks flowing by such villages. The compiler has been told that Rancheria Creek was named because of the Indian village not far from its mouth and also not far from the old military freight road from Jacksonville to Fort Klamath.

Rand, Josephine County. Rand is a community on Rogue River three miles north of Galice. Edith A. Keyte in *Josephine County Historic Highlights* states that it was the housing for the workers at the Almeda Mine a mile further downstream, and that it was named for the Rand, or more accurately the Witwatersrand, a ridge in the Transvaal of South Africa famous for its gold bearing soil. At one time there was a USFS ranger station at this site.

Randall Butte, Jefferson County. Zenery P. Randall took a homestead on the slopes of this Axehandle country butte in 1916.

Randleman Creek, Coos County. Randleman Creek, which flows into Bear Creek east of Bandon, was named for Michel Randleman, who settled near the stream in 1874. The Randleman family has been prominent in Coos County affairs for several generations.

Randolph, Coos County. Randolph is a community on the north side of Coquille River about three miles from the Pacific Ocean. Walling's *History of Southern Oregon,* page 492, says the place was established in the days of the Coos County mining excitement, by Dr. Foster and Captain Harris and was named for John Randolph of Roanoke, Virginia. Randolph was first situated several miles northwest of the present location, near the mouth of Whisky Run, a small stream flowing into the ocean. Nearby sands were mined with feverish activity between 1853 and 1855. A dreary picture of Randolph in October, 1855, after the fever, is given in an article by William V. Wells, in *Harper's Magazine,* October, 1856, page 595.

Range, Grant County. This post office was established June 4, 1908, and was named by its patrons because of the good stock range in the vicinity. Craig Thom was the first postmaster.

Rann, Grant County. Rann post office was established April 8, 1886, with William D. Baker first of two postmasters. The office was closed to

Canyon City, February 29, 1888. Rann and Ryan were in the livestock business in the central part of the Silvies Valley, and Rann post office was at or near the Rann ranch. It may be assumed that the office was named for this stockman.

Ransom Creek, Curry County. This Ransom Creek is tributary to Bravo Creek near Palmer Butte. Hiram C. Ransom who homesteaded at its mouth was the father of Edwin Ransom who later lived on the Ransom Creek at Brookings.

Ransom Creek, Curry County. This creek entering the Pacific Ocean on the north edge of Brookings was originally named Iler Creek. Edwin Ransom, son of Hiram Ransom, bought the Iler homestead prior to World War I and the creek name changed with the land title.

Rattlesnake Creek, Lane County. Rattlesnake Creek flows into Middle Fork Willamette River east of Pleasant Hill and west of Trent. Rattlesnake Butte, elevation 1374 feet, is just east of the south end of the stream. The creek was named by Elijah Bristow in pioneer days because of the prevalence of rattlesnakes in the vicinity. See Walling's *Illustrated History of Lane County,* page 447. The place now called Trent was once called Rattlesnake because it was on the banks of Rattlesnake Creek.

Rattlesnake Grade, Morrow County. Don McElligott wrote the compiler in 1969 regarding the name of this stretch of county road up McElligott Canyon. He stated that when the present road was built in 1923, his father and several other local ranchers contracted the grading which they did with fresnoes and horse teams. There were a lot of rattlesnakes in the canyon and after the crews uncovered one exceptionally big den, the road was known as Rattlesnake Grade.

Ray Gold, Jackson County. This was the railroad name for Gold Ray. Colonel Frank Ray built a power plant on Rogue River nearby and named the place for himself with Gold added because it was hoped the enterprise would be a gold mine. The power plant is still known by its original name, but the railroad reversed the order of things because of confusion with Gold Hill nearby.

Rebel Hill, Grant County. This small eminence in the southeastern part of Canyon City was named during the Civil War because some southern sympathizers lived on the hill and made their presence in the community very much noticed.

Rebel Rock, Lane County. Rebel Rock is on the west slope of the Cascade Range near South Fork McKenzie River. It is said to have been named for a pioneer sheep herder who boasted that he was the only rebel who had never been whipped, captured or surrendered.

Rector, Tillamook County. When the Wheeler Lumber Company established a logging camp at this place about 1909, it was named after Edward Rector, the manager of the company. The post office was established August 1, 1913, with Mrs. Elizabeth M. McClure first postmaster.

Red Blanket Creek, Jackson and Klamath counties. Red Blanket Creek flows into Middle Fork Rogue River south of Prospect. Mrs. Frances Aiken Pearson, who was born in Prospect in 1885, told the compiler in 1979 that she understood it received its name when early settlers gave the Indians red trade blankets for the fertile land east of Prospect. This became the site of the Red Blanket Ranch which in turn gave the name to the creek and Red Blanket Mountain.

Red Creek, Hood River and Wasco counties. This creek rises on Bonney Butte and flows southwest to White River. Lewis D. Reavis who worked for the USFS in the 1920s told the compiler that this is a descriptive name.

Redboy, Grant County. Redboy post office was established to serve the Redboy mine in the Blue Mountains a few miles southwest of Granite. The office was put in service December 5, 1907, with Percy W. Brick first of two postmasters. It was closed out to Granite December 15, 1910.

Redess, Harney County. Redess was named for "Red S" brand of the Pacific Live Stock Company's ranch nearby. It is between Burns and Crane on the Union Pacific Railroad. The stock company had acquired large acreage through the Swamp Act implementation of 1870 when overflow federal lands were marked with a capital "S" in red ink on land maps and deeded to the state. The administration of this law was marked by large scale abuse and some cases of outright fraud. The lands were generally known as Red S and it is probable that this was the origin of the brand.

Redland, Clackamas County. Redland is a locality six or seven miles east of Oregon City, so called because of the color of the soil. Redland post office was established March 21, 1892, with William J. Johnson first of five postmasters. The office was closed October 12, 1903, apparently because of the extension of rural free delivery.

Redmans Tooth, Douglas County. This is a prominent tooth shaped rock on the end of Ragged Ridge above the junction of Steamboat Creek and North Umpqua River. According to Fred Asam, an early USFS ranger, nearby Redman Creek was originally known as Buck Tooth Creek for the rock, but for some unknown reason it was changed to Dead Indian Creek. Asam combined the two elements and gave the present names to both creek and rock.

Redmond, Deschutes County. Redmond was named for Frank T. Redmond, who settled near the present site of the town in 1905. His house was a stopping place for transients. The town was laid out in 1906. For history of Redmond see University of Oregon *Commonwealth Review,* April-July, 1924. Redmond post office was established on August 29, 1905, with Carl N. Ehret first postmaster.

Redne, Marion County. Redne post office was established January 10, 1918, with Gladys Grafe first postmaster. The office was discontinued August 31, 1921. The writer was told in January, 1947, that the office was at a logging camp or headquarters on North Santiam River between Niagara and Detroit. It is said that the name was coined by spelling the proper name Ender backward. Ender was also a logging station, previously in service just east of Niagara, but it was not a post office.

Reed, Lane County. Reed post office was established February 8, 1900. John L. Taylor drew up the petition for the post office and suggested the name Reed in honor of Thomas Brackett Reed, for many years speaker of the United States House of Representatives.

Reed Creek, Douglas County. This creek in Camas Valley was named for Alexander Reed who took up a donation land claim along its banks in 1854.

Reeder Point, Multnomah County. Reeder Point is on the west bank of Columbia River and on the east shore of Sauvie Island in the extreme northwest corner of Multnomah County. It is about a mile south of the north boundary of the county. It is not a sharply defined point, in fact no more than a simple bend in the river. It bears the name of pioneer settlers in the locality, Simon M. and Catherine Reeder. The Reeders established themselves on their donation land claim in the 1850s. See under Sauvies.

Reeds Creek, Baker County. Reeds Creek empties into Burnt River southwest of Dooley Mountain. It was named for Tabor M. Reed, an early settler and prospector.

Reedsport, Douglas County. This town was named in honor of Alfred W. Reed, a pioneer resident of the western part of the county. The name was first applied about 1900 when the townsite was platted. The post office was established July 17, 1912.

Reedville, Washington County. This town was named for Simeon G. Reed, who was a prominent figure in Columbia River transportation during the years 1859-79. He was a leading member of the Oregon Steam Navigation Company, and a large part of his fortune came from the sale of that company to the Villard syndicate in July, 1879. Reed was born at East Abington, Massachusetts, April 23, 1830, and came to Oregon in 1852. In 1859 he became a partner in the mercantile firm of Ladd Reed & Company. He engaged in various activities after the sale of the Oregon Steam Navigation Company. He died at Pasadena, California, November 7, 1895. For his biography, see the *Oregonian*, November 8, 1895, page 10; June 26, 1904, page 33. Reed operated a blooded stock farm at what is now Reedville. For description of the farm and the livestock, *ibid.*, October 12, 1875. His property became the endowment of Reed College after the death of his wife, Amanda Wood Reed. Mrs. Reed was born at Quincy, Massachusetts, August 26, 1832; was married to S. G. Reed in October 1850, and came to Oregon in 1852. She died at Pasadena May 16, 1904. Reedville post office was established January 2, 1877, with George Thing postmaster. The office was closed January 31, 1954.

Reid Glacier, Clackamas County. This glacier is on the west slope of Mount Hood. It was named in 1901 for Professor Harry Fielding Reid, of Johns Hopkins University, an authority on glaciers. For his article on Glaciers see *Mazama*, July, 1903; Glaciers of Mount Hood and Mount Adams, *ibid.*, December, 1905. Professor Reid was born in Baltimore, May 18, 1859; died June 18, 1944.

Reinhart Creek, Curry County. In the spring of 1854 Herman and Charles Reinhart homesteaded on this creek about three miles north of Sisters Rocks. Herman Reinhart was born in Prussia in 1832 and emigrated with his family to the United States. In 1851 he and his brother came west and for the next eighteen years followed most of the important mining discoveries from the Siskiyou country to Fraser River in Canada and the Rocky Mountains in Montana. His recollections published in *The Golden Frontier*, University of Texas Press, 1962, are a classic description of day to day life on the frontier and contain innumerable references to people and events in southwest Oregon. Reinhart died in Chanute, Kansas, January 14, 1889. At the instigation of the OGNB the spelling Reinhart was approved by USBGN *Decision List 6801*.

Remote, Coos County. Remote was named in pioneer days because of the location, which was well isolated from other settlements. The post office was established June 1, 1887, with Herman S. Davis first postmaster.

Renfrew Glacier, Lane County. This glacier, on the northwest slope of the Middle Sister, bears the name of P. C. Renfrew, one of the incorporators of the McKenzie toll road project.

Reserve, Lane County. This station on the Cascade line of the Southern Pacific was named many years ago when national forests were called reserves. It was at the boundary of the Cascade Forest Reserve.

Rest, Harney County. A post office with the agreeable name Rest was established on the Harney County list on April 3, 1890, with Samuel F. Hutton first and only postmaster. This office was closed to Riley on April 29, 1891. In March, 1947, Archie McGowan wrote the compiler as follows: "Samuel F. Hutton was a pioneer settler in the vicinity of Wagontire Mountain. This area became quite famous during the last homestead era because of the feuds between the pioneer stockmen and the later settlers over the famous Wagontire waterholes. Mrs. America Sutherland, daughter of S. F. Hutton, reports that there were very few patrons for this early post office. It was situated in her father's home, and since patrons had to come so far for their mail, they had to rest before starting on their return journey. The name Rest was applied on that account."

Reston, Douglas County. This place is said to have been named by a traveler who sat on the front porch of Edmond E. Weekly's stage station. Weekly was considering a name for the post office, which was established August 25, 1890, and the stranger suggested Rest because of the conveniences furnished to tired travelers. Weekly found there was another post office named Rest and he added an additional syllable. The place has been called Reston ever since, but it was not a post office in 1941.

Retlaw, Washington County. This station was on the line of the Southern Pacific Company and was named by spelling the word Walter backward. The place was named for H. L. Walter, a member of the operating department of the company in Portland.

Retz Creek, Curry County. M. S. Brainard wrote the compiler in 1967 that this creek south of Port Orford was named for William Rhetz who lived near its banks. Rhetz was a long time local resident and a county commissioner in 1873. Posterity decided that his memory be preserved in four letters instead of the original five.

Reuben, Columbia County. On February 29, 1940, the Rainier *Review* published a short article about Goble and Reuben. Reuben is a place about a mile south of Goble and apparently it was named for Reuben R. Foster who was the second postmaster. The post office was established September 5, 1890, with Eli G. Foster the first postmaster. The office ran with one interruption until it was discontinued to Goble October 25, 1923. Members of the Foster family were prominent in the history of Goble and vicinity.

The place called Reuben is at or near a locality once known as Enterprise. It was planned to name the post office Enterprise in 1890, but that proposal fell by the wayside because there was already an Enterprise in Wallowa County, where the post office was established in 1887.

Reuben Creek, Josephine County. Reuben Creek is a tributary of Grave Creek west of Leland. It was named for Reuben Field, who fought in the Rogue River War. See under Mount Reuben.

Rex, Yamhill County. Rex is a community in Chehalem Gap a few miles east of Newberg, very near the Washington-Yamhill county line. The writer has not been able to learn why the name was selected. Some time in the 1890s Charles F. Moore, a local landowner, platted some property in the place and named it Charleston, presumably for his own given name. A railroad station was installed with the name Charleston and on March 27, 1900, Charleston post office was established with Harry L. Ward postmaster. Very soon confusion developed with the town of Carlton in the same county. Mail and railroad shipments went astray. The railroad changed the station name from Charleston to Rex and on May 14, 1901, the name of the post office was changed to Rex. Local residents say the railroad selected the name Rex, but no one seems to know why.

Rhea Creek, Morrow County. The name Ray Creek is incorrect. The stream was named for Columbus Rhea, son of Elijah Rhea, pioneer of Lane County. Columbus Rhea settled in eastern Oregon about 1870, near the junction of Willow and Rhea creeks. Other brothers settled in the neighborhood. Columbus Rhea was engaged in a number of enterprises beside farming and was living in Heppner in 1928. He died on July 11, 1934.

Rhinehart, Union County. Rhinehart is a small community and formerly a flag stop on the Union Pacific Railroad a few miles south of Elgin, but the name is misspelled. Henry Rinehart and other members of the family were early and prominent settlers in the locality, and the place is supposed to bear the family name, but has too many of the letter "h." For information about members of the Rinehart family, see *Illustrated History of Union and Wallowa Counties,* pages 337, 344, and 411.

Rhoda Creek, Coos County. This stream flows into South Fork Coquille River south of Myrtle Point. It was named for William Rhoda, one of the so-called Baltimore party that settled nearby in pioneer days. Rhoda is said to have been a skilled cabinet maker.

Rhodes Creek, Lane County. Rhodes Creek empties into Lookout Point Lake near the site of the onetime community of Blakelyville. It was named for William Rhodes, an early settler.

Rhodes Creek, Wallowa County. This stream flows into Lightning Creek in the northeast part of the county. It was named for one Doc Rhodes, a local resident.

Rhododendron, Clackamas County. Rhododendron is on the Mount Hood Loop Highway. It was once a popular summer colony but with the increased popularity of skiing it has become a year round community. The place was originally called Rowe for Henry S. Rowe, who was one time mayor of Portland and interested in the development of Oregon's scenic attractions. Later the post office was known as Zigzag. Still later the name was changed to Rhododendron because of the large number of rhododendron shrubs growing in the neighborhood.

Ribbon Ridge, Yamhill County. Ribbon Ridge is a spur in the southwest part of the Chehalem Mountains, about east of Yamhill. The top of the ridge twists like a ribbon, hence the name. A story in the Newberg *Graphic,* April 25, 1940, says that Ribbon Ridge was named by Colby Carter, who came to Oregon from Missouri in 1865, and was an early settler in the Chehalem Mountains.

Rice, Wasco County. Horace Rice settled on upper Fifteenmile Creek in the 1860s. He planted the first crop of wheat in upland Wasco County and through subsequent years increased his land holdings to 1000 acres. When the Great Southern Railroad was built up Fifteenmile Creek in 1905, Rice's name was given to the station near the mouth of Dry Creek. In 1980 there was little evidence of urban activity.

Rice Creek, Douglas County. Rice Creek is east of Dillard. It was named for Harrison Rice, who settled near this creek in 1852.

Rice Hill, Douglas County. Rice Hill was named for I. F. Rice, who settled there in 1850. It is a summit on the Southern Pacific Company line on the watershed between Elk Creek and Umpqua River. For many years Rice Hill was the bugaboo of pioneer travelers and it even presented a problem in railroad construction. The elevation of the government bench mark near the top of Rice Hill is 710 feet.

Rich Gulch, Malheur County. This gulch is in the very north part of the county, and drains south into Willow Creek a few miles west of Malheur. It was named during the gold fever in the 1860s when rich placers were found in the vicinity.

Richard G. Baker Park, Douglas County. This is a county park on North Umpqua River ten miles east of Glide. It was named for R. G. Baker, a long time Douglas County employee and county commissioner at the time of his death.

Richards Butte, Douglas County. This butte is about four miles north of Wilbur, and west of the Pacific Highway. It was named for James Richards, one of the earliest settlers in the lower Calapooya Creek section of the county.

Richardson Butte, Lane County. This butte is northeast of Elmira. It was named for a pioneer family. See *OHQ,* volume V, page 136. Richardson Butte has an elevation of 812 feet.

Richardson Gap, Linn County. Richardson Gap is east of Franklin Butte and southeast of Scio. It was named for a family of early settlers who resided nearby. Plats dated 1878 show several members of the family owning land in the vicinity of the gap. The principal man in the clan was W. W. Richardson. This gap connects the valleys of Thomas and Crabtree creeks.

Richland, Baker County. W. R. Usher platted this community and named it Richland on account of the character of the soil.

Richmond, Wheeler County. Richmond was named by R. N. Donnelly. He gave the site and was the prime mover in establishing the community. The writer is informed that Donnelly selected the name as a result of a controversy he got into with William Walters, another pioneer resident, who objected to Donnelly's selection of the site for a school building. Donnelly called Walters "Jeff Davis" because of Walters' rebellious tendencies about the school, and applied the name Richmond because it was the name of the capital of the confederacy.

Rickard, Benton County. Rickard post office was named for John Rickard, a well-known Benton County pioneer. The office was established April 28, 1879, and was closed October 5, 1880. Robert S. Brown was the only postmaster. The office was situated on the Rickard claim about two miles east of Bruce.

Rickey, Marion County. The community of Rickey was southeast of Salem and about a mile south of the Penitentiary road. The locality, which was not incorporated, was named for James Rickey, a very early settler. Rickey School was the principal landmark. For a short account of the place, see Salem *Statesman*, October 10, 1931. After World War II, Rickey was absorbed into growing southeast Salem.

Rickreall Creek, Polk County. Few geographic names in Oregon have caused such a dispute as the name of this stream, which rises in the Coast Range and flows eastward through Dallas and Rickreall to the Willamette River west of Salem. Members of pioneer families living along its banks have written fully on both sides of the subject, without converting those of opposite belief. The controversy deals with two problems, one concerning the original, pioneer name of the stream, and the other about the meaning of the word Rickreall. One group of early settlers is of the opinion that the pioneer name of the creek was La Creole, and that this name had its origin in the fact that an Indian was drowned at the ford near the present site of Dallas. The French-Canadians referring to the event used the word *la creole*, meaning the native. Another group insists that the first name of the stream was Rickreall, an Indian word. The matter is complicated by the belief by some that Rickreall is a perversion of *la creole*, and not an original name, while others insist that Rickreall comes from *hyak chuck*, Chinook jargon for swift water. It has also been suggested that the word Rickreall was an Indian name for a locality near the stream. As far as the compiler knows, the first use of the name is in Wilkes *Narrative*, 1841, volume V, page 222, Creole Creek. Joel Palmer uses the name Rickreall in 1845-46 in his *Journal of Travels*, published in 1847. A school at Dallas (La Creole Academy) retains the early name. This school was founded by Horace Lyman. See letter of J. T. Ford in the *Oregonian*, August 4, 1916, page 8, on Indian origin of the name Rickreall. The school was chartered with the name Rickreall, by the territorial legislature in December, 1853. The name is given Ricrall in an advertisement in the *Oregonian*, February 7, 1852. The references given above indicate that there was a difference of opinion about the name of the stream in the early days of pioneer settlement. It seems to the writer that different localities near the stream might have had different names, and while La Creole was used to refer to the creek near Dallas, Rickreall might have been an Indian name for another place on its banks. This would explain some of the discrepancies. The USBGN has adopted the name Rickreall Creek, and Rickreall is the name of the post office. Rickreal post office was established June 30, 1851, with Nathaniel Ford postmaster, but was discontinued April 11, 1857. The office was reestablished June 19, 1866, with the spelling Rickreall and with Colonel Ford again postmaster. It has been in continuous operation since it was reestablished. The controversy over the name Rickreall was particularly acute during the summer of 1916. Letters on the subject were printed in the *Oregonian* July 23, 26, 30, August 4, 5, 11, 13, 14, 18, 19, 20, 21, 24, September 10, October 2 and 8, 1916. During the Civil War and for some time thereafter Rickreall village was frequently referred to as Dixie because of Southern sentiment in the community. The name Dixie was used colloquially for several decades, but it was never the name of the post office.

Riddle, Douglas County. Riddle is a town on the Siskiyou line of the Southern Pacific, south of Roseburg. It was named for William H. Riddle, who came to Oregon from Springfield, Illinois, in 1851, and settled near the present site of the town. The old form Riddles is wrong. For information about the Riddle family, see the *Oregonian*, March 29, 1925.

Riddle Creek, Harney County. This creek and Riddle Mountain, just to the north, were named for Stilley Riddle, an early settler. The mountain is about ten miles southeast of Malheur Lake and has an elevation of 6351 or 6352 feet, according to the USGS Anderson 15' or 7½' quadrangles, both dated 1974. The compiler assumes that government map makers will reconcile this difference in due course. The highest point is near the east end. T. S. Riddle was a member of a pioneer family of Oregon. For his biography, see Walling's *History of Southern Oregon,* page 539.

Ridge, Umatilla County. Ridge post office was given a name descriptive of its situation which was about a dozen miles southwest of Pilot Rock. The ridge was the watershed between the Birch Creek and Butter Creek drainages, and there was sufficient local timber to provide business for a sawmill and for an output of poles and posts. Ridge post office was established October 5, 1882, and was in service until May 15, 1906. William R. Stansell was the first postmaster.

Ridgeway, Wasco County. Ridgeway post office was established March 3, 1892, with Mary S. Cooke first postmaster. The office was finally closed October 31, 1905, with papers to Shaniko. The locality called Ridgeway was west of Antelope in the southeast part of the county. In May, 1946, Judge Fred W. Wilson of The Dalles wrote the compiler in part as follows: "Mrs. D. V. Bolton, wife of our county clerk, was the daughter of H. C. Rooper and raised right in the Ridgeway country. She remembers all about it. When she was a girl, the stagecoaches going to Canyon City on the one hand and to Prineville on the other used one road from The Dalles to Bakeoven. Then at Bakeoven the roads branched and the road for the Canyon City coaches went by way of Antelope, Cold Camp, Burnt Ranch and Mitchell, while the other road to Prineville went from Bakeoven to the head of Cow Canyon and then through Cross Keys and Hay Creek. Mrs. Bolton says that when she was a little girl there was a post office at Ridgeway and that she used to ride a horse to get the mail. The reason for the name is easily explained. The road, after it left Bakeoven, went along a rather high ridge until it reached the head of Cow Canyon, and it was by reason of this ridge that the office got the name Ridgeway, and the area out there is still called the Ridgeway country, though the post office has long since been abandoned."

Ridgeway Butte, Linn County. This butte, east of Lebanon, was named for a pioneer settler, James Ridgeway. The name Chamberlain Butte is incorrect.

Rieth, Umatilla County. When the railroad company constructed new shops and terminals west of Pendleton, the station was named Rieth after a family of pioneer settlers who owned land nearby. The postal authorities named the post office Reith. This discrepancy in spelling prevailed for some time until the writer made an investigation of the matter, and found that local opinion was in favor of Rieth, and the post office name was accordingly changed. For obituary of Louis Rieth, one of the two brothers who owned the land where the town now stands, see the *Oregonian,* September 23, 1926. Rieth post office was closed in June 1971. The principal Union Pacific yard in eastern Oregon is now located at Hinkle.

Rietmann Canyon, Morrow County. Ernst and Paul Rietmann homesteaded in the late 1880s in this canyon tributary of Willow Creek at Ione.

Rigdon Guard Station, Lane County. This guard station on the Middle Fork Willamette River was once the site of a station or stand of Steve Rigdon of Pleasant Hill. During the times of the emigrations he traded there with the pioneers. Rigdon Lakes and Butte north of Waldo Lake were named for the same man.

Riggs Lake, Linn County. Riggs Lake is on Scar Creek a mile and a half southeast of Scar Mountain. It was named for Albert Riggs who was born in Missouri in 1857 and came to Oregon in 1862. Riggs trapped in the Scar Mountain area in the 1880s and later worked as a lookout for the USFS prior to World War I.

Riggs Meadow, Lane County. This meadow is just northwest of Odell Lake. Dee Wright of Eugene informed the compiler that it was named for Dave Riggs, a sheep man of central Oregon, who pastured his flocks nearby.

Riley, Harney County. William Hanley of Burns told the compiler that this place was named for Amos Riley, an early stockman. Archie McGowan, also of Burns, wrote the compiler as follows: "This rural post office was named about 1885 for Riley of Riley and Hardin. Prior to the birth of Riley post office there was an office located about 75 miles north and west named Hardin, which was named for Mr. Hardin of this firm, so it was suggested by residents of Silver Creek that the new office be named Riley."

Riley Camp, Union County. This spot in section 36, township 3 south, range 33 east, was the site of a cabin built by one Riley, the railroad station agent at Pilot Rock. There are several stories about the facilities which were in the heart of good elk country but the most intriguing says that one of Riley's associates, Ed Smith of Pilot Rock, put the torch to the building to stop its continued use by a superior force of intruders.

Riley Creek, Curry County. Riley Creek flows under the Oregon Coast Highway at Gold Beach. It was named for Judge Michael Riley, who was born in New York state in 1827 and came to Curry County in 1853. He was a well-known pioneer citizen. He served as sheriff and also in the state legislature. For many years he was county judge of Curry County. Additional biographical information will be found in Dodge's *Pioneer History of Coos and Curry Counties*. Riley Creek is about a quarter of a mile south of the main part of Gold Beach. The stream should not be confused with Dean Creek which flows through the main part of town.

Ringo Point, Clackamas County. In pioneer days a locality about 15 miles southeast of Oregon City was called the Ringo settlement, named for the Ringo family. It was near the place that was later called Clarke. Ringo Point post office was established May 16, 1876, with William J. Allison first postmaster. The office was closed April 3, 1878. The compiler has not been able to identify the exact geographic feature called Ringo Point and it does not appear on available maps.

Ritter, Grant County. The post office at Ritter was named for the Reverend Joseph Ritter at whose ranch it was first established. The office has not always been in its present location. It is now near hot mineral springs, formerly known as McDuffee Hot Springs, but now known as Ritter Hot Springs. Joseph Ritter was a pioneer Baptist minister of the John Day Valley. The springs were discovered by William Neal McDuffee, an early day packer between Umatilla and the John Day mines.

Ritter Creek, Baker County. Ritter Creek is tributary to Powder River five miles southeast of Keating. It was named for Andrew J. Ritter who settled in Lower Powder River Valley at the turn of the century.

River Mill, Clackamas County. This station and power plant north of Estacada were so named because they were established near a sawmill on the banks of Clackamas River.

Riverdale, Tillamook County. Shortly after the turn of the century a post office with the descriptive name Riverdale was in service for a little over a year at a point about three miles north of Tillamook. This office was close to Kilchis River and was named on that account. The office was not far from the locality later called Cloverleaf. Riverdale post office was established in June, 1901, and was closed in August, 1902. Theodore P. Bowlby was the postmaster.

Rivergrove, Clackamas County. This community is south of Lake Oswego just east of I-5. On January 27, 1971, 105 voters of a population of 319 voted 57 to 48 to incorporate. The name is taken from Tualatin River on the south and the old Lake Grove area on the north. Rivergrove is another example of a small area and population group incorporating to avoid ultimate annexation into a larger community.

Rivers, Deschutes County. Rivers post office was in the extreme north part of township 20 south, range 19 east, a little to the northeast of Brothers. Post route and other maps show this place as on the north border of Deschutes County, just over the line from Crook County. An office with the descriptive name Highland was established on the Crook County list September 6, 1913, with Mrs. Mary T. Rivers postmaster. This was before Deschutes County was established. On March 9, 1914, the name of the office was changed to Rivers in compliment to the family of the postmaster. The office was discontinued December 21, 1918. The later record of this office was put on the Deschutes County list by postal authorities and it is assumed that the Highland-Rivers office was always in what is now Deschutes County, but by a narrow margin.

Riverside, Malheur County. Riverside was given a descriptive name because the place was on the banks of Malheur River near the junction of the South Fork. Riverside post office was established November 21, 1889, with Teresa E. McRae first postmaster.

Riverton, Coos County. Riverton is a community on the Oregon Coast Highway about 12 miles east of Bandon. It is on the east bank of Coquille River and got its name on that account. Riverton post office was established June 30, 1890, with Orlando A. Kelly first postmaster. Riverton was laid out by E. Weston, a civil engineer, in 1889. The townsite was originally part of the Nathaniel Thrush property. Kelly, a teacher, is said to have been the first settler in the place. For more information about Riverton, see Dodge's *Pioneer History of Coos and Curry Counties,* page 249.

Roaring Springs, Harney County. These springs are at the western foot of Steens Mountain. They are so called because of the peculiar noise they make.

Robert W. Sawyer State Park, Deschutes County. This 41 acre park just north of Bend along Deschutes River was named to honor one of central Oregon's most distinguished citizens. Robert William Sawyer was born May 12, 1880 in Bangor, Maine. He was a graduate of Harvard University and practiced law in Boston until 1912 when he moved west to Bend. Shortly after his arrival he took a job writing for the Bend Bulletin then owned and edited by George Palmer Putnam. In 1914 Sawyer took over the management and continued as editor and publisher until 1953. His position on the paper provided him with a base for many other activities. He was county judge of Deschutes County from 1920 to 1927 and then a member of the State Highway Commission. During his tenure on the Highway Commission he showed particular attention to the parks program and was instrumental in the establishment of the Parks Engineer and the initial appointment of Samuel H. Boardman to this post in 1929. Sawyer was active in irrigation affairs and served as president of both the Oregon Reclamation Congress and the National Reclamation Association. He was a member of the Capitol Reconstruction Commission in 1935 and later served on the Capitol Planning Commission.

Robert W. Sawyer was an active outdoorsman with a great interest in nature. He was a tireless worker for both conservation and the proper and orderly development of central Oregon, his adopted home. He died in Bend on October 13, 1959 after a long and useful life.

Roberts, Crook County. Roberts, on Alkali Flat between Crooked River and Bear Creek, was named for an early settler in Crook County, J. E. Roberts, who was for a time postmaster, but not the first. The post office was established May 6, 1910, and closed February 29, 1940.

Roberts, Linn County. Roberts is a place on Quartzville Creek not far above the mouth. It seems to have been named for John Roberts, a miner and prospector, who lived beside the stream for many years, mining at various localities. For an account of his activities, see Sweet Home *New Era,* July 3, 1941.

Roberts, Marion County. Roberts was a station on the Oregon Electric Railway four miles southwest of Salem. When the railway was built south of Salem about 1911, the station was named Livesley in compliment to T. A. Livesley, a prominent hop grower of the locality. Livesley was associated with John J. Roberts and the style of the firm was T. A. Livesley & Company. In 1925 Roberts bought the Livesley interest and the firm became John J. Roberts & Company. The name of the station was changed to Roberts at that time.

Roberts, Yamhill County. Roberts post office was in service in the north part of the county from April 5, 1892, to August 28, 1895. It was about east of Wapato and near the south end of Wapato Lake. James H. Robertson was the first postmaster of Roberts post office and the name of the office is said to have been derived by abbreviation from the postmaster's family name.

Roberts Butte, Wallowa County. This butte is about 14 miles north of Enterprise and was named for Mrs. Nellie (Stillwell) Roberts Averill, who ranged stock nearby about 1885.

Roberts Mountain, Douglas County. This mountain, and Roberts Creek, just to the north, were named for Jesse Roberts, a pioneer landowner. The mountain is important because the early stage road passed through a gap on its summit and the steep grade and narrow road resulted in many accidents and not a few deaths. In modern times, I5 also traverses the same gap to avoid the circuitous route along South Umpqua River through Dillard. The *Sketch Map of Military Road from Myrtle Creek to Scottsburg,* prepared by 1st Lieutenant Jonathan Withers, 4th Infantry, shows the feature as Burnett Hill, apparently for John S. and James E. Burnett, father and son, who arrived in the area in 1853 and 1852 respectively and who both took donation land claims.

Robinette, Baker County. James E. Robinette, born in Maryland in 1852, emigrated to Nevada about 1870 and came to Union County, Oregon, in 1884. He was associated with various mining enterprises, and in October, 1887, settled at what was Robinette on the west bank of Snake River. When the railroad was built from Huntington down Snake River about 1909, a station and a townsite were named for Robinette. A post office was established about the time the railroad was built. For biography of James E. Robinette, see Gaston's *Centennial History of Oregon,* volume III, page 715. The spelling Robinett is wrong. The townsite was inundated when Brownlee Dam was built.

Robins Nest, Clackamas County. Robert Moore, who came to Oregon from Illinois with the Peoria party in 1840, used the name Robins Nest for his little settlement on the west bank of the Willamette River across from Oregon City. The place was later called Linn City and now is known as West Linn. On December 20, 1945, Ernest E. East of the Illinois Historical Society wrote the Oregon Historical Society as follows: "It is not impossible that Robert Moore got the poetic inspiration for 'Robin's Nest' from the name of the log house in which lived Philander Chase, first bishop of the diocese of Illinois, Protestant Episcopal Church. Chase bought land in the valley of Kickapoo Creek about 12 miles west of Peoria and established

Jubilee College. His first house was called 'Robin's Nest,' because, as he said, it was 'built of mud and sticks, and filled with young ones.' Robin's Nest was a United States post office. Philander Chase was the first postmaster. Robin's Nest Farm today occupies part of the original Jubilee College farm. The chapel and dormitory, erected in or about 1839, with 90 acres is maintained by the State and Jubilee College Park."

Robinson, Washington County. Robinson was a station where the Scholls Ferry Road crosses the Southern Pacific line south of Beaverton. It was named for William J. Robinson, whose donation land claim was situated nearby.

Robinson Canyon, Wheeler County. Granville C. Robinson homesteaded in this canyon off Pine Creek in 1881.

Robinson Ridge, Jefferson County. Robinson Ridge near the headwaters of Currant Creek was the scene of a strange murder. In 1923, Alvin Robinson left his ranch home near Coyote Mountain for a days work on the range. His horse returned riderless and no trace was found of the missing man until his wife told of a dream which showed in unbelievable detail her husband dead on the trail. Deputies found Robinson in the exact spot, shot through the back, but as of 1971 his murderer had not been discovered nor has there been any explanation of Mrs. Robinson's remarkable extra-sensory powers. Phil Brogan describes this incident in *East of the Cascades,* page 226.

Robisonville, Grant County. Robisonville was one of the early post offices in the Blue Mountain mining region, in the extreme east part of Grant County. The post office was established June 27, 1878, and was discontinued July 23, 1884. Charles W. Daggett was the only postmaster. The name of the office has been spelled in several different ways on government maps, but Miles F. Potter in *Oregon's Golden Years,* page 78, says that the place was named for William Robinson and that the form Robisonville is incorrect. The post office records all use Robisonville but the USGS Greenhorn quadrangle of 1972 shows the site as Robinsonville. William Robinson is long gone and the compiler must leave it to others to determine whether the Post Office Department erred originally or if later history altered William's name from Robison to Robinson.

Roby Hill, Marion County. Roby Hill lies in the bend between Willamette River and Santiam River and is just south of Ankeny Bottom. It has an elevation of 345 feet. It was named for R. Roby, who took up a donation land claim nearby in pioneer days.

Rocca, Polk County. Rocca post office was on Rock Creek in the extreme southwest corner of the county, and during its entire existence it was in the Hampton home. The office was established April 30, 1895, with Miss Maggie Hampton first of four postmasters. The office was closed on August 31, 1918. When the office was first proposed it was planned to have Sam Center act as postmaster, but as he was moving from the neighborhood, other arrangements were necessary. Center asked to have the office named for his daughter, Mary Rocca Center. This girl had been named for a friend of her mother who had married an Italian.

Rock Creek, Baker County. There are at least seventy streams in Oregon called Rock Creek, a name applied by early-day residents with the greatest of ease and not without reason. One of the best known of these creeks is that which flows eastward out of the Blue Mountains to join Powder River near Haines. This Rock Creek was named during the days of the mining excitement of the 1860s. There is a community area about six miles west of Haines that goes by the name Rock Creek. A post office was established in this locality shortly after the turn of the century, with Edward P. Castor postmaster, but available information about its life history is meager. The compiler finds it listed as Rockcreek in the *Postal Guide* as of December 1, 1903, but elsewhere the style Rock Creek is used. The office doubtless gave way to rural free delivery.

Rock Creek, Gilliam County. A post office called Rockcreek was established in 1906. There was an earlier office farther down stream which operated with the name Rockville. Information about a post office called Rock Creek has come to light. It was established June 3, 1872, with Alexander Smith postmaster. The second postmaster was James R. Alfrey. The office was discontinued March 11, 1874. While it is obvious that this post office was on or near Rock Creek the compiler does not know if it was in the same location as Rockcreek office.

Rock Creek, Hood River and Wasco counties. This stream is west and south of Wamic. Joel Palmer crossed a stream in this vicinity on October 4, 1845, and named it Rock Creek. See his *Journal of Travels*. While exact identification is impossible, it may be assumed that the stream now called Rock Creek is the one Palmer named.

Rock Creek, Jackson County. This stream is north of Lower Table Rock and flows westward into Sams Creek. It has been known in the past as Table Rock Creek, but in 1937 Paul B. Rynning recommended that the name Rock Creek was more suitable and that is the form used on the Medford topographic map of the USGS. See also under Snider Creek.

Rock Creek, Washington County. Early maps show the stream as Stony Creek, but for many years Rock Creek has been the universally accepted name. The name Dawson Creek, applied to the lower part of the stream, is incorrect, and was ruled against by the USBGN on October 6, 1926.

Rock Mesa, Lane County. The word *mesa* is Spanish for table, and is used in geographic nomenclature to describe hills and peaks with more or less flat tops. Rock Mesa is south of the Three Sisters.

Rock Point, Jackson County. Rock Point is now principally famous because of a fine concrete arch over Rogue River carrying the old Pacific Highway. It is two miles west of Gold Hill, and is named because of the geological formation. In pioneer days this general locality was known as Dardanelles, and there was a post office by that name established October 19, 1852, with William G. T'Vault first postmaster. It was also an important travelers' station and the tavern building built in the 1870s, and similar to the Wolf Creek Tavern, is still standing. The T'Vault place was on the south bank of the river about two miles east of the Rock Point bridge. Dardanelles post office operated intermittently until December, 1878. There was also a post office named Rock Point, established in November, 1859, with John B. White first postmaster. This office operated until October, 1912. Early writers sometimes referred to this locality as Point of Rocks.

Rockaway, Tillamook County. Rockaway is north of Tillamook Bay. The Rockaway Beach Company projected this summer resort and named the townsite. The place is obviously named for Rockaway, Long Island, New York, a famous eastern seashore resort.

Rockcreek, Gilliam County. Rockcreek takes the name of the longest creek in the county. The name of the creek is accurately descriptive. The community name is generally used in two words, but the post office used the form Rockcreek.

Rockford, Hood River County. This is a community on the west side of Hood River Valley and is said to have been named because of the rocky character of the surroundings.

Rockland, Douglas County. Rockland post office was given a name descriptive of the surroundings. It was a few miles southeast of Dixonville, and in the southeast quarter of township 27 south, range 4 east. The office was established June 28, 1910, with Alfred Mathews first and only postmaster. The office was discontinued to Dixonville on October 15, 1913.

Rockville, Gilliam County. Rockville was a place on Rock Creek not far above the mouth, probably not more than two or three miles and not as far as the railroad station now known as Rock Creek. The writer cannot determine the exact location. The first post office in this locality was called Scotts, and it was established February 4, 1867, with Daniel G. Leonard first postmaster. This office was at or close to the mouth of Rock Creek near the place known as Leonards Bridge. Leonards Bridge was over John Day River and was a toll enterprise. The name Scotts seems to have been derived from a local settler or landowner. There is a Scott Canyon making into John Day River a few miles south of Rock Creek. The name of the post office called Scotts was changed to Rockville on November 26, 1878, and Thomas S. Lang became postmaster. It was in operation until August 2, 1889. It is apparent from a War Department map of 1887 that when the name was changed to Rockville, the office was moved eastward two or three miles. Thomas Lang was an early day sheep raiser in the Heppner area and he carried on part of his activities near lower Rock Creek in what is now Gilliam County. Later he was a well-known citizen at The Dalles. He used a canyon to the northeast of Rockville to get his wool down to the Columbia River boats, and this canyon is still known as Lang Canyon. Scotts post office referred to above was apparently the first post office in what is now Gilliam County.

Rockville, Malheur County. Rockville is on the east border of the county in the Succor Creek drainage and about fifteen miles north of Sheaville. There is plenty of rock in the area and the name is descriptive. Rockville post office was established January 27, 1912, with Etta E. Mullinax first postmaster. The office was discontinued June 30, 1948.

Rockwood, Multnomah County. Rockwood community at the intersection of Southeast Stark Street and Burnside extension was named for the rocks and trees that characterized the locality in earlier days. The post office was established March 14, 1882, with Cyrus C. Lewis first postmaster.

The office was closed February 28, 1903, with the advent of rural delivery. Lewis, the first storekeeper, wanted a post office to help his mercantile establishment. Francis Tegart, frequently called Lord Tegart, local landowner, is said to have applied the name Rockwood in the hope of impressing members of his family in Ireland with his "estate." When the post office was established, he insisted on the selection of the name Rockwood.

Rocky Butte, Multnomah County. This butte has been known in the past as Wiberg Butte, but that name has fallen into disuse. The present name is appropriate because of the quarry on the east face.

Rocky Point, Klamath County. Rocky Point bears a descriptive name for a place on the shore of Pelican Bay of Upper Klamath Lake. It is an area that has been used for some years by summer residents. A post office called Pelican was established in this vicinity on July 5, 1888, with Charles Stidham first of five postmasters. This office ran along until October 29, 1907, when it was closed to Ashland. The next office for the Pelican Bay area was named Recreation, established October 15, 1913, with May D. Willson first postmaster. This office operated on and off until February 11, 1924, when the name was changed to Pelican Bay. The name Pelican Bay was changed to Rocky Point on June 30, 1924, and this persisted until October 1, 1947, when it was changed to Harriman. See under that heading. It may be noted that there was at one time a railroad station on the east side of Upper Klamath Lake opposite Pelican Bay with the name Pelican.

Rocky Ridge, Umatilla County. The old Indian Treaty boundary ran along this ridge just north of East Birch Creek. The ridge was a natural stock driveway for this part of the route from Pilot Rock to Starkey and Tom Gibson and others constructed a series of drift fences with the rails blocked by rock cribs. In many spots the continuous trample of hooves removed the soil to bedrock and the naming of the ridge logically followed both these circumstances.

Rocky Top, Marion County. This conspicuous mountain is near Niagara. It was named in 1863 by Thomas J. Henness, a pioneer of the North Santiam Valley, because of its formation at the summit. See the Salem *Capital Journal,* June 18, 1927, page 1.

Rodeo, Harney County. This railroad station was named with the Spanish word for roundup. It was a cattle shipping point. The correct pronunciation is with accent on the "e." Rodeo was on the Union Pacific Railroad just southeast of Burns.

Rodgers Creek, Marion County. Rodgers Creek rises in the hills south of Salem and flows eastward to join Battle Creek near Turner. The Pacific Highway East crosses this stream a little to the east of Jackson Hill. Rodgers Creek has been known as Taylor Creek, but on April 12, 1940, the USBGN adopted the name Rodgers Creek. The name of the stream commemorates Clark and Sarah Adams Rodgers, pioneers of 1852, who were married in Marion County in 1856 and settled near the banks of the stream in 1857. In 1939 residents of the vicinity petitioned to have the name Rodgers Creek officially adopted, and this petition was approved by the county commissioners and by various state agencies.

Rodley Butte, Douglas County. Rodley Butte, elevation 6838 feet, is

about two miles west of the north end of Diamond Lake and bears the
name of Oscar Rodley, a fire guard of the USFS who was drowned while
swimming in Diamond Lake on July 14, 1928. He was brought up near
Lookingglass and was a graduate of Lookingglass High School and had
worked for the USFS several seasons. The name Rodley Butte was adopted
by the USBGN on January 8, 1930, in place of Bald Butte on the theory
that there were more than enough Bald buttes in Oregon to meet existing
needs.

Rodman Rim, Crook County. William Rodman and his son Seth homesteaded near the east end of this rim north of Brothers in the 1880s.

Rogers Peak, Tillamook County. This 3700 foot peak south of Blue
Lake Guard Station in township 2 north, range 7 west, is one of the two
highest points in the Coast Range north of Marys Peak. It was named for
Nelson S. Rogers, Oregon state forester from 1940 to 1949, who played a
prominent part in the rehabilitation of the Tillamook Burn. For further
information on Rogers see the *Oregon Journal* for September 19, 1949.

Rognes, Wallowa County. Rognes post office was short lived. It was
established in August, 1909, with Louis O. Roggs postmaster and was discontinued in November, 1910. It was situated in the north part of section
10, township 2 north, range 44 east, about 18 miles airline north of Enterprise. The office was named for Rognes Sever, a Norwegian Lutheran minister, who lived in the locality.

Rogue River, Curry, Douglas, Jackson, Josephine and Klamath counties. Rogue River rises in the extreme northwest corner of Klamath County
at Boundary Springs near the northern boundary of Crater Lake National
Park. On December 20, 1904, Max Pracht wrote a letter to the *Oregonian*
giving a well-known but incorrect version of the origin of the name Rogue
River, ascribing it to the French word *Rouge* on account of the alleged red
color of the water during flood seasons. This letter was printed in the *Oregonian* for December 22, 1904, page 11. Harvey W. Scott wrote a spirited
reply to the Pracht letter, giving the real source of the name and printing it
on the same page with the communication. The reply is as follows: "This is
fanciful, purely so, though the 'Rouge' story is old. There would have been
reason for calling the Klamath River Rouge River, or Red River; for its
waters are much discolored by the marshes of the lake basin which it drains.
But Rogue River is one of the clearest of streams, and even in flood its
waters are not red. An old French map has been mentioned—though no
such map is known to be in existence—whereon the Klamath and Rogue
rivers are united and called Rouge-Clamet, or Red Klamath. But Rogue
River, as an individual stream, has been known by its present name ever
since white men first visited the country. Bishop Blanchet's account of the
Catholic Church in Oregon says the French were first to call it by this name.
The Indians there were a peculiarly troublesome lot; 'hence,' says Blanchet,
'the name "Les Coquins" (the Rogues) and "La Riviere aux Coquins" (The
Rogue River) was given to the country by the men of the brigade.' So far
then is it from the fact, that Rogue River is a corruption or change from the
alleged 'Rouge' River of the French. The actual truth is that the French
called it Rogue River themselves. Everything is against the assumption that

it once was 'Rouge River'—changed by Missourians to Rogue River, on the theory that 'them French couldn't spell.'" In his journal for Monday, September 16, 1833, John Work of the Hudson's Bay Company uses the name River Coquin, referring to what is now known as Rogue River, and the text indicates that the name Coquin was already in use by the fur brigades. In September, 1841, Henry Eld of the Wilkes Expedition used the names Rogue River and Rascally River in his journal. Wm. P. McArthur charted this stream as Rogue River for the USC&GS in 1850. Rogue River was called by the Indians *Trashit,* and by act of the territorial legislature, January 12, 1854, Gold River. See *Session Laws,* page 29; also the *Oregonian,* November 15, 1883; letter by "Pioneer." The old name was restored in 1855. For history of the name, see the *Oregonian,* November 15, 1883. For entertaining editorial about name Rogue River, larded with poetry, *ibid.,* May 23, 1935.

Rogue River, Jackson County. Rogue River is the name of a town on Rogue River at the mouth of Evans Creek. It was for many years known as Woodville, but about 1912 the name was changed to Rogue River, presumably on account of the better advertising the community would get with that name. In the early 1850s the settlers near the mouth of Evans Creek and west to Evans Ferry were served through Gold River post office, which was at the ferry about three miles from the present site of Rogue River office. See under Evans Creek. Woodville post office was established February 8, 1876, with John Woods first postmaster. Presumably the place was named for Woods. The post office was changed to Rogue River on March 11, 1912.

Rogue River, Polk County. This stream flows into South Yamhill River. It was named because Rogue River Indians lived along its banks after they came from southern Oregon to Grand Ronde Agency.

Roland, Coos County. Roland post office was established February 12, 1880, with William N. Warner first and only postmaster. The office was closed November 20, 1882, and what business there was turned over to Myrtle Point. The name of the office was intended to compliment William Rowland, a noted pioneer settler in the south end of the county, but there was a slip in the spelling. Information about William Rowland will be found under Rowland Prairie and Fort Rowland.

Rolling Grounds, Douglas County. These are about 15 miles west of Diamond Lake. They are so called because stock comes from some distance to roll in the light volcanic soil that abounds thereabout.

Rolyat, Deschutes County. Rolyat is Taylor spelled backward. The post office was established in what was then Crook County on September 15, 1910, and closed July 1, 1929. It is said that Taylor was the name of a postal official in Washington who had something to do with establishing the office. Victor Schreder was first postmaster and the office was near Hampton in township 22 south, range 21 east.

Roman Nose Mountain, Douglas County. This name is said to have been applied by government surveyors, who determined its elevation, 2856 feet (USGS). The pioneer name was Saddle Mountain, which was considered unsatisfactory because of frequent duplication.

Rome, Malheur County. This post office was established July 26, 1909. The first postmaster was Leonard R. Duncan. The writer is informed that the place was named by Wm. F. Stine because the peculiar geological formations nearby suggested the ruined temples of Rome, Italy.

Rome, Marion County. Rome post office was established June 30, 1851, with Christopher C. Cooley postmaster. It was discontinued March 19, 1852. It is not shown on early maps available to the writer but the Cooley claim was a little east of the present site of Woodburn and it may be assumed that the office was in that locality. There seems to be no record of the reason for the name.

Rondeau Butte, Douglas County. This butte four miles north of Tiller was named for John Rondeau, an early USFS employee and member of a pioneer Douglas County family who homesteaded nearby.

Rondowa, Wallowa County. Rondowa is a made up name. The station was at the junction of the Grande Ronde and the Wallowa rivers and railroad officials coined the name by taking parts of the names of the two streams.

Roney Creek, Lane County. Roney Creek was named for Peter Runey, onetime owner of Foley Springs. It flows into Horse Creek.

Rooper Ranch, Wasco County. Herbert C. Rooper was an early settler on Ward Creek southwest of Shaniko where his family is still well known. Rooper was born in England in 1852 and died at Antelope in 1935.

Roosevelt Beach, Lane County. For some years this community was known as Heceta, in honor of the Spanish explorer who is mentioned under the heading Heceta Head. Heceta post office was near the lighthouse, but a few years ago the office was moved several miles north to a ranch near the mouth of Big Creek. The name was changed to Roosevelt Beach in 1922, at the suggestion of Mrs. Gladys Murrow of Portland. This was because the Roosevelt Coast Military Highway was projected through the ranch, and the name Heceta seemed no longer appropriate because the office had been moved from the cape. The name comes of course from Theodore Roosevelt. The place was not on the post office list in 1939. The 1900 post route map shows a post office named Samaria near the mouth of Big Creek, but the compiler has no information about the origin of the name.

Rooster Rock, Clackamas County. This conspicuous peak, elevation 4663 feet, is in the south part of the county near Molalla River. It was named by Bob Ogle of Molalla, a prospector of the early 1860s, because of its resemblance to a rooster's comb. This information was furnished by Dee Wright of Eugene.

Rooster Rock, Multnomah County. This is probably the rock mentioned by Lewis and Clark as their camping place on the night of Saturday, November 2, 1805. Wilkes, in *U. S. Exploring Expedition,* volume XXIII, Hydrography, refers to it as the Obelisk, a name that has not persisted. The modern name is of phallic significance. A post office called Rooster Rock was established in May, 1876, with John Gilstrap first postmaster. The name was changed to Latourell Falls in August, 1887. There is nothing in the records to show that the office was always in the same place. In 1938 the

OSHD acquired the immediate area as part of the right of way for the water level highway, and after World War II developed the beach and adjoining low ground. Rooster Rock State Park is now one of the popular bathing and boating spots near Portland.

Roots Creek, Lincoln County. This stream flows into Siletz River from the east about a mile north of Mowrey Landing. It was named for a local settler. Roots post office was established in this locality on May 24, 1897, with Thomas A. Roots first postmaster. The office was closed on October 15, 1906. The post office seems to have been moved from time to time if maps of that period are to be relied on.

Ropers Bunion, Jackson County. This eminence at Ashland bears an unusual name derived from a local resident. It is just south of the business center of the city and east of Lithia Park.

Rosa, Linn County. Rosa post office was established April 4, 1892, with Joseph D. Cosgrove first postmaster. The office was closed October 17, 1895. The compiler has been informed by Rex Peery of Bay City that the office was named for his sister, Rosa Peery. The office was a few miles southwest of Scio, in an area previously served by Dotyville office.

Rosary Lakes, Klamath County. These lakes are in the extreme northwest corner of the county and are very close to the summit of the Cascade Range. They are in a series, simulating to some extent a string of beads and are named on that account. The lakes are very popular among summer residents around Odell Lake. A stream heading at the lakes was formerly known as Maiden Creek because it headed near Maiden Peak, but about 1939 the USBGN changed the name to Rosary Creek to fit popular use.

Rose Lodge, Lincoln County. Rose Lodge post office was established February 8, 1908, at the home of Julia E. Dodson, the first postmaster. Mrs. Dodson had a rose bower or "gazebo" over her front gate, and named the office on that account.

Roseburg, Douglas County. Roseburg was named for Aaron Rose who settled at the site of the community September 23, 1851. Rose was born June 20, 1813, and came to Oregon from Michigan in 1851. During many years his house at Roseburg was a public tavern. He was a well-known character in southern Oregon. He died March 11, 1899. The locality, Roseburg, was first known as Deer Creek, being at the junction of Deer Creek and South Umpqua River. Roseburg's rival was the town of Winchester. In 1854 Roseburg won the county seat by popular vote, aided by settlers of Lookingglass Valley. Rose gave three acres of land and $1000 for the court house. The important buildings of Winchester were moved to Roseburg prior to 1860. For references to Roseburg, see Scott's *History of the Oregon Country*, volume II, page 299. Deer Creek post office was established September 28, 1852, with William T. Perry postmaster. Lewis L. Bradbury became postmaster March 31, 1854. The name of the office was changed to Roseburgh on July 16, 1857. It operated with that name until March, 1894, when the spelling was changed to Roseburg. During that time people of the community generally used the form Roseburg and not Roseburgh.

Rosedale, Marion County. Rosedale, which is about six miles south of Salem, has borne its descriptive name for many years. It is at the point

where the old highway from Salem to Albany crosses Battle Creek and its
pleasing little dale. There are plenty of wild roses in the vicinity. Rosedale
post office was established April 20, 1892, by change of name from Dencer,
with James M. Lawrence first postmaster. The Dencer office had been in
operation since February 12, 1889, at the home of Jacob Dencer about two
miles northwest of Rosedale.

Rosland, Deschutes County. The origin of the post office name Rosland is one of the mysteries of central Oregon nomenclature. This office
was just a little north of the present location of La Pine, on the old stage
road, west of The Dalles-California Highway. Rosland post office was established April 13, 1897, with B. J. Pengra first of seven postmasters. It is
probable that Pengra named the office, but so far the compiler has failed to
discover the reason. The name of the office was changed to Lapine on
September 21, 1910.

Ross Flat, Wheeler County. Howard Ross was an early settler near
West Branch and his homestead was near this flat.

Ross Island, Multnomah County. This island was named for Sherry
Ross, who owned and lived on it in pioneer days. See the *Oregonian*, December 23, 1926, and *Oregon Journal*, editorial page, July 12, 1927. The name
Ross Island is correctly applied to the northwestward of two islands that lie
near each other. The southeast island is known as Hardtack Island by decision of the USBGN. There is a third small island, not more than a gravel
bar, lying westward of the south end of Ross Island. These islands are
shown as Oak Islands in the atlas accompanying Wilkes' *U. S. Exploring
Expedition*, volume XXIII, Hydrography. Early in 1943 Henry E. Reed of
Portland sent the compiler additional information about the small gravel-
bar island. A special plat of this island, approved by Surveyor-General E. L.
Applegate on January 23, 1869, shows it as Toe Island, obviously because
of its shape. Another survey was made in 1883 and the gravel bar was
shown as Island No. 3. For additional information, see under Hardtack
Island. A good deal has been written about the famous Blue Ruin whisky of
pioneer days and some narratives say it was made on Ross Island. It was a
fluid of high voltage. Some early settlers drank it neat, or barefoot, as the
saying goes. Others reduced its ferocity by making it into long toddy. Blue
Ruin was probably made from a mash of wheat, shorts or middlings and
molasses. The topers played bean poker for Blue Ruin. Every now and
again temperance enthusiasts swooped down on the stills and dumped the
stuff in the river. It may be a coincidence that the steelwork of the Ross
Island Bridge is painted blue.

Ross Mountain, Multnomah County. Nelson Ross brought his family
to Oregon from Michigan in the 1870s. About 1877 he moved to the Crown
Point area and cleared a homestead on what is now known as Ross
Mountain.

Ross Slough, Coos County. This is a tributary of Catching Slough,
southeast of Coos Bay. It was named for Frank Ross, a respected pioneer
resident of Coos County.

Rouen Gulch, Baker County. Rouen Gulch drains northward from a
spur of the Blue Mountains at a point about six miles west of Baker and

whatever water it carries finds its way into Salmon Creek. According to Isaac Hiatt in *Thirty-one Years in Baker County,* page 33, the creek was named in the summer of 1862 by a prospector who found paying gold in the gulch. Hiatt does not give this man's name, but says that he named the stream Ru Ann Creek for his eldest daughter. This is an unusual name for a girl, but of course not impossible. There is nothing to explain how the spelling got changed by later users, but Rouen has been the style for many years and is doubtless here to stay.

Rough and Ready Creek, Josephine County. Rough and Ready Creek rises in the Siskiyou Mountains and flows eastward to join West Fork Illinois River. It flows under the Redwood Highway about two miles north of O'Brien. Rough and Ready Creek was named in the mining excitement of the fifties when Waldo was a boom area in the Illinois Valley. Rough and Ready was the affectionate nickname given to General, later President, Zachary Taylor. The stream was probably named by a veteran of the Mexican War who admired General Taylor, or perhaps for some miner named Taylor who appropriated the nickname. The former is more likely. General Taylor died in 1850 and the Josephine County goldrush began but a few years after that.

Round Butte Dam, Jefferson County. This dam on Deschutes River west of Madras was completed in 1964 by Portland General Electric Company for hydro-electric power generation. It is an earth and rock fill structure 440 feet high which holds a reservoir of 535,000 acre feet of water and can generate 300,000 kilowatts of electric energy. The dam is named for Round Butte, a prominent cone rising from the high ground directly to the east.

Round Prairie, Douglas County. Round Prairie is a well-known place on South Umpqua River between Roseburg and Myrtle Creek. It bears a descriptive name. Round Prairie post office was established November 22, 1853, with James D. Burnett postmaster. This office has operated intermittently.

Rover Creek, Tillamook County. This creek empties into the Pacific Ocean about one mile south of Cape Lookout. It is on Camp Meriwether, Boy Scout property, and was named because the mounted troop of "Rover Scouts" had their camp site on its banks.

Row River, Lane County. This stream rises on the western slopes of the Cascade Range and flows into the Coast Fork Willamette River at Cottage Grove. In the early days it was known as East Fork Coast Fork, but its present name came after a dispute between George Clark and Joseph Southwell over a stock trespass. The two men were brothers-in-law as well as neighbors but the disagreement ran so deep that Clark lost his life as a result. The present name, of course, rhymes with *cow* not *slow*.

Rowe Creek, Wheeler County. In 1868, J. W. Rowe moved into what is now Wheeler County and engaged in the stock business on the banks of a stream flowing into John Day River. The stream is south of Fossil and its name commemorates this early settler.

Rowena, Wasco County. Pierce Mays, for many years a resident of Wasco County, told the compiler that this place was named for H. S. Rowe, in the early 1880s. Rowe was an official of the railroad company that was building along the south bank of the Columbia River. Mrs. Lulu D. Crandall of The Dalles confirmed this statement, but Miss A. M. Lang, also of The Dalles, thinks Rowena was the name of a girl who lived in the vicinity. Rowena is near the center of Rowena Gap where the Columbia River has cut four miles through the Columbia Hills anticlinal ridge. This geologic formation is easily discernible from the highway.

Rowena Dell, Wasco County. This is a peculiar canyon in the basaltic rock on the Columbia River Highway between Rowena and Mosier. In early days it was known as Hog Canyon, but after the highway was built, a more elegant name was desired, and residents of The Dalles selected Rowena Dell.

Rowland, Linn County. Rowland is a station on the Southern Pacific Company Springfield line five miles east-northeast of Harrisburg. It was named for a local resident. Rowland post office was established December 29, 1886, with Jere T. Rowland postmaster. The office continued in operation with various postmasters until February 15, 1905, when it was closed out to Harrisburg. Rural free delivery brought an end to the establishment.

Rowland Prairie, Coos County. In 1853 William Rowland and his wife, who was a dusky maiden of the forest, settled in the valley of South Fork Coquille River on what has become known as Rowland Prairie. Rowland was a well-known pioneer, and a fragment of his history is found in Dodge's *Pioneer History of Coos and Curry Counties,* pages 187-88. During the Indian troubles of 1855-56 the Rowland place was provided with some defense works and was called Fort Rowland. Rowland Creek, a tributary of South Fork Coquille River, is named for the same family.

Roxy Ann Peak, Jackson County. Will G. Steel was authority for the statement that this well-known feature in the Rogue River Valley was at one time known as Skinner Butte. He said that the present name was bestowed by pioneer packers in 1854 in honor of Roxana Baker, an early settler nearby.

Roy, Washington County. Railroad officials applied this name to a station about 1906, which became a post office in 1907. It came from the Roy family, pioneer settlers of the vicinity.

Roy Creek, Tillamook County. Roy Creek flows into Nehalem River a mile or so east of Mohler. It was named for Felix Roy, a local landowner.

Royal, Lane County. The USGS map of the Cottage Grove quadrangle shows a place named Royal about five miles northwest of and up Silk Creek from Cottage Grove. There is not much left of this little community except the school. Royal post office was established April 6, 1887, with Royal H. Hazleton postmaster. The office operated until September 19, 1899, and it was doubtless named for the first postmaster. Incidentally Silk Creek was at one time known as Hazleton Creek. Royal H. Hazleton received two patents for government land in this vicinity in 1867.

Royce Mountain, Klamath County. This mountain is northeast of Crescent Lake. It was named for George Royce, an early day stockman of the Deschutes Valley.

Royston, Klamath County. Royston was a post office in the east part of the county about eighteen miles northeast of Bonanza. The name Royston is still preserved at Royston Spring which is a little to the east of Yainax Butte on the old road from Bonanza to Bly. Royston post office was established December 14, 1892, and operated continuously until August 6, 1908, with Mrs. Lura E. White the only postmaster. Mr. and Mrs. Sanders White moved to a ranch in that part of Klamath County in the early nineties and soon felt the need of a post office. Erle R. White, a son, wrote the compiler from California in June, 1948, saying that his mother wanted the name Agnes for the office but this name in the form Agness was already in use in Curry County. Mrs. White selected the name Agnes in compliment to a sister living in Illinois. The name Royston was then suggested and accepted. Mr. White is of the opinion that his mother selected the name because she found it in a book she was reading. There are at least two places in England named Royston and it is possible that one of them may have been the source of the name of the Klamath County post office.

Ruby, Douglas County. Ruby post office, which was in operation from June, 1895, to August, 1901, was just east of Tahkenitch Lake in the extreme west part of the county. It was on the old Coast wagon road. The office was named at the request of Myrtle E. Wilson, daughter of Joseph E. Wilson, the first postmaster. This young lady liked the name Ruby because it had a pretty sound. Mrs. Mary Slonecker was postmaster at Ruby from 1898 to 1901. Ruby was ten or twelve miles north of Gardiner, and when Mr. Wilson had the office it was on Perkins Creek. When Mrs. Slonecker was postmaster the office was on Fivemile Creek.

Ruch, Jackson County. Ruch was named for C. M. Ruch who bought a small tract of land in 1896 where the community is now situated and built a blacksmith shop, a store and a house. In 1897 he was appointed postmaster and was given the privilege of naming the post office, which he did, for himself.

Ruckel Creek, Hood River County. This was formerly Deadman Creek, a melancholy designation. At the request of the OGNB, federal authorities adopted the name Ruckel in honor of J. S. Ruckel, who built the portage tramway on the south side of the Columbia River at the Cascades, completing the project in May, 1861. He was an original incorporator of the Oregon Steam Navigation Company. Ruckel signed his name as here written and not Ruckle nor Ruckles. See also under Thomas Creek, Umatilla County.

Ruckles, Douglas County. This place was named for M. C. Ruckles, who owned land where the Southern Pacific Company now has its station. The community was formerly known as Oak Grove, but when the post office was established this name could not be used on account of duplication so Ruckles was selected. The railroad station is Dole. It is understood that the railroad objected to the use of the word Ruckles because it sounded so much like Riddles and this presented the possibility of confusion in train orders. Riddles was the former name of the station now known as Riddle. Ruckles does not appear on the 1935 post office list.

Ruckles Creek, Baker County. Ruckles Creek rises near the Virtue Mine northeast of Baker and flows northeast to Powder River at Keating. It takes its name from Colonel J. S. Ruckel who after he sold his interest in the Oregon Portage Railway at Cascade Locks, moved to Baker County and operated a mine and stamp mill. Ruckel shares with Binger Hermann the distinction of bestowing two spellings of the same name on two different features.

Ruddock, Umatilla County. Ruddock post office was established July 25, 1888, with Isaac Ruddock postmaster. The office was closed October 12, 1895, and the business turned over to Gibbon. The office was at or near the railroad station North Fork, at the junction of that stream and Meacham Creek. The writer has been told that Ruddock, which was obviously named for the postmaster, was a post office established to serve people engaged in wood cutting operations in the Blue Mountains.

Rudio Mountain, Grant County. Rudio Mountain is in the west part of the county and Rudio Meadow and Rudio Creek are in the same general locality. Rudio Creek flows into North Fork John Day River. About 1930 J. E. Snow of Dayville wrote the compiler that these features were named for one Rudio, a cattleman, who settled near the mouth of the creek in the early 1870s. His first name was probably Peter.

Rufus, Sherman County. Rufus was named for Rufus C. Wallis, the original settler in the community. Wallis later moved across the Columbia River and settled in Klickitat County, Washington. He received a U. S. patent for the Klickitat County land on December 13, 1876, for 163.75 acres.

Rugg Canyon, Umatilla County. Alfred H. Rugg was born in Franklin County, Massachusetts in 1831. He moved gradually west coming to Oregon in 1882 and Umatilla County in 1885. Two of his sons, Alby and Emery took up property near Nye in the 1890s and members of the family are still active in the area.

Ruggs, Morrow County. This community on Rhea Creek was named for Ed Rugg who ranched nearby after World War I and at one time operated the local store and service station. It has now fallen victim to the urban migration.

Rujada, Lane County. Rujada was a lumber camp at the eastern terminus of the Oregon, Pacific and Eastern Railway, east of Cottage Grove. It is said the name was taken from a telegraph code book, and means "a considerable body of standing timber is available." Another theory is that it was made up from the first letters of Reserve and United States followed by those of several involved individuals. Rujada does not appear on recent maps, but the name is preserved in Rujada Point Lookout on Rose Hill nearby.

Rural, Coos County. The community called Rural was named for its surroundings, which were well described by the name. The place is in the south part of the county on South Fork Coquille River near the mouth of Salmon Creek. Rural post office was established August 21, 1890, with James D. Hayes first postmaster of a series of ten. The post office was discontinued September 30, 1915.

Rush Creek, Wallowa County. This stream is near Paradise. It received its name because of bulrushes growing on its banks.

Russ Creek, Clackamas County. This creek is a tributary of Collawash River. It was named for Hiram R. Wilcox of Estacada, formerly of the USFS, and universally known as Russ.

Russell Creek, Clackamas and Marion counties. This stream which flows into Molalla River, was named for Henry Russell of Molalla who, with several friends, prospected in this part of the state for a number of years.

Russell Lake, Marion County. North of Mount Jefferson, wedged in between living glaciers on the south and a rough precipitous mountain wall a thousand feet high on the north, lies Jefferson Park, a natural playground, invitingly level, directly athwart the Cascade Range. There is snow in this park even as late as the first of September, but generally during August the park is a mass of flowers. There are several lakes in the park, and the largest is but a few hundred feet in diameter, but looking down into it from the north, one gets a fine reflection of Mount Jefferson. This lake was named in honor of Dr. Israel C. Russell, one of the early geologists of the USGS, who was an investigator in Oregon beginning in the early 1880s. His principal contribution to the knowledge of Oregon geology is USGS Bulletin 252, *Geology and Water Resources of Central Oregon.* Russell Lake forms South Fork Breitenbush River until late in the season, when evaporation reduces its level to a point below the outlet. Its elevation is about 5900 feet.

Russellville, Multnomah County. Russellville is an area on Southeast Stark Street about a mile east of Montavilla. The best information available to the writer is to the effect that the locality was named in compliment to Russellville, Illinois. In July, 1947, Mrs. H. A. Lewis, a resident of the Russellville community, wrote the compiler that in 1888 Leander Lewis circulated a petition for a post office, and it was planned to use the name Lewisville. Officials at Washington would not approve this name because it duplicated the name Lewisville in Polk County. Mr. Lewis then suggested Russellville in compliment to a place in Illinois where he had relatives. The Multnomah County office was established February 11, 1889, with George W. Stafford first of a long list of postmasters. Russellville post office was closed as of July 15, 1904, probably as the result of rural delivery. According to Mrs. Lewis the Russellville post office was for most of its life in a store on the north side of Southeast Stark Street near the present Southeast Ninety-seventh Avenue.

Rustler Peak, Jackson County. This peak in the Cascade Range is said to owe its name to an incident connected with stock rustlers in early days.

Ruthton Point, Hood River County. Ruthton Point is on the Columbia River just west of Hood River. Joseph W. Morton bought a farm including this point in 1886 and applied the elided name of his daughter, Ruth Morton. This information was uncovered by Ruth M. Guppy of Hood River.

Rutledge, Sherman County. Rutledge post office was established June 6, 1884, with Joseph H. Rutledge first postmaster. This office continued in service until March 23, 1908. It served a territory a few miles east-southeast of Grass Valley. For information about the Rutledge family, see *Illustrated History of Central Oregon,* page 520. "Uncle Joe" Rutledge and his family came to central Oregon from California in the fall of 1882 and took up land south of Moro. However, actual residence on the land did not begin until the spring of 1883.

R. W. Spring, Malheur County. This spring three miles west of Harper owes its name to a change in government policy. When the Bureau of Land Management became responsible for the administration of federal lands outside the national forests, all lands with water resources formerly administered by the Bureau of Reclamation were among those turned over to the BLM. This typical perennial spring was properly coded R. W. for "reclamation withdrawal".

Ryan Ranch Meadow, Deschutes County. This meadow along Deschutes River near Benham Falls was named for John Ryan, an early day lumberman.

Rye Valley, Baker County. When the immigrants and miners came to Oregon, natural forage was more suitable than gasoline to the motive power then available. A good many geographic features in the state have been named for the native grains and grasses that have grown so abundantly in favorable places. Rye Valley is a name that had its start in the mining boom in northeastern Oregon in the 1860s. This valley is in the Dixie Creek drainage about thirty miles southeast of Baker. Rye Valley post office was established September 27, 1869, with Nayson S. Whitcomb first postmaster. This office operated on and off for many years, but was not in service in 1945. A prominent mesa in eastern Crook County just southeast of Paulina bears the descriptive name Ryegrass Table. The writer does not know just what types of ryegrass grow in the locations mentioned. Peck, in his *Manual of Higher Plants of Oregon,* lists no less than thirteen varieties of ryegrass native to Oregon, but a number of them do not grow east of the Cascade Range. While contemplating the fascinating subject of rye it should be noted that there is a locality in Sherman County known as Bourbon. Geographic nomenclature plays no favorites.

Sacajawea Peak, Wallowa County. This mountain is one of the highest points in the Wallowa Mountains south of Enterprise. It bears the name of the famous Shoshone Indian woman who was with the Lewis and Clark party. It was once called Legion Mountain in compliment to the American Legion. There has been ample controversy about Sacajawea, about the value of her services, the place of her death and even about the spelling of her name, a matter which doubtless bothered her but little. Grace Raymond Hebard's *Sacajawea* gives a general account of her story. An editorial by Albert Hawkins in the *Oregonian,* October 13, 1929, ably discusses some of her problems. See also C. S. Kingston's article in *Pacific Northwest Quarterly,* January, 1944.

Saddle Bag Mountain, Lincoln County. In 1980, William Erdmann of the State Forestry Department wrote to give the origin of the name of this high ground south of Salmon River between Otis and Grand Ronde. About 1900 the mail was delivered out of the Butler store in Grand Ronde. The mail route ran along Salmon River near the base of the mountain but as local residents were widely scattered, the letters were left in an old saddle bag which hung on a prominent snag. Mail service improved over the years and the saddle bag is long gone. However, after World War II the name mysteriously changed to Saddleback Mountain. Mr. Erdmann brought the matter to the attention of the OGNB in 1980 and the USBGN corrected the matter in *Decision List 8104*.

Saddle Creek, Wallowa County. Saddle Creek is so named because it heads near Freezeout Saddle, on the divide between the waters of Snake River and Imnaha River.

Saddle Mountain, Clatsop County. Gustavus Hines, in *Oregon and Its Institutions*, says the Indian name of this prominent landmark was *Swallalahoost*. There was an Indian tradition that one of the great chiefs, after being killed by enemies, assumed the form of an eagle and became the creator of thunder and lightning at the top of this peak. Hines further says that the name Saddle Mountain was applied by Wilkes in 1841. The name is unusually descriptive. Saddle Mountain is one of the highest peaks in the north part of the Coast Range in Oregon and has an elevation, according to the USCE, of 3283 feet. Lewis and Clark mention the mountain but give it no name.

Saddlebutte, Harney County. Saddlebutte post office was established September 26, 1916, with T. C. Albritton first postmaster, to serve the area near the physical feature Saddle Butte not far from the northeast shore of Malheur Lake. Saddle Butte is a prominent point a few miles west-southwest of Crane. Saddlebutte post office was closed May 15, 1920, and the business turned over to Crane. The butte was named for its shape.

Sage Hen Creek, Harney County. The sagehen or sage grouse, *Centrocerus urophasianus,* was formerly plentiful throughout the West, and its name has been applied to a number of geographic features, but as far as the compiler knows, the only place the name has been used in Oregon is in Harney and Lake counties. We have a good description of the sagehen as it is found near the Oregon creek that bears its name in U. S. National Museum Special Bulletin No. 1, *Life Histories of North American Birds,* by Captain Charles Bendire, page 106. This bird is, next to the wild turkey, the largest game bird found in the United States. During the winter the sagehen feeds largely on the leaves of the sagebrush, but that is not its exclusive diet, and some authorities assert that sage leaves are only eaten when other food is not available. Captain Bendire spent several years studying the birds of Oregon, particularly in the Harney Valley. The USBGN adopted the two word form in *Decision List 6202*.

Sageview, Harney County. Sageview post office served an area in the sage plains west of Catlow from February, 1916, until November, 1918. It would be most difficult to suggest a better name for an office in such surroundings.

Saginaw, Lane County. R. A. Booth, vice-president of the Booth-Kelly Lumber Co., informed the compiler that this place was named by J. I. Jones for Saginaw, Michigan. The community was established about a year before the lumber company began to operate there. Gannett says that Saginaw is an Ojibwa Indian word meaning Sauk place, referring to the Sauk or Sac Indians. Saginaw post office was established March 4, 1898, with Laura Weaver first postmaster, and closed July 31, 1957.

Sahale Falls, Hood River County. These falls of East Fork Hood River are on the original Mount Hood Loop Highway just east of Bennett Pass. They bear the Chinook jargon word for high. The name was bestowed on the falls by George Holman of Portland, as a result of a prize competition conducted by the Portland *Telegram,* in which it was judged that Mr. Holman had suggested the best name. The word *sahale* is composed of three syllables with the accent on the first.

Sahalie Falls, Linn County. This 140 foot waterfall on McKenzie River is between Carmen Reservoir and Clear Lake. At one time they were called Upper Falls but the present name came into general use about 1950 with the development of the Clear Lake recreation area. The USBGN confirmed this in *Decision List 6202. Sahalie* is a variant spelling of the Chinook jargon word for high.

Sain Creek, Washington County. This creek rises in section 33, township 1 north, range 5 west, and flows generally southeast into Scoggins Creek. It was named for Thomas W. Sain who settled there in 1875 and owned much of the land on the creek. The forms Sein and Seine are both incorrect and the USBGN adopted the present spelling in *Decision List 6402.*

Saint Benedict, Marion County. In 1881, a Benedictine monk, the Rev. Adelhelm Odermatt, came to Oregon and soon established a Benedictine community, which is now known as St. Benedicts Abbey. This community was first started at Gervais, but in 1884 it was moved to the town of Mt. Angel. Since it was less than a mile from the Mount Angel post office, the authorities would not establish a new post office for the abbey. In 1903 a new abbey was completed on the butte southeast of Mt. Angel town and in 1914 the post office of Saint Benedict was established at the abbey. The first postmaster was Wendel Neiderprum. Father Odermatt came from Engelberg, Switzerland. He translated this name into Mount Angel, thus naming the town and the butte although the town was incorporated with the form Mt. Angel. Saint Benedict was named for the founder of the Benedictine Order, who was born in Nursia, Italy, in the year 480, and died at Monte Cassino, Italy, in 543. For additional information see under the name Mount Angel. The butte on which St. Benedicts Abbey is built has an elevation of 485 feet.

Saint Helens, Columbia County. The community of Saint Helens was founded by Captain H. M. Knighton, a pioneer of 1845. Available records seem to indicate that Knighton, who was a mariner, was born in New England, which may have been the reason he first applied the name Plymouth to the new townsite. There is a tradition that this name was suggested by a prominent rock which Knighton found on the river bank. It made a natural wharf. The name Plymouth appears in an advertisement in the *Oregon Spectator,* July 22, 1847. The Rev. George H. Atkinson mentions the little Plymouth community on June 18, 1848, and says there were but two people there. See *OHQ,* volume XL, page 180. Theodore Talbot calls the place New Plymouth in his *Journals,* page 88, on May 13, 1849, and mentions two houses. On August 25, 1849, Knighton signed a deed in which he refers to "Plymouth and now called Kasenau." This new name was in compliment to Chief Cassino, a prominent Indian who lived nearby. This name is spelled in many ways. For Omar C. Spencer's article about Chief Cassino, see *OHQ*, volume XXXIV, page 19. It is hard to determine the exact status of the name Kasenau mentioned by Knighton, because within a year he was using the name Plymouth for the post office. See below. Also on May 6, 1850, Knighton refers to "Casenau now called St. Helens" at the very time he was using the name Plymouth for his post office. In any event, the name of the place was changed to Saint Helens in the latter part of 1850, apparently because of the proximity of Mount Saint Helens, Washington. Saint Helens is advertised in the *Oregon Spectator*, November 28, 1850, as a terminus of a proposed railroad from Lafayette because of its deep water for ships. Vancouver named the mountain in honor of Baron Saint Helens (Alleyne Fitzherbert, 1753-1839), British ambassador to Spain in 1790-94, who negotiated the Nootka treaty in Madrid. For information about Baron Saint Helens see article by Professor Edmond S. Meany, *Washington Historical Quarterly*, volume XV, page 124. Saint Helens post office was established with the name Plymouth, April 9, 1850, with Henry M. Knighton postmaster. The name was changed to Saint Helen November 4, 1850, with William H. Tappan postmaster. Saint Helen was an error in spelling at Washington, D. C. The name was later changed to Saint Helens. Tappan, a native of Massachusetts, came to Oregon in 1849 with the Mounted Rifles. He may have had a hand in naming Saint Helens, as he became interested in the townsite, but he was not in Oregon when Plymouth was named.

Saint Johns, Multnomah County. James John crossed the plains to California in 1841, with General John Bidwell, and came to Oregon in 1843. He settled first at Linnton, and several years later moved to the site of the town that bears his name. He operated a ferry there in 1852. He died May 28, 1886. For history of the town and of James John, see the *Oregonian*, August 29, 1907, page 11; March 29, 1903, page 40; May 29, 1886, page 5. The plat for Saint Johns was filed July 20, 1865, and of an addition thereto November 28, 1868. Efforts to change the name to Saint John have been unavailing, and the style Saint Johns has been approved by USBGN. The town was annexed to Portland in 1915.

Saint Joseph, Yamhill County. This place was named by Ben Holladay, probably for Saint Joseph, Missouri, but Mrs. Harriet McArthur informed the compiler in 1926 that she was once told that Holladay selected the name on account of his brother, Joseph Holladay.

Saint Louis, Marion County. Saint Louis is a very old settlement in the Willamette Valley about three miles northwest of Gervais. In 1844 a Jesuit missionary, the Reverend Aloysius Verecuysee, visited the early settlers and in 1845 he built a log church at Saint Louis. In November, 1847, the parish was first organized with a resident priest, the Reverend B. Delorme. The parish was named for Saint Louis, King of France, and not for the metropolis of Missouri. The compiler has been to Saint Louis, Oregon, many times and has always been impressed by the quiet simplicity of the place. Saint Louis post office was established October 26, 1860, with S. C. Matthieu first postmaster. With a couple of intermissions this office remained in service until the summer of 1901 when it was closed to Gervais. The remains of Madame Marie Dorion, famous member of the Astor overland party, are buried at Saint Louis Church.

Saint Marys, Washington County. Saint Marys, once a separate community but now part of Beaverton, is close to the Tualatin Valley Highway and SW 148th Avenue or Murray Road. The locality is well known because of the girls school, Saint Marys of the Valley, and a little to the west of the girls school is Saint Marys Home for Boys. These institutions are in charge of the Sisters of Saint Mary, an order founded in 1886 at Sublimity. In 1891 the Sisters assumed charge of the Saint Marys Home near Beaverton. That institution is no longer in its original location but has been moved westward toward Huber. On May 31, 1902, Saint Marys post office was established on the Washington County list with Dominic Faber first postmaster. However, this office was never completely organized and the appointment was rescinded in June, 1903.

Saint Paul, Marion County. Saint Paul was named by Archbishop Francis Norbert Blanchet, who came to Oregon in 1838, and established Saint Paul Mission in 1839 at the Catholic church on French Prairie. The mission was named for the Apostle Paul. The writer has been told that the first postmaster was John F. Theo. Brentano. The post office was established June 24, 1874.

Saint Peters Dome, Multnomah County. This basalt monolith in the Columbia Gorge near Dodson was a conspicuous challenge to the mountain climbing fraternity for many years. In 1940 it was first climbed by Joe Leuthold and five others including a woman, Ida Darr. For details see the *Mazama*, 1940. In early days this was called Cathedral Rock and the name Saint Peters Dome described the higher summit to the south now called Yeon Mountain. The name is most descriptive but the compiler has not been able to learn when it was first applied to the present peak.

Salado, Lincoln County. The post office Salado was established in April, 1891. The compiler has been told that George Hodges named the place for Salado, Texas, where he had formerly lived. *Salado* is a Spanish word meaning salty or saline, or a plain encrusted with salt.

Salem, Marion County. The Indian name for the locality of Salem was *Chemeketa*, which is said to have meant meeting place or resting place or possibly both. Chemeketa also may have been the name of one of the bands of the Calapooya Indians. In 1840-41 the Jason Lee Mission was moved from its old location near the Willamette River up stream about ten miles to the Chemeketa plain and extensive improvements were started. While the new establishment was called Chemeketa, it was probably better known as the Mill, on account of the installation on Mill Creek. In 1842 the missionaries established the Oregon Institute and a building was started. From that time the place was often spoken of as the Institute. There is argument as to who selected the name Salem. Bancroft, in *History of Oregon*, volume I, page 222, says that after the mission was dissolved in 1844, it was decided to lay out a townsite on the Institute lands. This was done and David Leslie, president of the trustees, named the place Salem. Leslie came to Oregon from Salem, Massachusetts. Leslie M. Scott, in *History of the Oregon Country*, volume II, page 298, says the place was named by W. H. Willson. The late R. J. Hendricks of Salem, a diligent student of the community, was strongly of the opinion that Leslie named the place. See articles in the Salem *Statesman*, March 8, 1931, and March 28, 1940. Salem post office was established

November 8, 1849, with J. B. McClane postmaster. Three plats forming
what is now the main part of Salem were filed in 1850-51. Salem is the
anglicized form of the Hebrew word *shalom,* meaning peace.

In December, 1853, efforts were made in the territorial legislature to
change the name from Salem to Thurston or Valena. Chester N. Terry
petitioned to have the name changed to Corvallis, but after spirited debate
the name Corvallis was given to the Benton County community then known
as Marysville. The names Chemawa, Willamette and Bronson were also
suggested. Pike and Victoria were mentioned, but by this time the members
concluded that they had wasted enough time over the matter and the various bills were postponed. The final vote was in January, 1854. The name
Valena is said to have been suggested because it was the name of Velina
Pauline Nesmith, later Mrs. Wm. Markland Molson, but she was not born
until 1855. In 1907 a station on the Oregon Electric Railway north of Salem
was named Chemeketa to perpetuate that name, but it was later changed to
Hopmere because of local sentiment. The location of the Oregon capital
caused a spirited contest that lasted for nearly fifteen years. The first legislative assembly of the provisional government met at Oregon City (Willamette Falls) in 1844. By an act of 1851 the capital was moved to Salem, and in
1855 it was moved to Corvallis, only to be moved back to Salem in the same
year. Destruction of the Capitol at Salem, December 29, 1855, was considered as an incendiary part of this controversy. For history of this squabble,
see article by Walter C. Winslow, OHQ, volume IX, page 173. For many
references to the history of Salem and the capital controversy, see Scott's
History of the Oregon Country, volume II, pages 298 and 312.

Salem Hills, Marion County. These hills form the high ground south
of Salem bordered generally on the east by the Southern Pacific Company
main line, on the south by Santiam River and on the west by Willamette
River. They have been variously known as the Salem Hills, Red Hills and
Illahee Hills. In 1963 the OGNB voted to recommend the name Chemeketa Hills, an Indian name of historic significance now applied only to a
Salem street. This action provoked a spirited dissent from a large group
who claimed that the area had been known as the Salem Hills for many
years. In December 1964 the matter was given a full hearing and the proponents of Salem Hills led by ex-Governor Charles A. Sprague and state geologist Hollis Dole carried the field as the board rescinded their action of 1963
and voted to approve the present form. In this case, as in many others, long
usage prevailed over an excellent historic name.

Salene Lake, Columbia County. This lake is near the west bank of Multnomah Channel north of Scappoose. It was named for the Salene family,
pioneer residents of the neighborhood.

Saleratus Creek, Lane County. Saleratus Creek is in the west part of
the county. It drains south into Wolf Creek, a well-known tributary to Siuslaw River southwest of Austa. The compiler has been told that the stream
was named to commemorate the baking of a batch of biscuits by some
accomplished surveyor. Saleratus is the common name originally for bicarbonate of potash but now also used for bicarbonate of soda, both when
used as an ingredient in baking powder. In bygone days *saleratus* was used

frequently and interchangeably with *baking powder* when describing biscuits.

Salineville, Morrow County. Salineville was thirteen miles northwest of Heppner and was undoubtedly named for the alkaline soil in the valley of Willow Creek. If early maps are to be relied on the place was a little to the northwest of the community now known as Lexington. Salineville post office was established January 9, 1884, with Mrs. Mary L. Benefiel postmaster. The office was discontinued April 2, 1886, and the records were turned over to Heppner. Lexington post office was established in November, 1885, and doubtless supplied the post office needs of the area.

Saling Creek, Tillamook County. Saling Creek was named for William Saling who homesteaded along it in 1892. It flows into Nestucca River about a mile below Beaver.

Salisbury, Baker County. Salisbury was a place on the Sumpter Valley Highway near Powder River about ten miles southwest of Baker. The locality was once known as Bennett, probably for a local resident. A post office called Salisbury was established March 23, 1906, with Charles R. Foster postmaster. This office was closed May 31, 1907, but the locality still retains the name Salisbury, which came from Hiram Salisbury, who lived nearby. In 1980 there was little evidence of commercial activity.

Salisbury, Umatilla County. Salisbury post office was established August 18, 1894, with Francis M. Salisbury postmaster. The office was closed January 24, 1896. It was named for the postmaster. A railroad map dated July, 1903, shows Salisbury on McKay Creek near the western boundary of the Umatilla Indian Reservation. It was about midway between Pendleton and Pilot Rock.

Salishan, Lincoln County. In 1964 John Gray of Portland began the development of a planned community and resort motel at the south end of Siletz Bay. The careful planning of architect John Storrs and landscape architect Barbara Fealy integrated the public facilities east of US 101 into the rolling terrain and typical coast vegetation. The name was taken from the *Salish* Indian, the linguistic group that included the Tillamook and Siletz languages. Salishan is an excellent example of a well chosen name for a commercial development.

Sallal Springs, Curry County. These springs are about five miles east of Humbug Mountain. Sallal is an Indian name for the fruit of the *Gaultheria shallon,* called by white people the sallal bush or sallal berry. This shrub grows in dense thickets in the Coast Range, and in other parts of the state as well. The berry is a purplish black, and not particularly palatable. The name has been used in a number of places in Oregon and Washington to describe geographic features. Sallal is spelled in several ways but the style here given is that used by government map makers.

Salmon, Clackamas County. Salmon post office was established to serve the area at the mouth of Salmon River, where that stream flows into Sandy River on the Mount Hood Loop Highway. The office was named for the river, but the naming of Salmon River is a matter probably lost to history. Salmon post office was established April 2, 1891, with Winnie McIntyre first postmaster. The office was discontinued May 6, 1910. Salmon post office was moved and the name changed to Brightwood when it was discontinued. The two places are very close together.

Salmon River, Lincoln, Polk and Tillamook counties. Considering the importance of the salmon in the history of Oregon, it is not surprising that a number of geographic features should be named for the fish. Salmon River mentioned in the heading rises in the Coast Range and flows into Pacific Ocean just south of Cascade Head. The Salmon River Highway follows the stream for many miles. George Davidson, in *Coast Pilot,* 1889, says the Indian name for this Salmon River was *Nechesne.* Another well-known Salmon River rises on the south slope of Mount Hood and flows into Sandy River. It is in Clackamas County. There are streams named for the salmon in other counties. A good deal has been written about the various varieties of salmon frequenting Pacific Coast waters. The opinions of some of the experts are highly controversial, and the compiler does not feel that he has the energy to join the battle. He knows but four sorts of salmon—fresh, salt, tinned and kippered, and if the reader requires information, he will have to look elsewhere.

Salmonberry, Tillamook County. There are several geographic features in Oregon named Salmonberry, the most important being Salmon-berry River, in Tillamook and Washington counties, and the railroad station near its mouth. They are named for the *Rubus spectabilis.* The form Salmon Berry is wrong when used as a geographic name. Preston's *Map of Oregon,* 1856, gives Salmonberry Creek for the stream mentioned above. Salmonberry post office was established March 15, 1923, with Ernest B. Graham postmaster, and closed February 28, 1924.

Salt Butte, Crook County. *A History of the Ochoco National Forest,* says that this butte north of McKay Creek was named for nearby Salt Spring. The spring was not named because the water was brackish but by a party of hunters camped there who found they had forgotten this essential commodity.

Salt Creek, Lane County. This large tributary of Middle Fork Willamette River has been called Salt Creek since pioneer days because of the salt springs along the stream used as licks by deer.

Salt Creek, Polk and Yamhill counties. Salt Creek rises in the foothills north of Dallas and flows northeast into South Yamhill River. John Ford of Dallas told the compiler that it was named in pioneer days because of the salt licks found on its banks. The advance of civilization has apparently obliterated the licks. Preston's *Map of Oregon,* 1856, shows Salt Creek post office six miles northwest of Dallas. This office was established July 6, 1852, with James B. Riggs first postmaster.

Salt Creek Falls, Lane County. These falls are among the finest in the state. They are estimated to be 300 feet high, and were discovered by Frank S. Warner and Charles Tufti in March, 1887. See the *Oregonian,* section 4, page 5, July 3, 1927. The rock at the top of the falls is so shaped as to make the water form a letter "s" as it plunges over. Warner was a member of a pioneer family of the valley of the Middle Fork Willamette River, and Tufti was his Indian friend. Tufti Mountain was named for the Indian.

Sam Davis Spring, Wheeler County. This spring in the southwest corner of township 13 south, range 24 east, was named for Sam Davis who ranged sheep nearby from his ranch on John Day River.

Sampson, Douglas County. Sampson post office was named for Rear-Admiral William Thomas Sampson, famous American naval officer who made a remarkable record in the war with Spain. Sampson post office was established August 27, 1898, and was in service until September 15, 1912. George B. Balderree was the first postmaster. Admiral Sampson was at the height of his fame in the summer of 1898. Sampson post office was six or seven miles south of Gardiner. The town of Reedsport had not yet been founded.

Sampson Mountain, Jefferson County. Sampson Mountain forms the south end of Blizzard Ridge south of Ashwood. It was named for Frank F. Sampson who homesteaded there in 1886.

Sams Valley, Jackson County. Chief Sam of the Rogue River Indians formerly lived in this valley and it was named for him.

San Antonio Creek, Lane County. This stream is tributary to Siuslaw River near Beecher. The form San Antone is not considered correct.

Sand Creek, Crater Lake National Park, Klamath County. This stream heads in the park and flows east toward Klamath Marsh. Captain O. C. Applegate wrote on July 21, 1911, as follows: "The old Indian trail and later the wagon road crossed Sand Creek in the valley of the Klamath Marsh. The pumice and sand was a menace to travel and teams and saddle horses were mired there. Even until a bridge was constructed over the stream a couple of months ago, the crossing was treacherous on account of the quicksands. The danger from these uncertain sands gave the name to the stream and was a reminder of the need of vigilance."

Sand Hollow Battleground, Morrow County. In 1964 Judge John F. Kilkenny proposed this name to commemorate the battle between the Cayuse Indians and troops under the command of Colonel Cornelius Gilliam in February 1848. The site is east of Finley Buttes and about a mile north of the OSHD marker indicating where the Oregon Trail crossed Sand Hollow.

Sand Ranch Well, Morrow County. This well is at the site of John S. Kilkenny's 1911 Sand Hollow ranch house. John F. Kilkenny tells of the housewarming party and other details of this establishment in "Shamrocks and Shepherds," *OHQ,* volume LXIX, number 2. It appears congenial combat was not confined to Donnybrook.

Sand Ridge, Union County. On April 6, 1875, a post office with the name Sand Ridge was established in the Grande Ronde Valley with Cyrus G. Enloe first postmaster. This office was in service only until July 9, 1877, and even at that there was a period of several months when it did not function. It was named for a local topographic feature. The post office was in the northeast part of section 16, township 2 south, range 39 east, at a station on the old stage route from Union to Summerville. See also under Slater.

Sanders Creek, Tillamook County. This creek which flows into Nestucca River at Cloverdale was named for Americus D. Sanders who raised goats nearby. He homesteaded near the mouth in 1882.

Sandlake, Tillamook County. Sandlake post office was not far from Sand Lake, which is near the shore of the Pacific Ocean. As is customary, many names of this type were telescoped into one word by postal authorities. The post office was established with the name Hembree on July 10, 1890, with A. J. Hembree first postmaster. The name was changed to Sandlake on January 18, 1898.

Sandy, Clackamas County. Sandy is near Sandy River and received its name on that account. See under that heading for the origin of the name of the stream. J. H. Revenue, of Boring, sent the compiler information about the history of the town. His father settled near the present site of Sandy in 1853, and in those days of pioneer influx over the Barlow Road, all that territory lying north and east of Eagle Creek was known as Sandy, and the particular place where the community now stands was called Revenue. About 1870 Richard Gerdes, who had been operating a store at Eagle Creek with Henry Wilbern, bought property near the Revenue farm and opened a store. He soon applied for a post office, which was established February 13, 1873, and it is generally believed Gerdes suggested the name Sandy, as he was more familiar with that name than with Revenue. On June 1, 1854, a post office named Sandy was established, apparently near the present site of Troutdale, with Emsley R. Scott postmaster. This post office was discontinued February 26, 1868.

Sandy, Multnomah County. In 1977 the Union Pacific Railroad, as part of their track modernization program, replaced the limited siding facilities at Troutdale with a new long siding east of Sandy River. The new station, Sandy, takes its name from the nearby river.

Sandy Creek, Coos County. This stream is a tributary of Middle Fork Coquille River just west of Remote. It was named for a pioneer settler, "Sandy" Brown.

Sandy River, Clackamas and Multnomah counties. Sandy River was discovered by Lieutenant W. R. Broughton of Vancouver's expedition and was named Barings River on October 30, 1792. This was probably for the great English family of bankers and financiers. Francis Baring (1740-1810) was for many years a director of the East India Company, and his second son Alexander (1774-1848) was better known as Lord Ashburton. Lewis and Clark passed the mouth of Sandy River on Sunday, November 3, 1805, and made the following notation in their journals: "we coasted and halted at the mouth of a large river on the Lard. Side, this river throws out emence quantitys of sand and is very shallow, the narrowest part 200 yards wide bold current, much resembling the river Plat." The presence of the two mouths of the river was noted, and the stream was called Quicksand River. This name continued nearly fifty years, in American and British maps and writings. The name seems to have shortened to Sandy River on the tongues of Americans, between 1845 and 1850. Joel Palmer's *Journals of Travel*, written as of 1845, mentions Quicksand, Big Sandy, and Alexander Ross gives Quicksand River.

Sanford Canyon, Morrow County. This canyon in Rhea Creek drainage south of Heppner was named for an early settler, one Sanford, who married a member of the Ayers family.

Sanger, Baker County. This place bears the name of one of the owners of the mining property nearby. The early name for this place was Hogum. See editorial page the *Oregonian,* October 7, 1927, and the Baker *Morning Democrat,* October 19, 1927. Dunham Wright of Medical Springs told the compiler that the place was named Hogum because of the greediness of some prospectors. The name was changed to Augusta in honor of Miss Augusta Parkwood. This change in name came about as the result of an agreement on the part of some of the miners to name the place for the first unmarried woman resident. The name Sanger has been established for many years, having displaced Augusta. Augusta post office was in operation for about a year in 1871-72. Sanger post office was established August 17, 1887, with William R. Aldersley first postmaster. Augusta and Sanger may not have been in exactly the same place. See also under Augusta.

Santiam, Linn and Marion counties. The name Santiam, with varied spellings, has been used for several Oregon post offices. For the derivation of the word, see under Santiam River. An office called Santyam Forks was established in Linn County, April 9, 1850, with Jacob Conser postmaster. John Crabtree became postmaster October 4, 1850, and the office was discontinued July 27, 1852. It is known that Jacob Conser was living near the present site of Scio early in 1850, and John Crabtree lived in the same general locality. It may be assumed that the office was in the neighborhood. Santyam post office was established in Linn County March 14, 1851, with Russel T. Hill postmaster. For the history of this office, see under Lebanon. An office named Syracuse was established in Marion County October 4, 1850. The place was about two miles downstream from the present site of Jefferson, but all available records show that it was really in Linn County and not Marion. See under Jefferson for details. On July 27, 1852, the name of the office was changed to Santiam City, and in the official records is a note that on October 16, 1852, the office was in Linn County, but here again, the record at Washington, D. C., does not fit early maps and records in Oregon, which show Santiam on the Miller claim and in Marion County. These discrepancies may have been due to shifts in the Santiam River channel, here the boundary between Linn and Marion counties. The office was later moved to Jefferson, with a change in name. The post route map for 1900 shows an office called Santiam near South Santiam River between Lebanon and Sweet Home. This office has been discontinued and the community has almost evaporated.

Santiam Pass, Jefferson and Linn counties. In earlier days Santiam Pass was considered to be that used by the old South Santiam road which crossed the summit of the Cascade Range just east of Big Lake. Hogg Pass was about three miles to the north and was the point selected by Col. T. Egenton Hogg for his railroad location. As a result of the topographic mapping of this area by the USGS in 1928-29, and also of the building of the Santiam Highway through the Cascade Range, the USBGN on April 3, 1929, adopted the name Santiam Pass for both of these routes of travel. This was done on the theory there was one wide pass and not two narrow ones, which is generally substantiated by the topographic map of the Three Fingered Jack quadrangle. The name Hogg Pass, as applied to the location of Santiam Highway, is now obsolete. For editorial on this change, see Salem *Capital Journal* for June 13, 1929. The name Santiam Pass appears to have been accepted very rapidly by the traveling public. The name of Colonel Hogg is perpetuated at Hogg Rock, a prominent point west of the pass and just north of Santiam Highway, which skirts its base. Andrew Wiley went through Santiam Pass as early as 1859. See under Wiley Creek and Hogg Rock.

Santiam River, Linn and Marion counties. Santiam River and North Santiam River form in part the boundary between Linn and Marion counties. In addition to the two streams named, other important tributaries to the Santiam drainage are the South Santiam, Little North Santiam and Breitenbush rivers, and Crabtree, Thomas and Quartzville creeks, all heading in the western slope of the Cascade Range. The stream was named for the Santiam Indians, a Kalapooian tribe, living near the Santiam River. The remnants were moved to Grand Ronde Agency in 1906. Variant forms of the name are *Ahalapam, Sandeam, Santiams, Santainas, Santian, Santians, Sandeham.* A detailed map of the North Santiam River and some of its tributaries may be found in USGS Water-Supply Paper 349.

Sardine Creek, Jackson County. Sardine Creek flows into Rogue River west of Gold Hill. In a letter signed "Pioneer," published in the *Oregonian* for November 15, 1883, it is said that this stream was named by J. W. Hayes of Rock Point. Hayes was a gold seeker, and his pack mule one morning kicked him into the creek. Hayes jumped up with the remark that he was no sardine. Some of the information contained in "Pioneer's" letter mentioned above is erroneous, and the data on Sardine Creek may be incorrect. Walling, in *History of Southern Oregon,* page 380, has another story of the origin of the name, to the effect that prospectors used sardines for food near the stream in the 1850s. Possibly the name had its start in both events.

Sardine Creek, Marion County. This tributary of North Santiam River was named in 1867 by Thomas J. Henness because he found an empty sardine can in the stream while he was on a prospecting expedition from his home near the present site of Gates. Sardine tins were unusual in the Oregon mountains in those days. The name spread from the creek to Sardine Mountain nearby. For information about the Henness family, see the Salem *Capital Journal,* June 18, 1927, page 1.

Sargent Butte, Wheeler County. This 3300 foot butte is just north of the mouth of West Branch. It was named for Allie E. Sargent who homesteaded nearby in 1893. Grover Blake, who knew Sargent well, told the compiler in 1968 that he was unable to find any relationship between A. E. and I. N. Sargent, the man who made the original plat of Mitchell.

Saunders Creek, Curry County. This stream, which flows into Rogue River about four miles from Pacific Ocean, was named for John Saunders who, with a man named Hastings, settled there about 1860 and built a saw and grist mill on the creek. This information was furnished by F. S. Moore of Gold Beach, Oregon.

Sauvie Island, Columbia and Multnomah counties. This is the largest island in the Columbia River, and is for the most part low land and lakes. The highest point on the island is only about 50 feet above sea level. Lewis and Clark called it *Wap-pa-to* and *Wap-pa-too* in 1805-06, the Indian name for the arrowhead or sagittaria. This was the wild potato, a valuable article of Indian food. There have been several forms of this native word, now generally spelled wapato. N. J. Wyeth built Fort William on this island in 1834-35 and some early maps have the name Wyeth Island. Wilkes used the name Multnomah Island. The name Sauvie Island comes from a French-Canadian employee of the Hudson's Bay Company who worked at the dairy farm on the west side of the island. The lettering Sauvies Island appears on Preston's *Map of Oregon*, 1856. Bancroft's *History of the Northwest Coast*, volume II, page 599, is authority for the statement that the island was named for one Jean Baptiste Sauve, but information has transpired that indicates this statement is wrong. In the files of the Oregon Historical Society is a letter from George B. Roberts to Mrs. F. F. Victor, dated November 7, 1879, in which he says that Sauve Island bears the name of a Canadian, Laurent Sauve, also called LaPlante. Many of the French-Canadians were known by two names. Mrs. Victor was one of the authors of Bancroft's history. The parish register of Saint James Catholic Church, Vancouver, has the marriage of Laurent Sauve to Josephte (Indian) on February 11, 1839, and records that Sauve was from the district of Montreal. The burial of Laurent Sauve is entered in the parish register of Saint Paul Catholic Church on August 3, 1858. In these registers the name of Laurent Sauve occurs a number of times, as godfather or burial witness. The name of Jean Baptiste Sauve does not occur at all. George B. Roberts came to Fort Vancouver in the service of the Hudson's Bay Company in 1831 and knew well the employees of the company. It may be inferred that Mrs. Victor erred in transcribing Roberts' letter. The USBGN has adopted the style Sauvie Island rather than the possessive Sauvies Island. It is interesting to note the following in a letter from Roberts to Mrs. Victor on July 5, 1882: "We say Sauvie (an old Canadian), not Sauvies—Puget, not Pugets, as we say Washington and not Washington's Territory."

Sauvies, Multnomah County. A post office named Sauvies was established in the extreme northwest corner of Multnomah County on April 3, 1882, with J. L. Reeder postmaster. This office was on the west bank of Columbia River and on the east shore of Sauvie Island, at Reeder Point, and it was of course named for the island. Reeder ran the office until it was closed April 6, 1906. Omar C. Spencer has informed the compiler that mail was brought to this and other Columbia River post offices by boat.

Savage Creek, Jackson and Josephine counties. This creek, together with Little Savage Creek in Jackson County, and Savage Rapids in Rogue River in Josephine County, were named for a pioneer settler, and not for Indians. James Savage came to Oregon from Illinois in 1853, and took up a donation land claim near the geographic features that now bear his name.

Savage School, Benton County. This school, north of Corvallis near Soap Creek, was named for Morgan R. Savage who once owned a donation land claim nearby. See land office certificate 2326.

Sawmill Canyon, Morrow County. When Heppner was being built in the 1870s, the closest lumber came from Van Armen's mill located where this canyon opens into Little Butter Creek east of Freezeout Ridge. In common with most Mill Creeks, all that now remains is the name.

Sawyer Bar, Lane County. The Pacific Crest Trail crosses the outfall of

Collier Glacier two miles northwest of the North Sister. Ray Engels of the USFS named this creek crossing Sawyer Bar in honor of Robert W. Sawyer of Bend. Sawyer had a great love for the outdoors and a tremendous knowledge of the geography and history of the Cascade Range. For additional information see under Robert W. Sawyer State Park.

Scappoose, Columbia County. Scappoose post office was established April 25, 1872. The name is of Indian origin and is said to mean gravelly plain. In addition to being used for the post office the name is also used for a well-known stream nearby, which drains the southern part of Columbia County. This stream is composed of two main branches, the correct names of which are North Scappoose Creek and South Scappoose Creek. "The History of Scappoose" is the title of an article in the Rainier *Review,* October 23, 1931, which says among other things that the Scappoose post office of 1872 was at what is now known as Johnson Landing. It was moved to the present community about 1886. Samuel T. Gosa was the first postmaster of the Scappoose post office. Records of this office are confusing. It may have been in operation previously for a short time with the name Columbia. Gosa was also postmaster of the Columbia office.

Scaredman Creek, Douglas County. Scaredman Creek flows into Canton Creek about three miles north of North Umpqua River. USFS ranger Fred Asam stated that the name came from Scaredman Camp near the headwaters. A group of hunters had camped at this spot in the days when wolves were still plentiful in the mountains. The nocturnal howlings so disturbed the nimrods that at daybreak they hastily packed and departed to more civilized surroundings.

Schaff, Marion County. This was a railroad station two miles south of Aumsville. It was named for Walter Schaff who owned the land on which the station was built.

Schieffelin Gulch, Jackson County. This draw is about a mile and a half southeast of the town of Rogue River and south of the river. It is named for the Schieffelin family who took a donation land claim nearby. The spelling Shefflein is incorrect.

Scholfield Creek, Douglas County. This is an important tributary of the Umpqua River at Reedsport. It was named for Socrates Scholfield, a member of the party that came to the Umpqua River in 1850 in the schooner *Samuel Roberts,* and founded Umpqua City. He was the son of Nathan Scholfield of Norwich, Conn. There is a discrepancy in the way the name is spelled by Bancroft in his *History of Oregon,* volume II, page 176, and in *OHQ,* volume XVII, page 341. Bancroft uses the form Schofield, but Scholfield himself uses the style with a second "l." Scholfield family papers and letters at the Oregon State Library all confirm the spelling here used. Nathan Scholfield was one of the leaders of the party, and it is not clear why the stream was named for the son rather than the father, although Bancroft says such was the case. Possibly some incident of the exploration connected the name of the younger man with the stream. Attention is called to the fact that there is a discrepancy in the name of the schooner, the form *William Roberts* sometimes being used. However, the contemporaneous newspaper accounts, marine records, and George Davidson of the

USC&GS all use the form *Samuel Roberts*, and it may be assumed that that style is correct.

Scholls, Washington County. Scholls, Scholls Ferry and Scholls Ferry Road are all well-known geographic names in the Tualatin Valley. These features were named for Peter Scholl, a pioneer of 1847, who took up a donation claim nearby. In early days Scholls Ferry was one of the important crossings of the Tualatin River. Peter Scholl was born in Kentucky October 20, 1809. He was related to the family of Daniel Boone. He died in Portland in November, 1872. For information about Peter Scholl, see OPA *Transactions*, 1887, page 80. Scholls Ferry post office was established September 12, 1871, with J. R. Bennett first postmaster. The name was changed to Scholls on February 2, 1895, and the office was discontinued in November, 1905.

School Creek, Lane County. A. J. Briem, in his notes on file at the OHS, says that when the railroad was built up the Middle Fork Willamette River in 1909, the old Eula School was torn down to clear the right of way. The USFS then gave a permit to build a new school on government land alongside what at once became known as School Creek.

School Section Cabin, Wheeler County. School Section Cabin is appropriately located in section 16, township 10 south, range 22 east, some ten miles north of Mitchell. This application of "School Section" applies to a number of features and originated with one of the earliest grants of public lands by the Federal Government to the State. The Oregon Territorial Act of 1848 provided that sections 16 and 36 of each township were to be reserved to the Territory for the support of common schools. Where these sections were already occupied by donation land claim or other valid possession, an equivalent area of "lieu land" could be selected from other Federal lands. This grant totaled 3,457,340 acres the bulk of which were sold prior to 1910. For an excellent and concise report on this and other land laws, see *The Disposition of the Public Domain in Oregon*, Jerry A. O'Callaghan, a doctoral dissertation printed for the U.S. Senate Committee on Interior and Insular Affairs, Government Printing Office, 1960.

Schoolmarm Spring, Wasco County. Schoolmarm Spring is on Mill Creek Ridge southwest of The Dalles. It was not named for a popular pedagogue but for a forked tree or *schoolmarm* in logger's parlance. There is also a Schoolmaam Creek in Jackson County west of Prospect.

Schooner Creek, Lincoln County. Schooner Creek is a well-known stream that flows into Siletz Bay just south of Taft. In 1945 Andrew L. Porter of Newport told the compiler that the stream was named for a schooner that came in over Siletz Bar about 1890 and ran aground on the rocks on the east side of the bay just south of the creek. Mr. Porter reported that some of the ship's ribs were still showing above the sand at low tide. Mr. Porter also said that he understood that about 1894 the ship's bell was taken to Grand Ronde and used at the Indian school.

Schooner Creek, Lincoln County. This paragraph refers to a stream called Schooner Creek that flows into Pacific Ocean about a mile north of Yaquina Head. The stream was named for a small schooner that came ashore on the beach near the creek about 1890. The writer has not been able to identify this vessel and little is known of her except that she was about 50 feet long. The schooner was hauled above high tide by means of oxen and tackle and in 1944 it was reported that some of her remains were on the ground. A small point of rocks about a quarter of a mile north of the mouth of the creek is called Schooner Point.

Schott Canyon, Gilliam County. Schott Canyon is southwest of Condon. It was named for Conrad Schott, a pioneer settler.

Schreiner Peak, Clackamas County. Schreiner Peak, elevation 5678 feet, is a point in the Cascade Range near the headwaters of Collawash River. It was formerly called Pikes Peak, a name without local significance, but in 1935 the USFS recommended that the name be changed to Schreiner Peak in honor of the late Professor Fred J. Schreiner, a member of the faculty at Oregon State University. Beside being held in public esteem, Professor Schreiner had spent much time in the Mount Hood National Forest in the vicinity of the peak carrying on surveys for fire control. The USBGN adopted the name Schreiner Peak March 29, 1935.

Schweitzer Creek, Lane County. This creek flows northeast from Hardesty Mountain. It is named for homesteader Jacob Schweitzer who settled near its mouth in the early 1900s.

Scio, Linn County. Scio was named for Scio, Ohio, which was in turn named for Scio, or as it is also known, Chios, an island off the west coast of Turkey in Asia. Mrs. C. A. Davis of Turner told the writer that Henry L. Turner and William McKinney built the flour mill at Scio, and when the work was completed, Turner suggested that McKinney give the new community a name. McKinney chose the name of his former home in Ohio. Another version of the story is to the effect that Mrs. McKinney really chose the name. Having been married, the compiler inclines toward the latter tradition. Scio post office was established October 3, 1860, with Euphronius E. Wheeler first postmaster. See also under Santiam.

Scissors Creek, Crook County. The writer has had several requests for information about the origin of the name Scissors Creek for a stream east of Prineville, flowing into Ochoco Creek. So far no data about this odd name have come to light. A map of 1889 shows a place called Scissorsville near this stream, with the probability that it was a mining locality.

Scoggins Creek, Washington County. Scoggins Creek was named for Gustavus Scoggin, a pioneer settler. The use of the terminal "s" without the possessive was so prevalent that the USBGN adopted the present form in *Decision List 6402*.

Scorpion Mountain, Marion County. According to Dee Wright of Eugene, this mountain received its name at the time the USFS trail was built nearby, because there were so many small wood scorpions in the rotting logs that were moved.

Scotch Creek, Wallowa County. Scotch Creek is west of Joseph. It was named by Mat Inglehorn, who was a Scotsman, in the 1870s. He and his brother had a homestead on the stream.

Scott Butte, Wheeler County. Scott Butte is east of Girds Creek and is 4304 feet high. It bears the name of Raleigh E. Scott who came from Tennessee and settled here before the turn of the century. Scott called his ranch "Fairview".

Scott Canyon, Sherman County. Owen, Elihu and John Scott were the sons of Polly Scott, a widow who homesteaded the upper reaches of this canyon near Rufus. The Scott brothers were among the earliest wheat farmers in what is now Sherman County.

Scott Creek, Curry County. Raleigh Scott settled on this creek east of Carpenterville in 1882. Although there was no established community, he operated a store and trading post for residents of the area.

Scott Mountain, Douglas County. This peak was originally known as Scotts Point, but nearby settlers changed the name to Scott Mountain. It is about 4300 feet in elevation and is clearly seen from the neighborhood of Sutherlin. It was named for Captain Levi Scott, the founder of Scottsburg. See under that name.

Scott Mountain, Lane County. This peak is in the Cascade Range west of McKenzie Pass. Scott Lake is nearby. These two geographic features were named for Felix Scott, the younger, who was one of the promoters of the McKenzie toll road project. See Hodge's *Mount Multnomah* for information on the subject. Felix Scott was the brother of Mrs. John E. Lyle, a pioneer resident of Dallas. This Scott family was not related to that of Captain Levi Scott of Scottsburg. About a mile east of the summit of the Cascade Range is Scott Pass, in Deschutes County. It is a gap in the ridge between Black Crater and North Sister. Scott Trail goes through Scott Pass. These two features were also named for Felix Scott.

Scott Spring, Umatilla County. In 1895 William Scott took up land near this spring in township 5 south, range 33 east.

Scotts Mills, Marion County. Robert Hall Scott and Thomas Scott had a sawmill and a flour mill at this place in early days, and the settlement was named Scotts Mills about 1866. The post office was established November 1, 1887, with Thomas Scott first postmaster.

Scottsburg, Douglas County. Scottsburg was founded in 1850 by Levi Scott, a pioneer of Oregon of 1844, from Iowa. Scott led the party that went into southern Oregon and thence to Fort Hall in 1846, locating the southern or Applegate route. Scottsburg became the metropolis of southern Oregon, but the establishment of Crescent City in California in 1852, and other diversions of transportation, caused the decline of the community. Scott was a member of the territorial council from 1852 to 1854, and of the constitutional convention in 1857. He died in Malheur County in 1890, aged 93 years. Mount Scott in Crater Lake National Park was named in his honor. For detailed information about the Scott family, see editorial page, *Oregon Journal,* November 25, 26, 27, 1926. Copies of Scott family records in the possession of the compiler do not substantiate the statement that Levi Scott died in Lane County in 1878. Historical information about Scottsburg is contained in an article in *Oregon Journal,* Portland, for May 21, 1939, compiled by Ben Maxwell. There appear to have been two parts to the community, separated by about a mile of river, and Lower Scottsburg was the port of entry. The big flood of 1861 is the important event in the history of the place, and is said to have obliterated Lower Scottsburg. The names Myrtle City and Scottsburg seem to have been applied to this locality at first, but whether they were for the separate places the compiler cannot determine. The early history of the post offices is confusing. Myrtle City post office was established June 30, 1851, with Levi Scott postmaster. It was discontinued July 27, 1852. In the meantime Scottsburg post office was established October 8, 1851, with Stephen F. Chadwick postmaster. Eugene R. Fisk became postmaster October 12, 1852. Preston's map of 1851 shows Myrtle City just east of and very close to Scottsburg. A place called Gagniersville is shown just east of Myrtle City, but Scottsburg is the only one of the three shown on Preston's map of 1856. The other two places did not persist. Postal records are not consistent about the name Scottsburg, and in a number of instances the spelling is Scottsburgh, but the public generally has used the style Scottsburg and that is the official spelling at present.

Scotty Creek, Grant County. This creek, south of Mount Vernon, was named for a pioneer sheep man, Scotty Hay, who had a camp and cabin on the stream. Scotti is incorrect.

Scout Lake, Hood River County. After the Boy Scout camp was built at Wahtum Lake about 1918, many of the young campers would hike to this small lake about one half mile south for undisturbed fishing or swimming. The name Scout Lake became fixed by association although the Boy Scout camp was always at Wahtum Lake.

Scout Lake, Marion County. This is one of the larger lakes in Jefferson Park. It was named in August, 1931 by a group of Boy Scouts from Troop #20, Albany, who camped by it for several days. Before they left they marked "Scout Lake" with a heavy pencil on a split limb pointer and wedged it into a tree alongside the Skyline Trail. On a subsequent trip they found the pencil markings unreadable so the words were carved into the limb. This troop was redesignated Troop #21 in December, 1931.

Seaforth, Curry County. Seaforth post office was established November 12, 1890, with Robert McKenzie postmaster. The office was closed March 8, 1892, and mail sent to Port Orford. According to Dodge in his *Pioneer History of Coos and Curry Counties,* appendix page 66, McKenzie lived on a large farm near the mouth of Elk River and it may be assumed that was the site of the post office Seaforth. Dodge gives a short biography of McKenzie on the page indicated. Members of the Mackenzie family have at various times been the earls of Seaforth in Scotland and the Mackenzies and McKenzies have a strong sentimental interest in the Scottish name.

Seal Rocks, Lincoln County. These form a ledge of partly submerged rocks extending parallel to the coast for about two miles and a half and a distance of half a mile from the beach. The highest rock rises about twenty feet above water. The *Coast Pilot* uses the name Seal Rocks, and that was the style used in pioneer days for the locality along the shore about ten miles south of Newport. There is one large rock at the shoreline and several smaller ones. The place was called Seal Illahe, Chinook jargon for seal place or seal home. The post office, which is on the Oregon Coast Highway, is named for the rocks, but is called Seal Rock. This form of name is not completely descriptive and seems to refer only to the large rock at the shoreline. The post office was established April 25, 1890, with J. W. Brasfield postmaster. In those days the rocks were well covered with seals and sea lions.

Seaside, Clatsop County. Silas B. Smith, in *OHQ,* volume I, page 321, says that the Clatsop Indian village at the site of what is now Seaside was called *Ne-co-tat*. The name Seaside came from Ben Holladay's famous hostelry and resort, the Seaside House. The first post office in the locality seems to have been Summer House, established December 1, 1871, with A. J. Clontire first postmaster. The name was changed to Seaside House on July 23, 1873, with Charles H. Dexter postmaster. The name was changed to Seaside on March 29, 1882. The old Seaside House was about a mile south of the present business section of Seaside. Seaside was at one time divided into two municipalities, east and west of the Necanicum, but they are now consolidated. Lewis and Clark sent a detail of men who established a salt-making cairn at the present site of Seaside about January 1, 1806. This site is now a detached section of Fort Clatsop National Monument. For a description of the cairn in 1899, see the *Oregonian*, August 19, 1899, page 8. For narrative of Lewis and Clark expedition to the salt cairn, by L. B. Cox, *ibid.*, June 17, 1900, page 8.

Seaton, Lane County. Seaton was an early-day post office in western Lane County, a little to the north of what was later Mapleton. Seaton office was established November 13, 1885, with William W. Neely first postmaster. The name Seaton was suggested by a Mr. Anthony, in compliment to a place in England called Seaton. There are several places in England called Seaton and the compiler has no means of knowing which one Mr. Anthony had in mind in 1885. Mrs. Julia A. Bean was appointed postmaster at Seaton April 1, 1889, and the name of the office was changed to Mapleton on March 26, 1896. It is believed that the office was moved to the present site of Mapleton in 1889, seven years before the name was changed.

Second Lake, Linn County. Second Lake is the name applied to the second of a series of four lakes on the east bank of Willamette River northeast of Albany, and it is so named because of the position it occupies.

Seekseequa Creek, Jefferson County. Seekseequa Creek is a tributary of Deschutes River and drains the south part of the Warm Springs Indian Reservation. Indians have informed the compiler that the word is from the Piute language and means a variety of coarse rye grass that grows near the stream. The spelling *Psuc-see-que* is used in Pacific Railroad Surveys *Reports*, volume VI, and there are several other forms. The USBGN originally adopted the form Seekseekwa but this was altered to the present spelling in *Decision List 6302*.

Seeley Creek, Douglas County. Seeley Creek is a small stream flowing eastward under the Territorial road and into Pheasant Creek in section 19, township 21 south, range 4 west. This creek or brook flows through the ranch of Mr. and Mrs. Ernest J. Martin, which lies a few miles north of Anlauf and south of Lorane. Seeley Creek was named to commemorate Seeley Douglas Martin, a young son of Mr. and Mrs. Martin. Seeley was a seaman first class in the United States Navy, reported missing in action May 23, 1942, while on duty in the Pacific area in the Midway campaign. He was a graduate of the Navy Communications School at San Diego. The application of the name Seeley Creek was approved April 12, 1947, by the Douglas County court and shortly thereafter the USBGN approved the selection.

Seghers, Washington County. Seghers is a station on the Southern

Pacific line north of Gaston. It was named for the Most Rev. Charles Seghers, Catholic archbishop of Oregon in the early 1880s, who was murdered in Alaska in 1886. See *Catholic History of Oregon,* page 152 *et seq.* Seghers post office was established June 21, 1898, with Augustine A. Roth postmaster. The office was closed June 14, 1924.

Selah, Marion County. This station was on the Southern Pacific Company Springfield branch west of Silverton. *Selah* is a Hebrew term meaning to pause, and is used as a place name to indicate a place of rest.

Sellwood, Multnomah County. This part of the city of Portland was named for the Rev. John Sellwood. The name was first applied about 1882, and the post office was established in October, 1883. Sellwood was taken into the city of Portland in 1893.

Selma, Josephine County. Selma post office was established by change of name from Anderson on July 10, 1897. When the name of the Anderson office was changed to Selma the office was moved south a few miles. The first postmaster at the new office was Robert C. Churchill. Mrs. Churchill selected the name Selma in honor of the little town Selma, in Van Buren County, Iowa, near where she was raised.

Seneca, Grant County. This post office was named for Judge Seneca Smith of Portland. The name was given by Minnie Southworth, the first postmaster. The office was established September 17, 1895. Postal authorities wanted a short name, and the word Seneca suggested itself to Mrs. Southworth because her sister-in-law was Mrs. Seneca Smith.

Senecal Spring, Hood River County. This spring near Lookout Mountain was named for John Batiste Senecal who was USFS ranger in Dufur from 1895 to 1913. He was commonly called Batt and at one time ran horses in the meadow near Red Hill that now bears his nickname. Senecal's father, Gideon, came to Oregon in 1840 with the Hudson's Bay Company and subsequently took a donation land claim near Champoeg. He later moved to eastern Oregon and left a substantial family in Wasco and Crook counties.

Senoj Lake, Deschutes County. Senoj Lake is near the summit of the Cascade Range and about four miles west of Lava Lake. The name is in compliment to some person called Jones, with the spelling reversed.

Sentinel Peak, Clackamas and Hood River counties. R. S. Shelley of the USFS named this peak for its commanding position overlooking West Fork Hood River. According to Ralph Lewis who was with him, this took place in July 1906.

Sepanek, Morrow County. Sepanek post office was established August 2, 1917, with Bertha Sepanek first and only postmaster. The office, which was obviously named with the postmaster's family name, was closed September 14, 1918. It was about six miles northeast of Lexington, in the southwest part of township 1 north, range 26 east.

Separation Creek, Lane County. Separation Creek heads west of the South Sister, and flows westward, its waters eventually reaching McKenzie River. The creek was so named because it flows between The Husband and The Wife, two lesser peaks, west of the summit of the Cascade Range and members of the Three Sisters group.

Serrano Point, Harney County. Serrano Point is between Alvord Desert and Alvord Lake, on the west side of Alvord Valley. *Serrano* is Spanish for mountaineer or highlander.

Service Buttes, Umatilla County. Service Buttes, which lie about eight miles southwest of Echo, have an extreme elevation of 1685 feet. Service Canyon is southwest of the buttes, and Service Springs to the north. These features are named for the serviceberry, otherwise called shadbush or Juneberry. The bush is of the *Amelanchier* family. The name is probably the most mispronounced botanical word in the West, the uneducated invariably making it sarvis berry.

Service Creek, Wheeler County. This is the name of a post office near the mouth of Service Creek, a tributary of John Day River. The creek was formerly called Sarvis Creek, spelled as pronounced colloquially. The post office was established on May 23, 1918, with the name Sarvicecreek and with May Tilley first postmaster. At the request of the compiler of these notes the name was changed to Servicecreek on December 4, 1918. The 1941 *Postal Guide* lists the office as Service Creek, the change to two words having taken place early in 1929. The post office was not operating in 1980.

Serviceberry Camp, Douglas County. This out of the way spot in township 30 south, range 1 east, was named by Durk Van Dike, a USFS employee and part time trapper in the early days, apparently for the abundance of serviceberries or *Amelanchier florida*.

Seufert, Wasco County. Seufert station is east of The Dalles. It bears the name of the two Seufert brothers, Frank A. and Theodore J. They were natives of New York, and came to Oregon in the early 1880s. They were engaged in various branches of the packing business, principally of salmon and fruit. For biography of Theodore J. Seufert, see *History of Central Oregon*, page 327.

Seven Devils, Coos County. In describing the coast south of Cape Arago, George Davidson in the *Coast Pilot* of 1889 says: "The hills are covered with dense forests and underbrush, and are cut by deep ravines running at right angles to the shore-line. From the number of these ravines the coast is locally known as 'the *Seven Devils*'." R. R. Monbeck of the USGS furnished the compiler with information about this name in 1943 and it seems apparent that the name Seven Devils was originally applied because of the difficulty in cutting the coast trail across these ravines. The earliest mention of these ravines that the compiler has seen is in the Harrison G. Rogers journal in *The Ashley-Smith Explorations* on July 4, 1828: "The travelling pretty bad, as we were obliged to cross the low hills, as they came in close to the beach, and the beach being so bad that we could not get along, thicketty and timbered, and some very bad ravines to cross."

Sevenmile Creek, Coos County. Sevenmile Creek flows into Coquille River about seven miles upstream from the river's mouth and is so named on that account.

Sexton Mountain, Josephine County. This mountain is a prominent peak north of Grants Pass and Interstate 5 crosses its western flank at an elevation of 1960 feet. It takes its name from a family of early settlers. William M. Colvig of Medford wrote the compiler on July 1, 1927, as follows: "In about the year 1853 a widow by the name of Niday settled on a location at the foot of the mountain. She kept a wayside tavern on the road and travelers were delighted to enjoy the restful hospitality of the place. In the 1850s she married David Sexton and the stopping place became known as Sextons. Their son Charles Sexton now lives there." Later investigation shows that Hiram and Caroline Niday took a donation land claim in what is now section 40, township 34 south, range 6 west. Hiram Niday died in March 1856, and David Sexton came to this spot in Pleasant Valley, presumably, shortly thereafter.

Sexton Mountain, Washington County. Edward S. Sexton was born in Ohio in 1822, and settled on land southwest of what is now Beaverton in the spring of 1853. Sexton Mountain was named for him. It is erroneously spelled Saxton on some maps.

Shady Cove, Jackson County. Shady Cove is on Rogue River between two and three miles south of Trail. The post office is on the Crater Lake Highway near the concrete bridge which carries the highway over the river, but the cove itself is up river a few hundred yards and on the southeast side of the stream. The name is descriptive of a little nook on the river bank, but is not particularly applicable to the locality of the post office and the highway bridge. Shady Cove post office was established in September, 1939, with Mrs. Lillian F. Hukill postmaster. The compiler has been informed that the name Shady Cove was applied to the place upstream from the post office some years before the office was established, by one J. Powell of Medford.

Shamrock Creek, Wallowa County. Shamrock Creek and Shamrock Flat are near Flora. These features are said to have been named by some soldiers who crossed the Grande Ronde River at Hanson Ferry from Walla Walla about 1885 or 1886. These soldiers had difficulty in fording the river and lost part of their equipment. After traveling near Bear Creek and Buford Creek they camped on a small flat at the head of what is now known as Shamrock Creek. When they left they painted a sign on a tree with a shamrock on it, and the flat has been known by that name ever since.

Shanahan Place, Lake County. Shanahan Place on the west edge of Antelope Flat was the homestead of Tom Shanahan. He settled there after World War I.

Shaniko, Wasco County. Shaniko was named for pioneer settler, August Scherneckau. Scherneckau came to Oregon after the Civil War and bought a farm near the present site of Shaniko. Indians pronounced the name Shaniko, and that is how the locality got its name. The Scherneckau ranch was on the stage route from The Dalles to central Oregon and August Scherneckau opened a stage station and kept the travel. Scherneckau some years later moved to Astoria, and after residing there several years moved to California, where he died. This locality was first called Cross Hollows, and a post office with that name was established May 23, 1879, with Scherneckau first postmaster. The office was closed May 27, 1887. The words Cross Hollows were descriptive of the local topography. Shaniko post office was established March 31, 1900, with John D. Wilcox first postmaster. For additional information about Shaniko, see Bend *Bulle-*

tin, September 24, 1930, and for story about early days in Shaniko by Giles L. French, see news section of the *Oregonian,* December 12, 1943.

Sharps Creek, Lane County. This stream was named for a well-known pioneer character, James H. "Bohemia" Sharp. He was an early prospector and road builder. For an interesting account of some of his activities see the Cottage Grove *Sentinel,* July 13, 1967.

Shasta Costa Creek, Curry County. Shasta Costa Creek is a tributary of Rogue River. It bears the name of the *Shas-te-koos-tee* Indians. Orvil Dodge spells the name of the Indian tribe in this manner and says that it numbered about 145 in 1854. The name of the creek does not seem to have anything to do with either Mount Shasta or the Spanish word *costa* meaning coast, but is merely the white man's convenient method of writing the Indian name. The *Handbook of American Indians* lists the tribe or band as the *Chastocosta,* part of the Tututni Indians, in volume II, page 857.

Shasta Gulch, Malheur County. Shasta Gulch is in the extreme north end of Malheur County, and drains south into Willow Creek. This gulch was named in the gold rush of the 1860s by miners from the Shasta region of northern California.

Shattuck, Multnomah County. Erasmus D. Shattuck was one of the foremost jurists of Oregon. He came to Oregon in 1853 from New York, and conducted the Oregon City College and the Clackamas County Female Seminary in 1853-55. He served at Pacific University as professor of ancient languages, beginning in 1855, and was elected superintendent of schools for Washington County in 1855, and probate judge for the same county in 1856. In 1857 he was a member of the constitutional convention, and, in 1858, a member of the territorial legislature; in 1862-67 he was supreme and circuit judge; in 1874-78 he was judge of the supreme court; in 1886 he was elected to the circuit court, and served until 1898. He also served in the Portland city council and on the school board of Portland. Judge Shattuck was born at Bakersfield, Vermont, December 31, 1824; died at Portland July 26, 1900. See various estimates of his work and character in the *Oregonian,* July 6, 1898. For tributes to him in 1896, *ibid.,* January 1, 1896. Judge Shattuck owned a farm on the Southern Pacific about two miles west of Hillsboro, and the station at the crossing with the Shattuck Road was named for him.

Shaw, Marion County. This is a station east of Salem. It was named for Angus Shaw. Shaw came to Oregon from Ontario, Canada, and bought a farm near the present site of Shaw in 1876.

Shaw Stewart Ditch, Baker County. Daniel Shaw filed on government land in Bowen Valley on January 11, 1875.

Sheaville, Malheur County. Sheaville is in the cattle country on the extreme east edge of the county and just about midway north and south. It was named for Con Shea, a pioneer stockman. Sheaville post office was first established November 3, 1887, with Morris Oberdorfer first postmaster. The office was not in continuous operation and was closed permanently prior to 1980.

Shedd, Linn County. A post office near the place now known as Shedd was established with the name Boston Mills, on September 22, 1869, with

William Simmons first postmaster. The name of the office was changed to Shedd on August 28, 1871, at the time when the railroad was being built south from Albany. The new name came from Captain Frank Shedd, upon whose land the community was started. For a time the place was called Shedds, but that form has passed into oblivion. For information about the Shedd family, see editorial page of the *Oregon Journal,* October 18, 1930.

Sheep Rock, Grant County. Sheep Rock is in the south part of Butler Basin, north of Picture Gorge. J. E. Snow of Dayville told the writer that this rock was not named because of any fancied resemblance to a ram's head, but because of the prevalence of mountain sheep nearby in pioneer days. The rock has an elevation of 3360 feet. See editorial page the *Oregonian,* December 10, 1925. There is another Sheep Rock in Grant County about 7 miles south of John Day. It is between US 395 and Strawberry Mountain and has an elevation of 6400 feet.

Sheep Rock, Jefferson County. This Sheep Rock is west of Trout Creek near the Maupin Cemetery. It is so called because from certain angles it resembles the head of a sheep.

Sheepshead Mountains, Malheur County. These mountains separate Wildhorse Valley east of Steens Mountains from Owyhee River. In the early days they were the haunts of large bands of rimrock sheep, *Ovis canadensis californiana,* that ranged most of eastern Oregon. In the 1880s domestic sheep entered this range and infected the wild animals with "sheep scab". This quickly exterminated the bighorns and the mountains were named because for many years thereafter large numbers of horned skulls were scattered throughout the area. Vernon Bailey in *Mammals and Life Zones of Oregon* describes this fine animal and its unfortunate demise.

Sheet Iron Jack Creek, Wheeler County. The compiler was told by Mrs. Lily Collins of the Fopiano Ranch that many years ago an early settler named Jack built a cabin covered with sheet iron in the meadow where this creek heads northwest of Waterman.

Shelburn, Linn County. In April, 1927, the postmaster at Shelburn wrote the compiler that the name Shelburn was supposed to be a combination of parts of the names of two pioneer residents, Shelton and Washburn. Riley Shelton of Scio, in 1927, confirmed the statement and told the compiler that the name was made up by Rosa and Mary Miller.

Sheldon Ridge, Wasco County. Joseph L. Sheldon settled on this ridge east of Mosier Creek in 1910.

Shell Rock, Hood River County. A post office with the name Shell Rock was established on the Wasco County list April 14, 1873, with David Graham postmaster. This office was in what is now Hood River County and was in the vicinity of Shellrock Mountain on the south bank of the Columbia River between Cascade Locks and Hood River. The office was of course named for the mountain. Shell Rock post office later was moved north across the Columbia River into Washington Territory and the name changed to Collins Landing, but the compiler cannot tell when. Shell Rock post office was in operation again on the Oregon side between May 20 and August 19, 1878, with John Cates postmaster. John Cates, of a well-known Wasco County family, operated a sawmill at a point a couple of miles west of the present site of Wyeth. The post office was apparently reestablished to serve people connected with the Cates mill. It was about three miles west of Shellrock Mountain, but named for that feature nevertheless.

Shellrock Creek, Clackamas County. Shellrock Creek, which takes its rise in Shellrock Lake, is in the east part of the county. It flows into Oak Grove Fork Clackamas River. The lake and stream were so named because they were near Shellrock Mountain, which had shale slides on its slopes. Several years ago the name of this mountain was changed by the government to Frazier Mountain because there were too many other Shellrock mountains in the state, but the name of the lake and creek remained as before because there was no duplication.

Shellrock Mountain, Hood River County. Mountains of this name are so called because the rock of which they are composed breaks off in platy chunks and piles up in long slopes, like shelled corn. There are several Shellrock mountains in Oregon, the best known being on the Columbia River Highway east of Cascade Locks.

Shepperds Dell, Multnomah County. This dell on the Columbia River Scenic Highway just west of Bridal Veil was presented to the public in May, 1915, by George Shepperd, as a memorial to his wife. The tract consists of eleven acres. The creek is spanned by a fine concrete arch about 100 feet long.

Sherar Burn, Clackamas County. This clear area north of Salmon River about five miles west of Salmon River Meadows was burned over by one of the big fires of the middle 19th century. It went to grass and Joseph Sherar grazed sheep there before it became National Forest. For a biography of Sherar see under Sherars Bridge.

Sherars Bridge, Wasco County. Peter Skene Ogden took an exploring party into central Oregon in 1826-27, and on Thursday, September 22, 1826, he noted in his journal that his party reached the River of the Falls [Deschutes] at the "Falls where we found an Indian camp of 20 families. Finding a canoe, also a bridge made of slender wood, we began crossing, 5 horses were lost thro' the bridge." See *OHQ,* volume XI, page 205. Apparently in pioneer times there was no bridge at the present site of Sherars Bridge, for Bancroft, in his *History of Oregon,* volume I, page 787, says that it had to be forded or crossed in Indian canoes. John Y. Todd built a bridge in 1860, but it was carried away and had to be rebuilt in 1862. For Todd's reminiscences, see *OHQ,* volume XXX, page 70. Todd later took in Ezra L. Hemingway and Robert Mays as partners. Hemingway bought out the other two, and then sold to O'Brien, who sold out to Joseph Sherar in 1871. Sherar was a prominent character in central Oregon. He was born in Vermont on November 16, 1833, of Irish parentage, and was reared in St. Lawrence County, New York. He came by sea to California in 1855. He mined in northern California, and in 1862 he started with passengers and freight by pack train to the John Day mines, and on this trip his party named Antelope Valley, Muddy Creek, Cherry Creek and Burnt Ranch, and laid the foundation for Bakeoven. Sherar married Jane A. Herbert in 1863 and settled in Wasco County. He paid $7040 for Sherars Bridge and spent $75,000 improving roads leading to it. He was interested in various milling enterprises on White River and kept a stage station at the bridge which bears his name. He died at The Dalles on February 11, 1908. Apparently there was a post office at this locality as early as 1868 with the name Deschutes. See under that heading.

Sheridan, Yamhill County. Sheridan is on the South Yamhill River and was named for Philip Henry Sheridan, who as lieutenant, did efficient and courageous work against the Indians at the Cascades in 1856. He arrived at Fort Vancouver in October, 1855, from California, and remained in Oregon and Washington until the outbreak of the Civil War. In April, 1856, he was ordered to Grand Ronde Agency, and was stationed not far from the town that now bears his name. He was stationed at Fort Hoskins in 1857, fourteen miles from Corvallis, as quartermaster and commissary. He went east in September, 1861, and as a result of his great work in the Civil War was made lieutenant-general in 1869, and general before he died, August 5, 1888. He visited Portland, Salem and Yamhill County in 1875; arrived at Portland August 31; left for California September 8. See his *Memoirs* for narrative of the Yakima War; also the *Oregonian*, December 9, 1888, December 23, 1888. Sheridan post office was established April 4, 1866, by change of name from Willamina, with Thomas N. Faulconer postmaster. The office had been serving an area a few miles west of Sheridan, and was moved eastward to the new location. Another office was established for Willamina in August, 1878.

Sheridan Mountain, Deschutes County. Sheridan Mountain, elevation 6948 feet, is a prominent point in a string of craters that extends south from Bachelor Butte. It is about five miles from Bachelor Butte and the same distance from Lava Lake. It was formerly called Tent Mountain, because of its shape when seen from the west, but on March 4, 1931, the USBGN adopted the name Sheridan Mountain, in honor of General Philip H. Sheridan, who, in 1855, as a second lieutenant with the Pacific Railroad Surveys, explored central Oregon. It seems probable that Sheridan ascended this peak on August 30, 1855. See also under Williamson Mountain.

Sherman, Sherman County. This station west of Biggs was once known as Deschutes Junction, because it was at one end of the railroad branch line up Deschutes River. Fred S. Stanley later asked to have the name Deschutes given to a point between Redmond and Bend, and it then became necessary to change the name at the north end of the line. The name Sherman was selected because it was in Sherman County. This was in 1912. In 1930 the name Sherman was changed to Ainsworth, because Sherman duplicated the name of other stations. See under Ainsworth for additional information. The north end of the Deschutes Canyon line was abandoned in 1936 and as a result the junction at Ainsworth was eliminated. There was no station there in 1940.

Sherman County. Sherman County was created February 25, 1889, by the state legislature. It was taken from the northeast part of Wasco County, as that county was then organized, and in 1940 had a land area of 830 square miles. Sherman County was named for General William Tecumseh Sherman, the great northern leader in the Civil War. W. T. Sherman was born at Lancaster, Ohio, February 8, 1820, and graduated from West Point in 1840. He resigned from the army in 1853. He accepted a colonelcy in the

Union army in 1861, and gained rapid promotion on account of his recognized ability. He was made a lieutenant-general in 1866 and general in command of the army in 1869. He died February 14, 1891, at New York City. It was first planned to name this county Fulton County for Colonel James Fulton, a pioneer resident, and the bill providing this name went through two readings in the house of representatives, but before it was passed, the name Fulton was changed to Sherman, at the instigation of J. W. Maxwell of Tillamook and Yamhill counties. It is said that this was done because Colonel Fulton objected to extending an invitation to General Sherman to visit the house of representatives some years previously when General Sherman was a visitor in Oregon. For editorial about naming Sherman County, see the *Oregonian*, November 27, 1942.

Sherod Meadow, Wallowa County. Sherod Meadow is in the northwest corner of township 2 north, range 43 east, and bears the name of William Sherod, who ranged his sheep there in 1887-88.

Sherrard Point, Multnomah County. Sherrard Point was named in honor of Thomas H. Sherrard who was associated with the USFS for more than forty years. It comprises the viewpoint on the northeast extremity of the summit ridge of Larch Mountain and is marked with a bronze plaque. During his tenure with the USFS, Sherrard served as supervisor of the Mount Hood National Forest from 1907 to 1934 and took a keen interest in the development of recreation facilities as well as assisting in the establishment of the Bull Run water preserve. He was born in Brooklyn, Michigan and studied forestry at Yale. After graduate study, he went to Washington, D. C. to be Gifford Pinchot's first assistant. Sherrard died in Portland on January 22, 1941. See the *Oregon Journal*, January 22, 1941 and editorial comment the following day in the same paper.

Sherrill, Lake County. Elmer Sherrill was the first postmaster at Sherrill and the office bore his family name. Sherrill post office was established September 17, 1914, and operated until June 29, 1918. It was situated about 15 miles southwest of Wagontire Mountain.

Sherwood, Washington County. Sherwood was founded and laid out as Smockville by James C. Smock in 1889. The post office was established in that year with George B. Seely first postmaster. The name of the place was changed to Sherwood in the summer of 1891. The new name was adopted at a meeting of the citizens and was suggested by Robert Alexander, and it is supposed he did so because he had formerly lived near Sherwood, Michigan, although there is a local tradition that the name was chosen in compliment to Sherwood Forest, England.

Shevlin, Deschutes and Klamath counties. From time to time Shevlin post office was in the news because of its mobility. It served loggers for The Shevlin-Hixon Company, and when logging was completed for a local area, the camp buildings were put on cars and moved to a new location. Most of the buildings were glorified trailers. When the compiler first knew the camp, it was about ten miles south of Lava Butte and two or three miles east of The Dalles-California Highway. It was later moved to a point about three miles southeast of La Pine. Both of these sites were in Deschutes County. The next move was to Summit Stage Station on the Fremont Highway in the very extreme east border of Klamath County. Shevlin post office was established in Deschutes County June 27, 1931, with William J. Baer first postmaster. It first appears on the Klamath County list in September, 1936. The office was discontinued April 1, 1951, with business transferred to Chemult. For illustrated story about Shevlin, see section 2, *Sunday Oregonian*, June 15, 1947.

Shevlin Park, Deschutes County. This natural park along Tumalo Creek is west of Bend. The land comprising the park was given to the city of Bend by a deed dated December 22, 1920, by The Shevlin-Hixon Company. The idea of setting this land aside for a park originated with T. A. McCann, then general manager of the company at Bend, who had witnessed the cutting over of an entire lumber district in the Middle West, and did not want to see the operation repeated. The park was dedicated to the memory of Thomas H. Shevlin, famous football player and former president of the lumber company.

Shirk, Harney and Lake counties. Members of the Shirk family were among the early settlers in Catlow Valley and for a time lived at the famous Home Creek Ranch. Shirk post office was established at or near this ranch September 22, 1890, with Leonore Mott first postmaster. Frances M. Shirk, the wife of Dave Shirk, was appointed postmaster August 31, 1892. The office was closed to Diamond May 31, 1902. Later some members of the family transferred their ranching operations to eastern Lake County, and Shirk post office was reestablished in that area September 10, 1903, with Olive G. Shirk, a daughter of Dave and Frances, postmaster. The office was closed to Cedarville, California, May 5, 1905.

Shirttail Gulch, Baker County. Shirttail Gulch is north of Rye Valley. J. Tracy Barton, in *OHQ*, volume XLIII, page 228, gives a glowing account of the origin of the name. In 1869, John Richardson, a rancher in Rye Valley, went foraging about five miles for a load of wood. He unhitched his team in a likely spot and began to assemble the load, when suddenly he was surprised by the singing of bullets from the guns of a band of rambling Snake Indians. Richardson abandoned his equipment and ran for home. His speed was so great that his shirttail fanned out behind him and even the jackrabbits were amazed. The place has been called Shirttail Gulch since that episode.

Shitike Creek, Jefferson County. This stream is in the south part of the Warm Springs Indian Reservation. It heads in a magnificent gorge cutting into the Cascade Range north of Jefferson Park. The stream is mentioned in the Pacific Railroad Surveys *Reports,* under date of 1855, as Chit-tike Creek, but the meaning of the name is not given. The Klamath Indians used the name *Sidaikti* to indicate the general locality of the Warm Springs Indian Reservation, and also the stream mentioned above. The compiler has been unable to get a satisfactory translation of the name. Indians indicate that it is a very old locality name.

Shivigny Mountain, Douglas County. Shivigny Mountain is a prominent summit with an elevation of 3782 feet in township 26 south, range 2 west. It is near the confluence of Emile Creek and Little River. Both the mountain and the creek were named for Emile Shivigny, a native of France, who settled nearby about 1875.

Shobe Creek, Morrow County. Shobe Creek is south of Heppner. Allen J. Shobe was educated as a druggist in New Mexico and came to Heppner about 1873. He eventually bought the local drugstore and was universally known as "Doctor" Shobe while he prescribed IXL and other popular remedies of the times. Shobe died in Heppner in 1901 at the age of 81. Shobe Creek watercourse is called Shobe Canyon until just south of Heppner. Here it enters Donaldson Canyon but the name of the creek is unchanged.

Shonquest Ranch, Deschutes County. The name of this pioneer ranch on the old road south of Bend is frequently misspelled.

Shortridge Butte, Lane County. James Shortridge came to Oregon in 1851 and in 1853 with his wife, Amelia, settled on Coast Fork Willamette River near the present Cottage Grove Dam. The butte just to the east bears their name as does a park with an historical marker. Shortridge Creek near London School was named for James' brother, William Wallace Shortridge, who built a sawmill nearby about 1883 and took up a homestead. He was postmaster at the community which was then called Wallace. The form Short Ridge for the creek is incorrect.

Shotpouch Creek, Benton and Lincoln counties. According to Jerry E. Henkle, Benton County pioneer, Shotpouch Creek was named in 1856 when a party of Benton County settlers was exploring the Coast Range looking for grazing land. George Knowlton, a member of the party, lost a shotpouch near the stream, which was named on that account. This story was reported to the compiler in 1937 by Mark Phinny of Philomath, who interviewed Henkle about Benton County history. Shotpouch Creek flows northwest from Marys Peak.

Showalter Creek, Lane County. This stream is in the Mohawk Valley west of Mabel. The creek bears the name of W. B. Showalter, who built a cabin on its banks in early days and operated as a hunter in the locality.

Shroyer Ridge, Benton County. This high ground between Marys and Tumtum rivers was named in 1969 in honor of Oliver J. Shroyer, local teacher and landowner. Shroyer lived there from 1910 until shortly before his death in 1961.

Shuck Mountain, Coos County. Shuck Mountain, a ridge with a maximum elevation of nearly a thousand feet, lies southeast of Coquille in the big bend between Coquille River and North Fork Coquille River. The mountain was named for Samuel Shuck, who came to Oregon in 1863 and settled in Coos County in 1872. See Dodge's *Pioneer History of Coos and Curry Counties,* supplement page 90.

Shutler, Gilliam County. Shutler is a place in Alkali Canyon about eight miles south of Arlington. Shutler Flat is in the same locality. In April, 1947, Mark V. Weatherford of Albany wrote as follows: "Schuttler Flat was named for the Schuttler wagon. The first plowing was done on the flat by W. W. Weatherford and A. H. Weatherford in 1880, and the first crop was raised in 1881. . . . Most of the early settlers moved from Willow Creek to Schuttler Flat and this movement was coincident with the building of the railroad along the Columbia River. Most of them had been cattle men." Peter Schuttler, 1812-1865, a native of Germany, came to the United States in 1834. He learned wagonmaking, and tried several ventures in the business. Finally he established himself in Chicago and supplied many of his wagons to emigrants and gold seekers en route to Oregon and California. His wagon was lighter than the old prairie schooners and easier running. It commanded a premium over other makes, and was widely used in many parts of the West. The compiler does not know the reason for the discrepancy in spelling for the name used in Oregon, except that it was simpler. A post office called Shutlers was established June 5, 1914, with May Piper postmaster. It was apparently named for the nearby railroad station, also called Shutlers. In November, 1915, the name of the post office was changed to Shutler, and the office was discontinued December 14, 1918. The name of the railroad station was changed to Shutler about the same time as the change in the post office name.

Shy Creek, Curry County. Early road surveys show a crossing of this creek on the property of Henry Shigh just north of Brookings. Curry County probate records refer to him as "Henry Schaich, also known as Shy or Shigh".

Siah Butte, Deschutes County. This butte southwest of Bend was named by the USFS with the Chinook jargon word for far or far off, indicating its more or less inaccessible position. The name should be pronounced as though spelled Si-ya with accent on the last syllable.

Siboco, Lane County. Siboco is a station on the Southern Pacific Company railroad at the mouth of South Inlet on the south side of Siuslaw River about two miles south of Cushman. The name was made synthetically by taking parts of the name of Siuslaw Boom Company which operated in those parts.

Sickfoot Creek, Wallowa County. This stream is about twenty miles north of Wallowa. It was named for David Rochester, a clubfoot, who lived on the creek. The Indians named him Sickfoot. Sickfoot Creek drains into Grande Ronde River in township 5 north, range 42 east.

Sidney, Marion County. Sidney is a station on the Burlington Northern in Ankeny Bottom. J. M. Wallace started a flour mill at Sidney in pioneer days and is said to have named the place because of his wife's family name.

Sidwalter Buttes, Wasco County. The Sidwalter Buttes lie on a northwest-southeast axis between Badger and Mill creeks in the south part of the county and near the west edge of the Warm Springs Indian Reservation. The maximum elevation of about 3600 feet is near the northwest end of the series. The buttes are named for an old Wasco Indian family of the vicinity. There are several spellings, including Sid Walter, Sidwalter, Sidwallo, Sidewalder and other styles. Sidwalter is the spelling used on the USGS map of the Fort Butte quadrangle and reflects the general modern usage.

Signal Buttes, Clackamas County. Signal Buttes are near the head of Roaring River. T. H. Sherrard of the USFS told the compiler that the name was intended to be descriptive, because as far as he knew there never were any signals of any kind on these buttes. The pointed summits gave rise to the name.

Signal Buttes, Curry County. M. S. Brainard told the compiler that this descriptive name was applied because of early Indian activity and that remnants of fire pits are still visible.

Signal Hill, Wasco County. Signal Hill is the rounded bluff one mile east of and overlooking the east abutment of The Dalles Dam. It was first named in 1956 in the U. S. Army Engineers *Foundation Report on The Dalles Dam.* Since then it has been the site of numerous radio and other electronic installations that make the name more significant.

Silent Creek, Klamath County. This creek rises in the northeast corner of Crater Lake National Park and flows east to Beaver Marsh. R. A. Long of Fort Rock told the writer in 1969 that despite a fairly rapid current the stream was so quiet as to be a curiosity.

Siletz River, Lincoln and Polk counties. The Siletz Indians were the southernmost Salishan tribe on the coast. The name now designates all the tribes on the former Siletz reservation—Athapascan, Yakonan, Kusan, Takilman, Shastan and Shahaptian linguistic families. The name had been called *Celeste, Neselitch, Sailetc.* Leo Frachtenberg, the philologist, in a letter to Professor Franz Boas from Siletz, Oregon dated September 5, 1915, states that Rogue River Indians first applied the name *Silis* meaning black bear to what is now known as Siletz Lake. The Indians and the river took their name from the lake. There was for many years a Siletz Indian Agency in Oregon. For editorial on the closing of this agency, see the *Oregonian,* November 18, 1925. It is estimated there were 2000 Indians at Siletz Agency in 1867. The Siletz reservation is described in the *Oregonian,* May 22, 1862, by Philip Ritz. For description of the Siletz Indians in 1869, *ibid.,* September 24, 1869, page 3. A writer in the *Oregonian,* February 2, 1877, page 3, identifies the word with the French *celeste.* This theory is controverted by James W. Nesmith (*ibid.,* February 7, 1877, page 2). The town of Valsetz was named for the Valley & Siletz Railroad.

Silica, Gilliam County. This station east of Arlington was named by the railroad company because of the presence of so much sand.

Silica Mountain, Douglas County. Silica Mountain is just south of the Lane County line on the headwaters of Mosby Creek. It was originally named Quartz Mountain but USFS ranger Fred Asam changed it to Silica about 1920 to avoid duplication with the more prominent Quartz Mountain near Little River. Much of the surface of western Oregon is covered with volcanic material and in some areas, usually associated with mining activity, the centers or sources of the volcanism are exposed. Because of the importance of early-day mining in local history, the author asked Hollis M. Dole, state geologist, for a few comments on this type of formation. He replied as follows: "Silica Mountain probably represents a center of volcanism to the early Tertiary volcanics of the Western Cascades. Due to uplift and erosion, these former sources of volcanism have been exposed and are represented by coarsely crystalline rocks. Silica Mountain is complex but its core is dacite porphyry. Altered rocks and highly siliceous rocks occur close by. The dacite may be related to the implacement of the larger nearby Bohemia Mountain intrusives and therefore also to the mineralization of that area."

Silk Creek, Lane County. This stream flows into Coast Fork Willamette River at Cottage Grove, and according to Elbert Bede, was once known as Hazleton Creek. A letter by Frances E. Morss Baker in the Eugene *Register,* April 17, 1929, says that a miner named Turpin returned from California, where he had been forced to take part of his wages in merchandise, which included enough handsome silk to make a dress. A woman living on the stream liked the silk so much that she traded a cow for it and the name Silk Creek had its origin in this swap.

Siltcoos Lake, Douglas and Lane counties. Not much is known about the origin of this name, except, of course, that it is Indian. It is said to be the name of a local chief and also that it is an Indian family name. This version seems to be substantiated by an entry under Kuitsh, a small Yakonan tribe on the lower Umpqua River, in *Handbook of American Indians,* volume I, page 732, where the village *Tsiakhaus* is listed. The proximity of Coos Bay could easily produce a distortion in the name of the lake, although the Indians of the two regions were not related. The name was formerly spelled Tsiltcoos, but the USBGN adopted the shorter form. The lake is a fine body of water covering several square miles, and has an elevation of eight feet. Siltcoos River connects it with the Pacific Ocean.

Silver Butte, Curry County. Silver Butte is a small point close to the Oregon Coast Highway about two miles north of Port Orford. On June 1, 1946, Louis L. Knapp, of Port Orford, told the compiler an amusing story about the origin of the name, a story that was told him when he was a small boy. The butte was named in the very early days at a time when there was plenty of panning for gold on the black beach sands. Some enthusiast got the notion of starting a silver stampede to property that he owned or controlled. He melted up some small silver coins and poured the metal so that it would resemble silver grains. He used these to salt the property and then announced a discovery of silver bearing ground. Wise prospectors soon exposed the scheme, but the name Silver Butte has remained attached to the feature to this day.

Silver Creek, Harney County. Silver Creek heads in the northwest part of the county and flows southeast to Harney Lake. A little to the northwest of Harney Lake is Silver Lake, which at times receives water from Silver Creek. The compiler has not been able to get definite information about the origins of the names of these features, but is of the opinion that they are the result of mixed identity with Silvies River, an important stream just to the east. Early in July, 1859, Captain H. D. Wallen, of the Fourth Infantry, in charge of a military expedition, passed Silver Lake and called it Whatumpa Lake, but gave no explanation of the name. See 36th Congress, 1st Session, Senate Executive Document 34, which gives an account of this expedition. For early history of this area by Robert C. Clark, see *OHQ,* volume XXXIII, page 101.

Silver Creek, Josephine County. This stream is in the western part of the county. Walling, in *History of Southern Oregon,* page 452, says the stream was named because of a pretended discovery of silver ore on its banks in 1879.

Silver Creek, Marion County. Silver Creek was named in pioneer days, and the town of Silverton was named for the stream. There are two stories about the origin of the name. The first is to the effect that a traveler on horseback had some silver in his saddle bags and tried to ford the stream near where the town of Silverton now stands. His horse got into deep water and in the struggle that ensued the saddle pockets were lost, silver and all. The loss was not recovered, and as a result the stream was named Silver Creek. The second and more probable story is that the stream was named for James Smith, who was called "Silver" Smith because he brought a quantity of silver dollars into the locality, possibly a bushel of them. Smith and John Barger built a sawmill at Milford, two miles above Silverton, about 1846. Old-timers generally favor this version. A post office with the name Silver Creek was established in Marion County November 16, 1854, with E. M. Waite postmaster. The compiler has not been able to get its location, but it was doubtless not far from the present site of Silverton.

Silver Creek Falls, Marion County. These falls are about fifteen miles southeast of Silverton, in Silver Creek Falls State Park. They constitute one of the important scenic attractions of Oregon and in ordinary times are visited by large numbers of sightseers. North and South Silver creeks join to form Silver Creek in the park, and the larger falls are on the two streams above the forks. In April, 1943, S. H. Boardman, state parks superintendent, had the heights of the falls accurately measured with the following results: North Falls, 136 feet; Winter Falls, 134 feet; Middle North Falls, 106 feet; Drake Falls, 27 feet; Double Falls, 178 feet; Lower North Falls, 30 feet; Lower South Falls, 93 feet; Twin Falls, 31 feet; South Falls, 177 feet. Below the junction of North and South Silver creeks are five small falls within the park, with the following heights; Crag Falls, 12 feet; Elbow Falls, 20 feet; Canyon Falls, 10 feet; Lisp Falls, 5 feet; Sunlight Falls, 5 feet. A community called Silver Falls City sprang up near these falls many years ago. The town was platted in 1888, with ambitious dimensions, but the enterprise folded up. See story by R. J. Hendricks, Salem *Statesman,* May 16, 1937.

Silver Falls, Coos County. These falls are on Silver Creek, northeast of Allegany. They were named in contradistinction to Golden Falls nearby, in the belief that Golden Falls were named for the metal. According to information from S. B. Cathcart in 1929 Golden Falls were actually named for Dr. C. B. Golden, first Grand Chancellor of the Knights of Pythias of Oregon.

Silver King Mountain, Marion County. This mountain, elevation 5238 feet, is in the north part of the county, north of Detroit. It was named for a mining claim nearby which was located by some Portland men.

Silver Lake, Lake County. Silver Lake is about six miles east of Silver Lake town. It formerly had an area of about 20 square miles, but is now quite dry. The lake apparently bears a descriptive name, but it is not known who first applied it. Residents of central Oregon attribute the name to John C. Fremont, but the compiler cannot find that Fremont had anything to do with it, and certainly did not see or name Silver Lake on his first trip into Oregon in 1843. The Klamath Indian name for Silver Lake was *Kalpshi.* This appears to have been derived from the word *kalapsh,* meaning a decayed log, and was used because of the presence of petrified wood near the lake.

Silver Lake, Lake County. Silver Lake post office was established on

December 9, 1875. It was first in the home of G. C. Duncan at a point considerably east of the present site of the town of Silver Lake. Duncan was the first postmaster. The office was discontinued in March, 1880, and reestablished in July, 1882, at the ranch of C. P. Marshall one and one-half miles west of where the town now stands. The most important happening in the history of the community was a fire which occurred on December 24, 1894, in which 43 people lost their lives in the burning of one building. *The Oregon Desert* by Jackman and Long, pp 126-127 has an account of the tragedy and Ed O'Farrell's 100 mile ride to Lakeview for medical help. Silver Lake town was named for Silver Lake, six miles to the east. See under that heading. Silver Lake town has an elevation of 4345 feet. For history of the community, see *History of Central Oregon,* pages 853-57.

Silver Point, Clatsop County. Silver Point is sometimes erroneously referred to as Sylvan Point. This small promontory on Cannon Beach was called Silver Point because of the characteristic color of the weathered spruce trees on its face. The land adjacent to the point was platted and recorded as Silver Point Cliff on April 21, 1894. On February 16, 1898, Sylvan Park was platted and recorded a half a mile north of Silver Point. In 1929 Rodney L. Glisan, long familiar with the geography of this part of Oregon, recommended that the name Silver Point be adopted, and this style was also favored by the compiler of these notes. On December 4, 1929, the USBGN adopted the name Silver Point rather than Sylvan Point.

Silver Wells, Crook County. The compiler has had an inquiry for the history of the place called Silver Wells. A post office with this name was established on the Wasco County list August 16, 1878, with Joseph J. Brown postmaster. The office was finally closed in 1881. It was on Camp Creek south of the east end of Maury Mountains. The name is intended to be descriptive, probably of the white sand near the wells.

Silverton, Marion County. Silverton took its name from the fact that it is situated on Silver Creek. The early history of the community is given in Down's *A History of the Silverton Country,* page 223. The first settlement was at a locality called Milford, where James Smith and John Barger established a sawmill about 1846. This was about two miles up stream from the present site of Silverton. Down says that the town of Silverton itself dates from 1854, but that the name did not come into use until the following year. Various milling and mercantile establishments along Silver Creek as far south as Milford were finally concentrated in Silverton, the other locations being abandoned. The name Bargerville was suggested for the new community in honor of John Barger, a nearby landowner. This was rejected because of confusion with Parkersville nearby. Mrs. T. R. Coon, a member of a pioneer Silverton family, has written the compiler that Polly Crandall Coon Price actually selected the name of Silverton. She came to Oregon in 1852, following her husband, T. L. Coon, who had arrived shortly before. Her husband died January 10, 1854, before securing title to his donation land claim. Mrs. Coon remained on the land and secured the title and sold town lots, naming the place Silverton. This was probably in the fall of 1854 or early in 1855, as the Silverton post office was established July 16, 1855, with Charles Miller postmaster. Mrs. Coon married Stephen Price in September, 1855.

Silvies River, Grant and Harney counties. Silvies River was named for Antoine Sylvaille, who, with a party of trappers, was sent into central Oregon by Peter Skene Ogden in 1826. See *OHQ*, volume X, page 354, and volume XI, page 202. Sylvaille, on his return from central Oregon, reported finding a stream very rich with beaver, to which the name Sylvailles River was at once given. The Arrowsmith maps published between 1830 and 1850 showed the stream as Sylvailles River. In the Ogden journals, under date of October 8, 1826, mention is made of the fact that Sylvaille discovered this river. On November 1, Ogden mentions the river as flowing into a lake, now known as Malheur Lake. Dr. Robert C. Clark, in *OHQ*, volume XXXIII, page 113, says that the party under Major Enoch Steen, 1860, named this stream Cricket River, because of the swarms of insects. That name did not supplant the older name, Sylvailles River, or its anglicized form, Silvies River, which had been in general use for many years. Silvies post office was established near this stream in the extreme north part of Harney County in February, 1892, with Adelaide Cross first postmaster. The office was closed in July, 1906, but was reestablished in 1915 in the south part of Grant County. It was not in operation in 1980.

Simax Bay, Klamath County. This bay is at the northern end of Crescent Lake. It is reported that the word *simax* is an Indian expression meaning landing place. The compiler has been unable to find the word in the Klamath Indian language, or any other language for that matter.

Simmons Creek, Tillamook County. Homer Simmons of Tillamook informed the writer in 1968 that this creek five miles south of Tillamook was named for his grandfather, Leonard Simmons, who came to Oregon from Indiana in 1865 and settled along its banks in the 1870s.

Simmons Draw, Wallowa County. Simmons Draw is east of Maxville. It was formerly known as Deadhorse Draw because a horse was drowned therein.

Simnasho, Wasco County. This was a post office on the Warm Springs Indian Reservation. Pierce Mays is authority for the information that the original Indian word was pronounced as though spelled *Sini-massa*. Warm Springs Indians have corroborated this and inform the compiler that the word means thorn bush.

Sinamox, Wasco County. A station on the Burlington Northern named with the Chinook jargon word for seven, since originally it was the seventh station from the north end of the line up Deschutes River. Sinamox post office was established January 2, 1914. The office was closed December 31, 1914, with papers to Moody.

Sink, Lake County. Sink post office, in the extreme north part of the county, took its name because it was near the sink of Peters Creek. It was established in April, 1911, and operated until August, 1920. Anna M. Long was the first postmaster.

Sink, Sherman County. Sink railroad station was named for George P. Sink who was born in Illinois June 2, 1847, and came west in 1876. He took up a homestead in Spanish Hollow in 1882.

Sinker Mountain, Lane County. Sinker Mountain, elevation 4752 feet, is the highest point on Alpine Ridge between Christy Creek and Fall Creek. George H. Kelly of Portland told the compiler that the peak received its name as the result of a camping experience of some hunters who were there forced to eat biscuits made with soda, popularly known as sinkers. A. J. Briem in his notes on file at the OHS, page 37, says the men were Jack and John Hills.

Sinnott, Morrow County. Sinnott post office was established in the southwest corner of the county, on one of the headwaters of Rock Creek, and about six miles south of Hardman, on April 29, 1916. Scott H. Osborn was the first postmaster. Sinnott post office was discontinued effective February 28, 1918. Sinnott was named in compliment to Nicholas Sinnott of The Dalles, a representative in Congress from Oregon from 1913 to 1928, who doubtless assisted in getting the post office established. N. J. Sinnott was one of Oregon's most esteemed citizens. He was born at The Dalles December 6, 1870, and was graduated from the University of Notre Dame in 1892. He was admitted to the bar and practiced law at The Dalles. He was a member of the Oregon state senate in 1909 and 1911. His service in Congress at Washington was brought to a close by an appointment to the United States Court of Claims. However, his term on the court was cut short by his death on July 20, 1929.

Sisi Butte, Clackamas County. Sisi Butte, elevation 5614 feet, is a prominent point in the Cascade Range in the southern part of the county, just west of Lemiti Butte. *Sisi* is the Chinook jargon word for blanket or cloth. Gibbs gives the form *pa' see-sie*, but it is the same word. In 1927, Dee Wright, who was a walking encyclopedia about Cascade Range place names, told the compiler that he had never been able to get a good explanation as to why the name was applied to Sisi Butte, although Indians told him that it was correct.

Siskiyou, Jackson County. The name Siskiyou as applied to a post office did not appear until April, 1895, well over a half a century after Hudson's Bay Company trappers had named the pass through the Siskiyou Mountains. The compiler does not know the exact location of the first Siskiyou post office, which was in charge of Alice E. Ager, but for many years this office was near the Southern Pacific Company station Siskiyou at the northeast end of the Siskiyou tunnel and very close to the Pacific Highway. This post office was closed October 31, 1932. The compiler has been asked about where the golden spike was driven on completion of the Siskiyou line of the Southern Pacific Company. In March, 1947, G. H. Kilborn, superintendent of the Southern Pacific Company's Shasta Division at Dunsmuir had a search made of the old records and reported that the golden spike was driven on December 17, 1887, at about 5:04 P. M. on the east side of the track at the south end of the Ashland yard at mileage 428:8. The spike was driven at survey station 1154 + 05. The driving of this spike completed the Siskiyou line of the Southern Pacific.

Siskiyou Mountains, Jackson and Josephine counties. George Gibbs, in his *Dictionary of the Chinook Jargon*, 1863, gives the following version of the origin of this name: "Siskiyou. Cree. *A bobtailed horse.* This name, ludicrously enough, has been bestowed on the range of mountains separating Oregon and California, and also on a county in the latter state. The origin of this designation, as related to me by Mr. Anderson, was as follows: Mr.

Archibald R. McLeod, a chief factor of the Hudson's Bay Company, in the year 1828, while crossing the mountains with a pack train, was overtaken by a snow storm, in which he lost most of his animals, including a noted bob-tailed race horse. His Canadian followers, in compliment to their chief, or 'bourgeois,' named the place the Pass of the Siskiyou,—an appellation subsequently adopted as the veritable Indian name of the locality, and which thence extended to the whole range, and the adjoining district." Alexander C. Anderson was connected with the Hudson's Bay Company. On page 598 of Lacombe's Cree dictionary, Montreal, 1874, published in French, is the Cree word *sisikiyawatim,* which refers to a spotted horse or possibly a pack-horse. The obvious similarity between the first part of this word and the word *Siskiyou* is too great to need comment. The compiler feels that when Gibbs attributed Siskiyou to the Cree, he was on firm ground. The story that the name Siskiyou comes from the French *six cailloux,* meaning six stones, has always seemed fanciful to the compiler. It is alleged that the six stones were used in fording various streams, but there are several versions of the story, and none is well authenticated. They cover too much territory and are very indefinite. Professor A. L. Kroeber of the University of California says of this etymology: "(it) looks too much like a typical case of folk-etymology to engender much confidence. The usual assumption of an Indian origin, though not necessarily from a tribal name, is more credible." The Siskiyou Mountains are part of what geologists call the Klamath Mountains, which lie as a connecting uplift between the Coast Range and the Cascade Range. Joseph S. Diller, in his *Topographic Development of the Klamath Mountains,* USGS Bulletin 196, gives an interesting description of the geography and geology of this part of Oregon. Attention is called to the fact that there is some confusion about the given name of the McLeod, referred to by Gibbs. Presumably this is the same person generally mentioned as Alexander R. McCleod, for whom McCloud River in northern California is said to have been named.

Sisters, Deschutes County. Sisters is just east of the summit of the Cascade Range, and is named for the imposing nearby peaks, the Three Sisters. There was previously a post office at Camp Polk, about three miles away, and in 1888 it was found advisable to move the office, and as a result of the move, the name was changed, as Camp Polk was no longer significant. It is said that Jacob N. Quilberg selected the new name, and John J. Smith was the first postmaster in the new office. The townsite plat was filed for the record July 15, 1901, by Alex and Robert Smith. For news story about 40th anniversary of the town of Sisters, see Bend *Bulletin,* September 24, 1941.

Sitkum, Coos County. About 1873, J. A. Harry established a tavern or roadhouse about half way between Roseburg and what was known as Coos City. As a result of a competitor putting up another halfway house nearby, a new name was selected, Sitkum, which is the Chinook jargon word for half. The post office got its name from the name of the tavern. It was established on May 9, 1873, with Wm. H. Flook first postmaster.

Sitkum Creek, Lane County. Sitkum Creek flows into Salmon Creek from the north about eleven miles east of Oakridge. *Sitkum* is the Chinook jargon word for half, and in this case means that the stream is rather piddling.

Siuslaw River, Lane County. Siuslaw was the Indian name of a locality, tribe or chief, and has become the name of a river in western Oregon. The Siuslaws are classed as a Yakonan tribe. The first mention of the name that the compiler has seen is by Lewis and Clark, in *History of the Expedition,* Biddle edition, volume II, page 118, where it is given as *Shiastuckle.* Alexander R. McCleod in his journal of 1828 gives *Saoustla;* Samuel Parker in his *Journal of an Exploring Tour* gives *Saliutla;* Hale gives *Saiustla* in Wilkes' *U. S. Exploring Expedition,* volume VI, page 221. The name has many other variations. See *Handbook of American Indians,* volume II, page 584. The forms Linslaw and Linslow are probably due to misreading of poor handwriting, mistaking S and u for L and n. A post office with the name Siuselaw was established April 23, 1852, with James Heatherby postmaster. Henry Coleman became postmaster June 1, 1854. Preston's *Map of Oregon,* 1856, shows this office at a point five miles north of the present site of Lorane, but with the spelling Siuslaw. Postal records of later dates show an office called Siuslaw, but the compiler does not know when the spelling of the name was changed. See also under Linslaw and also Lorane.

Sixes River, Curry County. Sixes River is an important stream flowing into Pacific Ocean just north of Cape Blanco, and draining a considerable part of northern Curry County. L. B. Spurgeon, postmaster at Sixes office in 1926, wrote that it was named for a local Indian chief. George Davidson, in the *Coast Pilot* for 1869, has a different history of the name, and says that in 1851 it was usually called Sikhs River, the Chinook jargon word for friend. On some maps he found the name of a stream in that locality shown as Sequalchin River. The Indian village on Sikhs River was known as *Techeh-kutt.* Captain Wm. Tichenor, in *Pioneer History of Coos and Curry Counties,* page 26, says the Indian name of Sixes River was *Sa-qua-mi. Handbook of American Indians,* volume I, page 746, under the heading Kwatami, a subdivision of the Tututni, lists a number of alternative forms of the tribe name. One of these forms, *Sik-ses-tene,* is said to mean "people by the far north country." This is probably the real origin of the name, but the form of spelling, Sixes, was doubtless applied during the southern Oregon gold rush by miners who were familiar with the Chinook jargon word for friend. The spelling Sixes was used as early as October, 1855. See *Harper's Magazine,* October 1856, page 591.

Sixmile Canyon, Morrow County. This canyon, opening onto Columbia River, was so called on the assumption that it was about six miles east of the mouth of Willow Creek.

Sixmile Creek, Gilliam County. This stream flows into Rock Creek east of Condon. The headwaters average about six miles from Condon and the stream is said to have been named on that account.

Sixteen Butte, Lake County. Sixteen Butte was named by W. O. Harriman of the USFS, because the butte was largely in section 16, township 23 south, range 15 east.

Skeeters Flat, Jackson County. Skeeters Flat is southeast of Butte Falls some eight or ten miles and Skeeters Creek is nearby. These two geographic features were named for Isaac Skeeters, who was one of the first white settlers in the vicinity and operated a rived shingle camp. Skeeters was one of the party that discovered Crater Lake on June 12, 1853. The name Skeeter Flat is wrong, as the etymology has nothing to do with the unpopular insect. The USFS maintained a guard station at this point called Mosquito Guard Station which seems to carry dignity a little too far.

Skeleton Cave, Deschutes County. Skeleton Cave, three miles north of Arnold Ice Cave on the Deschutes Plateau, was named for the accumulation of fossil and modern bones that were found in a natural sink near its mouth. Phil Brogan has an interesting article about this cave in the *Oregonian,* January 1, 1956.

Skell Head, Crater Lake National Park, Klamath County. A point on the east shore of Crater Lake named by Will G. Steel in 1908 for a Klamath Indian deity of the plains, represented by the marten.

Skelley, Douglas County. See under Kelleher.

Skinner Butte, Lane County. This butte is between the main business section of Eugene and Willamette River and has an elevation of 681 feet. It was named for Eugene F. Skinner, who settled at its foot in 1846. For references to Eugene F. Skinner and his family, see under the heading Eugene. The University of Oregon at one time maintained an observatory near the east end of the top of this butte. The Indian name was reported to be *Yapoah.*

Skipanon River, Clatsop County. Lewis and Clark called this stream Skipanarwin Creek on their charts, and for a century most maps used that form and Skeppernawin Creek. These spellings did not lend themselves to easy use, and for many years the stream has been locally known as Skipanon, a fact that the USBGN finally took notice of, and included in a decision: Skipanon Creek. Subsequently (April 1, 1925) the decision was changed to Skipanon River, which fits the universal Oregon use. Preston's map of 1856 uses the form Skippenon Cr. There was a station named Skipanon on the railroad south of Warrenton. Skipanon was originally known as Lexington. Lexington was surveyed in 1848 by W. Hall and the plat recorded April 19, 1854. It was part of the Jeremiah G. Fuller donation land claim. The place was also known as Upper Landing. Silas B. Smith is authority for the statement that the Clatsop Indian name *Skippernawin* referred to a point at the mouth of the stream rather than to the stream itself, *OHQ,* volume I, page 321. See under Warrenton. Lexington post office was established November 28, 1850, with David E. Pease first postmaster. It was discontinued February 24, 1853. It was in operation again with other postmasters from April, 1856, to September, 1857. Skipanon post office was in service from August, 1871, to April, 1903.

Skiphorton Creek, Umatilla County. Kirk Casper of Walla Walla wrote the compiler in 1975 regarding this tributary of South Fork Walla Walla River. He said that supposedly well before 1900 a man named Horton came to Milton and built a cabin near the mouth of this creek. Word came to the sheriff that Horton was wanted for murder but before the law caught up with him, he fled the country. The sheriff returned empty handed to report that Horton had skipped so the creek became known as Skiphorton.

Skookum Lake, Clackamas County. This small lake on the north slope of Thunder Mountain drains into Fish Creek, a tributary of Clackamas River. It is named with the Chinook jargon word which originally meant a strong or powerful malign deity, and later came to mean simply strong or stout. When used in connection with localities, the word *skookum* generally indicated a place inhabited by a skookum, or evil god of the woods. It sometimes meant a place used as a burial ground. There are several geographic features in Oregon described with this name. Indians avoided skookum places and considered them haunted. A Skookum Chuck did not mean a strong, swift stream, but a place to stay away from. The modern meaning of the word skookum is quite different from the earlier connotation. In contradistinction to a skookum, a hehe was a good spirit and a Hehe Chuck was a fine place for games, races and other sports and festivities.

Skookumhouse Butte, Curry County. Indians near the mouth of Rogue River built a fort or stockade on the south bank of the stream about fifteen miles from the ocean. It was named with the Chinook jargon word *skookum* for stout or strong, and the name has been applied to various geographic features nearby. White settlers drove the Indians out and took the fort. See Port Orford *News,* December 14, 1926. Skookumhouse was also a word used by early settlers to describe a jail.

Skull Spring, Malheur County. Skull Spring was so called long before the post office was established. The compiler was told many years ago that the name was applied because the bleached skull of a melancholy steer lay near a useful spring. Skullspring post office was established June 13, 1902, with Anna G. Riley first postmaster. The office was finally closed in October, 1927. It was in the high country about 20 miles east-southeast of Riverside, possibly not always in the same location. The name of the post office was in one word.

Skunk Creek, Josephine County. It is surprising how many people have the notion that a geographic feature may be made more attractive by changing its name. Every now and again someone wants to change the name of Skunk Creek, which is an agreeable brook flowing through the city of Grants Pass. Up till now champions of the old name seem to have had the best of the argument. If the compiler lived on Skunk Creek he would be glad of the publicity and would print a picture of the little black and white animal on his letterpaper. The skunk is independent, brave and capable He produces, among other things, a fine fur that is made into coats for beautiful women who don't object to the name skunk. There are several varieties of skunk in Oregon, which are ably described in Vernon Bailey's *Mammals and Life Zones of Oregon,* beginning on page 308. The skunk is an animal of distinction.

Slagle Creek, Jackson and Josephine counties. Slagle Creek is a tributary of Applegate River about ten miles southeast of Grants Pass. It was named for Conrad Slagle, a pioneer settler. A letter by Logan Wooldridge, of Murphy, Oregon, printed in Grants Pass *Bulletin* on June 4, 1937, says that Slagle was born in Tennessee and came across the plains to Oregon in 1852. He first settled in Lane County, but sold out and went to Jackson County in 1858, where he took up a claim on the creek which now bears his name. He died many years ago and was buried in the Sparlin cemetery on Williams Creek.

Slater, Union County. Slater was a post office with an unusually short life. It was situated in the Grande Ronde Valley, probably near the middle of township 2 south, range 39 east, on the old stage road from Union to Summerville. The post office was established June 9, 1881, with Stowell L. Payne first and only postmaster. The office was discontinued January 31, 1882, and the business turned over to Summerville. The office was at or near the site of an older office, Sand Ridge. See under that heading. At the time the post office was established James H. Slater of Union County was United States senator from Oregon and it was doubtless named in his honor.

Sled Springs, Wallowa County. These springs in township 3 north, range 44 east, were named for a broken-down sled that lay nearby for many years. It was abandoned about 1883 by James Alford and George Allen.

Sleepy Creek, Wallowa County. This is a tributary of Lightning Creek. It was named by James and Charles Rice, Fred Gaylord and Len Snell, who had a camp there, and since the sun did not fall on the camp until late in the morning they lay abed and snoozed.

Slick Creek, Douglas County. This creek flows into Boulder Creek in section 1, township 29 south, range 1 west. Grover Blake, who tried unsuccessfully to ride a horse down the creek in the 1930s, told the writer in 1968 that it was named for its slippery bed.

Slick Rock Creek, Lincoln County. Elmer Calkins of Otis told the compiler that in the early days there were seven important fords on the trail down Salmon River. The last of these was at Slick Rock Creek and was so named because the smooth, mossy rock of the streambed was a bad spot for horses.

Slide Mountain, Clackamas County. Slide Mountain is in the northeast part of the county and was named because of a large landslide on the southwest shoulder.

Sloan Creek, Tillamook County. This tributary of Neskowin Creek was named for John S. Sloan who patented land nearby in 1901.

Slough, Multnomah County. Slough post office was one of the first in what is now Multnomah County, and was put in service just about a year after the Portland office was established. Slough office was established November 25, 1850, with John Switzler postmaster, and was in operation until January 6, 1852. It was near what was then called Oregon Slough on the south bank of the Columbia River. Oregon Slough is now North Portland Harbor. Switzler was an early settler in that area.

Sluice Creek, Wallowa County. This stream heads near Hat Point and flows into Snake River. It was named by Alex Warnock because a miner named Corby sluiced for gold there in the early days.

Slusher Canyon, Umatilla County. This canyon empties into Butter Creek south of Echo. It was named for William M. Slusher who settled north of Vinson in the 1890s. Slusher was one of the early members of the Umatilla Wool Growers.

Sly, Deschutes County. A post office with the name Sly was established on the Crook County list as of January 17, 1900, with G. Sly first postmaster. The order was rescinded May 12, 1900, and the office was never put in operation. George Sly had a place in the extreme south part of what is now Deschutes County, and the Sly office would have been about four miles south of La Pine, on Long Prairie within a few hundred feet of the Klamath County line.

Smith, Harney County. Smith post office in Harney County was near the stream known as Smyth Creek. Smith was the correct spelling of the post office, which was established March 2, 1895 with Ida C. Smith first postmaster. The creek was named for D. H. Smyth, but the post office was named for another family. The office was closed October 31, 1913, with mail to Diamond.

Smith Canyon, Deschutes County. This canyon five miles north of Millican was named for several members of the Smith family who settled there in 1919. The father, John A. Smith, built a fine home that was a local showplace but it was a dry homestead and hauling water during the arid years after World War I was too great a problem. Vandals have since largely destroyed another early landmark.

Smith Creek, Multnomah County. Smith Creek flows into Sandy River south of Springdale. It was named for Fred Smith, a native of London, England. Smith came to Oregon in the 1860s and settled along Smith Creek in 1879 where he later developed one of the early prune orchards. He died on February 28. 1927.

Smith Hill, Benton County. Smith Hill is southeast of Airlie. It was named for Green Berry Smith, a prominent pioneer settler of the county. Smith, who was frequently called Greenberry Smith, was born in Grayson County, Virginia, in 1820 and came to Oregon in 1845 with the Meek party. He settled in Benton County in 1846 on a claim near the butte that now bears his name. See land certificate 2322. He later moved to a farm south of Corvallis and then to Corvallis. For biography, see *History of Benton County,* page 526. See also in this book under Greenberry.

Smith Hill Summit, Josephine County. Smith Hill Summit, elevation 1730 feet, is the pass on Interstate 5 between Wolf Creek and Sunny Valley. It takes its name from Henry Smith who came to the Leland area prior to 1870 and took up land at Wolf Creek in 1872. Smith was a prominent local citizen. Smith Hill is not identified on current maps so the name may have been applied either to the high ground east of the highway or to the grade on the old stage road where it ascended 500 feet from Wolf Creek to the pass. The historic Wolf Creek Tavern, restored in 1979 by the Oregon State Parks Division and now operated under their supervision, is built on land originally owned by Henry Smith.

Smith Hollow, Wheeler County. Smith Hollow five miles east of Waterman was named for Leander R. Smith who bought government land there in 1885.

Smith Lake, Clatsop County. Smith Lake is at the north end of Clatsop Plains, west of the Oregon Coast Highway and a short distance south of Skipanon. It was named for Solomon Howard Smith, one of the early American settlers in Oregon. Solomon H. Smith was employed by Dr.

McLoughlin to teach schóol at Fort Vancouver in 1832, a few weeks after John Ball had quit school-teaching there. He settled near the mouth of Chehalem Creek, and afterwards at Clatsop Plains. Ball was a member of Wyeth's first party and returned eastward in 1834. Smith taught school, also, at French Prairie, near the home of Joseph Gervais. Smith was one of the organizers of the provisional government in 1843. He died at Skipanon June 19, 1891. For biographical narrative, see OPA *Transactions*, 1887, pages 81-89. The name of Smith Lake was *O-mo-pah*. See *OHQ*, volume I, page 322.

Smith Point, Clatsop County. Smith Point is at the western extremity of Astoria, and was named for Samuel C. Smith, who took up a donation land claim that included the point. The Indian name for this point was *O-wa-pun-pun*. See *OHQ*, volume I, page 321. Vancouver's expedition named it Point George, for George III of England. Wilkes charted this with the name. Youngs Point. See the atlas for *U. S. Exploring Expedition*, volume XXIII, Hydrography.

Smith Ridge, Douglas County. This ridge south of Red Butte was named for William C. Smith, an early USFS employee and native of the area.

Smith River, Douglas County. Smith River is a large tributary of Umpqua River, into which it flows at a point opposite Reedsport. It was named for Jedediah Strong Smith, a western fur trader and explorer, who was born in the Mohawk Valley, New York, June 24, 1798, and was killed by Comanche Indians in the summer of 1831 while on the way from St. Louis to Sante Fe. When he was thirteen years old Smith obtained a position on a freight boat on the Great Lakes, and when he was about 18 he was in St. Louis, attracted by the fur trade. In 1826 Smith started from St. Louis with William Henry Ashley on the first stage of what was to be the first journey of a white man from the Mississippi to the Pacific Ocean over the midland route. He traveled to southern California by way of Great Salt Lake, then returned to Utah and in 1828 started for northern California and southern Oregon. His party made its way up the Pacific Coast, and reached the Umpqua River, which was crossed very close to the mouth early on July 12, 1828. The party then made its way up the west and the north side of the river until the evening of July 13, where camp was pitched on the north bank just west of the mouth of what is now Smith River. Gordon's land office survey of 1857 gives the location as about a quarter of a mile west of the east line of section 26, township 21 south, range 12 west, or about the same distance southwest of what is now Gardiner station on the Southern Pacific railroad. On the morning of Monday, July 14, Indians attacked the party, while Smith and two companions were away from camp. Arthur Black was the only man who escaped from the camp. He made his way north to Tillamook, thence to Fort Vancouver. Smith and his two companions escaped toward Willamette Valley. Fifteen men were killed. These figures are from the account by R. C. Clark, *OHQ*, volume XXXVIII, page 115. Through the aid of Dr. John McLoughlin, Smith's furs were recovered and the dead were buried. Smith eventually returned to St. Louis and continued in the fur trade until his death. He was a devout Christian, and a reliable geographer, and entitled to great credit for his explorations. For details of his life see *The Ashley-Smith Explorations* by Harrison C. Dale; *The Travels of Jedediah Smith* by Maurice S. Sullivan and *Jedediah Smith, Trader and Trail Breaker,* also by Sullivan. The main tributary of Smith River is North Fork Smith River, not West Fork. A tributary of North Fork is known as West Branch. There is another Pacific Coast stream named Smith River, for Jedediah Smith. It is in northern California. The north fork of this stream rises in southern Oregon, so that there are two North Forks Smith River in this state, but not two Smith rivers, named for Jedediah Smith.

Smith Rock, Deschutes County. This interesting formation is in the extreme northeast corner of the county. Here Crooked River is forced by geologically recent lavas on the west bank to undercut Clarno ash and tuff formations on the east. The name Smith Rock is strictly applied to the 3200 foot ridge in the southwest end of the large bend in the river. However, Smith Rock State Park, acquired in 1960, now includes most of the land west of North Unit Main Canal. A small day park site has been established south and west of Crooked River but the more inaccessible rock formations on the opposite bank are frequented by mountaineers who find climbs of every degree of difficulty. There is a popular story that the name comes from one Smith, a soldier who in the 1860s fell to his death while his company was camped nearby. However, a letter in the Albany *States Rights Democrat,* August 10, 1867, signed "Ochoco" describes a trip made in July 1867 over Santiam Pass to what is now the Prineville area. The five travelers, Captain J. A. White, Jackey Settle, W. S. Elkins, John Smelser and W. Usher, described Smith's Rocks and state specifically that they were named for their discoverer, John Smith, then sheriff of Linn County. "Ochoco" describes the 4200 foot high point east of the present irrigation canal rather than the lower ridge but it is this high ground along with Gray Butte that is visible from the north and west. John Smith was born in Kentucky and came to Oregon in 1852. He settled in Linn County where he was sheriff from 1855 to 1859 and then representative in the 1862 legislature. He was appointed Indian agent at Warm Springs Indian Agency and occupied that position with one short exception from 1866 until just before his death in 1884.

Smith Springs, Douglas County. In 1889 Owen E. Smith took up a homestead on North Umpqua River east of Glide at the springs that now bear his name.

Smith Well, Deschutes County. Smith Well is on the south edge of Millican Valley. It was named for Levi Smith who homesteaded the land in 1913.

Smithfield, Lane County. Daniel Smith came to Oregon in 1852 and shortly thereafter settled in Lane County on the Territorial road southwest of what is now Junction City. In 1857 R. V. Howard built a store in the vicinity and began to call the place Smithfield. In the meantime Franklin post office had been established in the same general locality. This has resulted in a controversy about the names Franklin and Smithfield that has at times been acute. For a history of the business see under Franklin-Smithfield.

Smithfield, Polk County. Smithfield, formerly a railroad station about five miles northeast of Dallas, bears the name of Absalom Smith, a pioneer settler. Smithfield post office was established July 28, 1893, with Ira Kimball postmaster, but the railroad station was in service before that date. The compiler cannot tell when the post office was closed, but it was before March, 1900. The railroad through this place was originally the narrow gauge line of the Oregonian Railway Company, later standardized by the Southern Pacific Company. The track has been removed.

Smoky Creek, Grant County. J. E. Snow of Dayville told the writer that this stream probably received its name because of mist and fog that collects against the mountain where it heads.

Smuggler Cove, Tillamook County. This snug little harbor is between Cape Falcon and Neahkahnie Mountain, and its shore has been called Short Sand Beach for many years. It is not a landing place, but fish boats sometimes anchor there in rough weather. The name Smuggler Cove is purely romantic as there is nothing to indicate that Smugglers ever used the place. See also under Treasure Cove.

Smyth Creek, Harney County. Smyth Creek was named for D. H. Smyth, a pioneer settler near Malheur Lake. Darius Hynson Smyth was born in Lincoln County, Missouri, October 29, 1844, and came to Oregon in 1853. He spent nearly twenty years in Lane County, but also roamed in Nevada and California. He settled in Harney County in 1872 and established himself in Happy Valley in the winter of 1873-74. His father and brother were killed in Happy Valley in June, 1878, by Indians. For reminiscences of D. H. Smyth, see *OHQ,* volume XXXIII, page 125. He died at his home in Happy Valley, May 13, 1942.

Snake River, Baker, Malheur and Wallowa counties. Snake River forms the north part of the eastern boundary of Oregon. Its name comes from the Snake Indians (Shoshones and Piutes). The Lewis and Clark journals called the Indians *Choshonnes* and *Sosonees.* The name Snake came out of the fur trade period. Alexander Ross, in *Fur Hunters of the Far West,* volume I, page 275, comments on the facility of these Indians in concealing themselves, and adds: "They are very appropriately named Snakes." De Smet said the Indians were called Snakes because of their poverty, and necessity of digging in the ground for food. See Chittenden and Richardson's *Life, Letters and Travels of Father De Smet,* page 217; also *OHQ,* volume XX, page 3, "The Snake River in History," by Miles Cannon. The habitat of these Indians was extremely barren, and their eating habits were repulsive to the early writers. Snake River has had various names: Lewis, for the explorer; *Shoshone, Nez Perce, Sahaptin, Kimeonim.* Captain William Clark named the river Louis, or Lewis, when a few miles below the confluence of the Salmon and Lemhi rivers. See Thwaites' *Original Journals of the Lewis and Clark Expedition,* volume III, page 10. For editorial by Harvey W. Scott on the name of Snake River, see Scott's *History of the Oregon Country,* volume II, page 209. For notes by Leslie M. Scott and comments by T. C. Elliott of Walla Walla about the application of the name Lewis River and other references, *ibid.,* page 324, *et seq.*

Sneddon Creek, Coos County. Charles Sneddon came to Coos County in 1861 and patented land east of Libby that included this creek. The form Snedden is incorrect.

Snell Creek, Wallowa County. Snell Creek was named for George Snell, a nearby rancher. This stream is in township 1 south, range 48 east.

Snell Lake, Klamath County. This lake three miles west of Crescent Lake was named in 1948 by a fish planting crew of the Oregon State Game Commission for Earl W. Snell, the 23rd governor of Oregon, who was killed in a plane crash on October 28, 1947.

Snider Creek, Jackson County. For some years there has been a difference in the names applied to the stream that flows southward between Upper and Lower Table rocks, and it has been shown on maps as Snider Creek, Table Creek, and Table Rock Creek. In 1937 the USGS adopted the name Snider Creek for this stream, apparently for an early settler. This was the recommendation of Paul B. Rynning, county engineer. The name Rock Creek is now given to the stream north of Lower Table Rock which flows into Sams Creek to the west. The geography of the area is shown on the map of the Medford quadrangle.

Snow, Klamath County. The post office called Snow was in the extreme southwest corner of Klamath County. It was established June 22, 1894, with Adelbert B. Smith first of four postmasters. The office ran along with its original name until November 22, 1898, when it was changed to Pokegama. This change doubtless came about because the Pokegama Lumber Company projected a railroad north into Oregon from Thrall, a station on the Southern Pacific near Klamath River, California. For a time this railroad was an important factor in the development of Klamath County. Snow post office was probably named for Snow Peak, a point about twelve miles to the northeast. In recent years Snow Peak has been called Chase Mountain, but the compiler does not know when the change was made. Emphasis must be called again to the fact that when the names of post offices were changed the offices themselves were frequently moved, sometimes a considerable distance. The compiler does not know if the Snow post office was in the same building as the Pokegama office or not. The situation is further complicated by the fact that the Pokegama office had more than one location before it was closed in 1911.

Soap Creek, Benton and Polk counties. This stream rises in the eastern foothills of the Coast Range and flows into Luckiamute River about two miles from the junction of that stream with the Willamette. There is a belief that Soap Creek was so called because of its white, soapy appearance, but David L. Stearns of San Francisco in a letter in 1963 recalled hearing both from his grandparents and at Oregon Pioneer Association gatherings how the early travelers stopped at Soap Creek ford to do the laundry as it was well known that the waters contained some detergent mineral which eliminated or reduced the need for soap. In view of relative impurity of 1972 surface water in the Willamette Valley, chemical analysis would probably add little to the pioneer's empirical knowledge. Soap Creek post office was established in Benton County November 4, 1854, with David D. Davis postmaster. The compiler does not know its location, but it was doubtless near the stream. The name of this office was changed to Tampico December 3, 1854, and it was closed November 3, 1860. The compiler has not learned the significance of the name Tampico as applied to this office.

Soap Creek, Deschutes County. This stream flows east from North Sister. Hodge, in *Mount Multnomah,* says it was named because of the white, glacial silt carried by the water.

Soap Flat, Wallowa County. This flat is in section 18, township 5 north, range 45 east, and was named because of the soapweed that grew there. William Ralls took up the first homestead there about 1890.

Social Ridge, Morrow County. This high ground lies north and east of Rhea Creek. Rachel Harnett of Heppner told the compiler in 1969 that it was named in the 1880s by Mrs. William L. T. Benge, the widow of a pioneer Walla Walla doctor, who homesteaded there with a large family. The few neighbors of that time were so helpful that the widowed mother chose to call it Social Ridge. Her son, Ralph L. Benge, was later county judge.

Soda Creek, Deschutes County. This stream is tributary, from the north, to Sparks Lake. It was named for a well-known soda spring about three miles from its mouth.

Soda Springs, Jackson County. There are several places in Jackson County with the name Soda Springs, but only one had a post office of the same name. Soda Springs office was on Emigrant Creek ten or twelve miles southeast of Ashland, in the extreme north part of township 40 south, range 2 east. The locality is often called Wagner Springs because of the ownership. Soda Springs post office was established in September, 1886, with John Marshall Wagner postmaster. The office continued under Wagner's direction until May, 1911, when it was closed to Ashland. The Wagner family was among the early settlers of the valley.

Soda Springs, Linn County. The valley of South Santiam River has been well endowed with mineral springs and it is not surprising that the localities of these springs have had communities and some post offices, such as Soda Springs, Soda Stone, Sodaville, Lower Soda, Upper Soda, and others. Soda Springs is shown on old maps in the east part of township 13 south, range 1 east, northeast of the present community of Foster. This was the first of the springs to have an office. Soda Springs post office was established September 24, 1869, with Daniel D. Gibson first and only postmaster. The office was discontinued December 7, 1873.

Sodaville, Linn County. Sodaville was named for a cold mineral spring situated nearby.

Soldier Camp Mountain, Curry County. This is a well-known point on the north side of Rogue River about ten miles airline east of the Pacific Ocean. It was named during the local Indian disturbances of the 1850s. The north end of the ridge is known as Sawtooth Rock Mountain, which is a little higher than Soldier Camp Mountain, a mile to the south. Troops under the command of Captain C. C. Augur, U.S.A., camped at the point on March 17, 1856, and an account of the event is given in Glisan's *Journal of Army Life,* page 295, *et seq.* On March 20 the detachment returned to the place and Glisan mentions it specifically as "Soldiers' Camp." The name appears in other contemporaneous records. The compiler thinks that the name was in use before Glisan's visit, although that may be debatable.

Soldier Creek, Harney County. This stream is just west of Harney. It was named because soldiers camped there in the Indian wars in the 1860s.

Soloman Butte, Klamath County. Soloman Butte, 5763 feet high, is located just east of Williamson River near Kirk. It and the nearby flat were named for Sam Soloman Lalakes who had an Indian Land Allotment nearby. Soloman was the son of the well-known and powerful regional chief, Lalakes.

Somerange, Harney County. When the petition was sent in for the establishment of this post office local residents suggested the name Steens because of Steens Mountain nearby. The name was not acceptable to the postal authorities so another name, Somerange, was suggested. This name had its origin in the words "summer range," the stockmen's term for summer feeding grounds. Somerange post office was established December 19, 1923, with Robert W. Bradeen first postmaster. Bradeen was a member of the firm of Bradeen Brothers, merchants in the Catlow Valley, who kept a supply camp in Steens Mountain during summer months for the accommodation of their customers. About 1926 the Bradeens abandoned this project, and Somerange post office was moved off the mountain to a point a little west of the P Ranch. On the death of Robert Bradeen, Jesse L. Bradeen became postmaster June 30, 1930, and on October 1, 1930, the name of the office was changed to Frenchglen, with Jesse Bradeen continuing as postmaster. See under Frenchglen.

Somers Creek, Wallowa County. This is a tributary of Snake River in the east part of the county. It was named for Frank P. Somers, who ran stock near this creek for many years.

Sonny, Hood River County. This station, west of Hood River, bore an unusual name. It was formerly called Mitchell, but owing to confusion with another place in the state of the same name, it was decided by railroad officials to make a change. Mr. and Mrs. Charles Parker, owners of the Little Boy ranch, just west of Mitchell Point, tried to have the station named Little Boy, but this was not acceptable to the railroad because it was awkward in telegraphy. Mrs. Parker's nickname Sonny was finally selected as the next best thing.

Soocup Canyon, Morrow County. This tributary of Balm Fork south of Heppner was named for William Soucup who settled there before World War I. The form Soocup has been in general use for many years.

Soosap Peak, Clackamas County. This peak, elevation 4693 feet, lies east of North Fork Molalla River. Dee Wright, for many years a packer in the Cascade Range, told the compiler that it was named for Soosap, a well-known Indian of Oregon City, who occasionally hunted in the neighborhood of the mountain. This Indian was also known as Joe Suisap and Joseph Andrews, and was part Klickitat and part Molalla, according to Wright. Soosap died January 18, 1916, and his obituary is printed in the Oregon City *Enterprise,* January 21, 1916. He was 61 years old at the time of his death. Soosap Peak was at one time known as Arquette Point, for a settler who lived nearby, but the name has not persisted.

Southbeach, Lincoln County. This is a descriptive name for a community near the south side of Yaquina Bay. It has been so known since the turn of the century, although the post office was not established until May

18, 1916. Harborton is the name of the place on the official plat, but that name is not in general use. Margaret F. Conrad was the first postmaster.

South Canyonville, Douglas County. Under the heading Canyonville mention is made of a place called South Canyonville. South Canyonville was the name used for a locality, but not for a community, about ten miles south of Canyonville, in the Cow Creek Valley where the road from Canyonville first reaches that valley. It was at the Hardy Elliff place, later called Johns. It was at this locality that pioneer settlers "forted up" at Camp Elliff at the time of the Indian wars of the 1850s. South Canyonville was not a post office, but the use of the words as a locality name made it necessary to use the name North Canyonville for the post office at Canyonville, ten miles to the north. The post office name North Canyonville was changed to Canyonville in 1892, as by that time South Canyonville was no longer used as a place name.

South Dickey Peak, Clackamas County. This peak, elevation about 5300 feet, lies in the Clackamas drainage basin in the extreme south part of the county. North Dickey Peak and Dickey Creek are nearby. These geographic features were named for J. K. Dickey, a native of Pennsylvania, who came to Oregon from Missouri in 1845 and settled in a small valley near the present site of Molalla, in the spring of 1846. He hunted a great deal near Collawash River, and it is thought that government surveyors named the features for him because of this fact. This information was furnished the compiler of these notes in October, 1927, by J. O. Dickey, a son of J. K. Dickey.

South Inlet, Coos County. South Inlet post office was established April 18, 1912, with Lillian Saunders first and only postmaster. The office was closed December 15, 1914. It was situated near the head of South Slough, about twelve miles by road south of Empire. The name was supposed to be descriptive.

South Junction, Wasco County. When the two railroads were built up Deschutes Canyon, an arrangement was made for the use of joint track for a distance of about twelve miles in the south part of Wasco County. The station at the north end of this joint track was named North Junction and the station at the south end was named South Junction. Subsequently one of the duplicate tracks between South Junction and Metolius was abandoned, so that South Junction is no longer a junction point, although the original name has been retained.

South Santiam River, Linn County. This is the correct name of the southern large tributary of Santiam River. The name South Fork is wrong.

South Scappoose Creek, Columbia County. This seems to be the form of name in general use, not South Fork.

South Umpqua River, Douglas County. This is the correct name of the southern branch of Umpqua River, not South Fork.

South Yamhill, Polk County. This was a pioneer post office situated near the present site of Broadmead. It was named for South Yamhill River nearby. This office was established July 6, 1852, with Marshall B. Burke first postmaster. The name was changed to Lawn Arbor on April 12, 1855, and the office was discontinued February 22, 1865.

South Yamhill River, Polk and Yamhill counties. This is the correct name of the southern branch of Yamhill River. It was so named in pioneer days.

Souvies Island, Multnomah County. This was the name of a pioneer post office near the mouth of Willamette River. The office was established under the name Mouth of Willamette on June 30, 1851, with Ellis Walker first postmaster. The name of the office was changed to Souvies Island on March 5, 1852. The office was discontinued August 1, 1860. The island is now officially known as Sauvie Island. For information about the island see under that heading. See also under Post Office Bar.

Spanish Charlie Basin, Malheur County. This spot is near the headwaters of Succor Creek just west of the Idaho border. In 1978 Jeffrey Ford of Ontario was kind enough to turn up some information on this name during an interview with Alfred McConnell. McConnell spent most of his early years in the area and he said that in the old days the land was owned by two Charlies, Spanish and Scarface. Spanish Charlie was shot to death on his own doorstep by a neighbor and he was commemorated by having the basin named for him.

Spanish Gulch, Jackson County. This gulch is on the extreme west edge of the county and drains into Wooldridge Creek, a tributary of Slagle Creek. In a letter published in Grants Pass *Bulletin* on June 4, 1937, Logan Wooldridge says that the gulch was named for a company of Spaniards who mined there during the Rogue River Indian War. The Spaniards deserted their camp in 1855 and never returned.

Spanish Hollow, Sherman County. This is the hollow that opens upon the Columbia River at Biggs. It is said to have received its name because a Spanish ox died in the canyon during the days of the immigrations. The name Spanish Gulch for this hollow is incorrect.

Sparks Lake, Deschutes County. This is a long, kidney-shaped lake just east of the summit of the Cascade Range. Its weedy banks originally provided a rendezvous for many varieties of water fowl, some of which have unfortunately been driven away by automobile travel. The lake was named for "Lige" Sparks, a pioneer stockman of central Oregon.

Sparta, Baker County. Sparta was named for Sparta, Illinois, by William H. Packwood, a prominent Oregon pioneer. Packwood and others visited the diggings near lower Powder River in 1871 and the name of Sparta was selected at that time. Sparta post office was established October 29, 1872, with William W. Ross postmaster. This office was first established with the name Gem on August 7, 1871, with William Lynn White postmaster, and the Sparta office was provided by changing the name. The office may have been moved, possibly some little distance, when the name was changed. Facts about these changes in early post offices are not always clear from the records. Gem was the name of a mine. The compiler has a copy of a statement made by Packwood on June 26, 1916, the substance of which is that Packwood, I. B. Bowen, Ed Cranston and C. M. Foster left Baker on January 8, 1871, to visit the locality where Packwood was preparing to build what is now the Sparta Ditch. They laid out a townsite and decided to name the place by spinning a four-sided wooden top with a proposed name on each face. Packwood wrote Sparta for his home in Illinois, and that side of the top turned up. H. S. Daly, in a letter on the editorial page of the *Oregonian*, October 7, 1927, says that Packwood did not name Sparta, but Dunham Wright, of Medical Springs, takes issue with him in a letter in the Baker *Morning Democrat*, October 19, 1927. Wright says he got his information first hand from Packwood. Irving Rand, of Portland, a grandson of Packwood, confirms the Packwood story. In view of all this the compiler thinks that Packwood was responsible for the name. Both Daly and Wright say that the locality was first called Koster, for Tom Koster, who discovered gold nearby. Daly also says the place was called Eagle City before it was named Sparta.

Speaker, Josephine County. Josephine Speaker was the only postmaster this office ever had and it was named in her honor. The office was on Wolf Creek about six miles east of and upstream from Wolf Creek community. It was in the northeast part of the county and depended on farming, lumbering and mining. The office was established September 20, 1905, and was discontinued March 31, 1925.

Specht Rim, Wheeler County. Specht Rim east of West Branch was named for the Henry Specht family. Specht was an early settler and his son, Henry Jr., homesteaded near the rim in 1907.

Speece, Gilliam County. Speece was a railroad station north of Condon. It was named for William Speece, a local resident.

Speelyais Columns, Multnomah County. These rock columns are on the south bank of the Columbia River near Shepperds Dell. They are the cores of old basalt volcanic vents, the softer coverings of which have been eroded away. They are named with the Indian word *Speelyai,* the name of the coyote god of the mid-Columbia region. See Lyman's *Columbia River,* page 8, *et seq.*

Spencer Butte, Lane County. Spencer Butte, elevation 2065 feet, is just south of Eugene and is a well-known landmark in the south part of the Willamette Valley. Spencer Butte was named in July, 1845, by Dr. Elijah White, while making an exploration along the foothills of the Cascade Range for the purpose of locating an emigrant road to the eastern states. Dr. White and a companion, Batteus Du Guerre, climbed the mountain, and the following passage quoted from his book, *Ten Years in Oregon,* (compiled by Miss A. J. Allen and published in 1848), describes their experiences on the summit: "They now took a delightful survey of the general features of the landscape before them. On one hand was the vast chain of the Cascade mountains, Mt. Hood looming in solitary grandeur far above its fellows; on the other hand was the Umpqua Mountains, and a little farther on, the coast ridge. Between these lay the whole magnificent panorama of the Willamette valley, with its ribbon streams, and carpet-like verdure. The day was fine, and such was the clearness of the atmosphere that the scene was very distinct, grand and imposing. In enthusiastic admiration of the noble site, the doctor named the elevation Mt. Spencer, in compliment to John C. Spencer, the then secretary of war . . ." For additional information about the discovery of Spencer Butte and Baptiste (Batteus) Du Guerre, see article by Fred Lockley on editorial page *Oregon Journal* June 7, 1927. This article indicates that Du Guerre's nephew used the spelling DeGuire. Walling, in *History of Lane County,* page 327, has quite a different story about the naming of Spencer Butte, based on tradition, to the effect that the butte was named for a young Englishman, Spencer, who had wandered away from a Hudson's Bay Company party and was killed on the mountain by Indians. The compiler inclines to Miss Allen's version, which was written nearly 40 years before Walling's and was not based on a legend. Spencer's Butte post office was established July 14, 1853, with Milton S. Riggs postmaster and was discontinued April 2, 1855. It was near the west base of the butte.

Spencer Creek, Klamath County. Captain O. C. Applegate in 1926 informed the compiler that Spencer Creek was named for an early settler who lived on a ranch on the creek.

Spencer Creek, Lincoln County. Spencer Creek flows into Pacific Ocean at Ocean Park about a mile south of Otter Rock. The creek was named for Doke Spencer, an Indian who lived near its mouth. Spencer and his family were allotted land in this locality.

Spencer Well, Deschutes County. This well northwest of Pine Mountain was on the homestead of Frank S. Spenser. The compiler has been unable to determine if the form Spenser was an error in the early records or if it changed through continued use of the more usual spelling.

Spicer, Linn County. Spicer, about five miles northwest of Lebanon, was first called Leng, apparently for a local landowner. The Oregonian Railway narrow gauge line was built south through the area in 1880, but the compiler does not know if the station Leng was established at that time or not. In any event, Leng appears as the station name in Polk's Directory of 1886-87, but Spicer post office was established August 17, 1886, with Adam A. Bashor first of a long series of postmasters. The post office was named for a local resident, W. E. Spicer, and the railroad adopted the post office name for its station. The post office was closed November 30, 1904, as the result of the extension of rural delivery. The railroad through this part of the county was abandoned in 1910.

Spikenard, Jackson County. The reason for the application of the name Spikenard to a Jackson County post office is another puzzle in Oregon geographic nomenclature. On November 21, 1879, a post office called Thomas Mill was established in the north part of the county with Thurston T. Thomas postmaster. The name of the office was changed to Spikenard on March 22, 1883, with Joseph Satterfield postmaster, and the office was finally closed in October, 1903. Old maps show Spikenard on the upper reaches of Evans Creek in township 34 south, range 2 west, but the exact location is a little indefinite. Dictionaries give several definitions of the word spikenard, including an ancient aromatic ointment, an essential oil or one of a number of plants allied to the valerian. The compiler does not know which of these was in mind when the post office was named, although the place was probably christened for a plant.

Spikes Gulch, Umatilla County. Spikes Gulch runs north to Echo Meadows. Elting J. Spike took up land near its upper end in 1909 but it is possible the name was applied for his nephews, Robert and Steve Spike, who farmed the property for many years.

Spinning Lake, Wasco County. This small lake east of Bonney Meadows is named for early USFS employee Bill Spinning.

Spino Spring, Umatilla County. This spring on Little Johnson Creek in the southeast corner of the county was named for an early Indian family.

Spirit Mountain, Yamhill County. This mountain, about a mile north of Grand Ronde, was so named because the Indians thought spirits or skookums lived on it. It was at one time called Cosper Butte for a family of early settlers. Dr. Rodney Glisan and other officers stationed at Fort Yamhill climbed this mountain on October 30, 1856, but Glisan does not mention a name in *Journal of Army Life,* pages 374-75.

Splintercat Creek, Clackamas County. This stream is a tributary from the south to Roaring River in range 7 east. It received the fantastic name of the legendary flying cat of the woods which was supposed to splinter branches from trees and tear out dead stumps. See editorial page of the *Oregonian,* April 17 and 24, 1944.

Split Falls, Clackamas County. This double falls on Salmon River is about one mile downstream from the mouth of Linney Creek. It is the second of six falls between Linney Creek and Welches and was named because it is divided into thirty-five and fifty-five foot drops. For details of this group see under Stein Falls.

Spores Point, Lane County. When Interstate Highway 5 was built it crossed McKenzie River at the site of the old Spores Ferry. In 1967 at the suggestion of the OSHD the OGNB recommended the name Spores Point for the high ground just east of the highway. Jacob C. Spores, a native of Montgomery County, New York, came to Oregon in 1847 and was one of the earliest settlers in Lane County. He operated a pioneer ferry on McKenzie River south of what is now Coburg a few hundred feet upstream from the Southern Pacific Company railroad bridge. This enterprise was of course named Spores Ferry in compliment to the owner. For information about Spores, see *Illustrated History of Lane County,* page 481 and also under Mohawk River.

Travelers on the highway should note the Southern Pacific Company railroad bridge, an historic structure. It is a 400 foot single span double intersection, pin connected, Pratt through truss constructed of wrought iron and as of this writing in 1979, probably the only wrought iron bridge of any size in the state. The bridge was originally erected at the OWR&N crossing of John Day River about 1887. In 1907, when the Columbia River line was rebuilt, it was sold to the Southern Pacific Company and relocated on the Springfield branch. This accounts for the incongruity of the date, 1887, cut into the headplates at each end.

Sprague River, Klamath County. There have been two different post offices in Oregon with the name Sprague River, established at different times and places. They were both named for the stream. The first Sprague River office was established November 12, 1873, with John W. Gearhart postmaster. The office was at first on the Jackson County list, but since it was east of the Cascade Range, it was not in what is now Jackson County. Later the office was moved to the Lake County list. John A. Smith became postmaster on March 24, 1876, and the office operated with other postmas-

ters and with some intermissions until January 31, 1883, when the name
was changed to Bly. The record does not show if the office was moved
when the name was changed. The Gearharts were stock raisers on the
upper reaches of Sprague River, but probably not as far east as what is now
Lake County. The compiler is of the opinion that this office was in what is
now Klamath County and never far from Bly. The second Sprague River
office was established September 14, 1923, with Benjamin E. Wolford first
postmaster, to serve a well-known lumber community. The office is much
further west of and downstream from the old office and is about fifteen
miles westward of Beatty.

Sprague River, Lake and Klamath counties. Sprague River was named
for Captain F. B. Sprague, who was a participant in various phases of the
Snake and Piute Indian wars, and who was in command at Fort Klamath in
1866. His name was applied to the stream at least as early as 1864. The
Klamath Indian name for Sprague River was *Plai,* or *Plaikni Koke. Koke* was
the general word for river, and *plai* indicated that the stream came from
the upper or higher country. See under Bly.

Spray, Wheeler County. Spray was named for its founder, John Fremont Spray, and his wife, Mary E. Spray. Spray was born in Iowa in 1859,
and came to the Willamette Valley in 1864. After living in various localities
in Oregon, he came to the site of Spray in 1900. The town plat was filed for
record May 19, 1900, by Mrs. Spray. Spray post office was established May
31, 1900, with John F. Spray first postmaster. For information of the Spray
family, see editorial page of the *Oregon Journal,* December 13, 1934. John F.
Spray died at Fossil January 11, 1930. See the *Oregonian,* January 18, 1930,
for obituary.

Spring Hill, Benton County. Spring Hill is a prominent landmark west
of the old wagon road between Albany and Independence. It has several
tops, the highest 519 feet in elevation. A fine spring fed a water trough by
the roadside, and for many years travelers pulled up their tired horses for a
drink.

Spring Valley, Polk County. Spring Valley is in the northeast corner of
the county, between the Eola Hills and Willamette River, and has been so
called since pioneer days. The name is descriptive. Spring Valley post office
was established March 5, 1852, with Sanford Watson postmaster. Solomon
Allen became postmaster November 30, 1854. When Watson was postmaster, the office was at his home on the extreme west edge of the valley in the
north part of section 26, township 6 south, range 4 west. When Allen
became postmaster, he moved the office to his home near the middle of
section 33, township 5 south, range 4 west, about two miles southeast of
Amity and a considerable distance from Spring Valley. The office was
closed on September 1, 1855. See under Valfontis.

Spring Valley, Wheeler County. A post office with the descriptive
name Spring Valley was established on the Wasco County list February 28,
1876, with Henry H. Wheeler first and only postmaster. The office was
discontinued April 14, 1880. Old maps show the place in the extreme northeast corner of what is now Wheeler County, on the south bank of John Day
River between Spray and Kimberly. H. H. Wheeler, for whom Wheeler

County was named, was a prominent pioneer character of the John Day country. His biography appears in *History of Central Oregon,* page 688. In 1864 he started the stagecoach service between The Dalles and the newly discovered mining area near Canyon City. In the early 1870s he located in the John Day Valley where he was associated with French Brothers in the stock business at the place called Spring Valley. About 1880 he bought property at a point six miles northwest of Mitchell where he lived until he sold out in 1904 and retired to Mitchell, where he died in 1915.

Springbrook, Yamhill County. Springbrook was for several years called Hoskins, for Cyrus E. Hoskins, a pioneer settler. When the post office was established June 30, 1893, it was impossible to use the name Hoskins because of confusion with a place of the same name in Benton County. Hoskins' farm was known as Springbrook and the name of the community was therefore changed to Springbrook. Hoskins was one of the pioneer horticulturists of the state.

Springfield, Lane County. Springfield appears to have been named for a natural spring, which sent up its water in a prairie or open field. In the early 1850s the spring and the land near it were fenced off, and the place came to be known by its present name. Elias Briggs was the first settler there in 1849. During many years he ran a ferry on the Willamette River. The town is described in the *Oregonian,* April 23, 1903; also *ibid.,* September 4, 1867, by Preston W. Gillette. Springfield post office was established May 15, 1868, with Albert G. Hovey first postmaster.

Springville, Multnomah County. The following note by Leslie M. Scott in Scott's *History of the Oregon Country,* volume II, page 328, is a good summary of the history of Springville: "Springville was south of Linnton, one mile, and north of Portland, six miles, at the place known (1922) as *Claremont.* At that place C. B. Comstock and Lafayette Scoggin established a warehouse, which served as a shipping point for farmers of Tualatin Valley, and which, about 1860, was regarded with jealousy by Portland and Saint Helens. It was the nearest shipping point to North Plains of Washington County, and Comstock and the farmers opened a road across the hills to Springville. The Springville road, from Tualatin, was a favorite route to the Willamette River before the Canyon Road to Portland was improved. When the west side railroad was opened, the Springville road fell into disuse, and, in 1872, the buildings there burned." Springville was named for a well-known spring on the slope of the hills to the west. The place was near the old Saint Johns ferry landing and just north of the modern Saint Johns bridge. Springville post office was established February 27, 1860, with C. B. Comstock first postmaster. The office was discontinued April 18, 1873.

Springwater, Clackamas County. The locality known as Springwater, about three miles south of Estacada, has borne the descriptive name since early days. Springwater was one of the first places on the upper Clackamas River to have a post office, which was established June 24, 1874, with George A. Crawford first postmaster. The office called Zion, later Currinsville, was established the same day. Springwater office was discontinued May 31, 1914.

Spruce, Tillamook County. Spruce post office, named for the Sitka spruce trees in the vicinity, was established at a point about twelve miles south of Tillamook in November, 1894, with Henry Peters first postmaster. The office was not far from the place later called Hemlock. Spruce office was moved around to suit the postmasters and was finally moved a few miles to the north to Pleasant Valley. It was discontinued in May, 1907. In the meantime the locality now called Hemlock was left without an office, so Hemlock office was established in April, 1906, with James W. Beaty first postmaster. Hemlock post office was closed in November, 1921.

Squaw Back Ridge, Jefferson County. This name is supposed to be descriptive, but the compiler has been unable to see the similarity between the ridge and what the name describes.

Squaw Creek, Deschutes and Jefferson counties. Fremont camped on this stream on December 2, 1843, but gave it no name. Lieutenant R. S. Williamson camped on Squaw Creek on September 1, 1855, and wrote that the Indian name was *Why-chus*. See Pacific Railroad Surveys *Reports,* volume VI, page 78. The compiler has been unable to learn who gave Squaw Creek its modern name.

Squaw Gulch, Wallowa County. This gulch drains into Sheep Creek in township 1 north, range 48 east. It was named in the early 1880s by Elisha Chase for an old Cayuse mare called Squaw, generally found ranging in the gulch.

Squaw Island, Coos County. One of the islands at the mouth of Sunset Bay southwest of the mouth of Coos Bay is called Squaw Island. There is a fairly well authenticated account of an Indian battle near Sunset Bay. The Indian women were put on the island so that when the tide came up they could not be captured. This encounter was between a roving band of Chetco Indians in war canoes and some Indians living near what is now Sunset Bay.

Staats Creek, Benton and Polk counties. This creek and Staats Hollow nearby were named for Isaac Staats, who was born in Albany County, New York, in 1814, and settled on his donation land claim near the creek in September, 1849. He married Orlena M. Williams May 10, 1846. See land certificate 4710.

Stacey, Douglas County. Stacey post office was established January 19, 1901, with T. B. Fagan first postmaster. This office, which was named for a local family, was situated on Elk Creek a few miles northeast of Yoncalla. The office was closed October 31, 1906.

Stafford, Clackamas County. This place was named by George A. Steel, a prominent pioneer of Portland, for his native town, Stafford, Ohio.

Stahlbusch Island, Benton County. This island is the upper part of a land-area in Willamette River above Corvallis. The lower part is Fischer Island, and the two are separated by water at high river stages. About 210 acres of the land were deeded to John and Herman Stahlbusch in December 1888, and Robert Johnson of Corvallis informed the compiler that this is the correct spelling, not Stallbush.

Stahlman Point, Linn County. This point overlooking the east end of Detroit Reservoir was named for Fred Stahlman, the first USFS ranger at Detroit.

Staley Ridge, Douglas County. This ridge is in the Calapooya Mountains. Just to the east is Staley Creek, a tributary to Middle Fork Willamette River. Staley Creek flows into the Middle Fork in Lane County. These features were named for W. F. Staley of the USFS. Staley Creek was known in early days as South Fork Middle Fork.

Stalter Canyon, Morrow County. Stalter Canyon four miles southeast of Heppner was named for Daniel B. Stalter who took up government land near its mouth in 1891. Stalter's wife and six of his seven children were drowned in the Heppner flood of 1903.

Stanfield, Umatilla County. Stanfield was first known as Foster. Mrs. J. M. Cornelison of Pendleton wrote in 1959 that John R. Foster was a Portland associate of Allen & Lewis who had commercial interests at Umatilla. They bought 4000 acres northeast of Echo where they established a large farm followed by a small community and branch store all named for one of the proprietors. Foster post office was established May 14, 1883, with Frank B. Clopton first postmaster. The name of the place was later changed to Stanfield, for Robert N. Stanfield, subsequently U. S. senator from Oregon. Senator Stanfield owned land nearby, hence the application of his name to the community. Stanfield post office was established in 1907.

Stanley, Clackamas County. The locality called Stanley is in the extreme north edge of Clackamas County about two miles northeast of Milwaukie. When the interurban line was built along Johnson Creek the company asked John H. Gibson, a local resident, to name the place. This he did in compliment to his son, George Stanley Gibson. Stanley post office was established November 16, 1904, and was discontinued April 29, 1905. Mary A. Morris was the only postmaster. The office was about a third of a mile west of Wichita.

Stanley Lake, Clatsop County. Stanley Lake is a short distance northeast of Seaside. It was named for S. K. Stanley, an early settler on Clatsop Plains.

Stanley Rock, Hood River County. This is a prominent rocky bluff on the south bank of the Columbia River just east of the mouth of Hood River. It is surmounted by a steel transmission tower of the Pacific Power & Light Company. The top of the rock is about 140 feet above the river level. It was named for John Stanley, who operated a farm at this point, and also a ferry to the Washington side.

Stapleton, Polk County. This station, near Independence, was named for John Stapleton, who came west from Canada in 1863, and after spending a few years in Idaho, settled in the Willamette Valley, near the place that now bears his name. His sons, George Stapleton and James P. Stapleton, were prominent members of the Oregon bar for many years.

Starkey, Union County. Starkey was a post office in the west part of the county near, but not on, Starkey Creek. Both were named for the first postmaster, John Starkey, who settled there in the 1870s. The post office was established December 10, 1879 and closed in the early part of 1935.

Starr Creek, Benton County. Starr Creek is southwest of Corvallis. It bears the name of a pioneer family. See under Monroe.

Starr Creek, Lane County. Starr Creek is tributary to South Fork McKenzie River from the west at a point just about due south from

McKenzie Bridge. It flows into South Fork about a half mile north or down-stream from the mouth of Augusta Creek. It bears the family name of a former forest assistant who was stationed at McKenzie Bridge. The compiler has been informed by competent authorities that young Starr began to pay his respects to (was a settin' of) Miss Augusta Young, daughter of Carl Young, an early day forest ranger in the neighborhood, and by the time their engagement was announced, their names had been joined in a sort of nomenclative couple. The two streams were named Starr Creek and Augusta Creek and thus sylvan romance has been preserved for posterity.

Starr Spring, Wheeler County. This spring above Stone Cabin Creek southwest of Fossil was named for early homesteader Felix Starr.

Starvation Creek, Hood River County. This creek was originally called Starveout in December 1884 when two trains of the recently completed railroad were snowbound nearby. There is a story that men were paid $25.00 per day to pack food on skis from Hood River and that the railroad offered the stranded passengers who were willing and able $3.00 per day to shovel snow. For more information on this intense, early storm see The Dalles *Times Mountaineer,* December 20 and 27, 1884.

Starvout, Douglas County. The locality called Starvout is on a stream of the same name which flows into Cow Creek a few miles east of Galesville. The place has been called Starvout since early days. Early in 1946 Miss Bess A. Clough of Canyonville was able to get the history of this name from her uncle, George Elliff, then mining gold in northern California. The Elliff family were well-known Douglas County pioneers. Some time in the 1850s Hardy Elliff grubstaked one George Walton and sent him up on the creek to prospect. Gold was scarce and when Walton came out in the spring, neighbors said he had starved out, hence the name of the stream. Some good diggings were found later on, farther up the creek. Starvout post office was established on the banks of this stream on February 18, 1888, with H. L. Miser postmaster. For the subsequent history of this office, see under the heading Azalea.

Stauffer, Lake County. Stauffer was in Lost Creek Valley, and local residents wanted the post office called Lost Creek, but the postal authorities objected to the name because of duplication, and instead selected the name Stauffer, for C. J. Stauffer, the first postmaster. The post office was established September 13, 1913, and closed to Hampton on June 30, 1950.

Stavebolt Landing, Clatsop County. This landing was named because it was the place where bolts or logs were dumped into Lewis and Clark River and towed away to the mills. Stavebolt Landing is about eight miles airline south of Astoria. Stavebolt Creek flows into Lewis and Clark River about a half mile above the landing. These names have been in use for many years.

Stayton, Marion County. Stayton was named for Drury S. Stayton, who founded the community. The following news item printed in the *Oregonian* for November 18, 1875, tells of early days in Stayton: "The new town of Stayton in Marion County has grown rapidly during the past season. A new flourmill and a sawmill have been built. It now contains 20 families." Stayton was platted in 1872, and the post office established on May 7 of that year. Samuel D. McCauley was first postmaster.

Steamboat, Jackson County. Many old mining camps have this name applied to one or more geographic features, and it does not mean that a steamboat has ever been in the neighborhood. When mines have been worked out, or where prospects do not come up to expectations, either naturally or through fraud, they are said by miners to have been "steamboated." In addition to a place and a mountain in the southwest part of Jackson County bearing this name, there is also a creek named Steamboat which rises in the Calapooya Mountains in Lane County and flows through Douglas County into North Umpqua River. It is said to have received its name in this manner.

Steamboat Creek, Wallowa County. Steamboat Creek flows into Snake River in township 4 south, range 49 east. This is near the site of the Copper Ledge Falls where the steamer *Shoshone* temporarily came to grief in 1870 and the *Norma* also had difficulty in 1895. These two steamers were the only boats to successfully make the trip from the upper Snake River down to Lewiston.

Steamboat Lake, Wallowa County. So called because of a rock in the lake resembling a steamboat. The lake is about 18 miles airline south of Lostine.

Stearns, Deschutes County. Harry Stearns of Prineville wrote the compiler in 1969 to say that this station on the Great Northern Railway north of La Pine was named for his brother Cecil. Their father, Sidney Stearns, had large land and cattle holdings near both La Pine and Prineville.

Stearns Butte, Crook County. This butte, four miles south of Prineville, is at the S. S. Stearns ranch, and got its name on that account. A prominent tree on the summit was for many years a surveyor's bearing mark.

Steel Bay, Crater Lake National Park, Klamath County. This bay is in the north shore of Crater Lake, and was named in honor of Will G. Steel, for a half a century a prominent explorer, mountaineer and nature lover of Oregon. William Gladstone Steel was born in Stafford, Ohio, September 7, 1854, the son of William and Elizabeth Steel. His father's mother, Jean Gladstone, was a sister of Thomas Gladstone, Jr., and was therefore the great aunt of William Ewart Gladstone who became premier of England. Steel moved to Pittsburgh with his parents in 1865 and in 1868 to Kansas. Here the boy read an account of the discovery of a mysterious lake in Oregon. This fired his imagination and filled him with a desire to come to this state and see the natural wonder. He reached Oregon in 1872, and it was nine years before he could get authoritative data about the lake he was looking for. He finally visited Crater Lake in 1885, and immediately started a movement to have the locality made into a national park. He was successful in this after 17 years of effort. Steel devoted a large part of his life to matters pertaining to the natural history and attractions of the Pacific Northwest and was the authority on Crater Lake. He died at Medford October 21, 1934.

Steel Cliff, Hood River County. This cliff is on the south face of Mount Hood, and was named for Will G. Steel by E. L. Coldwell, better known as Jerry Coldwell, for many years a reporter on the *Oregonian*.

Steens Mountain, Harney County. The first reference to this moun-

tain that the writer has seen is in the journal of John Work, for Friday, June
29, 1831. See *OHQ,* volume XIV, page 308. Work describes the mountain
as covered with snow. Pioneer maps use the name of Snow Mountains for
the range. In 1860 a joint expedition was sent into southeastern Oregon
under the command of Major Enoch Steen, U.S.A. Steen reached the
mountain that now bears his name early in August, and drove a band of
Snake Indians over its summit. See Bancroft's *History of Oregon,* volume II,
page 467. The name Steens Mountain has been in general use ever since,
although it is frequently misspelled Steins Mountain. The USBGN has
adopted the form Steens Mountain. The mountain is the highest in southeastern Oregon, and is much longer north and south than east and west. Its
east face is a notable escarpment that extends for 5000 feet above Alvord
Valley. Enoch Steen was born in Kentucky, and was commissioned second
lieutenant in the mounted rangers in 1832. He reached the rank of lieutenant-colonel on September 28, 1861, retired from the army on September
23, 1863, and died January 22, 1880. He was brevetted major in 1847 for
gallant conduct in the battle of Buena Vista, Mexico.

Stein Falls, Clackamas County. These are a double falls on Salmon
River just below the mouth of Linney Creek. They were named in honor of
Bobby and Johnny Stein of Welches who were killed in World War II. In
1963 W. Kirk Braun proposed this name along with six others on Salmon
River and Tumbling Creek. In order downstream from Linney Creek they
are Stein Falls, Split Falls, Hideaway Falls on Tumbling Creek, Little Niagara Falls, Vanishing Falls, Frustration Falls and Final Falls. There is a trail
from the end of the road above Welches to the upper reaches of Salmon
River, but it traverses some of the roughest country in Clackamas County.
A subcommittee of the OGNB consisting of Herbert Stone, Thomas Vaughan and Donald Sterling made a field inspection of this area in the summer of 1963. They reported that names such as Frustration and Vanishing
were most appropriate as much of the river bank is almost inaccessible
from the trail. For further information see under the individual headings.

Steinman, Jackson County. Steinman station south of Ashland was
established in 1887 when the Central Pacific completed the railroad north
into Ashland. It was named for Ben Steinman, a jeweler, pawnbroker and
money lender of Sacramento. He was well known to railroad officials and
employees, who wished to perpetuate his memory in a kindly way by naming a station for him.

Steinnon Creek, Coos County. This stream, which is southeast of Coos
Bay town, flows south from Blue Ridge. In 1929 S. B. Cathcart of Coos Bay
told the compiler that it was named for a Belgian farmer who settled
nearby about 1900.

Steins Pillar, Crook County. Steins Pillar is a 350 foot high monolith
south of Mill Creek and northeast of Mahogany Butte. Tradition has it that
it bears the name of Major Enoch Steen, USA. In 1860 Steen commanded
an expedition from Fort Dalles against the Snake Indians in the Harney
Basin. On June 3, 1860 camp was made on Mill Creek not far from the
pillar which is plainly visible from the valley. In the report by Lieutenant
Joseph Dixon of the U. S. Topographical Engineers who accompanied the

expedition Mill Creek is called Cottonwood Creek. On June 6, 1860 Dixon writes, "Road good with the exception of a few narrow and rocky places in the canon of Tooth Rock." However, this was along Crooked River well east of Post.

The Pillar is 120 feet in diameter and 350 feet high with a slight over-hanging cap. It obviously offered a major rock climbing challenge but it was not until 1950 that it was first climbed by a party of five men, Floyd and Glenn Richardson, Don Baars, Leonard Rice and Rodney Shay. The sur-face has been hardened by weathering but the rock immediately beneath is soft and friable. This makes the use of pitons and other direct aids difficult and dangerous.

Stephens, Douglas County. Stephens is a place on Calapooya Creek about four miles west of Sutherlin and was named for the family of Ebe-nezer Stephens who took a donation land claim nearby. Stephens post office was established January 6, 1890, with Mrs. Eliza Ottinger postmaster. The office operated until October 31, 1912, when it was closed out to Oak-land. Stephens was never a large community. The post office list for Ump-qua County contains the name of an office called Stephensville, which operated in the late 1850s with Winslow P. Powers postmaster. This list appears to be for that part of Umpqua County which was added to Douglas County in 1862. It may be that Stephensville was an early name for what was later Stephens.

Stephenson Mountain, Jefferson County. This mountain and adjoin-ing lake were named for Thomas J. Stephenson who homesteaded the old Stephenson Ranch in 1870. The mountain is in the extreme southeast cor-ner of Jefferson County while the ranch was in Wheeler County. Stephen-son was the first settler in the area. He died in 1898 but his family retained the property until 1967.

Sterling Creek, Jackson County. There have been a number of geo-graphic features in southwest Jackson County with Sterling as part of the name, including Sterling Peak, Sterling Creek, Sterling Mine and Sterling-ville. Many years ago the writer was told by Will G. Steel that these names all came from one James Sterling, presumably a miner, who operated in the area in the 1850s. Sterling Peak was named in 1853, according to Steel, but the name Dutchman Peak has supplanted the older name. Sterling Creek flows into Little Applegate River near Buncom, and Sterling Mine was well known because of its hydraulic works, shown on popular picture post cards. Sterlingville post office, a short distance upstream from the mine, was estab-lished April 21, 1879, with George Yandes first and only postmaster. This office was closed to Jacksonville on July 31, 1883.

Steve Fork, Jackson and Josephine counties. Steve Fork is a tributary of Carberry Creek. The name Steamboat Creek is incorrect.

Stevens Gulch, Baker County. Stevens Gulch empties into Ruckles Creek south of Keating. Azor L. Stevens settled near its mouth during World War I.

Stewart Lake, Benton County. This lake, northeast of Corvallis, was named for Archimedes and John Stewart, who took up donation land claims around it. See land office certificates 175 and 176.

Still Creek, Clackamas County. This stream flows into Zigzag River at Rhododendron. It was named in pioneer days because emigrants coming down the Zigzag, which is turbulent, noted the difference in the character of the flow of the two streams.

Stillwell Creek, Tillamook County. This creek which flows into Little Nestucca River about one mile above Dolph was named for Fred Stillwell, an early USFS ranger.

Stinger Gulch, Douglas County. This draw a mile west of Days Creek was named for Leonard Stinger, an early day prospector and settler. Stinger took up donation land claim #354 near Canyonville in 1854.

Stinkingwater Creek, Harney County. William Hanley of Burns told the compiler that this stream had been so known since the 1870s, because of the disagreeable fumes that are prevalent near some of the mineral springs along the creek. These disagreeable fumes are said to contain arsenical gases. The late George E. Davis, corporation commissioner of Oregon, who died in November, 1927, informed the compiler that, according to his understanding, the name of the stream was a corruption of the name of a pioneer German settler who lived on its banks. Hanley denied this, however, and said he never heard of such a settler and was positive this version was incorrect. Stinkingwater Mountains lie west of the creek.

Stipp, Marion County. Among the pioneer settlers in Marion County was John L. Stipp, who took up a claim just west of the community now known as Macleay. Stipp was pastor of the local Baptist Church, and was referred to as Elder Stipp. He gave land for what is called the J. L. Stipp Memorial Cemetery, just west of the community. Stipp post office, named for Elder Stipp, was established May 4, 1880, with William Taylor postmaster. The name of the office was changed to Macleay February 3, 1882. See also under the name Macleay.

Stone Bridge, Lake County. Stone Bridge is a well-known place near the south end of Hart Lake in the Warner Valley. The bridge was built in the summer of 1867 under the direction of Major-General George Crook, then a lieutenant-colonel in the regular army. In the previous year Old Camp Warner had been established on the east side of the Warner Valley and not in the place specified in the orders. When Crook arrived in the valley in 1867 he wanted to know why the camp had been built on the wrong side of the valley and was told that the troops were on the east side and could not get across the lakes. Crook immediately ordered the army wagons and carts to haul chunks of lava out to the narrowest crossing, and, using rock for a foundation, built a causeway to the west side. A new Camp Warner was then established. See *History of Central Oregon,* page 812. Stone Bridge is listed in the National Register of Historic Places. It is difficult to locate as in the 1980s the roadway is under water but still passable at low water stages.

Stookey Flat, Deschutes County. This flat west of Horse Ridge was named for Seth Stookey who settled there in 1917.

Stotts Landing, Multnomah County. This landing, just west of the mouth of Little Sandy River, was named for J. M. Stott, who took up a donation land claim nearby.

Stout Creek, Marion County. Stout Creek was named for Ephraim Stout and his son Lewis, who emigrated from Iowa in 1852 and operated pioneer sawmills near this stream. Lewis Stout was born in 1829 and died in 1922. His donation land claim was at the mouth of Stout Creek, and his sawmill was operated by water from the creek.

Stouts Creek, Douglas County. Stouts Creek is an important tributary of South Umpqua River from the south at Milo. Benjamin Stout took a donation land claim just east of the creek and probably gave his name to the stream. However, his brother, Milton, is mentioned in the 1860 census and Reinhart in *The Golden Frontier,* page 158, mentions seeing Ben and George Stout in 1858. He later adds that George Stout was killed by George Green in 1860 so all three brothers may have contributed.

Straightsburg, Hood River County. Straightsburg was the name given to a post office established on the Wasco County list October 19, 1888, with Henry D. Straight postmaster. The office was in the Hood River Valley and within the limits of what is now Hood River County. Straightsburg post office operated only until November 18, 1891. Old gazetteers say the office was on Neal Creek about seven miles south of Hood River town.

Strait Spring, Morrow County. This spring in section 22, township 2 north, range 25 east, was on the property of Alpheus L. Strait who settled there about the time of World War I.

Stranahan Ridge, Hood River County. Stranahan Ridge is on the northeast side of Mount Hood and divides the drainages of Eliot and Coe branches. It was named for Oscar L. Stranahan, one of the organizers of the Mount Hood Trail and Wagon Road Company along with Captain Henry C. Coe and David R. Cooper.

Strassel, Washington County. Strassel was named for Mrs. Mary Strassel. She was an early settler, who took up a homestead, and with pioneer spirit made a home in what had been a wilderness. When the railroad was built near her place, E. E. Lytle, president of the Pacific Railway and Navigation Company, named a station for her, and later a post office was established with the same name.

Straw Fork, Wheeler County. This stream flows into Butte Creek southeast of Fossil. It was named for Al Straw who settled there about 1869. See *History of Central Oregon,* page 640. Stories to the effect that the stream was named for strawstacks are wrong.

Strawberry, Morrow County. Strawberry is a locality about nine miles north of Lexington, supposedly named for the wild strawberries that grow there. The place has not grown into a community. Strawberry post office was established March 7, 1904, with Jesse C. White first and only postmaster. The office was discontinued December 31, 1908. Expected development did not become a fact.

Strawberry Mountain, Grant County. Patsy Daly of Prairie City, for many years a resident of the John Day country, told the compiler in 1927 that white settlers and miners first called this mountain Logan Butte for Camp Logan, nearby. This was in the 1860s. To the north of the butte was Strawberry Creek, so called because of the wild strawberries growing on its banks. Gradually the name Strawberry spread to the valley and to the butte, so that the forms Strawberry Valley and Strawberry Butte came into universal use. The name Logan Butte became obsolete. During the past three decades the name Strawberry Mountain has supplanted Strawberry Butte, and the form with the word "Mountain" now appears on official maps. It seems to be in general use. It is the highest point in the southwest part of the Blue Mountains. The elevation determined by the USGS is 9025 feet.

String Creek, Clackamas County. This stream is in the Salmon River drainage basin. It was so named because of its small, stringy appearance.

Stringtown, Clackamas County. There are several localities in Oregon called Stringtown, generally because they are or were strung out along a road or highway. One of the best known with this name is about a mile southwest of Canemah. It was called Stringtown long ago, long before there was a through highway. There were a number of houses built on the narrow strip between the railroad and the steep bluff to the southeast, and these houses were called Stringtown, especially by people living in more thickly settled areas such as Oregon City and Canemah. The place is now well known because it is on the Pacific Highway East.

Stukel Mountain, Klamath County. Stukel Mountain was named for Stephen Stukel, a pioneer settler. It is about ten miles southeast of Klamath Falls, and is shown on some maps as Laki Peak, but it is not known by that name locally. Laki is probably derived from the Klamath Indian word *laki* meaning chief.

Stulls Falls, Coos County. Stulls Falls are on West Fork Millicoma River thirteen miles southwest of Scottsburg. They bear the name of Walter Stull who settled nearby in the early 1900s. For a number of years they were incorrectly shown on various maps as Stalls Falls but this was corrected in USBGN *Decision List 7302.*

Sturgeon Lake, Columbia and Multnomah counties. Omar C. Spencer of Sauvie Island in a letter of January 18, 1946, says *inter alia:* "Before the hand of man despoiled its natural characteristics through the medium of the public levee built at government expense, Sturgeon Lake was a large body of water consisting of approximately 2500 acres, through which Gilbert River found its way to an outlet in Multnomah Channel of the Willamette River. Now the upper part of Gilbert River has been cut off from flowing through Sturgeon Lake, but the lake still has its Gilbert River outlet to Multnomah Channel. Originally Sturgeon Lake was of sufficient importance that it had its Little Sturgeon Lake, which has been taken from it by the levee above mentioned." Sturgeon Lake was named in very early days, but the exact circumstances of the event are not known to the compiler. The white sturgeon, *Acipenser transmontanus,* is the largest fish found in fresh water in North America. The biggest specimen on record was taken from the Columbia River near Vancouver in 1929. It was over twelve feet long and weighed 1285 pounds. These big sturgeon in the Columbia River are largely a thing of the past, and the fish now caught seldom exceed five feet in length. Sturgeon is much appreciated locally as a food fish, but is relatively scarce. Squire Spencer's letter contains a lively tradition that Sauvie Island sturgeon came ashore from the lake and stripped the fruit from the nearby apple trees. A fish weighing 1285 pounds might be able to do anything, even reach up into an apple tree.

Sturgill, Baker County. In 1925 railroad company officials wrote that this station was named for an early settler and prospector.

Sturgill Peak, Wallowa County. Sturgill Peak in the Wallowa Mountains was named for Jåke Sturgill.

Sturgis Fork, Jackson and Josephine counties. This stream is a tributary of Carberry Creek, and is named for an old settler. Sturges is wrong.

Sturtevant Creek, Lane County. This stream flows into Coyote Creek not far from Crow. It was named for Joseph K. Sturtevant, an early settler.

Sublimity, Marion County. According to information furnished the writer Sublimity was named by James M. Denny who established the town and said he called it Sublimity "for the sublime scenery in the hills around the town." Sublimity post office was established September 29, 1852. Denny was the first postmaster.

Substitute Point, Lane County. Substitute Point, elevation 6340 feet, is just west of the Three Sisters. It was named in 1916 by a USGS party in charge of J. G. Staack, which was extending triangulation in that part of the Cascade Range. Two unnamed peaks were selected for possible stations, where but one was to be used. The other peak was called Proxy Point. See under that heading. The station was installed on Substitute Point and later a lookout was established there.

Succor Creek, Malheur County. There has been a good deal of controversy over this name and it is to be hoped that the OGBN decision of December 1965 and the USBGN decision of June 8, 1966 will finally lay the matter to rest. The stream rises north of Sheaville and flows northward near the east border of the county, then northeast into Idaho, where it empties into Snake River near Homedale. The decision in favor of Sucker Creek was made by USBGN on June 6, 1906. Postal history shows that there was a post office called Sucker established on the lower reaches of the stream on October 4, 1895, with Sara McConnell postmaster. This office was close to the Idaho line. It was closed October 13, 1899. Apparently the name was changed and the office moved to DeLamar, Idaho. The existence of a post office with the spelling Sucker seems to indicate that that style was acceptable to local residents about the turn of the century. In the summer of 1929 the problem was presented again and after another study, the USBGN decided to stand by the earlier decision. The style Sucker Creek appeared to be based either on the prevalence of sucker fish or a story to the effect that some miners were played for suckers during early day mining excitement, and the spelling adopted by the Post Office Department in 1895. In 1965 the Oregon State Highway Department announced plans to establish a recreation area in the Succor Creek canyon between S. H. 201 south of Adrian and U. S. 95 north of Sheaville. The canyon contains spectacular rock formations, fossil plants and petrified wood, and is a favorite hunting ground for thundereggs, the Oregon state rock. The resultant publicity stirred up the old controversy as most of the local civic organizations and elder citizens protested that because of the intermittent nature of the stream there were few piscatorial suckers and there was no evidence of the gullibility of the early inhabitants. Horace L. Arment of Ontario and L. E. George of Salem took up the cudgel in behalf of Succor and unearthed references spelled in this manner as early as the John Tucker Scott diary entry for August 19, 1852, and the diary of Major G. G. Kimball in 1865. The account of the 1860 Vanorman massacre in *OHQ*, volume XX, page 16, and the reminiscences of Wm. Schnable printed in the *Malheur Enterprise* on March 8, 1930 also use this spelling. As Scott uses the name eight years before the Vanorman incident, it was not applied because the survivors of the massacre were saved by hiding in the willows along the bank. The origin of the name is obscure but there is a legend that travelers south of the Snake were saved by the fresh water found in the creek and applied the name as a corruption of the Spanish word *socorro,* meaning aid or help.

Sucker Creek, Josephine County. Sucker Creek flows into East Fork Illinois River. Walling, in his *History of Southern Oregon,* page 454, says the stream was named on account of some Illinois miners who prospected nearby. Illinois is known as the Sucker State.

Sugarbowl Creek, Umatilla County. This stream rises on the Butter Creek divide five miles south of Gurdane and flows north ultimately to North Fork John Day River. It was named because the meadow at its source is bowl shaped.

Sugarloaf, Polk County. Sugarloaf post office served the Siletz Basin in the locality of what is now Valsetz. The office was named for a conical point just north of South Fork Siletz River, called Sugarloaf Mountain. Sugarloaf post office was established on April 16, 1895, with John S. Wright first postmaster. It continued in operation until April 30, 1904, when it was closed out to Rocca.

Sugarpine Mountain, Klamath County. There are few geographic features in Oregon named for the sugar pine, *Pinus lambertiana,* and of these features Sugarpine Mountain north of Klamath Indian Reservation is probably the most important. The sugarpine is the largest of the Pacific pines, from 160-180 feet tall with a diameter as great as six feet. The long, chestnut brown cones are characteristic, reaching a length of sixteen inches. The range of the tree does not generally extend north of the latitude of Mount Jefferson.

Sullivan Creek, Baker County. This stream is in township 6 south, range 44 east. It was named for a pioneer prospector who is buried on its banks.

Sullivan Gulch, Multnomah County. Timothy Sullivan, for whom this gulch in east Portland was named, settled on a donation land claim in the eastern part of section 35, township 1 north, range 1 east, on January 27, 1851. The record of this claim, certificate 1478, shows that Sullivan was born in Ireland in 1805. He appears to have traveled extensively, for he was married to Margaret, last name unstated, in Van Dieman's Land (Tasmania), January 8, 1841. He was made a citizen of the United States by Judge Cyrus Olney on April 16, 1855, and appears to have received title to the claim about 1863. His house was on the south edge of the gulch, in the north part of his claim. For additional information about the Sullivan family, see editorial in the Portland *Telegram,* May 3, 1927, and article in *Oregon Journal,* May 15, 1927, section 1, page 10.

Sullivan Gulch, Union County. Sullivan Gulch is west of Starkey. it was named for Andrew Sullivan who came to the Starkey area in 1888 with 2500 horses. He also had a large horse ranch on Juniper Creek in Umatilla

County where a band<of cowboys broke the animals raised near Starkey. This information came from John Evans and Jon Skovlin of La Grande.

Sulphur Springs, Douglas County. Sulphur Springs are close to the north bank of Smith River a couple of miles east of North Fork. These springs, which flow cold mineral water, have been known from pioneer days. Sulphur Springs post office was one of the earliest offices in the west part of the county. It was established February 6, 1878, with John Cowan first postmaster. That was the same day that Norfolk post office was established not very far away. Sulphur Springs post office was closed to Reedsport on March 31, 1920.

Sumac Creek, Wallowa County. Sumac Creek is near Chico, in township 3 north, range 45 east. The stream was named for the sumac, *Rhus glabra occidentalis.*

Summer Lake, Lake County. Summer Lake is one of the larger lakes of the arid part of the state and has an area of about 60 square miles. Its main source of supply is Ana River which is a spring-fed stream attaining great volume within a short distance from its source. Summer Lake has no outlet and as a result its water is strongly impregnated with salts, particularly of sodium. The lake was discovered and named by then Captain John C. Fremont, of the U. S. Topographical Engineers, on December 16, 1843. As he looked down from the ridge which his party had climbed from the west he saw the sun shining on the lake, bordered with the green grass and the contrast was so great that he named the mountain Winter Ridge and the lake Summer Lake.

Summerville, Union County. William Patten, one of the founders of this community, named it for his friend and neighbor, Alexander Sommerville. The two had lived about six miles from Harrisburg in the Willamette Valley. They moved to Grande Ronde Valley in 1857, according to information furnished the compiler by Edgar J. Sommerville of Pendleton in 1926. Summerville post office was established on May 30, 1865, with Patten first postmaster. The compiler does not know why the spelling was changed from Sommerville to Summerville. There may have been a mistake somewhere along the line or Patten and the postal authorities may have concluded that the public would prefer the usual style and adopt it sooner or later instead of the family name.

Summit, Benton County. Summit is on the watershed between Willamette Valley and Yaquina River and the name is descriptive. One time the place was called Summitville.

Summit Lake, Klamath County. Summit Lake, elevation 5554 feet, is in the extreme northwest part of the county and drains eastward into Crescent Lake. It is very close to the summit of the Cascade Range, hence its name. Summit Lake must have been known in the days of the immigrations, but the first use of the name that has come to the compiler's attention is in a report on the Oregon Central Military Road, by B. J. Pengra, dated November 29, 1865. Part of this report is on file at the Oregon Historical Society. The report seems to indicate that the name Summit Lake was applied in July, 1865, by Pengra and W. H. Odell while making a reconnaissance of that part of Oregon.

Sumner, Coos County. Steel says this community was founded in 1888 by John B. Dalley and named for Charles Sumner, (1811-1876), Massachusetts statesman. The date must be wrong, for the post office was established on September 18, 1874, with Dalley first postmaster.

Sumpter, Baker County. C. A. Moore of Baker informed the compiler in 1927 that Sumpter was settled during the early days of the Civil War, and was named for Fort Sumter, South Carolina, because of the prominent position occupied by the name in the news dispatches. Post Office records show that an office with the name Sumter was established on the Grant County, Oregon, list June 24, 1874, with Joseph D. Young first postmaster. The office was soon changed to the Baker County list and was discontinued October 1, 1878. It was reestablished December 13, 1883, with the spelling Sumpter and F. Beagle postmaster. However, the records are obviously in error for the compiler has a photo-copy of Joseph D. Young's commission as postmaster of Sumpter dated December 13, 1883. His grandson, Frederick Young of Cove, supplied this in 1981 along with the information that his grandfather was told he could not use the form Sumter. As all supplies were packed in by mule train, he stayed as close as possible to the original form by changing to Sumpter as in sumpter mule. A news item in the Baker *Democrat-Herald,* May 3, 1929, says that the immediate reason for selecting the name for the Oregon town was that a local resident found a rock, as perfectly spherical as a cannon ball, and this, along with the name of Fort Sumter in the news, suggested the use of the name. This rock was on display in Baker in 1929.

Sundial Lake, Multnomah County. This lake is on the south side of the Columbia River near Fairview. It was named for the Sundial Ranch nearby. Charles F. Swigert of Portland told the compiler that the ranch was named by his business associate, the late Homer C. Campbell, also of Portland. Swigert said he did not know why Campbell chose the name Sundial Ranch, because as far as he knew, there never was a sundial on the place.

Sunny Valley, Josephine County. Sunny Valley post office was established in the summer of 1945 at the point where the Pacific Highway crosses Grave Creek, about 18 miles north of Grants Pass. The name takes the place of several that have had great historic significance in Oregon. The first establishment in this vicinity was the Grave Creek House of Harkness and Twogood, also called Fort Leland in the Indian wars of the 1850s. The first post office here was Leland, on March 28, 1855, with McDonough Harkness first postmaster. For the history of the name Leland, see under that name. Some time after the railroad was extended from Roseburg south in the 1880s, Leland post office was moved about four miles west to the railroad location. There had already been a railroad station at Altamont at or near the station later called Leland. The compiler cannot learn when the name Leland was moved to the railroad, but it must have been in the early 1890s. On July 24, 1894, a post office named Grave, with Samuel B. Pettengill postmaster, was established to serve the locality on Grave Creek from which Leland post office had been moved. Grave office was operated until October, 1913. It was opened again in March, 1928, with the name Grave Creek, and with Mrs. Nora Dunham postmaster. This office continued to serve the locality until the office Sunny Valley was established by change of name from Grave Creek. Local residents were apparently a little morbid about the old name and selected Sunny Valley because the locality is often free of the low fogs that frequent the general area. For the origin of the name Grave Creek, see under that heading.

Sunnyside, Clackamas County. The area called Sunnyside lies south of Mount Scott and is rather loosely defined. There is a Sunnyside Road, well known and also a Sunnyside School about two miles west of Damascus. These features are all near the north border of the county. Sunnyside post office was established December 17, 1888, with John R. Welch first postmaster. The office was closed August 12, 1903, probably because of the extension of rural free delivery. The compiler does not know the exact location. The fact that this office was in operation in the early 1890s made it impossible to have a Sunnyside post office to serve Sunnyside, now a part of Portland. Accordingly the Sunnyside addition in Multnomah County was served by an office called Sunnyview.

Sunnyview, Multnomah County. That part of Portland known as Sunnyside in the vicinity of Southeast Belmont Street between Southeast Twenty-ninth and Southeast Thirty-seventh avenues was once served by a post office with the name Sunnyview. The name Sunnyside could not be used because there was already a Sunnyside office in neighboring Clackamas County. Sunnyview office was established August 21, 1890, with Queen M. Bower first of three postmasters. The office was closed December 4, 1894, with all papers to Portland. The name was optimistically descriptive.

Sunriver, Deschutes County. This is a planned resort and residential community fifteen miles southwest of Bend on the site of World War II Camp Abbot. Sunriver post office was established with Lawrence J. Doherty first postmaster on July 18, 1969, at the same time that the first public facilities were opened. Sunriver is a coined name selected by John Gray and Donald V. McCallum, developers of the project. For information on Camp Abbot, see under that heading.

Sunset, Coos County. Sunset post office was named for Sunset Bay, where it was situated, about three miles west of Charleston. The office was established January 24, 1910, with William S. Denning postmaster. It was closed March 31, 1911. Sunset Bay is a little cove on the north part of Cape Arago and is said to have been named by Thomas Hirst.

Sunset Bay, Coos County. Sunset Bay is a snug little cove on the north part of Cape Arago, at the mouth of Big Creek. According to an article in the Marshfield *Coast Mail,* August 14, 1892, the name was first suggested by Thomas Hirst.

Sunset Highway, Clatsop, Columbia, Multnomah, Tillamook and Washington counties. Sunset Highway is the official name of the state road, which was built largely with the name Wolf Creek Highway. The name Wolf Creek was derived from a small stream flowing eastward into Nehalem River near Sunset Camp. For many months during the construction period the name Wolf Creek Highway was used for this important link in the state road system but it became apparent that the name caused confusion because of other Wolf creeks in Oregon. Accordingly on January 17,

1946, the Oregon State Highway Commission adopted a resolution changing the name to Sunset Highway. This was in compliment to the 41st or Sunset Division of the United States Army which played a conspicuous part in both World War I and II. The late M. R. Chessman of Astoria suggested the name Sunset Highway because the Sunset Division had such a large proportion of men from the Pacific Northwest. Chessman was a member of the Highway Commission. Sunset Camp in Washington County was named long before the name Sunset was applied to the highway. Sunset Camp was named for a logging enterprise that had nothing to do with the Sunset Division. Sunset Tunnel to the southeast was named for the camp. All this presents an interesting coincidence.

Sunset Shelter, Douglas County. This trail shelter on the west slope of Big Squaw Mountain was built in 1930. Fred Asam named the camp because of its exposure to the evening sun.

Suntex, Harney County. W. F. Sturges, of Scio, Oregon, was the first postmaster of Suntex. Sturges informed the compiler in January, 1927, that postal authorities selected the name of this post office and he did not know why they chose the word Suntex. It has no local significance. The office was established on February 7, 1916.

Suplee, Crook County. Annie Senecal, postmaster at Suplee, informed the compiler that the name was suggested by Charles Dorling because his mother's maiden name was Suplee. The office was established October 31, 1894, with Joel C. Abbott first postmaster.

Susanville, Grant County. Was settled in 1865 as a mining community on Middle Fork John Day River near the mouth of Elk Creek. A Canyon City correspondent signing himself "Bruney" wrote in the *Oregonian,* May 9, 1865, that John N. Reid had discovered the Elk Creek lode and that the new town was named Susanville in compliment to Mrs. Susan Ward, one of the earliest inhabitants. Susanville post office was established September 12, 1888, but in 1901 was relocated some two miles up Elk Creek while Galena post office was established at the original location. Susanville office was closed December 31, 1952 with papers to Bates.

Sutherlin, Douglas County. Sutherlin was named for Fendel Sutherlin, who was born in Greencastle, Indiana, in 1822, and after graduating from Greencastle College in 1846 came to Oregon in the following year. In 1849 Sutherlin joined the gold rush for California, but soon returned to Oregon. Fendel Sutherlin's parents came to Oregon, arriving in the fall of 1850, and in 1851 moved into the valley that now bears his family name. Sutherlin spent much time and energy in developing the valley and irrigating fruit land. Fendel Sutherlin died in 1901. See University of Oregon *Extension Monitor* for September, 1924.

Suttle Lake, Jefferson County. C. H. Stewart of Albany wrote the compiler in August, 1927, as follows: "This lake was named for John Settle, or Uncle Jackie, as he was familiarly known. He was one of the pioneers of the Lebanon district, where he took up a donation land claim about two miles north of that town. He was one of the organizers and directors of the Willamette Valley and Cascade Mountain Military Wagon Road project in 1866. He was one of the men who had actual supervision of the building of the road. It is said that while out on this expedition he went hunting one day and found the lake which was named for him and also Blue Lake in the same vicinity." This lake has been known for many years as Suttle Lake, a corruption of the correct name, but the compiler is of the opinion that it would be useless to attempt to revert to the spelling Settle. The form Suttle has been used in many legal documents, including irrigation district records, and is firmly established.

Sutton Lake, Lane County. This lake is about five miles north of Florence. It was named for Orrin W. Sutton, a pioneer homesteader who settled on its banks in early days.

Sutton Mountain, Wheeler County. Sutton Mountain, which has an extreme elevation of 4680 feet, lies north of Mitchell. It was named for Al Sutton, a pioneer stockman who settled in The Dalles in 1858 and moved to what is now Wheeler County in 1865. He was a native of England and well known throughout central Oregon.

Suver, Polk County. Joseph W. Suver, who was born in Virginia in 1819, was a pioneer of Oregon, and settled on a donation land claim at the present site of Suver in 1845. The community bears his name. His wife was, according to land office records, Deliley Suver. For history of the community, see Independence *Enterprise,* January 27, 1939.

Svensen, Clatsop County. This is the correct spelling and not Svenson. The USBGN has adopted the form Svensen for the community and also for an island nearby near the south bank of Columbia River. These features were named for Peter Svensen, a seafaring man, who settled near the Columbia River in early days.

Swaggart Buttes, Morrow County. This high ground east of Lexington was named for Benjamin F. Swaggart who was born in Creswell in 1854 and homesteaded on the buttes which bear his name in 1879.

Swallow Lake, Linn County. There are conflicting stories concerning the origin of the name of this body of water east of Marion Lake. A story in the Eugene *Register Guard,* October 11, 1959, says that one John Cooper found an unidentified body in Swallow Lake and buried it marking the grave with a combination of his given name and the lake as a patronym. Why he buried the man a mile and a half from the lake and why the lake was named Swallow to begin with are both unexplained. Another tale claims that John Swallow was an early sheepherder who drowned in the lake. His friends attempted to pack out his body but the delay in discovering the corpse coupled with summer heat caused them to abandon the project and perform a hasty burial. Swallow's grave alongside the Skyline Trail has apparently made him better known in modern times than at his death near the turn of the century.

Swan, Klamath County. Swan post office was about twelve miles northeast of Klamath Falls in the Swan Lake Valley. Swan Lake was once much larger than it is now and was much frequented by wild swan. It was named on that account. Arthur Cleveland Bent, in his splendid series of bulletins of the U. S. National Museum, *Life Histories of North American Wild Fowl,* and similar titles, has painted a graphic picture of the tragedy of some of the most picturesque of our birds. Bulletin 130, pages 281 to 301, contains a fine account of *Cygnus columbianus,* the whistling swan, and *Cygnus buccinator,* the trumpeter swan, both of which use the western United States for winter range. The ruthless destruction of these birds has been without the slightest excuse. As Bent says, no opportunity has been neglected to kill these magnificent swans, by fair means or foul, until they have been sadly reduced in numbers and are now confined to certain favored localities. For letter about swans along Columbia River, see editorial page the *Oregonian,* May 4, 1927.

Swan Island, Multnomah County. The origin of this name is obvious, but the compiler has been unable to find out by whom the name was applied. The island was charted by Wilkes in the atlas accompanying *U. S. Exploring Expedition,* volume XXIII, Hydrography, as Willow Island, but the name has not persisted. For editorial protest against changing the name of Swan Island, see the *Oregonian,* September 27, 1927. For similar editorial, *ibid.,* November 2, 1939. Despite the fact that the land is no longer an island, the name Swan Island is firmly and affectionately fixed in the public mind.

Swart, Umatilla County. Swart post office was established September 15, 1897, and was closed to Duncan on May 31, 1902. John H. Swart was postmaster all this time, and the office was named for his family. It was about seven miles south of Gibbon. The Swarts were well known in the Blue Mountain area, and several of the family were in the railroad service. Swart post office was established to serve people in the vicinity of the railroad spur which was installed on Meacham Creek to allow for the shipment of cordwood. At the time two of the Swart family were loading and shipping wood from this area.

Swastika, Jackson County. Swastika post office was in the extreme east part of the county, in the northeast part of township 38 south, range 4 east, at or near Deadwood. The office was established December 11, 1909, with Clayton E. Burton first of two postmasters. The office was discontinued September 15, 1912. The name of the office was derived from the stock brand of C. E. Burton, who branded his livestock with a swastika. It is apparent that the name Deadwood could not be used for this office because that name was already in use in Lane County. Hitler had not yet been heard of and there was no objection to the use of Swastika as a place name.

Sweet Creek, Lane County. Sweet Creek rises in the Coast Range in the west part of the county and flows generally northward to join Siuslaw River near the locality called Point Terrace, a few miles down stream from Mapleton. The name of the stream came from one Sweet, a local resident of those parts, and was not applied because of any excellence of the water.

Sweet Home, Linn County. At the approach of spring in 1930 Oswald West applied his talents to the early history of Sweet Home. His kindly letter on the subject and an equally sympathetic editorial appear in the *Oregonian* for March 5 of that year. Both are well worth reading. Governor West says, and it has not been disputed, that an early name for the locality of Sweet Home was Buckhead. This name, savoring of pioneering days, finally gave way to Sweet Home. There is nothing to indicate the date of this transition, but the post office of Sweet Home was established on March

13, 1874, with John B. Hughes first postmaster. It is apparent that Governor West could not have had much to do with the boisterous behavior of the young men of Buckhead which he so well describes. The calendar proves otherwise. In December, 1926, B. H. Watkinds told the writer that the place was called Sweet Home in the 1840s by Lowell Ames, Sr., but in October, 1927, C. H. Stewart of Albany wrote that this could not be true, because Ames did not arrive in the vicinity of Sweet Home until about 1860. Ames may have applied the name to his homestead. A letter in the Sweet Home *New Era,* March 28, 1930, by Mrs. O. Feigum, a well-known local resident, says that the name Sweet Home was first applied in the form Sweet Home Valley. The first community to be called Sweet Home was in the east part of what is now the town. Buckland was the name of a saloon on Ames Creek west of the community. It was decorated with a large pair of antlers over the front door. Mrs. Feigum says that about 1880 the community buildings were moved west to Ames Creek and the name Sweet Home supplanted the name Buckhead.

Sweetbrier, Multnomah County. Sweetbrier post office was established January 10, 1900, and was in service until August 31, 1901, with Robert G. Combs postmaster. This office was a little to the west of the center of section 1, township 1 south, range 3 east, about a half a mile south of the Base Line Road at the 15-mile post on the old road down to Sandy River. This was before the Base Line extension was cut through. The office was named for the well-known Sweet Briar farm then owned by Emmet B. Williams, Portland attorney, and in 1947 owned by Mr. Williams' daughter, Mrs. Lenore W. Althaus. Variations in the form of this name for one of the most popular bushes in Oregon are familiar to most people. Sweet Briar Farm is the style in the registration certificate held by Mrs. Althaus. Frequently one meets the forms Sweetbriar, Sweet Brier and Sweetbrier. The last spelling was the one used by postal officials at Washington, but Mrs. Althaus says that a signboard nailed to a maple tree in front of her house uses the form Sweet Brier for the old post office. This gives a fourway choice. In addition, there is the romantic name eglantine also used for this wild rose. For editorial comment about the sweetbrier, see the *Oregonian,* June 27, 1947, and for letters on the subject, *ibid.,* June 25, July 3 and July 4, 1947.

Sweetser, Harney County. A map of 1889 shows a place called Switzer a few miles southeast of Crane, but whether it was a real community or a proposed station for the projected Oregon Pacific Railroad the compiler does not know. In any event the name appears to be misspelled. Alphene Venator, J. W. Biggs and Phil Metschan say the place was intended to be named for Frank Sweetser, who, with Stauffer, operated horse ranches in the Harney Valley, and elsewhere in eastern Oregon. Sweetser died in 1895, and his widow, maiden name Meriah Sutherlin, married Phil Metschan, Sr., in 1896.

Swim, Clackamas County. The name Swim was given to this post office early in 1925. Boyd Summers was the first postmaster and the originator of the name. There was a large, outdoor, warm mineral-water swimming pool nearby

Swiss Spring, Klamath County. Swiss Spring is in section 29, township 27 south, range 7 east. It was at one time called Coyote Spring, but due to duplication with another Coyote Spring in the neighborhood, the USFS asked to have the name changed to Swiss Spring in compliment to a Swiss who was associated with the locality. The style Swiss Spring was adopted by the USBGN in 1940.

Swisshome, Lane County. The name Swisshome originated because a Swiss family, Mr. and Mrs. Heinrich Zweidler, lived about a mile west of the present site of the post office. The locality where they lived was called Swisshome and when the post office was established on March 5, 1902 with Mrs. Zweidler postmaster, the name followed naturally.

Switchback Falls, Hood River County. These falls were named May 6, 1925, by the USBGN because the title suggested was unusually descriptive. They are near where the Mount Hood Loop Highway crosses Iron Creek, southeast of Mount Hood.

Switzler Lake, Multnomah County. This was a slough lake on the south shore of the Columbia River near Portland. It has long since been reclaimed for industrial land but it was centered about the present intersection of Vancouver and Union avenues. The lake was named for John Switzler, who brought his family to Oregon, from Missouri, in 1845, and on September 30, 1846, settled on the south side of the Columbia, opposite Vancouver, and north of Woodlawn, which is a part of the city of Portland. This was the old landing of the Vancouver ferry. See map of W. W. Chapman, surveyor-general of Oregon, dated September 20, 1860, Eugene, Oregon, in the surveyor-general's office at Portland, Oregon. Switzler was born in Virginia and served in the War of 1812. He died in 1856. See Scott's *History of the Oregon Country,* volume II, page 289, and land office certificate 137. Slough post office was established in the vicinity of Switzler Lake November 25, 1850, with John Switzler postmaster. The office was discontinued January 6, 1852.

Sycamore, Multnomah County. Sycamore is a locality on Johnson Creek about three miles east of Lents, near the south border of the county. A story about George Flinn, in Fred Lockley's column of the *Oregon Journal,* July 16, 1927, tells of the origin of the name. Sycamore State is a name used in referring to West Virginia. The Flinn family came to Oregon about 1844 from West Virginia and settled at the present site of Sycamore. Nelson A. Flinn, the head of the family, named the locality Sycamore. A post office with that name was established May 29, 1889, with Flinn first postmaster. This office was closed March 23, 1901. Some of the family later moved to the vicinity of Cherryville east of Sandy.

Sycan Marsh, Klamath and Lake counties. Sycan Marsh gets its name from the Klamath Indian words *saiga* and *keni,* literally, the level, grassy place. The marsh covers a considerable area west of Summer Lake, and its outlet is Sycan River, a tributary of Sprague River. Most of it was aquired in 1980 by the Nature Conservancy to be preserved as a natural area. The best information about Sycan Marsh may be found in the cooperative report issued by the state engineer entitled *Silver Lake Project.* There are many spellings of the name, but the USBGN has officially adopted Sycan. It seems probable that the name Thompson Valley was at one time applied by white people to Sycan Marsh as well as to what is now known as Thompson Valley, to the north. The name Sycan has become applied to Sycan River as a result of the association of the stream with the marsh, and also rather inappropriately, considering its literal Indian meaning, to Sycan Butte, near the northeast corner of Sycan Marsh. There are many other examples of this misapplication of names by association and proximity. See under Lemiti.

Sylvan, Multnomah County. Nathan B. Jones, a pioneer of 1847, settled at the pass at the head of Tanner Creek in 1850 and lived there until he was murdered early in 1894. He called the locality Zion Town and platted lots with that name in 1892-93. Whether he chose the Bible name for religious reasons or because of the place called Mount Zion about a mile to the southeast the writer cannot tell. There was no community at Mount Zion, which was named about 1860-61. Jones may have adopted the unusual form Zion Town to show that it was the community or trading center for Mount Zion. When a post office was desired in the late 1880s postal authorities would not use the name Zion, on the grounds of confusion that might result from duplication. There had already been at least two Zions in Oregon and the names had been changed because of difficulties with the mails. T. H. Prince, resident of Zion Town, suggested the name Sylvan and an office with that name was established June 6, 1890, with Charles C. Prince first postmaster. This office was closed October 11, 1906. The locality is now generally called Sylvan. The name is derived from *Silvanus,* the Italian deity of the woods. For additional information see under the heading Mount Sylvania. Nathan B. Jones was born in Salem, New Hampshire, in 1819. Four years after he settled at the place now called Sylvan he built a dwelling called the Hermitage, which was destroyed by fire in 1893. Jones was considered to be an eccentric hermit. It is said that one of his schemes was to develop a town that would become Oregon's seat of government. The outside of his home was decorated with weird paintings that anticipated the modern fad for fantastic murals. In January, 1894, Jones disposed of some property to Henry E. Reed of Portland and took a check for the balance due, which he promptly deposited in a Portland bank. He was supposed to have retained the cash in his house, and was clubbed on January 17, apparently with the idea of robbery. He died January 25, 1894, and was buried at the little cemetery at Sylvan.

Symbol Rock, Lane County. Symbol Rock is on the divide between McKenzie River and Fall Creek south of Nimrod. USFS ranger A. J. Briem said that it was named because of the distinctive, almost geometric, formations of rock on the west face. It was used by Indians for ceremonial vigils prior to the coming of the white man.

Syracuse, Polk County. Syracuse post office was established in the valley of Luckiamute River on February 8, 1885, with Frank K. Hubbard first of two postmasters. James P. Starr became postmaster on January 9, 1889. On October 28, of the same year the office was moved westward about two miles to Falls City. When this move was made Starr was appointed postmaster of Falls City and retained the position until the summer of 1890. The origin of the name Syracuse is not based on water-tight evidence, but it is generally thought that the word was applied by some of the first settlers, who are said to have come from Syracuse, New York. However, there is another theory that should be mentioned. The Oregon post office may have been named by someone interested in classical history. There were several such students in the area.

Table Creek, Douglas County. Table Creek flows into Cow Creek from the north at a point about a mile due west of Peck. The stream got its name because it drained the south slopes of Table Mountain. Table Mountain is a conspicuous landmark north and west of Cow Creek Canyon. It has an elevation of 3335 feet. The name is of course descriptive.

Table Mountain, Lincoln County. This mountain, elevation 2804 feet, has a characteristic flat top and has been known as Table Mountain since pioneer days. Except for the fact that it is much too far south it might be La Mesa of Heceta. See under the heading Cape Falcon.

Table Rock, Jackson County. For nearly a century Upper Table Rock and Lower Table Rock have been well-known landmarks north of Central Point in the Rogue River Valley. They are real mesas, standing nearly a thousand feet above nearby Rogue River. The historic meeting between Rogue River Indians and white soldiers and settlers took place on the southwest slope under Upper Table Rock on September 10, 1853. Table Rock post office was in service near these two landmarks from April 25, 1872, until September 14, 1895, when in a fit of efficiency postal authorities changed the name to Tablerock, and that was the style until the office was discontinued November 15, 1906. Thomas Gianini was the first postmaster in 1872. After inspecting the list of postmasters of this office, Judge J. B. Coleman of Medford, long familiar with Jackson County history, gave it as his opinion that the office did a good bit of moving about to suit the convenience of the postmasters, but it was never far from the valley between the two rocks.

Taft, Lincoln County. The community of Taft was named for William Howard Taft, 27th president of the United States. The post office was established January 22, 1906, and was named when Mr. Taft was secretary of war. John W. Bones was first postmaster, and is said to have suggested the name. On December 8, 1964, Taft voted to become part of a new community to be called Lincoln City.

Taft Mountain, Douglas County. Former USFS ranger Fred Asam supplied the following information about the mountain north of Little River. He said that a huge Douglas fir stood about a half mile from the summit. It was known far and wide as the Taft tree and apparently had been named by then district ranger Oscar Houser before World War I for President William Howard Taft. The mountain and creek to the south took their names from the tree.

Taghum Butte, Deschutes County. This butte in the Paulina Mountains is named with the Chinook jargon word for six, it being the sixth of a series all named at the same time by the USFS.

Tahkenitch Lake, Douglas County. Tahkenitch Lake is in the western part of the county. It is of very irregular shape, and the Indian name is said to mean many arms.

Takilma, Josephine County. Takilma is on East Fork Illinois River about a mile southeast of Waldo. It was formerly called Taklamah, and is said to have been named by Colonel T. W. Draper of the Waldo Copper Company, for an Indian chief. Since 1902 the place has been called Takilma, a modification of the name Takelma, applied to an Indian tribe that lived on the middle course of Rogue River. See *Handbook of American Indians,* volume I, page 673. Takilma post office was established August 2, 1902, with George F. Morgan first postmaster. The writer was told in 1926 that the style Taklamah could not be used for a post office in Oregon because it duplicated the name of a place in Oklahoma. However, available post office records do not substantiate this statement.

Talapus Butte, Deschutes County. This butte, west of Sparks Lake, is named with the Chinook jargon word for coyote. See under Mount Talapus.

Talbot, Marion County. Guy W. Talbot was the first vice-president and general manager of the Oregon Electric Railway Company, and after he resigned and entered the public utility business, the new owners of the railway extended it south from Salem and this station near the Santiam River was named for him. Talbot station was at first known as Roby, for a pioneer family of the vicinity, but this name was confused with Ruby, a station in Multnomah County, so the change was made.

Talent, Jackson County. This place was named in the early 1880s by A. P. Talent, who platted the town. Talent suggested the name of Wagner, but postal authorities gave the place his own name. He came to Oregon about 1876 from Tennessee. In pioneer days the place was known as Wagner Creek for a family of early settlers.

Tallman, Linn County. This station northwest of Lebanon was named for a nearby settler, James Tallman.

Tallow Butte, Douglas County. Tallow Butte is on the divide between South Umpqua River and Jackson Creek in township 29 south, range 1 east. Grover Blake of Roseburg told the compiler this was so named because in early days some very fat deer were found nearby.

Tallowbox Mountain, Jackson County. Tallowbox Mountain, elevation 5021 feet, is a prominent point in the Siskiyou Mountains a little south of Applegate. Thomas V. Williams of Medford has submitted a story about the name, which he says may be fact or fiction, but in either event it is the best available. About 1880 some hunters in the locality shot more deer than they were able to get home with facilities available. They wished to save the tallow for future use, so they packed it in a box to keep it from birds and animals and fastened the box up in a tree. The story is to the effect that the tallow was never salvaged and the box gave the name to the mountain.

Tam McArthur Rim, Deschutes County. This prominent ridge runs east from Broken Top and is clearly visible from Lava Butte on the south to Madras on the north. It was named by the USBGN in *Decision List 5401* to honor Lewis A. "Tam" McArthur, the author of the first three editions of this book. After McArthur's death in 1951 many people felt that some geographic feature in Oregon should have his name and one of his oldest friends, Robert W. Sawyer of Bend, was instrumental in selecting this particular ridge. In retrospect it is interesting to note two curious facts; the Broken Top alpine uplands was one of the few spots in central Oregon that McArthur had not visited, and he probably would have expressed some dissatisfaction at the inclusion of a nickname in otherwise serious nomenclature. The introduction to this edition of *Oregon Geographic Names* contains a biography of Lewis A. McArthur and the background of this book.

Tamanawas Falls, Hood River County. These falls on Cold Spring Creek a mile west of Mount Hood Loop Highway were named by the USFS. *Tamanawaas* or *Tahmahnawis* is the Chinook jargon word for friendly or guardian spirit. The name was first applied with the curious spelling Tamanawaus, but in December 1971, the OGNB decided upon the present form. See USBGN *Decision List 7301.*

Tamarack, Umatilla County. Tamarack was the name given a post office in the Blue Mountains, about fifteen miles east of Weston on the road to Elgin. This office was established June 2, 1896, with Lewis A. Rambo first postmaster. It was finally closed after the turn of the century, but the writer does not know the exact date. In the Blue Mountains the name tamarack is generally given to the western larch, *Larix occidentalis,* which is not a true tamarack at all. There are many of these western larch trees near the locality of the Tamarack post office and that is how it got its name.

Tamarack Creek, Wallowa County. This creek is in township 5 north, range 45 east. Other geographic features in Oregon are also named for the tamarack, which is correctly, the western larch, *Larix occidentalis.* This tree has a variety of common names. It grows in many places in Oregon, particularly in the Blue and Wallowa mountains.

Tamolitch Falls, Linn County. This sixty foot waterfall on McKenzie River is about two miles downstream from Carmen Reservoir. Before the development of the Clear Lake recreation area, they were known as Lower Falls but the USBGN confirmed the present name in *Decision List 6103. Tamolitsh* is the Chinook jargon word for tub or bucket.

Tandy Bay, Klamath County. This bay is at the southwest end of Crescent Lake. In 1925 the USFS made a detailed map of Crescent Lake, and at the suggestion of Lewis A. McArthur, this bay was named for William Tandy, who was a member of the pioneer road exploration party sent out by the state in 1852. For information about this exploration see Scott's *History of the Oregon Country,* volume IV, page 8.

Tandy Creek, Lake County. Tandy Creek is south of Lakeview and flows westward into Goose Lake. It is about four miles north of the Oregon-California state line. William and Robert Tandy, pioneer settlers in the Willamette Valley, moved into the Goose Lake Valley about 1869, and Tandy Creek was named for some member of the family. The style Tansy Creek is wrong.

Tangent, Linn County. This station on the Southern Pacific line south of Albany was named because of the long stretch of straight track to the north and south. This tangent is over twenty miles long.

Tanks, Umatilla County. This was a summer settlement near the summit of the Blue Mountains on the road between Walla Walla and Elgin. It was named for water tanks used by freight haulers, and not by a railroad, as there is no railroad near the place. Tanks post office was established June 2, 1896, with DeWitt C. French first postmaster. It was discontinued May 14, 1906.

Tanner Creek, Multnomah County. Daniel H. Lownsdale settled on what was later the King claim, now in the city of Portland, in 1845 and built a tannery. Tanner Creek got its name from this enterprise. The creek drained the canyon at the head of Jefferson Street, and flowed under the present location of the Civic Stadium, and through a ravine where upper Alder Street is situated. Canyon Road, an important factor in the development of Portland, was named because it was built up the canyon of Tanner Creek.

Tanner Creek, Multnomah County. J. T. Tanner took up a donation land claim near the mouth of this stream in pioneer days, and his name became attached to the creek. It is just west of Bonneville. Tanner Butte near the headwaters of the creek was once known as Tanner Creek Butte, but the government has eliminated the unnecessary part of the name.

Tanners Pass, Douglas County. In 1948, U. S. Plywood Company was building a private road north of Sampson Butte heading toward Evarts Creek. The powderman, one Tanner, encountered so much difficulty because of bad rock and limited equipment that crew members referred to the place where the work was delayed as Tanners Pass.

Tansy Point, Clatsop County. The name Tansy Point is applied to a place on the south bank of Columbia River just north of Warrenton, and has been is use for many years. The tansy plant, *Tanactum huronense,* grows there in abundance and the name of the point is appropriate. Tansy ragwort is extremely harmful to cattle and in some areas much time and effort has been spent in attempted eradication. Sir Edward Belcher's chart of 1839 uses the name Racoon Point, presumably in commemoration of the visit of H. M. S. *Racoon* in 1813.

Target Spring, Wallowa County. Target Spring, southeast of Wallowa Lake, was named because of the fact that the ground nearby was used as a hunting camp and hunters practiced there, shooting at marks on trees.

Tartar Gulch, Josephine County. Tartar Gulch drains into Althouse Creek southeast of Holland. It is shown on various maps as Carter Gulch and Tarter Gulch, but in May, 1943, USFS officials wrote the compiler that these forms were wrong and that Tartar Gulch was correct. An old time resident of Selma is authority for the statement that the gulch bears a name applied in mining days indicating that gold in this gulch was in very spotted pockets and the term "tartar" was used to describe that condition. A tartar gulch was considered not good for mining. The compiler has not been able to verify this meaning for the word, but assumes it to be correct.

Tate Spring, Wheeler County. Grover Blake, the first USFS ranger in the area, told the compiler that this spring north of Spanish Peak was named for one or more of the several Tate brothers who ranched nearby.

Taylor, Multnomah County. Taylor was a siding west of Corbett on the south bank of the Columbia River. Land office records indicate that E. J. Taylor took up a homestead nearby, entry 76, in pioneer days, and it may be assumed that the place was named for him or his family. A post office named Leader was established in this locality July 15, 1881, with Joseph H. Leader first postmaster. The name was changed to Taylor on May 25, 1882, at which time Ervine J. Taylor was postmaster. The office was discontinued in June, 1895.

Taylor Butte, Lane County. Taylor Butte has an elevation of 5835 feet. It is west of the summit of the Cascade Range, three miles north of Waldo Lake. It and other nearby geographic features were named about 1898 for one Joe Taylor, a stockman of the Deschutes country, who ranged sheep in the neighborhood. This information was furnished the compiler by Geo. H. Kelly of Portland and W. P. Vandevert of Bend, both of whom were familiar with central Cascade Range history.

Taylor Creek, Curry County. This creek entering the Pacific Ocean two miles north of Brookings was named for William Taylor who settled near its mouth about 1870.

Taylor Creek, Lane County. Most of Taylor Creek is in the extreme west part of township 16 south, range 9 west. It flows west over the township line into Indian Creek. The stream was named in compliment to John L. Taylor, who settled on its banks in 1888 and lived there for nearly twenty years. John L. Taylor named Reed post office that operated for forty years on Taylor Creek. This was to honor Thomas B. Reed of Maine. Mr. Taylor was the father of ten children, several of whom, including Smith L. Taylor of McKenzie Bridge, were well known in Lane County.

Taylor Lake, Linn County. This is an enlargement of Courtney Creek and is northeast of Halsey. Land plats of 1878 show that S. Z. Taylor owned land nearby, and the lake was probably named for him.

Taylor Sands, Clatsop County. These sands in the Columbia River are just northeast of Astoria. They were named for Tom Taylor, who owned the grounds and seined them for salmon.

Taylors Ferry Road, Multnomah and Washington counties. John A. Taylor was born in New York state September 12, 1825. He crossed the plains with an ox team in 1852, and, upon arrival in October of that year, took up a donation land claim ten miles from Portland on the Tualatin River, and installed a ferry there. Afterwards he built a toll bridge to take the place of the ferry. He was at one time the county judge of Washington County. He died in Walla Walla, Washington, February 12, 1919. Taylors Ferry Road led from the south part of Portland over the north end of Palatine Hill to the ferry. Most of the road southwest of West Portland is now incorporated in Capitol Highway and Barbur Boulevard leaving the name to be applied only to a short section of the old road between Fulton and West Portland. The long tangent west of the intersection of Capitol Highway and Barbur Boulevard is of recent construction and has nothing to do with the original Taylors Ferry Road. Taylors Ferry post office was in service from October 8, 1869, to December 13, 1869, with John A. Taylor postmaster.

Taylorville, Wasco County. Taylorville is a locality on Fifteenmile Creek about eight miles southwest of Dufur. For the geography of the place see USGS map of the Dufur quadrangle. At late reports there was not much stirring in Taylorville. Taylor post office was established on August

20, 1909, and discontinued September 30, 1910, with Albert Taylor postmaster. The community was apparently named for the postmaster. According to Judge Fred W. Wilson of The Dalles, who wrote the compiler in 1946, a sawmill was established in the timber near this locality, and to accommodate the employees, Taylor opened a store and had the post office established. When the mill stopped operating, the post office was closed.

Teal Creek, Polk County. Teal Creek rises in the Coast Range south of Black Rock and flows generally eastward to join Little Luckiamute River near Bridgeport. In pioneer times the stream was called Brown Creek in compliment to Adam Brown, through whose farm it ran. Later John B. Teal moved into the mountains south of Falls City and gradually the name Teal Creek supplanted the name Brown Creek. The change in name took place during the 1890s. Teal was a carpenter, wagonmaker and also a sawmiller. He was at times county commissioner and also county judge. He was a much respected resident of Polk County. The spelling Teel is wrong.

Teaser Creek, Wallowa County. This creek, which was named for a stallion that ranged thereabouts, flows into Deep Creek in township 3 north, range 50 east.

Techumtas Island, Umatilla County. This was the Indian name for an island in the Columbia River east of Umatilla. It was also known as Switzler or McComas Island, for men who had owned land on it. In the fall of 1940 the compiler mentioned this name to William Switzler of Umatilla, and was told that Techumtas was the name given by the Cayuse Indians to J. B. Switzler, father of William Switzler, and one time owner of the island. J. B. Switzler always referred to the island as Techumtas Island, not Switzler Island, and that was the family custom. In 1941, USBGN adopted the name Techumtas for this island and applied Switzler to another island slightly upstream. Both Techumtas Island and Switzler Island were inundated when Lake Wallula was impounded behind McNary Dam.

Tecumseh Creek, Klamath County. Tecumseh Creek is a stream about one and one-half miles north of Klamath Agency. It is sometimes erroneously known as Spring Creek, which is unsatisfactory because this duplicates the name of a stream not far to the east. Klamath County pioneers used the expression Tecumseh Creek because a well-known Klamath Indian, Tecumseh, was found dead near the stream many years ago in circumstances that indicated that he had been murdered. He was of course named for the famous chief in Ohio.

Telephone Flat, Klamath County. Telephone Flat, in section 2, township 36 south, range 7 east, is named because an important long distance telephone line crosses this ground. The many wires on multiple crossarms are a distinctive feature.

Tellurium Peak, Douglas County. Tellurium is a rare, metallic element, generally found associated with other elements such as silver and gold. This peak, just southwest of Canyonville, was so named because tellurium has been found thereon.

Telocaset, Union County. This place was once called Antelope stage station. When the railroad was built through the Blue Mountains, Dr. William C. McKay was asked to suggest new names for stations that had names duplicating others in Oregon. Among those he suggested was Telocaset. This word is from the Nez Perce language and means a thing at the top, or put on top, such as a tree growing on a hill, summit or plateau, overlooking a valley. The Indians pronounced the word *Taule-karset,* according to O. H. Lipps, of Fort Lapwai Indian Agency, Idaho, in a letter dated March 2, 1927. Telocaset post office was established February 25, 1885, with William A. Cates first postmaster.

Temperance Creek, Wallowa County. This stream flows into Snake River in township 1 north, range 50 east. It was named by Ben Johnson and others with him as a result of the coffee giving out. The party had nothing but water to drink and named the stream on that account.

Templeton, Coos County. Templeton post office was established June 21, 1898, and was discontinued February 28, 1917. Albina Coleman was the first of five postmasters. When a petition was circulated asking for a post office Robert Templeton, a local resident, sponsored the document and the office was thereupon named in his honor. Templeton was in the extreme north end of the county, east of Tenmile Lake. It was in several locations, at least twice on Benson Creek and twice on Johnson Creek, but as far as the compiler knows it was always in township 23 south, range 12 west.

Ten O'Clock Church, Clackamas County. This is not the name of a community although it is so indicated on road signs and maps. It is a church two miles southeast of Beavercreek founded by a German reform congregation in 1880 and more recently used by the United Church of Christ Congregational. When the original building was erected a clock tower was included but the congregation could not afford the machinery, so a dummy face was installed with hands fixed at ten o'clock, the time of Sunday service.

Tenasillahe Island, Clatsop County. The name Tenasillahe is composed of two Chinook jargon words, *tenas* meaning small or little, and *illahe,* meaning land, hence, "little land." There are many ways of spelling Chinook words, but the USBGN as a matter of standardization has adopted the form shown at the head of this paragraph. This island is low, and marshy in places, which doubtless accounts for the Indian name. Maps prepared by Lewis and Clark show this and other islands nearby in the Columbia River marked *marshy islands,* but the expression was apparently not used as a geographic name. W. R. Broughton passed Tenasillahe Island on October 25, 1792, and describes it as a "long, sandy, shallow spit." His report on this part of the Columbia River is not entirely clear, but it may be that he camped on the island that night as he mentions "the dampness of the situation." Wilkes used the name *Kathlamet* for this island, a form of Cathlamet. See under Cathlamet.

Tencent Lake, Harney County. This is a small lake at the extreme north end of Alvord Valley. It is fed largely by ditches, which are also its outlet. It has an elevation of about 4400 feet. It was so named because it was small and round like a dime.

Tenino Creek, Jefferson County. This stream on Warm Springs Indian Reservation bears the name of the Tenino Indians, a Shahaptian tribe of the Columbia and Deschutes valleys. They are now classed with the Warm Springs Indians. See *Handbook of American Indians,* volume II, page 729. In December, 1942, J. W. Elliott, superintendent at Warm Springs Indian Agency, wrote the compiler that he had discussed with several older Indians the origin of the name. At the time of the treaty of 1855 the Teninos had as their habitat a locality on the Columbia River a few miles down stream from Celilo. This locality was known as the Tenino Fishery, and as nearly as Mr. Elliott could understand the translation, the name meant a river channel where the water was confined by steep rock walls. When the Teninos were moved to the Warm Springs Indian Reservation they took the name with them to the new location. Many of them return to the Tenino Fishery during the fishing season.

Tenmile, Douglas County. The name of the post office of Tenmile is derived from the fact that a man who lived in Happy Valley drove cattle from the valley and grazed them at the place now known as Tenmile. The distance was about ten miles, hence the name. This incident happened in pioneer days. The office was established June 13, 1870, and was still in operation in 1980 about halfway between Winston and Camas Valley.

Tenmile Creek, Coos County. This creek was undoubtedly named because it emptied into the Pacific Ocean about ten miles south of Winchester Bay, at the mouth of Umpqua River. It is also about ten miles north of the northern bend of Coos Bay, but Winchester Bay was settled earlier than any settlement on the northern part of Coos Bay, and the compiler thinks that the first explanation is the correct one. Tenmile Creek has given its name to Tenmile Lake, to Tenmile Butte, southeast of Tenmile Lake, and to North Tenmile Lake.

Tenmile Creek, Lane County. This stream, which flows into Pacific Ocean south of Cape Perpetua, was named by surveyors because it was about ten miles long. Tenmile Ridge to the north was named for the stream.

Tenmile Lake, Coos County. This lake was once known as Johnson Lake. The USBGN has officially named it Tenmile Lake. North Tenmile Lake is nearby. Both lakes probably received their names from Tenmile Creek, which connects Tenmile Lake with the ocean. Tenmile Creek was named because it was supposed to be about ten miles south of the pioneer settlement at Winchester Bay. The name South Tenmile for this lake is incorrect. It was approved by the USBGN, but subsequently the decision was revised.

Tenmile Rapids, Wasco County. These rapids of the Columbia River were named by USCE because of their distance east from the boat landing at The Dalles. They formed part of The Dalles of the Columbia, and were formerly known as the Little Narrows, Short Narrows, and *Les Petites Dalles.* See under The Dalles in this book, and *OHQ,* March, 1926, page 115. Part of Tenmile Rapids was in the state of Washington. They were inundated after The Dalles Dam was completed.

Tepee Camp, Wallowa County. This is an old Indian campground in township 5 north, range 46 east. It was used generally during hunting seasons.

Tepee Draw, Deschutes County. This is a draw on the northeast slopes of Paulina Mountains. It was so called because remains of Indian tepees were found therein.

Tepee Springs, Wallowa County. These springs are about six miles north of Enterprise and about a mile west of the Lewiston Highway. They were named for a group of tepees, the poles of which were left standing by Indians. They are on a piece of land reported filed on by Chancy Akin, but Akin did not prove up for title. A post office named Teepy Springs was established August 3, 1886, with Akin postmaster. This spelling is from Post Office Department records and does not agree with local style. The office operated until the summer of 1890.

Terrebonne, Deschutes County. The community of Terrebonne was first known as Hillman, a word made by taking parts of the names of two prominent railroad men, James J. Hill and E. H. Harriman, whose lines ran a race to see which could reach central Oregon first. Shortly after the town was founded a man named Hillman, a prominent real estate operator in the Deschutes Valley, got into trouble with the government, amidst unpleasant notoriety. This was disquieting to the good people of Hillman, who changed the name of the place to Terrebonne, a French expression meaning good earth. It is said that a Mr. Stevens suggested the new name. The name of the post office was changed in September, 1911.

Terry, Multnomah County. On October 13, 1899, a post office named Bement was established at or near the road intersection at Twelvemile Corner on Southeast Stark Street north of Gresham. Francois M. Graham moved a store building from Fairview and set it up at the Twelvemile Corner. He was appointed first postmaster at Bement. Shortly thereafter the name of the office was changed to Terry, and it was closed October 31, 1903. The patrons were then served by rural delivery. It has been reported that Terry was named for some postal official, but the compiler has not been able to identify any such official.

Testament Creek, Tillamook County. This creek flows into Nestucca River in the south part of the county. It was named by association with Bible Creek just to the south. See under that heading.

Tetherow Butte, Deschutes County. Tetherow Butte is about three miles north of Redmond, and Tetherow bridge across Deschutes River is three miles west of the butte. These geographic features were named for a local settler, A. J. Tetherow, a pioneer stockman and a member of a prominent early pioneer family of the Willamette Valley. He had a farm on Crooked River and a ferry on Deschutes River, near the present site of the bridge. This information was furnished by J. N. Williamson of Prineville.

Texas Bar Creek, Umatilla County. This creek flows into North Fork John Day River east of Dale. In the days of the mining excitement, a man named Tex kept a saloon and roadhouse at the mouth of the creek and the place was known as Tex's Bar. The change to present form occurred sometime during the intervening years.

Thatcher, Washington County. Thatcher is a cross-roads community about three miles northwest of Forest Grove and close to the northeast slope of David Hill. The place was named for Harmon and Jemima Thatcher who took up a homestead in the locality in early pioneer days.

The Thatchers were married in Indiana in 1847 and came to Oregon soon afterward. Thatcher post office was established August 3, 1895, with Thomas J. Clark first postmaster. The office was closed August 21, 1902.

Thayer Glacier, Deschutes County. This glacier is on the eastern part of the North Sister. It was named by Professor E. T. Hodge of the University of Oregon for Eli Thayer, representative in Congress from Massachusetts, who assisted in securing the passage of the bill admitting Oregon to the Union. See *Mount Multnomah,* page 75. For information about Oregon's debt to Thayer, see Scott's *History of the Oregon Country,* volume V, page 3.

The Dalles, Wasco County. The name The Dalles is derived from the French word *dalle,* meaning flag-stone, and was applied to the narrows of the Columbia River, above the present city of The Dalles, by French-Canadian employees of the fur companies. Among other things, *dalle* meant a stone used to flag gutters, and the peculiar basalt formation along the narrows doubtless suggested gutters. The word *dalles* signified, to the voyageurs, the river rapids flowing swifty through a narrow channel over flat, basaltic rocks. The name is common in America. Well-known *dalles* are those of the Saint Louis, Saint Croix, Wisconsin, and Columbia rivers. The best-known *dalles* were those of the Columbia. The name is not derived from the French *dale* meaning trough. As far as the compiler knows the first use of the name Dalles in Oregon is in Franchere's *Narrative,* on April 12, 1814, where it is used to describe the Long Narrows. John Work, in his journal of 1825, speaks of *Dalls.* The name *La Grande Dalle de la Columbia* became established. The incorporated name of the community is now Dalles City, but the postal name, and the one in universal use is The Dalles, this style being adopted not only for historical and sentimental reasons but also to avoid duplication with Dallas, Polk County. The post office was established with the name Dalles on November 5, 1851, with William R. Gibson first postmaster. On September 3, 1853, the name was changed to Wascopum, and on March 22, 1860, it was changed to The Dalles. The narrows of the river were generally known as The Dalles of the Columbia, and this collective term described the geographic features from the Big Eddy on the west to Celilo Falls on the east. All these rapids were inundated in March 1957 when The Dalles Dam was completed, forming Lake Celilo. Just east of Big Eddy was Fivemile Rapids, formerly known as the Long Narrows, The Dalles or The Great Dalles. Further east was Tenmile Rapids, formerly known as the Short Narrows, Little Narrows or *Les Petites Dalles.* For information about The Dalles of the Columbia, see *OHQ,* March, 1926, in the article by Henry J. Biddle entitled "Wishram." The neighborhood of Mill Creek at The Dalles was called *Quenett* by the Indians, which was a word for salmon trout. Lewis and Clark camped at the mouth of this stream on October 25, 26 and 27, 1805, and recorded the form *Que-nett* in their journals and maps. In April, 1806, they named this place "rockfort camp." Dr. William C. McKay, in an article in The Dalles *Mountaineer,* May 28, 1869, gives the Indian names of a great many places in the vicinity of The Dalles. Dr. McKay says that long before the white men came, the Indians called the locality of what is now the city of The Dalles *Win-quatt,* signifying a place encircled by rock cliffs.

The Dungeon, Clackamas County. This locality is on the east side of

Molalla River about three miles southwest of Table Rock. The place was named by Andy Wyland and Joe Davis of Molalla, who built a rough shelter of cedar shakes there in the early 1880s. Most of the structure has since disappeared, but the place is still known by its original name. The building was low and without windows and 'this name was quite descriptive. Joe Davis, a well-known character of Molalla, was a prospector and trapper. He died on Molalla River and was buried about 150 feet south of the original site of The Dungeon. Dee Wright of Eugene furnished this information.

The Flatirons, Jefferson County. These flat top rocks three miles east of Willowdale are named for their resemblance to the sad irons of pioneer days.

The Watchman, Crater Lake National Park, Klamath County. The Watchman, elevation 8025 feet, is one of the highest points on the western rim of Crater Lake. It was named because a party of topographic engineers was placed on its summit in 1886 to take observations while the lake was being sounded. It had previously been christened Bentley Peak by Captain O. C. Applegate in honor of A. Bentley of Toledo, Ohio, who visited Crater Lake in 1871 with Sir (then Mr.) William F. Maxwell, of Edinburgh, Scotland, and a Dr. Munson of Klamath Agency. Munson died of over-exertion and Maxwell faithfully watched his body all night while Bentley went for assistance. For an account of this event, see Klamath *Record,* March 22, 1918. See also under Glacier Peak and Munson Valley.

Thelake, Harney County. Thelake post office was in service from November 3, 1914, to March 1, 1919, with Rose G. Balcomb the only postmaster. It was at the east border of the Mann Lake Ranch, about ten miles south of the old Alberson post office. The name was intended as an allusion to Mann Lake, an intermittent feature named long ago. Mann Lake was named for a local settler, Phillip Mann.

Theora, Lake County. Theora post office, situated near the middle of section 7, township 40 south, range 19 east, was established December 4, 1916, with Hubert E. Koons first and only postmaster. The office was discontinued to Lakeview on March 15, 1918. Theora office was named for Theora Swift, sister of Alvin J. Swift. Swift was secretary of the local irrigation district.

Thief Valley, Union County. This little valley east of North Powder, was the place where John Wetherly was hanged in December 1864, for stealing mules from an emigrant at Boise.

Thielsen, Polk County. This is a station on the Southern Pacific line between Salem and Dallas, and is near the farm of the late Henry B. Thielsen, who was for a number of years engaged in railroad surveying and construction work in Oregon and in Washington, and subsequently conducted a farm near the site of Thielsen station. For several years before his death Mr. Thielsen resided in Salem. He was a son of Hans Thielsen, a prominent Oregon pioneer railroad builder for whom Mount Thielsen in the Cascade Range was named.

Thimble Mountain, Clackamas County. This point in the northeast corner of the county was named by T. H. Sherrard of the USFS because of its resemblance to a thimble.

Third Lake, Linn County. Third Lake is the third of a series of four lakes extending along the east bank of Willamette River north of Albany. These lakes are named in accordance with their position, First Lake being the one nearest Albany.

Thirsty Creek, Douglas County. This creek rises southeast of Lemolo Lake. It is intermittent and finally goes underground, presumably to form Spring River. It was named in 1919 when a fire crew found the stream dry when they needed it the most. The compiler believes "thirsty" is temperate language for men in this situation.

Thirty-two Point Creek, Wallowa County. This creek is in the extreme southeast part of the county. There are two theories about the name, one to the effect that a pair of antlers with 32 points was found nearby, and the other to the effect that there are 32 points of land fronting on the creek between its mouth and its source. The reader may take his choice.

Thomas, Linn County. Thomas was a railroad station on the Oregon Pacific Railroad, later the Corvallis & Eastern, near the mouth of Thomas Creek. Edwin D. Culp in *Stations West* has a picture of the building on page 89. Thomas post office operated from May 4, 1898 until January 31, 1921 in the same vicinity. Both were named for the Frederick Thomas of Thomas Creek.

Thomas Creek, Linn County. Thomas Creek is one of the important streams of the county. It was named for Frederick Thomas who in 1846 settled on the banks of the stream, where he took up a donation land claim. Other nearby settlers named the stream.

Thomas Creek, Umatilla County. George F. Thomas and J. S. Ruckel established the stage line from Walla Walla to the Grande Ronde Valley in 1865. South of Bingham Springs on Umatilla River the Ruckel Road, as it is still called, follows Thomas Creek to the summit of the Blue Mountains at an elevation of about 4500 feet. The compiler believes this Thomas Creek bears the name of the first partner as the second is also commemorated by Ruckel Ridge and Ruckel Spring immediately adjacent to the pass.

Thomson, Lane County. Thomson was an early-day post office on McKenzie River, but should not be classed as a pioneer establishment. Mary C. Thomson was appointed postmaster April 15, 1891. She ran the office until June 24, 1893, when it was closed to McKenzie Bridge. An effort was made to revive the office in May, 1895, when Cynthia J. Isham was appointed postmaster, but the order for some reason or other was rescinded in July, 1895. The C. W. Thomson homestead was in section 17, township 16 south, range 5 east, just across the McKenzie Highway from Belknap bridge, but bridge and highway were not there when the Thomsons settled. Thomson post office was between Blue River and McKenzie Bridge.

Thorn Hollow, Wallowa County. Thorn Hollow drains into Cougar Creek in township 4 north, range 45 east. In 1885 J. Pern Averill and James Alford killed two bears there that were found feasting off the thornberries, and the name Thorn Hollow resulted.

Thorn Prairie, Douglas County. Thorn Prairie is on North Umpqua River just above Toketee Lake. It is a comparatively level bench covered with thorn brush which sprang up after the area was burned over many years ago. G. C. Blake of Roseburg informed the compiler that the name was applied in 1917 by Perry and Jessie Wright of Caps Illahee.

Thornberry, Sherman County. This station, formerly known as Grebe, was named for a local resident and stockman. It is south of Biggs. Grebe post office was established in February, 1916, with Henry Grebe postmaster. Harvey B. Thornberry became postmaster in January, 1919, and the name of the office was changed to Thornberry in October, 1920. The office was discontinued in November, 1923.

Thornhollow, Umatilla County. Thornhollow was the name of a post office situated in the natural geographic feature Thorn Hollow about eighteen miles east of Pendleton. The name Thorn Hollow was applied in the 1870s, but the post office was not established until 1923. Marietta Jones was the first postmaster. Postal authorities made the name one word. Thorn Hollow was originally named by a stage driver because of an abundance of thorns along the road. Thornhollow post office was closed November 30, 1926, but Thorn Hollow railroad station lasted until the 1970s.

Thornton Lake, Benton County. This is a narrow lake about a mile northwest of Albany. It is on what was the donation land claim of J. Quinn Thornton, one of Oregon's prominent pioneers, and was named for him. Thornton was born in Mason County, West Virginia, August 24, 1810. He came to Oregon in 1846. He rendered important service toward creation of Oregon Territory. He wrote *Oregon and California in 1848,* in two volumes. Harper & Brothers, New York, 1849. He died at Salem February 5, 1888. His address on the migration of 1846 to Oregon appears in OPA *Transactions,* 1878, pages 29-71; history of the provisional government, *ibid.,* 1874, pages 43-95. Thornton was a member of the emigration that came by the Applegate Route in 1846, and for many years was especially bitter against Jesse Applegate and other members of the party who went from the Willamette Valley to prepare a road for the emigration. Particulars of this difficulty may be found in Bancroft's *History of Oregon,* volume I, page 542, *et seq.* Thornton challenged the integrity of David Goff, a member of the Applegate party, and James W. Nesmith, Goff's son-in-law, challenged Thornton to a duel. As a result of Thornton's failure to accept Nesmith's challenge, the latter prepared a poster and tacked it up on trees about Oregon City in June 1847, calling Thornton a variety of names. Judge Deady describes the poster as "a wealth of adjectives." C. H. Stewart, of Albany, calls attention to the fact that Thornton called this lake Fairmount Lake, presumably for a small hill to the north. The name Fairmount has not persisted for the lake, although it is applied to a school nearby. When Thornton settled on his homestead in November, 1846, he called the place Forest Grove. The name seems to have been unusually attractive to him, for on January 10, 1851, he suggested it for the locality which is now a town in Washington County. See under Forest Grove for details.

Thorp Creek, Wallowa County. Thorp Creek is just southwest of Wallowa Lake. It was named for C. H. Thorp by Fred McClain.

Three Creek Lake, Deschutes County. This lake is about seventeen miles south of Sisters and three miles east of Broken Top. It is directly below and to the north of Tam McArthur Rim and is a favorite fishing lake as well as the site of a USFS Forest Camp. About a mile north of the lake is a meadow where three streams, the outfall of Three Creek Lake, that of Little Three Creek Lake and Snow Creek Ditch come together to form Three Creek. This flows north past Three Creek Butte into Squaw Creek but the bulk of the water is diverted south of Three Creek Butte into the continuation of Snow Creek Ditch and thus eventually into Tumalo Canal.

Three Fingered Jack, Jefferson and Linn counties. While this peak is one of the lesser ones of the Cascade Range, as far as altitude is concerned, its unusual appearance has given it much prominence. Its elevation is 7848 feet, or practically the same as that of its neighbor, Mount Washington. Its name is in a way descriptive, but the writer has been unable to learn who named it, or when. It has three main rock spires. It is not mentioned by any writer of the exploratory period. Some time in the 1870s it was called Mount Marion because of the activities of a Marion County road locating party under the leadership of John Minto, who investigated passes over the Cascade Range nearby. The writer was told about 1900 that the present name had been applied because of a three-fingered trapper who lived nearby, whose name was Jack. As far as known the first ascent made of Three Fingered Jack was on Labor Day, September 3, 1923, when six men from Bend, some of whom had made the first ascent of Mount Washington on August 26, reached the summit. This party found a series of lava chimneys to ascend in mounting the almost perpendicular walls of the highest finger. For particulars about Three Fingered Jack, see *Mazama*, for December, 1917.

Three Lynx Creek, Clackamas County. This stream, a tributary of Clackamas River below Oak Grove Fork, bears a name that has provoked much controversy. Old maps show the name Three Links, and there is a legend in eastern Clackamas County to the effect that this name was the result of loss, by a surveyor, of three links out of a surveying chain. Ernest P. Rands and William C. Elliott of Portland, for many years civil engineers in Oregon, both informed the compiler that there was no truth in the three links story. They were in the neighborhood of the stream at the time it was named. They are authority for the statement that one of the Austen family, early settlers nearby, named the stream Three Lynx Creek because he saw three bobcats on its banks. The USBGN has adopted the name Three Lynx.

Three Rocks, Tillamook County. This community on the north bank of Salmon River takes its name from three prominent rocks just offshore. The form 3 Rox was fortunately only a temporary affectation.

Three Sisters, Deschutes and Lane counties. These peaks are among the most interesting in Oregon. There are but two higher mountains in the state, and the Three Sisters, together with Broken Top, comprise the most majestic alpine group in the Cascade Range in Oregon. The writer has been unable to learn who named the Three Sisters, and they are not frequently mentioned either by explorers or pioneers. The earliest mention of these mountains, as far as known, is by David Douglas, as follows: "Thursday 5th. [October 1826.] After a scanty breakfast proceeded at nine o'clock in a south course. Country more hilly. At one o'clock passed on the left, about twenty-five or thirty miles distant, Mount Jefferson, of Lewis and Clarke, covered with snow as low as the summit of the lower mountains by which it is surrounded. About twenty miles to the east of it, two mountains of greater altitude are to be seen, also covered with snow, in an unknown tract of country called by the natives who inhabit it 'Clamite'." (*Journal Kept by David Douglas*, London, 1914, page 216.) From certain positions the Three Sisters appear as two mountains, and Douglas' mistake was natural. The mountains appear as the Three Sisters on Preston's *Map of Oregon*, 1856. There is a story to the effect that at one time the three mountains were known as Mount Faith, Mount Hope and Mount Charity, beginning at the north. In 1927 William P. Vandevert of Bend, a native son of Oregon, confirmed this, and informed the compiler that when a youth, he was often told that the name Three Sisters was originally applied by members of the Methodist mission at Salem in the early 1840s, and that the individual peaks were given the names mentioned above. In 1928 John C. Todd of Bend told the compiler that in early days he heard the Three Sisters called Faith, Hope and Charity many times. The best information about the Three Sisters is that contained in USGS Bulletin 252, by Dr. I. C. Russell; in *Mineral Resources of Oregon*, volume I, No. 1; in *Mazama* for October 1912 and December 1916 and 1922; in *Mount Multnomah* by Professor E. T. Hodge and in *National Geographic Magazine*, June 1912. In the summer of 1944 the University of California Press issued Howel Williams' *Volcanoes of the Three Sisters Region*, a valuable contribution to the knowledge of the area. It contains some very fine plates. Williams controverts the notion that there was a Mount Multnomah.

Three Trappers, Deschutes County. The Three Trappers are three adjoining buttes about six miles east of Crane Prairie Reservoir. They were named in the 1920s to commemorate Roy Wilson, Dewey Morris and Ed Nichols who were murdered in the early spring of 1924 while tending a fox farm at Little Lava Lake. Circumstantial evidence pointed strong suspicion at an escaped convict who had been seen near Bend, but no direct link was established and the crime remains unsolved today. Phil Brogan, who covered the story as a young reporter for the Bend *Bulletin*, gives more details in *East of the Cascades*, page 224.

Threebuck Creek, Wallowa County. This stream flows into Little Sheep Creek in township 2 south, range 46 east, and was named by J. J. Blevans and his son Murat Blevans, in 1878, because the two had good luck there hunting. They were getting food for the white people who were in the Prairie Creek stockade.

Threemile Canyon, Morrow County. Threemile Canyon is about three miles east of the mouth of Willow Creek, and is so called on that account.

Threemile Creek, Coos County. The Coos County gold rush of 1853-55 was largely centered at Randolph, a mining town near the mouth of Whisky Run north of Coquille River. Threemile Creek was named because it was about three miles north along the beach from Randolph.

Threemile Creek, Douglas County. This is a small creek flowing into the Pacific Ocean north of the mouth of Umpqua River. It was named on the assumption that its mouth was three miles from the river. As a matter of fact it is about four miles.

Threemile Creek, Harney County. Threemile Creek flows westward from Steens Mountain into Catlow Valley at a point about three miles south of Home Creek and the Home Creek Ranch. It got its name on that account.

Threemile Creek, Wasco County. This stream was so named because the pioneer road from The Dalles into central Oregon crossed it about three miles from town. The mouth of the stream is also about three miles east of The Dalles, but the compiler is of the opinion that this fact was not the original reason for the name.

Threepines, Josephine County. Threepines was the name of a post office on the Southern Pacific line a few miles south of Hugo that operated from November, 1910, until November, 1921. W. E. Daniel was the first postmaster. The place was named for three prominent pine trees nearby.

Thunder Rock, Clackamas County. This rock, in the northeast corner of the county, was named by R. S. Shelley of the USFS in the fall of 1906 because he was caught there in a violent thunder storm.

Thurston, Lane County. Geo. H. Kelly of Portland told the compiler in 1926 that this town was named for George H. Thurston, a pioneer settler of Lane County. Among other things, he was one of the early day land surveyors of the county. He was born in Burlington, Iowa, December 2, 1846, and was the son of Samuel R. Thurston, who was later Oregon's first territorial delegate in Congress. George H. Thurston was brought to Oregon before he was a year old. For biographical information, see Hines' *Illustrated History of the State of Oregon,* pages 475 and 1272. Thurston post office was established March 16, 1877 and operated until July 1, 1973. An earlier post office named Thurston was established December 31, 1853, with Gamaliel Parrish postmaster. It was near the present site of Harrisburg, Linn County, and had nothing to do with the place in Lane County. It was discontinued December 3, 1856.

Tiara, Harney County. Tiara was a word originally used to refer to an ancient royal Persian headdress, but the meaning has been extended to include several forms of head ornament, including a style of coronet. On May 18, 1916, Tiara post office was established in Harney County with Mrs. Minerva Benson first and only postmaster. The office was closed January 15, 1917. It was in township 32 south, range 31 east, near the north end of Catlow Valley. In June, 1947, Mrs. Benson, then living in Albany, wrote the compiler that the name Tiara was selected for the post office by her son, Hill M. Benson, because it was at the head of the valley.

Tichenor Rock, Curry County. Tichenor Rock is south of The Heads and southwest of Port Orford, and is a well-known landmark. It was named for Captain William Tichenor, who was born at Newark, New Jersey, in 1813. In 1843 he settled in Illinois and in 1848 was elected state senator from Edgar County. In 1849 he started for California and engaged in the sea trade. In 1851 he commanded the steamer *Sea Gull,* one of the first in the San Francisco-Columbia River trade. He lost the steamer at Humboldt Bay on January 22, 1852, but saved the lives of all on board and was given a gold watch for heroism. Captain Tichenor founded the town of Port Orford, Oregon, in 1851, and brought his family there in May, 1852. For history of the first attempts at settlement, see under Battle Rock. He gave up sea life in 1868 and settled down at his home in Port Orford. He died in San Francisco July 28, 1887, and was buried in the family cemetery at Port Orford. He was a public spirited and highly respected citizen of southwest Oregon.

Tidbits Mountain, Linn County. This mountain is an important triangulation station and lookout north of Blue River. It received its name because the top is shattered into fingers or tidbits.

Tide Creek, Columbia County. The name Tide Creek as applied to a stream in the east part of Columbia County is very old and doubtless resulted from the fact that there were manifestations of small tides in the creek. Tidecreek post office was established near the lower reaches of this stream on November 29, 1902, with Fred A. Bucher first and only postmaster. Mr. Bucher was apparently not able to develop a heavy postal business as the office was closed to Goble on June 24, 1903.

Tidewater, Lincoln County. Tidewater lies east of Waldport, and received its name because it is near the head of tide on Alsea River.

Tiernan, Lane County. The post office at Tiernan was established about 1919. It was named for R. Tiernan of San Francisco who at the time was leasing a sawmill in the neighborhood. Some maps use the name Beck Station, so called because of an early railroad station master, but this was never the name of the community.

Tierra Del Mar, Tillamook County. This community was named by Marie F. Pollock who started the real estate development. *Tierra Del Mar* is Spanish for land by the sea.

Tigard, Washington County. Tigard was named for Wilson M. Tigard, who came from Arkansas to Oregon in 1852 and took up a donation land claim near the present site of the town. The community first bore the name of Tigardville and was situated about a half a mile west of the railroad station at Tigard. The village of Tigardville existed many years before the development at the railroad station.

Tiger Creek, Umatilla County. Tiger Creek flows northwest into Mill Creek about three miles east of where that stream passes into Washington. Kirk Casper of Walla Walla wrote in 1975 to say that in the early days a Swede went up the creek looking for timber to cut ties. On his return he reported seeing a tiger though the locals assumed it was actually a cougar.

Tillamook, Tillamook County. For the origin of this name, see under Tillamook County. The locality of the town of Tillamook was, in early days, called Lincoln, Hoquarton, the Landing and Tillamook Landing. The word Tillamook by itself generally meant the county. Hoquarton was an Indian word the meaning of which is unknown to the compiler. This word, now spelled Hoquarten, is applied to a slough at Tillamook. Even though the place was called by other names, a post office named Tillamook was established March 12, 1866, with George W. Miller first postmaster. Stories to the effect that the office could not be named Lincoln because of another Oregon office with that name are wrong, because the Lincoln office in Polk

County was not established until more than a year later, on May 31, 1867. It is possible that at some later date an effort was made to change the name of Tillamook to Lincoln but the existence of the Polk County office may have put a stop to the proposal. The Tillamook airbase for blimps was put in commission December 1, 1942, with the name U. S. Naval Air Station, Tillamook, Oregon. It was closed after World War II, but the two immense hangars are prominent landmarks.

Tillamook County. *Tillamook* was the name of a large tribe of Salish Indians whose habitat was near and south of Tillamook Head. In the journals of Lewis and Clark, this name is spelled *Kilamox* and *Killamuck*. Gass' journal gives it *Callemeux* and *Cal-a-mex;* the journals of Henry and Thompson, by Coues, give it *Callemex.* For references to various spellings used by early writers, see *OHQ*, volume XXVIII, page 183. Tillamook County was created by the territorial legislature December 15, 1853, and has a land area of 1115 square miles according to the Bureau of the Census. For further information about its name and establishment, see Holman's "Oregon Counties," *OHQ*, volume XI, page 1-81. Apparently the initial K was changed to a T about the time the county was created. In addition to the county, the name is used for Tillamook (city), Tillamook Bay, Tillamook Head and Tillamook River. Dean Collins' book *Cheese Cheddar,* Portland, 1933, contains information about the early history of Tillamook County and a popular account of the Tillamook cheese industry, a business of great importance.

Tillamook Head, Clatsop County. For the origin of the name Tillamook, see under Tillamook County. The first white man of record to visit Tillamook Head was William Clark, who spent the night of January 7-8, 1806, near the top of the head, and in his journals comments on the fine view to be had, which gave the place the name of Clarks Point of View. Clark was on his way to what is now called Cannon Beach on a short exploring expedition. The wording of his diary has caused several authorities, notably Greenhow and Thwaites, to confuse Tillamook Head with other features further south along the coast. Clark crossed over but one head though his journal seems to indicate two. For additional information see under Capes, Cannon Beach and Ecola Creek. Tillamook Head triangulation station, on the highest point, has an elevation of 1136 feet. Steel says the Clatsop Indian name for Tillamook Head was *Nah-se-u'-su.*

Tillamook Rock, Clatsop County. Tillamook Rock takes its name from Tillamook Head. It is famous because upon it is built Tillamook Rock lighthouse. An act approved June 20, 1878, made an appropriation of $50,000 for a first-class light on Tillamook Head. Subsequent appropriations of 1880-81 added $75,000 to this sum. The heavy cost of a road, and the fact that the light would be a thousand feet above the sea led Major G. L. Gillespie, U.S.A., then Light-House Engineer for the 13th District, to recommend a light on Tillamook Rock. An inspection was made of the rock, and H. S. Wheeler, superintendent of construction, was landed on the rock from the revenue-cutter *Corwin* on June 26, 1879. This was probably the first time a white man ever stood on the rock. An attempt by Wheeler to land on June 22 was a failure. John R. Trewavas, of Portland, a mason who had had experience in England working on lights, tried to land on September 18, 1879, to make a preliminary survey, but was drowned in the attempt. Construction was started in October. A little over 29 feet of rock was blasted off the pinnacle to provide a platform for the station. The rock was originally 80 feet high and a mile from shore, and had a sharp overhang to the west. All materials and supplies were landed by derricks. After World Was II, improved navigation systems and high maintenance costs combined against the installation and the light was finally extinguished at 12:10 AM on September 1, 1957. It was replaced by a radar buoy. The lighthouse and rock were designated surplus property and in 1959 sold to a pair of Las Vegas businessmen. They did not use it and after several changes of ownership, it was purchased in early 1980 by a Portland real estate consortium headed by Mimi Morisette. Work began at once to restore the exterior and convert the interior to a columbarium or repository for the ashes of cremated persons. The proprietors intend to deliver the permanent residents about twice a year by helicopter, a modern device which will disturb no one except the hordes of seabirds. The compiler can only quote Gray's *Elegy*, composed upon a similar theme—"of such as wandering near her secret bower, molest her ancient, solitary reign".

Tiller, Douglas County. Tiller was named for a pioneer settler, Aaron Tiller. The post office was established October 15, 1902, with Alfred B. Marquam postmaster.

Tilley Canyon, Wheeler County. Tilley Canyon is in Horse Mountain east of Girds Creek. Albert N. Tilley homesteaded there in 1893.

Tillicum Creek, Lane County. *Tillicum* is a Chinook jargon word that has been in popular use in the Pacific Northwest for well over a century, but not always with exactly the same meaning. The early Chinook use referred to people, or tribe or even relatives. With the passage of time the word came to mean also friendly people or even a friend. It also means friendly, or agreeable, as in the case of Tillicum Creek. The older Chinook jargon word for friend, applied to persons rather than things, is *siks* or *six*. Tillicum Creek flows into Salmon Creek northeast of Oakridge.

Tilly Jane Creek, Hood River County. This stream, east of Mount Hood, was named for Mrs. William M. Ladd of Portland. See under Ladd Glacier. The Ladd family spent many summers at Cloud Cap Inn, and the stream heading near the inn was given Mrs. Ladd's nickname.

Timber, Washington County. When this post office was established a number of local residents suggested names and a list was sent to the government. Postal officials chose the word Timber. The name was suggested on account of the heavy forests in the neighborhood.

Timber Culture Gulch, Jefferson County. Columbus Friend, a well-known early settler, filed a Timber Culture claim in 1886 near the mouth of this canyon in Trout Creek drainage north of Ashwood. Timber Culture filings were authorized in 1873 when Congress passed "An act to encourage the growth of timber on western prairies." The act provided that a man could file on a quarter section of 160 acres and put 40 acres into a tree farm of prescribed standards. At the end of ten years if the trees had shown adequate growth and care, the claim could be patented at no additional cost. It also provided that certain homesteads under the 1862 law could be patented in like manner. Proper administration and supervision were difficult and the results were not too satisfactory. The bill was amended at various intervals and finally repealed in 1891 but isolated stands of poplar, locust and other trees still mark the locations of these claimants.

Timberline, Clackamas County. Timberline and Timberline Lodge are names that have developed naturally and spontaneously because such names fit the physical conditions. The writer had some correspondence from Francis E. Williamson, Jr., of the USFS, which gives some interesting history about the origin of this name. The following quotations are from Mr. Williamson's letter of January 31, 1947: "The popularity of Timberline Lodge, combined with the public's idea that the area was new and possibly unexplored until recent years, causes me to assume that many people claim the distinction of naming it. Historically, I believe that you will find the following steps in the development of the lodge are correct and have some bearing on the actual naming. Plans and drawings for the formal compilation of a recreation plan for the south slope of Mount Hood were started by me in 1927. My ideas were the result of several trips over the area with Fred Cleator and a reconnaissance with Cecil Lord in which we ran a P-line for a road. The plan, as developed, authorized a *lodge at the timberline* along with ski club and mountain climbing club chalets." E. J. Griffith became interested in the project and soon thereafter became head of the W.P.A. in Oregon. Timberline Lodge as it now stands was a cooperative project and had the name Timberline Lodge from the very first. The name was natural and undoubtedly came about as the result of conferences between the USFS and the W.P.A. The post office was first called Timberline Lodge and established August 19, 1939, with Arthur V. Allen first postmaster. This office was officially closed as of December 19, 1943, but the compiler has been informed that due to war conditions the place was shut up in the latter part of 1942. The office was reopened in 1946 with the name Timberline and finally closed July 31, 1951. The lodge is now a National Historic Landmark and receives large numbers of visitors throughout the entire year.

Timon, Coos County. In the spring of 1894 J. H. Timon opened a vein of coal on the east side of Coquille River about four miles south of the community called Riverton. The Timon mine was diligently operated for a number of years and coal was shipped to California. For an account of this enterprise, see Dodge, *Pioneer History of Coos and Curry Counties,* page 250. The place was near what is now known as Lampa Creek. On January 22, 1902, Timon post office was established in this locality, with James L. Bean postmaster. The office was closed October 9, 1902. The compiler does not know if the mine was in operation at the time the post office was established or not. Bean also ran a store. Three years later Bean had a new office established with the name Lampa, at or close to the site of the Timon office.

Timothy Lake, Clackamas County. This artificial lake was formed when Portland General Electric Company dammed Oak Grove Fork Clackamas River for hydro-electric power and the impoundment flooded Timothy Meadows. In 1967 Lige Coalman told the compiler that before the

National Forest the meadows were a favorite summer sheep graze and sheepherders sowed timothy seed to augment the natural grass.

Timpanogas Lake, Douglas County. This lake, so named on the map of the Summit Lake quadrangle, is the principal source of Middle Fork Willamette River. The compiler has been informed that the name was applied to the lake in the Cascade Range by J. G. Staack, formerly topographic engineer for the USGS and later chief topographic engineer. The name was used in 1913-14 when Mr. Staack was mapping the area. It is reported that he found the name while reading in the Library of Congress, Washington, D. C., apparently in one of the Hall J. Kelley publications. Kelley published a *Geographical Sketch of Oregon* in Boston in 1830, and in this book it is stated that the Multnomah River, now known as the Willamette, had one of its sources in Lake Timpanogos. This is the name used by Mr. Staack, with slightly different spelling. Timpanogos was an early name for Great Salt Lake, derived from the name of a stream. Fremont says the word means Rock River. See his *Report,* Washington, 1845, page 273.

Tioga, Douglas County. The name Tioga is probably taken from an Iroquois Indian word meaning "where it forks," referring to a place in Bradford County, Pennsylvania, which was the southern gateway to the Iroquois country. Several important trails met there. For a discussion of the word, see *Handbook of American Indians,* volume II, page 755. Tioga, as a post office name, has been popular throughout the country. Tioga was once a post office on North Umpqua River about six miles northeast of Glide. The office was established April 3, 1890, with J. S. Williams postmaster, and was discontinued November 28, 1892. The name may have been selected because it was near this point that a trail forked away from the river and followed up Rock Creek. A later post office, Idleyld Park, has been established at this place. Tioga Fork is the name given a stream in the east part of Coos County, tributary to South Fork Coos River. It is probable that the name was used in this case because of its pleasing sound. There is a locality on this stream called Tioga, but it was not a post office in 1945.

Tipsoo Peak, Douglas and Klamath counties. This peak is on the summit of the Cascade Range north of Mount Thielsen. It is named with the Chinook jargon word for grass. *Tipsoo* also meant hair.

Tipton, Baker County. Tipton post office was established at the summit of the Blue Mountains near the Baker-Grant county line west of Whitney at a high point on the Sumpter Valley Railway, and was named on this account. The office was put in service February 13, 1904, with Robert W. Cecil first of two postmasters, and was closed January 17, 1906. The locality has an elevation of a little over 5100 feet.

Tiptop, Lane County. Tiptop post office was named with the nickname of the first postmaster, Isaac Hamner, who was frequently called Tiptop because of some hunting incident that suggested the name. The post office, which was established May 16, 1895, was in section 36, township 21 south, range 3 east, on or near Hills Creek. Isaac Hamner was the first and only postmaster. The office was discontinued April 5, 1901. The locality of Tiptop post office is frequently called The Boulders and in 1948 the place was owned by Cliff Morgan.

Tire Creek, Lane County. In May, 1943, USFS ranger C. B. McFarland of Oakridge wrote the compiler as follows: "Tire Creek was named during the early days soon after the old military wagon road was constructed. A traveler broke his wagon wheel. The wagon tire rolled to the lower side of the road and was abandoned in the small creek bed. It lay there for many years and the creek was referred to as Tire Creek." The stream rises on the mountain of the same name and joins Middle Fork Willamette River about two miles east of the head of Lookout Point Reservoir.

TNT Creek, Lane County. This is a tributary of Hills Creek. It is named because a USFS pack mule bucked off a box of TNT at this creek when the trail was being built.

Tobin Cabin, Klamath County. Tobin Cabin and Tobin Spring near Antelope Mountain bear the name of William Tobin who took up the surrounding land in 1902.

Todd Lake, Deschutes County. Formerly called Lost Lake because of the difficulty in finding it. Citizens of Bend asked to have the name changed because of confusion with other Lost lakes, and the name Todd Lake was selected in commemoration of Uncle John Y. Todd, an early settler of central Oregon. John Young Todd was born in Carroll County, Missouri, November 30, 1830, and died at Salem, November 8, 1919. He fought in the Mexican War and arrived in Oregon in 1852, by way of California. He packed goods to the mines and engaged in other business, and settled on a homestead in Tygh Valley. He built Sherars Bridge in 1860 and rebuilt it later. Todd later moved to the Farewell Bend ranch at the present site of Bend and lived in that vicinity for many years. For additional data, see *OHQ,* volume XXX, page 70.

Toketee Falls, Douglas County. These falls are on the North Umpqua at the mouth of Clearwater. *Toketee* is the Chinook jargon word for pretty, or graceful. The word is pronounced Tuck-et-tee, with the accent on the first syllable.

Toketee Lake, Douglas County. This is a reservoir with a normal elevation of 2430 feet formed by damming North Umpqua River above Toketee Falls but below the mouth of the Clearwater. It holds water for hydroelectric power and is named for the nearby falls.

Toledo, Lincoln County. Toledo is on the homestead of John Graham, a pioneer resident, who emigrated from Ohio. It is said that when the post office was established in 1868, Joseph D. Graham, a son, was told that he could name the place. He said: "I am homesick for Ohio. We will call the place Toledo." Toledo post office was established on July 14, 1868, with William Mackey first postmaster.

Tollgate, Umatilla County. Sometime in the 1870s the proprietor of the toll road over the Blue Mountains in the northeast part of the county established a toll gate and for many years the locality of this barrier was called Tollgate. With the development of Langdon Lake close by, the name Langdon Lake came into general use as the locality name. However, when a post office was established in September, 1941, the old name Tollgate was revived and used for the post office. Mrs. Harry (Gertie) Hunter was the first postmaster. The toll road was generally referred to as the Woodward road. Its west end was at the junction of the Lincton and Weston mountain roads and the southeast terminus was at Summerville. The gate was at Woodward Meadow in section 32, township 4 north, range 38 east. The meadow is the site of the Tollgate Ranger Station of the USFS. The locality is now on the main Weston-Elgin highway.

Tolo, Jackson County. Will G. Steel is authority for the statement that this place was named in error by postal authorities. Cleophas C. Ragsdale, formerly a resident of Yolo, California, was living in Willow Springs, Oregon, in 1885, and as he disliked the commonplace name of his adopted home, he petitioned to have it changed to Yolo. The Y was misread as a T in Washington, and on March 30, 1886, postal authorities changed the name of the office from Willow Springs to Tolo, and so it has been ever since. *Yolo* or *Yolay* was the name of an Indian tribe in California. The word is said to mean a place abounding in rushes. Willow Springs post office was established August 12, 1864, with Samuel P. Dean first postmaster.

Tolovana Park, Clatsop County. Tolovana Park is a place on Cannon Beach, named for Tolovana, Alaska. The town in Alaska is on Tanana River, about a hundred miles above Fort Gibbon, established in 1905 as a telegraph station and post office. This Indian name was selected by the Signal Corps, but the compiler has been unable to get the exact meaning. Some say it is an Indian tribe name, others that it means a wooded country and another version is that it means a pile of driftwood or log jam. Mark Warren and his brother, William E. Warren, spent some time in central Alaska, and, after their return, they platted property on Cannon Beach. Mark Warren chose the name Tolovana Park for his tract, because he fancied the sound of the word as used in Alaska.

Tom Dick & Harry Mountain, Clackamas County. This is the half mile long ridge about one mile southwest of Government Camp that forms the cirque now called the Ski Bowl. Lige Coalman told the writer that the name was in use when he first came to Government Camp in 1897 and that he thought it was so called because it has three distinct summits. The form Tom Dick Mountain is an incorrect abbreviation.

Tom East Creek, Curry and Josephine counties. While Tom East probably was no more peripatetic than many other early day miners in southwest Oregon, he accomplished wonders in leaving his mark on the land. There are at least three Tom East Creeks, one in Curry County tributary to Rogue River near Potato Illahe Mountain and two in Josephine County tributary to Grave Creek, near Galice and further upstream near Placer. East was born in England and came to the United States as a young man. He was mining in Josephine County in 1855 and lived in southwest Oregon until his death July 14, 1897.

Tom Taylor Canyon, Douglas County. This canyon east of Camas Valley was named for a homesteader of 1895.

Tomahawk Island, Multnomah County. This name was originally given by Lewis and Clark to a small island between what is now known as Hayden Island and the north shore of the Columbia River. The name was the result of an incident that took place on November 4, 1805, when William Clark's tomahawk pipe was stolen. The incident is mentioned several times in Thwaites' *Original Journals of the Lewis and Clark Expedition.* While the theft took place on the mainland, a small island was a silent witness and received its name on that account. See atlas volume, plate 34. Eventually the island disappeared. After the construction of the interstate bridge between Portland and Vancouver another island gradually emerged from the river not far from the original Tomahawk Island. In 1927 a group of students from the Catlin school in Portland petitioned the USBGN to attach the name Tomahawk Island to the new island in the Columbia River, which occupies a position between Ryan Point and Hayden Island. The USBGN made the requested decision on April 6, 1927, and thus perpetuated the old name.

Tombstone Gap, Jackson County. Tombstone Gap is at the north edge of the county, about a mile south of Richter Mountain. It is a pass through the watershed between the Umpqua and Rogue river drainages. It was named for an outcrop of gray rock nearby, which in a small degree simulates a gravestone.

Tombstone Lake, Union County. Tombstone Lake, in township 5 south, range 43 east, was not named because of a tombstone. In January, 1944, J. F. Irwin, for many years connected with the USFS, wrote the compiler that the lake was named because a prominent mountain peak stands immediately at one end, like a gravestone.

Tombstone Prairie, Linn County. This is a pleasant place on the South Santiam Highway, despite its melancholy name. Hackleman Creek flows eastward from the prairie into Fish Lake, and just west of the prairie the highway crosses Tombstone Summit, the watershed between the South Santiam and the McKenzie River drainage. On the south edge of the prairie is a tombstone with the inscription: "JAMES A., son of J. W. & C. M. McKnight. From an Accidental Shot. Oct. 17, 1871. AGED 18 Y's 9 M's 9 D's." Below this inscription there are eight stanzas of poetry, apparently composed by Mrs. McKnight.

Tomlike Mountain, Hood River County. This mountain is south of Wyeth. According to H. D. Langille of Portland, it bears the name of Tomlike, or Indian George, a familiar character in the Hood River Valley. He was the son of Chinidere, the last Indian chief in that part of Oregon.

Tomlinson Slough, Tillamook County. This waterway near the mouth of Tillamook River was named for Samuel Tomlinson who settled nearby about 1883.

Toney Butte, Wheeler County. Toney Butte near the headwaters of Girds Creek was named for Jonathan Toney who took up a homestead near its base in 1882. The form Tony is incorrect.

Tongue Point, Clatsop County. As far as the writer knows Tongue Point was the first geographic feature in Oregon not fronting on the Pacific Ocean to be named by white men. Captain George Vancouver, at the head of his expedition, attempted to sail into the mouth of the Columbia River in his sloop *Discovery* on October 19 and 20, 1792, but was forced to abandon the attempt on October 21, and sailed southward, leaving Lieutenant William Robert Broughton on the armed tender *Chatham* safely inside the bar.

On the day that Vancouver sailed south, Broughton noted "a remarkable projecting point, that obtained the name of Tongue Point, on the southern shore, appearing like an island." No one has ever suggested a better name. It speaks for itself. Lewis and Clark tried to attach the name Point William, for William Clark, but the name has not prevailed. See under Youngs Bay. Silas B. Smith says that the Indian name for Tongue Point was *Secomeetsiuc*. See *OHQ*, volume I, page 321. About 1920 a submarine and destroyer base was authorized for Tongue Point but it was not finished. Prior to World War II, the name of the installation was changed to U. S. Naval Air Station, Tongue Point, Oregon. The station was developed rapidly and was commissioned December 15, 1940. After World War II the station was decommissioned and the Navy declared the property surplus in 1961. After several alternate proposals, a federal Job Corps center was established in 1965. Tongue Point again figured in the news in 1980 with a discussion of the transfer of part of the area to the state or county for industrial use.

Tonquin, Washington County. When the Oregon Electric Railway was built in 1907-08, it was the policy of the company to establish stations with names of historic interest to Oregonians and the station Tonquin was named for the ship that brought the Astor party to Astoria. The *Tonquin* entered the Columbia River, with the Astor sea party from New York, March 24, 1811; was destroyed at Clayoquot Sound, Vancouver Island, in June 1811, and all the crew were killed through treachery of Indians. Its fate makes one of the most terrible and heroic tales of the Pacific Coast. For description of the place where the vessel was destroyed, see the *Oregonian*, April 17, 1887. For narrative of the tragedy, *ibid.*, April 23, 1887, page 3.

Tony Creek, Hood River County. Tony Creek, north of Mount Hood, was named by members of the Langille family for their Cayuse pony, Tony. The stream was named about 1885. This information was furnished by H. D. Langille of Portland, who told the compiler that stories to the effect that the stream was named for Thornton Ladd of Portland, better known as Tony, were wrong.

Tony Creek, Tillamook County. Homer Simmons of Tillamook told the writer in 1970 that this tributary of Nestucca River upstream from Beaver was named for an early resident, Antone "Tony" Dotesauer. He added that the spelling of the family name was questionable.

Toomey Gulch, Wallowa County. Toomey Gulch drains into Imnaha River from the west in township 4 north, range 49 east, and bears the name of Michael Toomey, who with Hamilton Vance, had some mining claims there.

Top, Grant County. Top is in the extreme northwest corner of the county. The post office was established October 22, 1915, with James Porter postmaster. Porter resigned, however, without actually having served and S. V. Cochran was the first postmaster who really conducted the office. Local residents who signed the petition for the post office sent in six names and Top was selected. It was suggested by one of the prospective patrons of the office because it was the first name of a prominent local resident, Top Reasner.

Tope Creek, Wallowa County. This stream is north of Wallowa and flows into Mud Creek. It bears the name of William A. Tope and was named for him in 1883 when he had a homestead near the head of the stream.

Topsy, Klamath County. Topsy post office got its name from the Topsy grade on the old road from Ager in northern California northeast to Linkville, now Klamath Falls. The post office, which was established January 9, 1884, was at the Overton ranch at the top of the grade leading up from Klamath River, not far north of the California-Oregon state line and east of the river. This establishment was about fifteen miles southwest by road from what was later Keno. The name Topsy was descriptive and was doubtless applied by freight haulers. Major Overton was listed as the only postmaster and the office was closed February 2, 1885. The compiler does not know if the first part of Overton's name was a military title, or whether it was his veritable given name.

Tot Mountain, Deschutes County. Tot Mountain is not a mountain at all, but a butte or point on the south slope of Bachelor Butte. It is named with the Chinook jargon word for uncle. The word was applied by the USFS because it was necessary to have a name for the butte for convenience in fire fighting. A little to the south is Kwolh Butte, and *kwolh* is the Chinook jargon word for aunt. These two names were doubtless selected because of Bachelor Butte, Three Sisters, The Husband and The Wife in the same general locality.

Tower Mountain, Umatilla County. Tower Mountain is in section 13, township 6 south, range 34 east, and was formerly known as Lookout Mountain. There is another Lookout Mountain 66 miles northeast, and on June 2, 1925, the USBGN changed the name of the mountain here considered to Tower Mountain because that was the name used by the USC&GS for a triangulation station on the summit. This was done to avoid confusion with the other Lookout Mountain. The triangulation station is about a quarter of a mile east of the USFS lookout.

Townsend, Marion County. This station was named for a pioneer family of the vicinity.

Trail, Jackson County. Trail is a post office on Rogue River at the mouth of Trail Creek. Trail Creek is so known because an Indian trail from Rogue River to Umpqua River traversed its banks, forming a short-cut between the military road and Roseburg in pioneer days. Will G. Steel is authority for the statement that the earlier name of Trail Creek was Stewart Creek, but it does not now go by that name.

Trail Creek, Wallowa County. Trail Creek flows into Camp Creek west of Imnaha. J. H. Horner told the compiler that it was named for an important Indian trail extending west from Imnaha River to camps on Camp Creek. The Indian name for the creek and trail is *Wa-lim-isk-kit*, with the accent on the second syllable.

Trailfork, Gilliam County. Trailfork is a descriptive name for a locality situated about ten or twelve miles southeast of Condon. The name came into use in pioneer days, but the post office was not established until July 1, 1902, with Nancy M. Mattingly first postmaster. This office was discontinued January 31, 1916. Government maps use the style Trail Fork, and there is a Trail Fork Canyon shown on the map of the Condon quadrangle.

Trapp Creek, Lincoln County. Trapp Creek in the Coast Range flows into Yaquina River from the south in the extreme southwest corner of township 10 south, range 9 west, at a point a little over a mile west of Chitwood. The stream was named for a well-known family of pioneer settlers of the vicinity. The spelling Trap is wrong.

Trask River, Tillamook County. Elbridge Trask, a native of Massachusetts, first came to Oregon in Wyeth's brig *May Dacre* in 1834, and in the fall of 1835 he went to the Rocky Mountains to trap and hunt. He returned to Oregon in 1842 and settled on Clatsop Plains probably in 1843. Silas B. Smith says Trask worked on Hunt's Mill, pioneer sawmill of Clatsop County, built at Hunts Mill Point in the winter of 1843-44. He moved from Clatsop Plains to Tillamook County in August, 1852. Trask River bears his name. Trask's land title certificate was number 3926. He died June 22, 1863, aged 49 years.

Traverse Ridge, Wallowa County. This ridge is south of Lostine and east of Lostine River. It was named by R. L. Hensel about 1915 during some mapping operations, and on account of a survey traverse.

Treasure Cove, Tillamook County. This is an almost inaccessible cove in the northern base of Neahkahnie Mountain. It is said to have a cave in its face not far above the waters of the Pacific Ocean. The name was bestowed because of the many legends of pirate treasure in the neighborhood of Nehalem. See Cotton's *Stories of Nehalem.* Just north of Treasure Cove is a similar indentation called Devils Cauldron, and the much larger Smugglers Cove is still further north.

Tremont, Multnomah County. The plat for the addition called Tremont was filed June 4, 1892, covering an area in what is now southeast Portland, and about a mile westward of Lents. There are other additions with Tremont as part of the name, including Tremont Park and Tremont Place. The name Tremont is familiar to Bostonians and refers to three hills or mounts. It is possible that someone from Massachusetts named the Tremont additions. In the summer of 1892 a post office was petitioned for, and it was established August 18, 1892, with J. A. Forbes postmaster, but to the surprise of the local enthusiasts the name turned out to be Fremont. Whoever wrote the petition did not have the benefit of the Spencerian method of handwriting. The mistake was soon corrected and the name of the office was changed to Tremont on October 15, 1892. The office was closed to Lents on February 18, 1903.

Trent, Lane County. Rattlesnake post office was established near Rattlesnake Creek in 1868. The office name was changed to Trent on October 8, 1875, but the compiler has been unable to learn why. The office was closed June 7, 1963.

Trester, Grant County. Trester was at one time a post office in Grant County at a point about six miles west of Fox, named for a local resident. The office was established August 6, 1913, with Gertrude Trester first postmaster. The office was discontinued June 29, 1918, and the business turned over to Fox.

Triangle, Curry County. Triangle post office was in the extreme north end of the county on the old mail road between Myrtle Point and Langlois. It was in service from September 29, 1914, to December 15, 1916. Mrs. Elinor Lehnherr was the only postmaster. The office was named for the Triangle ranch, operated by the Lehnherr family, where a triangular stock brand was used.

Triangle Hill, Deschutes County. A descriptive name, applied on viewing the hill from the east. The point is in the foothills of the Cascade Range east of the Three Sisters.

Triangle Lake, Lane County. This prominent lake west of Blachly is named because of its shape. Before the completion of Fern Ridge Reservoir, it was the most popular local spot for water sports and it still has a large following. Mrs. Elma Rust of Blachly wrote in 1971 to give some of the early history which is paraphrased as follows. It seems to have had various names as an 1878 map shows it as Loon Lake while Walling's 1884 *History of Lane County* also has a map with Loon Lake but a text reference to Lake of the Woods. An early Eugene newspaper, *Oregon State Journal,* September 23, 1882, mentions Echo Lake, formerly called Loon Lake and this is reiterated in an 1887 road petition that uses the form Echo Lake. This interesting variety appears to have ended with the advent of the motor car and the geometric forms of the age mechanical.

Triangle Moraine, Clackamas County. This glacial moraine on Mount Hood is at the 9000 foot level between Zigzag and White River glaciers and above Palmer Glacier. It is a conspicuous spot on the upper slopes and is the terminus of the snow cat run for spring skiers. Fred H. McNeil says in *Wy-east "THE Mountain",* page 142 that it was named not because of its shape but by the Triangle Club, a Y.M.C.A. organization of climbers who went that way in 1896.

Trolan Grade, Jefferson County. This grade on the old Teller Creek road was named because it ran by the property of Daniel Trolan who settled in the area just after the turn of the century.

Trout Creek, Jefferson County. Trout Creek post office was one of several established in the stock pioneering days northeast of what is now Madras. Cross Keys was another and also Hay Creek and Heisler. They were well-known places and have left a legacy of pioneer lore. Trout Creek post office was established July 3, 1878, with Jasper A. Friend postmaster. William Heisler became postmaster October 17, 1878. It seems probable from an inspection of postal records that the name of this office was changed to Cross Keys on February 13, 1879, but the record is not clear and the two offices may not have been in the same place, but they were both near the stream Trout Creek.

Troutdale, Multnomah County. The community of Troutdale was once known as Sandy. Sandy post office was established June 1, 1854, with Emsley R. Scott postmaster. The office was discontinued February 26, 1868. It was apparently near the present site of the town Troutdale. Captain John Harlow, an Oregon pioneer from Maine, originated the name Troutdale, because of the fact there was a small dale near his house where he had a fish pond, which he stocked with trout. This occurred about 1880. Shortly thereafter he secured the establishment of Troutdale post office.

This office was for a time discontinued. When the railroad built through this section of the country the station was named Troutdale, at the request of Captain Harlow, and so it has been known ever since.

Troy, Wallowa County. The postmaster at Troy informed the compiler in December, 1926, that at the time the post office was established, which was in 1902, several names were suggested, but the Post Office Department rejected them all. Finally the department suggested a list which included the name Troy. This was adopted. However, in 1931, J. H. Horner of Enterprise told the compiler that the place was probably named for Troy Grinstead, son of A. L. Grinstead. Mormons settled in the locality about 1898 and the place was generally called Nauvoo.

Truax Island, Linn County. Truax Island is northeast of Corvallis, on the south side of Willamette River and north of Dead River. It was named for Wallace and Maud Truax, landowners. The spelling Traux is wrong.

Tryon, Columbia County. Tryon, the name of a locality in Columbia County, came from the family name of Socrates Hotchkiss Tryon, son of an Oregon pioneer of 1850. Dr. Socrates H. Tryon, Sr., settled near Oswego and Tryon Creek just west of Palatine Hill in Clackamas and Multnomah counties bears his name. The younger Tryon was left fatherless in 1855 and had to shift for himself most of his life. In 1869 he became a fisherman on the Columbia River and later engaged in logging and farming. Tryon post office was established near the Columbia River at a point between Rainier and Mayger on December 1, 1884, with S. H. Tryon postmaster. The place was about a mile and a half south of Walker Island. The office was discontinued in September, 1894. There is an account of the activities of S. H. Tryon in Fred Lockley's column in the *Oregon Journal,* August 25, 1928, editorial page. Records at the Oregon Historical Society do not substantiate the statement that Dr. Tryon was an Oregon pioneer of 1849. That was probably the year he arrived in California. He reached Oregon in 1850.

Tryon Creek, Clackamas and Multnomah counties. Dr. Socrates Hotchkiss Tryon was born in Vermont about 1815 and came to Oregon by way of Panama about 1850. He settled near Oswego, and Tryon Creek is named in his memory. He died in 1855. Tryon Creek drains the west slope of Palatine Hill and flows into Willamette River just north of Oswego. For information about the Tryon family, see article by Fred Lockley, *Oregon Journal,* August 25, 1928.

Tryon Creek, Wallowa County. Tryon Creek flows into Snake River in township 3 north, range 50 east. It bears the name of Nate and James Tryon, who ranged sheep there and built a two-story cabin.

Tualatin, Washington County. The town of Tualatin is near Tualatin River and was named on that account. There was formerly a discrepancy in spelling between the post office name and the railroad station name. The USBGN finally decided on Tualatin, which is now in universal use. The post office with the spelling Tualitin was established November 5, 1869, with Marcellus S. Dailey first postmaster. The name was changed to Tualatin on September 25, 1915. In the 1880s the place was sometimes called Bridgeport probably because of the construction of one of the first bridges over Tualatin River nearby.

Tualatin River, Clackamas and Washington counties. Tualatin is probably an Indian word meaning lazy or sluggish, this being the character of the river's flow; other meanings are "land without trees," signifying the plains of Tualatin and "forks" or "forked" for the numerous upper tributaries including Gales and Dairy creeks. The "treeless plain" was vouched for by Tolbert Carter, pioneer of 1846, whose home was near Wells, Benton County to Geo. H. Himes. *Tualatin* was *Twha-la-ti*, according to Silas B. Smith in the *OHQ*, volume I, page 323. John Work gave *Faladin* in 1834. The name has had many variations, among them *Twality, Quality, Falatine* and *Nefalatine*. There is a town named Tualatin in Washington County. The settlements near what are now known as Hillsboro and Forest Grove were in pioneer days called East and West Tualatin precincts. One of the original districts or counties of Oregon was called Twality. See *OHQ*, volume XI, page 11, volume XVI, page 278 and volume XXVIII, page 56. The spelling Tuality was also used officially.

Tub Spring, Wallowa County. Tub Spring is in township 2 north, range 41 east, and is so called because it was lined with a tub to keep the water clean. This was done about 1890 when McDonald brothers had a cattle camp nearby.

Tub Springs, Jefferson County. This spring and canyon of the same name are tributary to Trout Creek just south of the Wasco County line. John Silvertooth of Antelope told the compiler in 1969 that there was a fine spring near the head of the canyon that was lined with an old wood tub to clarify the water.

Tub Springs, Morrow County. This spring in Juniper Canyon five miles north of McDaid Springs was named in early days because the hole resembled a round tub. It was on an alternate trace of the Oregon Trail some two miles north of the main route and for fifty years was the home of James Carty, a pioneer sheepman.

Tucker Bridge, Hood River County. B. R. Tucker built a bridge and a sawmill at this place about 1881, and the locality was named Tucker Bridge for him. Tucker post office was established January 15, 1892, with B. R. Tucker postmaster. The office was discontinued June 2, 1900.

Tucker Creek, Baker County. Tucker Creek empties into Powder River at Keating. It was named for John A. Tucker, an early settler.

Tucker Creek, Clatsop County. J. B. Kilmore of Astoria wrote the compiler in 1927 that this stream, southeast of Astoria, was named for a wood scow operator who cut wood near the stream and brought it to Astoria for sale.

Tufti Mountain, Lane County. Tufti Mountain is about six miles southeast of Oakridge. It was named for a local Indian celebrity, Charlie Tufti.

Tule Lake, Klamath County, Oregon, and Modoc and Siskiyou counties, California. Tule Lake was discovered May 1, 1846, by then Captain John C. Fremont, and was later named Lake Rhett for his friend, Barnwell Rhett of South Carolina. See Fremont's *Memoirs of My Life*, Chicago, 1887, page 480. On July 6, 1846, the Applegate exploring party first saw this lake. See *OHQ*, volume XXII, page 1. It is possible that members of the exploring party named the lake Tule Lake at that time, because of its surroundings, although the article does not specifically say so. The article was not written at the time of the exploration. In any event, the name Tule Lake has come into general use and has been adopted by the USBGN in preference to Lake Rhett. Tule is the name of a certain kind of rush. Due to the fact that the waters of Lost River have been diverted, the lake is being gradually reclaimed and at the time of this writing does not exist in Oregon. See *Oregonian*, September 16, 1923, page 2. There has been a post office called Tule Lake at various locations in Klamath County, but it was not in service in 1945. In 1944 there was a Tulelake post office just over the line in California, serving among others, a Japanese relocation center frequently in the news. Gatschet, in *Dictionary of the Klamath Language*, gives a number of Klamath and other Indian names for this lake. One was *Mayaltko E-ush*, meaning the lake overgrown with rushes or tule-grass. *Moatak* and *Moatokni E-ush* were words used by the Klamaths in referring to this lake, indicating that it was in the neighborhood of the Modoc Indians. The Pit River Indians, according to Gatschet, used the word *Lutuami* when speaking of this lake.

Tulley Creek, Wallowa County. Tulley Creek drains into Imnaha River in township 3 north, range 48 east. It was named for James Tulley, who, with Aaron Wade, drove cattle to the mouth of the stream in 1880 or 1881 for winter range.

Tumalo, Deschutes County. The original name of the community of Tumalo was Laidlaw. It was named for W. A. Laidlaw, one of the promoters of the place, and Laidlaw post office was established December 17, 1904 with William G. Stiles first postmaster. At that time the state was active in the development of the Tumalo irrigation project and a post office with the name Tumalo had been established near the construction camps on October 15, 1904 with George W. Wimer postmaster. In 1913 after the work was terminated and the camps abandoned, Tumalo post office was closed with mail to Laidlaw. Meanwhile, the name Tumalo was coming into general use for the locality and on January 20, 1915, the name of the Laidlaw post office was changed to Tumalo. The compiler is indebted to Mrs. May D. Fryrear of Salem for the preceding facts. Mrs. Fryrear's mother was acting postmaster at the first Tumalo post office when it was closed.

Tumalo Creek, Deschutes County. Satisfactory information about the origin of Tumalo has not been forthcoming, but the compiler is inclined to the belief that it is from the Klamath Indian word *temolo,* meaning wild plum. This shrub was once quite plentiful in south central Oregon. The Klamaths had another word *temola* meaning ground fog, which may have been used to describe the vicinity of Tumalo Creek, but this is conjectural. Robert B. Gould of Bend informed the compiler that an old settler told him the original name was *Tumallowa,* and meant icy water. Any one of the above explanations might fit the facts, so there you are.

Tumalt Creek, Multnomah County. This stream in the eastern part of the county was formerly called Devil Creek and Devil Slide Creek, but at the instigation of the Mazamas in 1915 the name Tumalt was adopted by the government to commemorate an Indian who was killed by Sheridan's command during the Cascade engagement in 1856.

Tumia, Umatilla County. In 1928 the Union Pacific Railroad established a new station just west of Gibbon and called it Tumia. The word is an abbreviation of the Indian name Toom-hi-ya. The accent is on the middle syllable. Toom-hi-ya was an Indian woman living near the siding, the wife of Charles Shaplish. The station was closed before 1970.

Tumtum River, Benton and Lincoln counties. *Tumtum* is a Chinook jargon word meaning heart, and Tumtum River was so named because it was considered to be the heart of the valley through which it flowed. Mrs. H. G. Downing, of Burnt Woods, wrote the compiler in 1927 that, when a post office was proposed, an effort was made to have the place called Tumtum, but the post office department selected the name Burnt Woods because of the forest fires that had swept over that part of the country many years ago.

Tunnel Canyon, Umatilla County. Tunnel Canyon is just west of Battle Mountain Summit and empties into East Fork Butter Creek. Prior to World War I O. D. Teel started the Teel Irrigation Project to bring water from Camas Creek to Butter Creek drainage. This included a tunnel under the pass south of Battle Mountain Summit with the north portal in what is now known as Tunnel Canyon. In the 1920s after about a quarter of the tunnel was completed, the company went bankrupt so we must conclude that in oil drilling parlance they ended with a 'dry hole'. Teel was the son of Dr. John Teel, the first physician on the Umatilla Indian Reservation.

Tunnel Creek, Marion County. Tunnel Creek flows into North Santiam River just downstream from Whitewater Creek. The name is descriptive for the stream, despite a substantial watershed, flows underground in the vicinity of SH 22.

Tunnel Point, Coos County. Tunnel Point is a natural rock formation on Bastendorff Beach at the south side of the entrance to Coos Bay. It has a hole in it, hence the name.

Tupper Rock, Coos County. This was a well-known landmark near Bandon, and just south of Coquille River. It was named for John P. Tupper, who kept a hotel at Bandon for many years. Most of the rock has been removed and used to build the Coquille River jetty. There is a snappy picture of J. P. Tupper's Ocean House and Tupper Rock in Walling's *History of Southern Oregon,* page 268.

Turner, Marion County. When the railroad was built through this part of the state the officials shipped a load of construction material to the present site of Turner, with instructions to build a station and warehouse to be known as Marion. A man in charge of the shipment unloaded it at the wrong place and built a station some six miles farther south which was called Marion and is in the present location of the station of that name. When the railroad officials discovered the material had been sent to the wrong place they sent a new consignment to the place originally intended to be called Marion, and after building a station named it Turner, for Henry L. Turner, a well-known pioneer resident of this vicinity.

Turner Creek, Yamhill County. The stream heading near the Yamhill-Washington county line and flowing south into North Yamhill River near Pike is generally known as Turner Creek. The name came from a family of pioneer settlers who at one time operated a small water driven sawmill on

the upper reaches of the stream. This creek has also been called Hay Creek
and Hayes Creek, but local sentiment at Pike seems to be in favor of Turner
Creek. That is the name used by the USGS on the Turner Creek quadrangle while Hay Creek is a small tributary north of Pike.

Turner Mountain, Grant County. Turner Mountain is in the extreme
northwest corner of Grant County, in the southwest part of township 7
south, range 27 east. It was named for Joseph A. Turner, a pioneer homesteader on the Howell ranch nearby.

Turtle Cove, Grant County. Turtle Cove is east of John Day River in
the John Day Fossil Beds National Monument. It was named in 1864 by
Professor Thomas Condon for the abundance of fossil remains of Miocene
turtles. The area has also been known as Blue Basin because of the distinctive coloration. This latter name was first applied by the John C. Merriam
party of 1899.

Tuskan, Wasco County. This is a railway station on the Burlington
Northern near Sherars Bridge. The Indian name of the locality near Sherars Bridge was *Tush-kan-ee,* and the modern form is derived from the old
name. The form Tuscan is incorrect.

Tustin Lake, Yamhill County. This intermittent pond was named for
Charles S. Tustin, a pioneer settler. The lake is near the North Yamhill
River west of St. Joseph.

Tuttle Creek, Douglas County. This tributary of Cavitt Creek was
named for Walter Tuttle who homesteaded near its source in 1912.

Tutuilla Creek, Umatilla County. Information about the origin of this
name is conflicting. Judge Fred W. Wilson of The Dalles told the compiler
in 1927 that there was a family tradition that this stream was named about
1870 by his father, the late Judge Joseph G. Wilson, because of some child-
ish remark made by his sister, Lucy Wilson, later Mrs. Joseph T. Peters of
Portland. Lucy Wilson's nickname was Toots and the story is that Judge
and Mrs. Wilson and their little girl were camped near the mouth of this
stream and the child referred to it as Toots Creek. Judge Wilson then made
up the name Tutuilla Creek. Residents of the Umatilla Indian Reservation
do not agree with this version. One old Indian says that the stream has been
known as Tutuilla Creek by the Indians for several generations and that
the word *tutuilla* means a thorn bush which grows along its banks. There is
another story in circulation in Umatilla County to the effect the stream was
named for a place in the South Seas, by an old resident. It is of course
possible that the Indians originally named the stream and Miss Wilson or
the old resident or both of them applied their own versions. Such coinci-
dences are not unknown in geographic nomenclature.

Tututni Pass, Crater Lake National Park, Klamath County. This pass
is in Vidae Ridge, south of Crater Lake. It bears the name of a tribe of
Indians that lived near the mouth of Rogue River. The name has no especial significance near Crater Lake, and was probably chosen for sentimental
reasons.

Twelvemile Creek, Lake County. This stream flows generally east-
ward back and forth across the California-Oregon state line southeast of
Lakeview. Its waters eventually find their way into the Warner Valley.
Twelvemile Creek was so called because the old wagon road north from

Fort Bidwell, California, crossed the stream about twelve miles north of Fort Bidwell. Fifteenmile Creek flows into Twelvemile Creek.

Twentymile Creek, Lake County. Twentymile Creek flows into the Warner Valley south of Adel. The stream received its name because the old road from Fort Bidwell, California, crossed it about twenty miles from the fort.

Twentythree Creek, Lincoln County. For most of its course Twenty-three Creek flows through section 23, township 10 south, range 10 west, and for that reason was named for the section number. The stream is about six miles northeast of Toledo and is tributary to Simpson Creek.

Twickenham, Wheeler County. Twickenham is a place on John Day River about twenty miles south of Fossil. In August, 1943, W. H. Steiwer of Fossil wrote the compiler that the locality was formerly called Contention, and that there was once a post office of that name, apparently commemorating a quarrel between Anthony "Pike" Helms and Jerome H. Parsons, local celebrities. Contention post office was established July 8, 1886, with Edward F. Horn first postmaster. Miss Frankie Parsons, daughter of Jerome H. Parsons, is said to have been responsible for changing the name of the office to Twickenham. While away at school she appears to have become familiar with Theophile Marzials' poem, *Twickenham Ferry,* the scene of which is laid at Twickenham, a western suburb of London on the River Thames. Upon her return from school, Miss Parsons is said to have objected to the name Contention as being undignified and she determined to get rid of it. Whatever the reason, the facts are that Twickenham post office was established on June 6, 1896, with Anthony Helms as postmaster. It is not clear whether this was a new office or a change of names, and the available records are not conclusive. Twickenham post office was discontinued on February 28, 1917, and mail is now sent through Fossil.

Twilight Creek, Clatsop County. This stream is east of Astoria. It was named for W. H. Twilight who took up land on its banks in pioneer days. He was one time sheriff of Clatsop County.

Twin Cities. The compiler has had several requests for information about a locality in Oregon known as Twin Cities. It may have been a mining camp.

Twin Lakes, Deschutes County. The correct names for these two lakes are North Twin Lake and South Twin Lake. They straddle the center north-south section line in township 21 south, range 8 east. Thornton T. Munger, who started with the USFS in 1908, told the writer in 1972 that about 1911 he was surveying certain boundaries for the proposed experimental forest near Crane Prairie. This section line had been previously surveyed but no mention was made of its crossing any lakes so he was not only surprised to find these two bodies of water but also surmised that the previous surveyor had made generous use of the "armchair transit". Munger stated that he applied the name Twin Lakes at that time.

Twin Rocks, Tillamook County. Twin Rocks post office serves a summer resort, and was named for two large rocks more than a hundred feet high in the Pacific Ocean just below low tide line. The office was established in the summer of 1914, with William E. Dunsmoor first postmaster.

Twin Sisters Creeks, Douglas County. These streams are in the northwest part of the county, in the Coast Range. They converge into one stream just before they flow into Smith River in section 18, township 20 south, range 8 west. The two creeks are very much alike, and of about the same size. They are known as North Sister Creek and South Sister Creek, and Twin Sister Guard Station is situated at the junction of the two streams. According to H. R. Oglesby, district fire warden, the names are very old and were applied in natural consequence of the similarity of the two creeks.

Two Corral Creek, Wallowa County. This stream flows into Snake River in township 1 north, range 50 east, and was named because W. H. Winters had two stock corrals there in the early days.

Twobuck Creek, Wallowa County. This stream is called Twobuck Creek because the Warnock brothers once killed two deer nearby at a time when they badly needed meat. It is in township 2 south, range 49 east.

Twocolor Creek, Baker County. This stream is in township 6 south, range 43 east. It was named because of the contrast in color of the two main forks.

Twomile Creek, Coos County. This stream is about ten miles north of Bandon. It was named during the Coos County gold rush of 1853-55 because it was about two miles north along the beach from Randolph and Whisky Run, one of the important points of the excitement.

Twomile Creek, Coos County. Twomile Creek south of Bandon is said to have been named because it was that distance south of the town and of the mouth of Coquille River. However, maps do not support this theory. The stream is more than five miles south of Bandon. See under Fourmile Creek.

Tycer Creek, Josephine County. Tycer Creek is about five miles southeast of Kerby. It was named for James E. Tycer who settled in Brownsville in 1853 and moved to Josephine County in 1866. He owned a ranch near the stream.

Tyee Mountain, Douglas County. *Tyee* is the Chinook jargon word for chief, and this mountain was so named because of its important position in its surroundings. The word comes from the Nootka language. Until 1939 there was a post office near the mountain called Tyee.

Tygh Valley, Wasco County. Tygh Valley is a post office in the valley of the same name on the banks of Tygh Creek. To the north is an imposing range of hills over 3000 feet high, known as Tygh Ridge. The name comes from the Tygh Indian tribe, now part of the Warm Springs Indians. The Pacific Railroad Surveys *Reports,* 1855, use the form Tysch Prairie. Fremont in his *Report* of 1845 gives Taih Prairie. *Handbook of American Indians,* volume I, page 860, gives other forms.

Ukiah, Umatilla County. This post office was established September 22, 1890, with DeWitt C. Whiting first postmaster. E. B. Gambee, of Portland, informed the writer in 1926 that he suggested the name of the Oregon community which had been platted August 6, 1890, by the Camas Land Company. Gambee had previously lived in Ukiah, California, and offered the name on that account. The place in California was named for the Yokaia Indians, a division of the Pomo. The word is said to mean South Valley. Gambee was born in Michigan about 1852 and came to Oregon from California about 1881. He died in Portland October 8, 1939. For obituary, see Pendleton *East Oregonian,* October 10, 1939.

Ulvstad, Jackson County. Ulvstad post office was on or near Sugarpine Creek, which flows into Elk Creek twelve or fourteen miles northeast of Trail. Martin Ulvstad served as the postmaster from July 16, 1904, to October 4, 1905, and the office was given his name. There was no community, just a very few small mountain ranches.

Umapine, Umatilla County. This place in the north part of the county was formerly named Vincent, but when a post office was applied for, it was found that there was another Vincent in the state. This was doubtless Vincent in Wallowa County. Citizens of Vincent in Umatilla County then changed the name of their community to Umapine, for a Cayuse or Umatilla Indian chief of some prominence. Umapine post office was established in June, 1916, with Edgar Holm first postmaster. The office was not in service in 1980.

Umatilla, Umatilla County. The town now known as Umatilla was surveyed by Timothy K. Davenport in 1863. It was first known as Umatilla Landing, and later Umatilla City. Eight miles west was the locality known for a time as Grande Ronde Landing, near the site of what is now Irrigon. Umatilla and Grande Ronde landings sprang up as stopping places for traffic with the Boise and Owyhee mines, but Umatilla Landing soon controlled the business and Grande Ronde Landing ceased to be of importance. Umatilla was known as Columbia about 1863, but soon resumed the old name. For information about the laying out of the town see *Oregonian,* May 16, 1863. Umatilla is at the mouth of Umatilla River and was named on that account. Postal records at Washington show that Umatilla post office was established September 26, 1851, with A. Francis Rogers postmaster. The office was discontinued January 6, 1852. See *OHQ,* volume XLI, page 69. This was the first post office in eastern Oregon. The *Oregonian* of August 2, 1851, says this office was at the Umatilla Indian Agency, about 150 miles east of The Dalles, on the route to Salt Lake. The news item gives the name of the postmaster as A. Francis Royer. Records at the Oregon Historical Society substantiate the name Royer and not Rogers. This pioneer post office was of course not near the present town of Umatilla, but probably near Echo. The post office for Umatilla town was established May 28, 1863, with Z. F. Moody postmaster.

Umatilla County. This county was created September 27, 1862, and was carved out of Wasco County as it existed at that time. It was named for Umatilla River, which see. It now has a land area of 3231 square miles. The temporary seat of government for the new county was put at what was then known as Marshall Station, on the north bank of Umatilla River near Houtama, William C. McKay's place at the mouth of McKay Creek. About 1863 Umatilla County citizens changed the name of Marshall Station to Middleton. This name was selected because it was thought that the place was about half way between Umatilla Landing and the Grande Ronde Valley. In 1865 Umatilla City was selected as the county seat and was continued so until 1868 when the legislature passed an act directing the citizens of the county to declare their choice between "the present location . . . and Upper Uma-

tilla, somewhere between the mouths of Wild Horse and Birch Creeks."
The election favored the new location, and it was accordingly made county
seat and named Pendleton, for George H. Pendleton, Democratic nominee
for vice-president. Umatilla tried to rescue the seat by legal means, on the
grounds of vagueness of the act of the legislature, but was not successful.
For additional information, see under Pendleton. See also Fred Lockley's
article in *Sunday Journal*, June 3, 1945.

Umatilla River, Umatilla County. Umatilla is the Indian name for a
river, given as *Youmalolam*, in Lewis and Clark journals; variously spelled in
early books of Oregon. Alexander Ross gives *You-matella* and *Umatallow;*
Townsend gives *Utalla* and *Ewmitilly;* Irving gives *Eu-o-tal-la;* Fremont gives
Umatilah; Parker gives *Umatella;* Wilkes and Nesmith give *Umatilla.* The
compiler knows of no reliable interpretation of the Indian name. For references to the name and to the locality, see *OGN,* 1928 edition, page 363-64.
The Umatilla Indians are a group of tribes formerly living on the Umatilla
River and on adjacent banks of the Columbia River. Umatilla, as a tribe
name, is of late application. These Indians were not originally Umatillas.
The name came to be applied after the extermination of many of the Cayuses and Walla Wallas.

Umbrella Falls, Hood River County. This descriptive name was suggested to the USBGN by Oregon residents, and adopted May 6, 1925. The
falls are on one of the sources of East Fork Hood River about a mile and a
half above the Mount Hood Loop Highway, southeast of Mount Hood.

Umpqua, Douglas County. Umpqua is an historic name in the state. It
was used by the Indians to refer to the locality of the Umpqua River and
came to be applied to Umpqua River. For a discussion of the name see
under Umpqua River. There have been several places known as Fort Umpqua. John Work visited the Umpqua River in 1834 and Fort Umpqua,
which was later established by the Hudson's Bay Company near the present
site of Elkton, did not then exist. Work mentions "umpqua old fort" which
appears to have been established in 1832 near Calapooya Creek. See under
Elkton for additional information. In the summer of 1850 a party of prospectors, originally planning to visit the Klamath River, explored the Umpqua River and established Umpqua City on August 5, 1850. It was on the
east side of the river, near its mouth. West Umpqua was the name selected
for the community planned for the other side. See *OHQ,* volume XVII,
page 355. There was some development at both places, but the towns had
petered out by 1867. See Scott's *History of the Oregon Country,* volume III,
pages 42 and 46. Umpqua City post office was established on September
26, 1851, with Amos E. Rogers postmaster. Samuel S. Mann became postmaster on February 24, 1852. This office may have been on the east side of
the river when first established but in 1860 the post office and community
of Umpqua City were on the west side of the river about two miles north of
the mouth. A military post was then at the same place. See under Fort
Umpqua. The present Umpqua post office is on Umpqua River near the
mouth of Calapooya Creek and a long way from the places mentioned
above. The post office now known as Umpqua was originally called Umpqua Ferry and was first established March 16, 1877, with John C. Sham-

brook postmaster. About 1905 the word Ferry was eliminated from the name.

Umpqua River, Douglas County. *Umpqua* was the Indian name of the locality of Umpqua River, and the name came to be applied both to the river and to an Indian tribe; given as *Umptqua*, or *Arguilas* River, by David Douglas, in 1825, *OHQ*, volume VI, pages 82, 84, 95. Peter Skene Ogden refers to *Umqua Mts.* on November 25, 1826, writing of the Cascade Range, which he was viewing from the Deschutes River, *OHQ*, volume XI, page 210. John Work used the style *Umquah Mountain* in his journal for October 3, 1833, referring to the divide between the Umpqua and Rogue rivers. Alexander Ross gives *Imp-qua* in his *First Settlers on the Oregon*, page 237, and *Umpqua* in his *Fur Hunters of the Far West*, volume I, page 108. Wilkes' map (1841) shows *Umpqua*. William P. McArthur uses the form *Umpqua* in his survey of the Pacific Coast in 1850. Hale gives *Umpquas* in *Ethnography and Philology*, 1846, page 198, and *Umpqua* and *Umkwa*, page 204. The Umpquas are classed as an Athapascan tribe of the upper Umpqua River. The territorial legislature created an Umpqua County January 24, 1851. It ceased to exist October 16, 1862, its area having been added to other counties. The Hudson's Bay Company had an establishment in the Umpqua Valley as early as 1832, probably on Calapooya Creek. It was generally called Old Fort Umpqua. The company later had another Fort Umpqua near the present site of Elkton. During the Indian wars there was a federal establishment called Fort Umpqua just north of the mouth of Umpqua River. For many references to Umpqua River and to Umpqua Valley, see *OHQ*, volume XLIV, page 357.

Uncle Dan Mine, Baker County. This mine in the Encina district was located in the early 1900s by Dan Cochrane, universally known as "Uncle Dan". This information was provided by Cochrane's daughter, Mrs. J. P. Jackson of Baker.

Union, Union County. Dunham Wright, aged 84 in 1926, of Medical Springs, informed the compiler that the town of Union was founded in 1862 by E. H. Lewis, Fred Nodine and Samuel Hannah, and was named for patriotic reasons during the Civil War. The town was named before the county was formed. Homemade flags from dresses and sheets were in the celebration on July 4, 1863. Union post office was established on May 8, 1863, with John A. J. Chapman first postmaster.

Union County. Union County was created October 14, 1864, and was taken from the north part of Baker County as that county then existed. Its name was taken from the town of Union, which had been established about two years. Union County has a land area of 2032 square miles.

Union Creek, Jackson County. The locality known as Union Creek is on the upper reaches of Rogue River, about twelve miles north of Prospect and about ten miles west of the entrance to Crater Lake National Park. It took its name from the stream, which was in turn named for Union Peak in the park. Union Creek post office was established April 22, 1924, with Mrs. Helen C. Herriott first postmaster. It was closed April 30, 1945 although it had actually ceased operation in October 1942.

Union Mills, Clackamas County. Union Mills is a well-known locality about three miles southeast by road from Mulino. It is adjacent to Milk Creek. The name of the place has had an interesting history. The Cutting family operated a post office in this vicinity as early as September, 1867. Charles Cutting, Sr., was the first postmaster and the office was named in his honor. It was called Cuttingsville. The office did not operate continuously. On December 28, 1875, the name Cuttingsville was changed to Union Mills and Gabriel J. Trullinger became postmaster. With one short interval he ran this office until August, 1904. In March, 1948, Isaac V. Trullinger, then living in Portland, and a son of Gabriel J. Trullinger, sent some information to the compiler. Gabriel J. Trullinger came to Oregon in 1847 and took up a donation land claim on Milk Creek in 1852. He built a sawmill and later added wool carding machinery. Still later he added a planing mill and as a result of these various activities he called his establishment Union Mills. A flour mill was built in 1877. In 1875 the post office had been moved from Cuttingsville. The post offices of Cuttingsville and Union Mills were not in exactly the same place. Isaac V. Trullinger adds an interesting note that the planer was bought from Dr. John McLoughlin, who imported it from England. It is said to have been the first power driven planer to operate on the Pacific Coast. This piece of machinery is now in the museum of the Oregon Historical Society at Portland.

Union Peak, Crater Lake National Park, Klamath County. This peak was named for patriotic reasons by a party of prospectors who climbed it on October 21, 1862. Will G. Steel gives their names as follows: Chauncey Nye, H. Abbott, S. Smith, J. Brandlin, James Leyman and J. W. Sessions. The elevation of Union Peak is 7698 feet.

Union Point, Linn County. Union Point post office was established February 18, 1854, with William B. Blain postmaster. Hugh Dinwiddie became postmaster March 2, 1855. The compiler suspects that the office was named for patriotic reasons but has no details. It was about four miles south of Brownsville. There is no longer a community with the name, but there is a Union Point School. Union Point post office was discontinued in August, 1859.

Uniontown, Clatsop County. Uniontown is in the west part of Astoria and got its name from the Union Packing Company, which began operations in the early 1880s, in the vicinity of Bond and Washington streets. The company was not successful and its real estate was platted into lots and deeded to the stockholders. The locality was called Uniontown and the name eventually spread until it included the entire west end of Astoria. For details, see *Astorian-Budget*, March 4, 1938.

Uniontown, Jackson County. Uniontown was an early post office on Applegate River near the mouth of Little Applegate River. Theodoric Cameron, a native of Madison County, New York, and a pioneer of 1852, was the only postmaster the place ever had. Cameron was a staunch Republican and during the Civil War had pronounced views on upholding the Union. The place was named on that account. Uniontown post office was in operation at the Cameron store from April, 1879, until September, 1891.

Unit Lake, Wallowa County. This lake is in township 4 south, range 44 east, in the Wallowa Mountains. It is somewhat separated from other lakes in the vicinity and is named because it is a unit by itself.

Unity, Baker County. Robert Murray, whose grandfather settled in the valley east of Unity in 1861, told the author in 1968 that the first post office in the area was at Tucker Swamp on Job Creek on the freight road to Baker, about one and one half miles from the present site. This was apparently not a convenient place for the settlers who were all ranchers throughout the valley, so they had a meeting to decide where to move it and what to name it. They all agreed on the location and were so pleased with their agreement that they decided to call it "Unity". Unity post office was established in September 1891 but the compiler has been unable to identify any previous post office in the immediate area.

University Park, Multnomah County. Portland has had a liberal supply of platted additions with fancy names, although many of them actually came into being before the city became a metropolis. In fact some of them antedated the Portland-East Portland-Albina consolidation of 1891. A number of them, then suburbs, had post offices. An office called Portsmouth was established April 17, 1891, with Chapman S. Pennock postmaster. This was to serve the area of Portsmouth addition, southeast of Saint Johns. It seems apparent that Pennock or the postal authorities were not satisfied with the name or location, for on August 25, 1891, the name of the office was changed to University Park to agree with that of an addition with that title. The plat for University Park had been filed in April, 1891. The post office may have been moved when the name was changed. University Park office was in operation until November 14, 1903, when it was closed out to Portland. In 1980 University Park was a station under the Portland office. The name of Portsmouth addition was doubtless suggested by the sight of waterborne commerce passing close at hand. University Park was named for Portland University, a Methodist institution established on the river bluff in 1890. This institution later became Columbia University, and is now University of Portland, both establishments of the Catholic church.

Unnecessary Mountain, Klamath County. Francis Landrum of Klamath Falls told the compiler in 1969 that Scott Warren named this small hill east of Algoma. A favorite fairy tale of his children related a long list of "unnecessary" items and the hill was a humorous addition.

Upper Astoria, Clatsop County. Upper Astoria post office was established March 19, 1877, with Christian Leinenweber first of five postmasters. The office was discontinued September 11, 1886, but was not in continuous service between the two dates given. Leinenweber was a prominent early-day citizen of Clatsop County, and probably named the office himself. It was about a mile and a half east of what is now the main business part of Astoria, but probably not always in the same place. The name was of course descriptive, as it was upriver from the older post office at Astoria. The general locality of what was Upper Astoria is now frequently called Alderbrook.

Upper Klamath Lake, Klamath County. The official and correct name of the largest lake in Oregon is Upper Klamath Lake and not Klamath Lake. There is a Lower Klamath Lake and a contradistinction is necessary. Beyond that, however, the name Upper Klamath Lake has a broad and deep historic background. In passing, it may be mentioned that John C. Fremont did not reach the shores of Upper Klamath Lake in the winter of

1843-44. In fact Fremont did not see the lake until his second visit to Oregon, in 1846. On December 10, 1843, Fremont reached and very accurately described Klamath Marsh, although at the time he supposed it was on "Tlamath lake." It can hardly be contended that Klamath Marsh is part of Upper Klamath Lake. The north end of the marsh is about 30 miles from the lake and approximately 400 feet greater in elevation. For the history of the name Klamath, see under Klamath County. Upper Klamath Lake has an area of about 142 square miles at high stages, and is quite the largest in the state.

Upper Land Creek, Coos County. This creek, together with Lower Land Creek nearby, was named for T. C. Land, a pioneer settler on South Fork Coquille River.

Upper Ochoco, Crook County. The early-day post office Upper Ochoco was not on the upper reaches of Ochoco Creek at all, but not more than about ten miles east of Prineville near the mouth of Mill Creek. It was near where the Claypool place was in 1946. Upper Ochoco post office was established April 13, 1871, with James H. Miller first of seven postmasters. The office was discontinued August 2, 1880.

Upper Table Rock, Jackson County. There are two table rocks, north of Central Point. They are prominent landmarks, and well named. Upper Table Rock is the eastern one of the two. It is famous because of the council between the white soldiers and Rogue River Indians held on its southwestern slope, at the foot of the vertical cliff, on September 10, 1853. For an account of this meeting by Colonel James W. Nesmith, see *OHQ*, volume VII, page 211.

Utopia, Wallowa County. The post office at Utopia was on the homestead of Charles N. Walker in section 24, township 4 north, range 42 east. Walker was not only a homesteader but also a schoolteacher and was so impressed with the surrounding country that he named the office for Sir Thomas More's imaginary paradise on earth. Utopia post office was established May 4, 1905 with Aurelia M. Walker postmaster, and it operated until May, 1911. The place was on Middle Point between Wallupa and Wildcat creeks about two miles southeast of Promise, and the name of the office at Promise may have suggested the name Utopia.

Utter City, Coos County. In January, 1946, Mrs. Mary M. Randleman of Coquille, who had an extensive knowledge of Coos County history, wrote the compiler as follows: "There were two brothers, Fred and William Utter, residents of San Francisco, who opened the Dale and Utter coal mine about a mile south of Coaledo. They had large holdings in Contra Costa County, but resided in Utter City while operating the mine here. Utter City was about a mile south of the Coos City bridge. The town was never recorded so it is hard to locate it geographically. Mr. Utter built the Isthmus Transit railroad from Coaledo to Utter City where the coal was put in bunkers and eventually shipped to San Francisco. Henry Sengstacken came from San Francisco to serve as bookkeeper, and store manager. There was a store, post office, hotel, brewery and a number of houses." Utter City was on Isthmus Slough south of the town of Coos Bay. A post office with the name Isthmus was established December 11, 1871, with Gilbert Hall postmaster. The name of the office was changed to Utter City on February 11,

1875, and the office was discontinued June 22, 1880. The compiler is told that the ravages of time have obliterated the community.

Utts Butte, Morrow County. George W. Utt was born in Missouri and came to Morrow County in 1885. In 1887 he applied for a Timber Culture claim on this 2185 foot butte north of Eightmile Canyon and ranched there until 1924. He died in Los Angeles in 1944 at the age of 85.

Valby, Morrow County. Valby, five miles north of Eightmile, is the site of the Swedish Lutheran Church built in 1897 by the large number of early Swedish settlers. Oscar Peterson, the son of one of the founders, offered the following information in 1970. *Valby* or *Vallby* was the Swedish term for a community or group of sheepherders and since many of the early members ran sheep, the name seemed humorously appropriate. After World War II a group of the younger members endeavored to change the name to one more dignified but fortunately the old tradition prevailed.

Vale, Malheur County. The compiler has never been able to learn who named this place or for what reason. Vale is on the Malheur River but its surroundings do not suggest a vale in the concise meaning of that word. Vale post office was established February 20, 1883, with Henry C. Murray first postmaster.

Valfontis, Polk County. This was a pioneer post office which eventually passed from the picture. Valfontis office was established September 29, 1854, with Andrew J. Doak postmaster. C. C. Walker became postmaster June 12, 1855. The origin of its name has not transpired, though its meaning may be surmised. It was just another term for Spring Valley. Doak and Walker had claims close to the present site of Lincoln, a community at the east edge of Spring Valley, and Valfontis office was in that neighborhood. The office was discontinued in August, 1865.

Valley, Columbia County. Valley was the name given to a locality and post office about eight miles by road east of Pittsburg, where the road crossed Clatskanie River. There was a vale of sorts and Omar C. Spencer says that was the reason for the name. Valley post office was established April 23, 1895, with Catherine Dupont postmaster. The office was discontinued March 20, 1905. The office was a little to the west of the place later called Trenholm.

Valley Falls, Lake County. C. W. E. Jennings named this community about 1908 because of a small fall in Chewaucan River a mile or so to the north. Valley Falls post office was established on June 25, 1909, with Ernest L. H. Meyer postmaster, but Jennings later took over the position. The office was first situated near the base of Abert Rim, about a mile east of its location in 1942, but was moved westward so as to be on the Fremont Highway at the junction with the highway northeast to Burns. The office was closed in the summer of 1943.

Valsetz, Polk County. Valsetz is a made-up name composed of parts of the title of the Valley & Siletz Railroad. Valsetz is the terminus of this road. The name was selected by officials of the railroad company.

Van, Harney County. The postmaster at Van wrote the compiler in December, 1926, that the office was named for Van Middlesworth, a local settler. The office operated from March 3, 1891 to August 31, 1953.

Van Horn Butte, Hood River County. This hill was originally called

Julia Butte for Mrs. Peter Neal, but in 1906 the Van Horn brothers purchased the surrounding property and it has been called Van Horn Butte ever since. Willes and Bert Van Horn were residents of Buffalo, and in the cold storage business there. Willes moved to Hood River Valley and built a home on top of Van Horn Butte. There was a nearby railroad station named Van Horn.

Vanderhoof Canyon, Wasco County. This canyon empties into Currant Creek in the extreme south part of the county. Gilbert Vanderhoof homesteaded near its upper end before World War I. J. A. Rooper of Antelope told the compiler in 1969 that after Oregon went dry in 1916, it was understood that Gilbert and his brother John enlarged the scope of their livestock operation to include liquid grain by-products.

Vandevert Ranch, Deschutes County. Vandevert ranch is on the old stage road south of Bend. It was for many years the home of William P. Vandevert. He was born near the place now known as Saginaw, Lane County, on April 22, 1854. His father, J. J. Vandevert, was a native of Ohio and came to Oregon in 1848. W. P. Vandevert was a forest ranger, rancher and stockman and an early settler in Deschutes Valley. He died February 24, 1944. For biography, see the Bend *Bulletin,* February 24, 1944.

Vanishing Falls, Clackamas County. This thirty foot high falls on Salmon River is about six miles downstream from the mouth of Linney Creek. It is the fourth of six falls between Linney Creek and Welches and was named because it vanishes into a narrow box canyon. For details of this group see under Stein Falls.

Vannoy Creek, Josephine County. James N. Vannoy took up a donation land claim near this stream, five miles west of what is now Grants Pass, about 1851. He operated Vannoy ferry across Rogue River. Bancroft, in *History of Oregon,* volume II, page 184, says that Perkins and Long operated ferries before Vannoy near this point. The spelling Vanoy is wrong. See also under Fort Vannoy. Vannoy post office was established September 4, 1856, with James N. Vannoy postmaster. The office was discontinued October 11, 1859.

Vanora, Jefferson County. The name Vanora was coined from the first two names of Ora Van Tassel. Vanora is a place on the east bank of Deschutes River about eight miles airline northwest of Madras. When the Oregon Trunk line was built through the area, there was a Vanora station in service, but the track in that locality has been torn out. Vanora post office was established March 22, 1911, with John T. Dizney first of four postmasters. The office was closed December 15, 1920, with mail to Madras. Ora Van Tassel was a real estate man and a farmer of the lands where Vanora railroad station and post office were situated. Later he was a grain buyer, active in civic affairs. He installed an elaborate water system, which was abandoned after he moved to Madras.

Vanport City, Multnomah County. Vanport City was the official name of the community built between Portland and Vancouver to house war workers. The name was made up in compliment to the two nearby cities. A page advertisement in the *Oregonian,* August 12, 1943, gives a history of the project. On that date the place had 9942 dwelling units, prepared for

40,000 inhabitants, and was the nation's largest single war-housing town. Construction officially started September 14, 1942, and from point of time, the development was remarkable. The place was frequently referred to as Kaiserville, an informal honor to the shipbuilder, Henry J. Kaiser. For an interesting account of the maintenance problems on a project of this sort, see the *Oregonian,* August 16, 1943. Vanport was destroyed on May 30, 1948, by a disastrous flood.

Vansycle Canyon, Umatilla County. This canyon opens into the Walla Walla Valley east of Wallula. The name is universally spelled Vansycle, and most historical records indicate that it was given for J. M. Vansycle, a local resident. However, T. C. Elliott of Walla Walla investigated the matter for the compiler and found the name signed to a deed in the form J. M. Vansyckle. An advertisement of Wallula Hotel, in the *Washington Statesman,* 1864, is printed over the name J. M. Vansyckle. Vansyckle may have used different forms of his name at different periods of his life. In any event it would probably be impossible to get the spelling of the name changed at this late date. Vansycle post office operated from 1882 to 1900.

Varco Well, Deschutes County. This well three miles east of Brothers was on the 1912 homestead of Joseph and Elva E. Varco. The latter brother was later Deschutes County commissioner.

Vaughn Creek, Lane County. Vaughn Creek flows into the upper reaches of Dorena Reservoir. Sidner H. Vaughn homesteaded near its mouth in 1891.

Veatch, Lane County. This was a station on the Southern Pacific Company line about three miles southwest of Cottage Grove at an elevation of about 700 feet. It was named for Frank Veatch, a nearby resident.

Veazie Creek, Crook County. Edmund F. Veazie came to Oregon from Maine about 1858, and in 1868 settled in the Ochoco Valley, near what is now known as Veazie Creek, but in a short time moved to Hay Creek where he lived until he was drowned in John Day River in 1877, in mysterious circumstances. His home on Hay Creek was approximately the same location as what was later known as Heisler. He married Harriet Lyle, a member of a pioneer Polk County family, and their four children have been prominent citizens of the Pacific Northwest. See editorial page *Oregon Journal,* December 17, 1926.

Veda Lake, Clackamas County. This small lake lies on the western slope of the Cascade Range, about five miles south of Government Camp. It has an elevation of approximately 4300 feet. It was named in 1917 when Vern Rogers and Dave Donaldson packed into the lake with a load of trout fry. George Ledford, local forest ranger, named the lake for these two men by appropriating the first two letters of the first name of each.

Venator, Harney County. Venator was named for Alphene Venator, (pronounced Venatta), a native of Linn County, who settled in the Harney Valley as a youth in 1872. He established himself on a stock ranch in the east part of the county in 1884, and the locality was soon known as Venator. The post office was established February 18, 1895, with Mrs. Louella Venator first postmaster. This office was later moved about two and a half miles north to a station on the Union Pacific Railroad.

Venator Canyon, Harney and Lake counties. Venator Canyon heads in Harney County and drains west into the Alkali Valley. It was named for Jezreal Venator, a pioneer settler in the vicinity of Albany, who crossed the plains in 1852. He took part in the Rogue River Indian War and was wounded. He moved to the Goose Lake Valley, in the fall of 1870, buying the Crane property on Crane Creek south of what is now Lakeview. In August, 1881, he started on a business trip to Harney County to pick up some horses. His saddle horse got away from him, and he died of thirst about a half mile west of the canyon which bears his name.

Veneta, Lane County. Veneta post office was established November 3, 1914, to serve a community which was started in 1913 by E. E. Hunter. He named the townsite for his small daughter, Veneta Hunter.

Verboort, Washington County. This place was named for William Verboort, who owned part of the Henry Black donation land claim. The place is about two miles north-northeast of Forest Grove.

Verdure, Linn County. This was a station on the Oregon Electric Railway. When the line was originally built the station was called Oakville, for the community of Oakville, a pioneer settlement about one mile to the west. Due to confusion with other places in the Pacific Northwest, the name of the station was changed to Verdure in December, 1916. The form Verdue is incorrect.

Vernie, Malheur County. Vernie post office, about five or six miles northwest of Ontario, was established March 29, 1909, with Cornelia Belknap first and only postmaster. The office was discontinued May 31, 1913, with mail to Payette, Idaho. In April, 1947, C. D. Warren of Chiloquin wrote that he was the son of the postmaster, and that the office was named for a boy named Vernie who was resident in North Carolina. A Mrs. Buchanan was to be served by the new Oregon office, and she wanted the place named Vernie for her grandson, who was the youth in North Carolina. Mrs. Buchanan's son Bert also put in a plea for the name Vernie, which was adopted, apparently to the annoyance of the postmaster elect.

Vernon, Marion County. Gill's Oregon map of 1874 shows Vernon post office a few miles northeast of Salem, near the west line of section 2, township 7 south, range 2 west. This office was established February 2, 1869, with Benjamin B. Wilson first postmaster. The office was closed April 6, 1874. The place was named for a local family.

Vernonia, Columbia County. The community of Vernonia was first settled by Judson Weed and Ozias Cherrington, of Ohio, in 1876. Sometime thereafter when the question of getting a post office came up for consideration the matter of choosing a name had to be settled. At a meeting held in the schoolhouse the name of Auburn was suggested for Auburn, Minn., and Cherrington suggested the name of Vernonia for his daughter in Ohio. The community was named Vernonia and the precinct was named Auburn. This arrangement continued for some years but as a result of the confusion that followed the county court changed the name of the precinct to Vernonia. Some interesting facts have come to light about Miss Cherrington, the most important of which is that her name was not Vernonia at all, but Vernona, so the place does not bear her exact name. Vernona Cherrington became Mrs. W. H. Dawson, and on March 15, 1942, she was living in Saxe, Virginia. On that day she wrote to Omar C. Spencer of the Portland bar and provided some biographic data. She was born March 30, 1868, apparently in Ohio. Her mother died when she was a small child, and her father emigrated to Missouri and on to Oregon about 1873, leaving Vernona with his stepmother. She never saw him again, as he never went back to Ohio and she never visited Oregon. Miss Cherrington was married to William H. Dawson in 1890 and moved from Jackson, Ohio, to North Carolina in 1902, and later to Virginia. Her father was thrown from a hay tedder about 1894, while working on Sauvie Island and died a few months later at the home of Judson Weed, apparently near St. Helens. Vernonia post office was established January 11, 1878, with David F. Baker, first postmaster.

Vesper, Clatsop County. Vesper is not now a post office, although it has been in the past. It is in the Nehalem Valley. It is said to have been named by William Johnston for the evening star. The name Vesper is generally applied to the plant Venus when it is east of the sun, and therefore shines brightly after sunset. Vesper post office was established January 30, 1879, with Johnston first postmaster. It was then on the Clatsop County list, but near the east boundary of the county, and at times the office has been in Columbia County, depending upon who was postmaster.

Vey Ranch, Morrow County. This ranch on Butter Creek south of Service Buttes was the headquarters for one of the largest and best-known early day sheep operations in Morrow County. John, Joe and Antone Vey came from the Isle of Graciosa, Azore Islands. After sundry travels, the first two settled along Butter Creek in the early 1870s where Antone soon joined them. In 1878, friendly Indians warned them of the impending uprising but John disregarded the advice and was murdered and scalped while tending the flock at Camas Prairie. Joe and Antone continued together for a number of years but broke up after a serious fraternal argument. Legend has it that the disagreement was so deep that they literally severed their ranch house into distinct halves.

Vey Spring, Umatilla County. Vey Spring just east of Service Buttes was apparently named for Joseph Vey, a son of one of the early Vey brothers, who took up government land nearby in 1928.

Victor, Wasco County. Victor was a post office serving an area on Juniper Flat about midway between Tygh Valley and Wapinitia. The office was established November 14, 1893, with Viola Jones first postmaster. The office was closed in November, 1912, and the business turned over to Maupin. The old USGS maps of the Dufur quadrangle shows Victor school in section 32, township 4 south, range 13 east, as of 1930. By 1980 the school and all other buildings had disappeared.

Victor View, Crater Lake National Park, Klamath County. Victor View is a natural viewpoint on the east wall of Crater Lake, north of Kerr Notch and above Sentinel Rock. It was named on January 4, 1933, by the USBGN in honor of Mrs. Frances Fuller Victor, Oregon poet and historian, who visited Crater Lake in 1872. For information about Mrs. Victor, see Scott's *History of the Oregon Country*, volume I, page 142, and *OHQ* article by Hazel Mills, volume LXII, December 1961. She was born at Rome, New York, May 23, 1826, and died in Portland, November 14, 1902. For many years a natural feature on the southwest rim of Crater Lake was called Victor Rock, but in 1930-31 the Sinnott Memorial was built on this rock, making it necessary to name another point for Mrs. Victor.

Vida, Lane County. The original name of this place was Gate Creek. This name resulted in confusion with Gales Creek in Washington County. The name Vida was selected because it was the name of the daughter of the postmaster, Francis A. Pepiot. Vida post office was established April 12, 1898. The community is where McKenzie Highway crosses Gate Creek.

Vidae Ridge, Crater Lake National Park, Klamath County. Vidae Ridge is a very prominent, rugged backbone extending south from the rim of Crater Lake. Applegate Peak is the highest point at its north end. The compiler has been unable to learn about the origin of the name.

Viento, Hood River County. Dr. T. L. Eliot of Portland, who was familiar with the history of Hood River and vicinity, told the writer that this railroad station was named by taking the first two letters of the names, Villard, Endicott and Tolman. William Endicott of Boston was a capitalist who was heavily interested in Henry Villard's railroad enterprise. Tolman was a railroad contractor. *Viento* is also a Spanish word meaning wind and this word is peculiarly fitting when applied to this station, but Dr. Eliot said the Spanish origin had nothing to do with the matter. Viento State Park on the banks of Viento Creek has both picnicking and overnight facilities.

Viewpoint, Lake County. Viewpoint was the descriptive name of a post office established during the homesteading wave just after the turn of the century. This office, which was in the south part of the Christmas Lake Valley, was established April 9, 1910, with Bertha C. Hach first postmaster. The office was discontinued September 30, 1918. In 1946 Mrs. Delbert Cloud, New Pine Creek, Oregon, wrote about the homesteaders' post offices in Lake County. Mrs. Cloud said she visited the vicinity of Viewpoint office about the time it was discontinued. She said that the people had all left. The newspaper mail had not been distributed and was still scattered around. The office door had blown away, but the post office books were still there. *Sic transit gloria* Viewpoint.

Villard Glacier, Deschutes County. This small glacier is on the north slope of the North Sister. It was named by Professor E. T. Hodge of the University of Oregon. See *Mount Multnomah*. Henry Villard was a great factor in the material development of Oregon, and did his share from a civic point of view as well, and he should have had something more than a small glacier named for him. Henry Villard was born April 10, 1835, in Bavaria. His family name was Hilgard. He came to the United States when he was 18 years old, and here entered upon a career as teacher, editor, war correspondent and finally railroad builder that lasted nearly half a century, and made him an outstanding figure in the history of transportation in America. For detailed accounts of his railroad construction work in Oregon, see many references in Scott's *History of the Oregon Country,* and also Villard's *Memoirs.* He died November 12, 1900. He was a firm supporter of the University of Oregon, where Villard Hall is named in his honor. See also under Hilgard.

Vincent, Wallowa County. J. H. Horner of Enterprise informed the compiler that this place was named for Vincent Palmer of the Palmer Lumber Company.

Vincent Creek, Grant County. This creek is west of Austin. Patsy Daly of Prairie City told the compiler that it was named for a nearby resident who was engaged in mining.

Vinemaple, Clatsop County. The vine maple or shrub, *Acer circinatum*, grows so abundantly and so persistently throughout western Oregon that it is surprising so few geographic features have been named for it, but such seems to be the case. About the turn of the century there was a post office in the Nehalem Valley called Vinemaple. This office was about six miles downstream, or southwest, from Jewell. Available records are not clear as to the opening and closing dates, but they were probably May 6, 1891, and May 12, 1902. The office was apparently closed out to Grand Rapids. Today the old name is retained by Vinemaple School and Vinemaple Log Church, both of which are a little south of the river on the road to Elsie.

Vineyard Hill, Benton County. Vineyard Hill, elevation about 1500 feet, is north of Corvallis, in the east part of section 3, township 11 south, range 5 west, on the boundary of the McDonald Forest of Oregon State College. It bears the name of an early settler who had a land claim nearby. It is the southward and larger of two hills of about the same height and about a half mile apart.

Vingie Creek, Lincoln County. This stream flows into Pacific Ocean about two miles north of Yachats. It bears the name of an early settler who owned land near the head of the creek. The name Divinity Creek is wrong and is due to a mis-hearing of the correct name.

Vinson, Umatilla County. Vinson was named for John S. Vinson, a pioneer settler, who once ran a store in the community. Vinson began operating as a merchant at Needy, Clackamas County, about 1854. In the early 1870s he preempted land at what was later Vinson and secured a post office. With Frank Newman he engaged in the livestock and farming business. Later they added a mercantile establishment and the place became an important stage station on the line between The Dalles and Pendleton by way of Heppner. Railroad development put a stop to the community. See editorial page of the *Oregonian*, March 17, 1928. A post office named Butter Creek was established at this place on July 28, 1873, with J. S. Vinson postmaster. The name of the office was changed to Vinson on September 15, 1881, and finally closed November 30, 1907.

Viola, Clackamas County. Viola is a place a few miles west of Estacada. It is said to have been named for Mrs. Violet O. Harding, the wife of an early settler in the locality. Clear Creek post office was established in this vicinity on October 30, 1867, with Oliver P. Mattoon first postmaster. The name was changed to Viola on January 25, 1876.

Virtue Flat, Baker County. This flat was named for James W. Virtue, for many years a resident of the county, and one-time sheriff. For additional information about Virtue, see under Ontario.

Vista Ridge, Hood River County. Vista Ridge is a long slope north of Mount Hood and northwest of Wy'east Basin. Its west face forms the east wall of the Ladd Creek Canyon. It was named in 1922 by an exploring party from Hood River because of the extensive views from its summit. This information is in a letter from C. Edward Graves, Arcata, California, dated July 5, 1943. The name has been approved by the USBGN.

Vistillas, Lake County. In February, 1944, Ida M. Odell of Klamath Falls kindly dug up some information about the history of this post office. In the late 1880s there was an office with the name Loraton serving an area in the Barnes Valley near the Klamath-Lake county line. This office was discontinued after a short life, and later, about 1890, local settlers tried to get it reestablished. The old name Loraton was objected to because it was so much like Lorella, also in Klamath County. The name Fairview was suggested to postal authorities, but it was not acceptable because there was another Fairview in Oregon. The Post Office Department is said to have suggested the name Vistillas, and that is what it has been for more than half a century. The office has been moved several times, depending on who would assume its responsibilities. It has been in both Klamath and Lake counties. Edward Tull was probably first postmaster. One of the Batchelders later took the office. It has been at the Lapham ranch and also at the Adams and other places. *Vistillas* is a Spanish word meaning an eminence affording an extended view, or a viewpoint. This is very much the same as a fair view. The compiler thinks that somewhere along the line, after the name Fairview was rejected for this office, somebody selected the Spanish word that is nearly equivalent.

Voltage, Harney County. Voltage was a post office just south of Malheur Lake. This is close to the site of Sodhouse which was for many years an important landmark in Harney Valley. The post office at Voltage was established on August 28, 1908, with Walter C. Botsford first postmaster. He suggested the name because he was interested in electricity and had the idea that sufficient "voltage" could be generated on Donner und Blitzen River to serve the entire Harney Valley. Botsford was not the first man to go astray and confuse force with power.

Voorhies, Jackson County. This station was named for Colonel Gordon Voorhies, who for many years operated an orchard nearby. Colonel Voorhies was a native of Kentucky and a graduate of West Point. He served in the Spanish-American War with rank of captain, and about 1899 retired from the army because of impaired health. He volunteered his services for World War I and reached the rank of lieutenant-colonel, serving with distinction. He died in September, 1940.

Vosburg, Tillamook County. Vosburg post office was established June 28, 1901, with J. L. Vosburg postmaster. The office was closed December 15, 1903. Vosburg was named for the postmaster, who was an early-day lumberman and was later connected with the Wheeler sawmill. The office was at or near the present site of the Wheeler mill and about a half mile west of what later became the community of Wheeler. Wheeler post office was established in August, 1910, and served the locality previously served by Vosburg office. Some years later the Wheeler office was moved eastward to the community of Wheeler and a third office, Hoevet, was established to serve the locality of the mill. Hoevet post office was closed January 31, 1944.

Waconda, Marion County. Waconda was a station on the Oregon Electric Railway north of Salem. It was named when the railroad was built about 1907, and the post office was established in 1912. Waconda is an old name in that part of the Willamette Valley, and was originally applied to a community about a mile south of Gervais, at the point where the present Pacific Highway East is crossed by the old road from Parkersville to Saint Louis. This old community has disappeared. The name Waconda was probably brought to Oregon from the Plains. *Wakonda* is used by tribes of the Siouan family to mean something consecrated and as a verb, it means to worship. It is hard to give an exact definition of *wakonda*. See *Handbook of American Indians*, volume II, page 897.

Wades Flat, Douglas County. Wades Flat is southwest of Reedsport. Captain Henry Wade and his brother settled on a ranch on this flat in early days, and the locality is named for them. For information about Henry Wade, see *Marine History of the Pacific Northwest*, page 185.

Wagner, Wheeler County. Wagner post office was established March 21, 1882, and was given the family name of the first postmaster, Carl N. Wagner. The office was then in Grant County, as Wheeler County had not yet been created. It was on or near the upper reaches of Kahler Creek and a few miles north of John Day River. The office was closed April 27, 1901.

Wagner Creek, Jackson County. This stream is northwest of Ashland. It was named for Jacob Wagner, who was born in Ohio in 1820 and came to Oregon in 1850. He settled on Wagner Creek two years later, and in 1862 moved to Ashland, where he ran the Ashland flour mills. For additional biographical information, see Walling's *History of Southern Oregon*, page 542. The community of Talent was once known as Wagner or Wagner Creek.

Wagontire Mountain, Harney and Lake counties. Wagontire Mountain is one of the important landmarks in central Oregon. It has an elevation of 6504 feet, according to the USC&GS. It received its name in pioneer days on account of the fact that a wagontire lay beside the road on its northern slopes for many years. This tire is said to have come from an emigrant wagon which was burned by Indians. There was a post office named Wagontire southeast of the mountain. This post office was formerly known as Egli, for a prominent local stockman. The name was changed to Wagontire in the fall of 1919 at the suggestion of Loretta M. Addington, who thought the new name more appropriate. The office was closed November 15, 1943 with papers to Burns.

Wahanna Lake, Lane County. Wahanna Lake, north of Waldo Lake, bears an Indian name imported from Clatsop County. Wahanna was the name used for many years for the stream flowing into Necanicum River north of Seaside, now officially known as Neawanna Creek. For the history of these names see under Neawanna Creek. The lake in Lane County was named at a time when several other nearby features were given Indian names for better identification. The name Wahanna Lake was probably used because it had a pleasing sound and not for any local reason.

Wahclella Falls, Multnomah County. These falls are on Tanner Creek, and were named by a committee representing the Mazamas and other organizations in 1915. Wahclella was the name of an Indian locality near Beacon Rock on the Washington side of the Columbia River, and was selected because of its pleasing sound.

Wahgwingwin Falls, Hood River County. Wahgwingwin or Wah Gwin Gwin Falls are produced by Phelps Creek when it plunges over the cliff west of Hood River town into Columbia River. The falls, which are about 207 feet high, are near the east end of the Columbia Gorge Hotel and are a well-known scenic feature of the vicinity. The name is said to be of some Indian tongue and means tumbling or rushing waters. There are a number of geographic names in the Pacific Northwest with the initial syllable Wah, and they generally refer to water features. The repeated syllables are used for emphasis. Walla Walla is a name of this type.

Wahkeena Falls, Multnomah County. These falls were once known as Gordon Falls, for F. E. Gordon, a pioneer landowner. On account of confusion with Gordon Creek near Sandy River, and Gorton Creek at Cascade Locks, a committee appointed by the Mazamas in 1915 to name points on the Columbia River Highway, changed the name to Wahkeena Falls and Wahkeena Creek. This name is said to be a Yakima Indian word meaning most beautiful. See *Wah-Kee-Nah, and her People,* by James C. Strong.

Wahtum Lake, Hood River County. H. H. Riddle told the compiler in 1922 that Wahtum Lake was named by H. D. Langille in 1901 while making a map for the USGS. *Wahtum* is a Sahaptin language word meaning pond or body of water.

Wake Butte, Deschutes County. This butte southwest of Bend was named by the USFS with the Chinook jargon word for no or none, indicating its unimportant character.

Wake Up Rilea Creek, Curry County. Peterson and Powers in *A Century of Coos and Curry,* page 201, say that this tributary of Rogue River near Agness was named indirectly for Michael Riley, an early settler. Riley grubstaked a miner only to be routed out at midnight by his enthusiastic partner with the words, "Wake up Riley. We're rich.". Unfortunately the bonanza proved to be iron pyrites so Riley lost both grubstake and sleep. While the foregoing may easily be correct, M. S. Brainard of Brookings told the compiler in 1968 that George Washington Rilea was a long time postmaster and school teacher at Agness in the early part of the century. Then in 1981 John Scharf of Burns added that he had been a forest ranger in Agness in the 1920s and knew Rilea. He said the postmaster would stay up listening to the news on the primitive radio which worked best at night. Rilea compensated by sleeping late in the mornings and early customers were forced to bang on the door to "Wake up Rilea".

Waldo, Josephine County. According to James T. Chinnock of Grants Pass, Waldo was a specific place in the general locality known as Sailor Diggings, so named because a party of seafaring men found gold there. However the legislative act of January 22, 1856, that created Josephine County, provided that Sailor Diggings was to be the county seat until the next county election. Waldo was not mentioned. This may mean that Sailor Diggings was also a specific place, or it may mean that the two names referred to the same locality. It is late in the day to determine the situation exactly. The name Sailor Diggings passed out of use; Waldo survived. Reports that Waldo was named for Daniel Waldo, prominent Oregon pioneer of 1843, do not seem to be true. Daniel W. Bass, a grandson of Daniel Waldo and a prominent citizen of Seattle, wrote the compiler in 1928 that the Josephine County town was named for William Waldo, brother of Daniel Waldo. William Waldo was nominated for governor of California by the Whig party in 1853. He had been of service to settlers and miners in northern California and the residents of what was later Waldo, Oregon, close to the state line, all voted for William Waldo with the notion that they were actually living in California. This origin of the name is confirmed by Walling in his *History of Southern Oregon*. There is nothing to indicate that Daniel Waldo ever held court in this part of Oregon. Waldo post office was established on September 4, 1856, with Lyman H. Guthrie first postmaster and closed December 15, 1928.

Waldo Gulch, Baker County. This gulch is southeast of Bowen Valley. In 1899 Charles A. Waldo filed on government land near Waldo Spring at the head of the gulch.

Waldo Hills, Marion County. The Waldo Hills are western foothills of the Cascade Range and lie east of Salem. Their geography is well shown on the USGS maps of the Stayton N.E. and adjoining quadrangles. They were named for Daniel Waldo who was born in Virginia in 1800; died at Salem September 6, 1880. For his funeral eulogy, by J. W. Nesmith, see the *Oregonian*, September 11, 1880; biography, by T. T. Geer, *ibid.*, May 7, 1905, page 19. He was a companion of the Applegates in the migration to Oregon in 1843. He was a member of the legislative committee of the provisional government in 1844, and a district judge for Champooick district in that government. He was a highly respected pioneer. "His name will be remembered as a synonym for independence and integrity" (Matthew P. Deady, Pioneer Address, 1875). Two of his sons, William and John B., were prominent in Oregon affairs. His daughters married James Brown, Samuel Bass and David Logan. In earliest pioneer days the name Waldo Hills was not generally used; the locality was referred to as the Waldo Settlement. The area was also called Lebanon, and Lebanon post office was in operation at a point about twelve miles east of Salem from 1851 to 1858. The name Lebanon was absorbed by the place in Linn County.

Waldo Lake, Lane County. This is one of the largest mountain lakes in the state, and lies in the Cascade Range at an elevation of 5410 feet. The geography of the lake and its surroundings is shown on the USGS map of the Waldo Lake quadrangle. The lake was named for Judge John B. Waldo, son of Daniel Waldo for whom the Waldo Hills were named. Judge Waldo sought his recreation in the Cascade Range, and Waldo Glacier on the southeast slope of Mount Jefferson was also named for him. Judge Waldo died September 2, 1907. This lake and others nearby were shown as the Virgin Lakes on a map dated August 24, 1863, by the surveyor general of Oregon. Frank S. Warner, a pioneer resident of Lane County, in a letter printed in the *Oregonian*, September 6, 1927, says that Waldo Lake was discovered by Charlie Tufti, and that its early name was Pengra Lake, for B. J. Pengra. Pengra was a pioneer railroad enthusiast, and championed the construction of a line approximately in the present location of the Cascade line of the Southern Pacific.

Waldport, Lincoln County. This community is said to have received its name in the early 1880s at the suggestion of P. V. Wustrow, then postmaster at Alsea. Waldport is a combination of the German word *wald*, meaning forest, and the English word port, referring to Alsea Bay. The name is descriptive, for the bay is closely surrounded by hills, once wooded. Waldport was founded by David Ruble, already in business in Alsea, and he is said to have asked Colonel Wustrow to suggest a name for the new community. Waldport post office was established June 17, 1881, by change of name from Collins. This office may have been on the north side of Alsea Bay. It was changed back to Collins on February 23, 1882. See under Nice. On August 15, 1882 another Waldport office was established with Thomas Russell postmaster. He was succeeded on September 27, 1883 by David Ruble who also had been postmaster of the earlier Waldport. Obviously there was some rivalry between the north and south side.

Waldron, Wheeler County. The compiler has not been able to get an explanation of the origin of the name of this early-day post office except that it was named for a person. The office was established on the Wasco County list on March 28, 1879, with William A. Helms postmaster. The place was on Shoofly Creek about ten or twelve miles northeast of Mitchell. Several members of the Waldron family have been prominent in central Oregon affairs and Henry J. Waldron was once postmaster at The Dalles. Waldron post office was closed out to Richmond in July, 1902.

Walker, Lane County. Walker post office was established in 1891. Francis Smith, first postmaster, had come from Crawford County, Iowa, to seek a western home and a place to open a small mercantile business. He secured some property from Mrs. J. F. Walker, a pioneer resident of the neighborhood north of Cottage Grove. Mr. Smith was instrumental in securing the post office and named it for Mrs. Walker. The post office at Walker was discontinued about 1925.

Walker Island, Columbia County. This island in the Columbia River below Rainier was discovered by Lieutenant Broughton on October 27, 1792, and was named Walkers Island for the surgeon of the ship *Chatham*. Modern usage, Walker Island, has been approved by the USBGN.

Walker Mountain, Joesphine County. Walker Mountain is east of Interstate 5 and south of Jumpoff Joe Creek. It was named for Wesley R. and Augustus Walker who took adjoining donation land claims in Pleasant Valley.

Walker Mountain, Klamath County. This is an important mountain a few miles south of Crescent. It is shown on maps as Walker Range, Walker Rim and Walker Mountain, but the last named is considered to be the best designation and the one in general use. In the opinion of the writer it was named for W. T. Walker, of the Middle Fork Willamette River road viewing party, who explored this part of the state in 1852. See under Diamond Peak. It appears that two peaks were named for Walker, one the mountain described herein, and the other a point on the summit of the Cascade Range north of Mount Thielsen. The name of the latter peak has been changed from Walker Mountain to Howlock Mountain for an Indian chief. This was done to avoid confusion that would result from two mountains of the same name so near together.

Walker Prairie, Multnomah County. Walker Prairie and Walker Peak are near Bull Run Reservoir. Ralph Lewis who was in the area in the early 1900s told the writer that an old trapper named Walker had lived on the prairie by one of the trails from Hood River to the Sandy drainage. The BLM plat book dated 1874 shows "Walkers Trail" in township 1 south, range 5 east.

Walker Road, Washington County. For many years the name Walker Road has been applied to a thoroughfare which extends westward from Canyon Road through the area south of the Sunset Highway toward Hillsboro. Walker Road was named for Mr. and Mrs. William E. Walker who took up a farm a little southwest of Cedar Mill in 1852. For an account of Walker family history, see Fred Lockley's article in the *Oregon Journal* for September 10, 1929, editorial page. In 1946 there was a painted sign over a gate on the north side of Walker Road near the crossing of Cedar Mill Creek, reading: "Mr. and Mrs. William E. Walker, 1852. The Old Meadow Farm."

Wall Creek, Grant County. Wall Creek is a tributary of North Fork John Day River. Little Wall Creek rises in Morrow County and flows into Wall Creek. J. L. Cochran, an early resident in the John Day country, informed the compiler that the stream was named because of the rimrocks or walls along its banks.

Wall Creek, Grant County. This Wall Creek is south of Canyon City and flows into Canyon Creek. Patsy Daly of Prairie City informed the compiler that it was named for a local resident.

Walla Walla River, Umatilla County. The sources of Walla Walla River lie in Oregon. South Fork Walla Walla River is the main tributary, and this stream rises in the extreme northwest corner of Wallowa County. The north and south forks join about seven miles southeast of Milton, and the stream flows into Washington north of Milton, after having been divided into several channels and ditches, one branch being known as Little Walla Walla River. "In several languages *walla* means running water, and reduplication of a word diminutizes it; so *Wallawalla* is the small rapid river." (Coues in *History of the Expedition of Lewis and Clark,* page 969.) According to Myron Eells, in *The American Anthropologist,* January, 1892, page 34, the word is Nez Perce and Cayuse, the root of which is *walatse,* which means running, hence running water. Wallula is probably an anglicized corruption of Walla Walla. Lewis and Clark use the name *Wallow Wallow,* with several variations, and other early travelers use different spellings. The pronunciation, however, is more or less the same. See *OGN,* 1928 edition, page 373. Old Fort Walla Walla (Fort Nez Perce), at the mouth of Walla Walla River, in Washington, was established in 1818 by the North West Company, and was abandoned in 1855. The city of Walla Walla, 33 miles east, came into importance in 1860-61, amid placer gold mining activities on Clearwater, Salmon, upper Columbia, Owyhee and Boise rivers. It was first settled upon in 1855. Whitman's mission, at Wai-il-at-pu, was six miles west of the city of Walla Walla.

Wallace, Clackamas County. Wallace was a station on the Oregon Electric Railway about two miles south of Wilsonville, named for Mrs. Guy W. Talbot, of Portland, whose maiden name was Wallace.

Wallace, Lane County. Wallace post office and what there was of a community were named for William Wallace Shortridge. The place was on Coast Fork Willamette River about ten or a dozen miles south of Cottage Grove, in township 22 south, range 3 west. The post office was established December 8, 1885, with Shortridge postmaster, and it continued in service until March 1, 1898. Shortridge had previously been postmaster at Ida, at or near the same place as Wallace. Shortridge was born in Iowa. He came to Oregon in 1852 and to Lane County in 1853.

Wallace Canyon, Wasco County. Nathan Wallace was born in Miami, Ohio, in 1832 and came to Oregon with the immigration of 1852. He settled near Currant Creek and was the second inhabitant of Antelope when he started a blacksmith shop at the old townsite in 1870. Wallace died in Antelope on September 10, 1904.

Wallace Hill, Polk County. Wallace Hill is a prominent landmark in the eastern part of the Eola Hills about three miles northwest of Salem. It has an elevation of about 400 feet and the highway between Salem and Dayton skirts its eastern shoulder. It was named for R. S. Wallace who planted nearby one of the largest orchards in Polk County.

Wallace Island, Columbia County. This is an island in the Columbia River north of Clatskanie. It is said to bear the name of an early settler who either lived thereon, or owned part of it. The compiler has been unable to get reliable information about the matter. Wilkes in *U.S. Exploring Expedition,* volume XXIII, Hydrography atlas, calls the western part of the island "Yapats I" and the eastern part "Kotse I," and the channel to the south, now known as Wallace Slough, is called by him "Natsox Run." Wilkes does not explain these names, though they are apparently of Indian origin.

Wallace Slough, Columbia County. This is probably the small river described by Broughton, which he named Swaine's River on October 26, 1792. Its appearance emerging from behind Wallace Island doubtless led Broughton to believe it was a real river.

Wallalute Falls, Hood River County. These falls of Eliot Branch are on the northeast slope of Mount Hood. They were named in 1893 by Miss A. M. Lang of The Dalles. The word is the Wasco Indian term for strong water. Miss Lang and Will Langille explored the falls on September 26, 1892. Langille and Will Graham had been there about a year before, but Miss Lang was the first white woman as far as known to visit the place. She asked Wasco Sally for a list of names from which to select, and Wallalute was the result. Sally told Miss Lang the word meant strong water, and her statement was confirmed by Sampson, a prominent Indian at the Warm Springs Agency. It should be noted that a number of old time Hood River residents claimed that Wallalute Falls were on Compass Creek, the next creek north of Eliot Branch.

Wallooskee River, Clatsop County. Wallooskee River is a tributary of Youngs River, southeast of Astoria. It bears in modern form the name of a small band of Indians that lived nearby. They were of the Chinook tribe. In 1851 Wallooska was the sole surviving member of this band. See *OHQ,* volume XXII, page 61. The stream is known as a river and not a creek. For many years the name was spelled Walluski but this was changed in *Decision List 7504.*

Wallowa, Wallowa County. Wallowa was the first post office in that part of Oregon that now comprises Wallowa County. The office was established April 10, 1873, with John Snodgrass first postmaster. It was on the Union County list at the time.

Wallowa County. Wallowa County is the extreme northeast county of Oregon. It has a land area of 3178 square miles. *Wallowa* is a Nez Perce Indian word used to describe a structure of stakes set in a triangle, used to support a network of sticks called *lacallas,* for catching fish. These traps were put in Wallowa River below the outlet of Wallowa Lake. This information was furnished the compiler by Levi Ankeny of Walla Walla, who was thoroughly familiar with the early history and tradition of the Wallowa Valley and on intimate terms with many Indians, who knew the facts of the matter. This origin of the name has been disputed, but the compiler is disposed to place great weight on Levi Ankeny's opinion, which was confirmed by J. H. Horner of Enterprise. Wallowa County was created February 11, 1887. See F. V. Holman's "History of Counties of Oregon," *OHQ,* volume XI, page 60. Wallowa River is a tributary of Grande Ronde River, which Lewis and Clark named *Wil-le-wah.* The explorers also gave the name to a tribe of Indians.

Wallowa Mountains, Baker, Union and Wallowa counties. The Wallowa Mountains are an important geographical feature in Oregon and represent a structure quite distinct from most of the other mountain ranges of the state. They are granitic and are not of volcanic origin, or the result of lava flows. They are rugged in character and alpine in appearance. They take their name from Wallowa River. These mountains were formerly known by a number of names, most of which were applied by prospectors. These names included Granite Mountains, Powder Mountains, Eagle Mountains. J. Neilson Barry, at the time living in Baker, recommended to the USBGN that these local names be eliminated and the name Wallowa Mountains be used to describe the features in question. This was done and the new name is now in universal use. Wallowa Mountains are separate from and are not part of the Blue Mountains.

Wallowa River, Union and Wallowa counties. Wallowa River is one of the important rivers of the northeastern part of the state. It is formed by the confluence of the east and west forks about a mile south of Wallowa Lake. The river flows into Wallowa Lake at the south end and out of the north end and joins Grande Ronde River at Rondowa. For the origin of the name see under Wallowa County. There is a post office in Wallowa Valley named Wallowa.

Walls Lake, Harney County. This is a small lake south of Harney Lake serving as a collecting place for spring runoff. It has an elevation of about 5000 feet. It was named for a pioneer stockman, Tom Walls.

Wallupa Creek, Wallowa County. J. H. Horner of Enterprise told the writer that *wallupa* was an Indian word and probably meant wildcat.

Walterville, Lane County. Walterville was named by George Millican, a pioneer resident, for his son Walter Millican. For further information see under Millican.

Walton, Lane County. The road from Eugene to Florence was started in 1881. It crossed the Coast Range near Noti and then followed a large tributary of Siuslaw River which was named Walton Creek to honor Judge Joshua J. Walton, a pioneer lawyer of Lane County and for some years county judge and secretary of the Board of Regents of the University of Oregon. Walton post office was established in 1884 to serve settlers along the new route and James L. Atkinson, the first postmaster, named the office for the stream. However, sometime after the turn of the century the name of the stream was changed to the mundane Wildcat Creek, the form now in universal use.

Walton Lake, Crook County. This artificial lake about twenty seven miles northeast of Prineville was formed by a dam near the headwaters of Camp Creek. The Prineville Chapter of the Izaak Walton League of America was instrumental in this work and the lake is named in honor of their well-known patron.

Waluga, Clackamas County. Indian tradition says that the lake now known as Oswego Lake by the town of Lake Oswego, was originally called Waluga Lake, *waluga* being an Indian term for wild swan. This name was used because of the peculiar sound made by these birds. When Waluga post office was established in March, 1916, near Oswego Lake, it was thought appropriate to use the old Indian name, but in June, 1923, the name of the office was changed to Lake Grove, a move of no improvement in the opinion of the compiler. Lake Grove was incorporated into Lake Oswego in 1959.

Wamic, Wasco County. Wamic was named for a family of early settlers named Womack. This family consisted of Asa and Levi, brothers, and a nephew Crawford. Pierce Mays, prominent resident of Wasco County, is authority for the statement that these three men had a remarkable plan of allowing each of the three in turn to determine what all should do during his day of leadership. Thus on Monday all worked in the blacksmith shop under the leadership of Asa. Levi was more socially inclined and on Tuesday all three sat in front of the shop and "chewed the rag and whittled." Crawford was the Nimrod of the family and on Wednesday the three went hunting or fishing. Thursday began the cycle anew.

Wampus, Klamath County. Wampus is a word used by timbermen to refer to a legendary monster of the forests. No one has ever seen a wampus but plenty of woodsmen will undertake to describe one. Wampus post office was established June 27, 1908, with Eugene Spencer first and only postmaster. It was put in service just a few months after nearby Forest post office was discontinued. According to a letter from Devere Helfrich of Klamath Falls, written in April, 1948, Wampus post office was probably at the old Spencer stage and freight station at the east foot of Hayden Mountain. This would make it about three miles southwest of Forest. Wampus post office was discontinued September 15, 1911.

Wampus Butte, Deschutes County. The wampus is a legendary monster of the forest, about which there are many stories. Wampus Butte, named for this creature, is about eight miles west-northwest of La Pine, near the Deschutes River.

Wanderers Peak, Clackamas County. Dee Wright of Eugene, a native of the Molalla Valley, told the compiler that this peak was named because a party of hunters got lost nearby and wandered around several days before it found camp.

Wanoga Butte, Deschutes County. Wanoga Butte, elevation 5740 feet, is about eight miles southeast of Bachelor Butte. It was named by the USFS with one form of the Klamath Indian word meaning son or male child. Other forms are *vunak, vunaga,* and *unak.* This butte was named about the same time as other nearby features were named with Indian words expressing family relationship. See under Tot Mountain and Kwolh Butte.

Wapato Lake, Washington and Yamhill counties. This intermittent lake, which covers considerable area in wet years, bears the Indian name for the arrowhead or sagittaria, commonly known as the wild potato. It grows in wet situations. For information about the wapato see under Chewaucan Marsh and under Sauvie Island. The form Lake Wapato was frequently used in earlier days, but Wapato Lake is now in general use. A post office with the name Wapatoo was established July 14, 1853, with William E. Molthrop postmaster, on the Washington County list. It was a little southeast of the present town of Gaston. The office was discontinued in August, 1865. On August 13, 1871, another post office, Wapatoe, was established in this vicinity. The name of the office was changed to Gaston on June 5, 1873. The office may have been moved at the time the name was changed. Both of the above offices were on the Washington County list. Wapato post office was established on the Yamhill County list on September 26, 1883, with Frederic Florey postmaster. This office was discontinued November 3, 1886. The railroad station at or near this place is shown on old time-cards with the spelling Wapato, but it was abolished prior to 1980.

Wapinitia, Wasco County. *Wapinitia* is a Warm Springs Indian word. The correct spelling is said to be *Wapinita.* The compiler of these notes has discussed the name with several Warm Springs Indians and finds that the word *Wapinitia* is difficult to translate but it suggests a location near the edge of something. One Indian says that it means the edge of the desert or cultivated land. Another version is that it means a point at the end of the brush, or coming out of the brush. These two meanings are not necessarily contradictory. In Wapinitia it is said the name means running water but this translation does not seem to be substantiated by Indians. Wapinitia was once known as Oak Grove because of the trees in the vicinity. One of the principal tributaries of Clackamas River is Oak Grove Fork, so called because it headed in the general direction of Oak Grove.

Wapiti Camp, Umatilla County. This forest camp on the Tower Mountain road was named by the USFS with a plains Indian word for elk or *Cervus canadensis.* Wapiti is used elsewhere as a placename and is a welcome relief from the surfeit of "Elk".

Ward Butte, Linn County. Ward Butte is east of Shedd and south of Plainview. Here there are two buttes, one on each side of the Southern Pacific Company tracks, and the name Ward is always applied to the westward one, which has an elevation of 858 feet. The eastern butte has no name, and an elevation of 442 feet. The compiler is informed that the hill known as Ward Butte is really on the Isom donation land claim, and should have been called Isom Butte, while the small hill is on the Ward claim and should be Ward Butte. Regardless of these facts, however, the larger hill to the west is always known as Ward Butte, and will probably continue to be so called. It was named for Thomas M. Ward.

Ward Butte, Umatilla County. This butte is west of Butter Creek south of Hermiston. It was named for Charles J. Ward who homesteaded near its base.

Ward Creek, Jackson County. Ward Creek is a tributary of Rogue River at Rogue River town, named for Oliver P. Ward, a pioneer settler.

Ward Creek, Wasco County. This creek rises southwest of Shaniko and flows into Antelope Creek. It was named for John H. Ward who was born in New York and came to California with the gold rush. About 1864 he moved to Oregon and located near Cross Hollows where he farmed and later kept the hotel and drove stage. Ward moved to The Dalles about 1874 and died there some three years later. His son, Thomas A. Ward, was a well-known citizen and later sheriff of Wasco County.

Wards Butte, Douglas County. William Ward came to Oregon from Ohio in 1852. He was an early settler where Ward Creek empties into Pass Creek near Comstock and was the operator of the toll road which passed near Wards Butte. He died in 1871 and was the first person buried in the Anlauf Cemetery near Comstock.

Wardton, Douglas County. Wardton, a place near Champagne Creek about six miles west of Roseburg, was named for a local resident, Frazier Ward. Wardton post office was established January 7, 1890, with Ward postmaster. The office was closed on February 28, 1907.

Warfield Creek, Lane County. This creek is a tributary of Hills Creek southeast of Oakridge. It was named for Mrs. B. B. Warfield, the owner of Kitson Hot Springs.

Warm Springs, Jefferson County. This place, the agency for the Warm Springs Indian Reservation, was named for natural features nearby. The name of the reservation was apparently taken from the much more important springs on Warm Springs River. Warm Springs post office was established February 7, 1873, with Michael Flinn postmaster. The name of the office was telescoped into Warmsprings in 1894, and later to Warmspring. All this was confusing, for people found it difficult to adhere to two styles, one for the agency and one for the reservation. About 1929 postal authorities changed the name again to Warm Springs, and at length all was brought into agreement.

Warner Lake, Lake County. Warner Lake post office was in the south part of Warner Valley. There never was a geographic feature in Oregon called Warner Lake. Instead the name Warner Lakes was used collectively for a string of lakes, ponds, and playas in the Warner Valley. However, there was a Warner Lake post office which was established August 28, 1889, with Alvin N. Bennett, first postmaster. This post office was about eight miles southwest of Adel. It remained in service until July 31, 1924.

Warner Mountain, Lane County. This mountain is in the big bend of Middle Fork Willamette River south of Oakridge. It was named for Fred Warner, an early settler on the stream. Warner was a hunter and came to

Oregon in 1853, according to information furnished by his granddaughter, Mrs. Lina A. Flock of Oakridge, in 1927.

Warner Valley, Harney and Lake counties. There are several geographic features in Oregon named for Brevet Captain William Horace Warner who was killed by Indians in September, 1849, just over the line in northern California. These features include, besides the valley, the Warner Lakes, former Warner Lake post office, and Warner Canyon just north of Lakeview. There is no Warner Lake in Oregon, the term Warner Lakes being a collective name. The peak east of Warner Valley, once known as Warner Mountain, is now universally known as Hart Mountain. Arrowsmith's map of North America, corrected to 1832-33, shows a string of lakes connected by Plants River in the locality of what is now called Warner Valley. Plants River and the lakes are also shown on the map of the Territory of Oregon, prepared by direction of Colonel J. J. Abert of the U. S. Topographical Engineers, 1838. The compiler is of the opinion that John Work of the Hudson's Bay Company visited the Warner Valley October 12-15, 1832. See *California Historical Society Quarterly,* September, 1943, page 203. Work left the main party to explore what "might with propriety be called the valley of the lakes," and there is an implication that the old hands had been there before. When Work made his little exploration, he took along C. Plante and J. Favel, two of his good men. Charles Plante was also known as Plant and it seems obvious that Plants River bears his name. Work gives a good description of Warner Valley and its string of lakes. Fremont explored what is now known as Warner Valley in December, 1843, and named one of the Warner Lakes Christmas Lake. This was probably Hart Lake of the present day. For many years the Warner Valley was known as Christmas Lake Valley, but the name of Christmas Lake was transferred to another and much less important body of water by a curious transfer that the writer is unable to explain. See under Christmas Lake. Captain Warner, together with Lieutenant R. S. Williamson, left Sacramento in August, 1849, for the purpose of exploring the upper reaches of Pit River. Unfortunate delays hindered the work. Finally the leaders separated, Williamson remained at Goose Lake, while Warner went north to Lake Abert, and then to Warner Valley. He worked south along the west edge of the valley until his party was ambushed and massacred. Williamson gives September 26, 1849, as the date of the massacre, and his map shows the place just south of the 42nd parallel. Williamson's map in Pacific Railroad Surveys *Reports* is on a large scale and shows the site of the massacre about four miles south of the state line. In 1864, Lieutenant-Colonel C. S. Drew of the First Oregon Cavalry, during the Owyhee Reconnoissance, visited and named Warner Valley for the murdered officer, in the belief that Warner had been killed in the valley itself. Drew says in his report that John S. Drum of Jacksonville told him later that Warner was killed in Surprise Valley, and not in Oregon. Drum was a member of the party that went to find Warner's remains in 1850. While it seems apparent that Warner was killed south of the state line, and not in Warner Valley, it also seems clear that he was not killed as far south as Surprise Valley. The massacre was possibly near Eightmile Creek. For additional information about Warner's death, see *Gold Rush,*

Columbia University, New York, 1944, page 624, *et seq.* The principal lakes and playas of Warner Valley, beginning on the north, are as follows:

Bluejoint Lake.	Flagstaff Lake.	Hart Lake.
Stone Corral Lake.	Mugwump Lake.	Crump Lake.
Lower Campbell Lake.	Swamp Lake.	Pelican Lake.
Campbell Lake.	Anderson Lake.	

The best information about Warner Valley may be obtained from the co-operative irrigation report issued by the state engineer entitled *Warner Valley and White River Projects.*

Warren, Columbia County. Warren post office was established on February 19, 1885. James Gill, later a resident of Newberg, named the place for his old home, Warren, Massachusetts. In 1888 the post office was discontinued and when it was reestablished two years later it was named Gillton, for Gill. This was due to the fact that there was another post office called Warren in Umatilla County. Some years later the post office in Umatilla County was discontinued and Gillton, Columbia County, was changed to Warren again. The place formerly called Warren in Umatilla County is now known as Myrick.

Warren, Umatilla County. Warren was a station on the Northern Pacific Railway about five miles southwest of Helix, named for a local family. The post office was in service from December 18, 1888, to March 26, 1895, with William O. Warren postmaster. From time to time there was confusion between this place and Warren in Columbia County. The name of the station in Umatilla County was changed to Myrick in compliment to another local family. Myrick post office was established August 1, 1902, with John W. Myrick first of several postmasters. The office operated, but not continuously, until March 31, 1908, but the compiler is informed that the station is still in service.

Warren Creek, Hood River County. Warren Creek and the lake of the same name were named for Warren Cooper, an early USFS ranger and son of David R. Cooper. The curious diversion tunnel was constructed by the OSHD in 1938 to control runoff water.

Warren Creek, Linn County. Warren Creek flows into Calapooia River east of Brownsville. It was named for Andrew J. Warren, a pioneer resident. He married Eliza Spalding, daughter of a pioneer missionary of the Oregon country, the Reverend Henry H. Spalding.

Warrendale, Multnomah County. Warrendale was a post office in eastern Multnomah County serving the territory west of Bonneville. Warrendale was named for Frank M. Warren, Sr., a pioneer fish packer of Oregon, and a prominent citizen of Portland. He was drowned in the wreck of the *Titanic* in April, 1912.

Warrenton, Clatsop County. Warrenton gets its name from D. K. Warren, an early settler. The community of Lexington, which was laid out in 1848, was the forerunner of Warrenton and was the first county seat of Clatsop County. Lexington was a post office in the early history of the state. The site of Lexington was near the south limits of Warrenton and about where Skipanon station is now situated. The name Lexington fell into disuse and for many years the territory where Warrenton is now was known as Skipanon. Small boats went up Skipanon River to the place called Skipanon, or Upper Landing, and there unloaded passengers and goods for Clatsop Plains. Warrenton near the mouth of the river was platted by its proprietor in 1889 and the development of the community immediately began around Warrenton, with the result that Skipanon ceased to be of equal importance. For additional information see under Skipanon. Most of Skipanon is now within the city limits of Warrenton, although it is about a mile away from the business part of Warrenton. For reminiscences of D. K. Warren, see *OHQ*, volume III, page 296.

Warrior Point, Columbia County. Warrior Point is the north end of Sauvie Island, and Warrior Rock is on the Columbia River side of the island a little to the south. The following quotation from Vancouver's *Voyage of Discovery* for October 28, 1792, indicates the reason for naming this point: "About three and a half miles from Oak Point Mr. Broughton arrived at another, which he called Point Warrior, in consequence of being there surrounded by twenty-three canoes, carrying from three to twelve persons each, all attired in their war garments, and in every other respect prepared for combat." Lieutenant Broughton made peace with these Indians, and no bloodshed ensued. The modern use Warrior Point has been approved by the USBGN. It is not possible to tell at this time if Broughton had his adventure at the point or at the rock not far away, but the latter is more likely.

Wasco, Sherman County. Wasco owes its inception to the fact that the old Oregon emigrant trail and the road south from the Columbia River, intersected at this point. Despite its early establishment, it was not incorporated until 1898. It was named for Wasco County, in which it was formerly situated, before Sherman County was formed. The first post office in the locality was called Spanish Hollow. It was established March 2, 1870, with Jesse Eaton postmaster. The name of the office was changed to Wasco on March 17, 1882.

Wasco, Wasco County. The postal history of Wasco County is complicated by the fact that when the county was established, it was of magnificent proportions. It is difficult to localize some of these early offices, as they may have been anywhere in eastern Oregon. Many are not shown on available maps. Some of the names are in duplicate. A post office called Wasco was in operation in Wasco County from August 26, 1868, until June 3, 1872, with William D. Gilliam postmaster. This office was apparently not for the locality now named Wasco, in Sherman County. It was a few miles east of what is now Dufur, and it was of course named for the county.

Wasco County. When Wasco County was created, January 11, 1854, it comprised all the area of Oregon Territory between the Cascade Range and the Rocky Mountains, an empire in itself. By successive takings for other states and counties, the land area of Wasco County has been reduced to 2387 square miles. Wasco is the modern name for a tribe of Indians. Early writers used the name in many forms. Ross in *Fur Hunters of the Far West*, volume I, page 186, speaks of the *Wiss-co-pam* tribe. Lee and Frost in *Ten Years in Oregon*, page 176, give *Was-co-pam*. For references to various

spellings, see *Handbook of American Indians*, volume II, page 918. About the
time of the immigrations white people shortened the name to *Wasco*. The
Wasco Indians were a Chinook tribe, formerly living on the south side of
the Columbia River, in the vicinity of The Dalles. The name *Wasco* is said to
be derived from the Wasco word *wacq-o*, meaning a cup or small bowl made
of horn. The *Handbook of American Indians*, volume II, page 917, says this
referred to a cup-shaped rock near the main village of the tribe, but Dr.
William C. McKay, in an article in The Dalles *Mountaineer*, May 28, 1869,
says that the name *Wasco* meant makers of basins, and that the literal meaning of the word was horn basin. Some of these basins were fantastically
carved. Both of the explanations may be correct. Dr. McKay says that the
locality of the city of The Dalles was called *Winquatt*, signifying a place
surrounded by bold cliffs.

Washboard Ridge, Lane County. This ridge is near the summit of the
Calapooya Mountains just north of the Douglas County line. The descriptive name was given by USFS ranger Fred Asam.

Washburn Butte, Linn County. This butte is in the southwest part of
section 18, township 13 south, range 2 west. It was named for James A.
Washburn, a pioneer landowner nearby. It is about three miles north of
Brownsville.

Washington, Yamhill County. There have been but two post offices in
Oregon using the name of the first president. The first of these offices was
known as Washington Butte. Its short history will be found under the name
Lebanon. This post office, strictly speaking, was named for George Washington indirectly, because it was named for a nearby geographic feature. A
post office called Washington was in service in southern Yamhill County
from September 30, 1858, to October 13, 1860. Edward Dupuis was the
only postmaster. While it is probable that Dupuis selected the name of this
office the compiler has no written record to that effect. The name of the
Dupuis family has been applied to a Yamhill County stream which flows
into Deer Creek a little to the northeast of Sheridan. The name of this
stream is generally given as Dupee Creek due to the inability of later settlers to struggle successfully with the French spelling. The compiler has not
been able to determine the exact location of the Washington post office in
Yamhill County.

Washington County. When the Oregon country was divided into counties by an act approved July 5, 1843, four districts were created. That part
of the country between the Willamette River and the Pacific Ocean, north
of Yamhill River, was called Twality. This is an Indian name and it is
spelled in many different ways. For information about the origin of the
name, see under Tualatin River. That part of Oregon originally lying in
Twality District was subsequently divided into several counties. The first of
these districts, or counties, to be cut off of Twality District was Clatsop
District, which was created June 22, 1844. On September 3, 1849, the territorial legislature passed an act changing the name of Twality County to
Washington County, in honor of the first president of the United States,
the act providing: "That the name of the county commonly called 'Twality'
or 'Falatine' be and the same is hereby changed to Washington." The name
Twality is so spelled in the written bills introduced in the legislature in

1849, but in the endorsements on the backs of the bills the word is Tuality. The law as printed in *Local Laws,* 1850 session, page 54, uses the spelling Tualitz. The z is probably a typographical error for a written y.

Wasson Creek, Coos County. Wasson Creek was named for George Wasson, a pioneer settler. The creek flows into Winchester Creek southeast of Cape Arago. See Dodge's *Pioneer History of Coos and Curry Counties,* page 16.

Wastina, Lake County. The postmaster at Wastina in 1925 wrote the compiler that Wastina was a name of Indian origin and that it meant beautiful valley. He gave no indication as to what tribe used the word. *Wastina* is not found in the dictionary of the Klamath language. The office operated from 1915 to 1925.

Water Tower Mountain, Marion County. When the Oregon Pacific Railroad was built to Detroit in 1889, a water tank was built at the mouth of Mayflower Creek just west of Detroit Dam. For a time the creek was known as Watertank Creek but the original name prevailed and the only memento is Water Tower Mountain at the top of the watershed.

Water Trough Canyon, Crook County. This canyon emptying into McKay Creek takes its name from an old watering trough on the Gail Demaris ranch.

Waterloo, Linn County. W. H. Klum of Lebanon informed the writer in December, 1926, that he was born and reared on the Klum donation land claim, and one of his first recollections was the saw and grist mill built by Elmore Kees at the falls of South Santiam River. The place was known as Kees Mill. After Kees died his widow leased the property to John F. Backensto. There was litigation among the Kees heirs and other persons. John Ambler, a local wit, suggested the name Waterloo after a court decision was handed down giving a substantial victory to one party to the contest. See story in Lebanon *Express,* September 16, 1937. Waterloo post office was established by change of name from Harris Ranch on January 5, 1875, with S. D. Gager postmaster. Harris Ranch office was established June 18, 1874, with W. S. Harris postmaster. The writer does not know if it was at the same location as Waterloo or not.

Waterman, Wheeler County. Waterman is in the south central part of Wheeler County. It was named for John W. Waterman, better known as "Doc." He settled on the land where the post office was subsequently established. The place was known as Waterman Flat. Waterman belonged to the cattle firm of Smith & Waterman. There was at one time a post office not far from this place known as Caleb, for Caleb N. Thornburg. Thornburg at one time had stock at Spanish Gulch in John Day Valley and was receiver of the land office in The Dalles.

Waterman Mine, Wheeler County. This mine and a homestead both near Antone were another center of operations for John W. Waterman, the founder of Waterman.

Waters Creek, Curry County. M. S. Brainard of Brookings told the compiler in 1967 that this creek entering Rogue River just north of Illinois River was named for George M. Waters who lived nearby at the turn of the century.

Waterspout Creek, Wallowa County. This stream occupies a canyon that drains into Snake River in township 2 south, range 50 east. It was named by the Warnock brothers because of the heavy floods that washed so much material down to Snake River.

Waterspout Gulch, Grant County. Waterspout Gulch drains into John Day River just north of Picture Gorge. It is common practice in certain sections of Oregon, Washington and Idaho to name streams and gulches Waterspout, not because of the frequency of waterspouts, but because of the excessive flood discharge after cloudbursts. The terrific effect of these floods is nowhere more noticeable than along the canyon of Snake River between Riparia and Huntington. Great masses of boulders and earth are swept down narrow defiles and into the main stream in quantities sufficient to form serious obstructions in the river.

Watkins, Jackson County. For nearly thirty years Watkins was a post office in the upper Applegate River Valley near the mouth of Squaw Creek. The office was established in March, 1893, with the name of the first postmaster, Mark Watkins. The office operated in this locality until November 30, 1920, when it was closed out to Jacksonville.

Watson, Malheur County. The post office at Watson was established in July, 1898. It was named for Harry Watson, a local stockman. Robert J. Ivers was the first postmaster.

Watson Cabin, Douglas County. Alma Watson wrote the compiler in 1967 that this cabin a mile and a half northwest of Red Butte was built in 1903 by Clair Watson, her husband's cousin, to prove up a timber claim. She said: "It was a nice one room cabin with a separate screened cooler over the creek, a nice place to keep a deer so the flies couldn't get it." She added that the hunters always stayed there the first night out from Wolf Creek but the author imagines the venison was more often poached than fried.

Watson Mountain, Douglas County. This 2288 foot peak three miles southeast of Glide was named for James Watson who took up a donation land claim near its base in 1854.

Waucoma Ridge, Hood River County. Waucoma Ridge is a spur off the main divide of the Cascade Range. It is in the northwest part of the county and separates the drainage of Hood River on the east from that of Eagle and Herman creeks to the west. Around the city of Hood River *waucoma* is said to be an Indian word meaning cottonwood tree, and it was used sometimes to refer to the locality because of the trees near the Columbia and Hood rivers. The compiler has not been able to learn what tribe used the expression. There are probably no cottonwood trees on Waucoma Ridge and the name seems to have been applied to that feature by white people because it has a pleasing sound.

Waud Bluff, Multnomah County. Old maps show this as Waid Bluff, but an investigation by government authorities disclosed the fact that Waud Bluff is correct, the name coming from an old settler, John Waud. Waud Bluff is on the east bank of the Willamette River north of Swan Island. Waud's donation land claim was north of the bluff.

Wauna, Clatsop County. For the origin of the name Wauna, see under Wauna Point. The name was applied to the Clatsop County community by Alfred W. Clark. Wauna post office was established January 21, 1911, with James Pollock first postmaster, and closed prior to 1980.

Wauna Point, Multnomah County. Wauna is an Indian name, probably Klickitat. It describes a mythological being supposed to represent the Columbia River. See *The Bridge of the Gods,* by F. H. Balch. Wauna Point is on the Columbia River Highway between Tanner Creek and Eagle Creek. The highest point of the bluff near the river is about 2500 feet in elevation.

Wauneka Point, Multnomah County. This point is just south of the Columbia River Highway between McCord Creek and Moffett Creek. It bears the Indian name of a locality on the south bank of the Columbia River west of Bonneville.

Waverly Lake, Linn County. This lake is not large, but it has a pleasing aspect. It is just east of Albany, and came into being largely because of the construction of the grades of the old and new locations of the Pacific Highway East. It lies between the two alignments and is an attractive feature of the locality. It was named Waverly Lake at the suggestion of Charles Childs, well-known Linn County resident.

Wawa Creek, Clatsop County. Wawa Creek is a small tributary to Youngs River about a mile south of Youngs River Falls. *Wawa* is the Chinook jargon word for talk and may have been applied to the stream because the water makes a noise flowing over the gravel.

Weaver, Douglas County. This small community about two miles south of Myrtle Creek on South Umpqua River was named for William and Anna Weaver who settled nearby in 1851. Weaver Creek, a tributary of South Myrtle Creek, was named for the same family.

Weaver Creek, Lane County. This tributary of Brice Creek north of Elephant Mountain was named for one Weaver who got lost and died nearby in the early days. This information was supplied by Loren W. Hunt of Cove who spent his boyhood near Disston.

Weaver Gulch, Marion County. Weaver Gulch lies just east of Pacific Highway East, a mile north of Looney Butte. It was named for David Weaver, who took up a donation land claim nearby.

Web, Yamhill County. This station, northeast of Newberg, was named by consolidating the initials of W. E. Burke, a well-known politician of Portland, who owned land nearby. The station was not in service in 1940.

Webfoot Creek, Baker County. Webfoot Creek is near the old mining community of Auburn and lies just east of California Gulch. It was the favored area of the Oregon miners while the California Tarheads stayed on the other side of the ridge. See also under the heading California Gulch.

Wecoma, Lincoln County. John Gill in his *Dictionary of the Chinook Jargon,* 1909, says that *wecoma* is the jargon word for sea. The community of Wecoma is in the north part of Lincoln County, overlooking the ocean.

Wedderburn, Curry County. Wedderburn was established by R. D. Hume, a prominent Pacific Coast business man, who had fishing interests at the mouth of Rogue River. He named the community for an ancestral home in Scotland. Literally, Wedderburn means Sheep Creek. *Wedder* is an old form of wether, and *burn* is of course a stream or brook.

Weekly, Douglas County. A post office named Weekly was established on the Coos County list on September 24, 1883, but about the same time it was moved to the Douglas County list and there it remained until it was discontinued February 25, 1884. Smith Baily was the only postmaster. All

the evidence available is to the effect that the office was at the west edge of
Douglas County, probably about twenty miles west of Roseburg on the Rose-
burg-Coos Bay stage road. The Weekly family was well known, especially in
Coos County and some members were interested in the construction of the
road. It is probable that Weekly post office was at or near the place called
Reston, a stage station on the road and a post office from 1890 to 1934.
Edmond E. Weekly was the first postmaster at Reston and was the proprie-
tor of the station.

Weekly Creek, Coos County. The correct spelling of this name is
Weekly and not Weakly, as sometimes written. The stream is a tributary of
East Fork Coquille River about one mile east of Gravelford. It was named
for a pioneer family of the Coquille Valley.

Wegner Creek, Umatilla County. Julius F. Wegner was born in Wallin,
Germany in 1845 and came to this country as a young man. After living in
Pilot Rock for a number of years, he homesteaded on the upper reaches of
the creek near Wegner Spring in 1885.

Wehrli Canyon, Gilliam County. William Wehrli came to Gilliam
County from California in 1884 and filed on a homestead northwest of
Mayville. For a brief biography see *Illustrated History of Central Oregon,* page
587.

Welches, Clackamas County. Welches was named for Samuel Welch,
who took up a homestead nearby in 1882. The post office was established
in 1905.

Wellen, Jackson County. Wellen is the neighborhood of the home of
H. von der Hellen. He named it for the estate of his ancestors in Germany.

Well Spring, Morrow County. Well Spring has been well known since
the days of the immigrations. It is south of Boardman and close to Juniper
Canyon, and the exact location may be found on the USGS map of the Well
Spring quadrangle. Well Spring is mentioned in several early journals written on the Oregon Trail, and was probably named because it was enlarged
into a well. The compiler has been unable to associate the name of anybody
called Wells with the spring.

Wells, Benton County. Wells was named for a man locally known as
"Red" Wells, who owned a donation land claim nearby in pioneer days.
Wells post office was established February 24, 1880, with James Gingles
first postmaster. The railroad station was put in service about the same
time, but some years later the name of the station was changed to Wellsdale
to avoid confusion with another Wells 'on the Southern Pacific railroad.
Wells post office was continued with that name until February, 1936, when
it was closed to Corvallis. The station name is still Wellsdale as of 1980.

Wemme, Clackamas County. Wemme is a place on the Mount Hood
Loop Highway about four miles west of Rhododendron, named for a public spirited citizen of Portland, E. Henry Wemme, who was instrumental in
getting the Barlow Road into the possession of the State of Oregon. This
road was for many years a toll road, but in 1912 Wemme bought it for
$5400. After making a number of desirable improvements, Wemme died,
but not before making arrangements to bequeath the road to the public. It
is now incorporated in part in the Mount Hood Loop Highway. Wemme

post office was established June 21, 1916, with Leonard A. Wrenn first postmaster.

Wenaha River, Wallowa County. This stream is also called Salmon River, but that name is unsatisfactory because of the more important Salmon River nearby in Idaho. J. H. Horner of Enterprise informed the compiler that the name Wenaha is derived from the Indian family or sub-tribe name Wenak, with a ha added to indicate the land governed by the sub-chief Wenak. See under Imnaha.

Wenaka, Wallowa County. This place was to have been called Wenaha, but postal authorities at Washington mistook the spelling and changed the "h" to "k."

Wendling, Lane County. Wendling was named for Geo. X. Wendling, a prominent Pacific Coast lumberman and at one time a director of The Booth-Kelly Lumber Company. The post office was established in 1899 and the first postmaster was Geo. H. Kelly.

Wendson, Lane County. Wendson is a railroad station northeast of Cushman. The name was condensed from that of the Wendling-Johnson Lumber Company.

Wendt Ditch, Baker County. Henry Wendt came to Baker County in the 1860s and eventually filed on land near Bridgeport in 1885.

Wesley, Benton County. Wesley got its name from the given name of the first postmaster, Wesley C. Keeton. The office was established in September, 1900, and was discontinued in October, 1903. It was on the extreme west edge of the county and about five miles east of Harlan. Some maps show Wesley on the extreme east edge of Lincoln County, but the postal records in Washington put the office in Benton County.

West Buker Spring, Wheeler County. This spring southwest of Antone near the Crook County line was named for Hal Buker, one of a number of brothers who ranched near the head of Pine Creek. The compiler has been unable to locate East Buker Spring.

West Chehalem, Yamhill County. West Chehalem is an area name, given in contradistinction to East Chehalem or Chehalem as it was more generally known. Chehalem meant the locality now usually called Newberg and vicinity. West Chehalem was on the upper reaches of Chehalem Creek six or eight miles northwest of Newberg. West Chehalem post office was established as early as November 20, 1865, with Isaac Rogers first postmaster. The office operated until July 31, 1900, when it was closed to Gaston. West Chehalem post office moved to fit the availability of postmasters, but it was generally in the northwest part of township 3 south, range 3 west. In recent years there has been no specific community called West Chehalem.

West Creek, Clatsop County. West Creek is near Westport and was named for John West, who settled in the vicinity in pioneer days. See under Westport.

West Creek, Tillamook County. West Creek near Beaver was named for a local settler, Walter West.

West Fork, Douglas County. West Fork was a railroad station on the Southern Pacific line in Cow Creek Canyon at the mouth of West Fork Cow Creek. The post office name was Dothan. See under that heading.

West Lake, Clatsop County. This is a long, narrow lake on Clatsop Plains south of Carnahan station. It was named for Josiah West, a pioneer landowner. The Oregon Coast Highway crosses the north end of this lake north of the old West homestead. For story about Josiah West and the building of the West house, see *Sunday Oregonian,* December 1, 1946, magazine section.

West Linn, Clackamas County. This is the successor to Linn City, which was established as Robins Nest by Robert Moore, a pioneer of 1840. Moore took a prominent part in organizing the provisional government, and bought the *Oregon Spectator* in 1850. In 1844 the legislature authorized him to operate a ferry between Oregon City and Robins Nest. On December 22, 1845, the legislature named the locality of his home Linn City, for Lewis F. Linn of Missouri. See under Linn County. A flood swept away the place in 1861. Linn community is now incorporated with the name of West Linn. Linn City post office was established January 8, 1850, with James M. Moore postmaster. The name was changed to West Linn on February 18, 1854.

West Portland, Multnomah County. The name West Portland is used to describe the area near the crossing of Barbur Boulevard and Capitol Highway. There was a West Portland School and the name is otherwise perpetuated in West Portland addition that lies generally south and southwest of Multnomah. In the 1890s a steam motor carline extended into the territory by way of Fulton Park. West Portland post office was established July 21, 1890, with Henry J. Osfield first postmaster. This office continued in service until March 15, 1907, when it was closed out to Hillsdale. In August, 1946, Werner Raz, superintendent of the Multnomah branch of the Portland post office, wrote that for a time the old West Portland office was housed in a building numbered 4623 Southwest Taylors Ferry Road, a short distance west of Capitol Highway. Mr. Raz added that the building was being demolished.

West Side, Lake County. This post office was named by Will C. Fleming, who was the first postmaster when the office was established in June, 1923. It was named for the West Side Store, which was on the west side of Goose Lake. The office was closed July 31, 1942.

West Stayton, Marion County. West Stayton railroad station was established on the Oregonian Railway narrow gauge line in the 1880s to serve the locality about four miles west of Stayton. The railroad did not go through Stayton, and West Stayton was the nearest shipping point on the narrow gauge. The station was of course named in contradistinction to Stayton. For origin of name see under Stayton. In the latter 1880s a post office was petitioned for to serve the locality of West Stayton, but postal authorities refused to establish an office with the name West Stayton for fear of mail confusion and suggested that the local people interested should choose another name. A meeting was held and Hugh McNeil suggested the name Ale which was short, and duplicated no other post office in the country. Mrs. Maude Porter Boone of Aumsville informed the compiler that the name was suggested by the finding of an empty ale bottle beside the road near the station. Ale post office was established on December 18,

1888, with Levi J. Hollister postmaster. The office was discontinued on July 26, 1890. It was opened again on January 21, 1891, with Henry B. Condit postmaster. Mr. Condit ran the office, in conjunction with the railroad station West Stayton, until September 3, 1902, when Ale post office was closed due to the extension of rural free delivery from Aumsville. The later development of the locality brought new demands for a post office, and West Stayton office was established October 12, 1911, with D. M. McInnis first postmaster. This office was closed July 31, 1953.

West Union, Washington County. The name West Union, applied to various places in Washington County, is of great historic interest and has been in use over a century. On May 25, 1844, a few members of the Baptist Church met in the cabin of David T. Lenox, a pioneer of 1843, who had taken up a claim on the north part of Tualatin Plains. A constitution and covenant was drawn up for the West Union Baptist Church, the first Baptist Church established west of the Rocky Mountains. The text of this document, as printed in the *OHQ* for September 1935, contains the express statement that the churchmen "have been thrown together in these Wilds of the West, and . . .Agree that we Constitute and come into union." West Union Baptist Church was built in 1853 on a site given by Lenox on the east edge of his claim. The congregation met in the new church on December 24 and 25, 1853. The church still stands on the Germantown Road about a mile northwest of the community of West Union. West Union post office was established January 27, 1874, with Stephen A. Holcomb first postmaster. This office was in operation until March 17, 1894. The writer does not know its exact location, but it was probably near the present community of West Union, which is close to the Holcomb claim. West Union community does not now have a post office. It is at an intersection just south of the Germantown Road and about a mile and a half northwest of Bethany.

West Woodburn, Marion County. West Woodburn originated when the Oregon Electric Railway was built in 1907. The line ran on a tangent that missed Woodburn by about two miles and a spur was built east to the downtown area by the Southern Pacific tracks. This spur has long since been torn up while a large, new, populated section of Woodburn has grown around the I5 freeway exit which is about halfway between the two places. For information about origin of the name, see under Woodburn. West Woodburn post office was established in May, 1912, with M. J. McCormick first postmaster. The office was closed in March, 1934.

Westfall, Malheur County. Westfall was named for Levi Westfall, a pioneer who settled in Bully Creek Valley. The post office was first established with the name Bully in April, 1882, but was changed to Westfall in February, 1889. It was at one time on the old Westfall ranch about two miles east of the present site of the town of Westfall.

Westfir, Lane County. Westfir was named for the Western Lumber Company. The name was first used July 19, 1923, according to a letter written the compiler by W. J. Norris. The Western Lumber Company was a large producer of fir lumber. The post office was established in November, 1923. Subsequently the lumber operations were taken over by the Edward Hines Lumber Company and the community was operated as a company town. Hines closed its mill in 1977 and sold the town along with the public facilities including water, sewers and the like. The new owners wished these utilities in public ownership and in January, 1979 the residents voted to incorporate.

Westimber, Washington County. Westimber, a post office and railroad station west of the town of Timber, was named on that account. The railroad station was formerly called West Timber but about 1918 the railroad company changed the name to one word to agree with the post office name. The post office was established in 1916 with L. R. Kern postmaster, and closed January 25, 1935.

Westlake, Lane County. Westlake post office derives its name from the fact that the town site it serves is on the west shore of Siltcoos Lake. This community was established by W. P. Reed in 1914 and the post office was installed in September, 1915. The community was incorporated in 1962 with the name Dunes City. See under that heading.

Westland, Umatilla County. Westland was a railroad station near the west bank of Umatilla River, about eight miles west of Stanfield, named because of its westward position as compared with other communities in the lower Umatilla River area. Westland came into being as a result of the construction by the railroad of the Messner-Hinkle cutoff. Westland post office was established August 17, 1917, with Henry T. Schroeder first postmaster. This post office was closed January 14, 1922, and the railroad station was no longer in service as of February 1972.

Weston, Umatilla County. Weston was named for Weston, Missouri, by T. T. Lieuallen. Lieuallen came from the Missouri town and named his home in Oregon after his old home in the middle West. He was first postmaster at Weston, Oregon. The writer has been informed by those who say they knew that Lieuallen said on several occasions that he intended to name the place Western, but the postal authorities circumvented him. In Carey's *History of Oregon,* it is said that Western was the name Lieuallen picked on, but this does not agree with other reports that have been received by the compiler. A post office named Mitchell's Station was established in February, 1867, with W. H. Abell postmaster. The name of this office was changed to Weston in September, 1869, at which time Lieuallen became postmaster. The compiler has been unable to learn if Mitchell's Station was at the present location of Weston, or if it was moved in 1869 when the name was changed.

Westport, Clatsop County. John West settled in this locality about 1850, and the place was named for him. West was born in Linlithgowshire, Scotland, in 1809, and came to Oregon by way of Quebec and California. He was known as Captain West and was a millwright and lumberman. He ran a sawmill at Westport and also a salmon cannery. He died in 1887 and his widow, Margaret West, also a native of Scotland, died in 1894. For information about John West, and his large family, see article by Fred Lockley in the *Oregon Journal,* January 31, 1943. Westport post office was established in December, 1863.

Wests Butte, Clackamas and Wasco counties. This butte is on the summit of the Cascade Range about five miles southeast of Timothy Lake. It was named for John I. West who settled near Wapinitia about 1880.

according to the Bureau of the Census, has a land area of 1707 square miles. It was named for Henry H. Wheeler, who was born in Erie County, Pennsylvania, September 7, 1826, of English and German ancestry; went to Wisconsin in 1855; drove an ox team from Wisconsin to Yreka, California, by way of Salt Lake, in 1857, in company with a family named Wells; came to Oregon in 1862 and located at The Dalles in 1867, but soon went to the Salmon River mines in Idaho. Mining being unprofitable, he secured work driving a stage. He returned to The Dalles, and began farming and stock raising in the vicinity of Mitchell, Oregon, where he remained until his death, March 26, 1915. He was married December 19, 1875, to Dorcas L. Monroe, who died at Mitchell in March, 1911.

Wheeler Creek, Curry County. This creek rises on the south slopes of Mount Emily and flows into East Fork Winchuck River. It was named for James P. Wheeler who settled near its mouth before the turn of the century.

Wheeler Creek, Crater Lake National Park, Klamath County. This stream was named for James H. Wheeler, of Fort Klamath, one time deputy sheriff. Wheeler was a trapper and spent a great deal of time, often alone for long periods, in the mountains with his traps.

Whelpley, Jackson County. Whelpley post office was established in July, 1882, and ran along to the following April when it was discontinued and the business turned over to Deskins post office. Whelpley post office was named for the postmaster, Thomas H. Whelpley. The compiler has not been able to find this place on any map. It is apparent from the fact that the office was closed to Deskins that it must have been in the upper Rogue River country. The name Deskins post office was later changed to Prospect.

Whetstone Creek, Clackamas and Marion counties. This stream is on the northeast slope of Whetstone Mountain and flows northward. The creek was named by John Paine and Preston Pendleton, familiarly known as Doc Pendleton, because of the prevalence of a rock that could be used to sharpen knives.

Whetstone Point, Jackson County. This point is a prominent place near the south end of Bald Mountain, west of Rogue River and a few miles southwest of Prospect. It was named because of the local occurrence of a slate rock which forms a good abrasive whetstone for sharpening blades. The rock splits into suitable shapes and sizes.

Whiskey Creek, Tillamook County. Mrs. Mildred Edner of Netarts told the compiler the humorous incident concerning the naming of this creek. One Charles Wiley had a campground on Netarts Spit. This was an eight or nine mile trip with a team and wagon and late starters would often spend a night along the way. Two couples travelling together were benighted at this stream and while the wives made camp, the men took the whiskey keg to cool in the creek. The cooling apparently required continuous supervision and the wives were unable to get the men to perform the routine chores such as gathering firewood. The matter was resolved and the creek named when the ladies dumped the whiskey in the creek and broke up the keg for the campfire.

Whisky Creek, Jackson County. This stream is a tributary to Rogue

Wetmore, Wheeler County. Wetmore community was establish
1942 about eleven miles northeast of Kinzua at a location used by the
zua Pine Mills Company in handling logs in northeast Wheeler Cou1
was named for the late E. D. Wetmore of Warren, Pennsylvania, a
stockholder in the logging and lumbering concern who had prev
named Kinzua for Kinzua, Pennsylvania. The post office was establis1
the summer of 1945, and discontinued July 8, 1948.

Weygandt Canyon, Hood River County. In 1899 Marcus W.
gandt homesteaded near the mouth of this canyon between Evans
and East Fork Hood River. Weygandt, usually known as Mark, was
the early guides on the north side of Mount Hood.

Whale Cove, Lincoln County. Whale Cove is a well-known place
Oregon Coast Highway at the north base of Cape Foulweather. The
ler was told about 1930 that it was named many years before by a p
white people who found some Indians busy at work on the carcass of
whale. Despite the aroma, Indians were enthusiastic over a whale ste2

Whalehead Island, Curry County. This rocky islet is in the
Ocean, close to the shore twenty miles south of Gold Beach. It is ho
seaward and has a hole in the top so that at certain stages of the tid
rushes into the cavity and spouts out the hole, simulating a whale.
head Island has been so known since very early pioneer days. The
the name has included such forms as Whaleshead, Whale Head an
variations, but in 1943 the USBGN adopted the name Whalehead I≀
being the most desirable arrangement. A nearby stream is called
head Creek. Orvil Dodge, in *Pioneer History of Coos and Curry Count*
that Frances Fuller Victor's statement that Gold Beach was once kr
Whalehead is wrong.

Wheatland, Yamhill County. Wheatland is in the extreme so
corner of the county and was named in pioneer days because it
important shipping point for wheat grown on nearby lands. The pl
also called Wheatland Landing and sometimes Matheny Ferry. Wl
post office was established January 29, 1867, with Marion B. Hend1
postmaster. The office was discontinued January 31, 1903, doubt
to the extension of rural free delivery from larger offices. The are
tary to Wheatland has been extensively developed by intensified an
sified field and fruit crops.

Wheeler, Tillamook County. This place was named for Cole
Wheeler, of Portland, a prominent lumberman and sawmill opera
operated a mill in the community shortly after the railroad w
Wheeler died about 1920. For his biography, see Carey's *History of*
volume II, page 72.

Wheeler, Wheeler County. Wheeler post office was establishec
15, 1890, with Lafayette Frizzell postmaster, and continued in o
until September 5, 1895, when it was closed to Waldron. Lafe Friz:
at the Frizzell Ranch on Girds Creek about six miles north of Mitc
reported that the office was named for Henry H. Wheeler, promi1
neer resident of central Oregon, for whom Wheeler county was r
1899.

Wheeler County. Wheeler County was created February 17, 1

River, not a great way from Crater Lake. Will G. Steel says that it was named as a result of an enterprising pioneer bootlegger, who planned to take a load of whisky from Jacksonville over the mountains to Fort Klamath. Snow impeded his progress and he buried his load for the winter. Someone discovered his cache and the soldiers of Fort Klamath gradually cleaned out his stock so that when he returned in the spring there was nothing left. All this is said to have occurred about 1883. Times have not changed much.

Whisky Creek, Wallowa County. Whisky Creek drains an area northeast of Wallowa. The *Illustrated History of Union and Wallowa Counties,* page 674, gives the origin of the name. Raz Tulley, a resident of Wallowa, is authority for the statement that in the summer of 1872 traders brought a supply of whisky by pack train from Walla Walla and began to barter the firewater to the Indians for Indian goods. Local residents, including Tulley, Masterson, White, Cox, and several others, became much alarmed and went to the camp to put a stop to the business. A three-cornered fight ensued, which was won by the settlers. The kegs were broken and the whisky ran into the stream, which has been known as Whisky Creek ever since. In 1931 J. H. Horner confirmed this story, and said he got his information from W. W. White.

Whisky Hill, Clackamas County. Whisky Hill is a locality about four miles south of Aurora, on the Meridian Road just east of Pudding River. On March 9, 1945, the Oregon City *Banner-Courier* printed a letter from Mrs. Wilda Elliott Fish of Woodburn to the effect that when she was a small girl she drove through this neighborhood with her father and asked about a strange looking building with steam coming out. Her father explained it was a distillery where whisky was being made from apples. This sounds more like applejack than whisky, but either fluid carries a stout kick.

Whisky Run, Coos County. Whisky Run, just north of Coquille River, was named at the time of the Coos County gold rush of 1853-55. Excitement in the locality was at a high pitch, and it hardly seems possible that liquid stimulants were needed, but the name of the stream indicates otherwise. Remarkable stories are told of the results of panning the beach sands. The community of Randolph was established near the mouth of Whisky Run but was moved to Coquille River after the gold fever subsided.

Whitaker, Deschutes County. Whitaker post office was a short-lived establishment on the High Desert about ten miles east of Millican. The office was named for John O. Whitaker, a property owner in eastern Deschutes County. The office was established March 28, 1911, with Mary E. Gray first and only postmaster. It was discontinued August 15, 1912, with mail to Bend. Mary E. Gray later became Mrs. John O. Whitaker.

Whitcomb, Linn County. Whitcomb is a locality on Quartzville Creek about fifteen miles northeast of Sweet Home. It was named for George B. Whitcomb, who had some interests there. A stream flowing in from the northwest is called Whitcomb Creek. Whitcomb post office was established December 26, 1889, and was closed May 15, 1899. George B. Whitcomb was the postmaster. The office was out of service from April 13, 1893, until August 12, 1896.

White Bull Mountain, Linn County. White Bull Mountain, east of the site of Quartzville, was the location of one of the big gold strikes of 1864, the White Bull Ledge. A stock certificate of the Santiam Gold and Silver Mining Company dated 1864 and now in the possession of the University of Oregon Library lists the White Bull Ledge along with Dry Gulch and Driggs ledges. Quartzville community was located in Dry Gulch and Jeremiah Driggs made the first gold discovery in the area in August 1863.

White Butte, Wheeler County. George Nelson of Mitchell told the compiler that this 5664 foot high conical butte was named because it was colored white by the thick cover of dead bunchgrass. It held this cover because it was too steep for easy grazing.

White Creek, Linn County. This stream flows into Little Muddy Creek east of Harrisburg. It was named for Luther White, through whose donation land claim the creek runs. White was a pioneer surveyor for that part of Oregon.

White Horse, Baker County. The name White Horse as applied to a post office in Baker County was long a puzzle in Oregon nomenclature. The office was established February 13, 1867, with W. A. Mix postmaster and was closed on August 6 of the same year. In 1980 information from Keith and Donna Clark of Redmond and Priscilla Knuth of Portland, the meticulous investigators of early matters military, indicates beyond a doubt that the office was at or near Camp C. F. Smith on Whitehorse Creek within the confines of what later became the Whitehorse Ranch. The *Owyhee Avalanche*, Ruby City, Idaho Territory, under date of March 10, 1866 tells of Captain Walker, Mr. William Mix and others on their way through the area along with Walker's efforts to relocate Camp Alvord. This was accomplished shortly thereafter and Captain J. H. Walker, 23rd U. S. Infantry, assumed command at Camp C. F. Smith. The same paper on April 21, 1866 tells of forty men moving onto ranches along White Horse (*sic*) Creek and again, on April 13, 1867 says "Documents for the postmaster at White Horse, Baker County, Oregon, are in the Ruby City Office, which makes it probable that an office has been established at that place." At that time Baker County included all this area as Harney County was not created until 1889.

White Lake, Klamath County. This lake was so named because of the color of the lake bottom, which apparently consisted of some white diatomaceous material. The lake was an extension of the original Lower Klamath Lake, and much of its area was south of the Oregon state line and therefore in California. It was two or three miles southwest of Merrill. Irrigation and drainage projects have eliminated White Lake. White Lake City was named for the lake. One of the original promoters of the city, Mr. Bert C. Hall, was a resident of Klamath Falls in April, 1947, and kindly submitted some interesting information about the project. The Oklahoma and Oregon Townsite Company was organized to market a large number of lots which were to be made available by the passage of a bill in Congress to dispose of some Indian lands near Klamath Falls. The bill failed to pass and the company acquired the White Lake City area as a substitute townsite. The nucleus of the town was in section 16, township 41 south, range 10 east. White Lake

City boasted a bank, built by Mr. Hall, a restaurant, a newspaper and small piers for waterborne traffic. Lots in the project were sold for $15 each, assignment made by lottery. When the Southern Pacific Company extended its line from Weed northeast to Klamath Falls and Kirk, White Lake City was left off the main route of travel, and the town expired. Most of the buildings have been salvaged for nearby farm structures. Whitelake post office was established September 20, 1905, with Lillian H. Stilts first postmaster. The office was closed to Merrill December 15, 1913.

White Pine, Grant County. White Pine post office was about five miles northeast of Austin, on the Sumpter Valley railroad, near the summit of the Blue Mountains. It was established April 6, 1912, with Julius Gardinier first postmaster, and was discontinued March 15, 1918, with mail to Austin. The post office was named for the Baker White Pine Lumber Company, then operating in those parts. The mill was doubtless cutting western yellowpine rather than western whitepine.

White Point, Jackson County. White Point was a post office on the old stage road from Ashland south over the Siskiyou Mountains to Yreka. It was about sixteen miles south of Ashland. The post office was established August 8, 1883, with Edward J. Farlow first postmaster. Byron Cole took office October 17, 1883, and was apparently the cause for changing the name of the office to Colestin on April 8, 1892. Colestin office was in service for many years. The name White Point came from a conspicuous outcrop or ledge of white rock, probably some form of granite, visible from many parts of the Cottonwood Creek Valley. The Southern Pacific Company had a railroad station in this locality called White Point, shown on the USGS map of the Medford quadrangle. This station was abandoned about 1938-40. The compiler does not know if this station was in the same location as the old White Point post office or not, but is of the opinion that the old White Point post office was in about the same location as the place called Colestin, also shown on the above map. White Point station and Colestin station were about a mile apart.

White River, Hood River and Wasco counties. This stream has a descriptive name, resulting from the color of the water when glacial silt and sand are present. William Clark's map accompanying the Biddle edition of the journals of the Lewis and Clark expedition published in 1814, shows the stream with the name Skimhoox River, but the compiler has been unable to find any mention of the name in the text. Peter Skene Ogden saw the stream on Monday, December 5, 1825, and Fremont mentions it under date of November 26, 1843, but neither of these explorers commented on its color. This is not remarkable, because in the winter the amount of silt carried by White River is small. Joel Palmer, in his *Journal of Travels,* as of 1845, mentions the river in a number of places, as a branch of the Deschutes, but does not use the name White River. He makes a note of the sand. White River, as a name, probably came into use in the late 1840s, but it is not known who was the first to apply it.

White Rock, Douglas County. This is purely descriptive. The mountain has an exposed white rock formation on the west side.

Whiteaker, Marion County. Whiteaker post office was named for John

Whiteaker, first governor of Oregon, but probably not because he held that position. Governor Whiteaker was Oregon's representative in Congress when the post office was established and was probably of some help in getting the new facility. Doubtless the office was named for some such reason. Whiteaker post office was established May 3, 1880, with George W. Hunt first of four postmasters. George W. Hunt was a well-known local resident who owned property in section 23, township 8 south, range 1 west. There was a store on the east-west road near the north part of his property and this is said to be the first location of the Whiteaker post office. The Hunt place was known as the Beaver Glen farm because it was in the vale of Beaver Creek. Old maps show that this post office was moved around from time to time but it was generally a few miles north or northeast of Sublimity. The office was discontinued July 20, 1903. John Whiteaker was born in Indiana in 1820 and came to Oregon in 1852. He was first state governor of Oregon. He served one term as representative in Congress and also in several sessions of the Oregon legislature. He died in Eugene in 1902.

Whitehill, Lake County. Whitehill post office was about ten miles northwest of Paisley and just south of the south end of Summer Lake. It was named for a local topographic feature, apparently composed of some chalklike substance. The office, with one short intermission, operated from December 9, 1875, to April 28, 1879. The four postmasters were: William H. Miller, Mrs. Julia D. Hayes, William T. Hill, and Peter Withers.

Whitehorse Creek, Crater Lake National Park, Klamath County. Will G. Steel informed the compiler in 1927 that when the government forces were constructing the road from Annie Spring west toward Rogue River in 1865, a white horse was used to carry supplies, and the stream and Whitehorse Bluff nearby were undoubtedly named for this animal.

Whitehorse Ranch, Harney County. Whitehorse Ranch is one of the historic landmarks of southeast Oregon and much has been written about it. The ranch is on Whitehorse Creek, southeast of Steens Mountain. John S. Devine came to this part of Oregon about 1868 and soon was a member of the partnership of Todhunter and Devine. These two stockmen assembled a fine collection of blooded animals of one sort and another and the Whitehorse Ranch became famous throughout the West. A weather vane simulating a white horse was put on the cupola over the barn and there it has stood for many decades. This weather vane is kept carefully painted and is an object of considerable veneration. In May, 1946, James F. Abel then at Berkeley, California, wrote the compiler that the name Whitehorse Creek appears as early as 1866 on Colonel R. S. Williamson's map of the Steens Mountain country. Mr. Abel continues: "Some thirty years ago a vaquero from the ranch told me that it was named for a beautiful white horse ridden by an Indian chief who frequented that section in the early days. His statement is to some extent verified by the *Humboldt Register.* The issue of September 23, 1865, in telling of an Indian fight in Quinn River Valley has the following: 'One horse, which had often before attracted notice, was again conspicuous on this occasion—a white animal that defied all efforts to approach its rider.'" There is another mention of this white horse in the issue of December 30, 1865, where it is said that he was ridden by Black Rock Tom, a local sub-chief who was captured and killed at the Big Meadow on Humboldt River December 26, 1865. The newspaper account says that Tom did not ride his "pale horse" in the last foray and as a result the animal remained with other Indians. It is Mr. Abel's belief that Whitehorse Creek and Whitehorse Ranch owe their names to Tom's pale horse, which appears to have ranged as far north as the Alvord Valley.

Whiteman Bar, Marion County. Whiteman Bar is on the east bank of Willamette River about one mile southwest of Sidney. It was named for S. J. Whiteman who owned land nearby in pioneer days.

Whiteson, Yamhill County. The postmaster in 1926 wrote the compiler that this place was named for Henry White, who gave the right-of-way to the railroad, and laid out the townsite. Steel says it was named for William White. The reader may do his own guessing. Possibly there were two men, of the same family. A post office called Whites was established here on October 3, 1889, with Dennis A. Browne first postmaster. The name of the office was changed to Whiteson on October 2, 1890. The writer recalls that when he was a very small boy, the railroad station was also called Whites. This was the place where the old narrow gauge railroad from Portland to Airlie crossed the standard gauge line from Portland to Corvallis.

Whitewater Creek, Linn and Marion counties. This stream was named by the Marion County road surveying expedition in 1874. See article by John Minto, *OHQ*, volume IV, page 249. The name was applied because of the light colored glacial silt held in suspension by the water.

Whitewater River, Jefferson County. This stream rises on the northeast shoulder of Mount Jefferson and flows into Metolius River. It carries much glacial silt in suspension, and the name is descriptive. It was named many years ago, and for a time was known as Whitewater Creek, but this caused confusion with Whitewater Creek, a tributary of North Santiam River west of Mount Jefferson. As a result, the eastern stream is now generally known as Whitewater River.

Whitford, Washington County. This station was named for W. A. White and A. C. Bedford, prominent capitalists of New York City, who were directors of the Oregon Electric Railway Company during the early history of the line.

Whitney, Baker County. This town was named for C. H. Whitney, a pioneer landowner of the county.

Whittaker Flats, Umatilla County. In 1969 Charles Kopp of Pilot Rock informed the compiler that these flats south of Nye were named for Harry Whittaker who settled there just before the turn of the century.

Whorehouse Meadow, Harney County. In the early days "sin" was considered an unavoidable adjunct of life in the cattle and sheep country. During the summer one or more of the female entrepreneurs from Vale would set up facilities under canvas in this accessible but secluded meadow a mile east of Fish Lake. Houses of this category, wood and canvas, passed with the end of open cattle range and all that remained was the name on the slopes of Steens Mountain. In the 1960s the BLM issued a recreation map and in deference to the moralists substituted a namby-pamby name, Naughty Girl Meadow. The USGS advance sheet of the Fish Lake quadrangle followed suit but in 1971 the OGNB took strong exception to the change. As this is written, the final decision is pending before the federal arbiters. *O tempora! O mores.* The compiler is happy to add in 1981 that the old name has been restored.

Wichita, Clackamas County. Wichita station was on the interurban line about two and a half miles northeast of Milwaukie at the extreme north edge of the county. The Wichita property was developed by George Parry, who had formerly lived in Wichita, Kansas. Mr. Parry applied the name of his old home in the Midwest.

Wickiups, Deschutes County. This is an old stockman's name for a point on Deschutes River south of Crane Prairie. The place was a camp ground for Indians who gathered there to hunt and fish in the fall. They left their wickiup poles standing which gave the place its name. Wickiup Butte, elevation 4913 feet, is nearby and got its name from the locality. Wickiup Dam is also named for the locality. In 1939 the USBGN adopted the spelling Wickiup rather than Wikiup.

Wicopee, Lane County. Wicopee is a station on the Southern Pacific Company Cascade line, situated in the Salt Creek Valley southeast of Oakridge. It was named at the time the railroad was built. Wicopee is an Indian word transplanted from New York state. It is said to mean "long hill," and it probably refers to a long grade or steep climb, rather than to an elongated hill or mountain standing by itself. The compiler has no idea how the name happened to be dug up in far away New York. As far as the Indian meaning is concerned "long hill" is strictly accurate for the Lane County railroad station. It is about midway of the long climb from Oakridge up the summit of the Cascade Range. Wicopee in Lane County is not a community nor does it have a post office. It is just an operating point on the railroad with some company facilities. The name may be found in USGS Bulletin 258, *Origin of Certain Place Names in the United States,* by Henry Gannett.

Widby Loops, Clatsop County. Before World War II the lower Columbia River Highway ascended from the river level up to Clatsop Crest and part of the ascent was made by a series of hairpin bends called the Widby Loops. In 1914 J. L. Widby was resident engineer of the OSHD during the construction of these loops and an assistant, Earl Withycombe, prepared a sign reading "Widby Loops," which was nailed to a tree nearby. The name became permanently attached to this interesting example of engineering.

Widows Creek, Grant County. This stream east of Dayville was named for a widow, Mrs. S. E. Heim, who lived on the creek, and was, according to reports, a typical frontierswoman.

Wilark, Columbia County. The name of Wilark post office was made by taking the first part of Wilson and the last part of Clark. These two names occur in the Clark & Wilson Lumber Company which operated a mill at Linnton and owned timber lands in Columbia County. The post office was established in 1924 and served the camp which was logging the company timber lands.

Wilbur, Douglas County. Wilbur was named for James H. Wilbur, D. D., who was born in Lowville, New York, September 11, 1811, and died at Walla Walla, October 8, 1887. He was universally known as Father Wilbur and was one of Oregon's best-known pioneer Methodist ministers. He came to Oregon by way of Cape Horn in 1846-47. He was instrumental in founding several educational institutions, among others Umpqua Academy at Wilbur. The first building was a rough log structure on Father Wilbur's land claim upon which he settled September 8, 1853. For short history of Father Wilbur and Umpqua Academy, see *OHQ*, volume XIX, page 1. A pioneer post office with the name Laurel was established near the present site of Wilbur on October 14, 1854, with Willis Jenkins postmaster. It was discontinued in November, 1855.

Wilbur Mountain, Umatilla County. Wilbur Mountain is a prominent feature in the Blue Mountains about ten miles east of Meacham. It is almost on the southwest corner of section 6, township 1 south, range 37 east. It was named for Erastus J. Wilbur, who, as a member of the firm of Wilbur and Son, cut and milled a great deal of railroad timber from the vicinity of Wilbur Mountain.

Wild Rose Point, Douglas County. This point north of Illahee Rock was named by USFS ranger Fred Asam for the thicket of wild roses around the nearby spring.

Wilderville, Josephine County. Wilderville was named for Joseph L. Wilder, a local resident. Postal authorities inform the compiler that the first post office established at this place was called Slate Creek. It was established on September 30, 1858, with Oliver J. Evans first postmaster. The name of the office was changed to Wilderville on August 12, 1878. Joseph L. Wilder was then postmaster.

Wildhorse Creek, Umatilla County. This name is an old one. It occurs as Marron's Fork in Brouillet's *Account of the Murder of Dr. Whitman,* New York, 1853, page 55. *Marron* is a French word, meaning, among other things, a domesticated animal gone wild. Brouillet uses the name as of 1847. Kip, in *Army Life on the Pacific,* 1859, page 25, uses the form Wild Horse Creek. The origin of the name obviously had some connection with an early day experience with stock, probably by fur traders. Government map makers use the form Wildhorse.

Wildwood, Lane County. For a good many years Wildwood, with its descriptive rustic name, was an important locality in the Row River area. Wildwood post office was established January 6, 1888, with Sarah E. Kerr first of a long series of postmasters. The office was closed December 31, 1914, with papers to Disston. The office was a mile or so southeast of what was later Culp Creek post office.

Wilelada Creek, Lane County. This creek west of Foley Springs has a composite name. Ray Engels, longtime USFS ranger at McKenzie Bridge, stated that the middle section, "ela" was for Mrs. Ella Haflinger of Foley Springs. He did not know the source of the first and last syllables. Mrs. Haflinger's first husband was Peter Runey and they had two children, a son, William, and a daughter who died at an early age. It is possible that son Will provided the first syllable.

Wiley Creek, Linn County. This stream flows into South Santiam River near Foster. It bears the name of Andrew Wiley, a pioneer settler. It is also known as Rock Creek, but there are already too many creeks of that name in the state. C. H. Stewart of Albany wrote the compiler in 1927, as follows: "Andrew Wiley was a great hunter and was the pioneer explorer of the old Indian trail up the South Santiam River. Each year on his hunting expeditions he would penetrate farther into the recesses of the mountains, and in the year 1859, accompanied by two others, he made his way entirely across the Cascade Range and arrived in the locality of the present town of Sisters. He was thus the first man to discover the famous Hogg Pass. He was the chief pilot of the locators of the Willamette Valley and Cascade Mountain road project in 1866 and 1867, and the road followed the route of his memorable trip of 1859. Some surveyor has tried to change the name of Wiley Creek to Rock Creek, but the people of the vicinity still cling to the old name, and you never hear the other mentioned anywhere in the county." John Minto, in *OHQ*, volume IV, page 241, mentions this pioneer trail, but misspells it Wyley. County records substantiate the spelling Wiley.

Wilhoit, Clackamas County. John Wilhoit took up a land claim at the present location of Wilhoit post office about 1866. There were attractive mineral springs in the vicinity and Wilhoit took up the property on that account and operated a health and pleasure resort. The post office was established in 1882, and closed on September 29, 1928.

Wilkesboro, Washington County. The community of Wilkesboro was named about the time the United Railway was built through that part of Washington County. The post office was established in 1916, but the town was platted about four years before that. Wilkesboro was named for Peyton G. Wilkes, a pioneer of 1845, who settled at the present site of the community in pioneer days.

Wilkins, Lane County. Wilkins is a station north of Coburg. It was named for Mitchell Wilkins, who settled near there in 1848. See *OHQ*, volume V, page 136.

Willamette, Clackamas County. This town is on the west bank of Willamette River at the mouth of the Tualatin. It takes its name from Willamette River, which see. The locality of Oregon City was first known as Willamette Falls, and in pioneer days a community was projected on the west bank of Willamette River not far from the mouth of Clackamas River, to be called Willamette. These two places should not be confused with the town now known as Willamette, which is farther south. See under Willamette River for information about the name. A post office named Willammette Forks was established on the Linn County list on January 10, 1851, with William Spores postmaster. It was changed to the Lane County list on March 4, 1852, with the style Willamette Forks, with Mitchell Wilkins postmaster. Preston's map of 1856 shows the place close to the foothills about three miles north of Coburg. The office was operated until about 1884. Willamette post office was established in Yamhill County March 14, 1851, with John M. Forest postmaster. It was discontinued July 27, 1852. A pencil correction in the postal records changes the spelling to Willammette. John M. Forrest, who spelled his name thus, had a claim at the north bend of Lambert Slough about four miles southeast of Dayton and the office was probably in that locality. A post office named Wallamette was established August 19, 1853, with Robert V. Short postmaster. It was on the Yamhill

County list and was closed late in 1857. The Short claim was about a mile west of the present site of Wilsonville, in what is now Clackamas County.

Willamette Pass, Klamath and Lane counties. When SH 58 was completed in 1940, it was the most convenient route from the Willamette Valley to southeastern Oregon. It was also popular with California bound travelers anxious to avoid the then curvacious Douglas and Josephine county sections of US 99. The initial stretch from Goshen to Oakridge follows Middle Fork Willamette River and the road was promptly and commonly called the Willamette Highway. It crosses the Cascade Range at elevation 5126 feet about one half mile north of Odell Lake and one mile northwest of the Southern Pacific summit tunnel under Pengra Pass. On December 2, 1960 the OGNB moved to designate this Willamette Pass and the USBGN concurred in 1961 *Decision List 6103*. Historically Willamette Pass was the emigrant route crossing about one half mile west of Summit Lake and one and one half miles north of Emigrant Butte, several miles south of the present location. This original pass was renamed Emigrant Pass in simultaneous action.

Willamette River, Benton, Clackamas, Lane, Linn, Marion, Multnomah, Polk and Yamhill counties. This is the largest river entirely in the state of Oregon. Controversy over the spelling of the name continued many years. *Wal-lamt* was an Indian word, according to H. S. Lyman in *OHQ*, volume I, page 320, designating a place on the Willamette River near Oregon City on the west bank. Three ways of spelling the name have had their respective champions: *Willamette, Wallamette* and *Wallamet. Wilarmet* is the form used in David Thompson's *Narrative*, Toronto, 1916, page 493, under date of July 9, 1811. Ross Cox, in his *Adventures on the Columbia River*, gives *Wallamat* (volume II, page 135), and *Wallamut* (volume II, page 164). Alexander Ross, in *Fur Hunters of the Far West* and *First Settlers on the Oregon*, gives *Wallamitte;* Franchere gives *Wallamat* and *Willamett;* Townsend's *Narrative* gives *Wallammet;* David Douglas, 1826, gives *Willamette;* Arrowsmith's map of North America, corrected to 1832-33, gives *Wallamatte*. A map of the Territory of Oregon, prepared by direction of Colonel J. J. Abert, U. S. Topographical Engineers, 1838, and attached to several government documents, shows the lower part of the stream as *Multnomah* or *Wilhamet*. The upper part is lettered *Walla Matte*. In 1841 Charles Wilkes used the spelling Willamette and this is the style throughout *U. S. Exploring Expedition* and atlas, 1845, as well as on the large charts prepared by Wilkes. Wilkes appears to have crystallized government use in favor of Willamette. For many references to the controversy over the spelling of the name, see *OHQ*, volume XLIV, page 360. Harold Mackey in *The Kalapuyans*, page 15 *et seq*, also gives references generally supporting the various forms of *wal.* . . . The meaning of the word Willamette is not known, although there are several theories, including Mackey who says *Wallamet* means "spill water" and was applied to the river above the falls. Broughton discovered the river on October 29, 1792, and named it the River Mannings, possibly for Boatswain's Mate Samuel Manning, a member of Vancouver's expedition. Lewis and Clark did not observe the stream on their westward trip, nor on their eastward trip either until their attention was called to it by Indians after they had gone as far as Sandy River. Clark went back and entered the Willamette on April 2, 1806, calling it the Multnomah.

Willamette Slough, Multnomah County. Willamette Slough post office was in service from February 10, 1873, to February 8, 1887, at a point on the mainland northwest of Linnton, and about opposite the south end of Sauvie Island. The office may have moved from time to time depending on who was postmaster. Thomas J. Howell, Oregon's famous botanist, was first to hold the office. The office was named for the channel on the west side of Sauvie Island, formerly Willamette Slough, now officially known as Multnomah Channel.

Willamette Stone, Multnomah and Washington counties. The Willamette Stone is a surveyor's monument at the intersection of the Willamette base line and the Willamette meridian in the hills west of Portland. The mark was established on June 4, 1851, by John B. Preston, the first surveyor general of Oregon. The original mark was not a stone but a stake. This stake was officially replaced on July 25, 1885, by the present Willamette Stone. The replacement was carried on by another surveyor, W. B. Marye, and other officials, who made the replacement the occasion of a small ceremony. Preston selected the site of the Willamette Stone because it was thought at that time the meridian surveyed north from the stone would pass through the mouth of the Willamette River. The base line was established in its present location so that it would not cross the Columbia River and thus produce difficulties in surveying. In 1903 the USC&GS extended the triangulation net to include the Willamette Stone. The geographic position of the stone, based on the 1927 datum, is 45° 31' 10.831'' in north latitude and 122° 44' 33.551'' in west longitude.

Willamina, Yamhill County. The community of Willamina was named for Willamina Creek, and the stream was named for Mrs. Willamina Williams, who is said to have been the first white woman to ride a horse across it. Some written reminiscences of Enos C. Williams are on file at the Oregon Historical Society. He says that Mrs. Williams was born in 1817 in Ohio and was married to James Maley in March, 1837, apparently in Illinois. Mrs. Maley came to Oregon in 1845 with her husband and her stepdaughter and in the spring of 1846 the Maley family and a man named Burden went prospecting for land on which to settle. They found a stream flowing into South Yamhill River in the foothills of the Coast Range and named it in compliment to Mrs. Maley. Maley died in 1847 and on February 24, 1848, Enos C. Williams and Willamina Maley were married, probably in Polk County. They settled on the land on which the town of Amity was built. They were much respected citizens of Amity and are buried at the old churchyard at that place. Willamina post office was established May 29, 1855, with James Brown first postmaster. The office was on the Brown claim about a mile east of the present town of Willamina. On January 1, 1863, Jeremiah Lamson became postmaster and the office was moved to his claim nearly two miles west of the Brown place. Brown had the office again on March 24, 1865. On April 4, 1866, the office was moved to and the name was changed to Sheridan, with Thomas N. Faulconer postmaster and there it has been ever since. This shift left Willamina Creek without a post office, and on August 29, 1878, a new office was established with the name

Willamina and with Jackson Monroe postmaster. From December, 1880, to March, 1891, Willamina post office was operated just over the line in Polk County.

Willard, Marion County. The Willard area is about four miles east-southeast of Pratum and was named for Abner S. Willard, a pioneer of 1847. Willard was born in Ohio in 1827, and after reaching the Willamette Valley, settled near the middle of township 7 south, range 1 west. He died there in 1851. The Willard school district was organized as early as 1855 and in 1893 the Willard church was established. Willard post office was established in April, 1889, with Mary H. Starmer first postmaster. This office was finally closed in April, 1904.

Willbridge, Multnomah County. This station is the junction of the Astoria branch and the main line of the Burlington Northern Inc. It is southwest of the bridge over the Willamette River, and it has a composite name on that account.

Williams, Josephine County. Williams is one of three post offices in southern Oregon named because of the proximity of Williams Creek. See under Williamsburg and Williams Creek in this series of notes. In 1981 Williams post office was situated six miles southwest up Williams Creek from Provolt. Williams post office was established October 11, 1881, with David John first of a long string of postmasters. The office is still in service as this note is being written. It is about two miles west of the Jackson-Josephine county line.

Williams Canyon, Morrow County. Williams Canyon is in the south part of township 1 south, range 23 east. It apparently was named for Nathaniel Williams who filed a Timber Culture claim in the canyon in 1883. However, John A. Williams who lived near Sand Hollow in the 1880s also bought land near the canyon in 1898.

Williams Creek, Douglas County. Williams Creek rises north of North Umpqua River and flows into it about two miles west of Steamboat Creek. A USFS Forest Camp of the same name is located at the confluence of the two streams. The creek was named for Joe Williams who came from Ohio with several other families in the 1890s and settled near Lone Rock.

Williams Creek, Jackson County. Williams Creek post office was established March 14, 1876. It was out of service for a time and the compiler does not know the dates of its later history. The first postmaster was John A. Lewman. This post office was very close to the center of the northwest quarter of section 7, township 38 south, range 4 west, and was therefore about a quarter of a mile east of the present Jackson-Josephine county line. It was also about the same distance southeast of the present Provolt post office. See also under Williams and Williamsburg. The Williams Creek post office was not exactly on Williams Creek but not far from it.

Williams Creek, Josephine County. This stream flows into Applegate River. Walling, in *History of Southern Oregon,* page 458, says that it was named for Captain Robert Williams, an Indian fighter of local fame, who skirmished with the natives on the creek in 1853. Williams post office took its name from the stream.

Williamsburg, Josephine County. Williamsburg was a pioneer post office on Williams Creek, named in compliment to Captain Robert Williams, a well-known Indian fighter in the Rogue River War. In June of 1948, the compiler had some interesting correspondence about early post offices in this area with R. F. Lewman, an old time resident of the vicinity. Mr. Lewman wrote that Williamsburg was in the north part of northeast quarter of section 26, township 38 south, range 5 west. Mr. Lewman says that at one time there were several hundred people in Williamsburg. The place was on a slight rise of ground at a point about three miles southwest of Provolt and about three miles northeast of the community presently called Williams. Williamsburg was a little to the east of the present highway from Grants Pass to Williams, but not much. Williamsburg post office was established November 16, 1860, with P. C. Wood first and only postmaster. The office was discontinued July 5, 1861. The compiler has been informed that there are a very few remains of the old post office structure, in fact just a little of the roof. The post offices called Williams Creek in Jackson County and Williams in Josephine County were also named for the stream and for Captain Williams, although they were not all in the same place.

Williamson Creek, Crook County. This stream rises in the Bear Creek Buttes and flows northwest to disappear into Dry River near the Deschutes County line. It was named for John N. Williamson who homesteaded near its headwaters in 1893. Williamson, who was born in Lane County in 1855, served as sheriff of Crook County and later was both state representative and state senator.

Williamson Mountain, Deschutes County. Williamson Mountain, elevation about 6300 feet, is just west of Lava Lake and near the summit of the Cascade Range. It was named for Lieutenant R. S. Williamson for whom Williamson River was named. See under that heading. Williamson and Lieutenant P. H. Sheridan, attached to the Pacific Railroad Surveys, were in this part of central Oregon in the latter part of August, 1855, and Williamson Mountain was named to commemorate the event. The mountain was formerly known as Leloo Mountain. *Leloo* is the Chinook jargon word for wolf, derived from the French *le loup*. The name Williamson Mountain was adopted by the USBGN on March 4, 1931.

Williamson River, Klamath County. Williamson River drains a large part of northern Klamath County, and its enlargement forms Klamath Marsh. It empties into Upper Klamath Lake. The Klamath Indian name for the river was *koke,* and this word was generally used alone in referring to Williamson, Sprague, Lost and Klamath rivers, because of their importance. Sometimes the Williamson River was called *Ya-aga-Koke, ya-aga* being the word for willow trees not far from the mouth of the stream. This name was generally applied to that locality only. Lieutenant Robert Stockton Williamson explored parts of central Oregon for the Pacific Railroad Surveys in 1855, and Williamson River was named in his honor. He was the first man to determine with reasonable accuracy the height of Mount Hood, which he did in 1867. Fremont's party fought the Klamath Indians on this stream on May 12, 1846, and Fremont named it Torrey River for his friend Professor John Torrey, the botanist. See Fremont's *Memoirs of My Life,* pages 493-5. The battleground was up stream from the former highway crossing, probably near the old Indian trail ford.

Willits Ridge, Jackson County. Willits Ridge is in the north part of the county a little southeast of Persist and about six miles airline west of Prospect. The ridge took its name from William W. Willits who in 1884 settled on a homestead at the place later called Persist. For a brief mention of Mr. and Mrs. Willits see under Persist.

Willoughby, Jefferson County. Willoughby post office was established on the Wasco County list on May 20, 1872, with Robert Warren first of a series of five postmasters. The office was not in continuous operation, and was finally discontinued March 7, 1879. It served a locality on Willow Creek not far from what is now known as Grizzly, Jefferson County. The compiler has not been able to learn the reason for the name of the office, though it has been suggested that it represents a play on the words willow by, that is, by Willow Creek. No other explanation has been suggested. There seems to be no record of any family with the name Willoughby ever having lived in the district.

Willow Bar Point, Columbia County. This point is on the northeast part of Sauvie Island. In the opinion of the writer, it is the place mentioned by Broughton in his report to Vancouver for the day of October 28, 1792, when he stated that "he proceeded up what he considered the main branch of the river, until eight in the evening; when under the shelter of some willows, they took up their lodging for the night on a low sandy point." This was just after Broughton had passed the lower end of Sauvie Island.

Willow Creek, Gilliam and Morrow counties. Lewis and Clark mention this stream as a "riverlit" in their journals for Sunday, October 20, 1805. On the sketch map by Clark, in Thwaites' *Original Journals of the Lewis and Clark Expedition,* volume IV, page 308, it is shown as *Choch.* It has been known as Willow Creek since pioneer days. There are many Willow creeks in the state, which is not surprising, as Sudworth in *Check List of Forest Trees of the United States,* lists at least ten of this family that grow in Oregon.

Willow Creek, Jackson County. Willow Creek heads in the hills west of Central Point and flows northeast into Bear Creek. It received its name in the early 1850s and it was a prominent locality in the early Indian wars and also in the mining days. After it flows out of the hills, it receives Lane Creek from the west and it was at this point that the pioneer community of Willow Springs was established. See Walling's *History of Southern Oregon,* page 377.

Willow Lake, Jackson County. Willow Lake was created in 1952 when Willow Creek, a tributary of Butte Creek, was dammed about eight miles east of Butte Falls by the Medford Water Commission as part of the municipal water system. The USBGN adopted the name Willow Lake in *Decision List 6303.* This drainage is in no way connected with the Willow Creek west of Central Point.

Willowcreek, Malheur County. Willowcreek post office took its name from the natural feature, Willow Creek, one of the prominent streams of the county. Willow Creek got its name in pioneer days, and it is doubtless too late to learn the circumstances. Willowcreek post office was established August 19, 1937, at a point on Willow Creek about a dozen miles northwest of Vale. Mrs. Dorothy Sappe was the first postmaster. It was not in service in 1980.

Willowdale, Jefferson County. Willowdale is in the north part of the county, a few hundred feet south of the bridge which carries The Dalles-

California Highway over Trout Creek. The locality has been called Checkerboard because of the style of painting once used on the service station at
that point. Willowdale post office was established May 23, 1928, with Mrs.
Edna Chesnut first of five postmasters. The office was closed to Gateway on
March 11, 1937. Willowdale is in the same general locality as the pioneer
post office Cross Keys. It was of course named for one of the many varieties
of willow that grow in central Oregon.

Willows, Gilliam County. Willows post office, named for the many
trees of that species that grow in Oregon, was established December 17,
1878, on the Umatilla County list. Morrow and Gilliam counties had not
then been created. The first Willows post office was very near what was
later to be the Gilliam-Morrow county line, and the exact location is not
clear from the available data, though it seems probable that the office was
on the south bank of the Columbia River near the mouth of Willow Creek
or just to the east. J. W. Smith was the first postmaster. This office was
closed June 29, 1885, in the same year that Gilliam and Morrow counties
were established. Willows office was reestablished on January 29, 1895,
with James A. Vawter postmaster. This time it was in Gilliam County, and it
was at or near the mouth of Willow Creek, sometimes a little to the west.
The railroad station at the mouth of Willow Creek is known as Heppner
Junction.

Willsburg, Clackamas County. Willsburg is a junction point on the
Southern Pacific line between Sellwood and Milwaukie. It was named for
George W. Wills and his son, Jacob Wills, who emigrated to Oregon in 1848
from Iowa. They took up adjoining claims near Johnson Creek, the Jacob
Wills claim being near the present site of Eastmoreland. Jacob Wills was a
pioneer sawmill operator along Johnson Creek. His father was a "hard-
shell" Baptist preacher, and he did not allow his business of farming and
building to interfere with soul saving activities. Willsburgh post office was
established nearby in Multnomah County on January 15, 1883, with Jacob
F. Rhodes first postmaster. This office was in operation until September,
1900. The post route map for 1900 uses the spelling Willsburg for this
office.

Wilson, Tillamook County. Wilson post office, named for Wilson
River on which it was situated, was about twenty-five miles upstream from
Tillamook and near the mouth of North Fork. The office was established in
July, 1896, with Walter J. Smith first postmaster. The office was discontinued officially in December, 1917, when it was closed out to Gales Creek.
Wilson post office was apparently served over nearly twenty-five miles of
mountain road from Gales Creek. Wilson post office actually went out of
service in 1916 because no one would make a bid to carry in the mail from
the outside. It was feared that there might be too much parcel post for a
bidder to take chances. Wilson post office served Glenora station of the
United States Weather Bureau. Postal officials would not accept the name
Glenora for an office because of possible confusion with such places as
Glenwood, Glendale and others with similar names. See also under
Glenora.

Wilson Creek, Clackamas and Marion counties. Wilson Creek is in the
Molalla River drainage basin and in the south part of Clackamas County. It

was named for an early day prospector who visited the vicinity of the stream and prospected there. His home was in the North Santiam Valley.

Wilson Creek, Douglas County. In 1918 Abraham Wilson homesteaded on this creek near where it flows into North Umpqua River just west of Copeland Creek. Wilson was an old time USFS packer and Abes Mountain near Red Butte was also named for him.

Wilson Lake, Linn County. This lake is near the east bank of Willamette River north of Albany. It was named for a nearby resident, John P. Wilson. Stories to the effect that it was named for Woodrow Wilson are not founded on fact, because the lake was called Wilson Lake before President Wilson came into political prominence.

Wilson Prairie, Curry County. In 1892 George Wilson homesteaded near Bravo Creek northwest of the prairie and creek which now bear his name.

Wilson River, Tillamook County. Miss Lucy E. Doughty, one of the early residents of Tillamook County, wrote the compiler in June, 1927, that much obscurity surrounded the origin of the name Wilson River. The stream was called Georgie or Georgia River in pioneer days. The name was later changed to Wilson River, in honor of an early settler who drove the first cows into the county from Seaside. Wilson was apparently the founder of the great Tillamook dairy industry. Warren N. Vaughn, a pioneer resident of the county, wrote a memoir in 1891-92, which was published in the Bay City *Tribune,* and in the series of articles mentions Wilson and tells about cattle being driven from Astoria about 1851. The story about Wilson is questioned in a letter on the editorial page of the *Oregonian,* September 17, 1927, signed Mary Alderman Bird. Miss Doughty's reply, with quotation from Vaughn, is printed in the *Oregonian,* September 26, 1927. Henry W. Wilson was an English printer. After leaving the Tillamook country, he moved to Salem, and was employed on the *Oregon Statesman.* There is a story to the effect that he secured the passage of the bill creating Tillamook County, but the compiler has been unable to secure confirmation. Wilson was not a member of the legislature in 1853, although his name is signed to the petition to establish the county. Miss Doughty calls the attention of the compiler to the fact that there was a Wilson River road project as early as 1875. After the plan was organized, a party consisting of William T. Baxter, Jacob E. Elliott and William T. Doughty explored the Kilchis and Wilson rivers, got lost, and nearly starved to death. The idea of a road was given up.

Wilsonia, Clackamas County. This station north of Oswego was named for A. King Wilson, a well-known attorney of Portland, who made his home nearby.

Wilsonville, Clackamas County. The name of this community was derived from a local resident, Charles Wilson. R. V. Short suggested the name. This was in 1880. A post office named Boons Ferry was established in this locality on December 7, 1876, with Charles Wilson postmaster. The name of the office was changed to Wilsonville on June 3, 1880. For information about the origin of the name Boones Ferry, see under that heading in this volume. The writer does not know why the style used by postal authorities did not agree with the family name. A post office called Boon was in operation in Clackamas County from April, 1868, to March, 1869. The writer has been unable to learn its location. It seems probable it was at Boones Ferry, but that is just an assumption. Wilsonville was incorporated October 10, 1968.

Wilts Creek, Union County. This small tributary of Grande Ronde River near the mouth of Meadow Creek was apparently named for George P. Wilt who filed on nearby government land in 1898.

Wimer, Jackson County. Wimer is a place on Evans Creek. On July 1, 1927, William M. Colvig of Medford wrote the compiler: "In 1886-7 William Wimer edited a paper at Grants Pass, 12 miles distant. He had something to do with getting a post office for the people there. He had a relative named Wimer who lived in the neighborhood. I do not know which one gave the name, but I think William Wimer did."

Winans, Hood River County. Winans was a station on the Mount Hood Railroad near the forks of Hood River. It was named for Ross Winans who settled nearby about 1880, and operated a hotel for hunters.

Winant, Lincoln County. Winant post office was named for Captain James J. Winant who made his home nearby. Winant was the post office name for Oysterville station, and it operated from 1902 to 1946. For biography of Captain Winant, see *History of Benton County*, page 530.

Winberry, Lane County. Winberry post office was near the mouth of Winberry Creek. Winberry is simply another name for whortleberry, and is applied more or less indiscriminately to various species of *Vaccinium*. The form windberry is wrong. Winberry Creek is an important tributary of Fall Creek, but Winberry post office was discontinued in 1933.

Winchester, Douglas County. This place, which was founded by the Umpqua exploring expedition of San Francisco in 1850, was laid out by Addison R. Flint. See Bancroft's *History of Oregon*, volume II, page 183. For a number of years it was the largest settlement in the Umpqua Valley. It was the county seat until 1854, when Roseburg won that distinction. Winchester post office was established November 3, 1851, with A. R. Flint first postmaster. There were two Winchesters in the expedition, Heman and John. The party sailed from San Francisco on July 5, 1850. Heman Winchester was captain. The expedition was headed for Klamath River, but actually first landed at Rogue River, and later established a settlement at the mouth of Umpqua River. Nathan Scholfield, a member of the party, kept a diary and used the form Heman Winchester, which is also the form used by Bancroft, and it may be assumed that the spelling Herman is wrong. The compiler has been unable to substantiate stories to the effect that Winchester was named for the younger brother John. Attention is called to the fact that there is also a discrepancy in the name of the schooner used by the party, various accounts giving *William Roberts* and *Samuel Roberts*. George Davidson of the USC&GS, authority on Pacific Coast marine history, used the name *Samuel Roberts,* Bancroft uses that form, and *Samuel Roberts* appears in Lewis & Dryden's *Marine History of the Pacific Northwest,* which seems conclusive. Nathan Scholfield's diary is in the State Library at Salem. His son, Socrates Scholfield, wrote a summary of this diary, which was published in *OHQ*, volume XVII, page 341.

Winchester Bay, Douglas County. Winchester Bay is a town on Winchester Bay on the Umpqua River, near its mouth. Winchester Creek flows into Winchester Bay. These geographic features were all named for Heman Winchester, a member of the expedition that came to Oregon from San Francisco in 1850 and established itself on Umpqua River. See under Winchester.

Winchester Creek, Coos County. Winchester Creek, which flows into South Slough, drains a considerable area southeast of Cape Arago. Its geography may be found on the USGS topographic atlas sheets for the Charleston and Riverton quadrangles. It was named for T. D. Winchester, a pioneer who tried to develop a logging and milling project at the head of the slough. See Dodge's *Pioneer History of Coos and Curry Counties,* page 16.

Winchester Lake, Lane County. Winchester Lake is northwest of Waldo Lake. Mrs. Lina A. Flock of Oakridge wrote the compiler in July, 1927: "I think Winchester Lake was named for a gun of that make that was found near the lake. It was lost by some prospector who was killed or lost near there."

Winchuck River, Curry County. F. S. Moore, in *Curry County Reporter,* December 16, 1926, says this stream was called by the Indians *Hasonta,* for the tribe living nearby. Moore had a theory that the modern name is derived from the Chinook jargon, *wind chuck,* or windy water. The compiler has been unable to identify the Hasonta Indians. Old maps show Windchuck, but modern use is generally Winchuck River, which seems to be the accepted local style. George Davidson in the *Coast Pilot,* 1889, page 361, says that *winchuck* was the local Indian word for woman, and that the Indians called the stream *Neh'-saw,* but he does not explain that word. Davidson spent much time working on the Oregon coast and his observations are generally reliable. The compiler has been unable to reconcile the information under this heading.

Wind Cave, Deschutes County. This cave is a mile north of Arnold Ice Cave on the Deschutes Plateau. It is named for the breeze that on warm summer days roars from its 5000 foot tube through the small surface opening.

Windmill Canyon, Umatilla County. This canyon empties into Jack Canyon three miles east of Nye. Charles Kopp of Pilot Rock said in 1969 that the canyon was named for an old fashioned windmill located near its mouth.

Windsor Island, Polk County. Windsor Island is in the Willamette River in the extreme northeast corner of the county. It bears the name of a family of pioneer settlers that lived in the locality.

Windy, Harney County. Windy Point is a projection westward onto the floor of Harney Valley, just east of Malheur Lake. It bears a descriptive name. On August 3, 1908, a post office called Windy was established in this locality, with August Haarstuch postmaster. The order was rescinded October 9, 1908, and the office accordingly never functioned. Waverly post office had just been established a very short distance south, which may account for the failure of Windy to get blowing.

Windy Brown Spring, Jefferson County. This spring south of Priday Agate Beds was named for an early and apparently loquacious settler, William Brown, who took up his homestead nearby in 1913.

Windy Point, Crook County. John Beoletto whose family has been in the area since the turn of the century stated in 1969 that this spot north of Alkali Butte bears a descriptive name. It is an excellent spot to hold stock for branding as there is a good spring nearby.

Windy Spring, Union County. This spring is in the extreme west part of the county near the headwaters of McCoy Creek. Helen Stangier of Pendleton said in 1969 that it was named for William Porter, an early and well-known but extremely talkative settler.

Wineglass, Crater Lake National Park, Klamath County. This peculiar rock slide on the northeast part of the inside rim of Crater Lake was named by J. S. Diller of the USGS. From across the lake the slide looks like a huge wineglass.

Winema, Klamath County. The compiler does not know the exact location of Winema post office. It was some ten or twelve miles north of Kirk, but whether on the highway or on the railroad the compiler has not been able to learn, and there is nothing in the record to give a reason for its existence. Winema post office was established January 27, 1928, with Mrs. Mae Allen postmaster. The office was closed to Kirk November 30, 1929. Irrespective of its location there is no doubt that the office was named in compliment to Winema, otherwise Mrs. Frank Riddle, the Indian heroine of the Modoc Lava Beds massacre.

Winema Pinnacles, Multnomah County. These basalt spires high above the Columbia River Highway, are about half a mile east of Multnomah Falls. They were named for Winema, Mrs. Frank Riddle, the heroine of the Modoc Lava Beds massacre. For information about her, see Jeff C. Riddle's *Indian History of the Modoc War.* She did not live near the Columbia River, but the pinnacles were named because it was thought her memory should be perpetuated somewhere in the state.

Wing, Baker County. This station is near the community of Wingville. See under that heading. The railroad company shortened the name because of awkwardness in telegraphing.

Wing Ridge, Wallowa County. This ridge, southeast of Wallowa Lake, was named by surveyors because of its shape. It lies between Sheep Creek and Little Sheep Creek.

Wingville, Baker County. Major-General Sterling Price, of the Confederate army, was active in Missouri and Arkansas in 1861-64. He was finally defeated by the Union forces in 1864. Many Southern Democrats thereafter migrated to Oregon. Numbers of them had been soldiers in Price's campaigns. The newcomers in Oregon were derisively termed by Republicans, "The left wing of Price's army." They contributed largely to the southern admixture in the pioneer population of Oregon. A community of these people near Baker was referred to as Wingville. Wingville post office was established June 23, 1871, with John R. McLain first postmaster. The office was closed in July, 1879.

Winino, Lane County. The name Winino appears to be of Indian origin, but the compiler cannot find it in any available Indian dictionary. The place is now known as McCredie Springs. The hot springs on Salt Creek have long been known. In 1914 John Harding of Portland obtained a lease on the springs property and applied the name Winino. Later, Judge William Wallace McCredie of Portland acquired an interest in the springs and used the resort as training quarters for his Portland baseball club. For additional information, see under McCredie Springs. Winino post office was established July 8, 1924, with Vivian Cartwright postmaster. This office was discontinued December 31, 1925, with mail to Railhead. This was at the time of construction of the Southern Pacific Cascade line.

Winkle Bar, Curry County. This bar on Rogue River was named for William Winkle, a pioneer prospector. Winkle has long since passed into obscurity but his name is well preserved because his claim was later purchased by Zane Grey, the author, who built a summer cabin on the bar. Grey used his experiences there as background for some of his later novels. In 1962 the property was sold to Walter Haas of San Francisco who was still using the cabin during the 1970s.

Winkle Butte, Benton County. This butte is just east of the Pacific Highway West about nine miles south of Corvallis. It is on the donation land claim of Isaac W. Winkle, and was named for him. Winkle Lake, just to the east, is on the claims of Isaac W. Winkle and Wiley Winkle and may have been named for either or both of them. Winkle Butte has been known in the past as Irwin Butte for another pioneer family of the vicinity, but that name has not prevailed.

Winlock, Wheeler County. Winlock post office was named for Winlock Steiwer, a pioneer settler in eastern Oregon. Steiwer was instrumental in having the office established about 1888, but not at its later site. See under Steiwer Hill.

Winniford, Douglas County. This office was just east of the Umpqua River at a point about eight miles west of Wilbur. It was established in April or June, 1890, with Thomas W. Winniford postmaster and was closed in January, 1891, with papers to Oakland. The office was situated in the Winniford home, which was still standing in December, 1945.

Winona, Josephine County. A recent number of the *Postal Guide* shows more than a dozen post offices in the United States named Winona, a word of the Santee Indian dialect meaning first-born (if a girl). The name was well known for its use at Winona, Minnesota, and was apparently introduced to the reading public by Keating in his *Narrative* of Long's expedition, 1823. The musical sound of the word has made it popular as a name. The principal use of the name in Oregon has been for a place on Jumpoff Joe Creek, Josephine County, a few miles north of Grants Pass. A post office called Winona was established here in June, 1897, with Herbert M. Gorham first postmaster. The office was closed on January 31, 1905. The name Winona has also been applied to a place in Polk County between Salem and Eola.

Winopee Lake, Deschutes County. This lake is just east of the summit of the Cascade Range and northwest of Cultus Lake. *Winopee* is a Chinook jargon word meaning by-and-by or wait. The name was applied to the lake by someone who was in no hurry to leave the place.

Winslow, Wallowa County. Winslow post office was situated in section 13, township 1 north, range 45 east, about ten miles northeast of Enterprise, airline. It was established in May, 1890, with Fannie Root postmaster. The office was discontinued in December, 1900. The office was named directly for Edward Winslow Rumble, a teacher in the neighborhood, and indirectly for a General Winslow who fought in the Civil War. J. A. Rumble, father of E. W. Rumble, served under General Winslow and named his son for the officer. There were several generals named Winslow who served in the Civil War, but it may be presumed that the one complimented was Brigadier-General Edward Francis Winslow, who entered the forces from Iowa.

Winston, Douglas County. Winston is a locality a couple of miles north of Dillard and just west of South Umpqua River. A little further north is the Pacific Highway bridge over the river, generally called Winston Bridge. Winston post office was established June 16, 1893, and bore the name of the first postmaster, Elijah Winston. The office was closed July 14, 1903. It was reestablished in 1948.

Winter Knight Camp, Douglas County. Winter Knight Camp is on Thorn Prairie near North Umpqua River. Jessie Wright of Caps Illahee stated that the spot was named for a man of this name who used it as a hunting camp prior to World War I.

Winter Ridge, Lake County. Winter Ridge is the rimrock west of Summer Lake. It was discovered and named on December 16, 1843, by then Captain John C. Fremont of the U. S. Topographical Engineers. Fremont applied this name because of the bad weather he encountered at the summit of the ridge, where he looked down to the sunshine on the green grass around Summer Lake. He named Summer Lake at the same time. See under that heading.

Winters Spring, Wallowa County. This spring, sometimes called Mormon Spring, is in the northwest part of township 2 north, range 50 east. It was named for W. H. Winters, an early settler. Winters was of the Mormon faith and Mormon Flat in the same township was named on his account. The style Winter Spring is wrong.

Wise, Clatsop County. Wise post office, south of Astoria, was in what is known as the Tucker Creek district. The office was established in June, 1895, with Hugh McCormick postmaster, and was discontinued in May, 1903. Herman Wise was the postmaster at Astoria when the office was established and it is more than probable that it was named in compliment to him.

Witch Hazel, Washington County. Witch Hazel was a place on the Tualatin Valley Highway and on the Southern Pacific railroad about a mile west of Reedville. Van B. DeLashmutt of Portland had a farm there in earlier days and is said to have named the place. In fact the writer once heard a statement to the effect that DeLashmutt named the farm for one of his racehorses. Oswald West was the authority on Oregon bang-tails and in October, 1945, told the writer that he never heard of an Oregon racehorse named Witch Hazel. That settles it as far as the writer is concerned. However Governor West said that Mayor DeLashmutt once owned a building at Southwest Front and Madison streets in Portland, called the Witch Hazel Building. DeLashmutt seems to have had a fancy for the name. The witch hazel tree or shrub, *Hamamelis virginiana,* is not native to Oregon and has nothing to do with the hazelnut bush. Witch hazel wands are said to have the power of pointing to buried gold and silver and even to underground water. Oddly enough Jonathan Carver was one of the very first American authors to mention this belief, which he did in 1778. A post office was established at Witch Hazel in August, 1904, with Earl W. Anderson postmaster. It was closed in November, 1905.

Witches Cauldron, Crater Lake National Park, Klamath County. The crater at the top of Wizard Island was named Witches Cauldron on August 17, 1885, by Will G. Steel, because of its weird appearance.

Wizard Island, Crater Lake National Park, Klamath County. This island in Crater Lake has a weird appearance, and was named on that account by Will G. Steel on August 17, 1885. The top of the island is 763 feet above the surface of the lake.

Wocus Bay, Klamath County. Wocus Bay, near the southeast part of Klamath Marsh, is named with the English form of the Klamath Indian word used to describe the seed of the yellow pond lily, *Nuphar advena*. This seed was roasted and ground for food. The Indians pronounced the word as though spelled *Wokash*.

Wolf Creek, Josephine County. The post office for Wolf Creek community and railroad station was Wolfcreek but in 1951 it was changed to two words to conform. There were plenty of wolves in Oregon in early days, and a number of streams are known as Wolf Creek. This community was the locality of the famous Six Bit House, frequently mentioned in pioneer history. In 1936 James T. Chinnock of Grants Pass wrote the compiler about this establishment, transmitting information from James Tuffs and George Riddle of Grants Pass, both familiar with the history of southern Oregon. The original Six Bit House was built during the Indian wars, probably about 1853, within the sharp hairpin curve of the Southern Pacific Company railroad about a mile east of town. It was at the mouth of a gulch on the old road location north of the present Pacific Highway. There are several stories about the origin of the name. The most probable explanation is that 75 cents was charged for a night's lodging, compared with a dollar charged elsewhere along the road. Another story is that the proprietor interrupted some white men who were hanging an Indian nearby and declined to let them proceed with the business until the melancholy brave paid the inn-keeper six bits, then past due. This story seems fanciful to the compiler because of the improbability that a local Indian ever had six bits in currency. The building has long since disappeared, but Mr. Tuffs recalled seeing the remains during his youth. The second Six Bit House, built of logs, was in the north part of the town, close to the railroad. Mr. Tuffs lived in it several years. The present Wolf Creek Tavern was built later and had no connection with either of the Six Bit houses.

Wonder, Josephine County. About 1902 a man by the name of John T. Robertson started a store at the present site of Wonder. He began to call this store Wonder store because neighbors wondered where he would get his trade as the territory was sparsely settled. Later postal authorities used the name of the store for the name of the post office, which was established in December, 1903.

Wood Lake, Wallowa County. According to J. H. Horner of Enterprise, this lake in township 3 south, range 43 east, was named for John Wood, who helped J. H. Jackson stock it with young salmon in 1914.

Wood River, Klamath County. Wood River is part of the west boundary of the Klamath Indian Reservation and flows into Agency Lake. During the early days of Fort Klamath, contractors cut wood for the fort in a lodgepole pine grove on the banks of the stream, hence the name. The Klamath Indians called it *Eukalksine Koke.*

Wood Village, Multnomah County. Wood Village was built during World War II as a housing project for the employees of the Troutdale plant of Reynolds Aluminum Company. Lester J. Wood of Commonwealth Inc., a Portland real estate firm, told the compiler in 1967 that while he arranged the financing, originally the Long-Bell Lumber Company was to have had charge of the actual construction. Supposedly the name was selected by them to go with a number of streets named for native trees, but in view of the major part played by Mr. Wood, the author suspects more than mere coincidence. The town was incorporated February 9, 1951, with a mayor and commission form of government.

Woodburn, Marion County. Woodburn was platted in 1871 by J. A. Settlemeier and the post office was established December 28, 1871 with Adolphus Mathiot postmaster. It is said that when the railroad came through the place was first called Halsey, presumably for a railroad official. See under Halsey. However, in 1981 Charles E. Nebergall of Portland told the writer that in the 1880s his grandfather had been a close friend of Settlemeier's and that a brochure in his possession, *Woodburn, Oregon,* Stewart & Doud, Printers, undated but apparently printed during the 1890s, gives the following origin of the name. Settlemeier platted the town and left a large grove of fir trees surrounded by cleared fields. When the railroad came through, their right of way went directly through the middle of the grove. The felled trees and brush were left alongside the track until winter when they were burned. The fire got out of hand and a substantial quantity of the standing timber was destroyed along with the brush. The name Woodburn commemorates this happening.

Woodcock Creek, Josephine County. Woodcock Creek is about five miles south of Kerby and flows into the Illinois River. It was named for Horace Woodcock, a pioneer rancher.

Woodlawn, Multnomah County. Woodlawn was an outstanding separate community in the 1890s and rated a post office of its own. It was an important stop on the steam, later electric, railway from Portland to Vancouver. Woodlawn post office was established December 24, 1890, with Hiram Parrish first postmaster. That was before the Portland-East Portland-Albina consolidation. The office was finally closed on November 14, 1903. It was out of service for about a year in 1897-98. The name of the office followed Woodlawn addition, which was of course the product of real estate activity. The plat for Woodlawn was filed in October, 1889.

Woodley, Union County. Woodley post office was established February 1, 1896, with Daniel M. Griffith first postmaster. The compiler does not know when the office was discontinued, but apparently it did not last long. Woodley is not shown on the post route map of 1900. The post office was named for the Woodley mine, located by Frederick Woodley. The property was in the northwest part of township 6 south, range 36 east, near Grande Ronde River.

Woodrow, Lake County. A post office named Woodrow, apparently in compliment to Woodrow Wilson, was in operation during the last wave of homesteaders in northern Lake County. It was situated about ten miles east of Fort Rock and was established April 24, 1914, with George W. Craig postmaster. The office was closed May 15, 1916.

Woodruff Creek, Douglas and Jackson counties. Woodruff Creek flows into Rogue River from the west eight miles north of Prospect. Anne and Newton Woodruff both patented homesteads in the area during the 1890s.

Woodruff Mountain, Douglas County. This mountain is on the west side of the Umpqua River, west of Wilbur. It was named for Jonathon W. Woodruff, a donation land claim owner nearby. His musical talents made him famous in pioneer days in Douglas County.

Woods, Tillamook County. Woods was named for Joseph Woods, who settled there about 1875. The post office was established in April, 1886, with William Booth first postmaster. Booth suggested the name in honor of Woods. The post office was closed on August 29, 1935.

Woodson, Columbia County. Woodson got its name from Woods Landing on Westport Slough. Many years ago a man named Wood hauled logs to the locality and dumped them into the slough, where they were made up into rafts. Woodson post office was established April 2, 1929, with Mrs. Alice Brooks first postmaster. It was in the northwest corner of the county, about a mile east of Kerry.

Woodstock, Multnomah County. Woodstock was a station of Portland post office. It bears the name of a real estate tract platted in 1889. At that time there was a vogue for naming tracts after Sir Walter Scott's novels, and in the southeast part of Portland we have Woodstock, Ivanhoe, Kenilworth, Waverly, *sic.,* and even such flights of fancy as Waverleigh. The word *stoc* came from the Anglo-Saxon and means a stockaded place, and woodstock means a place fortified with wooden posts. Woodstock was an independent post office from 1891 to 1912.

Woodward Creek, Coos County. This creek is a tributary to South Fork Coquille River. It was named for Henry H. Woodward, a pioneer settler nearby.

Wooldridge Butte, Lane County. This low hill, elevation 380 feet, is about a mile east of Cheshire and bears the name of a well-known pioneer family of the vicinity. The spelling Waldridge is wrong. Wooldridge Creek, a stream in Jackson County flowing into Slagle Creek, is named for members of the same family. See letter by Logan Wooldridge in Grants Pass *Bulletin,* June 4, 1937.

Woolley, Douglas County. The Woolley family is very well known in northern Douglas County and when a post office was established September 20, 1905, with Anna L. Woolley first postmaster it was natural that the office should be given the family name. Woolley was about fifteen miles northwest of Drain on the Smith River road. It was also about eight miles east of Gunter. The office was discontinued June 30, 1912. In February, 1948, Mrs. May Brown Woolley of Drain, sent the compiler an interesting letter about early day conditions in the upper Smith River area. Mrs. Woolley's letter with other useful information will be found in the Roseburg *News-Review,* March 6, 1948.

Woolly Horn Ridge, Hood River County. According to Ralph Lewis of Parkdale this ridge north of Tomlike Mountain was named by the Odell and Lenz brothers who once shot a buck in velvet on its slopes.

Worden, Klamath County. William S. Worden was a member of a family of early settlers in Klamath County and during the time the Southern Pacific Company built a railroad into Klamath Falls Worden acted as right-of-way agent and while doing so purchased the land and laid out the present townsite of Worden. The post office was established in 1910. Worden was subsequently elected county judge of Klamath County.

Wren, Benton County. This place bears the name of George P. Wren, a pioneer settler.

Wrentham, Wasco County. Wrentham was named by the Daniel Farrington family, which came to Oregon from Maine. It is said that the family had lived in New York near a point once known as Wrentham Hill and Wrentham, Oregon, was named on that account. Wrentham post office was established in 1900 but has been discontinued.

Wright, Jackson County. Nicholas B. Wright was the only postmaster that Wright post office ever boasted and the place was named in his honor. It was about nine miles up Applegate River, or south, from the place called Uniontown, which was near the mouth of Little Applegate River. Wright post office was in service from April 25, 1878, to December 22, 1888, when it was closed out to Uniontown.

Wright Creek, Clackamas County. Wright Creek is a small stream just north of Liberal, flowing into Molalla River. It was named in compliment to Harrison Wright, a pioneer of 1844, who settled near the present site of Liberal. He was instrumental in getting a pioneer post office, which was named Molalla, and Wright was first postmaster. This office was established April 9, 1850. The office was not at the present town of Molalla, but was moved to that place in the 1870s. The highway bridge over the Molalla River north of Liberal is also named for Harrison Wright.

Wright Point, Harney County. This is a long neck of solid land extending into the flats north of Malheur Lake. It was named for Camp Wright, which was established in October, 1865, by Captain L. L. Williams, and named for Brigadier-General George Wright. For details concerning Captain Williams and his operations in the Shoshone War, see Bancroft's *History of Oregon,* volume II, page 514. George Wright was born in Vermont, and graduated from West Point in 1822. He served in various Indian campaigns and in the Mexican War, with distinguished gallantry, receiving three brevets. He came to the Pacific Coast in 1852, and was identified with operations in Oregon and Washington, finally reaching command of the Department of the Pacific in 1861, with the rank of brigadier-general. He and his wife were drowned in the wreck of the *Brother Jonathan,* which foundered off Crescent City, California, July 30, 1865, with a loss of about 300 lives. See under Camp Wright.

Wroe, Douglas County. Wroe post office was on North Fork Smith River about four miles up stream from the mouth. The office was named for the family of the first postmaster. It was established November 27, 1922, with Floyd A. Wroe first and only postmaster. The office was discontinued June 20, 1923. In April, 1948, William M. Wroe of Reedsport, brother of Floyd A. Wroe, wrote from Reedsport that by the time Wroe post office was set up for business it was found that a number of the prospective customers had moved away from the valley of the North Fork. In these circumstances it was concluded not to operate the office, so it never actually functioned.

Wyatt Creek, Lane County. Wyatt Creek flows into Brice Creek in the Bohemia district. It was named for one Wyatt, an early day prospector.

Wy'east Basin, Hood River County. Wy'east Basin is north of Mount Hood. Wy'east is said to be the legendary name for Mount Hood, but the word does not appear in available books on Chinookan dialects. H. H. Riddle of Portland, an authority on the names of the Columbia River Gorge, told the compiler that he was unable to get facts about the origin of the name, but that it was used in Indian myths. In 1943, C. Edward Graves, Arcata, California, wrote that the basin was named Wiyeast in 1922 by an exploring party from Hood River. Graves was the organizer of the party and was in 1922 living in Hood River. In June, 1973, the OGNB voted to adopt the now current form, Wy'east, and this was duly approved by the USBGN in *Decision List 7402*.

Wyeth, Hood River County. Oregon has seen fit to honor one of her notable explorers by attaching his name to a railroad station that achieved fame largely because it was for some years the site of a "tie pickling plant." Other than that, not much has been done to commemorate Nathaniel J. Wyeth. Wyeth, trader and patriot in one, had a definite plan to counteract the British fur-trading influence in the Pacific Northwest. Inspired by Hall J. Kelley, but compelled to dissolve a compact with him because of Kelley's procrastination, Wyeth crossed the plains without the Boston school teacher in 1832, the first American after the Astor overlanders to make the journey to the Willamette. On a second expedition, in 1834, he convoyed the missionaries, Jason and Daniel Lee, built Fort Hall, near the present site of Pocatello, and named it for one of his financial backers. He established on Sauvie Island the trading post which he called Fort William. With him came Thomas Nuttall and J. K. Townsend, naturalists who share with David Douglas the honor of being pioneers in science in Oregon, and John Ball, first school teacher in the Pacific Northwest. Wyeth planned a more diversified program than that of the Hudson's Bay Company, studied salmon packing and visioned an American trade with the Orient by way of the Pacific Coast, asking no exclusive privilege for his company. "Nothing on our part is desirable," he wrote, "excepting aid to get men out there and enacting some laws for their regulation when there, and leave us to ourselves." Wyeth's *Correspondence and Journals,* edited by Professor F. G. Young, have been published by the University of Oregon. For other information about Wyeth, see editorial in the *Oregonian,* December 13, 1925. See also under Kelley Point in this book.

Ya Whee Plateau, Klamath County. This plateau is southwest of Saddle Mountain. The name is derived from a Klamath Indian word meaning eastern. Various forms have been in use, including *ye-wat, yah-wa*, etc. The name is properly written in two parts in order to indicate the proper pronunciation, as *Yawhee,* written as one word, is not satisfactory.

Yach, Tillamook County. Yach post office was in service from March,

1907, to January, 1908, when it was closed out to Dolph. Frank Yach was the postmaster. The Yach homestead was about four or five miles westward of Dolph, on Little Nestucca River. The office was manifestly named for the postmaster.

Yachats, Lincoln County. This post office was established in 1887 about a mile north of its present location with the name of Ocean View. George M. Starr was the first postmaster. In 1916 the name of the post office was changed to Yachats for a tribe of Indians. These Indians had previously been moved to Siletz and they are now practically extinct. The name is pronounced Ya-hats. Indians say that the word means "at the foot of the mountain." This interpretation fits the facts. The name of the post office was changed to Yachats at the suggestion of J. K. Berry because it was at the mouth of Yachats River. See *Handbook of American Indians,* volume II, page 982.

Yager Creek, Tillamook County. Lon Yager was a cattle buyer who lived near Netarts after the turn of the century and this creek bears his name.

Yainax, Klamath County. This place was for a number of years a sub-agency for the Klamath Indian Reservation. It took its name from the Klamath Indian word *Yainaga,* meaning little hill, which was the name the Indians used in referring to a little butte about two miles away, now known as Council Butte. The name Yainax Butte, originally applied to this feature, has become transferred to a mountain twelve miles southeast. See under Yainax Butte.

Yainax Butte, Klamath County. The government has officially adopted this name for a mountain, elevation 7226 feet, about twelve miles southeast of Yainax, and just south of what was the Klamath Indian Reservation. The butte has also been known as Modoc Mountain, Bald Mountain, and Yonna Butte. *Yainax* is a Klamath Indian word meaning little hill, and the name is not strictly suitable for a mountain, yet it has been used so long for the feature in question that the USBGN finally adopted it as official. *Yainax* was originally the name used for what is now Council Butte, near the settlement of Yainax.

Yakso Falls, Douglas County. This seventy foot fall is on Little River in section 16, township 27 south, range 1 east, near its source. *Yakso* is a Chinook jargon word meaning "hair of the head", and the falls resembles the long hair of a woman. The name was applied by USFS officials and approved by the OGNB on December 2, 1966.

Yamada, Lincoln County. Yamada post office was in operation for a few months near South Beaver Creek, north of Alsea Bay. The office was established March 26, 1898, with Newton L. Guilliams first and only postmaster, and was closed to Ona on December 26, 1899. It is reported that Yamada post office was established as the result of some "feudin" between the people on South Beaver against the patrons of Ona post office, which was on the main Beaver Creek, or north branch. In any event, Yamada office had a short life. There are two places in Japan named Yamada, and this fact tends to substantiate the story that members of the Guilliams family ran across the name while sealing in Alaska and cruising off the coast of

Japan. They liked the sound of the word and later applied it to the Oregon post office. The Japanese word *yamada* means a mountain field.

Yamhill, Yamhill County. The name Yamhill, in various forms, comes of course from the Yamhill River, but the exact meaning is a matter of doubt. A post office with the name Yam Hill Falls was established January 8, 1850, with Jacob Hawn postmaster. This office, which was the first post office in Yamhill County, was closed January 6, 1852. Yamhill Falls are directly south of the park square in Lafayette and not downstream near Yamhill Locks. Hawn's home was south of Hawn Creek on his donation land claim but old records show that Joel Perkins sold him "a certain mill seat at or near the town of Lafayette known as Falls of Yamhill River". He built a tavern or hotel on this property where on at least one occasion in 1850 Judge Deady held court so this was probably the site of the post office. Apparently it was replaced by the office of Lafayette established nearby on March 14, 1851. Yam Hill post office was established September 4, 1856, with Thomas Bailey postmaster. The office was closed September 25, 1857. The writer has been unable to find this place on any old map, but Bailey's donation land claim was across the Willamette River from J. V. Boone in what was then Yamhill County near present day Wilsonville. Bailey sold his property to Boone in 1857 and moved to McMinnville so it is possible this post office was actually on the Willamette River. North Yam Hill office was established March 14, 1851, with Benjamin E. Stewart first postmaster. With one break, this office was in operation for more than a half a century at or near the North Yamhill River on the route of travel from McMinnville to Forest Grove. On May 9, 1908, the name of the office was changed to Yamhill and that has been its official title ever since.

Yamhill County. This county was created July 5, 1843, and now has a land area of 709 square miles according to the Bureau of the Census. It was one of the original four districts of Oregon and embraced the southwest part of the territory. Several counties have been taken from it. The origin and meaning of the name are uncertain, but the best evidence indicates that it is the white man's name for the Yamhill Indians. The Yamhill Indians were of the Kalapooian family, formerly living on Yamhill River, in Yamhill County. The remnants of the tribes were sent to Grand Ronde agency. The Henry-Thompson *Journals*, page 812, under date of January 23, 1814, refer to the *Yamhelas*, "who dwell in houses on Yellow river, a branch of the Willamette. They are great rogues, but not very numerous." John Work uses the name *Yamhill* in 1834. Lee and Frost, in *Ten Years in Oregon*, page 90, give *Yam-hill*. The early pronunciation of the word was *Yam-il*. Nothing very definite is known about its meaning. In *All Over Oregon and Washington*, by Mrs. F. F. Victor, the origin is given as from *Che-am-il*, Indian word for bald hills, this being the character of the hills near the falls of Yamhill River, where there was a convenient ford. John Minto discusses the history of the word in the *Oregonian*, October 7, 1890, page 4. There is a town with the name Yamhill, formerly known as North Yamhill, presumably because it was near North Yamhill River.

Yamhill River, Yamhill County. For the origin of this name, see under Yamhill County. The two main branches of Yamhill River are North Yamhill River and South Yamhill River, the latter being the larger. South Yamhill River has part of its course in Polk County.

Yampo School, Yamhill County. Yampo School is in the Eola Hills about a mile north of the Polk-Yamhill county line. The name is synthetic and is made up of parts of the two county names.

Yamsay, Klamath County. Yamsay post office was established February 28, 1930, with Claude Houghton postmaster. This office was about forty miles by road northeast of Chiloquin and it was established to serve a lumbering activity. The office was near Yamsay Mountain and was named on that account. Yamsay post office should not be confused with Yamsay railroad station on the Southern Pacific Cascade line about ten miles south of Chemult. The origin of the name of the railroad station is the same as that of the post office. Both are in Klamath County but some distance apart.

Yamsay Mountain, Klamath and Lake counties. This is a well-known geographic feature with an elevation of over 8000 feet. It is east of Klamath Marsh and just west of the Lake County line. The mountain and its extension to the south are drained to the west by Williamson River and its tributaries. The Klamath Indian name was *Yamsi,* a form of *Yamash,* the north wind, referring possibly to the abode of the north wind. The Weaslet was supposed to live at Yamsay Mountain. See under Chaski Bay. Yamsay Mountain was also supposed to be the abode of *Kmukamtch,* the supreme being of Klamath mythology, who at times appeared as the Marten, elder brother of Weaslet.

Yankton, Columbia County. This community was settled about 1890 by several families from the state of Maine. It was known as Yankeetown. About 1894 a post office was petitioned for and local residents suggested the name Maineville. Postal authorities did not like this name, and when Yankeetown was suggested they shortened it to Yankton and Yankton it has been ever since.

Yapoah Crater, Deschutes and Lane counties. This crater has an elevation of 6737 feet and lies on the summit of the Cascade Range halfway between McKenzie Pass and the North Sister. *Yapoah,* signifying an isolated hill, was the Indian name for Skinner Butte near Eugene. Professor Edwin T. Hodge of the University of Oregon applied the name to this isolated crater in 1924 when he was studying the Three Sisters area.

Yaquina Bay, Lincoln County. Yaquina Bay, Yaquina station and Yaquina River which heads near the Benton-Lincoln county line, and flows into the bay, bear the name of the Yaquina Indians. The Yaquinas were a small tribe of the Yakonan family, formerly living about Yaquina Bay. Hale gives the name as *Iakon* and *Yakone,* in *Ethnography and Philology,* 1846, page 218; Lewis and Clark give *Youikeones* and *Youkone;* Wilkes' *Western America,* 1849, gives *Yacone.* Another form of the word is *Acona.* (*OHQ,* volume I, page 320.)

Yaquina John Point, Lincoln County. Yaquina John Point is on the south side of the entrance to Alsea Bay just southwest of Waldport. It was named for Yaquina John, a chief or councillor of the Yaquina Indians, who lived in the vicinity of Alsea Bay.

Yarnell Canyon, Morrow County. Yarnell Canyon, west of Utts Butte, is named for Henry Yarnell who came to Morrow County in the 1920s and bought the ranch at the head of the canyon.

Yellow Jacket Spring, Umatilla County. This spring east of Carney Butte was on the old road between Pilot Rock and Ukiah. Lester Hurst of Pendleton said that it had the first water on the way to Lehmam Springs and was also a fine campsite with huckleberries in season. In the spring and fall it was also plagued with the well-known *Vespa vulgaris* or common yellow jacket which has given its name to so many similarly supplied features.

Yellowstone Creek, Linn County. This stream flows into Quartzville Creek about twenty-five miles northeast of Sweet Home and bears a descriptive name. The creek was named in the early 1890s when there was a good deal of mining excitement along Quartzville Creek. The miners became attracted by the abundance of a yellowish, quartz-like bedrock in the channel of a branch entering Quartzville Creek from the northwest and crossed by the old Quartzville trail near its mouth. This side stream became known as Yellowstone Creek, the name by which it is still called. Yellowstone Mountain was named in 1919 when it was first used as a forest lookout station. It was named for the creek. Yellowstone Mountain, elevation 4320 feet, is a little to the west of Yellowstone Creek.

Yeon Mountain, Multnomah County. Yeon Mountain is a prominent point on the south bank of the Columbia River east of Saint Peters Dome and west of Tumalt Creek. It is conspicuous from the Columbia River Highway. It was named for John Baptiste Yeon, who was born in Canada on April 24, 1865. After working in various places, he came to Oregon in 1885, and began his career as a logger at $2.50 a day. He accumulated a large fortune, and for many years was interested in the good roads movement in Oregon. He was among those who developed the idea of the Columbia River Highway. He served as roadmaster of Multnomah County, and also as state highway commissioner. John B. Yeon State Park to the east along the Columbia River was named in his honor. Yeon died on October 15, 1928. For obituary, see *Oregonian*, October 16; for editorial, *ibid.,* October 17.

Yeoville, Grant County. All the available evidence shows that Yeoville was a post office in Bear Valley or vicinity, but old timers in the valley disclaim knowledge of the place. Yeoville post office was established February 23, 1887, with Aaron Wickiser first and only postmaster. The establishment did not last long, for it was closed out to Canyon City May 18, 1887. The reason for the unusual name is not known.

Yoakam Point, Coos County. For many decades this name has been applied to a small promontory about a mile west of Coos Head just south of the entrance to Coos Bay. It commemorates a family well known in the history of the county. John Yoakam settled in Coos County in the early fifties. He was the father of seven children, five of whom were killed by a large tree which fell one night, March 27, 1855, on the Yoakam cabin. This was the most unexpected and unusual tragedy in the early history of the county. It took place at a point sometimes called Yoakam Hill southwest of Coos Bay town and west of Libby. The family also lived for a time at

Empire and also other places in the county. Dodge in *Pioneer History of Coos and Curry Counties* mentions John Yoakam in several places and spells the name in several ways. George Bennett in *OHQ*, volume XXVIII, page 334, mentions John Yoakum, in the late 1850s living near Coquille. In 1943 Mrs. Mary M. Randleman, authority on Coos County history, wrote the compiler that Yoakam was the correct spelling of the name.

Yoakum, Umatilla County. This spot on Umatilla River ten miles southeast of Echo was named for Hughy G. Yoakum who was born in Tennessee and came to Pendleton in 1867. Yoakum bought a stock ranch on Umatilla River and was elected county judge in 1872. He moved to Idaho in 1889 and the community after a decent interval passed into obscurity.

Yocum, Lake County. Yocum post office, in Yocum Valley, was in the extreme southwest corner of the county and was in service from August, 1917, to June, 1937, when it was closed to West Side. An earlier office called Kriegh was established March 8, 1915, with Margaret E. Kriegh postmaster. Belle Pardue became postmaster August 4, 1917, on which date the name of the office was changed to Yocum. Yocum Valley bears an old name, the history of which has not been unravelled by the writer. The name has been in use for well over fifty years, apparently to commemorate an early settler or squatter who departed long ago. There was once a cabin in the west end of Yocum Valley called Yocum cabin, and the owner of the name apparently lived there many years ago.

Yocum Ridge, Clackamas County. This ridge is a western spur of Mount Hood. It bears the name of Oliver C. Yocum, who came to Oregon as a small boy with the emigration of 1847, and after residing in Yamhill County and in Portland for many years, he developed the Government Camp hotel and resort in 1900, and lived there for 22 years. He probably took more persons to the top of Mount Hood than any other guide, and was admired and respected because of his affection for the mountain. He returned to Yamhill County about 1922. Yocum Falls also bears his name. For additional information see editorial page, *Oregon Journal,* July 3, 4, 1927.

Yoder, Clackamas County. This place was named for a pioneer family. It was formerly known as Yoderville, but that form has fallen into disuse.

Yoncalla, Douglas County. Yoncalla is in a small valley called Yoncalla Valley. It was famous for many years as being the home of the Applegate brothers. The valley and the town were named for a prominent bald mountain to the northwest, which was known by the Indians as Yoncalla, or the home of the eagles. Eagles made their nests and reared their young on this butte. It is said that Jesse Applegate applied the name to the community. Bancroft, in *History of Oregon,* volume II, page 225, footnote, says the word is composed of *yonc,* eagle, and *calla or calla-calla* meaning bird or fowl in the Indian dialect. The compiler has been unable to identify the word *yonc* in any Indian dictionary available. The Chinook jargon borrowed the word *kal-lak'-a-la,* meaning bird, from the Chinook Indian language. The accent given by George Gibbs is on the second syllable, but the compiler heard the word frequently in the Willamette Valley in the 1880s and 1890s pronounced as though spelled *cully-cully,* with the accent on the first syllable of each part. This word was used by Indians in referring to birds generally but more especially to game birds such as grouse and quail. It seems to have been the same word used by Applegate in his name Yoncalla. Yoncalla post office was established on March 14, 1851, with James B. Riggs postmaster. Jesse Applegate became postmaster on September 15, 1851.

Yonna Valley, Klamath County. Yonna Valley was at one time known as Alkali Valley, but that name was abandoned some time ago for the Klamath Indian name. *Yonna* may come from *yana*, meaning below, or low down, referring to the lower altitude of the valley, or it may be from *yaina*, meaning mountain. There are mountains nearby. There was at one time a post office at Yonna, in Yonna Valley northeast of Dairy.

Youngs Butte, Grant County. This butte, elevation 5330 feet, southwest of Dayville, was named for John M. Young, a Civil War veteran who lived on Youngs Creek, under the butte.

Youngs Canyon, Morrow County. Youngs Canyon spills into Eightmile Canyon. Alex Young settled near a small spring two miles up this canyon in the 1880s. Members of his family owned the ranch until after World War II.

Youngs River, Clatsop County. Lieutenant William Robert Broughton of Vancouver's expedition, discovered and explored Youngs Bay and Youngs River on October 22, 1792. He named Youngs River for Sir George Young of the royal navy. The bay took its name from the river. Lewis and Clark named the bay Meriwether Bay for Meriwether Lewis, just as they named Tongue Point, Point William for William Clark, but neither of these new names was able to supplant the names attached to the features by Lieutenant Broughton in 1792. The Lewis and Clark maps indicate that Youngs River was called Kilhowanahkle River by the explorers, apparently from the Indian name, but Silas B. Smith is authority for the statement that this was the name of a place on the river and not of the river itself. Admiral Sir George Young was born in 1732 and became a midshipman in the royal navy in 1757. He served at various important stations and reached the position of flag captain to Sir Edward Vernon in the East Indies in 1777. He was knighted in 1781 and became an admiral in 1799. He was a fellow of the Royal Society and actively supported a proposal of Jean Maria Matra for establishing a colony in New South Wales in 1784. He was the promoter and one of the first proprietors of the Sierra Leone Company in 1791. He died in 1810.

Youtlkut Butte, Lake County. This butte is just south of the Paulina Mountains. It was named by the USFS with the Chinook jargon word for long.

Zena, Polk County. Zena is a community in the southeastern part of Eola Hills. It was named for Arvazena Cooper, wife of Daniel Jackson Cooper. The Coopers moved to this place in 1863 and lived there until 1875, when they moved to Salem. Mrs. Cooper was living in The Dalles in 1927. This information was furnished by Norman Cooper of The Dalles, a son of D. J. Cooper.

Zigzag River, Clackamas County. On October 11, 1845, Joel Palmer crossed the deep ravine of Zigzag Canyon near timberline on Mount Hood. In his journal for that day he uses the following description. "The manner of descending is to turn directly to the right, go zigzag for about one hundred yards, then turn short round, and go zigzag until you come under the place where you started from; then to the right, and so on, until you reach the base." The members of the Barlow party, who crossed south of Mount Hood without wagons in October, 1845 used a trail that ascended White River nearly to timberline and then traversed west not far from the 1975 alignment of the Timberline Trail. After crossing Zigzag Canyon they descended one of the ridges of Zigzag Mountain. It is obvious that the principal stream was identified by the crossing. The river is no more crooked than adjoining streams and there is no reason to believe it was named for an especially irregular alignment. For a detailed account of the investigation of the south side of Mount Hood and the discovery of Barlow Pass see the entries for October, 1845 in Joel Palmer's *Journal of Travels over the Rocky Mountains,* a photographic reproduction of which was made in 1966. The name Zigzag has also come to be applied to Zigzag Glacier on Mount Hood. The form Zig Zag is wrong. See decision of USBGN. For discussion of the name Zigzag, see *OHQ*, volume XIX, page 75, where it is held that the use of the name for a stream east of Mount Hood is not likely.

Zinc Creek, Douglas County. Zinc Creek flows into South Umpqua River above Dumont Creek. It was named for a zinc mine development that has long since passed into obscurity.

Zion, Lane County. Zion post office operated for more than a decade in the Lost Creek Valley south of Dexter. It was named because of the proximity of Mount Zion just to the east. Mount Zion was named in pioneer days by Elijah Bristow. It has an elevation of 2660 feet and is a prominent point. Zion post office was established March 11, 1899, with Thomas H. Hunsaker postmaster. The office was finally closed November 30, 1913, and the business turned over to Dexter. There is still a Zion School in the Lost Creek Valley.

Zollner Creek, Marion County. Robert Zollner settled near this stream in pioneer days and it was named for him. Zollner Creek flows into Pudding River northwest of Mount Angel.

Zosel Hill, Marion County. Zosel Hill is about five miles southwest of Salem. It has an elevation of about 600 feet. It was named for William Zosel, a landowner nearby.

Zuckerman Island, Klamath County. Francis Landrum of Klamath Falls informed the writer in 1969 that this high ground in Lower Klamath Lake near Worden was named because nearby land was owned or farmed by Weyl-Zuckerman, a California agricultural corporation.

Zumwalt, Wallowa County. Zumwalt got its name from Henry Zumwalt, a local resident. The community is northeast of Enterprise. The post office was established August 25, 1903, with Josie Zumwalt first postmaster.

Zwagg Island, Curry County. M. S. Brainard of Brookings provided the following curious information about the early days on this island just offshore from Brookings. Folker Von Der Zwaag was born in The Netherlands in 1835 and came to Curry County in 1889. He was obviously fond of solitude as he lived alone on the island with his dog Sniff. The island had no fresh water and the local mechanical marvel was the trolley with the self filling attachment by which he drew water from the mainland.

Index

This index does not include names that may be found directly by alphabetical reference to the text. The main purpose of the index is to help the reader find names that have been discarded for various reasons. For further assistance, multiple references have been included, where applicable. However, space has not permitted the inclusion of all the variations in spelling of Indian names taken from early writers. Most of then are not important.

Also since names beginning with the words "Camp," "Cape," "Fort," "Lake," "Mount," and "The," are printed in the text under those headings the index lists the last words of all such compound names with their page numbers. Thus, Hood, Mount Hood is on page 513, under the name Mount Hood.

Checkerboard, page 802, **Willowdale**
Chehalem, **West Chehalem,** page 783
Chemay-way, page 149, **Chemawa**
Chemeketa, page 372, **Hopmere**
Chemeketa, page 645, **Salem**
Chemeketa Hills, page 646, **Salem Hills**
Chenoweth Flat, page 149, **Chenoweth Creek**
Chetco, page 344, **Harbor**
Chetco Peak, page 512, **Mount Emily**
Chetlo, **Lake Chetlo,** page 427
Chichester Falls, page 16, **Andy Creek**
Chinook, **Lake Billy Chinook,** page 427
Chintimini, page 474, **Marys Peak**
Chitwood, page 91, **Bull Run Lake**
Chopunnish, page 99, **Butteville**
Cienega Creek, page 495, **Mill City**
Cincha Lake, page 435, **Latigo Creek**
Cincinnati, page 259, **Eola**
Citizen Fort, page 290, **Fort Miner**
Civil Bend, page 84, **Brockway**
Clackamas, page 572, **Park Place**
Clackamas River, **Oak Grove Fork Clackamas River,** page 551
Clark Glacier, **Newton Clark Glacier,** page 543
Clark River, **Lewis and Clark River,** page 443
Clarks Point of View, page 122, **Cape Falcon**
Clarks River, page 218, **Deschutes River**
Clarksville, page 158, **Clarks Creek**
Classic Lake, page 159, **Classic Ridge**
Clatsop, Camp, page 113, **Camp Rilea**
Clatsop, **Fort Clatsop,** page 284
Clatsop, Port, page 284, **Fort Clatsop**
Clatsop River, page 535, **Necanicum River**
Clay River, page 327, **Grande Ronde Valley**
Clear Creek, page 763, **Viola**
Cleone, page 267, **Fairview**
Cline Buttes, page 162, **Cline Falls**
Clinger Spring, page 421, **Klingers Camp**
Clover, page 255, **Elsie**
Clover Creek, page 163, **Clover**
Clyde, page 478, **Mayville**
Coast Fork, East Fork, page 636, **Row River**
Coast Highway, **Oregon Coast Highway,** page 563
Cockscomb, The, page 609, **Pulpit Rock**
Coe, page 220, **Detroit**
Cold Creek, page 319, **Gold Creek**
Cole Collier Creek, page 169, **Collier Creek**
Colestin, page 791, **White Point**
Colfax, **Camp Colfax,** page 107
College, **Brush College,** page 88
Collins, page 235, **Drift Creek**
Collins, page 544, **Nice**
Collins, page 768, **Waldport**
Collins Mountain, page 169, **Collings Mountain**
Columbia, page 364, **Hillsboro**
Columbia, page 654, **Scappoose**

Columbia, page 751, **Umatilla**
Columbus, page 364, **Hillsboro**
Conant Creek, page 172, **Conant Basin**
Condit, page 28, **Aumsville**
Connley Hills, page 173, **Connley**
Conser Ferry, page 394, **Jefferson**
Contention, page 749, **Twickenham**
Cook Point, **Captain Cook Point,** page 127
Cooper Lake, page 174, **Cooper Creek**
Coos River, North Fork, page 497, **Millicoma River**
Copper Camp, page 176, **Copperfield**
Copper Creek, page 176, **Copper**
Copper Mountain, page 176, **Copper**
Coquin, page 632, **Rogue River**
Corral Creek, **Double Corral Creek,** page 232
Corral Creek, **Two Corral Creek,** page 750
Cosper Butte, page 693, **Spirit Mountain**
Costa Creek, **Shasta Costa Creek,** page 663
Cougar Creek, page 183, **Cougar Lake**
Cougar Dam, page 183, **Cougar Lake**
Council Butte, page 814, **Yainax**
Cowhorn, Big, page 523, **Mount Thielsen**
Cowhorn, Little, page 186, **Cowhorn Mountain**
Coyote Spring, page 714, **Swiss Spring**
Crabtree Lake, page 187, **Crabtree Creek**
Cracker, page 343, **Hanover**
Crag Falls, page 673, **Silver Creek Falls**
Craigs, page 483, **McKenzie Bridge**
Crail, page 188, **Crale**
Crale Creek, page 188, **Crale**
Crapper, page 551, **Oak Grove**
Crater, page 436, **Lava**
Crater Lake, **Little Crater Lake,** page 450
Creighton, page 550, **Oak Grove**
Creole Creek, page 621, **Rickreall Creek**
Creswell Butte, page 192, **Creswell**
Cricket River, page 675, **Silvies River**
Crims, page 337, **Gull Island**
Criterion Summit, page 193, **Criterion**
Croisan Gulch, page 193, **Croisan Ridge**
Cross Hollows, page 662, **Shaniko**
Crossing, The, page 244, **Echo**
Crow Creek, page 197, **Crowcamp Creek**
Crowcamp Hills, page 197, **Crowcamp Creek**
Crowcamp Mountain, page 197, **Crowcamp Creek**
Crown Rock, page 159, **Clarno**
Cub Peak, page 570, **Palmer Peak**
Cueter, page 424, **Kuder Creek**
Cultus Mountain, page 200, **Cultus Lake**
Cummings Lake, page 171, **Comegys Lake**
Cummins Ridge, page 200, **Cummins Creek**
Currey, **Camp Currey,** page 108
Currey, page 361, **Hershal**
Cuttingsville, page 754, **Union Mills**
Cynthia Ann, page 205, **Dallas**

Dahlgren, **Camp Dahlgren,** page 109
Dale, page 231, **Dorman**
Daley Prairie, page 205, **Daley Creek**

Dalles, **Fort Dalles,** page 284
Dalles, **The Dalles,** page 725
Dalles, The Great, page 278, **Fivemile Rapids**
Dan, page 363, **Hilgard**
Daneville, page 297, **Freebridge**
Dark Cabin, page 38, **Bark Cabin Creek**
Darrow Chute, page 207, **Darrow Rocks**
Dave Fulton Canyon, page 303, **Fulton Canyon**
David Douglas, **Mount David Douglas,** page 511
Davis Creek, **Jeff Davis Creek,** page 393
Davis Creek, **Mart Davis Creek,** page 473
Davis Creek, page 483, **McKay Creek**
Davis Mountain, page 209, **Davis Lake**
Davis Spring, **Sam Davis Spring,** page 648
Dawson Creek, page 628, **Rock Creek**
Day, **Camp Day,** page 109
Day, John, page 209, **Day**
Day, **John Day,** page 396
Day Point, John, page 397, **John Day River**
Day River, **John Day River,** page 397
Day River, **John Day River,** page 397
Dead Indian Creek, page 616, **Redmans Tooth**
Dead Indian Mountain, page 210, **Dead Indian Creek**
Deadhorse Butte, page 210, **Deadhorse Canyon**
Deadhorse Draw, page 675, **Simmons Draw**
Deadhorse Lake, page 210, **Deadhorse Ridge**
Deadman Creek, page 638, **Ruckel Creek**
Deadman Slough, page 387, **Iowa Slough**
Deardorff Creek, page 212, **Deardorff Mountain**
Deathball Mountain, page 212, **Deathball Rock**
Dedman Canyon, page 212, **Dedman Ranch**
Deep Blue Lake, page 189, **Crater Lake**
Deep Canyon Creek, page 60, **Big Canyon**
Deer Creek, page 60, **Big Canyon**
Deer Creek, page 634, **Roseburg**
Deer Island, page 326, **Grand Island**
Deerhorn, page 439, **Leaburg**
Defiance, **Mount Defiance,** page 512
Delmar Creek, page 214, **Delmar**
Delmar Gulch, page 214, **Delmar**
DeMoss Springs, page 31, **Badger**
Dencer, page 635, **Rosedale**
Deschutes Bridge, page 217, **Deschutes**
Deschutes Junction, page 6, **Ainsworth**
Deschutes Junction, page 666, **Sherman**
Deschutes River, **Little Deschutes River,** page 450
Deschutesville, page 496, **Miller**
Deskins, page 607, **Prospect**
Devil Creek, page 746, **Tumalt Creek**
Devil Slide Creek, page 746, **Tumalt Creek**
Devils, **Seven Devils,** page 661
Devils Cauldron, page 742, **Treasure Cove**

Devils Ladder, page 221, **Devils Stairway**
Devils Lake, page 221, **Devils Lake Fork**
Dewars, page 72, **Bolon Island**
Dewie, page 241, **Duwee Canyon**
Diablo Canyon, page 222, **Diablo Mountain**
Diamond, page 222, **Diamond Craters**
Diamond Island, page 324, **Government Island**
Dickey Creek, page 689, **South Dickey Peak**
Dicks Run, page 603, **Prairie Channel**
Dillon, page 272, **Ferry**
Divers trail, page 226, **Divers Creek**
Divinity Creek, page 763, **Vingie Creek**
Dixie, page 603, **Prairie City**
Dixie, page 622, **Rickreall Creek**
Dixie Mountain, page 226, **Dixie**
Doane Point, page 227, **Doane Lake**
Dog Mountain, page 228, **Dog Creek**
Dog Mountain, page 228, **Dog Lake**
Dog River, page 370, **Hood River**
Dogleg Lake, page 228, **Dog Lake**
Dole, page 638, **Ruckles**
Dollar Mountain, **Eight Dollar Mountain,** page 247
Donaca Creek, page 229, **Donaca Lake**
Donahue, page 230, **Donahue Creek**
Dorena Dam, page 231, **Dorena**
Doten, page 410, **Keno**
Doty Creek, page 149, **Chehulpum Creek**
Double Falls, page 673, **Silver Creek Falls**
Douglas, page 506, **Morgan**
Douglas, **Mount David Douglas,** page 511
Downey Saddle, page 234, **Downey Gulch**
Drake Butte, page 235, **Drake Peak**
Drake Falls, page 673, **Silver Creek Falls**
Drift Creek, page 544, **Nice**
Drouthit, page 233, **Douthit Springs**
Drum, Camp, page 285, **Fort Dalles**
Drury Butte, page 236, **Drury Creek**
Drusy, page 235, **Drewsey**
Dry Gulch, page 610, **Quartzville**
Dry Lake, page 236, **Drylake**
Dry Lake Flat, page 236, **Drylake**
Dry Point Creek, page 210, **Dead Point Creek**
Duckworth, page 254, **Elmira**
Dundee Junction, page 238, **Dundee**
Dungeon, **The Dungeon,** page 725
Dupee Creek, page 778, **Washington**
Durhams Mills, page 239, **Durham**
Dusty, page 53, **Bellfountain**
Dutcher Creek, page 434, **Lathrop Creek**
Dutchman Cabin, page 240, **Dutch Flat**

Eagle Bar, **Gray Eagle Bar,** page 332
Eagle City, page 691, **Sparta**
Eagle Creek, page 1, **Abbot Creek**
Eagle Creek, **Little Eagle Creek,** page 450
Eagle Creek, Little, page 417, **Kirby Creek**
Eagle Creek Butte, page 241, **Eagle Butte**
Eagle Mountains, page 241, **Eagle Cap**
Eagle Mountains, page 771, **Wallowa Mountains**

East Creek, **Tom East Creek,** page 738
East Fork, page 450, **Little Deschutes River**
East Fork Coast Fork, page 636, **Row River**
East Marshfield, page 244, **Eastside**
East Side, page 243, **East Morrison Street**
East Tualatin Plain, page 364, **Hillsboro**
Eastland, page 65, **Blakeley**
Eastport, page 445, **Libby**
Eaton Ridge, **Nick Eaton Ridge,** page 545
Echo Lake, page 743, **Triangle Lake**
Eckman Creek, page 245, **Eckman Slough**
Eddy, **Big Eddy,** page 60
Eden Ridge, page 246, **Eden**
Edgewood, page 363, **Hildebrand**
Edwards Butte, page 247, **Edwards Creek**
Egan, page 95, **Burns**
Egan Lake, **Finney and Egan Lake,** page 275
Egli, page 765, **Wagontire Mountain**
Ehrck, page 259, **Erk Hill**
Eightmile Canyon, page 247, **Eightmile**
Ekins, page 238, **Dundee**
Elbow Falls, page 673, **Silver Creek Falls**
Elijah, **Mount Elijah,** page 512
Elijah Caves, page 562, **Oregon Caves**
Eliot Branch, page 250, **Eliot Glacier**
Elk Creek, page 245, **Ecola Creek**
Elk Creek, page 245, **Ecola Point**
Elk Creek, page 581, **Perdue**
Elk Head, page 253, **Elkhead**
Elk Mountain, page 505, **Moolack Mountain**
Elk Trail, page 77, **Boyer**
Elk Trail Creek, page 77, **Bowman Creek**
Ella Butte, page 253, **Ella**
Ellensburg, page 319, **Gold Beach**
Ellicks Butte, page 10, **Alecs Butte**
Elliff, **Camp Elliff,** page 109
Elliston, page 308, **Gate Creek**
Ellwood, page 255, **Elwood**
Elyville, page 255, **Ely**
Emery, Mount, page 512, **Mount Emily**
Emigrant, page 257, **Emigrant Springs**
Emigrant Lake, page 256, **Emigrant Creek**
Emigrant Pass, page 797, **Willamette Pass**
Emily, **Mount Emily,** page 512
Eminence, page 613, **Rainier**
Emma Trail, page 257, **Emma**
Emmons Peak, page 588, **Pilot Rock**
Empire, page 175, **Coos Bay**
Empire City, page 257, **Empire**
Emrick, page 67, **Blodgett**
Encampment, page 487, **Meacham**
Ender, page 616, **Redne**
Endersly, page 258, **Endersby**
Enger, page 604, **Pratum**
Engles, page 258, **Engels Creek**
Ensign Creek, page 480, **McCoy Creek**
Enterprise, page 619, **Reuben**
Erskine Springs, page 260, **Erskine**
Erskineville, page 260, **Erskine**
Estacado, page 260, **Estacada**
Esto, page 501, **Mist**

Etalka, page 262, **Etelka**
Eugene City, page 263, **Eugene**
Eureka Bar, page 263, **Eureka**
Eureka Creek, page 263, **Eureka**
Evergreen, page 541, **Neverstil**
Ewauna, **Lake Ewauna,** page 427
Ewing Harbor, page 120, **Cape Arago**
Ewing Harbor, page 599, **Port Orford**
Express, page 239, **Durkee**
Express, page 265, **Express Ranch**
Express Ranch, page 239, **Durkee**

Fairfield, page 259, **Enterprise**
Fairgrounds, page 266, **Fair Grounds**
Fairmount, page 183, **Council Crest**
Fairmount Lake, page 728, **Thornton Lake**
Fairview, page 372, **Hoquarten Slough**
Fairy Creek, page 273, **Ferry Creek**
Faith, Hope and Charity, page 548, **North Sister**
Falcon, **Cape Falcon,** page 122
Fall Creek, page 3, **Adams Creek**
Fall Creek, page 38, **Bare Creek**
False Tillamook Head, page 122, **Cape Falcon**
Fanny, **Mount Fanny,** page 512
Fannys Bottom, page 551, **Oak Point**
Fannys Island, page 193, **Crims Island**
Fannys Island, page 551, **Oak Point**
Farewell Bend, page 54, **Bend**
Ferrelo, **Cape Ferrelo,** page 123
Fielder Mountain, page 273, **Fielder Creek**
Fields Creek, page 273, **Fields Peak**
Fiester, page 271, **Feasters Rocks**
Fillmore, page 509, **Mount Angel**
Finger Prairie, **Crooked Finger Prairie,** page 195
Finn Creek, page 275, **Finn Rock**
Fir Clearing, page 525, **Mountain Home**
Fir Creek, page 275, **Fir**
Firglen, page 17, **Anglersvale**
First Periwinkle Creek, page 582, **Periwinkle Creek**
Fish Trap, page 606, **Pringle Falls**
Fisher, page 277, **Fischer Island**
Fisher Creek, page 530, **Murder Creek**
Fishtrap, page 249, **Elgin**
Flagstone Creek, page 279, **Flagstone Rock**
Flatirons, **The Flatirons,** page 726
Fletcher Lake, page 205, **Daley Lake**
Flettville, page 279, **Fletts**
Flicks Bar, page 280, **Flickbar**
Floreys Creek, page 280, **Floras Creek**
Flournoy, **Fort Flournoy,** page 285
Foley Butte, page 281, **Foley Creek**
Foleysprings, page 282, **Foley Springs**
Folley, page 281, **Foley**
Forest Cove, page 185, **Cove**
Forest Crossing, page 557, **O'Neil**
Forest Grove, page 728, **Thornton Lake**
Forks of Mary River, page 180, **Corvallis**
Fort Astor, page 285, **Fort George**
Fort George, page 26, **Astoria**
Fort Miners, page 290, **Fort Miner**
Fort Umpqua, page 253, **Elkton**

Foster, page 697, **Stanfield**
Foulweather, **Cape Foulweather,** page 123
Four Mile, page 295, **Fourmile Creek**
Fourmile, page 294, **Fourmile Creek**
Frank Brice Creek, page 81, **Brice Creek**
Frank Fulton Canyon, page 302, **Fulton Canyon**
Frankfort, page 509, **Mount Angel**
Franklin, page 296, **Franklin-Smithfield**
Franklin, Mount, page 378, **Humbug Mountain**
Franklin, page 259, **Enterprise**
Freeport, page 498, **Milton-Freewater**
Fremont, page 742, **Tremont**
Frieda, page 207, **Dant**
Frissell Creek, page 301, **Frissell Point**
Frissell Crossing, page 301, **Frissell Point**
Fultonville, page 302, **Fulton Canyon**
Fultonville, page 496, **Miller**

Hart Lake, page 155, **Christmas Lake**
Gagniersville, page 658, **Scottsburg**
Gale Butte, page 340, **Hale Butte**
Gales City, page 304, **Gales Creek**
Gales Peak, page 304, **Gales Creek**
Gardiner City, page 305, **Gardiner**
Garrison Lagoon, page 307, **Garrison Lake**
Gasburg, page 586, **Phoenix**
Gatch Falls, page 321, **Gooch Falls**
Gate Creek, page 762, **Vida**
Gauldy, **Mount Gauldy,** page 513
Gauls, page 305, **Galls Creek**
Gem, page 690, **Sparta**
George, **Fort George,** page 285
George W. Joseph State Park, page 435, **Latourell Falls**
 Wilson River
German Settlement, page 67, **Blooming**
Gherkin, page 311, **Gerking Canyon**
Gibbs, **Camp Gibbs,** page 110
Gibbs Creek, page 195, **Crooked Creek**
Gibraltar Rock, page 312, **Gibraltar Mountain**
Giddings, page 312, **Gettings Creek**
Gilhooley, page 493, **Middle Mountain**
Gilhouly, page 493, **Middle Mountain**
Gillton, page 776, **Warren**
Girkling, page 311, **Gerking Canyon**
Gittings, page 312, **Gettings Creek**
Giveout Mountain, page 217, **Derby Creek**
Glacier Peak, page 363, **Hillman Peak**
Glaise River, page 328, **Grande Ronde Valley**
Glasgow Point, page 401, **Jordan Point**
Glass Hill, page 183, **Council Crest**
Glenbrook, page 179, **Cornutt**
Glenn, page 369, **Home**
Gods Valley Creek, page 318, **Gods Valley**
Gold, Ray, page 320, **Gold Ray**
Gold River, page 264, **Evans Creek**
Gold River, page 632, **Rogue River**
Gooch Falls, page 308, **Gatch Falls**
Goose Creek, page 206, **DaMotta Branch**
Goose Island, page 352, **Hayden Island**
Goose Island, page 324, **Government Island**

Goose Lake, page 375, **Hot Springs**
Gooseberry Spring, page 322, **Gooseberry**
Gordon, **Camp Gordon,** page 110
Gordon Butte, page 322, **Gordon**
Gordon Falls, page 766, **Wahkeena Falls**
Gordon Ridge, page 322, **Gordon**
Gouge Eye, page 235, **Drewsey**
Governors Island, page 2, **Abernethy Creek**
Grade, page 95, **Burnt Ranch**
Graham Corral, page 326, **Graham Butte**
Graham Ferry, page 325, **Graeme**
Grand Ronde, page 97, **Butler**
Grand Ronde Blockhouse, page 209, **Dayton**
Grande Ronde Landing, page 751, **Umatilla**
Grande Ronde River, page 327, **Grande Ronde Valley**
Granite City, page 328, **Granite**
Granite Creek Mines, page 328, **Granite**
Granite Hill, page 329, **Granite**
Granite Mountains, page 771, **Wallowa Mountains**
Granny View Point, page 329, **Granny Creek**
Grant, **Camp Grant,** page 110
Grave Creek House, page 440, **Leland**
Graves Butte, page 98, **Butte Creek**
Graves Butte, page 510, **Mount Angel**
Gray Flat, page 332, **Gray**
Graystone, page 266, **Face Rock**
Great Dalles, The, page 278, **Fivemile Rapids**
Great Sandy Desert, page 362, **High Desert**
Grebe, page 728, **Thornberry**
Green Mountain, page 210, **Dead Mountain**
Green Peter Creek, page 333, **Green Peter**
Green Peter Dam, page 333, **Green Peter**
Green Point Creek, page 210, **Dead Point Creek**
Greenleaf Creek, page 334, **Greenleaf**
Greenville, page 37, **Banks**
Greenwood, page 350, **Haskin Butte**
Gregory, Cape, page 120, **Cape Arago**
Gregory Point, page 176, **Coos Head**
Grenville, Cape, page 122, **Cape Falcon**
Grenville, Cape, page 124, **Cape Meares**
Griffith Canyon, page 335, **Griffin Canyon**
Ground, **Camp Ground,** page 110
Grouse Creek, page 301, **Fruita**
Grouse Flat, page 336, **Grouse**
Guano Creek, page 337, **Guano Lake**
Gull Island, page 193, **Crims Island**
Gumboot Butte, page 337, **Gumboot Creek**
Gurney, **Mount Gurney,** page 513
Independence, page 328, **Granite**
Hagerhorst Mountain, page 339, **Hager Mountain**
Hailey Ferry, page 104, **Camp Alden**
Hale Ferry, page 340, **Hale Butte**
Hall Creek, page 229, **Dogwood Creek**
Hall Creek, **Mack Hall Creek,** page 464

Indian Point, page 385, **Indian Beach**
Indian Slough, page 449, **Lint Slough**
Indian Valley, page 249, **Elgin**
Ingles, page 142, **Centerville**
Ingram Butte, page 386, **Ingram Point**
Institute, page 645, **Salem**
Ireland, **Mount Ireland,** page 517
Iron Dyke Mine, page 369, **Homestead**
Irwin Butte, page 807, **Winkle Butte**
Isaac, **Mount Isaac,** page 517
Isabel, page 470, **Marcola**
Isabelle, **Mount Isabelle,** page 517
Isom Corral, page 9, **Alder Springs**
Isthmus, page 390, **Isthmus Slough**
Ivie, page 253, **Elkhorn**

Jack Springs, page 337, **Gumjuwac Saddle**
Jackass Creek, page 391, **Jack Creek**
Jackson, Mount, page 451, **Llao Rock**
Jackson Creek, page 392, **Jacksonville**
Jackson Falls, page 392, **Jackson Creek**
Jap Hollow, page 393, **Japanese Hollow**
Jarboe Creek, page 393, **Jarboe Meadow**
Jawbone, page 413, **Kilchis Point**
Jefferson, **Mount Jefferson,** page 517
Jeffries, page 393, **Jeffers Slough**
Jett Gulch, **Dixie Jett Gulch,** page 227
Jim Ridge, **Poker Jim Ridge,** page 596
Jim Town, page 264, **Evans**
Joe Creek, **Jumpoff Joe Creek,** page 403
John B. Yeon State Park, page 817, **Yeon Mountain**
John Day, page 209, **Day**
John Day Point, page 397, **John Day River**
John Mule Creek, page 527, **Mule Creek**
Johnson Creek, page 399, **Johnson Mountain**
Johnson Creek, page 483, **McKay Creek**
Johnson Lake, page 723, **Tenmile Lake**
Johnson Slough, page 479, **McCaffery Slough**
Jones Bridge, **Ben Jones Bridge,** page 53
Jordan, page 401, **Jordan Valley**
Jordan Canyon, page 400, **Jordan Butte**
Jordan Cove, page 401, **Jordan Point**
Jordan Creek, page 401, **Jordan Valley**
Joseph, Point, page 152, **Chief Joseph Mountain**
Joseph, **Saint Joseph,** page 644
Joseph Creek, page 402, **Joseph**
Joseph Mountain, **Chief Joseph Mountain,** page 152
Joseph State Park, George W., page 435, **Latourell Falls**
Josephine Caves, page 562, **Oregon Caves**
Joy, page 274, **Findley Buttes**
Julia, page 316, **Glendale**
Julia Butte, page 758, **Van Horn Butte**
Julianna Creek, page 138, **Catherine Creek**
Junction House, page 32, **Baird**
June, **Mount June,** page 518
Juniper Mountain, page 141, **Cedar Mountain**
Juniper Ridge, page 404, **Juniper Mountain**

Kaiserville, page 759, **Vanport City**
Karlson, page 405, **Karlson Island**
Keeney Pass, **Captain Keeney Pass,** page 127
Kees Mill, page 779, **Waterloo**
Kees Precinct, page 439, **Lebanon**
Kellogg Lake, page 408, **Kellogg Creek**
Kelly Creek, page 479, **McCord Creek**
Kentuck Creek, page 410, **Kentuck Slough**
Kerbyville, page 410, **Kerby**
Kerr Valley, page 412, **Kerr Notch**
Kettle Rock, page 412, **Kettle Creek**
Keyes Mountain, page 412, **Keyes Creek**
Keys, **Cross Keys,** page 196
Kilchis River, page 413, **Kilchis Point**
Kilhowanahkle, page 819, **Youngs River**
Killamacue Lake, page 413, **Killamacue Creek**
Killamook, page 733, **Tillamook County.**
Kimball Creek, page 414, **Kimball Hill**
Kinak Passage, page 78, **Bradbury**
King Mountain, page 558, **Onion Springs Mountain**
Kinzel Lake, page 417, **Kinzel Creek**
Kirbeyville, page 411, **Kerby**
Kirk Spring, **Johnny Kirk Spring,** page 398
Kirkford, page 417, **Kirk**
Kist Creek, page 418, **Kist**
Kitchen, **Fort Kitchen,** page 288
Kitson Ridge, page 418, **Kitson Hot Springs**
Kiwa, **Lake Kiwa,** page 428
Kiwanda, **Cape Kiwanda,** page 123
Kiwanda Lake, page 494, **Miles Lake**
Klamath, **Fort Klamath,** page 288
Klamath, page 491, **Merganser**
Klamath Lake, **Lower Klamath Lake,** page 460
Klamath Lake, **Upper Klamath Lake,** page 755
Klickitat Ridge, page 420, **Klickitat Mountain**
Klickitat Trail, page 421, **Klickitat Mountain**
Klondyke, page 421, **Klondike**
Klovdahl Lake, page 421, **Klovdahl Bay**
Knighttown, page 117, **Canby**
Konapee, page 279, **Flavel**
Koster, page 691, **Sparta**
Kotse I, page 770, **Wallace Island**
Kriegh, page 818, **Yocum**
Krumbo Mountain, page 424, **Krumbo Creek**
Kusa, page 470, **Maplewood**

La Butte, page 99, **Butteville**
La Creole, page 621, **Rickreall Creek**
La Mesa, page 122, **Cape Falcon**
La Rosa, page 459, **Louse Canyon**
Labeasche, page 370, **Hood River**
Labish, **Lake Labish,** page 428
Lackemute, page 461, **Luckiamute**
Ladd Creek, page 426, **Ladd Glacier**
Laidlaw, page 746, **Tumalo**

Lower Pony Creek Reservoir, page 428, **Lake Merritt**
Lower South Falls, page 673, **Silver Creek Falls**
Lower Table Rock, page 716, **Table Rock**
Luckiamute River, **Little Luckiamute River,** page 450
Lugan Flat, page 461, **Lubbing Flat**
Lutgens, page 235, **Drift Creek**
Lutgens, page 544, **Nice**
Lynn, page 260, **Estacada**
Lytle, **Lake Lytle,** page 428

Macy Cove, page 464, **Macey Cove**
Madison, page 456, **Long Tom**
Maiden Creek, page 634, **Rosary Lakes**
Majesty, page 189, **Crater Lake**
Majors Creek, page 466, **Majors Prairie**
Maklaks Mountain, page 466, **Maklaks Pass**
Mannings, page 797, **Willamette River**
Marble, page 368, **Home**
Marble Gulch, page 470, **Marble Creek**
Marble Halls, page 562, **Oregon Caves**
Marble Point, page 470, **Marble Creek**
Maria, Villa, page 473, **Marylhurst**
Marion, Mount, page 729, **Three Fingered Jack**
Marion Creek, page 471, **Marion Lake**
Marks Ridge, page 471, **Marks Creek**
Marr, **Lake Marr,** page 428
Marr Flat, page 472, **Marr Creek**
Marron Fork, page 795, **Wildhorse Creek**
Marshall Station, page 580, **Pendleton**
Marshfield, page 175, **Coos Bay**
Marshfield, East, page 244, **Eastside**
Marshville, page 157, **Clackamas**
Marysville, page 180, **Corvallis**
Marysville, page 475, **Marys River**
Mason Dam, page 585, **Phillips Lake**
Masterson Butte, page 349, **Hartshorn Butte**
Matheny Ferry, page 787, **Wheatland**
Matney School, page 476, **Matney Flat**
Maury, **Camp Maury,** page 112
Maury Mountain, page 24, **Arrowwood Point**
Maxwell, page 361, **Hermiston**
Maxwell Peak, page 363, **Hillman Peak**
May Basin, page 478, **Mays Canyon Creek**
Mayborn Hill, page 587, **Piety Knob**
Mays Rock, page 478, **Mays Canyon Creek**
Maywood Park, page 573, **Parkrose**
Mazama, **Mount Mazama,** page 519
McAlister Ridge, page 479, **McAlister Creek**
McAlister Spring, page 479, **McAlister Creek**
McArthur Hill, page 375, **House Rock**
McArthur Rim, **Tam McArthur Rim,** page 717
McBee Slough, page 479, **McBee Island**
McCrady River, page 458, **Lost River**
McDermid Cone, page 322, **Gordon**
McDowell, **Camp McDowell,** page 112

McDuffee Hot Springs, page 624, **Ritter**
McKenzie, page 23, **Armitage**
McKibbin, page 350, **Haskin Butte**
McKinley, **Camp McKinley,** page 112
McKinzie Bridge, page 483, **McKenzie Bridge**
McLoughlin, **Mount McLoughlin,** page 519
Meacham Hill, page 140, **Cayuse**
Meadow View, page 326, **Grand Prairie**
Meadows Ranch, page 15, **Anchor**
Meadowville, page 487, **Meadows**
Meares, **Cape Meares,** page 124
Memaloose Park, page 147, **Chatfield**
Menominee, page 490, **Meno**
Menzies Island, page 352, **Hayden Island**
Meriwether, **Camp Meriwether,** page 113
Meriwether Bay, page 819, **Youngs River**
Merritt, **Lake Merritt,** page 428
Meva, page 80, **Braymill**
Meyersville, page 532, **Myrtle Point**
Middle Bridge, page 605, **Prichard**
Middle Falls, page 423, **Koosah Falls**
Middle Fork Wallowa River, page 459, **Lostine River**
Middle Mountain, page 73, **Bonneville**
Middle Mountain, page 511, **Mount Bonneville**
Middle North Falls, page 673, **Silver Creek Falls**
Middle Sister, page 730, **Three Sisters**
Middleton, page 580, **Pendleton**
Mikecha, page 312, **Gibbon**
Mikecha, page 405, **Kamela**
Milford, page 674, **Silverton**
Mill, page 645, **Salem**
Millard, **Camp Millard,** page 113
Miller, page 6, **Ainsworth**
Miller, **Lake Miller,** page 428
Miller Island, page 324, **Government Island**
Miller Island, page 496, **Miller Hill**
Miller stage station, page 380, **Huntington**
Millican Crater, page 497, **Millican**
Millicoma Tract, page 254, **Elliott State Forest**
Millra, page 260, **Erskine**
Mills, Ashland, page 25, **Ashland**
Mills, Aurora, page 29, **Aurora**
Mills, **Boston Mills,** page 74
Mills, Boston, page 663, **Shedd**
Mills, Durhams, page 239, **Durham**
Mills, ONeals, page 254, **Ellendale**
Mills, **O'Neals Mills,** page 557
Mills, **Pattersons Mills,** page 574
Mills, **Scotts Mills,** page 657
Mills, **Union Mills,** page 753
Milton, page 375, **Houlton**
Milton, page 498, **Milton Creek**
Minam Creek, page 60, **Big Canyon**
Minam Lake, page 499, **Minam River**
Minam River, **North Minam River,** page 547
Miner, **Fort Miner,** page 289
Miner Fort, page 290, **Fort Miner**

Miners, Fort, page 290, **Fort Miner**
Miners Fork, page 168, **Collawash River**
Mink, page 49, **Beaver Creek**
Minnehaha, page 17, **Anglersvale**
Minto Island, page 500, **Minto Mountain**
Minto-Brown Island, page 500, **Minto
    Mountain**
Mission, page 501, **Mission Creek**
Mission Landing, page 500, **Mission Creek**
Mitchell, **Mount Mitchell,** page 520
Mitchell Station, page 786, **Weston**
Modoc Mountain, page 814, **Yainax Butte**
Mohawk, page 502, **Mohawk River**
Molalla, page 445, **Liberal**
Moloch Creek, page 505, **Moolack Creek**
Monroe Creek, page 504, **Monroe Roughs**
Monument Mountain, page 505,
    Monument
Moriah, **Mount Moriah,** page 520
Mormon Spring, page 808, **Winters Spring**
Morrison, page 590, **Pioneer**
Morrison Street, **East Morrison Street,**
    page 243
Mount Bonneville, page 73, **Bonneville**
Mount Emery, page 512, **Mount Emily**
Mount Faith, page 548, **North Sister**
Mount Franklin, page 378, **Humbug
    Mountain**
Mount Jackson, page 451, **Llao Rock**
Mount Marion, page 729, **Three Fingered
    Jack**
Mount Multnomah, page 730, **Three
    Sisters**
Mount Pisgah, page 267, **Fairview**
Mount Pit, page 519, **Mount McLoughlin**
Mount Pleasant, page 267, **Fairview**
Mount Vancouver, page 518, **Mount
    Jefferson**
Mount Zion, page 332, **Green Hills**
Mount Zion, page 522, **Mount Scott**
Mount Zion, page 820, **Zion**
Mountain View, page 255, **Ely**
Mouse Mountain, page 474, **Marys Peak**
Mouse River, page 474, **Marys River**
Mouth of Willamette, page 601, **Post
    Office Bar**
Mowry, page 477, **Maury Mountains**
Mt..Angel, page 510, **Mount Angel**
Mud Flat, page 269, **Fangollano**
Mud Lake, page 347, **Harney Lake**
Mud Lake, page 374, **Hosmer Lake**
Mud Lake, page 467, **Malheur Lake**
Muddy, page 10, **Alford**
Muddy, page 53, **Bellevue**
Muddy, page 526, **Muddy Creek**
Mule Mountain, page 527, **Mule Creek**
Muleshoe Creek, page 527, **Muleshoe
    Ridge**
Multnomah, Mount, page 730, **Three
    Sisters**
Multnomah, page 798, **Willamette River**
Multnomah Creek, page 528, **Multnomah
    Falls**
Multnomah Island, page 653, **Sauvie
    Island**

Munsel Creek, page 529, **Munsel Lake**
Munson Falls, page 529, **Munson Creek**
Murderers Harbour, page 46, **Bays**
Murphy Creek, page 530, **Murphy**
Muskrat Camp, page 382, **Idanha**
Myrtle City, page 657, **Scottsburg**
Mysterious Lake, page 189, **Crater Lake**
Mystery Lake, page 189, **Crater Lake**

Namanu, Camp, page 91, **Bull Run River**
Namanu, **Camp Namanu,** page 113
Nansene, page 274, **Fifteenmile Creek**
Nansene Creek, page 274, **Fifteenmile
    Creek**
Napoleon, page 411, **Kerby**
Natsox Run, page 770, **Wallace Island**
Naughty Girl Meadow, page 793,
    Whorehouse Meadow
Nauvoo, page 744, **Troy**
Naylox Ridge, page 533, **Naylox**
Neacoxie Lake, page 534, **Neacoxie Creek**
Neal Creek, page 61, **Bilyeu Creek**
Neal Folly, page 282, **Follyfarm**
Nebo, **Mount Nebo,** page 521
Nellies Point, page 537, **Nellies Cove**
Nelson Reservoir, page 538, **Nelson Creek**
Nenamusa Falls, page 538, **Nenamusa**
Nesmith, page 540, **Nesmith Point**
Nesmiths, page 254, **Ellendale**
Nesmiths, page 557, **O'Neals Mills**
Nestucca Bay, page 540, **Nestucca River**
Nestucca River, **Little Nestucca River,**
    page 450
Netul River, page 443, **Lewis and Clark
    River**
New Albany, page 7, **Albany**
New Astoria, page 415, **Kindred**
New Castle, page 244, **Eckley**
New Plymouth, page 643, **Saint Helens**
New Walla Walla, page 298, **Freewater**
Newellsville, page 145, **Champoeg**
Newton, page 251, **Elk City**
Newtown, page 554, **Odell**
Ney Slough, **Joe Ney Slough,** page 396
Niagara Falls, **Little Niagara Falls,** page
    450
Niagora, page 544, **Niagara**
Nice, page 236, **Drift Creek**
Nichols, page 577, **Peck**
Nicolai, page 490, **Meno**
Nicolis, page 544, **Nichols Canyon**
Nigger Ben Mountain, page 536, **Negro
    Ben Mountain**
Noonday Mine, page 18, **Annie Creek**
North Beach, page 239, **Dunes City**
North Canyonville, page 120, **Canyonville**
North Dickey Peak, page 689, **South
    Dickey Peak**
North Falls, page 673, **Silver Creek Falls**
North Fork Applegate River, page 449,
    Little Applegate River
North Fork Coos River, page 497,
    Millicoma River
North Fork River, page 547, **North Minam
    River**

North Lake, page 548, **North Tenmile Lake**
North Powder Lakes, page 19, **Anthony Lakes**
North Santiam River, **Little North Santiam River,** page 450
North Sister Creek, page 750, **Twin Sisters Creeks**
North Slough, page 350, **Hauser**
North Twin Lake, page 749, **Twin Lakes**

Oak Cut, page 258, **Encina**
Oak Grove, page 638, **Ruckles**
Oak Grove, page 773, **Wapinitia**
Oak Grove Mountain, page 520, **Mount Mitchell**
Oak Islands, page 345, **Hardtack Island**
Oak Islands, page 635, **Ross Island**
Oak Mountain, **Live Oak Mountain,** page 451
Oaks, **Fair Oaks,** page 266
Oakville, page 760, **Verdure**
Obelisk, page 633, **Rooster Rock**
Ocean View, page 814, **Yachats**
Oceanlake, page 447, **Lincoln City**
Ochoco, page 487, **Meadow**
Ochoco, **Upper Ochoco,** page 756
Ochoco Mines, page 375, **Howard**
Odell Butte, page 554, **Odell Lake**
Odell Creek, page 554, **Odell Lake**
Ogden Park, **Peter Skene Ogden Park,** page 583
Olalla Creek, page 555, **Olalla Slough**
Old Bailey, page 510, **Mount Bailey**
Old Baldy, page 510, **Mount Bailey**
Olds Ferry, page 270, **Farewell Bend**
Olney Creek, page 150, **Chenoweth Creek**
ONeals Mills, page 254, **Ellendale**
Oneonta Creek, page 557, **Oneonta Gorge**
Onion Peak, page 537, **Nehalem**
Oppie Dildock, page 559, **Opie Dilldock Pass**
Ord, page 242, **Earl**
Oreana, page 563, **Orejana Canyon**
Oregon Slough, page 547, **North Portland Harbor**
Oregon Slough, page 681, **Slough**
Orford, Cape, page 121, **Cape Blanco**
Orford, **Fort Orford,** page 290
Orford, **Port Orford,** page 599
Orient Mill, page 564, **Orient**
Orla Falls, page 308, **Gatch Falls**
Orton, page 453, **Logsden**
Osborn Grove, page 336, **Grove City**
Oseola, page 553, **Oceola**
Oswego, **Lake Oswego,** page 429
Ott, page 532, **Myrtle Point**
Ouxy Spring, page 566, **Ouxy**
Owl Creek, page 98, **Butte Creek**
Owyhee, page 567, **Owyhee River**
Owyhee Ferry, page 567, **Owyhee**
Owyhee Ridge, page 567, **Owyhee River**
Oxford, page 356, **Helix**
Oyster Bay, page 540, **Netarts**
Oysterville, page 804, **Winant**

P. O. Saddle, page 578, **Peepover Saddle**
Pacific City, page 430, **Lakeport**
Paddys Marsh, page 569, **Paddys Valley**
Painted Rock, page 152, **Chiloquin**
Palisades State Park, The Cove, page 184, **Cove**
Palmain, page 465, **Madras**
Palmer Peak, page 570, **Palmer Creek**
Pamelia Lake, page 571, **Pamelia Creek**
Panky Lake, page 571, **Panky Spring**
Paper Mill, page 572, **Park Place**
Parawa, page 574, **Patawa Creek**
Parkdale, page 513, **Mount Hood**
Patch Bridge, **General Patch Bridge,** page 310
Paulina Basin, page 575, **Paulina**
Paynes Butte, page 296, **Franklin Butte**
Pearcy Slough, page 576, **Pearcy Island**
Pebble, page 18, **Anoka**
Pebble Springs Camp, page 577, **Pebble Springs**
Pelican, page 578, **Pelican Bay**
Pelican Prairie, page 579, **Pelican Creek**
Pengra Lake, page 767, **Waldo Lake**
Perdue, page 251, **Elk Creek**
Perdue, page 498, **Milo**
Periwinkle Creek, First, page 582, **Periwinkle Creek**
Periwinkle Creek, Second, page 186, **Cox Creek**
Periwinkle Creek, Second, page 582, **Periwinkle Creek**
Perpetua, **Cape Perpetua,** page 125
Pete Creek, **French Pete Creek,** page 300
Peter, Bald, page 333, **Green Peter**
Peter, **Bald Peter,** page 34
Peter, **Bald Peter,** page 35
Peter, **Green Peter,** page 333
Peters Creek, page 675, **Sink**
Philippi Park, Albert, page 585, **Philippi Canyon**
Pierce Creek, page 479, **McCord Creek**
Pikes Peak, page 656, **Schreiner Peak**
Pilot Knob, page 34, **Bald Mountain**
Pine City, page 3, **Acton**
Pine City, page 589, **Pine Creek**
Pine City, page 595, **Pocahontas**
Pine Creek, page 198, **Crown Rock**
Pine Creek, **New Pine Creek,** page 541
Pine Valley, page 588, **Pine**
Pioneer, page 590, **Pinehurst**
Pioneer Mountain, page 591, **Pioneer City**
Pioneer Summit, page 591, **Pioneer City**
Pisgah, Mount, page 267, **Fairview**
Pisgah, **Mount Pisgah,** page 521
Pit, Mount, page 519, **Mount McLoughlin**
Pit Lake, page 322, **Goose Lake**
Pitt, page 519, **Mount McLoughlin**
Pivot Mountain, page 64, **Black Butte**
Plants River, page 775, **Warner Valley**
Pleasant, Mount, page 267, **Fairview**
Pleasant, **Mount Pleasant,** page 521
Pleasant City, page 328, **Granite**
Pleasant Creek, page 594, **Pleasant Valley**
Pleasant Home, page 564, **Orient**

Ruckel Spring, page 727, **Thomas Creek**
Rudio Creek, page 639, **Rudio Mountain**
Rudio Meadow, page 639, **Rudio Mountain**
Russell, Battery, page 292, **Fort Stevens**
Russell, **Camp Russell,** page 113
Ryan Camp, page 383, **Idiot Creek**
Ryegrass Table, page 641, **Rye Valley**

Saddle, page 506, **Morgan**
Saddle Butte, page 642, **Saddlebutte**
Saddle Mountain, page 632, **Roman Nose Mountain**
Saddleback Mountain, page 642, **Saddle Bag Mountain**
Sailor Diggings, page 766, **Waldo**
Saint Helens, page 375, **Houlton**
Salmon, page 83, **Brightwood**
Salmon River, page 783, **Wenaha River**
Salmon River Glacier, page 570, **Palmer Glacier**
Salt Lake, page 347, **Harney Lake**
Salt Lake, page 427, **Lake Abert**
Salt Spring, page 648, **Salt Butte**
Salt Springs, page 52, **Belknap Springs**
Sam Tomeleaf River, page 456, **Long Tom River**
Samaria, page 633, **Roosevelt Beach**
Samuel H. Boardman State Park, page 455, **Lone Ranch Creek**
San Sebastian, Cape, page 126, **Cape Sebastian**
Sand Canyon, page 597, **Polallie Creek**
Sand Cape, page 123, **Cape Kiwanda**
Sand Creek, page 597, **Polallie Creek**
Sand Mountain, page 512, **Mount Elijah**
Sandwich Island River, page 567, **Owyhee River**
Sandy, page 743, **Troutdale**
Sandy Desert, Great, page 362, **High Desert**
Santiam City, page 394, **Jefferson**
Santiam River, **Little North Santiam River,** page 450
Santiam River, **Little Santiam River,** page 450
Santiam River, **Middle Santiam River,** page 493
Santiam River, **North Santiam River,** page 548
Santiam River, **South Santiam River,** page 689
Santyam, page 439, **Lebanon**
Santyam, page 651, **Santiam**
Santyam Forks, page 651, **Santiam**
Sardine Mountain, page 652, **Sardine Creek**
Saroute Creek, page 307, **Garoutte Creek**
Sarvis Creek, page 661, **Service Creek**
Sauvies Island, page 525, **Mouth of the Willamette**
Savage Creek, page 88, **Brush Creek**
Savage Creek, page 262, **Euchre Creek**
Savage Rapids, page 653, **Savage Creek**
Sawmill Creek, page 597, **Pole Gulch**

Sawtooth Rock Mountain, page 687, **Soldier Camp Mountain**
Sawyer State Park, **Robert W. Sawyer State Park,** page 625
Saxton, page 662, **Sexton Mountain**
Scappoose Creek, **North Scappoose Creek,** page 548
Scappoose Creek, **South Scappoose Creek,** page 689
Scaredman Camp, page 654, **Scaredman Creek**
Schindler Hill, page 146, **Chapman Hill**
Scholls Ferry, page 655, **Scholls**
Schoolmaam Creek, page 655, **Schoolmarm Spring**
Schooner Point, page 656, **Schooner Creek**
Scissorsville, page 656, **Scissors Creek**
Scott, **Mount Scott,** page 522
Scott Lake, page 657, **Scott Mountain**
Scott Pass, page 657, **Scott Mountain**
Scott Spring, **Minnie Scott Spring,** page 499
Scott Trail, page 657, **Scott Mountain**
Scotts, page 629, **Rockville**
Scotts Point, page 657, **Scott Mountain**
Seal Illahe, page 658, **Seal Rocks**
Seaton, page 470, **Mapleton**
Sebastian, Cape San, page 126, **Cape Sebastian**
Sebastian, **Cape Sebastian,** page 125
Sebastopol, page 319, **Gold Beach**
Second Periwinkle Creek, page 186, **Cox Creek**
Second Periwinkle Creek, page 582, **Periwinkle Creek**
Sequalchin River, page 678, **Sixes River**
Service Canyon, page 661, **Service Buttes**
Service Springs, page 661, **Service Buttes**
Seven-springs Ranch, page 51, **Bedfield**
Shake, page 590, **Pinehurst**
Shamrock Flat, page 662, **Shamrock Creek**
Shasta Gap, page 249, **Eldorado**
Shaw Island, page 352, **Hayden Island**
Shawpatin Mountains, page 68, **Blue Mountains**
Sheeny Creek, page 148, **Cheeney Creek**
Sheep Creek, page 60, **Big Canyon**
Sheep Creek, page 456, **Lookout Creek**
Sheep Creek, **Mountain Sheep Creek,** page 525
Sheep Rock, page 29, **Awbrey Mountain**
Shellrock Lake, page 665, **Shellrock Creek**
Shellrock Mountain, page 297, **Frazier Mountain**
Shellrock Mountain, page 523, **Mount Talapus**
Shelter, **Sunset Shelter,** page 710
Sheriff, Point, page 333, **Green Point**
Sherman, page 6, **Ainsworth**
Sherman, **Camp Sherman,** page 114
Shevlin Park, page 299, **Fremont Meadow**
Shinglebolt, page 139, **Caulkins Creek**
Shobe Canyon, page 669, **Shobe Creek**
Shoestring, page 253, **Elkhead**
Short Narrows, page 723, **Tenmile Rapids**

Short Sand Beach, page 685, **Smuggler Cove**
Shortridge Creek, page 669, **Shortridge Butte**
Shubel, page 49, **Beaver Creek**
Shutler, page 32, **Baird**
Shutler Flat, page 669, **Shutler**
Sidney, page 18, **Ankeny Bottom**
Signal, page 431, **Landax**
Signal Peak, page 517, **Mount Howard**
Sikhs River, page 678, **Sixes River**
Siltcoos River, page 672, **Siltcoos Lake**
Silver Falls City, page 673, **Silver Creek Falls**
Silver Lake, page 402, **Joseph**
Silver Lake, page 672, **Silver Creek**
Silver Point Cliff, page 674, **Silver Point**
Simax, page 192, **Crescent Lake**
Simtustus, **Lake Simtustus,** page 429
Siskiyou Peak, page 510, **Mount Ashland**
Sister, **North Sister,** page 548
Sister Creek, North, page 750, **Twin Sisters Creeks**
Sister Creek, South, page 750, **Twin Sisters Creeks**
Sisters, **Three Sisters,** page 729
Sisters Creeks, **Twin Sisters Creeks,** page 749
Six Bit House, page 809, **Wolf Creek**
Skeeters Creek, page 678, **Skeeters Flat**
Skeppernawin Creek, page 679, **Skipanon River**
Ski Bowl, page 738, **Tom Dick & Harry Mountain**
Skimhoox River, page 791, **White River**
Skinner, page 263, **Eugene**
Skinner Butte, page 637, **Roxy Ann Peak**
Skinner Butte, page 816, **Yapoah Crater**
Skipanarwin Creek, page 679, **Skipanon River**
Skipanon, page 679, **Skipanon River**
Skookum, page 575, **Paunina**
Skunk Cabbage Flat, page 473, **Marshland**
Slab Creek, page 539, **Neskowin**
Slate Creek, page 795, **Wilderville**
Slough, page 714, **Switzler Lake**
Smith, **Camp C. F. Smith,** page 107
Smith, Camp C. F., page 790, **White Horse**
Smith, **Fort Smith,** page 291
Smith Island, **John Smith Island,** page 398
Smith River, **North Fork Smith River,** page 546
Smith River, **North Fork Smith River,** page 546
Smithfield, page 296, **Franklin-Smithfield**
Smockville, page 667, **Sherwood**
Snake, page 214, **Dell**
Snipe, page 7, **Albee**
Snipe Creek, page 7, **Albee**
Snow Mountains, page 700, **Steens Mountain**
Snow Peak, page 686, **Snow**
Snowy Butte, page 60, **Big Butte Creek**
Snowy Butte, page 519, **Mount McLoughlin**

Sodhouse, page 764, **Voltage**
Somerange, page 301, **Frenchglen**
South Canyonville, page 120, **Canyonville**
South Falls, Lower, page 673, **Silver Creek Falls**
South Falls, page 673, **Silver Creek Falls**
South Forest Grove, page 129, **Carnation**
South Fork, page 459, **Lostine River**
South Lookout Mountain, page 268, **Fairview Peak**
South Sister, page 730, **Three Sisters**
South Sister Creek, page 750, **Twin Sisters Creeks**
South Twin Lake, page 749, **Twin Lakes**
Spanish Hollow, page 777, **Wasco**
Sparta, page 310, **Gem**
Spencer, **Camp Spencer,** page 114
Spores Ferry, page 693, **Spores Point**
Sprague, page 103, **Calimus**
Sprague River, page 70, **Bly**
Spring Creek, page 721, **Tecumseh Creek**
Springer, page 532, **Narrows**
Squally Hook, page 371, **Hook**
St. Theresa, page 550, **Oak Grove**
Staats Hollow, page 696, **Staats Creek**
Staley Creek, page 697, **Staley Ridge**
Stalls Falls, page 704, **Stulls Falls**
Stampede, Lake, page 347, **Harney Lake**
Stampede, Lake, page 467, **Malheur Lake**
Stanford, page 235, **Drift Creek**
Stanford, page 544, **Nice**
Stanley, page 583, **Perry**
Starkey Creek, page 487, **Meadow Creek**
Starkey Creek, page 697, **Starkey**
Starrs Point, page 504, **Monroe**
Starveout, page 698, **Starvation Creek**
Starvout, page 30, **Azalea**
Stavebolt Creek, page 698, **Stavebolt Landing**
Stayton, **West Stayton,** page 784
Steamboat Creek, page 127, **Carberry Creek**
Stearns Ranch, **Carey Stearns Ranch,** page 128
Steele, Camp, page 286, **Fort Harney**
Stephensville, page 701, **Stephens**
Sterlingville, page 701, **Sterling Creek**
Stevens, **Fort Stevens,** page 291
Stewart Creek, page 741, **Trail**
Stewart Ditch, **Shaw Stewart Ditch,** page 663
Stinkingwater Mountains, page 702, **Stinkingwater Creek**
Stokes, page 389, **Irrigon**
Stone, page 131, **Carver**
Stony Creek, page 628, **Rock Creek**
Stranahan Glacier, page 426, **Ladd Glacier**
Strawberry Creek, page 703, **Strawberry Mountain**
Strawberry Island, page 79, **Bradford Island**
Strawberry Prairie, page 483, **McKenzie Bridge**
Strawberry Valley, page 704, **Strawberry Mountain**

Stringtown, page 493, **Middleton**
Stuart, **Camp Stuart,** page 114
Stuart Creek, page 47, **Bear Creek**
Stuart Creek, page 114, **Camp Stuart**
Stubblefield Mountain, page 521, **Mount Moriah**
Stumptown, page 583, **Perry**
Sucker Creek, page 566, **Oswego Creek**
Sucker Creek, page 705, **Succor Creek**
Sucker Lake, page 566, **Oswego Lake**
Sugarloaf Mountain, page 378, **Humbug Mountain**
Sugarloaf Mountain, page 706, **Sugarloaf**
Summer House, page 659, **Seaside**
Summit, page 57, **Bertha**
Summit House, page 433, **Larch**
Summit station, page 405, **Kamela**
Summitville, page 707, **Summit**
Sumter, page 708, **Sumpter**
Sunlight Falls, page 673, **Silver Creek Falls**
Sunset Lake, page 534, **Neacoxie Creek**
Sunset Valley, page 454, **Loma**
Swaine River, page 770, **Wallace Slough**
Swan Bay, page 138, **Cathlamet Bay**
Swan Creek, page 397, **John Day River**
Swan Lake, page 711, **Swan**
Swift Station, page 580, **Pendleton**
Switzerland, page 604, **Pratum**
Switzler Island, page 721, **Techumtas Island**
Sycan Butte, page 715, **Sycan Marsh**
Sycan River, page 715, **Sycan Marsh**
Sylvailles River, page 675, **Silvies River**
Sylvan Park, page 674, **Silver Point**
Sylvan Point, page 674, **Silver Point**
Sylvania, **Mount Sylvania,** page 522
Syracuse, page 269, **Falls City**
Syracuse, page 394, **Jefferson**

Table Creek, page 686, **Snider Creek**
Table Mountain, page 716, **Table Creek**
Table Rock Creek, page 628, **Rock Creek**
Table Rock Creek, page 686, **Snider Creek**
Tabor, **Mount Tabor,** page 523
Taih Prairie, page 750, **Tygh Valley**
Takenah, page 7, **Albany**
Taklamah, page 717, **Takilma**
Talapus, **Mount Talapus,** page 523
Talbot State Park, **Guy W. Talbot State Park,** page 338
Tamanawaus, page 718, **Tamanawas Falls**
Tamarack Mountain, page 524, **Mount Wilson**
Tamarack Point, page 386, **Ingram Point**
Tampico, page 686, **Soap Creek**
Tanner Butte, page 719, **Tanner Creek**
Tansy Creek, page 718, **Tandy Creek**
Tarter Gulch, page 719, **Tartar Gulch**
Tater Hill, page 602, **Potato Hill**
Tay, page 268, **Fall Creek**
Taylor, page 720, **Taylorville**
Taylor Canyon, **Tom Taylor Canyon,** page 738
Taylor Creek, page 630, **Rodgers Creek**

Teepy Springs, page 724, **Tepee Springs**
Tell Tale, page 244, **Eckley**
Tenmile Butte, page 723, **Tenmile Creek**
Tenmile Lake, **North Tenmile Lake,** page 548
Tenmile Ridge, page 723, **Tenmile Creek**
Tent Mountain, page 666, **Sheridan Mountain**
Tetherow bridge, page 724, **Tetherow Butte**
The Basin, page 465, **Madras**
The Boulders, page 736, **Tiptop**
The Chute, page 164, **Coalman Glacier**
The Cockscomb, page 609, **Pulpit Rock**
The Cove Palisades State Park, page 184, **Cove**
The Crossing, page 244, **Echo**
The Great Dalles, page 278, **Fivemile Rapids**
The Hill, page 521, **Mount Pleasant**
The Hogsback, page 164, **Coalman Glacier**
The Point, page 198, **Crown Point**
Theresa, St., page 550, **Oak Grove**
Thielsen, **Mount Thielsen,** page 523
Thomas Mill, page 692, **Spikenard**
Thompson Valley, page 715, **Sycan Marsh**
Three Brothers, page 125, **Cape Meares**
Three Creek, page 729, **Three Creek Lake**
Three Creek Butte, page 729, **Three Creek Lake**
Three Links, page 729, **Three Lynx Creek**
Three Notches, page 193, **Criterion**
Thurston, page 349, **Harrisburg**
Tichenor Cove, page 537, **Nellies Cove**
Tichenors Humbug, page 378, **Humbug Mountain**
Tillasana Creek, page 60, **Big Creek**
Tillicum Creek, page 579, **Pelican Creek**
Tilly Ann Creek, page 60, **Big Creek**
Tilly Jane Creek, page 60, **Big Creek**
Timothy Meadows, page 735, **Timothy Lake**
Timpanogos, Lake, page 736, **Timpanogas Lake**
Tinanens Creek, page 274, **Fifteenmile Creek**
Tinanens Creek, page 532, **Nansene**
Tioga Fork, page 736, **Tioga**
Toad Lake, page 598, **Poole Lake**
Tobin Spring, page 737, **Tobin Cabin**
Toe Island, page 345, **Hardtack Island**
Toe Island, page 635, **Ross Island**
Tom Dick Mountain, page 738, **Tom Dick & Harry Mountain**
Tombstone Summit, page 739, **Tombstone Prairie**
Tomeleaf River, Sam, page 456, **Long Tom River**
Torrey River, page 800, **Williamson River**
Tower Mountain, **Water Tower Mountain,** page 779
Trail Creek, page 741, **Trail**
Trail Fork Canyon, page 742, **Trailfork**
Trail Road, **Logie Trail Road,** page 453
Trapper Creek, page 88, **Buck Creek**

Notes

Notes

Notes

Notes

Notes

Notes

Notes

Notes

Colophon

The Fifth Edition of *Oregon Geographic Names* is typeset in Baskerville, a Transitional typeface designed by John Baskerville in 1757. The composition was done by Nelson Composition Systems located in San Bruno, California. The book was printed and bound by BookCrafters, Inc. of Chelsea, Michigan.

124° 123°

●Astoria

46° — C L A T S O P

Nehalem River

COLUMBIA

St Helens●

COLUMBIA 122° 121°

Hood River●

Tillamook● WASHINGTON Portland● MULTNOMAH HOOD The Dalles●

TILLAMOOK Hillsboro● RIVER

W A S C O

YAMHILL Oregon City●

McMinnville● C L A C K A M A S

Dallas● Willamette River SALEM●

45° — P O L K M A R I O N

North Santiam River J E F F E R S O

Newport● Albany● L I N N Madras●

LINCOLN Corvallis● South Santiam River

BENTON

McKenzie River

Siuslaw Eugene●

44° — River L A N E Bend●

Umpqua D E S C H U

River

Deschutes

Coquille● Roseburg●

C O O S D O U G L A S

43° — Crater Lake

Williamson R L A

CURRY KLAMATH

Rogue River JACKSON Sprague River

Grants Pass● Upper Klamath Lake

Gold Beach● Medford● Klamath Falls●

JOSEPHINE Lost River

42° —